ART SINCE 1980
Charting the Contemporary

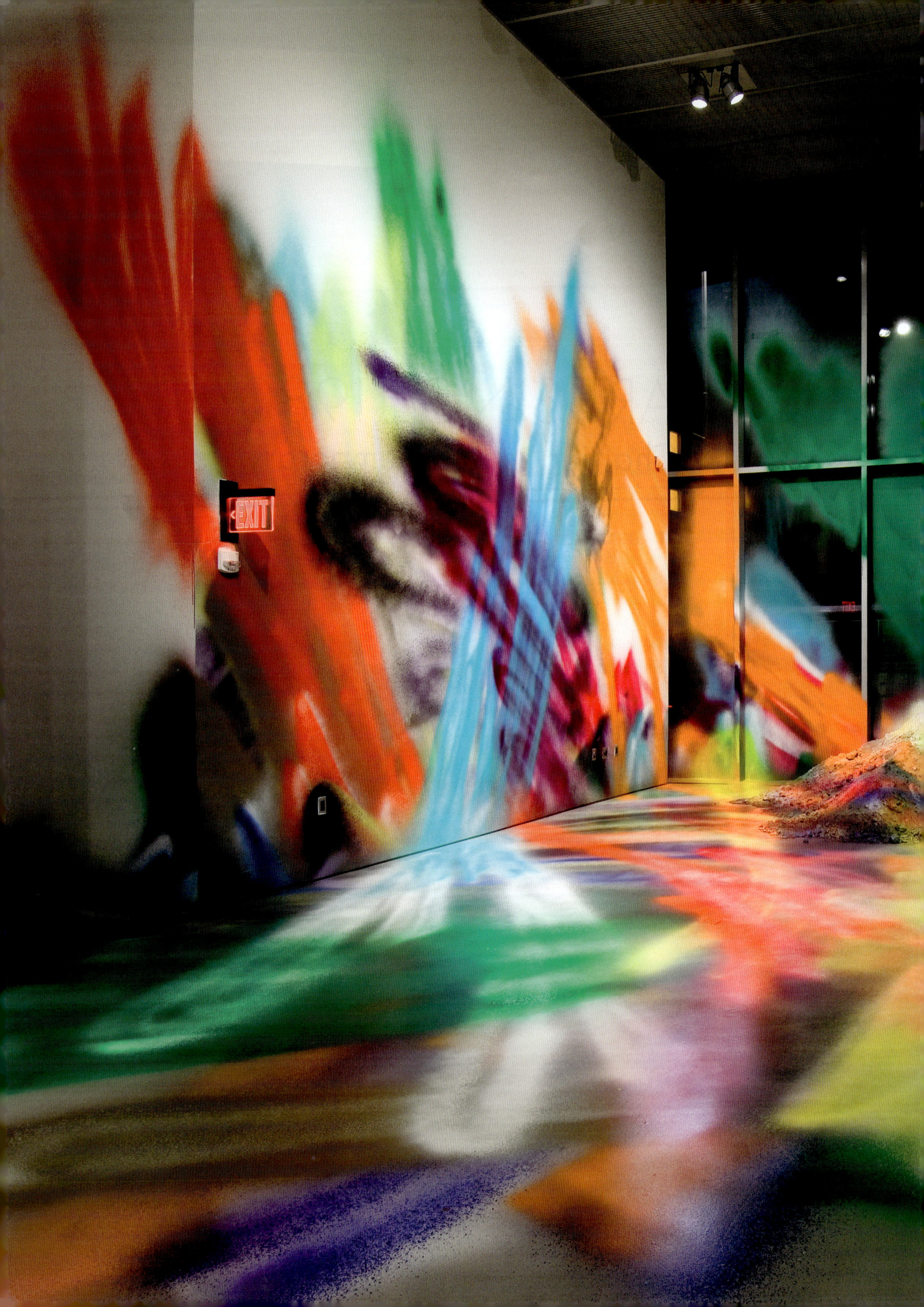
EXIT

ART SINCE 1980
Charting the Contemporary

Peter R. Kalb
Brandeis University

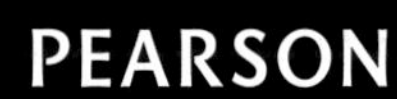

Boston Columbus Indianapolis New York San Francisco Upper Saddle River
Amsterdam Cape Town Dubai London Madrid Milan Munich Paris Montréal Toronto
Delhi Mexico City São Paulo Sydney Hong Kong Seoul Singapore Taipei Tokyo

Editor in Chief: Sarah Touborg
Editorial Assistant: Victoria Engros
Director of Marketing: Brandy Dawson
Executive Marketing Manager: Kate Mitchell
Production Liaison: Lynne Breitfeller
Senior Managing Editor: Laurence King Publishing/
Melissa Danny
Senior Operations Supervisor: Mary Fischer
Operations Specialist: Diane Peirano
Text and Cover Designer: Nick Newton
Photo Researcher: Ida Riveros
Senior Digital Media Editor: David Alick
Lead Media Project Manager: Rich Barnes
Full-Service Project Management: Laurence King Publishing/
Kara Hattersley-Smith
Composition: Laurence King Publishing
Text Font: ITC New Baskerville Std/Futura
Printed in Hong Kong

This book was designed by
Laurence King Publishing Ltd,
361–373 City Road
London EC1V 1LR
www.laurenceking.com

To Jessica, with love.

Cover image: Cao Fei, *A Mirage* from *COSPlayers* series, 2004. Detail. Digital C-print, 29¼ × 39¼" (74.3 × 99.7 cm). Courtesy the artist and Lombard Freid Gallery.

Frontispiece image: Katharina Grosse, *Cincy*, 2006. Installation using spraypaint, styrofoam, and soil at the Contemporary Arts Center, Cincinnati, Ohio. Image courtesy BUREAU N. Photo: Tony Walsh © Katharina Grosse and VG Bild-Kunst, Bonn 2013/DACS 2013.

Credits and acknowledgments borrowed from other sources and reproduced, with permission, in this textbook appear on the appropriate page within the text or on the credit pages in the back of this book.

Library of Congress Cataloging-in-Publication Data

Kalb, Peter R.
Art since 1980 : charting the contemporary / Peter R. Kalb. – 1st edition.
pages cm
Includes bibliographical references and index.
ISBN-13: 978-0-205-93556-7
ISBN-10: 0-205-93556-7
1. Art, Modern–20th century. 2. Art, Modern–21st century. I. Title.
N6490.K284 2014
709.04'8–dc23

2013006663

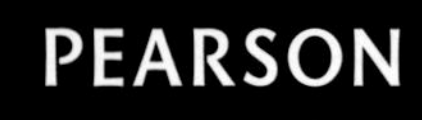

10 9 8 7 6 5 4 3 2 1
ISBN 10: 0-205-93556-7
ISBN 13: 978-0-205-93556-7

Acknowledgments

While working on the following text I have been the beneficiary of intellectual and economic largess from a variety of sources. Representatives of all the artists discussed in this book were graciously forthcoming with information, insight, and images both in the research and production stages of creating this book. Over the course of the last few years many artists and colleagues have shared ideas, corroborated or contradicted observations, and in several cases opened their studios and archives to me, and for this I am immeasurably grateful. Often a quick email, that may even have been quickly forgotten by the sender made a significant impact on the course of this book. Such is the nature of discussing art: a fleeting impression and single facts merge with lifelong friendships and days of debate to create a history. There is no doubt that I will leave out the names of some of those who helped shaped this book. I hope they will forgive me.

It is first to the students who have taken my various contemporary art history courses over the last decade or so that I owe my appreciation. Working through the history of art with students at Middlebury College, The New School, Ursinus College, and for the last seven years at my home institution of Brandeis University has been both a challenge and pleasure. It is with these collaborators that the need for this book was made clear and the form it has taken was hammered out. The students in my seminars at Brandeis were especially helpful in offering their insight into how much contemporary art resonated with their lives. Several students including Sara Chun, Amanda Deibert, Amanda Di Santo, Daniella Gold, Emily Leifer, Rebecca Pollack, and Hannah Rothstein are owed individual acknowledgment for assisting with research and reading sections of manuscript drafts.

As my courses became a laboratory for writing this book, several institutions provided financial support essential for the necessary travel and research. Middlebury and Ursinus College provided travel grants. I owe a great debt to Lisa Tremper Hanover who, as Director of the Berman Museum of Art at Ursinus College, provided funding for research in Cuba that proved critical to the course of this study. At Brandeis I have received generous funding through the Tomberg Research Fund, the Norman Faculty Research Grant, and the Center for German and European Studies. Introductions to collections and artists were provided by the generosity of the Rose Museum of Art under Director Michael Rush and the Rose Board of Overseers, on which I served under Chair Jonathan Lee from 2007 to 2009. Thanks too, to Cynthia L. and Theodore S. Berenson for providing singular support of contemporary art history here at Brandeis. Finally at the university, I am pleased to be able to thank colleagues in my department for their ongoing support and enthusiasm for this project, in particular Charles McClendon, Nancy Scott, Graham Campbell, Susan Lichtman, Jonathan Unglaub, Tory Fair, and Talinn Grigor, as well as Aida Wong and Gannit Ankori who offered many insights from their own specialties. Support from Joy Vlachos and Jennifer Stern, the latter providing numerous visual and administrative resources, was invaluable. A particular acknowledgment goes to Joe Wardwell with whom I spent hours discussing art, often with large groups of students in New York galleries, studios, and restaurants.

Over the course of working on this book I have had the pleasure of many conversations with artists, galleries, and art historians, among them Janine Antoni, Shimon Attie, Andrea Bowers, Ingrid Calame, Chang Tsong-zung (Johnson), Chen Chieh-Jen, Phil Collins, Hasan Elahi, Omer Fast, Paul Gladston, Joanne Huang Chi-Wen, Silvia Kolbowski, Sally Mann, Ibrahim Miranda, Rene Francisco Rodriguez, Tom Sachs, and Shahzia Sikander. I will no doubt be missing names, but a word of gratitude is owed to a number of people for their willingness to confer about their personal histories as well as their scholarship. As I embarked on this project and at various points along the way, I received sustaining encouragement and advice from Linda Nochlin and often returned to kernels of practical wisdom from Nan Rosenthal and Bill Hood.

As with any project, this one was supported by friends and interlocutors, many of whom have been fellow travelers in the world of contemporary art for decades and who have sharpened my eye and mind. Thanks to Claudia Bucher, Ilana Cepero, Anna Indych, Leslie Jones, Bill Kaizen, Karen Kurczynski, Justin Lieberman, Karen Overbey, Tricia Paik, Lizzy Pergam, Katherine Smith, Eugene Tan, Greg Williams, and Andrew Witkin. And finally Joe Lin-Hill is owed a personal thank you for years of debating the aesthetics, ethics, and economics of contemporary art from studios in Havana to long nights of wine and conversation in New York. This book is better for his influence.

Almost ten years ago Lee Greenfield, then of Laurence King Publishing came into my office and asked who I would like to see write a book on contemporary art. I replied, "Besides me?" Since then Kara Hattersley-Smith and the team at Laurence King have been enthusiastic, supportive, and patient as this project turned from proposal to book. From the beginning Laurence King has been eager to push the limits of what it meant to write a history of contemporary art and encouraged me to let the variables of an as-yet-unwritten history—rather than market expectations—determine the shape of this book. They have allowed for the considerable time necessary to adequately research work only just created, and encouraged a macroscopic view that challenges both thematic and chronological structures. As the text has become the final book they have also been generous in providing a team of anonymous readers to which I am humbly grateful, as well as editors. Many thanks are owed to Michael Bird and Robert Shore who at various points tore chapters apart for me, and to Robert for providing the final editorial support. For leading the book through the final stages I thank Melissa Danny and Ida Riveros. The ambitions for this project required participation not only of many individuals but also two publishing houses. *Art Since 1980: Charting the Contemporary* could not have been produced without the partnership with Pearson and the support of Sarah Touborg. To Sarah and the readers she enlisted— Bill Anthes, David Hart, Sarah Hollenberg, Ellen Hoobler, Monica McTighe, Doreen Maloney, Soraya Murray, and Alisa Swindell—thank you.

To my family, extended and immediate, who have supported me I am grateful. Thanks to Marty and Joan Kalb for starting me on this journey and helping along the way and to Leah and David Roland for their enthusiasm. Finally, a profound and most heartfelt debt of gratitude is reserved for my wife, Jessica Roland, to whom this entire effort is dedicated. Jessica has lived with this project for years and has read every word of the following text and many more besides. Time and time again she provided emotional support, intellectual challenge, and common sense, all of which I desperately needed on many occasions. With my children, Talia and Lev, Jessica has been an anchor that helped me tread further into this project while maintaining my bearings in art and in life.

Contents

Preface

I grew up going to museums and galleries. My father taught painting in a small college in Ohio and art took us to Chicago or New York and a couple of times to Europe. On a few memorable occasions, contemporary art also brought exciting people to us. I have a distinct childhood memory of watching Andy Warhol standing in front of a projected image of one of his famous portraits of Mao. Years later, in college, I realized that what I understood best about history or politics or theory came to me from art. My biblical and historical education was rooted in painting and sculpture. My growing understanding of the transformations of the modern era came via Romanticism, Realism, and Dada. Most important was the sense that art taught what it meant to be engaged with one's life and times. This understanding, that creative manipulation of materials and images had the power to convey the sense and nonsense of life, came first in front of Abstract Expressionist painting. Quickly, however, an admittedly selfish impulse took me to the art of the 1960s and 1970s, work created in my lifetime. As my art historical knowledge and aesthetic taste caught up with my own moment, at some point in the 1980s, it was clear to me that the art of our own age speaks to far more than our own lives. The art that fills the first chapters of this book transformed my thinking about culture, self, and politics. Here are conceptual and formal practices that invited the viewer into intellectual critiques of power and injustice while lavishing him or her with the sensual power of everything from the oil paint with which I had grown familiar to media as diverse as lead, chrome, video, bodies, and breath. Contemporary artists took me into my own time but also far from my own place or experience; their art forced me to consider how I related to the world. This book was written to invite readers to the world of beauty and politics, and the discovery of self and others that is art at the turn of the millennium.

The art discussed here links societal shifts and the individuals and communities who live through them. It represents a cultural and intellectual history, written in many languages, materials, styles, and perspectives reaching from New York to London, Lagos, Havana, Beijing, and on around the globe. Artists' power to reflect upon and affect the world around them depends on viewers who are able to comprehend specific details of both form and content. There are many ways to introduce the variety of practices and subjects found in the contemporary art world. One can create categories according to place of origin, media, subject matter, or chronology. *Art Since 1980: Charting the Contemporary* is fundamentally a chronological survey, but in the course of telling the story of the transformation of the contemporary art world it enlists all of these methodologies. This narrative documents regional productions, thematic concerns, and formal developments as they made their imprint on the history of art and it was written to be read from front to back. This story of the increased breadth and self-consciousness of the contemporary art world is, I believe, compelling. However, there are very good reasons to be skeptical of such narratives. Much of the art and theory discussed in the first third of this book challenges the impulse to layer plot lines on the past and this warning must be taken seriously. Moreover, there are clearly many themes that join the art that is separated by the temporal and geographical span of this story. In response to this concern, I have attempted to weave thematic threads in and out of the chronology. One can trace the relationship of abstraction and representation across a wide variety of times and places, or compare the integration of mass culture into fine art in New York in the 1980s with similar experiments in Cuba or Europe at the same time, or China in the 1990s, or Japan in the 2000s, to name a few examples. The urgency of creating politically effective art is addressed across the scope of the book. Likewise, I have tried to highlight traditions of feminist and activist art, as well as art analyzing issues of class, warfare, and social injustice. While one might come across these moments as the chronology of the book unfolds, one might also use the book to teach in a very different way, calling attention to various themes within the text. Finally, it must be said that *Art Since 1980* does not aspire to be an exhaustive study—there could be no such history of contemporary art; instead it is an introduction to many of the ideas and solutions that artists have pursued, and a series of examples of how one might engage with the art of our time.

Digital Resources for Teaching and Learning

Image PowerPoints

Instructors who adopt this text may receive access to a PowerPoint set featuring most of the images in the text. To request access, visit the instructor resources area for this text on www.pearsonhighered.com

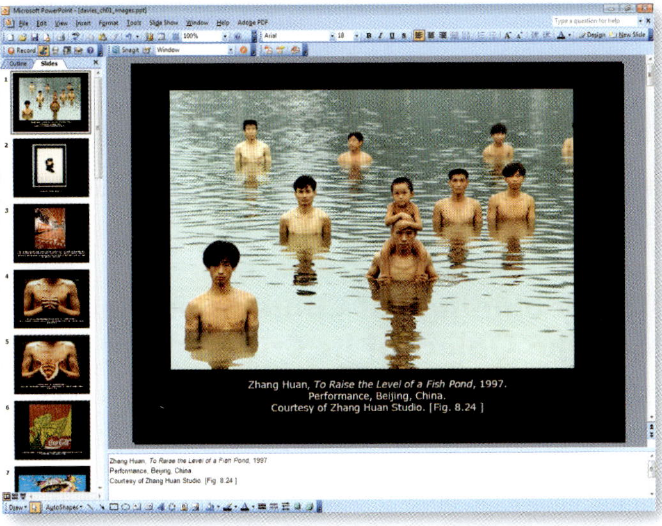

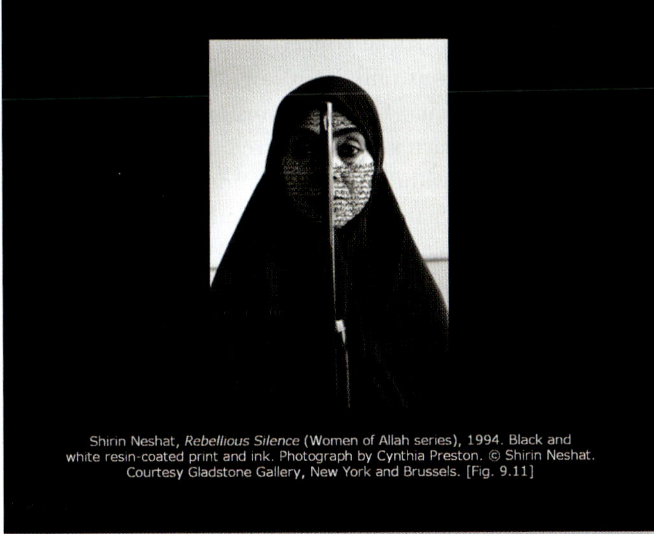

MySearchLab with Pearson eText

MySearchLab contains a Pearson eText and several helpful research and writing tools:

- The **Pearson eText** lets students access their textbook anytime, anywhere, and any way they want. Just like the printed text, students can highlight relevant passages and add their own notes. For even greater flexibility, students can download the eText to a tablet using the free Pearson eText app.
- **Research and writing tools** provide access to various academic journals, census data, Associated Press news feeds, and other rich media links. A wide range of composition and citation tools is also available to help students throughout the writing process.

The eBook version of this title is also available in CourseSmart, Kindle, Nook, and iBooks.

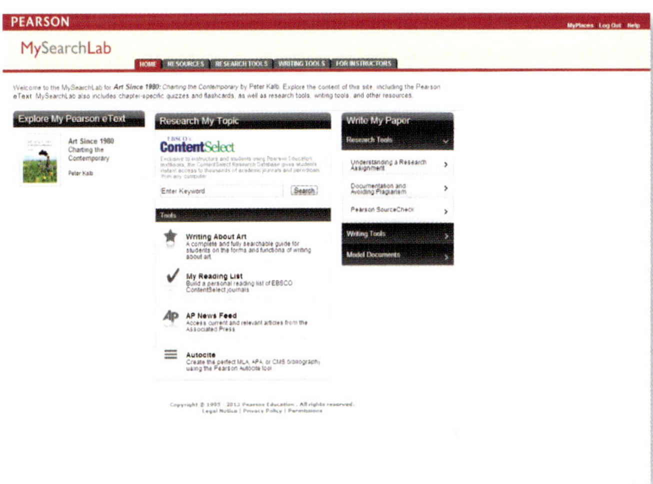

Introduction

In the first decades of the twenty-first century, the question "What is contemporary art?" has been posed with surprising frequency, leading historians, theorists, and critics to re-examine the character and consequences of artistic production at the turn of the millennium. The question is really three questions: What is "the contemporary"? What is "art"? And what constitutes the intersection between the two? Those asking the questions are highly invested in the answers; it is central not only to their professional lives, but also to their own passions and politics as citizens of the contemporary world and advocates of art. We can all, as citizens of the present, weigh in on the nature of the contemporary and on the significant issues that matter in today's world. However, defining contemporary art is neither strictly a matter of common sense nor is it exclusively philosophical: It refers to a body of objects accepted as art and labeled contemporary about which one can pose questions of identity, meaning, and consequences. Parsing why this work matters, to whom, and for how long presumes a familiarity with art and artists that is not shared by all. This book does not answer the question "What is contemporary art?" Rather, it is an introduction to a body of work that might set some useful parameters and provide material for a debate on just that issue.

Art Since 1980 introduces examples of painting, photography, sculpture, installation, performance, and video art that can be called upon to help us define both the contemporary and art; it is a history that joins these two terms. The intellectual, political, cultural, and aesthetic history of the turn from the twentieth into the twenty-first century is expressed and imprinted upon the art discussed in this book. The story of art in contemporary global culture provides a record of our society and the processes of change through which we are living. While the book aims at inclusivity, it is also structured in a way that suggests that the limits of the text do not indicate limitations in its subject matter. Every work that is discussed is intended to provide a model for exploring art that is not directly addressed in the book. By providing examples of contemporary art from many artists, cultures, and locations, I hope that this book serves as an invitation to contribute to the conversation about the significance, character, and future of art.

The Beginnings of Contemporaneity and the Object of Its Critique

This history of late twentieth- and early twenty-first-century art really begins after the protracted debates about Modernism that fill accounts of post-World War II art. Art and criticism in the immediate postwar decades offered challenges to the paradigms of Modernism: its formalist pursuits, its priority on unifying narratives, and its construction as an avant-garde removed from wider social concerns. Artists, along with the rest of the world, confronted not only the atrocities of Auschwitz and Hiroshima, but also transformative events of a very different character that occurred in the wake of the war, including the withdrawal of the British from India, the foundation of the State of Israel, and the establishment of the People's Republic of China, followed by a surge of liberation struggles and protest movements in the 1950s and 1960s. All these events undermined the certainties both of colonial power and of Modernist artistic judgments.

As the world changed, historians and theorists, particularly a group of French intellectuals including Michel Foucault, Roland Barthes, Louis Althusser, Jacques Derrida, and Jean-François Lyotard, were reconceptualizing history and ideas about subjectivity to accord with the shifting ground of contemporary reality. Labeled Poststructuralists and Deconstructionists, these writers described political and intellectual activity as contingent on social actions rather than as historical inevitability. Thus, institutions from marriage to medicine as well as forms of governance and means of communication were described not as permanent structures around which people could order their lives, but as conditional agreements that were continually being renegotiated and manipulated in the process of being used. Lyotard summed up the state of thinking in *The Postmodern Condition: A Report on Knowledge* (1979) by contrasting modern disciplines and institutions, which legitimate themselves by appealing to a "grand narrative" such as "the emancipation of the rational or working subject or the creation of wealth,"[1] with "Postmodern" ones that are skeptical of such appeals. "Grand narratives" might include the spread of Western civilization, the assertion of individual freedom, or the growth of democracy. Postmodern life exists as a nest of intersecting pursuits that may or may not contribute to such grand narratives of official Western history and in either case cannot claim to be justified by them.

Lyotard concluded that efficiency was the sole remaining justification for our actions. As the protest, feminist, and revolutionary movements of the postwar decades made clear, his dismantling of the authoritarian narratives of Modernism was very much in keeping with the spirit of the times. But replacing the compromised truths of the past with the idea of simple efficiency satisfied few people. The resulting challenge—of creating meaning and validity for our actions without appealing to higher authorities, be they gods or governments—continues to motivate many artists and thinkers in the new millennium. Lyotard's book represented a moment of what has been called "Deconstruction," but his observations also take note of what would become tools for construction. At the end of his introduction to *The Postmodern Condition*, he writes: "Postmodern knowledge is not simply a tool of the authorities [as modern knowledge was appearing to be]; it refines our sensitivity to difference and reinforces out ability to tolerate the incommensurable."[2] Artists and thinkers in the subsequent period have striven to produce such Postmodern knowledge, cultivate the ability to see the unfamiliar, the alternative, and the Other, and enable themselves and others to exist in states that the foregoing Modernist generation would have considered unacceptably unstable, tenuous, and confusing.

Though the roots of Modernism as an art-historical movement can be traced back to the economic and colonial expansion of the seventeenth century or even to the Italian Renaissance in the fifteenth century, the immediate starting point for any history of modern art is provided by nineteenth-century Paris. By the 1860s, when the poet and critic Charles Baudelaire proclaimed the greatness of the painter Edouard Manet, and the 1870s, when the Impressionists took their place at the head of the avant-garde, the French capital was securely established as the capital of modern art. The Postimpressionist flight from the urban center only reconfirmed the importance of Paris, as Paul Cézanne, Vincent van Gogh, and Paul Gauguin were faced with making their reputations in the city even as they made their homes elsewhere—it was still from Paris that their work influenced artists all over Europe. Thus, the early twentieth-century migrations from Spain to the Parisian stage by the likes of Pablo Picasso, Joan Miró, and Salvador Dalí were merely later episodes in an already familiar story. Well into the new century, the exhibitions, sales, collections, and conversations that mattered most took place in the French capital. On occasion, other cities—the Vienna of the Secessionists or the Moscow of the Constructivists and Suprematists, for instance—might momentarily draw attention from Paris, but it was not until World War II that global politics shifted eyes decisively away from France and onto a new art capital, New York City.

Until the 1950s, New York had been merely one of the many artistic satellites orbiting Paris, with exhibitions such as the Armory Show (1913) and the Society of Independent Artists exhibition (1917), galleries such as Alfred Stieglitz's 291 (1905–17) and Marius de Zayas's Modern Gallery (1915–21), as well as the Museum of Modern Art (established 1929), the Museum of Non-Objective Painting (established 1939), which became the Solomon R. Guggenheim Museum (1959), and Peggy Guggenheim's Art of This Century (1942–47), all providing important stages for the products of European Modernism. But if, in these years, it was the French capital that conferred ultimate cultural validation on the work, New York was nonetheless beginning to function as an art capital in its own right. Indeed, Picasso's Cubism was embraced by Stieglitz in New York in 1911 before Parisian galleries really began to take notice of it (**fig. 0.1**). In 1929, Stieglitz opened his third gallery, calling it An American Place and choosing to use it to foreground the work of U.S. artists in a show of

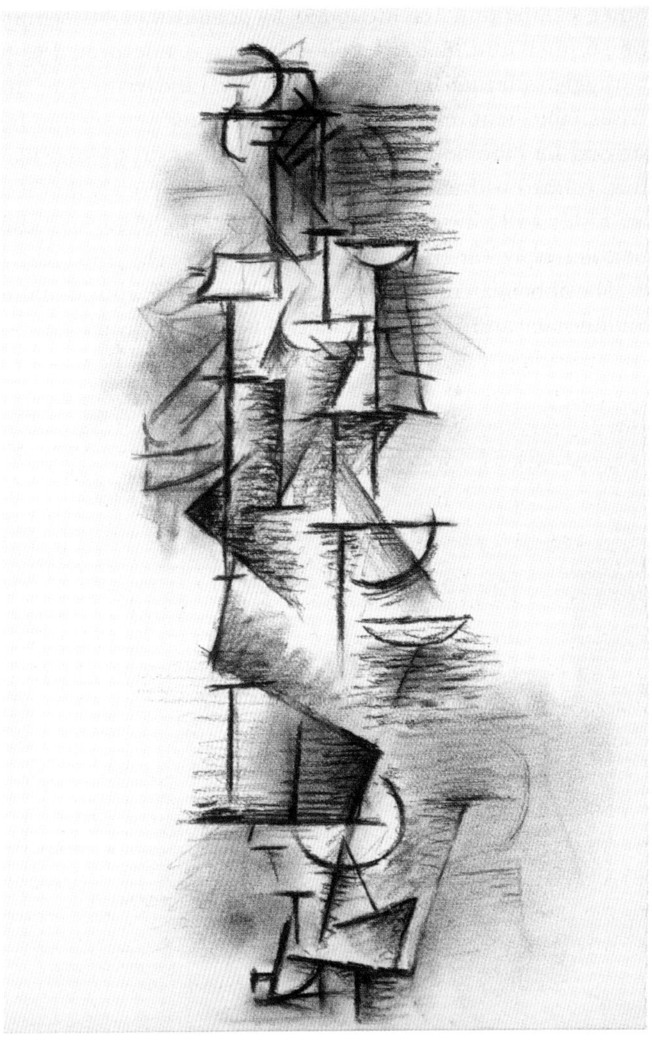

0.1 Pablo Picasso, ***Standing Female Nude***, 1910. Charcoal on paper, 19 × 12⅜" (48.3 × 31.4 cm). The Museum of Modern Art, New York, Alfred Stieglitz Collection, 1949. Acc.n.: 49.70.34.

confidence in the quality and importance of non-European Modernism. In the buildup to World War II, artists from Europe feeling threatened by the rise of fascism began emigrating to the U.S., joining the domestic flow of artists into New York to produce a vibrant art community that operated increasingly independently of Europe. As the U.S. took on the role of political superpower in the 1940s and 1950s, New York became the capital of the twentieth-century world and its art came to represent the cultural complement to its financial and political hegemony.

In 1958, as if to confirm this rise to power, the Museum of Modern Art mounted an exhibition to demonstrate what its chief curator of paintings, Alfred Barr, referred to as the "anxiety," "commitment," and "dreadful Freedom" of postwar American painting.[3] Curated by Dorothy Miller, "The New American Painting" (**fig. 0.2**) toured Europe as a celebration of U.S. Abstract Expressionism and as a cultural counterpart to the U.S.-sponsored campaign to rebuild postwar Europe and challenge Soviet influence in the early years of the Cold War. It had been argued since the late 1940s that Abstract Expressionism was proof of the depth of U.S. culture and "New American Painting," in conjunction with several other exhibitions, was designed to demonstrate its significance. In Berlin, Jackson Pollock's art was interpreted as a "struggle with the elements, with society, [and] with fate." In Basel, "the great reach of American painting" was seen to be striving for "the domination of space."[4] It was responses like this, echoed with even louder voices by U.S. critics, that led art historian Irving Sandler to title his 1977 chronicle of the period simply *The Triumph of American Painting*.[5]

The abbreviated history told here, with its repetition of the nation-state and military models—its capitals, avant-gardes, and sorties binding the fate of art history to geopolitical victories and defeats—illuminates the imperialist conception of Modernism that would be critiqued in the second half of the twentieth century. In the face of this apparently inexorable connection between modern art and political power, its practitioners and advocates, from Manet to the Abstract Expressionists, took pains to define themselves in contrast to the politicians and businessmen. The conviction of the Dada artists in World War I Europe that their art was made "to remind the world that there are independent men, beyond war and nationalism, who live for other ideals," demonstrated a powerful politics of negation.[6] Kazimir Malevich's Suprematism, created in tandem with the Russian Revolution, demonstrated a parallel between avant-garde art and revolutionary politics. "I think [artistic] freedom can be attained only after our ideas about the organizations of solids has been completely smashed," Malevich proclaimed, echoing the sentiments of those seeking to transform Russian society on a more practical level.[7] Art of the twentieth century, he wrote, "will become a new architecture: it will transfer [its] forms from the surface of the canvas to space."[8] Whether nihilist or revolutionary, modern art was defined from the inside as a campaign toward a world apart from the intellectually and aesthetically impoverished state of daily life.

Negation continued as the dominant voice of modern art at mid-century. Mark Rothko explained that, though the New York School of Abstract Expressionist painters had been strongly influenced by the Russian avant-garde, it was not for its political idealism. The new American painting, he asserted, was in fact aimed to escape the binds of the society, even a more perfect one. "The progression of a painter's work," he wrote, was "toward the elimination of all obstacles ...

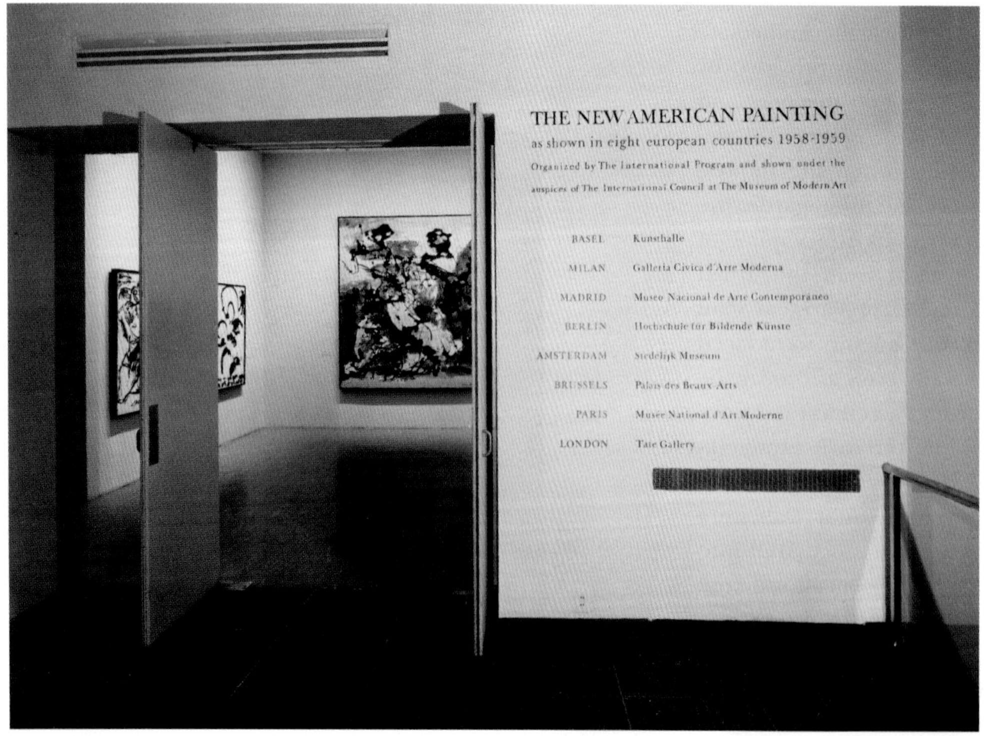

0.2 Installation view of the exhibition "The New American Painting as shown in eight European countries 1958–1959." The Museum of Modern Art, New York, May 28 through September 8, 1959.

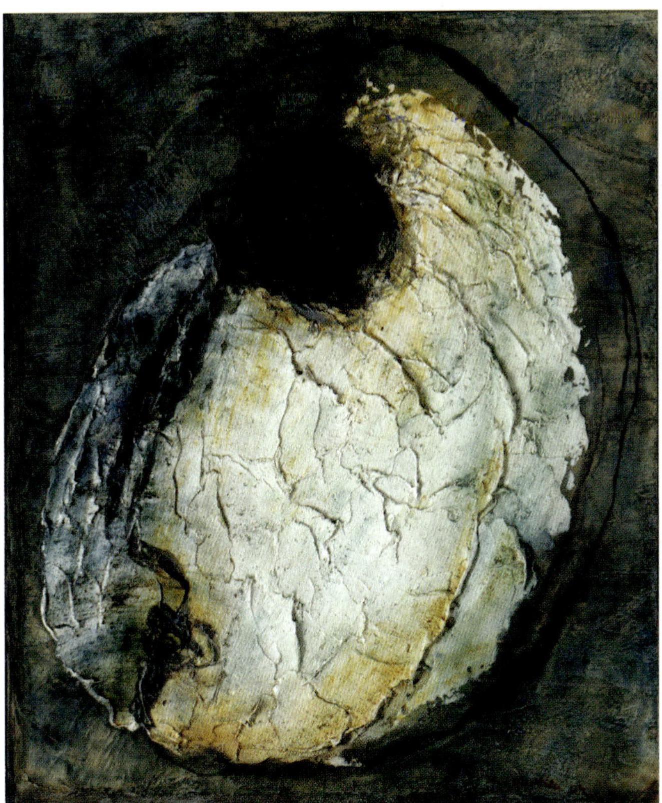

0.3 Jean Fautrier, ***Head of a Hostage #1***, 1944. Oil and pigments on paper mounted on canvas, 25³⁄₁₆ × 21¼" (64 × 54 cm). The National Museum of Art, Osaka. Courtesy Malingue S.A., Paris.

[including] memory [and] history."[9] In Europe, art critic Michel Tapié, a strong advocate for the postwar avant-garde European painters including Jean Dubuffet (1901–85) and Jean Fautrier (1898–1964) (**fig. 0.3**), explained that the Dada reaction to World War I was significant for its "total liquidation of form" and corresponding obliteration of moral as well as aesthetic foundations.[10] Post-World War II artists, Tapié asserted, had merely to repeat the Dada message. "[W]ithout possible recourse to our personal ethic," the contemporary artist, he wrote, "pulverizes our domestic reflexes too long conditioned by the undiscussed routine of our habits."[11] Everything about life and culture as it was, Tapié suggested, must be violently cast aside.

Artists and writers of the 1960s and 1970s would challenge the aggressive disengagement of the modern artist. Recognizing that art history was not only following political history by analogy, but was also actively engaged in the political life of nations, demanded a change in perspective. Swedish-born US Pop artist Claes Oldenburg captured this new attitude in 1961 when he said: "I am for an art that embroils itself with the everyday crap & still comes out on top."[12] As will be discussed in Chapter 1, and throughout the book, once artists, critics, and historians presented art as an integral and engaged part of society, narratives of resistance, exception, and difference became visible and alternative histories were written.

Clement Greenberg: Objects of Concern

Before modernist negation became an obstacle to artists such as Oldenburg in the 1960s, its was envisioned as a productive force of almost unlimited capacity. Nowhere was the historical urgency of modernism more forcefully argued than in the writing of U.S. critic Clement Greenberg (1909–94). Greenberg's critical output from the 1930s through the 1960s was the dominant expression of art theory in the twentieth century, establishing the criteria against which critics and artists would define their practices well into the 1970s. Describing the fate of culture in the 1930s, Greenberg famously wrote: "A society, as it becomes less and less able, in the course of its development, to justify the inevitability of its particular forms, breaks up the accepted notions upon which artists and writers must depend in large part for communication with their audience."[13] Western society, according to Greenberg, had reached this point. In the context of 1930s New York welcoming refugees from European fascism, it is not surprising that he would recognize meaning itself to be under siege. Greenberg continued: "All the verities informed by religion, authority, tradition, style, are thrown into question and the writer or artist is no longer able to estimate the response of his audience to the symbols and references with which he works." Though written in the face of the crises of the 1930s, this description suits the state of affairs during the social unrest of the 1960s and 1970s and by the turn of the millennium, the idea that truths are not absolute but instead depend on variables of culture and history would be taken for granted by artists.

Greenberg, however, unlike late-twentieth-century historians assessed the crisis of meaning before him and found fault with society. He objected not to the idea of inevitable forms that would trouble the Poststructuralists, but to the manner in which Western civilization had destroyed them. Indeed, Greenberg's primary contribution was to argue that Western artists, by basing their work on the materials with which it was being created, an approach called "formalism," were able to produce new forms of reliable communication, reassert an inevitable form of expression, and thereby advance civilization. Greenbergian formalism further asserted that true artists by conscience and necessity separated themselves from middle-class society and isolated their art from society's weaknesses. Rejecting the appearances as well as the content of the fickle, petty, and destructive world of bourgeois life, the artist thus embraced abstraction. However, as Greenberg notes, abstract art "cannot be arbitrary and accidental, but must stem from obedience to some worthy constraint or original." Daily life having been deemed unworthy, artists were instructed to look instead to his or her materials. "The excitement of their art," he concluded," lie[s] most of all in its pure preoccupation with the invention and arrangements of spaces, surfaces, shapes, colors etc." Greenberg's legacy rests on in his conviction that quality in art and the survival of culture was determined by the perceptivity with which artists considered and revealed the properties of their materials.

In the final lines of his foundational essay "Avant-Garde and Kitsch" (1939), Greenberg declared that "advances in culture ... no less than advances in science and industry corrode the very society" that make them possible. Thus an art seeking independence from society holds the power to change it. A decade after World War II, however, one can perceive in Greenberg's writing a shift as the social mission of the artist is traded for increased attention on the individual. In his 1955 "American-Type Painting," written in support of New York School painters such as Jackson Pollock (1912–56) and Willem de Kooning (1904–97) (**fig. 0.4**), Greenberg, characterized the artist as an isolated figure struggling "to maintain the irreplaceability and renew the vitality of art in the face of a society bent in principle on rationalizing everything."[14] In the context of the 1950s Cold War and curatorial efforts such as "New American Painting," however, the rugged individualism of such criticism took on a rather doctrinaire tone. In fact, by the 1960s, *The New York Times* could credit Greenberg with being largely responsible for the success of U.S. art on the world stage. With such power, statements such as "It seems to be the law of modernism—thus one that applies to almost all art that remains truly alive in our time—that the conventions not essential to the viability of a medium be discarded as soon as they are recognized" came to be read as proscriptions and led to generations of artist and critics treating formalism as a new faith.[15] Nonetheless, in many artists' studios, from the late 1950s through the 1970s, formalism was being questioned. As art historian Leo Steinberg wrote of responses to the painted numbers, letters, symbols, and things of Jasper Johns (b. 1930) (**fig. 0.5**), "Even those whose long-practiced art appreciation had educated them to ignore a picture's subject as irrelevant to its quality talked and could talk about little else—though they tried."[16] A "half-century of formalist indoctrination" was being brought to a close.[17]

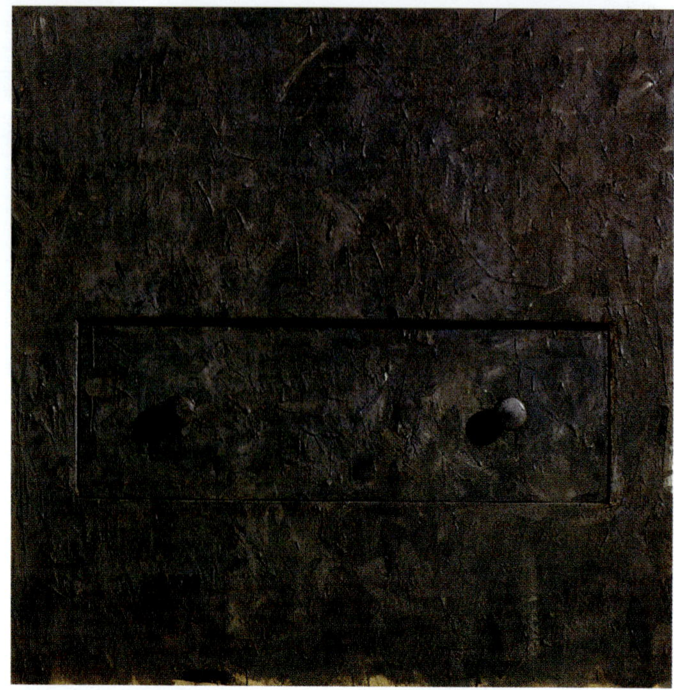

0.5 Jasper Johns, ***Drawer***, 1957. Encaustic and assemblage on canvas, 30¾ × 30¾ × 2" (78 × 78 × 5 cm). The Rose Museum of Art. Gevirtz-Mnuchin Purchase Fund.

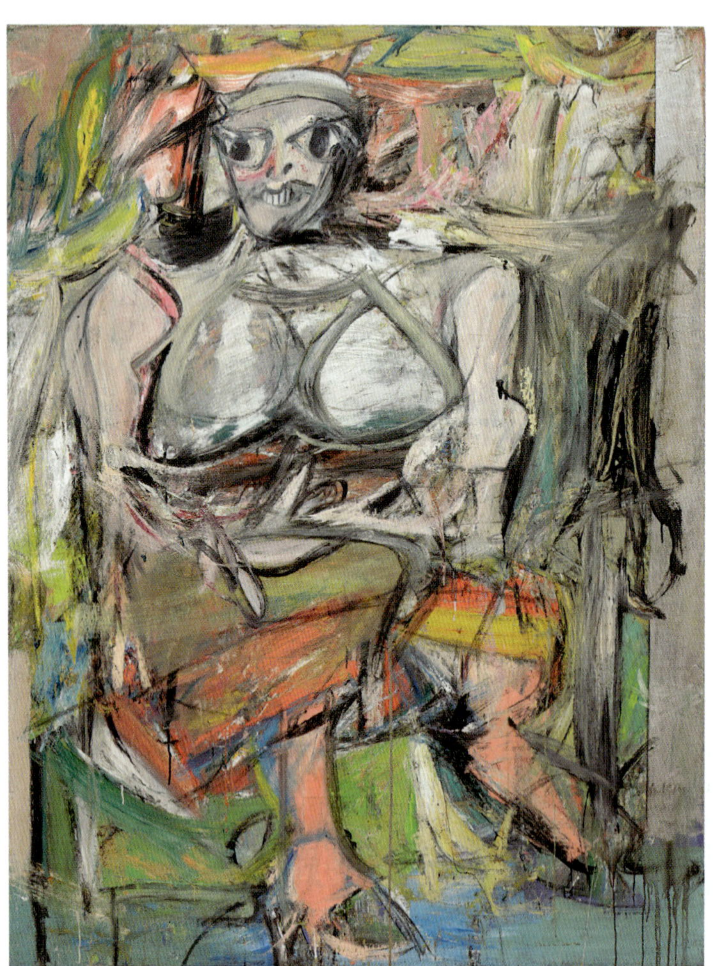

0.4 Willem De Kooning, ***Woman I***, 1950–52. Oil on canvas, 6' 3⅞" × 58" (192.7 × 147.3 cm). The Museum of Modern Art, New York. Purchase. 478.1953.

Beginning the Contemporary

Johns's and Oldenburg's generation faced the problem of deconstructing Modernism, breaking down its assumptions about universal truths and necessary forms. As a result of their efforts, artists beginning their careers later, in the 1970s and after, were faced with an abundance of alternative histories and conflicting realities as the once-dominant narrative of progressive or evolutionary Modernism was being swept aside. Some of their work will be presented in the pages that follow, and the art history it tells extends around the globe. Looking critically at contemporary reality was as important to artists newly liberated from the restriction of the Cultural Revolution in China hanging their work at the "Stars Arts Exhibition" in Beijing in 1979 as it was for appropriation artists testing the nature of representation in media-saturated New York for the "Pictures" exhibition in 1977 or for the "Volumen" generation crafting a contemporary identity for Cuban artists in Havana in 1981. Likewise, once the forms of modern art appeared no longer inevitable in Greenbergian terms, but ideological—to use Althusser's term referring to the role culture plays in reinforcing existing power relations—artists faced the question of what their efforts to create with abstract form might mean. Numerous so-called "neo" styles developed, the first being Neo-Expressionism, which had a prehistory in Germany in the 1960s before being catapulted, controversially, to artworld stardom at the German Pavilion at the 39th Venice Biennale and at several New York galleries in 1980.

The late 1970s and early 1980s also provided a dramatically changing political terrain. In addition to China initiating reforms that would turn it into an economic superpower by the end of the century, the Middle East was asserting itself, first as the linchpin in the oil crisis of the 1970s that nearly crippled portions of the Western economy, and then by reshuffling religious and nationalist priorities with the Islamic Revolution in Iran in 1979. The societal effects of these changes provide a foundation for a range of artistic investigations at the turn of the millennium. Meanwhile, both the U.K. under Margaret Thatcher (elected 1979) and the U.S. under Ronald Reagan (elected 1980) embraced policies that led to a reassertion of national power and a redistribution of wealth that exacerbated the gap between the rich and poor, especially in the U.S. The impact of Reagan-era politics became a magnet for radical art in New York. Independent arts organizations such as Collaborative Projects (CoLab), founded in 1977, and Group Material, Fashion Moda, and ABC No Rio, founded in 1979, provided a platform for aggressive and innovative reinventions of realist and political art in the 1980s, as well as a counterpoint to the more financially driven galleries in the lower Manhattan SoHo district.

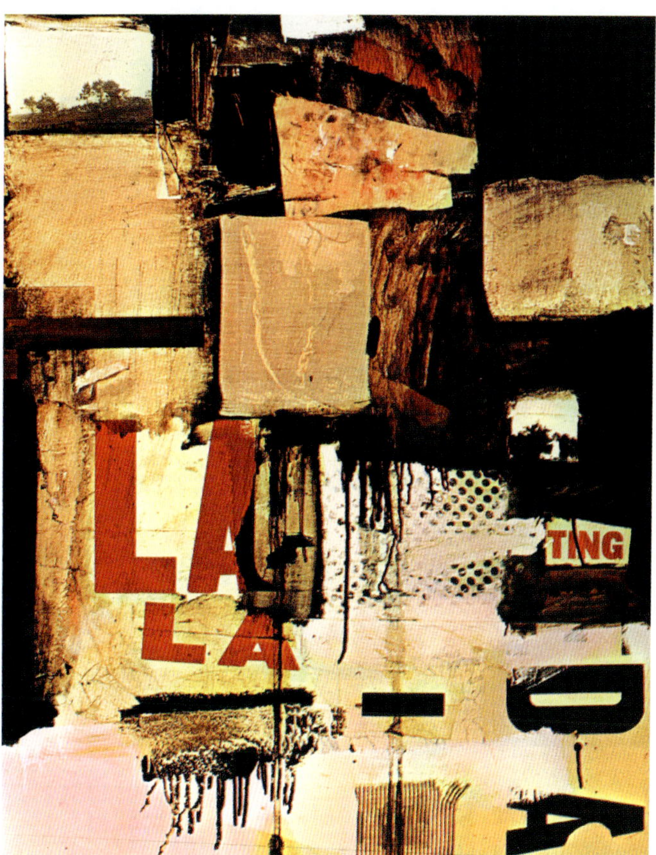

0.6 Robert Rauschenberg, *Thaw*, 1958. Oil, printed paper, printed reproductions, map, and fabric on canvas, 50¼ × 40" (127.6 × 101.6 cm). Whereabouts unknown.

Exhibitions and the Art Market

As artists and intellectuals were challenging the habits and limits of the art world, the art market was being reinvented as well. While artists, theorists, and historians were contesting the very models for global culture that had conferred victory upon the new capital, the place of New York as the center of the art world was—and to a degree still is—being vigorously asserted. In the 1970s, the primary market—where artworks are sold for the first time, usually through galleries, at relatively fixed prices—and the secondary market—responsible for the sale of art that has previously been purchased, with values based on auction results—dovetailed dramatically for the first time, breathing life into the economic machine that continues to this day to generate wealth from art. In 1973, the art world watched with a mixture of excitement and dismay as Robert and Ethel Scull sold highlights of their collection of Pop art at Sotheby's auction house for a seven-figure profit. Prior to the Scull sale, auction houses rarely concerned themselves with the work of living artists, especially young ones, because established values had not been determined. Much of the Scull collection had been bought directly from the artists for very little money in the first years of their careers. *Thaw* (1958) by Robert Rauschenberg (1925–2008) (**fig. 0.6**), which had been purchased by the Sculls for $900 right after it was painted, sold for $85,000. The sale thus established contemporary art as an investment item. The artists did not directly benefit from this financial appreciation, but they did get a firsthand look at the future, and ultimately saw the value of their work on the primary market increase accordingly. The pace of inflation has hardly slowed in the twenty-first century. *200 One-Dollar Bills* (1962) (**fig. 0.7**) by Andy Warhol (1928–87), which was first seen at auction in the 1986 Scull estate, when it realized $385,000, sold at Sotheby's New York in 2009 for $43,762,500. U.S. Pop art, which has a fascination with the commodity at its heart, has proved itself to be a reliable asset. Over the past decade, the status of New York as the center of contemporary art may have been called into question, but its position as the capital of the art market has remained stable.

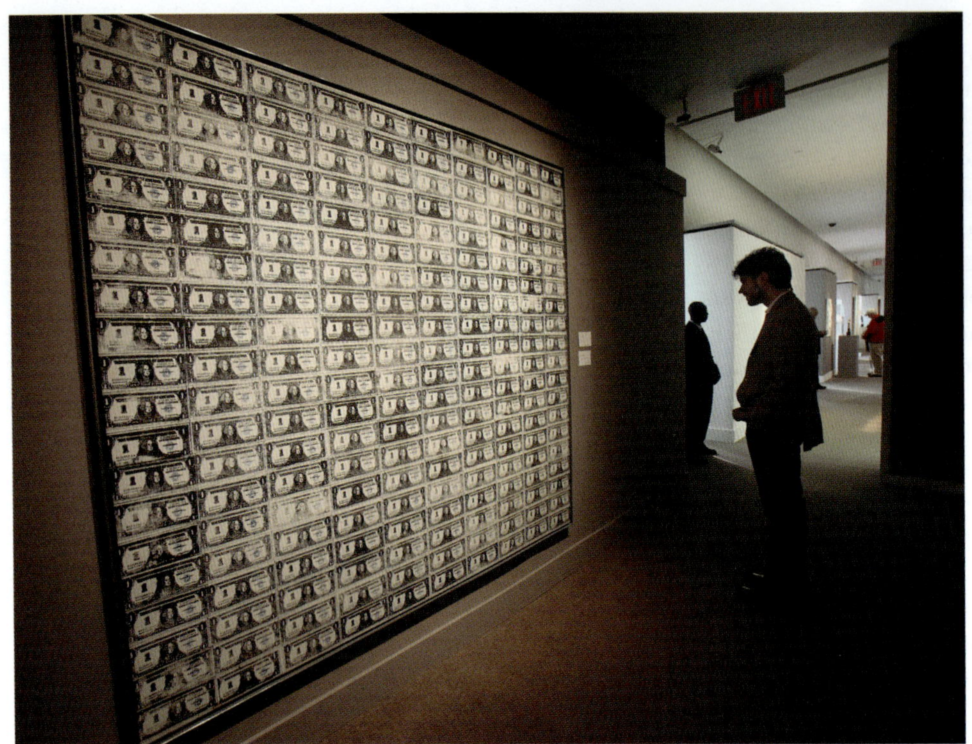

0.7 Andy Warhol, ***200 One-Dollar Bills***, 1962. Silkscreen ink and pencil on canvas, 80¼ × 92¼" (203.8 × 234.3 cm). Displayed during a preview of Sotheby's Evening Sale of Contemporary Art in New York City, 30 October 2009; sale November 11, 2009.

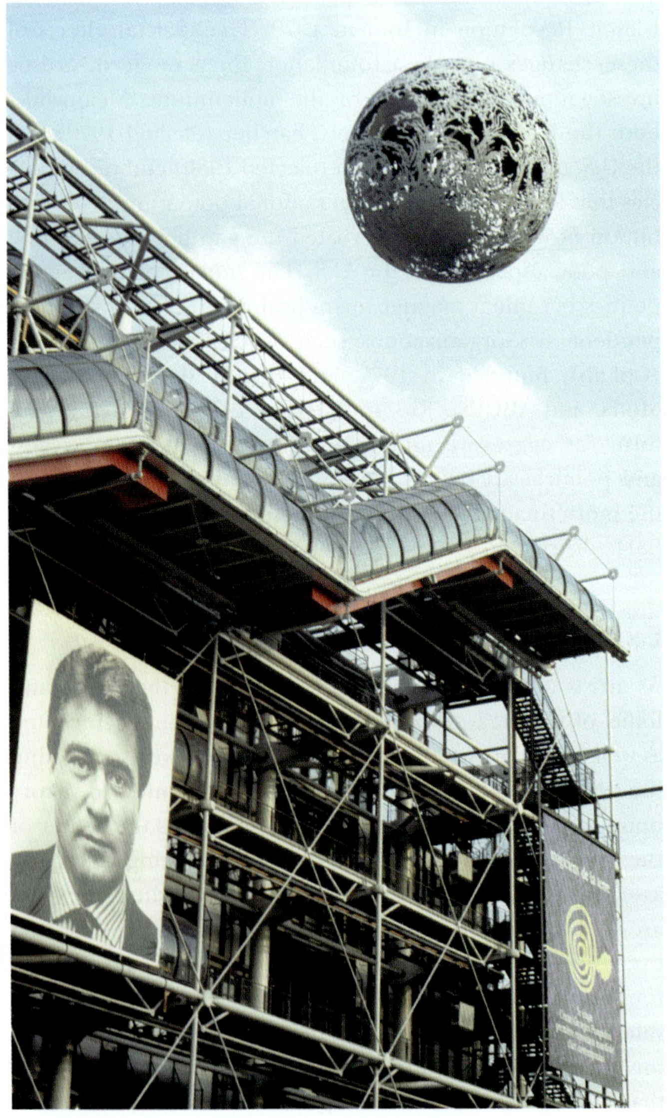

0.8 "Magiciens de la Terre" exhibition at the Centre Georges Pompidou, Paris, 1989. The poster on the side of the building is ***The Casual Passer-by I met at 11.09 a.m. Paris*** (1971) by Braco Dimitrijevic (b.1948), and hanging above is ***Globe*** (1989) by Neil Dawson (b.1948).

The market responded to the growing interest in contemporary art by seeking out new styles in unexplored regions of the art world and celebrating them, first with exhibitions, then with sales. Throughout the 1980s and 1990s, the cycle of biennials, largely invitational and international showcases of contemporary art, grew exponentially. Cities including Havana, Johannesburg, and Shanghai joined established venues such as Venice and New York to host these temporary exhibitions of contemporary art, and the arts calendar filled up with events attended by a cadre of curators, critics, and collectors. The exposure provided by these exhibitions, which often integrated local work with that of international art stars, drew attention to the limits of museum programming in the major Western museums. The first Havana Biennial in 1984, founded as a gesture of unity among Third World nations, proved a touchstone event, demonstrating the depth of artistic production beyond the borders most often surveyed by the art world. Parisian curator Jean-Hubert Martin remarked in the mid-1980s that museums in Europe and the U.S. seemed blind to 80 percent of the planet. His response was "Magiciens de la Terre" (1989) (**fig. 0.8**), held in several venues in Paris including the Centre Pompidou. As a challenge to standard museum practice, Martin juxtaposed installations and objects created by artists from all over the world: Established artworld figures were displayed in the company of Tibetan sand painters. By the turn of the millennium, international exhibitions with long histories such as the Venice Biennale (founded in 1895) and Documenta in Germany (1955), which both rose to prominence as venues for asserting national identity and power, were handed over to curators intent on turning them into platforms for rethinking contemporary art, its display, and its audience.

In the twenty-first century, the biennial circuit has become intertwined with those of art fairs and auctions. The work of artists shown on the former is often then bought and sold on the latter. In 2007, the 52nd Venice Biennale, Documenta 12, and Sculpture Projekte Munster 07, three of the most prestigious international art exhibitions, collaborated with the most prominent art fair, Art Basel, to promote what they called "Grand Tour 2007," a package deal providing visitors with travel to and accommodation at all four events. New art markets have opened at the turn of the millennium. Significant sales and collecting communities have developed all over the world, with particular concentration in the growing sectors of Asia, Russia, and the Middle East. The established auction houses have responded to this growth, achieving, for example, significant sales of Russian contemporary art in Moscow, Middle Eastern contemporary art in Dubai, and Asian and Southeast Asian contemporary art in Hong Kong. In 2012 mainland China entered the global market with the joint venture initiative between state-owned Beijing GeHua Art Company and Sotheby's. Those same auction houses are now also buying galleries, handling sales for living artists, and sponsoring art fairs. Galleries, paying equal attention to the emerging economies, have been strategically opening branches far from their traditional New York, London, or Berlin bases, and selectively importing international artists. Meanwhile, configurations of dealers, curators, and collectors outside the West connect art communities in Beijing, Shanghai, Guangzhou, and Hong Kong, or Havana, Mexico City, and São Paulo.

This centrifugal movement has been complemented by a centripetal impulse illustrated by the 2010 and 2011 BRIC sales at the London auction house Phillips de Pury. "BRIC" is a term used by economists and investors to designate the four emergent markets of Brazil, Russia, India, and China. In contrast to the internationally based sales that mimic the biennial circuit, the London BRIC sale reinvented the capital/periphery model, bringing the cultural products of far-flung and culturally diverse economic powers to a single venue for exhibition and evaluation. Moreover, the list of lots read like a checklist for a contemporary biennial. Though the metaphor of intersecting and changing networks reflects the organic and social aspects of contemporary art, earlier models have not entirely disappeared. Like artists and art historians, the art market has established its own network of interests untethered by, but not indifferent to, the previous artworld cartography.

Narrative and Methods

Art Since 1980 is organized roughly chronologically and uses a number of strategies to discuss contemporary art. While the book presents a historical narrative, it also addresses how artworks are formally produced, critically received, theoretically constructed, socially defined, and historically situated. In discussions of some works, issues of the biography, history, class, race, or gender of the artist(s) will take priority, while in others technique, craft, and materials will have precedence. Enlisting a variety of perspectives in this way is intended to respond to the heterodox nature of contemporary artistic production and to suggest the intellectual advantage of examining art, and sometimes a single artwork, from different positions. The text is intended to document and illustrate a history of art within changing conditions of production and viewing.

The main narrative starts in the United States, widens its view first to include those cities that once constituted satellite art centers, and then to consider contemporary art in a global context. As with any art-historical survey, there is far more art left out than there is included. This is not intended to be an exhaustive study; there is too much interesting art being made today for any book to address it all. Rather, this survey is designed to raise enough issues of form, content, and context to illuminate any work the reader might encounter in exhibitions of contemporary art. I have chosen examples that reflect significant movements and themes in contemporary art and that, between them, can be seen to constitute a history of the period. There will be readers who search the index in vain for a particular artist they love. Great artists have been left out. There will be readers who puzzle at the attention devoted to one artist rather than another. In selecting works for discussion, I have chosen to write primarily about art that students and museum visitors can actually go and see, and it is here that the institutional forces of the art world are certainly at play in the choices I have made. *Art Since 1980* is a companion to the efforts of thousands of arts professionals around the world who do not make art but who live for it, spending their intellectual, emotional, and economic lives putting it in front of audiences.

Each discussion of a particular piece of art in this book is intended to be taken as a more general model of how art can be examined, what questions can be asked, and what kind of answers one might expect to glean. Every work opens into different, intersecting histories. For clarity's sake, many works are presented in the context with which they are most often linked. As such, most of the contemporary Chinese art here appears as part of a discussion of the history of art in China and its introduction to the world stage in the early 1990s. Likewise, a number of African-American artists rose to prominence in the same decade due not only to the quality of their work, but also to a more general emerging interest in themes of identity and race within the art world and culture at large. It is hoped that the depth such work adds to the discussion of art and politics in China or race in the U.S. will not keep readers from asking what the same work also tells us about painting or experience, two of the themes taken up elsewhere in the text. Each encounter with a work in this book is intended to invite the reader to engage, interrogate, and enjoy art that is not found here.

1

Discovering the Contemporary

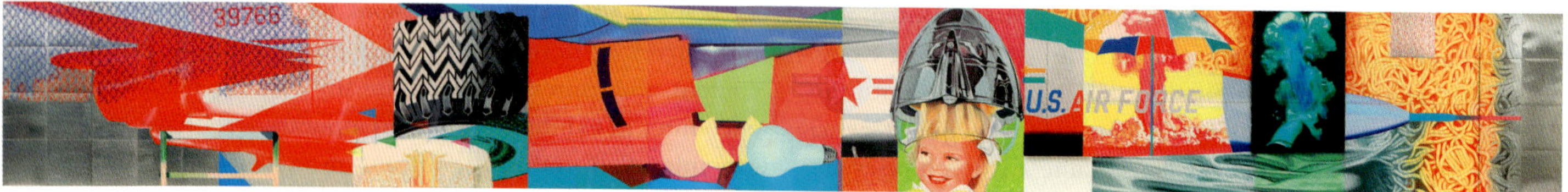

1.1 James Rosenquist, *F-111*, 1964–65. Oil on canvas with aluminum, 10 × 86' (3.04 × 26.21 m). The Museum of Modern Art, New York. Purchase Gift of Mr. and Mrs. Alex L. Hillman and Lillie P. Bliss Bequest (both by exchange). Acc. n.: 473.1996.a-w.

In 1968, the Metropolitan Museum of Art in New York displayed *F-111* (1964–65) by James Rosenquist (b. 1933) in the company of works by European masters of the seventeenth, eighteenth, and nineteenth centuries (**fig. 1.1**). The painting is a monumental expression of U.S. Pop art, a full-scale image of an F-111 military aircraft overlaid with overlapping images drawn from U.S. culture, mixing the innocuous—a girl getting her hair done, cake, spaghetti—with the destructive and horrific—a mushroom cloud and the plane itself. The imposing size of the piece and its ominous juxtapositions were intended by the artist to express the sense of fear he felt in the face of nuclear proliferation. He also created it to serve as a rebuttal to those who thought that the threat of war was a thing of the past and that contemporary Pop art "had nothing to say."[1] Here were the details of life as it was being lived presented in the billboard advertising style in which it was being represented on the streets outside the museum. The event marked a change in the perception of contemporary art. The curators and directors of the Metropolitan Museum pronounced the work a commentary on the omnipresence of the military in American society and hung it with such well-known images of politics and power as Jacques-Louis David's *Death of Socrates* (1787), Emanuel Gottlieb Leutze's *Washington Crossing the Delaware* (1851), and Nicolas Poussin's *Rape of the Sabine Women* (1633–34). By juxtaposing Rosenquist's work with classic history paintings, the museum invested Pop art with the gravity of history, history with the immediacy of Pop, and the Met itself with the cachet of the contemporary.

Within a few years of Rosenquist's Metropolitan Museum debut, all of the other institutions of high culture in New York had begun to embrace contemporary art. Every prominent American Pop artist was given a major museum retrospective, despite the fact that their careers were less than a decade old. Paintings such as Roy Lichtenstein's (1923–97) *Golf Ball* (**fig. 1.2**), which in 1962 had inspired his dealer, Leo Castelli, to exclaim enthusiastically, "Look at that picture! There is not an idea in it," were being compared to the work of David and Mondrian.[2] Not everyone was pleased. "Pop Art at the Met? Sire, this is no longer the revolution, it is the Terror," stated the critic Sidney Tillim, comparing the situation to the worst excesses of the French Revolution.[3] Even if overstated, Tillim's critique raised issues that remain contentious. If it was now museums, rather than churches or aristocrats, that determined the cultural value of art, he argued, works such as *F-111* reflected not true resistance but instead the result of career-minded artists compromising with publicity-seeking museums. After the efforts of modern artists from Courbet to Pollock to evade existing power structures, Pop now appeared to be collaborating with them enthusiastically. Tillim and others felt that artists had sacrificed the outsider position that, following the logic of Clement Greenberg, had permitted the Modernist avant-garde to challenge the status quo.

In truth, Tillim's objections to Rosenquist's inclusion in the Met lay in large part in the Pop artist's style. He disliked Rosenquist's use of montage, which involved layering independent graphic elements and thus resisting the custom of treating the painting as a unified whole. The broken rhythms

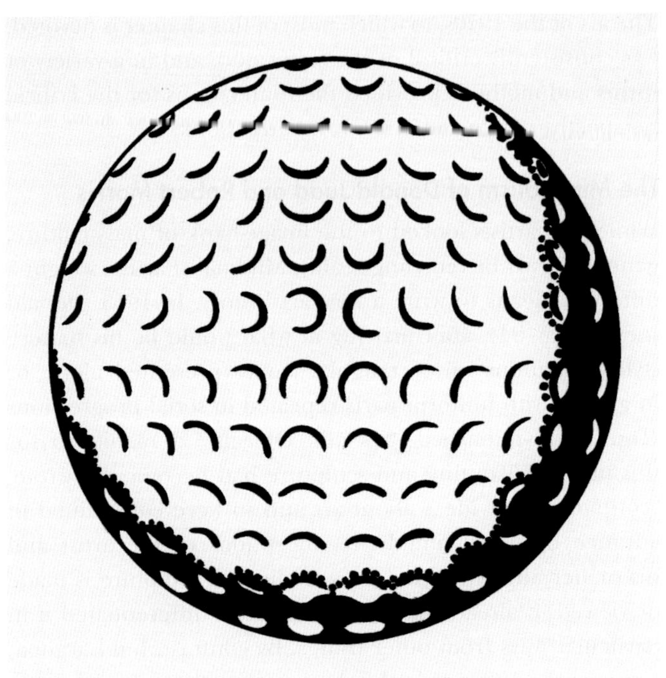

1.2 Roy Lichtenstein, *Golf Ball*, 1962. Oil on canvas, 32 × 32" (81.3 × 81.3 cm). Courtesy The Estate of Roy Lichtenstein.

of advertising imagery and disruptive juxtapositions of scale and color in *F-111* can be read as a deliberate rejection of the compositional devices of traditional painting. This style also rebutted the expectation that art should make order out of the world rather than repeat its chaos. Four years later, in 1972, when Rosenquist was given a retrospective at the Whitney Museum of American Art in New York, the discord and disjunction of his paintings was interpreted as a metaphor for contemporary experience.[4] In effect, the contemporary was perceived as those experiences, in art and life that were being dislodged from narratives either of progress or of formalist distance upon which modernists had relied for understanding the world. Critics increasingly pointed to a correspondence between the formal properties of 1960s art and the nature of the radically changing world that surrounded them. In fact formalism, the commitment to prioritizing formal qualities of a work of art over its content, was being transformed in these years into a means of discovering content. Leo Steinberg described Rauschenberg's work as "flatbed painting," one of the lasting critical metaphors invented in response to the art of the immediate post-World War II period.[5] The collisions across the surface of Rosenquist's painting and the collection of materials on Rauschenberg's surfaces were being viewed as models for a new form of realism, one that captured the relationships between people and things in the world outside the studio. The lesson that formal analysis could lead back into, rather than away from, content, often with very specific social significance, would be central to the creation and reception of late-twentieth-century art.

New Movements and New Metaphors

Artists all over the world shared U.S. Pop artists' interest in creating new metaphors from the appearances and experiences of everyday life. The international artists' group Fluxus directed its attention to the artistic potential of the everyday. From the Latin term for "flow," Fluxus was a loose grouping of progressive international artists who worked in diverse media. "Why does everything I see that's beautiful like cups and kisses and sloshing feet have to be made into just a part of something fancier and bigger? Why can't I just use it for its own sake?" asked Fluxus artist Dick Higgens.[6] In a similar spirit, Fluxus member Nam June Paik created *Zen for Film* (1964–65) (**fig. 1.3**), which consists of twenty-three minutes of leader—the blank strip at the beginning of a reel, used to

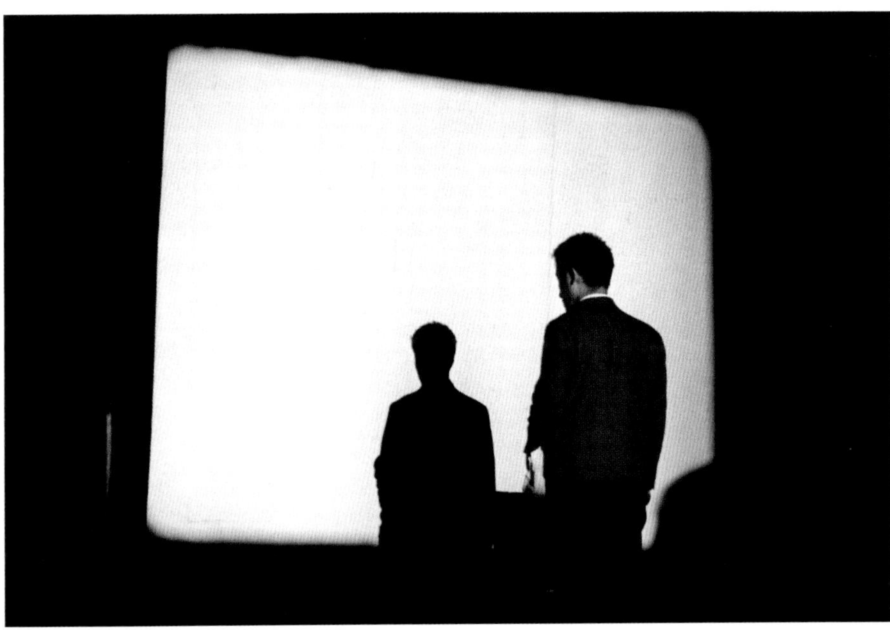

1.3 Nam June Paik, *Zen for Film*, 1964–65, Photo by Peter Moore © Estate of Peter Moore/ Licensed by VAGA, NY. Courtesy the Nam June Paik Estate.

help threading in a projector—so that the viewer watches an imageless movie made of just the physical film itself. Meanwhile, the Japanese collective Hi Red Center marked off a section of the Ginza financial district of Tokyo and, dressed as surgeons, began the absurd task of sterilizing it. *Cleaning Event (Campaign to Promote Cleanliness and Order in the Metropolitan Area)* (1964) (**fig. 1.4**), announced with a sign reading "Be Clean!" in English and "Soji-chu" ("Cleaning Now") in Japanese, used ordinary, even official-looking actions in a real place to direct viewers' attention toward larger political events: in particular, the Japanese government's attempt to brighten its image in advance of the forthcoming summer Olympics.

While artists such as Rosenquist, Paik, and Hi Red Center utilized the products of contemporary society, isolating and examining its component parts, other groups, specifically Minimalist and Process artists, carried out investigations into the processes of art making and explored the properties of new non-traditional art materials. Such artists represented an urgent desire to redefine the focus of art and the role of the artist. As the 1970s wore on, many artists came to feel that Pop, Minimalist and Process art were only addressing part of the issue; these movements interrogated the nature of reality as it was, but left questions regarding how existing forms acquired meaning and how reality might be changed unanswered. Questions of meaning are philosophical, social, and political and the 1970s ended with artists having begun to inflect their practice according to each of these terms. Conceptual, feminist, and political artists of this second postwar generation set out toward a wider examination of the relationships between history, society, and art. The art of the 1970s, to which most of this chapter is devoted, was consistently critical of the status quo, and in a variety of forms and methods provided the foundations for the critical perspectives discussed in the rest of this book.

The Minimalism of Donald Judd and Robert Morris

While Pop artists looked to the image-bank of mass culture, generating art by recycling reality, Minimalist artists sought a different means to write a new art history. In 1965, Donald Judd (1928–94), after arriving at what would be his mature style—variations on rectangular boxes presented alone or in groups with uniform parts repeated in serial progressions (**fig. 1.5**)—published "Specific Objects," a manifesto for this new art. Painting and sculpture had become, he wrote, "containers" for ideas about art and so were constrained in advance by unexamined preconceptions of the artist and his or her audience.[7] Before a traditional sculpture is made or viewed, it already had an identity that differentiated it in particular ways from other things. By contrast, Judd argued, artists of the 1960s wished to be free of such a priori assumptions and so avoided resemblance to sculptural traditions. As these new works forged a new history of art they activated the space around them in a very particular and even aggressive fashion. A "specific object," he explained, did not sit passively waiting to be observed; it interrupted the serenity of the gallery or museum, eschewed the hieratical platform of the pedestal, and claimed real space as its own. Like the careening images in *F-III* or the flatbed of Rauschenberg's combine, Judd was describing not only a contemporary approach to art making but also a new metaphor for understanding contemporary life.

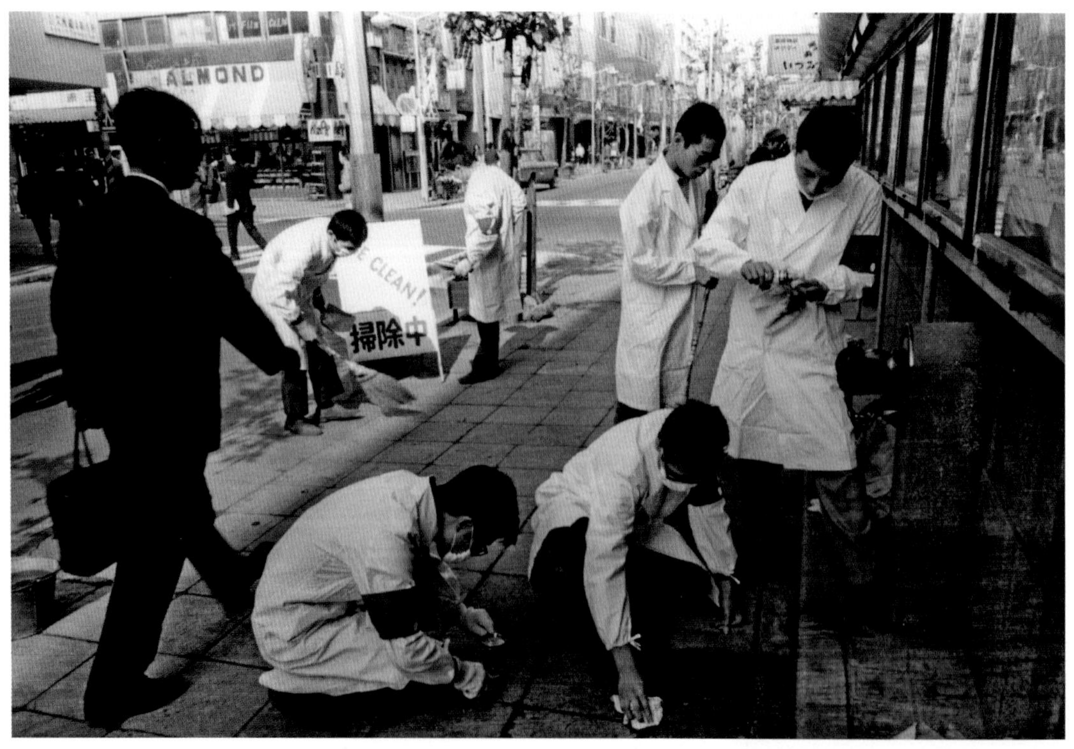

1.4 Hi Red Center, ***Hi Red Center's Cleaning Event*** *(Campaign to Promote Cleanliness and Order in the Metropolitan Area)*, October 16, 1964. Performance piece. Photograph courtesy the artist and sepiaEYE.

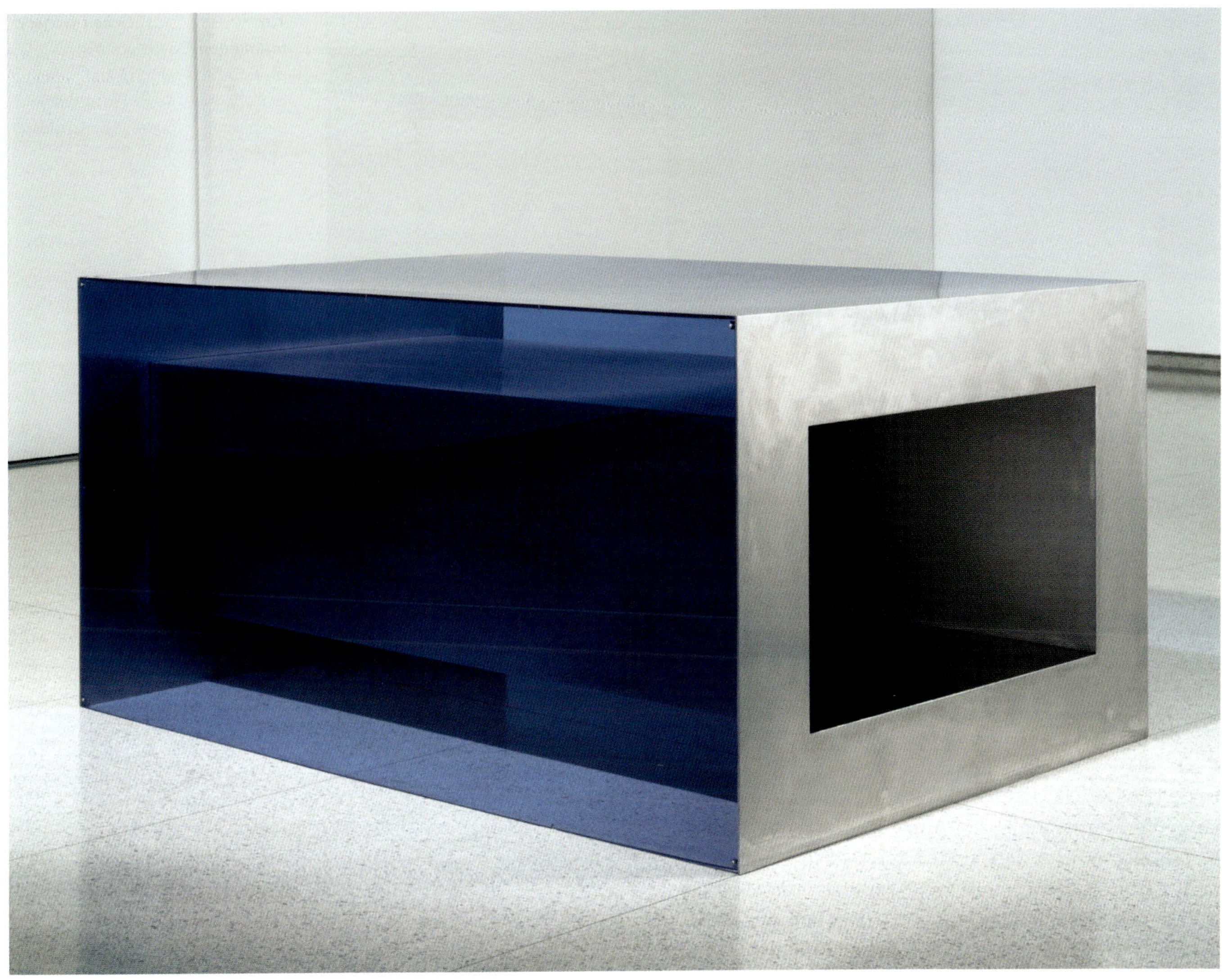

1.5 Donald Judd, *Untitled*, 1968. Stainless steel, plexiglass, overall 33 × 67⅞ × 48" (83.82 × 172.4 × 121.92 cm). From the exhibition "Art in Our Time: 1950 to the Present," Walker Art Center, Minneapolis, 5 September 1999 to 2 September 2001. Collection Walker Art Center.

Judd, himself, created objects where the dimensions, the character of the materials, and the relationships between the parts were all immediately self-evident. Anything suggested by one part of the work, must be born out by the whole. There were to be no mysteries to which the artist held a secret key, or any unique point of view that would explain the work. Likewise for works with multiple parts, any arrangement must be made so that the viewer could independently glean its logic; there were to be no complicated patterns, symbolic arrangements, or random or intuitive compositions. To borrow a quote from the Minimalist painter Frank Stella, "what you see is what you see."[8] Judd's intention was to disengage from the oppressive weight of history to present something that could be known completely and experienced directly. Yet even his abstract boxes could be seen as connecting to life. In a 1965 exhibition review, fellow artist Robert Smithson (1938–73) identified Judd's sources—a rather traditional art-historical endeavor. Behind Judd's abstractions, however, which Smithson found exquisitely beautiful, "Saturnian" even, lay references neither to earlier artists nor even to images from popular culture, but rather to commercial suppliers: Bernstein Brothers, Tinsmiths; Allied Plastics; Rohn Haas Plexiglas; and Galvanox and Lavax finishes.[9] Judd trawled contemporary culture as eagerly as did the Pop artists, suggested Smithson; he just looked for different things.

Smithson's review hints at the emotional, even mystical, quality of Judd's work. The boxes are often optically complex sculptures that convey unpredictable effects through their knowable form. Robert Morris's (b. 1931) work resists this visual pleasure and transcendental potential in favor of a more physical brand of Minimalism. Morris's work of the mid-1960s is characterized by boxes that are as simple as Judd's, but they are made of wood and painted gray. The simplicity of the work and its lack of surface interest forces the viewer to pay less attention to the object itself and more to the relationship between it, the viewer, and the context—usually a gallery, sometimes a stage. Morris's sculptures

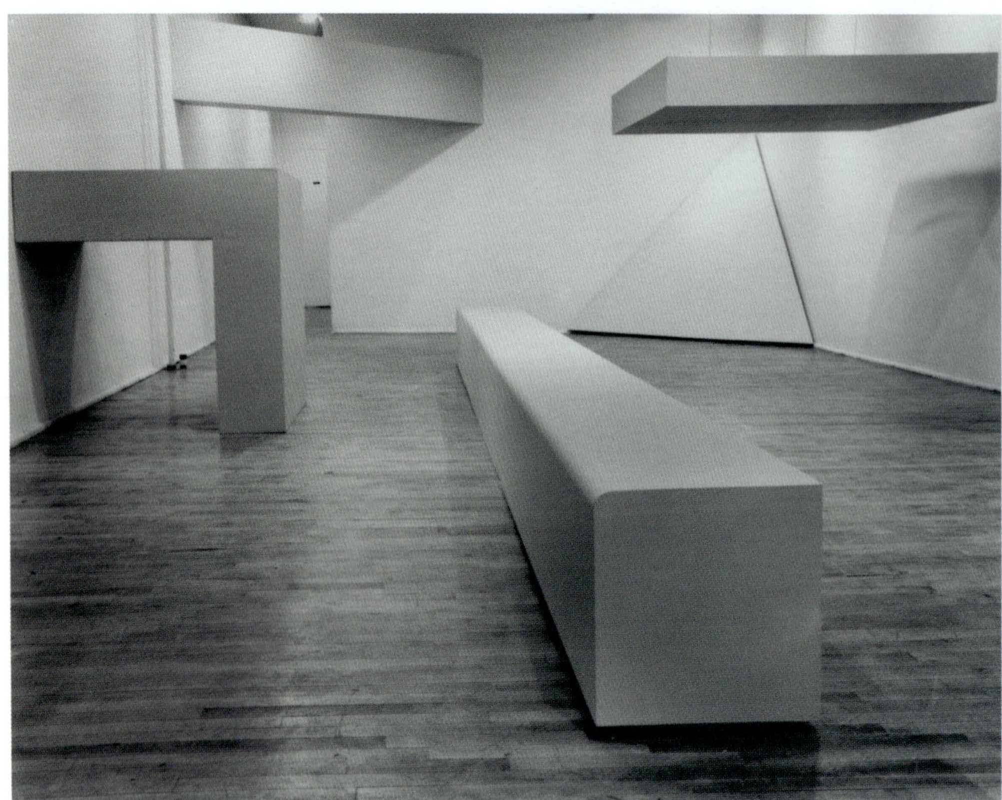

1.6 Robert Morris, ***Green Gallery Installation***. Seven painted plywood sculptures at the Green Gallery, New York, 1964. Varying dimensions. Courtesy Leo Castelli Gallery, New York.

were closely related to his interest in dance, particularly the choreography of Anna Halprin and Merce Cunningham, who were both interested in generating dance from ordinary movements. Installations such as that at the Green Gallery in 1964 (**fig. 1.6**) produce situations in which the viewer is made aware of his or her physical presence in the environment. Morris's objects exert themselves in the room, forcing the visitor to navigate through, under, and around the objects and any other people in the space. Morris explained his interests, noting that the "better new work takes relationships out of the work and makes them a function of space, light, and the viewer's field of vision. The object is but one of the terms in the newer aesthetic."[10] This is a Minimalism to be experienced, not merely observed.

Neo-Concrete Art

The Minimalists' interest in geometric compositions and the occupation of real space was shared by a variety of artists. Brazilian Neo-Concrete artists, of whom Lygia Clark (1920–88) and Hélio Oiticica (1937–80) were chief representatives, offer a particularly dynamic expression of these concerns. Moving beyond the isolated interest in geometry that they felt had limited the Concrete Art movement that preceded them, Neo-Concrete artists studied the relationships between materials, form (often but not exclusively geometric), and the environment. For Clark, geometry was a means toward the creation of spaces and incidents that inspired free movement and participation. Her early

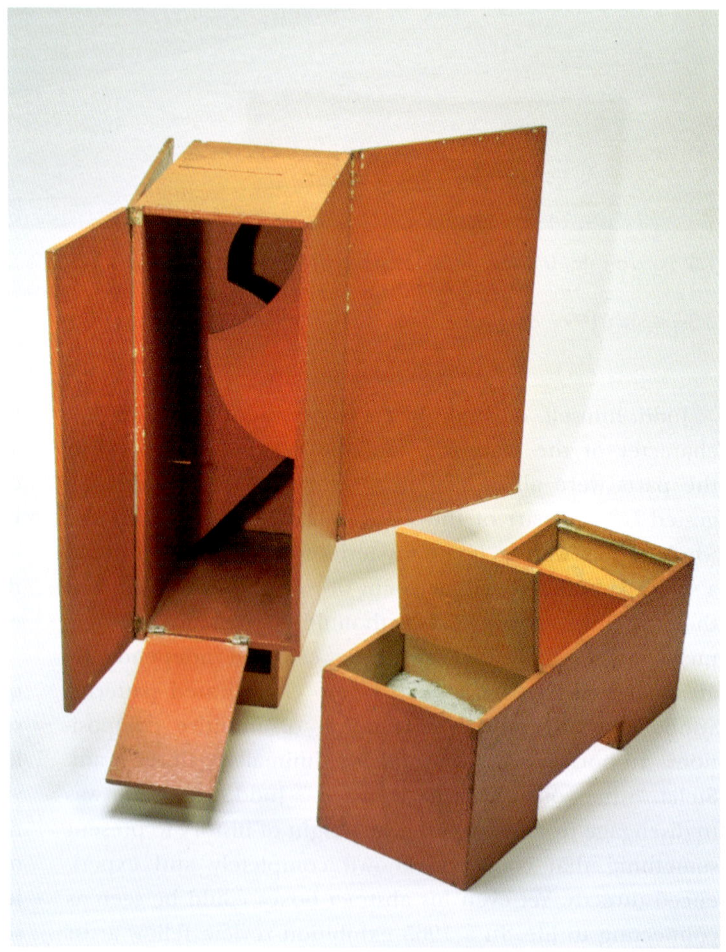

1.7 Hélio Oiticica, ***B3 Bólide Box 3 "Africana,"*** 1963. Oil on wood, 23⅝ × 9⅜ × 11¾" (59.9 × 23.8 × 30 cm). Image courtesy Projecto Hélio Oiticica.

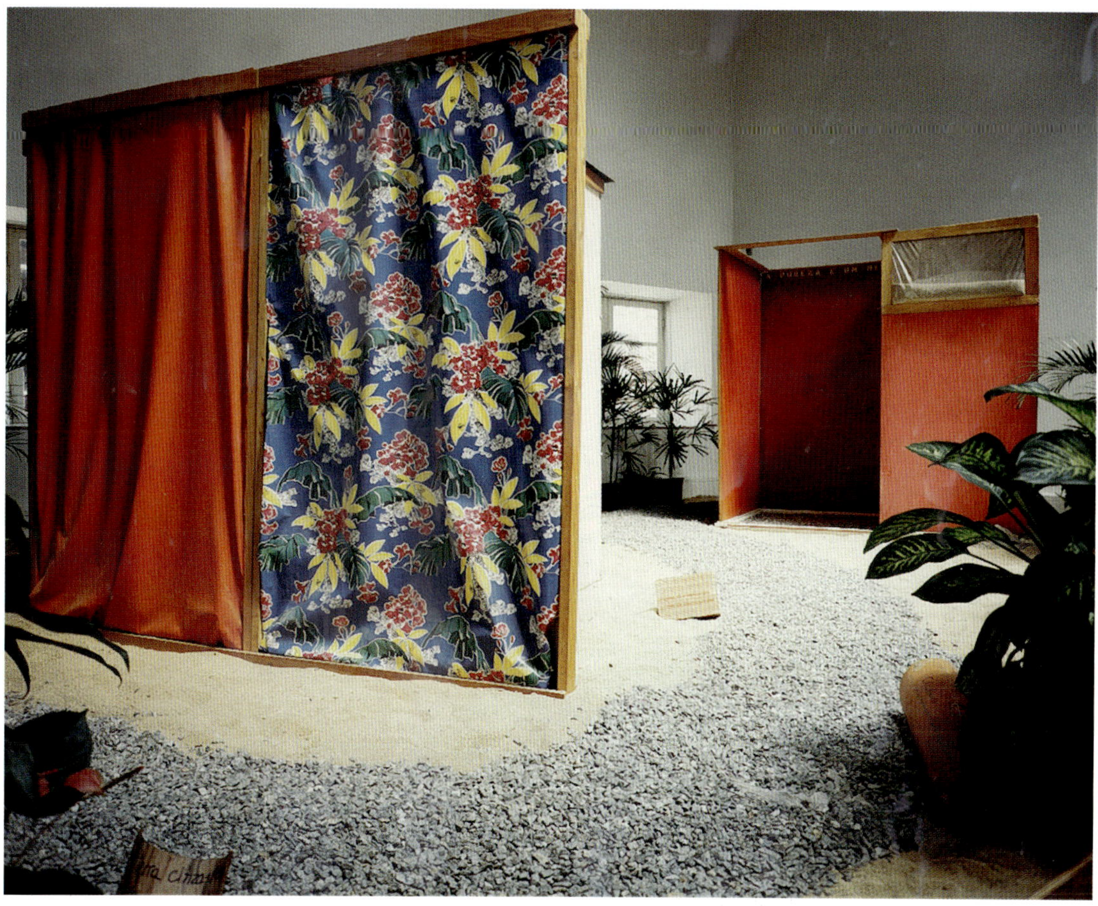

1.8 Hélio Oiticica, ***Tropicalia***, 1967. Showing Penetrables PN2 and PN3 as installed at Centro de Arte Hélio Oiticica, Rio de Janeiro in 1996. Mixed media. Image courtesy Projecto Hélio Oiticica.

works, called *Counter Reliefs* and dating to the late 1950s, are quite modest: simple compositions built of panels of black, geometric shapes hung flat on the wall but layered so they extend, like Judd's "specific objects" a few years later, into the space of the viewer. From the *Counter Reliefs*, Clark and soon Oiticica pushed geometric forms into the rooms and even the streets, assembling boxes and hinged assemblages (**fig. 1.7**) that are intended to be handled by the viewer, who in so doing activates the object and the space around it.

In 1967, Oiticica created *Tropicalia* (**fig. 1.8**) in Rio de Janeiro (and in 1969 created similar installations in London), in which viewers were invited into the art rather than asked to manipulate it with their hands as Clark had done. His inspiration was the spaces of the favelas, the slums of Brazil, which exemplified the integration of aesthetic form and social content. In the gallery, Oiticica constructed a series of small rooms, boxes opening up into each other and occasional interstitial spaces, some with floors of sand or straw, and one set up like a small pond. The walls were adorned, and in places constructed, using brightly colored and patterned fabrics. Tropical plants and birds populated the installation. The different spaces, all of which were open to the visitor, were inspired by different features of the favelas. Exhibition-goers were invited to take off their shoes and wade in the water, walk across the sand, and lie in the straw. There were books to read and music to hear. In *Tropicalia*, the Neo-Concrete desire to "begin with geometry" and end with "an organic space" was realized by adopting details from the real spaces of Brazilian daily life and culture.[11]

Process Art

In his 1968 essay "Anti-Form," Morris argued that the problem with Minimalism was that, although it had pointed to the need to interrogate the assumptions that inform artistic production and reception, and compelled artists to focus directly on the specific properties of the object, much Minimalist art ended up indifferent to its own material specificity. Morris's own blocks, for instance, could have been made of anything—there was nothing in the way he presented or even shaped his Green Gallery exhibition that responded directly to the materials with which he had chosen to work. The piece hanging from the ceiling even seemed to defy its own materiality. Much had been learned about the relationships with and beyond the work, but what about the object itself? In response, Morris and others began to look closely at their materials to provide both the form and content of the work, letting the process of making rather than the finished object take priority. Sculptor Lynda Benglis (b. 1941) described how these artists created what would be termed Process art: "When I learned what the material could do, then I could control it, allowing it to do so much within the parameters that were set up. So the material could and would dictate its own form, in essence."[12]

1.9 Lynda Benglis, ***Quartered Meteor***, 1969 (cast 1975). Lead, 57½ × 65½ × 64¼" (146.1 × 166.4 × 163.2 cm). Edition of 3. Courtesy Cheim & Read, New York.

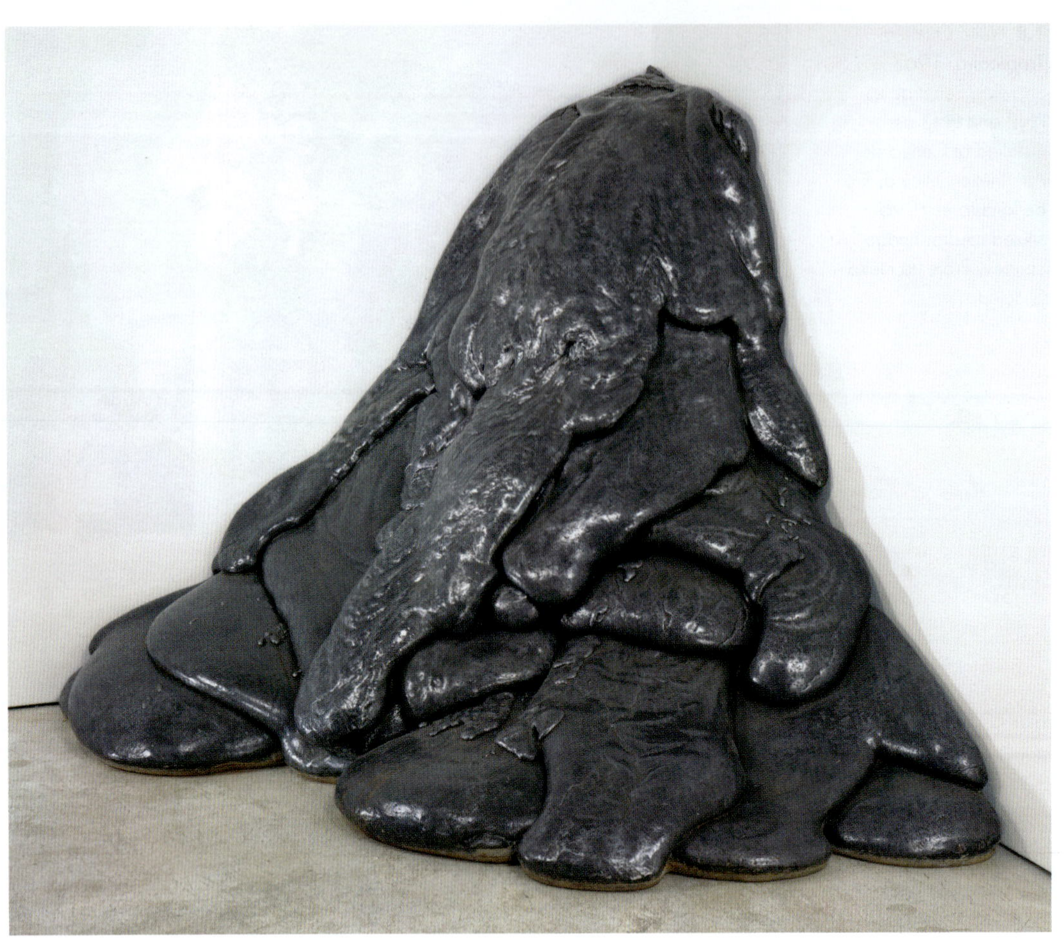

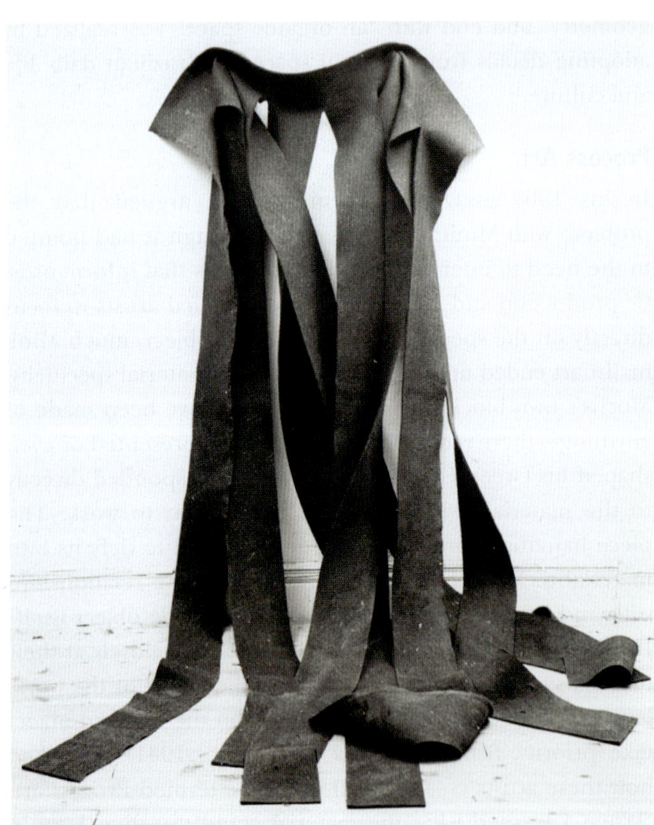

1.10 Robert Morris, *Untitled*, 1967. Felt, 12 × 6' (3.65 m × 182.88 cm). Archives of American Art, Smithsonian Institution. Collection of Ellen Johnson. Photo Rudy Burckhardt.

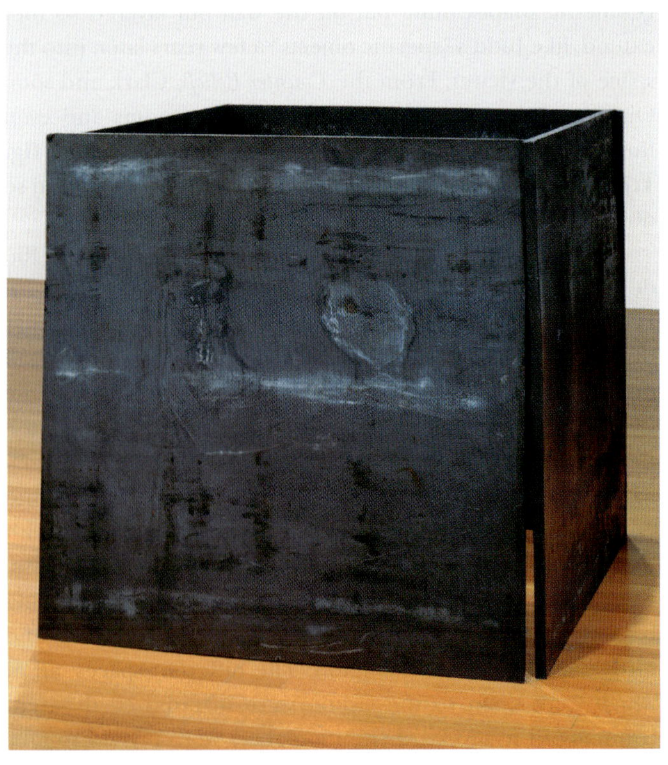

1.11 Richard Serra, *Prop*, 1968. Lead antimony, four plates, each 48 × 48 × 1" (122 × 122 × 2.5 cm). The Museum of Modern Art, New York. Gift of the Grinstein Family. Acc. num. 286.1986.a-d.

For *Quartered Meteor* (1969) (**fig. 1.9**), Benglis poured pigmented polyurethane foam into the corner of a room. The amorphous fluidity of the foam hardened into an object with both organic shape and a hard edge as it dried in mid-cascade. Benglis then cast the form in lead for the work we see here. Morris cut, hung, and dropped pieces of felt to create works such as *Untitled* (1967) (**fig. 1.10**), in which gravity and the qualities of the fabric determined the composition. Richard Serra (b. 1939) created a text piece (1962–68) consisting of a handwritten list of verbs that might serve as instructions for Process art: "To roll/ to crease/ to fold/ … to crumple/ to shave/ to tear/ to chip/ to split/ to cut/ to sever/…"[13] The shock of Serra's sculpture lay in his single-minded application of such actions to materials and his commitment to letting the process define the product. Splitting, cutting, suspending, or forcing lead, steel, rubber, and timber resulted in evocative, often poetic, even frightening results, such as his sculptures in which massive sheets of metal are supported without fixings by gravity alone (**fig. 1.11**). By deeply experimenting with a wide variety of materials, often foreign to the art museum, Process artists created work that could not be readily integrated into existing modes of thinking about and displaying art.

Alternative Logics: *Spiral Jetty* and Conceptual Art

One of the most radical Process art proposals was made by Robert Smithson during the creation of *Spiral Jetty* (1970) (**fig. 1.12**), an enormous spiral constructed in Great Salt Lake, Utah, from rock, earth, and salt crystals. As the artist walked toward the still red water of the lake, he said that the stability of the deserted mining operations that flanked the water and the hot desert that surrounded everything seemed to give way to a spinning movement that inspired the winding form of the spiral that he eventually realized there. "No ideas, no concepts, no systems, no structures, no abstractions could hold themselves together in the actuality of that evidence … It was as if the mainland oscillated with waves and pulsations, and the lake remained rock still."[14] In Smithson's film documenting the project, geological and historical time intersect in the basements of natural-history museums, maps blowing across the desert, and toy dinosaurs marching through dioramas of the Paleolithic era. Footage of massive earth-moving vehicles is spliced with scenes showing crystal growth, sunspots, and Smithson's editing table. The loss of dialectical distance between past and present, history and actuality, enacted by *Spiral Jetty* would become an increasingly important theme throughout the 1970s.

In 1972, two years after *Spiral Jetty* was completed, the French philosopher Gilles Deleuze (1925–95) and psychotherapist Pierre-Félix Guattari (1930–92) published *Anti-Oedipus: Capitalism and Schizophrenia*, the most far-reaching statement of the anti-dialectical trend. Deleuze and Guattari were interested in erotic desire and the unconscious as creative forces. They saw the key to understanding the psyche not

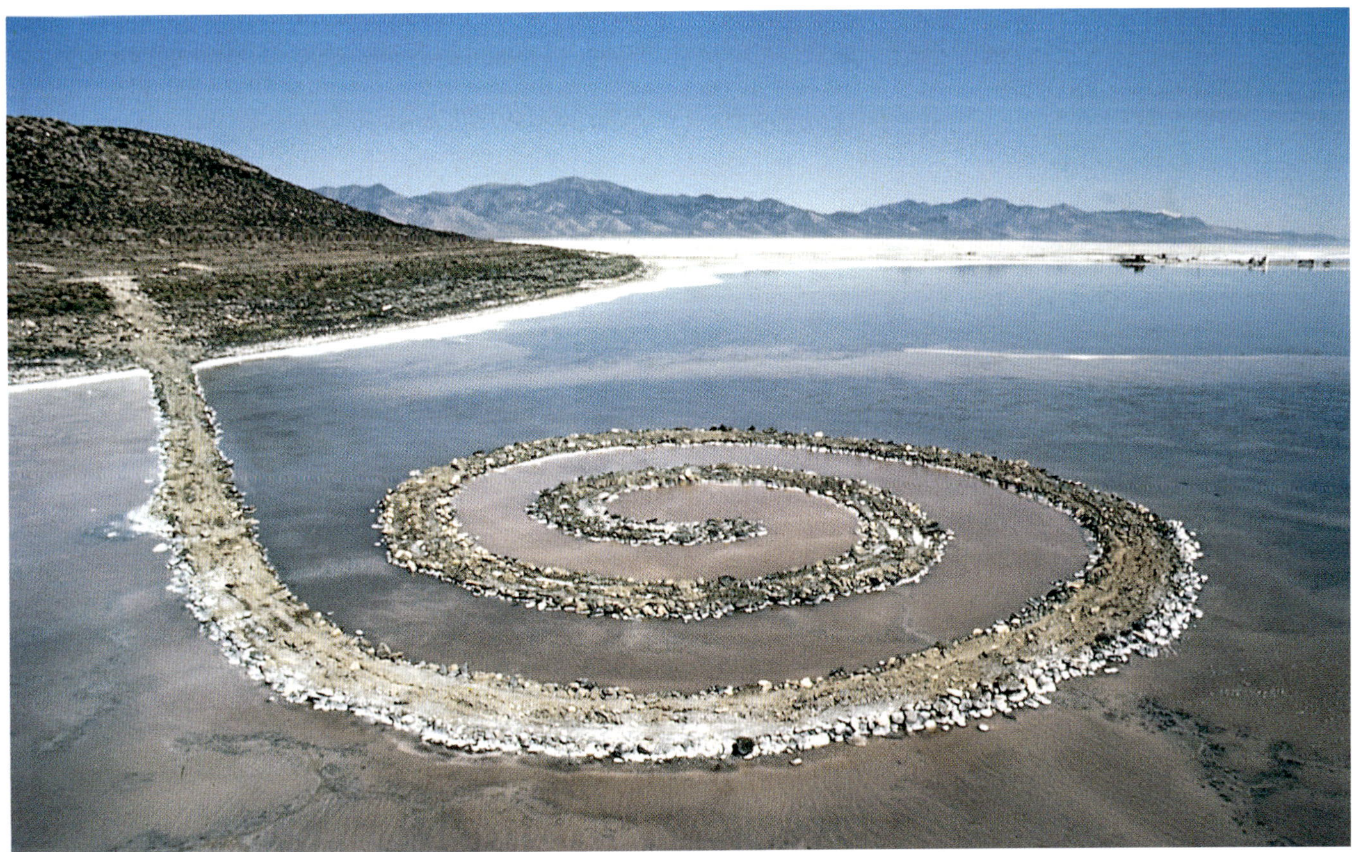

1.12 Robert Smithson, *Spiral Jetty*, 1970. Black basalt, limestone rocks, earth, and salt crystals, length 1,500' (457.2 m). Great Salt Lake, Utah. Photograph by Gianfranco Gorgoni, courtesy John Weber Gallery, New York.

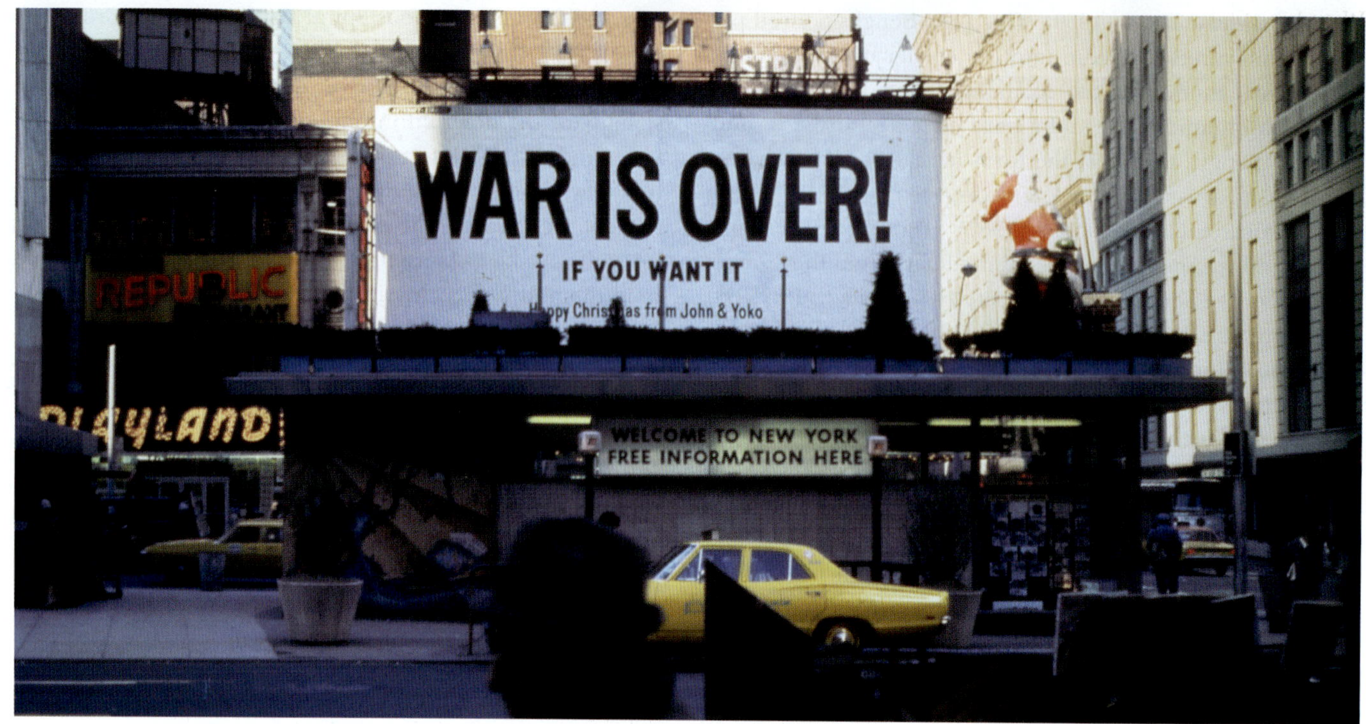

1.13 John Lennon and Yoko Ono, *"War is Over! If You Want It,"* 1969. Billboard, New York. Photo by Yoko Ono © Yoko Ono.

in decoding hidden meanings based on past events, in the Freudian manner, but rather in asking questions about production: "The question posed by desire is not 'What does it mean?' but rather 'How does it work?'"[15] By putting the emphasis on creation, Deleuze and Guattari saw opportunities to merge the arts, psychoanalysis, and social revolution. Their sentiment is reminiscent of Susan Sontag's injunction at the end of her 1964 essay "Against Interpretation" that "in place of a hermeneutics we need an erotics of art."[16] Efforts to translate, define, and explain art, Sontag argued, obscure and overlook its productive power. One can see a similar turning away from history and conventional logic to embrace the generative potential of sensuality, desire, and action in the billboards announcing "War is Over! If You

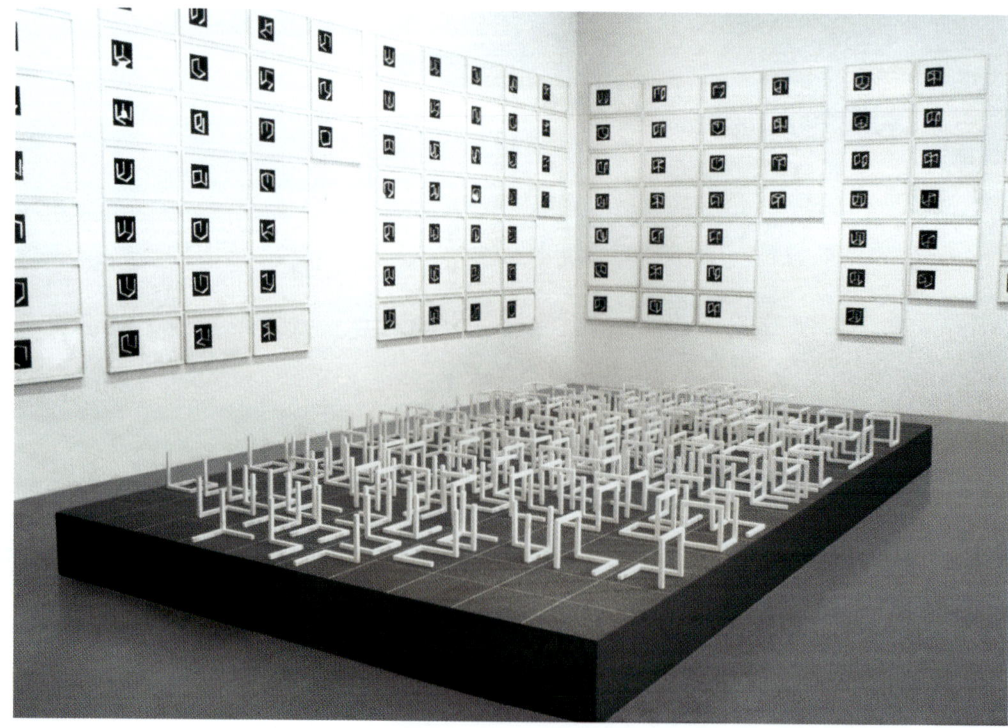

1.14 Sol LeWitt, *Variations of Incomplete Open Cubes*, 1974. Wood sculptures with white paint (122 pieces), each piece 8" (20.3 cm) square. Framed photographs and drawings (131 pieces), each piece 26 × 14" (66 × 35.6 cm). Base 12 × 120 × 216" (30.5 × 304.8 × 548.6 cm). Courtesy the Saatchi Gallery.

Want It" (1969) created by John Lennon (1940–80) and Yoko Ono (b. 1933) (**fig. 1.13**), and the couple's *Bed-In* (1969), a repeated performance in which press and guests were invited to discuss politics with them as they lay in bed in their hotel room.

Relinquishing history and logic, however, did not always require that one lose oneself in the desert or the bedroom. As Smithson was moving earth in Utah, Sol LeWitt (1938–2007) was composing texts on Conceptual art that initiated a new form of secular mysticism. In his 1969 writing "Sentences on Conceptual Art," he pronounced: "Conceptual artists are mystics rather than rationalists. They leap to conclusions that logic cannot reach."[17] That leap depended on following a consistent "irrational" choice through to its completion.[18] LeWitt's conceptual processes, like those of Judd, are generally quite simple: The point of the object is to communicate the operations that produced it. *Variations of Incomplete Open Cubes* (1974) is an example (**fig. 1.14**). The title provides a description of the idea that has generated the work. The minimum requirement for a visual description of an open cube is three lines, one each along the axes of height, width, and depth. As the title does not specify how the variations are to be presented, LeWitt produced two- and three-dimensional renderings. On the floor are sculptures of every possible combination, from the three three-piece models to the single eleven-piece one. Images of the open cubes are framed and hung on the wall. In the end, LeWitt depicted the concept in three ways, through words, objects, and images, thus diagramming both the geometrical concept and the threefold manner in which artists typically communicate their ideas.

LeWitt's art would always include a physical component, but this was not the case for every Conceptualist. Many utilized text to suggest an idea that would become the work of art as the viewer contemplated the words. Robert Barry's (b. 1936) *All the Things I Know But Am Not Now Thinking* (1969), consisting of the title written across a white canvas, or Yoko Ono's *Breath Piece* (1966), for which the artist circulated a card among spectators with the word "Breathe" written on it, were such works, initiated by text and completed by the viewer's mind and body.

On the Social Meaning of Form

At Cornell University in 1970, the artist, writer, and curator Willoughby Sharp (1936–2008) presented an exhibition titled "Earth Art" that celebrated the examination and manipulation of over forty kinds of organic matter. Sharp listed the materials used in alphabetical order, from "air, alcohol, ashes," through "felt, fire, flares," all the way to "twigs, twine, water and wax."[19] Sharp presented the actions to which the materials had been subjected in a similarly ordered list, beginning with "bent, broken, curled" and ending with "spread and sprinkled."[20] While clearly drawing on Morris's notion of "Anti-Form" and the Abstract Expressionist drip paintings of Jackson Pollock (1912–56), he suggested that his show had wider implications. Audiences were to understand that art was engaged with the outside world; the exhibition consequently included pieces that could be found in the woods and rivers around the Cornell campus.

The artist and critic Allan Kaprow (1927–2006), who created performances that drew both on the ritualistic process of Abstract Expressionism, as exemplified by Pollock, and on the materials and spaces of the real world, shared Sharp's expansive vision. Happenings, the name Kaprow gave to his performances, included any number of participants engaged in activities ranging from rearranging furniture in *Push Pull* (1963) and piling-up tires for *Yard* (1961), to more complex scenarios including building towers and bonfires, and spreading strawberry jam on a Volkswagen Beetle and licking it off in *Household* (1964). As he explained in his landmark essay "The Legacy of Jackson Pollock" (1958), artists had learned that if they wanted to evoke sensations from the real world, they need not imitate them in paint: If the artist wants to suggest something hot or sweet, a bonfire and jam are more suitable materials. Kaprow went as far as asserting that the only significant art was that which rejected the geometric, sanctioned spaces of the gallery. He claimed that purportedly anti-aesthetic work, such as Process art, by situating itself in galleries and museums, actually reinforced conventional Western views of art, including the "conventional dualism of the stable versus the unstable, the closed versus the open, the regular versus the organic, the ideal versus the real and so on."[21] For example, we may find interest in dropped felt, but it looks interestingly chaotic only in relation to the square room in which it is installed. Worse than that, its value depends on the importance assigned to it by the owners of that room. The concern with exploding conventional binaries such as order/chaos became more urgent as artists, especially feminist artists, moved away from formal issues to address social ones.

In a 1970 article on an exhibition of Minimalist, Process, Conceptual, and Earth art called "Spaces" at the Museum of Modern Art, New York, the artist and critic Gregory Battcock (1937–80) extended the line of critique presented by Kaprow, proposing that it was one's moral responsibility to examine the context of contemporary art when interpreting its content. "One characteristic of modern man and of his art is his new awareness of the repressive function of boundaries," he announced. "There are sexual boundaries, familial, administrative, governmental, geographical, and social boundaries and they all diminish man's desire for freedom and subsequently reduce the chances for authentic social change."[22] Battcock identified certain forces that influenced the way work was shown and viewed in "Spaces," including the corporations that had funded the exhibition and individual works within it: General Electric, Kimberly-Clark, RCA, and Sylvania to name a few. These "[i]ndustrial and research giants, electronic and data-oriented companies," wrote Battcock, "encouraged ... artists to incorporate their discoveries into art works. Instead of contributing to the church,

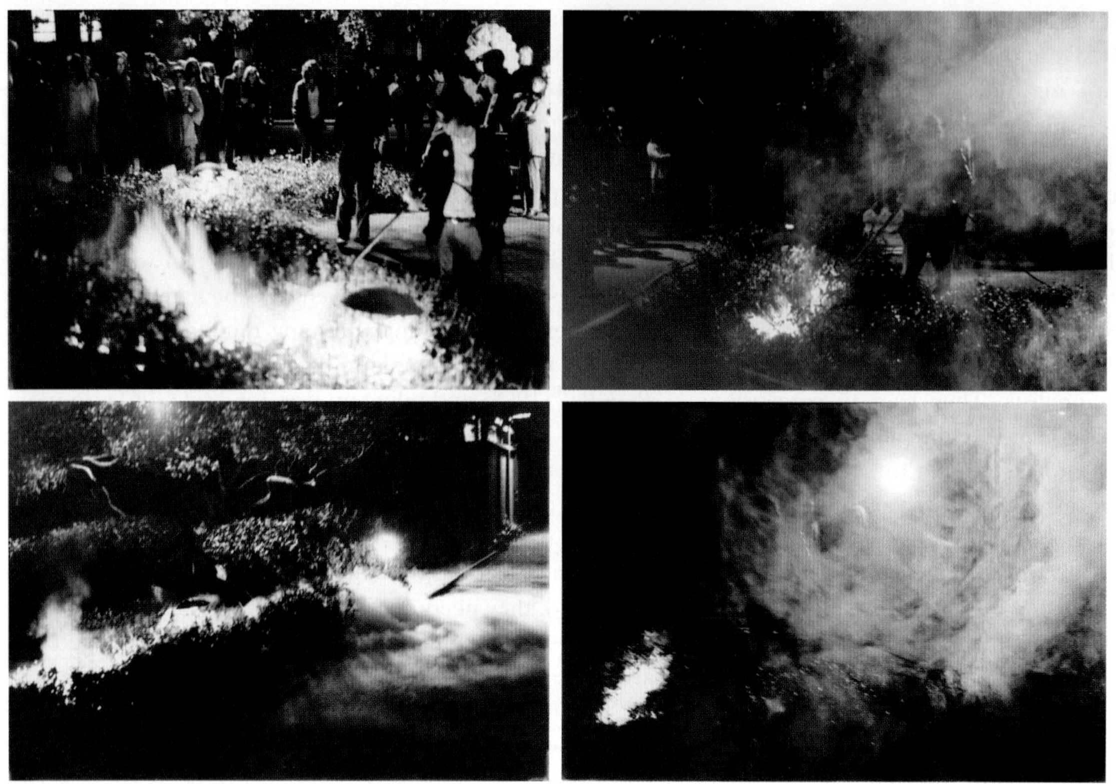

1.15 Terry Fox, ***Defoliation Piece***, 1970. Four black-and-white photographs, 8 × 10" (20.32 × 25.4 cm) each. Performance documentation of "The Eighties" exhibition, 17 March 1970, at the Powerhouse Gallery, University Art Museum, University of California, Berkeley. © Estate of Terry Fox, Köln. Courtesy of Marita Loosen-Fox.

they contributed to artists, and it all had the same effect. The corporate conscience was appeased."[23] His charge was not simply that MoMA provided industry with public-relations opportunities, but that certain artists were also masking the nature of their corporate production. In contrast to the convictions expressed by Process artists, "the properties of the materials and inventions that are donated by the companies are not exploited for their unique and peculiar effects. Rather these properties are sublimated."[24] To illustrate this point, Battcock cited Robert Morris's use of trees provided by Kimberly-Clark which suggested that forest care, rather than paper-making, was the company's business. He further noted that one (unnamed) artist had solicited one of the Defense Department's largest suppliers for his materials, thus presenting the public with arms dealers in the guise of art suppliers. Such art concealed the social significance of its materials and the corporations that produced them.

In contrast to the sublimated violence and whitewashed history Battcock perceived at MoMA, the performances of Terry Fox (1943–2008) enacted real violence with historical consciousness. In *A Sketch for Impacted Lead* (1970), Fox attempted to create a small bar of lead by firing several bullets at the same spot. *Impacted Lead* is a variation on a theme explored in lead Process pieces by Richard Serra, but by using a gun to reveal the properties of his material, Fox bound the meaning of the piece to social issues relating to firearms rather than formal ones concerning the inherent qualities of his materials. The performance was photographed: We can see Fox at the gun shop and the shop owner holding the gun, before Fox takes aim at a target behind the counter. In the same year, Fox created *Defoliation Piece* (1970) (**fig. 1.15**), in which he set fire to a rectangular plot of jasmine flowers outside the University Art Museum, Berkeley, California. To get the garden to burn he used agent orange, a defoliant then in daily use in the Vietnam War (1959–75). In this case, Fox was able to invest what resembled a piece of Minimalist and Earth art with poignant political content. Fox wrote of *Defoliation Piece*: "Everyone likes to watch fires. It made a beautiful roaring sound. But at a certain point people realized what was going on—the landscape was being violated ... Suddenly everyone was quiet. One woman cried for twenty minutes."[25]

Joseph Beuys

One of the loudest voices demanding that artists respond to the entirety of human experience rather than to exclusively aesthetic questions was Joseph Beuys (1921–85), who left Fluxus in 1965 because, as he put it, "they held a mirror up to people without indicating how to change things."[26] Artists were obliged to participate, not simply to observe, he argued. His art was rooted in his experiences as a German air-force pilot in World War II and the personal crisis that he had subsequently undergone. In 1944, according to his account, his airplane was shot down over the Crimea and he was left stranded in the snow. Discovered barely alive by a group of local people called Tatars, he was kept warm with felt blankets and animal fat, and tenderly nursed back to health. Although the truth of these experiences has never been confirmed, when he finally started to make art again after the war, Beuys drew heavily on the story, creating art from felt and fat and casting himself in the role of healer, providing for Europe the assistance he had received from the Tatars.

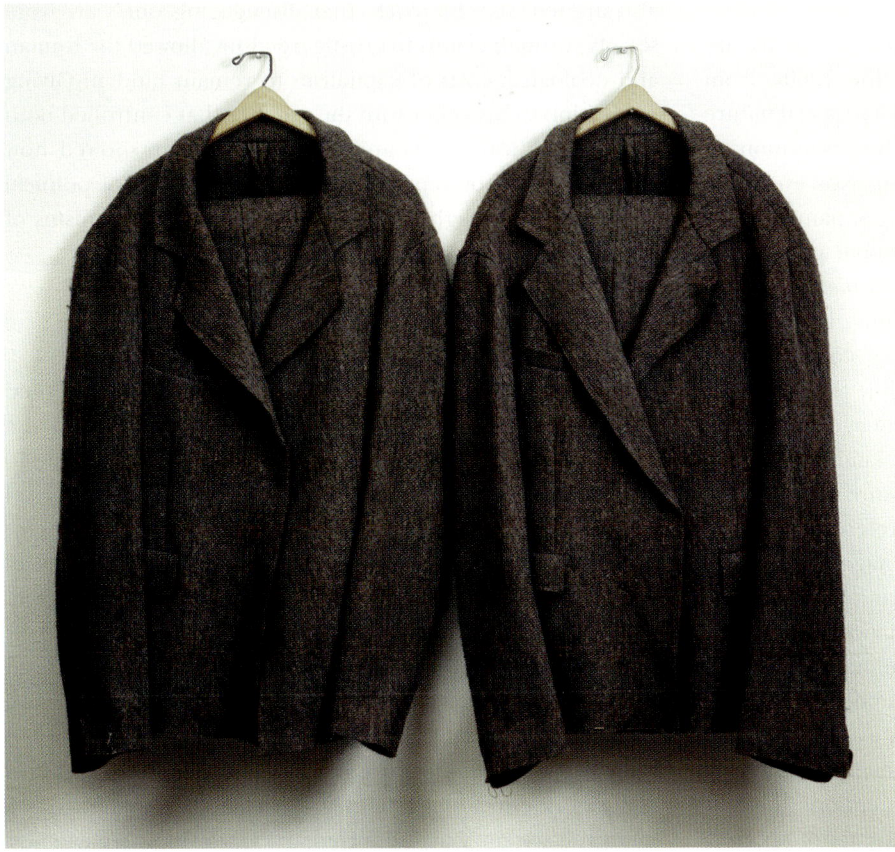

1.16 Joseph Beuys, ***Felt Suit***, 1970. Edition of 100. Two lifesize felt suits. Courtesy Ronald Feldman Fine Arts, New York.

By the 1970s, Beuys had created an identity for himself that was equal parts shaman (mystical healer), politician, and art professor. His mission was to develop forms of engagement with the world rather than to add more things to it. His work was intended to lead students from ideas to action; any "art objects" as such were no more than by-products: "I am not a teacher who tells his students only to think. I say: Act; do something; I ask for a result. It may take different forms."[27] In Beuys's case, these included evocative non-art objects and alchemical combinations of fat and felt, sticks, stuffed animals, wires, toys, cars, bicycles, chalkboards, and himself, dressed almost invariably in a hunting vest and felt hat. As in Process art and Arte Povera (the Italian movement based in Turin that made use of "poor" materials from nature and industry, as opposed to traditional fine-art ones), these materials, which he selected on the basis of their relative determinacy (including iron, tin, and wood) or indeterminacy (fat, honey, gelatin, watercolor, and blood), communicate first through their physical properties. Beuys's materials quite often degrade before the viewer's eyes, and evoke complex associations with organic and geometric forms, ideas of creation and decomposition, and biographical and biological elements. Beuys's work, from his suits and stacks of felt (**fig. 1.16**) to his performances with live and dead animals, pointed to a dimension beyond rational materialism.

Beuys's theory of art depended, he famously announced, "on the fact that every human being is an artist,"[28] a claim that celebrated the potential for creativity in all human beings. He explained that his audience must be intellectually and politically alive, since art produced through thoughtful action required an equally engaged response from its recipients. Although Beuys is best known for his use of fat and felt, the materials for which he advocated most strongly were actually "Thinking Forms" and "Spoken Forms," which produce "Social Structure."[29] By "sculpting" with thought, speech, and human relationships, artists could reshape society and history. This formulation suggested a radical extension of the artist's role into a combination of activist, teacher, sculptor, painter, performer, and politician. One manifestation of Beuys's "expanded concept of art" was the Organization for Direct Democracy, which he founded in Düsseldorf in 1970. The group advocated a united Europe with a single electorate. In place of representational legislative bodies and political parties, the organization promoted direct democracy as a means of governance that treated everyone as fully active social beings. After the crises of fascism and the hubris of contemporary democracies, the Organization for Direct Democracy insisted that citizens be able to represent themselves in the political arena. The Organization also offered free education, to provide an informed and active electorate.

Beuys's political activities were integral to his artistic production, providing a context in which the viewer was accorded agency and creative power, serving as a collaborator with the artist to generate significance for his sculptures, to turn the fragmentary objects he created into tools for the creation and exchange of ideas. Beuys's suits of felt, of which he made many, achieve artistic depth as a conceptual artwork that invites the viewer to re-imagine the relationship between contemporary urban society, as alluded to by the garment, and the compassion and knowledge of the natural world revealed to the artist through the felt of the more ancient Crimean communities. Although few artists would pursue all the implications of Beuys's practice, his influence remains palpable today. The generation of German artists who dominated the international scene in the 1980s and 1990s were almost all products of Beuys's teachings, and his conviction that every human being is an artist continues to resonate through artistic circles worldwide.

Leon Golub

Beuys's Organization for Direct Democracy shared its distrust of representation with much art of the 1960s, from Minimalism to Process. The clearly political and social nature of Beuys's Organization is useful for calling attention to the political connotations of this suspicion. Not everyone, however, had given up on representation. U.S. painter Leon Golub (1922–2004) embraced representational painting as a means, he said, to "get at the real."[30] In *Vietnam II* (1972) (**fig. 1.17**), he cut away parts of the painting, inviting real space into the carefully rendered images of contemporary warfare. Nailed to the wall like a tarpaulin, the image of bodies in violent confrontation appears damaged by gashes that the eye falls into, moving through the skin of the canvas as though each cut were a wound or a fissure between the realms of art and life. Golub's work made reference to existing figurative traditions and mass-media imagery, including photographs from newspapers and popular military magazines such as *Soldier of Fortune*. Bodies, often awkwardly posed and imperfectly formed, act out scenes of military aggression and almost inhuman malaise. Soldiers pause between killing and smoking to look out at the viewer. Their expressions, suggesting a range of emotions from self-satisfaction to sadistic pleasure, seem to seek out the camera's attention. As such, Golub insists that viewers consider their own act of observation as well as the acts they observe.

Some of the most striking works of the 1970s were texts and images presented in art magazines, particularly *Artforum* and *Arts Magazine*. In the U.S., Sol LeWitt's "Sentences on Contemporary Art" discussed above was published in the British journal *The Fox* as well as the U.S. *0-9*, and the German periodical *Interfunktionen* will be discussed in Chapter 3 for providing a similar platform for German conceptualism. Golub took advantage of this medium, writing essays addressing the relationship between art and society, and criticizing the dissociation from real-world concerns that had generally defined avant-garde art throughout the twentieth century. Golub argued that claims for the freedom of art were in fact a means to neutralize its revolutionary potential. He also argued, like Battcock, that disengaging one's art from society through claims to artistic freedom allowed the human and ecological costs of capitalism to remain hidden. Giving expression to his anger with the regimes that controlled both current political events and art history, Golub showed how art could resist by representing the human cost of political choices and highlighting its own role in the mechanisms of political control.

Institutional Critique

"Institutional critique" is the name given to art designed to examine the conditions of its own existence, from the museums that show it to the groups of people that value it. One of the most suggestive examples of such art appeared in Sharp's "Earth Art" exhibition at Cornell University. This was a pile of dirt deposited by the German artist Hans Haacke (b. 1936) in the center of one of the galleries. The mound, titled *Grass Grows* (1969), was seeded and watered, and by the end of the exhibition had become a small grassy hill—an indoor landscape. To see the work through to its completion, Haacke relied on what he called the "systems" that connected his materials to their environment. The museum, with its staff of curators, educators, administrators, and custodians, constituted the system that supported art. However, the particular requirements of *Grass Grows*—water, light, consistent temperature, and fresh air—collided with those of display and security that museums are generally designed to meet. As curators became gardeners, the contrast between cultural and natural systems became apparent. Soon after *Grass Grows*, Haacke shifted his attention away from issues of nature and culture to investigate increasingly complex social systems.

Haacke's most notorious investigation, *Shapolsky et al., Manhattan Real Estate Holdings, a Real-Time Social System, as of May 1, 1971* (**fig. 1.18**), caused his scheduled 1971 Guggenheim Museum exhibition to be canceled. The piece included publicly available information about poorly maintained apartment buildings owned by Harry J. Shapolsky and his associates. When housed in their original archives,

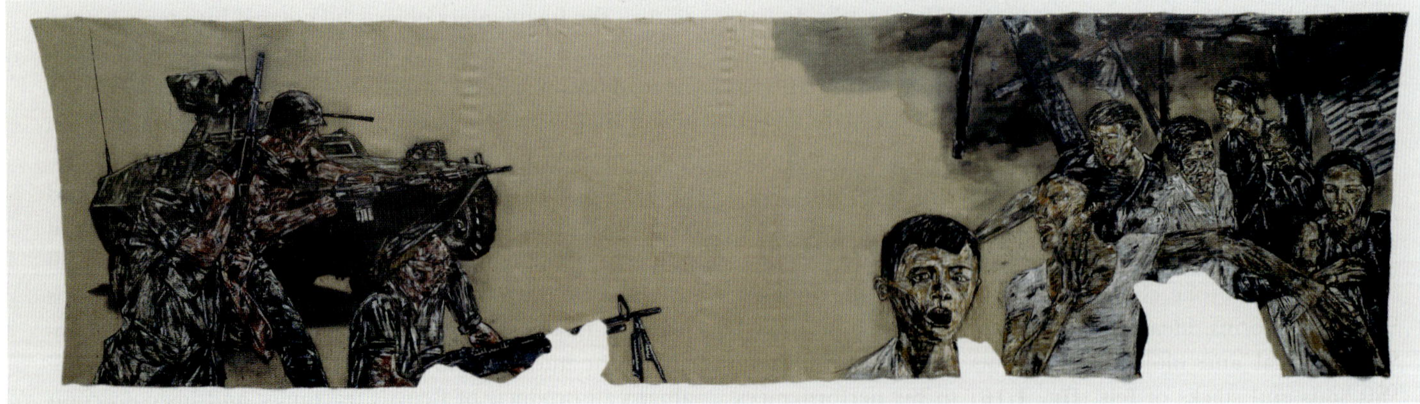

1.17 Leon Golub, *Vietnam II*, 1972. Acrylic paint on linen, 115¾" × 37' 9⁵⁄₃₂" (2.94 × 11.51 m). Presented by the American Fund for the Tate Gallery, courtesy of Ulrich and Harriet Meyer (Building the Tate Collection), 2012.

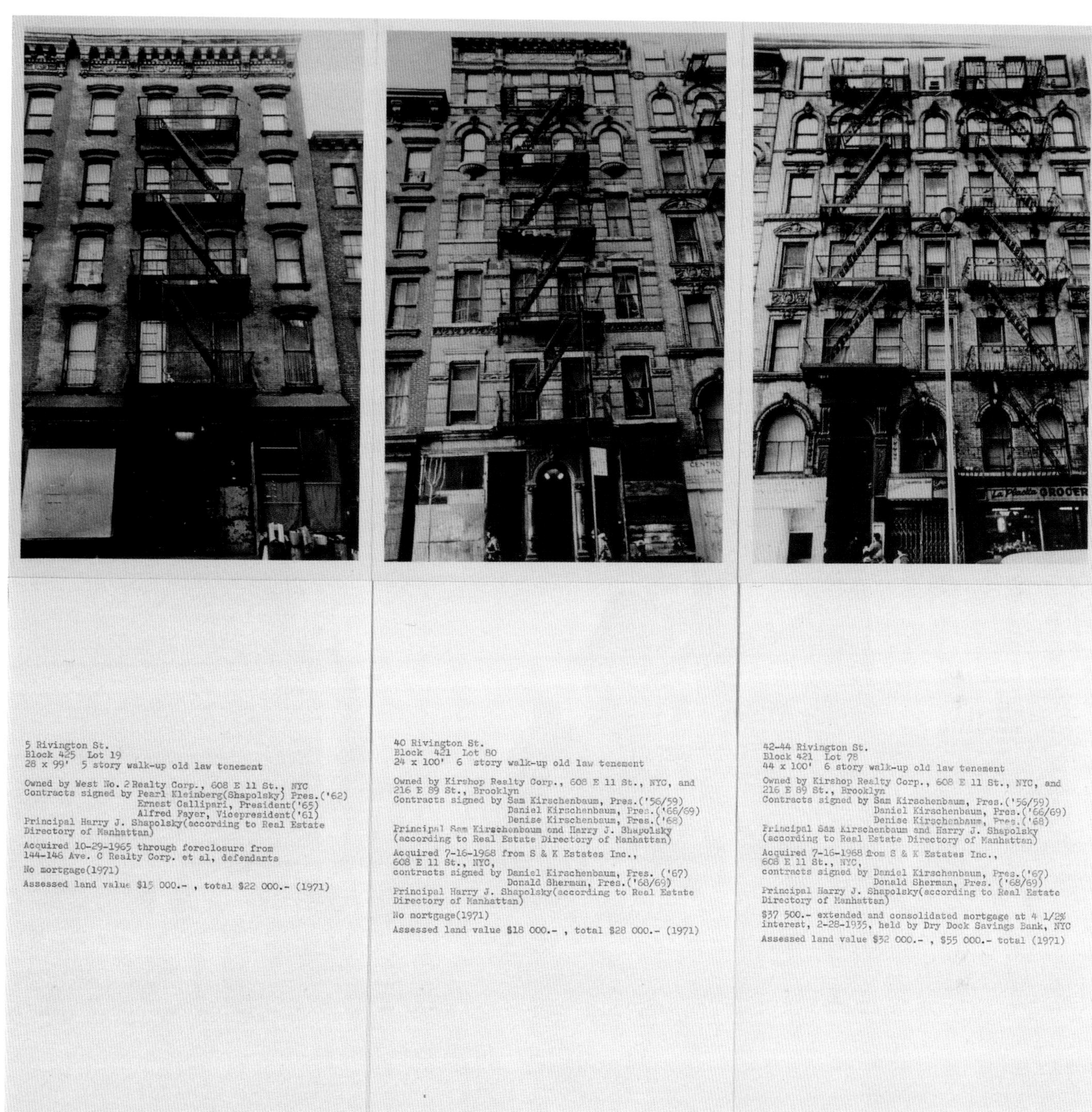

1.18 Hans Haacke, *Shapolsky et al., Manhattan Real Estate Holdings, a Real-Time Social System, as of May 1, 1971*, 1971. Showing three of 33 panels; 146 black and white photographs, 146 typewritten pages, 2 plans, 6 tables of transactions, 1 explanatory panel. La Musée National d'Art Moderne, Centre Georges Pompidou, Paris.

the photographs and records Haacke assembled were seen only by the few lawyers who might look through them in the course of their work. Presented on the wall of the museum, however, they became public displays of economic injustice. As one writer explained, "At a gut level Haacke is asking this question: is there really any difference between the power of money to control the direction of art and the power of money to keep rotten slums in existence?"[31] By reaching out through the doors of the museum into the streets, Haacke upset the Guggenheim, which suddenly found that its status as a treasure box for valuable art objects had changed into being a flashpoint for the real-world social politics of real-estate speculation and tenants' rights in New York City. As Haacke said of the role of an artist whose practice is informed by politics: "One's responsibilities increase; however, this also gives the satisfaction of being taken as a bit more than a court-jester, with the danger of not being forgiven."[32]

Haacke was not alone in his concern with creating politically engaged art. For a 1974 show at the Claire Copley

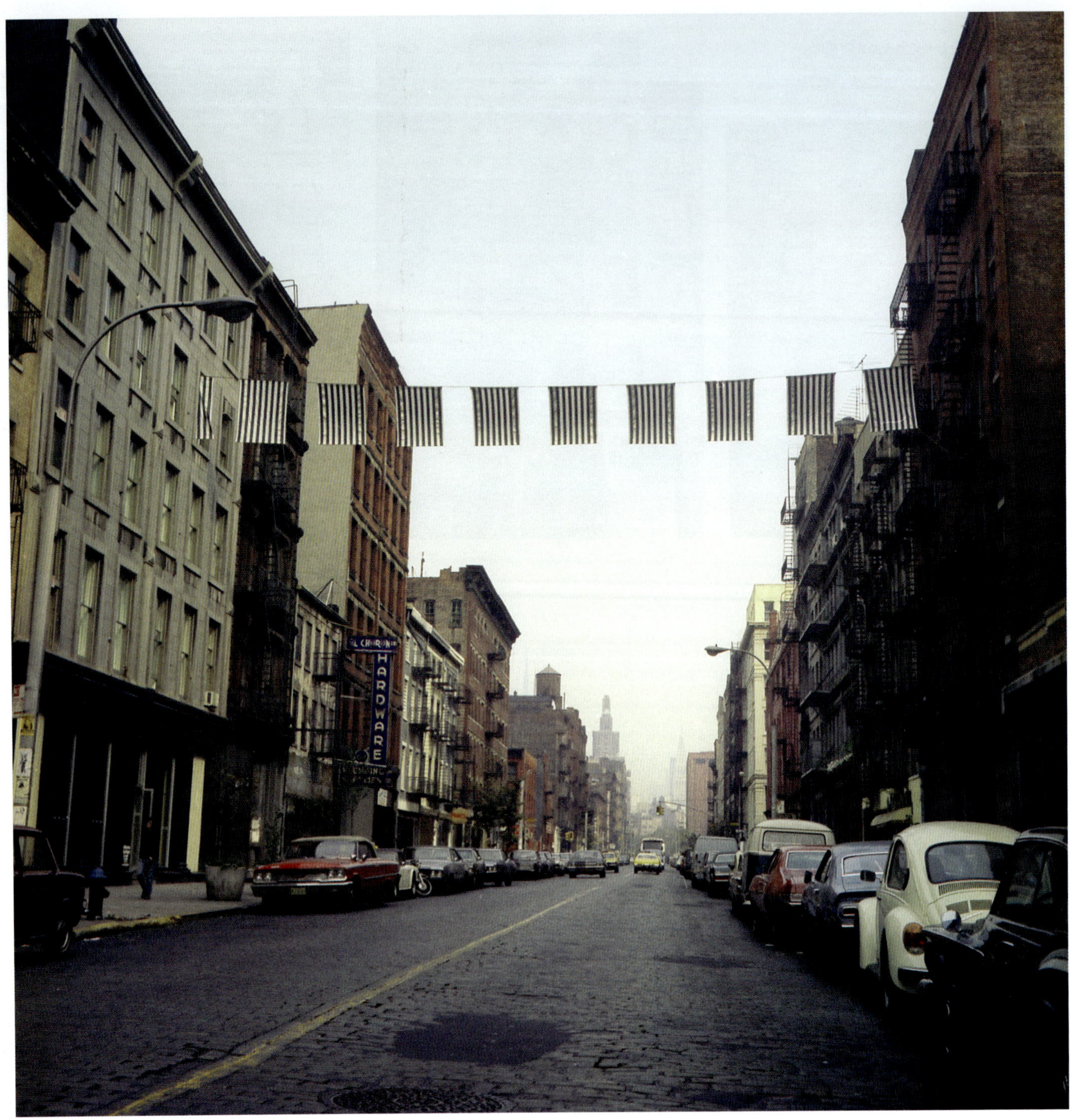

1.19 Daniel Buren, ***Photo-souvenir: Within and Beyond the Frame***, 1973. Detail, work in situ. John Weber Gallery, New York. Image courtesy the Buren Studio.

Gallery in Los Angeles, artist Michael Asher (b. 1943) removed the dividing wall between the exhibition space and the offices behind it, revealing the commercial side of the business. Meanwhile U.S. artist and philosopher Adrian Piper (b. 1943) called on artists and audiences to consider political awareness as integral to all artistic practice. She called such political awareness "meta-art" and defined it as "the activity of making explicit the thought processes, procedures, and presuppositions of making whatever kind of art we make."[33] Piper (see Chapter 7), like Haacke and others, did not demand that an artist's practice be limited to such politically conscious reflexivity, only that it be informed by it.

French Conceptual artist Daniel Buren (b. 1938), with colleagues Olivier Mosset (b. 1944), Michel Parmentier (b. 1938), and Niele Toroni (b. 1937), used uniform painted marks and complex critical analysis to argue that even a Minimalist box communicated its meaning within a socially defined discourse, which ultimately had more influence on the nature of the art experience than properties such as color or form. Buren's work consisted exclusively of selectively placed alternating 3½-inch-wide bands of white and another color in, out of, and between spaces where art was displayed, including gallery walls and windows, art magazines, and out in the streets. Art objects, Buren argued, take their place in the museum as signs of value based on economic, political, and social factors as well as aesthetic and mystical considerations. By eliminating the individuality of the image, giving the viewer no form or content within the work to contemplate, attention is shifted to the context around it instead, those external features that define certain objects as art.

In works such as *Photo-souvenir: Within and Beyond the Frame* (**fig. 1.19**), Buren's stripes drew attention to non-artistic sources of value, much as Piper's "meta-art" required. This installation inside, on, and outside the Weber Gallery in New York was set up in 1973 and then re-created for the gallery in a new location in 1978 as *Change of Scenery*, thus pulling the viewer's eye and mind not only through the art gallery and out into the street but also through time. Like Haacke, Buren had trouble with the Guggenheim Museum in 1971, when he suspended a banner of stripes down the center of the museum. Waving gently in Frank Lloyd Wright's rotunda, Buren's work implicated the space of the building in processes of cultural politics, connecting the museum to the other contexts to which Buren's stripes had previously drawn attention, to galleries that sell art and the neighborhoods that invest in it. Buren's work was removed by the museum authorities after just a day on the premise that it blocked views of other works—a somewhat perplexing argument considering that the sightlines are already obstructed by the spiraling architecture of the museum.

In the 1970s, voices drawing attention to the connections between art and politics were becoming increasingly forceful. In 1971, protesters marched in front of MoMA in New York to urge Picasso to remove his painting *Guernica* from the city. The artist had entrusted his 1937 memorial to the victims of fascism in Spain to the United States for safekeeping until a republican government was re-established in Spain and the painting could be returned, which it was in 1981. However, the protesters argued that the American bombing of civilians during the war in Vietnam had rendered prominent U.S. institutions such as MoMA inappropriate caretakers for a painting expressing the artist's anger at similar actions by the Spanish fascists.

Institutional critique as practiced by Haacke, Buren, and others would be developed into a distinct genre in the subsequent decades. Artists discussed in later chapters including Group Material, Fred Wilson, Krzysztof Wodiczko, Santiago Sierra, and Alexander Brener have created object-, image-, and performance-based practices that point to the complex ways in which cultural institutions participate in politics and how art can assume both complicit and resistant positions. By the 1980s, museums were opening their doors to artists to perform what approximated to a form of public self-critique. The work of Andrea Fraser, in which the artist or a surrogate steps into various institutional roles including docent, keynote speaker, and curator, demonstrates the critical detail and historical nuance being presented by institutional critique inside the museum. For *Museum Highlights: A Gallery Talk* (1989), performed at the Philadelphia Museum of Art, Fraser took on the identity of Jane Castleton, a professionally attired college-educated young museum professional who provided docent tours of the museum. Her talk took in the membership desk, where she recited passages from museum statements about the importance of membership, and the great hall, where she discussed the history of the Philadelphia Museum and its relation to other municipal services and civic institutions including local hospitals, prisons, libraries, and zoos. Her walk through the period rooms took visitors from the display of eighteenth-century French work, where she quickly recited art-historical descriptions, to the men's room, where she rehearsed early twentieth-century tracts on health. In the galleries she indicated highlights from the collections but, as she did in the bathroom, focused more on early-century descriptions of social types and urban issues than art-historical texts.

In the 1970s institutional critique was one expression of the growing impulse among artists and critics in the labor, anti-war, and minority rights and women's rights movements to make the connection between art and politics evident and instrumental. In the subsequent decades the lesson that the museum is connected to every other political and social institution had become standard fare, giving Fraser's generation the opportunity to move beyond needing to point to the fact of complicity. Such a critical and comprehensive approach to making art has been a continued means of maintaining the connection between the often-sanctified rooms of the art museum and the spaces and issues that surround them.

African-American Critiques

In the U.S., many African-American artists felt with particular urgency the need for engagement with daily life on the streets as well as artistic experimentation in the studio. By the late 1960s, artists such as Romare Bearden (1911–88) and Benny Andrews (1930–2006) in New York had already created a substantial body of work exploring intersections of abstraction and figuration in the context of racially focused subject matter (**fig. 1.20**). Few venues existed for them to show their work, however, and there was a clear divide between black and white art worlds. Mobilized by the disparity not only between black and white artists, but between the level of racially conscious discourse occurring every day in the streets and newspapers and the virtual silence on the same subject in museums, artists of color, with Andrews in a leading position, followed the model of grassroots activists and formed the Black Emergency Cultural Coalition (BECC) in 1969 in direct response to the Metropolitan Museum of Art exhibition "Harlem on My Mind." Presented as a commemoration of the New York borough and its celebrated arts scene,

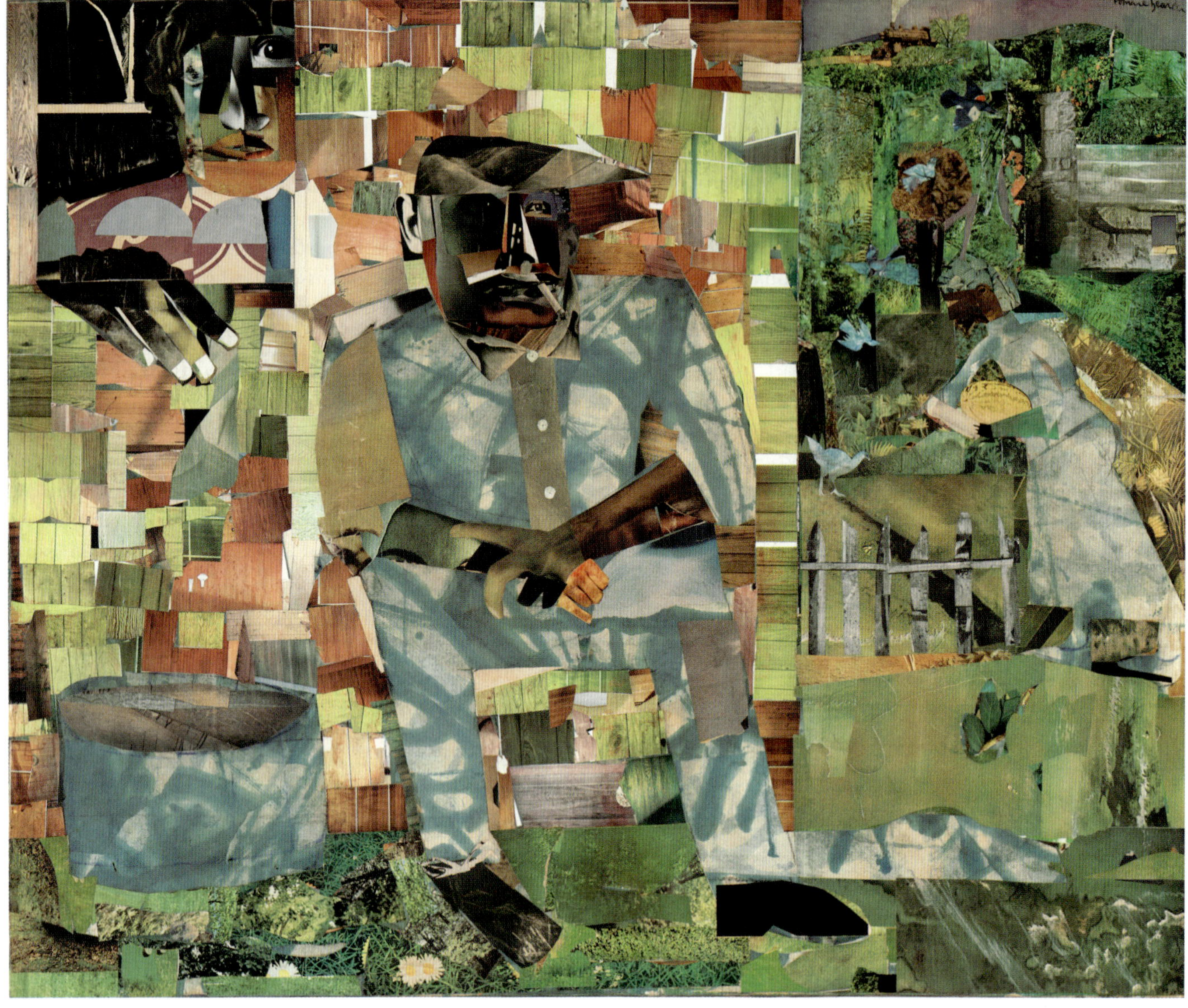

1.20 Romare Bearden, ***Tomorrow I Might Be Far Away***, 1967. Collage of various papers with charcoal and graphite on canvas, overall 46 × 56" (116.8 × 142.2 cm). National Gallery of Art, Washington, D.C. Paul Mellon Fund.

it consisted exclusively of photographs of the neighborhood and showed no interest in Harlem artists themselves. Many painters and sculptors who had been working in Harlem since the 1920s and 1930s lived just a short walk from the museum, but were not included in the show. The BECC argued that, since the museum had no experts on black art on its staff and had failed to enlist any such specialists to help curate the exhibition, the only thing "Harlem on My Mind" revealed was institutionalized racism and a deep desire to keep the existing Met power structure intact. Bearden's group Spiral took a less confrontational stance, but also criticized the show's exclusions.

The BECC made public its objections to the racism of current museum practices and entered into negotiations with the Met and other museums. Conversations with the Whitney Museum of American Art in New York resulted in plans for an African-American art exhibition to be produced with the help of an African-American guest curator. Similar, if smaller, shows were being held at the Brooklyn Museum (1969) and the Museum of Fine Arts in Boston (1970); the time was thus obviously ripe for the Whitney Museum to make a national statement. When the "Survey of Black Art" opened in 1971, however, there was no guest curator and limited participation by the African-American arts community. Major figures, including painter Sam Gilliam (b. 1933) and sculptor Melvin Edwards (b. 1939), publicly boycotted the show on the grounds that it "negate[d] a coherent viewing and analysis of the creative content, context, influence, and general value of the works of African American artists."[34] Although the groundwork for representing non-majority art was beginning to be laid, decades would pass before satisfactory exhibitions would result.

New York might play the dominant role in the exhibition, sale, and production of American art, and indeed in art activism, but it was not the only important center. Black arts received steadily growing attention throughout the late 1960s

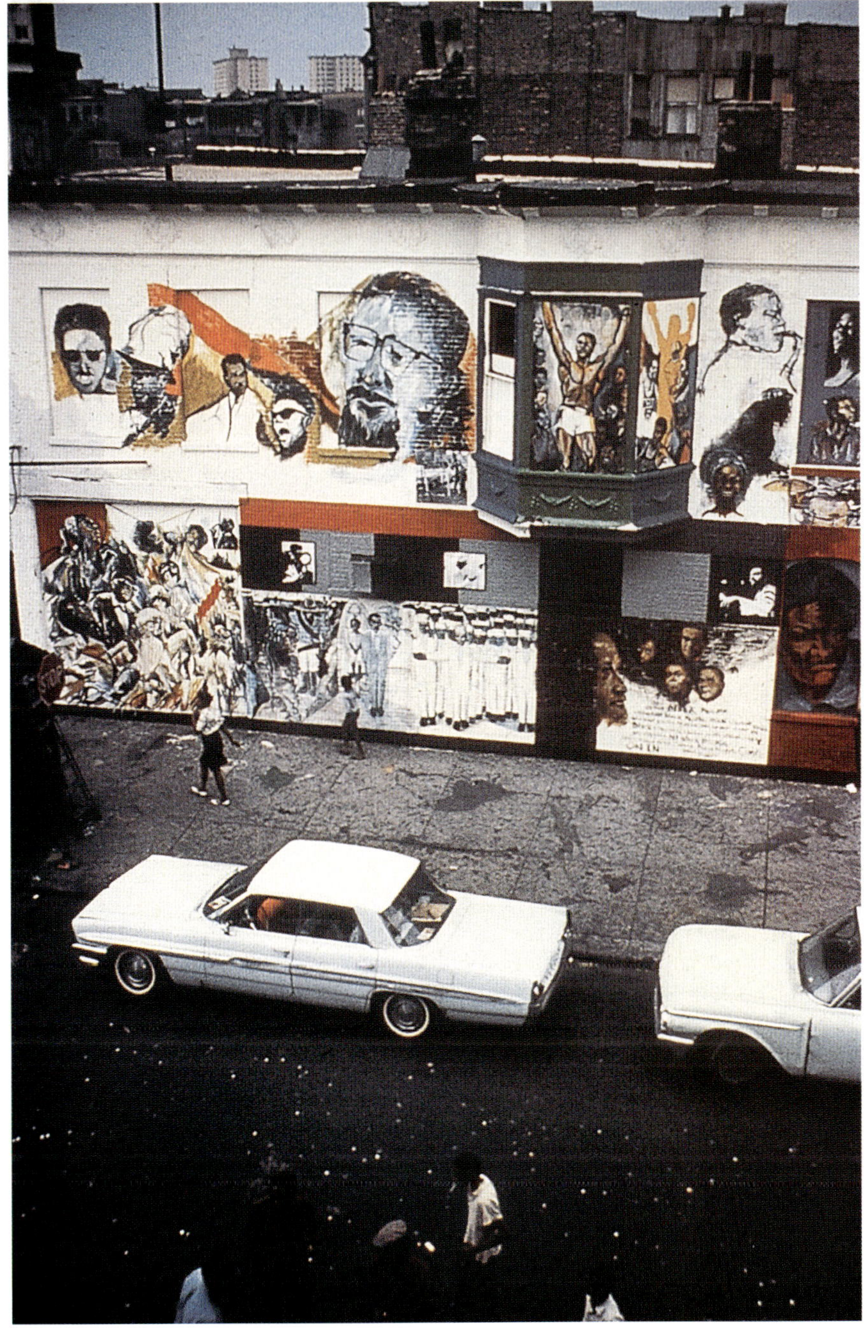

1.21 OBAC Visual Arts Workshop, *Wall of Respect*, 1967. Oil on brick, 30 × 60' (9.1 × 18.2 m). Chicago.

and 1970s across the U.S. By the end of the 1960s, the Organization for Black American Culture (OBAC) had sparked significant activity in Chicago. OBAC (pronounced "oba cee," to suggest the Yoruba word *oba*, or "ruler"), the primary organ of the Black Arts Movement, a national cultural organization that promoted intellectual production by and about African-Americans, formed a visual-arts workshop to complement its literary activities. The result was the 1967 *Wall of Respect* (**fig. 1.21**), a mural depicting African-American luminaries selected by the artists in a dialogue with residents of the city's South Side neighborhood, where it was painted. Among those represented were Martin Luther King, Jr., Malcolm X, Muhammad Ali, and Aretha Franklin. The wall was among the first of many expressions of local and racial politics to be painted in U.S. cities across the following decade. It responded to sentiments such as those expressed by Black Arts Movement writer Larry Neal that the "political liberation of the Black Man is directly tied to his cultural liberation."[35]

AfriCOBRA

In 1968, Jeff Donaldson (1932–2004), Jae Jarrell (b. 1935) and her husband, Wadsworth Jarrell (b. 1929), and Gerald Williams (b. 1926) brought together other OBAC participants and like-minded African-American artists to "transcend the 'I' of the 'me' for the 'us' and 'we' in order to create a basic philosophy which would be the foundation of a visual Black Arts movement."[36] This gathering resulted in the formation of COBRA (Coalition of Black Revolutionary Artists), which took as its mission the need to address the challenges facing the black community at home in Chicago and nationally. The group selected subject matter that it would address collectively (the first such theme was the black family) and outlined aesthetic parameters for its output, such as the use of figurative composition, the inclusion of text, and the production of low-price prints that could be made available to a wide audience.

In the process of inventing appropriate means to match its message, the group's message changed. It remained committed to a "shared collective concept" and a "black aesthetic," but soon these concerns led members to look beyond their original local, distinctly U.S., setting.[37] In 1969, COBRA thus became AfriCOBRA, the African Commune of Bad Relevant Artists. With this new name came a new audience, defined not by where it lived but by its African heritage. Successful work was still judged on its ability to convey "to its viewer a statement of truth, of action, of education, of conditions and a state of being to our people."[38] Those conditions were clearly expressed in the assertion that "all Black people, regardless of their land base, have the same problems, the control of their land and economics by Europeans or Euro-Americans."[39] The combined themes of race, class, and power produced imagery replete with the signs of the Black Power movement, such as raised, clenched fists, paramilitary garb, afros, portraits of Malcolm X, and revolutionary texts.

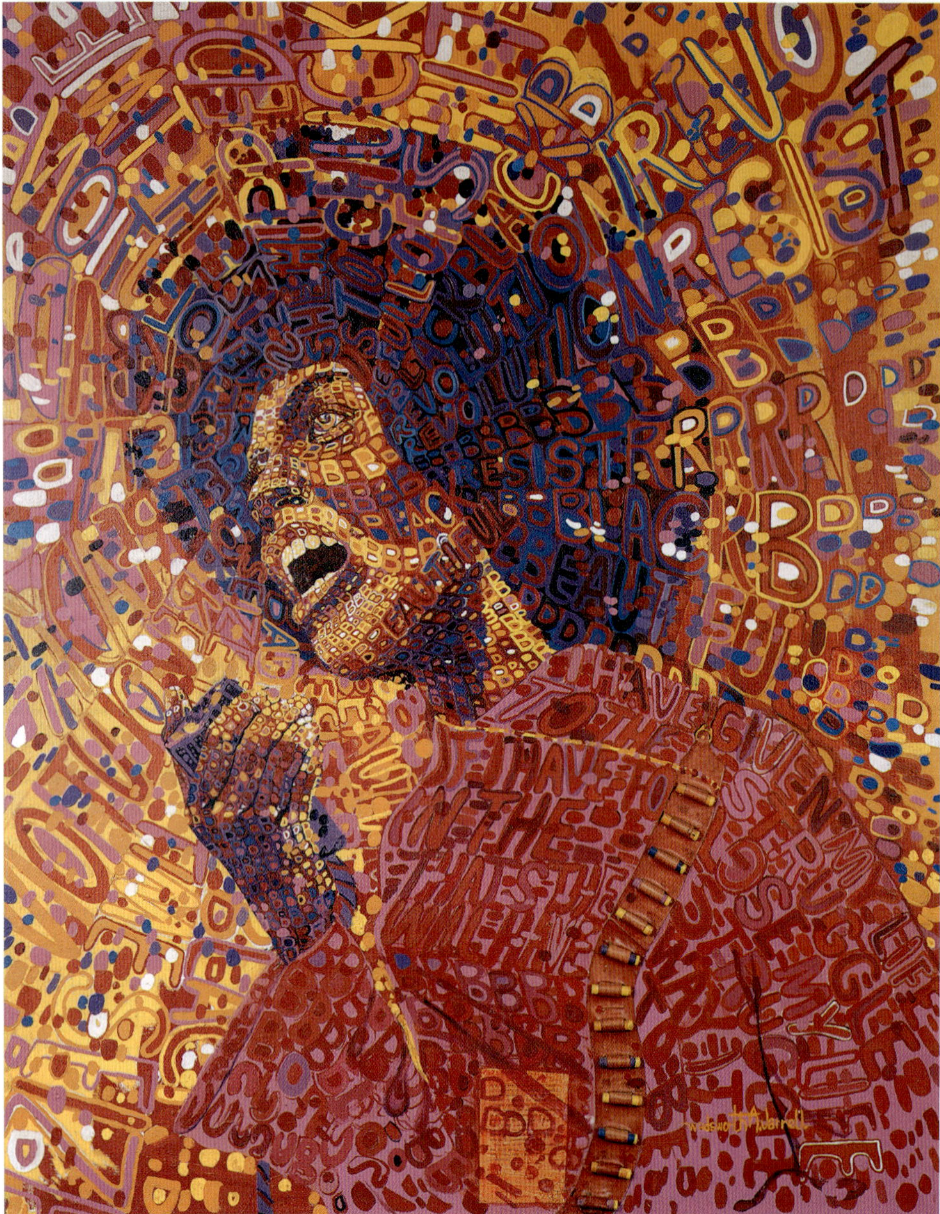

1.22 Wadsworth Jarrell, ***Revolutionary***, 1971. Acrylic on canvas, 50½ × 63½" (128 × 161 cm). Collection of the Brooklyn Museum, New York. © Wadsworth Jarrell.

In Wadsworth Jarrell's *Revolutionary* (1971) (**fig. 1.22**), a portrait of African-American activist Angela Davis, the subject's body, clothing, and the space around her vibrate with words: "BLACK," "BEAUTIFUL," "REVOLUTION," "RESIST," and long lines of "B"s and "R"s. Her loose-fitting blouse with facsimile ammunition belt projecting off the canvas was based on Jae Jarrell's "Revolutionary Suit," which integrated pan-African and paramilitary references in a skirt-suit design with real bullets affixed to the top. In the painting the fabric is covered with the words: "I have given my life to the struggle. If I have to lose my life in the struggle that is the way it will have to be." In 1971, after being accused of providing weapons used in an ambush on a California courtroom intended to free Black Panther organizer George Jackson, Davis was placed on the Federal Bureau of Investigation's list of most-wanted criminals and went into hiding. Four people were killed in the ambush, including a judge. There was little evidence that Davis had been a participant and her case inspired a nationwide campaign for her exoneration; in 1972, she was tried and acquitted. Wadsworth Jarrell's use of the hero's words to represent her body in *Revolutionary* reflected a political reality as well as a formal artistic solution.

The impact of such politically volatile content was further amplified in *Revolutionary* by Jarrell's explosive use of "Coolade Color" and "Shine," terms employed in AfriCOBRA texts to discuss the aesthetic qualities of their art. Jeff Donaldson defined "Shine" as "a major quality, a major quality. We want the things to shine, to have the rich luster of a just-washed fro, of spit shined shoes, of de-ashened elbows and knees and noses. The Shine who escaped the Titanic, the 'li'l light of mine,' patent leather, Dixie Peach, Bar-BQ, fried fish, cars, *ad shineum*!"[40] "Shine" was not a word found in art establishment-sanctioned texts about formalism or the history of the avant-garde. And that, of course, was the point: It was a term coined by black-art theorists for exclusive use in relation to black art. In her declaration about its history and philosophy, AfriCOBRA artist Barbara Jones-Hogu (b. 1938) explained that the group's art and theoretical standpoint were the outcome of "rap[ping] about the hip aesthetic things that a 'negro' group could do."[41] Like much feminist work of the period, AfriCOBRA made clear that aesthetics were culturally specific. Even if they strove to praise AfriCOBRA art, white critics often felt shut out by it. As Donaldson noted, though he and his peers were of the same generation and trained by the same people as the Pop artists, their goals were very different.

Celebration of the specific associative qualities of form and color in a black context, however, did not exclude more formalist discussions of art. The AfriCOBRA theory of representation is particularly striking. Rather than understanding representation as the reflection of an appearance or experience, AfriCOBRA style was presented as a resolution of competing interests, "mimesis at mid-point" as it was dubbed for the group's third exhibition. The appearance of the world in an AfriCOBRA work "marks the spot where the real and the un-real, the objective and the non-objective, the plus and the minus meet. A point exactly between absolute abstractions and absolute naturalism."[42] As in Photorealist work of the period, abstraction was enlisted as a means to produce naturalism. Chuck Close (b. 1940), the best-known Photorealist, began painting by taking a photograph, plotting a grid across it and a corresponding one across his canvas, then transcribing the image by copying it square by square. In 1969, his paintings closely resembled photographs; in the 1970s, the process itself became his subject matter as much as the actual appearance of his sitters. Though AfriCOBRA artists were less methodical, they also conceived of the canvas as a field of abstractions that coalesced to form clear images. As mentioned above, several members of AfriCOBRA marked a further contest between abstraction and representation by including text, often imitating the cadence of spoken words. In a painting such as *Revolutionary*, for instance, forms combine to produce images at the very point where letters and words join to deliver a message about the world.

Emory Douglas and the Black Panther Party

Across the country, in Oakland, California, institutional critique of a very different sort could be found in the work of Emory Douglas, creator of the media-savvy style and iconography of the Black Panther Party. Douglas's training was in commercial art at City College, San Francisco, in the late 1960s. While using his talents to promote the City College Black Students' Association, he met Huey Newton and Bobby Seale, who were then developing the Black Panther platform and strategy. Named minister of culture for the party, Douglas created a public image for the Panthers that would be imitated by liberation movements all over the world. The pages of the Black Panther newspaper provided a gallery of what Douglas called "revolutionary art," that "enlightens the party to continue its vigorous attack against the enemy, as well as educate the masses of black people."[43] Addressing a community that Newton described as highly visual, Douglas integrated graphic design, portraiture, caricature, text, and photography to demonstrate "the Correct Handling of the Revolution."[44] Images in the newspaper revealed how the conditions of daily life demanded social upheaval and how black men, women, and children possessed the moral and physical strength to carry it out. By the early 1970s, the newspaper had a circulation of over 100,000 copies.

Douglas designed the format of the newspaper to maximize its visual impact, including detachable posters that showed black Americans suffering garbage-filled streets and police brutality, and that could be used to spread the Black Panther message. In an image from April 1971 (**fig. 1.23**), this bullet-riddled photograph of a seventeen-year-old boy who was shot by Oakland police gives evidence of the need for community control of the police. By the mid-1970s, Douglas had introduced a more sensitive visual style which used line drawings that were nuanced in detail and soft in effect. Like his earlier collage aesthetic, the drawings demonstrate another face of revolutionary representation and the heterogeneity of both political art and black identity.

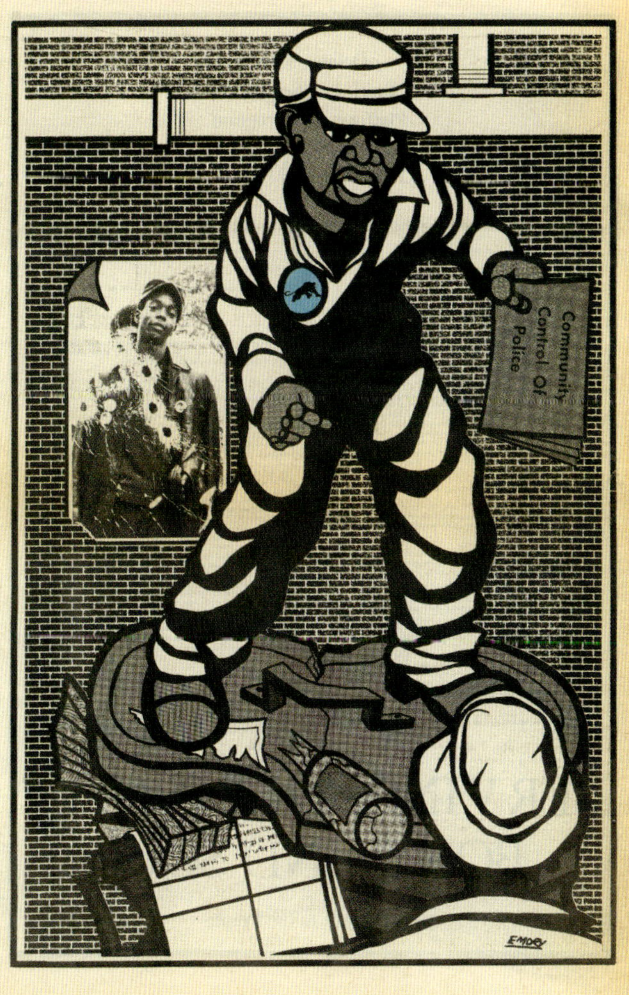

1.23 Emory Douglas, *The Black Panther, April 3*, 1971. Pen, ink, and collage on board, 17 × 11" (43.2 × 27.9 cm). Courtesy the artist.

Feminist Statements

In her 1971 essay "Why Have There Been No Great Women Artists?" the art historian Linda Nochlin (b. 1931) concluded that the idea of "greatness" depended on a set of social practices that by definition excluded women. The institutions that conferred value on a work of art or enabled a young artist to gain skills were all structured in such a way as to make it difficult for women to succeed. Educational opportunities, the customs of workshops and studios, not to mention the venues for patronage, exhibition, and sales, were all shaped to suit men. The few women who did "make it" were exceptions whose success often relied on help from a male guide. The route to change, Nochlin suggested, was not to be more attentive to women within the existing system, but to alter the art system and the structures of society altogether.

Concern about gender difference in the production, reception, and definition of art can be seen in work made at various times and in different places after World War II. Women artists inflected postwar movements including Fluxus, Actionism, and Gutai with gender consciousness. In some cases the feminist politics were explicit. For example, in 1969, VALIE EXPORT (b. 1940), an artist associated with Austrian Actionism, whose participants experimented with ritualistic performances, created *Genital Panic*. For this aggressively confrontational piece, the artist forced viewers to consider the discrepancy between the real and represented worlds of sexuality by entering a cinema wearing crotchless pants and standing directly in front of the seated audience. Photographs taken later and titled *Aktionshose: Genitalpanik (Action Pants: Genital Panic)* showed the artist wielding a machine gun. The gun makes explicit the connection, asserted by EXPORT's performance, between issues of representation and issues of power. However, contrary to rumors that have grown up since, EXPORT denies having this weapon with her on the occasion of the original performance. Other works, such as Yoko Ono's performance *Cut Piece* (1964) (**fig. 1.24**) or film *Fly* (1970) (**fig. 1.25**), demonstrate a more implicit feminist politics through their embrace of the Fluxus interest in simple acts: in this case, cutting clothes and watching a fly. As the viewer realizes that the object on which these acts are being performed is a woman's body, revealed slowly as her clothes are cut away or as the fly and the camera traverse the contours of her body, the content becomes more pointed and political. Throughout the 1970s, feminists would focus on the interplay between the social and the individual, and the represented and the real, to great effect.

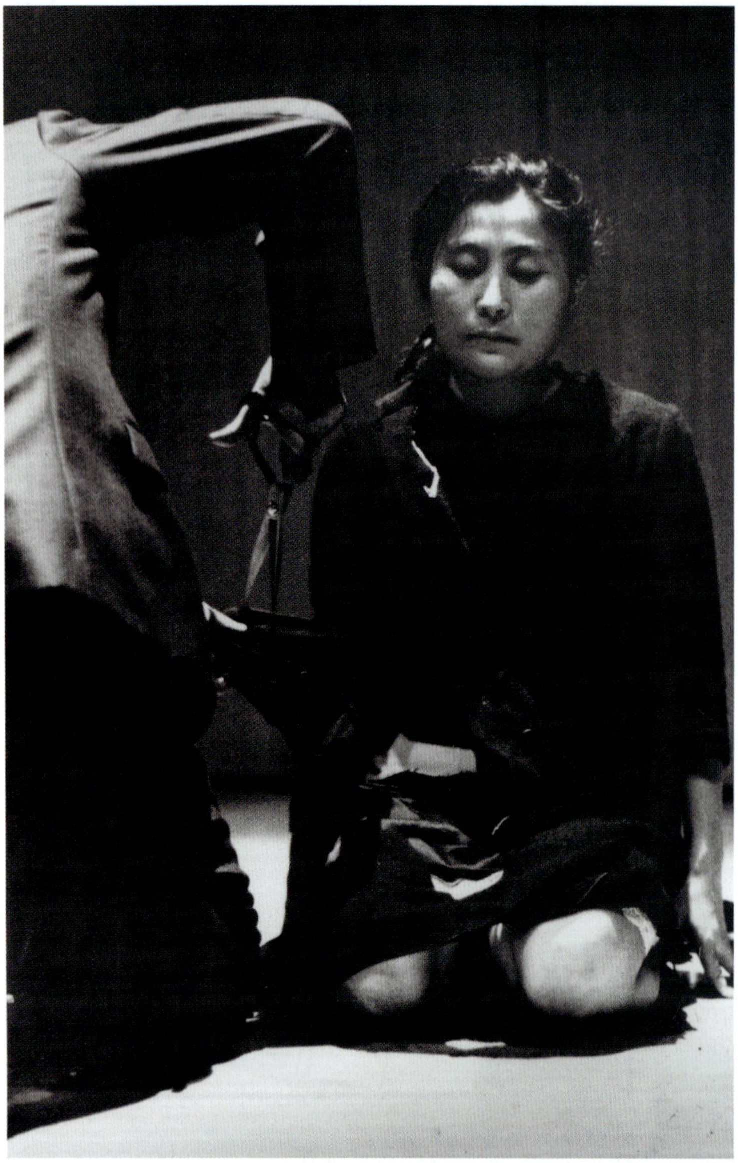

1.24 Yoko Ono, *Cut Piece*, 1964. Performance at Yamaichi Hall, Tokyo, 1964. Courtesy of Yoko Ono.

The Role of Theory

By the 1970s, political and social criticism had become as much a part of an artist's practice as painting or sculpting. This expansion of the artist's purview took place initially in the context of the debates over Minimalism and Process art in texts such as Morris's "Anti-Form," but was increasingly adopted by artists concerned with clarifying the political terrain that they considered relevant to an understanding of their work. Turning to French Poststructuralist theorists such as historians Michel Foucault and Louis Althusser, linguists Roland Barthes and Jacques Derrida, and psychoanalyst Jacques Lacan, as well as different elements of feminist and socialist theory, artists and critics began a process of redefining artistic production as a significant strand of intellectual and political history. As a theory of culture and meaning, the earlier Structuralism had posited that there were patterns within human societies and psyches that could be isolated and shown to repeat across history. The search for and creation of such unifying structures typified twentieth-century intellectual pursuits across the disciplines. The foremost

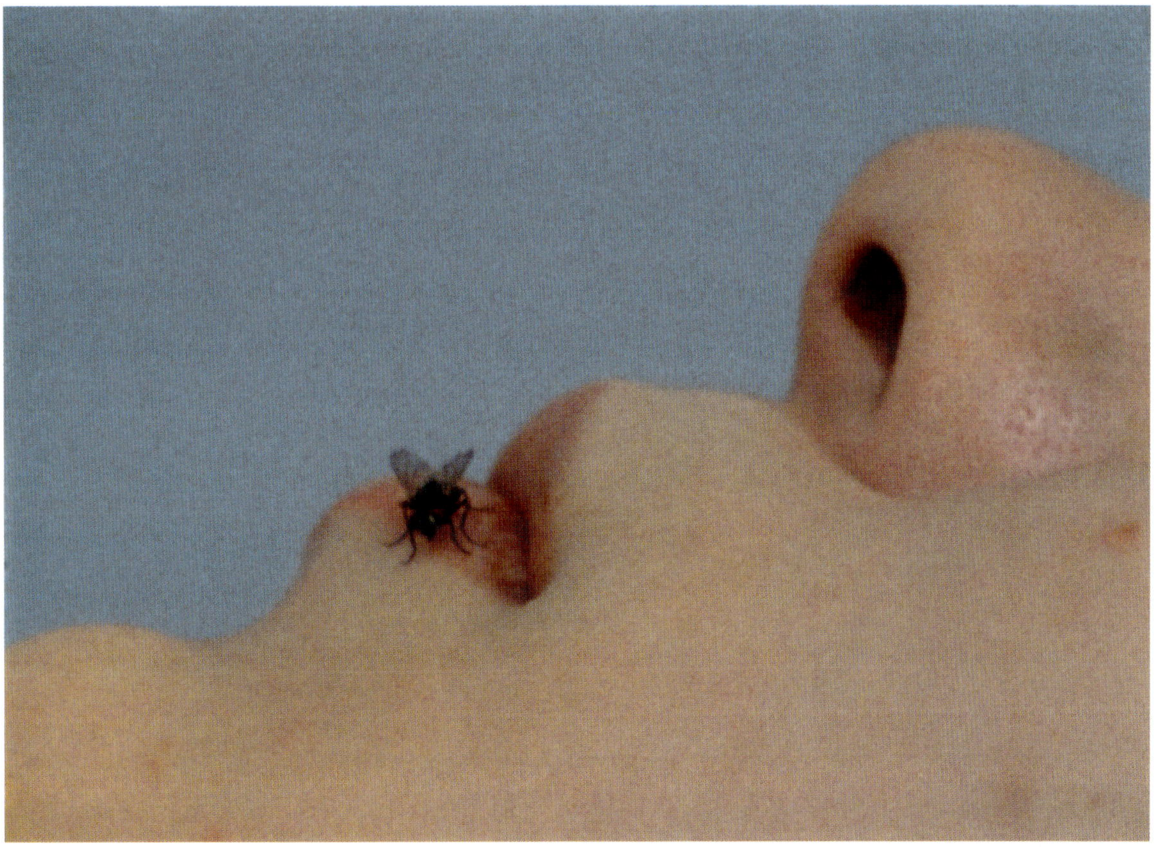

1.25 Yoko Ono, *Fly*, 1970. Film still. Courtesy of Yoko Ono.

Structuralist thinker was the anthropologist Claude Lévi-Strauss, whose analysis of kinship relations led to his articulation of structures of familial and social relations that were seemingly repeated in communities across the spectrum of contemporary and historical humanity. By the 1960s, however, faith in the existence of such universal structures and in our ability to correctly discern and define them had faltered—hence the turn to Poststructuralist analyses.

Drawing on their experience of the radicalism of the 1960s as well as on political theory, European historians and philosophers such as Foucault and Althusser examined the role of power in history. Foucault believed that categories organizing knowledge, from criminal codes to the methods and objects of historical study, functioned to maintain existing power relations; artistic greatness was one such category. By identifying certain practices—technical virtuosity, for instance—as the measure of artistic success, artists could be corraled to work in line with, rather than against, prevailing power structures. Althusser interpreted power in Western society through his theory of the Ideological State Apparatus (ISA), showing how the assumptions one made about society were largely ideological products reflecting the way society was organized. Social norms are thus not collective wisdom but ideological devices that enforce "subjugation to the ruling ideology or the mastery of its practice."[45] Whether one learned to be docile, as did most girls, or active, as did most boys, depended on one's position in society. In addition, corresponding to feminist insights, Althusser's analysis was explicitly Marxist: The labor force was taught submission, while the "agents of exploitation and repression" learned mastery.[46] In Althusser's view, individuals do not choose their own path, as society is structured to preclude options that might upset its balance. Culture plays a role here. For instance, contained in the notion that art is either a form of pure, personal expression or equally pure, formal experimentation, two typical Modernist convictions, there is the assumption that art and society are separate. Such ideas are part of an ISA that keeps the work of artists isolated from that of politicians. In the context of nineteenth- and twentieth-century capitalist industrialism, such beliefs about the separation of art and politics coincided with the disenfranchisement of the working class. Activist artists in the 1960s used the theories of Foucault, Althusser, and others to demonstrate the common cause of artists and the working class.

Nancy Spero

As is evident in EXPORT's and Ono's work, feminist politics often encouraged new formal solutions. In the U.S., Nancy Spero's (1926–2009) creation of an explicitly feminist practice drew on her earlier oil-on-canvas works, which had explored the intersections between figuration and abstraction. By the late 1960s, Spero had turned to hand-printing fragments of personal testimonies, news and police reports, poetry and roughly drawn female forms, which she applied to single pages, scrolls, and eventually walls and ceilings. In this new working practice, Spero—like Leon Golub, to whom she was married—addressed overtly political content. She explained: "I decided to address the issues I was actively involved in—women's issues. I wanted to investigate the more palpable realities of torture and pain."[47] After several years of research and production, Spero completed two series of works, *Torture of Women* (1974) and *Notes in Time on Women* (1979). For *Torture of Women,* she used blocks of texts recording horrific abductions, tortures, and murders of women that she had culled from a variety of public and personal sources. Spero then hand-printed the narratives using a variety of typefaces, generating a formally inventive combination of highly legible and emotionally and morally excruciating content. In *Notes in Time on Women* (**fig. 1.26**), Spero used imagery from a range of historical periods and cultures to expose past and present violence against women. She juxtaposed documentation of assaults on women with images of Greek and Aztec goddesses, fashion models, and athletic nudes. Words and bodies, letters, lines, and colors collide and caress each other in a rhythm that fluctuates from earthly to airborne, from graceful to damaged.

Spero's desire to create a visual language for women's experience of and resistance to societal oppression was shared by and explored in the work of a number of intellectuals and activists. The French literary critic and philosopher Hélène Cixous's account of "women's writing" in her 1975 manifesto "The Laugh of the Medusa" is a key text for interpreting Spero's work. Here, Cixous explained that a woman "must write her self, because this is the invention of a new insurgent writing which ... will allow her to carry out the indispensable ruptures and transformations in her history." Women's textual insurgency required, Cixous argued, a new relationship to the body one that resisted translating sensation into the limiting structures of existing language. She implored women: "Write your self. Your body must be heard. Only then will the immense resources of the unconscious spring forth."[48] Cixous's writing, like Spero's art, was based in a political and sensual experience of the body. It aimed to expose and destroy existing social orders and to envision a previously unimagined future.

Spero enlisted women's experiences to generate the symbols with which to share sensations, emotions, and ideas that up to that point had lacked access to language. Simultaneously destructive and constructive, women's art of this type crossed the formal boundaries between writing, painting, criticism, and theory. "Women's writing," Cixous asserted, was a product of women who had been liberated from the example of history and as such could not truly be "theorized, enclosed, or encoded."[49] Throughout the 1970s Spero produced just such a language of unprecedented form and subversive content. In 1981, she completed *The First Language,* the first of her large-scale print works without text. The piece consisted of images of women dancing, running, threatening, contemplating, even roller-skating. After a decade of explicitly feminist work, she had created a lexicon that, variously using text and imagery separately or together, communicated in the realm of activist politics and feminist theory.

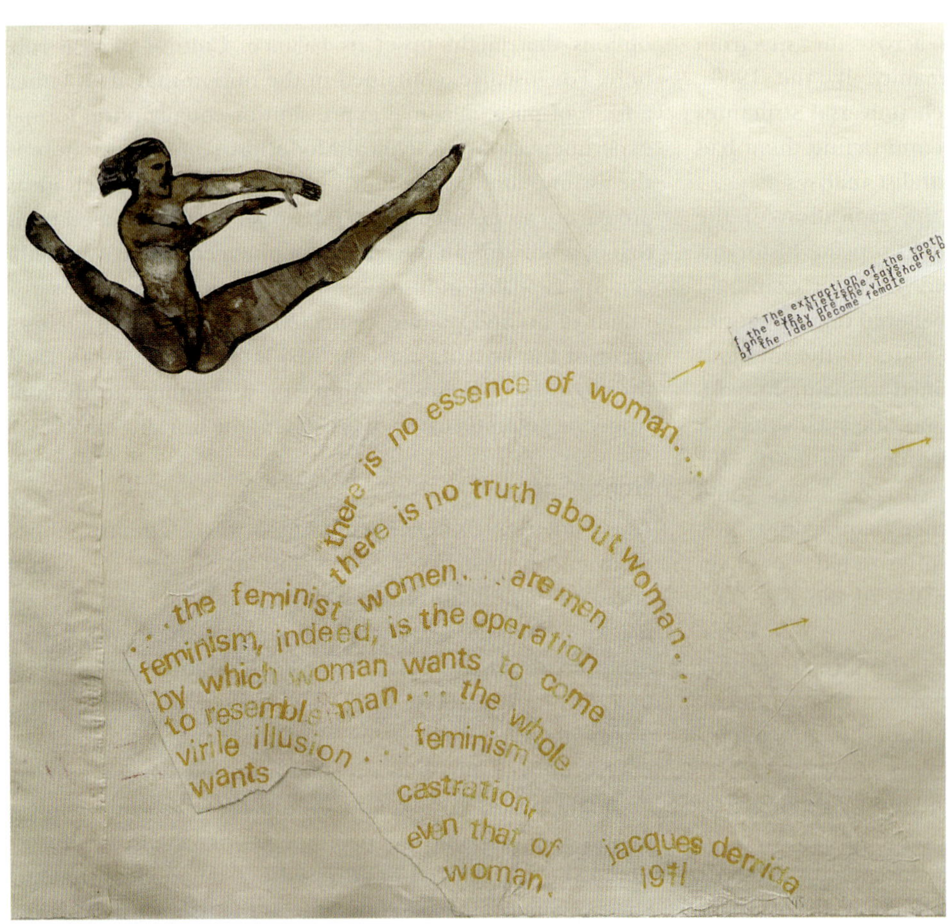

1.26 Nancy Spero, *Notes in Time on Women,* 1979. Detail. Hand-printing, gouache, and collage on paper; 24 panels, overall 20" × 210' (50.8 cm × 64 m). Collection Museum of Modern Art, New York. Courtesy Galerie Lelong, New York.

The Feminist Art Program

By the mid-1970s, U.S. feminist artists could be divided into two groups loosely based on their attitudes toward three issues: belief in a shared female artistic practice; relations with the existing art world; and the balance between social critique and personal expression. Opinion tended to divide along regional lines, with feminists on the West Coast advancing a distinctive female style, a separatist approach to the art world, and a personally expressive art, while their East Coast counterparts by and large argued the reverse.

One major source of this dichotomy was the early and lasting success of the Feminist Art Program (FAP), begun in 1970 by Judy Chicago (b. 1939) at California State University Fresno, and then developed by Chicago and Miriam Schapiro (b. 1923) at the California Institute of the Arts, Valencia, beginning in 1972. The FAP was a response to its founders' (and many other women's) experience of sexism in the art world. Women were making art in basements and bedrooms after coming home from work, cooking meals, and caring for husbands and children. Art schools, then as now, were full of female students, but galleries and museums showed almost no women's art. The FAP's mission was "to help women restructure their personalities to be more consistent with their desires to be artists and to help them build their art-making out of their experiences as women."[50] The concept of training women artists to value their experience and to base communities and artistic identities upon it contrasted with the highly individualistic and competitive approach of contemporary art schools. The FAP encompassed consciousness-raising sessions, performances, discussions, and opportunities to practice painting, sculpture, film, weaving, crafts, collage, assemblage, and installation. It developed a resource center containing a catalogue of images and projects initiated by women artists across the U.S. (Donaldson had set up a similar archive of African-American arts in Chicago.) To some—Judy Chicago in particular—the images in the FAP database revealed a female aesthetic to match the circumstances of female artists.

The most influential FAP production was *Womanhouse: Nurturant Kitchen* (1971–72), a Hollywood mansion converted into a stage, installation, workshop, and community space. *Womanhouse* was a showcase for the alternative processes and products created by self-identified "women artists," and the rooms were turned into materialized fantasies and fantastic metamorphoses of their realities. In *Womanhouse: Nurturant Kitchen* of 1972 (**fig. 1.27**), an installation designed for the house by FAP participants Vicki Hodgetts, Robin Weltsch, and Susan Frazier, the walls, ceilings, windows, and appliances glowed with warm, enveloping shades of pink, while eggs appeared to have migrated from the stovetop directly to the ceiling, where Hodgetts had sculpted dozens of them hovering over the visitors. As the eggs reached the edge of the ceiling and headed down the walls, they turned into breasts, capturing the sensuality many in the group associated with the kitchen, but also the sense of exposure and

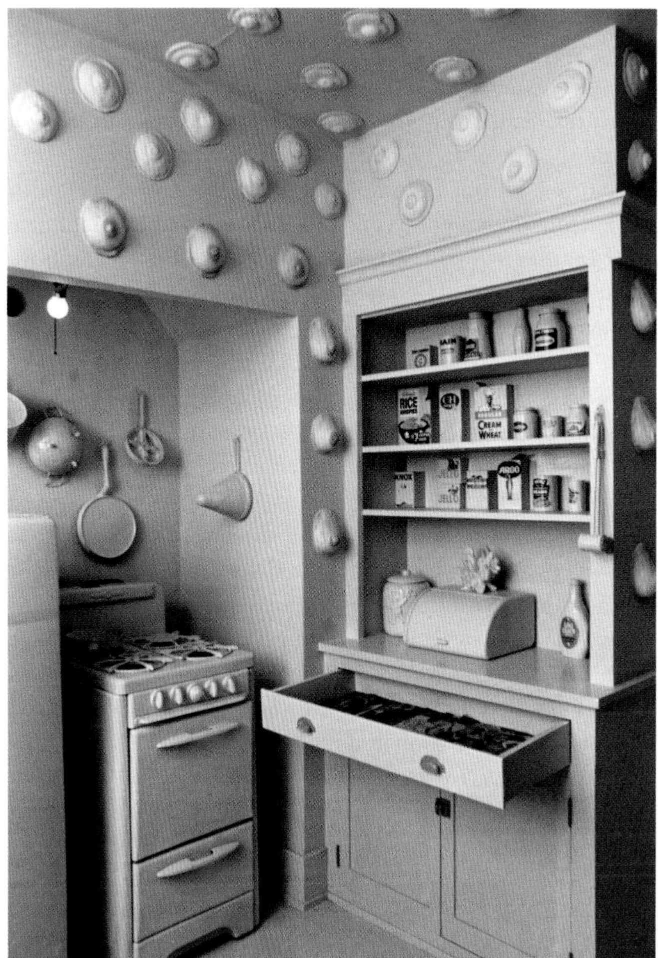

1.27 *Womanhouse* installation in Los Angeles featuring Robin Weltsch's *Kitchen* and Vicki Hodgetts's *Eggs to Breasts* (sponsored by the Feminist Art Program at CalArts), 1972. Gelatin silver print, $9\frac{15}{16} \times 7\frac{15}{16}$" (25.3 × 20.2 cm). The Getty Research Institute, 2000.M.43.1.

danger. Though the piece, subtitled *Eggs to Breasts*, was attributed to Hodgetts, it was designed collaboratively, matching personal inspiration to group vision.

Integrating anatomy with architecture was a common motif of the *Womanhouse* installations, as was the works' ambivalent combination of sensual pleasure and social anxiety. Faith Wilding's (b. 1943) *Crocheted Environment* (1972) enveloped audiences in "womb-shelters," while Sandy Orgel's *Linen Closet* (1972) featured a nude female mannequin walking through shelves of sheets and towels and out into the room.[51] *Womanhouse* exemplified the type of alternative institution that feminist practice could generate. Audience members walked out of the building exhilarated and often quite upset as a result of experiencing the sensations of confinement, restriction, and liberation so dramatically visualized within. As such, *Womanhouse* politicized many of its visitors.

Judy Chicago

Critic Anne-Marie Sauzeau (b. 1938) argued that the key to representing femininity did not lie in using images drawn from reality to challenge stereotypes, since such a strategy allowed the existing order to define the terms of reference, "which means betraying the basic ... OTHERNESS of women's experience."[52] Proposing a radical language of otherness, Sauzeau posited: "The actual creative project of [women] ... involves BETRAYING the expressive mechanisms of culture."[53] From 1974 to 1979, Judy Chicago worked with a team of women to create the monumental collaborative work *Dinner Party* (**fig. 1.28**) as both a real and a metaphorical attempt to bring women to the table and to wrest the expressive mechanisms of culture from the grip of men. The work consists of a triangular table with place settings for thirty-nine named female "guests of honor," each with an individually designed plate in the form of a symbolic vagina. The names of a further 999 women are painted on the tiled floor around the table. Like *Womanhouse* before it, *The Dinner Party* laid claim to the empowering capacity of artistic expression on behalf of women. It replaced the exclusively male cast of traditional "Last Supper" paintings—Jesus flanked by his twelve disciples—with a celebration of vaginal power. Perhaps this amounted to a "betrayal" of male-dominated (or phallocentric) cultural forms—the controversy that the piece spurred upon its initial exhibition and the reticence, until 2002, for any museum to take *The Dinner Party* into its collection suggests that it was perceived as such. However, Chicago's inadvertent mirroring of the phallocentric hierarchical order, as represented by the provision of "places of honor" at the table, has been seen to undercut the work's liberating quality.[54]

Mary Kelly

In England, the work of the American-born artist Mary Kelly (b. 1941) represented a very different approach to making art about experience, arriving at emotion and politics through a highly conceptual and analytic practice. In her striking contemporary portrait of a mother and child, *Post-Partum Document* (1973–79), Kelly combined psychoanalytic explanations of identity formation with records of the growth of her own newborn son and her personal experience as a new mother. Kelly's investigation drew on the work of Jacques Lacan, who developed Freud's ideas in wide-ranging intellectual contexts including linguistics and philosophy. She also observed the stages of child-rearing with methodical rigor, including such things as notes on her child's linguistic development, food intake, topics of conversation, drawing and writing, and even his soiled diapers. In the image shown here (**fig. 1.29**), we see how Kelly combined different elements from her analysis, insisting, for instance, that scientific observation is literally sullied by the physicality of child-rearing. As we read this and other sections of *Post-Partum Document* we come to know Kelly as the artist/mother who is both emotionally sensitive to the subtle changes in her son's life and intellectually brilliant in her careful analysis and selective accumulation of data. Although Chicago's hijacking of the expressive mechanisms of male-dominated culture also continued to be reflected in feminist practice, Kelly's more distanced, analytical approach, with its concern for issues of

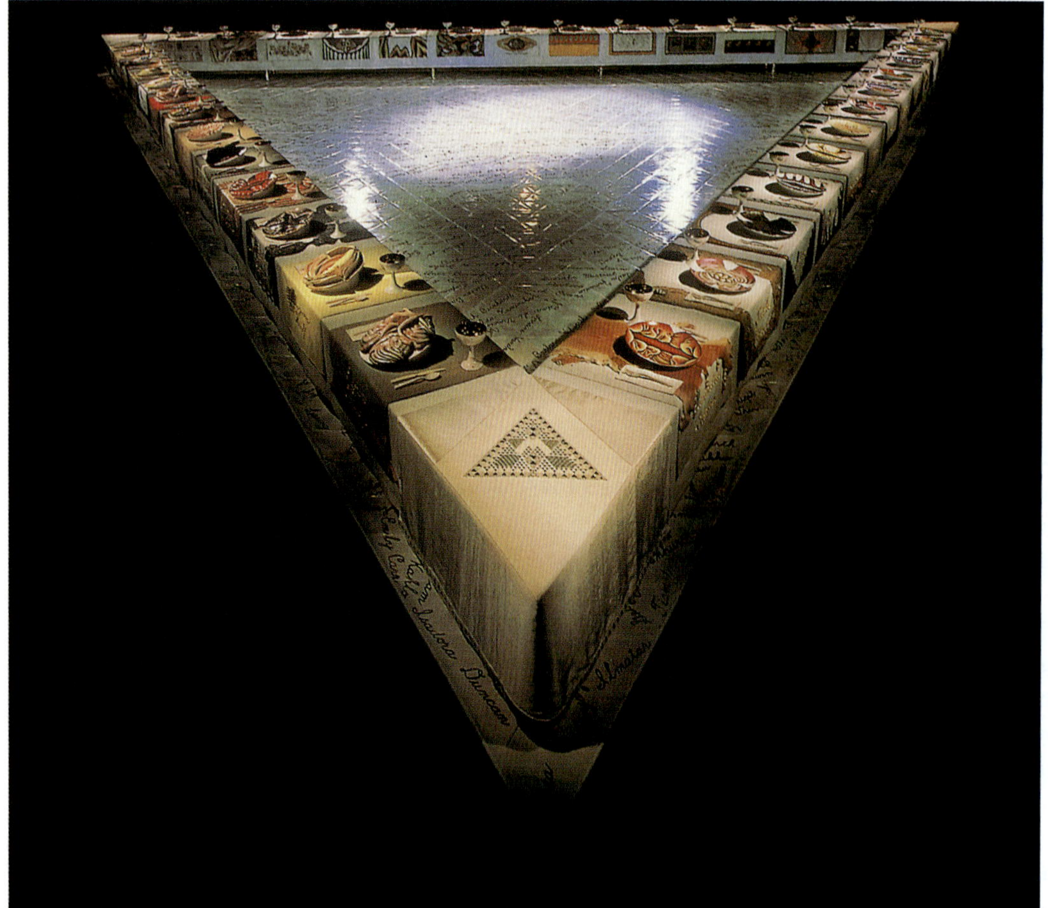

1.28 Judy Chicago, *Dinner Party*, 1974–79. White tile floor inscribed in gold with 999 women's names; triangular table with painted porcelain, sculpted porcelain plates, and needlework, each side 48" (14.6 m). The Brooklyn Museum of Art, New York.

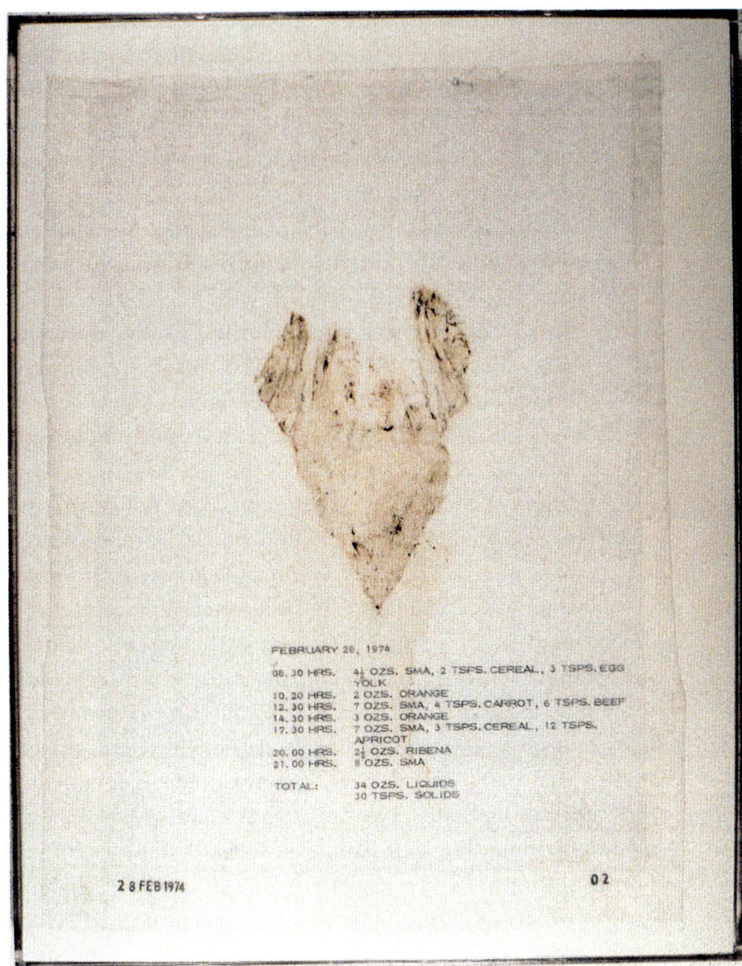

1.29 Mary Kelly, ***Post-Partum Document, Analysed Faecal Stains and Feeding Charts***, 1974. Detail. Perspex unit, white card, diaper linings, plastic sheeting, paper, and ink; 1 of 31 units, each 13⅞ × 11" (35.5 × 28 cm). Collection, Art Gallery of Ontario. © Mary Kelly.

psychoanalysis, identity, and representation, would prove to be more in tune with the critical art of the 1980s.

Martha Rosler

Almost immediately upon its creation, *Womanhouse* became a reference point by which feminists identified their own particular brands of feminism. To artist and critic Martha Rosler (b. 1943), the FAP appeared to practice Abstract Expressionism "by other means," thus committing more to expressing the self than transforming society.[55] When asked in 1973 about their relationship to *Womanhouse*, members of AIR (Artists in Residence), the New York women artists' cooperative gallery co-founded by Nancy Spero, either rejected the comparison entirely or used it to draw distinctions between the East and West Coast projects. Agnes Denes (b. 1931) noted that work produced in California reminded women of their accomplishments and encouraged them to create art from their experiences. AIR, on the other hand, was "trying to get out, to go forward to do innovative art and art of any kind, not looking backwards to what we left."[56] While the FAP was raising feminist consciousness and creating new languages to express it, members of AIR were doing studio visits and opening a gallery; AIR responded more directly to practical problems facing working artists. As the critic Lucy Lippard (b. 1937), who had helped give a voice to Minimalist and Process art in the 1960s and to feminist art from the 1970s on, observed, women artists who began to show their work in the 1970s had often been artists for a long time. Because they had had few professional opportunities after art school, however, their careers had been shaped in the absence of the artistic, personal, and professional benefits that usually came with being part of the art community. The agenda of groups such as AIR, WAR (Women Artists in Revolt), and increasingly vocal groups of curators and historians was to provide a context for this work and to generate a dialogue about it in feminist terms.

In a 1977 essay on feminist art in California, Rosler argued that the most pressing issue for feminist and other contemporary artists was to set their work in a political context. She observed that art by women was shown and discussed only in contexts where the political challenge of the women's movement could be neutralized. In such circumstances, said Rosler, feminist art could be presented as "valorizing, in the name of 'women's culture,' [practices] developed under conditions oppressive to women" and might "wind up serving repressive ends."[57] As critics of Process and Earth art noted in the late 1960s, and as the Black Emergency Cultural Coalition found in the early 1970s, radical art often needed partisan writers to help prevent it from being presented in ways that merely served dealers, museums, and the status quo. Making art was up to the artists; making it dangerous required critics and historians.

Rosler's conclusion cut two ways. Not only was "wider attention to feminist theorizing" required, but also "new theory needs new practice."[58] Her *Semiotics of the Kitchen* (1975) (**fig. 1.30**) illustrates one form of this new practice. The six-minute film features Rosler wearing an apron and standing at a kitchen counter as though she were on the set of an advertisement or cooking show. From this stage, Rosler presents and demonstrates a series of kitchen utensils, beginning with her apron and proceeding alphabetically through the rest of the items around her. She raises the objects, pronounces their names, and demonstrates their use, giving physical expression to the dominance that tools of the kitchen exert over the woman who use them. As Rosler continues, the letters of the alphabet themselves make an appearance among these conventional kitchen instruments: When she reaches "U," "V," and "W," Rosler holds her arms up, knife and fork in hand, to form the letters. She thus turns language into just one more object shaping and controlling women's daily activities and even their bodies. As the demonstration progresses, however, the viewer becomes aware

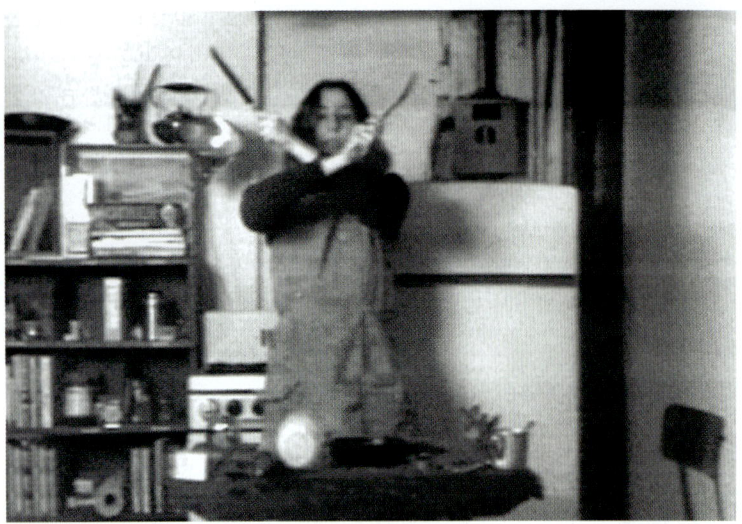

1.30 Martha Rosler, ***Semiotics of the Kitchen***, 1975. Video, 6:09 minutes. Courtesy Mitchell-Innes & Nash.

of an uneasy relationship between the tools and the woman. Some objects—the hamburger press and juicer, for instance—reveal their expected kitchen functions. Others, however—such as the knife, fork, and icepick—are presented like weapons. These momentary glimpses of possible violent disruption in the otherwise peaceful routine of a woman's life are quite different from the cathartic expressions of *Womanhouse.* There is no drama and no personal expression—potential action is simply pointed to, before the rhythm of the alphabet resumes, and the presentation and the presenter are both kept in order. *Semiotics of the Kitchen* points to the collusion between language and sexism, but it also demonstrates resistance and humor. Often, Rosler turns very utilitarian gestures, such as serving or stirring, into slapstick comedy, as when she pretends to throw the contents of a ladle or spoon off-camera. Such humor lightens but also emphasizes the seriousness of the project. In a spirit akin to the social protest movements of the 1950s and 1960s, Rosler's film suggests that the first step toward changing power relations is to make them visible, while her threatening gestures with sharp objects indicate the urgency of the matter.

Suzanne Lacy

The challenge facing artists seeking to reveal the political nature of daily experience was that, as Beuys said in relation to Fluxus, presenting reality was not enough. Injustice is not always self-evident; it must be labeled as well as shown. Without visible and political self-consciousness, art risks leaving the viewer unsure how to interpret what he or she sees. Instructions and labels, however, reveal an artist's point of view and thus tend to run counter to the expectations that most viewers have for art. The work of West Coast artist Suzanne Lacy (b. 1945) and East Coast-based Hannah Wilke (1940–93) demonstrate different options for a critical feminist representation.

Lacy's integration of performance, installation, and community outreach is on vivid display in works such as *Three Weeks in May* (1977), which typifies the practice she has continued to develop since the 1970s. Each day of the three-week project, Lacy went to the central office of the Los Angeles Police Department to gather information about the number and locations of rapes reported the previous day. In a gallery space, she then assembled the police reports in a systematic manner, repeating a format used in work such as Haacke's *Shapolsky et al.* A second public venue was created at City Hall, where Lacy presented a large map of Los Angeles County with markers to indicate where each rape had taken place. Around each location was a ring of smaller notations signifying the number of rapes that go unreported for every call made to the police. These visual components were accompanied by demonstrations, educational and political activities, and performances including dramatic productions as well as rituals of catharsis and healing. The events added the emotive and personal features of West Coast feminism to the analytical, intellectual quality typical of East Coast work. In 2012, Lacy reinvented the piece as *Three Weeks in January* (**fig. 1.31**), again creating a map of violence against women and facilitating a series of public events. Lacy collaborated with Los Angeles organizations including Code Pink and Peace over Violence, and

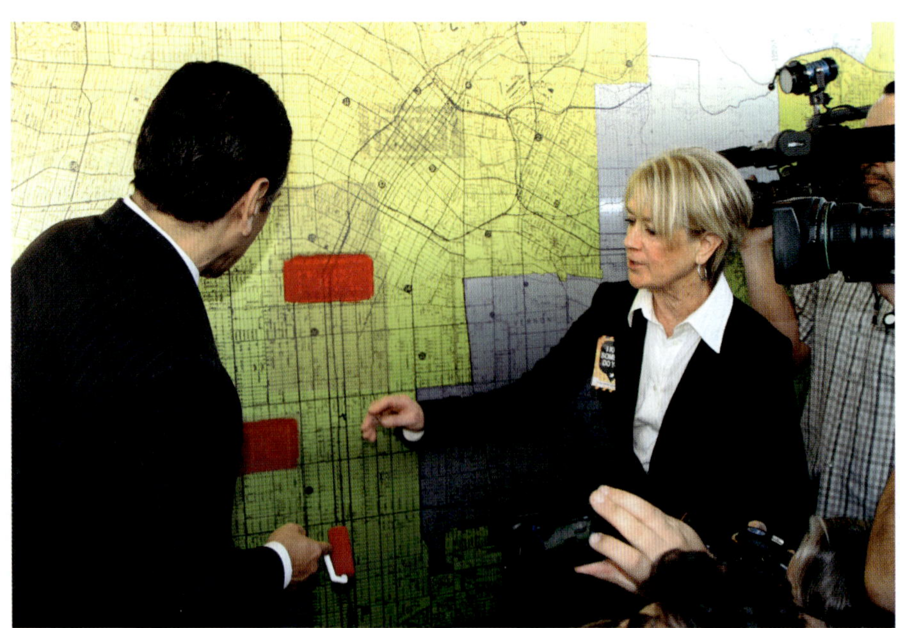

1.31 Suzanne Lacy, ***Three Weeks in January***, 2012. Lacy and Mayor Antonio Villaraigosa at the opening press conference of this performance piece. Produced by Los Angeles Contemporary Exhibitions for the Getty Pacific Standard Time Performance and Public Art Festival, January 2012. Courtesy of the artist.

held press conferences, vigils, panels, and performances. The comparison with the epidemic of violence in the late 1970s was significant: 2,387 sexual assaults were reported in 1977; in 2011, there were fewer than half that number, with a higher percentage of the crimes being reported. Lacy's strategy of making art about political issues by utilizing means often associated with organizing and protest has been termed "public practice" and constitutes the focus of the graduate program that she now runs at Otis College of Art and Design in Los Angeles. Lacy's program and projects such as *Three Weeks in January* demonstrate the continued urgency with which contemporary artists are creating socially engaged art.

Hannah Wilke

On the East Coast, Hannah Wilke used a mix of performance and sculpture to reflect social, personal, and aesthetic concerns. As described in 1975 by critic Cindy Nemser, Wilke's work sounds as though it would be at home in *Womanhouse*: "Hannah Wilke ... currently produces vaginal forms out of pastel-tinted latex, pink pigmented terra cotta, multi-colored lint, and grey-toned kneaded erasers."[59] Despite at first appearing personal and emotive, however, these small sculptures became more ambivalent when viewers were invited to survey the large series, choose their favorite vagina, pay for it, and take it home. The impact of the work rested on its identity as a carefully sculpted form and an individually priced commodity, a comment on the commercialization of art as much as the objectification of women. The feminism of Wilke's work become more apparent in *S.O.S. Starification Object Series* (1974–82) (**fig. 1.32**), for which Wilke presented the vaginal forms in a variety of ways: presented in frames, display cases, and, most memorably, made out of gum and applied like three-dimensional tattoos on the artist's face, neck, and torso. The vagina in these works is both star and scar, a label for the socialized sexuality that empowers women as sexual beings and the brand that defines them as sex objects. Wilke's sculptures explore the process of objectification in an awkward yet alluring way. On the one hand, the forms epitomize rejection: They are chewed up and spat out. On the other, they are produced by the action of lips, tongue, fingers, and saliva, and so allude to physical intimacy. In photographs of the work, Wilke strikes fashion-model poses with the vaginal objects thus combining pop-culture and conventional norms of beauty, which Wilke satisfies, with more complex issues of objectification, repulsion, and desire, as well as those of politics, feminism, and representation.

By the end of the 1970s, hotly contested questions of the social dimensions of artistic production and the politics of representation remained unresolved. The following chapters address the response to the appeal made by Rosler, Sauzeau and others for new art and new theory. Chapter 2 examines appropriation art, while Chapter 3 looks at the more visceral productions of Neo-Expressionism. Although the debates that had shaped art in the 1960s and 1970s continued into the following decade, their tenor changed. The activist politics of the Vietnam years and the social movements that developed in their wake lost ground to the political and social conservatism of the Reagan/Thatcher era. In addition, a boom in the art market introduced the topic of price. Radicalism in contemporary art remained but, as will be discussed, politics looked different in the 1980s than it had in the 1970s.

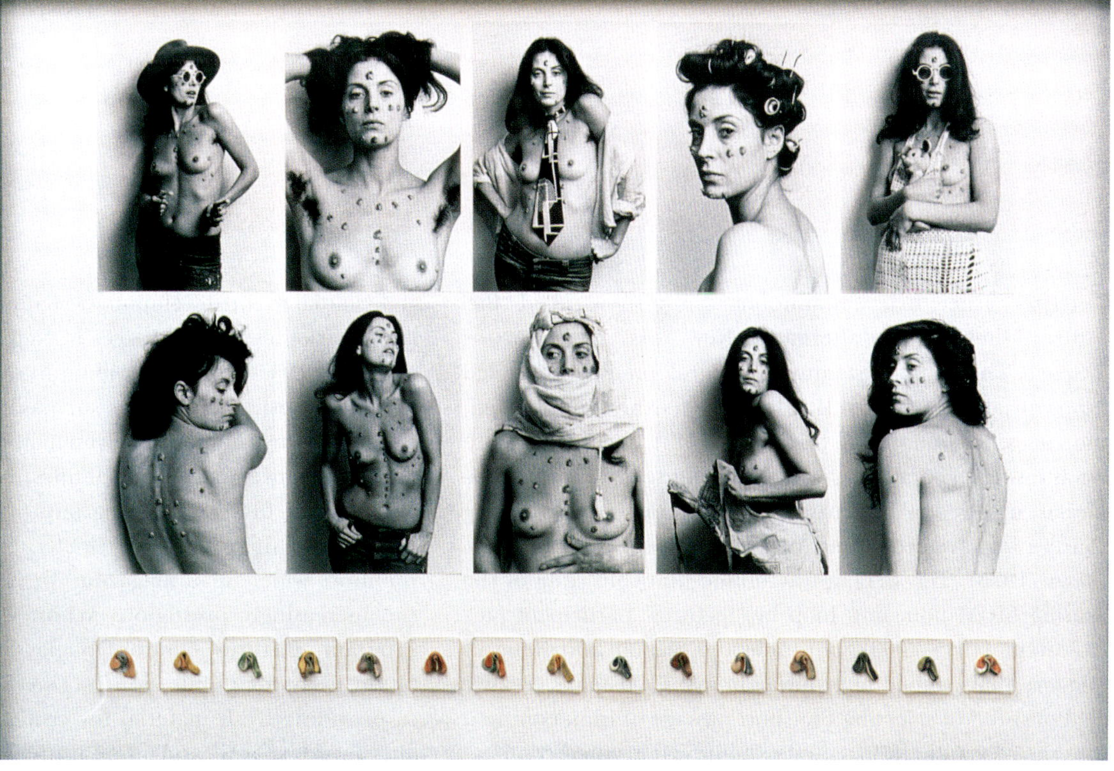

1.32 Hannah Wilke, *S.O.S. Starification Object Series*, 1974–82. Gelatin silver prints with chewing gum sculptures, 40 × 58½ × 2¼" (101.6 × 148.6 × 5.7 cm). The Museum of Modern Art, New York. Courtesy Ronald Feldman Fine Arts, New York.

2

Taking Pictures: Appropriation and Its Consequences

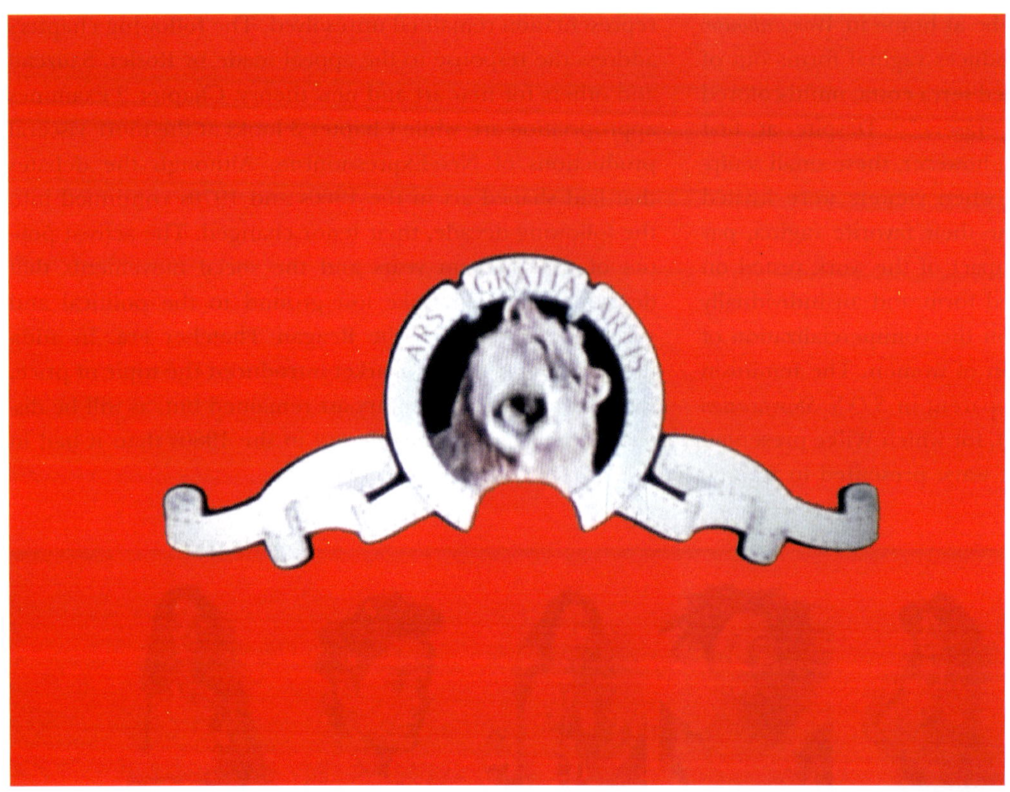

2.1 Jack Goldstein, *Metro-Goldwyn-Mayer*, 1975. 16 mm film, color, sound, 2'. Courtesy Galerie Buchholz, Berlin/Cologne and the Estate of Jack Goldstein.

In 1977, a new style was announced in a show called "Pictures," held at the alternative New York gallery Artists Space. This chapter examines the development of so-called "appropriation art" from this late 1970s exhibition through the 1980s. Responding to the idea that the meaning of both art and self is generated through social discourse, appropriation art involved taking imagery from a variety of pre-existing sources and "re-presenting" it as one's own. *Metro-Goldwyn-Mayer* (1975) (**fig. 2.1**), a two-minute film consisting of the roaring MGM lion on a loop by "Pictures" participant Jack Goldstein (1945–2003), illustrates the blatant borrowing of imagery that typified appropriation art. Goldstein's creative act consisted of selecting the short passage of film, editing it into the repeating format, and exhibiting it in a new context.

Essential to the development of appropriation was the proliferation of alternative spaces in New York in the late 1970s and early 1980s that were willing to show potentially confusing and abrasive art. Venues such as Artists Space sought to create an environment in which intellectual and political concerns outweighed financial ones. The new movement was also closely connected to a group of critics identified with the art and theory journal *October*, but who also wrote for the more widely read magazine *Art in America* and taught at the increasingly prestigious Whitney Independent Studies Program. "Pictures" curator Douglas Crimp adapted his exhibition essay for publication in *October* in 1979. In addition to providing fresh material for critical consideration within alternative spaces and the academy—"Pictures" traveled to the Allen Art Museum at Oberlin College, Ohio, the Los Angeles Institute of Contemporary Art, and the University of Colorado, Boulder—appropriation also contributed to the transformation of the commercial gallery world, beginning with the foundation of Metro Pictures gallery in 1980 by Janelle Reiring and Helene Winer, who had previously worked at Castelli Gallery and Artists Space, respectively. The first show at Metro Pictures was devoted almost exclusively to appropriation artists, including Sherrie Levine and Cindy Sherman, both of whom were discussed in Crimp's 1979 essay (Sherman had been working at Artists Space in 1977 but was not included in the original show), as well as Richard Prince. Soon after, Louise Lawler also joined Metro Pictures. The gallery enabled this group of young New York artists to have access to intellectual, critical, and commercial platforms, in the process demonstrating not only the power of their work, but also the continuing role of New York as the linchpin in the art world.

Douglas Crimp, the curator of "Pictures," chose the exhibition's title in large part for its easy familiarity.[1] Free of specific art-historical associations, "pictures" is a common word, used to refer to all kinds of images, from paintings in a museum to illustrations in a children's book. The "Pictures" artists took images and stripped them of the contexts—advertisements, movies, newspapers, art museums—that had helped fix their original meaning. Reframed, these appropriated images could be analyzed as functional parts of various different social systems much as one might take apart a machine to investigate its operation and examine its constituent parts.

Crimp, an art historian as well as a curator, defined the practice of appropriation in opposition to formalist critic Michael Fried's concept of "grace,"[2] which referred to the sort of spiritual experience that will be familiar to anyone who has stood wordlessly entranced in front of a work of art. For Crimp, and indeed for Fried as well, the definition of art in terms of "grace" had the effect of setting it apart from daily life. Since the late 1950s, however, many artists had objected to this separation of art and life; Crimp's exhibition took up the argument again. The "Pictures" artists, and appropriationists in general, he argued, perceived Modernist art and culture, due to its promise of transcendent experiences of the kind Fried had described, to have been responsible for fostering a desire to turn away from the world. Appropriation artists by contrast focused their attention on one aspect of daily life: the ubiquity of representation, whether in mass culture, as in Goldstein's *Metro-Goldwyn-Mayer* or Richard Prince's photographs of cigarette advertising, or in high culture, as in the reproduction of Modernist artworks in the practices of Sherrie Levine. By prioritizing copies over originals, appropriation artists directed the viewer's eye toward their source material, while simultaneously challenging its authority. By the end of the 1980s, political action groups such as ACT UP (see Chapter 4) and the Guerrilla Girls had made appropriation the dominant visual strategy for contemporary activist art. Even in the twenty-first century, though appropriation has been adopted by mainstream Hollywood moviemakers, the music business, and, inevitably, the advertising industry, artists of every ilk continue to renew its critical application.

Appropriation is based on the insight that our sense of self and community is constructed from the barrage of images that continually confronts us in the public sphere—on television, in art, and in almost every other form of social interaction. In this context, photography is particularly important, since it is the medium by which most messages are conveyed in public. Appropriation artists such as Sherrie Levine, Cindy Sherman, Silvia Kolbowski, and Richard Prince were not trained as photographers, but nonetheless used the camera to acquire source material from the image bank of contemporary society. The "amateur" qualities of their photographs, allowing flaws in the developing and printing process and eschewing formally precise compositions or technically polished final executions, laid bare the act of picture taking and, in theory, made the politics of picture making visible. Such concern with the process of interpretation—with how we give pictures meaning—was claimed by numerous critics to be a characteristic of contemporary art. Craig Owens, for example, thought that allegory had become the preferred artistic mode of the 1980s.[3] Allegory relies on the viewer's ability to equate concrete visual representations with more abstract meanings, such as a cigarette-smoking cowboy with North American masculinity. Appropriation, like allegory, requires its audience to be alert to the duplicity of images. Even with a sympathetic audience, however, and especially with one unfamiliar with contemporary art, appropriation artists take on a twofold responsibility: They must draw attention to the mechanisms of representation and convey their own particular analysis of them.

Power on Display

The act of creating finished works by copying, despite having been introduced to the art world first by Marcel Duchamp and then by Andy Warhol decades before, remained unsettling into the 1980s. Placing Levine's *Untitled (President 4)* (1979) (see fig. 2.2) alongside Warhol's *200 One-Dollar Bills* (1962) (see fig. 0.7) undoubtedly makes the latter appear comparatively artful and expressive, suddenly full of the signs of artistic transformation that some critics back in the 1960s had argued were missing. Moreover, in contrast to the nearly encyclopedic accumulation of imagery in the work of Warhol or Rauschenberg, the appropriation artists' archive was much more pointed in what it included: Images of sex, power, gender stereotypes, and tokens of U.S. power predominated. A visitor to the "Pictures" exhibition or to Metro Pictures gallery in the early 1980s would have been struck by the political nature of the art on view. Readers of commentaries on the work likewise could have found many connections to the activist art criticism of the 1960s and 1970s. As Silvia Kolbowski has pointed out, appropriation as an artistic strategy was intimately bound to the political struggle for ethical and just representation, not merely in the art world but beyond it as well. Appropriation was a means of taking control of the tools of power and repurposing the means of representation that, in the age of mass media, are the primary means of consolidating the ideology of the status quo. With this new movement, the social criticism that had been so central to the art of the previous decade was finding a new voice.

Sherrie Levine

In 1978, the year after she had exhibited in "Pictures," Sherrie Levine (b. 1947) began a series of untitled works consisting of images of fashionable women and sentimental mother-and-child groups cut to fit the silhouettes of U.S. presidents (**fig. 2.2**). This series, in which the feminine spaces of the U.S. middle class are framed by the masculine face of American power, typifies early appropriation practice. Levine took her images of motherhood from the women's magazines that shaped the idea of femininity for thousands of readers, and placed them within profile portraits of presidents Washington, Lincoln, and Kennedy. The photogenic charm of the models, the soothing prosperity of their settings, and the gentle authority of a magazine are thus reframed through the lens of political power. Levine's *Presidents* illustrate the intimate connection between the conventions of domestic life and the established forms of governance. In the Kennedy portrait, the idyllic image of a satisfied, attractive white mother at home with her daughter encapsulates the substance of early 1960s America, even as the presidential profile delineates the boundaries of its space. Such gender conventions—men of power and women in the home—Levine's work asserts, are not merely the unthinking results of contemporary society, they are the deliberate means by which the status quo perpetuates itself. If the power of the iconic image of Kennedy as Cold War victor staring down the communists is conveyed in the contour, it is stabilized, literally filled in, by the scene of female tranquility. The strength of the masculine public sphere is dependent on the passivity of this feminine private space. In Crimp's argument, the image demonstrates how U.S. society is thus defined by the relationship between two misleading myths of gender.[4] As if replaying the contest between contour and plane, between line and color, Levine presents a deadlock of gender politics. To breach this restrictive and reductive trap required a systemic critique that further violated the boundary between art and life; such an analysis is visible in Levine's later work.

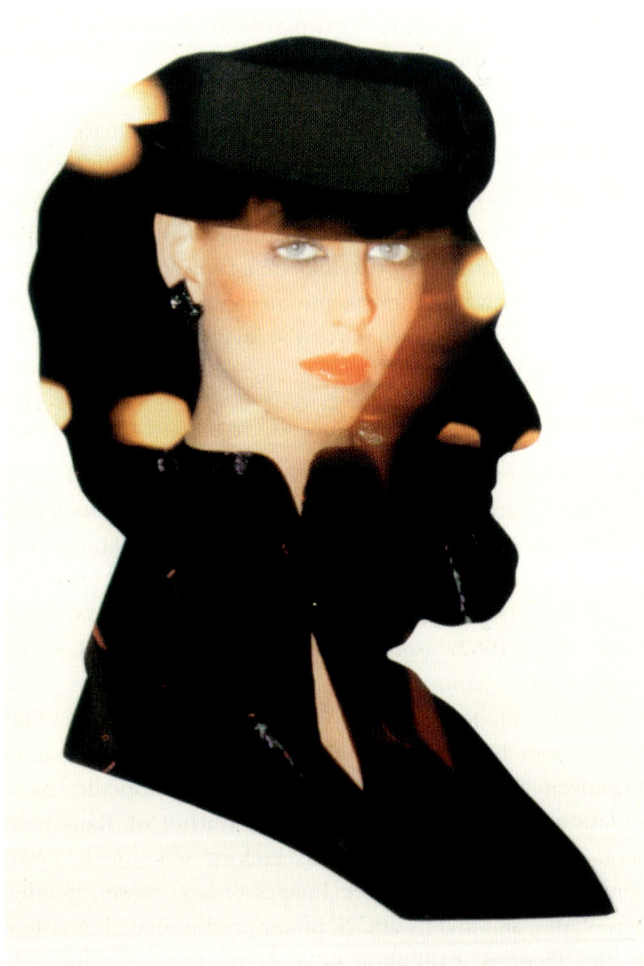

2.2 Sherrie Levine, *Untitled (President 4)*, 1979. Collage on paper, 24 × 18" (60.9 × 45.7 cm). The Metropolitan Museum of Art, New York. © Sherrie Levine. Courtesy Paula Cooper Gallery, New York.

Following the presidents, Levine turned from mass-media imagery to the archive of the museum, most famously by photographing the photography of iconic modern photographers. Disposing of the silhouette, which allowed the viewer to compare the image created by the contour and the one captured within, Levine's photographs of photographs, such as *After Walker Evans: 7* (1981) (**fig. 2.3**), align the frame of the copy with that of the original. *After Walker Evans: 7* is a single image, appropriated in its entirety. The creative act of selection and manipulation—gestures with which, thanks to Pop and Conceptual art, we are already quite familiar—has been reduced by half for the compositions are identical. *After Walker Evans: 7* is Levine's photograph of Evans's (1903–75) classic 1936 photograph *Farmhouse Hale County, Alabama* (**fig. 2.4**), one of a series taken by Evans illustrating Southern poverty during the Great Depression. The rephotographed photograph appears much as an art historian might present it during a lecture, not as evidence of Levine's aesthetic skill but as a piece of history, interesting both as a composition and for the meanings it possessed at its creation and that it has acquired since. Because it makes little sense to interrogate Levine's formal skills (her primary creative acts were selection and mechanical reproduction), *After Walker Evans: 7* raises questions about the intention of the artist and the meaning of the work, questions that critics of Levine's generation felt had yet to be forcefully asked of Modernist art such as Evans's.

In Evans's photograph, we see the meticulously ordered room which suggests the dignity of its resident and constituted

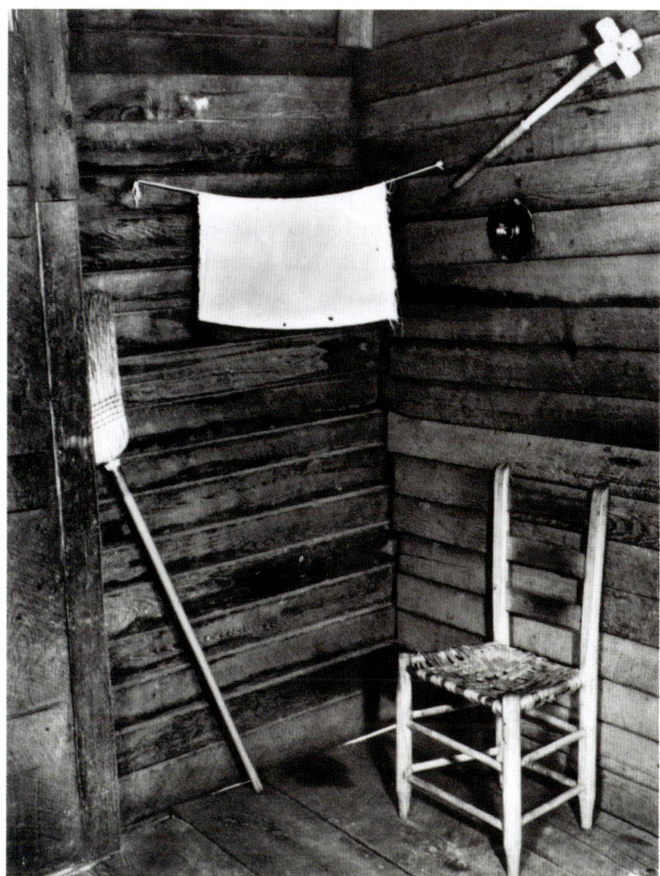

2.3 Sherrie Levine, ***After Walker Evans: 7***, 1981. Gelatin silver print, 5 1/16 × 3 7/8" (12.8 × 9.8 cm). The Metropolitan Museum of Art, New York. © Sherrie Levine. Courtesy Paula Cooper Gallery, New York.

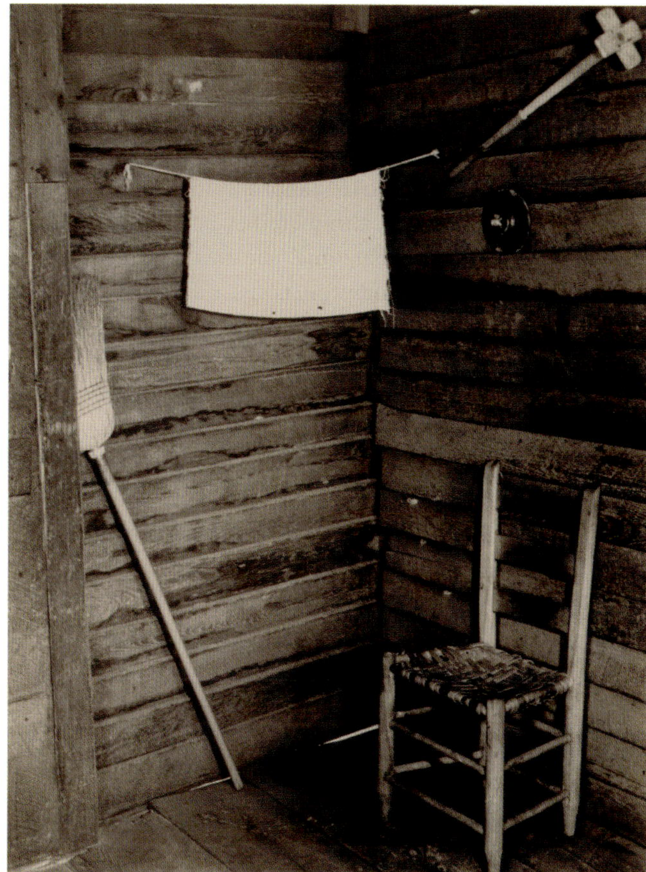

2.4 Walker Evans, ***Farmhouse Hale County, Alabama***, 1936. Gelatin silver print. 7 11/16 × 6 5/16" (19.5 × 16.1 cm). The Library of Congress.

the heart of the artist's appeal to Northern liberals to help fund renewal projects across the rural South. In such works, Evans demonstrated photography's role in the pursuit of social justice, while remaining faithful to the abstract compositions favored by other classic Modernist photographers such as Alfred Stieglitz (1864–1946) and Paul Strand (1890–1976). Walker Evans's photograph was the result of an encounter between Depression-era poverty and twentieth-century avant-garde aesthetics. Levine's *After Walker Evans: 7*, however, is not imbedded in a pursuit of justice, or invested in proving photography to be high art; rather, its context is the early 1980s art world, and Levine shares with her "Pictures" peers a commitment to challenging myths of originality and conventions of artistic creation. As several writers of the period, notably Rosalind Krauss (b. 1941), have pointed out, claims of originality have been tenuous throughout the modern era, despite the faith many artists have placed in them.[5] Evans's original photograph is itself full of challenges to its own claims to originality and authenticity. The aesthetic success of the image—its carefully coordinated lines of furniture and wooden planks juxtaposed against the planes of the hanging cloth and corner of the room—depend on Evans following the example of contemporary norms of avant-garde art. In addition, the political success of the work rests on the artist eschewing significant compositional invention: To convey its message that Hale County citizens are deserving, Evans relies on his audience believing that his photograph documents the room as he found it. Had the artist staged the image, then the photograph would be politically suspect. So, if Evans is following a given style and dependent on others to compose his subject for him, then what does his creative act consist of exactly? Evans's "originality" might be said to have been: seeing the house, framing the scene, and printing the photograph—in other words, selection and presentation. In her copy, Levine presents modern art as a cultural object that functions not as an isolated object of beauty, or even as a heroic gesture of independent journalism, but as an image produced within systems of aesthetic norms and national politics.

In a 1985 interview, Levine explained: "The pictures I make are really ghosts of ghosts … When I started doing this work, I wanted to make a picture which contradicted itself. I wanted to put a picture on top of a picture so that there are times when both pictures disappear and other times when they're both manifest; that vibration is basically what the work's about for me—that space in the middle where there is no picture."[6] As when the Belgian Surrealist René Magritte (1898–1967) opened up a space between things and the names we give them in his 1929 image of a pipe inscribed "*Ceci n'est pas une pipe*" ("This is not a pipe"), Levine's practice highlighted the uncertainties that images attempt to conceal. "I'm trying not to be tyrannized by the original image," she continued. "What I'm really interested in is constructing my relationship to the image."[7]

In the 1980s, Levine's interest in craft and the evocative and personal character of her appropriative impulse were not immediately apparent, although they have become much more evident since. At that time, she was typically praised for creating work with "only functional value for particular historical discourses,"[8] or for engaging in an "uncompromising rejection of all notions of self-expression, originality, or subjectivity."[9] Looking back in 1993, Douglas Crimp described what he felt had been his project in the 1980s; one he felt he shared with Levine. He wrote that he had wanted to "displace" the conventional subject of art, namely the humanist artist expressing his convictions in the name of "universal mankind." Instead: "I wanted to show that the creating subject was a fiction necessary to modern esthetic understanding, and that what took its place in post-modern knowledge was the institution, if by institution we mean a discursive system."[10] Certainly, Levine and others appropriated tactically, choosing source imagery that facilitated critiques of existing notions of self-expression and contemporary structures of power. It is useful to remember, however, that the art writing of the 1980s that addressed appropriation was (like all art writing) itself a tactical endeavor, which played the dual role of explicating art and challenging the rising popularity and prices of Neo-Expressionism (see Chapter 3). In this context, Levine's comments regarding the relationship between contemporary artists and Modernist art, and much of what appears to be the expressive dimension of appropriationist work, can be read as attempts to find new forms of subjectivity and even originality that were free from the repressive taint of Modernist art.

Richard Prince

Appropriation was not always so highbrow or self-consciously critical. Richard Prince's (b. 1949) first appropriations were drawn from what he called "art-directed and over-determined" magazine images that conveyed the anonymous perfection of the commercial American Dream.[11] Soon, however, he began to mine more lowbrow and unpolished material from biker magazines, fanzines, and softcore pornography. The result was an unsettling, if sometimes beautiful, collection of stylized, though rarely stylish, images of objects, ranging from watches, cigarettes, and monster trucks, to bikinis, bikes, and heavy metal bands. Prince described the appeal of popular culture as consisting of "signs, signals, things that didn't need to be explained."[12] Unlike the Dada or Pop gestures that raised pop culture to the status of fine art, or subjected high-art objects to the replicating processes of technological reproduction, Prince's work, like that of Jeff Koons (see Chapter 5), functions at a more emotional level, appealing to the pleasure his audience takes in visual material that lies outside the customary taste range of the art-buying public. Prince's art presents an archive of subcultural icons of beauty that constitute a portrait of desire that would appear to have little to do with the aesthetics and interests of most of Prince's sophisticated audience. His series of "joke" paintings—text pieces reproducing bad one-liners and sendups found in men's magazines—confirm his interest in giving viewers something that they don't usually get in an art museum. If there is a critical agenda in Prince's work, and unlike Levine's it was not at all

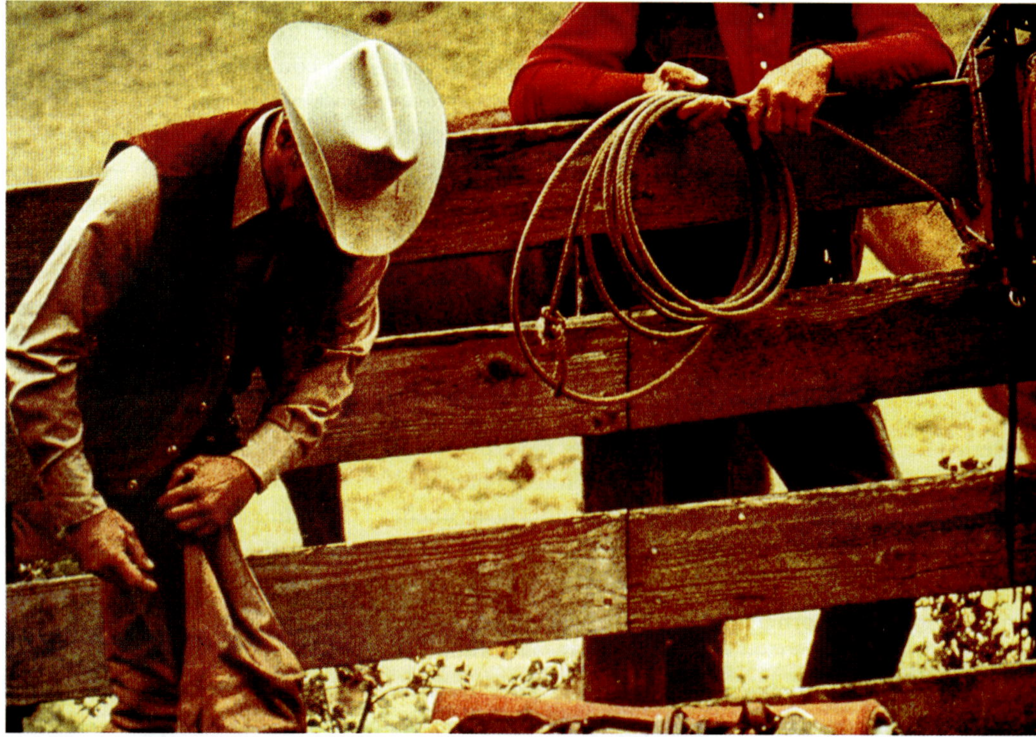

2.5 Richard Prince, *Untitled (Cowboy)*, 1995. Ektacolor photograph, 48 × 72" (121.9 × 182.9 cm). Courtesy Richard Prince Studio.

clear to critics that there was one, it lies in its implication that the desires of the collecting class is on a continuum with those who subscribe to the magazines in which Prince finds his imagery.

Prince began his career in New York cutting the editorials out of magazines for *Time-Life*. What was left after the text had been removed in this way were seductive visual fragments of advertisements—lips, eyes, hair, hands, watches, pens, cigarettes, and carefully cropped presentations of the men and women who inhabit the world these objects define. This material became the source for Prince's first experiments in appropriation. The "Marlboro Man" rides through many of his works of the 1980s (**fig. 2.5**) and continues to appear throughout his oeuvre. Captured in rich, often luminescent colors, amplified through Prince's rephotographing process, the cigarette-ad cowboy excites as much visual pleasure as he exudes macho allure. Prince's work celebrates the aesthetic tastes of those usually excluded from high art, such as commercial artists and lower-middle-class white Americans.

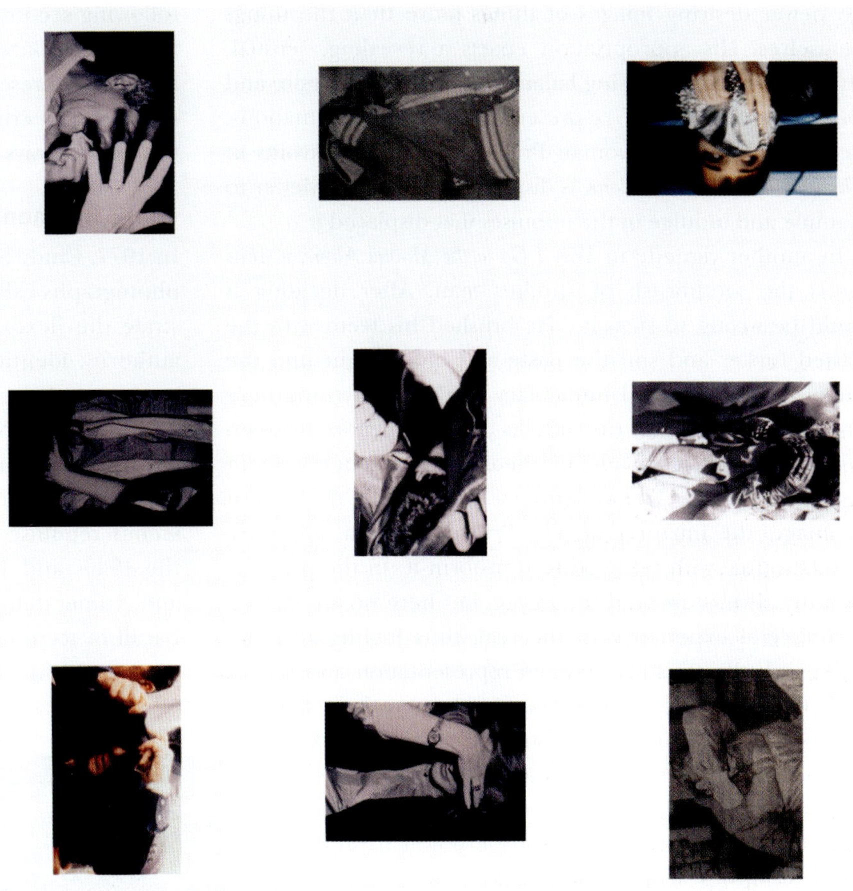

2.6 Richard Prince, ***Criminals and Celebrities***, 1986. Photographic paper with 9 Ektacolor photographs, 86 × 48" (218.4 × 121.9 cm). Courtesy Richard Prince Studio.

Prince's manner of re-presentation reveals, like the variety of Levine's means, the degree to which appropriation, like any other kind of mark making, was an aesthetic tool. Prince described his practice as "8-track photograph[y]," referring to a playback device popular in the 1970s before the invention of the cassette recorder. The eight tracks consisted of: the original, the rephotographed copy, the angled copy, the cropped copy, the focused copy, the out-of-focus copy, the black-and-white copy, and the color copy.[13] Most of Prince's appropriation work was produced using one or more of these procedures, which allowed him to achieve a variety of formal effects. In 1984, he began making "gangs," a term used by professional photo labs for a single page of photographic paper printed with a grid of nine or twelve images. Prince used this "gang" format to create groups of images and thus to curate his appropriations. "I realized I could have a whole show on one piece of paper," he explained.[14] Some of the resulting collections were themed in terms of the things represented, such as *Flames, Dragons, and Titles* (1985–86), which depicts decorations on the sides of trucks, or *Live Free or Die* (1986) featuring nine amateur photographs of girls on motorcycles submitted to biker magazines. Others show groups of related forms, as in *Untitled (For Catherine Deneuve)* (1987), which presents cascading waves, leaves, and women's hair. Combinations of the two include *Criminals and Celebrities* (1986), in which all the images show people hiding their faces with their hands (**fig. 2.6**). Though unfamiliar, and often alienating and aesthetically unsatisfying, Prince's gangs demonstrate artistic choices—selection of subject matter; balancing formal connections between unlike forms; conceptual relationships between similar forms—of the same kind as those made in more traditional art.

In his book *Why I Go to the Movies Alone* (1983), a collection of fictional vignettes, Prince discussed the function of photography, exploring the relationship between representation and desire. On the compulsion of one of his characters to acquire photographs of a particular woman, the narrator muses: "He had to have her on paper, a material with a flat and seamless surface ... a place that had the chances of looking real, but a place that didn't have any specific chances of being real."[15] Here, photography indulges a desire for possession that cannot be had in real life. Complicating his account of what appears at first to be a simple pathology, Prince explains that photography didn't serve "uncritical devotion," but permitted an active rather than passive adoration. The "image did seem to have," he writes, "a power he could willingly and easily contribute to."[16] One can engage photographic images with a confidence that disappears when encountering the real; in the end, Prince's work itself leaves the viewer desiring images of things more than the things themselves. His appropriation enacts a revealing, sensual, perhaps even embarrassing balancing act between desire and control. In a world of re-presentations of representations, the original, like the woman Prince's protagonist avoids in *Why I Go to the Movies Alone*, is displaced, leaving the viewer to examine and indulge in the impulses that displaced it.

In another vignette in *Why I Go to the Movies Alone*, a man covets the toothbrush of another man. After deciding it would be wrong to steal it, "He brushed his teeth with the blasted fucker and spit the paste and blood right into the mirror."[17] The fictional immediacy of Prince's writing here has little to do with the intellectual distinction between copies and sources made in theoretical statements about appropriation art. The violence of the scene is directed at an image, the mirror that, like Prince's camera, appropriates its source with no need to transform it. In the previous narrative, Prince favored the image, but here we are treated to a visceral experience of the real, thus highlighting the dialogue in Prince's art between representation and reality, analysis and desire, examination and evocation. This dialectic, present in Levine's attention to craft and the emotive power of materials, was reflected in the critical reception of appropriation. For critics such as Craig Owens (1950–90), the style held the power to shift art-world priorities from money-making to politics and theory. Others saw it as just one more modification of traditional, even Romantic, artistic practice.[18] A few critics struggled to synthesize these two, apparently mutually exclusive propositions.[19] Read as a demonstration of and appeal to such an unstable interpretive lens, Prince's work straddles both critical and indulgent positions while securely occupying neither.

Identity and the Gaze

The analysis of the image world of high art and mass culture initiated in works such as those of Levine or Prince contributed to wider debates over culture and politics in the 1980s. If, as Levine's work so eloquently argued, representation was an act of control and a statement of power, what was the act of looking? Reception as well as production of images was of critical importance, and an issue to which appropriation was well suited. Looking establishes relationships and creates meaning. Who looks at what, at whom, in what contexts, and with what consequences, were pressing concerns much discussed in the 1980s and 1990s under the label of "the Gaze." The Gaze constituted any act of looking that was understood as having social and political implications. Feminism and psychoanalysis provided the starting point for understanding looking as a generative act both in terms of enforcing cultural norms and shaping personal identity. Artists including Cindy Sherman and Silvia Kolbowski, as well as Barbara Kruger (discussed in the following section), used appropriation to examine the character of the Gaze. The stakes of interrogating how we look at, as well as represent, the world lay not only in the possibility of developing a critical vision, but in opening up the possibilities for new ways of seeing.

Cindy Sherman

In 1977, Cindy Sherman (b. 1954) began making a series of photographs called *Untitled Film Stills* (**fig. 2.7**) that demonstrate the flexibility of appropriation in engaging issues of authority, identity, and gender. Sherman has described this moment in her career, shortly after finishing graduate school and moving to New York, as one characterized by insecurity and a retreat from the art world into a studio full of costumes and props, where she would photograph herself posing in scenes reminiscent of European and Hollywood movies of the 1940s and 1950s. The images capture all the strength and vulnerability conveyed by actresses such as Lauren Bacall in scenes suggesting Sherman's melancholic vision of what it was like for a woman to grow up in America at this

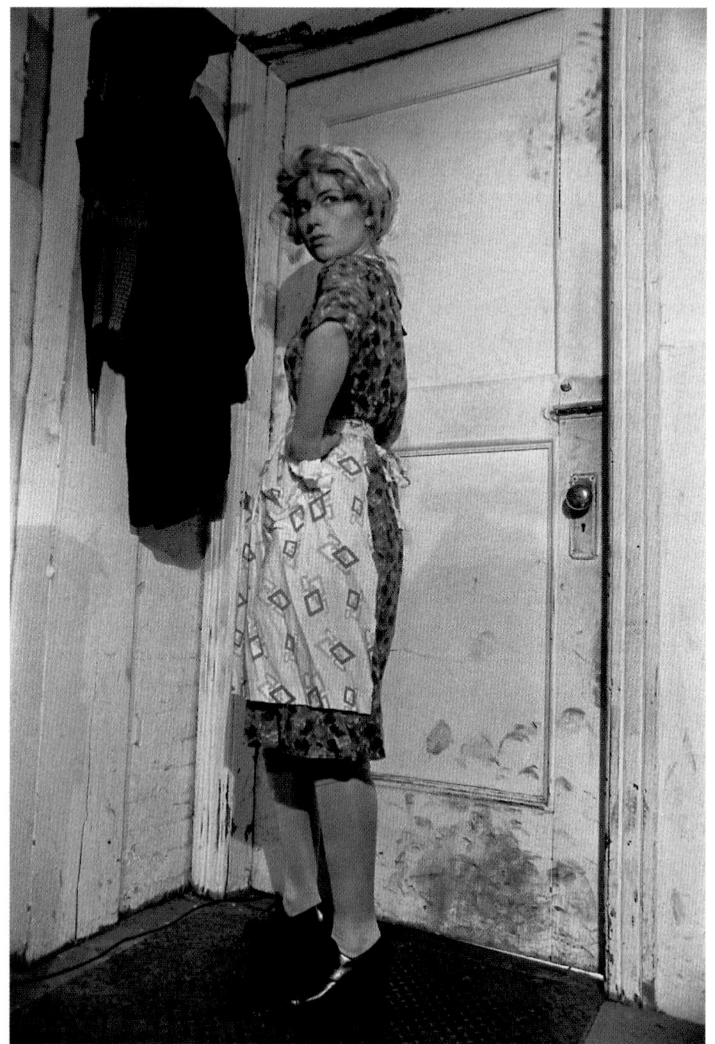

2.7 Cindy Sherman, ***Untitled Film Still #35***, 1979. Black-and-white photograph, 10 × 8" (25.4 × 20.32 cm). Edition of 10. Courtesy of the artist and Metro Pictures, New York.

time.[20] Appropriating scenes from popular cinema, she felt, would make it possible for a wide audience to "relate to [the work] without having read a book about it first."[21] The results brought a sense of playfulness and sentiment to contemporary art, but also, as Sherman had intended, the critical lens of contemporary theory.[22] This dualism animated Sherman's work and its reception through the 1980s and after.

Each of the *Untitled Film Stills* features a woman alone, caught in the middle of an action or thought, like the star of some vaguely remembered movie. These isolated instants invite contemplation, but the black-and-white photographs' format—8 by 10 inches, like a standard production still—and often grainy and imperfect quality challenge the viewer's impulse to dwell on a single image. Instead, we feel compelled to move on, either in our imagination to the next scene, or in the gallery to the next image, where we find the same actress, Sherman herself, in a different movie. Sherman moved on from the small black-and-white format to larger color photographs in the mid-1980s but continued to mine viewers' collective memory for its visions of women.

Untitled #152 (1985) (**fig. 2.8**) shows her mimicking the tropes of low-budget horror movies. As Levine did with her *Presidents*, Sherman appropriated conventional scenes of femininity and exposed their oppressive partiality: No single mass-media image could ever satisfactorily express the nature of a real person; neither could a catalogue of many identities add up to a single "true" portrait. In contrast to the conventional expectation that self-portraits should reveal inner truths, Sherman's photographs present identity as continually shifting among readily available stereotypes. The question "Who is Cindy Sherman?" is perpetually deferred, raising the further question of the work's subject. Is it about popular culture and the representation of gender, or is this a form of Postmodern self-portrait after all?

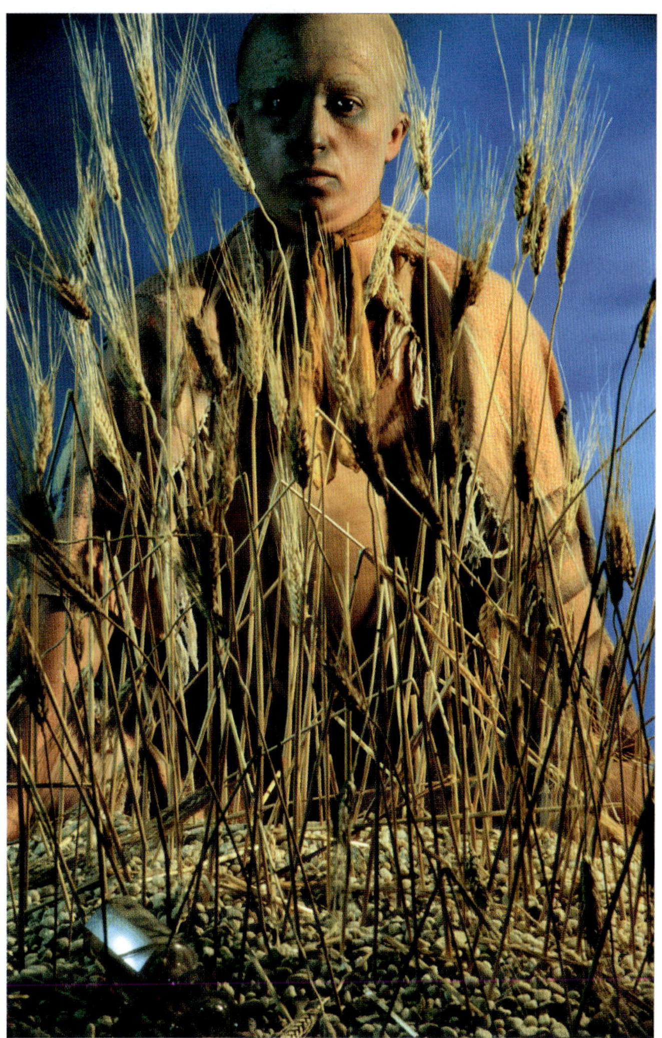

2.8 Cindy Sherman, ***Untitled #152***, 1985. Color photograph, 72½ × 49⅜" (184.2 × 125.4 cm). Edition of 6. Courtesy of the artist and Metro Pictures, New York.

Sherman's practice seemed to eschew traditional ideas about the artist as charismatic innovator. By the late 1970s, it was widely accepted in the art world that the idea of "creative genius" was an aggrandizement of art making that was complicit with oppressive features of Western society. In 1981, art historian Rosalind Krauss published "The Originality of the Avant-Garde and Other Modernist Myths," in which she argued that "modernism and the avant-garde are functions of what we could call the discourse of originality, and that that discourse serves much wider interests."[23] For Krauss, Modernism and the avant-garde, like the compulsion to be original, depended on the "repression" of any challenge to the power of the individual genius, the copy chief among them. Copying necessarily demonstrated a process by which the resulting artwork was not the product of one mind alone. Krauss and others demonstrated that the myth of the artist birthing his art assisted only by inspiration and intuition was contradicted by the many repeated ideas and forms found in modern art; she used the many grids such as those found in Cubist paintings (see fig. 0.1) or modernist architecture in twentieth-century art to make her point.[24] By embracing the copy, appropriation drew attention to this contradiction. Krauss concluded her essay with a reference to Sherrie Levine, suggesting that appropriation, by disavowing the contest between original and copy, provided a way out of the binary conflicts of Modernism (such as real vs. fake, high art vs. low art) and heralded a Postmodernism.[25]

Support for the importance of materialism over mystification was found in the writings of the philosopher Walter Benjamin, whose 1936 essay "The Work of Art in the Age of Mechanical Reproduction" was cited in nearly every 1980s critique of contemporary art for its brilliantly theorized argument that photography and mass reproduction had removed the mysterious and elitist "aura" from artworks. When more people had access to the works that had been reserved for the elite few, then the mysticism of cultural production would be lessened and its power to communicate would be enhanced. The corollary of this democratizing effect was that any cultivation of the aura in the age of mass media was a political act with dire consequences. As Benjamin explained, it was the fusion of aesthetics, politics, and mass media that had propelled the fascists to power in the 1930s. Thus contemporary culture must be self-consciously alert to the way reproduction and representation function. In the conclusion of his "A Short History of Photography," Benjamin writes: "'The illiterate of the future,' it has been said, 'will not be the man who cannot read the alphabet, but the one who cannot take a photograph.' But must we not also count as illiterate the photographer who cannot read his own pictures?"[26] Contemporary means of image production require updated practices of looking, a point seconded by appropriation.

Sherman's imagery, so obviously derived from popular culture, seems to confirm her opposition to traditional notions of creativity. The formal elements of her photographs, however, suggest a slightly different attitude. The apparent imperfections of her technique and careful manipulations of props draw attention to the activity of art making and even, like a painterly brushstroke, to the hand of the artist. Some critics thus located her work in the history of avant-garde portraiture, seeing its fragmentary, emphatically manipulated views of characters caught between self-expression and social conformity as offering a truthful presentation of the contemporary self in society. Others universalized what they saw as Sherman's portrayal of her personal experience. Peter Schjeldahl wrote in 1982 that her work was about "the universal state of daydream or reverie, the moments of harmless, necessary psychosis that are recurring mechanisms in anyone's mental economy."[27] This universalizing, expressionistic interpretation was repeated on the occasion of Sherman's 1987 retrospective at the Whitney Museum, where the exhibition catalogue referred to the artist as an "oracle ... a source of ambiguous messages that seem to tell us our nature and our fate."[28] *Arts* magazine likewise published an account of the show as "an archeology of the self," in which "Historic layers of early psychology ... are being exposed and revealed not as dead but as still living states." The review concluded: "Sherman is discovering what it might be like to go crazy."[29] Such responses to Sherman's work bore out Judith Williamson's 1983 observation that "so tenacious is the wish for this set of psychic garments to turn out to be actual skin, that almost every time Sherman's work is written about the issue of Cindy Sherman 'herself' comes into it."[30]

The praise of Sherman's photography as traditionally expressive did not go unchallenged. Art historian and critic Therese Lichtenstein declared that, rather than simply enlisting popular culture to reveal truths, Sherman "demythologizes" her sources with the aim of addressing the fantasy of "a unitary feminine essence."[31] To read Sherman as doing otherwise, even if the resulting feminine essence was complex, was nothing but an attempt to make a radical artist whose art challenged the status quo acceptable to the mainstream culture or, in Abigail Solomon-Godeau's phrase, "suitable for framing."[32] The institutional claims on radical art have always been forceful: As Allan McCollum's 1985 photo-essay "In the Collection Of ..." (see fig. 2.13) argued, there was a long history of taming antagonistic art in order to be able to present it in sites of power. In general, the critical view of Sherman's work has taken the side of Williamson and Lichtenstein and found that feminist analysis must play a part in viewing Sherman's photographs. It should be noted, however, that Sherman has courted viewers who do not generally read art criticism and theory. Her work with fashion designers and Hollywood, as well as her general reluctance to join the polemical debates about her work, have left a lot of room for interpretation. Sherman has said that she wants audiences to be able to engage with her work without reading about it, and it must be admitted that her work permits viewers to "know," if not the real Cindy Sherman, then at least a Cindy Sherman that feels real.

Laura Mulvey and the Theory of the Gaze

Like Levine and Prince, Sherman succeeded in repositioning the familiar. While Levine placed her appropriations in the context of art history and Prince organized his into subcultural gangs, Sherman's impact lay in infiltrating the histories of film and self-portraiture. Here it is useful to examine how film and spectatorship were theorized in the 1970s, in particular Laura Mulvey's 1975 essay "Visual Pleasure and Narrative Cinema." Mulvey (b. 1941) used psychoanalysis to dissect the extent to which Hollywood film perpetuates traditional gender roles, not only in social relations but also in identity development. Her essay, reprinted in the influential collection *Art After Modernism* (1984), provides an analysis of cinematic storytelling that is relevant to Sherman's work.

Mulvey argued that the pleasures offered by classic Hollywood films correspond to the description of identity formation in Freudian psychology. The latter model crucially refers only to the male; female identity is not theorized beyond its functionality in relation to the male, an imbalance Mulvey also detected in popular films. Cinematic pleasure is primarily experienced in two ways: first, the enjoyment of watching; and, second, the relief provided by the narrative arc. These two types of viewing correspond to Freud's categories of the scopophilic and the narcissistic.

Scopophilic viewing (from the ancient Greek for "watching" and "love") displaces sensations of touch with those of sight. The standard example is voyeurism and, though there is a difference between movie buffs and peeping toms, the prevalence of sex in popular entertainment suggests that it is one of degree rather than kind. The effect of the scopophilic Gaze, as it came to be called, is to objectify the thing observed, transforming it from a subject in its own right into an object that is important only for the pleasure it provides the viewer. The viewer, it should be recalled, is consistently theorized by Freud and imagined by filmmakers as male. In film, the transformation effected by the Gaze occurs in the close-up, as the camera zooms in on the actress, turning her into a series of fragments—for example, a high-heeled shoe and stockinged leg extended from car to street, or a cascade of hair falling over a shoulder. Just as Prince's character in *Why I Go to the Movies Alone* enjoyed the security of possessing his beloved as an image rather than in the flesh, the close-up permits the viewer to divorce himself from the whole person in favor of savoring the details.

To determine how scopophilic vision produces satisfaction, Mulvey turned again to psychoanalysis. In Freud's account of identity formation, there is a moment when the (male) child discovers that his mother, whom he had conceived of as an all-powerful extension of himself, is different from him: She has no penis. Difference is registered visually; it is the child's perception of absence that shocks him. Believing the penis to be a source of power or important in some not yet comprehensible way, the boy cannot accept that his mother does not possess one. The dismayed child looks away in desperation, and his redirected gaze invests whatever it falls on—a leg, stocking, foot, shoe, or other domestic object—with the power to stave off his mounting anxiety. This object masks both the mother's lack of a penis and the fact of sexual difference (between child and mother). Thus empowered, the ordinary object becomes the *fetish*. The mother, once a source of comfort but now a cause of fear, is exchanged for an object that, while inscribed with the fact of difference, exists to hide it. The classic film replays this search for comfort, denying a full development of the female character in favor of re-presenting her to the audience in fragments.

The second form of visual pleasure identified by Mulvey, which she termed narcissistic, involves the viewer sacrificing his subjectivity. Mulvey explained that our pleasure in seeing a Hollywood story reach its conclusion derives from a profound identification with its hero. This relates to the mirror stage in psychoanalysis, in which the child recognizes his appearance as an image in a mirror and invents an idealized self to inhabit it. Movie stars replicate this idealized self-image. In the comfortable dark of the theater, we are invited to do more than empathize with the figures on the screen. We are not simply happy to see Cary Grant or Hugh Grant get the girl, we take their conquest as our own. In this narcissistic transfer, the viewer erases his subjectivity in order to become, if only for a couple hours, the character in the movie. The familiar sigh of relief as the hero overcomes adversity thus becomes a form of self-congratulation.

These two devices, the close-up and narcissistic mirroring, exist in a state of tension throughout the viewing of a film, the one putting off or cutting short the pleasure the other provides. It is the same dance of anticipation, disappointment, and compensation that defines Freudian identity formation, in which the subject continually seeks, fails to find, and struggles to reconstitute a unitary and coherent sense of self in the world. In Freudian psychology and classic cinema, women are objects of both scopophilic and narcissistic pleasure. They are objects of desire for competing lovers, *femmes fatales* obstructing the hero's path, or helpless souls in need of rescue. Fay Wray, Jessica Lange, and Naomi Watts exist so that King Kong has to be defeated. In *Star Wars*, Princess Leia's *raison d'être* is to convince Obi-Wan, inspire Luke, and compel Han Solo to save the Federation. Classic cinema, like Freudian psychology, places woman at the intersection of male subjects' power and vulnerability. Both modes of representation depend on women to develop the identities of men.

In Mulvey's critique, classic cinema universalizes the pleasures that Freudian psychoanalysis sees as specific to the development of male sexual identity. By relinquishing their own subjectivity, women too can enjoy such films; unlike their male counterparts, however, they are unable to step into the idealized role of the hero. Women can star in films too, but only if their roles remain faithful to their male precedents. Two films from either end of the decade covered by this chapter, *Alien* (1979) and *Thelma and Louise* (1990), both directed by Ridley Scott, demonstrate how classic film can accommodate female actors. Sigourney Weaver in *Alien* (**fig. 2.9**) provided audiences with an action heroine who was as strong, if not as well paid, as the guys. In *Thelma and Louise*, Gina Davis and Susan Sarandon stepped out of suburbia to take on the roles of outlaws Butch Cassidy and the Sundance Kid. The movies were fun, the heroines were tough, but they remained safely contained within the format of classic Hollywood cinema. Mulvey was not interested in reversing conventional male and female roles in this way; instead, her goal was to find "the thrill that comes from leaving the past behind without rejecting it, transcending outworn or oppressive forms, of daring to break with normal

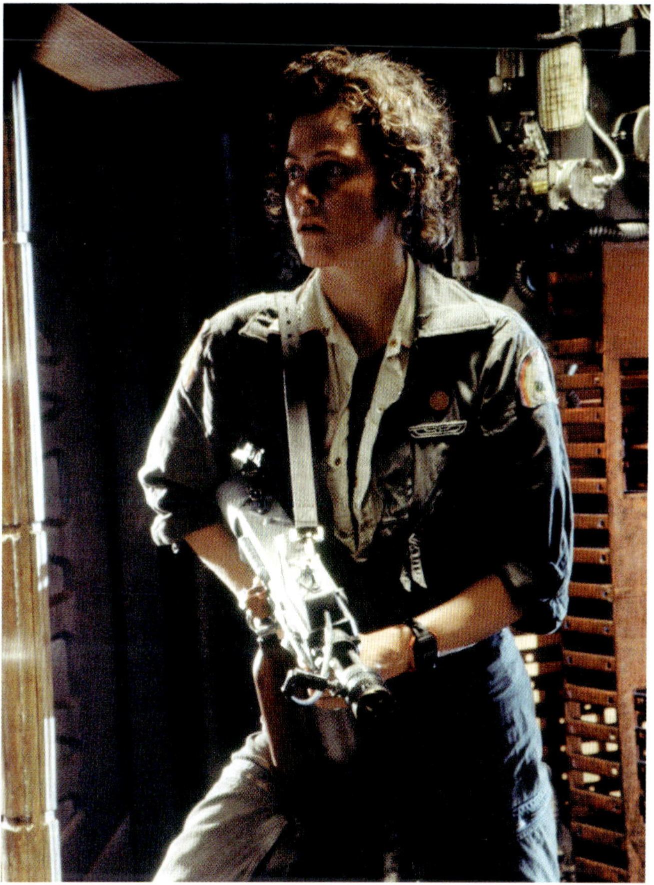

2.9 Sigourney Weaver in *Alien*, 1979. Film still. 20th Century Fox.

pleasurable expectation in order to conceive a new language of desire."[33] Sherman's *Untitled Film Stills* inspire such a thrill and can be said to help initiate discussion of new forms of the Gaze that exceed the binaries of Mulvey's diagnosis of narrative cinema.

In Sherman's images, scopophilic and narcissistic pleasures are framed and frustrated. Like the close-up, the *Untitled Film Stills* transform the actress into an object of the Gaze, providing satisfaction for viewers while they anticipate the next scene. An active being caught in mid-step or mid-thought becomes, for a moment, a passive object. By identifying the women in the photograph with the woman behind the camera, however, a Sherman photograph resists completely transforming the female into fetish. Whether the image seems to represent a working-class wife, B-movie starlet, or girl-next-door, it also presents an artist dressed up for a camera she herself controls. Sherman's work set up a dialogue between the woman-artist as subject and the woman-actor as object. Unlike the Freudian fetish, which protects the (male) subject from awareness of sexual difference, Sherman's images draw attention to difference. The artist herself juxtaposes the roles of model/actor/object and artist/director/subject, layering the notion of the artist who created the images with the multiplicity of feminine identities to which they attest.

Silvia Kolbowski

As the discussion of Sherman's *Untitled Film Stills* indicates, by the 1980s identity was understood to be significantly shaped by representation: Freudian theory, pop culture, mass media, and fine art all provided important examples of this process. By further dissecting and re-presenting the image of women in the media, the Argentine-born, New York-based artist Silvia Kolbowski (b. 1953) demonstrated how appropriation could be used to examine and challenge the psychically formative power of representation. *Model Pleasure* (1982–83) and *Monumental Prop/portions* (1983) demonstrated Kolbowski's strategy of appropriation, which includes selective copying from the mass media combined with imitations of commercial styles to question the relationship between body, image, and feminine identity.

Model Pleasure (**fig. 2.10**) is a series of compositions, arrangements of photographs, most representing cropped and framed images of women's faces, wet with moisturizer, lip gloss, and eyeliner, and often suggesting narratives. Additional images include still lifes of fruit, a dress, isolated hands and feet, occasional texts, and, in one case, machinery in a textile factory. Evoking the gridded and serial presentations of Minimalism and Conceptual art, the work confronts the viewer with sensuous masks of conventional femininity proffering themselves to be consumed like the cinematic close-ups deconstructed by Mulvey and Sherman. Punctuating the close-ups here are images of accessories and objects—some not appropriated but photographed by the artist, suggesting that the entire collection might be merely fetishes diverting our attention from a glaring absence. In this case, the absence is not the mother's lack of a penis but Western culture's lack of an adequate definition of the feminine. The faces in *Model Pleasure*, shaped by the ideals of the mass media, provide the closest thing the modern West has to a definition of feminine identity. They convey both the Freudian description of woman as "lacking," and more contemporary definitions of the feminine as a performance of socially generated roles designed to preserve the patriarchal status quo. The inclusion of the textile machine alludes to Marxist critiques of labor, both inviting economic analysis into the discussion and reminding the viewer of other theories that have failed to adequately address the particularity of women's experience.

Monumental Prop/portions (**fig. 2.11**), another series, this time of images of shadows, was first published as a photo-essay in the art journal *Wedge*. Each source photo of a shadow has been cropped so as to include just a hint of the object that cast it. In each case, that object is a female body, represented by a sliver of arm, shoulder, or leg. Like some uncanny afterimage, the shadow looms over the fragment. Across the final six pages of the essay, Kolbowski placed the words "A SHADOW OF HER FORMED SELF," underlining the metaphorical reading of the work. The final page presents a text in place of the shadow image. Over the word "self" is a description beginning: "She has been represented to death." The text describes how the societal ideal presented in *Model Pleasures* becomes a destructive product consumed by women. *Monumental Prop/portions* clarifies the interaction of fashion and fetish while insisting that the relationship is socially constructed rather than biologically given.

In her explication of cinematic pleasure, Mulvey showed how narcissistic identification compels the male to see himself in the image of the hero. Here, Kolbowski demonstrated that women are left with only objects in place of role models and must seek satisfaction by identifying with objectified, fragmented female figures. This process leaves only

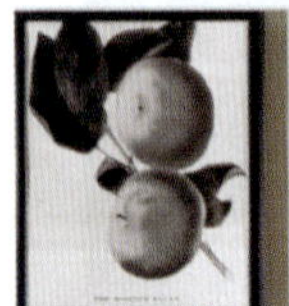
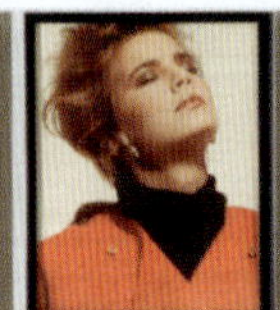
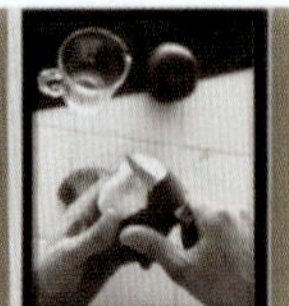
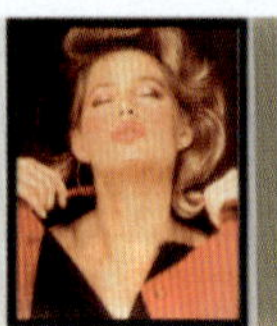
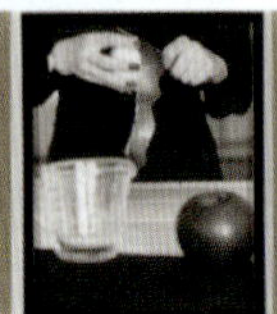
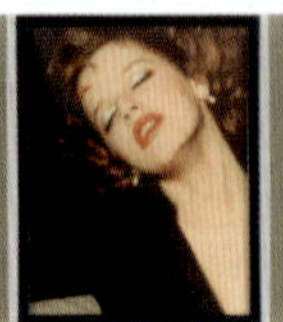
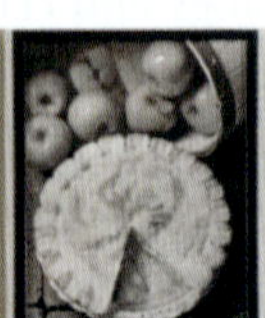
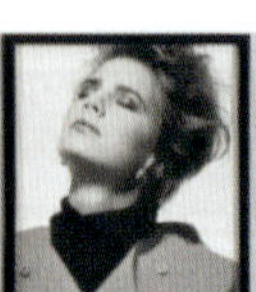
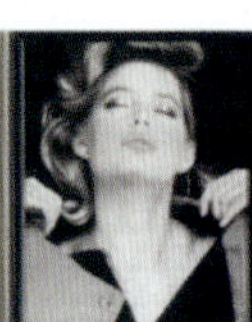
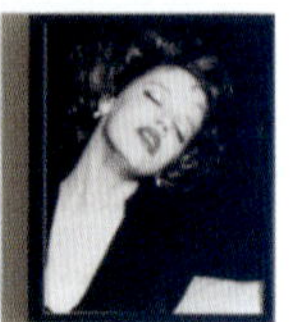

2.10 Silvia Kolbowski, ***Model Pleasure I***, 1982. 3 chromogenic and 7 gelatin silver prints, each 10 × 8" (25.4 × 20.3 cm). Collection: Walker Art Center. Image courtesy the artist.

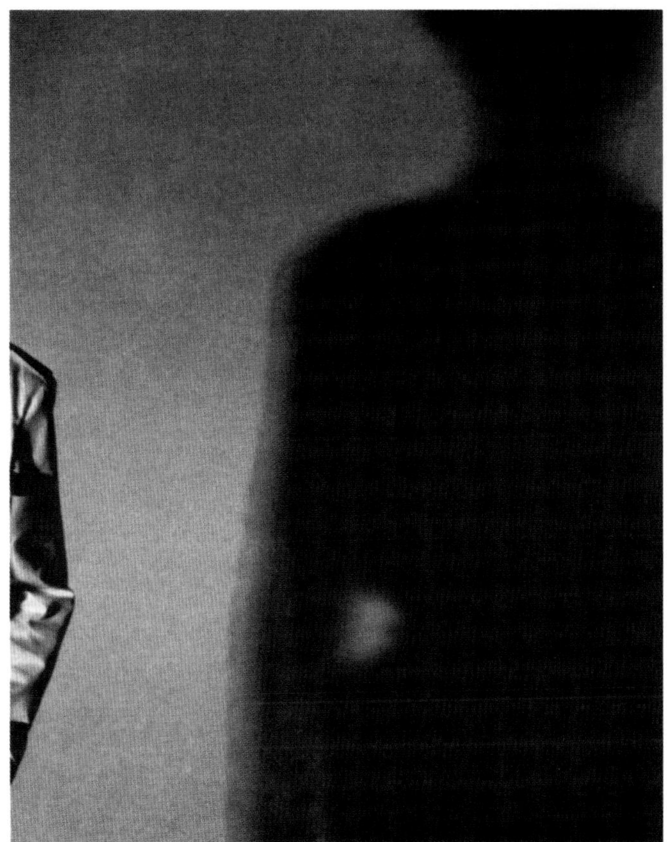

2.11 Silvia Kolbowski, ***Monumental Prop/portions***, 1983. Pamphlet #2 included loose with *Wedge*, issues 3/4/5, edited by Phil Mariani and Brian Wallis, 1983 (New York). Exact dimensions of this print unknown. Magazine 12 pp, 8.5 × 8.5" (21.59 × 21.59 cm). Collection MACBA, Centre d'Estudis i Documentació. Image courtesy the artist.

shadows, but it is complicated by the role contemporary women play within it. "Placed between the producer of the pose and the consumer of the pose," wrote Kolbowski, "she is consumed by both." Women end up being complicit; they are "self-consumptive, self-consumed. Done in. Finished. Only to be repeated in ... the mimicry of [their] assumed pose." Like Levine's *Presidents* or Sherman's *Untitled Film Stills*, the text of *Monumental Prop/portions* draws attention to the fact that this idea of femininity is defined from the outside, by society. At the same time, by cropping out the source of the shadow, Kolbowski gives viewers a glimpse of the possibility of resistance. With the source of the shadow relegated to a fragment, the viewer has the opportunity to imagine the body that cast it. Kolbowski's image depicts the uncanny spaces between the image of femininity created by society, as presented in *Model Pleasure*, and the inscription of that image on women's real bodies. It appropriates fashion photography from mass culture to create a space where we cannot see the social ideal or its effect, where, to use Levine's words quoted above, "both pictures disappear" and we are left with a "vibration ... in the middle where there is no picture." The next step is the viewer's, to become an active partner in the social construction of femininity. *Monumental Prop/portions* can be seen as an invitation to walk away from the limiting social ideal of femininity, to leave the past behind as Mulvey had advised.

Spaces of Action

Appropriation was used to create spaces for action as well as voices of protest. Artists including Allan McCollum and Louise Lawler used appropriation to demonstrate that the spaces in which art was usually found were highly political and often compromised, while the work of Barbara Kruger and Jenny Holzer, and the 1980s collective the Guerrilla Girls, pushed appropriation out of the usual spaces of art and into the streets. These artists occupied non-art spaces using media with which their new audiences were familiar, but delivered a message for which they were not prepared. Following the perception of performance artist Laurie Anderson (b. 1947) that "language is a virus"—a message she herself appropriated from author William S. Burroughs—appropriation artists understood mass-media and commercial communications to be aggressive carriers of potentially malignant messages.[34]

Allan McCollum

Allan McCollum's (b. 1944) exhibitions and objects in the early 1980s developed the ability of appropriation to raise questions about the relationship of art to power. His work also indicated how appropriation could be applied to more than just the details of an image. McCollum's œuvre is based on what he calls *surrogates* (**fig. 2.12**), cast and painted objects that, in the early 1980s, resembled a black frame enclosing a black image on a white matte ground. Deliberately lacking pictorial or sculptural interest, the surrogates

2.12 Allan McCollum, ***Collection of Forty Plaster Surrogates***, 1982–84. Enamel on cast Hydrostone. 40 panels ranging from 5 × 4⅛" (12.8 × 10.2 cm) to 20¼ × 16¼" (51.3 × 41.1 cm), overall 64" × 9' 2" (162.5 × 279.4 cm). The Museum of Modern Art, New York. Courtesy of the artist and Barbara Krakow Gallery, Boston.

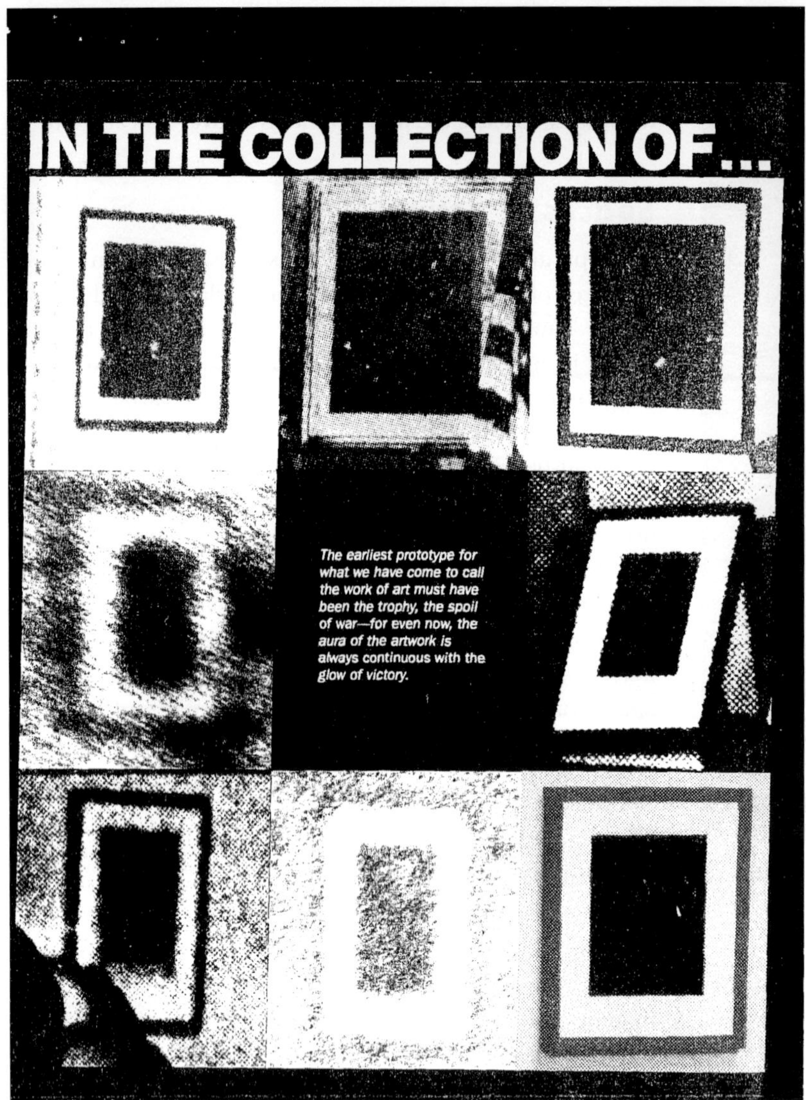

2.13 Allan McCollum, *In the Collection of ...*, 1985. Cover of photo/text essay. Courtesy of the artist and Barbara Krakow Gallery, Boston.

stood for a work of art and were exhibited (framed and presented on the walls of a gallery, corporate office, or museum, and reproduced in art magazines) in a manner that appropriated conventional modes of displaying art. Since casting the first of the surrogates, McCollum has created them in a variety of shapes and materials, pointing to the many different ways in which art is created and displayed.

McCollum's 1985 photo/text essay "In the Collection of ..." reveals the very specific and significant source from which he appropriated the black-field-on-a-white-ground-in-a-black-frame format of the first surrogates—press photos documenting political power (**fig. 2.13**). McCollum's essay outlines the genesis of the "surrogate," beginning from the works of art that are visible on the walls and desks seen in official photographs of figures such as presidents Truman and Ford or bodies such as the Warren Commission, which investigated the assassination of President Kennedy. The composition, lighting, focus, and resolution of McCollum's photographic sources insure that the art cannot be seen in detail. This is how artworks appear in the news—visible only as small but ever-present black rectangles, where it is the generic presence of art, not its specific form or content, that is judged important. The final image in the essay presents McCollum's own work adorning places of power—in this case, the walls of Chase Manhattan Bank, where art is made to appear as an attribute of power with no aesthetic detail at all.[35] In the accompanying text, McCollum defined modern art as essentially an appropriation of value, important for its status as a trophy rather than its visual qualities. "Modern art has always sought," McCollum asserted, "to assume the status of whatever treasures it is able to supplant; its history is no more than the perpetual reenactment of this interminable cycle of preemption."[36] McCollum's appropriation consisted of excising these artworks or trophies from images of power and re-presenting them stripped of those unique and identifying details we tend to celebrate when we use the word "art."

Louise Lawler

Louise Lawler (b. 1947) also took the operation of art and power as her subject, focusing on practices of display. She photographed art in galleries, museums, corporate offices, storage rooms, and collectors' homes. By capturing arrangements of artworks in such settings, she highlighted their owners' appreciation of how good an Abstract Expressionist painting might look in their dining room, or how Pop art could add interest to a lobby. She photographed the juxtaposition of a Jackson Pollock painting and fine china in *Pollock and Tureen* (1984) (**fig. 2.14**) and a Roy Lichtenstein and a Telex machine seen in the offices of the stockbrokerage Paine Webber in *Arranged by Donald Marron, Susan Brundage, Cheryl Bishop, Paine Webber, New York* (1982). The artist and critic Andrea Fraser, who has herself critiqued the institutional use of art (see Chapter 1), wrote: "For Lawler artistic production is *always* a collective endeavor: it isn't simply artists who produce esthetic signification and value, but an often anonymous contingent of collectors, viewers, museum, and gallery workers—and ultimately the cultural apparatus in which these positions are delineated."[37] In 1984, Lawler collaborated with Allan McCollum on the gallery installation *Ideal Settings: For Presentation and Display* (**fig. 2.15**), in which the props for commercial display—lights, pedestals, stands, and prices tags—were presented as sculptures in their own right. The artists set out to create a "gesture which tends to reflect upon the function of the art gallery as a presentational arena."[38]

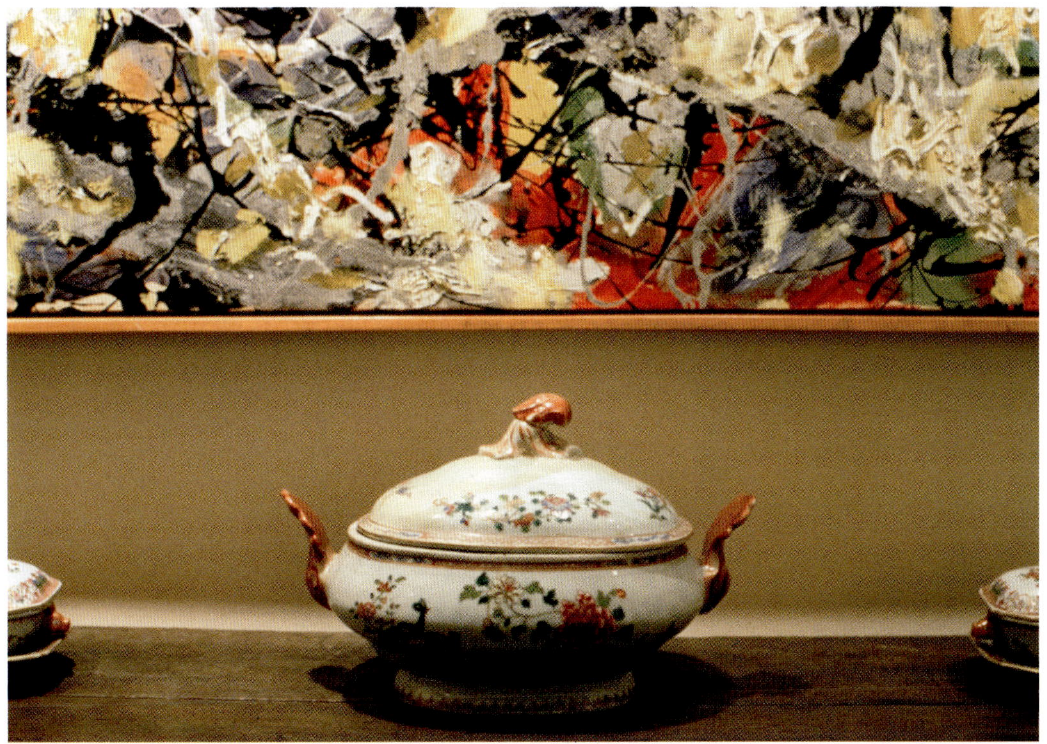

2.14 Louise Lawler, ***Pollock and Tureen***, 1984. Cibachrome, 16 × 20" (40.6 × 50.8 cm). Edition of 5. Courtesy of the artist and Metro Pictures, New York.

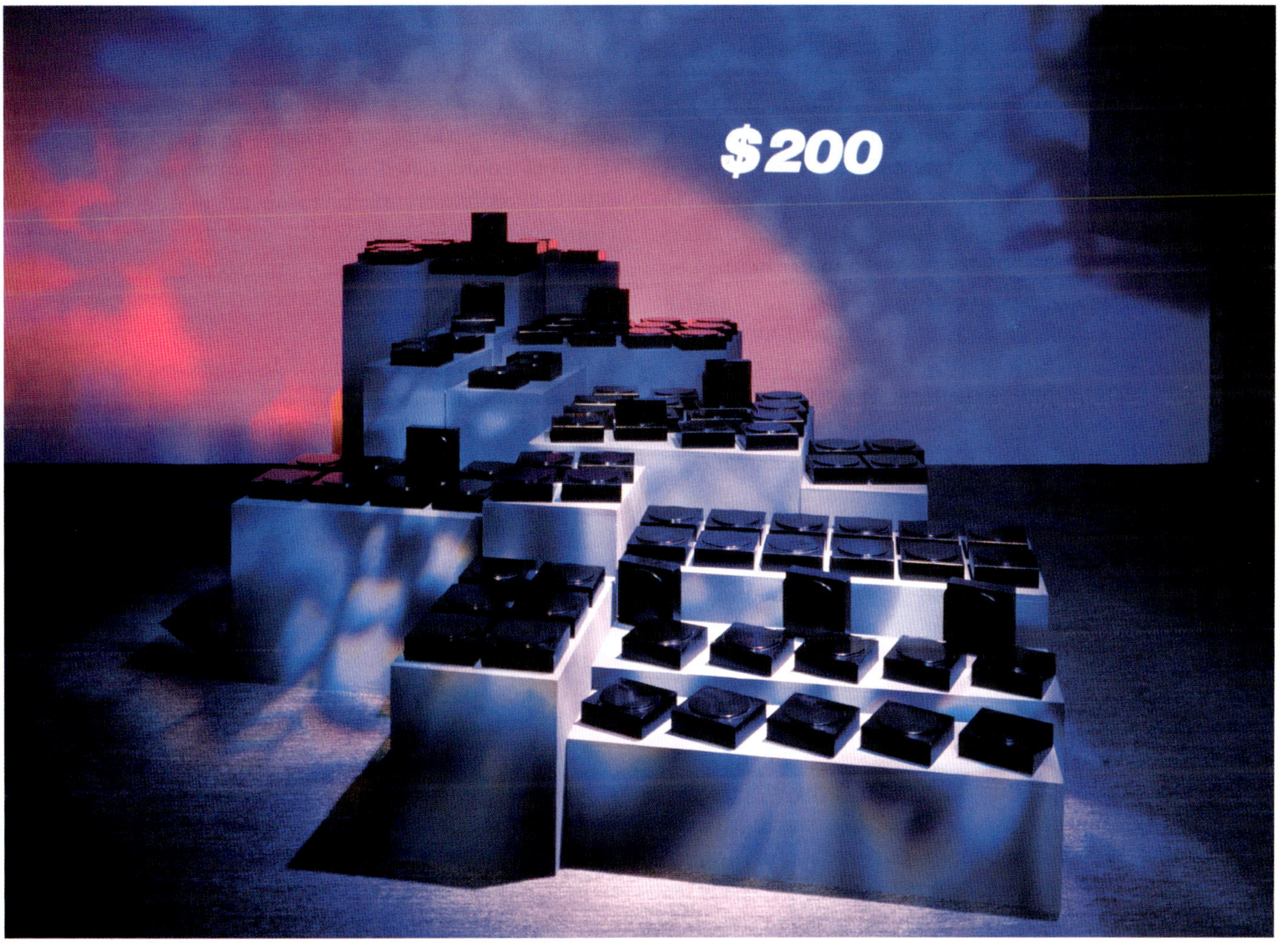

2.15 Louise Lawler and Allan McCollum, ***Ideal Settings: For Presentation and Display***, 1983–84. ca.100 objects of wax and shoe polish on cast, pigmented Hydrostone, each 9 × 9 × 2¼" (22.86 × 22.86 × 5.7 cm). Installation designed by McCollum and Lawler, with theatrical lighting and sales price projected on wall, at the Diane Brown Gallery, New York, 1984. Courtesy of the artists and Barbara Krakow Gallery, Boston.

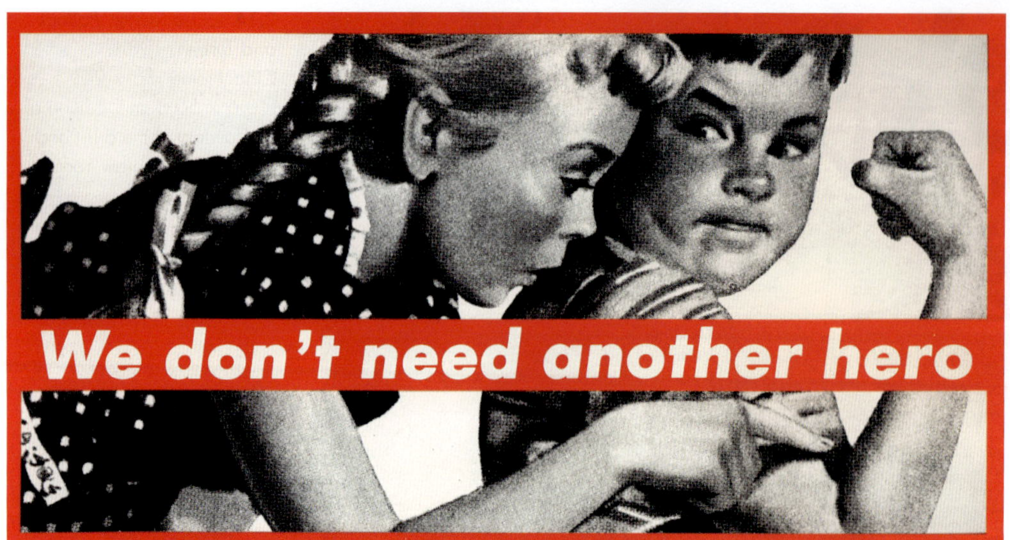

2.16 Barbara Kruger, *Untitled (We don't need another hero)*, 1986. Photographic silkscreen/vinyl. 109 × 210" (277 × 533 cm). © Barbara Kruger. Courtesy Mary Boone Gallery, New York.

Barbara Kruger

In the mid-1980s in cities across the U.S. and Europe, billboards appeared presenting a closely cropped image of a Caucasian girl aged around ten with ribbons in her braided blonde hair and polka dots on her 1950s-style dress (**fig. 2.16**). The girl admiringly rests an index finger on the arm of a figure who appears to be her little brother, posing with clenched jaw and flexed muscle. The picture mimics the illustrative style of the *Saturday Evening Post*, and evokes what the voters who elected then-president Ronald Reagan might have called "Traditional American Values." It resembles an advertisement for soap or cereal, except that printed across the image are the words: "We don't need another hero." The image was the work of Barbara Kruger (b. 1945), who set it up in billboard locations where messages about money and power were regularly delivered. Kruger adopted the mode of address of advertising to challenge the status quo on its own turf. The billboard next to hers might have been advertising a new car or *Cobra*, the latest Sylvester Stallone movie, promoted with an image of a heavily armed and sunglasses-wearing Stallone underneath the words: "Crime is a disease. Meet the cure." With Stallone's U.S. Vietnam War veteran character John Rambo dominating 1980s pop culture, and the White House actively intervening in Latin America and the Middle East, Kruger's message was both apropos and outgunned. In the popular imagination, America still wanted heroes whose main attribute was brawn.[39]

Fighting public-relations battles, however, was not Kruger's aim. Art historian and critic Rosalyn Deutsche argued that Kruger's work was significant for "Treat[ing] space as a relationship and then enunciat[ing] the mechanisms within it."[40] Just as Levine deconstructed the "neutrality" of the art museum, transforming a space of passive reception into one of active critique, and Sherman did the same for the movie theater and Kolbowski for the media, Kruger appropriated the means of the advertiser to expose the politics of urban space. By creating disjunctions between work and text and between message and context, *"We don't need another hero"* draws attention to the fact that our physical surroundings, like the media, actively generate meaning. Space, Deutsche explained, is an arena that we relate to either as passive receivers or, as we turn critically from a Kruger to a real ad, as active interpreters.

In most cases, Kruger raised awareness of social conditions at a general level. She described her work as existing in the realm of "time passing, but seldom [of] particular events."[41] Her work appropriated modes of communication designed to fill a soundbite or a fleeting glance, and used them to take a longer view of social change. In order to focus on more specific issues, Kruger readily lent her style, and sometimes her work, to direct-action political groups, thus practicing a form of secondhand production. She made or authorized posters, pamphlets, book covers, image-based "op-ed" pieces and other forms of public relations for campaigns including the prevention of domestic violence, women's health issues, such as abortion rights, and AIDS awareness. By donating her style in these ways, Kruger was able, both in and beyond art galleries, to engage in systematic social critique as well as more detailed problem-solving.

Examples of Kruger's work inside art institutions include her 1991 installation at the Mary Boone Gallery in New York (**fig. 2.17**). For this, Kruger covered the gallery walls, floor, and ceiling with disturbing texts and images documenting aggression and violence. A monumental photograph showing mirror images of a shouting head covered the wall at one end of the gallery. Between the two screaming faces Kruger inserted a red field several feet across containing a list of insults: "hebe kike yid hymie spic wop dago mex cunt gash snatch pussy spook sambo nigger bookie slant nip chink jap faggot homo fairy" repeated down the wall. Over the center of both image and list was placed the statement: "All violence is the illustration of a pathetic stereotype." Other parts of the installation similarly assaulted the viewer with aggressive invocations as well as condemnations of hate, encouraging people to contemplate injustices closer to their own lives.

Kruger's earlier work used pronouns such as "you" and "we" to force the viewer into the role of either accuser or accused, victim or perpetrator. Statements such as "Your comfort is my silence," "You substantiate our horror," and "We are your circumstantial evidence" left little safe space for the viewer. Using appropriated images of cloak-and-dagger intrigue, dental surgery, and high fashion, these works proved moral and ethical minefields. In comparison, the 1991 installation created the potential for a communal viewing experience, but shifted the ethical considerations outside the gallery. Kruger's walls created a community of victims. Once the shock of the violence was absorbed, the work induced a general shaking of the head and acknowledgment that the world is a hard place. The discomfort occurred as viewers left and had to decide how they might now act in the world outside the gallery. As this piece made clear, seeing injustice is easy, the responsibility for deciding what to do next is not.

In the 1980s, Kruger's work was commonly interpreted as social critique. More recently, her non-art world references have given rise to a very different reading. In the catalogue for a 1999 retrospective at the Museum of Contemporary Art, Los Angeles, critic Gary Indiana announced that Kruger enlisted the methods of "commercial media since these are, in fact, more persuasive and more authentically gratifying than a lot of contemporary 'fine art.'"[42] Indiana here identified persuasion and authenticity as the motivating forces behind her art. The first of these terms aligns well with the political force and moral certitude of much appropriation: Kruger had used the mass media's powers of persuasion, she explained, to "remove [the image] from the seeming natural position within the flow of dominant social directives [and present it in] the realm of commentary."[43] But what of authenticity? Appropriation by its very nature seems

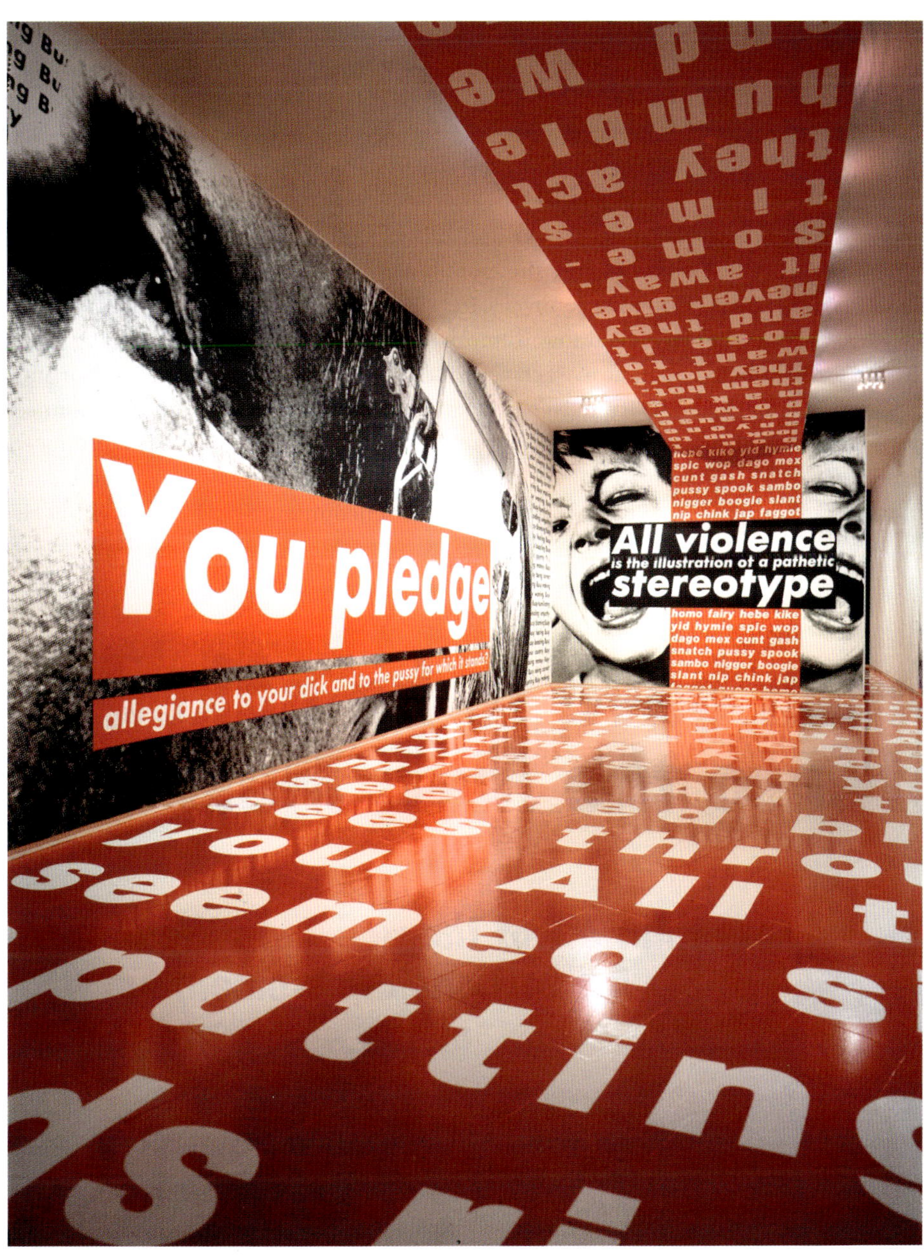

2.17 Barbara Kruger, ***Mary Boone Gallery installation***, New York, 1991. © Barbara Kruger. Courtesy Mary Boone Gallery, New York.

to undermine the idea of authenticity, arguing in favor of notions of social construction and against belief in authentic or essential notions of self. Indiana's essay suggests that, by the late 1990s, words such as "authenticity" and "faith" could be reintroduced into discussions of art, taking it for granted that they were inevitably now being read with critical awareness. It is a measure of the changing perceptions of art between 1979 and 1999 that appropriation could come to be viewed by the second of these dates as a means of creating art that was both evocative *and* analytical, emotional *and* intellectual.

Like Prince, Kruger began her career working for a magazine, as an art director for the women's publication *Mademoiselle*. By the 1990s, when magazines such as *Newsweek* and *Harper's Bazaar* featured work actually by or at least inspired by Kruger, her art was appearing in the very places from which she had appropriated its visual elements in the first place. The press used these images to address social and political issues. In effect, Kruger's persuasive and authentic presentation of contemporary life crafted from media imagery permitted her to re-enter the mass media with an effective critical stance. Her stylish intrusions into the public arena provided a valuable model that was adopted by activist artists in a wide range of political spheres.

The Guerrilla Girls

One political collective that became particularly adept at appropriation-based art actions was the Guerrilla Girls. The group formed in New York in 1985 in response to the unequal treatment of men and women in the art world. As one of their earliest works declared: "Women in America earn only ⅔ of what men do. Women Artists earn only ⅓ of what men do." In the Metropolitan Museum of Art's 1985 "International Survey of Painting and Sculpture" exhibition, slightly under 8 percent of the work displayed was by women. Noticing how few people responded to the traditional picket-line demonstrations with which other feminist groups were drawing attention to this significant underrepresentation, the group adopted the strategy that had worked for Kruger: They produced posters, books, and media events combining the savvy of advertisers with the intellectual consciousness of feminist art historians. The group maintained anonymity by wearing gorilla masks in public. In 1989, they produced a poster that featured a classic nude by Ingres wearing a gorilla mask and posed the question: "Do women have to be naked to get into the Met. Museum?" (**fig. 2.18**). Underneath were statistics showing that women represented less than 5 percent of the artists in the museum's Modern Art collection, whereas they were the subject of 85 percent of its nudes. In 2005, the Guerrilla Girls noted that these percentages had still not significantly changed, although it is worth noting that this time they made their announcement from within a major art institution, the Venice Biennale, where they had been invited to show their work. Through the work of Kruger and groups such as the Guerrilla Girls, appropriation came to be seen as an effective combination of politics, theory, aesthetics, and public address.

Jenny Holzer

While Kruger and others were adopting the tools of advertisers and the popular press, the New York-based Conceptualist Jenny Holzer (b. 1950) avoided visual imagery and looked toward more anonymous means of transmitting information, such as public-service announcements, aphorisms, D.I.Y. advertising, historical plaques, marquee announcements, and electronic billboards. Though Holzer produced material for museum settings in the late 1970s and early 1980s, most audiences encountered her work either in

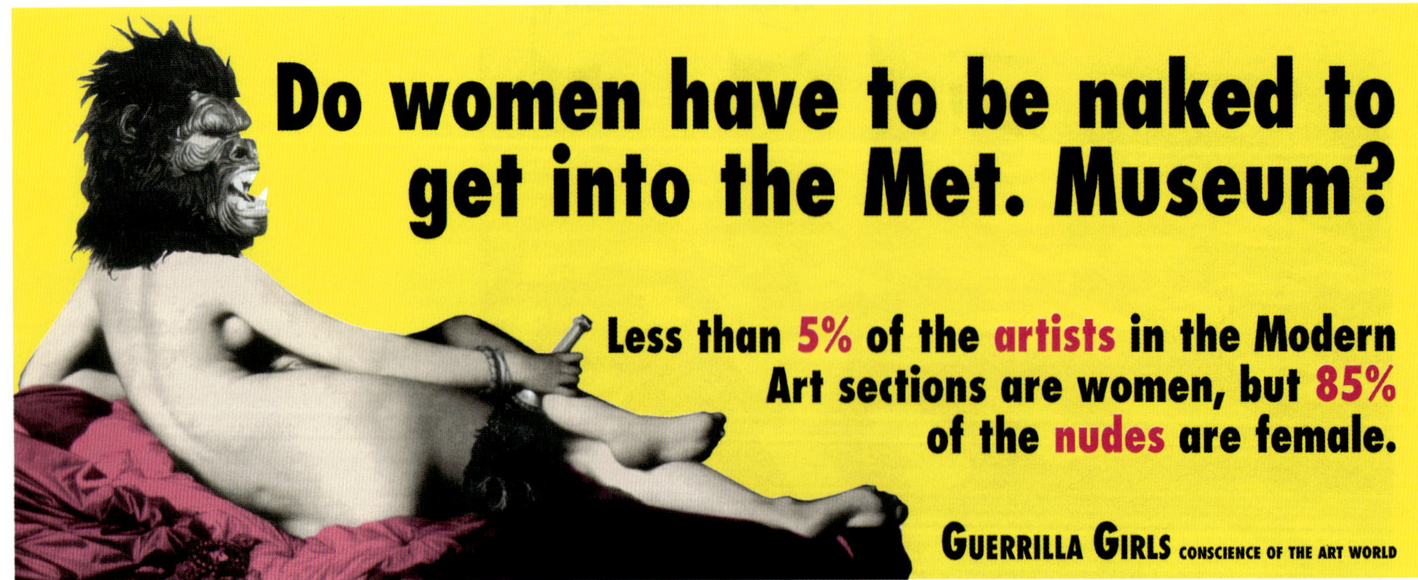

2.18 Guerrilla Girls, *Do women have to be naked to get into the Met. Museum?*, 1989. Poster, 11 × 28" (27.9 × 71.1 cm). Private collection. Courtesy Guerrilla Girls.

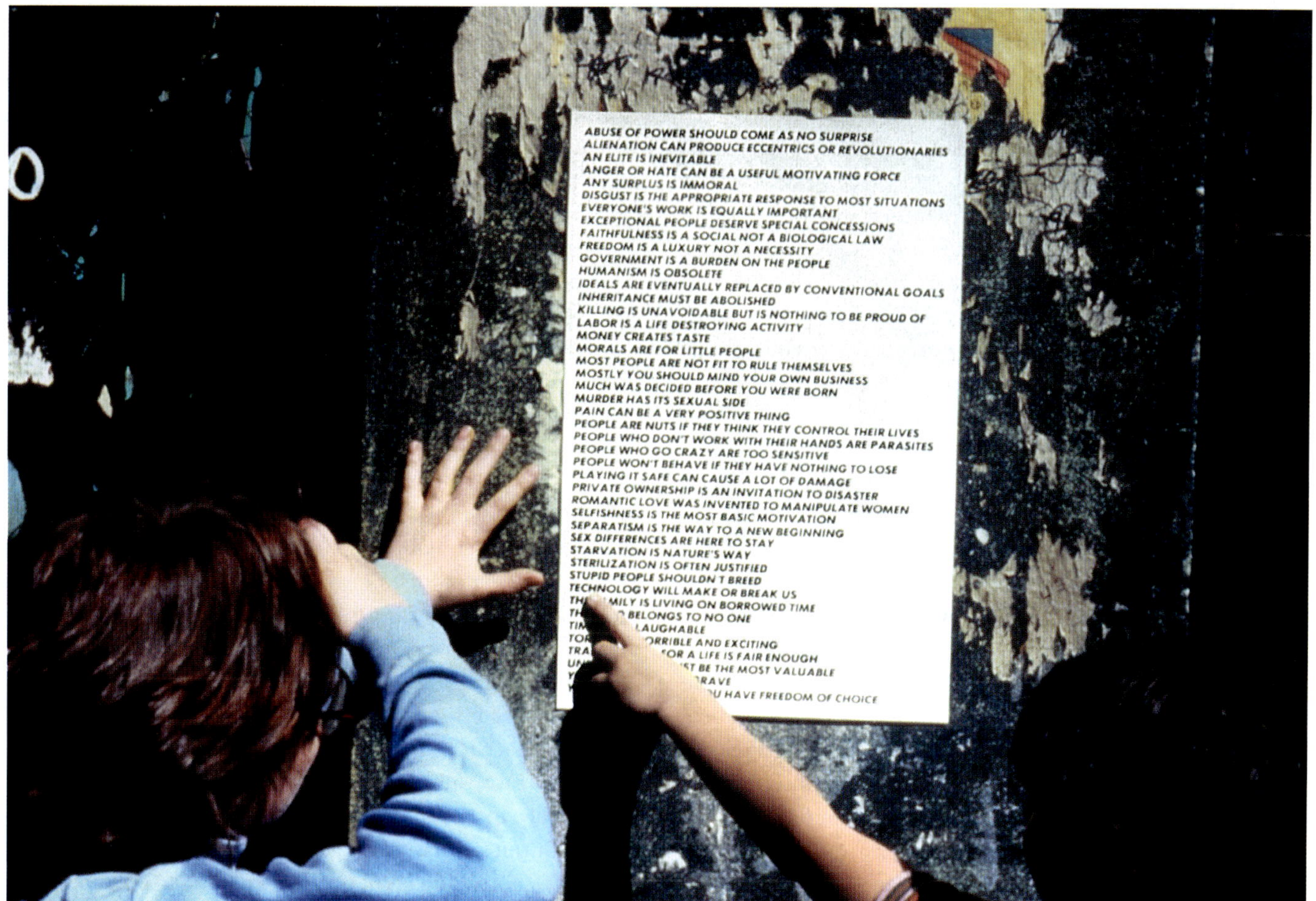

2.19 Jenny Holzer, from *Truisms (1977–79)*, 1977. Offset poster, 24 × 18" (61 × 45.7 cm). Installation in New York, 1977. Courtesy Jenny Holzer Studio.

the street or in art magazines—sites that suggested different interpretations.

Between 1977 and 1979, Holzer created her *Truisms* series. This consisted of statements written by the artist, brief assertions that, in their matter-of-fact manner, seemed to express the obvious and universal but that often contained controversial content: "ABUSE OF POWER COMES AS NO SURPRISE," "AN ELITE IS INEVITABLE," "MURDER HAS A SEXUAL SIDE." The several hundred *Truisms* were alphabetized and displayed in a range of formats, including posters, signs, T-shirts, stickers, bags, buttons, and in various forms of public address. The image reproduced here (**fig. 2.19**) shows the statements as they could have been encountered on the streets of the East Village, New York. Capturing a style of communication Holzer called "lower anonymous," the statements appeared among ads for parties, concerts, or rallies, or posters advertising apartments or guitar players, or seeking lost animals.[44] The effect of Holzer's statements is highly subjective and largely depends on context; they signify differently according to whether they are placed next to a movie advertisement, a political poster, a broken telephone, or a community garden. In each case, however, the viewer is directed to consider issues of inequity and violence that have real political consequences. Holzer explained in the mid-1980s that it was part of her intention to integrate her political and artistic life. It is thus appropriate to read as much as one can into her statements and their relationship with each other and their surroundings.[45] Like Kruger's billboards, this was public art that engaged the space of the city to activate its citizens.

It is not only context that generates Holzer's content. When she began the *Truisms*, she had recently completed her art studies, during which she had been greatly impressed by her readings in cultural theory and criticism. The *Truisms* consisted of her distillation of an intellectually challenging reading list into a format tailored to the attention span of an urban pedestrian. The method of the *Truisms*, enlisting one mode of address (slogan or soundbite) to express a form of analysis (critical theory) alien to it, proved fruitful for Holzer throughout the 1980s. Later series developed this method, incorporating snippets of personal narratives, common sense, and paranoia, as well as social, political, and art theory. In *Survival* from the early 1980s, for instance, emotional and intellectual responses were elicited by inserting such statements as "IT IS IN YOUR SELF-INTEREST TO FIND A WAY TO BE VERY TENDER," "THE BREAKDOWN COMES WHEN YOU STOP CONTROLLING YOURSELF AND WANT THE RELEASE OF A BLOODBATH," or "WITH ALL

THE HOLES IN YOU ALREADY THERE'S NO REASON TO DEFINE THE OUTSIDE ENVIRONMENT AS ALIEN" into huge public spaces from city squares to sporting arenas. The results are "alternative public service announcements" that suggest issuing authorities different than the customary ones of commerce and political power.[46]

The points of view that appear to underpin Holzer's statements fluctuate widely. One statement might suggest the sentiments of a left-wing revolutionary, another a fascist; one may evoke pathos, another disgust. Like Cindy Sherman's work, but unlike the messages one generally encounters in the public sphere, Holzer's series are multivocal and impossible to pin down. Again, as in Sherman's work, such a shifting authorial position suggests that Holzer was more interested in the movement between positions rather than in any single statement—she appeared to be enacting another challenge to the traditional idea of the artist as someone who seeks for and expresses truth, either about the self or about the world. Her statements read like announcements from a peripatetic, Postmodern subject moving through varied identities, wearing each like a costume that was useful for one situation but that was to be discarded for the next. Her critical reception is founded on the perception that she helped to articulate what was new about Postmodern identity: namely, its flexibility and rejection of notions of authentic, essential, unitary, or fixed identities.

Read aloud as convictions rather than caricatures, some statements from the *Survival* series might be deemed profoundly troubling. However, the viewer who chooses to stop and read has the opportunity to reflect not only on single statements, but also on the relationships between them. If we take just those listed above, themes start to emerge. There is a repeated invocation of physical violence and the suggestion of an intimacy between such violence and language. Physical crisis seems to inspire textual expression, which in turn generates physical unease.[47]

By the twenty-first century most people who have encountered Holzer's work have done so not in the street but in the very different public space of an art magazine, where it rubs shoulders with a particular form of cultural debate and promotion. Like Levine's, Holzer's work has been introduced with persuasive theoretical explanations that emphasized its critical operations over its expressive power; it was said to subject the "ideology of 'everyday life'" to "formal and linguistic operations."[48] In other words, Holzer, like Kruger, deconstructed the media, exposing its role as a tool of power. A formative critical essay on Holzer and Kruger (quoted earlier as forming part of the critical response to appropriation) was Hal Foster's "Subversive Signs" (1982), which identified one of the most striking features of both artists' work as its oppositional and linguistic character: "Indeed Kruger and Holzer are manipulators of signs more than makers of art objects—a shift in practice that renders the viewer an active reader of messages more than a contemplator of the esthetic."[49] Drawing on Conceptual art of the 1970s, with its skepticism about the aesthetic object, Foster found in Holzer's work an art of political content unhampered by conservative form. Art is presented as effective not for what it represents but for how it functions within the field of representation, just as Kruger's photo-collages, critic Craig Owens argued, revealed the machinery of stereotypes and offered viewers an opportunity to reject them.[50] Foster treats Holzer as a fellow traveler intent on demystifying contemporary culture. Asserting that "few of us are able to accept the status of art as a social sign entangled with other such signs,"[51] Foster presented the network of voices in Holzer's *Truisms* as an embrace of the signifying power of the urban environment and the successful presentation of what we tend to experience as a meaningless chaos as instead a chaos of meanings.

Conceptual artists of the 1970s had also defined art as an entangled social sign. Hans Haacke's *Shapolsky et al.* (see fig. 1.18) had forcefully argued that what hangs in museums is inescapably intertwined with what goes on outside them. Daniel Buren's work (see fig. 1.19) further postulated that there was no self-contained entity called "art" that existed to be contaminated by a likewise self-contained society: Art was part of the social and political networks in which it was valued. As Hal Foster indicated, appropriation took its cue from works such as those of Haacke and Buren. Artists adopted appropriation to explore how the networks of power spotlighted by their predecessors were perpetuated through representation. In addition to exposing the mechanisms of power, appropriation artists also explored how representation was complicit with that power. If artists were not free to select their means of expression, what choices were open to them? The answers were not always optimistic. Allan McCollum and Sherrie Levine cast a critical eye on formal innovation, while Barbara Kruger and Jenny Holzer suggested that the history of art was no longer a privileged source. Nevertheless, these artists adopted forms of expression that fell clearly in the category of art. In the spaces of Silvia Kolbowski's photo/text combinations, between the layers of Levine's copies, and in Cindy Sherman's presentation of self as both object and subject, lay fertile ground for contemporary art. Like realists before them, appropriation artists succeeded in reorienting the way people looked at both life and art.

3

Back to the Easel: Neo-Expressionism and the Return of Painting

Between 1980 and 1982, as appropriation was becoming a critical voice in New York, an international style that came to be labeled Neo-Expressionism emerged in a series of European exhibitions. Neo-Expressionist art was characterized by large-scale figurative oil-on-canvas paintings. After over a decade in which the trend in the art world had been away from painting in favor of Conceptual, performance, and installation practices, the return to painting came as something of a shock. To its supporters, Neo-Expressionism marked a renewed commitment to the psychological power of art and the pleasure of paint. To its detractors, it demonstrated a willful ignorance of critical developments of the 1960s and 1970s that had promised to liberate art from the restrictions of the male-dominated world of easel painting and elite commercial galleries.

The Neo-Expressionist label linked the work to the Expressionists, German artists who had expressed the anxiety of the early twentieth century through their aggressive and abstracted representations of modern life. The likes of Ernst Ludwig Kirchner (1880–1938) and Emil Nolde (1867–1956), members of the Dresden- and Berlin-based Die Brücke group, and Viennese Secession leader Oskar Kokoschka (1886–1980) mixed highly individualized styles with emotional and often spiritual content. Neo-Expressionism also evoked the painterly energy of the U.S. Abstract Expressionists such as Willem de Kooning (1904–97) (see fig. 0.4) and Jackson Pollock (1912–56) or the European Informel artists Jean Dubuffet (1901–85) and Jean Fautrier (1898–1964) (see fig. 0.3). It demonstrated that pictorial traditions widely presumed extinguished by the late 1970s were still relevant to the late twentieth century, and presented a formidable challenge to those who saw the critical approaches examined in Chapters 1 and 2 as the dominant tendencies in postwar Western art. The controversy in the early 1980s about the moral and artistic value of American and European Neo-Expressionist painting recalls the heated polemical debates of the 1930s, when avant-garde art was associated with the political resistance to fascism. Some critics did indeed reject Neo-Expressionism as nostalgic, elitist, and even fascistic, while the fact that this return was greeted with high prices and also that its participants were mostly male reignited feminists' critiques of the coincidence of patriarchal and capitalist forces in and beyond the art world. But others praised the emergent movement as honest, ironic, or as a liberating application of the past to the present that reopened the possibilities of paint to a new generation of artists. These competing attitudes to the "return to the easel" expressed deep-rooted concerns about the direction of contemporary art.

"A New Spirit in Painting"

In 1981, a major exhibition at the Royal Academy of Arts in London heralded "A New Spirit in Painting," as the show's title put it. The following year, members of the "New Spirit" curatorial team Christos M. Joachimides and Norman Rosenthal offered a similar show, "Zeitgeist," in Berlin, while Achille Bonito Oliva created a series of related exhibitions in Italy and christened the new movement there the *Transavanguardia*, or "Transavantgarde." Neo-Expressionism quickly became a significant force in both the art market and the museum world. There were high-profile New York gallery exhibitions of German artists Anselm Kiefer, Georg Baselitz, Markus Lüpertz, Rainer Fetting, Jörg Immendorff, and A.R. Penck, as well as Italians Francesco Clemente, Sandro Chia, and Enzo Cucchi, and Americans Julian Schnabel, David Salle, and Eric Fischl. The core male-dominated cast of Neo-Expressionist artists, along with the movement's selective internationalism, was quickly established. The common themes in the major exhibitions suggest that many artists and intellectuals in the United States and Europe were searching for the kind of "international style" that the pluralism of the previous decade had failed to generate.

Unlike appropriation, which was promoted as a new approach being explored by a particular group of young artists, Neo-Expressionism was presented as the logical

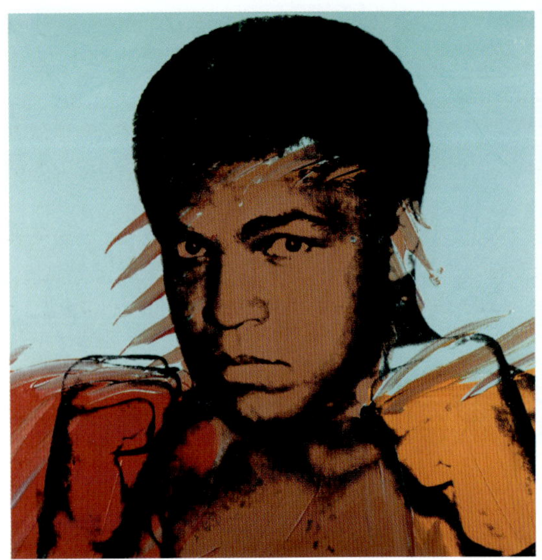

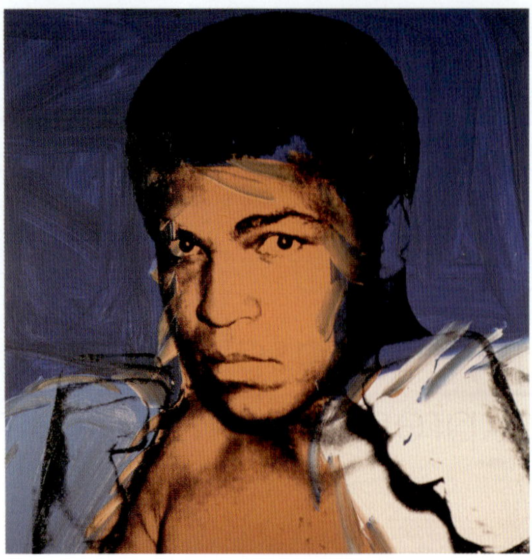

3.1 Andy Warhol, ***Muhammad Ali***, 1977. Synthetic polymer paint and silkscreen ink on canvas, 40 × 40" (101.6 × 101.6 cm). Courtesy the Andy Warhol Foundation.

outcome of art history. It was defined by blockbuster painting shows and exhibition catalogues that constructed a genealogy for Neo-Expressionism that extended from Cubism, through Expressionism, Abstract Expressionism, Art Informel, and Pop art, and into the 1980s. Picasso, de Kooning, Gerhard Richter, Joseph Beuys, and even Andy Warhol were all represented in these histories, suggesting the inevitability of the current trend and providing a pedigree for the younger artists. The shows set out to convey, as one curator explained, "the contemporary significance of the oldest form [of art]"[1]—an argument that dismissed challenges to painting made by some of the very artists included, notably Warhol and Richter. Warhol's gestural portraits of the mid-1970s such as *Muhammad Ali* (1977) (**fig. 3.1**) and Richter's blurred images including *Annunciation after Titian* (1973) (**fig. 3.2**), both shown at "A New Spirit in Painting," could have been read as critical commentaries on painting's expressive language; Warhol for reducing the gestural

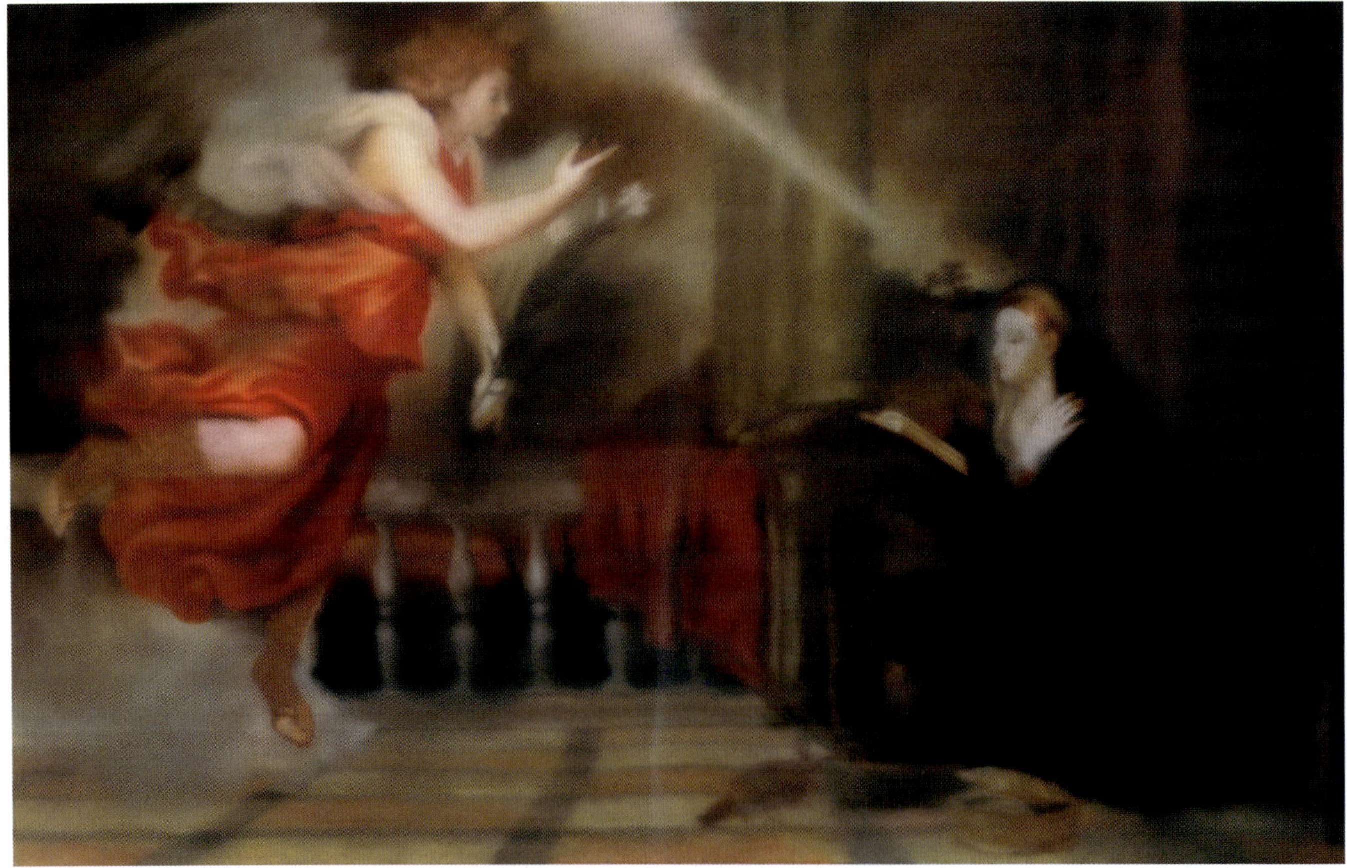

3.2 Gerhard Richter, ***Annunciation After Titian***, 1973. Oil on canvas, 49¼ × 78¾" (125 × 200 cm). Hirshhorn Museum and Sculpture Garden, Washington, D.C. Courtesy Atelier Gerhard Richter.

brushstrokes to conventional markings as repeatable as the photographic image, and Richter for basing his evocative blurred painting style on nothing more than an out-of-focus photograph. In neither case did the artist treat his painterly style as a conduit to personal expression, as Neo-Expressionists were said to do. Nonetheless, the assertive presence of painting in both artists' oeuvre, regardless of its content, served the return-to-painting agenda. The London "New Spirit" show was introduced with the bold claim: "The artists' studios are full of paint pots again and an abandoned easel in an art school has become a rare sight ... In the studios, in the cafes and bars, where artists or students gather you hear passionate debates and arguments about painting."[2] By the time "Zeitgeist," a second celebration of New-Expressionism, opened in Berlin in 1982, the style of Neo-Expressionism was said to provide proof that "Subjectivity, the Visionary, Myth, Suffering and Grace have all been rehabilitated."[3] It was such claims, with their hyperbolic restaging of Modernist tropes, that riled artists and critics who had been struggling for the past few decades to revise and reject the limits such priorities set for contemporary art.

Neo-Expressionism provoked a different style of commentary than appropriation. Rather than dispassionately dissecting the function of art, Neo-Expressionist criticism engaged in poetic forays. In 1979, poet and art critic René Ricard reviewed the first showing by Julian Schnabel of his notorious oil, plaster, wax, encaustic, bondo, and plate paintings (see fig. 3.4) in the following terms: "There comes a point in a painter's life where civilization abandons him; he looks at his brushes like a gorilla looking at a knife and fork, digs in with his hands, smashes the plate and makes a big mess."[4] Ricard then reversed the metaphor, transforming the painting rather than the painter into a beast locked away in the basement, exposed only to those with a taste for the monstrous side of artistic creation, whom he referred to as "gorillaphiles." Such hyperbole well captured the sensation that Schnabel's work generated, with its hundreds of square feet of broken plates and oil paints. Less sanguine commentators saw evidence that, after being diversified and critiqued since the late 1950s, artistic practice was not being advanced at all, but was rather being returned to a traditional bohemian setting that evoked the Parisian Left Bank garrets and artists' cafés of the early twentieth-century avant-garde. There was something familiar about this "New Spirit."

Critics of the new painting were appalled at the apparent victory of "high art public relations" over critical theory,[5] and at the willingness of curators to claim universalism for the work, despite the limited demographic of Neo-Expressionist artists. The catalogue for "A New Spirit" declared the typical heroic young painter to be "engaged in a search for self-realization ... as an actor on a wider historical stage";[6] it failed to mention that the new international movement was being represented at the London exhibition by thirty-eight white men, with negligible involvement from women or non-white artists. The monumental *Running Man* (**fig. 3.3**), painted by Jonathan Borofsky (b. 1942) on the Berlin Wall

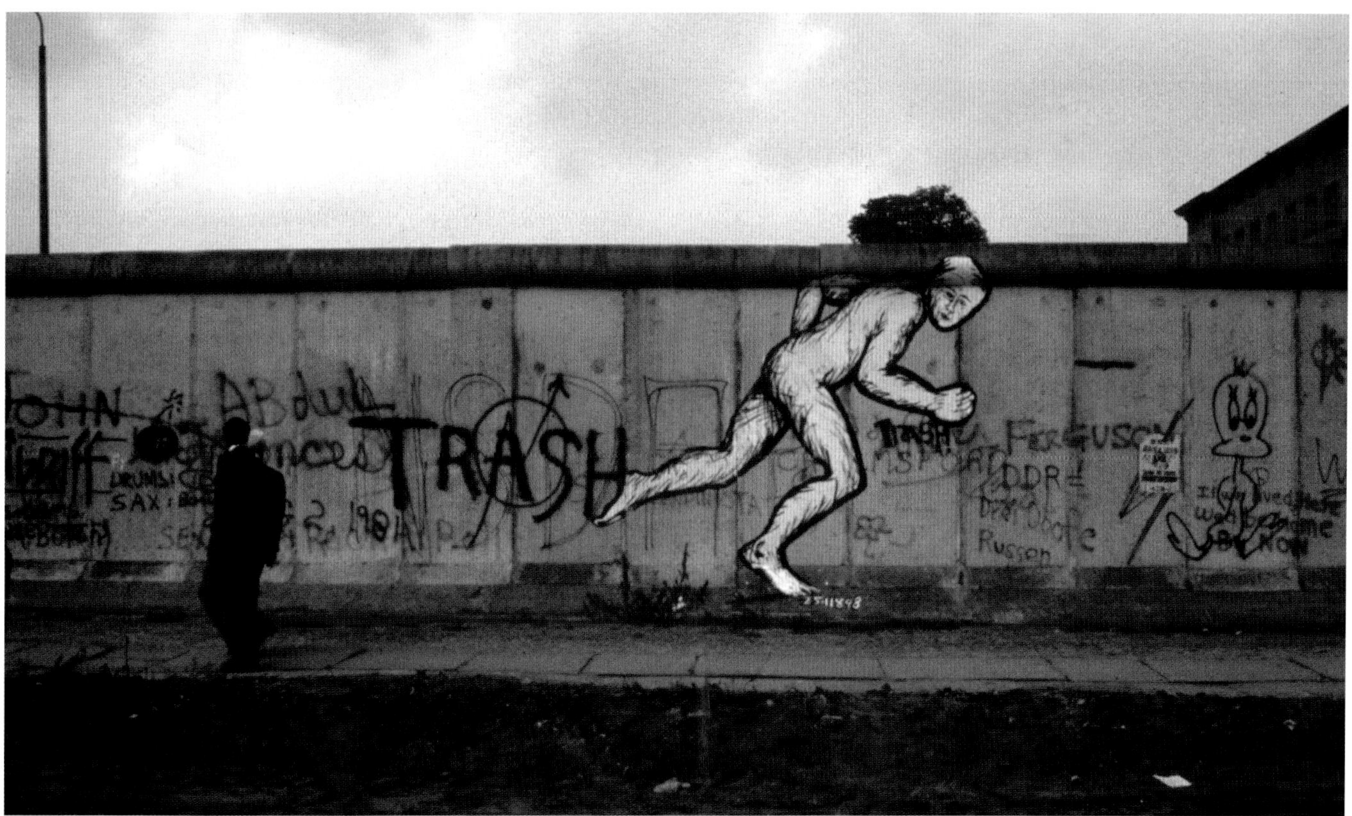

3.3 Jonathan Borofsky, on-site installation of ***Running Man at 2,541,898*** as part of the "Zeitgeist" International Art Exhibition, Berlin, Germany, 1982. © Jonathan Borofsky. Courtesy Paula Cooper Gallery, New York.

on the occasion of "Zeitgeist," offers a representative embodiment of the "New Spirit" actor: a white male fleeing the modern tragedies created by the Western world (the Wall, erected in 1961 and destroyed in 1989, divided democratic West Berlin from communist East Berlin). With its generic appearance and ID number instead of the traditional artist's signature, *Running Man* suggests an ambivalence toward identity rather than a "search for self-realization." In this case as in most others, the relationship between Borofsky's artistic concerns and the curatorial statements published alongside his work was unclear; crucially, it was the latter that were largely responsible for Neo-Expressionism's contentious quality. The promotion of Neo-Expressionism perhaps made the movement seem more limited than it actually was.

The United States

Despite the critical controversies raised by Neo-Expressionism, in terms of content and scale the works were undeniably striking. After a decade of art that had resisted and critiqued the economics of culture, problematizing art's relationship to commerce and display, here were painters making paintings that could be exhibited in spectacular shows and then purchased. A major strand of the story of Neo-Expressionism in New York concerns the changing relationships of art and society in 1980s. The financial crisis brought on in the 1970s in large part by the oil crisis was being met by President Reagan's supply-side economics rooted heavily in tax cuts, deregulation of government controls over private industry, and reduced government support for public service, excluding the military. Though the success of what came to be called "Reaganomics" has been debated, from the perspective of the arts it indisputably reduced the amount of funds available to non-profit arts organizations and increased the spending power of wealthier U.S. citizens. The result was to change the balance of how money entered the art world and where it was spent. With much less public funding to support experimental art, the gallery system, with its focus on sales, gained power as the ultimate arbiter of success or failure. Compounding the issues was the fact that the financial picture continued to look bleak. With less confidence in the stock market, art started to seem like a good addition to one's portfolio. By and large, those looking to art as an investment were not seeking to collect the more politicized and ephemeral art discussed in earlier chapters. Though by no means was all Neo-Expressionism socially conservative, its aesthetics nonetheless appealed to traditional tastes formed by the historical canon of oil-on-canvas paintings, and, in contrast to so much of the conceptual, earth, process, and performance art of the 1970s, it could be sold. Many of the artists who entered Neo-Expressionist circles in the early 1980s saw their prices skyrocket and the art world around them change dramatically.

Julian Schnabel

Julian Schnabel's (b. 1951) plate paintings were nearly 8 feet high but would be dwarfed by his subsequent paintings on tarpaulins and kabuki theater backdrops. His career followed a similarly expansive course. In 1979, he showed twice at the Mary Boone Gallery in New York. Within two years he was represented by both Boone and Leo Castelli, and in 1986 he had a retrospective at the Whitechapel Art Gallery, London, which subsequently toured through Europe and on to New York, San Francisco, and Houston, where Schnabel had begun his career. Schnabel's experience was typical of the Neo-Expressionists who, like the Pop artists a generation earlier, found themselves canonized before their careers were much more than ten years old.

A 7ft 6in by 10ft accumulation of broken plates, *The Death of Fashion* (1978) (**fig. 3.4**) is typical of Schnabel's early work and characteristic of the hubris of U.S. Neo-Expressionism generally. Thick oil paint has been pushed over the fractured surfaces, defining pictorial forms in one place while working against the image in others, diverting attention instead to the irregular shapes of the ceramic shards. The support for the picture consists of a central wood panel extending several inches toward the viewer. It is flanked by two smaller, stepped-back wings, which fill out the painting's horizontal dimensions. Two central motifs—a torso in rose, madder, pink, and alizarin on a pedestal, and a tall slender brown ovoid decorated with a gold cross balancing on a slight branch of green and yellow—hover against a field of black, grays, and purple. Behind the torso, set back upon the right wing, is an amorphous cone of pink and purple paint that recalls the flesh tones of a nude by de Kooning or the eighteenth-century French painter François Boucher. The effect of impulsive sensuality that this mass of organic fleshy paint evokes is, however, trivialized by the scattering of cheap red and yellow plates with which it is filled. The title, *The Death of Fashion*, suggests both physical violence and superficiality, denying the gravity of the image. This mix of aggression and indifference, emotional investment and glib ambiguity, characterizes Schnabel's work.

The pedestals, torsos, and ovoid that figure prominently in *The Death of Fashion* recur throughout Schnabel's early works. The prominent torso in *St. Sebastian Born 1951* (1979) creates a link between the martyred saint and the artist, who was born in 1951.[7] The appearance of the self-referential torso in *The Death of Fashion* echoes Schnabel's 1978 notebook entry, "I want my life to be embedded in my work, crushed into my painting,"[8] which in turn seems to warrant Ricard's image of bestial drama quoted above. In 1986, however, Schnabel's tone changed. "Art is not about self-expression," he wrote in a statement accompanying his Whitechapel retrospective.[9] He now asserted that "Neo-Expressionism doesn't exist"—"the political climate was different [for the original Expressionism], the concerns were different."[10] By the mid-1980s, Schnabel seemed to want his eclectic imagery, materials, and methods to be understood in relation to

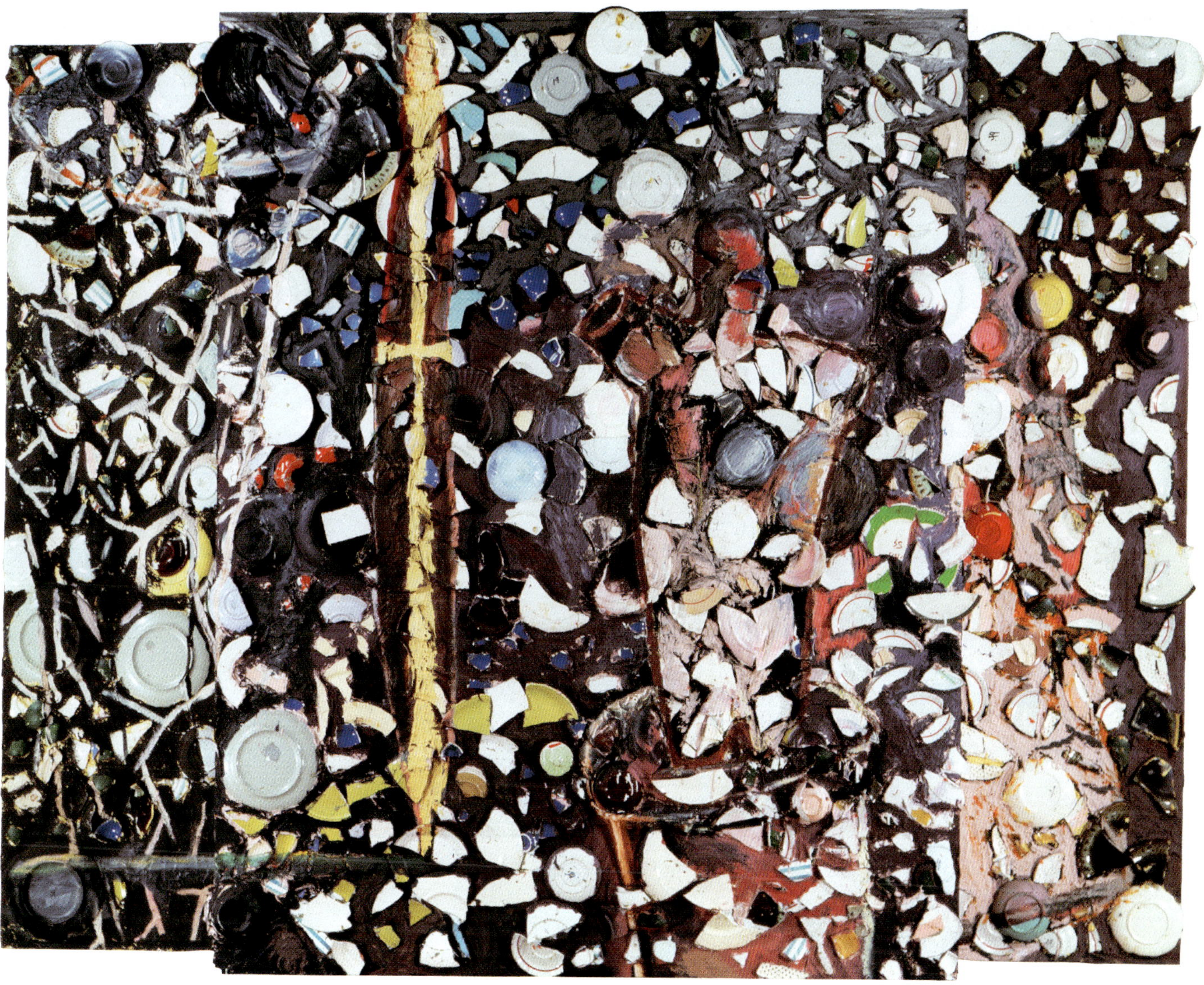

3.4 Julian Schnabel, *The Death of Fashion*, 1978. Oil, plates, and bondo on wood, 90 × 120 × 13" (225 × 300 × 32.5 cm). Image courtesy of Julian Schnabel.

contemporary cultural politics that eschewed the Modernist aim of creating universal truths from personal expression which had inspired early twentieth-century Expressionism. Some viewers accepted that Neo-Expressionists, like appropriation artists, were skeptical of the idea of art as a conduit to universal truths, but others felt that this new painting was the vessel into which the artist might pour his or her heart and soul, to universalizing effect.[11]

Eric Fischl

The education of the U.S. Neo-Expressionists was distinguished by the degree to which many of them trained in conceptually oriented art programs. Schnabel, after finishing a BFA at the University of Houston, enrolled in the Whitney Independent Study Program, the same program that Jenny Holzer and several Colab (see Chapter 4) members attended. Eric Fischl (b. 1948) and David Salle were both at California Institute of the Arts, where artists and teachers such as John Baldessari, Allan Kaprow, Douglas Huebler, and Michael Asher led a rigorously Conceptual program. Conventional training in painting or drawing was subordinated at CalArts, as Fischl said, to developing "a sense of knowing what we were doing, knowing what history was, knowing what strategies were, knowing that there was this great purpose behind what we were doing."[12] This form of artistic self-awareness, coupled with a willingness to "educate yourself in public," led to the emergence of artists in a wide variety of media.[13] Fischl's Conceptualist training is evident in his self-conscious detachment from his subject matter, as in his breakthrough paintings of the late 1970s. These narratives of suburban puberty are fictions for which his own life served, in his words as "an energy source," but not a direct model.[14] Preliminary studies consisted of layers of drawings on transparent glassine that could be arranged and rearranged until psychologically intricate compositions emerged.

One such work, *Bad Boy* (1981) (**fig. 3.5**), began with a still life, whose visual and narrative clues Fischl then followed until the scene was completed to his satisfaction. The artist

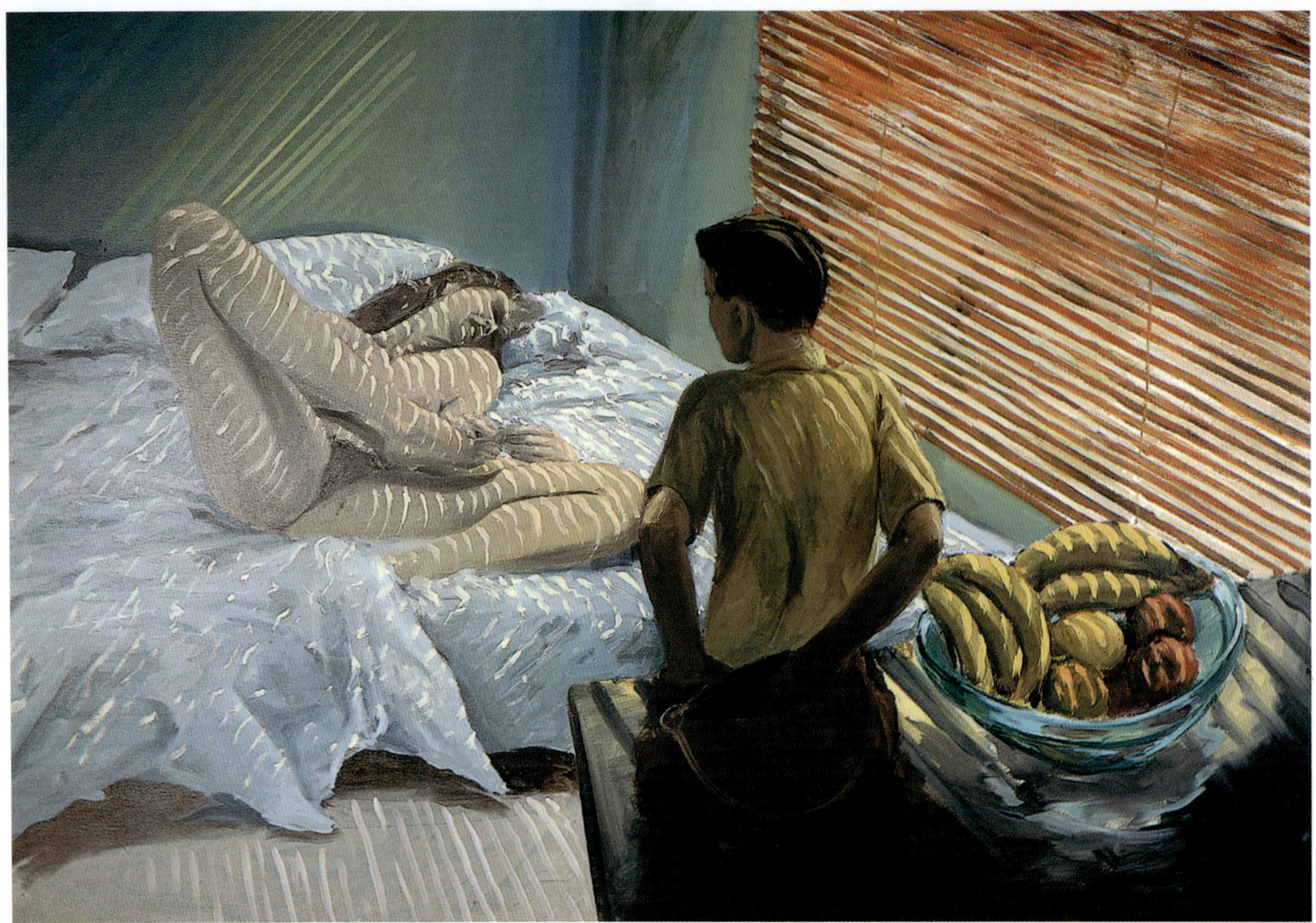

3.5 Eric Fischl, *Bad Boy*, 1981. Oil on canvas, 66 × 96" (167.64 × 243.84 cm). Image courtesy the Eric Fischl Studio.

noted how the stripes of light on the fruit implied a window with blinds that then defined the setting as a room. Its initial occupants were a couple in bed, but this pair was then resolved into a single woman lying nude on her back rubbing her foot. The viewer is invited to gaze from the parted legs of the woman, up to her foot, and then back to her distracted gaze. She is joined by a boy, perhaps her son, who stands in the foreground by the fruit bowl and stares. Here, the boy performs the action that earns him a reprimand and distinguishes his intrusion from the viewer's: He slips his hand into the open slit of the woman's purse.[15] A notable rumination on the power of the Gaze (see Chapter 2), *Bad Boy* is also one of Fischl's many pictures in which the status and meaning of the scene—reality or fantasy, seduction or warning?—remain ambiguous. The artist asserted that the alienation, insecurity, artificiality, and distance in his work expressed "the spiritual dilemma" of U.S. suburban life.[16] He was also willing to talk about how his paintings related directly to his own family's experience of dealing with the life and death of his alcoholic mother. While other artists spoke of culture and expression in general if often political terms, or, like Schnabel, rejected the role of the self in their paintings altogether, Fischl opened up Neo-Expressionism to content found in the daily lives of the middle class.

David Salle

Fischl's increasingly readable narratives made him one of the least contentious of the Neo-Expressionists. David Salle (b. 1952) and Julian Schnabel, by contrast, invited controversy with their invocation of conventional painting while, in Salle's case especially, attempting to empty its history and content of significance. Whereas Schnabel, even as he rejected the notion that his art was simply "self-expression," did assure viewers that contemporary painting sought to convey a "psychological resonance," Salle avowed that his art "participate[ed] in meaninglessness" and even pronounced it "dead."[17] Despite using imagery heavily loaded with references to sex, art, and popular culture, he presented his work as being about nothing.

Like the appropriation artists, Salle's practice was based on manipulated existing imagery, layering materials drawn from softcore pornography (often his own photographs replicating the appearance of their pornographic sources), geometric abstraction, amateurish line drawings and fashion illustrations, cartoons, and copies of Modernist masterpieces. Unlike Fischl, however, Salle frustrated critics by refusing to acknowledge relationships between his fragmentary images, insisting: "There's no narrative. There really is none."[18] Rather than generating content, he aimed for "extreme cancellation," or the "draining away of recognition or of meaning even as you look at it."[19] Salle's desire to "divide the meaning of the thing in the painting from the meaning of the thing in the world"[20] has troubling consequences. His painting *Géricault's Arm* (1985) (**fig. 3.6**), for instance, includes two images of a woman's body, underwear pulled down below her thighs, arms raised and lifting a cut-off T-shirt to just below her breasts. Her head is cut off by the frame in the first case and in the second covered by a copy of a study of severed limbs by the French artist Théodore Géricault (1791–1824). How were viewers to see such elements as meaningless, rather than as standard—if diverse—signifiers of sexual submission and violence with a high-culture twist?

Salle's attempt to free forms from their content follows logically from the work of Jasper Johns, an early and frequently cited influence (see Introduction). The everyday motifs in Johns's work—drawers, coffee cans, flags, numbers, paving slabs—were separated from their real-world functions and thus lost their customary significance. Salle's source material, however, was loaded with meaning that was far more provocative than Johns's. To deny that meaning appeared to many immoral, if not simply impossible. Unlike Johns or even Schnabel, Salle was not seeking to create alternative associations for familiar images.[21] As a result, as his images saturated the art market in the early 1980s, he faced accusations of trafficking in pornography rather than, as he claimed, examining its "mechanisms."[22]

Though Salle acknowledged that his images of women lacked "the neutrality [viewers] believe other painted images have," his work inspired critics to look closely at the consequences of Neo-Expressionism's non-neutrality.[23] The most thorough response was Mira Schor's 1986 essay "Appropriated Sexuality." Methodically surveying Salle's images of unclothed women in contorted, subservient poses, often pictured alongside weapons, vehicles, or other bodies, Schor analyzed the artist's attempt to render such images meaningless. She compared the anti-painting and anti-representational impulse of the CalArts program when Salle studied there to the critical engagement with painting and representation practiced in Judy Chicago and Miriam Schapiro's Feminist Arts Program (FAP) (see Chapter 1), which was based in Fresno, also in southern California. The work of the FAP, in which Schor participated, demonstrated how the relationship between imagery and meaning was intimate, political, and informed by gender. This observation, she argued, was disregarded by Neo-Expressionism: "Salle's lack of belief in the meaning of imagery [stands] in striking and significant contrast to much work by women artists."[24] This was significant because the paintings' critical success revealed the art world's willingness to join with Salle in seeing the "desecration of woman" as meaningless.[25]

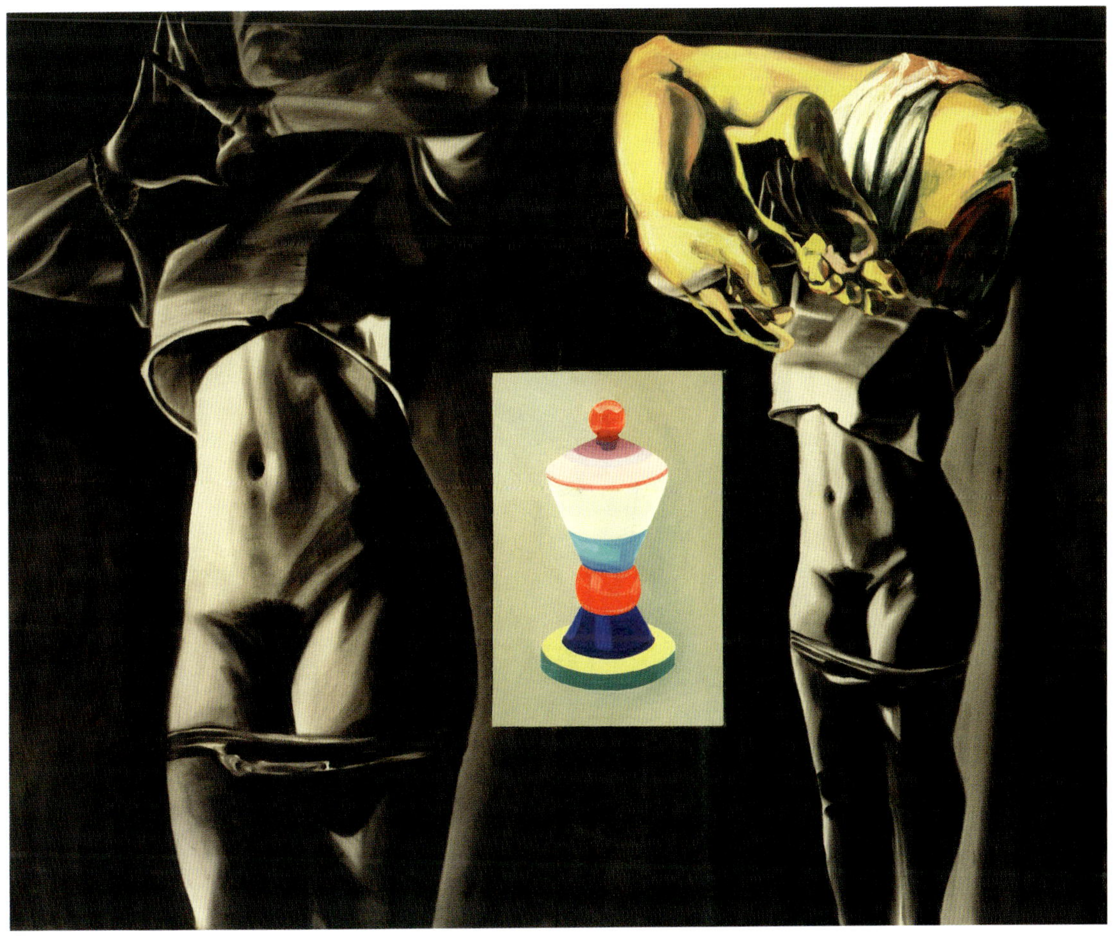

3.6 David Salle, *Géricault's Arm*, 1985. Oil and synthetic polymer paint on canvas, 6' 5⅞" × 8' ¼" (197.8 × 244.5 cm). The Museum of Modern Art, New York.

Schor was not the first critic to contrast the art education of the 1970s with the art produced in the 1980s. In a 1982 review of work by CalArts graduates, Craig Owens declared himself troubled by their turn away from Conceptualist traditions. He argued that museums and galleries alienate artists from their art, much as capitalism estranges workers from their labor: The work of art is transformed from an object of personal and social significance into a commodity in which such qualities as originality, individuality, and national pride are packaged and circulated. Revealing how this ideological process occurred and whom it served had been one of the key achievements of artists, theorists, and art historians of the previous two decades. Neo-Expressionism's apparent restoration of traditional forms of art looked, to Owens and others, like a return to the mystification of Modernist painting and a capitulation on the part of art criticism with regard to its social function.

As Douglas Crimp, curator of the "Pictures" exhibition (see Chapter 2), wrote in 1981: "The rhetoric that accompanies this resurrection of painting is almost entirely reactionary: it reacts specifically against all those art practices of the 1960s and 1970s that abandoned painting and worked to reveal the ideological supports of painting as well as the ideology that painting, in turn, supports."[26] Defenders of Neo-Expressionism such as Achille Bonito Oliva countered that the avant-garde, with its fetishization of the new and its notion of "progress," had always functioned in concert with capitalist power. He concluded that the 1960s avant-garde had merely proved that art was powerless in the face of politics and the economy. Rather than relegate the history of the 1960s and 1970s to one of failure and complicity, however, critics such as Owens, Crimp, and Hal Foster retorted that such analyses of post-World War II art were inadequate and merely symptomatic of the conservative tendency of Neo-Expressionism and its advocates.

Jean-Michel Basquiat

The myth of Jean-Michel Basquiat (1960–88) claims that he sprung forth untrained from the city streets, tagging the walls of New York with cryptic poetry, pictographs, and his signature "SAMO©." This story certainly fit the image of the "modern primitive" snatched from the fantasies and fears of the Western imagination. As such, the black, urban Basquiat appeared to provide a counterweight to the middle-class, often Jewish (Schnabel, Salle, and Fischl are all Jewish), white men who composed the New-Expressionist cadre. Coming from a very different background, Basquiat demonstrated the relevance of the new painting to a broad audience. Writers of different critical persuasions, both black and white, have pronounced his art to be truthful, "orphic," and even "fundamentally black"; others, meanwhile, have subjected such assertions to rigorous critical analyses.[27]

Parts of the myth that grew up around Basquiat were true. He was essentially untrained—though his mother was an amateur artist who encouraged his interest, and he had art lessons and as a six-year-old even had junior membership at the Brooklyn Museum. A child of a middle-class family, he attended the alternative City As School high school, where he participated in Family Life Theater, a community theater program. Though he dropped out and left home at eighteen, living for a time on the streets, it is clear that the idea of art as a worthy endeavor was instilled in him by his family and

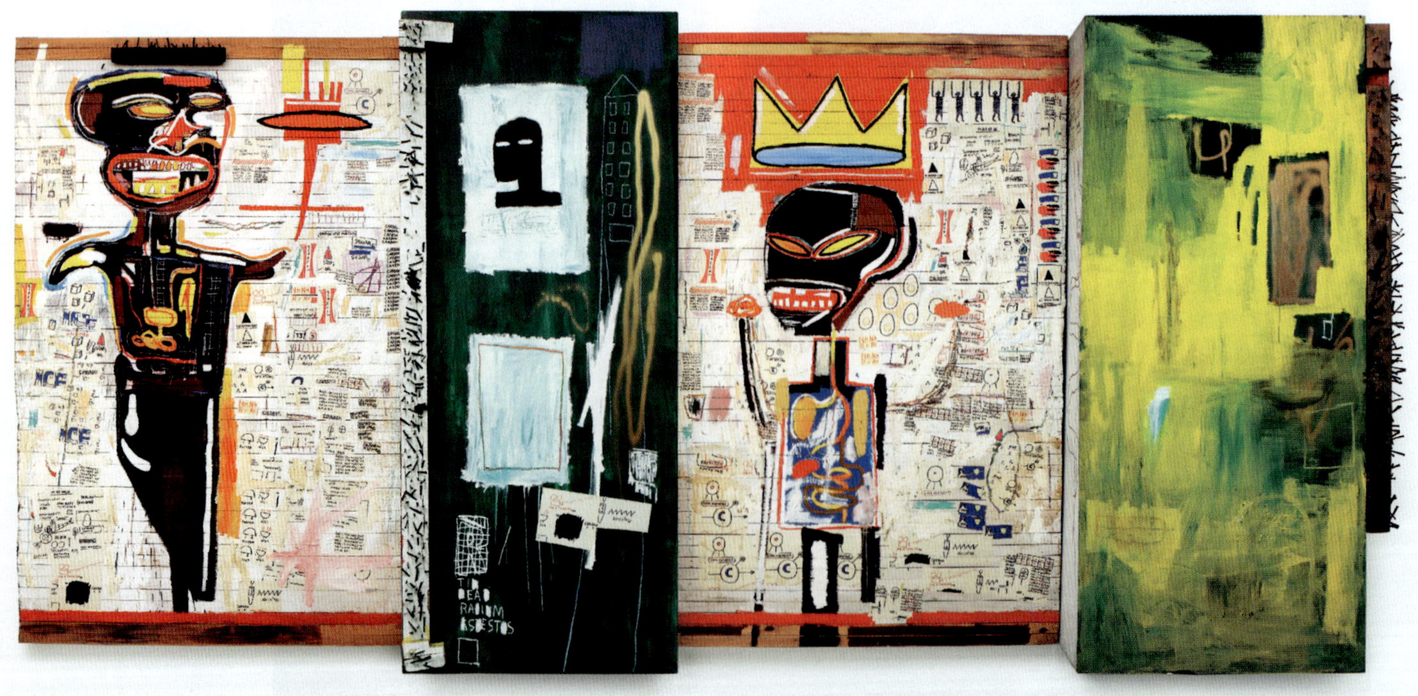

3.7 Jean-Michel Basquiat, *Grillo*, 1984. Oil, acrylic, oilstick, photocopy collage, and nails on wood (in four parts), 96 × 211½ × 18" (243.8 × 537.2 × 45.7 cm). Stefan T. Edlis Collection, Chicago.

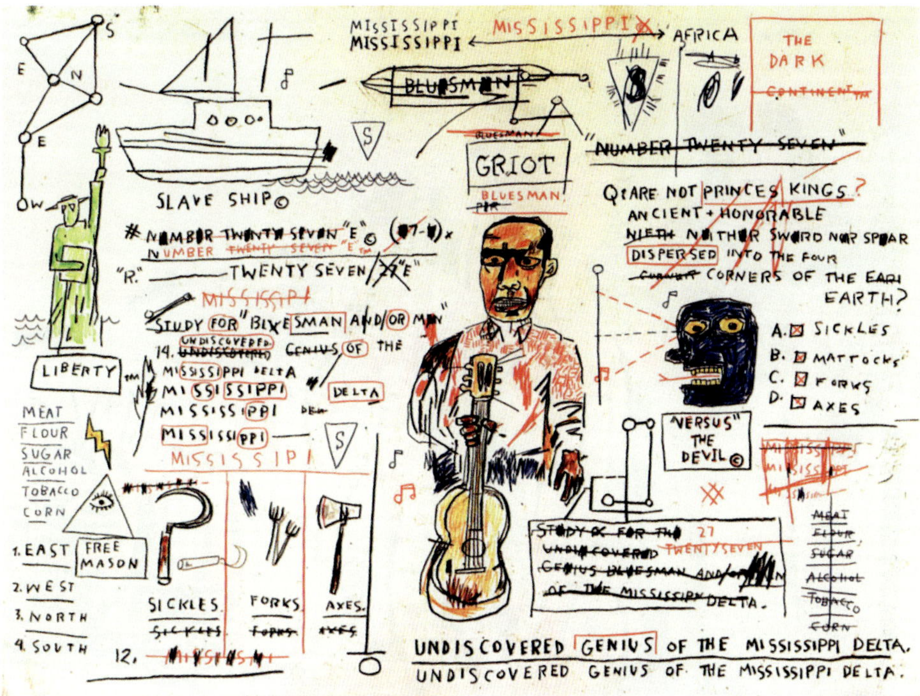

3.8 Jean-Michel Basquiat, *Undiscovered Genius* (from *Untitled: The Daros Suite of Thirty-two Drawings*), 1982–84. Acrylic, charcoal, crayon, pastel, and pencil, 22⅜ × 30⅛" (57 × 76.5 cm). Daros Collection, Switzerland.

early education. But even if the myth of Basquiat as a naïve painter and poor child of the streets wasn't exactly true, his mixed heritage was real: He was the son of a Haitian-born father and Puerto Rican mother, and had spent three years in Puerto Rico. When he became a fixture in the affluent world of the cultural elite, he brought with him a rare knowledge of African art and African-American culture as well as of the history of postwar American painting.

While Basquiat was one of the fixtures of the East Village scene, showing in "The Times Square Show" and at the Fun Gallery (see Chapter 4), he was also one of the first artists to make the move to the more business-oriented galleries in SoHo. On the streets, Basquiat spraypainted tags and text. In the gallery, he captured the semiotic heterogeneity courted by both appropriationist and Neo-Expressionist artists. Various painterly languages appear across the surface of canvases such as his 1984 multipanel tour de force *Grillo* (**fig. 3.7**). Here we find expressive de Kooningesque flourishes and linear scratchings that echo cave drawings or the paintings of Cy Twombly. Fields of color applied in broad brushstrokes balance expanses of white or black that evoke absence and erasure. Nails punctuate the boundaries between panels, while lists and notes that appear to catalogue thoughts, desires, research, history, aphorisms, and streams of consciousness cover the surfaces like notes on a page or chalk on a board. Typical of Basquiat's imagery, *Grillo* favors schematic and often skeletal figures in which contour is asserted over form and color. Drawing that suggests a stuttering, halting, and aggressive figuration is are often countered with passages of wet-on-wet paint, or traced hands and stick figures that evoke children's art.

Interpretation of Basquiat's oracular visions remains a bone of contention: Are they best understood, like Schnabel and Salle's work, to be about general concerns, or is there more specific content to be gleaned? Reading the text in Basquiat's pictures certainly suggests specific concerns. In *Grillo,* there are references to sugar plantations, physical combat, and colonization. Moreover, pronounced with a Spanish accent, as art historian and curator Kellie Jones suggests, the title of the work is actually "griot," a term meaning "poet and historian" in the West African oral tradition. Basquiat had used the word in earlier works including *Gold Griot* (1984) that featured a large iconic figure like those in *Grillo.* In one drawing, *Undiscovered Genius,* from *Untitled: The Daros Suite of Thirty-two Drawings* (1982–84) (**fig. 3.8**), the words "Griot Bluesman" are provided as a label for a solitary figure who faces forward out of a field of textual and symbolic references to the roots of African-American culture. Likewise, Jones points out, the nails hammered into *Grillo* allude to similar practices in African works, while the crown motif recurs throughout Basquiat's oeuvre as a self-referential symbol. Text and iconography address cultural and personal struggles in the wake of colonialism.

This agglomeration of styles, texts, images, and histories might constitute a personally pointed reflection on the multicultural identity of a young, black, middle-class Brooklynite of Puerto Rican and Haitian descent, but they also spoke the broader language of Neo-Expressionism. Basquiat's works were thus readily accessible to the collectors, dealers, and curators who promoted them into the rarefied spaces of Western culture. Basquiat chose his contacts well, moving from East Village celebrities at the Fun Gallery to more powerful brokers. Among his earliest supporters was René Ricard, whose emotional pronouncements had announced the arrival of Julian Schnabel and whose understanding of the scene helped Basquiat launch his meteoric career.

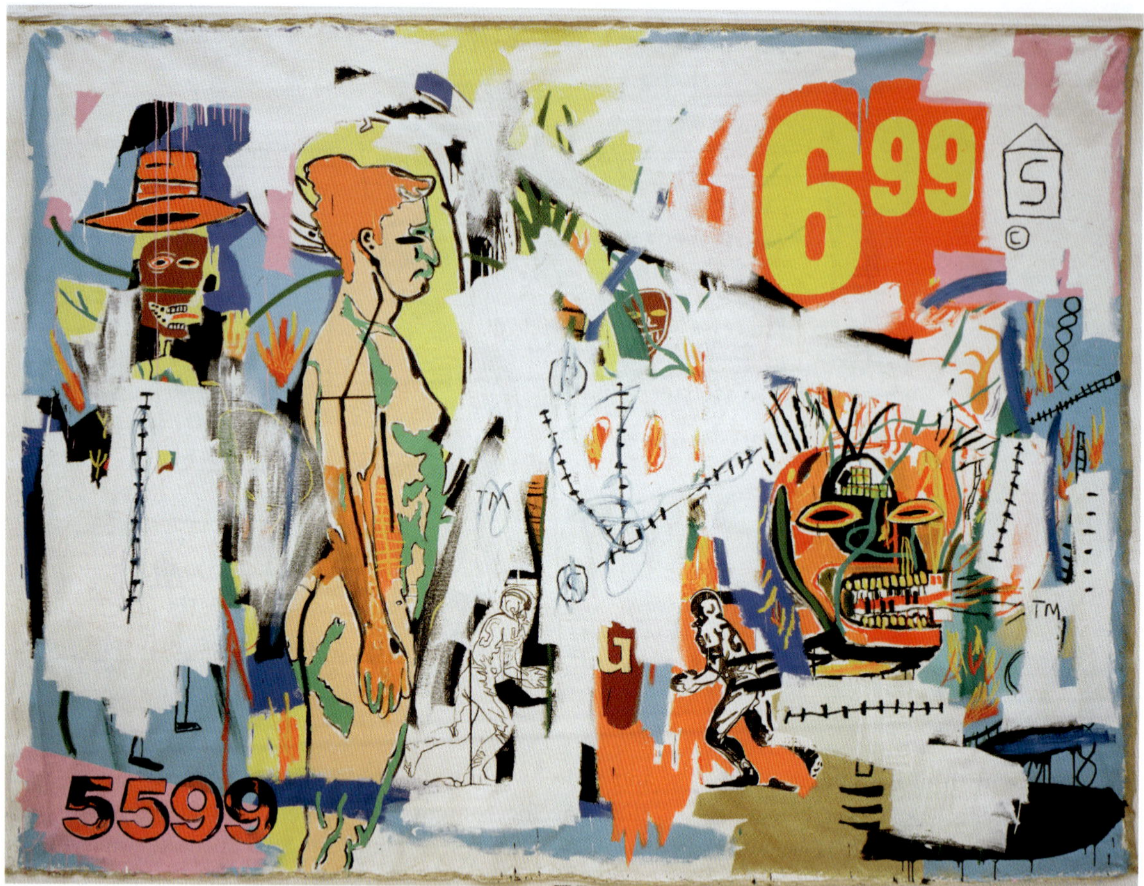

3.9 Jean-Michel Basquiat and Andy Warhol, ***Untitled***, 1985. Synthetic polymer paint on canvas, 116⅞ × 165⅜" (296.9 × 420.1 cm). Courtesy the Andy Warhol Foundation.

In an early encounter, Ricard encouraged the young artist to approach Andy Warhol with a society-page photographer and offer to trade works—graffiti for Pop, street for establishment, credibility for fame. The ploy worked and Warhol became one of Basquiat's most important supporters, even collaborating with him on a series of paintings in the mid-1980s. Such episodes show Basquiat as a master strategist, possessing skill and knowledge but also the drive to insert his art, name, and concerns into the history of American painting. Paintings such as *Grillo* and especially *Untitled* (1985) (**fig. 3.9**), one of the collaborations with Warhol, reveal that his success was far more than a question of ego. Side by side with Warhol—arguably the most influential artist since Jackson Pollock, if not Picasso—Basquiat injected themes of colonialism, African history, and identity into the history of Pop art, the canon of Western art, and nearly every major art collection.

Italy

Achille Bonito Oliva's critique of the avant-garde was part of his definition of the Transavantgarde. The Italian critic and curator drew on the work of several theorists including Jean-François Lyotard, Gilles Deleuze, and Felix Guattari (see Introduction and Chapter 1) in proposing an end to Modernism. The Modernist avant-garde adhered to the Enlightenment conception that history was progressive and that art contributed to, and was even able to direct, that progress. In this view, avant-garde art from early twentieth-century Cubism and Expressionism through to postwar Minimalism and Conceptual art fulfilled a historical function of leading society into an unknown and far better future. After the student revolts, free-speech movements, and anti-war demonstrations that exploded across the West in 1968 and their subsequent frustration in the 1970s, however, things changed. Artists of the 1970s, Oliva claimed, started to reject the identification of art with progress, and instead began a "process of de-ideologization, overcoming the euphoric idea of the creative experience as ... [the] coercion of the new."[28] No longer impelled to create new forms, artists were instead compelled to reach back into art history to realize their visions.

The Transavantgarde dedicated itself to manipulating existing styles, gleaning from past art to cultivate what Oliva termed an "ideology of the traitor."[29] Oliva contended that this tendency was based on an impulse first seen in sixteenth-century Italian Mannerism, which rejected authority, not by implementing new rules, but by making "oblique and tormented" use of the existing ones.[30] Like Giorgio Vasari (1511–74), the contemporary and admirer of Michelangelo and Italy's first art historian, Oliva located artistic greatness in "license," Vasari's term for individual creativity manifest in knowing manipulations of style. The Transavantgarde rejected idealist dreams of inventing new forms in favor of revisiting existing movements from Classical Greece to

1960s New York. Transavantgarde artists' disinterested attitude toward these diverse sources led to an art that Oliva described as "the product of a network of recoveries and renewals that shatter the proud and purist unity of a concurrent vision of art and the world."[31] The relationship between art and modern life that had been the focus of the historical avant-garde, one in which each is distinct but in dialogue with the other, was pronounced as being at an end. Art had become "intensity" without direction.[32]

The Italian Transavantgarde included a group of young painters dominated by Francesco Clemente, Enzo Cucci, Sandro Chia, and Mimmo Paladino. Like their U.S. Neo-Expressionist counterparts, they developed figurative iconography and produced almost no purely abstract work. Current events and history might appear briefly, but the emphasis was largely on illustrating personal narratives using pre-modern stylistic references and a languid sensuality. In Clemente's words, theirs was an art with "more joy and more hope and more light."[33]

Sandro Chia

Sandro Chia (b. 1946), as photographed in his studio with his paintings—"physical proof of metaphysical existence," as he called them—and motorcycle, perfectly embodied the Transavantgarde's fusion of the macho and the mystical.[33] In interviews, he seemed as eager to talk about his improving financial status as his art, which exemplified the eclectic pastiche advocated by Oliva. Chia's figurative compositions mingle Classical myths with personal references, and are painted in a lush, painterly style. *Water Bearer* (1981) (**fig. 3.10**) is typical of the Italian painters' use of iconography. It presents a male figure in profile walking slowly across the canvas with a fish that is larger than himself slung over his shoulder. The fish's bright red tail curls gently between the

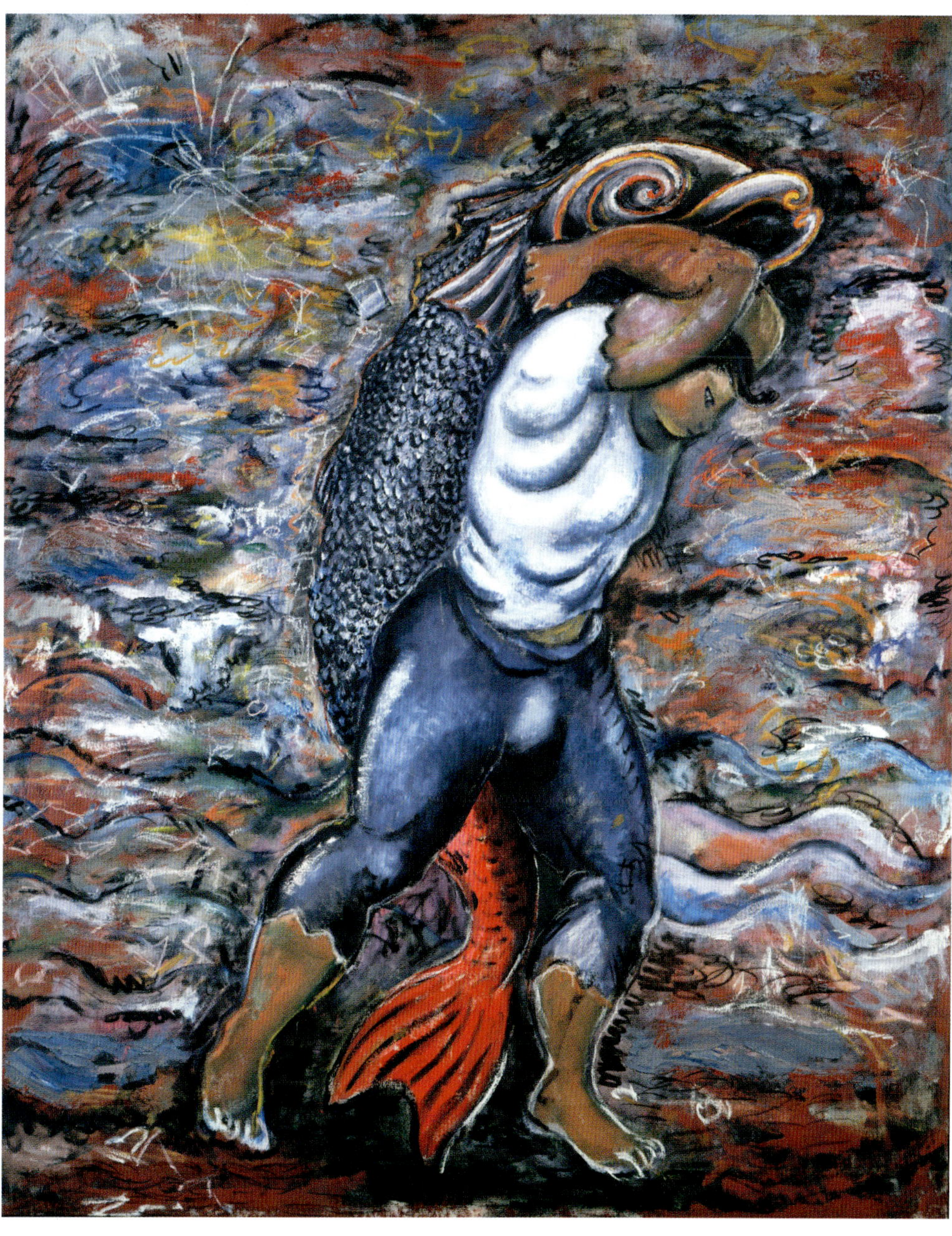

3.10 Sandro Chia, *Water Bearer*, 1981. Oil and pastel on canvas, 81½ × 67" (206.5 × 170 cm). Tate, London.

man's steady, slow-moving feet. The image confounds the reference to Classical and Renaissance sources in the title by replacing the water with the fish. This mixing of incongruous symbols that resist interpretation and of styles that resist history struck some viewers as a true expression of the contemporary artist's relationship to traditional painting and to meaning itself. "The conventions of iconography are bearable in our era so long as the artist retains his privilege of confounding them," wrote one supporter, who concluded that the meaning of Chia's work lay in "something about the ambiguity of any message."[35] Some Transavantgarde paintings and statements, however, were far from ambiguous. Describing America, for instance, Chia declared that there "man has more of a rapport with nature, and nature is the big city," where "a great struggle ... is fought by the individual" independent of ideological concerns.[36] This assertion denied the key perceptions of much art of the 1960s and 1970s that ideology pervades all parts of society, from foreign policy to personal relations. Such disregard for what had become a commonplace of cultural analysis suggested that Chia's readiness to associate his art with naïve recitations of rugged American individualism did not so much confound conventions as glorify Modernism's expansionist impulses.

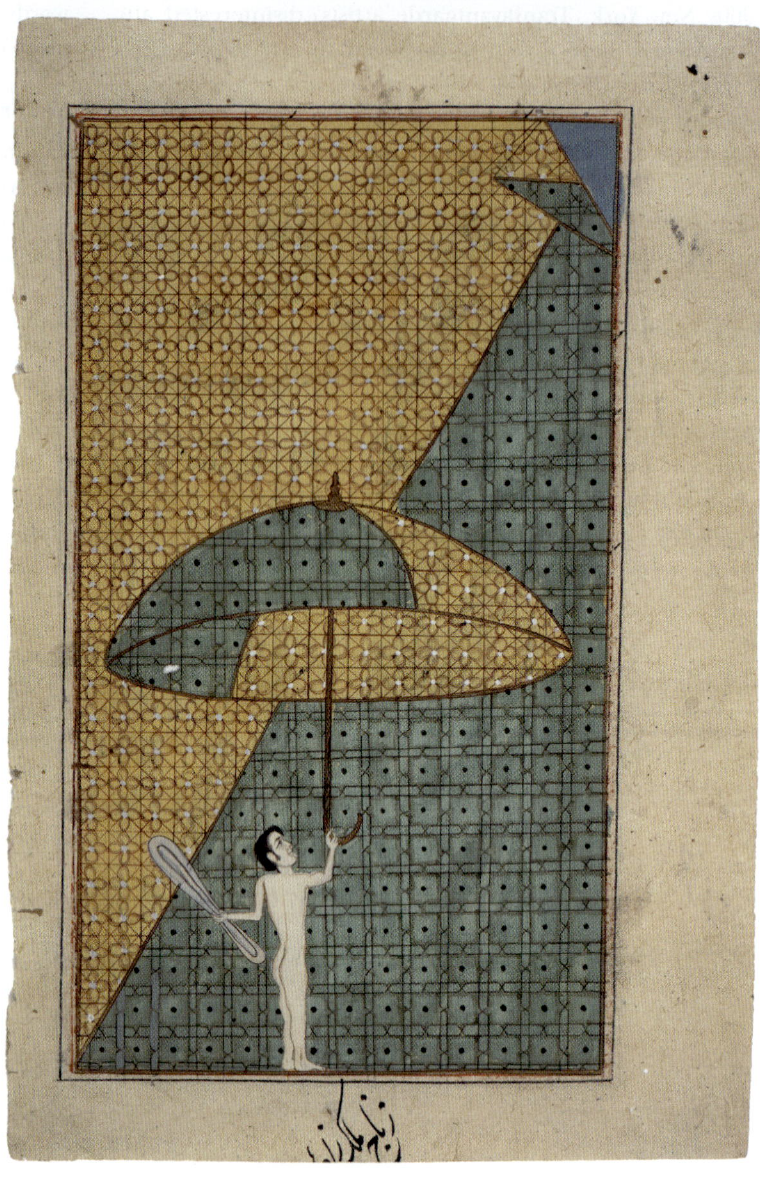

3.11 Francesco Clemente, from the ***Francesco Clemente Pinxit*** series, 1981. Gouache on paper, 8¾ × 6" (22.2 × 15.2 cm). © Francesco Clemente. Courtesy Mary Boone Gallery, New York.

Francesco Clemente

Oliva encouraged artists to strip historic styles and familiar objects of their contexts. He also suggested a radical relationship between history and geography. The Transavantgarde, he explained, drew inspiration and motifs from a wide field in terms not only of time but also of space. Francesco Clemente (b. 1952) provides a model of such a Transavantgarde traveler. Resisting the politicized discourse of art and society of the 1960s, he turned to a private examination of fine-art media including fresco, watercolors, gouache, tempera, and oil on canvas. By evoking historical periods through their associated techniques rather than their characteristic appearances, Clemente avoided confining his work to stylistic mimicry or anachronistic iconography. Though he expressed nostalgia for Italy before the radical movements of the 1960s and 1970s, his deepest affinities were for the ancient Roman and earlier eras, before the advent of the Catholic Church.[37] Moving that far back in time involved more than a revival of figurative art and ancient media. For Clemente, it also entailed travel to India, which by the late 1970s had become his second home. "The gods who left us thousands of years ago in Naples are still in India," he said, "so it's like going home for me. In India I can feel what it was like [in Italy] many years ago."[38]

Clemente turned to Indian miniature paintings as a culturally specific art form distanced from present-day Europe. The results can be seen in *Francesco Clemente Pinxit* (1980–81) (**fig. 3.11**), for which he collaborated with a workshop of Indian painters trained in the sixteenth-century Mughal miniature tradition. For the twelve gouaches that make up the work, members of the workshop executed the decorative motifs that were their individual specialties. These envelop Clemente's human narrative within the elegant fields of ornate geometries, detailed floral motifs, and abstracted landscapes of traditional Indian art. Clemente's use of local styles and techniques to expand the historical resonance of his work continued when, in 1981, he established a third studio and home, this time in New York. Like India and his birthplace, Naples, he felt that New York preserved the spirit of the pre-Christian world: "Naples is Ancient Greece. New

York is third-century, B.C. Rome."[39] Though mapping the history of the West in this way raises issues of cultural imperialism, it also exemplifies the eclectic connections that Oliva and others saw as generative forces in contemporary art.

Clemente's works, whether miniatures created in India, oil paintings in New York, or frescos in Italy, share a fascination with sensuality and the self. Bodies, often self-portraits, swim through fields of color, embracing and consuming one another in what critic and curator Robert Storr described as a "confusion of sexual preference and sexual function."[40] Arms, legs, fingers, tongues, even tails intertwine and enter bodies with a languid, dreamlike grace. *Abbraccio* (*Embrace*) (1983) (**fig. 3.12**) shows a profusion of bodies and body parts that seem to multiply and even bloom as they caress one another. Critics often responded with hyperbole, declaring Clemente a master or visionary, and celebrating his "romantic sensibility [which] can accept every facet of life" or which "restores our belief in the authenticity and power of the unconscious."[41] His intention, it was argued, was "simply the expression of raw moods with paint and canvas."[42] Such claims suggest that Clemente, like Chia, was appealing to the heroic myths of Modernism.

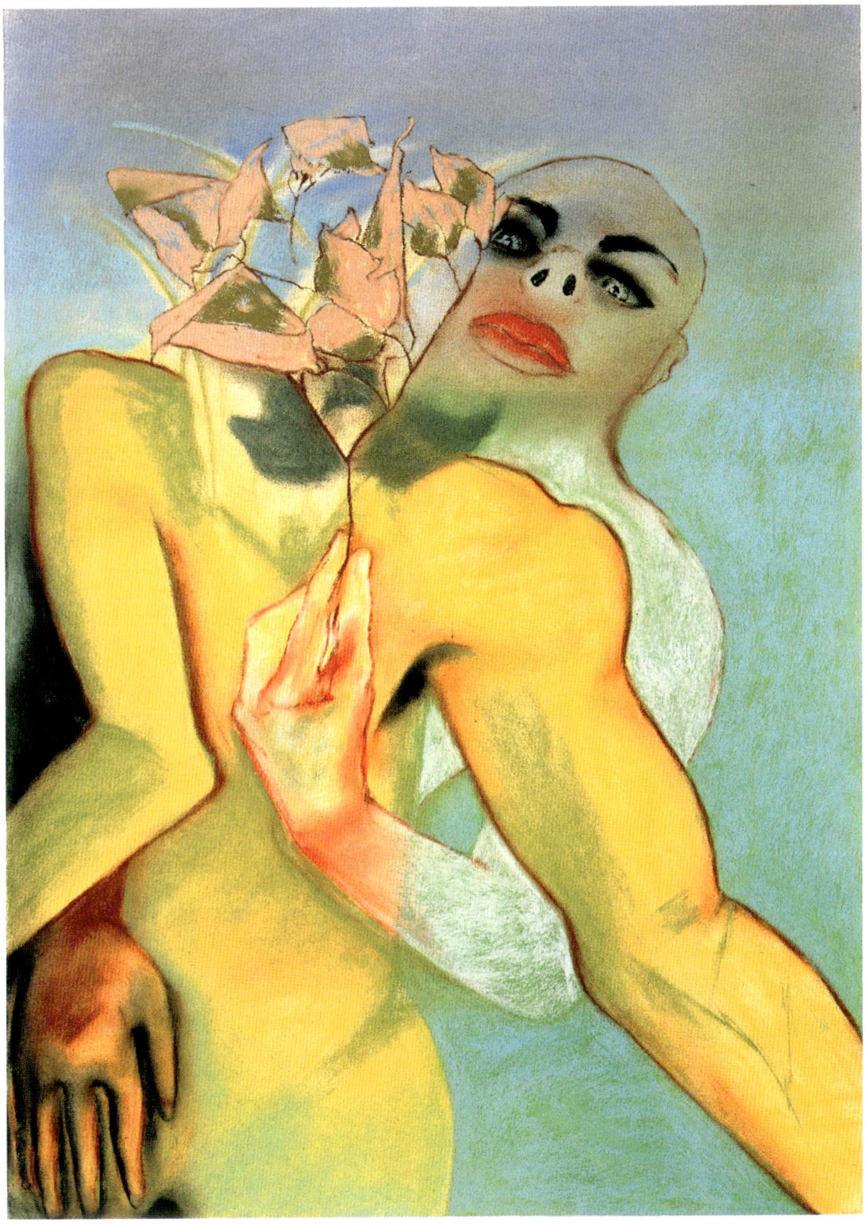

To some critics, Clemente's work was no more than the result of an aimless infatuation with sexual mystique or "empty formalism."[43] Others, however, felt that Clemente had transcended decadence to traffic in the abject, a philosophical category being discussed in light of French feminist thinker Julia Kristeva's *Powers of Horror*, written in 1980 and translated into English in 1982. Kristeva described the abject as those things such as cadavers, waste, and disease that elicit revulsion at their apparent rejection of the forces of life and coherency in favor of processes of chaos, degradation, and death. The abject repulses us, and yet, Kristeva argues, it is also compelling for the promise it offers to enlighten us about the realms beyond the limits of our experience and understanding. Within abjection lie "dark revolts of being" that reveal the human impulse to challenge life as it is and to reach through its pain to different, possibly better, ways of living.[44] It was, perhaps, toward such a place that Clemente's work was striving, but it was not at all clear. Edit DeAk, with something of the stylistic floridness of René Ricard, celebrated Clemente's facility for transforming images "from one internal venue to another, each ruminating with its own enzyme of fermentation."[45] From Robert Storr's perspective, Clemente's work could be imagined as an extended metaphor for processes of decay, fertilization, and regeneration, particularly as they intersect with human intimacy. The resulting imagery is often quite beautiful, but poses a challenge because, according to Storr, Clemente has "no tangible social vision," thus making it difficult to determine where the work, or the artist, stands in relation to such loaded content.[46] As was the case in the work of the U.S. Neo-Expressionists, particularly David Salle, Clemente presented potent imagery but appeared ambivalent toward its potential meanings.

How viewers interpreted Clemente's work depended on their sense of history. Those who agreed with Oliva's Transavantgarde vision of an end of history saw Clemente's images of polymorphous sexuality as a celebration of sensual

3.12 Francesco Clemente, *Abbraccio (Embrace)*, 1983. Pastel on paper, 26 × 19" (66 × 48.2 cm). © Francesco Clemente. Courtesy Mary Boone Gallery, New York.

experience. Those for whom the work represented the conservative trend in contemporary politics and culture were troubled by its ethical indifference, which they saw as characteristic of Neo-Expressionism in general. Others again saw in Clemente and Neo-Expressionism a parallel to the "return to order" spirit of European art immediately after World War I, in which avant-garde artists from French Cubists to Italian Futurists had briefly reverted to Classical representational styles of the kind later favored by 1930s fascist governments. Art historian Benjamin H.D. Buchloh forcefully articulated the argument that Neo-Expressionists opposed the revolutionary impulses of the avant-gardes they revived in a widely circulated essay, "Figures of Authority, Ciphers of Regression." Buchloh, as editor of the German art journal *Interfunktionen* in the 1970s, had challenged readers to re-evaluate the legacy of fascism in Germany and was sharply critical of what he saw as the conservative and cynical use of history in Neo-Expressionist painting. His distrust of both the painters and their advocates lent particular passion to his unfavorable comparisons between the 1980s and the 1930s.[47] Once again, social context was central to the interpretation of these tendencies.

Germany

In 1980, the American gallerists who had just begun promoting Schnabel and Salle as the new American painters discovered the Neo-Expressionism that had been germinating in Europe throughout the previous decade. Calvin Tompkins, the art writer for *The New Yorker* who had chronicled the career of Robert Rauschenberg and his generation of U.S. artists, saw work by Georg Baselitz and Anselm Kiefer in the German Pavilion at the 39th Venice Biennale and announced that the artworld dominance of New York was over.[48] Both German artists had been working since the 1960s, and their output bore clear signs of historical consciousness and, to U.S. viewers at least, gravity. German critics were less enamored, however, reflecting a growing desire within German academia and politics to create a national identity that was independent from the country's recent history of fascism. By mid-decade, this would take the form of a public call for the "normalization" of German life and history, a process that would attempt to draw a line between the Nazi past and the "normal" present.[49] By this stage, German Neo-Expressionism had been integrated into the narrative of normalization either as a Postmodern rejection of history or as a means of resuming pre-fascist art traditions that the Nazis had silenced as degenerate.[50] At the time of the 1980 Venice Biennale, however, these arguments were not yet in place. Most German writers then saw Baselitz's and Kiefer's work not as a reckoning with history but as symptoms of an obsession with the past and perhaps an attempt to relive it. Critics labeled the show fascist, imperialist, and embarrassing. Baselitz's contribution was particularly abrasive. His *Model for a Sculpture* (1980) (**fig. 3.13**) is a massive male figure with legs painted onto the lower section of a block of linden wood and a torso roughly carved out of the top part. The figure sat in the center of the pavilion and, bent at the hips as if rising from sleep, greeted visitors with a Nazi salute. Baselitz's aggressive style was branded neo-fascist, while Kiefer's mammoth prints and paintings of landscapes and various German historical figures were described as "being in dangerous proximity to glorifying German megalomania."[51]

Though it would take most of the 1980s for German critics to become at least ambivalent about, rather than overtly hostile to, Baselitz's and Kiefer's projects, Americans began collecting early. In addition to Baselitz and Kiefer, their countrymen A.R. Penck, Rainer Fetting, Helmut Middendorf, and Markus Lüpertz, would all be represented by New York commercial galleries by the next biennale. Many Americans saw their often awkward, visceral brushwork, violent landscapes, and luminous street scenes as honest confrontations with history. Art historian and critic Donald Kuspit, the most vocal and consistent U.S. advocate of the German painters, claimed that they "lay to rest the ghosts ... of German style, culture, and history so that the people can be authentically new."[52] Peter Schjeldahl saw a "reawaken[ing of] the glamour of European pastness," recast in the manner of Jackson

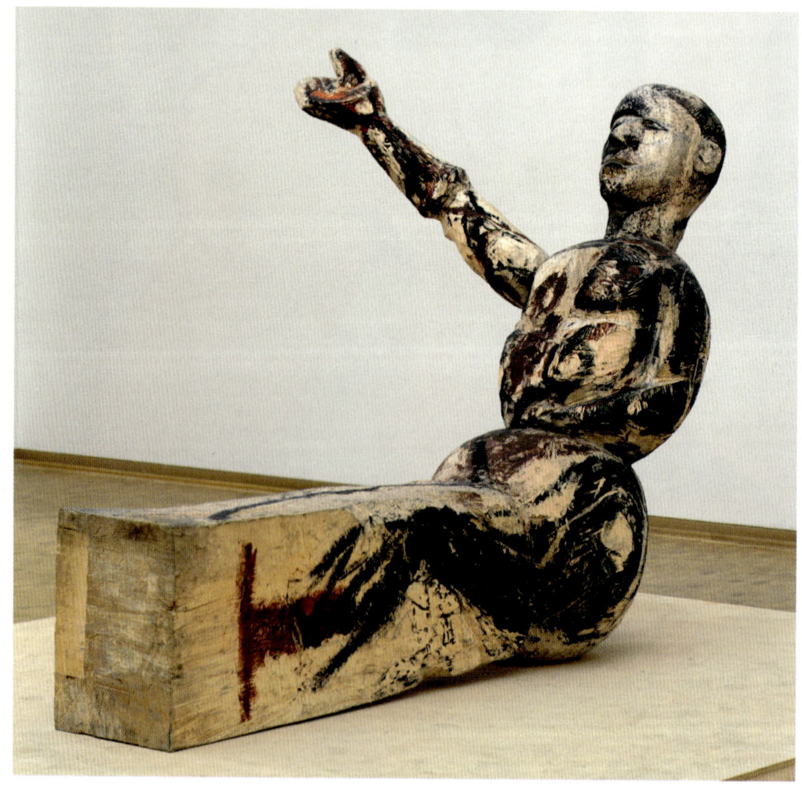

3.13 Georg Baselitz, *Model for a Sculpture*, 1980. Lime wood and tempera, 70 × 57⅞ × 96" (178 × 147 × 244 cm). Museum Ludwig, Cologne. © 2012 Georg Baselitz.

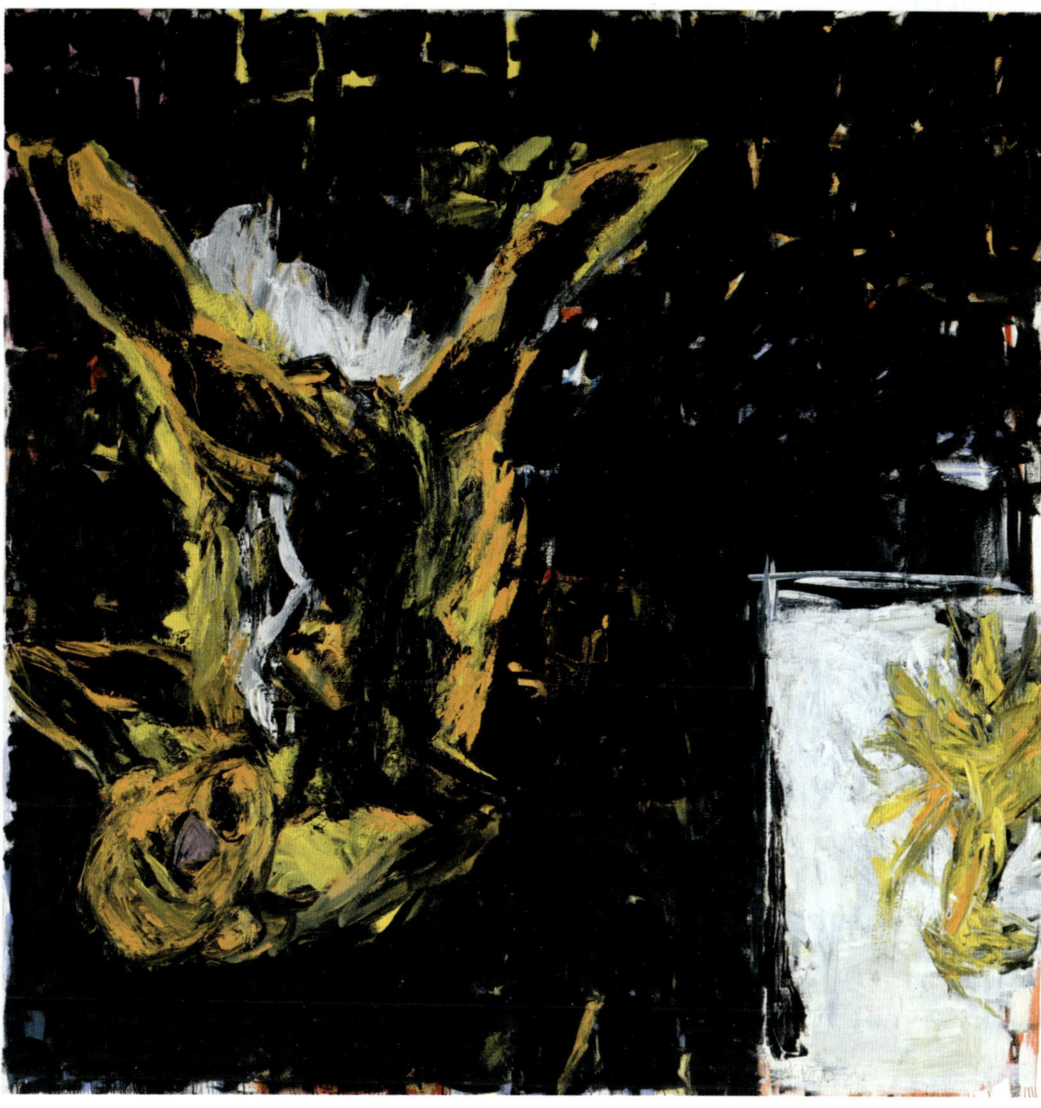

3.14 Georg Baselitz, ***Eagle in the Window***, 1982. Oil on canvas, 98⅜ × 98⅜" (250 × 250 cm). The Metropolitan Museum of Art, New York. Gift of The Jerry and Emily Spiegel Family Foundation, 2007. © 2012 Georg Baselitz.

Pollock.[53] With the groundwork laid in the New York galleries and museums in London and Berlin, it was as if European culture—blackened by World War II and dismissed as the art world shifted its capital to the U.S.—had suddenly been restored to view. The ghosts and glamour that seemed apparent to these U.S. eyes were less visible to many other critics. Moreover, despite being presented as a group, German Neo-Expressionists were hardly a uniform or united group. These artists held diverse opinions on issues of self, history, and style. Kiefer's work in particular interrogated the psychic weight of fascism and questioned the possibility or even desirability of becoming "authentically new."

The roots of Neo-Expressionism in Germany go back to the early 1960s. In the decades after World War II, a number of artists in both West Germany, which was politically part of democratic capitalist Europe, and East Germany, which lay within the Soviet bloc, attempted to resist the influence of both American Abstract Expressionism and Soviet Socialist Realism by re-examining expressionist traditions. East German-trained but West German-based artist Gerhard Richter (b. 1932) was painting from photographs, giving them a uniformly blurred appearance to make explicit the mediated relationship between image, style, and content. His contribution to "Zeitgeist," *Annunciation after Titian* (1973) (see fig. 3.2), was just such a work. East German born Georg Baselitz (b. 1938) meanwhile fused the abstract styles of the capitalist West with the Socialist Realism of the communist East in his expressionistic figure painting. In the 1960s, Baselitz was painting monumental images of the distorted bodies of German soldiers who had survived World War II and the damaged land to which they had returned. By the early 1970s, however, he was rendering the potency of his imagery, with its deformations and anxiety-ridden narratives, absurd by painting his subjects upside down. *Eagle in the Window* (1982) (**fig. 3.14**), with its screaming human figure, ambiguous interior, and aggressive paint handling, appears to locate expressionist terror and painterly catharsis in an environment overseen by the authority of the German state (symbolized by the eagle). When upended, however, the image becomes striking less for its narrative content than for its vigorous and bold color—exactly the effect Baselitz desired. The artist's position regarding the possible content of the work, and modern German history more broadly, is made highly ambiguous.

Anselm Kiefer

In the early 1980s, much thinking about art making after World War II was colored by the philosopher Theodor Adorno's statement that "to write poetry after Auschwitz is barbaric."[54] Anselm Kiefer's (b. 1945) work drew attention to this crisis, first by the simple fact of its existence but also because it took pains to remind viewers of the potential barbarism of postwar culture. His works in the German Pavilion at Venice in 1980 came from a series of massive compositions based on the empty interior of his studio and a forest clearing evoking the Teutoburg Forest, traditionally believed to be the birthplace of the German nation. These spaces are simple and cavernous—open rooms with torches illuminating exposed beams and boards, or shadowy wooded groves. Dwarfed by the great interiors are icons suggesting self and nation: An empty crib sits in one space, the sword of the legendary hero Parsifal in another. In works such as the interior *Germany's Spiritual Heroes* (1973) and the landscape *The Ways of Worldly Wisdom: Battle of the Teutoburg Forest* (1978) (**fig. 3.15**), Kiefer indicated the actors meant to occupy these spaces: Handwritten names line the great hall and faces fill the woods. The lineage these names establish, however, is contaminated by association with the Third Reich. In addition to national heroes such as philosophers Friedrich Schleiemacher and Johann Fichte, the list includes individuals whose only contribution to German history was as members of the Nazi party. The pavilion in Venice, designed as an expression of national pride, thus housed a genealogy of German consciousness, both worldly and spiritual, that ran directly through the crimes of recent history. Though a few critics were intrigued by the absences in Kiefer's compositions and the alluring material qualities of his paint use, most German commentators saw only provocation and embarrassment in its overt content.

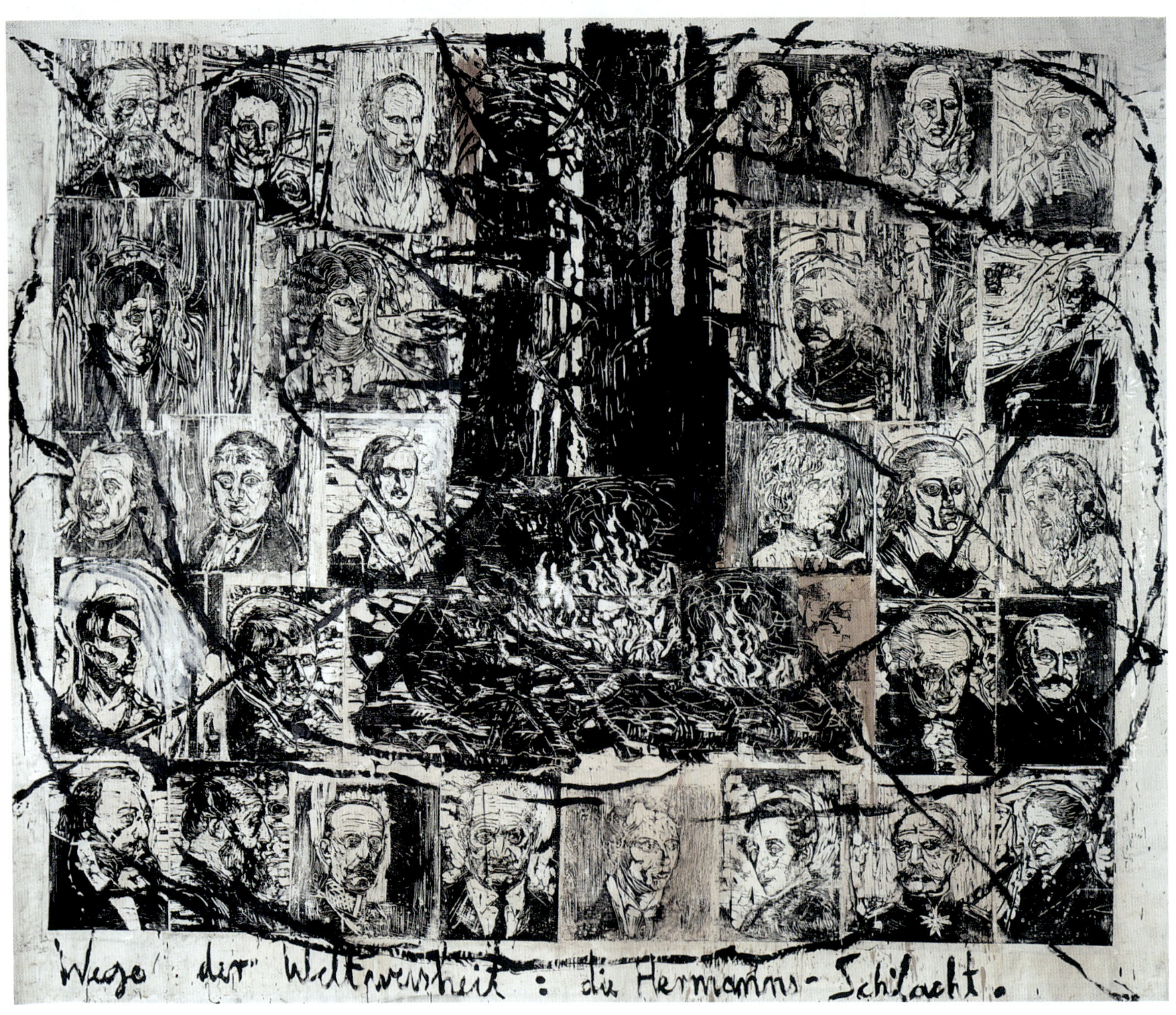

3.15 Anselm Kiefer, *Wege der Weltweisheit: die Hermannsschlacht (The Ways of Worldly Wisdom: Battle of the Teutoburg Forest)*, 1978. Acrylic resin and shellac on woodcutting on paper, 133⅞ × 161⅜" (340 × 410 cm). Courtesy White Cube.

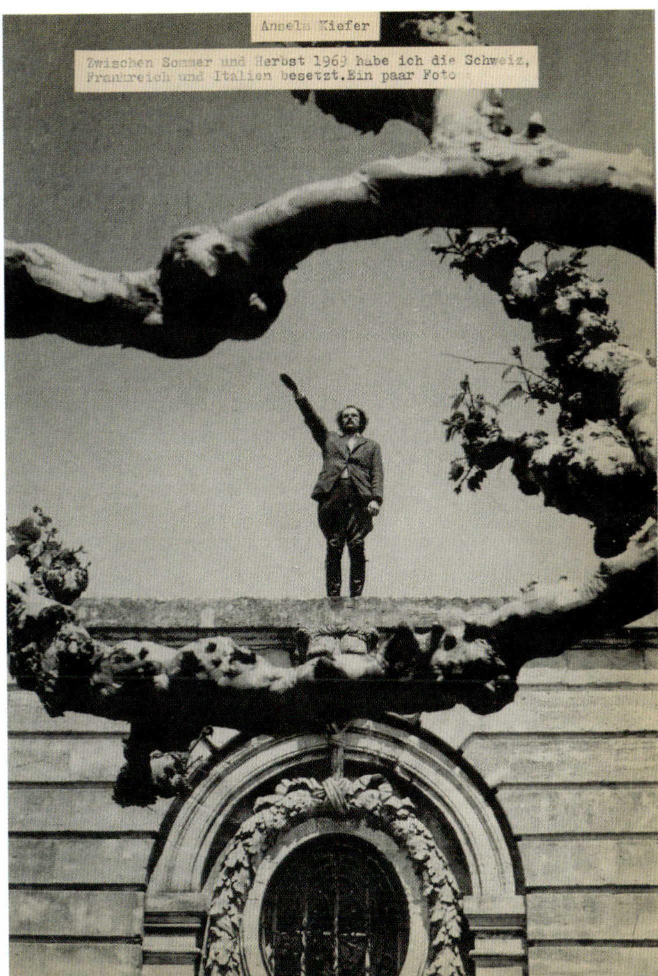

3.16 Anselm Kiefer, *Besetzungen (Occupations)*, 1969. Published in *Interfunktionen* #12, Köln, 1975. Collage. Black-and-white photograph. Courtesy White Cube.

This was not the first time Kiefer had angered German critics by pointedly integrating recent history and current national identity. In 1975, he had published *Occupations* (**fig. 3.16**), a series of photographs taken six years earlier in Switzerland, France, and Italy. The images resemble tourist photos, with Kiefer posing in front of iconic locations such as a coastline or the Roman Colosseum. Instead of smiling for the camera, however, Kiefer gives a Nazi salute. Though defended as farcical representations of Nazi imperial aspirations, the images in *Occupations* also seemed to demonstrate a deep ambivalence toward the fascist past and the contemporary self, and resulted in a boycott of the journal that published them.[55] Was Kiefer mocking Nazi ambition by assigning this lone, rather unthreatening, middle-aged man the task of securing the Reich? Was he accusing Germans of his generation of still harboring sympathies for the Nazi legacy? As a German born in 1945, Kiefer's life started in the aftermath of World War II; as an artist, in light of Adorno's assessment, he was incapable of anything but barbarism. *Occupations* examines this predicament. Kiefer explained it as a record of his belief that to understand history one must take part in it, even if that history is brutal and one's means of participating in it are secondhand. Like much of Kiefer's work of the 1970s and early 1980s, the series was created "to evoke the question from myself, Am I a fascist?"[56] As art historian Lisa Saltzman has commented, the German title for the series is *Besetzungen*, a psychoanalytical term referring to the psychic investment one makes in objects, particularly in relation to loss or mourning. Viewed as examinations of psychological rather than military "occupations," Kiefer's images become a meditation on the role of power, specifically fascist power, in the German psyche. Of the impulse to reject the fascist past, Kiefer said: "You cannot answer so quickly. Authority, competition, superiority ... these are facets of me like everyone else."[57] History and biography were to be intimately joined throughout Kiefer's career.

By the time his work reached the U.S., Kiefer had turned his attention to the seductive power of Nazi architecture in vast canvases showing emptied Nazi monuments and halls. These demonstrated his impressive handling of illusionistic spaces and painterly surfaces, which placed him, according to some, in the same league as Picasso and Pollock. Andreas Huyssen, a historian of the postwar transitions in European and U.S. culture, argued that such formal accomplishments increased the moral dilemma represented by Kiefer's work, which gave the viewer limited options for interpreting these historically significant and terrible places. The choice these paintings gave, Huyssen argued, was between "melancholy fixations on the dreamlike ruins of fascism" and the seductive aesthetic experiences that ensnare the viewer in a trap of fascination and horror—a parallel to the way Kiefer's elders had been seduced by the promise of a German empire.[58] Unlike the engagement of *Occupations*, these works seemed to convey a nostalgia and estrangement that protected the artist and viewer from history's moral dilemmas. Kiefer's viewer is trapped, nodding impotently at the awesome power of the spaces represented and the painterly means used to represent them; his or her moral being is pushed aside. To resolve this crisis, the viewer must theoretically be aesthetically sensitive enough to respond to the painterly allure of the image, while remaining morally vigilant enough to resist it. In practice, such conflicting reactions are nearly impossible to maintain as analysis spoils the seduction and emotion undermines judgment.

Kiefer's legacy, the artist asserted, will rest on "the way I handle the tension of German and Jew."[59] His engagement with Jewish/gentile tensions, as distinct from German identity, began in earnest after the 1980 Venice Biennale. In a series of the early 1980s, Kiefer began to occupy the empty pictorial spaces that had caused Huyssen to feel such ambivalence with evocations of the lost actors of the Holocaust, both German and Jewish. Engaging the relationship between Jews and Germans came to be intimately related in Kiefer's thinking to questions of reunifying East and West Germany. There could be no real reunification, he argued, because the destruction of the Jewish communities had irrevocably changed Germany. The country might become one nation again but it could no more reunify as the culture it had previously been than it could "normalize." Handling the tension in art as in politics meant crafting an identity for postwar Germany that included self-conscious references to the Holocaust and to the necessarily incomplete nature of contemporary German identity. For Kiefer, the pursuit of such a historically aware vision led him on a path through German history to biblical and mystical themes toward what he described in the later 1990s as a "global" or even "geological" history, evoked in monumental paintings heavy with earth, burnt wood, trees, tar and lead as well as paint.[60]

Despite his proclamation of the death of art, Theodor Adorno discovered in the poetry of Paul Celan (1920–70), a Jewish Romanian writer, an art that survived and he theorized the means for its continuation. In Adorno's view, Celan had created a way to "express unspeakable horror by being silent."[61] He refused to use art to replicate the experiences that inspired it: Such a mimesis of experience was suitable for love poems, not for the moral abyss of the Holocaust. In the early 1980s, Kiefer turned to Celan's poem "Death Fugue" to create works that led beyond the anxiety of his images of vast empty halls and landscapes in which Huyssen saw the perpetuation of melancholy. The poem contrasts two absent figures: Margarete, the lover of a German concentration-camp guard; and Shulamite, a Jewish woman incinerated in the crematorium. Their names are repeated throughout the poem and Kiefer uses them in his titles to refer the viewer back to Celan. The bodily presence of each woman is evoked in the poem by reference to her hair: golden for the living, ashen for the dead.

Kiefer followed Celan's lead, avoiding figurative representation in favor of allusions and synecdoche (using a part of something to express the whole). To the monumental landscape of a barren field, for example, he applied straw, cut from the fields and pasted onto the canvas in gentle contours evoking the absent lover's body. The dried yellow grasses evoke the blonde German gentile who, due to an accident of birth, survived the war far from the brutality of the camps. Margarete is a symbol of the German nation, estranged from

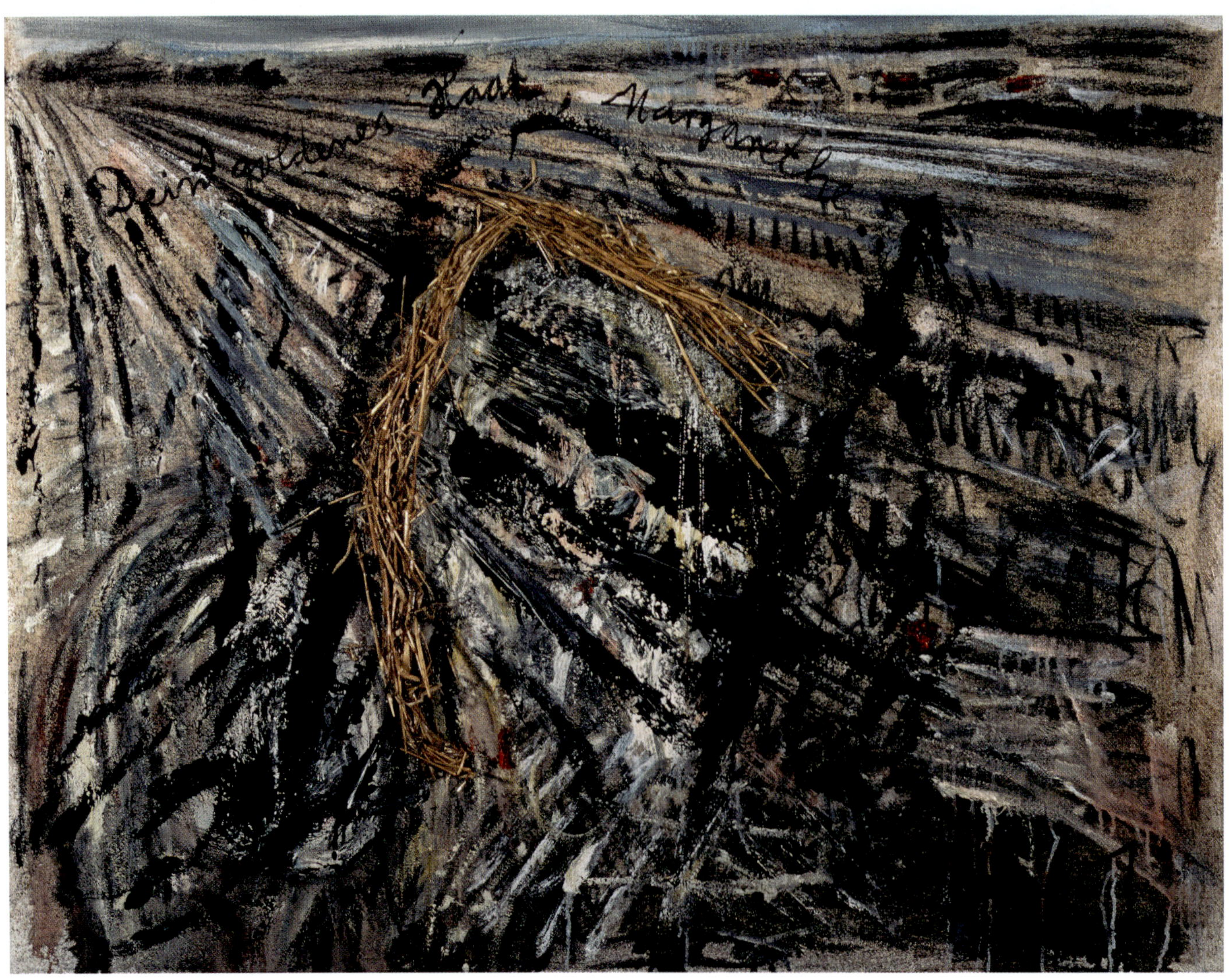

3.17 Anselm Kiefer, ***Dein goldenes Haar, Margarete (Your Golden Hair, Margarete)***, 1981. Oil, acrylic, emulsion, charcoal, and straw on burlap, 51 3/16 × 67" (130 × 170 cm). Courtesy White Cube.

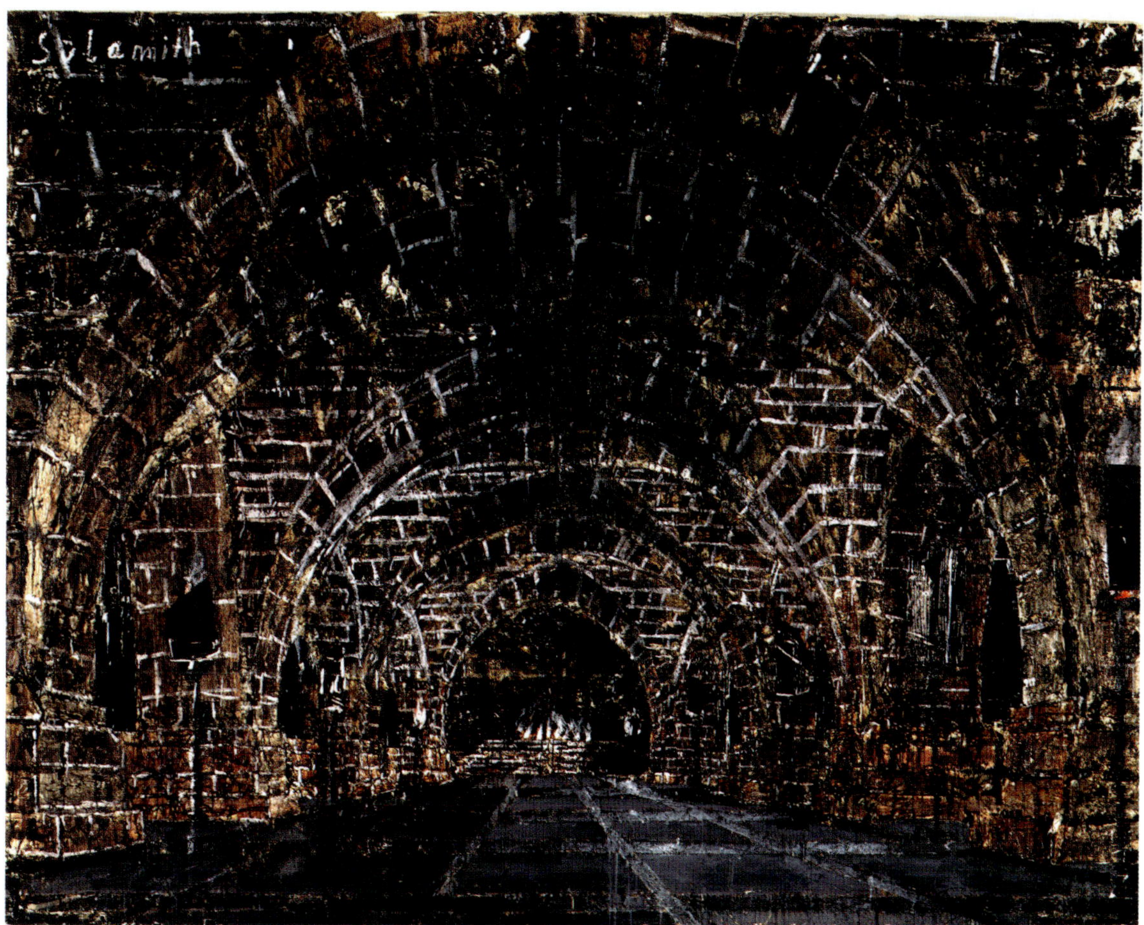

3.18 Anselm Kiefer, ***Sulamith (Shulamite)***, 1983. Oil, emulsion, woodcut, shellac, acrylic, and straw on canvas. 114⅛ × 145⅝" (290 × 370 cm). Courtesy White Cube.

its deeper identity and history due to the unfathomable immediacy of Nazi cruelty. Her Jewish counterpart, Shulamite, appeared first as a haunting echo of Margarete in Kiefer's 1981 *Your Golden Hair, Margarete* (**fig. 3.17**). Echoing the straw are black arcs of paint, suggesting a dark-haired, living Shulamite.[62] In *Your Golden Hair, Margarete—Midsummer Night* (1981), the field is now blackened by night and the golden hair is shadowed by silver lines evoking the ashes of the dead woman's burnt hair. German identity, represented in these images by fragile isolated stalks in a devastated field, is haunted by the companion it has destroyed. Still eschewing figuration, Kiefer placed his audience on a stage where they had to struggle with morality, as in his earlier work, but this time in the company of those who had had to face history as it occurred.

Kiefer further explored the allure and cost of fascism in *Shulamite* (1983) (**fig. 3.18**), where he addressed the absent Jewish woman directly. The setting of the painting is the Funeral Hall for the Great German Soldiers in the Hall of Soldiers in Berlin, built for the Nazis by Wilhelm Kreis (1873–1955). The space is depicted as a cavern made of methodically laid stones, with great arches spanning the hall and a niche at its end, into which Kiefer painted seven flames that appear to burn from a seven-branched candelabrum, representing the Menorah that stood in the Temple in Jerusalem. (Modern Jewish tradition has added two more candles to the Menorah.) All six windows are shrouded with pieces of paper darkly printed to look like wood. Five of six torches are similarly covered. The remaining torch burns at the far end of the room, accompanying the candles and transforming a space that had been built to honor the Nazi dead into a memorial for the murdered Jews. *Shulamite* indicts Germany for its history of fascism and anti-Semitism. The spectator is not sure how to respond, swept into the vast illusionistic space and enthralled by Kiefer's typically inviting surfaces. In *Shulamite*, an awareness of the absent lovers and their experiences forces the viewer to consider the lives of individuals as well as the course of history. Kiefer's work of the 1980s and since suggests paths through spiritual, psychic, and historical traditions that draw on the Hebrew Bible and the mysticism of various religions and cultures, proposing that the way to a post-Holocaust sense of self passes through many cultures.

Heftige Malerei ("Violent Painting")

According to many German as well as non-German critics, Kiefer's empty, stagelike spaces allowed both artist and viewer to enact a form of postwar mourning. Other German Neo-Expressionists, however, followed Baselitz's lead and painted actors on their dramatic canvases. The work of a group of Berlin painters illustrates this representational approach. Shown first under the label *Heftige Malerei* ("Violent Painting"), it includes such works as Helmut

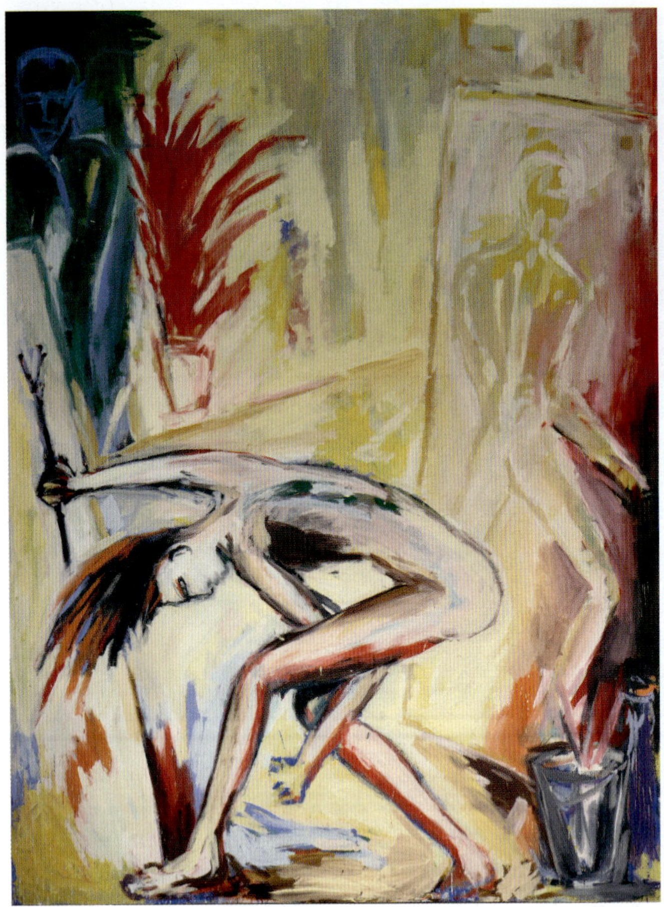

3.19 Helmut Middendorf, ***While Painting***, 1982. Acrylic on canvas, 13' 1" × 9' 10" (4 × 3 m). Private collection. Courtesy of the artist.

Middendorf's (b. 1953) *While Painting* (1982) (**fig. 3.19**). The *Heftige Malerei* were described as countering the "political-ideological" trends of Conceptual traditions with a "self-thematization of personal existence."[63] Although critics noted that defining painting in this way as the materialization of Romantic introspection was itself ideological, there was an undeniable interest in oil on canvas and the artists' experience of daily life.[64]

The Berlin group which included Rainer Fetting, Helmut Middendorf, and Berndt Zimmer (b. 1948) drew on the legacy of Baselitz, who had strong ties with the city, and the rhetoric of Markus Lüpertz (b. 1941). Lüpertz's series of *German Motifs*, begun in the 1970s, included monumental images such as *Black-Red-Gold I—dithyrambic* (1974) (**fig. 3.20**), which confront the viewer with Nazi relics and military machinery. In his work and statements, Lüpertz consistently enlisted the Dionysian rhetoric of the philosopher Friedrich Nietzsche, together with nationalistic claims for German painting, which he characterized as "violent," "genius," and "apolitical." As his imagery moved between agglomerations of weapons and Nazi paraphernalia in his *German Motifs* to other works representing imperfect, rather contemporary-looking figures in Classical poses, his insistence on political disinterest was tested.[65]

Compared to Lüpertz, the content of the *Heftige Malerei* painters was rooted in enthusiasm for Dionysian excess. They produced narrative and genre scenes that recalled the Expressionism of the Die Brücke artist Ernst Ludwig Kirchner and included visions of nightlife, artists' studios, landscapes, and fantasies of physical catharsis and destruction: Middendorf's *While Painting* shows the artist crouching before his easel like a lead singer holding a microphone and equates acting out with making art. Though clearly committed to an explosive public display of the lives of young artists, the group avoided political statements in favor of more personal admissions such as Rainer Fetting's (b. 1949) that "deep down we are all would-be rock stars."[66] *Heftige Malerei* painting left one unsure of the artists' intention in employing the painterly heroics of modern Expressionism to evoke nightlife and fantasy. Looking at Neo-Expressionism alongside the Expressionism of Die Brücke, art historian Rosalyn Deutsche argued that the later version lacked the specificity that had made Kirchner's paintings of modern urban life, for instance, so searching.[67] By comparison, *While Painting* seemed like adolescent play.

Others found such painterly theatrics liberating precisely because of their difference from the work of the original

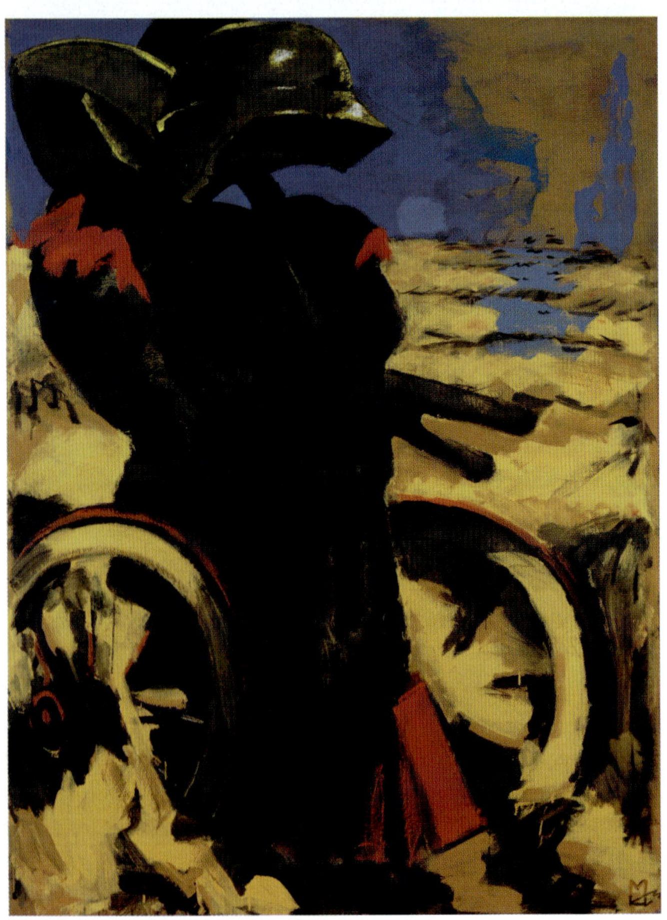

3.20 Markus Lüpertz, ***Schwarz-Rot-Gold I—dithyrambisch (Black-Red-Gold I—dithyrambic)***, 1974. Distemper on canvas, 102¼ × 78¾" (260 × 200 cm). Courtesy Galerie Michael Werner Märkisch Wilmersdorf, Cologne & New York.

German Expressionists. Donald Kuspit claimed that the "buried alive situation" of a walled and surrounded West Berlin led to the flowering of a "mannerist sense of fluidity—a loose artificial freedom" in the *Heftige Malerei* artists.[68] Neo-Expressionism in the 1980s was thus sincere in the degree that it differed from the sincerity of the 1910s. The paintings approached contemporary German life with the rawness of a punk band. Each painter used limited basic variations of fluid paint, bold colors, quick strokes, and simple figurative groupings. The paintings stuck to a format that encouraged clarity and power. Simple compositions, whether in Neo-Expressionist art or punk music, could carry challenging content. After all, it was punk icons the Ramones who sang about President Ronald Reagan's 1985 trip to the German military cemetery at Bitburg, which included graves of SS troops.[69] In the similarly rhythmic, pounding compositions of the Neo-Expressionist painters, Berlin audiences could recognize specific settings such as nightclubs the New York Anvil and SO36, and with them the alternative identities that such locations fostered. The art of the *Heftige Malerei* was problematic not, as in Kiefer's art, because of its evocative and political ambiguity, but because of the way it combined Modernist styles with contemporary content, emotive outbursts with references to popular and youth culture.

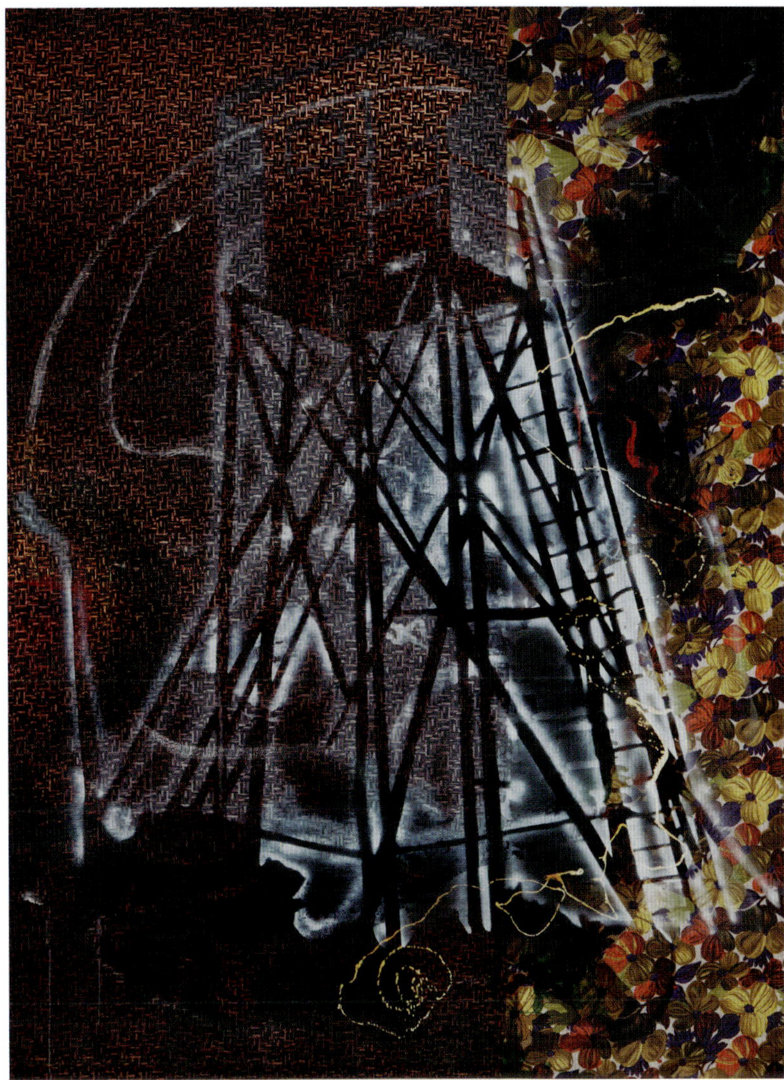

3.21 Sigmar Polke, *Hochsitz (Watchtower)*, 1984. Synthetic polymer paints and dry pigment on fabric, 9' 10" × 7' 4½" (300 × 224.8 cm). The Museum of Modern Art, New York.

Jörg Immendorff and A.R. Penck

Kiefer's shifting position contrasts not only with the "apolitical" violence of Lüpertz and the rock-star excitement of *Heftige Malerei*, but also with other German Neo-Expressionist painters such as Gerhard Richter and Sigmar Polke (1941–2010), whose work in the 1960s challenged the hegemony of American Pop art by adopting its mass-media source material to address the German political situation. In the 1970s and 1980s, both artists expanded their projects. Richter pursued his dialogue with photography, while Polke continue to challenge Modernist claims to universalism and formalist purity by exploring scores of different styles from appropriation to Abstract Expressionism in media ranging from bedlinen to meteorites. Paintings such as *Watchtower* (1984) (**fig. 3.21**) showed a stylistic inconsistency that undermined both the Modernist faith in artists' "signature styles" and the Neo-Expressionist desire to enlist them for new purposes. In addition, in this work and others, Polke developed his critique of style while raising the specter of the fascist past. Meanwhile, Jörg Immendorff (1945–2007) took a different path toward historical reckoning and political action, dispensing with the self-consciousness of Richter and Polke's dialogue with Modernism and avoiding Kiefer's monumentalism. By the 1980s, he was using a distinctive style based on theatrical artifice to address the politics of reunification, the movement to end the division of postwar Germany into communist German Democratic Republic (East Germany) and the capitalist Federal Republic of Germany (West Germany). His training with Joseph Beuys (see Chapter 1) contributed to his sense of the need for active political involvement (at one point he even briefly set aside his studio practice to run for a position on Düsseldorf city council). More important in the development of his aesthetic solutions, however, was his training with stage designer Teo Otto (1904–68). In 1977, he began his breakthrough series *Café Deutschland*. These works, which combine expressive representation, portraiture (often of the artist himself), and symbolism, exemplify Immendorff's particular brand of Neo-Expressionism.

In the foreground of his 1978 canvas *Café Deutschland I* (**fig. 3.22**), Immendorff painted himself extending his hand in friendship through a section of masonry wall toward a figure identifiable from his painted reflection as the

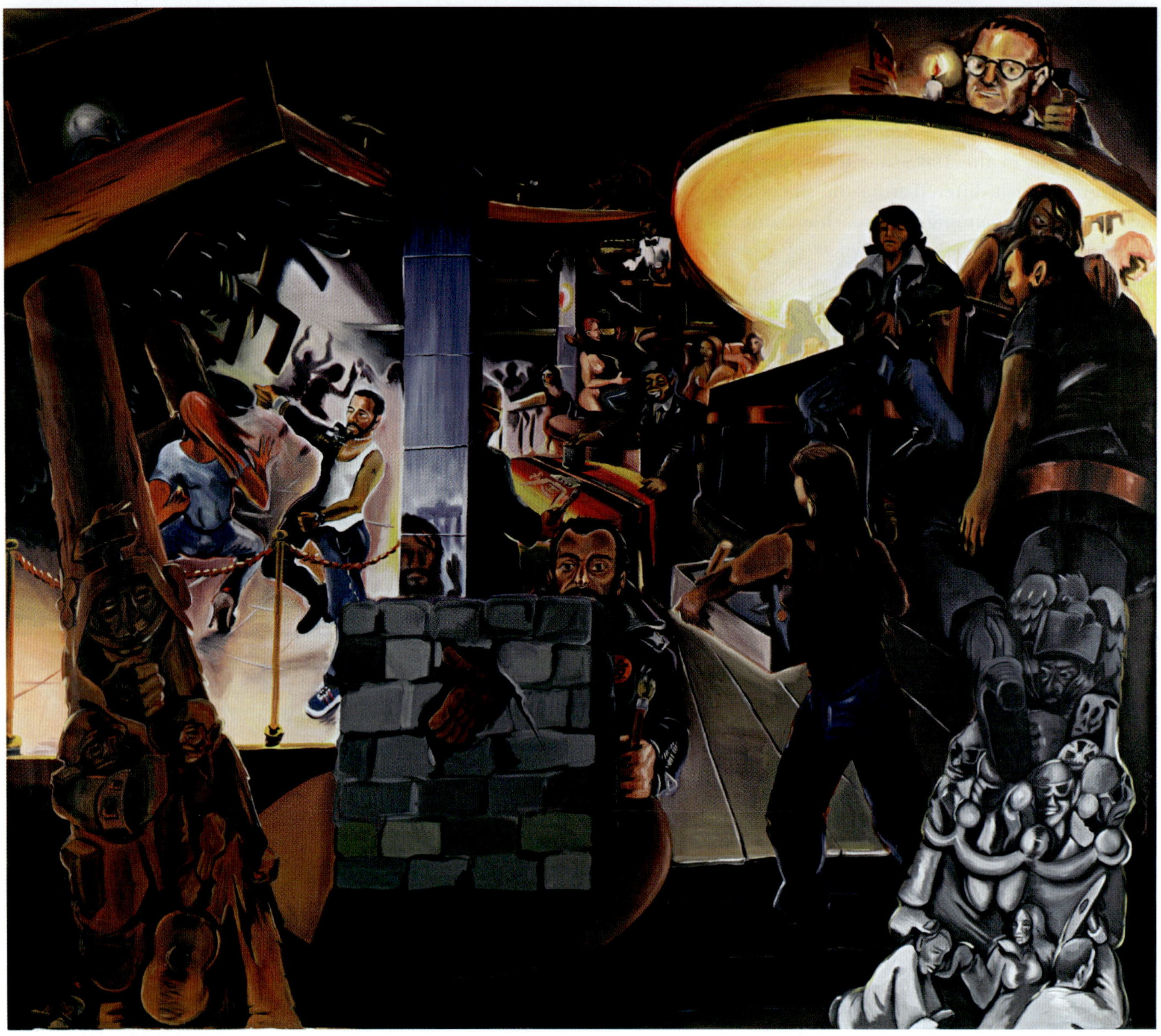

3.22 Jörg Immendorff, *Café Deutschland I*, 1977. Oil on canvas, 111 × 130" (282 × 330 cm). Courtesy Galerie Michael Werner Märkisch Wilmersdorf, Cologne & New York.

contemporary East German painter A.R. Penck (b. 1939). Immendorff had met Penck (an alias for Ralf Winkler) in 1976. The two men were equally concerned with resolving the political challenges facing Germany. Their dialogue on this question was the impetus for, and one of the subjects of, the *Café Deutschland* paintings. Since the 1960s, Penck had addressed the difficulty of painting a critical account of life in East Germany. His solution involved a type of painterly, expressive hieroglyphics that compressed contemporary life into pictographic stick figures analogous to Borofsky's anonymous men (see fig. 3.3). Such pictures, he asserted, were "essential criteria for determining the condition of the system," a system that for Penck, after his emigration to Kerpen, near Cologne, in 1980, included both East and West Germany.[70] *What Is Gravitation? III* (1984) (**fig. 3.23**) revolves around the flight of a man, shown as a stick figure walking among planets and stars. On his journey, the man navigates between a provocatively posed female and small stick figures, one carrying a sign reading "A=A," another a book and a cross, and several wielding clubs. These characters variously symbolize sex, education, religion, and violence. Meanwhile a monster looms over the man, and an eye appears on his hand, symbolizing for the artist different forms of the unknown and unknowable. Though an eagle evoking Germany flies into the scene at the upper left, *What Is Gravitation? III* largely approaches questions of dislocation and alienation without explicit political references. In his *Café Deutschland* imagery, Immendorff by contrast aimed to be politically specific. In the middle of *Café Deutschland I*, he painted the leaders of the two Germanies, Erich Honecker (East) and Helmut Schmidt (West), inscribing a Penck-like glyph on the German flag, while a woman with a tray circulates around the bar with tools rather than cocktails. In the *Café Deutschland* series, Immendorff discovered how to respond to the challenge he laid

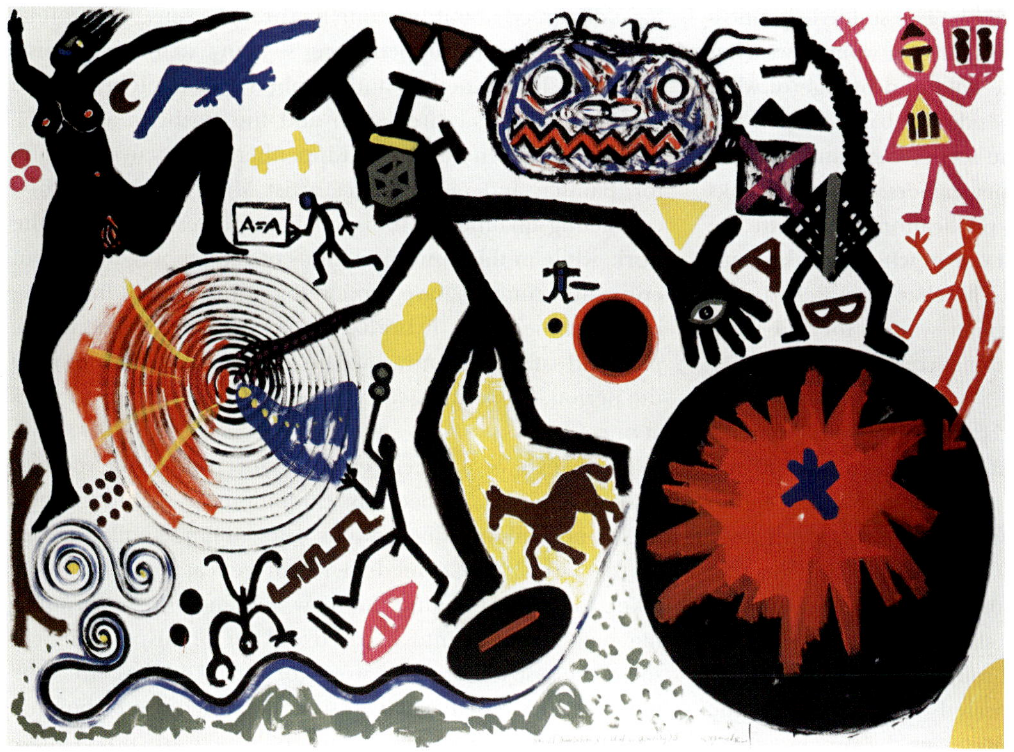

3.23 A.R. Penck, ***Was ist Gravitation? (What Is Gravitation?) III***, 1984. Acrylic on canvas, 98½ × 137¾" (250 × 350 cm). Courtesy Galerie Michael Werner Märkisch Wilmersdorf, Cologne & New York.

down to other European artists: "Make the themes of your works everyday problems, injustice, the threat of war between the two Imperial powers, [and] political violence."[71]

Put Germany in Order (1983) (**fig. 3.24**) is part of Immendorff's extended allegory of the struggle for German unification, which includes the *Café Deutschland* series and most of his other work of the period, and is typical of his theatrical manner of composition. It recalls the interwar *Neue Sachlichkeit* ("New Objectivity") German painters, such as Georg Grosz (1893–1959), Otto Dix (1891–1969), and Max Beckmann (1894–1950), and the morality tales of the eighteenth-century British painter William Hogarth (1697–1764), whose *Rake's Progress* series Immendorff would reinterpret in the 1990s. The setting for *Put Germany in Order* is a bar glowing

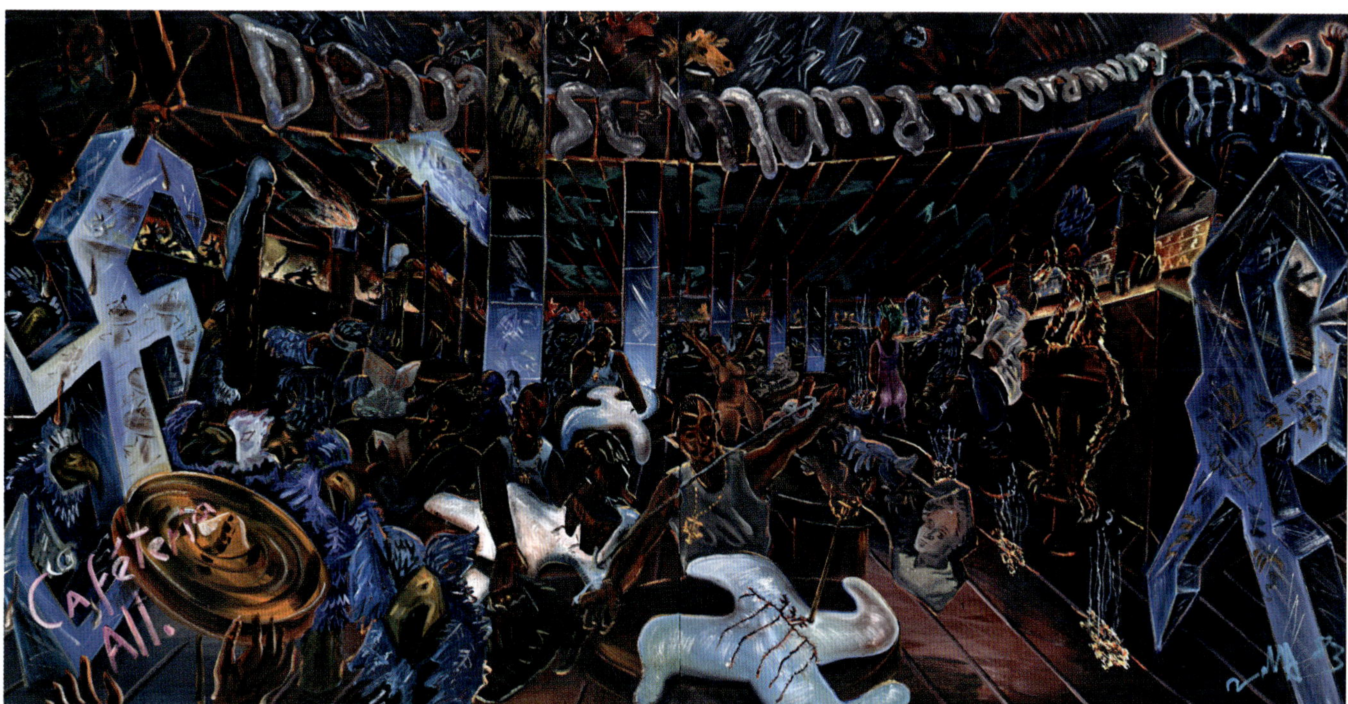

3.24 Jörg Immendorff, ***Deutschland in Ordnung bringen (Put Germany In Order)***, 1983. Oil on canvas in two parts, 98½ × 196" (250 × 498 cm). © The Estate of Jörg Immendorff. Courtesy Galerie Michael Werner Märkisch Wilmersdorf, Cologne & New York.

with electric neon blues and fiery reds. The stultifying atmosphere is punctuated by the green hair of a woman wearing a transparent pink dress, and the gold and orange of what look like steaming piles of shit beside the bar stools. In the lounge that fills the center of the scene, German eagles fly in from stage left as men read newspapers; one man looks up from his copy of the Soviet publication *Pravda*. In the back, animals and people, at least one of whom is naked, are caught in suspended animation. The chaos is watched over by an ice swastika, the East German symbol for the West, and an ice hammer and sickle, the corresponding icon for the East.

In the shadow of authoritarian power and hedonistic chaos, three images of the artist can be seen, all bearing Immendorff's signature closely shaven head. Each figure wears a pendant of the Brandenburg Gate around his neck and works diligently to fix an icy star marked with a scar resembling this landmark that marks the border between East and West Berlin. These stars acquire significance as icons of German identity through their repetition in Immendorff's work. Other repeated motifs include the doglike figure at the bar, who appears as the protagonist of three 1983 paintings called *The Collector*, and the spoon-wielding figure at the upper left. Objects and figures are all joined together in a theatrical appeal to rise above the current unseemly and immoral contest between East and West. The triple figure of the artist suggests that the political work is hard going. By 2000, however, with the Berlin Wall down and the two Germanys unified, Immendorff could claim: "I am the sole painter in art history who has worked on a utopia (reunification) which then became concrete."[72]

Epilogue, Addenda, Errata

While the story told in these opening chapters of painters and appropriators is accurate, it is also deceptive. As U.S. Minimalist sculptor Donald Judd wrote: "The history of art and art's condition at any time are pretty messy. They should stay that way."[73] In Germany in the 1980s, while the *Heftige Malerei* played at being rock stars and Kiefer, Baselitz, and Immendorff waged campaigns against history, others—notably Martin Kippenberger (1953–97)—rejected the primacy of painting, self, or history. Kippenberger put quotation marks around his status as an artist, described his primary activity as enabling others, and expressed a desire to be remembered for generating a good mood. To this end, he expended as much energy on managing the nightclub SO36, on running his workshop/distribution center/exhibition venue Kippenberger Bureau, and on drinking, as he did on making art objects. His studio practice was correspondingly eclectic, combining appropriative, painterly, performative, and Conceptual approaches. He assembled other artists' work, published books, took photographs, painted, sculpted, enlisted others to paint and sculpt for him, and made himself the center of an ever-growing spectacle. Critics have disagreed about how one might make sense of the relationship between Kippenberger's many activities. Artists including Jutta Koether and Stephen Prina celebrated the sense of perpetual circulation and the aesthetic and intellectual anti-essentialism of Kippenberger's oeuvre. Sculptor, painter, and performance artist Mike Kelley identified conflicting qualities of transgression and respect within the work, while in their interpretations of Kippenberger's output critics and curators have proposed guiding themes including inversion, negation, hybridization, connection to the world, play, and satire. In contrast to the contentious polarization of the period, Kippenberger's work seemed to embrace all sides at once.

In an extensive, often-reprinted interview with Koether, Kippenberger described his exhibitions as running gags, each one building on previous ones, telling similar stories in the way that a comedian might repeat and develop a joke, adapting it slightly for new audiences or incorporating new elements into it based on her or his experiences since the last telling. The works of art, like jokes, are integrated into larger narratives, some of which are elaborated in a particular exhibition, some of which are not. Unlike Neo-Expressionists such as Immendorff, Baselitz, and Middendorf, whose work tells a story, or Kiefer, Schnabel, and Salle, who provide objects and space for the viewer to create their own, Kippenberger presents pieces of stories from the world beyond the painting. The viewer may or may not recognize the allusions or get the joke. A painting such as *Self-Portrait* (1982) (**fig. 3.25**), with its dramatic presentation of cartoon martini glasses and musical notes orbiting Kippenberger's bandaged head, teases the viewer with hints of the artist's misadventures. The charisma of the work's subject, even when battered after a hard night of drinking, as well as Kippenberger's vigorous style, contrasting rough impasto on the figure's bandaged face with icons flatly applied across the work's surface, invite the viewer to spend time with the painting. Some viewers might have remembered the image from a photograph used as the invitation to the artist's 1981 exhibition "Dialogue with the Young" the previous year. Others may even have heard details about the events that left Kippenberger bandaged. Most will respond to the many easily legible symbols painted on the work and to the painter's willingness to show himself in such an unflattering light. But we also know there are things we are not being told. The work is both confessional and withholding, representational and abstract, iconic and psychological.

If the comedy of the running gag and the charisma of the comedian are Kippenberger's means for creating a good mood for the willing, his technical facility, Koether argues, is a trap for critics bristling at the apparent self-indulgence of his subject matter. Praise of his painterly invention on an otherwise skeptical viewer's part is, she says, tantamount to announcing: "This picture ... is quite acceptable in both its form and content and even in its execution ... but if I get involved with it I'll get carried away from the individual

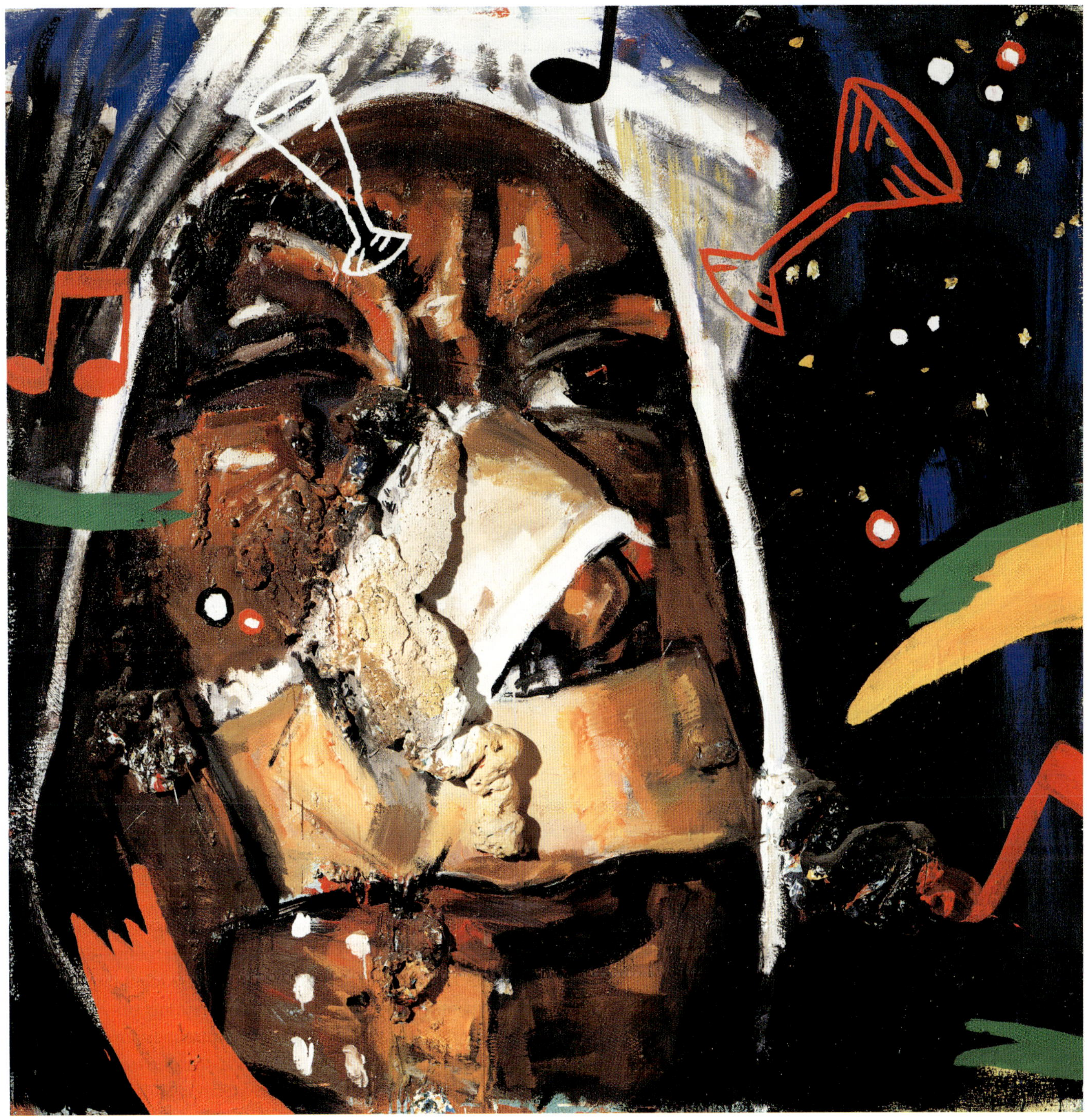

3.25 Martin Kippenberger, ***Self-Portrait***, 1982. Oil on canvas, 66⅞" × 66⅞" (170 × 170 cm).

object into a deluge of Kippenberger's scandalous or exhausting or otherwise threatening activities."[74] Prina, embracing the deluge, clarifies what happens if we keep looking: "I cannot escape the suspicion that I have been trapped in an elaborate plot [that has been begun but is] nowhere near complete."[75] *Self-Portrait* is an opening into activities and relationships that extend from the studio out into the streets and that involve a cast of initiates and strangers. The most productive approach to Kippenberger's work, Koether writes, is to accept the "embarrassment" inevitably created by it, "stay normal and quite open and try to get involved." "[I]n medical terminology," she continues, "allow group dynamic … [which] includes speaking, showing and drinking."[76] Prioritizing the world beyond the frame is a theme addressed in the critical and conceptual traditions that supported appropriation; the personal dimension, however, is akin to the spirit of Neo-Expressionism. Kippenberger's antipathy toward gravity pushes him away from either camp and makes it clear that taking sides is either impossible or beside the point.

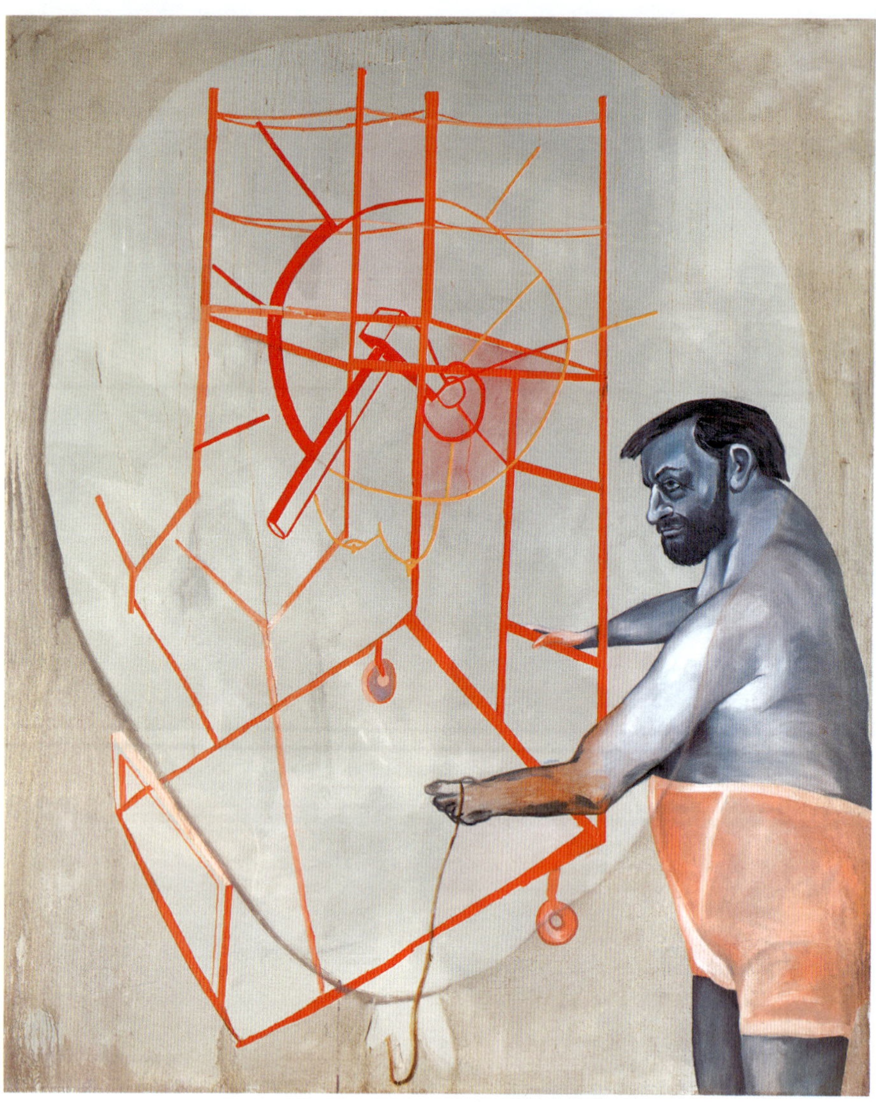

3.26 Martin Kippenberger, *Untitled*, 1988. Oil on canvas, 94½ × 78¾" (240 × 200 cm).

Categories and positions in Kippenberger's art are only temporary and contingent; his art is more of an aesthetic and intellectual flow. In many cases, Kippenberger represented the idea of art-as-contingent-network quite literally. His first paintings, done in Florence, Italy, in the late 1970s, were based on photographic snapshots taken during his daily wanderings. Throughout his career he would draw on hotel stationery, creating an archive of visually disparate images that registered his fleeting thoughts and mapped his peripatetic lifestyle. Kippenberger's circulatory system, to use one of Koether's metaphors for his art, is dramatically and humorously illustrated by his *Metro-Net*, a global subway system with stations in Greece, Canada, and Germany. *Metro-Net* was necessarily conceptual, suggesting a community of travelers imagining themselves on a global commute. Kippenberger's fellow travelers were many, and he also integrated other artists' work and ideas into his art through his generously acknowledged use of assistants and by collecting and curating. He complemented the network of his travels and friends with allusions to art-historical lineages, identifying himself through his actions and portraiture with Joseph Beuys, Andy Warhol, and Pablo Picasso, in each case with tongue in cheek and his own identity in quotation marks. In *Untitled* (1988) (**fig. 3.26**), Kippenberger paints a portrait of himself in the role of Picasso by mimicking a famous photograph of the Spanish master in a bathing suit. The large garment clings unflatteringly to Kippenberger's belly and thighs as he awkwardly maneuvers a sculpture adorned with the icon, a hammer, sun, and breasts in a spider web that can be found throughout the artist's oeuvre including several of the *Metro-Net* stations. Viewers are presented with a comparison of the two as aging men as well as artists, a comparison that is closer to deliberate humiliation on Kippenberger's part than hubris. As he declared: "I'm not a 'real' painter, nor a 'real' sculptor, I only look at all that from the outside and sometimes try my hand at it, trying to add my own particular spice."[77]

Kippenberger died of cancer at the age of forty-four, leaving a body of work containing visions of art, self, and history that in fragments seems to accord with much of the art discussed in this and the previous chapter, but that in its totality reminds us how problematic it is to imagine the past as possessing a coherent Zeitgeist that can be captured and explained in a single, unified narrative.

4

Into the Streets

In 1982, the seventh edition of Documenta, the highly influential twice-a-decade exhibition of international contemporary art held in Kassel, West Germany, found its tranquility interrupted by a concession stand installed outside the "official" exhibition space (**fig. 4.1**). This guerrilla exhibition was selling buttons, T-shirts, and low-priced souvenirs. A banner announced: "Great Art for Low Prices." The stall was an *ad hoc* exhibition space for Fashion Moda, an alternative art gallery based in the South Bronx, New York, and full of work by members of Collaborative Projects (Colab), a politically engaged group of artists based in New York.[1] Fashion Moda was created by Stefan Eins in 1979 to support art outside the art establishment. Its name, made up of the English word "fashion" and its Spanish equivalent, captured the gallery's multicultural context of the Bronx, while the art it promoted represented the intersection of graffiti, painting, fashion, and music (**fig. 4.2**). The gallery was one of many alternative spaces responding to new artistic practices that treated the streets as well as galleries as important venues exhibiting art. Fashion Moda had not been invited to participate in Documenta, a curated exhibition, but Jenny Holzer, one of the invited artists, co-produced the Fashion Moda

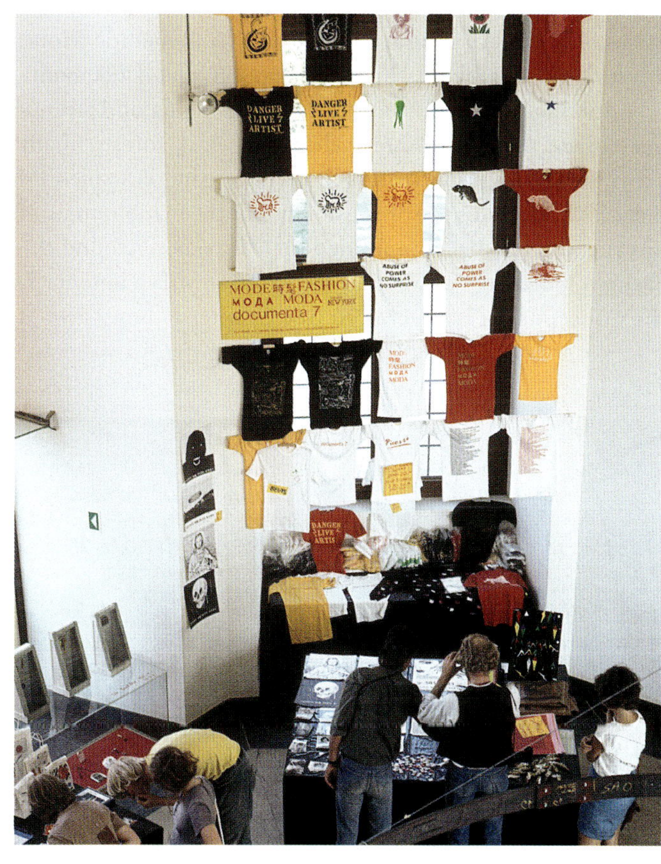

4.1 Fashion Moda, *Concession stall at Documenta 7*, 1982. Kassel, West Germany.

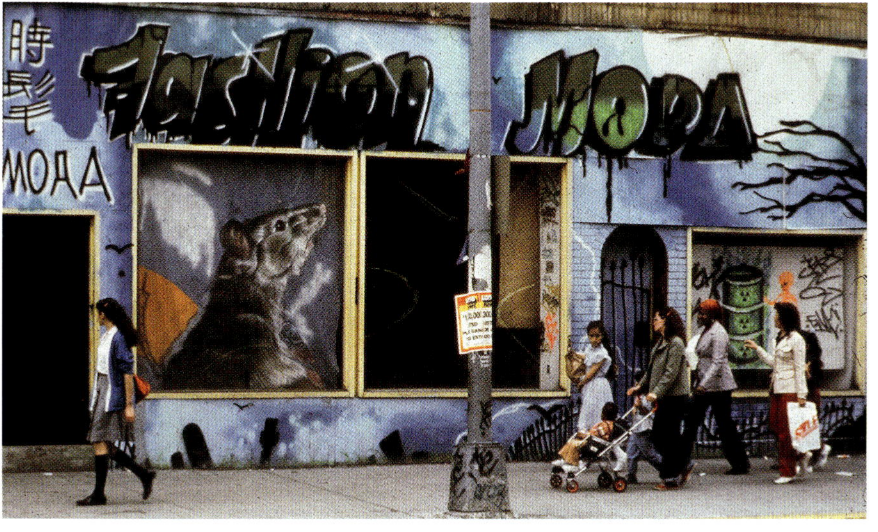

4.2 Fashion Moda, *gallery exterior*, 1980s. Mural by Crash. South Bronx, New York.

event as her contribution. Holzer's *Truisms* (see fig. 2.19) appeared on T-shirts at the stall. This intrusion exemplifies the exuberant—and often strongly politicized—early 1980s alternative art scene that thumbed its nose at the exclusivity of high culture. Often allied with political causes including AIDS activism, economic justice, and citizenship issues, galleries, outdoor public spaces, and eventually museums became stages for political debate. The location of the Fashion Moda concession at the edges of Documenta, enjoying at least the tacit support of the curatorial staff, conveys the desire of its creators to confront artworld institutions on their own territory, as well as from terrain less accustomed to the display of art.[2]

The work inside Documenta 7 was also symptomatic of its cultural moment. Many in the art press castigated Rudi Fuchs, the chief curator, for creating a Romantic cloud around the exhibition. Fuchs's proposal that Documenta 7 be subtitled "In which our heroes after a long and strenuous voyage through sinister valleys and dark forests finally arrive in the English Garden, and at the gate of a splendid palace" captures his poetic sensibility, but the exhibition itself was rife with art that complicated such fairytales. Around the Fashion Moda concession and the exterior of Documenta 7, the Conceptualist Daniel Buren (see Chapter 1) hung striped pennants that enveloped the event in his own critical project while also giving it the flavor of a carnival or car dealership. Once inside, meditative experiences were upset by the presence of the appropriation art of Sherrie Levine and Barbara Kruger (see Chapter 2), several *Café Deutschland* paintings by Jörg Immendorff (see Chapter 3), and a Hans Haacke installation dissecting the business activities of German art patron Peter Ludwig. Haacke's infamous *Shapolsky et al.* (see fig. 1.18) was even featured in the exhibition catalogue. Fuchs's comments notwithstanding, this was not "A New Spirit in Painting," Part II, but instead demonstrated that aesthetic, political, and theoretical critiques of art and power were beginning to infiltrate the very spaces they attacked. It is to this process of infiltration—by which art traveled from alternative spaces and the streets themselves into the machinery of high culture and mass media—that this chapter turns.

The East Village and the Alternative Scene

The emergence of appropriation and Neo-Expressionism together in New York in the early 1980s revealed the city's two very different functions within the art world: The former, shaped by critics, demonstrated it to be a hothouse for

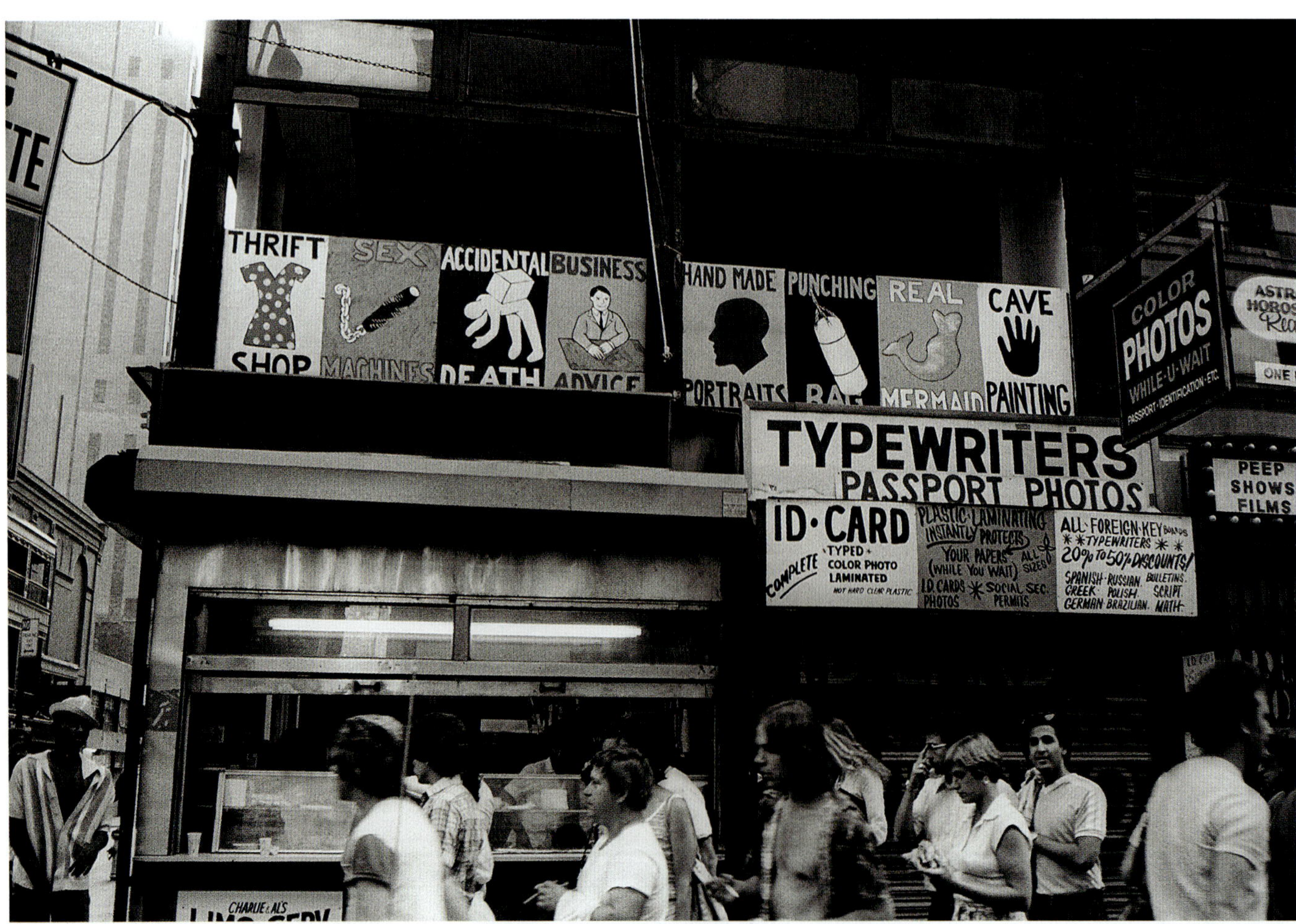

4.3 Colab, ***Times Square Show***, 1980. Collage by Terise Slotkin. Installation in Times Square, New York.

intellectual discourse and political critique; the latter, rooted in the entrepreneurial insight and energy of a new generation of gallerists, proved its importance as an engine turning contemporary art into an economically valuable and culturally visible product. While denizens of the art world took up positions around these two, often conflicting identities, artists of the kind who were showing at Fashion Moda or attending Colab meetings sought refuge in a third art world, one dominated by the everyday concerns of urban life and the invention of aesthetics that responded to them. Though it would be quickly subsumed by intellectual and economic concerns, this alternative scene—split between the East Village and the South Bronx—was home to an almost anarchic energy that in its zeal to redefine artistic practice would find sympathetic audiences and fellow travelers in other movements.

By the time its artists were hawking their wares at Documenta 7, Colab, formed in 1977, already had several controversial art interventions to its name. Two years before, in the summer of 1980, the group had occupied a dilapidated building in Times Square in New York for what one newspaper called the "first radical art show of the 1980s" (**fig. 4.3**). Earlier the same year, members had entered a vacant, city-owned building in Lower Manhattan and presented "The Real Estate Show," which featured art addressing the political causes and consequences of the housing shortage. It was shut down after a day. By way of contrast, the summer project, called "The Times Square Show," aimed at offering a less pointed analysis of metropolitan society, with the atmosphere tending toward the carnivalesque rather than the directly political. The run-down four-story structure on 41st Street occupied by the group became home to graffiti, murals, sculpted rats and printed weapons, slogans, spaceships, and mounds of debris that evoked 1960s assemblage art, the tenement housing of the destitute, and the adult theaters and sex shops that then filled Times Square. Colab artists including Holzer, John Ahearn, Jean-Michel Basquiat, Byron Kim, Tom Otterness, Kenny Scharf, and Kiki Smith took turns as barkers outside the building and blasted punk music from the windows to project the energy of their art into the street. As at Documenta, bargain-basement slogans encouraged passers-by to come in and shop: "Four jam-packed floors!! More than you bargained for." The appeal of the artists' brand of updated realism was not lost on critics, who celebrated the impulse to hold a mirror up to the city in this way. As one reviewer declared: "The hordes of half-wild, half-crazed, and fully degenerate individuals who keep pouring out of the 42nd street subway had occasion to check out a whole building full of art that was just as raw, raucous, trashy, and perhaps even as exciting as some of the [neighborhood's] more notorious attractions."[3]

Colab supplemented its lowbrow theatrics with references to cutting-edge art of the previous decades, from Picasso to Fluxus. In addition, "The Times Square Show" had financial support not only from alternative spaces such as Fashion Moda and Colab's own ABC No Rio, established in 1979 in the Lower East Side, but also federal and state arts funding, not to mention the permission of the occupied site's landlord. This time, building on the experience of the short-lived "Real Estate Show," its infiltration into the non-art world was fully sanctioned.

The new environs brought significant challenges. An examination of rape in a standard gallery context might look like a carefully judged exposure of brutality. Shown in a non-conventional space next door to a peepshow or an adult-movie house, however, collages made of pornographic sources and performances enacting edgy sexual activities such as were featured at "The Times Square Show" threatened to read as fantasy. A similar ambiguity was true of the multiple images of violence that filled the Colab show. On 42nd Street, then as now in its more Hollywoodified form, images of gun-toting young men teeter toward a glorification of violence rather than social critique. As had been noted before, not least by Joseph Beuys, a critical art practice needs to do more than merely reflect reality. If the fact that "The Times Square Show" resonated with its environment proved that contemporary art was suited to being displayed in spaces other than white-walled galleries, fitting in too well in such surroundings suggested that it might not be art at all. This was one of the new challenges facing artists whose aim was to articulate political and social options not sanctioned by normative society and whose venues lay outside the established art world.

The collective actions of Colab and Fashion Moda represent the outer reaches of what was emerging as a third tier in the New York art market. By the mid-1980s, a new group of eclectic galleries were competing with those on 57th Street, the historic center of art dealing in New York, or the blue-chip spaces of SoHo, which in the 1960s had been first an outpost of radical art but by the 1980s had developed into the economic heart of the art world. The new scene was rooted in the East Village, a neighborhood of Manhattan that had yet to be gentrified by developers. The area provided low rents and a haven for artists in search of a supportive space for their deliberately unrefined agitational work. The social issues being addressed were serious, but pleasure was also an important part of the scene. Art was made for display in nightclubs as much as galleries, and the openings were legendary for their duration, decibel level, and consumption of controlled substances. Clubs like the Palladium turned private rooms over to artists such as Keith Haring and Kenny Scharf to use for exhibitions and installations. The boom started with the opening of a core group of spaces including Fun Gallery in 1981, Nature Morte, Civilian Warfare, Gracie Mansion (named for its owner, who took her name from the residence provided for the mayor of New York), and Exit Art in 1982, and International with Monument in 1984. By the end of the latter year, there were over seventy-five galleries in the area. Feeding off what turned out to be an economic bubble, the East Village was a microcosm of the cultural economy and prime stomping ground for artists and collectors alike. As Carlo McCormick, an East Village critic and collaborator, noted as early 1984, the scene, as distinct from some of its productions, was never intended to subvert the business of culture. Rather, it was "right at the cutting edge ... cannily transform[ing] inspiration to commodity and willfully avoid[ing] the hypocrisy of denying its materialistic value."[4] In the journal *Art in America* in the same year, McCormick and painter/critic/editor Walter Robinson more bluntly asserted: "The East Village scene, incidentally, suits the Reaganite zeitgeist remarkably well."[5] By the end of the decade, most of the more successful artists had found more business-savvy dealers in SoHo and the few genuinely profitable galleries had relocated there as well. The scene thus vanished, leaving only a few holdouts, including ABC No Rio, Exit Art, and The New Museum, all of which had established enduring connections with the neighborhood, reputations in the art world, and, coincidentally perhaps, were positioned some distance from the center of East Village activities at their height.

The sense that East Village art might be complicit with the system it purported to resist and indifferent to the company it kept riled critics and many artists. In the context of art-world pressures to produce refined work for the Minimalist- and Pop-inspired blue-chip galleries, accumulations of color and kitsch such as Rhonda Zwillinger's (b. 1950) *Post-Minimal Glitz* (1985) (**fig. 4.4**) or the confounding efforts of David McDermott (b. 1952) and Peter MacGough (b. 1958) to live as Victorians with corresponding technology (e.g., no electricity) were cathartic and even liberating celebrations of artistic independence. Nonetheless, critics were anxious about the role artists were playing in raising neighborhood property values, and though few were ready to lay the blame for gentrification on artists, many were troubled by steadily rising rents and corresponding demographic changes. Living without electricity as an artistic statement was entirely different than having one's electricity cut off for non-payment of bills as a result of inescapable poverty.

Keith Haring

One of the most celebrated artists to come out of the East Village scene was Keith Haring (1958–90). His work could be seen in the subways of New York by the late 1970s, in Lower Manhattan nightclubs and galleries by the early 1980s, in museum exhibitions around the world after the mid-1980s, and at his own store, the Pop Shop, from 1986 to 2005. In the second decade of the twenty-first century, Haring's work maintains a vivid presence at auction and on the Internet, as well as in museums and galleries. He worked on campaigns for causes including AIDS research, famine relief, and drug awareness, but it is his subway drawings, often whimsical and fantastical in nature, that most concretely demonstrate his interest in the social context of his work. Arriving in New York in the late 1970s, Haring began to explore the city's art world and its social life. At the School of Visual Arts in Manhattan, he met Kenny Scharf (b. 1958) and Jean-Michel Basquiat, both of whom shared Haring's commitment to the blurred boundaries separating art and entertainment. Haring collaborated with graffiti artists as well as with art-school peers, at times

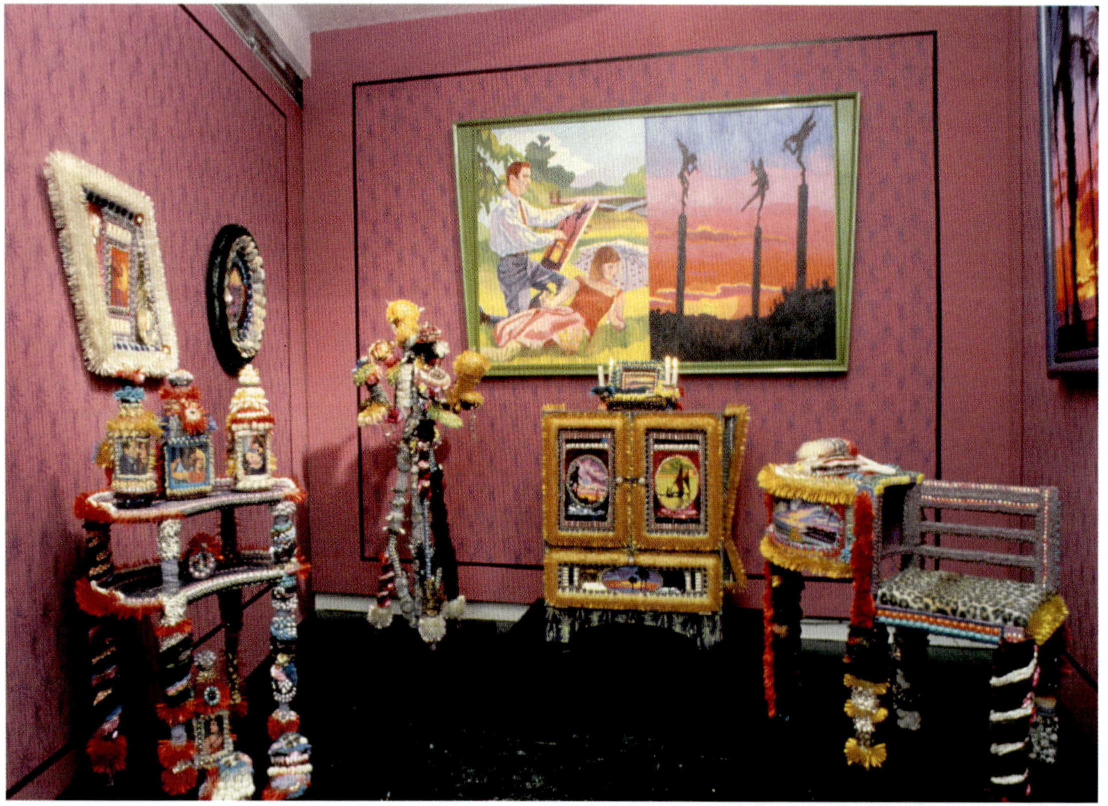

4.4 Rhonda Zwillinger, *Post-Minimal Glitz*, 1985. One-room view of two-room installation. Oil paint, glass beads, found furniture, drawings/colored pencils, painted walls with antique stencils, silicon caulking, and leopard fabric. Installation at Gracie Mansion Gallery, New York City. Courtesy the artist.

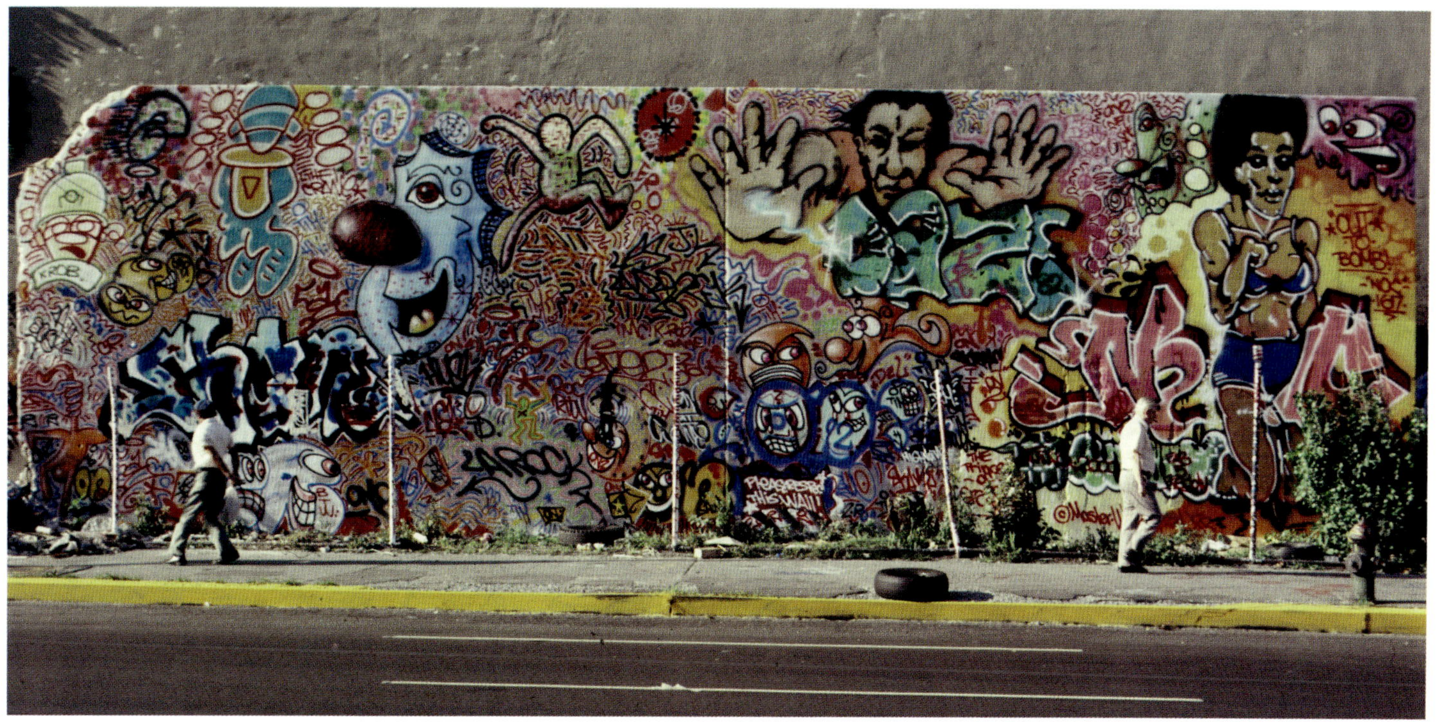

4.5 Keith Haring, Kenny Scharf, A-One, Daze, LA2, *Mural*, 1983. Houston Street mural, New York. Photograph by Tseng Kwong Chi. © Muna Tseng Dance Projects, Inc. New York.

all together on a single work (**fig. 4.5**). While his aboveground career included tagging, curating, and exhibiting in East Village and SoHo galleries, underground he was making chalk drawings on the black paper used to cover expired advertising posters in subway stations (**fig. 4.6**). Both bodies of work were socially engaged, graphically concise, and highly expressive.

The subway drawings were a way of taking possession of public space and becoming involved in the everyday activities of ordinary people. Haring began by defacing advertisements

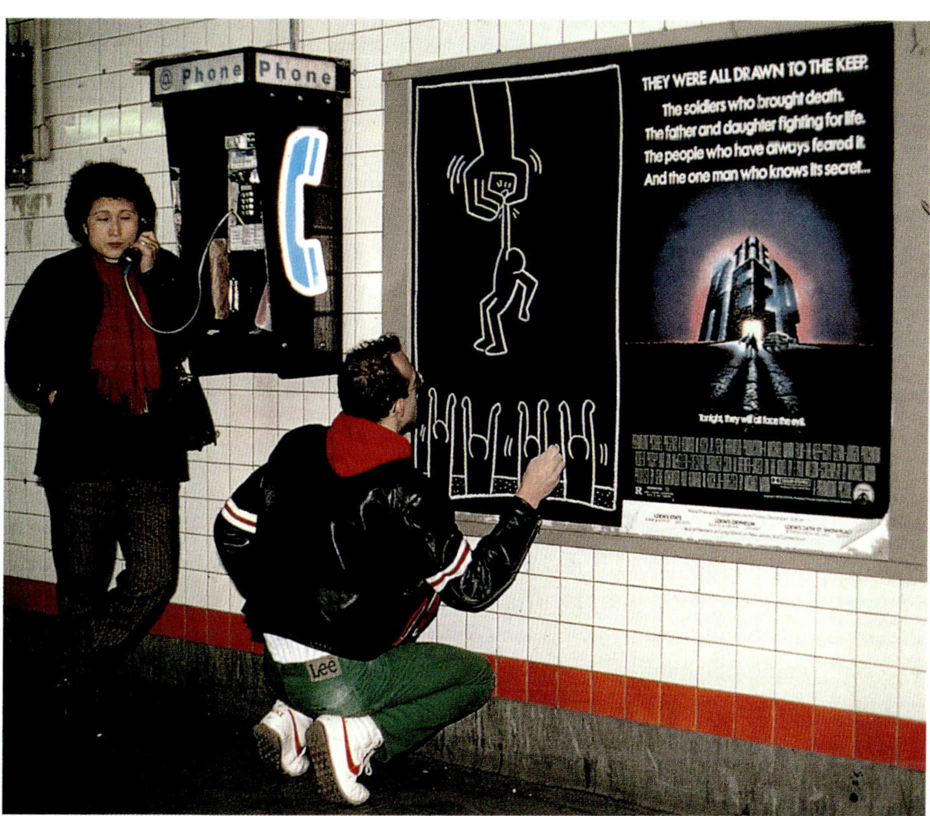

4.6 Keith Haring, *Untitled Subway Drawing*, 1983. New York subway. © Keith Haring Foundation. Photograph by Tseng Kwong Chi. © 1983 Muna Tseng Dance Projects, Inc. New York.

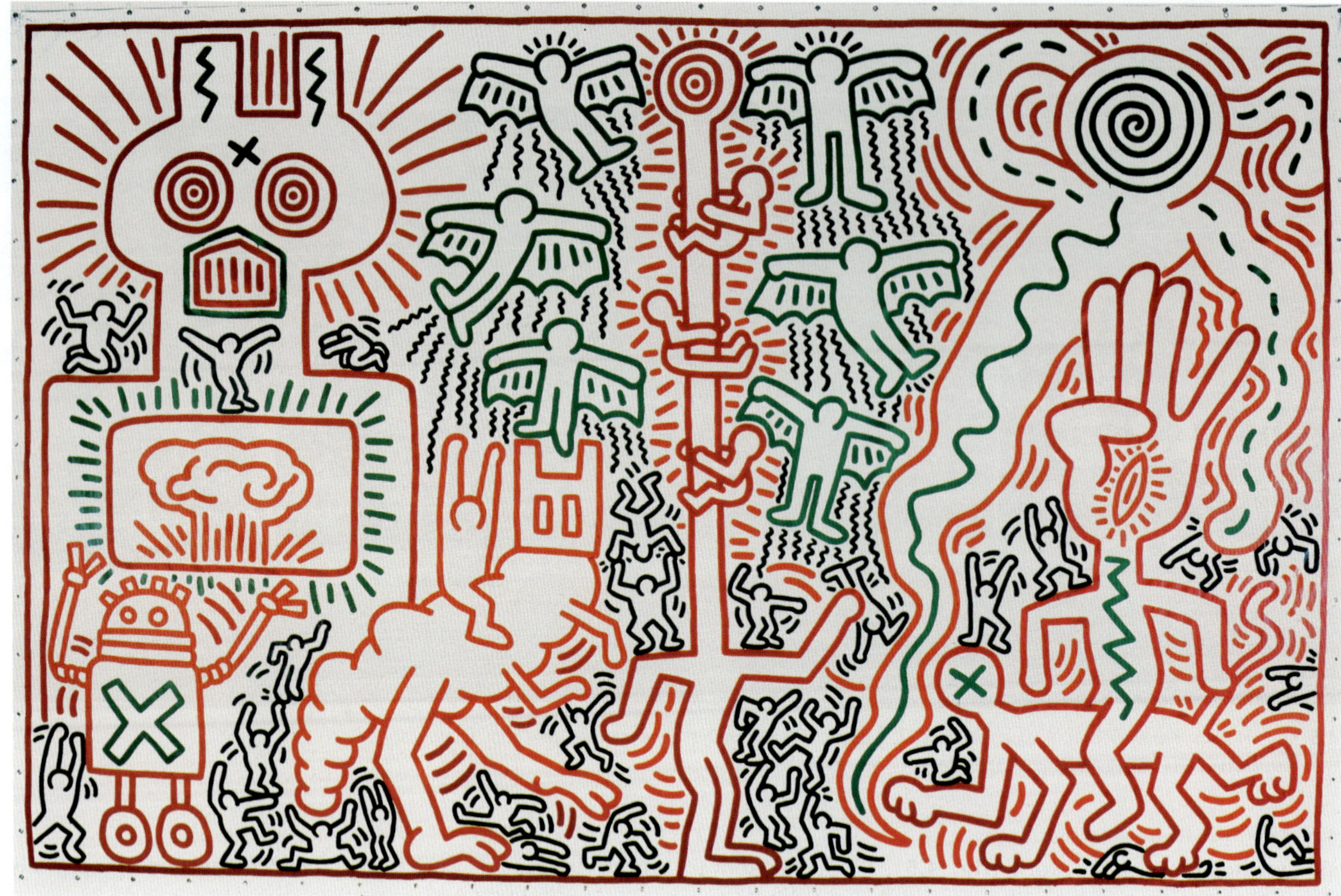

4.7 Keith Haring, *Untitled*, 1983. Vinyl ink on vinyl tarp, 180 × 276" (457.2 × 701 cm).

to draw attention to stereotypes and sexism in media images. Soon, however, he shifted to the more playful chalk-drawn visions that would be part of his oeuvre until his AIDS-related death in 1990. Haring's acts of petty vandalism created a sense of community among his fans, who became connoisseurs of his growing legions of dancing figures, flying saucers, and radiant children. As Haring became aware of the pleasure and sense of connection his work provided, he circulated pins of a "radiant child" figure that became so popular he was once mugged for them despite the fact that he was giving them away for free. The pins led to the establishment of the Pop Shop, a commercial venture of international scope which generated income for Haring as well as for a foundation that continues to support a variety of causes worldwide.

The attention Haring's work received in the subway was paired with growing artworld acclaim. On the streets and on gallery walls, Haring demonstrated his ability to cover huge surfaces with intricate patterns and exuberant references to sex and death, pleasure and play (**fig. 4.7**). His irrepressible style and the immediacy of his imagery lent themselves to easy commodification, a fact that colored his critical reception, but also permitted social issues, such as AIDS and homosexuality, to enter the public discourse as never before. As an openly gay artist, Haring's frank integration of homosexual content in his art and his vocal advocacy of gay rights provided a significant show of resistance to the homophobia then dominating public responses to AIDS. In the face of accusations that the disease was God's punishment for homosexuality, Haring's art bubbled over with life-affirming exuberance, even while it addressed sometimes painful content.

David Wojnarowicz

The work of David Wojnarowicz (1954–92)—often seen in the same spaces, even on the same streets as Haring's—expresses a very different attitude toward art and life in the 1980s. Wojnarowicz created drawings, paintings, graffiti, illustrations, constructions, writings, films, and photographs that responded to the perceptions and dreams of those cast aside by mainstream society for their differences—in his case, for being gay. His work is characterized by a relentless drive to challenge what he calls the "preinvented reality" of the conservative, suppressive biases of the status quo and to facilitate the creation, by himself and all of us, of spaces, visions, and artistic languages of our own making. "Bottom line," he declared in his memoirs, "every gesture carries a reverberation that is meaningful in its diversity; bottom line we have to find our own forms of gesture and communication."[6] Harking back to the eclectic chaos of early Colab and even further to Dada artists such as Hannah Höch (1889–1978) and John Heartfield (1891–1968), who

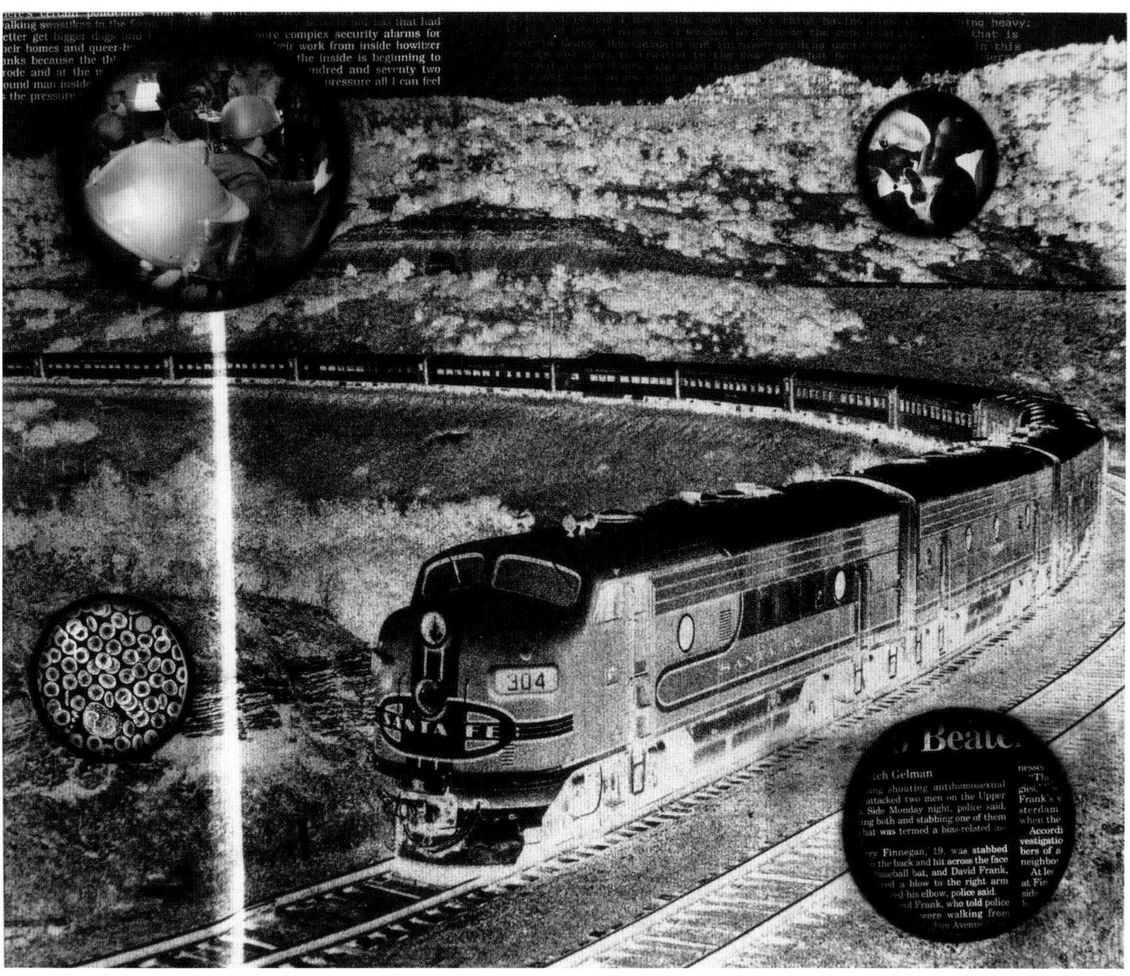

4.8 David Wojnarowicz, *Untitled from Sex Series (For Marion Scemama)*, 1988–89. Gelatin silver print, 37 × 34¾" (93.98 × 88.26 cm). Courtesy of the Estate of David Wojnarowicz and P.P.O.W. Gallery, New York.

manipulated images of technology to critique modernity, Wojnarowicz culled source material from newspapers, maps, science books, shop windows, and his own previous creations. His oeuvre looks as though it might be the output of several different artists, expressing in its diversity the variety within any one person. Unlike most of his peers in the New York art world of the 1980s, whose styles were often complex but obviously coherent, Wojnarowicz's oeuvre rejects a uniform appearance, looking instead like the product of a diverse community in search of many different means of expressing itself.

Wojnarowicz's career as a visual artist extended from the late 1970s until his death from AIDS-related complications in 1992. During this time he produced hundreds of images that forced the conventional symbols of American power and progress, such as gears, locomotives, cowboys, space travel, maps, and money, into intimate proximity with the uncertainties they were designed to overcome. In his *Sex Series* (**fig. 4.8**), trains, an icon of industry, and military planes, a symbol of war, rush through landscapes punctuated by riot police, blood cells, money, reports of gay-bashing, stories of love, and images of homosexual sex. Each fragment Wojnarowicz inserts into his compositions hints at larger worlds of terror, pathos, and sometimes joy, and each provides a counterweight to the myths of a homogeneous American empire. As we connect the components of his imagery to each other and the outside world we create stories in which their themes of gay existence, poverty, neglect, and death become laced with poetry, color, advertising imagery, and ideas from art history. The *Sex Series*, like all of Wojnarowicz's work, acts as a simple and often visceral reminder that contemporary American life is more complex than the mass media and the political mythmakers would have us believe.

Like many of the artists discussed in this chapter, Wojnarowicz produced opportunities to imagine societies not yet regulated by the usual divisions of "us and them." His own biography is a record of the violence enacted across such boundaries. He fled an abusive home, ending up in often violent, even life-threatening, situations on the streets of New York. Such brutal experiences inform but do not constitute the limits of his work. A particularly clear and emotionally effective combination of the personal and the political can be seen in *Untitled (One Day This Kid)* (1990) (**fig. 4.9**), created as an element of a installation. A simple juxtaposition of image and text, it features a black-and-white portrait of the artist as a child surrounded by phrases describing a startling coming-of-age story delivered in rather matter-of-fact tones. On the left a rhythmic series of statements begins the narrative: "One day this kid will get larger." The text then describes the discovery of sexuality—"One day this kid will come to

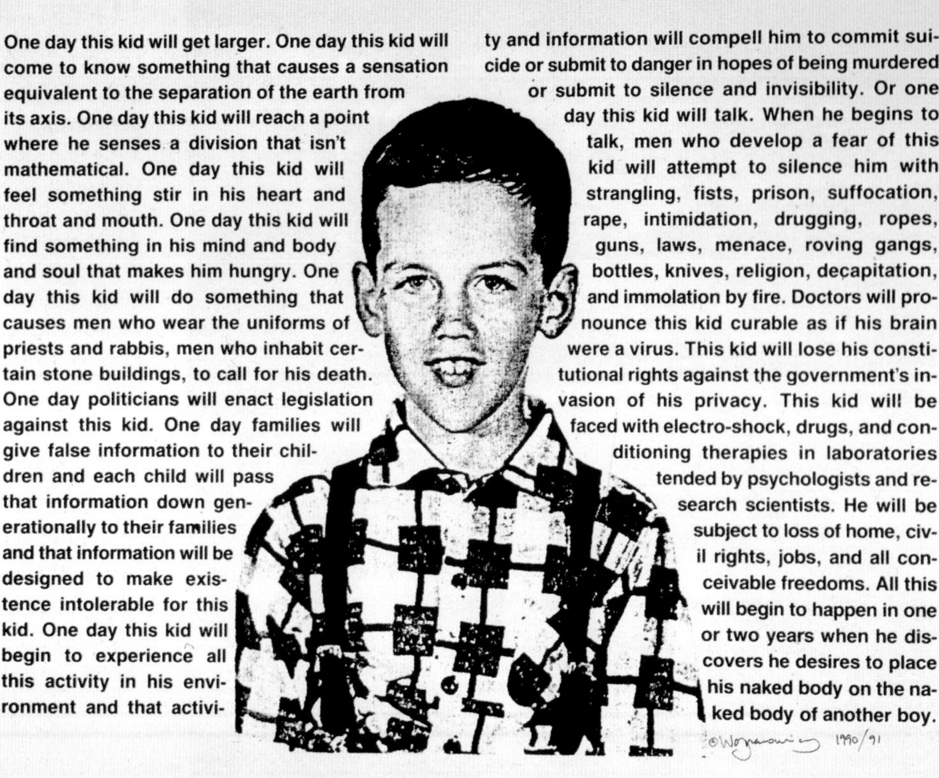

4.9 David Wojnarowicz, *Untitled (One Day this Kid)*, 1990. Photostat, 30¾ × 41" (78.1 × 104.14 cm). Whitney Museum of American Art, New York. Estate of David Wojnarowicz and P.P.O.W. Gallery, New York.

know something that causes a sensation equivalent to the separation of the earth from its axis;" and then the public control over such sensations—"One day politicians will enact legislation against this kid." The statements on the right-hand side of the portrait become increasingly violent and the repetition of "One day" stops. "When he begins to talk, men who develop a fear of this kid will attempt to silence him with strangling, fists, prison, suffocation, rape ... he will be subject to loss of home, civil rights, jobs, and all conceivable freedoms." Then the story ends simply: "All this will begin to happen in one or two years when he discovers he desires to place his naked body on the naked body of another boy." The nature of being cast aside is clarified in this work to be not merely a matter of biography or personality, but of the subjection of both to socially sanctioned hatred. The stakes for creating new spaces and languages are high.

A final defining element of Wojnarowicz's art is the artist's demand that it be made public. Alternative visions of reality had been kept private too long. As an artist, he felt he could raise an issue or express passions and ideas, but it remained for an audience to use what they found in the art to transform social reality. This did not mean that every work had to be shown on a bus or a billboard; rather, Wojnarowicz considered his oeuvre a valuable piece in the creation of a new history of, and new spirit for, the United States. "Bottom line, emotionally, even a tiny charcoal scratching done as a gesture to mark a person's response to the epidemic [of AIDS] means whole worlds to me if it is hung in public ... You can never depend on the mass media to reflect us or our needs or our states of mind; bottom line, with enough gestures we can deafen the satellites and lift the curtains surrounding the control room."[7] The importance of such exposure lay not so much in the display of the work as in the display of the reactions of those who saw it. Gestures become communication in public. Taking action demanded engagement with the public and, although, unlike Haring or Colab, Wojnarowicz did not give this process the popular appeal or a party atmosphere, he too presented the viewer with an opportunity to see and imagine a different world. Reflecting on Wojnarowicz's impact, John Carlin, art critic throughout the 1980s for the downtown *Paper Magazine*, wrote: "David was not just an artist ... He was a visionary whose work was deeply rooted in our collective daily lives yet constantly linked the everyday to some greater, unknowable force."[8]

Nan Goldin

In the summer of 1980, Nan Goldin (b. 1953), on the advice of her friend Kiki Smith (b. 1954), contributed a collection of slides to "The Times Square Show." She had began taking photographs as a teenager and later, while living in Boston and studying at the School of the Museum of Fine Arts, started using the medium to document subcultures within the city. The images she took of transvestites she befriended in Boston established an informal and intimate snapshot-approach to photography that she would continue to pursue in the late 1970s when she moved to New York. The slides she showed at "The Times Square Show" offer a scattered record of the people she knew and the places in which she lived. She photographed herself, her home, where she went at night, her friends, and what they all did. David Wojnarowicz and

Colab organizer Maggie Smith were particularly struck and drew Goldin's attention to the political nature of the themes explored in her photographs: It was at this time that Goldin began to draw out narratives within the material, transforming the collection into a slide show called *The Ballad of Sexual Dependency* that Goldin would continue to develop until 1994.

The lives she recorded throughout the 1980s and 1990s, with often shocking intimacy, were defined by meager resources, drug and alcohol abuse, and destructive relationships. The immediacy of images such as *Rise & Monty on the Lounge Chair, NYC* (1988) (**fig. 4.10**) captures Goldin's snapshot style, as well as the almost surgical skill with which she isolates emotionally gripping moments. We see Goldin and her friends lounging at the beach, drunk in bed, making love, beautiful, beaten, ecstatic, and miserable. An accompanying soundtrack featuring the likes of Maria Callas, Screamin' Jay Hawkins, Dean Martin, Yoko Ono, and Dionne Warwick helps to focus the narrative of the slideshow. Goldin refers to *The Ballad* as her *Leaves of Grass*, an apt comparison, not just because of Walt Whitman's own expansive editing process, but also because we come to know Goldin, as we do Whitman, less through self-descriptions than through the experiences and obsessions recorded in their work.

The Ballad of Sexual Dependency was published in book form in 1986. Goldin described the scope of the work, with its nearly seven hundred images, as well as its unifying themes:

> The photographs show people in terms of their images of themselves, their conditioning, their gender identification, and their relationships to each other. The women, then the men, are shown first outside in the world, then alone in their rooms; then women are shown together and men are shown together. Battered women are shown and women who have been abused, who have been subjected to violence. Some men are shown as violent. And the condition of violence is explored through things such as guns and dogs. The images of women are followed by images of prostitution, brides, and mothers, so there is a sequence of the mother, the whore, the bride, the sexual woman, and introspective woman ... The drag queens are shown as a third sex, not as men dressed as women. They are shown in a world of their own, in their clubs, in their jobs, on the street, in their home lives, and in their relationships with lovers ... It continues with couples. There are couples together and couples in bed having sex, followed by images of empty rooms, empty beds, and graves ... In spite of it all, people have a need to couple. Even when they're being destroyed, they're still coupling. The ballad of sexual dependency starts and ends with this premise, but in between there is the question as to why there is this need to couple and why it is so difficult.[9]

In the context of the early 1980s, whether we compare it with "The Times Square Show," the "Pictures" artists (see Chapter 2), or the Neo-Expressionists (see Chapter 3), *The Ballad of Sexual Dependency* seems exceedingly, almost overwhelmingly, personal. We come to know Goldin and her milieu almost too well. As its context changed to include the body and identity art of the 1990s, however, *The Ballad* changed in meaning too, appearing to open out to tell us about society and community more generally.

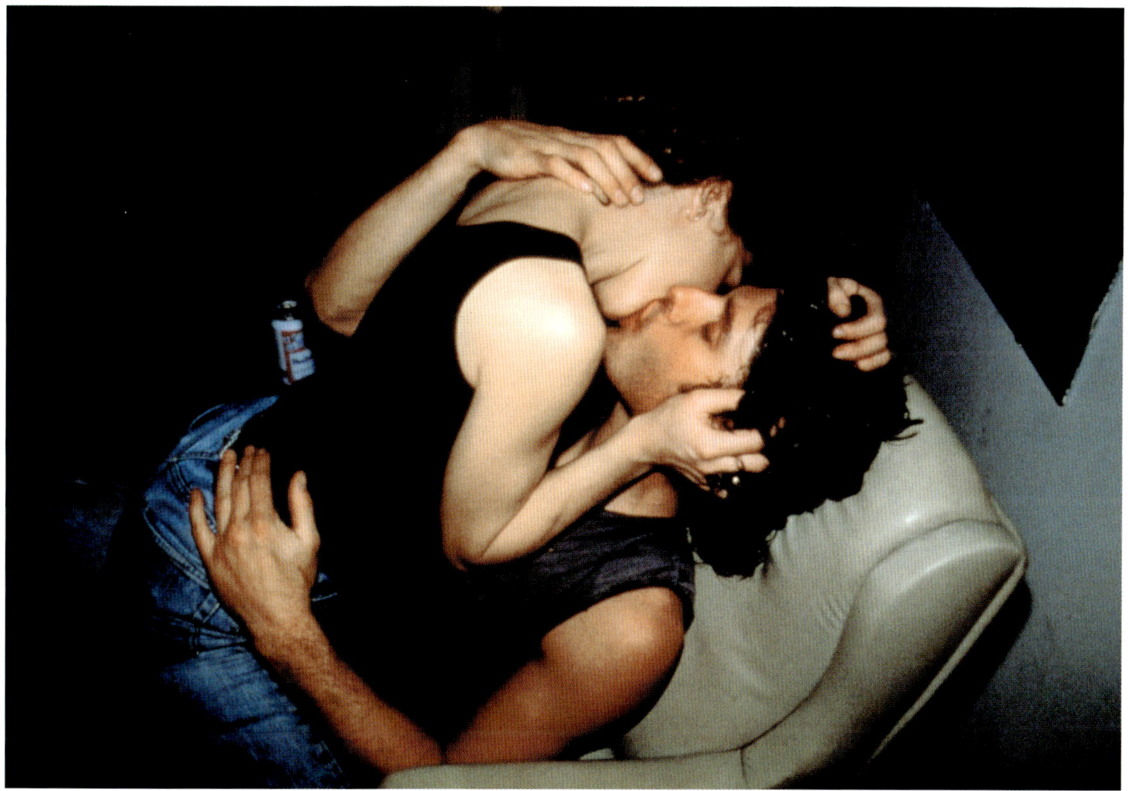

4.10 Nan Goldin, *Rise & Monty on the lounge chair, NYC*, 1988. Cibachrome, 30 × 40" (76.2 × 101.6 cm). George Eastman House Still Photograph Archive. © Nan Goldin, courtesy Matthew Marks Gallery.

Martin Wong

The work of Martin Wong (1946–99) further demonstrates the degree to which the East Village provided a destination for artists whose concerns and means of expression exceeded the Neo-Expressionist-cum-Pop stylistics and casual hedonism that dominated the U.S. art scene in the early 1980s. Like Wojnarowicz and Goldin, Wong produced art that reflects lives shaped but not defined by the official visions of American life. He arrived in New York in 1978, having been raised on the West Coast and taken a degree in ceramics before becoming involved with San Francisco-based performance groups. In New York, Wong painted and became a fixture in the East Village, orienting his life and career around the Puerto Rican art scene shaped by Miguel Piñero (1946–88), the leading figure of the Nuyorican poetry movement since the 1970s. Nuyorican was a self-conscious combination of the language and culture of Puerto Rico and New York: Its participants insisted that the roots of their art and identity were spread out amongst the buildings and streets of the neighborhood. Puerto Rico was an important reference and a source of inspiration, but New York was home. Nuyorican poetry and Wong's painting drew on and reflected the wide range of languages and cultures present in the city.

Wong's first opportunity to show in New York was at ABC No Rio in the gallery's "Crime Show" in 1982. He contributed several pieces that took sensational quotations such as "Psychiatrists Testify: Demon Dogs Drive Man to Murder" from tabloid newspapers and translated them into schematic renderings of hands signing the words, which he called "paintings for the deaf." It was at the show's opening that he met Piñero. Shortly after, the poet initiated a collaboration, suggesting Wong make a painting of a playground where a protégé of his had just finished a large graffiti mural. Wong agreed and the result was their first collaboration, *Attorney Street (Handball Court with Autobiographical Poem by Piñero)* (1982–84) (**fig. 4.11**). As the title indicates, the painting had evolved from Piñero's initial conception into a portrait of the poet in the form of an urban landscape and a painted poem. Piñero brought Wong the poem while he was painting and requested that it be included in the image. This established a pattern for collaboration between the two artists: Piñero would contribute a text and Wong would use it in a painting. In *Attorney Street*, Wong transcribed the poem in the gray sky above the tenements that surround the playground. Below, floating on the surface of the painting itself and partially obscuring the scene, Wong "signs" lines Piñero had recently spoken in a controversial film, *Fort Apache: The Bronx* (1981). This signed text is then translated below in a trompe-l'oeil plaque, itself placed on a trompe-l'oeil wooden frame. The script reads: "It's the real deal Neal I'm going to rock your world make your planets twirl, ain't no wack attack," and echoes the bravado of Piñero's autobiographical poem. This doubling of lines written by and for Piñero, like the combination of confessional and conventional language employed in the poem itself, is repeated in Wong's framing device. The entire scene appears doubly framed, once in a painted edge of bricks that surrounds the canvas, and again by the illusionistically painted wood on the frame itself. In this and

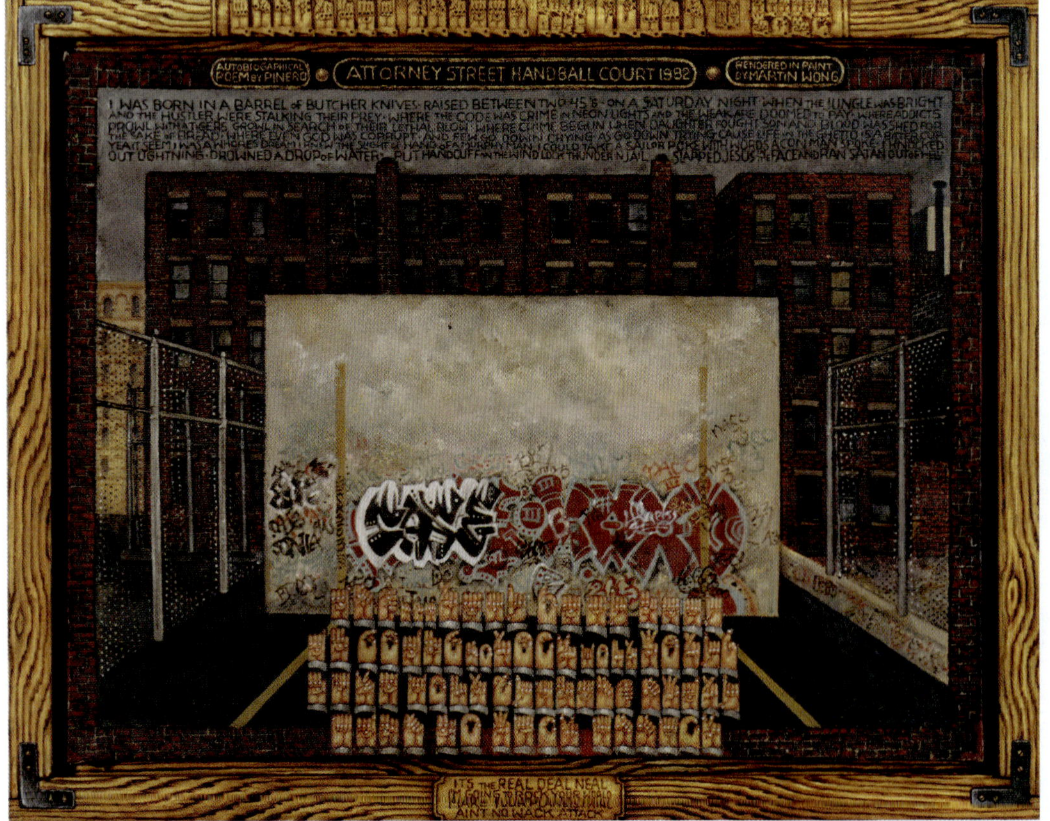

4.11 Martin Wong, *Attorney Street (Handball Court with Autobiographical Poem by Piñero)*, 1982–84. Oil on canvas, 35½ × 48" (90.2 × 121.9 cm). The Metropolitan Museum of Art, New York. Courtesy of the Estate of Martin Wong and P.P.O.W. Gallery, New York.

other Wong paintings, scenes of daily life in the Lower East Side become settings for the transcription of words from the neighborhood, both spoken and written. Wong's painting is a meditation on language and representation as well as a testimony to the self-conscious translation of art and culture.

Art in the Community

Goldin's and Wong's images of community were one form in which life on the streets appeared on gallery walls. Community engagement, however, took a variety of forms, many of which did not look or function like traditional art at all. In the case of Group Material, the art consisted of curating exhibits of what people in their working-class Latino neighborhood considered art, or publishing information about the history of AIDS. Group Material member Tim Rollins also adopted the strategy of creating institutional structures to address marginal communities. Rollins worked outside the art world, using his job as an art teacher in the public schools to create a collaborative project with his students. Called Tim Rollins and the Kids Of Survival, the group transformed the educational experience of its kids and thanks to Rollins's artworld experience put its art, with references to both middle-school curriculum and urban life, in front of a national and soon international audience. Between reshaping the art world and infiltrating the public sector there existed a range of options for artists eager to address the politics of daily life with everyday citizens. Sculptors and performance and multi-media artists took to the streets, creating works such as those of David Hammons and Pepón Osorio that drew on the aesthetics and iconography of local communities in order to make publicly accessible installations and monuments. Joining the institutional critique implied in the alternative practices of every artist discussed in this section with an interest in photography, architecture, and engineering, Krzysztof Wodiczko solicited homeless New Yorkers to help him create a proposal for multi-use vehicles for living on the streets. Simultaneously Wodiczko developed a projection system with which he covered public monuments with images of poverty and war. By the 1990s, artists had introduced a wide range of models for creating art that was embedded in the social lives of its viewers as well as the political ideals of its creators.

Group Material

In 1979, a dozen or so artists opened a storefront on East 13th Street. Like the other galleries coming to populate the East Village, Group Material, as both the group and the space were called, identified the neighborhood as hospitable to artists seeking to base their activities on the day-to-day life of the city, rather than on the ins and outs of the art market. It also viewed the community not as subject matter but as collaborators. The stalwarts of the group, Doug Ashford (b. 1958), Julie Ault (b. 1957), Tim Rollins (b. 1955), and Mundy McLaughlin (b. 1958), explained their mission:

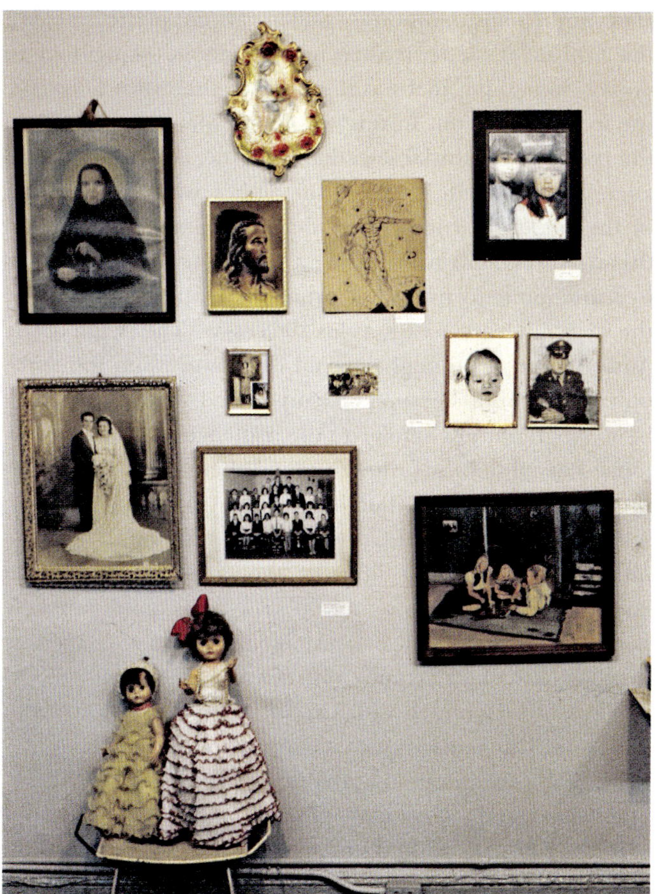

4.12 Group Material, *The People's Choice (Arroz con Mango)*, 1981. Exhibition view from Group Material's exhibition space on East 13th Street, New York. Courtesy Group Material.

> Group Material was founded as a constructive response to the unsatisfactory ways in which art has been conceived, produced, distributed, and taught in American society ... Group Material researches work from artists, non-artists, the media, the streets. Our approach is oriented toward both people not well acquainted with the specialized languages of fine art and an audience that has a long-standing interest in questions of art theory and practice. In our exhibitions, Group Material reveals the multiplicity of meanings that surround any vital social issue. Our project is clear. We invite everyone to question the entire culture we have taken for granted.[10]

Unlike the East Village scene and alternative spaces more generally, Group Material rarely produced objects and scrupulously avoided using its activities to advance individual members' careers. It aimed to be more of a community center than an art gallery. This contrast in focus between self and community can be seen in Group Material's approach to curating when compared to events such as "The Times Square Show."

The most celebrated exhibition held in the 13th Street space was 1981's "The People's Choice," or "Arroz con Mango" (a Cuban expression meaning "What a Mess") as it came to be subtitled (**fig. 4.12**). Taking inspiration from the

Dada and Fluxus traditions of making art out of the everyday, the group sent a letter to their new neighbors, asking them to donate something that was displayed in their own home for use in an exhibition. In this way Group Material transferred the power of curatorial selection from the artists to the audience. Honoring the death of the author with a celebration of the viewer, of course, was not new. Roland Barthes had theorized this shift from basing a work's meaning in the artist's intentions to finding it primarily in the experience of the viewer at least as early as his 1968 essay "The Death of the Author," and his thoughts would exert a growing influence on the art world. These newly empowered viewers tended to be demographically similar to the audiences that had always looked at modern art, however, and the objects they interpreted usually looked familiar as well. Handing over the selection process as did Group Material resulted in an exhibition that looked very different, though not entirely alien. Paintings, mostly amateur, and photographs, predominately portraits, hung near less conventional ornaments such as a collections of PEZ candy dispensers and toy animals. As Doug Ashford pointed out, Group Material's projects were not appeals to replace one category of object with another. Instead, they proposed that the various components of art—intellectual and emotional, political and aesthetic, avant-garde and kitsch—existed simultaneously and together could be oriented toward asserting the rights, identities, and agency of individuals. Such a conviction, Group Material claimed, had a long history, extending back to the Realist movements of the nineteenth century.

After Group Material presented "The People's Choice (Arroz con Mango)," it spent only a few more months on East 13th Street. Unlike Colab, it had never intended to create a long-term alternative gallery space. Its mission was to "direct ... our energies to the demands of the social conditions as opposed to the demands of the art market," yet soon after moving into the 13th Street location, group members had found themselves attending more to the logistics of running a gallery than to social concerns.[11] As a consequence, they gave up the lease and abandoned the space. Ashford claimed that what Group Material had always done differently from other groups was to attend to issues of context. Now that they had no physical space to manage, its members turned to other contexts, including uptown museums, buses and subways, and even Midwestern colleges. In 1987, with the group now consisting of Ashford, Ault, and Felix Gonzalez-Torres (1957–96), it launched a two-year project consisting of exhibitions, lectures, meetings, and publications investigating the state of contemporary society in the United States. Called *Democracy*, the event was housed and sponsored by the Dia Foundation, a private arts organization in Manhattan created to provide long-term support to artists working in the Minimalist tradition. In the late 1980s, Dia was expanding its identity and *Democracy* fit this agenda well. Ashford, Ault, and Gonzalez-Torres used the platform to address political issues and, just as importantly, to stretch notions about what constituted art as a category of objects and practices. *Democracy* was a startling example of their ability to manipulate a variety of forms, from theoretical lectures on topics such as race and representation, to public hearings addressing concerns such as AIDS and education, to objects ranging from abstract canvases to pamphlets. Communication was the basic material of *Democracy*. Though critics complained that the high-culture venue limited the efficacy of the project by insuring its audience was predominately artworld cognoscenti, choosing to speak about politics in an art gallery such as Dia transformed an established and well-heeled cultural institution into a political one.

If *Democracy* transformed a classic white-walled gallery into something that looked more like a series of counseling rooms, or even government offices, other projects undertaken by the

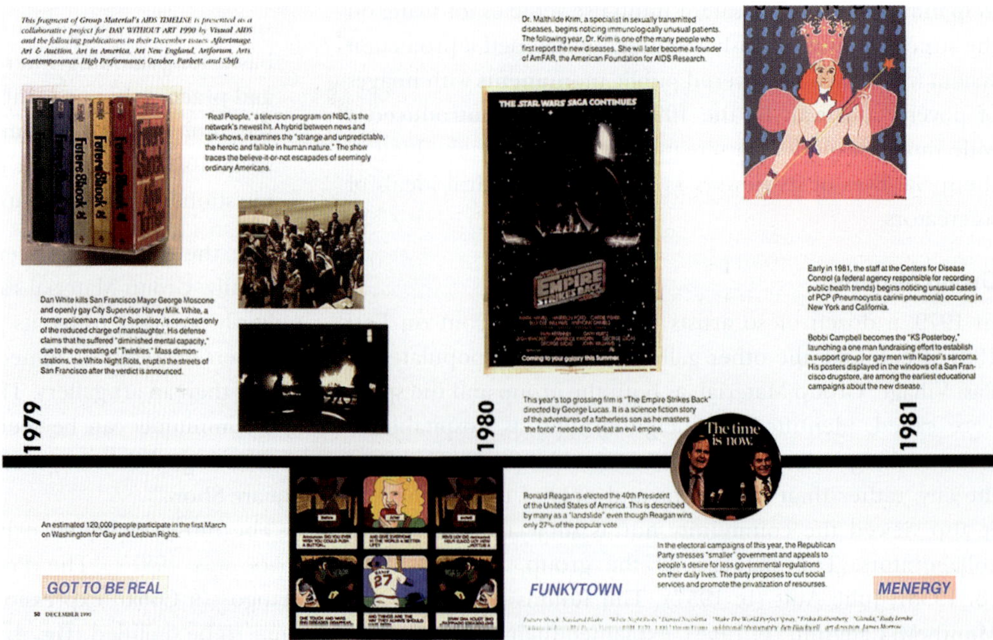

4.13 Group Material, ***AIDS Timeline***, 1990. This particular fragment was published in *Arts* magazine Vol. 50–51, December 1990. Courtesy Group Material.

artists fit more comfortably in their environments. In 1983, Group Material bought advertising space in the subways and, like Barbara Kruger or Jenny Holzer, enlisted the media of capitalism to circulate messages and materials that were not for sale. For this project, it invited 103 artists to design posters for display in the subway system, thereby creating a project that was fragmented, dispersed, and the product of different personalities. The work thus mirrored contemporary ideas about the fragmentation and heterogeneity of identity. In December 1990, Group Material created another fragmentary event, this time a single object, the *AIDS Timeline*, which was taken apart and presented in extracts in different places (**fig. 4.13**). Unlike a conventional timeline that condenses information for easy consumption, the *AIDS Timeline* was published in sections in different art journals. Short spreads presenting incidents in the history of the epidemic appeared in a variety of art journals including *Art in America*, *Artforum*, *Arts* magazine, *October*, and *Parkett*. Each portion was full of details, but, due to Group Material's decision not to publish the entire timeline in a single journal, necessarily partial, as if to remind the reader of the partiality of all mass media. With the *AIDS Timeline*, Group Material used art and the art industry to write a history of something that had been obscured by the mass media. Moreover, reconstructing these fragments of history leads into a story of politics and disease rather than the one of aesthetics generally expected in such a context.

David Hammons

David Hammons (b. 1943) was born in Springfield, Illinois, and educated in Los Angeles, where he sought out fellow African-American artist Charles White (1918–79), a veteran of the Harlem Renaissance. The latter's commitment to addressing African-American issues in the context of national discussions of race and economics, as well as his dedication to printmaking, impressed Hammons. Some of the most dramatic early pieces by Hammons were experimental prints made using his body as a stamp. He covered parts of himself in oils and then pressed them onto the paper, imprinting a crushed likeness of himself on the page. Additional elements from flags to weapons were similarly applied to the image, and these oil impressions were then dusted with ground pigment to produce a final image. Many of the prints evoke political oppression and were used in civil-rights activities in the 1970s. Hammons also began to explore sculpture, making use of materials with metaphorical, biographical, and linguistic relationships to the history and current reality of African-American life: A shovel blade with chain link, for instance, was titled *Spade with Chains* (1973). Objects, however, would soon appear as tangential to Hammons's art. Rejecting the conventions of art and eliminating elements such as frames and labels, Hammons threatened to eliminate the art object altogether: His work has included acts such as kicking a trashcan through the city, selling snowballs, and exhibiting a vast, empty, and darkened gallery. This condition of artlessness corresponds to the artist's disdain for the way society attributes value to art objects. Hammons has explained that the art is the process; once there is a finished work, "it becomes a political object, it's not even art anymore."[12]

In *Higher Goals* (1986) (**fig. 4.14**), Hammons produced what has become an iconic public work addressing African-American culture, African aesthetics, and American economic politics. The work consists of telephone poles decorated with bottle caps applied in geometric patterns reminiscent of African beadwork and textiles. At the top, raised 40 feet from the ground, are backboards and basketball hoops. Open to the sky and produced out of doors in

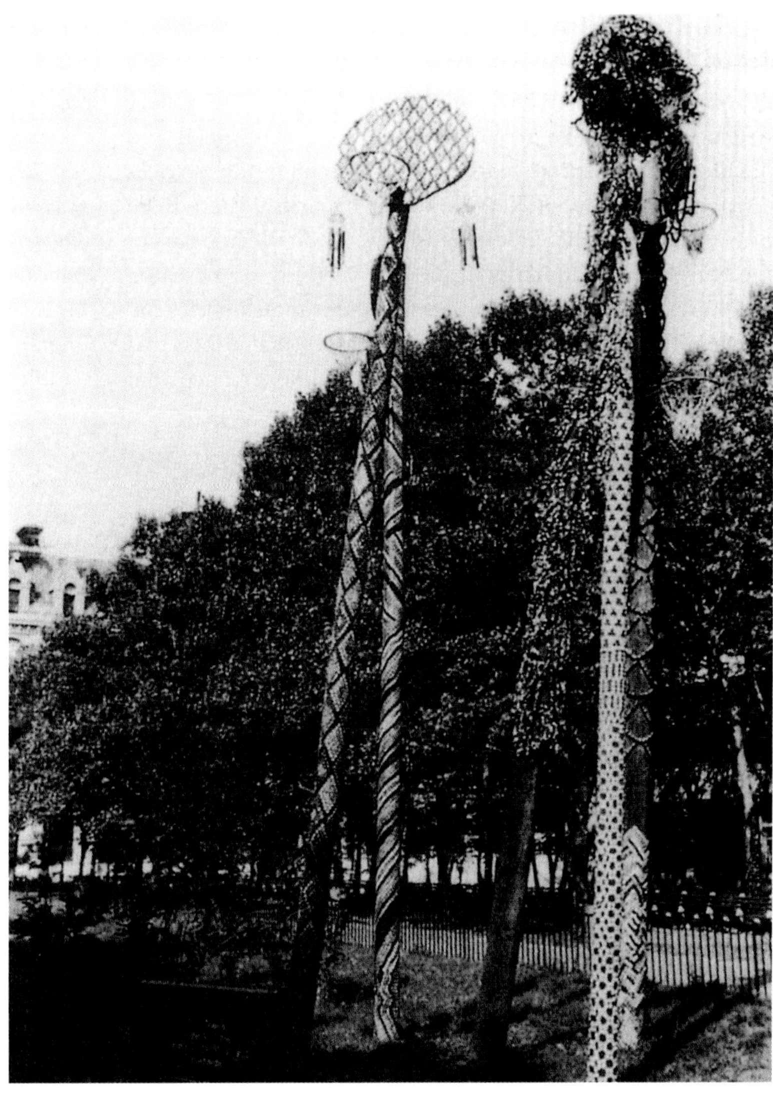

4.14 David Hammons, *Higher Goals*, 1986. Poles, basketball hoops, and bottle caps, height 40' (12.2 m). Shown installed in Brooklyn, New York, 1986. Courtesy Jack Tilton Gallery.

the very spaces the work would occupy, *Higher Goals* embodies a boundless spiritual quality Hammons finds outside the studio. The artist, an athlete and serious sports fan, identifies the grace and invention required of athletes as being akin to those required in other disciplines such as jazz, dance, and art. Likewise, the history of basketball as a sport adopted and reinvented by the African-American community conveys the culturally specific nature of Hammons's practice. The work is also anti-basketball—a critique of the cult of the sport that feeds African-American men with a fantasy of success that is rarely achieved and only at significant cost to the wider education of the community. A 1985 incarnation of the piece stood on the corner of 125th and Lenox Avenue in Harlem, where Malcolm X had given speeches, and in many ways the sculpture echoes the activist's concerns with its multivocal references to Africa and America, past and present, personal and public, the capacity for greatness and warnings about risk. *Higher Goals* conveys the sublime quality of a well-placed jump shot, the audacity of racial pride, and an exhortation to young men to strive for a future more accessible than a jump shot at a 40-foot-high hoop.

Pepón Osorio

Pepón Osorio (b. 1955) also stepped outside the gallery system both to make art and exhibit it. Osorio trained and practiced as a social worker for the children's services division of the City of New York after his arrival there from his native Puerto Rico in the mid-1970s. As he became part of the Nuyorican community in the mid-1980s, Osorio created sculptures and installations that reflected upon his circumstances. He focused his attention on issues that concerned the local community and embraced a studio practice that mimicked the accumulation and decoration he felt defined the Puerto Rican immigrant aesthetic. *La Bicycleta* (1985) (**fig. 4.15**), one of Osorio's first assemblages, exhibits characteristic qualities of humor and poignancy. The piece was created as part of a set for a performance by Merián Soto (b. 1954) called *Cocinado* (*Cooking*) about the evolution of Puerto Rican traditions. Osorio's objects brought features of Puerto Rican homes into the realm of art, exaggerating and underlining certain practices and tastes. Palm trees dot the mud flaps, evoking an island breeze on a city street as one imagines the bike coursing through Lower Manhattan, plastic branches bending in the wind. His sculptures of the 1980s often displayed a similar working process to that evident in *La Bicycleta*: simple domestic objects covered with hundreds of decorative elements including plastic flowers, jewelry, dolls, party favors, decals, glitter, plastic trees, toy animals, and all types of kitsch materials. In aesthetic terms, the work reflects the impulse Osorio found in the Puerto Rican community of "creating an abundance that is not there," masking the effects of poverty in large part forced on the community by economic inequities in the U.S. with an overload of inexpensive objects.[13] As such, in Osorio's hands vernacular aesthetics reveal economic and psychological realities. His content, however, like the decoration of *La Bicycleta* that even extends down to the pedals, exceeds such insular dialogues. *La Bicycleta*—as an object of, if not actually in, motion—was intended to evoke migration from the Caribbean to New York, while as a specific object it recalls the decorated bikes used by Puerto Rican tradesmen he remembered from his childhood. The sculpture thus serves as a general metaphor of a communal experience and as a specific emblem of personal memory. Critic and artist Coco Fusco

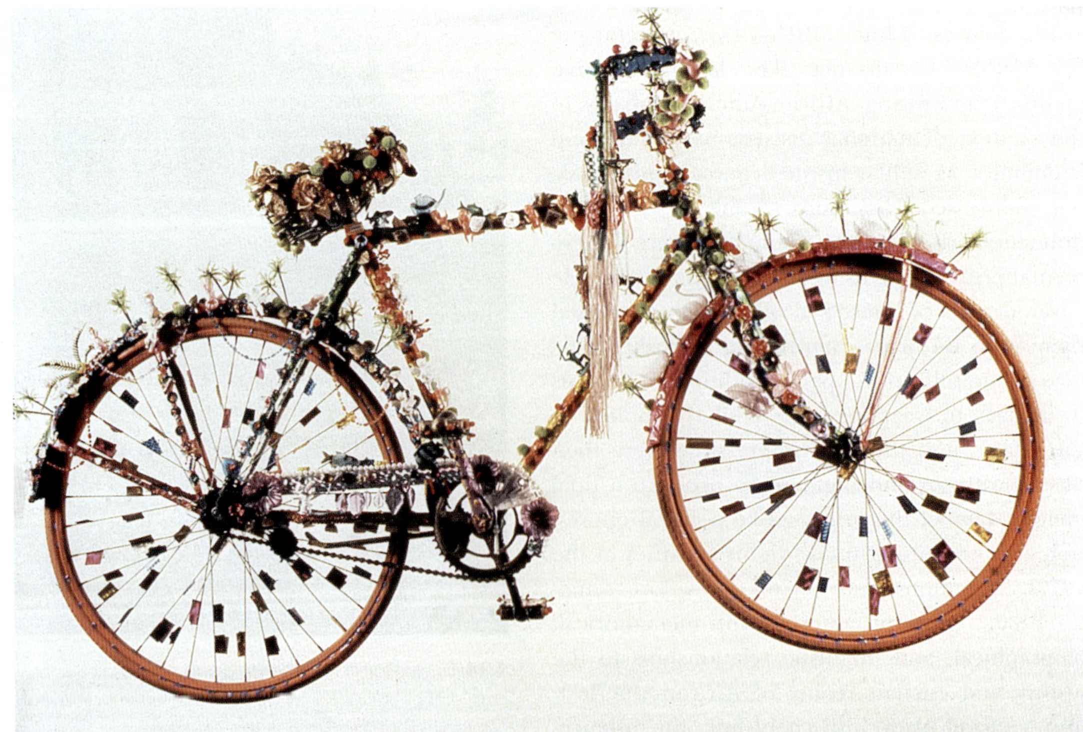

4.15 Pepón Osorio, *La Bicycleta*, 1985. Mixed media, 39 × 24 × 60" (99.06 × 60.96 × 152.4 cm). Courtesy Ronald Feldman Fine Arts, New York.

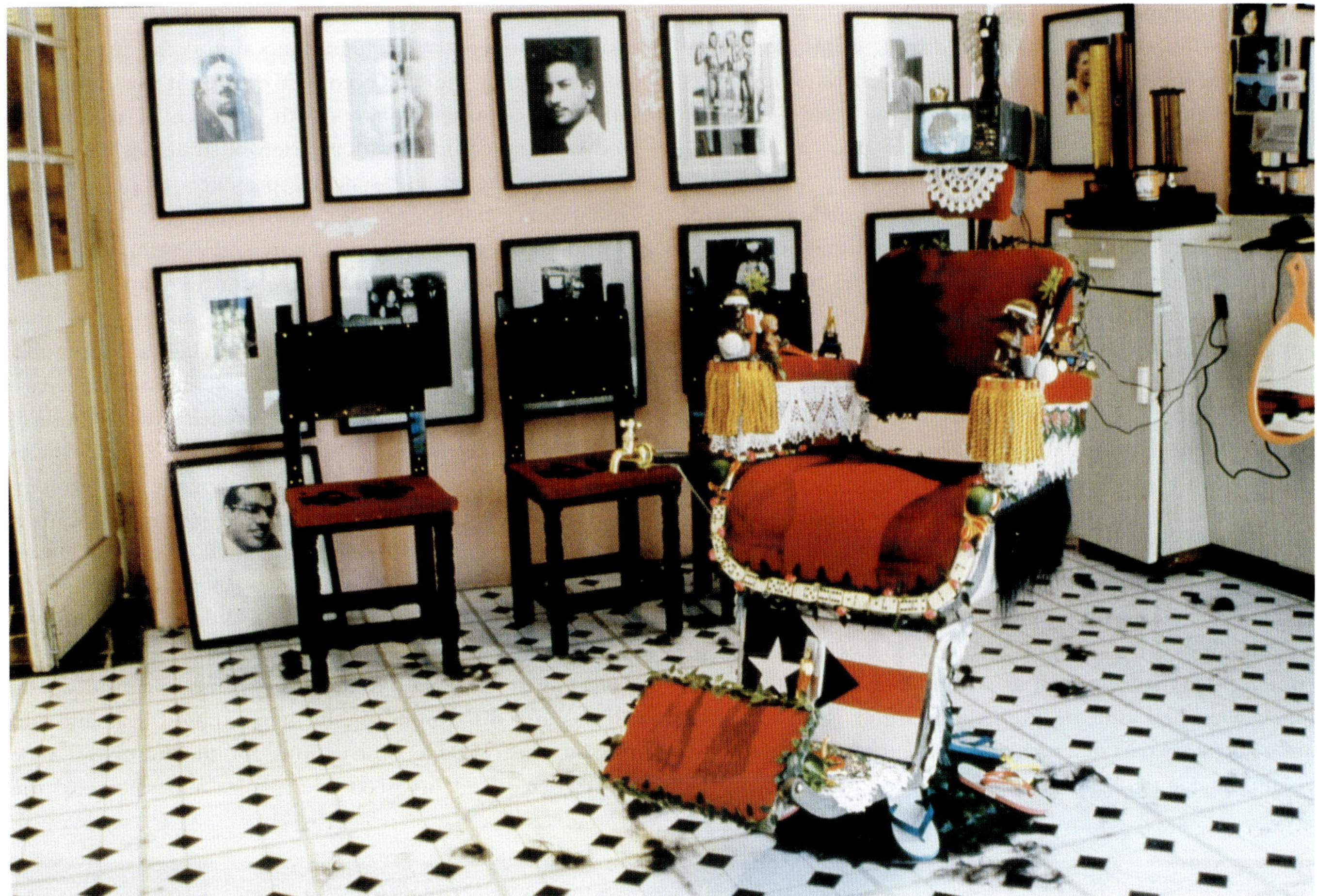

4.16 Pepón Osorio, *No Crying in the Barbershop*, 1994. Installation in a barbershop in Hartford, Connecticut. Courtesy Ronald Feldman Fine Arts, New York.

has seen this deliberate and multivalent use of kitsch as an act of resistance, parodying the outsider's view of Puerto Rican aesthetics as quaint folklore and demonstrating instead that a critical artistic practice can be rooted in the Nuyorican home.

Audiences from outside the Puerto Rican community, in New York and beyond, have consistently responded positively to Osorio's work. He was given a prominent position in the 1993 Whitney Biennial, is regularly reviewed in the mainstream art press, and was awarded the MacArthur "genius" grant, a $500,000 prize for his contribution to contemporary art. Nonetheless, Osorio has insisted that the potential for his work to transcend its local roots must not overwhelm its power to respond to the particularity of its sources in local cultures. To this end he creates very literally from within the community. *The Scene of the Crime (Whose Crime?)* (1993), Osorio's contribution to the Whitney Biennial, is an overloaded domestic setting cordoned off with police tape which reveals, through broken glass and overturned objects, that a crime has been committed at the museum. It brought, Osorio said, a piece of "the south Bronx to Madison ave." After the exhibition, however, he decided he no longer wanted to show his work first in museums; he felt the need to orient his exhibition practice, like his studio practice, to his Latino community. His next project after the biennial was *No Crying in the Barbershop* (1994), an installation commissioned by the Hartford, Connecticut public arts organization Real Art Ways (**fig. 4.16**). For the piece, Osorio occupied an abandoned barbershop in a Latino neighborhood in Hartford and filled it—overfilled it in his characteristic manner—with materials relating to the upbringing of Latino men. On every surface Osorio displayed signs of the growing male, posters of heroes, and portraits of loved ones. A mural depicting intertwined roses and bullets dominated one wall, asserting the presence of death in male-identity formation. Chairs were decorated with all sorts of objects—baseballs, Puerto Rican flags, baseball caps, hair-picks—all giving substance to stereotypes of Latino machismo. But, as Osorio pointed out, male identity is not the sum total of the stereotypes that form around it. Attitudes and emotions typically labeled feminine are also part of male life and signs of these were also present in the barbershop. Visible on the chairs were lace doilies, plastic flowers, garlands, and dolls, and the walls—bearing photos of baseball players, musicians, and father-figures—were painted pink. The most striking feature of the installation was the sound and sight, on small video monitors set in the headrests of each of the five red-velvet chairs, of men crying. At the heart of this male world there was sensitivity and emotion; in the midst of all this machismo was cathartic weeping. Since *No Crying at the Barbershop*, Osorio has presented work in storefronts, private homes, as well as in museums and galleries all over the world.

Krzysztof Wodiczko

One of the exciting possibilities offered by the kind of work discussed in this chapter is that it proposed that art did not require a specially designated space; it could be a process, a conversation that functioned in relation to an audience and an environment outside the confines of a gallery or museum. Polish-born multi-media artist Krzysztof Wodiczko (b. 1943) developed objects and imagery that display the unspoken mechanisms of urban life in the public spaces of the city. In the mid-1980s, after having emigrated first to Canada and then to the U.S., he began to produce a series of prototypes for vehicles designed with and for the homeless and to develop what has become his signature medium: large-scale images projected onto public monuments and city buildings. In both cases, Wodiczko makes visible facts of contemporary society such as poverty and war that are customarily pushed aside. If, as the artist argues, such social ills are a necessary part of a society such as ours, oriented toward economic competition, then it falls to the political artist to reveal their details much as the realist painters and muckraking documentary photographers did at the turn of the last century. By the late twentieth century it was no longer sufficient to present viewers with the face of poverty, so Wodiczko has come up with a variety of strategies for depicting the character and systemic presence of poverty and violence in contemporary life.

Wodiczko's vehicles were begun and developed in conjunction with the homeless people who were to use them. Essentially an elaborate and enlarged shopping cart, they provided their users with storage space, shelter, and mobility (**fig. 4.17**). They did not resemble houses or apartments, as though the needs of the homeless were those of the middle class in miniature. Neither were the vehicles the result of romantic visions of the homeless as wanderers unbound by the tether of material possession. Rather, Wodiczko and his collaborators designed a series of prototypes that articulate the sometimes startling relationship between the needs of the homeless and those of the housed as revealed by Wodiczko's project. Both have possessions to protect as well as health and security issues to consider. The vehicles and discussions about them exposed dramatic and morally unacceptable obstructions for the homeless. One interviewee noted his need to organize and safeguard the

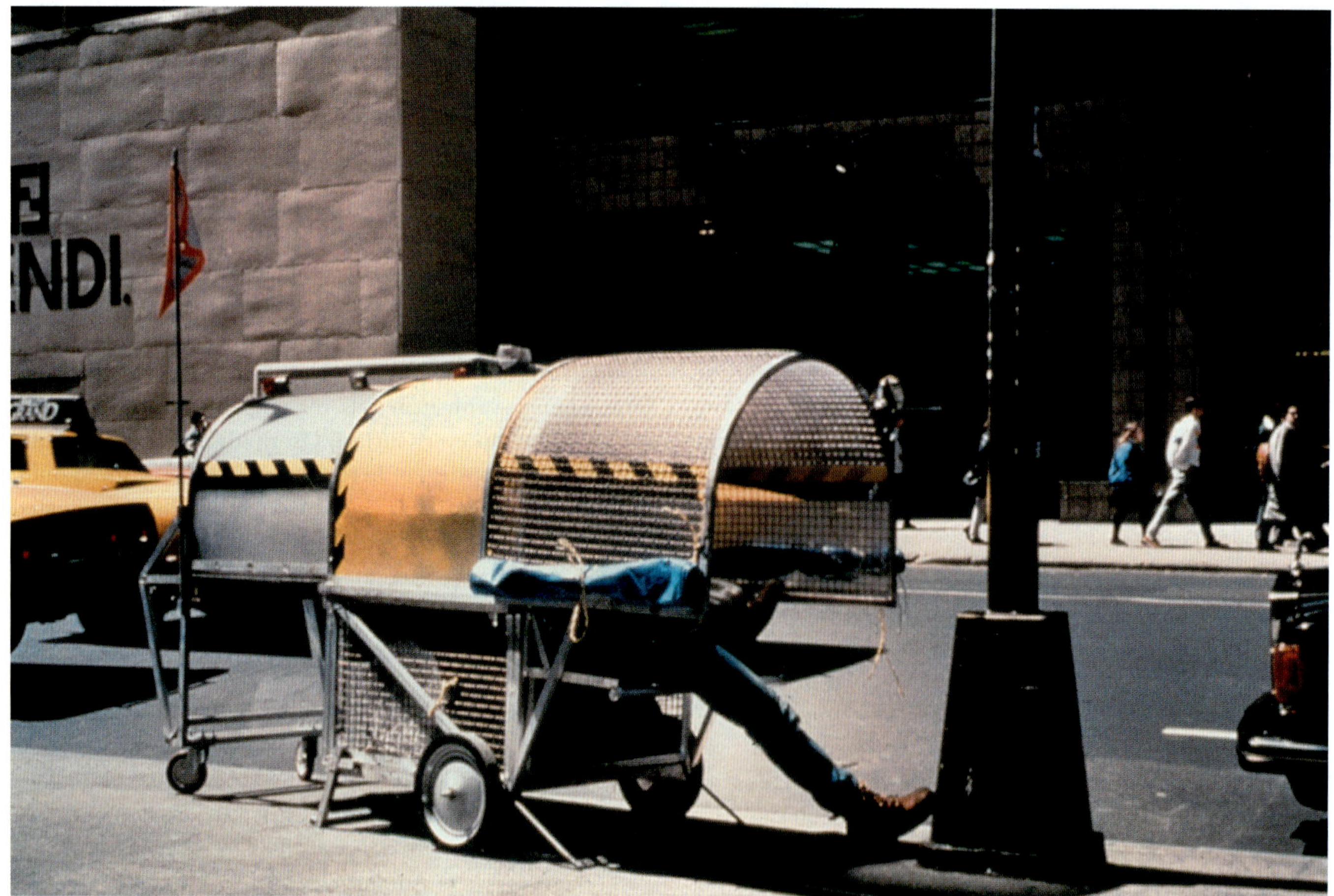

4.17 Krzysztof Wodiczko, ***Homeless Vehicle Project with David Lurie***, 1988–89. Aluminum and mixed media. Dimensions variable. Variant 3 of 4 pictured at Trump Tower, New York. © Krzysztof Wodiczko. Courtesy Galerie Lelong, New York.

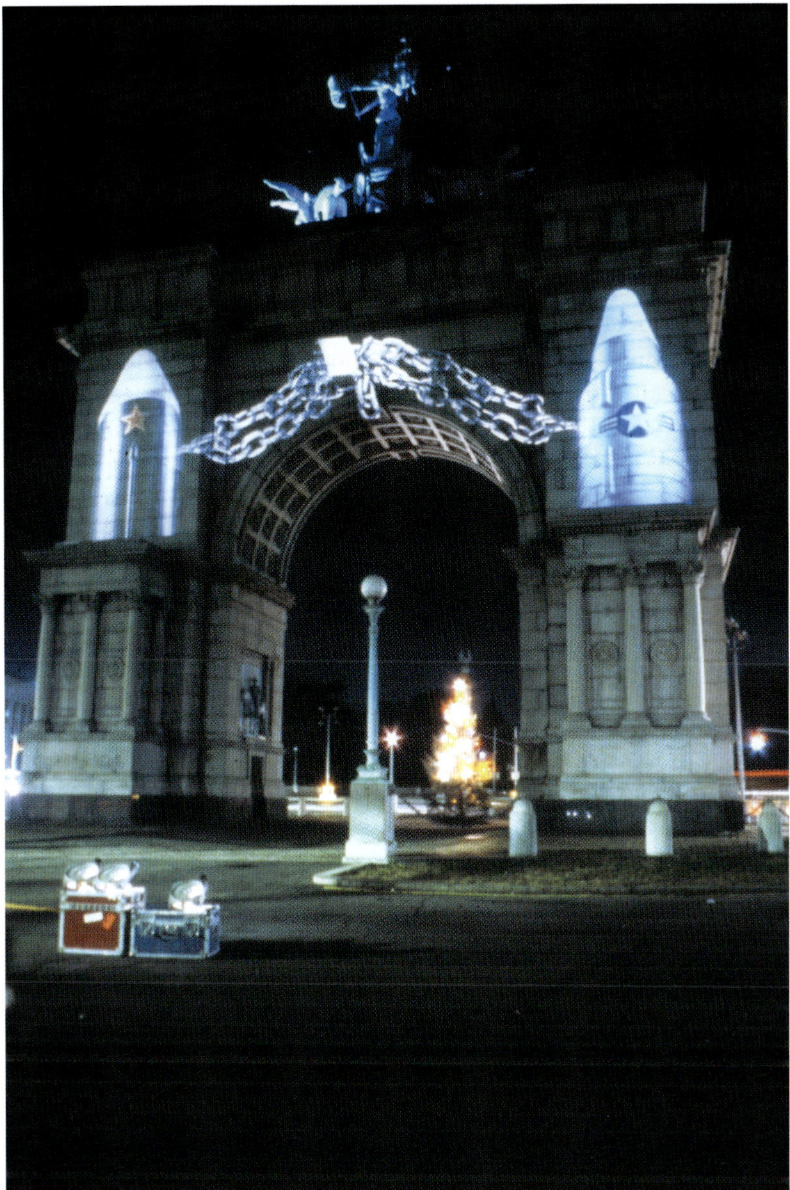

4.18 Krzysztof Wodiczko, ***Projection Soldiers and Sailors Memorial Arch, Grand Army Plaza***, 1985–86. Public projection at the Soldiers and Sailors Memorial Arch, Brooklyn, New York. © Krzysztof Wodiczko. Courtesy Galerie Lelong, New York.

cans and bottles he recycled for money. He also expressed concern that the vehicles should permit visibility and a ready exit so as to reduce the risk of being attacked or crushed in a garbage truck. Wodiczko's vehicles embody such concerns, but do not solve, and clearly cannot solve, all of them: Art cannot stop aggravated assault on a homeless person, nor can it fix the problem that part of the population lives in fear of actually being thrown into a garbage truck. This is part of Wodiczko's point. The homeless vehicles represented an effort to make issues and people who are otherwise overlooked momentarily visible.

Wodizcko's projections are equally responsive to their political and social context. At the Soldiers and Sailors Memorial Arch, Grand Army Plaza, Brooklyn, Wodiczko projected two images of missiles, one U.S., one Soviet, onto either side of the otherwise empty northern side of the monument (**fig. 4.18**). Joining the two was a third projection of a chain and padlock which conveyed the sense that as 1985 turned into 1986 (the projection lasted from 11:30 p.m. on December 31, 1985 to 00:30 a.m. on January 1, 1986) the futures of the two superpowers were inextricably bound together. Clearly the political message is dependent on a general knowledge of the relationship between the nations in what turned out to be the twilight of the Cold War. The work itself relies on the relationship between the images and their ground, the Soldiers and Sailors Memorial Arch, which was built to commemorate the victorious return of the Union troops after the Civil War. The arch is set apart from the surrounding city by a very busy circle of traffic, but it has a history that Wodiczko found significant. While the decorated south side of the monument proclaims victory in a burst of Neoclassical figures, inside the arch, two realistically rendered figures, President Lincoln and General Grant, look toward an unknown future. The two leaders appear calm, pensive, even exhausted as they face the work of recovery, a future that the sculptors, even many years later, in 1889, when the arch was commissioned, did not try to represent. Wodiczko noted in particular the sensitivity of the horses ridden by Lincoln and Grant, created by the American Realist artist Thomas Eakins (1844–1916). They are not the heroic chargers of the sort that usually proclaim victory; they look real. Once appropriated into the projection, the arch itself adds histories that deepen the relationship between the insecurity and fear of the Cold War period and the cost of wars past. At midnight, fireworks lit up the sky, giving an explosive accent to the military images from past and present. As the New Year celebrations then dimmed, the projection was turned off, leaving its future existence and interpretation entirely dependent on those who had seen it for themselves or heard about it from others. The work thus passed into the care of its audience.

John Ahearn and Tim Rollins and K.O.S.

The difficulty of producing socially engaged public art in the 1980s is conveyed in compelling terms by the experience and work of John Ahearn (b. 1951). In the later 1970s, Ahearn began working on sculptural murals in the Bronx. His medium was plaster casts taken from living subjects; he had begun his practice with Colab, making portraits of his friends in the East Village. After the opening of Fashion Moda, where he met Rigoberto Torres (b. 1960), he insinuated himself into the community in the South Bronx, to which, encouraged by Torres, he would soon move and where he continued to live and work. Outside the familiar community of the East Village and without a studio, Ahearn set up an *ad hoc* space to make art on the sidewalk near his new home. He reached out to the neighborhood, inviting kids and adults to join the project, which had what he has described as often approximating a summer-camp atmosphere. Though the spirit was light-hearted, the stakes were high for all involved. Ahearn's appearance—first as a visitor, then as a resident—was greeted with a curiosity not unlike that accorded to Group Material down on 13th Street, but also with a degree of hostility. Whites had left the Bronx for the suburbs years ago, and the borough now largely appeared in the public imagination through the lens of tabloid headlines such as those illustrated in Martin Wong's paintings and in movies such as *Fort Apache: The Bronx* (1981), which was shut down in New York and had its release delayed across the East Coast by the Bronx-based "Committee Against Fort Apache." This community action group objected to what it saw as its dehumanizing representations of Puerto Ricans and its legitimization of violence in the narrative of the film itself and by extension on the streets. As one of Ahearn's neighbors who would become a close friend and model for several works reported, everyone felt that whites would return to the Bronx only when they thought they could change the area to suit themselves. The perception that art-making of the sort Ahearn was engaging in was the first step in a process of gentrification—a concern being theorized at the time in critiques of the East Village scene, where artistic success had led to rising rents—underlay the suspicion directed toward the white artist. Consequently, even as Ahearn was welcomed into the neighborhood, in no small part due to the generosity of Torres and his family in whose building he lived, his home was broken into and some of his installations were vandalized.

Ahearn cast his lifelike sculptures in poses surprising for their snapshot-like immediacy and painted with great emotional sensitivity. Once they began to be seen, people quickly volunteered to be Ahearn's subjects and readily became collaborators, teaching him about the community and assisting in the creation of objects that were significant to them as well as to the artist. The casting process was difficult, requiring the subject to remain still and breathe through straws while his or her entire face was covered with plaster. The sitters received a copy of the resulting sculpture. Briefly, Ahearn recounts, between 1979 and 1983, there was a convergence of the needs and expectations of the neighborhood, himself, and the art world. Art could provide representation for a community that found an ally in the artist. Uptown, well past the blue-chip galleries and collectors' homes, it seemed, was suddenly the center of the art world. Ahearn was not the only one to feel this way. Fashion Moda thrived and the neighborhood was the subject

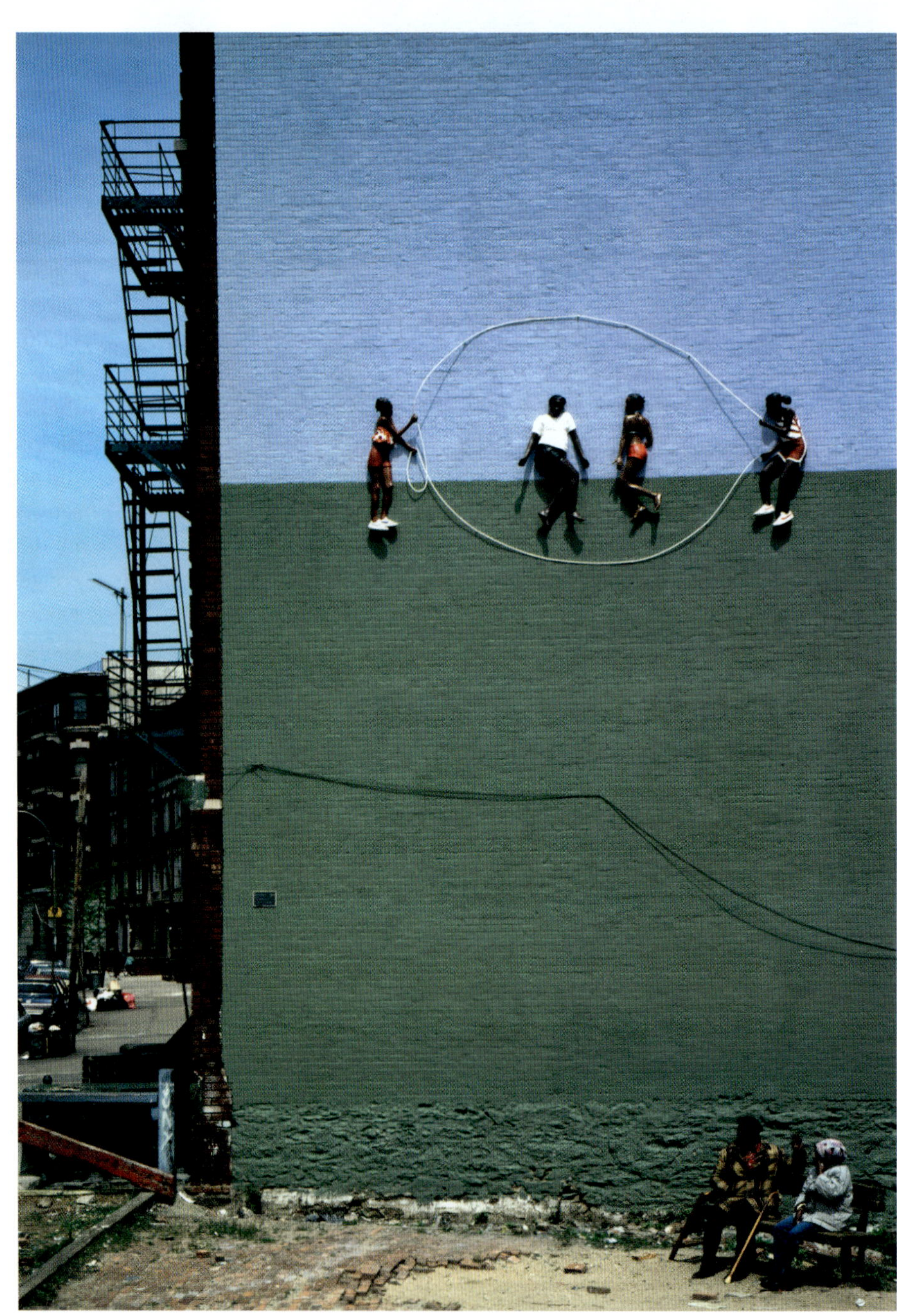

4.19 John Ahearn, *Homage to the People of the South Bronx: Double Dutch at Kelly Street 1: Freida, Jevette, Towana, Stacey*, 1981–82. Cast fiberglass, oil, and cable, each figure 54 × 54 × 12" (137 × 137 × 30.5 cm). Image courtesy Alexander and Bonin, New York.

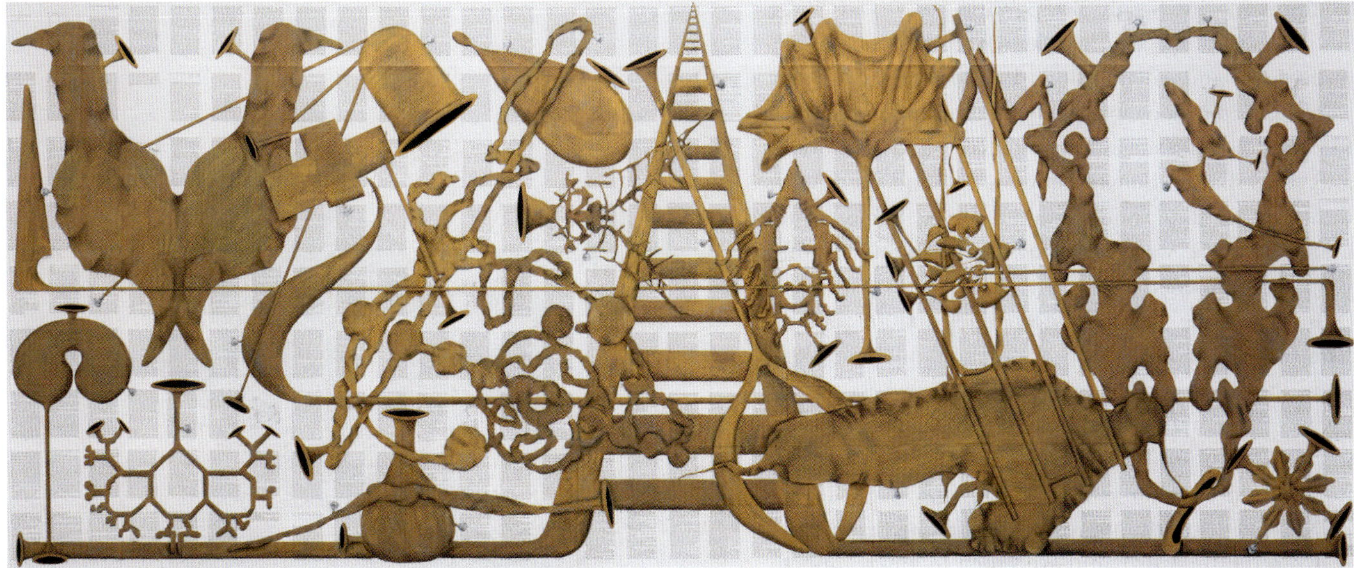

4.20 Tim Rollins and K.O.S., ***Amerika VIII***, 1986–87. Watercolor, charcoal, synthetic polymer paint, and pencil on bookpages on linen, 5' 9⅛" × 14' (175.6 × 426.7 cm). The Museum of Modern Art, New York. Jerry I. Speyer Fund and Robert and Meryl Meltzer Fund. Acc. n.: 30.1988. Courtesy the artists and Lehmann Maupin, New York and Hong Kong.

of *Wild Style* (1982), the instantly iconic film directed by Ahearn's twin brother, Charlie (b. 1951), which told of the birth of hip-hop and the entrance of graffiti into the art world.

Ahearn's work *Homage to the People of the South Bronx: Double Dutch at Kelly Street 1: Freida, Jevette, Towana, Stacey, 1981–82* (**fig. 4.19**), a multifigure composition showing Harlem girls jumping ropes, and installed beside a vacant lot high on one of the models' apartment building, was a high point of the period. Drawing their eyes up over the vacant spaces of urban blight to an image filled with vibrant, promising life provided viewers with a sense of empowerment. The figures floating several stories above the ground also have a certain uncanny quality. Cast from the front only, they appear slightly compressed into the wall, and their postures are contorted due to the difficulty of jumping two ropes at once as part of a game called Double Dutch. Their activity playfully provides a metaphor for the girls' graceful navigation of the difficulties of urban life.

Further north, in a public school in the South Bronx, Tim Rollins of Group Material was focusing his energies on a public-school art program he called Kids of Survival or K.O.S., which took books from the middle-school English curriculum and used them as both figurative and literal background for a series of collaborative paintings. The earliest pieces expressed an almost arrogantly vandalistic, rebellious spirit, as pages from George Orwell's *1984* were pasted to the canvas and covered with the kids' interpretations of life in the South Bronx, complete with references to crime, death, graffiti, and pop culture. The K.O.S. project was about bringing life and art together, relating the South Bronx to classic works of literature. As a group, Rollins and his collaborators would develop an aesthetic consisting of elegant abstracted symbols that related to literature and life, sometimes directly, sometimes at a poetic remove. One of the most striking of the K.O.S. motifs is the horns in the series of works based on Franz Kafka's *Amerika* (**fig. 4.20**). The group's fantastical instruments echo the motif that in Kafka's text had trumpeted a highly critical representation of American society, while the gold that forms them in the painting conveys the value of critique and more specifically the importance of the children's own voices. Rollins and K.O.S. succeeded in gaining gallery representation—*Amerika* was shown in 1985 in SoHo alongside pieces by Jenny Holzer and Leon Golub, among others—and their work was displayed in mural format on New York buildings. Sales of their work were used to create scholarship funds for the participants. Such material benefits were not the only measure of their success, either. Reflecting on the experience, Rollins asserted that K.O.S. "changed the fiber, the psychological fiber of the kids and what they think is possible. Not only that, but this belief in what is possible spreads to the parents and to the community as a whole."[14]

Unlike Rollins, who guided his students to an aesthetic consistent with contemporary art world interest in appropriation and abstraction, Ahearn's success depended on his ability to present his South Bronx neighbors with an image of the community they found empowering. After the moment of good faith in the early 1980s, the right of an artist, particularly a white male artist such as Ahearn, to represent a community that was racially different from him and that enjoyed fewer economic opportunities than him was challenged with increasing urgency. By the late 1980s, the conditions that had permitted Ahearn's success had changed. The oil crisis of the 1970s which struck all households across the U.S. was followed by a recession that created an unequal pattern of financial distress. Economic policies transformed the financial landscape, leaving the underrepresented and underemployed communities such as those in the South Bronx with fewer and fewer resources. Freeing up the spending power of wealthy individuals and corporations in the hope that they would pump money into the economy and create jobs further down the social ladder failed to reduce poverty and exacerbated the gap between rich and poor. With diminishing state and Federal funds being made available, there was increasing competition for what resources remained.

In this fragile and often desperate situation, people from already marginalized populations including gay men, intravenous drug users, and sex workers started dying of a mysterious illness. AIDS tested public policy to breaking point, witnessed by the fact that it would not be until over forty thousand people had died of AIDS-related conditions that President Reagan publicly uttered the word, and even then he did so only to assert that the government would remain silent with regard to sex education, a measure that could help slow the spread of the disease. The horror and mystery of the disease, the limited funds made available for health care in general, and the fact that it was, for the moment, focused on communities outside the perceived mainstream of U.S. culture heightened feelings further. Art that expressed discontent at the state of public life or clearly articulated a position from what were seen as the social margins became a magnet for controversy in what came to be known as the "Culture Wars." The fact that even a fractional amount of public money was spent on art at all, and an even smaller amount might support such oppositional voices, became a hot-button issue for conservatives. At the same time, much of the sense of community that had joined different groups in the previous decades was slipping away.

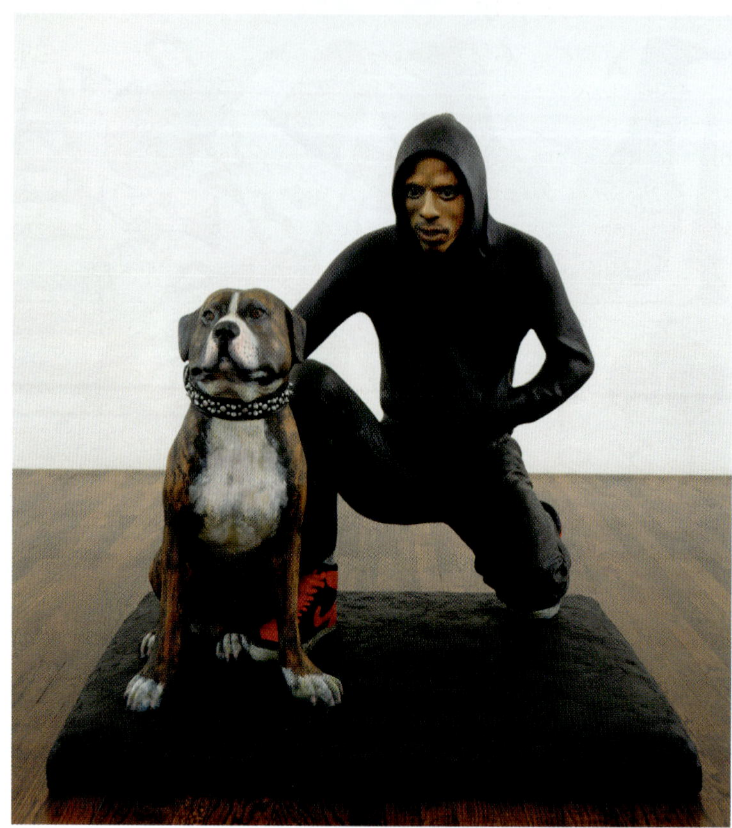

4.21 John Ahearn, ***Raymond and Toby***, 1986. Oil on fiberglass, 47 × 43 × 39" (119.38 × 109.22 × 99.06 cm). Collection of The Montclair Art Museum. Image courtesy Alexander and Bonin, New York.

With the stakes thus heightened, debates over who had the right to represent whom became increasingly common in the U.S., and in Ahearn's case the loudest challenge came from outside the immediate community. In 1986, Ahearn was commissioned to make a multifigure monument to adorn a police station in the Bronx. The body that invited him to create the work contained representatives of the Police Department, the City, the Bronx Museum of Art, and the community in which the work was to be installed. Ahearn designed and executed three statues from casts of people he had worked with before. The results, however—three life-size bronze polychrome statues showing local residents in everyday clothes and comfortable poses—presented a vision of the Bronx that for many viewers conformed too easily to stereotypes. Advocacy groups mobilized to protest the sculpture and five days after it was installed, Ahearn, anticipating that the controversy would only get more heated, hired a team to remove the work to a warehouse. It proved impossible, in 1989, to translate Ahearn's modestly scaled relief sculptures, shown within the neighborhood, into more monumental public sculptures that could be presented to the outside world. The image of Raymond Garcia and his pit bull terrier Toby proved particularly contentious. To Garcia, the work successfully captured the essence of daily life. Beyond the immediate community, however, the image of a Latino in hip-hop garb crouched down over his pit bull—a notoriously aggressive animal—suggested an extra in an urban crime movie (**fig. 4.21**). Though taken from life, Ahearn's subject matter, chosen for a monument erected in the shadow of a police station, seemed unsuitable for a public that extended well beyond the immediate neighborhood and the art world. Though Ahearn acknowledged that the site transformed the effect of his artistic choices it was as much the changes in how audiences were treating race and representation in the later 1980s that made the project so controversial.

From Marked Territory to the Mass Media

During the 1980s, the mass media, like the street, were perceived as more than just a source for content, an object of critique, or a place to discover new forms; they were also a staging ground as significant as any museum. This chapter will end with a discussion of artists from the 1980s who further destabilized the coherence of the art world's center by moving their practice into the spaces of the mass media and thus into the realm of national and international discourse.

Gran Fury and ACT UP

Group Material's *AIDS Timeline*, discussed above, reflected the growing politicization of factions within the cultural press and the increasing success of AIDS activists in coopting the mass media. The most prominent activist group was ACT UP (AIDS Coalition To Unleash Power). Angry at what appeared to be an official sanctioning of public ignorance and acceptance of the deaths of thousands of people with HIV, ACT UP mobilized a network of locally based activists. Learning from the anti-war and free-speech movements of the 1960s and 1970s, it kept a keen eye on opportunities to use the mass media. Early actions of the group included marches on political and economic targets that were designed to create imagery as well as to convey a message. Die-ins, in which protestors obstructed thoroughfares by lying on the ground as if dead, and other forms of passive resistance in the face of police hostility generated dramatic and hauntingly familiar images for the evening news and *The New York Times*.

In 1987, a spin-off group, Gran Fury, produced what has become the most recognizable icon of the movement. The opportunity came in the form of an invitation when William Olander (1950–89), a curator at the New Museum, New York, invited it to make use of the window by the museum entrance on Broadway (**fig. 4.22**). Like the billboards of Barbara Kruger (see fig. 2.16) or John Lennon and Yoko Ono (see fig. 1.13), the window became a point of intersection between popular culture and fine art. It was now surmounted by a pink triangle and the words "Silence=Death" in neon lights, like a commercial sign. Appropriating commercial language for political ends became the hallmark of the artists involved. The name Gran Fury, borrowed from the type of American car used by the New York Police Department, indicates the group's characteristic mixing of popular culture and political outrage. Its other projects included replacing copies of *The New York Times* in coin-operated dispensers with *The New York Crimes*—which looked like the *Times* but was full of news relating to the AIDS crisis. In 1989, Gran Fury took its politics to the streets with media savvy and a sense of joy in *Kissing Doesn't Kill: Greed and Indifference Do* (1989), which involved reworking an influential Benetton ad campaign. Featuring the heads of young, attractive, racially diverse couples wearing the company's clothes, the Benetton ads suggested in some degree that diversity rather than clothing was the product it offered for sale. For its version, Gran Fury made a few alterations. Youths were paired off—two men, two women, and a man and a woman

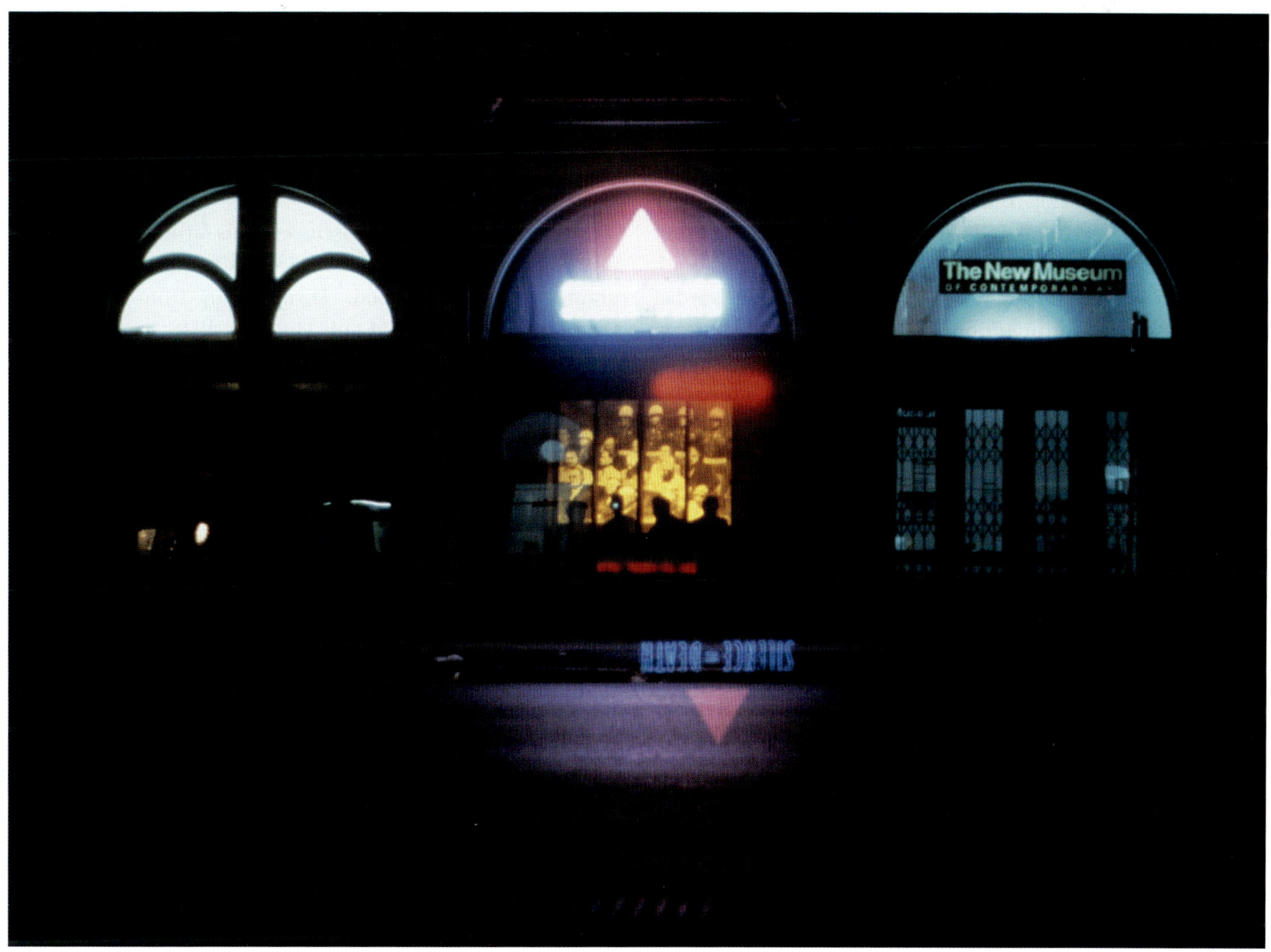

4.22 Gran Fury, *Let The Record Show*, 1987. Installation at the New Museum, New York.

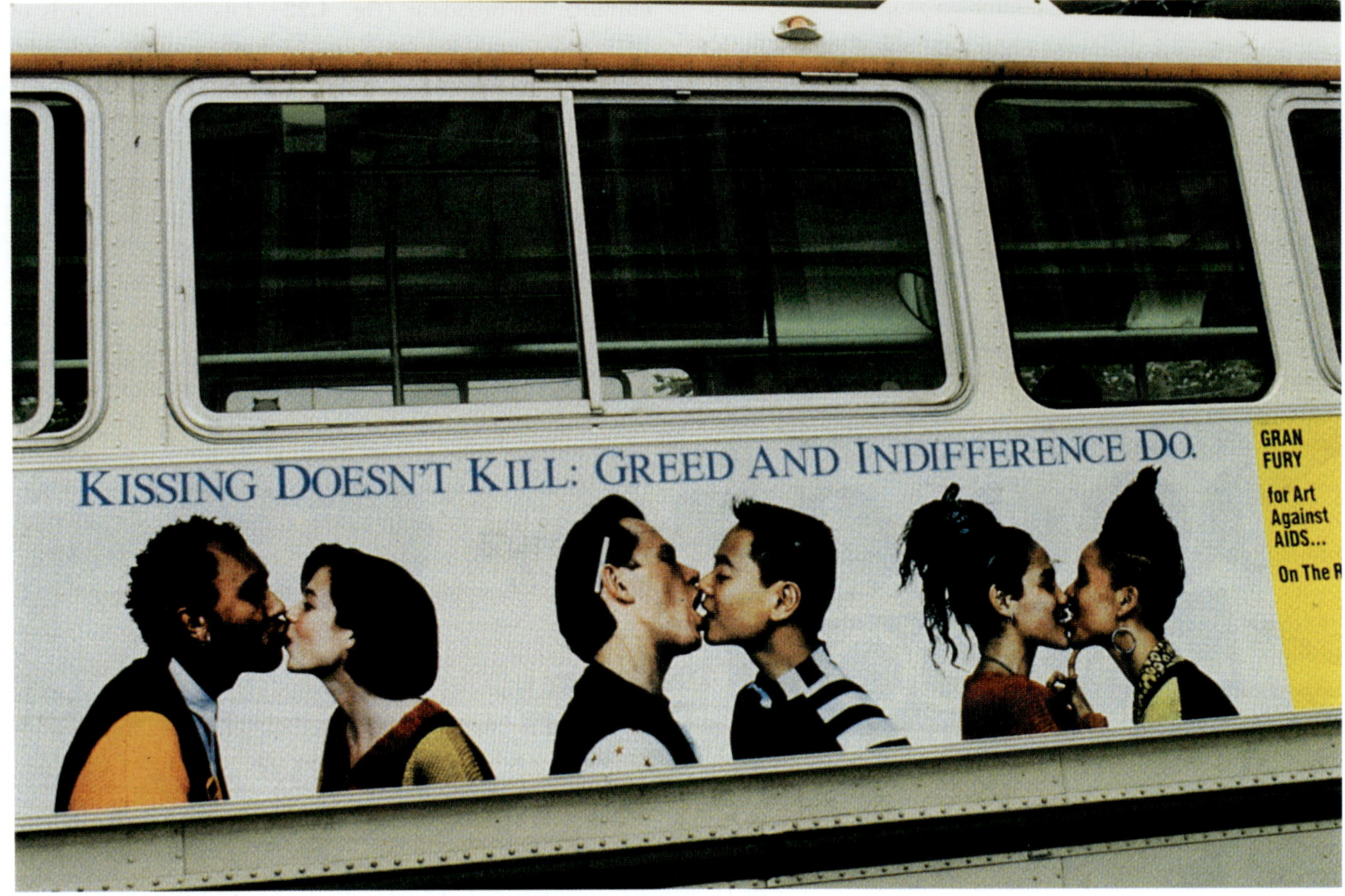

4.23 Gran Fury, *Kissing Doesn't Kill: Greed and Indifference Do*, 1989. Bus poster, New York.

(**fig. 4.23**). Above the couples appeared the text: "Kissing Doesn't Kill: Greed and Indifference Do." Carried on the sides of buses, the ads infiltrated the public space and confronted viewers when they were, in Gran Fury's words, "less defensive." The intention was to "Bring a whole new vocabulary—a whole new way of looking—to bear on the AIDS health crisis ... We want people to question what is out there."[15]

Meanwhile, ACT UP continued to expand the vocabulary of its actions. On one occasion it interrupted trading at the New York Stock Exchange by throwing fake money from the observation deck to which its members had chained themselves. In the streets, the demonstrations grew larger and tended to end in sit-ins that culminated in mass arrests and the spectacle of police lifting the limp bodies of passive resisters, all of which made for great footage on the evening news. Reflecting on a poster campaign presented at the 1990 Venice Biennale, Gran Fury member John Lindell (b. 1956) explained that its work only became art when it was the subject of press coverage: "It seems that artists can manipulate the baggage around the project as the real site ... the physical project is just a blasting-off point."[16] With words such as this, Gran Fury shifted the site for art not only out of doors and away from the museum, but into the mechanisms of information dispersal and retrieval.

David Avalos, Louis Hock, and Elizabeth Sisco

Though the activist work discussed thus far has been located primarily in New York, activist art was by no means so geographically circumscribed. Three artists from San Diego, David Avalos (b. 1947), Louis Hock (b. 1948), and Elizabeth Sisco (b. 1954), became adept at using the mass media as a site for their work. Avalos was a longtime Chicano rights activist, educator, and artist, as well as a founder of the Border Arts Workshop/Taller de Arte Fronteriza (BAW/TAF), in which Hock, a filmmaker, also participated. Sisco was a photographer, filmmaker, and activist. Their collaborations, like those of Group Material and Gran Fury, challenged the myths of the isolated and individual artist, but, unlike them, Avalos, Hock, and Sisco did not assert a group identity. Maintaining a macroscopic view of political and economic systems became increasingly difficult as identity issues came to the fore in the 1990s and clarity about authorship rather than self-effacement seemed most appropriate. Because they worked in San Diego and often examined the political and economic disenfranchisement of Latino populations in the region around the U.S./Mexican border, it was assumed that they aimed to empower or represent that particular community. But Avalos asserted that they did "not profess nor attempt to 'empower' anyone, but instead [tried] to reveal public policies that [were] implemented without public debate."[17] Identifying themselves as individuals—and from different cultures—helped to establish that their work was based on political allegiances, not personal identity. Like Wodiczko, their subject was not victims in need of assistance, but a system in need of transformation. Their aim had less to do with responding to existing communities than making it possible for individuals to form new communities. When they succeeded, it was in ways that had more to do with the future than the present. "We deal with the possibilities of communities," Avalos explained; "working as artists, within a community context, we create models."[18] This conviction—that art can be a conceptual stepping stone by which a viewer can imagine social change—was shared in numerous communities. Via the mass media, the art world, academia, and community outreach, Avalos, Hock, and Sisco elaborated a history of art that was committed to social, artistic, and critical engagement with the structures of contemporary society.

Two works that explore the politics of the U.S./Mexican border territory are *Welcome to America's Finest Tourist Plantation* (**fig. 4.24**), a 1988 bus ad campaign, and *Arte Reembolso/Art Rebate* (1993) (see fig. 4.26), a performance involving giving $10 bills to undocumented Latin American laborers. The first introduced a small event, in the form of a bus ad, into the urban fabric of San Diego. Enlisting the style of appropriation art, Avalos, Hock, and Sisco directed viewers' attention to what makes the city work: Dark-skinned hands wash dishes, provide maid service, and, in the center of the image, are handcuffed and pulled aside by a police officer. Across the image is the title "Welcome to America's Finest Tourist Plantation." The text drew the connection between the image of San Diego promoted by its tourism board—"America's Finest City"—and the reduction of its non-white population to a workforce with few resources or rights. Since San Diego was hosting Superbowl XXII that year, the increased media presence in the city gave extra publicity to the event and, like the bus routes that carried the work through the city, transported the issues it raised into a national and even international discussion of the economic factors underlying U.S. leisure. Avalos has cited courses at the University of California, San Diego on art, Russian film, and propaganda, specifically one taught by Martha Rosler (see fig. 1.30), as formative influences, and it is possible to see in the sensitivity here to image/image and text/image juxtapositions an echo of Rosler's practice as well as that of the Soviet filmmakers.

The style of *Welcome to America's Finest Tourist Plantation* relates it to the political work of appropriation-based artists and distinguishes it from the prevailing tenor of what was

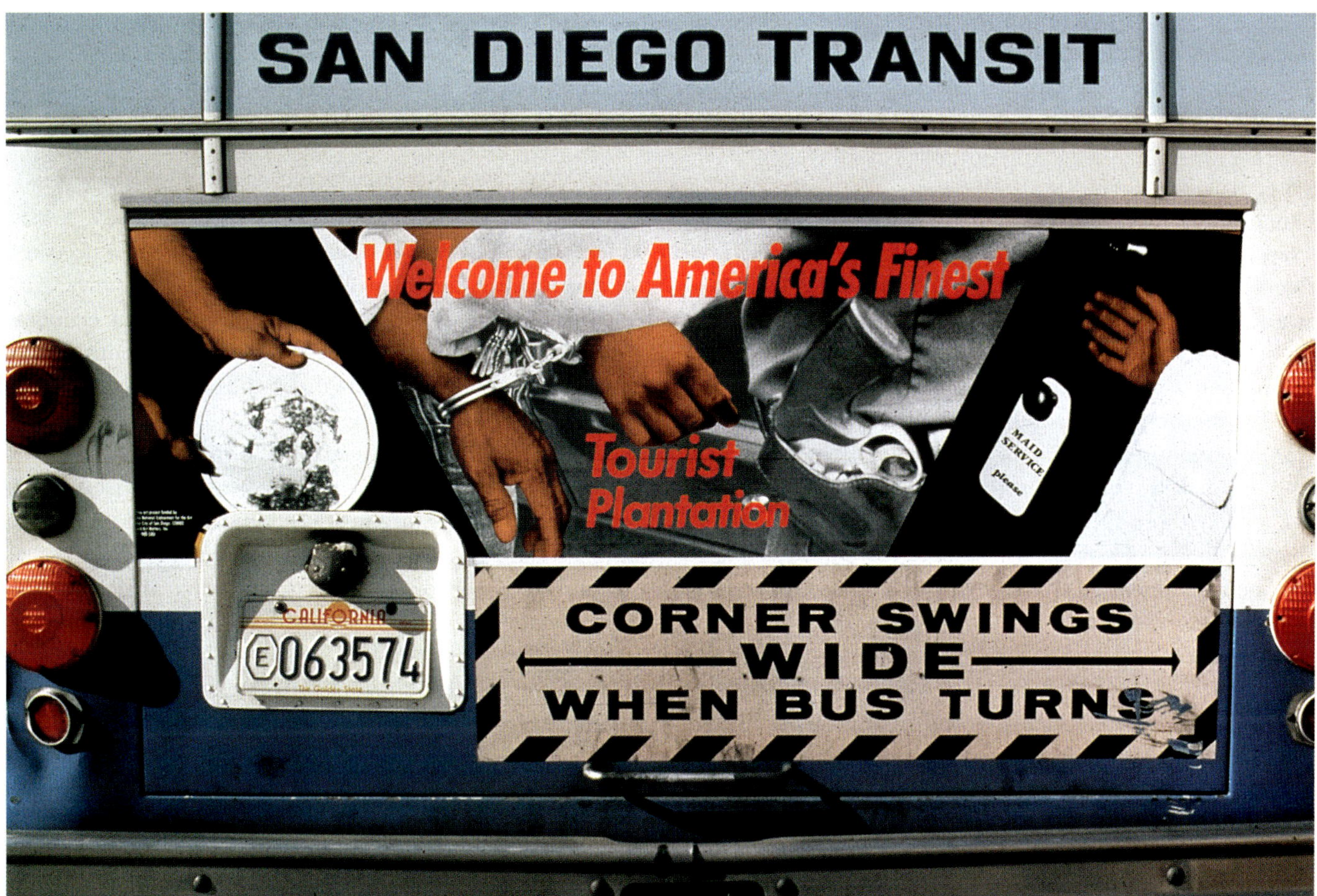

4.24 Elizabeth Sisco, Louis Hock, and David Avalos, *Welcome to America's Finest Tourist Plantation*, January 1988. Commercially screened photomontage, 21 × 72" (53.34 × 182.88 cm). One of 100 posters on San Diego Metropolitan Transit buses throughout San Diego County. Courtesy of the artists.

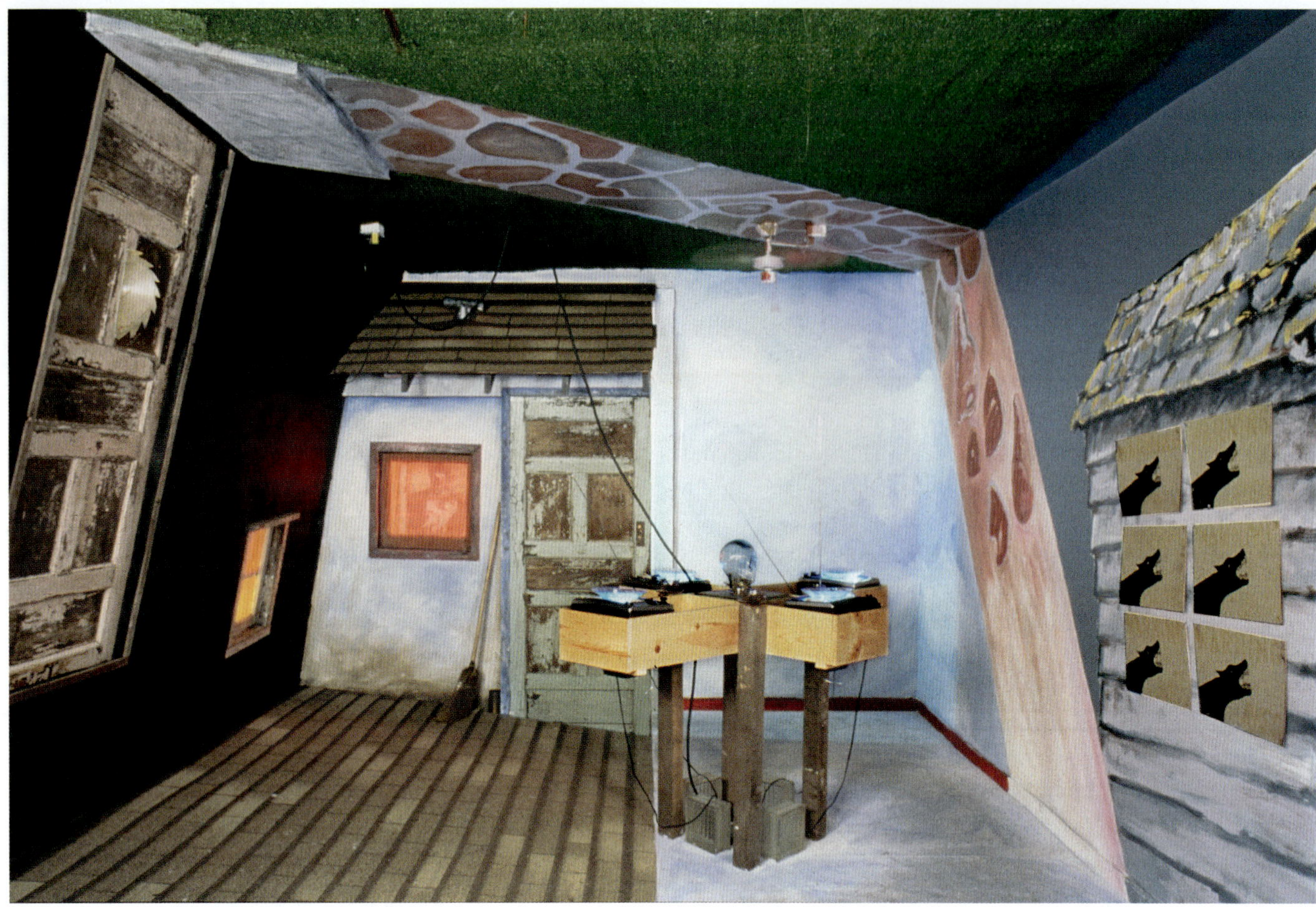

4.25 Border Arts Workshop/Taller de Arte Fronterizo, *911: A House Gone Wrong*, 1987. Mixed media. La Jolla Museum of Contemporary Arts, San Diego, April 3–June 28, 1987. Installation artists: David Avalos, Michael Schnorr, Robert Sanchez, Victor Ochoa with Sara-Jo Berman, Eriberto Oriol, and Ignacio Enloe. Courtesy the artists.

being called "Border Arts" in San Diego, the best-known example of which was BAW/TAF's installation *911: A House Gone Wrong* (1987) (**fig. 4.25**). Here, the artists combined stagecraft and sculpture, creating a world turned upside down, with a lawnmower cutting an Astroturf yard on the ceiling and a soundtrack of news bulletins about crises on the border or farther south punctuated by a busy signal from an unanswered 911 call. Beyond this front space, with its U.S. identity, complete with well-manicured lawn, was a shelter like those visible on the Mexican side of the border that was full of newspaper articles and editorials relating to life and law at the border. The installation evoked the tension and chaos of binational relations in San Diego in a dramatic and enveloping form, using surreal and expressionistic means.

In 1993, Avalos, Hock, and Sisco furthered their engagement with public policy by intervening directly in the economy and the news media. With *Arte Reembolso/Art Rebate* (**fig. 4.26**), they responded again to the symbiosis between what they were now calling undocumented taxpayers and the U.S. economy, and in doing so stepped even further from the expected visual language of contemporary art. The piece involved the transfer of money from the official economy of government-supported organizations to the unofficial economy of the U.S./Mexican border territory. Avalos, Hock, and Sisco argued that the reverse process occurred all the time as undocumented workers spent money, paid sales taxes, and provided labor for the national economy without receiving the benefits that the same contributions would earn an officially recognized citizen. In response, they turned $4,500 of a $5,000 grant they had won to participate in an exhibition, "La Frontera/The Border," produced by the Centro Cultural de la Raza and the Museum of Contemporary Art, San Diego, into new $10 bills, recorded their serial numbers, and distributed them to undocumented workers as "rebates" of a portion of the tax dollars that they had paid. The payment was accompanied with a signed document stating: "This ten dollar bill is part of an art project that intends to return tax dollars to taxpayers, particularly undocumented taxpayers. The Arte Reembolso acknowledges your role as a vital player in an economic community indifferent to national borders." To the recipients, the rebate expressed gratitude, while to U.S. citizens it was a reminder that their social services were paid for in part by the labor of those denied citizenship.[19]

As important as making such statements, however, was the fact that as an artwork, the *Reembolso* engaged a wide range of the population. The most obvious participants

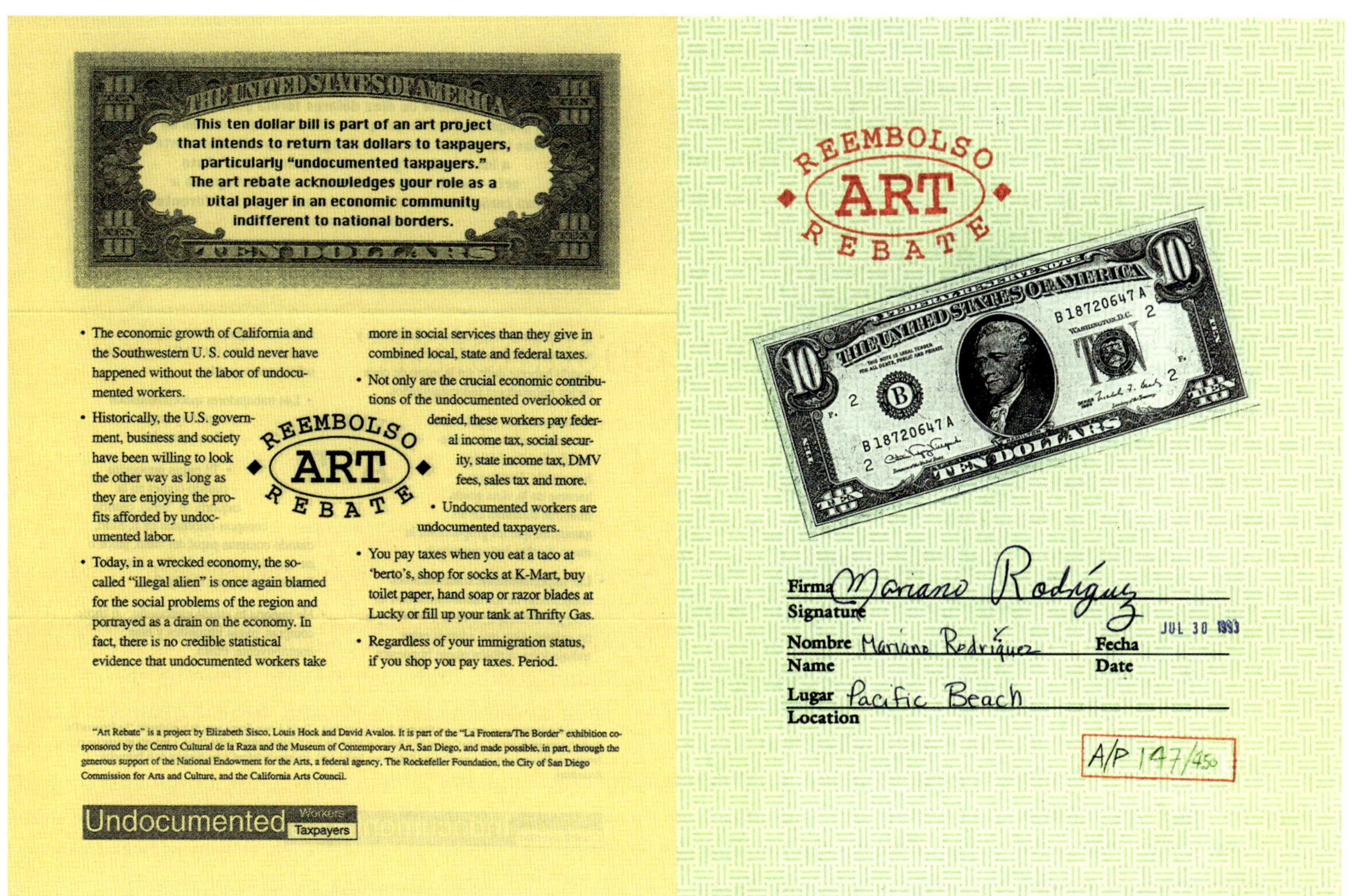

4.26 Elizabeth Sisco, Louis Hock, and David Avalos, ***Arte Reembolso/Art Rebate***, July–September 1993. Street performance/media event: ten-dollar bills signed by each artist, receipts signed by rebate recipients, English/Spanish language flyers, envelopes. Performed on street corners, highways, and migrant camps throughout San Diego County. Courtesy the artists.

were the artists, the arts institutions, and the individuals who received the $10 rebates. Beyond the exhibition or the action itself, TV news coverage and print journalism turned the semi-private exchange into a public debate. The ensuing discussions were extended through local Spanish- and English-language media outlets, often at the invitation of the artists, to penetrate even the national political discourse. Mass-media attention was not mere publicity. As the grant money provided the raw material rather than financial support for the project, television and radio were also the artists' media. With their 1988 bus-ad campaign, Avalos, Hock, and Sisco had influenced the discourse surrounding the border economy by placing an image in the city and watching the response it drew. *America's Finest Tourist Plantation* was, at root, a work of representation; *Arte Reembolso* was not. Since the artists had received funding from the National Endowment for the Arts (NEA), a Federal agency, the *Reembolso* was exactly, and not merely symbolically, what it purported to be—the return of tax dollars to taxpayers. In this way, the artists acted directly in the political economy, effectively redistributing money from the national coffers. Everyone who paid Federal taxes thus participated in some degree. Under pressure from forces both in and beyond government, ready to use any excuse to cut public funding to the arts, the NEA reacted with great displeasure. The Centro Cultural de la Raza and the Museum of Contemporary Art, San Diego were punished by having the portion of their grant that had been used for *Arte Reembolso* taken back.

Avalos, Hock, and Sisco's work created what Hock has described as a "conceptual social space."[20] The work mixed pragmatism and utopianism in a way that has facilitated its continuing relevance and development. Pushing beyond the confines of the traditional frame of the artwork and out into the wider public discourse has given these projects an afterlife. Even our discussions of the work today extend and expand the work, just as the initial debates in San Diego in 1988 or 1993 did. To talk about works such as *Arte Reembolso* or Group Material's *Democracy* is to contribute to their continuing growth, and since the issues they raised—citizenship and economic parity, the AIDS crisis, colonialism and postcolonial relations, homelessness, education, and more—are still with us, these works of the 1980s and early 1990s continue to be relevant in the 2010s. Discussed in the first decade of the twenty-first century, at a point in history when, in the U.S. at least, issues such as immigration and citizenship have been folded into discussions of terrorism and national security, and when the AIDS crisis has been pushed further from the national agenda even as it devastates populations and regions of the non-Western world, this body of work can continue to function just as it did when it was first created.

5

Commodities and Consumerism

At first glance, the 1985 season in the East Village (see Chapter 4) looked pretty familiar. Though there was a sense that a peak had been reached, new galleries were still opening and collectors were primed to move in and invest. One of the newer spaces, International with Monument, stood out from the D.I.Y. celebrations and alternative sincerity of its neighbors. Here was a polished gallery that looked like the franchise of a smart SoHo establishment. It showed art that reflected its professionalism in what appeared to be knowing references to art history and critical theory and a knowing attitude toward the market. Sculptor Jeff Koons and painter Peter Halley, who were both given solo shows there in 1985, along with Ashley Bickerton and gallery co-founder Meyer Vaisman, recast Minimalist and Pop aesthetics into what was quickly dubbed commodity art and Neo-Geo (neo-geometric). Rejecting the photo-based intellectualism of appropriation, the cathartic expressivity of Neo-Expressionism, and the *ad hoc* populism of installation, this new brand of contemporary art looked, like the gallery that promoted it, self-consciously polished. Koons, Halley, and company referenced consumer culture and modern art by featuring brand-new consumer goods, logos, and geometric compositions that clearly quoted Modernist precedents (see fig. 5.1). Rather than copying or paying homage to the earlier styles, however, these new works purported to be "simulations" in the spirit of the newly fashionable theories of French philosopher Jean Baudrillard. Sorting out the relationship between Neo-Geo theory and practice would take some time for contemporary onlookers, and will occupy a central place in this discussion.

"Commodities" is the name for goods in a capitalist system that we buy and sell, not only for the functions they fulfill, but also for the intangible satisfactions relating to status or sentiment that they provide. A car or a watch, for instance, is designed so that its form fits its function, but, as we know, there are far more reasons than transportation and time-keeping to buy either. Commodity artists such as Koons, but also those beyond the International With Monument stable including Israeli-born New York-based sculptor Haim Steinbach, and also European sculptors such as John M. Armleder from Switzerland and Rosemarie Trockel from Germany, appropriated commodities, fabricated replicas of consumer goods, and copied logos, choosing their sources for their social connotations and formal qualities. Unlike the appropriation artists, with whom they share aspects of their practice, but very much like both movements' Pop art predecessors, commodity artists drew criticism about their intentions: It was impossible to tell if the art was intended as Marxist critique or capitalist praise of its subject matter. Viewers did not know how to respond to a display of vacuum cleaners, a stainless-steel whiskey decanter, or fire tools. The artists' statements rarely clarified things. In Steinbach's view, there had appeared a "renewed interest in … taking pleasure in objects and commodities" and a "stronger sense of being complicit with the production of desire than being positioned somewhere outside of it."[1] Such insider status led to a pervasive ambiguity within commodity art and its reception. In Europe, Armleder, whose work consisted of arranging furniture and composing with store-bought fixtures and other people's art, was content to label his assemblages "pudding" and his subject matter "jello-culture."[2] In New York, Jeff Koons laid claim to social critique but couched his politics in pleasure, explaining that art that was not directed at society was "like sex without love."[3] This was not the expected language of social critique and failed to appease critics who saw signs of complicity in the rising prices and profiles of contemporary artists. Within a year, the four artists from International with Monument had been picked up by the legendary gallerist Ileana Sonnabend, formerly Andy Warhol's dealer, and Neo-Geo grew to include Sherrie Levine and Ross Bleckner. The financial success of the work was accompanied by a critical furor inflated, like the debates over Neo-Expressionism, by claims of conspiracy, bad faith, and ignorance. The issue, however, was more complex than such a response allowed. Artists faced the challenge of balancing critique of the art world with their desire to participate in it, a feat that, as Trockel acknowledged to her dealer and friend Monika Sprüth, was perhaps impossible.[4]

Market Forces

By the fall of 1985 those who frequented New York art galleries could be expected to understand that an appropriated image was, among other things, an invitation to contemplate the power of representation and the ubiquity of images in the fabric and function of contemporary society. Galleries and museums are, after all, places to look and think about what one sees; they are also, however, sites of commercial exchange and places to safeguard valuables. It is these latter functions that seemed to come alive when viewers found themselves standing before handsomely displayed merchandise or finely fabricated liquor bottles. Even after decades of seeing artists rely on found objects, re-presented commodities created a great deal of anxiety. The issue rested on ambivalence in the new work with regard to its politic message. On the one hand one might assume that a social critique was intended by the equation such art implied between shopping for luxury goods and collecting art. Andy Warhol had set the tone for such a reading by celebrating his use of copies as a means of simplifying the creative process and making it possible for everyone to own art thus setting the democratic promise of mechanization against the uniformity industrialized society forces upon human experience. How to read the 1980s generation of re-purposed commodities and carefully copied consumer goods, on the other hand, was not so clear. Unlike Warhol, commodity artists such as Koon and Steinbach emphasized the acts of buying and accumulating goods, rather than the acts of manufacture. It would take time before the degree to which commodity artists were concerned with production became clear, and likewise decades before any consensus could be reached on the creative power of consumption. In the meantime collectors and museums included commodity art, like Neo-Expressionism, in their collections, adding to the urgency and anxiety felt in its critical reception.

Jeff Koons

The most dramatic and controversial of the commodity artists was Jeff Koons (b. 1955), who had studied at the School of the Art Institute of Chicago with Ed Paschke (1939–2004). Though Paschke's subject matter, as seen in *Mid American* (1969) (**fig. 5.1**), tended to be drawn from the gritty underbelly of urban entertainments, his embrace of lowbrow pleasures and high-keyed color and corresponding delight in artifice and masquerade can be seen in Koons's work. Upon arriving in New York in 1977, Koons became a commodities broker on Wall Street and a remarkably successful membership sales associate for the Museum of Modern Art. His artistic career would likewise join the worlds of capital and culture. In the spring of 1980, Koons lavished a new kind of attention on commodities in the Broadway window of the New Museum of Art in SoHo, where he presented several brand-new vacuum cleaners smartly displayed in Plexiglas boxes illuminated by self-contained fluorescent lighting. The arrangement looked like a cleaning supply store as conceived by a Minimalist sculptor. Koons called the show

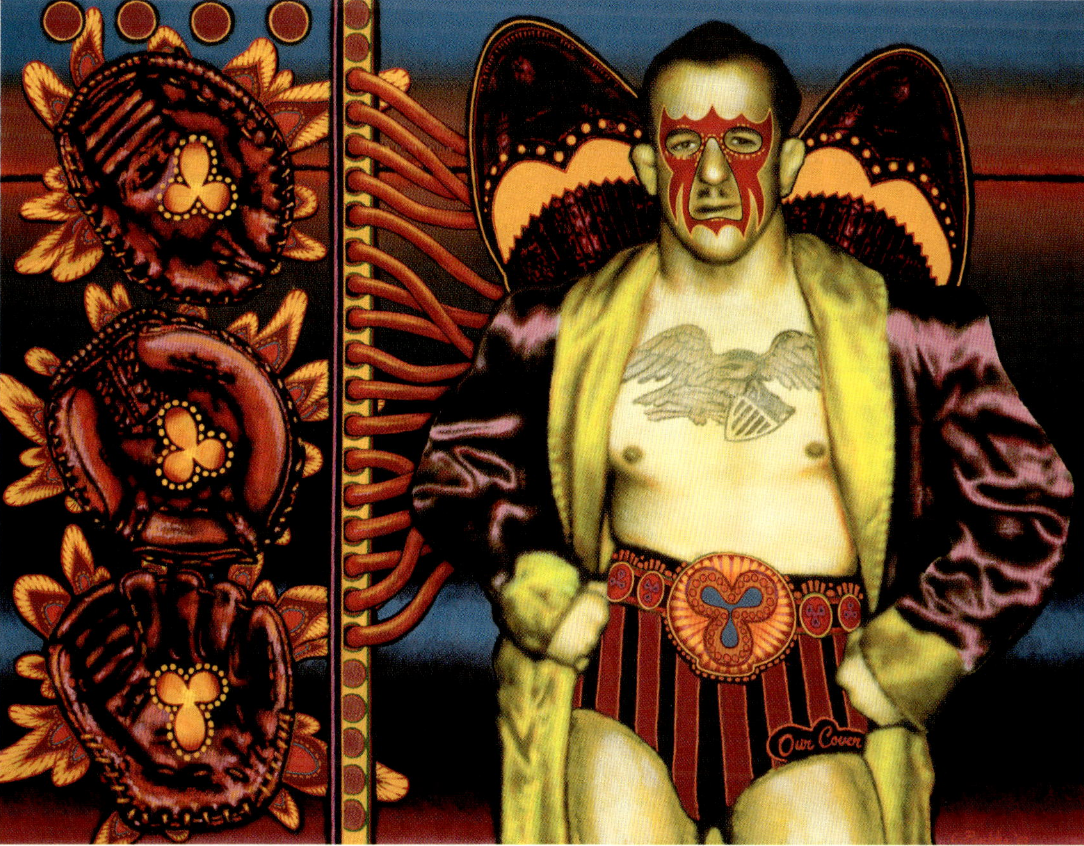

5.1 Ed Paschke, *Mid American*, 1969. Oil on canvas, 45 × 60" (114.3 × 152.4 cm). Art Institute Chicago. Courtesy of the Ed Paschke Foundation.

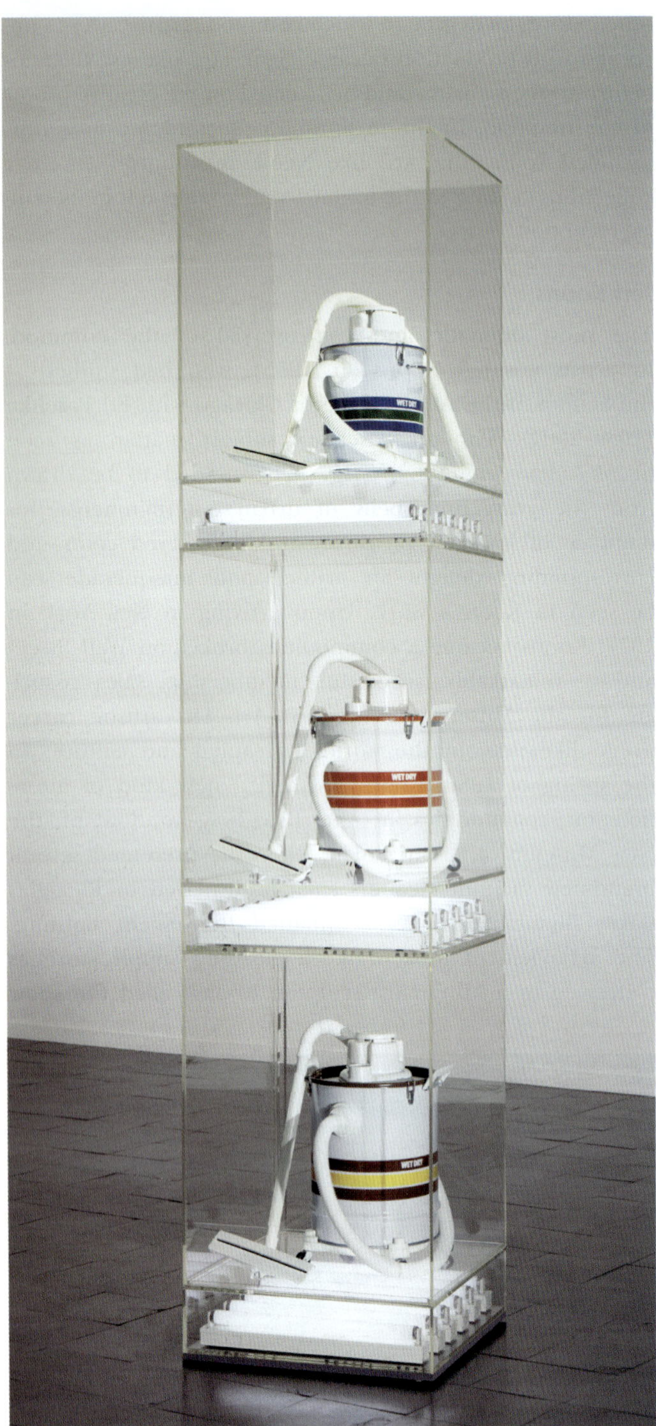

5.2 Jeff Koons, *New Shelton Wet/Dry Tripledecker*, 1981. Three vacuum cleaners, acrylic, fluorescent lights. 124½ × 28 × 28" (316.2 × 71.1 × 71.1 cm). Des Moines Art Center. © Jeff Koons.

"The New" in celebration of the pleasures stimulated and satisfied by novelty. As one stepped back from the New Museum window, the sculptures blended into the merchandise displayed in the windows of the surrounding stores: Art and commerce looked the same. Viewers had long been able to stand inside a museum and celebrate the equation of art and life or mourn the degradation of art into commerce, a discussion with a long history extending from the integration of popular imagery into Realist painting in the nineteenth century through Duchamp's readymades to Pop art in the 1960s. In the museum, however, artists were by definition in charge, but out on Broadway, facing the man or woman on the street, they had to cater to the public's needs and desires like any other salesperson. Koons relished this position—he declared himself eager to claim "the responsibility of manipulation and seduction" shouldered by the entertainment and advertising industries.[5] Like a good advertisement, a well-designed object, or a compelling work of art, Koons's sculpture strove to create and then meet consumer demand.

Koons's early work stuck closely to Pop and Minimalist precedents. The arrangements of upright household vacuums and heavy-duty shop vacuums in "The New," including *New Shelton Wet/Dry Triple Decker* (1981) (**fig. 5.2**), are formally akin to Minimalist artist Donald Judd's boxes (see fig. 1.5). Koons, however, attempted to pack more traditional content into his objects. Caught in a suspended state of immaculate newness, the vacuum cleaners in their sealed boxes were intended to be expressions of confinement, purity, life and death, and even nods to art history. In the artist's statements, the vacuums are anthropomorphic "breathing machines" that explore issues of personality, selfhood, and the "psychological state tied to ... immortality."[6] Koons even compared the vacuum to the Virgin Mary, in the process perhaps testing his audience's credulity, but also drawing on precedents such as Andy Warhol's *Gold Marilyn* (1962) to invoke the emotional and even spiritual power of popular culture.

In the mid-1980s, Koons stopped using "real" merchandise and started copying collectibles, both high- and lowbrow, employing materials traditionally associated with design and the decorative arts. To make the work, Koons hired the best craftspeople and technicians he could find, his own skills as a maker being judged inadequate. For *Jim Beam—J.B. Turner Train* (1986) (**fig. 5.3**), for instance, he had a collectible whiskey decanter emptied of its contents, cast, and then sent back to the Jim Beam distillery to be refilled and sealed with the authenticating label. As with the earlier pristine vacuum cleaners, the sanctity of the object's interior is preserved and used to convey an allusion to perfection and potential.

Just as Koons had earlier invested bought goods with spiritual content, so he now presented these new copied objects as political and even moral creations. A stainless-steel statuette of Louis XIV (made in the same year) or a whiskey decanter, such as in *Jim Beam—J.B. Turner Train*, could, Koons felt, provide an antidote to the crippling weakness, moral vacuity, and political cynicism he saw in contemporary art. Koons's logic worked like this: Kings and kitsch occupied opposite ends of the spectrum in Western culture, and casting them in highly polished reflective steel replicated the luxuriance of the former's fine silver while catering to the lower budget associated with the latter. By responding to the aesthetic and acquisitive impulses of consumers at different ends of the market, Koons claimed

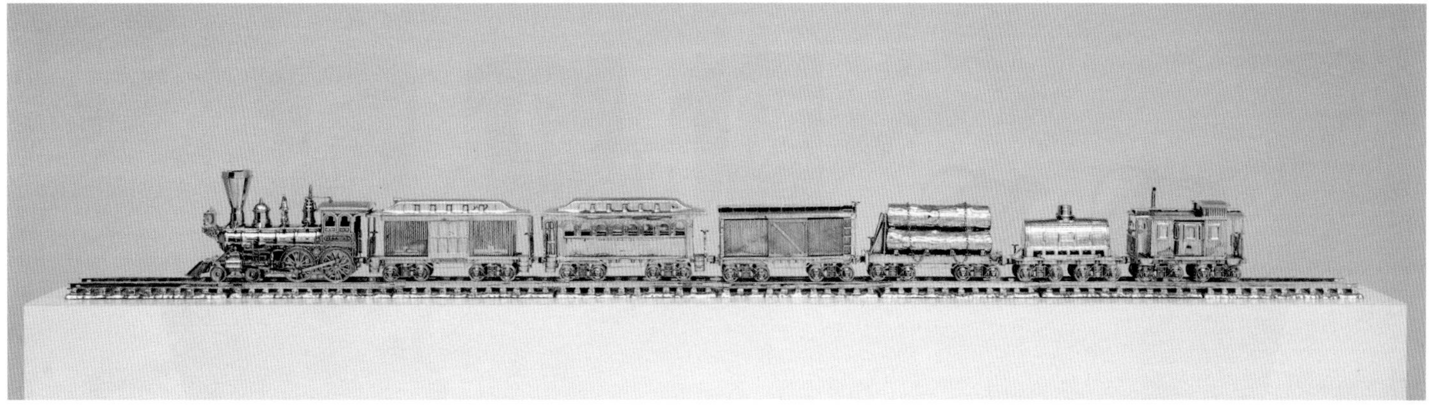

5.3 Jeff Koons, *Jim Beam—J.B. Turner Train*, 1986. Stainless steel, bourbon. 11 × 114 × 6½" (27.9 × 289.6 × 16.5 cm). © Jeff Koons.

his work exhibited a form of power sharing that he described as democratic. Whether this egalitarian impulse could be actualized through his art, especially as it became a high-priced luxury good in its own right, is a question. What is clear is that the work functioned by creating a relationship between the middle-class desire for upward mobility and the reality that most of the middle class, itself losing its economic security in the 1980s, could be satisfied with imitations. Rather than critique either the circumstances that contributed to this situation or bemoan the bad taste it begat, Koons celebrated the existence of desire and the ability for objects to satisfy it.

Jim Beam—J.B. Turner Train was one of several stainless-steel sculptures featured in Koons's second solo show at International with Monument, "Luxury and Degradation." On the walls of the gallery, the artist displayed billboard-sized appropriations of liquor advertisements. Translucent cascades of caramel-colored alcohol poured past the steel objects. These luxuriant flows enhanced the allure of the polished steel, permitting glimpses of an intoxicating interior to shimmer across the reflective exterior. If there was any question that this optical scintillation was meant to engage a physical response, Koons set the matter straight. "The surface of my stainless steel pieces is pure sex and gives an object both a masculine and feminine side: the weight of the steel engages with the femininity of the reflective surfaces."[7] Surrounded by the images, generated from the original negatives used by the advertising companies but printed on canvas instead of paper and using a more oil-rich ink, sex and surface make contact. The centrality and power of such a heroic vision of heterosexual sex repurposed from its role selling commodities and reproducing the capitalist status quo was cause for critical alarm. The ambivalence of the work became acutely problematic as Koons's output reached higher and higher prices, for, despite the conviction that commodity artists could draw attention to and even reorient our desires, the art market seemed to indicate that it was business as usual. The line between commodity art and art as commodity was being stretched thin.

Haim Steinbach

While Koons experimented with techniques of appropriation, Israeli-born, U.S.-educated and -based artist Haim Steinbach (b. 1944) refined his method of re-presenting merchandise. In the late 1970s and early 1980s, Steinbach was working in New York, creating room-sized installations consisting of what looked like the combined contents of apartments, fabric shops, and grocery stores. His aesthetic was defined by the same vigorous and chaotic energy that shaped East Village productions of the period, and garnered attention in exhibitions at Artists Space downtown and Fashion Moda uptown. Along the walls of the installations, he hung display shelves: sometimes rather baroque assemblages, sometimes just boards on brackets. These supported all manner of goods, from tabloid newspapers to teapots and shampoo to sailboats. The shelves would soon become the focus of Steinbach's practice. In the mid-1980s, like the cadre at International with Monument, Steinbach eliminated his references to East Village chaos in favor of more subdued and well-ordered style.

By 1984, Steinbach's shelves supported primarily new objects—lava lamps, kitchen pots, souvenir mugs, Halloween masks—unwrapped and arranged like colors on a canvas. The shelves themselves were uniformly shaped wedges, at times nested, laminated most often in single colors but occasionally with patterns, and even chrome finished. The effect was that of an abstract painting as much as that of a representational sculpture. *ultra red* (1986) is one of a series of studies in red that juxtapose towers of pots against rows of clocks and clusters of lamps. In *supremely black* (1985) (**fig. 5.4**), the reflective onyx glaze of two ceramic water pitchers highlights the black text on three red boxes of soap detergent. *untitled (walking canes, fireplace sets) #2* (1987) presents a more controlled palette of silvers and grays as canes and tools weave a surprisingly complex pattern offset by the room's colors reflected in the chrome-covered shelf. In works such as these, Steinbach produces aesthetic pleasure with means shaped by the supply and demand of the marketplace as much as by his art-school training.

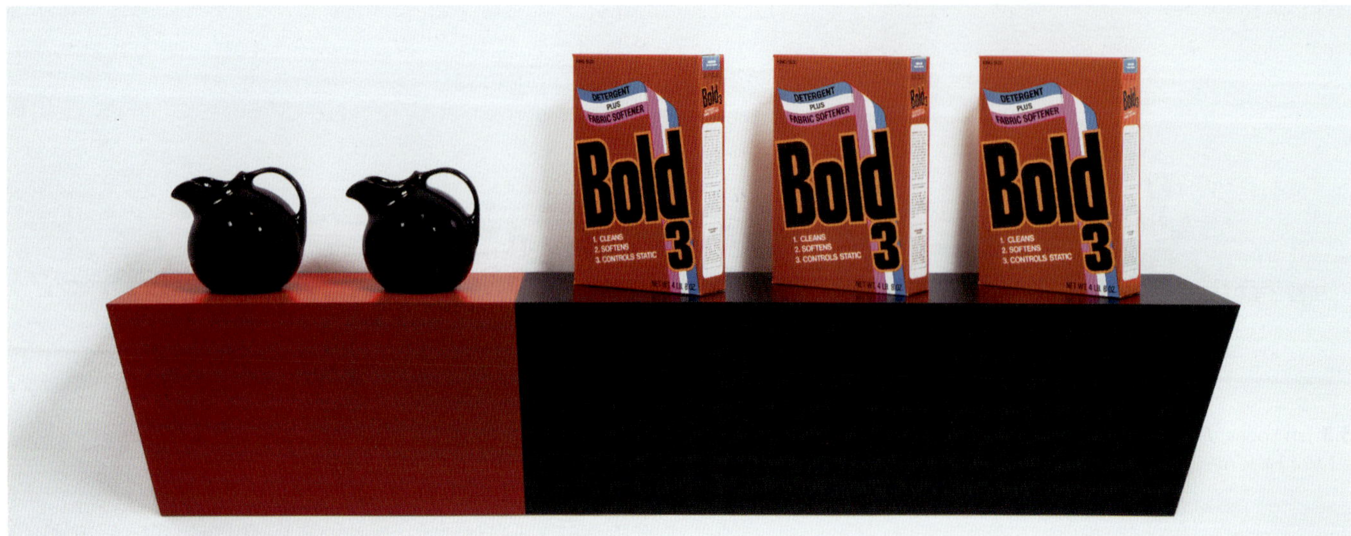

5.4 Haim Steinbach, ***supremely black,*** 1985. Plastic-laminated wood shelf; ceramic pitchers; cardboard detergent boxes, 29 × 66 × 13" (73.7 × 167.6 × 33 cm). Courtesy of the artist.

Steinbach supplemented his aesthetic refinement with a conviction that "all surfaces are social surfaces."[8] In common with all shoppers, he began with the undifferentiated mass of consumer products arranged on store shelves and transformed a selection of products into something of his own—possessions. Unlike products, possessions, Steinbach explained, "take on different characters, moving in an out of concreteness, mystery, fantasy, the troubling, the reassuring."[9] The various connotations created by juxtaposing such evocative objects make up Steinbach's subject matter. With a poetic sensibility attuned to the connotative and aesthetic potential of things you can buy in a store, Steinbach composed, in his words, a "map of human beliefs, necessities, and exploration."[10]

Ashley Bickerton

After graduating from CalArts in 1982, Ashley Bickerton (b. 1959) moved east to New York to create his own brand of commodity art. Rather than manipulate objects, Bickerton composed with logos. His works look like well-protected packages labeled with icons arranged like stickers on a suitcase. *Tormented Self-Portrait (Susie at Arles)* (1987–88) (**fig. 5.5**), for instance, looks like a box that has been custom-designed to hold lab equipment, firearms, or musical instruments. It has a rubber tarp rolled below it, seemingly providing additional protection, and is mounted on the wall with substantial metal brackets. At the top Bickerton's logos title the work, announcing it to be a self-portrait, and at the bottom act as a kind of artist's signature. Bickerton chose the rather anonymous female name of "Susie" to contrast with the authoritative signatures of modern painting, the "Picassos" and "Pollocks" that adorn great art. In Bickerton's work, however, critique goes hand in hand with complicity: Running up and down the edges of the box and clearly branding the work is the real artist's own signature

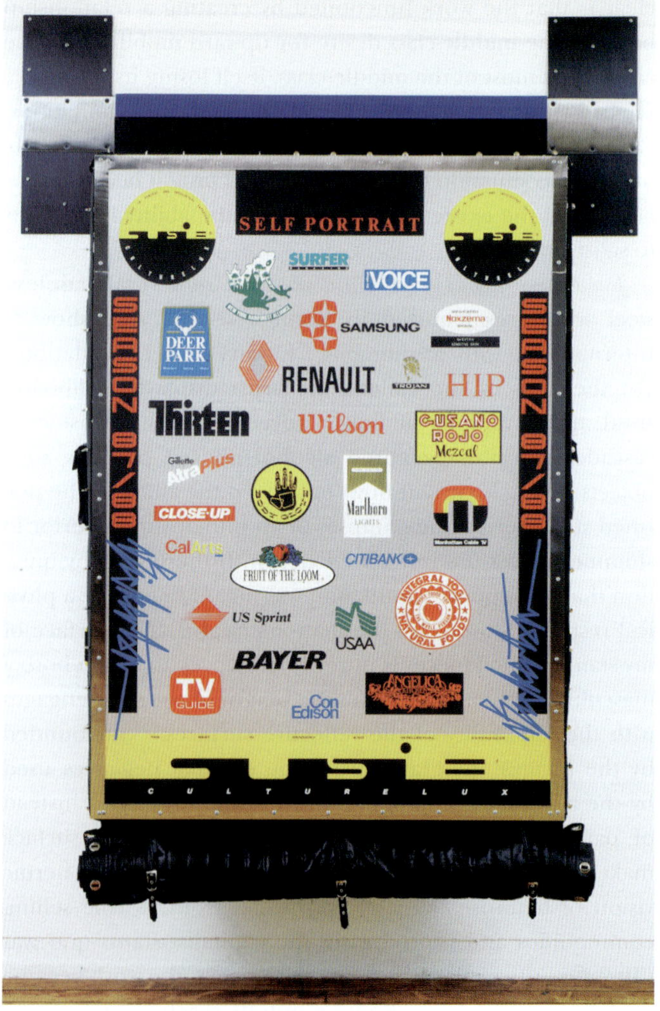

5.5 Ashley Bickerton, ***Tormented Self-Portrait (Susie at Arles)***, 1987–88. Synthetic polymer paint, bronze powder and lacquer on wood, anodized aluminum, rubber, plastic, formica, leather, chrome-plated, steel and canvas, 89⅜ × 68¾ × 15¾" (227.1 × 174.5 × 40 cm). Collection of the Museum of Modern Art, New York. Courtesy the artist and Lehmann Maupin Gallery, New York and Hong Kong.

stylized into a recognizable and repeatable logo. The title of *Tormented Self-Portrait (Susie at Arles)* heightens its ambivalent stance toward issues of genius by inviting comparison to the French town of Arles's most tormented self-portraitist, Vincent van Gogh. However, Bickerton evades any kind of artistic contest by avoiding all pictorial references. Brand names are all that he uses to convey the content of the work; they function like artifacts. The names "Renault" and "Marlboro" suggest a drive through southern France, cigarette in hand, while "The Village Voice," "Citibank," and "Con Edison" suggest the home Susie left behind in the U.S., "Gillette Atra Plus" hints at a male companion, while "Surfer Magazine" and "Body Glove" detail the couple's interests. The artist and his subject are nothing more than the sum total of what can be communicated by a brand name.

Mike Kelley

While Koons and company explored the gratifying surfaces and indulgent associations of the commodity, there were others exploring its underside. By the 1990s, LA-based artist Mike Kelley (1954–2012) had produced a body of work that arrived, he felt, at a compromise between the mode of the commodity artists sculpting out of consumer goods and the East Village or Colab crowd creating installations out of everyday waste (see Chapter 4). His paintings and sculptures such as *The Wages of Sin* and *More Love Hours Than Can Ever Be Repaid* (1987) (**fig. 5.6**), made of stitched-together and carefully arranged discarded stuffed animals, became instantly iconic. All told, he appropriated, purchased, re-presented, enlarged, copied, and arranged—all proven strategies of the appropriation and commodity artists. He also painted, performed, collaborated, vandalized, scrawled, and narrated—devices common to the assemblage installation artists and even the Neo-Expressionists. His training, first at a conventional painterly art school and then at the conceptually oriented CalArts in the late 1970s, suggests a pattern to Kelley's eclecticism. His performances, installations, films, videos, music, cartoons, prose, and criticism, however, demonstrate a

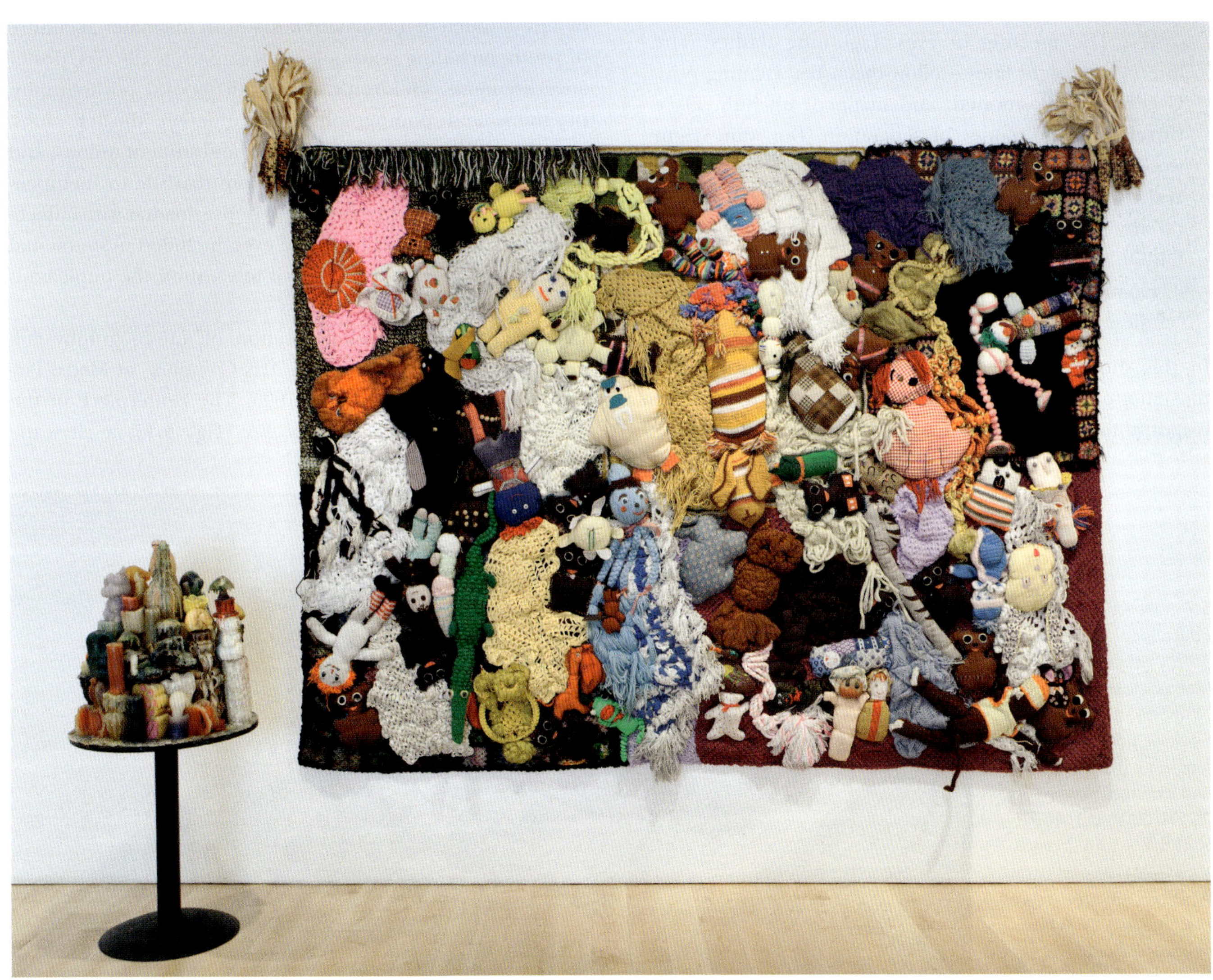

5.6 Mike Kelley, *The Wages of Sin* and *More Love Hours Than Can Ever Be Repaid*, 1987. Stuffed fabric toys and afghans on canvas with dried corn; wax candles on wood and metal base, 90 × 119¼ × 5" (228.6 × 302.9 × 12.7 cm) overall plus candles and base. Whitney Museum of American Art, New York; purchase with funds from the Painting and Sculpture Committee 89.13a-e. © Kelley Studio Inc./Mike Kelley Foundation for the Arts.

thought process that goes beyond a simple dialectic between painting and Conceptualism, or between Jeff Koons and Colab. By the late 1980s, he had directed his attention to, among other topics, the coincidence of art and crime, mysticism, pleasure, power, affection, abasement, and the body. Over the next two and a half decades, Kelley would pay particular attention to the processes and consequences of socialization and adolescence.

The 1989 statement used to introduce his second volume of collected writings, *Minor Histories* (2004), illustrates the ease with which Kelley moved through narratives of adolescent pathos to psychoanalytical speculation, cultural interpretation, and aesthetic appreciation, with even a nod to contemporary theoretical interests of center and periphery, masquerade, and the body:

> Wallflowers ... those shy ones! Oh! Cling! Cling thee to the furthermost borders—the hinterlands. Sublimate, oh sublimate thy libidinal impulses into decorative organic motifs ... ornamental hair growths, aesthetically placed tattoos. Beauty-mark thyself!
>
> Yes. The meeting of eyes. Lightning flashes. The intertwining sight lines—follow them. Yes. Glinting orbs. Gazes fixed, positioned, and mapped, uh huh. Place thyself in Polar Zones of separation. But wait! Tight wooden mind, chopped off from the body trunk. Oh! Yes! Yes! Fold the fruit away from the hard seed. Slough off thy mortal tarp and reveal thyself ... *in glory* ... Oh!Oh!Oh! ... the essential form lies beneath ... *timeless.*
>
> Floating, we are ... in the free area designated "endless periphery."[11]

In this short passage, Kelley performs his conviction that the emotions of the reticent U.S. teenager and his or her response to society coincide with the hermeneutic strategies of art—sensuality becomes decoration, masquerade permits revelation, and perception breeds comfort. Adolescence in Kelley's work appears as the time when the laws of culture and selfhood are struggled with and rejected, but also internalized. Embracing adolescence is also polemical for Kelley: Making art about teenagers, he feels, constitutes an art-historical rejection of what he sees as the Modernist idealization of childhood and the Postmodern hyperanalytic preoccupation with adulthood.[12]

It is perhaps not surprising in the context of identity and body art of the 1980s and early 1990s that Kelley's work would be read as confessional. Yet intimacy and self-exposure were processes and subject matter for Kelley, not a means of access to the artist's psyche. Kelley intended the hyperbolic style of his writing, like the absence of personal touch in his stuffed animals and explicitly neutral drawing style, to evade associations between the work and his personal life. Eventually Kelley would stop resisting and embrace his viewers' impulse to seek answers in biography. He did not, however, make confessional art, but instead mixed seemingly autobiographical details—"much of it is blatant lies"—with the material culture of youth, including yearbooks, newspapers, textbooks, poster advertisements, children's art, comic books, pornography, programs and photographs from amateur theater clubs, churches, universities, alumni clubs, and student unions, and testimonials of all sorts, ranging from diaristic to therapeutic in tone.[13] The result is an oeuvre overloaded with subject matter. In a 1991 installation he even included monumental crystalline room deodorizers as if to ward off the unpleasant odor of excess.

Kelley's embrace and fabrication of autobiography culminated in "Toward a Utopian Arts Complex" at Metro Pictures Gallery in New York in 1995. The centerpiece of the exhibition was *Educational Complex* (**fig. 5.7**), a cityscape

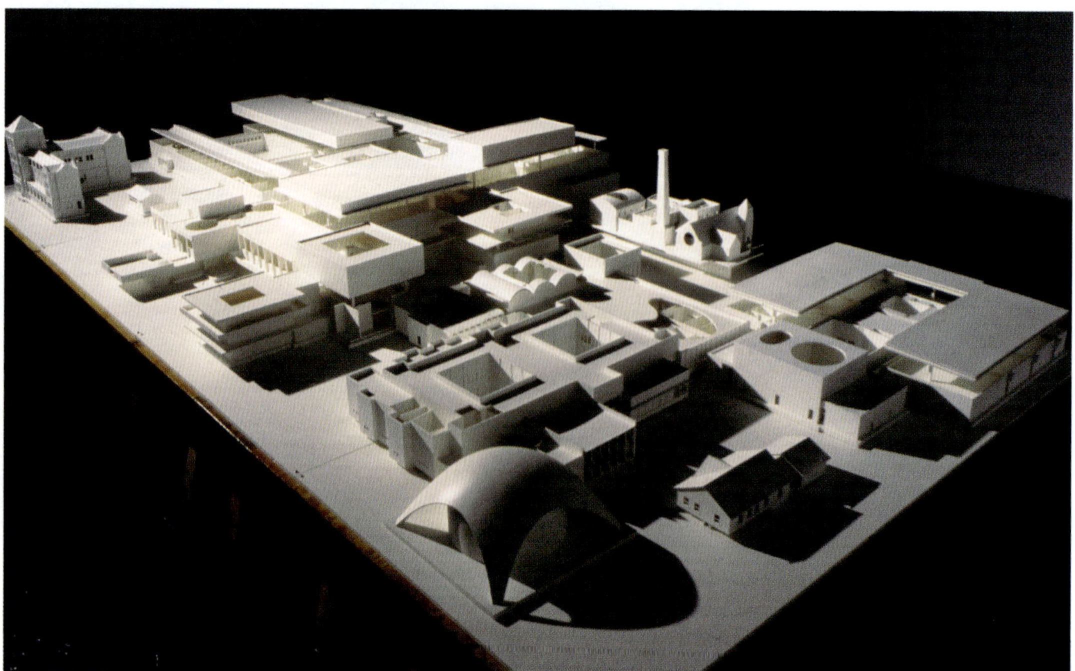

5.7 Mike Kelley, *Educational Complex*, 1995. Installation at Metro Pictures Gallery, New York, 1995. Synthetic polymer, latex, foam core, fiberglass, and wood, 57¾ × 192³⁄₁₆ × 96⅛" (146.7 × 488.2 × 244.2 cm). Whitney Museum of American Art, New York; purchase with funds from the Contemporary Painting and Sculpture Committee 96.50. © Kelley Studio Inc./ Mike Kelley Foundation for the Arts.

representing Kelley's induction into society. His childhood home is there, as is his local church, Catholic elementary school, public high school, college, and graduate schools. These buildings are modeled on Kelley's memories. Most are therefore only half-constructed and passages within are often hidden from view, blocked like the memories of a repressed trauma. The resulting work has the appearance of an architectural model made with insufficient information to actualize the structures. This is institutional critique made with tongue in cheek.

Kelley's turn to autobiography and its lapses coincided with a fascination in the U.S. with Repressed Memory Syndrome (RMS). Practitioners of RMS therapy argued that the sources of many mental illnesses lay in traumatic events that had been forgotten through a defensive coping mechanism. As with Freudian repressions, the lost memories plague the individual until they are exposed and discussed. RMS promised concrete causes for a host of mental-health issues and quickly became popular, not only as a treatment but as a form of entertainment on talk shows and in the mass media. Critics charged that recovered memories—most often involving scenes of childhood sexual abuse—were fictions created under the sway of eager therapists, television producers, and lawyers. The stories repeated by vulnerable individuals trying to account for the pain in their lives often became grounds for legal action. Though some people did manage to clarify painful events in their lives through the technique, the pressure placed on memory often led to the generation of fictionalized autobiographies—which had real consequences. Kelley explained: "this is where I become interested in the debate. For at this point, the whole drama of the law and the system of justice merges with the territory of aesthetics. The implication is that life at its most 'real,' where it intersects with the agencies of power, with that which controls you, also lies in the domain of art, of that which is created or fictional."[14] In RMS as in narrative art, storytelling regardless of its relationship to actual events was ascribed the power to create meaningful relationships between the individual and the world. In the "Toward a Utopian Arts Complex" show, the viewer could turn from the lacunae in *Educational Complex* to the walls of the gallery and read of horrors that truly warranted repression. Oversized clippings from newspapers published in cities where Kelley had lived or exhibited reported gruesome cases of violent and at times preposterous assaults. As a whole, "Toward a Utopian Arts Complex" provided a map of the traumatic passage from mythic childhood innocence into the damaged world of adult life. All that was missing were the actual memories.

In 2000, Kelley stepped up his practice of fabricating memories with the first part of the projected 365-part *Extracurricular Activity Projective Reconstruction*, in which anonymous high-school activities became the catalyst for fantastic explorations of those moments that stood out in adolescence. *Extracurricular Activity Projective Reconstruction #1* (2000) is a black-and-white film of a domestic scene based on a single yearbook photo of two boys in what looks like a coldwater flat in an unnamed city. Five years later Kelley presented *Day Is Done: Extracurricular Activity Projective Reconstructions #2–32* (2004–05) (**fig. 5.8**), with elaborate sculptural and video installations that fuse reinventions of religious rituals,

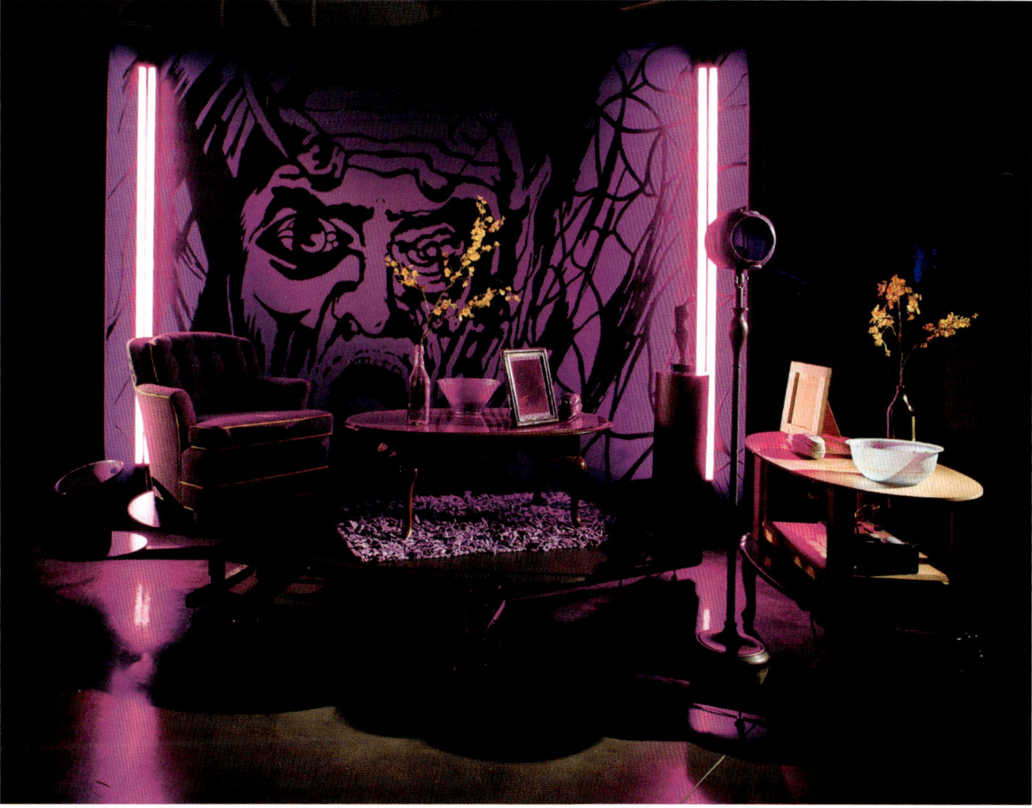

5.8 Mike Kelley, *Shy Satanist (Extracurricular Activity Projective Reconstruction #19)*, 2004–05. From the project *Day is Done*. Mixed media with video projection and photograph(s), 86 × 112 × 116" (218.44 × 284.48 × 294.64 cm). Exhibited at Gagosian Gallery, Chelsea (London) in 2005. © Kelley Studio Inc./Mike Kelley Foundation for the Arts. Courtesy of the foundation and Gagosian Gallery.

vampiric rites, and high-school musicals. As in the first *Extracurricular Activity Projective Reconstruction,* the production of *Day Is Done* began in yearbooks and school publications. For the ensemble of numbers 2–32, Kelley wrote lyrics and music for short theater productions that elaborated or explained the photographs. He then enlisted dozens of performers to step into the roles with all the heart and hyperbole of stereotypical high-school actors, but with the skills of professionals. The gallery is darkened and the viewer moves from station to station amid the cacophony of competing musical and theatrical performances. A photograph of two boys dressed as nineteenth-century dandies inspires a narrative of a young man's realization of his homosexual identity. Another photograph, this time of two boys awkwardly dressed as Nazis, is transformed into an uncanny conflation of hip-hop in the spirit of Sir Mix-a-Lot, *Baby Got Back* and the musical theater of *Cabaret.* In *Day Is Done,* the blockages that kept us out of the corridors of *Educational Complex* are cleared, and the repression, imaginary and real, that fueled RMS trauma is unleashed. We see the fictionalized memories, heroic and traumatic, artificial, absurd, and strangely poignant, played out to their utmost; the yearbook source photos are there to verify the truth of it all. The combinations of veracity and artifice, confidence and doubt, and accuracy and irrelevance that define adolescent productivity characterize the power and pleasure of *Day Is Done.*

Signs and Abstractions

While the commodity artists embraced the world of brands and goods as the tools for representing contemporary culture and the relationships that define it, a number of painters took up the iconic styles of Modernist geometric abstraction with similar zeal. Peter Halley and a group of artists who came to be called Neo-Geo appeared to take up the Minimalist mantle in much the same spirit as Koons and company appeared to be writing a sequel to Pop art and Dada. Unlike the Neo-Expressionist embrace of historical styles, which appeared either to assert the emotional depth and philosophical urgency of gestural paintings, as if they could still function as they had in the Expressionist or Abstract Expressionist movements, or—to the contrary—pronounce them dead, empty gestures devoid of content, Neo-Geo was acutely concerned with style as an ambiguous bearer of meaning. Like commodity artists, Neo-Geo practitioners held to the assumption that meaning in their work relied first and foremost on the socially determined significance of its contents. Formal and phenomenological qualities were still important, as demonstrated by Halley's centralized compositions and embrace of artificial Day-Glo paints or by Sherrie Levine's turn to the unusual and historical medium of casein. Surface and composition, however, were secondary to consideration of the work of art as a field of signification in which styles provided a record of past attempts to order society, the body, and the cosmos, much as commodity artists treated the things and labels in their art as placeholders for desire—for luxury, class mobility, adventure, satisfaction, and meaning. Both Neo-Geo and commodity art relished the instability of the individual components of their artistic vocabulary—of geometric shapes or found objects—and put great faith in viewers' inclinations, perhaps even against their will, to treat the things and forms in the art as referents to complex contemporary and historical meanings.

Peter Halley

Peter Halley (b. 1953) would be the most visible and vocal member of the International with Monument group in its first years, and it was he who provided the initial theoretical foundations of Neo-Geo. Halley began writing reviews and criticism before attaining prominence as an artist. The reception of his art and that of his peers was strongly influenced by his reflections on the writings of Michel Foucault, Jean Baudrillard, and Robert Smithson, and on a variety of historical and contemporary art. His paintings, however, were not simply illustrations for his theoretical texts. In many cases, their characteristic forms appeared on canvas years before being discussed in his writings. Both image and text were thus part of an intellectual and aesthetic investigation that drew on theory, experience, and observation, and that moved between diverse and at times contradictory positions.

His work, exemplified by *Two Cells with Circulating Conduit* (1985) (**fig. 5.9**), consisted of squares, rectangles, and bars that he called "cells" and "conduits" to draw attention to their technological and social as well as aesthetic roots. Here, in the form of electrical circuitry, urban grids, and cell blocks, were symbols of the networks of communication and power in contemporary society. Halley's compositions also refer to the history of geometric abstraction from the early twentieth-century Modernists to the more recent Minimalists. To viewers versed in the history of modern art, a painting composed of several squares conjured Suprematist compositions by Russian revolutionary painter Kazimir Malevich (1878–1935), for whom the geometric shape unlocked from traditional rules of composition was a key to imagining the modern citizen free of existing power structures. The same compositions also evoke the grids of Piet Mondrian (1872–1944) and his conviction that the proper placement of horizontal and vertical lines and blocks of primary colors allowed artist and viewer to reach an intellectually and spiritually productive life. Halley's abstraction also had sources in the architecture of the International Style, which appealed to the grid as a means of capturing in glass and steel, stone and space, structures most able to respond to modern needs for living, as well as in the phenomenological clarity of Minimalist sculptor Donald Judd's box forms (see fig. 1.5), used to elicit sensations outside the confines of either art history or social life. In reminding viewers of the range of uses to which artists have enlisted geometry, Halley makes the argument that forms, like commodities, do not have a single, essential significance, but rather take on different meanings through

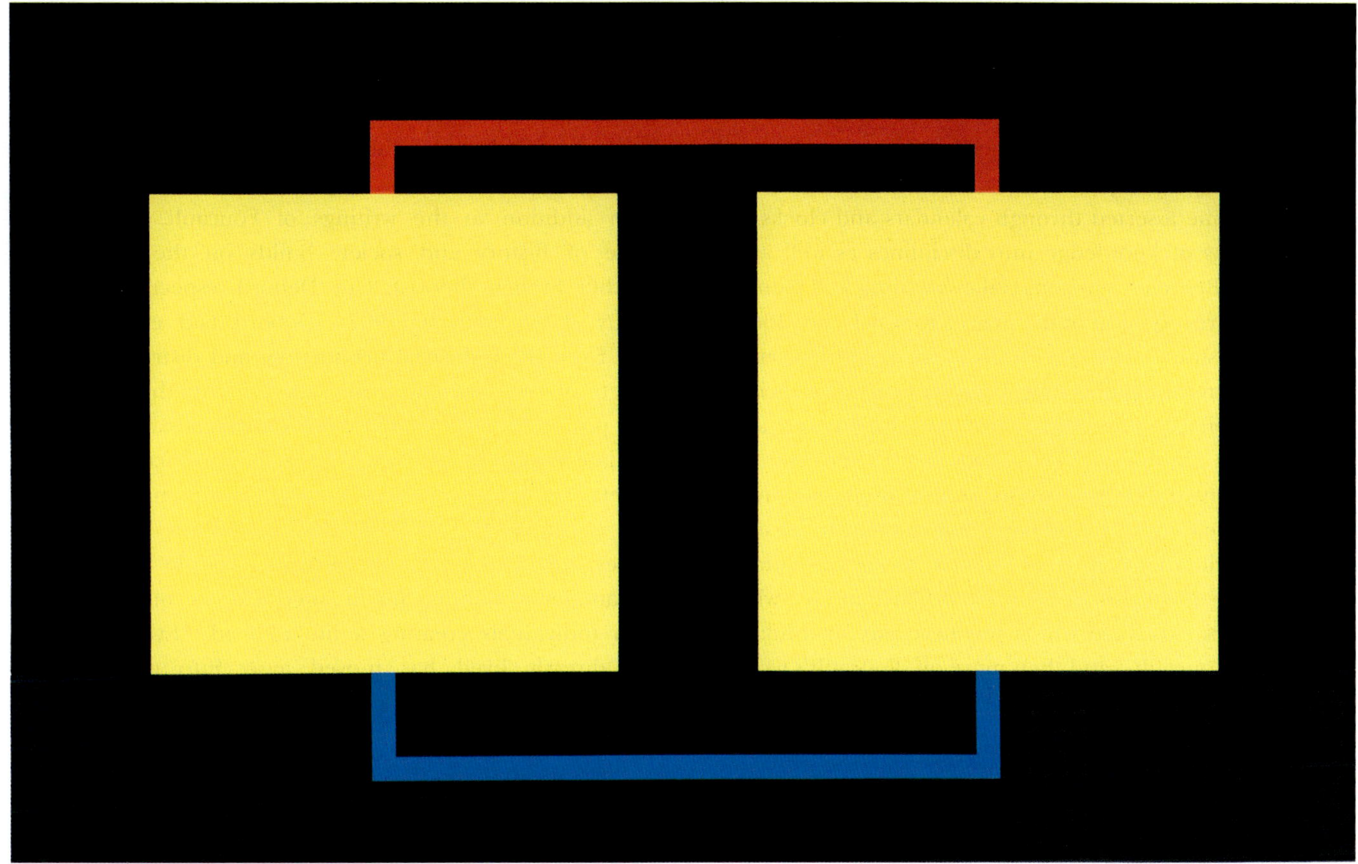

5.9 Peter Halley, ***Two Cells with Circulating Conduit***, 1985. Acrylic, Day-Glo acrylic, and Roll-a-Tex on canvas, 63 × 108" (160.02 × 274.32 cm). Courtesy the artist.

use and context. These meanings constitute the history of the style, and become material for the contemporary artist.

Halley grew up in New York in a left-wing, intellectual family, went to Yale, and after college moved to New Orleans. There, he began thinking about Modernism as a language one could interpret and analyze. He also began looking to the ubiquitous U.S. urban sprawl for inspiration. Upon returning to New York in 1980, he started painting geometric environments with Roll-a-Tex and Day-Glo paints, materials from the construction industry. His garish yet deliberately composed images parodied the idealist aspirations of Modernist geometric art by combining allusions to the idealized patterns of modern urbanism, architecture, and art, as well as to the realized appearances of middle-class real estate developments and cheap hotels. The geometric compositions and textured surfaces also had personal sources in the appearance of the artist's own apartment and unshaven face. Soon after returning to New York, Halley joined a theory and cultural criticism reading group where he read Foucault and discovered "in the square a prison, behind the mythologies of contemporary society a veiled network of cells and conduits."[15] Halley's thinking, which had begun as an intuitive reflection on modern art and his surroundings in New Orleans, was now becoming integrated into a topology of power relations that extended, as Foucault described it, from the buildings and operations of schools, hospitals, streets, and prisons to devices for organizing time and information including clocks, charts, graphs, and calendars. Halley's geometry was thus invested with direct social meaning.

In *Discipline and Punish* (1975), a touchstone text for the period, Foucault used the example of Jeremy Bentham's Panopticon, a design for a prison, to address the role of vision in the distribution of power in modern society. In 1785, Bentham conceived of a facility that would make it possible to incarcerate a maximum number of inmates with a minimum number of guards. He did so by replacing force with a new configuration and use of architectural space. The Panopticon consisted of a guard tower surrounded by a multistory ring of uniform cells; the central tower was illuminated from within in such a way that the guards could see the inmates without themselves being seen. In this way the burden of control shifted from the guard, who previously had to seek out infractions, to the inmate who, knowing he is never out of view, now becomes the agent of his own punishment. Bentham's design enlisted the psychology of the scrutinized subject as the primary means of maintaining order. Under threat of being seen, the prisoner guards himself. The Panopticon, Foucault suggested, made explicit a key organizing principle of the workplace, school, or hospital: Behavior is better controlled through isolation and the fear of being observed than by force or the bodily presence of authority. This new model of control took specific forms, all based on the repetition of geometrically defined units. Halley's interest as a painter and art critic led him to connect the appeal of geometric abstraction in Modernist art to patterns of modern social organization described by Foucault, including the design of factories, the ordered division of time asserted through calendars and clocks, and even divisions of knowledge into disciplines as well as the geometry of Bentham's prison. Halley's writing and paintings offer a bleak recognition of the degree to which the Modernist faith in abstract form, specifically geometry, might serve as a smokescreen for the ordering of modern capitalist society.

Halley soon expanded his analysis into the theoretical territory of Jean Baudrillard's simulacra. In his 1984 essay "The Crisis in Geometry," Halley argued that while the writings of Foucault were critical to understanding geometric art of the 1970s, Baudrillard's ideas were essential to interpretation of the art of the 1980s. It had been Baudrillard, in fact, who in the late 1970s explained why it was necessary to think seriously about Foucault—and then move on. Foucault's writing, in common with many of the theoretical reevaluations of culture, economy, psychology, and language since the late 1960s, rejected the existence of essential truths that could be discovered and promoted by the historian. History and language, he argued, must be understood as a series of tactical agreements dependent on the needs and creativity of the historian. This perspective was called "Poststructuralist" because it rejected stable forms of history or knowledge. Baudrillard embraced Foucault's arguments; however, he also sensed that they remained wedded to authority and an idea of truth, albeit in a more liberating way. Beginning with the treatise "Forget Foucault" (1977), Baudrillard forced Poststructuralist analysis to its logical conclusion. Even contingent and shifting histories, he argued, lay claim to a certain truth-value. In order to rid Foucault's critique of its residual faith in this idea of truth, Baudrillard theorized a construction of the world that was distanced not only from the truth, but from reality as well. He called it "the simulacra."

Baudrillard presumed that our experience of the world was so mediated that we had lost all contact with anything even approximating a conventional idea of "reality." In his 1983 essay "The Precession of Simulacra," Baudrillard provided a short history, an art history, which explained that images had once been representations of real things, but that all that had now changed. In a society of simulacra, images ceased to refer to something else, something real, and took on a significance all their own—references without referents, together making up a kind of hyperreality. Baudrillard writes:

> These would be the successive phases of the image.
> It is the reflection of a basic reality.
> It masks and perverts a basic reality.
> It masks the absence of a basic reality.
> It bears no relation to any reality whatever: it is its own pure simulacrum.[16]

There is a painful conundrum in Baudrillard's short history of the image; by its end, it is no longer possible to represent the path by which it has come to pass. A society of the simulacrum has lost the ability to represent itself. It is this idea that Halley found central to his work and the work of Neo-Geo artists generally.

In addition to the writings of Foucault, Baudrillard's sense of history and society builds on the thinking of another French theorist, Guy Debord, especially his book *Society of the Spectacle* (1967). Debord had examined the shift from the industrial production- and distribution-based society of the nineteenth and early twentieth centuries to the post-industrial service and information economy of the late twentieth century. The main product of this new society, he suggested, was the spectacle, an image that, like a commodity or a dream, intervenes between our senses and the world we perceive. People had become an audience waiting for a spectacle to observe rather than individuals creating a life to lead. "Everything that was directly lived has moved away into a representation," he wrote on the first page of *Society of the Spectacle*.[17] Representations, he elaborated, splinter off from any relation to reality and form their own realm of the non-real, which unifies late capitalist society under what he describes as the "spectral" power of the spectacle. This corresponds to the second phase of Baudrillard's history of the image and introduces the possibility of the third.

Foucault's and Debord's theories depicting Western society as one of representations created a foundation for theorizing the simulacra, a society-as-image with no representational relationship to anything at all. If Foucault's discursive histories still contained, according to Baudrillard, a lingering sense of Enlightenment truth, the spectacle, as Debord himself noted, still possessed the residue of the directly lived or the real. With his simulacra, Baudrillard pushed past Debord's image-world full of representations. Simulacra dispense entirely with truth and representation by rendering the real not lost, dead, or absent, but quite simply irrelevant. Unlike a copy, which validates the authority of the original through imitation, and unlike an appropriation, which recontextualizes and thus conceptually transforms the original, simulation puts to rest the competition between itself and any conception of the real. The simulacrum validates nothing beyond itself. As Baudrillard wrote, "It is the generation by models of a real without origin or reality, a hyperreal."[18]

Halley follows Baudrillard's lead in examining the conflict between reality and representation in contemporary life. His painting and writing treat the simulacra as the limit point against which he charts his own history of the image. His *The Place* (1992) (**fig. 5.10**) is a case in point, its cells and conduits referring both to the real—that is, Halley's observation of life in the city—and to his theoretical readings of Foucault and Baudrillard. Emphasizing this multiplicity is Halley's choice of title, which alludes to the way Andy Warhol referred

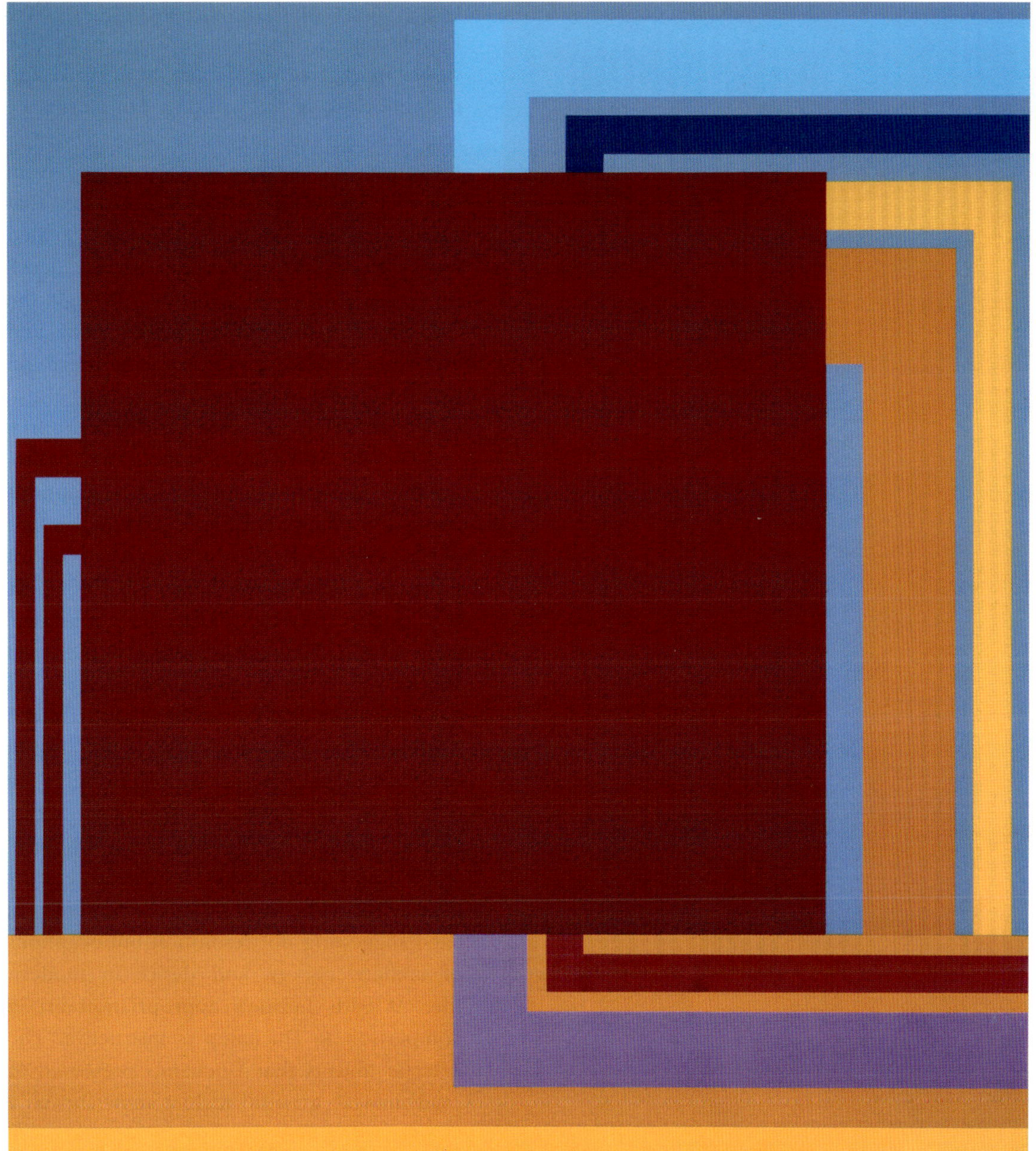

5.10 Peter Halley, *The Place*, 1992. Acrylic, Day-Glo acrylic, and Roll-a-Tex on canvas, 95½ × 86" (242.57 × 218.44 cm). Tate Modern, London. Lent from Mottahedan Projects, Dubai. On long-term loan since 2000.

to hospital, a word he would not say out loud. Thus Warhol, the artist known for holding a mirror up to contemporary culture, also reminds us of the power of naming and of the important distance between the representation, "the place," and the reality, the hospital.

Halley's work, both written and painted, can be seen as including all the stages of Baudrillard's history of the image. As such, it constitutes a library of often conflicting ideas about art and culture. For some, this indicated a lack of discipline and a streak of opportunism in the artist. Others were more generous in their assessments. The curator/writer team of Tricia Collins and Richard Milazzo, responsible for a number of East Village events, zeroed in on this abrasive conjunction of incompatible positions as a source of strength in Neo-Geo. In their eyes, presenting the viewer with problems, irregularities, and confusion meant making art that was instrumental and active, not instructive or directive. Here was art that juxtaposed conflicting propositions rather than telling us its conclusions, and thus mimicked life with its constant barrage of often irreconcilable oppositions. As fellow painter Ross Bleckner described it, painting was "an investigatory tool, a language to think thought and not just to locate it."[19]

Ross Bleckner and Sherrie Levine

Ross Bleckner (b. 1949) and Sherrie Levine (see Chapter 2) also saw painting as a means to reckon with the compromised and compelling history of Modernism. Bleckner borrowed heavily from Op Art, a movement of the 1960s that had experimented with graphic patterning to create optically surprising and often emotionally wrenching effects. In *Departure* (1986) (**fig. 5.11**), he combined a trancelike rhythm of stripes with a sensual application of paint. As the eye moves across the pattern, it is stalled by dissolving passages of paint, as though the clean lines and optical pleasure of Op Art are

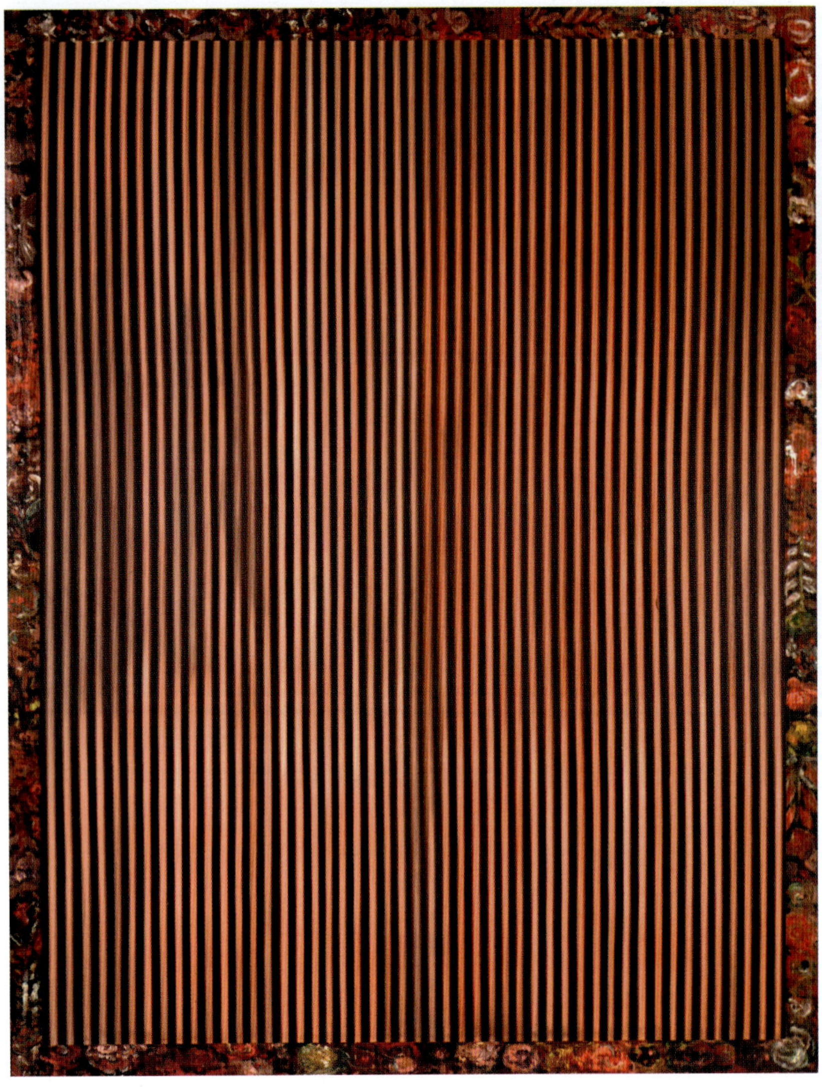

5.11 Ross Bleckner, ***Departure***, 1986. Oil on canvas, 108 × 84" (274.3 × 213.4 cm). © Ross Bleckner. Courtesy Mary Boone Gallery, New York.

being interrupted by the tactility of Neo-Expressionism. These disruptions invite the viewer to explore the depths, both visual and metaphorical, of the painting. On its surface and through its suggestive title, *Departure* transforms a repetitive pattern copied from the past into a dirge for personal loss that casts a pall over the optical pleasure created by Bleckner's paint. Bleckner further developed this theme of mourning through the floral border he painted onto *Departure*, and elsewhere in imagery he created based on urns and blood cells.

Sherrie Levine combined appropriation and painting differently. In her photographs, she had challenged presumptions about authorship (see fig. 2.3). Now, through her watercolor copies of reproductions of artworks, she critiqued other claims made for Modernism. Her target was what she called the "false promise" that art could and should reconcile oppositions of matter and spirit, content and form, desire and reality.[20] Among Levine's paintings are copies of Egon Schiele's Expressionism, Piet Mondrian's De Stijl, Joan Miró's Surrealism (**fig. 5.12**), and Fernand Léger's mechanical Modernism, chosen because they represent radically different combinations of such oppositions, each suggesting not resolution but eruptions of anxiety, energy, and desire in modern life. As with Levine's appropriation art, a comparison to Duchamp is instructive. The eclectic objects that Duchamp presented as readymades—a bottle rack, a snow shovel, a

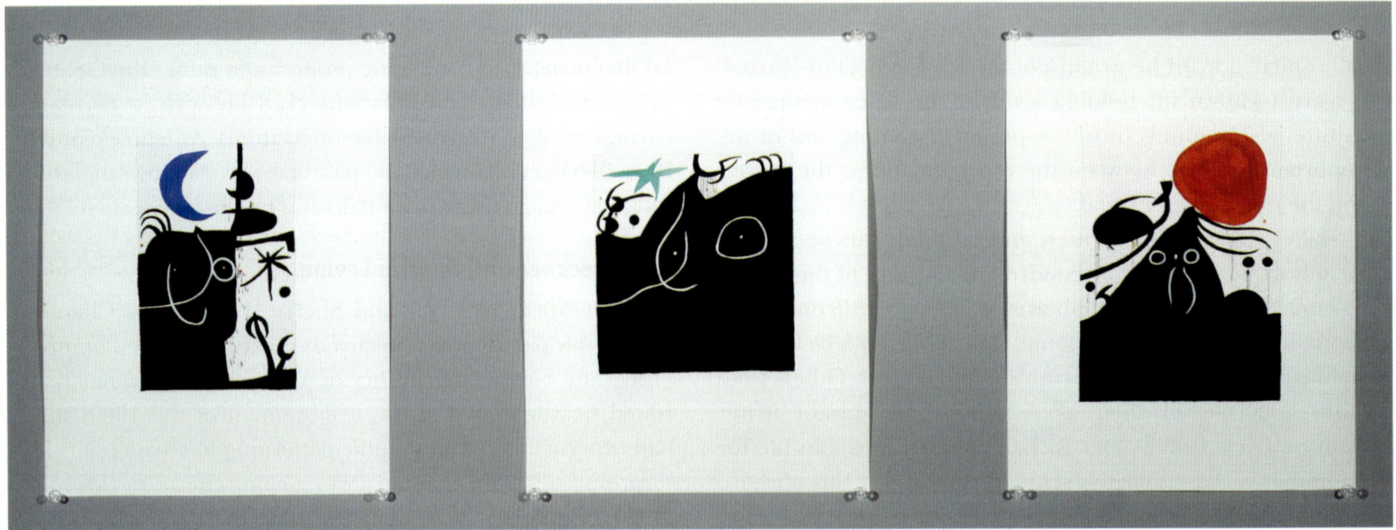

5.12 Sherrie Levine, ***After Joan Miró***, 1985. Three watercolors on paper, each 14 × 11" (35.6 × 27.9 cm). The Museum of Contemporary Art, Los Angeles. Gift of Councilman Joel Wachs and the artist in memory of Joe Bishop 86.6.1-.3. © Sherrie Levine. Courtesy Paula Cooper Gallery, New York.

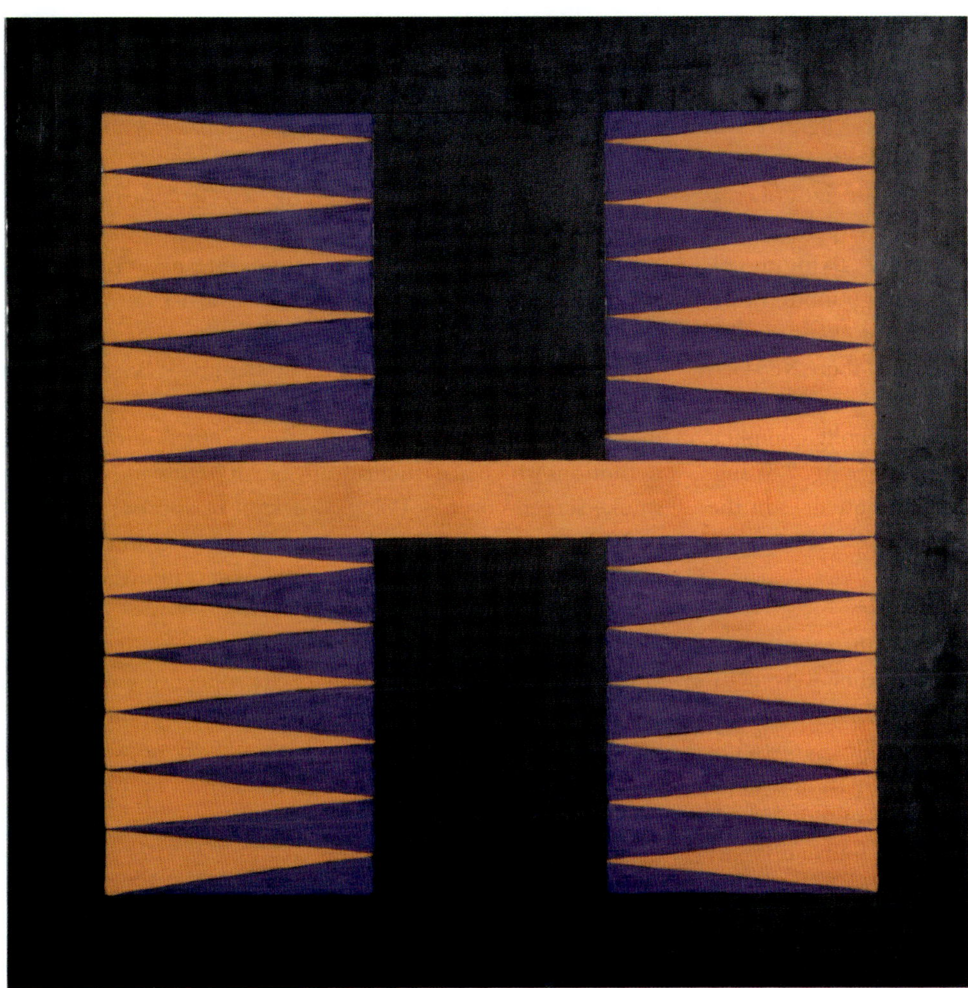

5.13 Sherrie Levine, *Lead Chevron: II*, 1988. Casein on lead, 20 × 20" (50 × 50 cm). © Sherrie Levine. Courtesy Paula Cooper Gallery, New York.

urinal, for example—were chosen not for their unique properties, but as demonstrations of the creative act of the artist. As appropriation, Levine's copies make a similar statement, reflecting on how creative acts of others can be diminished as they become history. The particularity of her subjects—Miró's biomorphic, highly personal, and often whimsical Surrealism or Mondrian's abstract universality—is sacrificed in favor of their general status as "works of art." Differences are glossed over and antagonisms are quieted by the urge to convey a cohesion in the Western artistic tradition's most recent chapter. Levine's appropriation shows modern art reduced to little more than a series of illustrations and the great variety of contradictions these works engaged—the irreconcilable forces of desire and reality in Miró's work or the universal and the particular in Mondrian's, for instance—have been reconciled, not in the active or confrontational synthesis that the artists strove after, but in the stasis of canonized history.

Levine's paintings themselves, however, do resist being reduced to illustrations of a theoretical or political point by introducing the very element that Duchamp had excised from his readymade and that textbook reproductions cannot replicate—the artist's touch. In a poetic twist, confounding in the context of appropriation, Levine replaced the equivocating gaze of the photographer with the subtle poignancy and personal expressivity of the handmade in her paintings. These handmade copies of machine-made representations of handmade objects are invested with a sense of craft and the connotations created by human contact. As if to focus our attention on the act of making, in the mid-1980s Levine created a second series that emphasized her choice of materials. With her series of works alluding to geometric abstraction, including *Lead Chevron: II* (1988) (**fig. 5.13**), Levine reduces her compositional activity to copying the mundane patterns of chess and backgammon boards. But her medium is highly unusual: Casein, a milk-based paint with a history extending back to ancient Egypt and conveying an organic quality, is applied to lead, which provides the work with a sensual and surprising presence. Levine thus brings together geometric abstraction and games, sensuality and criticality, history and contemporaneity.

Halley's work inspired ire because its appeal to Baudrillard's theory of the simulacra seemed to insulate it from real-world problems, while its sensually provocative surfaces and its creator's blue-chip gallery representation connected it to real-world pleasures. Levine's art struck a different chord. With the introduction of each new medium and material to her oeuvre, first watercolor, then casein, lead, wood, and gold, she embraced more nuanced and esoteric aspects of painting. If Halley's use of Day-Glo and Roll-a-Tex resisted the transcendence of his abstractions, Levine sought out a sublime and "auratic presence" in her new work.[21] Bleckner did a similar thing, investing what he deemed the "dead" style of Op Art with spiritual content, mystical light, and a mysterious aura to match that of the turn-of-the-century Symbolists.[22] Such emotive content, especially in the light of critical challenges to Neo-Expressionism, drew sharp responses. In such a context, hearing an artist speak of "trying to collapse the utopian and dystopian aspects of high modernism" could be harrowing.[23] If art was a conceptual exercise, or a game as *Untitled (Lead Chevron 1)* suggested, then Neo-Geo provided a safe space to examine the collisions of thought and action; if, on the other hand, art was wholly complicit with power, as Levine's *After Walker Evans: 7* (see fig. 2.3) suggested, then the art making had direct consequences in the realm of life.

General Idea

Though the techniques of Neo-Geo were thrust into the spotlight from the East Village and SoHo, they were actually being practiced across a much broader field. By the late 1970s, the Canadian artist group General Idea, consisting of A.A. Bronson (b. 1946), Felix Partz (1945–94), and Jorge Zontal (1944–94), had polished a strategy of mimicking, appropriating, and transforming advertising, journalism, art criticism, architecture, exhibitions, spectacles, camp, fine art, satire, and education. In a variety of works including performances, parties, sculptures, installations, images, books, videos, and seventeen years of *FILE Megazine* (1972–89), a send-up of *LIFE* magazine, General Idea made art containing a high dose of sex, comedy, and politics. Tired of the rules and constraints of society, one could sidle up to the bar in General Idea's *Colour Bar Lounge*, the set for the group's 1979 video *Test Tube*, and order a cocktail mixed to relieve "abstract repressionism." Or you could wave a flag featuring three brightly colored intersecting ziggurats and advocate turning the icons of power on their heads. General Idea's humor was rooted in the perception, shared by Neo-Geo artists, that the creative work of the 1980s would involve manipulating pre-existing symbols and integrating them into new critical contexts. Clive Robertson, a performance artist, curator, and critic based in Toronto, described the group's art as subjecting the everyday to a "logic of … ambiguity."[24] Borrowing its prose style, Robertson explained that General Idea created "a dense metaphorest cultivated for the production of sawn-off definitions which are ritualistically burnt to provide optimum smoke screen cover."[25] Using a cocktail of appropriated bits of high, mass, and sub-cultures, General Idea undermined mainstream values and conventional expectations about the relationship between art and society.

General Idea's origin story reads like a page out of Andy Warhol's philosophy. Reflecting on its collective journey, the group mused, "we wanted to be artists and we knew that if we were famous and glamorous we could say we were artists and we would be."[26] Making no reference to French theory or leftist politics, General Idea asserted that the key to artistic authority lay in style. "We knew Glamour was not an object, not an action, not an idea. We knew Glamour never emerged from the 'nature' of things … We knew Glamour was artificial. We knew that in order to be glamorous we had to become plagiarists, intellectual parasites."[27] Armed with the skills of the spy and the copyist, General Idea created a "superabundance of significant forms and gestures."[28] At its most refined, the group's art resembled the careful presentation

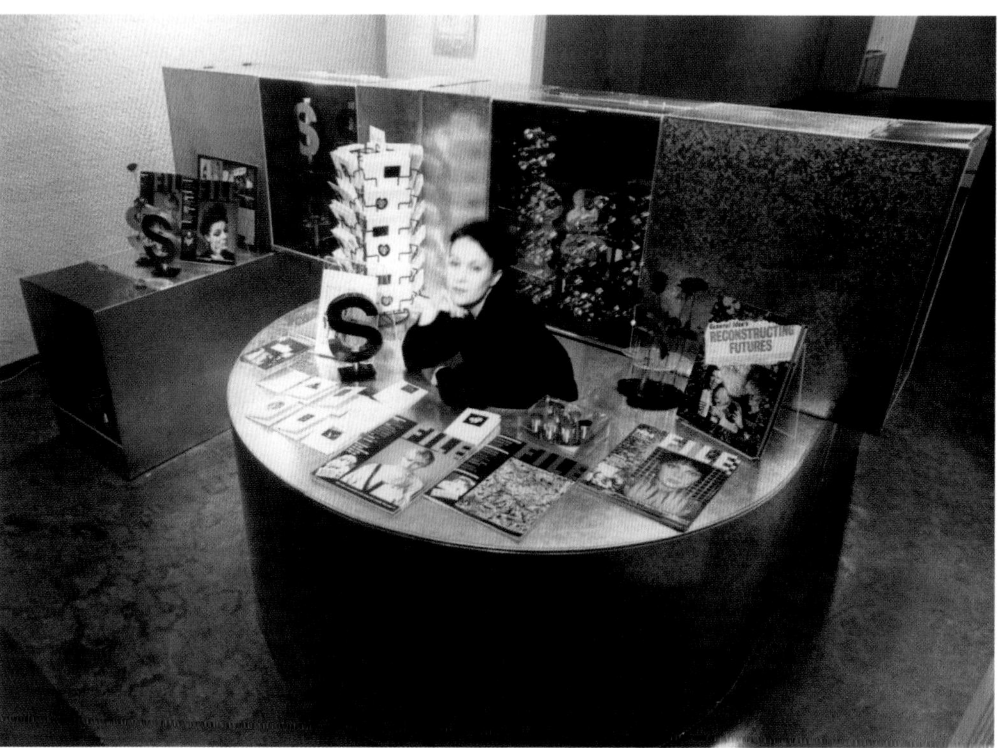

5.14 General Idea, ***Boutique from the Miss General Idea 1984 Pavilion***, 1980. Installation, counter in the shape of a dollar sign, constructed of galvanized metal and Plexiglas, containing various multiples, prints, posters and publications, 60¼ × 131⅞ × 102⅜" (153 × 335 × 260 cm). Collection General Idea, Toronto/New York.

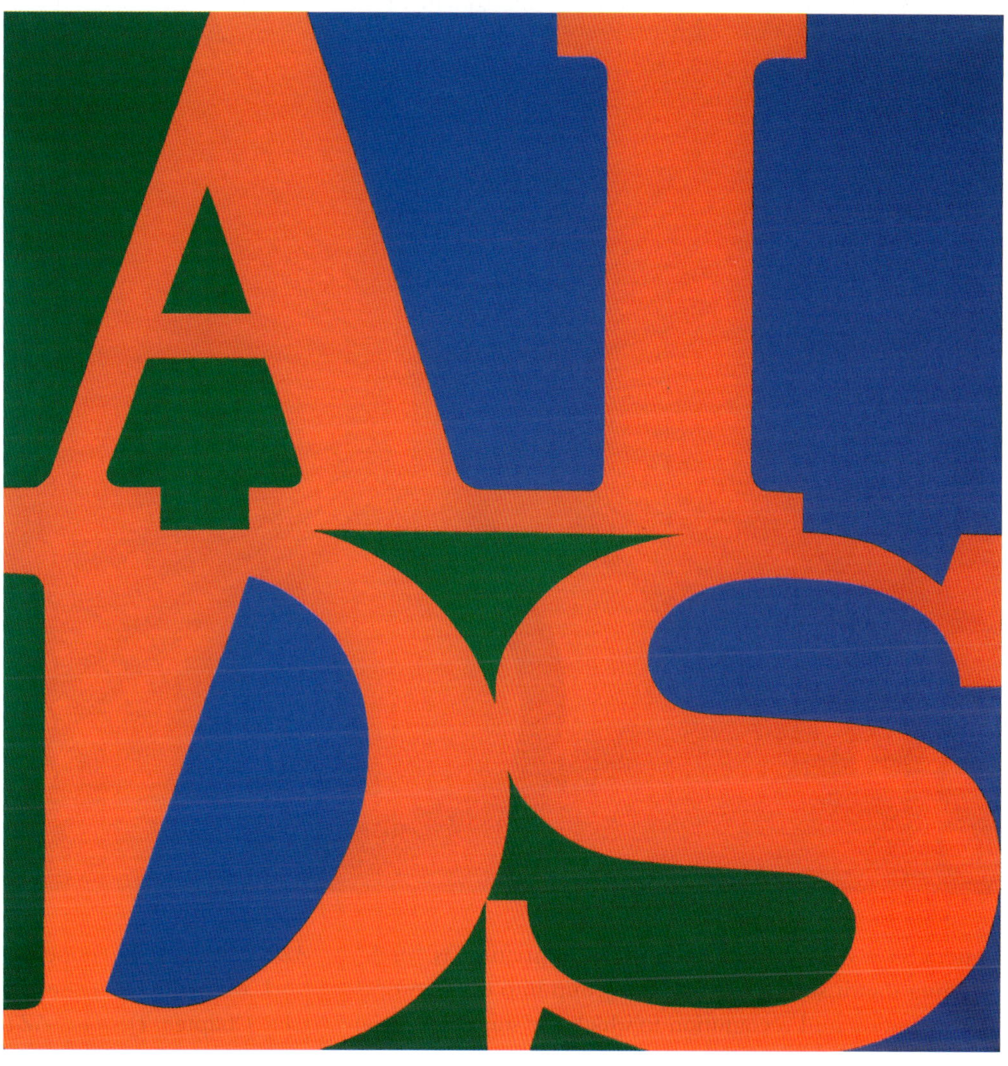

5.15 General Idea, *AIDS*, 1989. Acrylic on canvas, 72 × 72" (183 × 183 cm). (GI 155). Private collection. Courtesy BFAS Blondeau Fine Art Services, Geneva.

of geometric signs and styles of Halley or Levine, but refinement was not General Idea's point. Modernist geometry was only one of many symbolic forms the group transformed in its art. Its most famous concoction was the *Miss General Idea 1984 Pavilion* (ca. 1970–ca. 1986), a fragmentary simulation of a nonexistent beauty pageant accompanied in several incarnations by an actual gift shop, the *Boutique from the Miss General Idea 1984 Pavilion* (1980) (**fig. 5.14**). With *Miss General Idea,* the group created an elaborate three-dimensional fiction that struck a delicate balance between describing the condition of consumer desire, serving it, and mocking it, with the viewer invited to feel a confusing mixture of self-consciousness, self-critique, and self-indulgence.

In 1980, General Idea staged the simulated destruction by fire of the *Miss General Idea 1984 Pavilion* and began exhibiting artifacts from this nonexistent place as the *Miss General Idea 1984 Armoury.* Individual pieces included the *Mar-Bells,* marble barbells with which the artists "worked on problem areas and built up those flabby clichés into three-dimensional insights," or the *Seats of Power,* where they sat and relaxed.[29] Unlike much Neo-Geo work, General Idea's faux-relics frustrate one's search for clues. Confronted with a Halley, the viewer can find answers in the writings of Foucault or Baudrillard. The viewer of the *Miss General Idea 1984 Pavilion,* on the other hand, must find satisfaction in the deferral of any such clarifying theoretical positions. The point of *Miss General Idea,* the group explained, was to provide a "framing device for arresting attention without throwing away the key"; our attention is captured, but is also free and encouraged to roam.[30] General Idea cast this quest for continually shifting content in an altogether pleasurable context of disco lights, dancing, sex, and fashion, suggesting that the coincidence of pleasure and indeterminacy is at the heart of the project.

In the mid-1980s, General Idea joined International with Monument, which soon after regrouped with modified personnel in SoHo under the name Koury-Wingate. At this time, the character and content of General Idea's work changed significantly. In 1987, in response to the AIDS crisis, the group executed the first of many presentations of the letters "A," "I," "D," and "S" in imitation of Robert Indiana's (b. 1928) famous LOVE design (1989) (**fig. 5.15**). Indiana's work had both refined compositional clarity and pop-culture references. For General Idea, it was even more important that Indiana's LOVE icon was already part of mass culture through its adoption in numerous advertising campaigns.

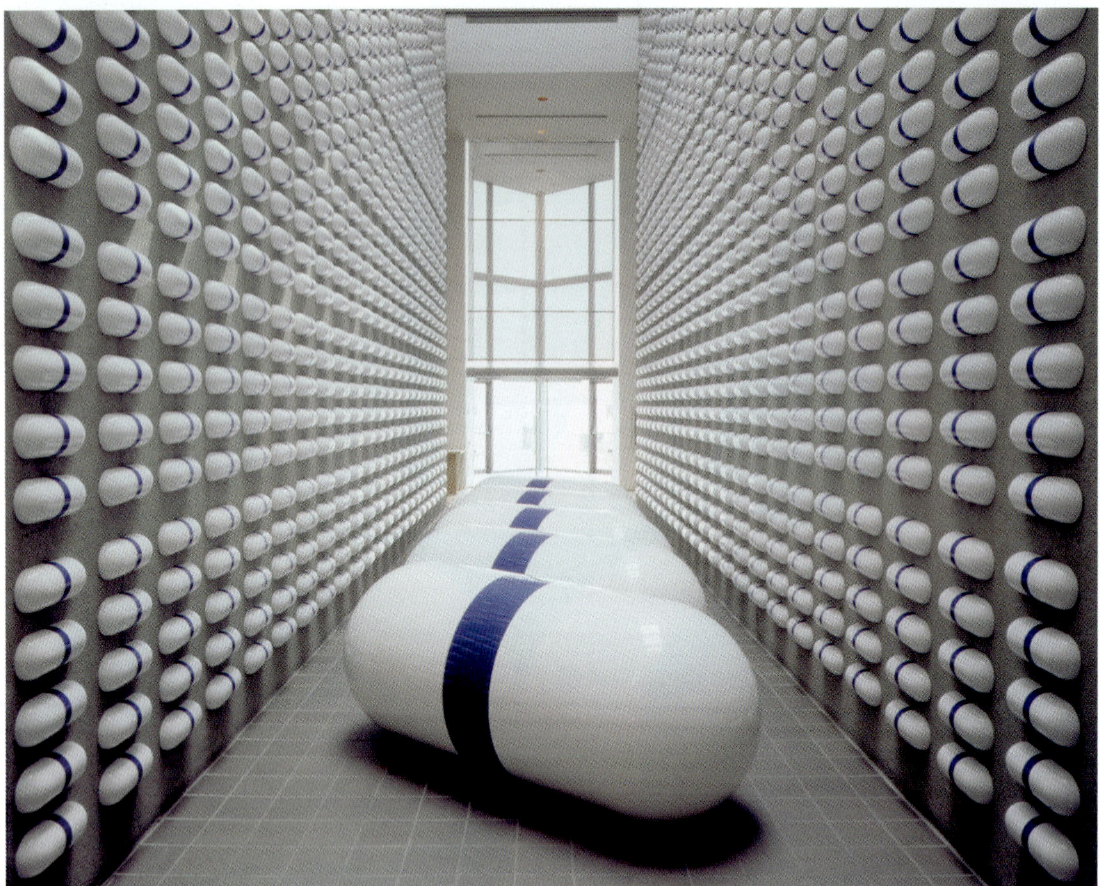

5.16 General Idea *One Day of AZT*, 1991, and *One Year of AZT*, 1991. Installation, 5 parts, fiberglass and enamel, each 33½ × 84 × 33½" (85 × 213.3 × 85 cm), and 1,825 vacuum-formed styrene with vinyl, each 5 × 12½ × 2½" (12.7 × 31.7 × 6.3 cm) (GI 003). Installation view, General Idea's "Fin de siècle," The Power Plant, Toronto, 1993. Both works from Collection General Idea, Toronto/New York.

General Idea described its brand of appropriation as "viral," meaning that it served to hook the group into the networks of distribution and recognition to which the source material was already connected. The already coopted LOVE image was thus ideal in permitting General Idea access to pre-existing cultural and commercial arenas. At a moment when AIDS was a public-health crisis but was not being discussed in constructive terms by national governments, General Idea's image could be seen in museums and galleries, on buses and in subways, on television news programs, at demonstrations, and in public-health campaigns across the globe.

In the early 1990s, General Idea created a series of Minimalist-inspired sculptures and wall reliefs—such as *One Day of AZT* (1991) and *One Year of AZT* (1991) (**fig. 5.16**)—about the treatments being developed for AIDS. AZT was (and is) the most widely discussed and distributed treatment for AIDS-related symptoms. In 1991, the treatment involved taking five pills a day at regular intervals and was very expensive. The combined installation of *One Day* and *One Year of AZT* presents a single day's dosage in the form of outsize pills, larger than a human body, resting in a narrow corridor, and then, climbing up the walls in an ordered grid, 1,825 smaller pills—the equivalent of one year's prescription. Not only does the work resemble the modular sculpture and reductive painting of Minimalism, it also evokes the regulating devices central to Foucault's histories and Halley's imagery. As AZT is not a cure, the treatment described in General Idea's works ends in death. *One Year of AZT* contrasts the hopeful optimism of most Pop-inspired work with echoes of the "Silence=Death" icon of Gran Fury (see Chapter 4). The AZT installation also demonstrates General Idea's interest in cultivating viral relationships with different types of hosts. Recognizing the museum as another form of mass media, much as Barbara Kruger had in the late 1980s (see Chapter 2), works such as the AZT pieces latch onto the language of fine art to take the discussion of health-care and politics to a wider audience.

Commodity and Form in Europe

European artists shared concerns over the intersection of capitalism and modern art, and of the commodity and style, with their North American counterparts. As discussed in Chapter 3, the coordinated presence in the decades after World War II of U.S. money and U.S. art inspired an urgent critique of aesthetics and art among many European artists and intellectuals. By the 1990s, nationalism had, to a great extent, faded from the picture, but the interest in the aesthetic and social power of brands, logos, and goods remained strong.

John M. Armleder

The Europeans most often linked to U.S. commodity concerns are the Fluxus-inspired mixed-media artist John M. Armleder (b. 1948) from Switzerland and the more politically oriented German artist Rosemarie Trockel. Armleder shares with the U.S. artists what he has described as a readiness to treat Modernism as a set of effects to be manipulated by collection, assemblage, and transformation. His work has been acutely attuned to the power and potential of using commodities to aesthetic and hermeneutic ends since the 1970s and he has even included curating, perhaps the ultimate appropriative art, in his toolbox.

Armleder began his career creating almost invisible interventions into everyday spaces—repainting walls the color they already were and rearranging waste paper in trash baskets. Composing by arranging the things that already circulate in our daily lives remained the foundation of Armleder's practice and led to a slightly broader range of sources than is found in U.S. Neo-Geo. Typical of his work is *Ne dites pas non! (Don't say no!)* (1986/2007) (**fig. 5.17**), a recurring collaboration between the artist and various museums. For this piece, Armleder instructs curators to buy furniture and display it with art from their collection. He provides a general guide for the kind of furniture or art that should be selected, but puts the museum professionals in charge of actually obtaining the materials and composing the installation. Curators thus become collaborators and fabricators, making decisions that affect the appearance and content of the work. The results share with Neo-Geo the appearance of the familiar re-presented, and offer aesthetic pleasures that both repeat and slightly modify those already inherent in their component parts.

Ne dites pas non! is a variation on a larger body of work that Armleder calls "furniture sculpture," begun in 1979. These works are composed of carefully placed chairs, couches, benches, bar stools, dressers, carpets, lamps, and occasionally non-furniture items such as musical instruments or paintings by Armleder and others. *Untitled Furniture Sculpture 144* (1986–87) (**fig. 5.18**), with its centrally presented canvas hung low between two cymbals liberated from their drum kits, displays the characteristically rigid structure of the series. The piece has a limited color palette of white, green, chrome, and brass. Deep green dots gridded across the white canvas provide ordered counterparts to the cantilevered arms and potential crash of the cymbals. Like most of the furniture pieces, it possesses a strong sense of balance which in this case counters the threatening anxiety that the cymbals might be struck by a visitor thus knocking the composition askew. The meaning of the work is likewise open to flux. For some viewers, it will evoke art history—Op Art or Dada for instance—for others the allusion to sound, accident, and rock-and-roll may dominate. For the artist, all interpretations are equally acceptable.

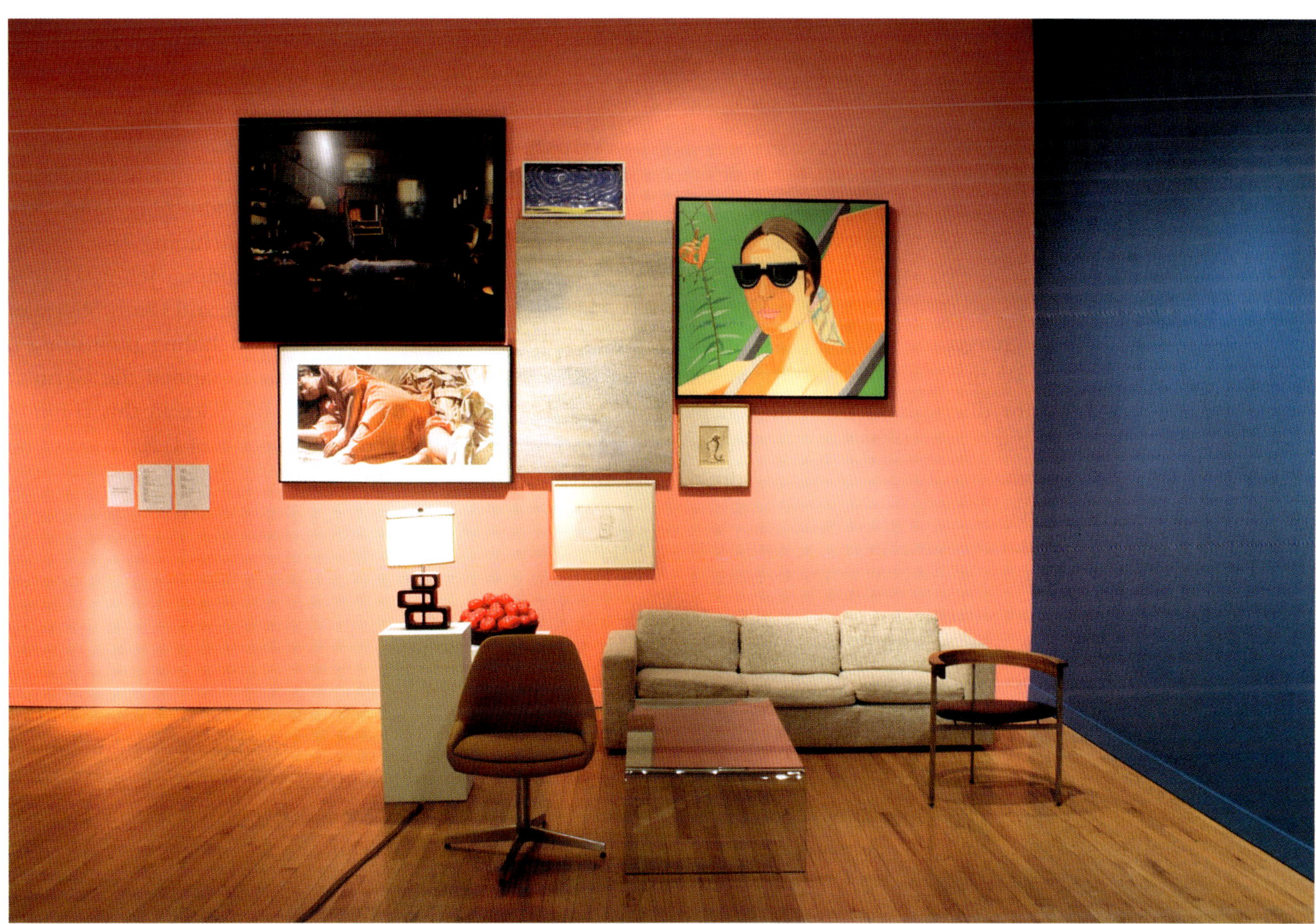

5.17 John M. Armleder, ***Ne dites pas non! (Don't say no!)***, 1986/2007. Selection of artworks from the permanent collection of The Rose Art Museum and furniture. Installation view at The Rose Art Museum, Waltham. Courtesy of the artist.

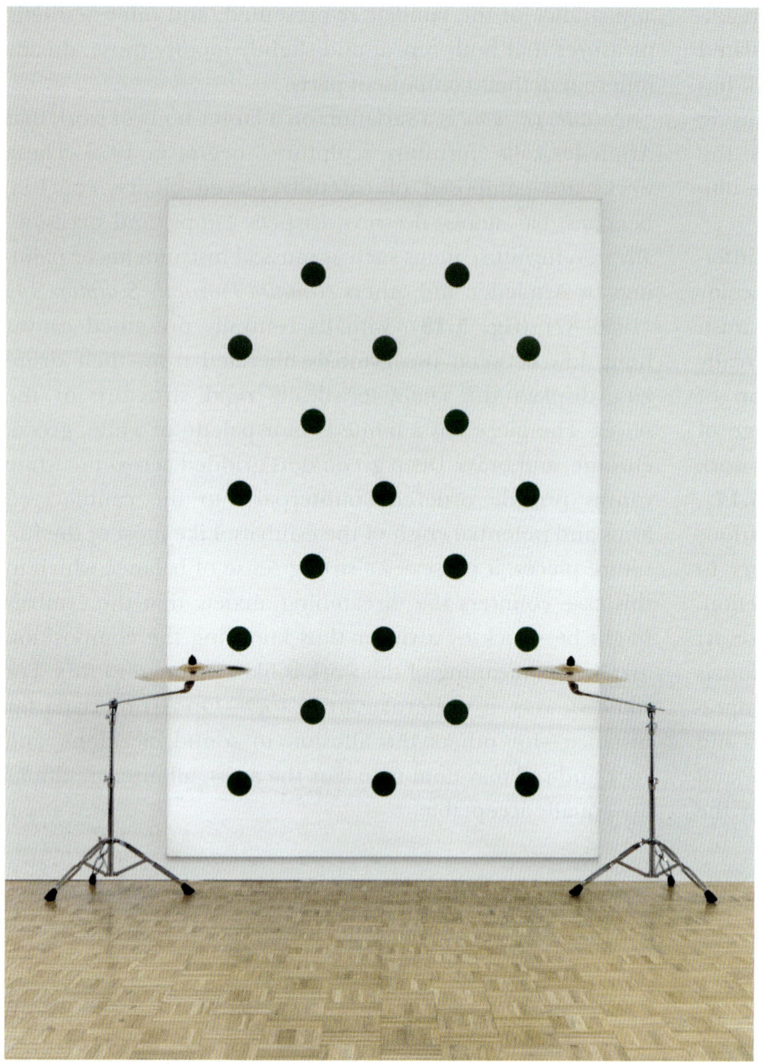

5.18 John M. Armleder, *Untitled Furniture Sculpture 144*, 1986–87. Acrylic on canvas and two cymbals. Painting 118 × 78¾" (300 × 200 cm); overall 118 × 118 × 59" (300 × 300 × 150 cm). Courtesy Galerie Andrea Caratsch, Zurich.

Though they denied the charge, the U.S. Neo-Geo artists were accused of making art about contemporary life that displayed neither judgment nor discrimination. Armleder, by accepting all interpretations as equal, describing his work as devoid of critique or even analysis, and invoking "pudding" as the most appropriate metaphor for it, seemed to aspire to just such a non-judgmental art. Nevertheless, certain very general hermeneutic guidelines do appear as one steps back from the aesthetic and emotional pleasures of Armleder's "pudding" to contemplate his carefully choreographed exhibitions. For instance, the 2006 *Ne dites pas non!* was integrated into an installation that included imitation second-generation Abstract Expressionist paintings hung on walls covered with stenciled rats, brains, and jellyfish near works by other artists that themselves looked down on examples of Armleder's furniture sculptures and arrangements of flowers, mirror balls, bricks, books, lights, and plastic Christmas trees. Such heterogeneous concoctions clarify Armleder's open-ended approach to meaning. It is not just that single works have changing meanings, but that every work is embedded in a context that is itself variable enough to generate multiple connotations for it. Reflecting on meaning in his work, Armleder said: "Materials work. They have a range of visual, acoustic, symbolic, decorative, associative, allegorical, and other programs that will snare various understandings for each and every user. And this will change depending on whether the visitors are alone, or with their kids, or after a good or terrible lunch, a rainy day, tax season, or an unhappy election outcome."[31] Artist, object, audience, and atmosphere all contribute to the meaning of Armleder's art.

Rosemarie Trockel

In Cologne in the late 1970s and early 1980s, Rosemarie Trockel (b. 1952) began crafting work that mixed expression and analysis and took aim at the nexus of art and the economy, with a particular focus on issues of gender and power. During this period, she observed what she described as the "mutual slaughter" of oneupmanship between the Mulheimer Freiheit, a Neo-Expressionist group that infused the painterly impulse of the *Heftige Malerei* with a sense of Dada nihilism, and the circle of self-consciously heterodox and stylistically inconsistent painters and sculptors around Martin Kippenberger (see Chapter 3).[32] The energy of the social life associated with these circles was invigorating, yet overwhelmingly male-dominated. It was in this environment, in 1983, that Monika Sprüth opened a new gallery with a heterodox feminist agenda, showing, publishing, and promoting many women artists including Trockel and significant U.S. figures including Jenny Holzer, Barbara Kruger, Louise Lawler, and Cindy Sherman (see Chapter 2). Sprüth's activities, including publishing a journal, *Eau de Cologne*, significantly expanded the German art world. Trockel occupied a central place in this community and her work engaged the concerns of U.S. artists while being rooted in the specific history of Cologne.

Untitled (1985) (**fig. 5.19**) illustrates Trockel's complex exploration of issues surrounding Modernist form, corporate capitalism, gender, and German history. As an image, it has three elements: 1) a symmetrical juxtaposition of two adjacent vertical rectangles, one red and one white; 2) a grid pattern; and 3) two commercial logos, white Woolmarks on the left side, red Playboy Bunnies on the right. The grid of *Untitled* joins geometric abstraction—one of the foundations of Modernist art—to branding, the signature of Western capitalism. Trockel explained that her interest in patterns such as the grid derived from the fact that they function as a "model to be copied."[33] Patterns, like models, are a means to an end: An architectural model projects what a building will look like, a pattern book guides the sewing of a dress. Trockel's pattern of logos raises questions about what her

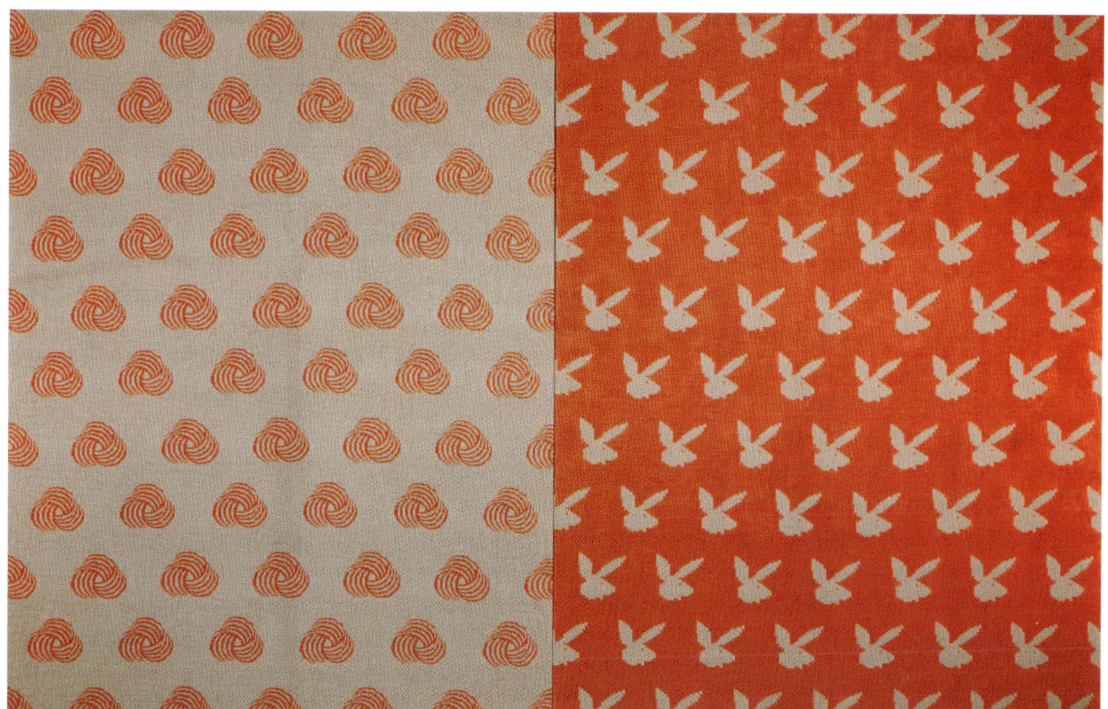

5.19 Rosemarie Trockel, *Untitled*, 1985. Wool, two parts, total 78¾ × 125⅞" (200 × 320 cm). Courtesy Sprüth Magers, Berlin/London.

model represents and what is being proposed through its execution. The geometry and brands of *Untitled* allude variously to categories of purity, beauty, and value, creating, in essence, a map of identity formation in which our values are guided by the combined forces of Modernist art, corporate power, and stereotypes of sex and gender.[34]

Untitled is an object as well as an image. As a blanket of knit wool, it connects to specifically German content. After World War II, German women were encouraged to reclaim the conventional roles of mother, wife, and homemaker as a means of rebuilding the German nation, much as women in the U.S. were encouraged to step back out of the workforce to make room for returning GIs. In Germany, wool was associated with this nationalist agenda as a modest and useful material. Trockel's knit pieces refer specifically to this history, but they also challenge it. *Balaclava* (1986) (**fig. 5.20**) connotes the handmade care that postwar propaganda encouraged; however, it also suggests the masks worn in the terrorist attacks that occurred with alarming frequency in the 1970s. Trockel thereby transforms patriotic domesticity and conventional ideas about gender into the masked face of anti-social violence, all the while knitting the defining shapes of Modernism and the logos of capitalism into the substance of her art. Moreover, the knit works are not handmade—they were produced to the artist's specifications on mechanical looms. The sense of handiwork is thus entirely simulated, or represented, with the knit wool being linked to the production line rather than the living room. These paths, from passive domesticity to violent revolt, and from home to industrialized workplace, were exactly those traversed by women at mid-century. Trockel described her process as taking the "material out of the [the context of women's work] and rework[ing] it in a neutral process of production."[35] The

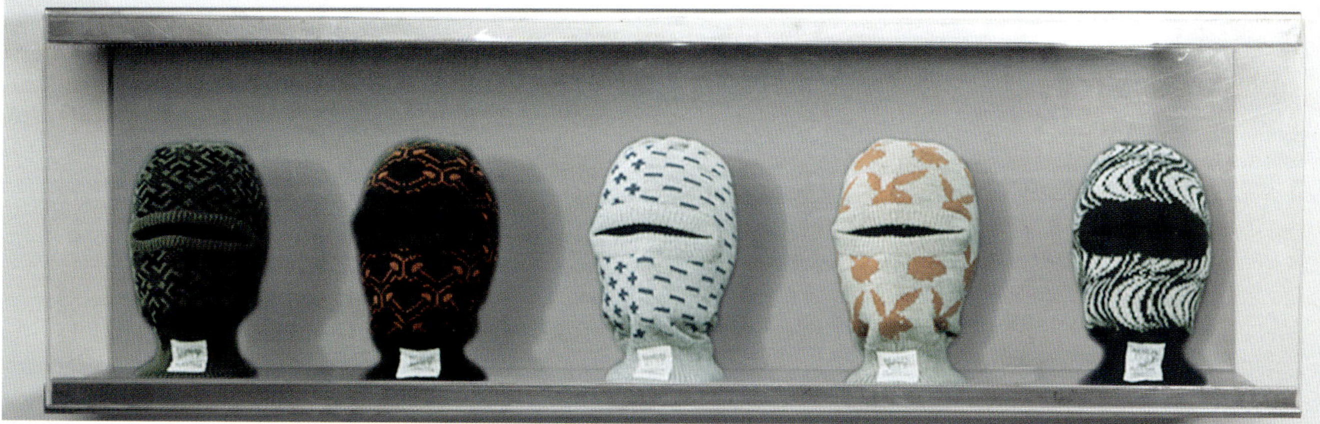

5.20 Rosemarie Trockel, *Balaclava*, 1986. Wool on styropor and metal shelf, ca. 13¾ × 51⅛ × 7⅞" (35 × 130 × 20 cm). Private Collection. Courtesy Sprüth Magers, Berlin/London.

results reveal the wool to be a site of the interaction between ideas about craft, modernity, gender, history, nationality, economy, violence, and crime.

Within her exploration of women and the history of production in postwar Germany, Trockel also hinted at the psychology and power of consumption. In their most common incarnation, Trockel's balaclavas appear supported from within, like hooded mannequins in a boutique window, thus merging the force of fashion with the fear of terrorism. The viewer is subjected to both. At their first display, in 1986 at the Monika Sprüth Gallery, however, they were presented in boxes, wrapped delicately in tissue paper like lingerie. Resting like luxury goods to be purchased rather than activated like fragments of the body, they accentuated the sensuality of purchase and possession, seducing rather than accosting the viewer. Cologne-based artist and critic Jutta Koether reported that the effect was an explosive mix of irritation and longing as the viewer was made aware of her role in perpetuating social forces and of her power to resist them. Trockel's work, like Sprüth's gallery, engaged the art world while challenging the ideological power by which it functioned. Trockel remarked in *Eau de Cologne* that an exciting moment was approaching—when the impact of women participating in the art world would actually change it.[36]

Sylvie Fleury

By the 1990s, after the very visible interventions of Sherman, Holzer, and Kruger, it became increasingly viable for women to create art and critique society from within the market economy. Nowhere was this more dynamically confirmed than in the shopping bags and high-fashion appropriations of Swiss artist Sylvie Fleury (b. 1961). Fleury established her reputation with her arrangements of shopping bags, their contents intact and often accompanied by furniture, floor coverings, shoes, and fashion magazines. In *C'est la vie! (That's life!)* (1990), a gold Estée Lauder cosmetics bag anchors a closely arranged group of seven shopping bags in garish tones of of red, yellow, pink, blue, and orange. Other pieces present more earthbound palettes, or more upscale products, as evidenced in the refined *Brave* (1994) (**fig. 5.21**), a composition of nuanced whites accented with the pink and almond tones of select fashion plates and a blond wood chair. While the care taken in constructing palette and composition reveals Fleury's formal concerns, the logos and contents of the bags point to the economic and social content of the work. In *Brave*, her consumption-based practice reinvents portraiture as something like a product-enhanced version of Bickerton's logo-based work. The label-title establishes the tone for the emotional content of the sculpture and the character of its heroine. Brave, the name of the label of

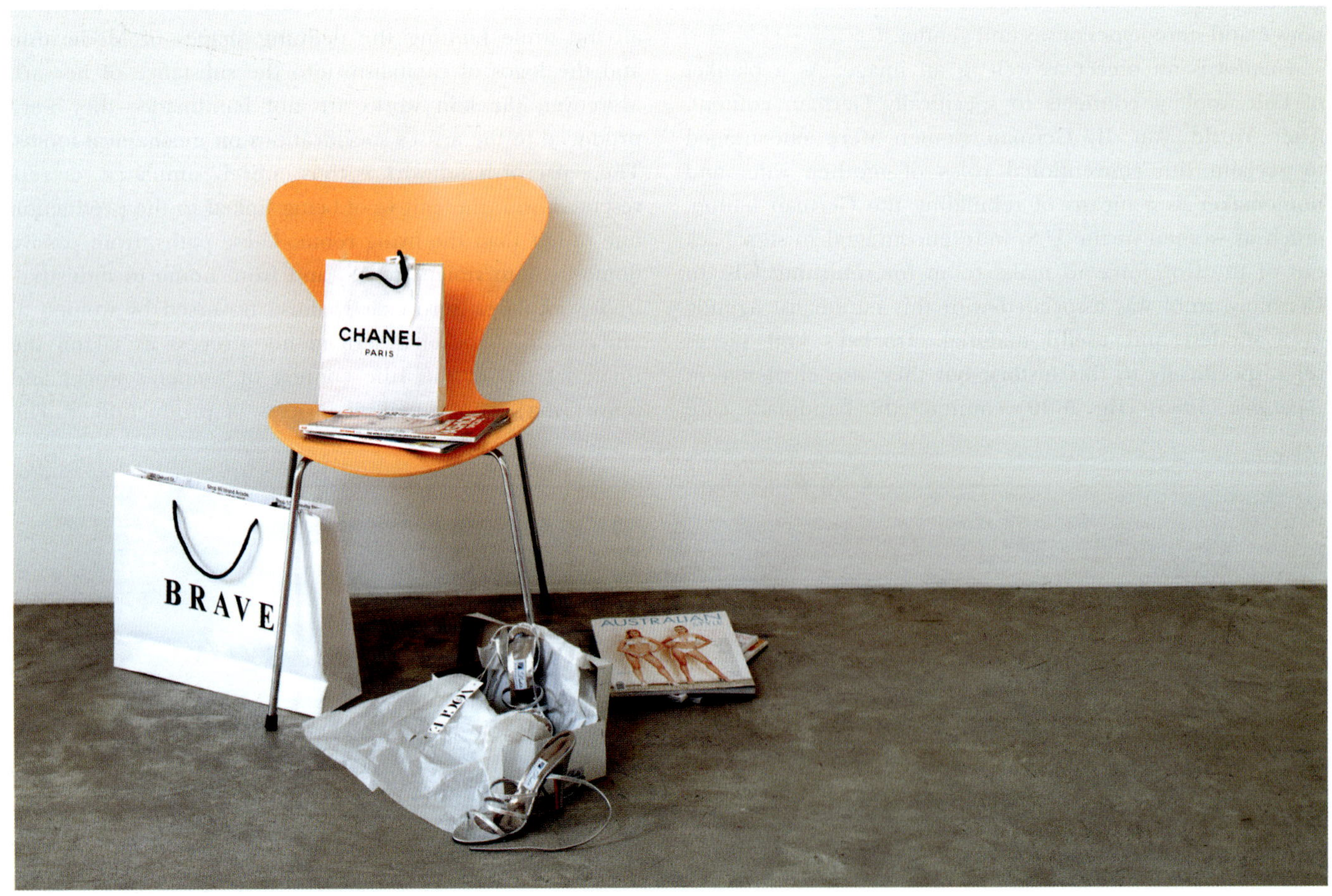

5.21 Sylvie Fleury, ***Brave***, 1994. Chair, magazine, shoes, and shopping bags, dimensions variable. Courtesy Sarah Cottier Gallery, Sydney.

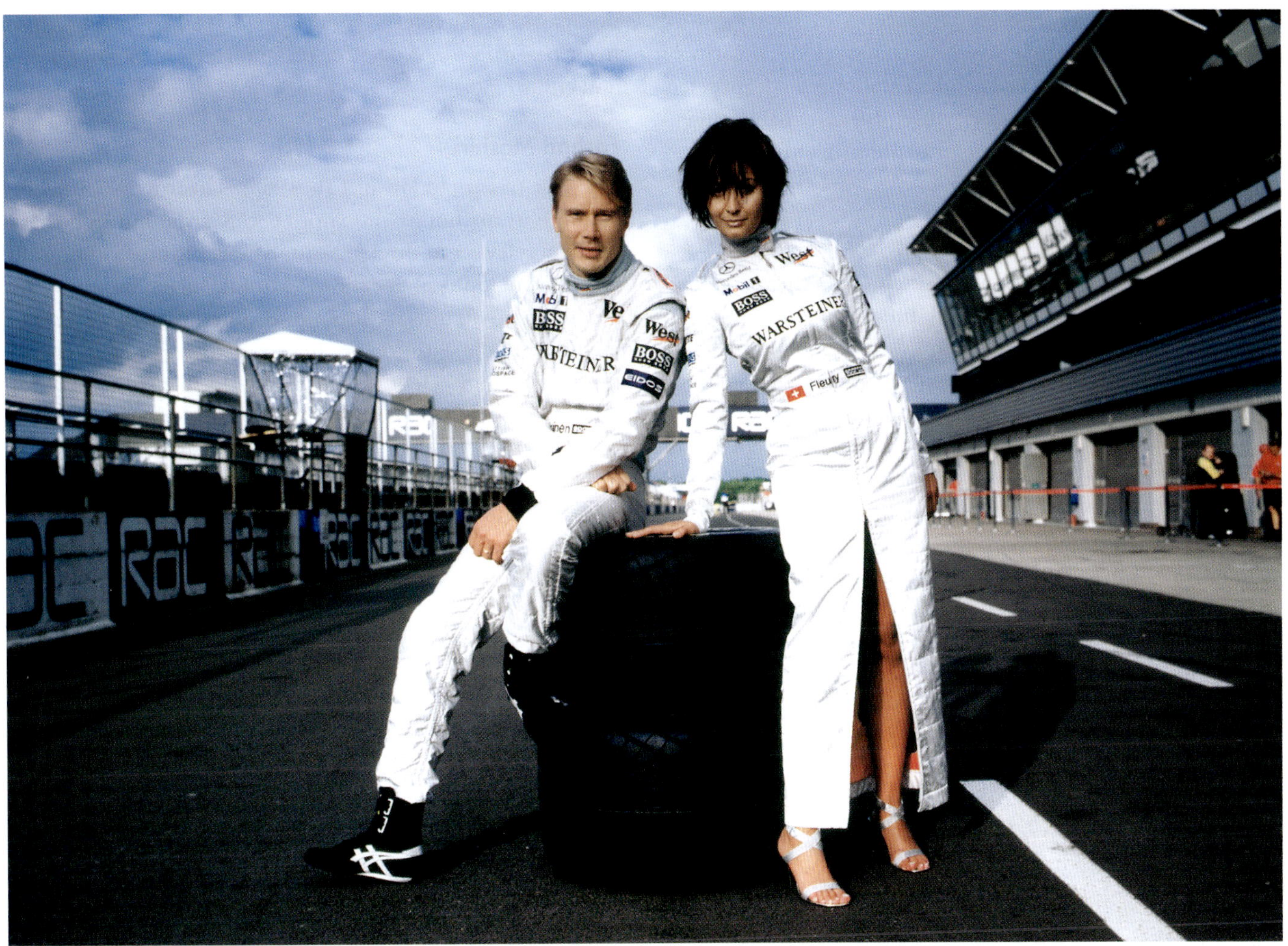

5.22 Sylvie Fleury, ***Formula One Dress***, 1998. Hand-tailored dress with original Formula One fabric, original Formula One logos, two-way zipper, and printed lining, manufactured by Hugo Boss. Edition of 100 dresses, 58 × 28½" (147.3 × 72.4 cm). Courtesy the artist and Hauser & Wirth & Presenhuer.

British-born, Australia-based fashion designer Wayne Cooper, also establishes the terrain in which courage is needed, the world of high fashion in Sydney. Fleury presents the required equipment: Dahto heels—perhaps custom-made, a specialty of the Australian designer—and Chanel scents. Copies of *Elle* and *Australian Style* serve as guidebooks to the local flora and fauna. Here are the relics of a high-fashion equivalent of a trip through the outback. This focus distinguishes Fleury's practice from that of peers such as Steinbach and Armleder even more than her choice of materials. Dealings with Armleder are well documented. In 1990, he and fellow Swiss artist Olivier Mosset (b. 1944) invited Fleury to join their two-person show. For a time afterwards, Armleder enlisted her to share responsibility for his work, much as he had done with curators in *Ne dites pas non!* In need of suggestions for paint color, he turned to Fleury, who proposed the shades of new lines of eye shadow. When she returned to the same solution the next time he asked, it became clear that, unlike Armleder, Fleury had a system and focused interests: Armleder declined her suggestion the second time.

In the context of most of the feminist work discussed in earlier chapters—Silvia Kolbowski's *Monumental Prop/portions* or Kruger's *Untitled (We Don't Need Another Hero)* (see figs. 2.11 and 2.16), for instance—Fleury's shopping pieces are confounding. They seem to embrace the mass-media imagery and consumer lifestyle that feminists had demonstrated were so debilitating. *Formula One Dress* (1998) (**fig. 5.22**), created with fashion house Hugo Boss, goes even further, wrapping the wearer in corporate logos, actualizing through the signs of sponsorship the equation of women with sports cars as objects of masculine desire. Jutta Koether, writing in 2000, reflected on her initial skepticism regarding Fleury's work, explaining that at the beginning of the previous decade there had been no reason to think that "declaring [oneself] the product of one culture industry or another or outing [oneself] as a construct" was at all progressive.[37] Though an investigation of consumption might be sanctioned, equating it with liberation was trite at best. With time, however, Koether found in Fleury's work a "call to rethink one's own part in the game" of culture and capitalism, and not simply a celebration of the privileges of membership.[38] Taken as such, *Brave* and *Formula One Dress*, like Sherman's photographs (see Chapter 2), upset the binary opposition between the acting subject who rebels against the dominant culture and a passive object who simply accepts it. Fleury's work turns to consumption as a means to challenge the polarity of passive consumer and active producer. Shopping, both selective and excessive, becomes a creative process capable of generating content and effects similar to drawing or painting.

The Internationalism of Commodity Art

Jeff Koons's transformation of even the cheapest consumer goods—balloon dogs and inflatable bunnies—into multimillion-dollar collectors' items was the kind of alchemy that made up the American Dream. Almost immediately, his works became icons of consumerist U.S. culture, celebrations, as was written in 1988, of "the apotheosis of corporate culture."[39] Discovering his work displayed on the rooftop of the Metropolitan Museum of Art or in the Hall of Mirrors at Versailles (**fig. 5.23**) in the early twenty-first century seemed to confirm that Koons had struck upon the house style of a U.S.-sponsored global capitalism. The accuracy of this perception has to be measured against the utility of the commodity for non-Western artists. In fact, the most spectacular careers in the twenty-first-century art world—those of Ai Weiwei in China (see Chapter 8), Takashi Murakami in Japan (see Chapter 9), and Farhad Moshiri in Iran—have been based in large part on the intersection of commodity and culture.

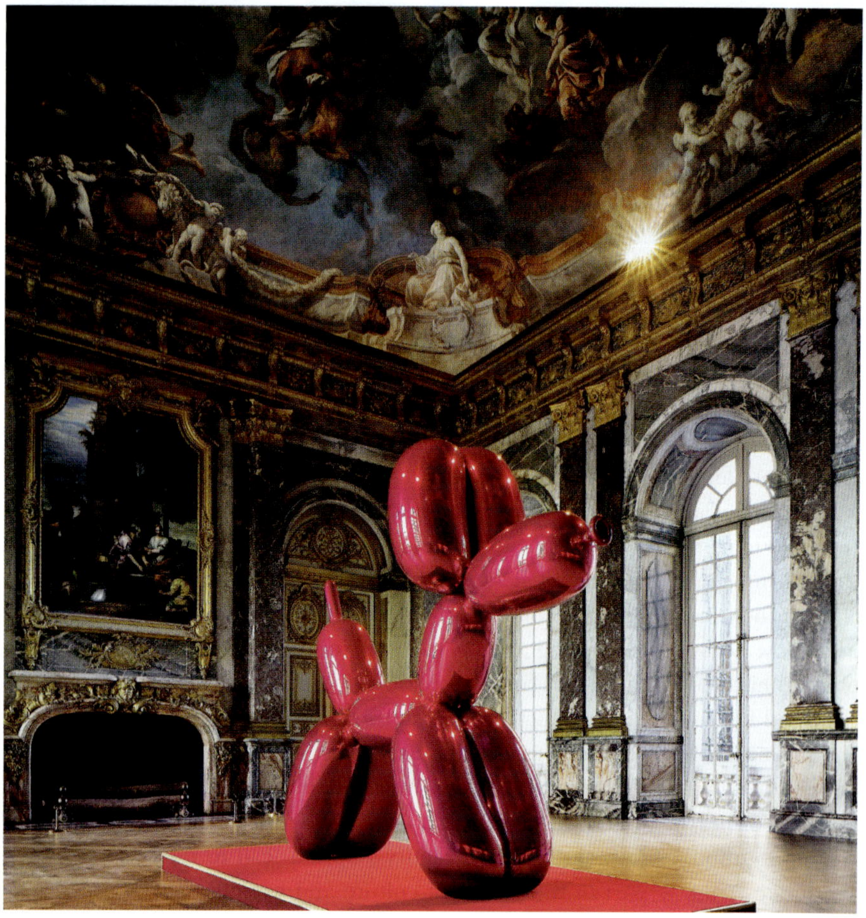

5.23 Jeff Koons, ***Balloon Dog (Magenta)***, 1994–2000. Shown at the "Jeff Koons Versailles" exhibition at the Château de Versailles, October 9, 2008–April 1, 2009. Mirror-polished stainless steel with transparent color coating, 121 × 143 × 45" (307.3 × 363.2 × 114.3 cm). © Jeff Koons.

Farhad Moshiri

The case of Farhad Moshiri (b. 1963) is instructive for seeing commodity art not as an exported U.S. style, but rather as a strategy relevant to diverse artists at various times and in different geographical locations. Moshiri plays on the same conjunction of fine-art aspiration and kitsch taste among wealthy Middle Eastern art buyers of the new millennium that Koons had celebrated in regard to the Western collectors of the 1980s. Critical responses to his work, including accusations of "amputating his Iranian heart and replac[ing] it with a cash register" in exchange for a career making "toys for the anaesthetized new rich," even replicate the bile that had met commodity artists.[40] Moshiri was born in Shiraz, Iran, but was sent to boarding school outside Los Angeles when the Western-leaning Shah was overturned by the Islamic Revolution in 1979. He spent three years at CalArts and moved back to Iran in the 1990s. Citing Koons, Bickerton, and the Neo-Geo painters as influences, Moshiri nonetheless struck a different balance between new money and high art as he took the pulse of the rising Middle Eastern collecting class. Works such as *Cradle of Happiness* (2004) (**fig. 5.24**), a gilded Louis XIV-style bedroom set with gold mattress and seat cushions comfortably supporting gilded CD and cassette players, celebrate the objects desired and acquired by successful Iranian families. Like Koons, Moshiri invites his audience to revel in the things that their culture covets; if that means glorifying imitations of European antiques or Japanese audio equipment, then so be it. In addition to conspicuously adding value to the objects the artist feels best represent Iranian taste, literally spraying them with gold, *Cradle of Happiness* offers an experience akin to Sylvie Fleury's consumer forensics, in which we learn about the psyche of the shopper by examining what she brings home. Celebration of the state of contemporary taste takes a slightly critical turn in what has become another of Moshiri's signature styles, evidenced by the Swarovski crystal and sequin on canvas *Eshgh* (*Love*) (2007) (**fig. 5.25**). Of this work, Moshiri explained: "An artificial make-believe lifestyle fascinates me. I use fake diamonds in paintings, and that's … related to the fact that some people want to believe that they're real diamonds. Art is about

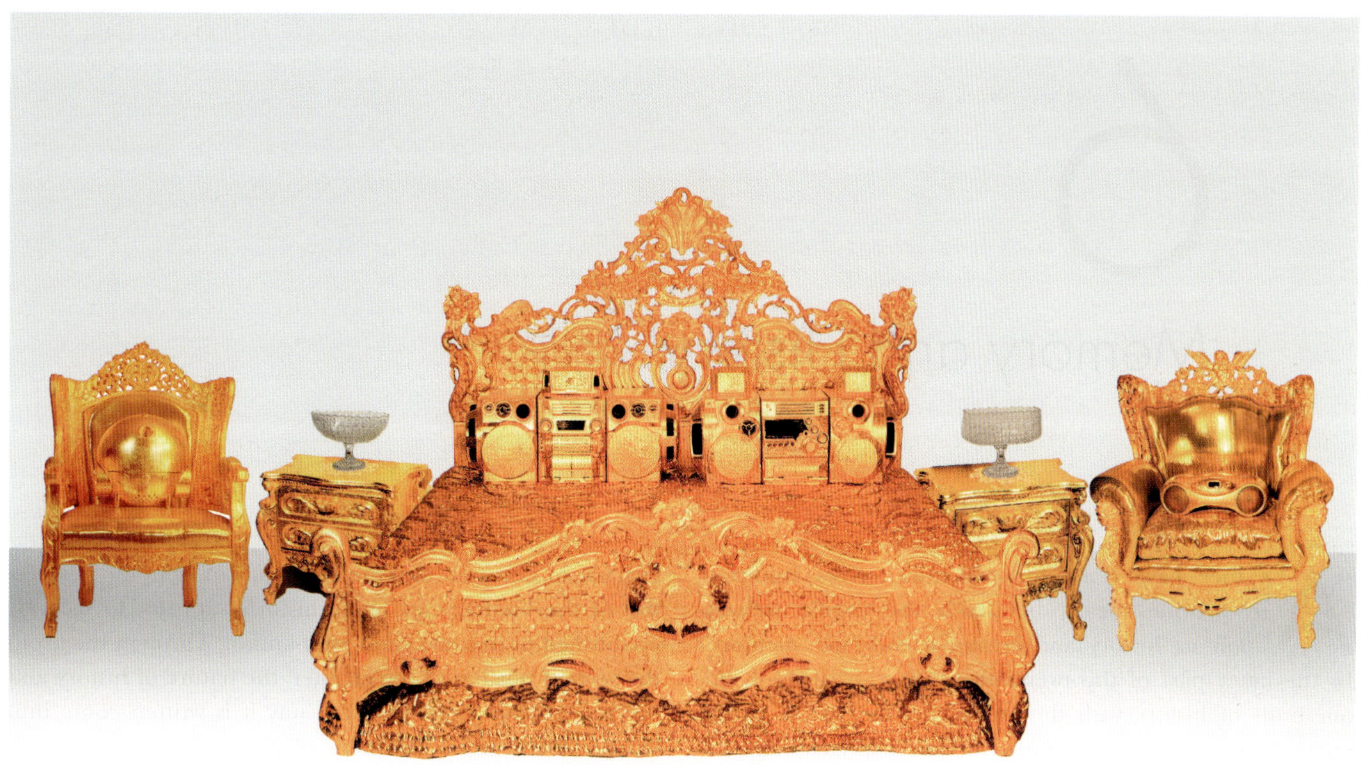

5.24 Farhad Moshiri, ***Cradle of Happiness***, 2004. Life-size installation of gold-leaved mixed materials. Courtesy of the artist and The Third Line.

illusion. It's a manufactured idea in order to reach a certain illusion and expression."[41]

With *Eshgh*, Moshiri jumped into the make-believe lifestyle being cultivated in the oil-rich nations of the Middle East. In March 2008, the painting sold for just over $1 million at auction in Dubai, making Moshiri the first Middle Eastern artist to have a work top the million-dollar mark. As artists around the globe have demonstrated, discussing capitalism—whether as a Western ideology or an international investment—is facilitated by an appropriative embrace of the commodity.

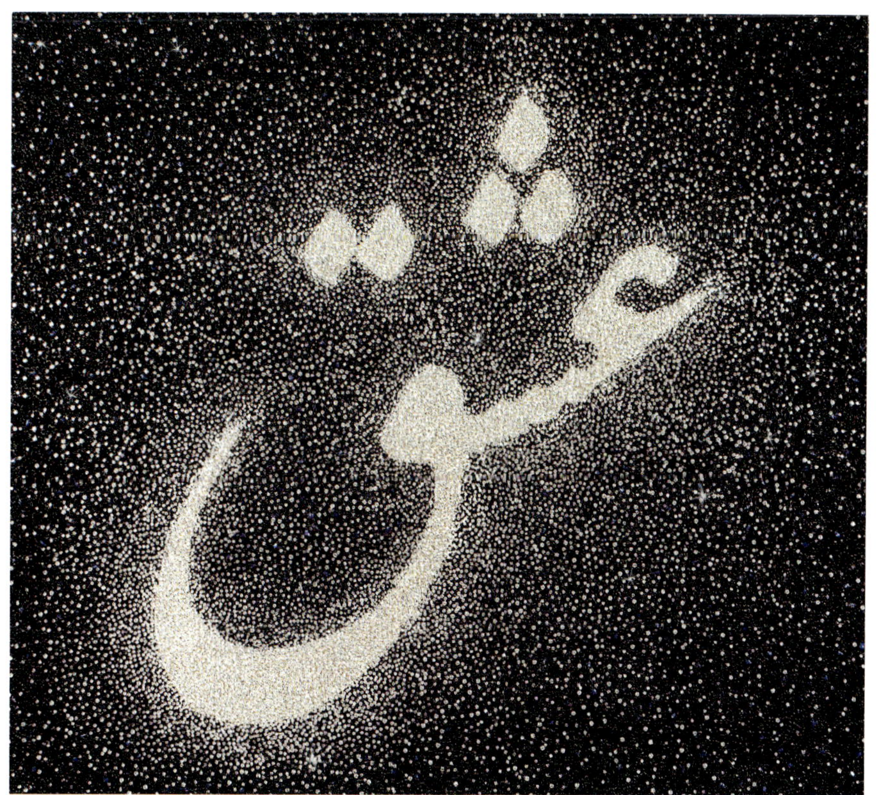

5.25 Farhad Moshiri, ***Eshgh (Love)***, 2007. Acrylic, Swarovski crystals, and glitter on canvas on board, 61 × 69¼" (155 × 176 cm). Courtesy of the artist and The Third Line.

6

Memory and History

As they have done for millennia, artists continue to provide means by which the public reflects upon its history and creates a collective memory. In the latter part of the twentieth century, artists took up questions of history with the critical debates of the previous decades in their minds. Criticisms expressed in the writings of Michel Foucault and Jean-François Lyotard, among others, that challenged the idea of history as a linear progression of master narratives and conveyed a skepticism toward authority, had become integrated into artists' working practices. Thus as a new generation stepped into the role of providing public memorials or more private historical investigations, they were expected and prepared to invent new forms of art to do so. The works discussed in this chapter range in medium from granite monuments to found clothing, cut paper, and video. The subject matter they address, in addition to "History" itself, will be taken largely from the history of the West and attempts to reckon with the traumas of World War II and the Vietnam War. Just as these events inspired a re-evaluation of the role of art and politics for earlier generations (see Chapter 1), they also continued to haunt artists well into the 1980s and 1990s. In this second moment of reflection, beginning with Maya Lin's *Vietnam Veterans Memorial* (see fig. 6.1), it will be the historical, psychological, and political dimensions of surviving trauma and rebuilding societies that will dominate the concerns of contemporary art about history. In every case, the artists have rejected the traditional aim of historical monuments—to assert essential identities for the victors or victims—and focused instead on the historical event as a confluence of different individuals, communities, and histories.

The first part of the chapter introduces Lin's memorial and discusses a body of work dealing with the Holocaust. In this case, the historical record is, by and large, accepted, leaving artists to grapple with its consequences and questions of how it should be publicly engaged. In the second part of the chapter, the discussion turns to art about the African-American experience, the covert wars in Latin America, the civil war in Lebanon, and the Vietnam War from the perspective of the Vietnamese. These histories are not so securely established or in some cases even known. Through the art in the second portion of the chapter, the nature of history and the politics that determine the way it is written come into sharper focus, while the status of the facts that comprise it become less and less clear. In its commitment to the past and its consequences, this work resonates with that of the artists who dealt with World War II, and it provides provisional answers as to what constitutes history or an art based upon it when facts, lives, records, images, and voices are often silent, missing, or lost.

Memorializing War

In the early 1980s, with the Vietnam War less that a decade in the past and its legacy still far from certain, a group of veterans enlisted the support of several U.S. Congressmen and others to build a memorial to the soldiers who had fought in the war. In the late 1960s and early 1970s, the conflict had divided the U.S. public, giving rise to a significant resistance movement. The nightly news put footage of the fighting into people's homes while reporters documented news of civilian massacres, chemical warfare, and increasing U.S. losses. The moral cost of the war came to appear a more serious threat to national security than a Communist Vietnam and the political pressure as the death count rose to nearly 60,000 U.S. and around 3 million Vietnamese deaths at the war's end became unsustainable. The polarizing nature of the war meant that returning G.I.s were confronted with anti-war sentiment that often manifested itself in resentment and disgust directed at them—an experience very different from the heroes' return that had greeted veterans of previous U.S. wars. Not only did any memorial have the grave responsibility of paying homage to the soldiers who died and those who returned home often to years of personal struggle, it was also called upon to contribute to the no less challenging task of repairing the national fabric and allowing those who had fought in the war to find common ground with those who had campaigned against it. Personally aware of the divisive nature of responses to the war, during and since, the Vietnam Veterans Memorial Fund, as the organizing group came to be called, held a design competition and specified that submissions should be contemplative and make no political statements. The results made it clear that the understanding of public and national art was at a turning point. The memorial that was handed over to the care of the National Park Service in 1984 was a testament to the successful resolution of artistic and political issues regarding the history of the war, and confirmation of a new relationship between contemporary art and its audiences.

Maya Lin

Maya Lin's *Vietnam Veterans Memorial* (1984) (**fig. 6.1**), in Washington, D.C., is a black chevron of polished black granite sunk into the earth upon which the names of all the U.S. citizens killed in Vietnam have been carved. Drawing on Minimalism and Conceptual art of the 1960s and 1970s, landscape architect and sculptor Lin (b. 1959) rejected the heroic statues of idealized men and women that had traditionally been used to memorialize the past when she submitted her design proposal for the competition. Despite the apparent coldness of its means—its formal abstraction and dependence on the written word—Lin's monument has overcome initial skepticism and controversy to serve as a highly successful invitation to emotional catharsis and intellectual contemplation. In the process, it has also transformed public art across the globe, continuing to be the touchstone for memorial art in the new century. Lin's example demonstrates the commitment made by artists to address the legacy of modern history using the means of contemporary art.

The *Vietnam Veterans Memorial*, finished so soon after the end of the war it commemorates, combines three features familiar in art since the 1960s. First, there is the recession cut into the earth, a gesture that evokes the dramatic outdoor monuments of the Land Art movement. This cut is faced with polished granite and recalls classic Minimalist art. On the stone surface are the names of the dead U.S. servicemen and -women listed on a timeline according to the date of their deaths, beginning in 1956 and ending in 1975, which references a tradition in Conceptual art of using graphs, lists, and other arrangements. In effect, Lin chose to reckon with the war by making use of artistic forms that had emerged while it was being waged. But she also complicated this art-historical model by incorporating aesthetic features that had been suppressed by those same movements—namely, theatricality and representation, the very qualities that guaranteed the Neo-Expressionists such a dramatic entrée into the art world at the same time (see Chapter 3). As visitors walk along the pathway that follows the wall down into the earth and then back up to the level of the surrounding parkland, the polished stone reflects their bodies and faces so that their forms flicker over the names of the dead (**fig. 6.2**). Such dramatic

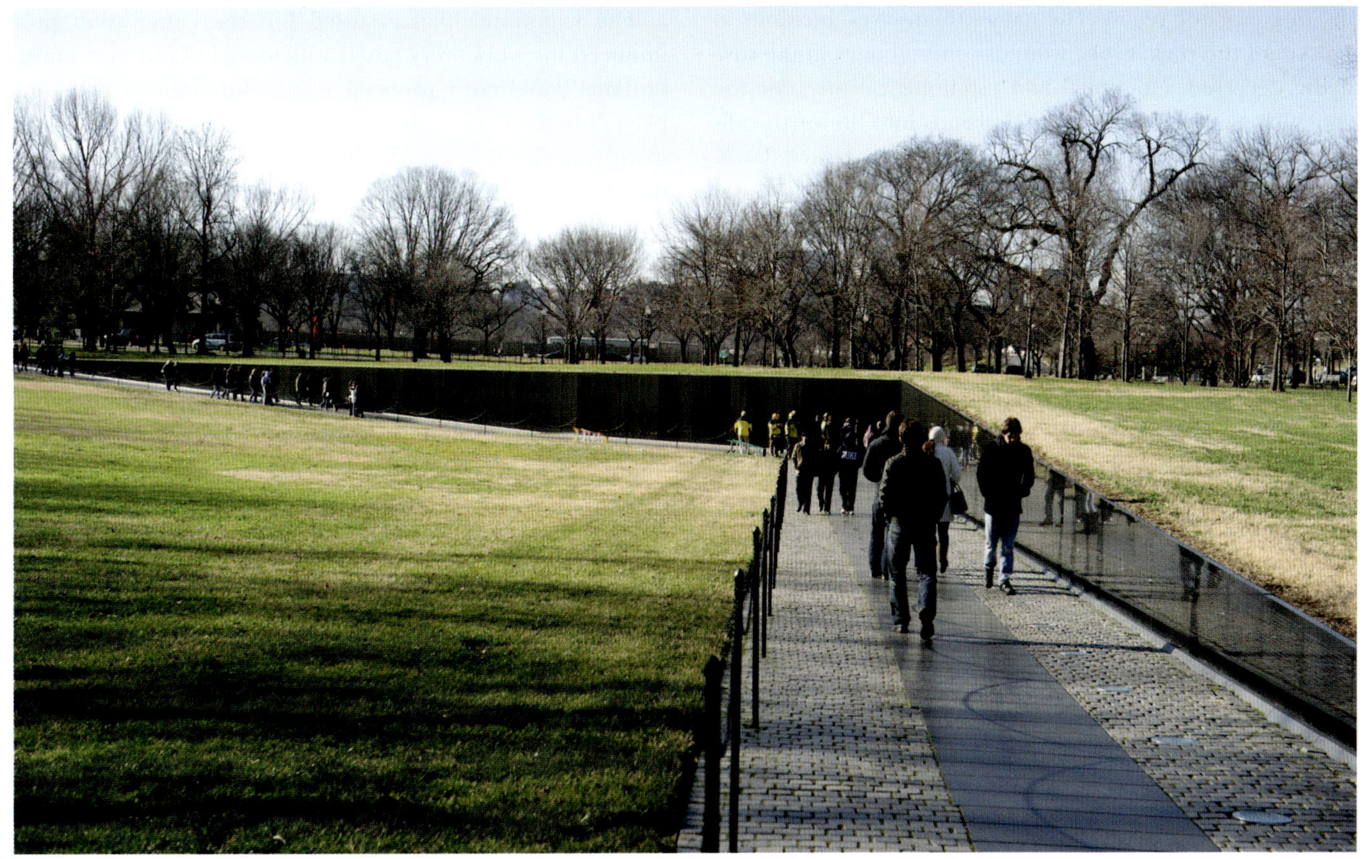

6.1 Maya Lin, ***Vietnam Veterans Memorial***, 1984. Black granite, two walls each 246' (75 m) long, rising to an apex of 10' 1" (3 m). Washington, D.C.

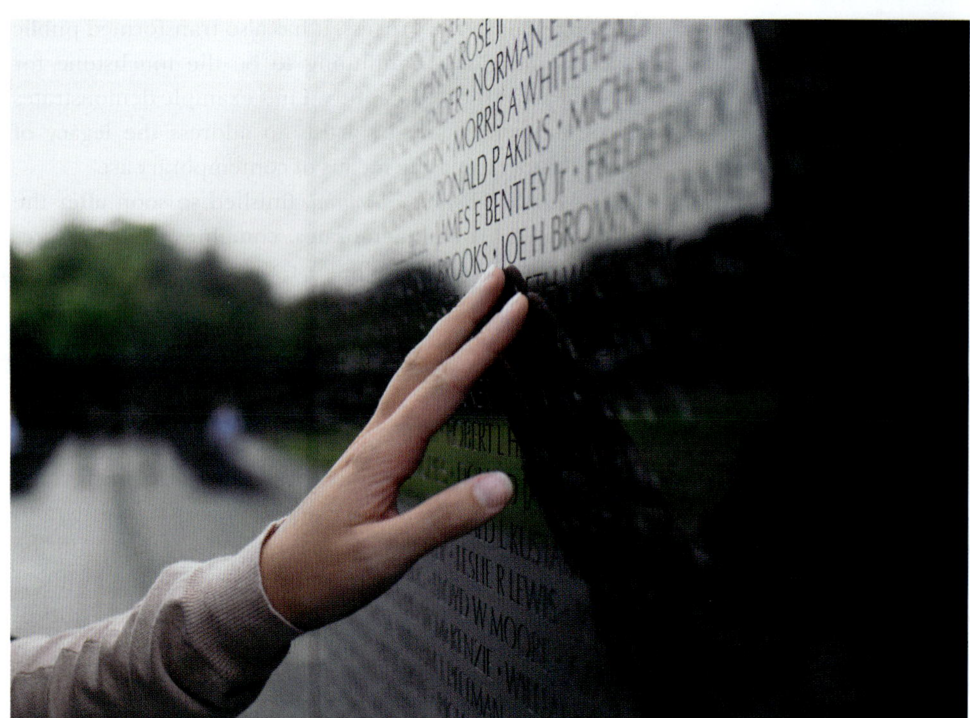

6.2 Maya Lin, ***Vietnam Veterans Memorial***, 1984. Detail.

pictorial effects heighten the emotional impact of the memorial but they remain tightly controlled, so that overall the wall balances somber gravitas with emotional release.

As one approaches the *Vietnam Veterans Memorial*, simple geometric forms, smooth surfaces, sharp cuts into cold black stone, and the accumulation and sculpting of the earth invite one into a poetic realm. The names themselves, incisions in the skin of the rock, evoke wounds—mortal ones in the case of the deceased, emotional and psychological ones for the living. The way the black stone descends into the earth calls to mind a gravestone. When the visitor is ready, the walkway leads him or her from the realm of reflection and memory back up into the light of day. It is essential to the process of mourning not only that survivors of the conflict or other visitors have the space to imagine the dead as present, but also that the living arrive at a psychic place where the dead remain apart from daily life. In response to Anselm Kiefer's paintings about the Holocaust (see Chapter 3), Andreas Huyssen had worried that the mourning viewers would be so overwhelmed that they would be lost in melancholy, unable to come to terms with their loss and so become incapable of returning to living fully in the present. Lin's memorial responds to this need exquisitely with the hopeful spiritual ascension of the pathway. In addition, as one looks back to the wall from a short distance, the list of names that had only moments before appeared so poetic now looks almost mundane. It is this affectless efficiency that had made such lists interesting to Conceptualists seeking to reduce their art to a bare presentation of facts. The forthright presentation of the casualties of war in the form of such a "timeline" may appear abrupt, but much of the success of the memorial rests on such frank simplicity. The memorial strikes one as consistent with the U.S. experience. Soldiers returned from Vietnam to a harsh reality with none of the adoration or postwar prosperity that had awaited those returning from World War II. Resisting the temptation to create a fantasy to compensate for that reality, Lin instead designed an experience oriented toward the emotional needs of the survivors.

The committee that awarded Lin the commission pronounced the work "very much a memorial of our own times, one that could not have been achieved in another time and place."[1] Indeed, it was almost not built at all owing to the controversy it stirred up as a result of a perceived ambivalence of the work toward the war. Lin had rejected the idea of using heroic figures such as those presented in the *Abraham Lincoln Memorial* or triumphal abstractions of the kind found in the *Washington Monument*. Without such familiar references to anchor the meaning of the work, many people found Lin's proposal illegible and its point of view impossible to determine. To others, it was simply an affront, an insinuation that the U.S. soldiers killed in Vietnam were not worthy of being honored in the traditional fashion. An alternative monument, *Three Soldiers* (1982–84) (**fig. 6.3**) by Frederick Hart (1943–99), a bronze figurative group representing three patrolling soldiers of different races which had come third in the original design competition, was thus installed nearby—though not, as its sponsors desired, at the apex of Lin's work.

Despite this controversy, Lin's *Vietnam Veterans Memorial* has won almost universal praise for the way it navigates the political and emotional challenge of memorializing a war that was resisted and resented by much of the country at the time it was being fought. The National Parks Service which oversees the memorial now presents the work with accompanying texts, including a statement from an artist who had

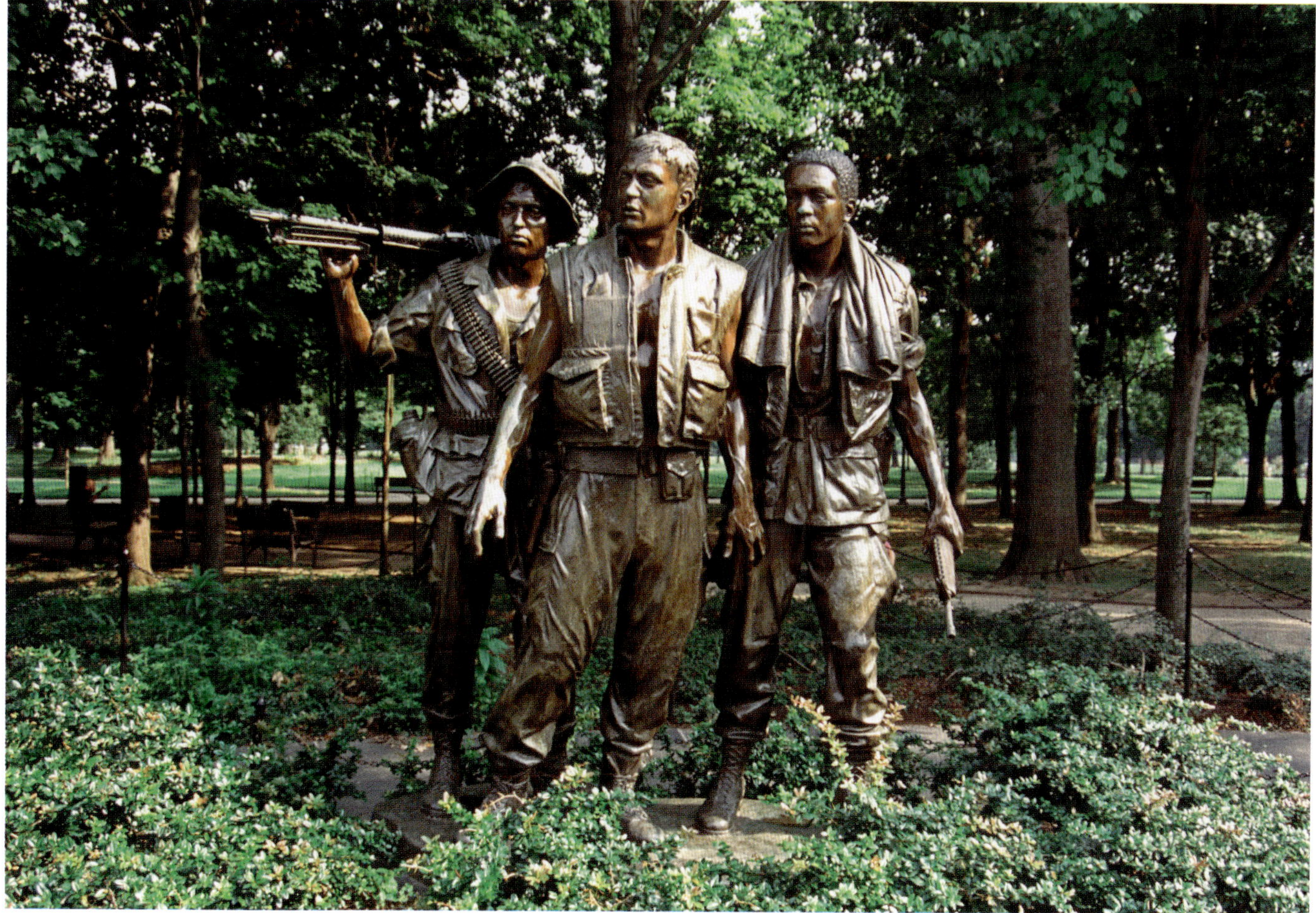

6.3 Frederick Hart, *The Three Soldiers*, 1982–84. Bronze sculpture with black Indian granite base, (sculpture only) 96 × 60 × 36" (243.8 × 152.4 × 91.4 cm). Washington, D.C.

initially strongly objected to Lin's design, saying that with its actualization the wall "became a bridge." Perhaps the fact that Lin was young—only sixteen at the end of the war—made her better attuned to the needs of those seeking new means to write history. Her memorial demonstrated that the formal and conceptual features of contemporary art, previously perceived to be comprehensible only to a small community, could be not only legible, but also emotionally and intellectually meaningful to an audience drawn from all walks of life. Public art could be an invitation to seek the significance of the past together.

The United States Holocaust Memorial Museum

Theodor Adorno's claim that there could be no art after Auschwitz hung over all attempts in the second half of the twentieth century to examine trauma through art. As discussed in Chapter 3, however, his assertion was by no means absolute. Adorno himself discovered in the post-Holocaust poetry of Paul Celan a response to his own anxiety over the place of art in the postwar world. Artists have not turned their backs on history or the challenges it poses. Those discussed below revisited the genocide and fascism that Adorno addressed and began to create a formal vocabulary, one sharing much with Lin's *Vietnam Veterans Memorial*, with which to engage it.

The success of Lin's memorial virtually codified her expressive Minimalism as the new official style for public art about national history. The United States Holocaust Memorial Museum, in Washington, D.C., opened in 1993 and included commissions by four artists long practiced in Minimalist traditions: Sol LeWitt (1928–2007), Joel Shapiro (b. 1941), Richard Serra (b. 1939), and Ellsworth Kelly (b. 1923). All four contributed work that fit well within the oeuvres that they had been creating since the 1960s, but that now, due to the experience of the *Vietnam Veterans Memorial*, was also seen to be attuned to contemporary history.

As a young artist in Paris, Kelly was one of the first U.S. painters to create Minimalist canvases by refining a severely reductive abstract vocabulary. His contribution to the museum was the two-part, all-white *Memorial* (1993) (**fig. 6.4**), consisting of a 27-foot-wide panel in the shape of an attenuated fan and three large vertical rectangles. The two parts—white panels that hang against the white walls of the museum—exude a graceful counterpoint of steady rhythm and expanding harmony. Uniformly monochrome, *Memorial* nearly fades into the background of the museum, evoking the fleeting and fragile nature of the human spirit as it ascends above the material world. But it is the context that really determines the content of *Memorial*. By reason of its being in the

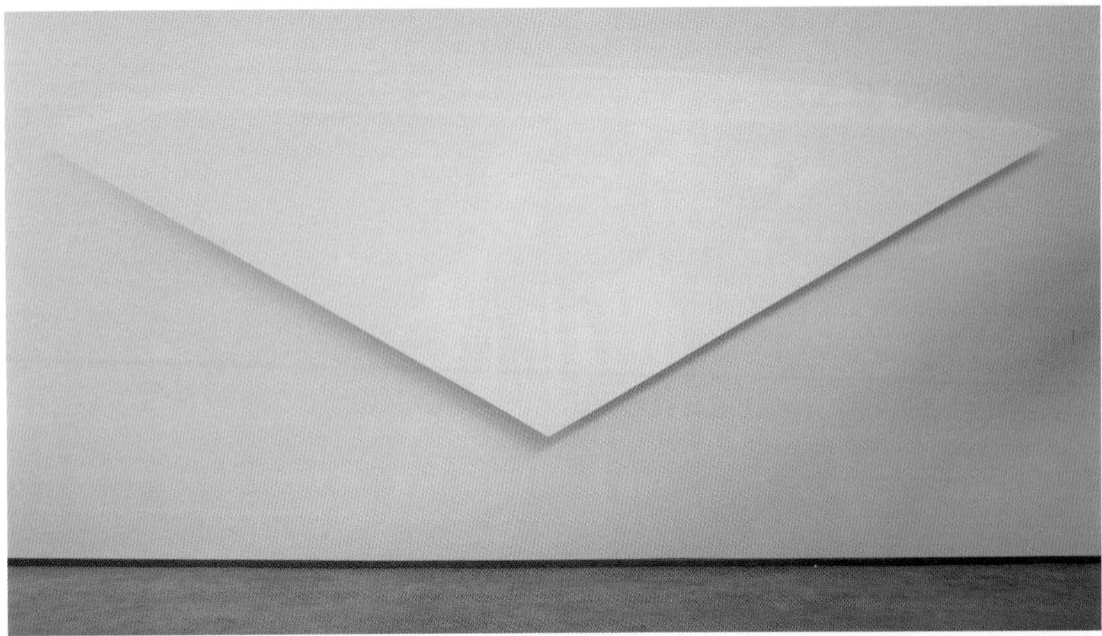

6.4 Ellsworth Kelly, ***Memorial***, 1993. Enamel on wood and composite in four parts. Top image: 114 × 330 × 2" (289.6 × 838.2 × 5.1 cm). Lower image: each of three panels 108 × 64 × 2" (274.3 × 162.6 × 5.1 cm). United States Holocaust Memorial Museum, Washington, D.C., artist commission and gift of Ruth and Albert Abramson and Family, 1993. © Ellsworth Kelly.

Holocaust Museum, *Memorial* automatically becomes a work about the Holocaust. Both the museum and the artist rely on the audience's understanding, thanks in large part to the *Vietnam Veterans Memorial* nearby, that evocative geometries such as Kelly's can be a means to address weighty content.

Jochen Gerz and Esther Shalev-Gerz

In Harburg, a suburb of Hamburg, Germany, Jochen Gerz (b. 1940) and Esther Shalev-Gerz (b. 1948) turned to Minimalist, Conceptual, and performance traditions to create their *Monument Against Fascism* (1986) (**fig. 6.5**). At its dedication on October 10, 1986, this hollow yet massive, 7-ton, 39-foot × 3-foot × 3-foot column of lead-plated steel stood on a raised terrace overlooking a small square near the local train station. Harburg is a town of working-class Germans and Turkish immigrants, the latter having begun arriving there after World War II to work on U.S.-sponsored projects. The Gerzes, intent on responding to the local population and to drawing attention to the varied audience for such a monument, placed a large placard bearing text in German, Turkish, English, French, Hebrew, and Arabic next to the column. The languages indicated both the range of communities likely to visit the site and those others the artists felt were essential participants in the discussion. The text explained what the monument was and how it was intended to function. It read:

> We invite the citizens of Harburg, and visitors to the town, to add their names here next to ours. In doing so, we commit ourselves to remain vigilant. As more and more names cover this 12-meter-tall lead column, it will gradually be lowered into the ground. One day, it will have disappeared completely and the site of the Harburg monument against fascism will be empty.

In the end, it is only we ourselves who can rise up against injustice.

The metal column was inscribed by the artists and accompanied by a stylus with which visitors were invited to carve their signatures in the soft lead of the monument. The list of names was to form a community united by a pledge of vigilance in the continued struggle against fascism. Entirely covered with writing, it was finally completely buried seven years later, on November 10, 1993, and a new plaque describing the monument and the event was then put up at the site.

Upon disappearing into the ground, the *Monument Against Fascism* began a new life. According to the artists, the monument can be said to "work" if it successfully sacrifices the permanence of a statue and commutes its memorial function to "where it belongs—that is, within the people for whom it was created."[2] For them, inviting the community to sign the column was a gesture that transferred responsibility for the work and its purpose from the city and state bureaucrats who commissioned it and the artists who created it to the ordinary people who live with it. If the column had remained unsigned, it would not have been buried and would have remained visible as a reminder of the unwillingness of the community to proclaim such vigilance; if it were signed, the monument would pass from the somber form of a dark obelisk to the invisibility of an oath. The degree of audience participation that the Gerzes intended for the *Monument Against Fascism* was new for a public monument. Those who come to pay their respects at Lin's *Vietnam Veterans Memorial* fleetingly transform the appearance of the stone by casting their reflections and leaving flowers and gifts. The visitors to the *Monument Against Fascism*, on the other hand, had the opportunity to alter the appearance of the column permanently and, indeed, determine whether it could be seen at all.

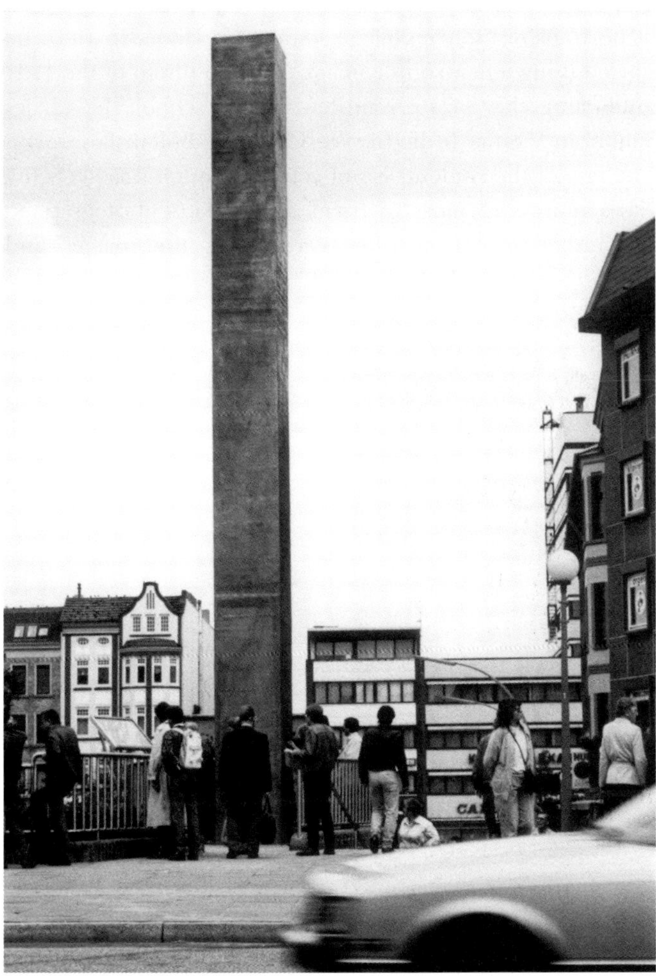

6.5 Jochen Gerz and Esther Shalev-Gerz, ***Monument Against Fascism***, 1986. Galvanized steel with a lead coating, 39' × 39⅜" × 39⅜" (12 × 1 × 1 m). Hamburg, Germany. Courtesy Gerz Studio.

However, when the monument was turned over to the community in the fall of 1986, something happened that surprised the artists and revealed the complex relationship of the citizens of Harburg to German national history. Signatures left during the day were vandalized at night. Under cover of darkness, people cut into the surface of the work, attempting to obliterate the messages of peace and solidarity, and often replacing them with messages of hate. Swastikas appeared on the monument, and someone even fired a bullet into it. Rather than a simple and orderly pledge of peace, the monument became a layered web of graffiti that gave form to a truly ambivalent response to history and memory. While it remained visible, the monument was an active element of city life. Jochen Gerz commented: "The filth brings us closer to the truth than would any list of well-meaning signatures. The inscriptions, a conglomerate of approval, hatred, anger and stupidity, are like a fingerprint of our city applied to the column."[3] The standing monument was an index of the best and worst in humanity and a testament to the fragility of our civilization. It was also a physical reminder of the violence to which many Europeans had succumbed in the 1930s and against which all nations needed to be vigilant in the 1990s.

Gerz began his career in Paris in the late 1960s as a poet, often using the streets to display his writing. One of the statements with which he plastered walls, streets, and public sculptures was "Art Corrupts." In the context of memorials, it was argued that art corrupted by seducing society into thinking that public sculpture could serve as public memory; in this way public art allowed individuals to forget. Contemporary life and its history required new means of engaging the public if art was to do more than corrupt. The *Monument Against Fascism*, by being first an object and then an absence, challenged the conventional memorial by becoming, in Gerz's words, a "site of social dialogue."[4] The French philosopher Jacques Rancière (b. 1940) cites the *Monument Against Fascism* as evidence against the argument that art was impotent in the face of horrors such as the Holocaust. Art, Rancière argues, draws attention to our capacity for experiencing and understanding new and unfamiliar sensations and enlists them to help change ourselves and the world. He begins his book *The Politics of Aesthetics* (2006) by asserting the role of the senses in discovering the common features shared by things in the world and also those qualities that are exclusive to individual entities. This ability to comprehend and navigate relationships based on similarities and differences is essential to the political tasks of building coalitions and negotiating conflicts. Adequately engaging with society, whether through communities and individuals or via ideologies and objects, requires constantly testing our capacity to perceive and comprehend our surroundings: It is here, Rancière explains, that art is essential. Art, as a way "of doing and making that intervene[s] in the general distribution of the ways of doing and making," holds the promise of change by providing opportunities to challenge and expand our ability to sense the world and to learn from our perceptions.[5] The inhumanity of societies in World War II was a painful challenge to art, but, Rancière insists, it was not the end of art. Writing in opposition to Adorno's famous claim, Rancière argues that horror "does not forbid images ... rather, it obliges [artists] to move and to explore new possibilities."[6] This process assumes not only that artists will work in new ways, but that images themselves will signify differently after a crisis; that words, objects, and images will carry associations that did not exist before. These new associations are part of the material with which artists can work. As is evident throughout this chapter, the meanings that accrue around images and objects in the wake of catastrophic events are of special interest to artists examining the character and consequences of the past.

Christian Boltanski

Of Jewish descent on his father's side and born in Paris in early September 1944, just weeks after the city had been liberated from the Nazis, Christian Boltanski was shaped by a war that he did not directly experience. In his early work, Boltanski trawled his memory for traces of his childhood. Finding little, he fabricated a past for himself complete with physical evidence: photographs, handmade replicas of toys and household objects, and descriptions of events and people. Boltanski's homemade relics, which he presented in books and archives, evoke a European childhood at the birth of the postwar age. In May 1969, Boltanski produced *Research and Presentation of All That Remains from My Childhood 1944–1950*, a slim volume of photocopied photographs and descriptions. Like all of his generation, his relationship to the events that had shaped the second half of the century was, in common with the copies in the book, secondhand. *Research and Presentation* was, however, a misrepresentation: Most of the images did not document the artist's own life but that of his nephew. Thus Boltanski's book, like most of the work that would follow, was not a reconstructed memory, but rather a meditation on the lacunae in personal and cultural histories and how we fill them.

Autel Chases (1988) (**fig. 6.6**) is an example of what has become Boltanski's signature practice of appropriating and slightly altering found photographs to create diverse, often site-specific installations. He often reuses groups of photographs, returning many times, for instance, to a collection of portraits of French college students in Dijon. In 1987, he started using a new source image, a group photo of the 1931 graduating class of a private Jewish high school, the Chajes School in Vienna (called Lycée Chases in Boltanski's work). The fate of the students is not certain, though it is likely the Nazis murdered most of them. Boltanski rephotographed the rather prosaic yearbook, cropping the images and

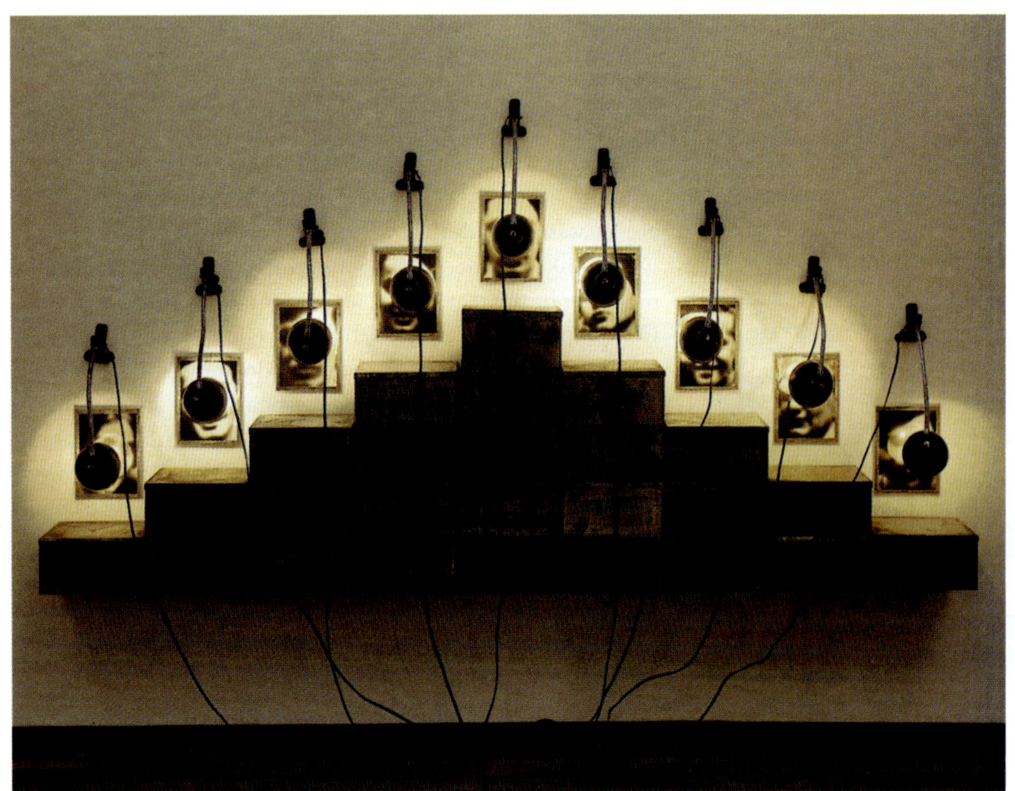

6.6 Christian Boltanski, ***Autel Chases***, 1988. Nine black and white photographs, 25 tin biscuit boxes, 9 lamps. Courtesy of the artist and Marian Goodman Gallery, New York/Paris.

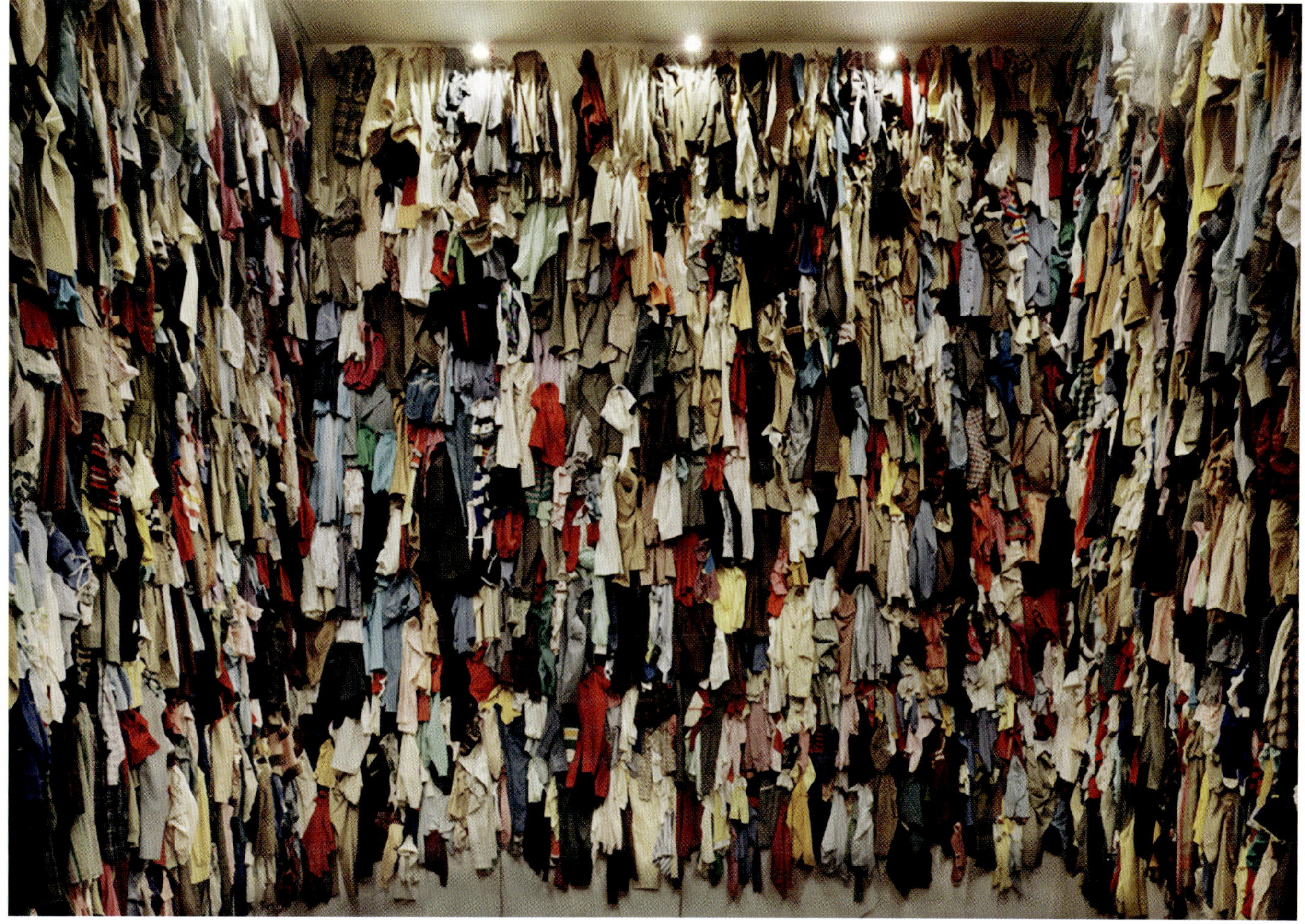

6.7 Christian Boltanski, *Canada*, 1988. Clothing and lamps. Courtesy of the artist and Marian Goodman Gallery, New York/Paris.

enlarging them to create blurred approximations of the individual faces shown in the original. In his installations, constructed using rusted biscuit tins, desk lamps, inexpensive frames, and extension cords, Boltanski transformed this familiar picture of middle-class childhood into one showing the ghosts of European Jewry. Stepping into *Autel Chases* is like walking into a holy space and standing before an altar (the meaning of the French word *autel* in the title). Accompanying Boltanski's allusions to death and mourning, however, is a conundrum created by the photographs at the center of his work. The artist blurred the faces, cropped them to exclude any identifying details, and even changed the spelling of the school's name. He also deliberately used too little emulsion so that the images lack the even surface, rich tones, and clarity that usually characterize silver gelatin prints. As a result, the images are incomplete, obscured by an imperfect printing process as well as by being enlarged past the point of clarity. Like memory, Boltanski's art distorts that which it calls to our attention.

Boltanski's work of the late 1980s—including his Lycée Chases work, a similar series based on a 1939 photograph of a Jewish Purim celebration, and an installation of secondhand clothing titled *Canada* (1988) (**fig. 6.7**) after the name given to the Nazi warehouses that held confiscated Jewish possessions—transformed perceptions of his art. The Holocaust, previously the "displaced and hidden" subject of his work, was brought into the light; everything he created was now seen through that lens.[7] Boltanski's attitude toward history, however, remained as ambivalent as his thoughts on memory. To answer questions such as who is being memorialized in his art and to what end, one can turn to a large archive of work and interviews, which inevitably leads to Jewish life in prewar Europe. But the exact connections between the artist and this source material are always as much a product of chance as of intention. *Autel Chases*, like nearly all of Boltanski's oeuvre, invites the viewer to clarify the ambiguities of rusting tins and obfuscated portraits by drawing on his or her own memories and knowledge. These blurred faces are meaningful in myriad ways, depending less on the artist's biography than on that of the viewers whose memories provide features and futures for these fading images.

Rachel Whiteread

The rejection of figurative monuments in the wake of Maya Lin's *Vietnam Veterans Memorial* implied that representational art might be less well suited to issues of war and injustice than had previously been thought. Boltanski's work revolved around the presumption that representation was compromised: His displays of failed attempts at depicting the past were enormously successful at addressing the relationship between the present and wartime past. As the United States Holocaust Memorial Museum commissions demonstrate, many artists embraced abstraction as the most effective means to reckon with historical trauma. British sculptor Rachel Whiteread (b. 1963) produced two monuments, *House* (1993) (**fig. 6.8**) and The *Holocaust Memorial*, Vienna, Austria, begun in 1995 and executed in 2000 (**fig. 6.9**), that provide another reflection on the relationship between representation, abstraction, and history. Like all of Whiteread's oeuvre, the latter makes use of inventive forms of casting to capture the profound strangeness of domestic objects and spaces. In this case, she cast the form of a private library and presented it as a monolithic cube finished with a decorative trim in a Viennese square. The book-filled shelves have been turned inside out, so that the books' spines face the walls; the room itself has been transformed from a warm domestic environment into an impenetrable mass. The memorial evokes nothing so much as a white tomb and is dedicated to the 65,000 Austrian Jews killed in the Holocaust. Around its base are carved the names of the Nazi concentration camps where they were murdered.

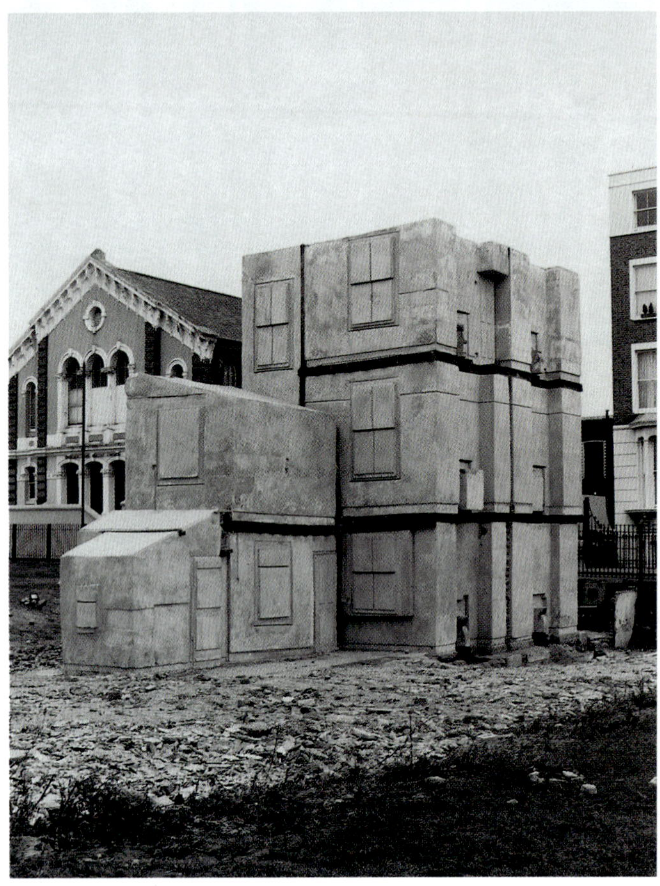

6.8 Rachel Whiteread, *House*, 1993. Grove Road, East London. Concrete, full size cast. Commissioned and produced by Artangel. Courtesy of the artist, Luhring Augustine, New York, and Gagosian Gallery.

Whiteread had been invited to submit a proposal for the Viennese memorial in large part owing to her proven adroitness at giving form to absence and loss, demonstrated most spectacularly in her 1993 London piece *House*. *House* was created by spraying concrete onto the interior walls of a condemned building. When the house itself was subsequently removed, what remained where it had once stood was Whiteread's monumental rendering of the space formerly inhabited by a typical London family. The massive form of *House* produced a poignant contrast to the empty spaces of the vacant lots around it. The house itself had been in a working-class neighborhood of London that was being demolished and reshaped by real-estate developers. By the time of its completion, *House* stood alone, the last uncleared

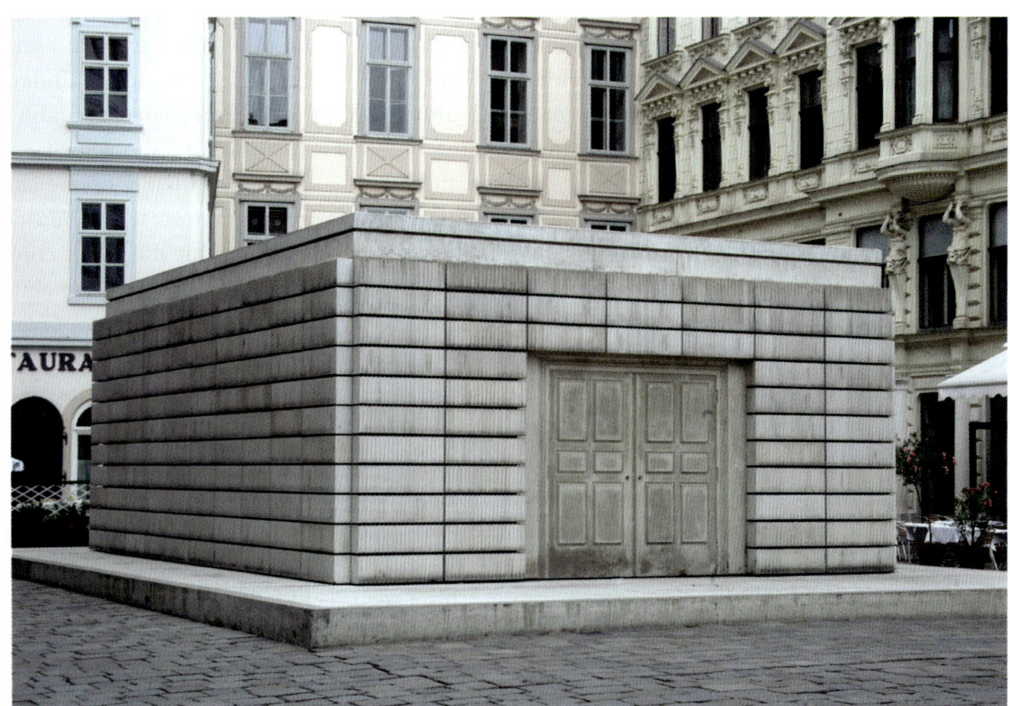

6.9 Rachel Whiteread, *Holocaust Memorial*, 1995–2000. Judenplatz, Vienna. Concrete, 153½ × 296⅛ × 416½" (390 × 752 × 1058 cm). Courtesy of the artist, Luhring Augustine, New York, and Gagosian Gallery.

plot of land in the path of gentrification. The metaphor of transforming the domestic spaces of the working class into intractable concrete blocks standing in the way of capitalist investors resonated with activists seeking to change the current trends in urban development.

For the Austrian memorial, Whiteread struck a balance between presence and absence that responded to the different families and histories being recognized in Vienna. Whiteread typically casts found objects in such a way that the resulting sculpture takes the shape of the negative space in and around the object. In the *Holocaust Memorial*, the negative space of the room is cast in this way, but the books are cast as positive forms. The visitor to the memorial thus confronts both the contents of the library and the space in which they were read as solid material. As in *House*, however, the architecture that would have supported and protected the room in reality is evoked, but not reproduced. Whiteread's sculpture approaches the very edge of the walls and ceilings, touches them, but then stops, leaving gaps where the structural supports should be. The missing architecture is most dramatically evoked at the edges of the books. Each volume is bonded to its neighbor and to the block of the room, but is suspended with no shelf beneath it—the books thus exist as unlikely objects whose means of support have been denied, whose substance has been changed, yet whose shapes remain. With a graceful coincidence of representation and Minimalist form, Whiteread's room makes reference to the Jews as "People of the Book" and their fate when the European communities they had called their own turned against them.

Shimon Attie

As the *Monument Against Fascism* was slowly sinking into the ground in Harburg, a young U.S. photographer, Shimon Attie (b. 1957), arrived in Berlin in search of pictures of Jewish life there before World War II. After hunting through archives, he selected a group of images, rephotographed them, and projected them, briefly, onto the buildings and streets that they depicted. The results, themselves photographed by Attie in works such *Almstadtstrasse 43, Berlin* (1993) (**fig. 6.10**), constitute a body of work called *The Writing on the Wall*. The projections were made in Sheunenviertal, a once-vibrant Jewish neighborhood that was never fully rebuilt after the war. When Attie arrived in Berlin, Sheunenviertal was starting to be gentrified, although the state of decay recorded in his photographs reveals that the current residents had benefitted little from German economic growth, either in the immediate postwar years of expansion or in the boom after Unification in 1990. *The Writing on the Wall* bears witness to the destruction of the war and years of disregard afterward.

During the few hours in which Attie projected his photographs, it was once again possible to see Jews walking along the streets dressed for temple or for work. They could again be seen in the windows of what had been their homes and stores. One man looks over the display at a Hebrew bookstore while around the corner a proprietor looks out from the Biograph Theater. Attie's carefully crafted photographs of the projections accent the juxtaposition of this vibrant past with the decaying present. As public works of art, Attie's

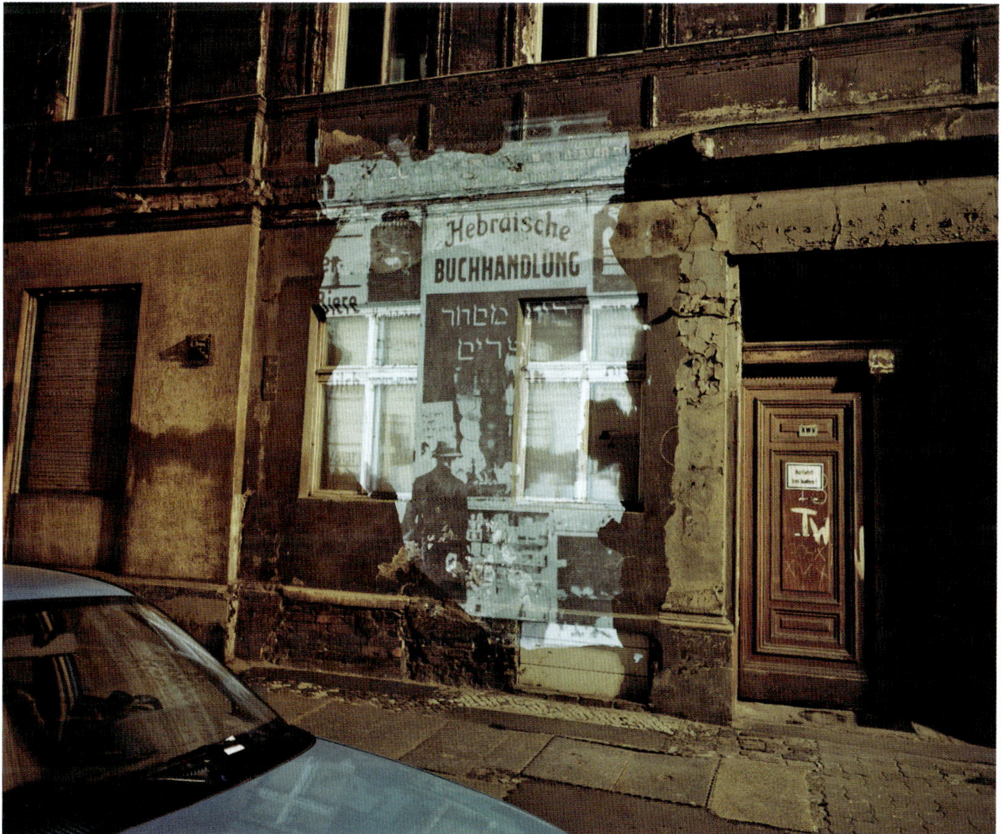

6.10 Shimon Attie, *Almstadtstrasse 43, Berlin*, 1993. Ektacolor photograph. The Museum of Modern Art, New York. Courtesy of the artist and Jack Shainman Gallery, New York.

projects were short performances with their own audiences whose reactions were at times quite volatile. Several residents of the now non-Jewish neighborhood, including the owner of Almstadtstrasse 43, were distraught at Attie's intervention. They felt it accused them of either profiting from the Nazi murders or of being Jewish—both, it turned out, were regarded as serious charges. *The Writing on the Wall*, like the Gerzes' monument and Whiteread's *Holocaust Memorial*, which was protested by nearly 2,000 people before its opening, raised the specter of fascism even as it evoked a tragic sense of loss. As an artful display of the pre-Nazi past, produced with great care and formal precision, *The Writing on the Wall* offered testimony against Nazi crimes and a memorial to the Jewish dead. Balancing nostalgia and reflection, it also illuminated contemporary attitudes that remained troublingly similar to those of the 1930s.

Eleanor Antin

Feminist filmmaker, photographer, and performance artist Eleanor Antin (b. 1935) addressed history by creating work in which, as she described it, "time collapses" and "layers of life flow simultaneously into a mesh of memory and dream."[8] The U.S. artist achieved an organic flow through time and consciousness by mixing archival research and theater. She began working with the idea of historical fiction in the 1970s, creating characters such as the King of Solano Beach, an erudite bum from another age who made his rounds through this southern California town interacting with his subjects and overseeing his domain. Other characters include Eleanor Nightingale, a nurse in the Crimean War (1853–56), and Eleanora Antinova, a black ballerina who danced for the impresario Sergei Diaghilev (1872–1929) in the Ballets Russes. In these early creations the historical setting provided a premise from which to explore possibilities for creativity, agency, and identity across time, as well as to investigate the parameters of female selfhood. It is the resulting proximity to the past, and Antin's viewers' ability to imagine themselves into other ages and other bodies, that drives her work.

In the early 1990s, Antin began to work on themes drawn from the early twentieth-century history of Eastern European Jewry. The first fruit of this was *Man Without a World* (1991) (**fig. 6.11**), a film written and directed by another of her characters, Yvgeny Antinov, a Yiddish-speaking Russian director from the 1920s. The film is particularly significant in Antinov's career. His previous work, *The Last Night of Rasputin*, supposedly made in 1924 (it was actually produced by Antin in 1989), had been about the fall of the Romanovs and the politics of the Russian Revolution. Announcements for it had declared: "In the dark night of Tsarism, the flame of idealism burnt in the ardent hearts of three friends from the productive classes—a worker, a student, and a ballerina."[9] The dancer was played by one Eleanora Antinova. *Man Without a World* stepped away from Russian political history to examine Jewish experience, but did so under the influence of the U.S. Jewish taste for romantic stories of shtetl life. Antin thus here examined the impulse to explore the past not as memory but as nostalgia, though, as she explains in the preface to the published screenplay of *Man Without a World*, Antinov couldn't refrain from including revolutionary politics in his film, thereby, she felt, spoiling its prospects in the U.S. market. Though Antinov undertook his foray into Jewish history in large part for financial reasons, Antin's commitment to Jewish themes arose from her changing relationship with her aging mother. With *Vilna Nights* (1993) (**fig. 6.12**), she set aside the fictive lens of Antinov and began to explore the past through her mother's memories.

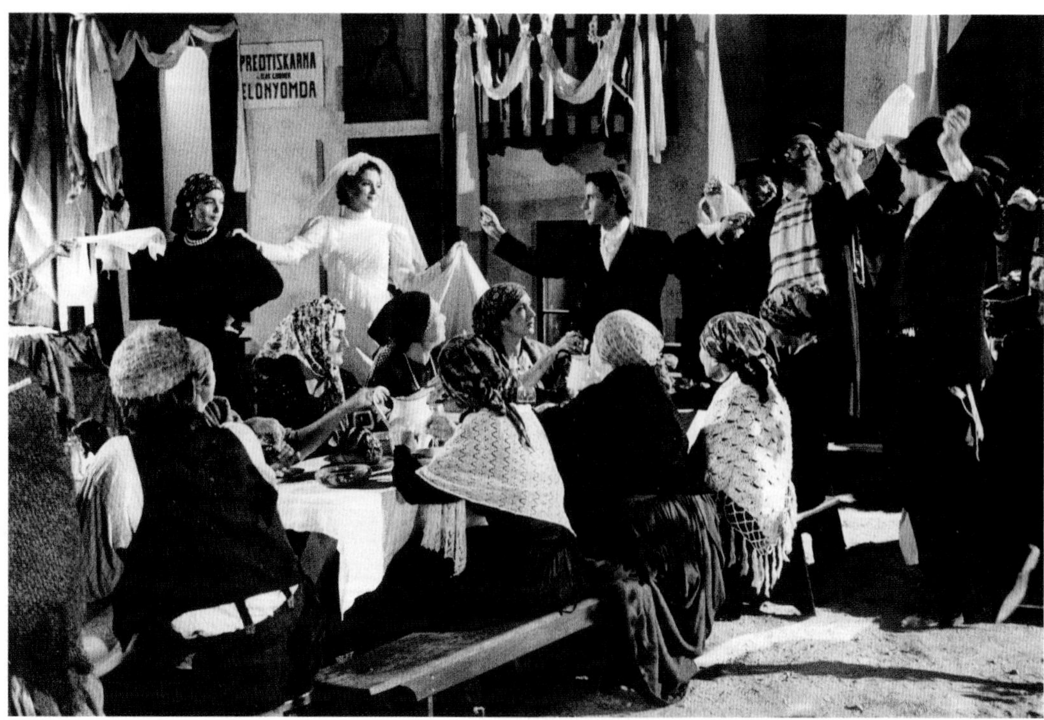

6.11 Eleanor Antin, *Man Without a World*, 1991. Film still. Courtesy Ronald Feldman Fine Arts, New York.

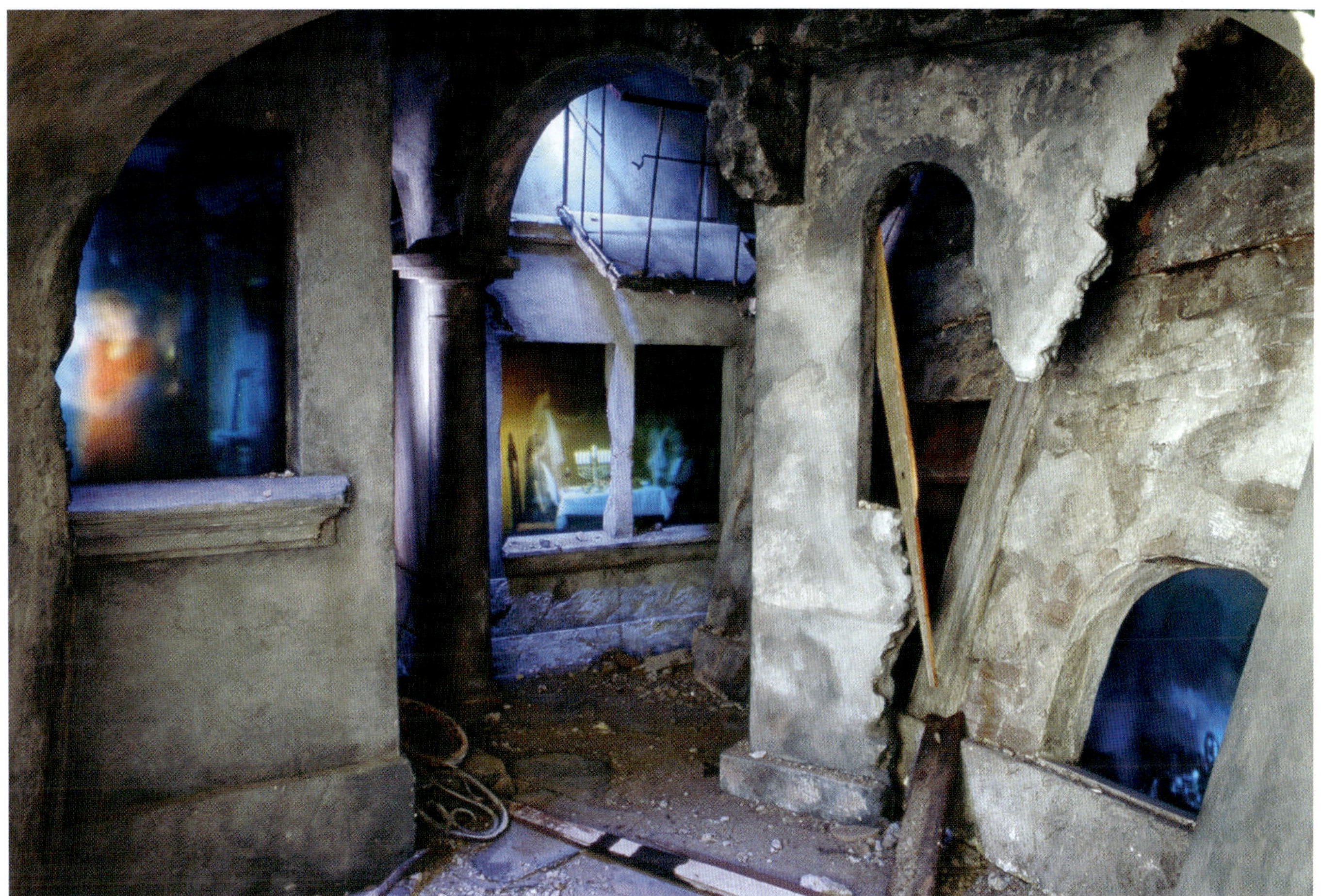

6.12 Eleanor Antin, ***Vilna Nights***, 1993. Mixed media installation, dimensions variable. The Jewish Museum, New York. Courtesy Ronald Feldman Fine Arts, New York.

Vilna Nights, a fabricated recollection of life in the Lithuanian capital before World War II, is an installation featuring a stage set showing the postwar ruins of the Jewish ghetto in Vilna on which are projected short films of life before the war. The work is somewhat exceptional among Antin's historical pieces in not focusing on a main character. Instead, Antin offers the viewer the chance to wander "through a history made up of [my mother's] romantic, probably embellished stories."[10] Antin's mother was in her late eighties and nineties and suffering from periods of memory loss when she recounted her life to her daughter. The stories, enhanced by research, provided the material from which Antin fabricated narratives that convey the temper of the period. Just as shtetl life was a site of collective nostalgia for Antinov's hypothetical U.S. viewer, Vilna in *Vilna Nights* is a screen not only in a literal sense for Antin's projections but also in a metaphoric and psychological sense for Antin's audience. Both the sculpted space and the acted scenes stand in for survivors' memories and visitors' fantasies. Unlike the other work discussed in this chapter, *Vilna Nights* invites us to leave the present behind. The viewer steps in and is surrounded by the fictionalized past. He or she looks in doorways, leans through windows, and peers down alleys into a lost world. Two Jewish children share bread, a woman burns letters, a tailor works steadily at his sewing machine, and a magical *challah*, a traditional braided bread, and a menorah dance through the air. Each scene suggests a memory from a life almost forgotten. Antin has said that *Vilna Nights* was partly an attempt to create a memory for her increasingly forgetful mother. The fragments proved sufficient to jog the memories of others. One reviewer described overhearing a couple identify the precise Vilna street that Antin had re-created, when, in fact, there was no direct visual or topographic source for the work. Images, fragments of stories, sculpted sets, and the invitation to step outside daily life led viewers to accept Antin's art as an amalgam of prewar Eastern Europe as it actually existed and as it is now remembered and imagined by the audience.

African-American Histories

The global reach of World War II and its shocking revelation that European civilization was hopelessly weak in the face of its own genocidal compulsion have made it a critical reference for examining the relationship of art and trauma in the twentieth century. Art about the war and its aftermath can also be understood as symptomatic of how late-twentieth-century artists engaged with the past more generally. The complexity with which history was being interrogated, and its effects being considered, can be seen in the paintings, sculptures, and installations by a number of artists making work about different aspects of the African-American experience. Informed by personal experience, historical research, political will and imagination, a number of young African-American artists challenged existing models for interrogating racial politics in the historical past and contemporary present. Their work drew on practices as diverse as appropriation, portrait photography, silhouette making, installation, and painting. In many cases the histories being told were not common knowledge and demanded significant research on the part of the artists—and, afterward, soul-searching on the part of the audiences.

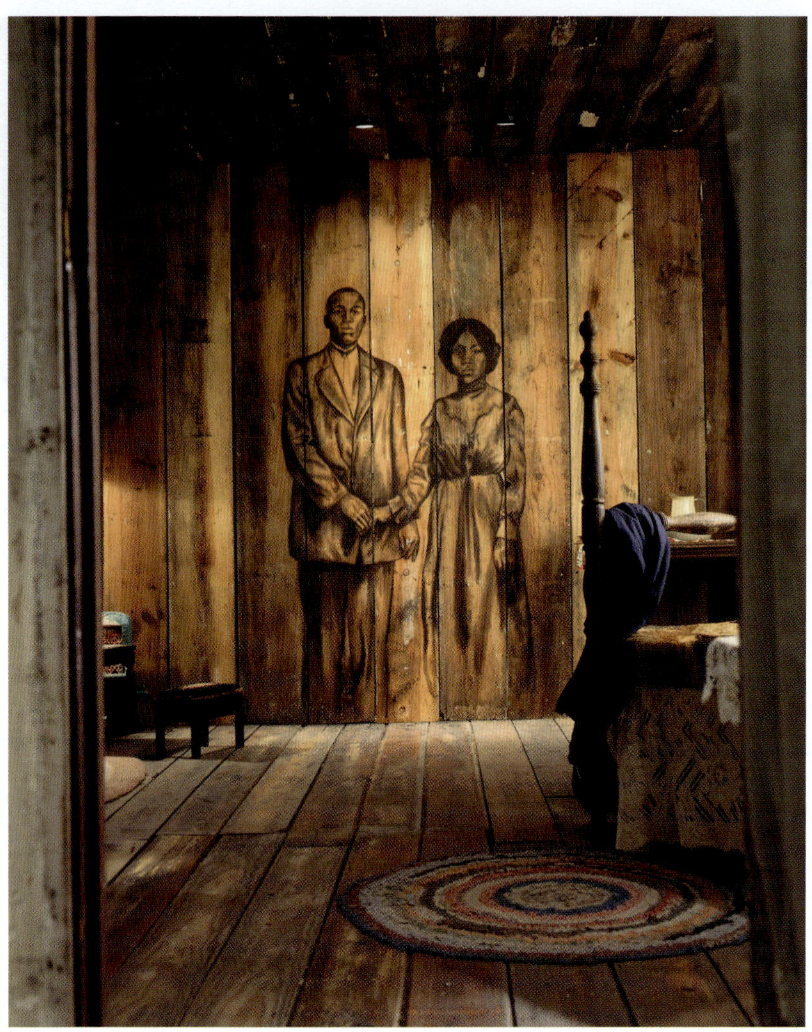

6.13 Whitfield Lovell, *Whispers from the Walls*, 1999. Installation view. Charcoal on wood with found objects. Courtesy of the artist and DC Moore Gallery, New York.

Whitfield Lovell

U.S. painter, sculptor, printmaker, and installation artist Whitfield Lovell (b. 1959) began what became a personal and historically searching body of work with the following premise: 'What were [black] people doing and who were they, between the Emancipation Proclamation to the Civil Rights Movement? Were they walking around barefooted and scrubbing clothes for white people? Or were they going about the business and the necessities of living their lives? ... Were they sitting around talking about how oppressed they were? No. They were living their lives. They were eating, breathing, cooking, having sex, reading, writing, and occasionally going to get their photos taken."[11] These photos became the key to Lovell's art. After a period of experimenting with expressive styles of painting, drawing, and printmaking, as well as learning from sources as diverse as Italian Renaissance art, African textiles, and Neo-Expressionist figuration, Lovell turned to photography for inspiration. Lovell's father had been an accomplished amateur photographer, and watching images—portraits primarily—appear almost magically in the chemical baths of the darkroom at home in Harlem had been a formative experience for the young Lovell. He began collecting photographs of his family as well as amassing portraits of anonymous African-Americans from the 1870s through to the 1950s. In addition to becoming a means of connecting to family and community, photography also suggested formal solutions for Lovell's practice as a painter and sculptor. The photographic portraits led him to wall paintings and then to full-scale installations built from found lumber, doors, windows, frames, furniture, pictures, clothes, and personal effects. These works might be as small as windowboxes or, in the case of *Whispers from the Walls* (1999) (**fig. 6.13**), as large as a house; like Antin's work, they are inventive while remaining faithful to the history they represent.

Lovell's style and content started to come together in a rather unlikely place, an Italian villa in the countryside near Milan. In 1993, he was granted a residency at the Villa Val Lemme in Capriatta d'Orba, once the home of a slave trader active into the early twentieth century. Fantasies of African tribal society were painted around the estate. Living among the spoils of the slave trade, Lovell felt compelled "to leave some dignified image of Black people in that space."[12] So he added his own pictures to the walls. He drew self-portraits, hands, and Yoruba figurines, thus challenging the depictions that permeated the villa with signs of African and African-American agency and identity. The experience in Italy led to other site-specific installations throughout the southern U.S. and one in Cuba. Lovell has served as visiting artist/historian across the U.S. and abroad, raising awareness of forgotten events and people while experimenting with visual means to integrate subject matter from the past into the experience of the present.

In 1999, he completed *Whispers from the Walls*, a tour de force that includes a small home furnished with objects from the 1920s and 1930s. An old turntable in the installation plays barely audible conversations that give voices to portraits painted directly onto the walls of the house. Lovell portrays the residents in sparse and sensitively rendered black line drawings based on photographs in his collection. They rise out of and seep back into the surfaces of the walls, asserting presence and loss with equal strength. Like the images Attie projected onto the streets of Berlin, Lovell's portraits both confidently claim the space and offer melancholic elegies to lost communities. *Whispers from the Walls* traveled across the United States, not only stopping at the predictable art spaces on the east and west coasts but also at venues in Texas, Alabama, North Carolina, and Kansas, thereby connecting Lovell's poetic and assertive vision of African-American history with the landscape in which some of its most dramatic episodes had occurred.

Nari Ward

The type of project in which a host institution invites artists to create work about its environs became increasingly popular in the 1990s. Artists who accepted these invitations faced technical challenges related to working in unfamiliar places and often in non-traditional media, as well as the difficulties inherent in carrying out community-based research. Equal parts anthropologists, sociologists, historians, and therapists, such artists-in-residence had to learn to select what was needed to realize their artistic visions from the vast amounts of personal narratives, local histories, and material culture they gathered on site. Making art about history at the end of the twentieth century, they discovered, demanded a special and new kind of creative practice.

Nari Ward's (b. 1963) *Rites of Way* (2000) (**fig. 6.14**) is a complex response to the challenge of creating historically oriented work as a visiting artist. Produced during a residency at the Walker Art Center in Minneapolis, Minnesota, it combined community outreach and research with formal and conceptual experimentation. For the project, Ward, who was born in St. Andrews, Jamaica, set out to learn about the community into which he had been invited. Using the museum as a platform, he set up a series of workshops and invited visitors to tell him their thoughts and stories about home. By the end of six months, he had discussed the subject with college students, Hmong immigrants from southern China, homeless teenagers, and African-American senior citizens, among others. To the stories provided by those living in the city, Ward added what he was learning from his own research about several neighborhoods that had disappeared from the Minneapolis and Saint Paul landscape. The first and

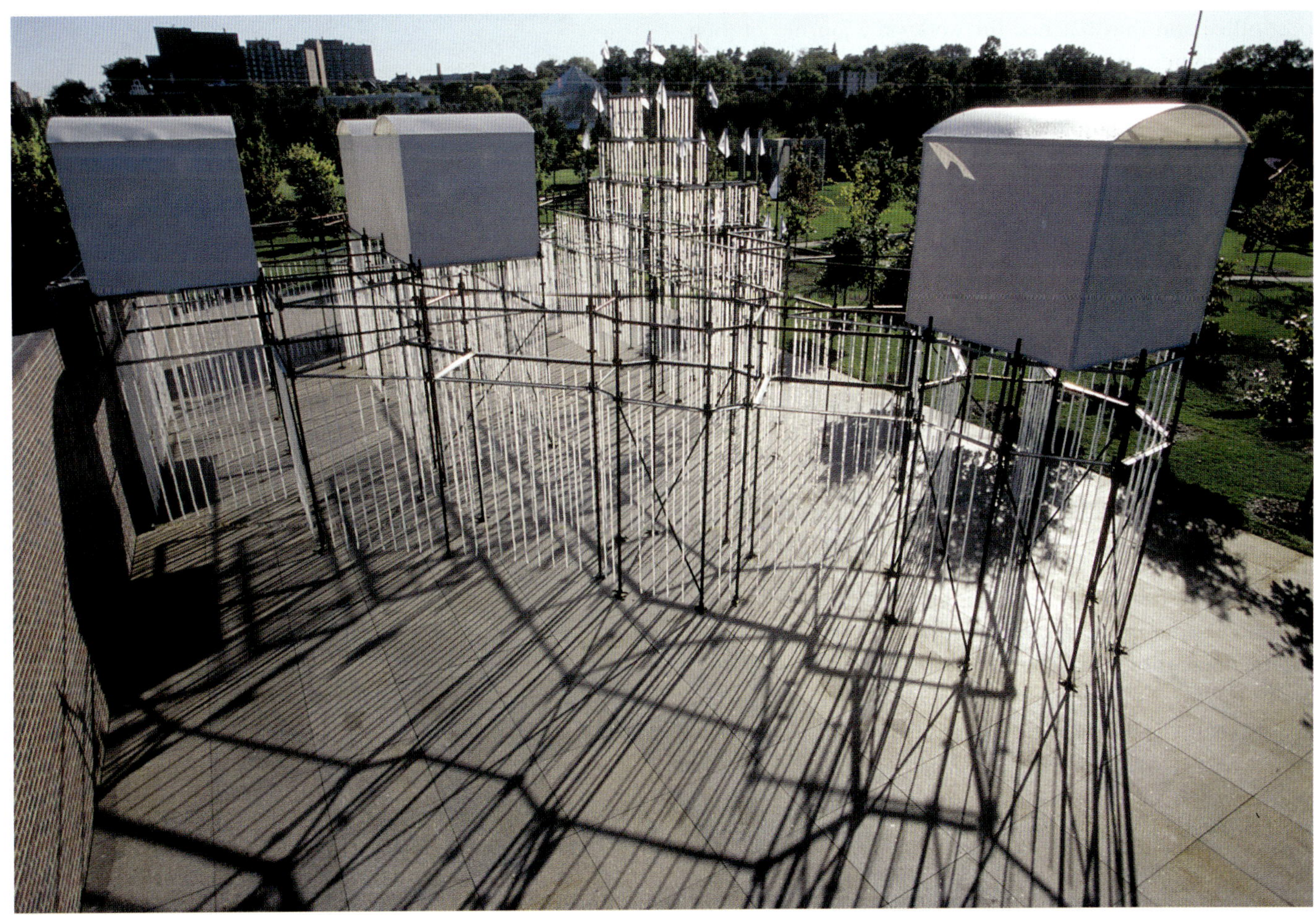

6.14 Nari Ward, *Rites of Way*, 2000. Installation view, Walker Art Center, Minneapolis. Courtesy the artist and Lehmann Maupin Gallery, New York and Hong Kong.

largest of these lost communities was Rondo, a center of the African-American community in St. Paul until it was largely demolished in the 1950s to expand the highway system. The second and third neighborhoods had been more fleeting in their appearances—clusters of ice houses built by fishermen on the frozen lakes of the region and equally transient ice palaces designed by architects in the 1930s and 1940s. Ward's installation joined the feelings of those making their homes in the present with a local history of urban change.

Rites of Way alluded in its title to the dispossession that occurred in Rondo when the city asserted municipal rights of way in order to reshape the Twin Cities metropolis. Ward's use of the punning word "rites" in the title invokes the rituals in which we engage to establish ideas of individuality and community, and to turn new places into "home." For the installation he constructed a cluster of small shelters evoking the temporary ice fishing huts, but raised them up on stilts, creating a floating village that rested briefly in the sky rather than on ice. The arrangement of the huts was based on the plans for an ice palace designed by African-American architect Clarence Wigington (1883–1967). Hanging from the huts were mementos contributed by the workshop participants to evoke their feelings about home. Before including them in the sculpture, however, Ward had mailed these domestic objects to long-vanished addresses in Rondo. These "home" objects were returned undelivered by the post office and thus reached the work via a journey of their own. Together, the three parts of the installation—the huts, their arrangement, and their decoration—each corresponding to communities from St. Paul past and present, contribute to a symbolic unity across time. Clearly indebted to Conceptual works from the 1960s and community work such as OBAC's *Wall of Respect* or the Feminist Art Program's *Womanhouse* (see Chapter 1) of the 1960s and 1970s, *Rites of Way* addressed the multiple local histories and communities that Ward encountered during his Minneapolis residency in eclectic terms specifically connected to them.

Michael Ray Charles and Fred Wilson

Lovell's *Whispers from the Walls* and Ward's *Rites of Way* came on the heels of a highly contentious national discussion about representation and race in U.S. contemporary art. The controversy was sparked by a body of work by young African-American artists who appropriated the caricatures of African-Americans common in nineteenth- and early-twentieth-century U.S. popular culture. Michael Ray Charles (b. 1967), for instance, took minstrel shows and lawn jockeys as models for paintings. The results, including *(Liberty Brothers Permanent Daily Circus) Blue Period* (1995) (**fig. 6.15**), call attention to the tenacity of racist attitudes that define African-American success in terms of entertainment value, whether on the stage or the basketball court. As with Fred Wilson's (b. 1954) appropriations and juxtapositions of racist memorabilia such as *Funny* (1995) (**fig. 6.16**), the work reveals the degree to which racism permeates U.S. society.

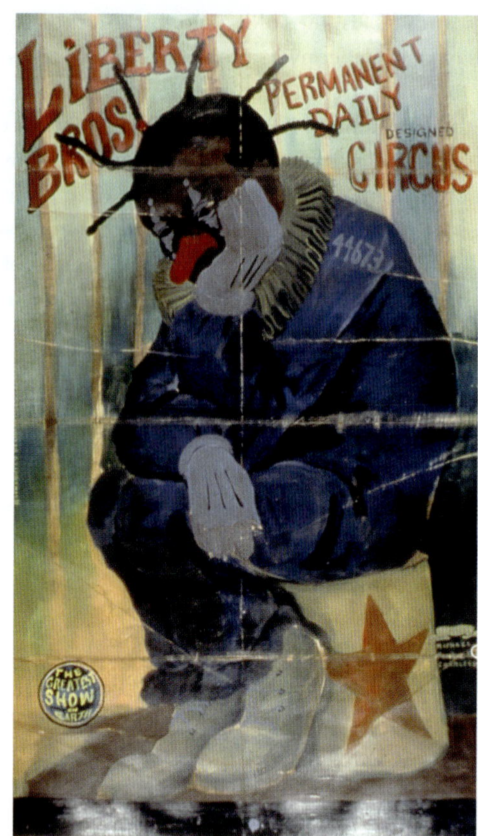

6.15 Michael Ray Charles, ***(Liberty Brothers Permanent Daily Circus) Blue Period***, 1995. Acrylic latex, oil wash, and stain, copper on paper, 60½ × 36½" (154 × 93 cm). Courtesy of the artist and the Tony Shafrazi Gallery, New York.

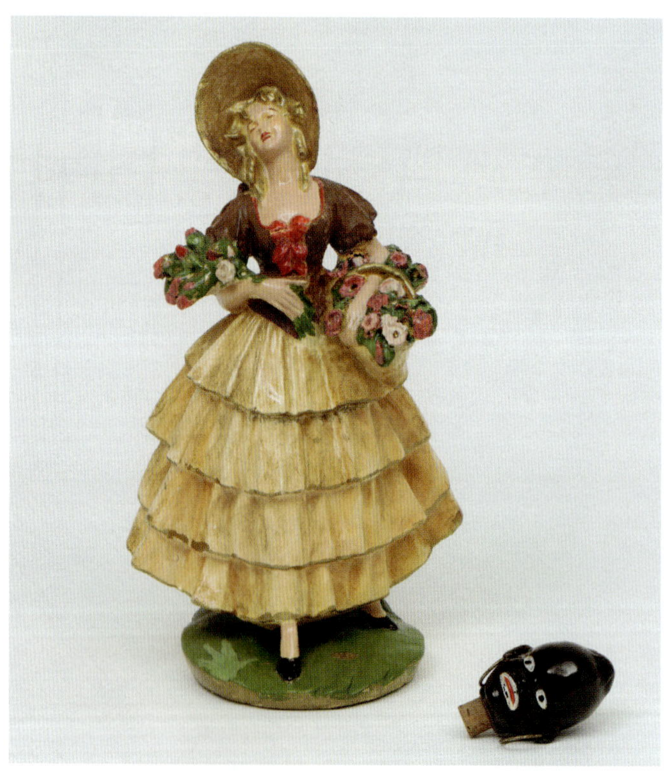

6.16 Fred Wilson, ***Funny***, 1995. Painted plaster and ceramic, cork and metal 14 × 7½ × 6½" (35.6 × 19 × 16.5 cm). Photograph by Kerry Ryan McFate, courtesy Pace Gallery. © Fred Wilson, courtesy Pace Gallery.

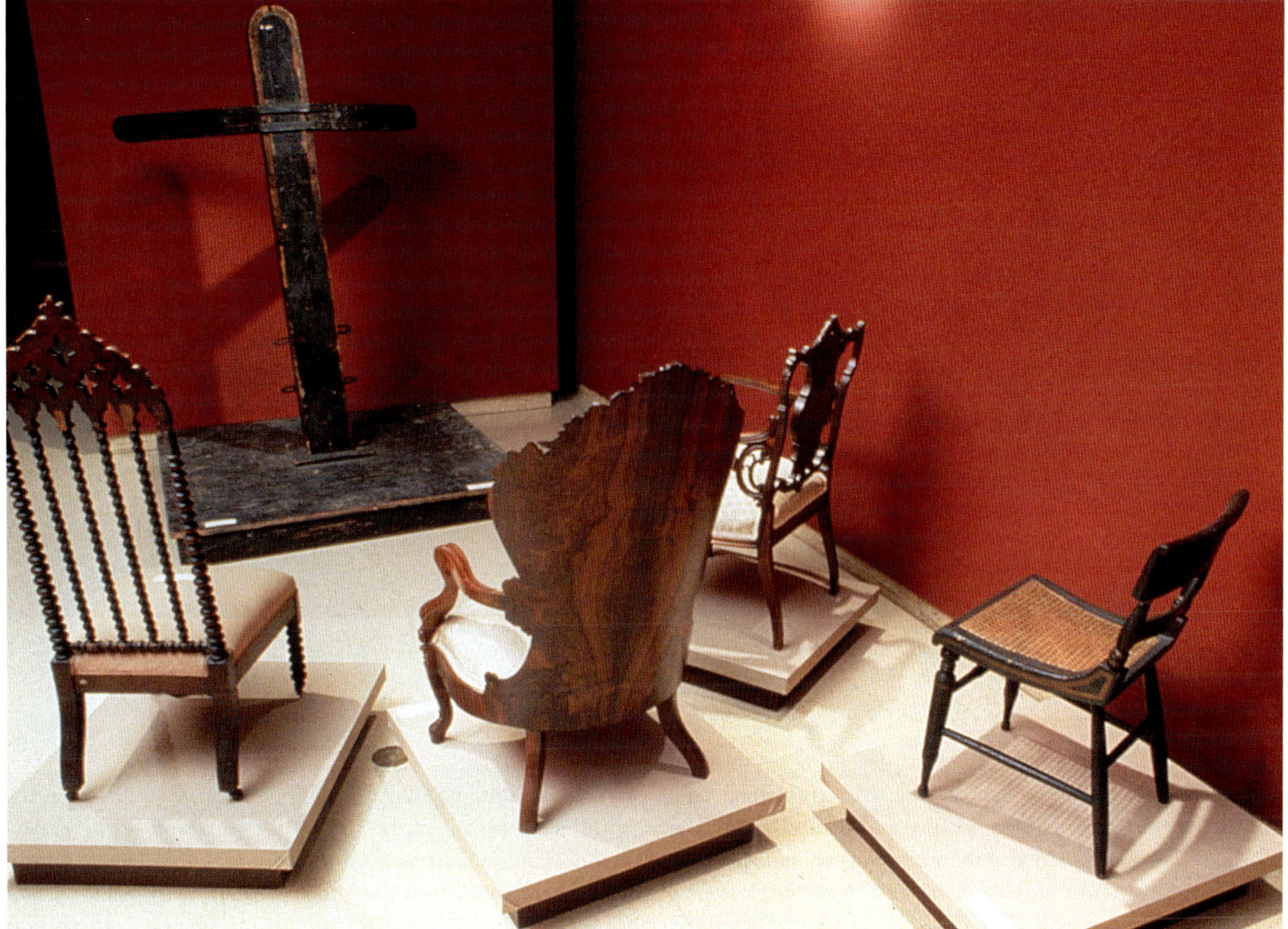

6.17 Fred Wilson, ***Cabinet Making 1820–1960*** from ***Mining the Museum***, an installation by Fred Wilson, The Contemporary Museum, and Maryland Historical Society, Baltimore, 1992–93. Whipping post, two armchairs dated ca. 1855 and ca.1896, and two side chairs dated ca. 1820–40 and ca. 1840–60. Photography courtesy the artist and Pace Gallery. © Fred Wilson, courtesy Pace Gallery.

Wilson made clear his historical interest in material culture in his groundbreaking intervention *Mining the Museum* (1992). For this piece, Wilson, at the invitation of the Maryland Historical Society, re-curated its galleries, juxtaposing objects from different installations and displaying unsettling items long since consigned to storage. Under headings that mimic conventional museological categories such as "Metalwork 1793–1880" and "Cabinet Making 1820–1960" (**fig. 6.17**), Wilson brought together objects generally treated as unrelated. Candlesticks were displayed with shackles, domestic furniture with a whipping post, raising uncomfortable yet accurate historical connections between the violence of slavery and the economic growth of the nation.

Kara Walker

Though both Charles and Wilson raised the ire of critics who were concerned that their work was too offensive to be effective, their intentions were at least understood with relative clarity. This was not the case with Kara Walker (b. 1969), whose hand-cut silhouettes repeat the exaggerated thick lips and prominent brows and buttocks that are the staple of racist representations of African-Americans. Room-sized installations such as *Gone: An Historical Romance of the Civil War As It Occurred Between the Dusky Thighs of One Young Negress and Her Heart* (1994) (**fig. 6.18**) featured scenes of life and love, creation and destruction, abasement and aggression in the slave-era South. Across a 50-foot wall, Walker applied life-sized silhouettes of a motley group of antebellum whites, blacks, masters, mistresses, slaves, children, and animals arranged in contorted narratives of commingling and catharsis that teeter on the edge of a moral and psychological abyss. There are no heroes and there are also no innocent victims as *Gone*—and the murals, drawings, installations, and films that have followed it—gives form to the distressing historical, emotional, and psychological entanglements that have grown up between white and black Americans since slavery.

When she was thirteen, Walker's family moved from a comfortable, racially mixed community in California to one in Atlanta permeated, she felt, by racism. Hurt and perplexed by the change in her environment, Walker described how, in order of comprehend and survive the racism of her daily life, she needed to create a place where she could experiment with the roles created for her as a black woman in white

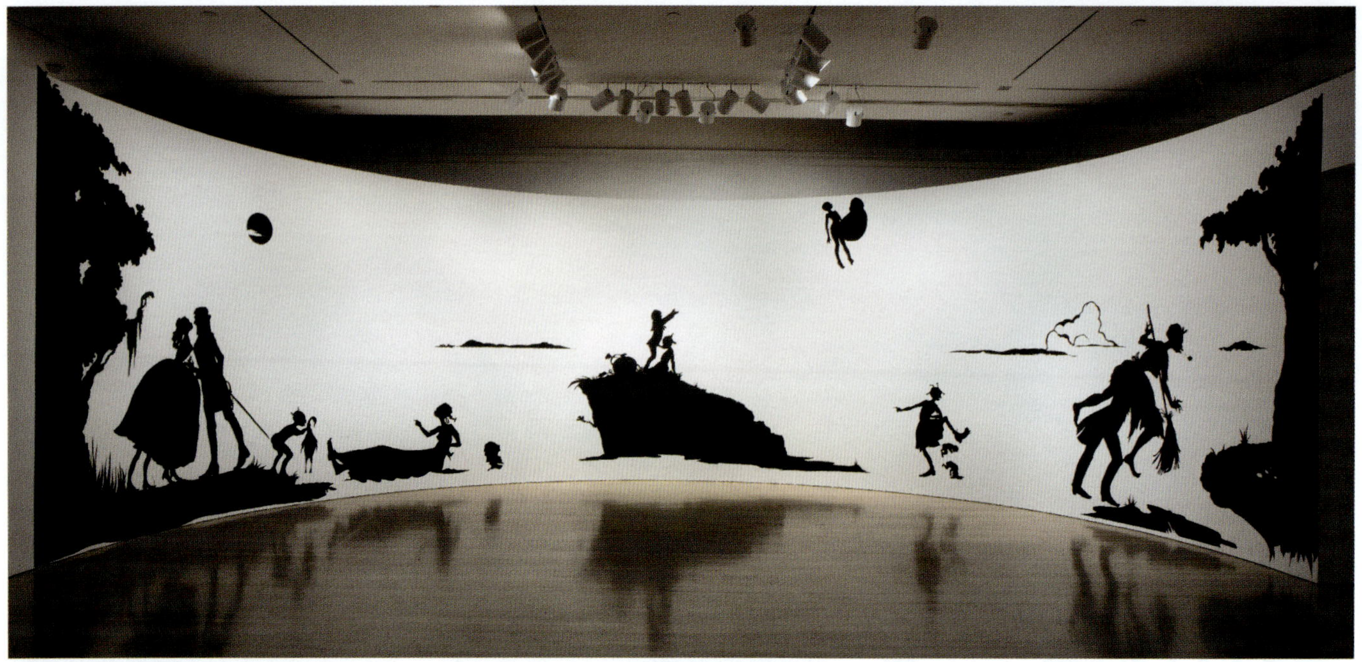

6.18 Kara Walker, *Gone: An Historical Romance of the Civil War As It Occurred Between the Dusky Thighs of One Young Negress and Her Heart*, 1994. Detail. Cut paper on wall, ca. 180" × 50' (396.2 cm × 15.24 m). Installed at the Museum of Modern Art, New York. © 2012 Kara Walker/Image courtesy of Sikkema Jenkins & Co., New York.

society. In her life she assertively resisted stereotypes of all kinds, first rejecting the introspective and painterly tradition in which she was trained and then standing up and speaking out as an African-American woman artist. In her art, however, she courted and embellished stereotypes. Like Charles and Wilson, Walker made art about race and racism, but, unlike them, she felt that appropriating evidence of racism was not enough. To truly understand her subject, she said: "I had to actually reinvent or make up my own racist situation ... In order to have a real connection with my history, I had to be somebody's slave."[13] Like Anselm Kiefer (see Chapter 3), though in a very different context, Walker attempted to step into the past to investigate its moral confusion on its own terms. Both artists acted out of a dissatisfaction with what they perceived as the false clarity with which their contemporaries condemned, glorified, or ignored the past, and both would be accused of immorality as a result.

After graduating from art school, Walker turned from painting to the silhouette, a traditional medium that evokes eighteenth- and nineteenth-century domestic environments. Silhouette making was a modest pre-photographic means for recording likenesses that was practiced by men and women, whites and blacks alike. In the 1970s, artists concerned with gender equality and racial justice often turned to such craft traditions to valorize those artisans who had traditionally practiced them—a much more diverse group than "fine artists," who were almost exclusively male. Though Walker's medium might suggest empowerment, her scenes of degradation refuse to provide any emotional uplift. In fact, the qualities of Walker's medium tighten the connection between the actors she represents and the actions they take. Like photography, the silhouette appears to transform an object into an image without the intrusion of the artist's hand. Shadow, not skill or interpretation, creates a silhouette. Attie and Lovell used this so-called "indexical" quality of found photographs to clarify the historical content and heighten the emotional power of their work. But Walker turned this effect against itself by juxtaposing the truth-value claimed by her medium with the hyperbole of her narratives. No cast shadow shaped Walker's silhouettes, her subjects take their forms from the history of racist visual culture filtered through the artist's imagination.

Walker's work suggests quite dramatically that this history of representation has become bonded to the identity of the individuals it represents. Racism in this case is not simply a distorting lens that could be removed through education or enlightenment to leave the true image visible. Walker's vision contrasts with the character of blackness suggested by Charles's *(Liberty Brothers Permanent Daily Circus) Blue Period*, for instance, which presents the African-American subject divided between an interior "true" self and the exterior costume he is forced to wear. In Walker's art, the legacy of racism in the U.S. has changed the very bodies of the people affected by it. This was a message, as one might expect, that many found difficult to hear.

The controversy over Walker's work exploded in 1997. That year she had a traveling solo show organized by the Renaissance Society in Chicago, further exhibitions at the San Francisco Museum of Modern Art and the Huntington Beach Arts Center, California, and was awarded the John D. and Catherine T. MacArthur Foundation Award, often called the "genius grant." The Chicago show presented her most comprehensive artistic statement to date, and was accompanied by an intricately produced catalogue declaring her intention to address a wide swath of U.S. history. The book began with an installation shot featuring PRESENTING NEGRO SCENES DRAWN UPON MY PASSAGE THROUGH THE SOUTH AND RECONFIGURED FOR THE BENEFIT OF ENLIGHTENED AUDIENCES WHEREVER SUCH MAY BE FOUND, BY MYSELF, MISSUS K.E.B. WALKER, COLORED (1997) (**fig. 6.19**). Above one vignette a floating female Gabriel figure, trumpet held between her legs, blossoms as her boot soles, skirt, breasts, hair, and fingers fan out around her. The spectator is then led by Walker's graceful lines and fluid compositions to view slaves' quarters and plantation grounds where figures dance, bathe, play, copulate, defecate, and vomit. "Now Reader prepare for Scenes of a more dusky nature," the book announces on page two, before, with a personal ad—"SBF, 23, painter, seeks tall, affectionate bastard, 30s, for coffee and paranoia"—the reader is invited inside. The book is a layered collection of reproductions of slavery-era prints, Walker's notes and sketches, cuttings from advertisements for 1970s blaxploitation films, and pornography. Many of the pages are translucent, permitting the texts and images to be glimpsed across and through one another. By the end of 1997, it was clear that Walker's vision of a turbulent and compromised history extended right up to the present.

To its critics, Walker's use of racist visual culture was doing nothing more than circulating the lowest forms of racism at the highest levels of culture. Her imagery was decried for celebrating the whitewash of history popularized by romantic fictions of the slave-era South such as *Gone with the Wind*, the racist iconography of texts such as *The Clansman*, source of D.W. Griffith's heroic portrait of the Ku Klux Klan in *Birth of a Nation*, or the hyperbolic stereotyping in blaxploitation films—all sources openly cited by Walker. The attention she now received catalyzed a segment of the African-American arts community already troubled by her art into castigating her work as "bestial fantasies about blacks created by white supremacy and racism, for the amusement and investment of the white art establishment."[14] When a call to censor her went out from a number of prominent artists, Walker and her advocates responded with the expected appeals to free speech. Even more significantly, however, writers including renowned literary and historical scholar Henry Louis Gates Jr. and the artist herself theorized the work as a proactive engagement with history and racism that took hold of the means used to perpetuate subjugation and hate. Walker's art, they said, was defined by aberrance and invention that took her bilious sources to expressive, even humorous extremes in order to pose questions about the reality of slavery and its aftermath.

As art historian and curator Robert Hobbs wrote of Walker's art, "It presents black as a destabilized term whose meaning ricochets back and forth among a number of variables"—some innocent and compelling, others horrifying and repugnant.[15] Identity and selfhood, African-American or otherwise, are defined in Walker's work by a perpetual mutation that draws on all manner of historical references and psychic possibilities. Her imagery bombards its audience with, in her own words, "contradictory desires and interpretations" that may "seduce" or "outrage"—and often do both at the same time.[16] Being caught between irreconcilable extremes is, for Walker, part of the realism of the work. Walker's work is upsetting to herself as well as her viewers for the way in which it gives form to the moral distortions that the history of slavery brought to U.S. culture.

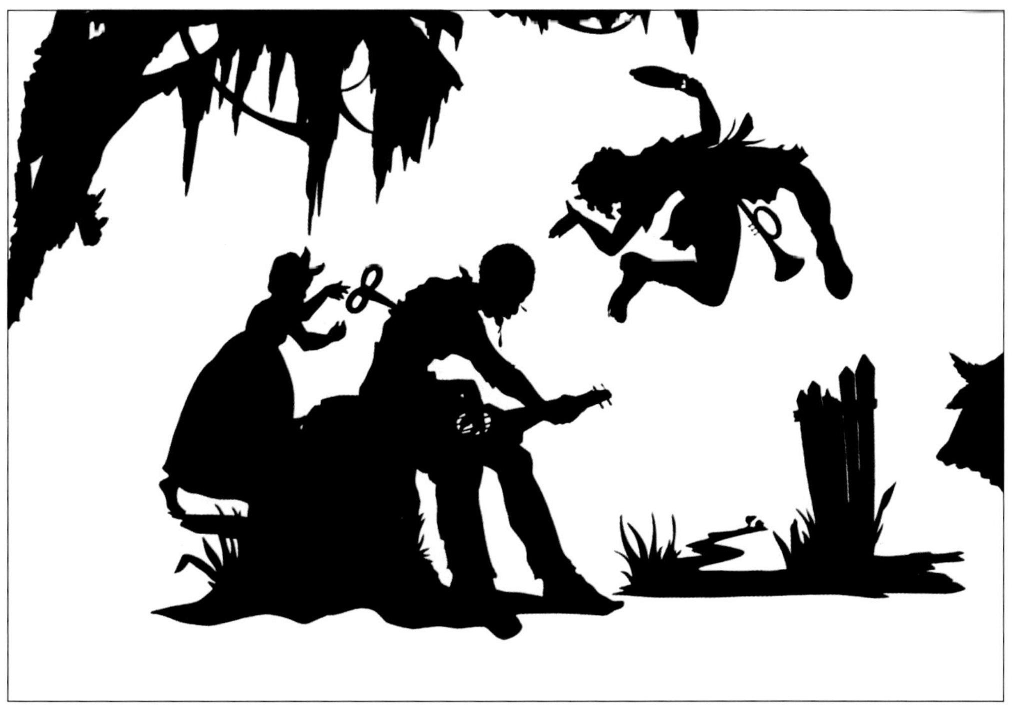

6.19 Kara Walker, *PRESENTING NEGRO SCENES DRAWN UPON MY PASSAGE THROUGH THE SOUTH AND RECONFIGURED FOR THE BENEFIT OF ENLIGHTENED AUDIENCES WHEREVER SUCH MAY BE FOUND, BY MYSELF, MISSUS K.E.B. WALKER, COLORED*, 1997. Detail. Cut paper on wall, cut paper on paper, ca. 144" × 155' (365.8 cm × 47.24 m). Installed at the Museum of Contemporary Art, Chicago. © 2012 Kara Walker/Image courtesy of Sikkema Jenkins & Co., New York.

Kerry James Marshall

In 1995, Chicago-based painter Kerry James Marshall (b. 1955) completed a series of paintings he called *The Garden Project.* In a palette of springtime hues, Marshall painted scenes of life in Altgeld, Stateway, Wentworth, and Nickerson Gardens, public housing projects in Chicago and Los Angeles, including the one in which Marshall himself had grown up. Marshall's flourishes of Neo-Expressionist brushwork hit the surface of the canvas with a force that evokes the violence of life in the projects and the theatrics of the local evening news. The tragedy that the housing projects cultivated some of the worst crime in the country was commonly acknowledged in public discussions of poverty in the United States. Marshall's painting style, however, also displays an ebullient energy and sense of potential that are rarely part of discussions of race and poverty in the U.S. Marshall depicts scenes of life in the projects with a sensitivity to their character that is unusual in the typically polarizing accounts of such places. The young couple who walk hand in hand through Wentworth Gardens in *Better Homes, Better Gardens* (1994) (**fig. 6.20**) are individualized and appear to represent real people navigating the complexities of life. The young black man looks toward the viewer and the path before him as he holds his girlfriend's hand. She extends her other arm behind him, revealing the tips of her fingers gently resting on his belt in a gesture that embraces and guides her companion. Around them, Marshall has created a complex setting that in its specific details and stylistic variety matches the psychological realism of the figures.

While *The Garden Project* provides insight into life as it is actually lived rather than perpetuating stereotypes, Marshall's work is not strictly realist. Like Kara Walker, Marshall uses indicators of race as symbols. At the Otis Art Institute in Los Angeles, Marshall studied with Charles White, a leading African-American painter rooted in the political and figurative traditions of the 1930s and 1940s. White's stylized black Everyman served as a model for Marshall, whose figures, he explains, "are literally and rhetorically black in the same way that we describe ourselves as black people in America; we use that extreme position to designate ourselves in contrast to a white power structure of the country or the white mainstream."[17] Marshall conveys the dichotomy implied by this statement—that African-Americans project a self-image that functions first and foremost in relation to the

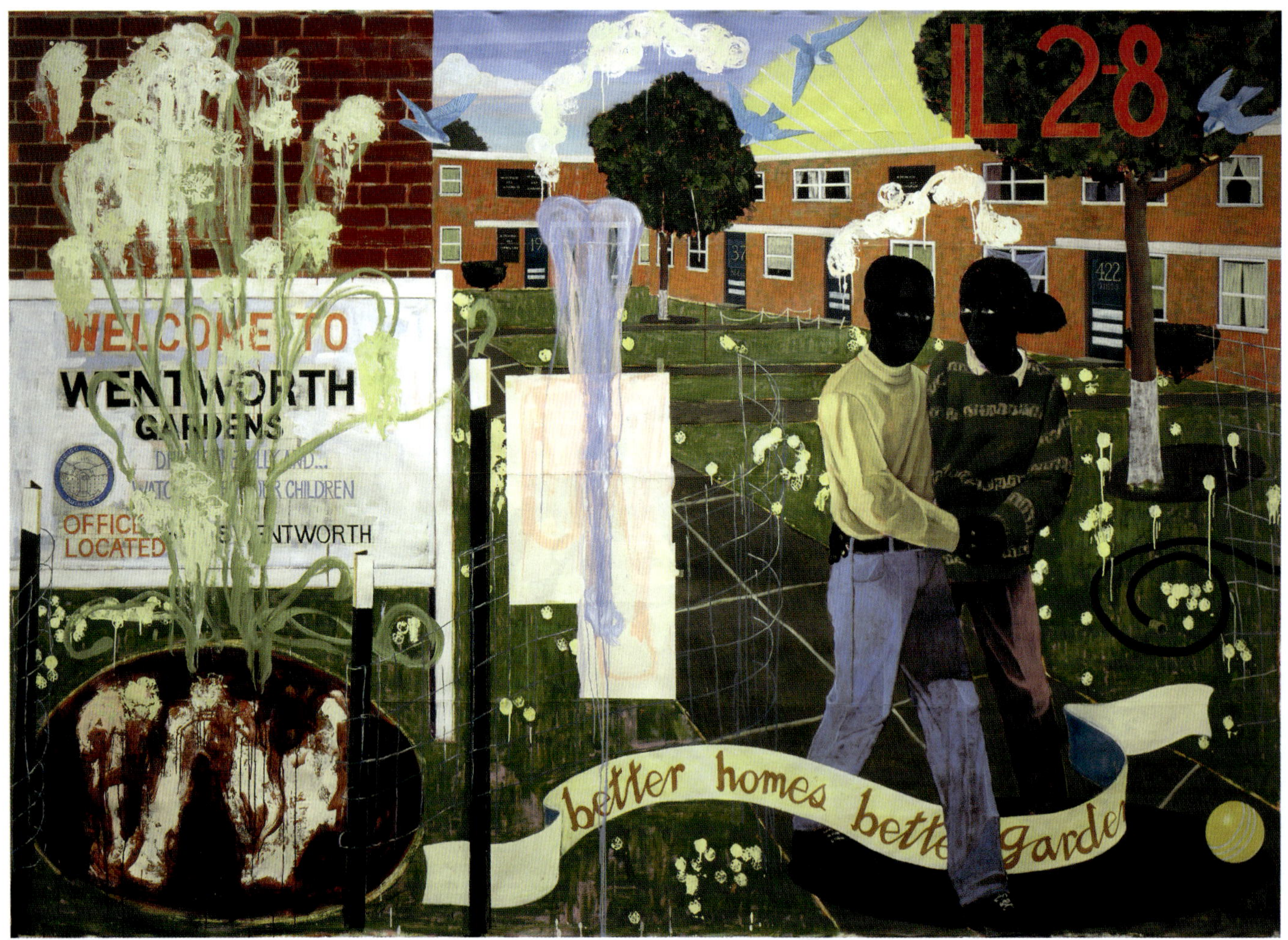

6.20 Kerry James Marshall, ***Better Homes, Better Gardens***, 1994. Acrylic and collage, 100 × 144" (254 × 365.76 cm). Denver Art Museum. Image courtesy of Koplin Del Rio Gallery, Culver City, CA.

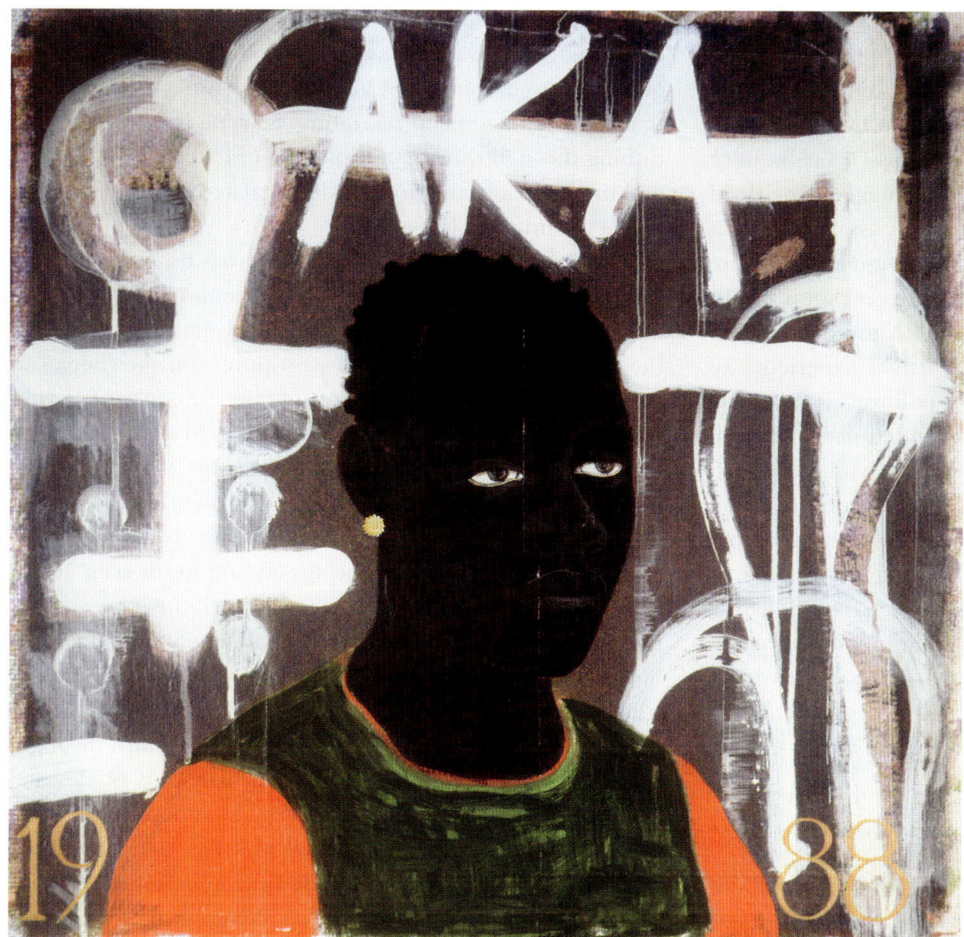

6.21 Kerry James Marshall, ***Lost Boys: AKA Black Sonny***, 1993. Acrylic, 24 × 25" (60.96 × 63.5 cm). Private collection. Image courtesy of Koplin Del Rio Gallery, Culver City, CA.

dominant culture rather than the self—in a second series, *Lost Boys*. Responding to the incarceration of his youngest brother, Marshall created a series of portraits that elide the fantasy in *Peter Pan* of the Lost Boys who never grow up to be adults with the plight of African-American men, so often kept from a meaningful adulthood by the inequities in U.S. society. Marshall was painting from personal experience and political outrage. In order to provide his own "Lost Boys" with individual personalities and simultaneously address a social crisis in more generalized terms, Marshall depicted his subjects with the features of real people but using a nearly impenetrable black palette that reveals its nuances slowly. The character of the portraits as renderings of actual people only emerges from the symbolic black forms upon close inspection. Aesthetically and emotionally, the deep blacks of the flesh tones of the *Lost Boys*, the painterly variety of their backgrounds, and their individualized modeling provide critical social content and invite the viewer to personalize Marshall's politics.

Conceptually and politically, portraits such as *Lost Boys: AKA Black Sonny* (1993) (**fig. 6.21**) represent people and issues usually excluded from the canon of art history. Such works, Marshall has argued, prove that with the simple materials of paint and canvas one individual can make a statement and so help transform national culture and art history itself. His own path took him from the projects in Los Angeles to Otis for a college degree and then out into the wider world, where Marshall set out to make art for the museum that could serve as an example to others in the black community. "I wanted to find a way to make sure that when young black kids went to the museum, that they didn't just have to be inspired by the work of European artists but could also be inspired by the work of a black painter and by work that didn't have to be segregated into a black section of the museum, like there must be something a little deficient or something about it."[18] In 2007, curators Roger M. Buergel and Ruth Noack included a mini-retrospective of Marshall's work in Documenta 12 that explicitly integrated it into European art history. In addition to providing a socially conscious lens through which to think about the exhibition that surrounded it, Marshall's work carried on a direct dialogue with the art of the Old Masters: At Wilhelmshöhe Castle, one of Documenta's venues in Kassel, the *Lost Boys* were hung in the baroque galleries near paintings by Rubens and Rembrandt.

Art Histories and Civil Wars

By the end of the twentieth century, even if the results proved controversial, artists were being asked publicly to engage the histories of World War II, Vietnam, and slavery. These events were being written about and debated elsewhere at the same time. The artists discussed in this final section also invented forms to address the trauma of the past, but the histories they speak about, and live with, had not been written at the time of their interventions—and, in some cases, have still not been formulated. The covert wars in Latin America, in particular the conflict in Colombia discussed below, were defined by the secrecy in which they were waged. The dead were not necessarily combatants while their assailants might be soldiers, police, criminals, or revolutionaries. Where very little of the past is recorded properly, reckoning with history becomes particularly challenging. A number of Lebanese artists and thinkers, reflecting on their experience of the constantly shifting psychological, political, even cartographic terrain of Beirut during its extended period of civil war, have raised the question of whether the violations such conflicts enact upon participants' memories render them un-recountable. The possible impossibility of writing history is a problem that is relevant to many of the instances of war, dislocation, and trauma occurring in the wake of globalization. A final return to the history of the war in Vietnam serves as a reminder to Western viewers that it too was a civil war with consequences that exceeded the military conflict, and as such shares many of the ambiguities present in the Colombian and Lebanese experiences.

Doris Salcedo

In the summer of 1985, sculptor Doris Salcedo (b. 1958) returned home to Bogotá, Colombia after finishing graduate school in New York City. That November, she witnessed the siege of the Palace of Justice by the insurgent M-19 militia, an event that transformed the political history of Colombia. The largely middle-class militants did not have a long history of carrying out guerrilla assaults, but were savvy about the power of the media. The capture of the Supreme Court was planned to provide an effective piece of political theater culminating in the trial of President Belisario Betancur for violating a 1984 ceasefire agreement he had negotiated with a collection of rebel groups, some of whom had been fighting the state for the past three decades. The government responded to the siege with overwhelming force, however, killing nearly all the rebels in a two-day battle that marked an end to the diplomatic engagement that had secured the ceasefire the previous year. The Colombian military now quickly moved south to Cali where it suspected, correctly, that the M-19 had been recruiting. Starting in 1985 and continuing through the 1990s, violent conflict based on politics, and in some cases the drug trade, escalated between the government and rebel forces.

The fighting at the Palace of Justice was traumatic for the nation and left Salcedo with visceral memories of buildings burning and people dying. She has said that in response to the attack and the brutality of its suppression she "began to conceive of works based on nothing, in the sense of having nothing and of there being nothing."[19] In retrospect, the incident stands out for its visibility since, by 1986, one of the most common and disturbing acts of violence experienced in Colombia was passing unseen: People would be taken from their homes or from the streets and never seen again. The disappearances were generally attributed to government forces seeking to silence and terrorize the populace. It has been estimated that nearly 20,000 people simply "disappeared" in the decade after the Palace of Justice attack. This form of violence, repeated in military dictatorships throughout Latin America, produces a particular kind of devastation that denies those left behind any resolution: There is no body, no proof of death, and no answers.

Beginning in the 1990s, Salcedo used her work to respond to this specific form of loss. Her challenge as an artist was to give form to absence or, in her own words, to "make a material object from nothing" that would correspond to the historical specificity of her subject.[20] Maya Lin had done this by mixing the evocative, abstract qualities of Minimalism with the very precise and human facts of the Vietnam War in the timeline of the *Vietnam Veterans Memorial* (see figs. 6.1–6.3). Salcedo started by collecting refuse from the streets of Bogotá, striving to create a connection between the discarded materials and the experience of loss. To link her art more clearly to the recent political history of Colombia, Salcedo then began interviewing families of the disappeared. The people left behind were primarily women, and Salcedo spent significant amounts of time with them, gathering

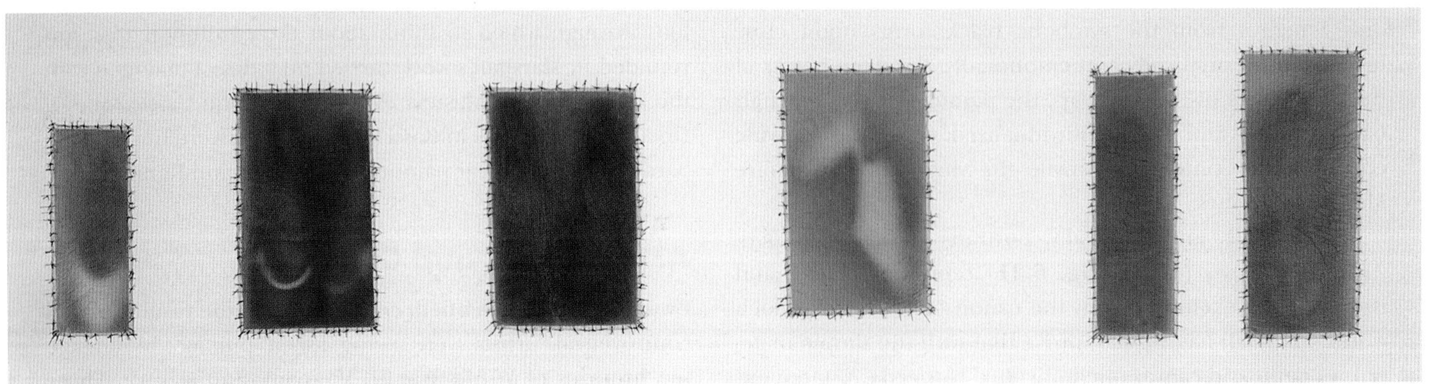

6.22 Doris Salcedo, *Atrabiliarios*, 1992–93. Detail. Wall installation with sheetrock, wood, shoes, animal fiber, and surgical thread in ten niches with 11 animal-fiber boxes sewn with surgical thread. Collection of The Pulitzer Foundation for the Arts, St. Louis. Image courtesy Alexander and Bonin, New York.

stories until she felt that she had internalized the narratives. Murder was not witnessed, death was never certain—what had definitely changed, however, was "home." It was here, in ordinary people's living rooms, kitchens, and bedrooms, that loss was most clearly and painfully evident, and it was in these homes that Salcedo sat and spoke with those who remained. To translate the intensity of her subjects' experiences, Salcedo collected materials that appeared to contain traces of the disappeared—shoes, chairs, beds, armoires, clothing, doors—with which she could build. From the late 1980s through to the new millennium, Salcedo has created an extensive oeuvre based upon reconfiguring domestic objects in light of the lives they touched

The first work to draw on the interviews was *Atrabiliarios* (1992–93) (**fig. 6.22**), an installation consisting of small niches covered with animal hide and containing shoes. The hides were translucent and stitched to the gallery walls with surgical thread. It took time to make out the forms behind them, so viewers were forced to get close enough to sense, even smell, the uncomfortable alliance of the medical and animal realms in the materials used. Salcedo explained that selecting shoes as the content of the work felt like a choice that had been made for her by the history of the area. When common graves were discovered, families would often confront bodies that were no longer recognizable and accompanying shoes were one means of identifying corpses. Almost hidden between the veils of animal skin in Salcedo's work, the shoes evoke the painful closure for the survivors who finally received confirmation of the fate of the disappeared by their recovery.

The shoes in Salcedo's work, however, are all women's shoes, so drawing attention to the fate of women who vanished but also alluding to the women who were left behind—Colombian widows' groups have been the most vocal in seeking justice for the dead. The title *Atrabiliarios* means "defiant," thus evoking resistance to the psychological and political paralysis created by fear and violence. Like all of the work discussed in this chapter, Salcedo's art is about the experience of enduring history, as well as addressing the events themselves. It alludes to the dead, but is directed to the community of survivors. Salcedo's work tells us of the struggle with the material world that remains after one's emotional world has been devastated. After people disappear, things often take on the status of relics of lost companions. In a 1999 interview Salcedo asserted, "My works are not memorials, they are not about remembering. I am not interested in telling stories; when you deal with violence words are no longer possible. These sculptures are empty, there is nothing there but silence: the silence of the victim, the silence of death, the silence of the artist and of the viewer."[21] Salcedo's work is both about and a means of coping with a violated world; it does not replace the devastation wrought by history with hope or heroes any more than do Walker's scenes or Lin's wall. Instead, *Atrabiliarios* provides an opportunity to reflect on surviving the world as it has become.

William Kentridge

Doris Salcedo's insights into trauma began in and return to silence. *Atrabiliarios* came into being as the artist asked what remains in the wake of acts of violence that have no witnesses and that often leave no means of verification at all. With a similar concern for representing the invisible scars of injustice, South African artist William Kentridge creates drawings and animated films that plumb the political history and psychological depths of his own country. As a child of middle-class Jewish lawyers who defended victims of apartheid, Kentridge had an unusual South African childhood. He experienced the privilege of being white under the apartheid system, which granted rights and power to South Africans of European descent, but at the same time he was also profoundly aware of the unethical foundation of his status. Most of his white peers lived separately from both black South Africans and critiques of apartheid. For them, as the artist points out, the "illogicalities" and "evils" of their society were "naturalized" when they were children.[22] For Kentridge, by contrast, ordinary activities such as going to whites-only swimming pools, movies, or schools were both normalized and at the same time recognized for the offenses that they were. His art can be seen as a representation and reflection upon the effect of such contradictory experiences. Even as he has often turned his attention to topics outside the history of South Africa, Kentridge has continued to examine the philosophical and emotional dimensions of the human quest for moral and ethical equilibrium.

In the late 1980s, Kentridge created a form of animated film that replaced the thousands of individual drawings that make up traditional animations with frame-by-frame documentations of the creation and modification of a few charcoal drawings. On a single page, lines are rendered and erased, landscapes appear and are populated, characters enter and act, and objects are formed and transformed. The first of the films, *Johannesburg 2nd Greatest City After Paris* (1989), introduced the city that serves as the primary setting and subject of a series of nine short films; the last, *Tide Table*, was completed in 2003. The films' two protagonists—an industrialist, Soho Eckstein, always presented dressed in a suit, and an artist, Felix Teitelbaum, shown naked—enable Kentridge to address a spectrum of experiences that intersect with his own. Initially it was Felix who was conceived as and appeared to be the artist's alter ego, expressing the sensibility of a white South African pained by the injustice of apartheid and eager for, if also anxious about, change. As the series continued, however, Kentridge found that the conflicted and poignant condition of his identity and that of much of the rest of the nation was also represented by Soho, a businessman who was invested in the political and economic realities of apartheid even if not necessarily in the ideologies that upheld it.

During the 1970s and 1980s, Kentridge had produced agit-prop theater and political prints that treated art as a means to intervene in politics. With his turn to animation,

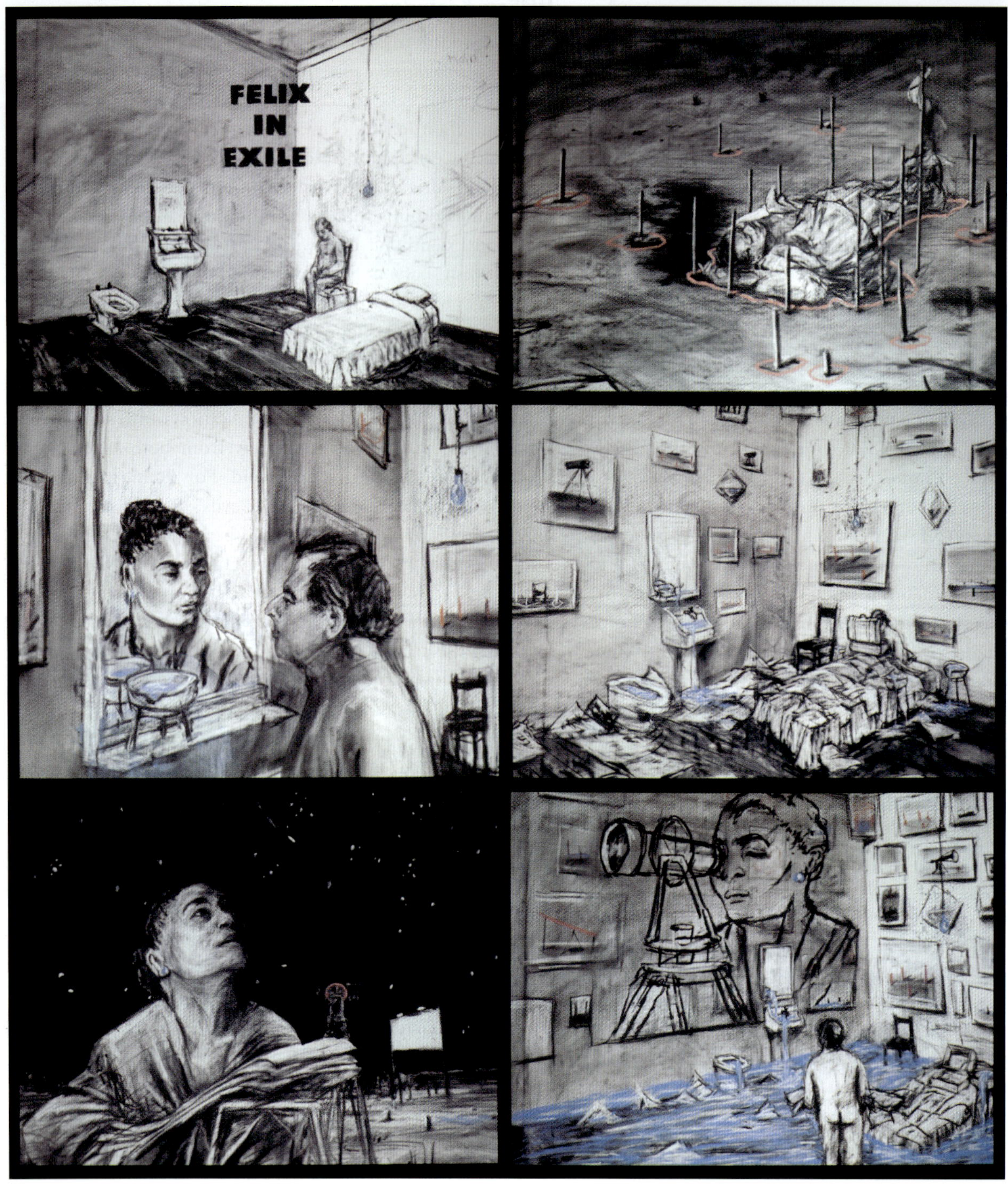

6.23 William Kentridge, ***Felix in Exile***, 1994. Video stills. Whole film 8 minutes, 43 seconds. Courtesy of the artist and Marian Goodman Gallery, New York/Paris.

however, his work started to become "more a reflection on the political world, in terms of the way it affects us personally, than an attempt to become part of it," he recounted.[23] The plots of his films take us into the daily lives of the two men. Soho struggles with the urgent economic, emotional, and political difficulties of running his business, while Felix lives the more distanced existence of an observer, only occasionally submitting to moments of passion, including a love affair with Soho's wife. In *Felix in Exile* (1994) (**fig. 6.23**), the naked artist is shown in a one-room flat that evokes a Parisian garret. In the drawings that fill his notebooks and cover his walls, Felix renders the recognizable terrain of Johannesburg and through them even appears to travel back from his exile. His drawings drift on a wind that blows through his room and out onto the South African landscape. In one particularly moving segment, a scene that Kentridge had conceived before he determined the plot of the film, Felix looks into the mirror that hangs above a small sink in the room and sees Nandi, a black South African surveyor, in place of his own reflection. Nandi measures and imagines new spaces for the city as we see massacred victims of the suppressed anti-apartheid uprisings through her eyes. Nandi's body, too, falls like the others. Back in Felix's apartment, water fills the sink and spills out into the room. Felix stands in the rising water as the walls around him vanish, the artist finding himself half-submerged in a pond in the desolate terrain where Nandi had died. *Felix in Exile* was completed just before the first fully democratic election in South Africa in 1994, at a moment when apartheid had been abolished but the next chapter of the nation's history had yet to be written.

Stereoscope (1999) (**fig. 6.24**) was produced after the 1994 election of Nelson Mandela as president and the 1995 establishment of the Truth and Reconciliation Commission, which sought to openly address the crimes of apartheid. In the film, Kentridge focuses on Soho in an effort to articulate the relationship between a white protagonist who stood to gain from the previous social order and the political transformation of the black population of South Africa. Unlike the exiled Felix, Soho occupies the actual space of Johannesburg, but he is distanced from the city by the walls of his factory and his own anxieties. He witnesses riots in the streets and his factory is bombed. The world of Johannesburg is transformed around him as he watches bodies and objects appear on the pages of his balance sheet, in the factory, and on the city streets. At several moments in the film, Kentridge divides the page on which he is drawing in two, repeating the same scenes as if they were to be examined in a stereoscope, a nineteenth-century viewing device that created from two identical photographs the illusion of a three-dimensional image. More than a nod to obsolescent technology, Kentridge's duplication—always imperfect and sometimes dramatically so—becomes a means of examining divided identities. "Mine is a desperate sort of naturalism," he has explained. "I question the cost and pain engendered by self-multiplicity ... There's a kind of madness that arises from living in two worlds ... Somehow the state is not so terrible or strange when it's named, fixed through its representation."[24] In the final scene of *Stereoscope*, it is Soho who stands alone in his room as blue water pours forth, cascading from his pockets as it had from the sink in *Felix in Exile*, leaving him standing head down, with water up to the knees of his striped suit.

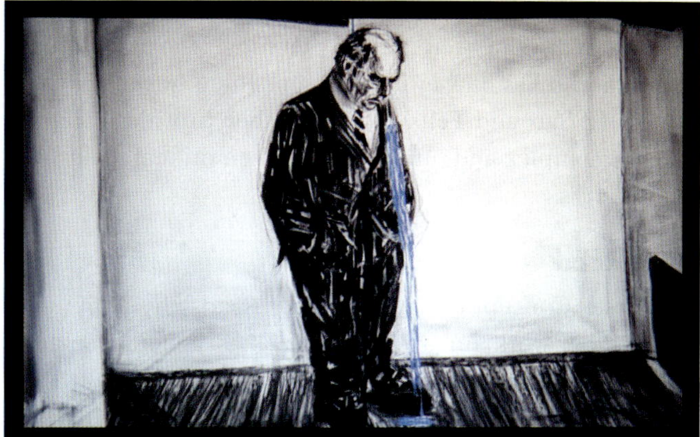

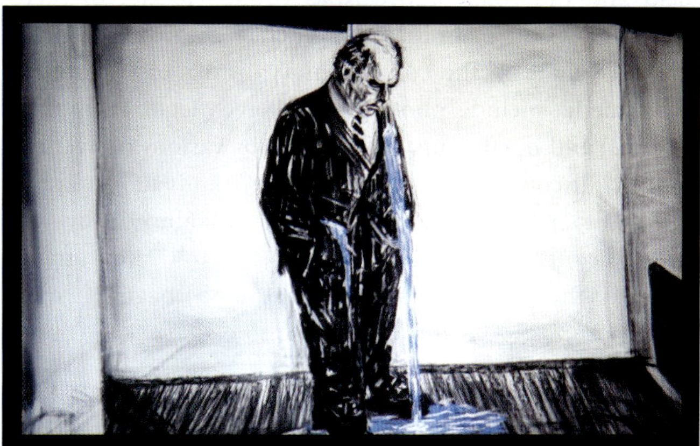

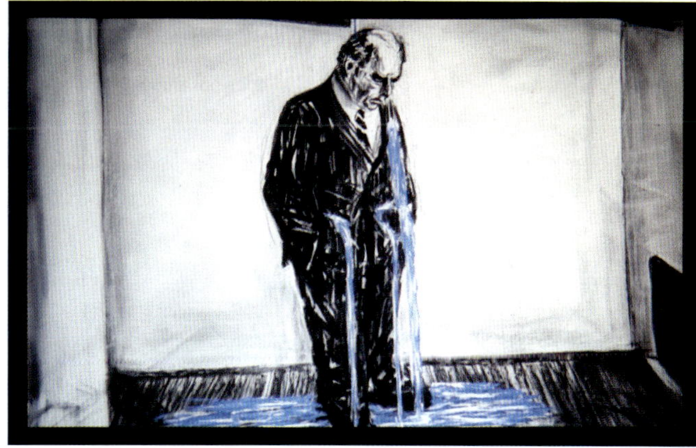

6.24 William Kentridge, ***Stereoscope***, 1999. Video stills. Whole film 8 minutes, 22 seconds. Courtesy of the artist and Marian Goodman Gallery, New York/Paris.

By the completion of *Stereoscope*, Kentridge's strategies for making art about South Africa were being interpreted as analogous to the aims of the Truth and Reconciliation Commission. The transfer of power from the apartheid state to the South African democracy was inspiring and the Truth and Reconciliation Commission, through which the nation sought to respond to its violent history with public reflection, appeared to provide an unprecedented means to avoid the purges and silences that plagued other twentieth-century attempts to transcend moments of social conflict. South Africa's success was duly celebrated. However, treating the airing of grievances as an end in itself had the unintended consequence of guilt being pronounced in the absence of any corresponding mechanism to inflict punishments or bring about redemption. Art historians Jessica Dubow and Ruth Rosengarten summarized the issue in their discussion of the complexity of Kentridge's presentation of South African identity and history: "...that a struggle of stark, but stabilizing, antagonisms ultimately resolved itself through the rationalization of political reconciliation foreclosed the clarity of any definitive catharsis. As the South African academic and writer Njabulo Ndebele has put it, what the liberation struggle was denied was 'the ultimate experience, the witnessing of the enemy's resounding defeat'. 'The Bastille', as he says, 'was not stormed.'"[25] Kentridge was able to give aesthetic expression to this lack of clarity. Soho's tears, transposed from his body to his clothing, transform the catharsis of weeping into the more ambiguous spectacle of being drenched in a scene that has been interpreted as representing both absolution and abjection. As with an antique stereoscope, Kentridge's manner of representation relies on viewing the same thing twice: The characters of Soho and Felix taken together provide a window into the complex and often conflictual emotional reality that follows crisis.

Walid Raad

Lebanese Conceptual artist Walid Raad (b. 1967) has focused his work on a history that has generally evaded understanding in hopes of answering one question: "How does one write the history of 'the Lebanese Civil War?'" Raad and the collaborative Atlas Group "locate, preserve, study and produce audio, visual, literary, and other artifacts that shed light on the contemporary history of Lebanon."[26] Their media include photographs, books, lectures, models, archives, and documents "constituted by various individuals, groups, discourses, events, situations, and more importantly by modes of experiences" produced by the civil war in Lebanon (1975–91).[27] How we are to evaluate these pieces of evidence is a nagging question posed by Raad's art. *Missing Lebanese Wars—Notebook Volume 72* (1996–2003) (**fig. 6.25**) typifies the conundrums created by the Atlas Group. The work consists of notebook pages on which historian Fadl Fakhouri recorded the gambling activities of himself and a group of Lebanese intellectuals. Each page features a photo-finish of a horse race with notes detailing the bets made, the individuals present and their personalities, and the result of the race. The historians, however, were not betting on the outcome of the horse race but on the amount of time between the end of the race and the moment the photographer was able to document the winner's victory. A complex calculation based on the speed of the horse and its distance from the finish line as indicated in the published photograph determined the winning historian. The images were always fractions of a second early or late so that the representation of the victory never coincided with the event itself. This discrepancy between the recording of history and the experience of it was of acute interest to the historians and to Raad.

A second twist to *Missing Lebanese Wars* and all of the Atlas Group's work involves the method by which the information was collected and the authorship of the final document. The Atlas Group's mission statement gives its founding date

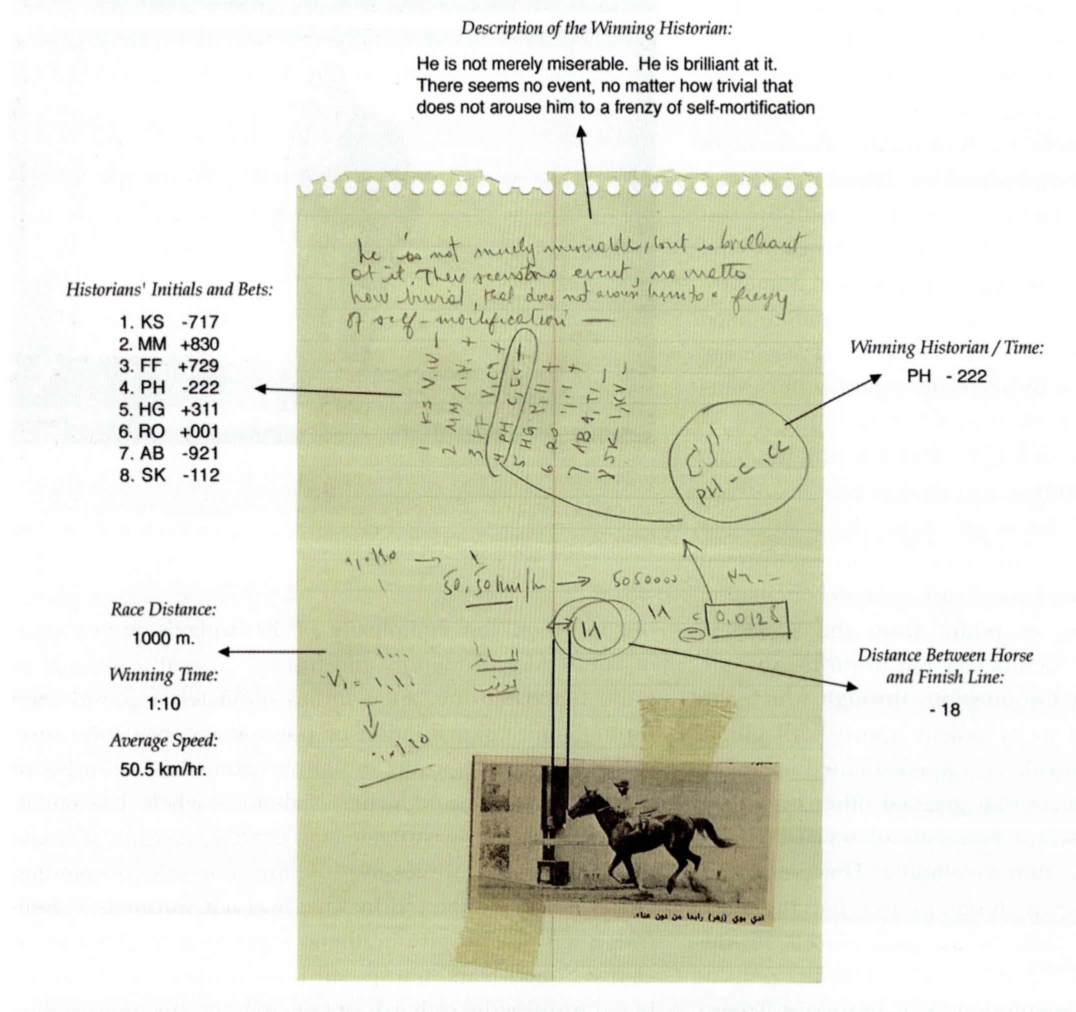

6.25 The Atlas Group in collaboration with Walid Raad, ***Missing Lebanese Wars—Notebook Volume 72***, 1996–2003. Detail. Framed digital color prints. 21 plates; each 13⅞ × 10¼" (35.2 × 26 cm). Private collection. Courtesy Anthony Reynolds Gallery, London.

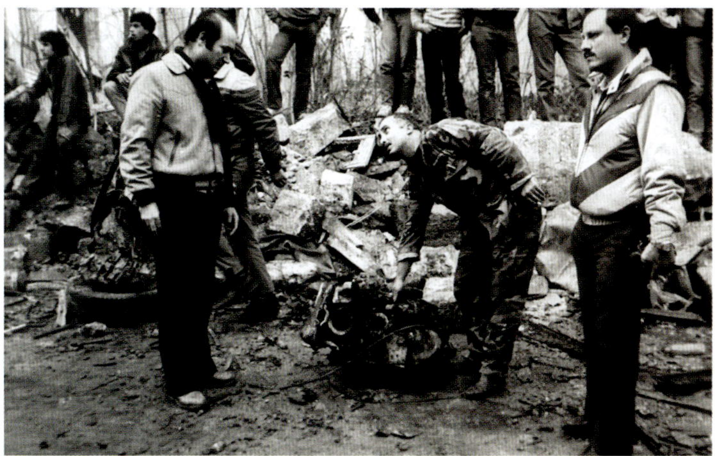

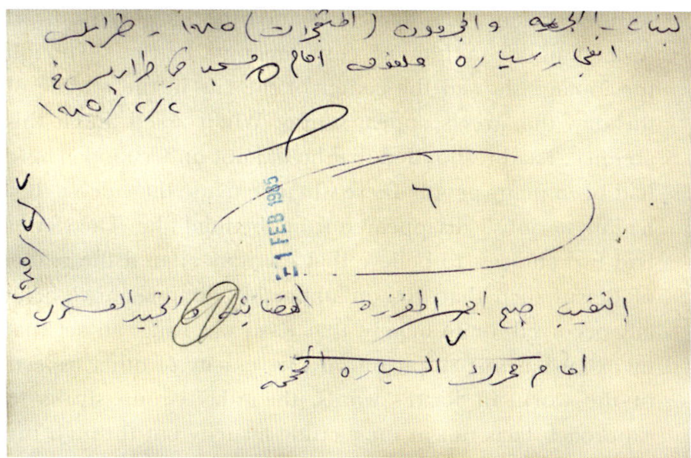

6.26 The Atlas Group in collaboration with Walid Raad, ***My Neck Is Thinner Than a Hair***, 2000–03. Detail showing front and back of one photograph. Digital prints. 100 plates; each 10 × 13⅞" (25.5 × 35.5 cm). Private collection. Courtesy Anthony Reynolds Gallery, London.

as 1999, whereas its website says 1989 and Raad has given a date as early as 1967. This is the first indication that history and facts in Raad's work do not follow ordinary logic. Collaborators on the project include architect Tony Chakar, journalist and poet Bilal Khbeiz, artist Maha Traboulsi, and co-founder Zainab Fakhouri. Writer Jalal Toufic, artist Waled Sadek, and historian Fadl Fakhouri are repeatedly referenced by Raad and the group. Fakhouri, who has served as source and subject in several Atlas Group works, is—like his widow, Zainab Fakhouri, and Maha Traboulsi—fictional. One piece of work might be credited to the Atlas Group, another to Raad in collaboration with the Atlas Group, a third to the Atlas Group/Walid Raad. The instability of authorship suggested by such changing attributions—made to both real people and fictional characters—reflects the illusory nature of the history of war and its effect on those who live through it.

In an essay addressing the peculiar conditions of communication in contemporary Beirut, Waled Sadek asserted that "the floating sign" had become the "condition and … prerequisite for any consequent critical activity."[28] History had rendered the relationship of the sign to its referent, between word and meaning, one of continual and irregular flux. Beirut's civil war was defined by diverse internal alliances that manipulated, and were manipulated by, a range of external forces. The treaties at the close of the war—the Ta'if Agreement in 1989, its amendment in 1990, and the general amnesty of 1991—ended the fighting but established only a fragile alliance among religious groups and militias which faced considerable pressure from Israel, the United States, Syria, and other Arab nations. Raad explained in an extended interview with Silvia Kolbowski (see Chapter 2) that during the Israeli incursion in 2006 the central government was unable to deliver basic services and the populace returned to civil-war allegiances and expectations. The ease with which postwar understandings were replaced by wartime relationships, even at a moment when one might have expected heightened nationalism, demonstrated how unstable even the most basic narratives of war and peace, alliance and conflict, had become. Sadek concluded that all communication had taken on the status of "rumor," which he defined as language in a state of "unchecked textual promiscuity," unleashed from customary or official relationships to meaning.[29] This condition has consequences for post-conflict regions around the globe. "Such demands invite art[ists] … to reconsider the conditions which govern and even promote an art practice based on the politics of protest."[30] Raad's exploration into writing a history of the Lebanese civil war is such a practice.

My Neck Is Thinner Than a Hair (2000–03) (**fig. 6.26**) takes car bombs as an entry point into Lebanese history. Car bombs transform the everyday into a threat to life. In the civil war, they altered the relationship of the Lebanese to their city and came to symbolize the conflict. After its repeated use in Lebanon and the concurrent violence in Northern Ireland, the car bomb came to define the character of urban warfare in the 1970s and 1980s. *My Neck* started with straightforward documentary research. Raad, with Chakar and Khbeiz, investigated a single car bomb detonated on January 21, 1986 in the Furn Ech Chuback district of East Beirut. After assembling considerable information, they expanded the project to include images and accounts of other car bombings. Unlike *Missing Lebanese Wars*, *My Neck* is based on period photographs of the conflict, several of which were taken by George Semerdjian, who was active in the region until his death by sniper fire in 1989. All the photographs reproduced in the work document engines thrown from exploded cars. Though there is often evidence of damage, the expected spectacle of wounded civilians, craters in the streets, broken glass, chaos, and death is absent here. Raad introduces *My Neck* with a text that claims it was a matter of pride among wartime photographers to be the first to find and photograph the ejected engine, the only part of the car to remain intact. These images are the result of journalists leaving the scene of destruction to investigate a site related to but removed from the actuality of the violence.

In Berlin in 2004, Raad presented the imagery from *My Neck* alongside a film of contemporary Beirut.[31] Though the footage showed the center of the city in the middle of the day, the streets appear empty. When asked about this absence, Raad responded that he did not understand: There had been many people there when he made the video—they had mysteriously disappeared from the final film. The viewer had two choices: to believe that the wars altered the reality of Beirut such that this unfathomable disappearance actually occurred, or to believe that Raad was lying, an act that by extension cast suspicion on the veracity of other aspects of the work. In Raad's words, the Atlas Group strives to "approach facts not in their crude facticity but through the complicated mediations by which they acquire their immediacy."[32] Facts, as Raad points out, come in all sorts of different categories, including aesthetic, emotional, political, material, and psychological, and in a post-crisis region like Beirut do not follow any simple logic.

Raad fashions his facts from what he calls "hysterical documents."[33] Hysteria is a psychological condition, discussed at length by Sigmund Freud, in which the individual generates fantasies regarding the world and reacts to them as if they were real. The world of the hysteric coincides with actuality but is not guided by its logic or limits. For the hysteric subject, as for Raad's audience, distinguishing between fact and fiction is difficult, if not impossible, and may even be destructive. In a remarkable exchange between Kolbowski and Raad recorded during his evacuation from Beirut in the course of the 2006 Israeli attacks, Kolbowski cites the following lines from historian and theorist of psychoanalysis Jacqueline Rose: "Paranoid impulses don't just project onto reality as delusion; they affect reality and become a component of it. At which point, to deny the real danger, even though you may have created it, would be as pathological as to imagine, falsely, that danger is there."[34] Rose's concerns here are with the destructive paranoia that produces wars, but her warning extends to those trying to reckon with the consequences of such violence. Facts exist independently of their relationship to reality. In the context of the psyche, they move in and out of delusions; in that of the Atlas Group, they occupy spaces of reality, fiction, history, memory, art, imagination, materiality, emotion, and desire.

In the same conversation, Raad quotes Lebanese theorist and video artist Jalal Toufic's thoughts on the character of post-crisis regions. Toufic discusses Beirut, Hiroshima, and Auschwitz in *Undying Love or Love Dies* (2002) and describes them as sites that "invoke an act of remembrance but [in which] ... concrete acts of memory become impossible."[35] To remember requires coherent connections between the past and the present, and those disappear during states of crisis. There are no formulas for mending the links required to mourn, but it is clear that citizens of post-crisis regions need to have access to the events that are to be overcome: If society is not providing it, then artists must. Toufic writes in *Undeserving Lebanon* (2007): "Against the prevalent post-traumatic amnesia encountered in postwar Lebanon, and which is exemplified by the unjust and scandalous general amnesty law ... writers and filmmakers should have devised affirmative scenarios and strategies either to remember or not to remember."[36] Toufic is not alone in seeing artists as having an important role to play in this process. Anselm Kiefer's and Kara Walker's very different efforts to step into the shoes of the aggressor, the Gerzes' invitations to community dialogue, and Doris Salcedo's exploration of silence all propose means of facilitating acts of mourning; Raad's attention to the actual, possible, and definitely fictional past illustrates another. André Lepecki, one of Raad's most insightful commentators, argues that the Atlas Group provides the means for "active remembering" by facilitating "imaginative actualization of an event's nameless multiplicities."[37] The plurality of Raad's solutions threatens the stability of any single response to his art or its subject matter. Hysterical documents such as *My Neck Is Thinner Than a Hair* constitute primary sources from which to begin a history written after crisis.

Jun Nguyen-Hatsushiba

The final image in this chapter returns us to the history of Vietnam, but this time as seen from a Vietnamese perspective. The work in question, *Memorial Project, Nha Trang, Vietnam: "Towards the Complex—For the Courageous, the Curious and the Cowards"* (2001) (**fig. 6.27**) by Jun Nguyen-Hatsushiba (b. 1968), is a thirteen-minute film showing bicycle taxis, called "cyclos," being ridden on the floor of the ocean in the waters off Nha Trang, Vietnam. The cyclos are maneuvered by local fisherman who dive down to the vehicles, pedal and push them along the sand, and then come back up to the surface to draw breath before returning below. The film follows the divers as they descend to the cyclos, which are clearly out of place immersed in the blue water, and exert considerable energy maneuvering them around coral and rocks. Most of the video is shot underwater, but there are moments when we see the ocean surface, broken by the men's heads as they come up for air.

In Vietnamese cities like Ho Chi Minh City (formerly Saigon), where Nguyen-Hatsushiba moved in 1996, cyclos were once a ubiquitous form of transportation, and they appear in a number of his works. Many of their drivers had been on very different career paths before the Vietnam War. Afterward they found themselves without resources and so took up this form of comparatively humble labor. By 2001, cyclos had been banned from much of the city due to traffic congestion, leaving their operators again at a crossroads. In response, Nguyen-Hatsushiba designed a small museum dedicated to bicycle taxis and has even designed cyclos. Transferring these vehicles from the street to the ocean floor dramatizes the difficulty of the work while emphasizing its beauty and pathos—qualities perfectly captured in *Memorial Project*. This new setting for the cyclos also connects them to the history of Vietnam and the sea, both of which have been

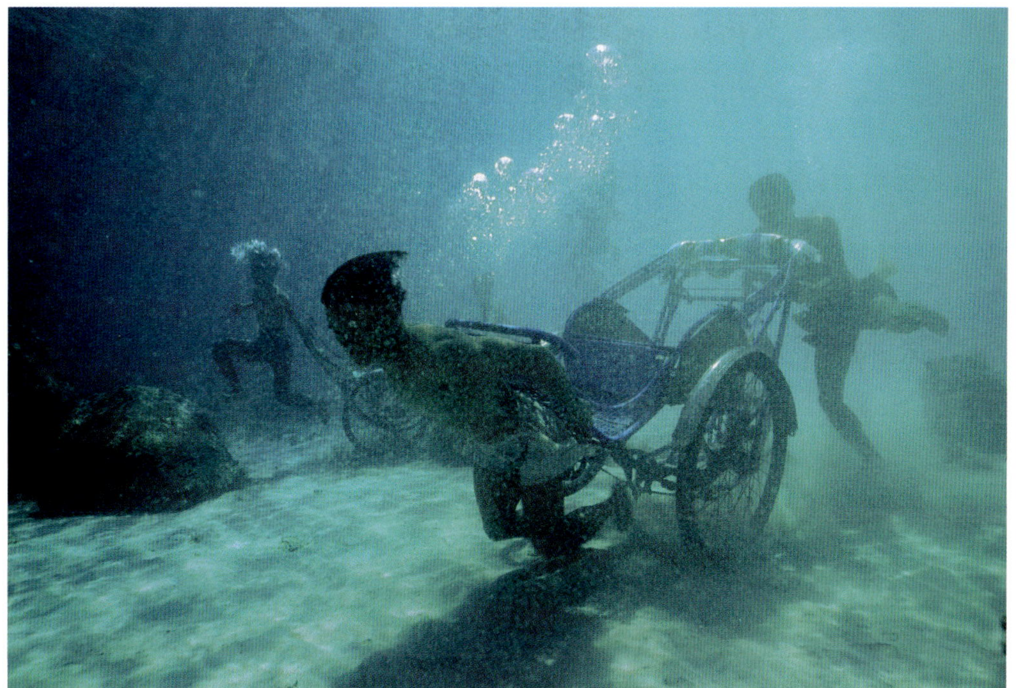

6.27 Jun Nguyen-Hatsushiba, *Memorial Project, Nha Trang, Vietnam: "Towards the Complex—For the Courageous, the Curious and the Cowards,"* 2001. Film, 13 minutes, looped. Single-channel projection on DVD with two unique sculptures: History-Xich Lo Cyclo sculpture 59⅛ × 86⅝ × 39⅜" (150 x 219.9 x 99.9 cm); unique Reflect-Xich Lo Cyclo sculpture 48 × 106 × 37" (121.9 × 269.24 × 93.98 cm). Unique dimensions variable. Edition of 10. Courtesy the artist and Lehmann Maupin Gallery, New York and Hong Kong.

shaped by the war and its aftermath. On the one hand, there are parts of the coast that still have mines left from the time of the U.S. blockade—Nguyen-Hatsushiba admitted to being concerned about the risk of encountering them while shooting the film. More important for *Memorial Project* is the connection between the cyclo drivers and the approximately 2 million Vietnamese boat people who, fearing persecution or poverty, fled the country between the end of the war in 1975 and the mid-1990s. These refugees set sail on treacherous waters in vessels ill-equipped for the trip. Many, even thousands, died in the effort.

Nguyen-Hatsushiba was born in his mother's native Japan. After the war, his family moved briefly to Vietnam, his father's homeland, but decided they could not stay: Nguyen-Hatsushiba left with his father for the U.S., while his mother and sister went to Japan. After graduating from art school, Nguyen-Hatsushiba moved back to Vietnam on his own. Looking at Vietnamese history from the position of a returning émigré, he saw those people who left and those who stayed as complementary, each living lives transformed by the political changes wrought by the war. Bringing the activity of the riders into the space of the boat people dramatized the struggle of postwar Vietnam, but also brought together these two groups of people, commemorating two different means of surviving the calamities of Vietnamese history. *Memorial Project* uses performance, sculpture, painting, video, and music to recount and reflect upon histories that have brought us to the present.

History, written as a teleological progression showing successive victories of civilization leading toward a deferred but implied final perfect state, had been one of the grand narratives that the French theorist Jean-François Lyotard witnessed being dismantled in the late 1970s. How to engage the past without reinforcing the power of those narratives, and how to reject the form those histories took but still address the past they strove to explain, were serious challenges to contemporary artists. James Rosenquist, OBAC, and Judy Chicago, all discussed in Chapter 1, provide examples of how contemporary artists might engage history even as that history was being deconstructed around them. Each sought to include more in the historical record than they felt was currently there. James Rosenquist, in his *F-111* (see fig. 1.1), linked the militarism of the mid-1960s with the horrors of World War II by juxtaposing images of the atomic mushroom cloud, a young girl, and the titular fighter bomber, flown for the first time in late 1964 while he was working on the painting. OBAC filled the *Wall of Respect* (see fig. 1.21) with heroes, both dead and living, who were being left out of the history lessons taught at school, and Judy Chicago invited women to the table of history (see fig. 1.28). As the turn of the millennium approached, artists who had been raised with history deconstructed turned back to its narratives to create networks of intersecting stories. Such histories are conveyed in the faces of surviving Vietnam War veterans reflecting off the names of the dead; they are written in the signatures of those committing themselves against fascism and in the defacing graffiti of those unready to join them; and they are spoken through the silence of cast-off clothing from Colombia or the waters off the shores of Vietnam. The art built of these stories tells of histories and speaks of History.

7

Culture, Body, Self

In the U.S., the late 1980s and early 1990s witnessed an intense backlash against the liberalism and particularly the feminism articulated in the previous decades. Having finally been obliged to acknowledge the specter of AIDS and the growing visibility of marginal communities, conservative forces initiated what have become known as the "Culture Wars" against contemporary art as a means to express frustration with society. Antagonists met in dramatic fashion on the occasion of a 1988 retrospective of U.S. photographer Robert Mapplethorpe (1946–89), "The Perfect Moment," curated by Janet Kardon, the director of the Institute of Contemporary Art, Philadelphia. The exhibition presented the full scope of Mapplethorpe's work, including still lifes, formal and informal portraiture, erotica, and even some collages and abstractions. It toured between 1988 and 1990, and was thus on view when the artist died of an AIDS-related condition in 1989, so becoming a magnet for Culture Wars combatants. "The Perfect Moment" drew particular fire for including a group of photographs depicting—in exceptionally controlled compositions, exquisitely printed with remarkable tonal range—subjects in sexually provocative and, in several cases, sadomasochistic poses. Despite the potentially upsetting imagery in some of his photographs, Mapplethorpe's sensitivity to the artist-photographer's traditional tasks of demonstrating aesthetic invention and revealing his subject's personality makes it clear that his intention is not simply to shock. Images such as *Larry and Bobby Kissing* (1979) (**fig. 7.1**) represent beauty, desire, and sexuality outside mainstream heterosexual society, and Mapplethorpe's graceful command of classical compositional techniques and his seductive tonal palette invite viewers to lavish attention on bodies sometimes—though hardly as often as critics claimed—engaged in taboo sexual behavior. That the exhibition also included Mapplethorpe's portraits of children in casual, informal poses and not always fully dressed further charged the controversy. Three weeks before its scheduled opening at Corcoran Gallery of Art in Washington, D.C., museum officials succumbed to pressure and backed out of participation in the tour. When the show then reached Cincinnati the city brought its host institution, the Contemporary Arts Center, to court on charges of violating state obscenity laws. The museum was found not guilty, but not before the exhibition had been transformed into the largest censorship scandal of the decade, thereby confirming

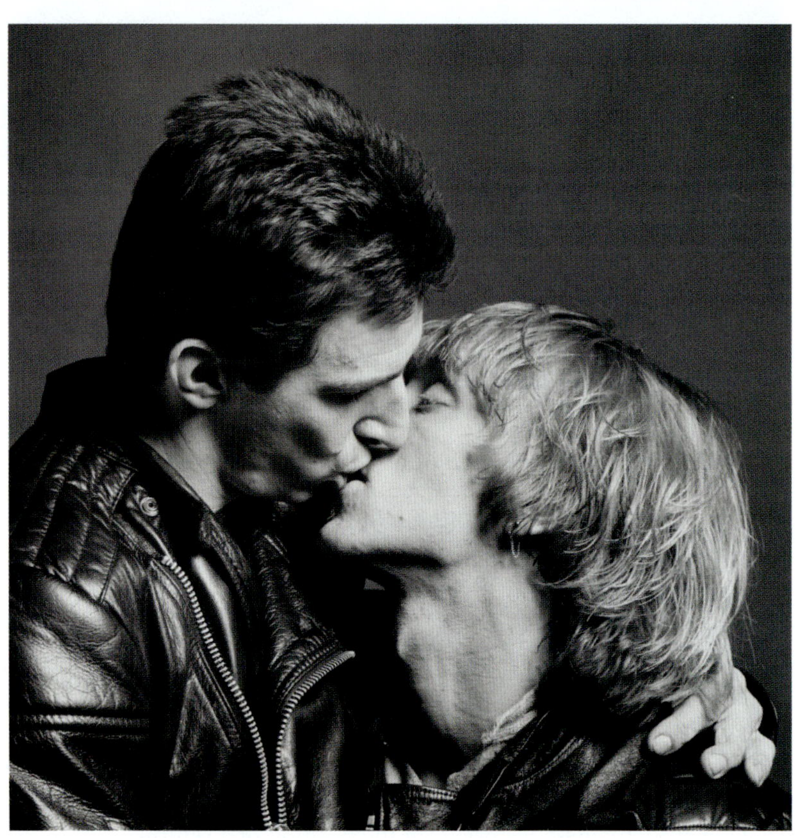

7.1 Robert Mapplethorpe, ***Larry and Bobby Kissing***, 1979. 13⅝ × 13⅝" (34.5 × 34.5 cm). © The Robert Mapplethorpe Foundation. Courtesy Art + Commerce.

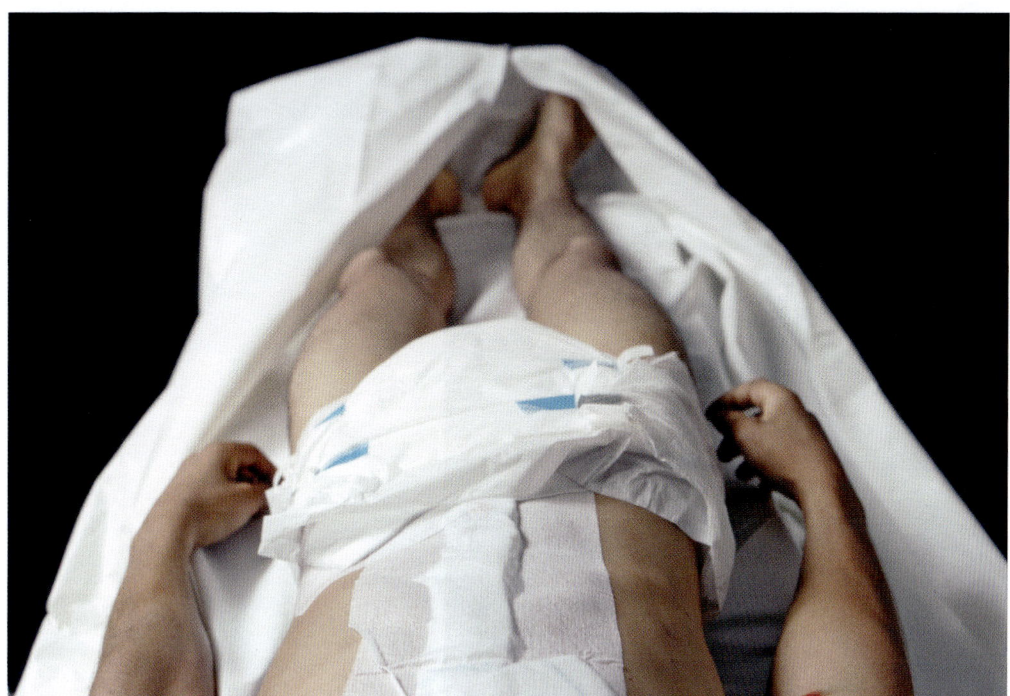

7.2 Andres Serrano, ***Gun Murder (The Morgue)***, 1992. Cibachrome and plexiglass, 50 × 60" (127 × 152.4 cm). Courtesy Yvon Lambert, Paris.

the vibrancy—but also the tenuous position—of contemporary art in U.S. public life.

Another photographer to draw fire during the early 1990s was Andres Serrano (b. 1950). Though his photographs lack the political engagement that informs Mapplethorpe's work, his manipulations of bodies and bodily fluids are seductive in their beauty and almost intuitively provocative in their subject matter. Serrano's work of the late 1980s and early 1990s included photographs of blood, milk, ejaculate, and urine. His most controversial works combined these fluids with religious objects including a crucifix—the much-attacked *Piss Christ* (1987)—and a statue of the Virgin Mary, but his imagery of real bodies was no less controversial. Among Serrano's subjects were Ku Klux Klan members and, in a 1992 series called *The Morgue*, dead bodies (**fig. 7.2**). To critics, such work were emblematic of how far artists had drifted from mainstream culture. Debates about contemporary art in newspapers, museums, academia, talk shows, and even in the U.S. Congress and Canadian parliament were punctuated by demands for reduced public funding for such artists, accusations of censorship, and political grandstanding. In the early 1990s, Mapplethorpe and Serrano were used by conservative politicians in the U.S. to pressure the National Endowment for the Arts to severely cut financial support and limit what artists could do with grant money. In a 2011 epilogue to the Culture Wars controversies, French Catholic protestors and ultra-right-wing Front National politicians, objecting to what they felt was the blasphemy of Serrano's *Piss Christ*, called for its removal from an exhibition at the renowned Yvon Lambert gallery in Avignon, France. When the gallery refused to oblige, several individuals attacked the work with a hammer and a sharp object that witnesses reported was an icepick.

This contentious atmosphere of the 1990s politicized all art about the body. Some artists, such as Serrano, used the controversy to play the role of provocateur. Others, including photographer Sally Mann (b. 1951), whose exquisitely rendered prints from an 8 × 10 inch-view camera of her children came under fire for what critics claimed was their undue attention to their subjects' sexuality and sensuality, felt that politicians and even art critics were distorting their work almost beyond recognition. Though the debates over censorship and NEA funding tended to revolve around issues of free speech, individual rights, and public responsibilities, the inclusion of Mann's work in the controversy reveals that its deeper roots lay in a struggle to define the character of U.S. society. At issue in a photograph such as *New Mothers* (1989) (**fig. 7.3**), presented family album-style in the artist's book titled *Immediate Family* (1992) and featured in an exhibition of the same year, was whether viewers recognized themselves and their own family in the image. Unusual in her ability to capture the liminal moments in which childhood and adulthood merge, and able to show her children as fully active agents in their lives, Mann struck a nerve among viewers trying to keep up nostalgic fictions of American family life and conservative myths about childhood. The photographs in *Immediate Family* originated with Mann's children. It was her daughters who chose the props and the poses in *New Mothers*—Mann merely asked them to hold still for the camera. As the photographer herself has said, these are scenes that loving parents witness as their growing children imagine themselves in adult society: This is play as it occurs, not as politicians might like to imagine it. Mann has continued to interrogate constructions of U.S. identity, turning from the family to the landscape, photographing often unremarkable features—a tree scarred by a knife cut, overhanging

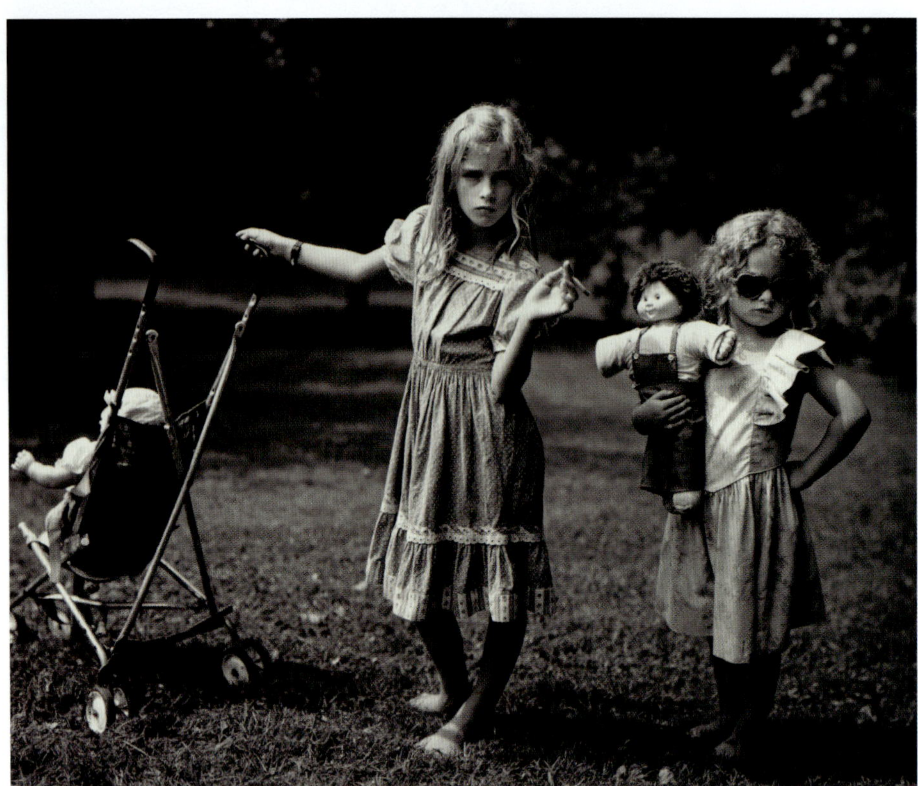

7.3 Sally Mann, ***New Mothers*** from the ***Immediate Family*** series, 1989. Gelatin silver print. © Sally Mann. Courtesy Gagosian Gallery.

vines, tangled roots—to convey a sense of the character or history of a place (**fig. 7.4**). Nationalism is no more the limit of these photographs than documentation was the justification for *Immediate Family*; both join in a national conversation about the role of art in crafting a sense of individual and collective identity.

In the face of steady attacks by conservative critics expressing the anxiety of mainstream culture toward difference, artists began to draw attention to their outsider identity as a source of inspiration and power. Curators, in turn, began exploring what constituted the individual. New York hosted exhibitions of art that variously examined contemporary African-American, Latino, Asian-American, female, and Jewish culture. The Whitney Museum of American Art turned to the identity politics of selfhood as its biennial theme in 1993 and the next year presented "Black Male," a survey of work by artists of all backgrounds that examined the representation of black men in a white-dominated society. In their focus on ethnicity and identity, the New York exhibitions were representative of global trends. In 1989, the Hayward Gallery in London opened "The Other Story: Afro-Asian Artists in Post-War Britain," curated by artist Rasheed Araeen, asserting the art-historical importance of various non-white art communities in the U.K. The 1990s witnessed a growing number of international exhibitions, including the Asia-Pacific Triennial (1993) and biennials in Jerusalem, Israel (1994), Johannesburg, South Africa (1995), Kwangju, Korea (1995), and Shanghai, China (1996), all of which joined the pioneering Havana Biennial (1984) to provide audiences with the opportunity to consider the relationship between self and society in a variety of international contexts. The Venice Biennale of 1993 featured identity art from artists and cultures across the globe.

This chapter presents a wide variety of work that asks who the "I" is at the intersection of social forces and layered

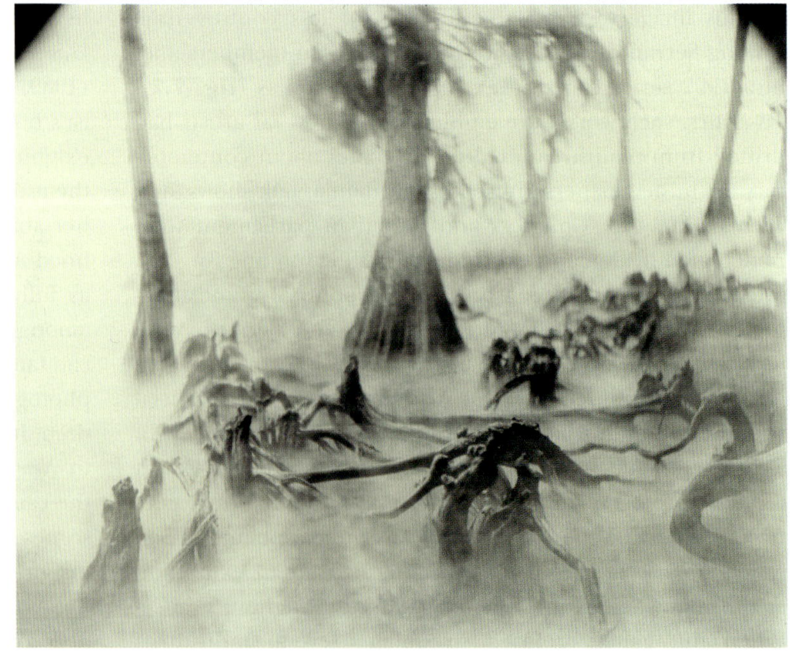

7.4 Sally Mann, ***Untitled (#30)*** from the ***Deep South*** series, 1998. Gelatin silver print, © Sally Mann. Courtesy Gagosian Gallery.

histories at the end of the twentieth century, and turns to the body to find an answer. At the end of the chapter, several examples of art that resist ready identification of body with self will be discussed. For these artists, body and self are significant due to their alienation from one another.

Body as Form and Content

Body art took form as an independent genre in the 1960s and 1970s as artists interested in creating work between the disciplines of theater, dance, and sculpture turned to their own bodies as a medium. These experiments, referred to generally as performance art, adopted narrative, ritual, or formal structures as the human body was treated as both object and subject. Artists discussed in earlier chapters represent moments in this history of body-oriented performance from different traditions in the U.S. and Europe. Movements outside the West, including Neo-Concrete art in Brazil and Gutai in Japan (see Chapter 1), reveal the international scope of the turn to the body as a means to generate form and content in contemporary art. Much of the work of the 1970s was informed by a feminist concern for how the body was contained and controlled by society. In some cases, including *Womanhouse* (see fig. 1.27) and Suzanne Lacy's *Three Weeks in May*, the body was represented, serving as significant content. In others, including Yoko Ono's *Fly* (see fig. 1.25), Martha Rosler's *Semiotics of the Kitchen* (see fig. 1.30), and Hannah Wilke's *S.O.S.* (see fig. 1.32), the body itself was the medium. *Interior Scroll* (1975) by Carolee Schneeman (b. 1939) was a touchstone performance piece in this respect: The artist stood naked before the audience, first painting, then removing a text that had been rolled and inserted into her vagina, and finally reading that text aloud. The positions of creative actor, experiencing subject, and object on display are all conflated in the body of the artist. All of these feminist works used the body to insist on the fact that in contemporary society women occupied such varied positions. By the 1980s, the body had been demonstrated to be as flexible and potent an artistic medium as any other, and uniquely suited to certain kinds of artistic expression.

In the 1980s, Ana Mendieta, Adrian Piper, and Tehching Hsieh created a new chapter in the history of body art. Though from very different backgrounds, all three artists drew on traditions of Minimalism, Process, and performance art as they established their reputations in the New York art world. The individual character or life experience of the performing body had made little difference in earlier body art. It was Joseph Beuys the healer and critic who was on stage, not Beuys the individual. Even in the feminist work of the 1970s the body tended to be used to address experiences shared by many people or political positions. Counting on audiences' awareness of the formal, political, and spiritual content addressed in earlier body art, Mendieta, Piper, Hsieh, and artists that followed directed their bodies and those of their viewers to objects and experiences that raised questions that intertwined personal and social identities.

Ana Mendieta

For her first solo show, held in November 1979 at the AIR Gallery in New York, Cuban-born sculptor Ana Mendieta (1948–85) presented photographs of small earthworks that were roughly the size and shape of her own body. The images, called *Silueta* (*Silhouettes*) (**fig. 7.5**), document performances done in Mexico, the U.S., and Cuba between 1973 and 1981 in which Mendieta lay down on the ground and drew the earth up around her body. She then rose and embellished the cavity created in this way. In one action, for instance, she poured gunpowder into the form and ignited it. In her

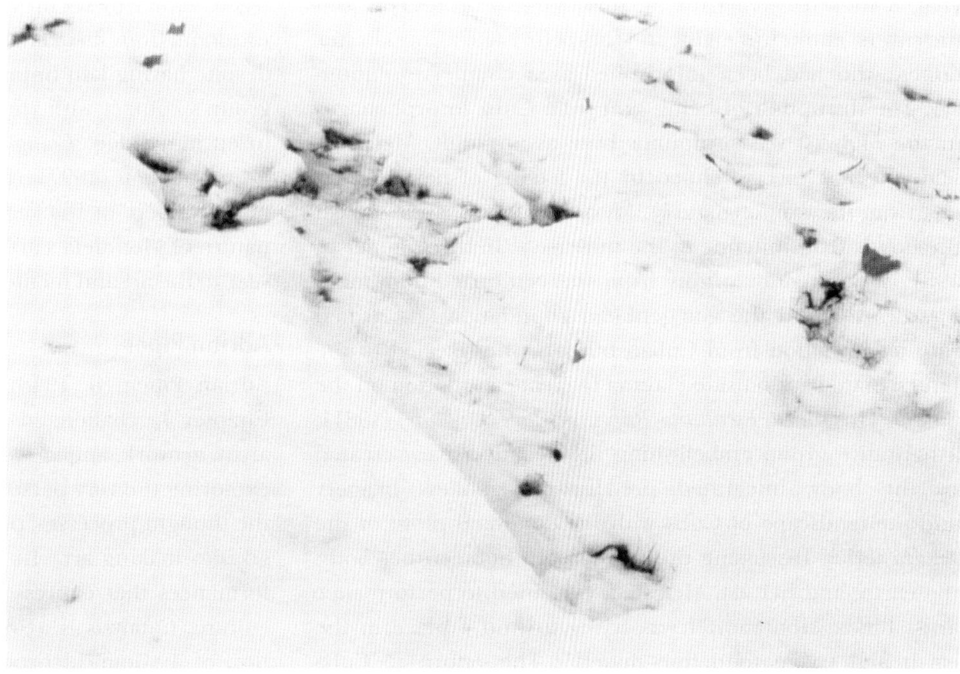

7.5 Ana Mendieta, *Untitled* from the *Silueta (Silhouette)* series, 1977. Color photograph, 10 × 8" (25.4 × 20.3 cm). © The Estate of Ana Mendieta Collection. Courtesy Galerie Lelong, New York.

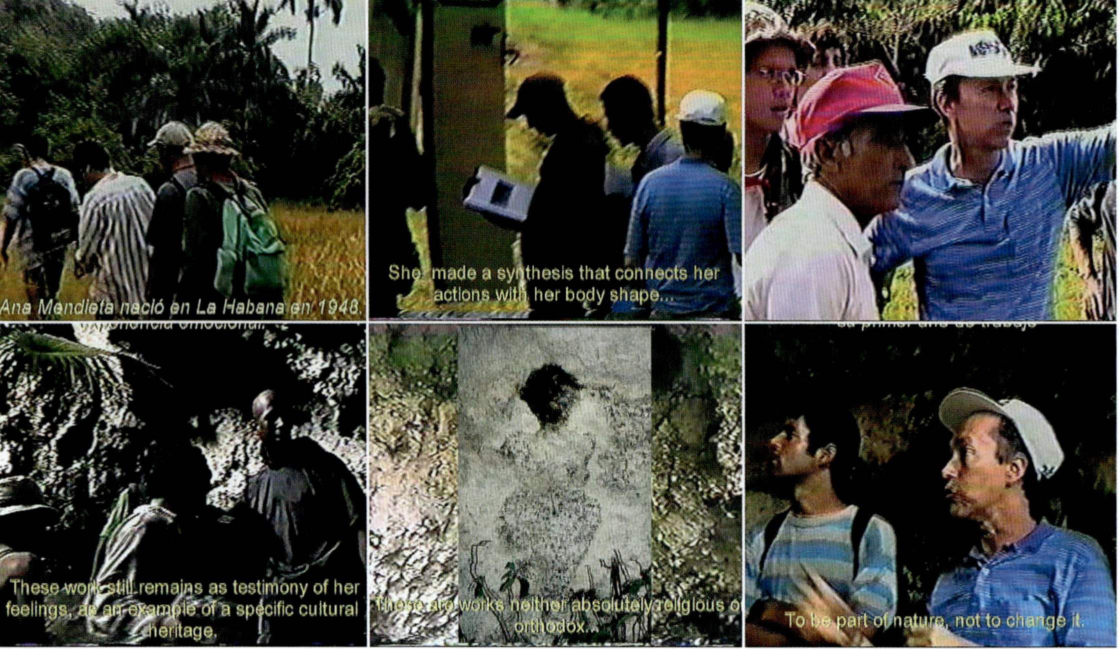

7.6 DUPP, *Going After a Trace: To Meet Ana Mendieta's Cave Sculpture*, 1997. Film. Courtesy Galería DUPP.

studio, she created related performances in which her body remained physically at the heart of the work, surrounded, covered, embraced, and constrained by various materials. She made short films of several of these performances. The work displays a strong sense of ritual, rooted in Mendieta's deep affiliation to the Afro-Cuban religion of Santería. In Miami, one of her sculptures was even integrated into a local Santería ritual.

According to Mendieta, her art was intimately related to the circumstances of her emigration from Cuba at age thirteen. She and her sister had been part of "Operation Peter Pan" (1960–62), a U.S.-sponsored evacuation of nearly 14,000 children between the ages of five and eighteen from Cuba. Though her family was eventually reunited in the U.S., it took five years for her mother and brother to join the sisters, and it was eighteen years before she again saw her father, who had been imprisoned as a counterrevolutionary. The disruption of being sent from Cuba to orphanages in the Midwest was profound. Even as an adult, Mendieta said, she was "overwhelmed by the feeling of having been cast from the womb (nature). My art is the way I re-establish the bonds that unite me to the universe."[1] In the summer of 1981, supported by grants from the National Endowment for the Arts and the Guggenheim Foundation and armed with an invitation from Cuban officials, she traveled to the Jaruco State Park outside Havana to create a variation on the *Silueta*. This piece, *Esculturas Rupestres (Cave Sculpture)* (1981), a figurative group embellishing the negative space created by the body, integrated pre-Hispanic goddess imagery and the landscape of Cuba with the dominant motif of the *Silueta* series. Discussing the relationship between her body, the earth, and her art, Mendieta explained to performance artist Linda Montano, "I was trying to find a place in the earth and trying to define myself."[2] The return to Cuba and the *Esculturas Rupestres* provided the spiritual and personal homecoming she had desired. The earth in Cuba, she explained, spoke to her; outside the island of her birth, the land was silent.

During the early 1980s, Mendieta acted as a conduit between U.S. and Cuban artists. In January 1981, she toured Cuba with a group of artists and critics including Suzanne Lacy, Martha Rosler, and Lucy Lippard. They saw "Volumen I" and met many of the artists featured, including José Bedia, Elso, and Flavio Garciandia (see Chapter 9).[3] In the aftermath of her early death in 1985, Mendieta's art has continued to be important for artists in search of connections between self, spirit, nature, and nation, especially those with connections to Cuba. In 1997, René Francisco and DUPP (see Chapter 9) set off into the Jaruco State Park to find the *Esculturas Rupestres*. The carved silhouettes were still visible despite having lain unprotected for nearly two decades. The group's contact with the relics of Mendieta's trip were captured in a video, *Going After a Trace: To Meet Ana Mendieta's Cave Sculpture* (1997) (**fig. 7.6**), which contrasts the communal aspect of the search with the private and individual nature of Mendieta's art. DUPP dedicated all of its work that year to the art and memory of Mendieta.

Adrian Piper

Adrian Piper (b. 1948), whose writing on "meta-art" (see Chapter 1) challenged the presumed relationship between artist, artwork, and viewer in the 1970s, created a body of art exploring the very personal ramifications of "making explicit the thought processes, procedures, and presuppositions" that go into making art.[4] In 1970, she created the *Catalyses*, performances that express the effect of difference in Western culture. Catalysis is a scientific term meaning the acceleration of a chemical process brought about by an agent, or catalyst. For *Catalysis IV* (**fig. 7.7**), Piper soaked her clothes in vinegar, eggs, milk, and cod-liver oil for a week and then rode the subway during rush hour; for another, she traveled in the Empire State Building elevator dressed in a business suit but with a red bath towel pushed deep into her mouth. Having thus created a very intrusive metaphor for difference and become a catalyst for the expected reactions of disgust, Piper tried to make eye contact, asked passers-by small questions, and muttered loudly. Her ability to break through the barrier created by her difference was insufficient to the task, her efforts far too ambiguous to be greeted with positive responses. Though in effect conveying the social effect of difference by metaphorically representing the isolation of being black and female in the United States, the *Catalyses* were, as she explained, about recognizing the boundaries of the self, becoming aware of the effect of one's difference on others. The *Catalyses*, like much of her subsequent work, were about the challenge of acting from within a position of difference, as well as reflecting the character of society more generally.

Afterward, Piper shifted away from metaphors to emphasize issues of race and gender more explicitly. She has recounted how, as a light-skinned African-American, she often suffered racism while those around her—sometimes those perpetuating it—failed to perceiving her as its object. Thus, unlike those for whom their racial status is immediately visible, the impact of difference on Piper's life was felt in irregular, drawn-out, and surprising, even if predictable, ways. In response, she created characters and portraits of herself that exaggerated the visibility of her racial difference. Like a catalyst, the image accelerated the process by which her difference was recognized and reacted against. Piper's most seamless and provocative integration of art, experience, and analysis is her "calling cards," short texts on small cards that she presented to people as appropriate circumstances arose. The cards read:

> Dear Friend,
>
> I am black.
>
> I am sure you did not realize this when you made/laughed at/agreed with that racist remark. In the past, I have attempted to alert white people to my racial identity in advance. Unfortunately, this invariably causes them to react to me as pushy, manipulative, or socially inappropriate. Therefore, my policy is to assume that white people do not make these remarks, even when they believe there are no black people present, and to distribute this card when they do.
>
> I regret any discomfort my presence is causing you, just as I am sure you regret the discomfort your racism is causing me.

As she had advocated in her appeal for "meta-art," this work directed attention to the context, in this case racism, that conditioned her career as an artist and our response to it as an audience. Through the cards, Piper transformed her experience and her analysis of it into a catalyst for a new experience, this time to be shared first, and with difficulty, with those who occasioned the need to present the card, and then later with the audience who learned of the work. The cards are displayed in museums and are given away freely so that viewers can take and use them when necessary

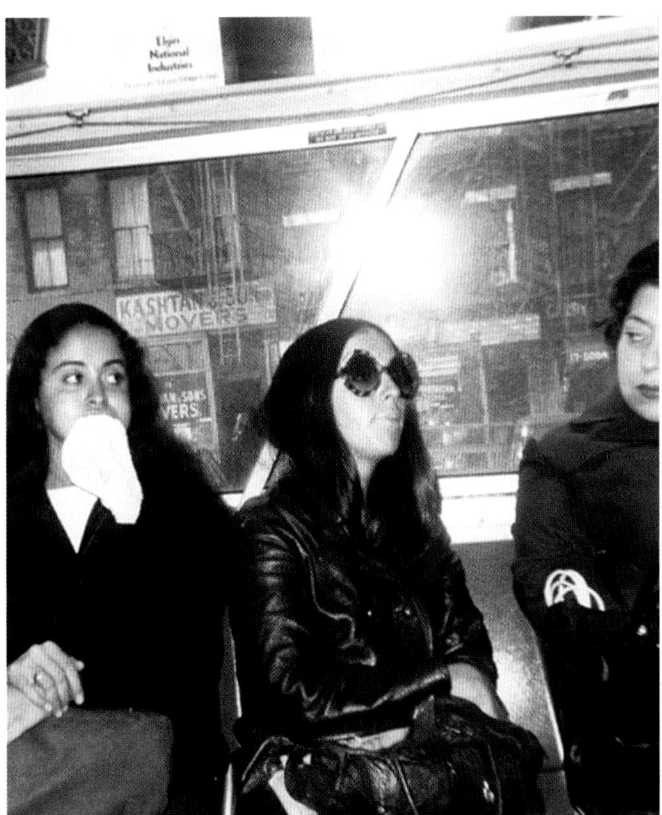

7.7 Adrian Piper, *Catalysis IV*, 1970. Performance documentation notebook: 2 silver gelatin prints and typescript, 5 × 5" and 9½ × 11½", (12.7 × 12.7 cm and 24.1 × 29.2 cm). Private collection, U.S.

Tehching Hsieh

In the fall of 1979, as Mendieta was preparing her exhibition at AIR, Tehching Hsieh had just completed the first of five year-long performances. The previous September he had circulated the following statement around New York (**fig. 7.8**):

> I, SAM HSIEH, plan to do a one-year performance piece, to begin on September 30, 1978. I shall seal myself in my studio, in solitary confinement inside a cell-room measuring 11'6" × 9' × 8'. I shall NOT converse, read, write, listen to the radio or watch television, until I unseal myself on September 29, 1979. I shall have food every day. My friend, Cheng Wei Kuong, will facilitate this piece by taking charge of my food, clothing, and refuse.

Hsieh (b. 1950) had been living in the U.S. illegally since 1974, when he had left his native Taiwan to come and live in what he felt was the center of the art world. His status as an illegal alien and his limited English, however, left him

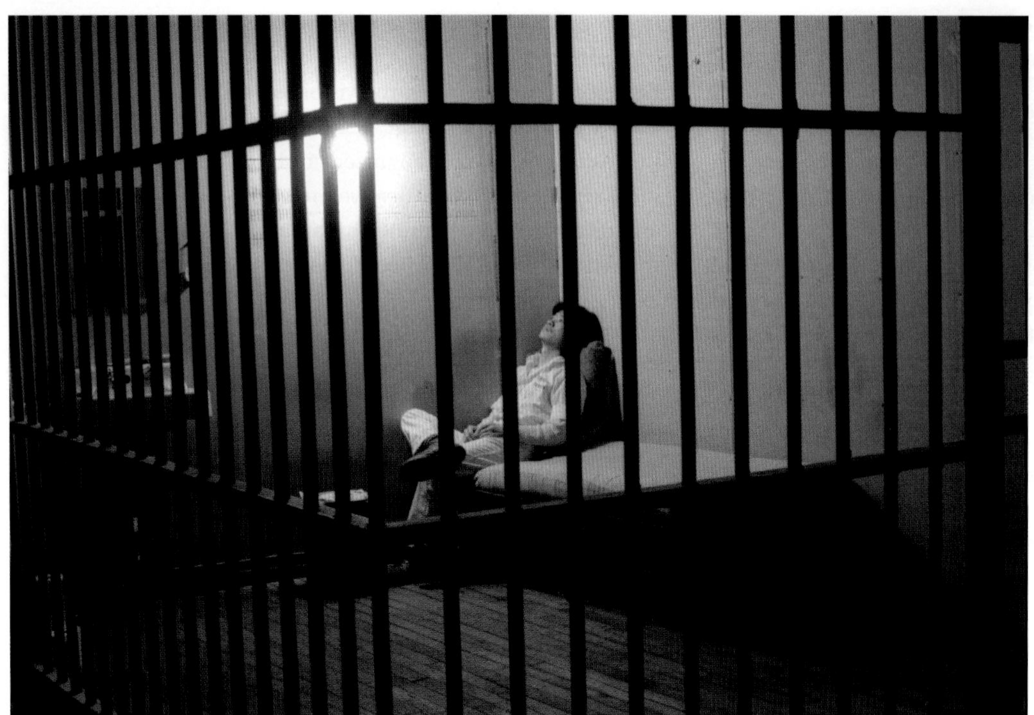

7.8 Tehching Hsieh, ***One Year Performance Cage Piece***, September 30, 1978–September 29, 1979. Tehching Hsieh, One Year Performance 1978–1979 Life Image © 1979 Tehching Hsieh. Courtesy the artist and Sean Kelly Gallery, New York.

profoundly alienated, depressed, and scared. "For me, life was a prison: not in a political sense, but in the isolation of being. Passing time and presenting the thinking process is the concept of this piece," he recollected.[5] The 1978–79 performance, documented and reported on, was a means of giving form to this feeling.

After *One Year Performance (Cage Piece)*, with its focus on experience measured only in the rhythms of the body and the pattern of meals consumed, Hsieh forced himself to be aware of living within the regimen of a smaller unit of time, the hour. For one year, starting on April 11, 1980, Hsieh punched a time clock in his studio every hour. Each time he clocked in, he filmed himself using a single frame of 16mm film. At the end of the year he had a short movie documenting his changing appearance over the course of the 8,627 times he had punched the clock. He also scrupulously documented the cause of each of the 133 missed punches—there are 8,760 hours in a year—most being the result of oversleeping.

After these two works about confinement and regimentation, Hsieh created a work that had boundaries as big as the city. Starting on September 26, 1981, he spent an entire year, with one brief exception, outdoors in New York City. He avoided all interior spaces, including buses, trains, and even restrooms. He documented the year in photographs and maps of his wanderings. These first performances were rigorously framed by society but were studiously anti-social. Forces external to artist, the authorities from which Hsieh was hiding, the friend who was keeping him alive, the ordered schedules of society, and the harsh confines of the city itself, provided the structure of the work, at the center of which was the individual, stoic and surviving.

In *One Year Performance (Rope Piece)* (**fig. 7.9**), by contrast, Hsieh put a relationship at the center of the performance.

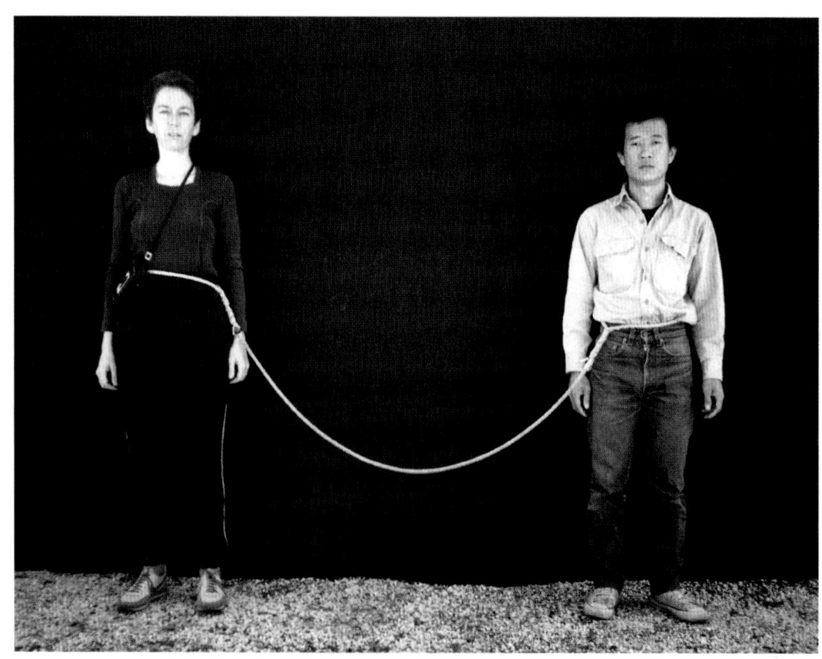

7.9 Tehching Hsieh and Linda Montano, ***One Year Performance (Rope Piece)***, July 4, 1983–July 4, 1984. Tehching Hsieh, Linda Montano, Art/Life One Year Performance 1983–1984 Life Image © 1984 Tehching Hsieh, Linda Montano. Courtesy the artists and Sean Kelly Gallery, New York.

The project was announced with the following statement signed by Hsieh and fellow performance artist Linda Montano: "We will stay together for one year and never be alone. We will be in the same room at the same time, when we are inside. We will be tied together at the waist with an eight-foot rope. We will never touch each other during the year."[6] Montano had done a three-day piece in 1973 in which she was handcuffed to artist and curator Tom Marioni. In *Rope Piece*, Montano said she honed the "survival skills" and "emotional conditioning" that contemporary life sought to destroy. For Hsieh, the project was less tactical. On the one hand, like *Cage Piece*, it was a metaphor: "I got the idea for this piece because there are problems about communication with people. I feel this is always my struggle. I wanted to do one piece about human beings and their struggle in life with each other. I find being tied together is a very clear idea, because I feel that to survive we're all tied up … So we become each other's cage … so this piece to me is a symbol of life and human struggle." In his explanation, the metaphor of the rope serves to express the condition of humanity while also reflecting his personal experience. There was also a very literal aspect for Hsieh. All of his work was "a mirror showing … my weaknesses, my limitations, my potentials." Hsieh's shocking feats of endurance and tightly focused performances established restricted situations that exposed aspects of his personality that were otherwise hidden.

Changing Strategies: Body as Social Medium

In the 1970s, ORLAN in France and Marina Abramović in Yugoslavia created art that, like that of their peers across Europe and the U.S., explored the body as a medium and used it to contemplate social conventions. Like the artists discussed thus far, even as the performative element of the work focused attention on the artist's body, the content of the work remained general. As with Piper or Hsieh's work, viewers discovered much about the world in which the artists lived but only by inference did they learn about the individual personality of the artist. At the end of the 1980s, however, both ORLAN and Abramović introduced new ideas about the relationship between body and self that raised the importance of individual experience and even autobiographical detail within the work, thus setting the stage for the next generation of body artists who embraced personal narrative as well as physical experience.

ORLAN

Early in her career, ORLAN (b. 1947) created what she called "body sculptures," in which she photographed herself mimicking poses from canonical works of Western art such as the *Grand Odalisque* by French Neo-Classical painter Jean-Auguste-Dominique Ingres (1780–1867). In another group of works called *MesuRages* (1972–83), she measured streets named after famous French men or sites such as the Vatican using her body as the unit of measurement. ORLAN's surveying involved lying on the ground and then crawling forward to repeat the gesture until she had supplicated herself across the whole length of the street or monument in question. In both series, the artist's body substituted for more traditional tools—marble or oil paint in the first, surveying equipment in the second—to visualize the argument that women's role in the history of art and architecture has been that of either represented object or invisible subject.

In 1971, she rechristened herself Saint-ORLAN, a new saint whose identity was split according to the misogynistic reduction of women into the two antithetical identities of virgin and whore. Saint-ORLAN was both and neither. For *The Artist's Kiss* (1977), ORLAN stood behind a cutout of a nude female torso and sold kisses to collectors at the French art fair FIAC. Offering a taste of her body for purchase was a commentary on the fusion of sex and money in the culture at large, and more specifically on the conflation of female artists with their bodies in the art market. Instead of buying kisses, participants in the performance could opt to donate their money to an icon of Saint-ORLAN's other persona, the virginal female, and then light a candle at her feet. They invariably favored the sensual option over the spiritual one.

After over a decade spent embellishing the personalities of Saint-ORLAN, the artist began work on one of the most controversial pieces of body art ever produced, the surgical remodeling of her own body. *The Reincarnation of Saint-ORLAN* (1990–93) involved a series of nine operations that reshaped ORLAN's face and body according to ideal types from the history of Western art: Botticelli's Venus, Leonardo's Mona Lisa, Boucher's Europa, a School of Fontainebleau Diana, and Gérôme's Psyche. Each surgical intervention was transformed into a performance and included the artist delivering monologues before and during the operation; the artist and the surgeons were often outfitted by couture designers such as Paco Rabanne and Issey Miyake. Objects from the procedures including tools, costumes, and even bits of removed flesh were saved and sold. The events were presented to gallery audiences in gruesome detail through videos and photographs that showed the artist's cut and bruised body during the surgery and her subsequent recovery. Indeed, the seventh operation was broadcast live to fifteen galleries, museums, and art centers around the world, including the Centre Pompidou in Paris, the McLuhan Center in Toronto, and the Sandra Gering Gallery in New York. Audiences could ask questions of the artist by fax, video or webcam, and she responded as best she could.

Critics have made use of the extreme nature of ORLAN's actions to discuss the violent way culture is often imprinted on the female body and to debate the role of pain, language, and theory in the construction of beauty and gender. The brutal reality of the surgery casts a pall over the glib manner in which Western society talks about getting nips and tucks to preserve one's youth. The artist, however, did not present the work as a critique of the superficiality of Western society. Rather, ORLAN argued that we have failed to explore the possibilities of plastic surgery with sufficient creativity or ambition. In an introductory text read before the seventh procedure, *Omnipresence* (1993) (**fig. 7.10**), she explained: "I never have the skin of what I am ... I thought that in our time we have begun to have the means of closing this gap [between appearance and identity]; in particular with the help of surgery ... that it was thus becoming possible to match up the internal image with the external one."[7] ORLAN's project was a demonstration of individual agency that reconciled the inner and outer facets of the human being, drawing on the technology of modern medicine and the image bank of fine art to resolve the disparity between self and body, between how we feel ourselves to be and how we and others interpret our external appearance.

The duality of ORLAN's work, its allusions to the submission of individuality to impossible ideals of beauty on the one hand and to women's ability to take hold of shape-changing technologies on the other, is evident in how she discusses the art that has guided her self-re-creation. The models she chose are ideal types that have exerted pressure on women for centuries, but they are also characters with personality traits and powers that ORLAN wanted to claim for herself. The goddesses Venus and Diana are incorporated into her face and figure to impart power; Leonardo's *Mona Lisa* is adopted for its associations, according to ORLAN, with both the mysterious female sitter and her brilliant male portraitist. By the end of the century, ORLAN was enlisting the power of digital photography to transform her representation (rather than her actual body) into a mélange of non-Western and Western identities. *African Self-Hybridization: Half-White Half-Black, Mbangu mask with face of European-St. Etienne woman in rollers* (2002) (**fig. 7.11**) captures the face of the artist midway between African tribal and French middle-class cultures. ORLAN's *Self-Hybrids* introduce a new element to her discussion of body and identity. No longer confined to the image bank of Western fine art, ORLAN submits her European body to transformations influenced by the wider spectrum of world culture, suggesting that the self cannot be expressed exclusively in the terms of the particular culture, race, or tradition into which it was born.

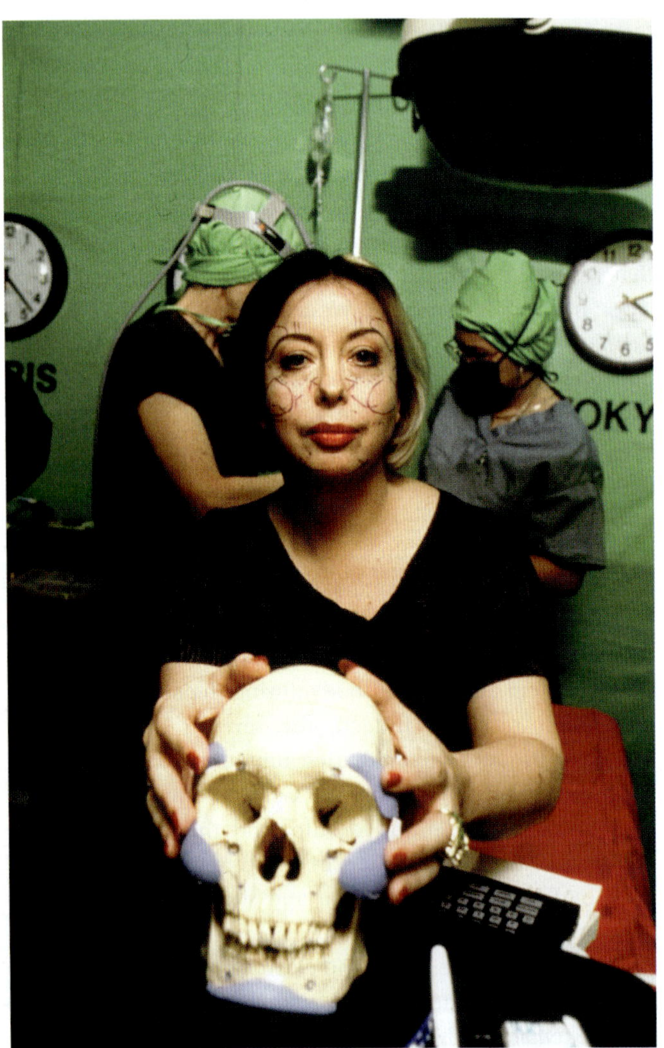

7.10 ORLAN, *Omnipresence*, 1993. Cibachrome in Diasec mount, 64⅞ × 43¼" (125 × 110 cm). Surgery-performance, New York. Courtesy the artist.

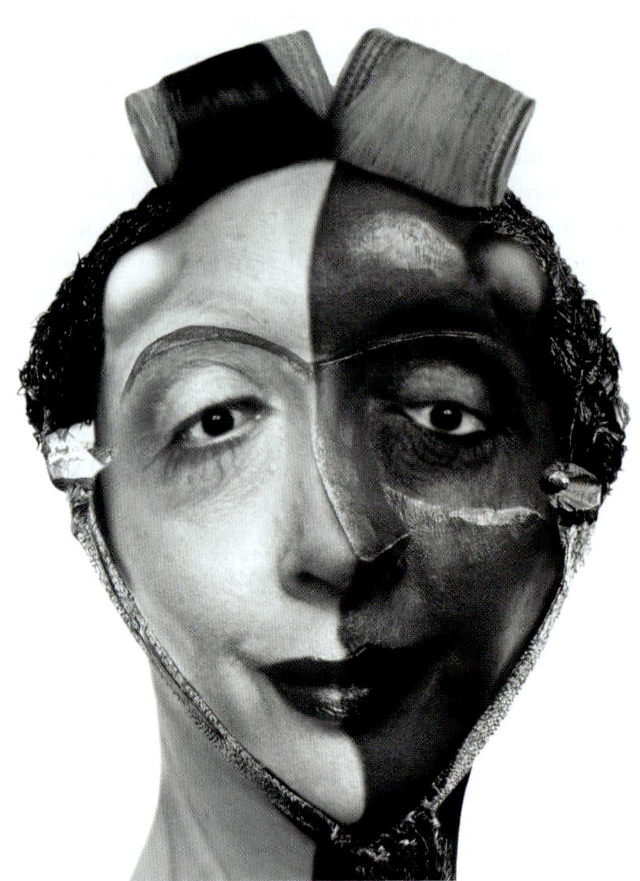

7.11 ORLAN, *African Self-Hybridization: Half-White Half-Black, Mbangu mask with face of European-St.Etienne woman in rollers*, 2002. Printed on photographic paper, 49¼ × 61⅜" (125 × 156 cm). Courtesy the artist.

Marina Abramović

In 1975, at the Student Cultural Center in Belgrade, Yugoslavia, a woman lay on the floor with her head tipped back and screamed until she lost her voice. The performer of the piece, *Freeing the Voice* (1975), was Marina Abramović (b. 1946). The same year she performed *Art Must Be Beautiful*, which involved her repeating the title of the work while brushing her hair violently with a metal brush. Abramović had previously participated in the Actionist events of Viennese performance artist Hermann Nitsch (b. 1938). Though she had since turned away from such collective rituals, she remained committed to using the body to address the human condition. In her works of the mid-1970s, endurance and pain were used to dramatize the position of the individual in society. Spectacles such as a woman screaming until her voice fails or grooming until she bleeds constitute painful metaphors for experiences outside the gallery.

On November 30, 1975, her birthday, Abramović met fellow performance artist Ulay (b. 1943), who was himself celebrating a birthday. For the next fourteen years, the two collaborated and lived together, creating works that explored the physical limits of the body and the psychological tension produced when those limits were approached. They often made art that addressed relationships and connections between individuals but they never integrated their own biographies into the work. Only the barest indications of personality were allowed; even gender was de-emphasized through androgynous costumes or deliberately asexual actions. Abramović and Ulay referred to their medium as the "hermaphroditic body." *Interruption in Space* (1977), a typical collaboration of the period, consisted of a temporary wall. This was constructed in the middle of a gallery that the two artists walked and then ran across as if they didn't even see the obstruction. Each time they attempted to cross the room, she from one side, he from the other, they collided with the wall until they were no longer able to continue. In an unsettlingly blunt fashion, the performers displayed the limits of the body. The same year also saw *Breathing In, Breathing Out,* a fifteen minute performance piece that reconfigured their two bodies into a single organism. With their noses pinched closed, the performers pressed their mouths together and inhaled each other's breath, creating a closed system with human features, but altered contours and a necessarily brief lifespan. In the early 1980s, the couple began their longest series of performances, *Nightsea Crossing* (1981–87), which integrated meditation into their work. For these pieces, the artists faced each other across a table, often accompanied by significant objects, including a diamondback python, Aboriginal boomerang, and 250 grams of gold, and sat still and silent for hours on end. Meditation as well as endurance became the central aspect of the work, thus layering the physical component of the earlier performances with a spiritual one. Body, mind, and spirit were now integrated into the closed system of the performance.

Abramović and Ulay ended their relationship in 1988. That year, they performed their final collaboration, *The Lovers—The Great Wall Walk* (**fig. 7.12**), for which each artist walked half the length of the Great Wall of China, approximately 1250 miles, she beginning from the Gulf of Pohai in the Yellow Sea and he from the Gobi Desert in Kunan province. Their meeting in the middle was to have been celebrated by a wedding, but, their relationship having suffered in the preceding years, it ended instead with a goodbye. Abramović has described her persona in the early performances as "very tough, very male, a going-forward-no-matter-what performance attitude."[8] The works she created with Ulay succeeded in revealing some aspects of her personality; however, after *The Great Wall Walk,* she found herself struggling with the residue of an emotionally wrenching experience, suddenly aware of large parts of her personality that had previously remained untouched and untapped by her art: Her work gave her no obvious way to express anything but a fraction of her sense of self. In this situation, she turned again to her body, but now surrounded it with narratives that had been excluded from her earlier work.

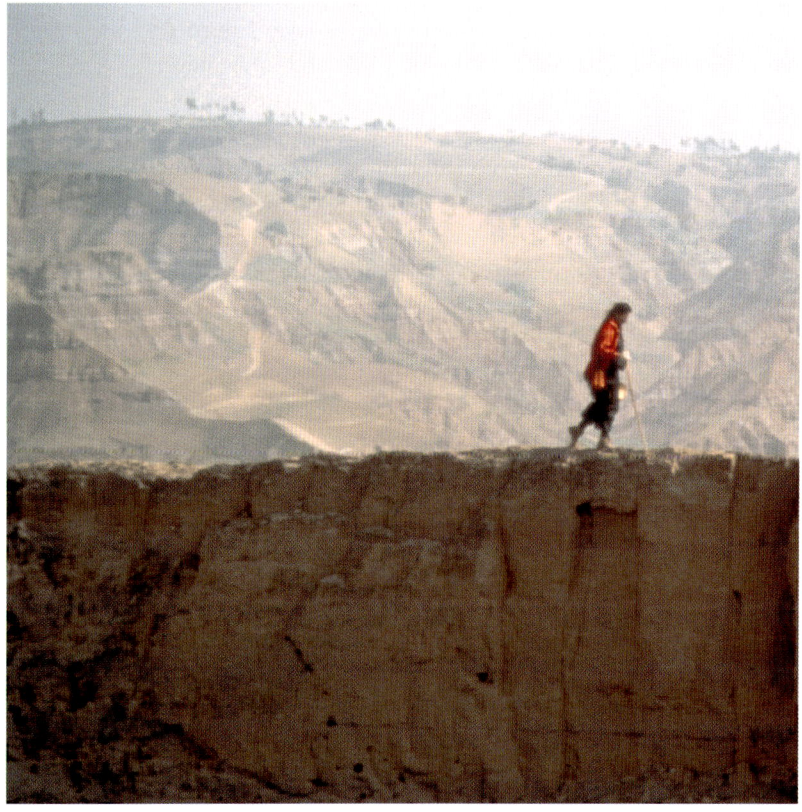

7.12 Marina Abramović and Ulay, ***The Lovers—The Great Wall Walk***, 1988. Performance piece walking the Great Wall of China. Courtesy The Marina Abramović Archives and Lisson Gallery, London.

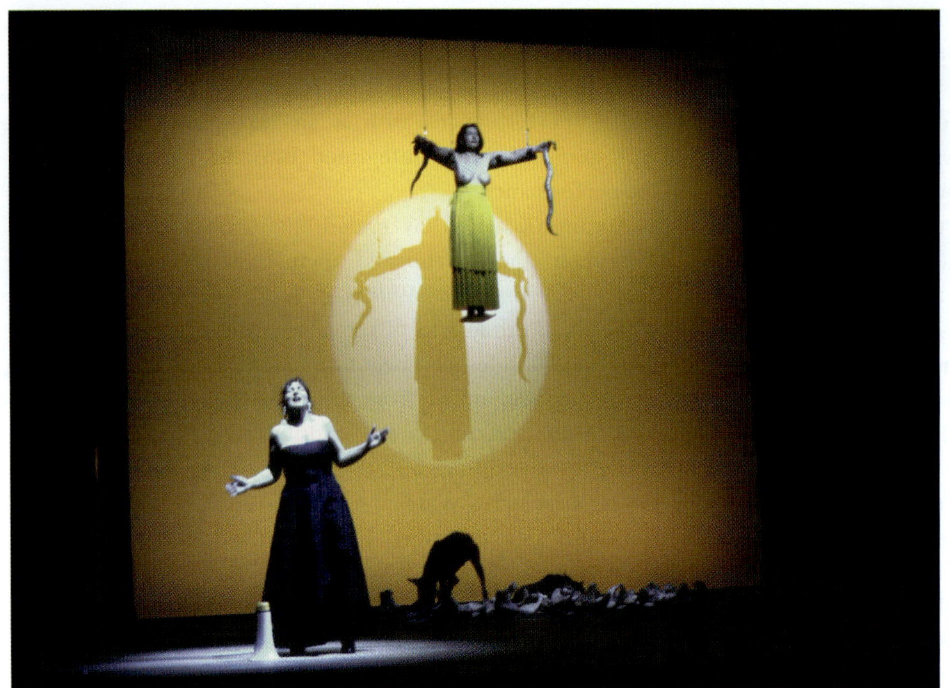

7.13 Marina Abramović and Michael Laub, ***The Biography Remix (Snakes)***, 2004. First performance 1993. Romaeuropa Festival, Teatro Palladium, Rome, Italy. Courtesy The Marina Abramović Archives and Lisson Gallery, London.

By 1993, Abramović had created the structure of an ever-changing performance called *The Biography* (**fig. 7.13**), which theatrically integrated elements from her personal, artistic, and emotional life. No longer refusing autobiography, Abramović used her body as a means to reflect upon and produce an image of her self that offered more legible details than her earlier work. In an interview in 1999 she explained: "Now I need glamour. I need something to love. I need to see all these other parts of me which I had absolutely never allowed to exist. I had been ashamed of this part of me and let them *[sic]* go. Then I created *The Biography*, in which I staged my life and played both sides, the tough one and the contradictory one, and when I exposed my shame, this was the biggest liberation I had in my life."[9] Using video, photography, and live performance, *The Biography* integrated fragments of Abramović's endurance pieces with these personal and fictive narratives. This willingness to draw on the physicality of the body as well as on the particularity of her personality, often with an appeal to the transcendence of spirituality, characterizes Abramović's work of the 1990s and since.

As she re-evaluated the content of her art, Abramović also created new ways to activate the viewer's experience through what she calls "transitory objects": furniture, clothes, even choreographed events that stimulate the body as well as the eyes and mind. One of the transitory objects Abramović considers particularly successful is *Shoes for Departure* (1991) (**fig. 7.14**), a series of sculptures created in the early 1990s that feature one to several pairs of 150-pound crystal shoes. Encountering these shoes in a gallery or museum, you are instructed to take off your own shoes and socks, put your feet into the sculpture, close your eyes, and depart. Physical motion is impossible due to the weight and shape of the shoe, so departure becomes a matter of the mind. Abramović explains that the viewer's physical contact with the crystal and an object defined as art is important, but that the experience is above all else one of entering into a meditative state of consciousness. The fresh awareness of the body brought about by putting on the precious, heavy shoes is intended to lead the participant to a new experience of the body and the mind in the world. In addition to using many different kinds of crystal in the transitory objects, she incorporates hair, copper, iron, clay, and obsidian mirrors to produce experiences rooted in the material world but stretching toward something else.

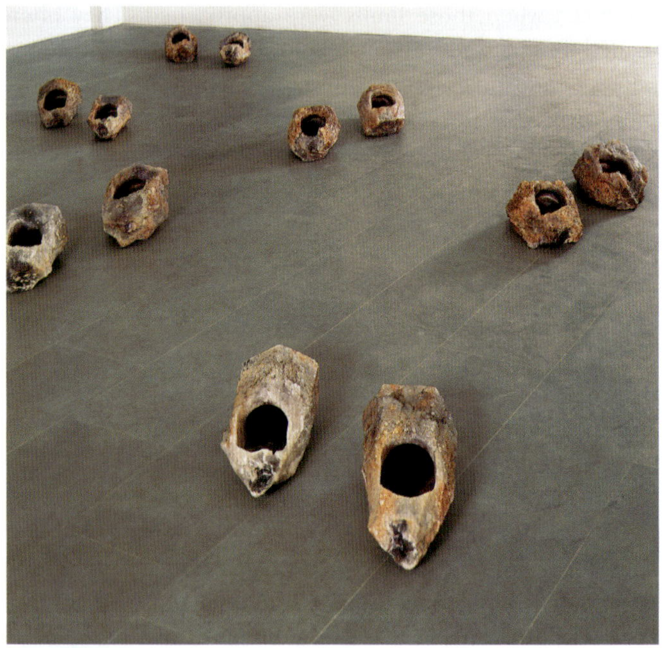

7.14 Marina Abramović, ***Shoes for Departure***, 1991. Amethyst sculptures. Galerie Enrico Navara, Paris. Courtesy The Marina Abramović Archives and Lisson Gallery, London.

Too Close: Personal Lives and Artistic Practice

Of the five artists discussed above, those who continued making art beyond their early careers, Piper, ORLAN, and Abramović, all developed strategies for creating intimate and directly personal works. Piper's calling cards, ORLAN's surgeries, and Abramović's *The Biography* all place the artist in an exposed position, revealing details of their lives that far exceed what audiences are generally shown. Not every mature work of these artists is so revealing, of course, but the use of biography as well as bodies to raise issues of identity and society is an important legacy of all three. The feminist injunction that the personal is the political, as well as the aesthetic intuitions of performance and Conceptual traditions of the 1960s and 1970s, are amply displayed here. By the 1990s, the drama of the Culture Wars and the surprise of witnessing duress as an artistic strategy was fading, leaving artists with a profound awareness of the body and biography as sensitive and productive artistic media. Learning to control an audience's interpretations was a challenge, but not to the point where it prevented the artist's body having an increasing presence in contemporary practice. In the U.S., a number of artists integrated their and others' bodies into two- and three-dimensional works that alluded to the recent history of art as well as to personal and political events of the present. This impulse to maintain the body as one among other available materials was shared by artists from many different locales, several of which—the Middle East, Europe, and Central America—will be discussed here, while the use of the body in work by Cuban, Chinese, and Russian artists will be addressed in subsequent chapters.

Tracey Emin

Art about human experience often directs attention to our emotional lives. The collages and paintings of David Wojnarowicz (see Chapter 4), the performance of Marina Abramović, and the photography of Sally Mann challenge viewers to think hard about how, whom, and under what conditions we love. British artist Tracey Emin (b. 1963) exploded onto the international art scene in the 1990s. Her work, most often based on personal diaristic material, reveals the events and entanglements of her emotional life. *Everyone I Have Ever Slept With 1963–95* (1995) is a tent appliquéd with the names of everyone with whom the artist had slept. Though the title suggests the promiscuity of a tell-all, a comparison of the names and dates on the list with the artist's biography reveals how literally the artist imagined this project—"slept with" in this case is not always a euphemism for "had sex with." The list therefore refers to moments throughout the artist's life, knitting together the innocence of infancy and early childhood with the complicated and at times painful entanglements of adolescence and adulthood.

Though Emin's gestures often seem calculated to cause maximum scandal—for instance, submitting an installation designed around her own bed for the Turner Prize competition or showing up drunk on live TV after failing to win it—the drama is the result of her displaying the raw emotion expected of an artist in a manner and setting considered ill-suited. Emin has simply resisted confining her expressions to the limits of a painting or sculpture. As if to tease the viewer with a possible, but uncertain, window into her motivations, Emin spells out the impulses behind so many of our actions, both noble and otherwise, in text pieces such as *Just Love Me* (1998) (**fig. 7.15**), or *You Should Have Loved Me* (2008). In

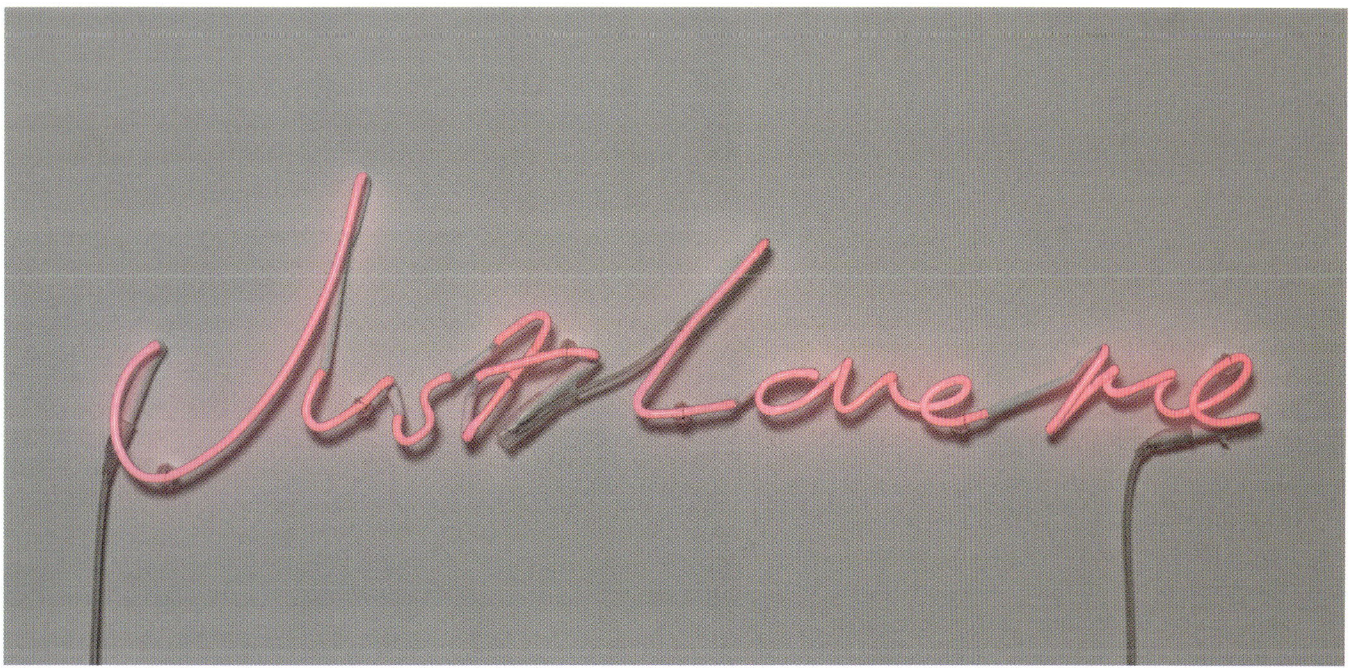

7.15 Tracy Emin, *Just Love Me*, 1998. Neon tubes, 14⅞ × 45 × 2½" (38 × 114.4 × 6.5 cm). © the artist, courtesy White Cube.

the case of these signs, emotional content takes the form of an advertisement or a piece of Conceptual art. By 2001, Emin could count on viewers' appreciation of the elision of art and commerce that artists from Andy Warhol to Barbara Kruger had traded on in their neon signs and billboards. The potency of Emin's text pieces lies, however, in her substitution of a nearly abject, exposed emotionalism for Nauman's or Kruger's comedy or political theory. There is no joke here, no theoretical or political argument. *Just Love Me* reads more as an embarrassing outburst than a knowing aside, and as such brings to the surface the emotional fury and desperation that is often harnessed for art, but rarely so blatantly exposed.

Sophie Calle

Though adopting a very different tone than Emin, French Conceptualist Sophie Calle (b. 1953) has used her personal life as the premise for works that examine the pain and confusion of, but also the relationships and communities that evolve from, the failures of love. The film *No Sex Last Night (Double Blind)* (1992) (**fig. 7.16**) documents Calle's poignant and often painful interactions with her co-filmmaker, Greg Shephard, as they drive across the United States. The car breaks down repeatedly, the couple meet strangers, they reveal personal insights, and they get married in Las Vegas. Calle and Shephard film each other and record private narratives of the trip. Shephard records his admiration for Calle's art and her ability to reinvent herself continually for the work. He is clearly seduced by Calle's chameleonlike abilities and her confidence, though equally he is nearly crushed by a feeling that he is being manipulated. The reasons for Calle's attraction to Shephard are less clear. He had failed to show up for their first date, a meeting at Orly Airport in Paris, and then waited an entire year to contact her again. This, Calle says, was exactly the right way to talk to her. In the less dramatic, day-to-day relationship that the film presents, Shephard proves unable to re-create the appeal of his first impression.

Despite the marriage at the end, *Double Blind/No Sex Last Night* is not a romance. The film contrasts the artists' reserves of self-awareness and profound emotional investments with their surprising lack of knowledge about each other. There is a grueling, almost brutal quality to the film as their relationship shows every sign of failing. Calle makes clear from the outset that the film itself was functional, serving to extend the relationship she felt sure would otherwise have ended earlier. Conversations between Calle and Shephard prove difficult and rare, and even the simplest acts of decision making are often torturous to watch. The elements of filmmaking, how and what each artist films, and the private thoughts each records, become their emotional as well as intellectual and artistic outlets, replacing conversation and sex. When Calle says, as she does many times, "no sex again last night," she both narrates the events and voices her feelings of loneliness. Speech, like the film itself, becomes simultaneously analytic and performative as *Double Blind/No*

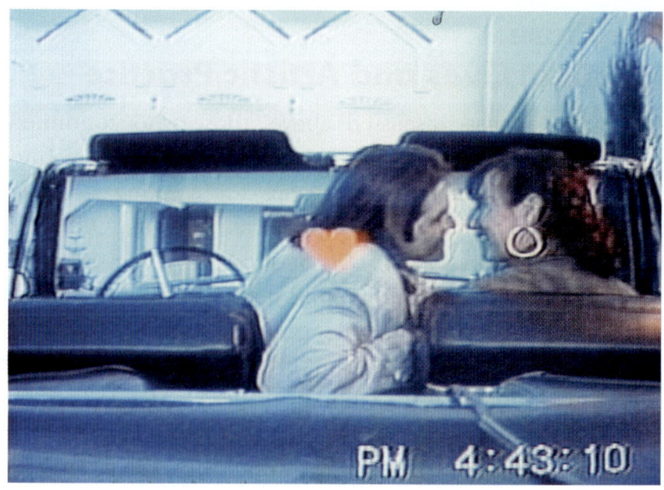

7.16 Sophie Calle and Greg Shephard, *No Sex Last Night (Double Blind)*, 1992. 35mm film in French and English with English subtitles, 76 minutes. Courtesy of Sophie Calle/Paula Cooper Gallery, New York.

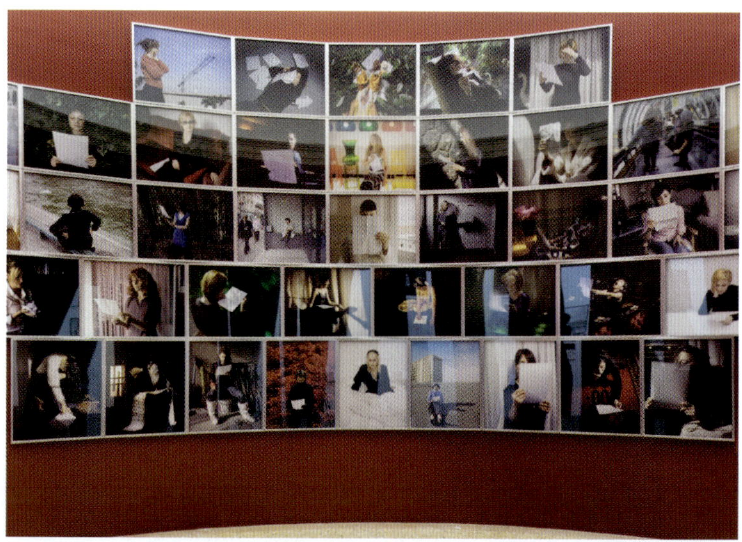

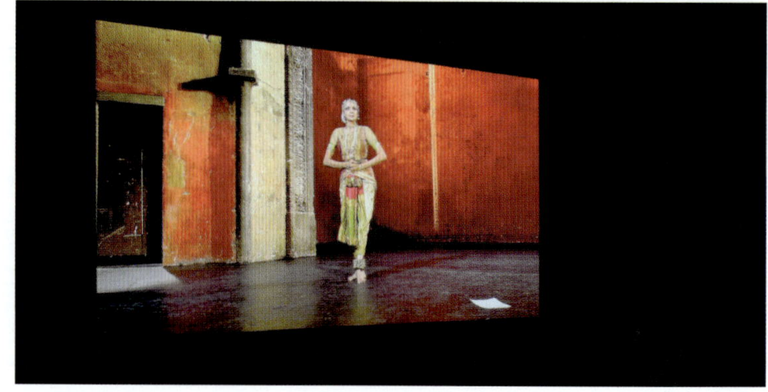

7.17 Sophie Calle, *Take Care of Yourself*, 2007. Top: exhibition view from French Pavilion, 52nd International Art Exhibition, Venice Biennale (June 10–November 19, 2007). Bottom: exhibition view from Paula Cooper Gallery, New York (April 9–June 6, 2009). Courtesy of Sophie Calle/Paula Cooper Gallery, New York.

Sex Last Night is revealed to be both about the experience of love and a means of representing it.

For the more recent *Take Care of Yourself* (2007) (**fig. 7.17**), Calle circulated copies of a breakup email she had received to 107 women, including doctors, actors, artists, musicians, intellectuals, and a clown. Like *Double Blind/No Sex Last Night, Take Care of Yourself* is functional as well as representational. Its title comes from the closing line of the email, and it is exactly what Calle does in the work. The artist had a great deal to say about Greg Shephard in the earlier work, but here she assigns the task of analyzing her new lover (he remains unnamed in the piece) to others. In the installation, which Calle created as the French representative at the 2007 Venice Biennale, she displays a copy of the letter alongside video testimony, photographs, and numerous written analyses by her female correspondents dissecting the email and speculating on its content, meaning, and ramifications. A handwriting analyst examines the letter, psychoanalysts elaborate on the insecurities of the writer, and friends and acquaintances offer Calle supportive readings of the failures of this ex-lover. Calle filmed the thoughts and reactions of most of the women and presented the results on banks of monitors. The letter is acted out and sung. Insights and performances, jokes and compassion, flow forth from the television screens, transforming the subject of the work from the email itself, which quickly becomes familiar, to the continually changing style and substance of its interpretations. As a final gesture, Calle advertised for a curator to take the material she had assembled and organize it into an exhibition. Daniel Buren (see Chapter 1) was chosen from among the applicants, thus reinforcing the Conceptualist lineage of Calle's engagement with emotional content.

Kiki Smith

Reflecting on the changes evident in art during her career, Marina Abramović noted that, by the 1990s, to make body art one needed to look beyond the body. Indeed, sculptors, photographers, and video artists as well as performers had developed eclectic means of exploring the intersection of self, body, and society without necessarily putting a body on display. Despite the overtly revealing, even confessional effect of Emin's *Everyone I Have Ever Slept With 1963–95* and Calle's *Take Care of Yourself,* the embroidered tent and rows upon rows of letters and talking heads are formally reserved and even modest. Kiki Smith (b. 1954), a member of Colab, showed her first piece of body art, a bedsheet printed with body parts, at "The Times Square Show" in 1980 (see Chapter 4). Two years later, similarly printed scarves appeared in the Fashion Moda concession at Documenta 7 in Kassel, Germany. After her initial interest in corporeal fragments and surfaces, Smith turned to the body's interior, a change evident in a small work called *Kiki Smith, 1983* (1983), a blood sample on a microscopic slide. The body, she felt, had been taken over by social forces such as religion and medicine, and art was a means of taking it back. In 1985, she and her sister took a three-month Emergency Medical Technician training course. After the course, her art underwent a shift and started to revolve around the organs and systems within the body.

Like many of her peers, Smith discussed her work in Foucauldian terms, emphasizing the changing meaning of the body and its parts within society. The heart, she noted, is essential in expressions of romantic sentiment, and is also integrated into religion, particularly in the Catholic tradition in which Smith was raised. Like all organs, it also has a position in medical discourse. Smith credited Nancy Spero (see Chapter 1) with impressing upon her the idea that the body functions as a language. Much as Spero had recontextualized individual figures, Smith isolated organs, separating them from their expected context, thus encouraging the viewer to reimagine the meaning of the heart, stomach, or brain. A bronze reproductive system evokes not only the intractable nature of gender in Western culture, but also demonstrates the uncanny results of turning fragile yet generative organs into a strong yet sterile form. Likewise, in the midst of the AIDS epidemic, when bodily fluids were identified as potentially lethal, the oversized lead-crystal sperm of *Untitled* (1989–90) (**fig. 7.18**) staked out an ambiguous middle ground between plague and pleasure. These sculptures take seriously the transformation of the human body in the late 1980s and early 1990s into a site of fear without sacrificing its fragility and elegance.

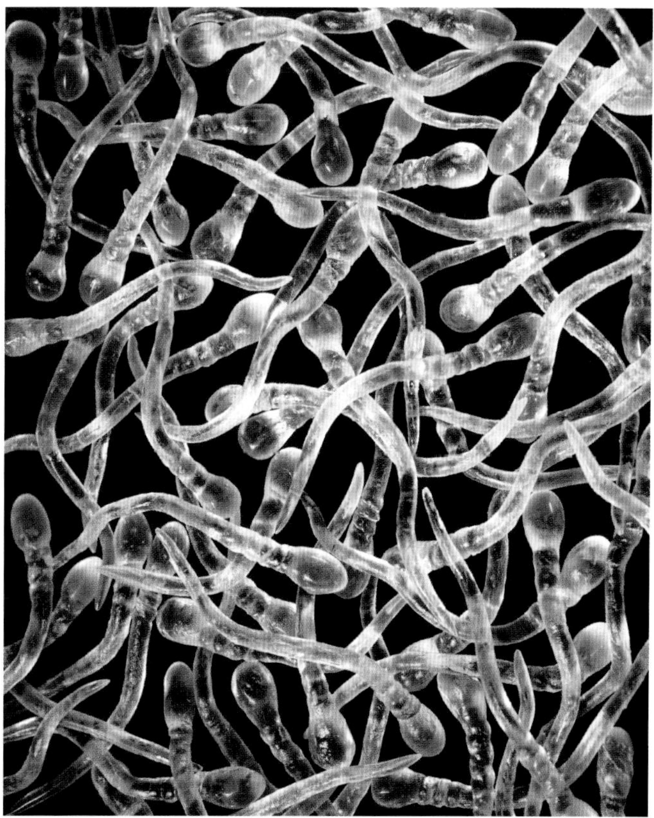

7.18 Kiki Smith, *Untitled*, 1989–90. Glass and rubber, 3 × 108 × 108" (7.6 × 274.3 × 274.3 cm). © Kiki Smith, courtesy Pace Gallery. Photograph courtesy the artist and Pace Gallery.

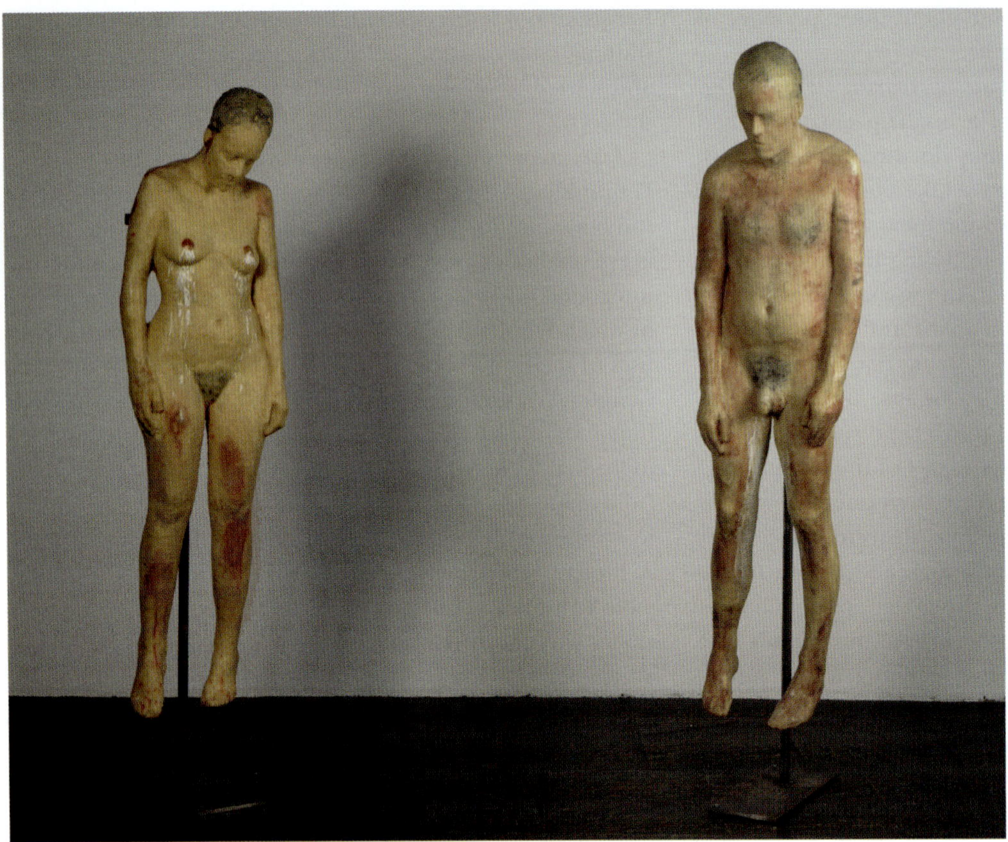

7.19 Kiki Smith, ***Untitled***, 1990. Beeswax and microcrystalline wax figures on metal stands. Height of female figure 73½" (186.7 cm); height of male figure 76¹⁵⁄₁₆" (195.4 cm). Whitney Museum of American Art, New York. © Kiki Smith, courtesy Pace Gallery. Photograph courtesy the artist and Pace Gallery.

Smith was attracted to the body in part because it is universally understood—we all have bodies—and yet remains absolutely unique: The body is thus the site of both our common humanity and our absolute individuation. Smith's first use of the full figure in her work was in *Untitled* (1990) (**fig. 7.19**), a pair of bodies—one male, one female—sculpted in wax and suspended on metal armatures by their underarms a few feet above the ground. The bodies are nude and their heads hang down as if sapped of strength. The female appears to leak milk from her breasts. In the shadow of the male's flaccid penis, ejaculate drips down his leg. The work conveys the human qualities of physicality and fertility, yet, Smith notes, "her milk nurtures nothing, his seed seeds nothing. So it was about being thwarted—having life inside you, but the life isn't going anywhere, it's just falling down."[10] This is a depiction of the body losing control and becoming "uncontainable," a word Smith uses to describe all of her body art.

Smith's interest in the expressive power of the figure led her to make increasingly personal work. She even created self-portraits, reaching the end of a journey that had begun with the broken bodies on bedsheets: "In 1979 I started making pictures of the body from *Gray's Anatomy*, microscopic images ... Slowly, I went from these images to organs, then to systems, and then at one point, I started thinking of skin as a system, and then I moved from the outside of the body to making figures. Now I am moving back and forth through the skin, going from internal portraiture to making new combinations of internal and external figures."[11] Several of these new combinations took the form of women from the Judeo-Christian religious tradition, including Lilith, Eve, the Virgin Mary, and Mary Magdalene. One such work was titled *Lucy*, after the name given to the 3-million-year-old skeleton of a hominid discovered in 1972. Smith thus made the human body a key to exploring not only contemporary life, but history and even prehistory as well.

Embodying Abstraction

Not all art that addressed the self and society so clearly utilized the body as a subject or medium. Many artists continued to find the aesthetics of postwar abstraction, from Abstract Expressionism to Minimalism and Process art compelling. Like the art discussed thus far, however, the work of Mona Hatoum, Felix Gonzalez-Torres, Janine Antoni, and Gabriel Orozco represented a widespread commitment to political and social content even as it took highly aesthetized form. As indicated in the discussions of Gregory Battcock, Terry Fox, and Joseph Beuys in Chapter 1, there were critics and artists for whom, as early as 1970, the practices of Minimalism and Process art were understood to have political and philosophical significance; by the 1990s, there was a ready audience with whom one did not have to argue the point. Critics in and out of the art world generated a variety of political interpretations of this new brand of abstraction. Hatoum's art, for example, was embraced as a profound expression of the experience of political exile and Gonzalez-Torres's work was championed as an assertion of the complexity of homosexual identity in an age of AIDS. This embodied abstraction introduced new discussions of the self, the body, and power to art audiences with work that combined formalist and activist traditions, demonstrating that the division between the two, never so clearly defined, was no longer respected.

Mona Hatoum

The work of Mona Hatoum (b. 1952) charts a particular engagement with the body and Minimalism that gives form to some of the complex intersections of self and space, and identity and globalism, at the end of the century. In the 1980s, Hatoum—a Beirut-born, London-based, Palestinian performance artist and sculptor with a British passport—chose to focus her work on the notion of the body as a threatened entity, confined and controlled by power structures. She had been stranded in London in 1975, unable to return home due to the civil war in Lebanon. This exile echoed the original exile of her parents from Palestine and their relocation to Beirut by the British in 1948 following the creation of Israel. Denied citizenship by the Lebanese, her family was granted British passports, thus multiplying the fragmented nature of their identity: Their citizenship, nationality, and place of residence were all different. After she relocated to London, Hatoum's alienation was compounded by a feeling of powerlessness and invisibility as an Arab woman in the U.K. The performance she created to make sense of her situation was *Under Siege* (1982), where the artist was immersed in a transparent plastic, square-bodied structure, approximately 8 feet tall and 4 x 4 feet at its base, and filled with brown clay slip. For seven hours she lashed out at the wet earth, attempting to stand, slipping and falling, and trying to right herself again. As she did so, excerpts from news broadcasts in English, French, and Arabic, along with revolutionary songs, blasted out from some speakers. The following year Hatoum wrote, "As a Palestinian woman this work was my first attempt at making a statement about a persistent struggle to survive in a continuous state of siege."[12]

Hatoum's focus on the body was informed by the history of her family, her experience as a foreigner in the U.K., and also by her interest in recent art. As a student at the Slade School in London, Hatoum had been impressed by Minimalism, as well as by the politics of feminism. She was troubled, however, by what she considered the "disembodied" quality of art-making going on around her, and the formalist debate that defined it it.[13] *Under Siege* addressed the body in two ways: as an active presence and as an image. Hatoum's struggle against the mud inside the transparent structure seemed to act out in abstract form the plight of Palestinians struggling against clearly visible obstacles, such as the Israeli occupying forces, or less immediately tangible barriers, such as political, social, and economic restrictions. As an image, *Under Siege* could evoke Hatoum's feeling of invisibility as an Arab woman in the West. Hatoum overlays and mixes together this complex set of meanings in the work just as they are blended in life.

Hatoum quickly became frustrated that critics interpreted her art exclusively in terms of her identity and a rather fixed idea of exile. In response, she shifted the focus away from her own body. The work that heralded this change was *The Light at the End* (1989) (**fig. 7.20**), a simple square consisting of six red cords strung vertically in a black frame and mounted in the corner of a red room. The work is lit from above, but

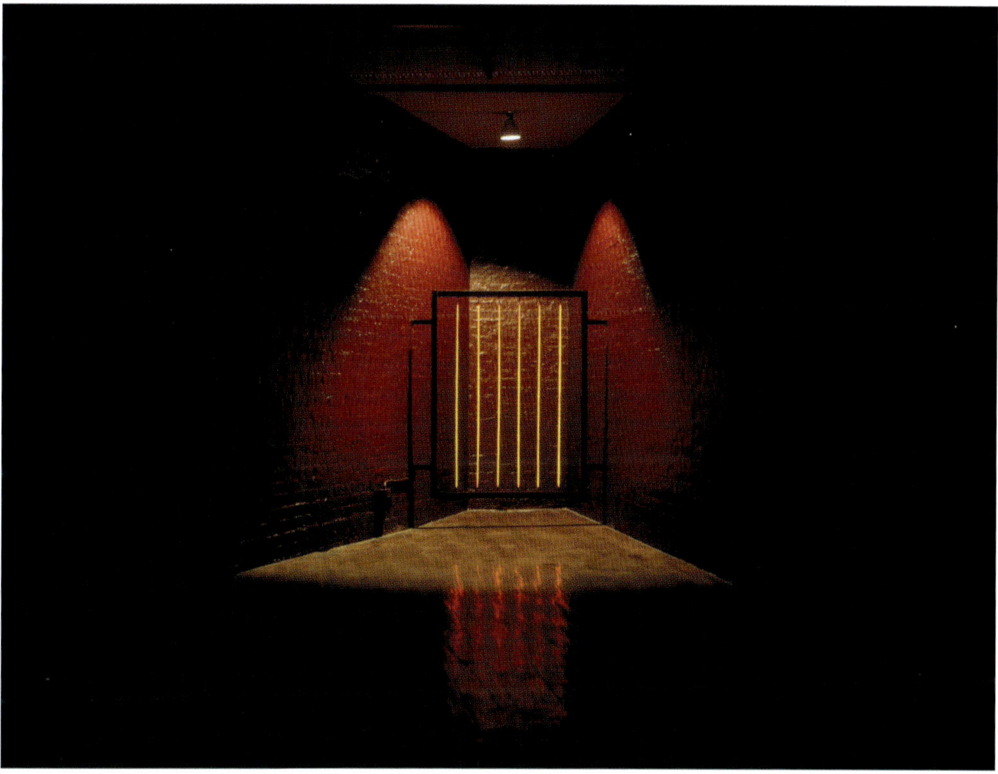

7.20 Mona Hatoum, *The Light at the End*, 1989. Angle iron frame and six electric heating elements, 65⅜ × 63¹⁵⁄₁₆ × 1¹⁵⁄₁₆" (166 × 162.4 × 5 cm). Courtesy White Cube.

also emits a glowing red light that brings to mind the Minimalist light works of Dan Flavin (1933–96). Hatoum's elegant installation accrues threatening allusions through its resemblance to a barred doorway and its dramatic color palette. The work, however, is not only an image or an object but also an experience. The red lights at the end of this tunnel are heating elements that, according to the artist, are capable of burning through flesh. Standing near the object, the proximity of possible pain overcomes one's compulsion to analyze—the viewer stops thinking about art history or geometry, and instead reflects on incarceration and the fear of exposure to the elements. *The Light at the End* and a series of related installations take up ideas inherent in Minimalism in quite different ways than *Under Siege.* Any metaphors drawn from the work are here generated by the sensations of the viewer, not the actions or appearance of the artist.

Hatoum did not leave her engagement with the body completely behind, however. In *Corps étranger (Foreign body)* (1994) (**fig. 7.21**), she paired an image of her own physical being with the viewer's corporeal experience. As with *Under Siege* and *The Light at the End,* this piece is structured like a Minimalist form—a cylindrical room, with two slits through which to enter and exit. Once inside, viewers stand with their backs pressed against the wall and their feet at the edge of what looks like a precipice over an ever-changing chasm of human tissue and hair. This abstract organic abyss is actually a video projection created with an endoscopic camera moving over and inside Hatoum's body. Viewers thus look down into the orifices and through the passages of the artist's body. The sound of her heartbeat fills the chamber while the heat and smell of the viewers fill the small room. The work's title, which translates as "Foreign Body," can be interpreted in a variety of ways—for instance, as referring to Hatoum as a foreigner or to the camera as a foreign body. Standing inside the work, however, one is overwhelmed by the sheer foreignness of the body itself. Like Kiki Smith's sculpted organs, this body seems to have little to do with what we think we know of our own physical being.

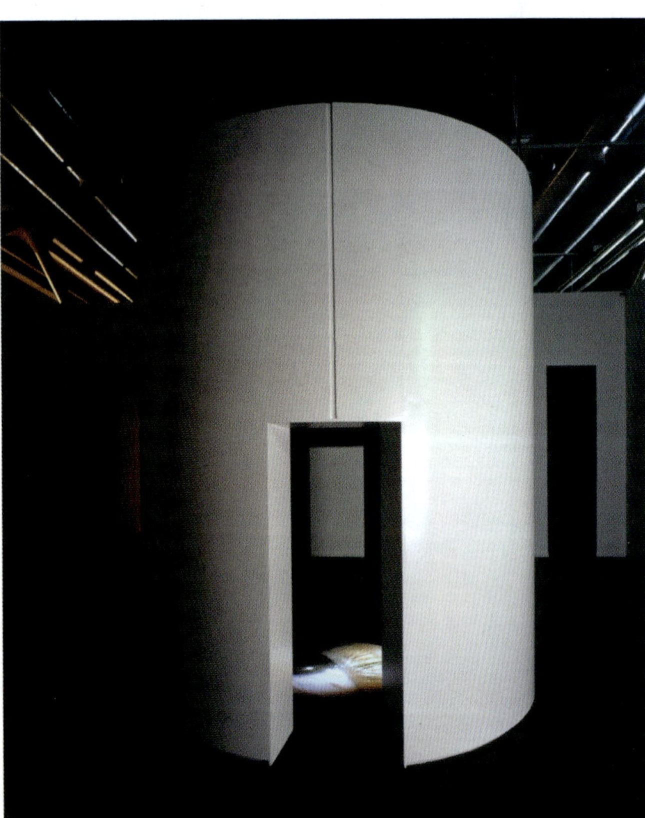

7.21 Mona Hatoum, *Corps étranger (Foreign body)*, 1994. Video installation with cylindrical wooden structure, video projector, video player, amplifier and four speakers, 137¹³⁄₁₆ × 118⅛ × 118⅛" (350 × 300 × 300 cm). Centre Pompidou. Courtesy Centre Pompidou, Paris.

Hatoum's work expresses her sense of "inbetweenness," the state of perpetual passage in which there is no home to return to and no being at home in the place where one is currently living.[14] Palestinian intellectual Edward Said, author of a groundbreaking text on Western perceptions of the East, *Orientalism* (1978), wrote that her work is "like a refugee's world, which is full of grotesque structures that bespeak excess as well as paucity ... [it] travest[ies] the idea of a single homeland," and expresses the nature of contemporary Palestinian existence.[15] Part of Hatoum's success at refuting singularity rests on this change of focus in the late 1980s from works centered on her own body to situations that affect the viewer's body.

Felix Gonzalez-Torres

Felix Gonzalez-Torres (1957–96), the Cuban-born, New York-based sculptor whose work as a member of the collective Group Material was aimed at changing the world (see Chapter 4), took a personal, poetic, exploratory turn in his solo work. Unlike Kiki Smith, whose work with Colab appears indistinguishable from the work she showed alone, Gonzalez-Torres seems to have experienced collective and individual practice in very different ways. Alone, he began integrating the presence of the body into abstract works that refer to the histories of Minimalist, Process, and Conceptual art. Like Hatoum, his practice began as an exploration of the styles of the 1960s and 1970s and took a specific interest in the sensations of the viewer. *"Untitled" (Portrait of Ross in LA)* (1991) (**fig. 7.22**) is an exemplary piece. The sculpture, a pile of candy possessing an "ideal weight," the wall label explains, of 175 pounds, looks like a rather light-hearted take on Process or Earth art. The fact that the audience is invited to take a piece of candy adds a participatory dimension and casts a sensual light on the work. Moreover, Gonzalez-Torres titles almost every one of his works "Untitled" to encourage the viewer to make personal associations and interpretations as they interact with the work. The parenthetical subtitle, however, indicates that the artist had some thoughts about the meaning of the work as well. Ross, one learns, was the artist's lover and in 1991 was dying of an AIDS-related condition; 175 pounds was Ross's weight when healthy. This knowledge complicates the playful gift of the candy, suggesting a twofold transubstantiation of Ross's body,

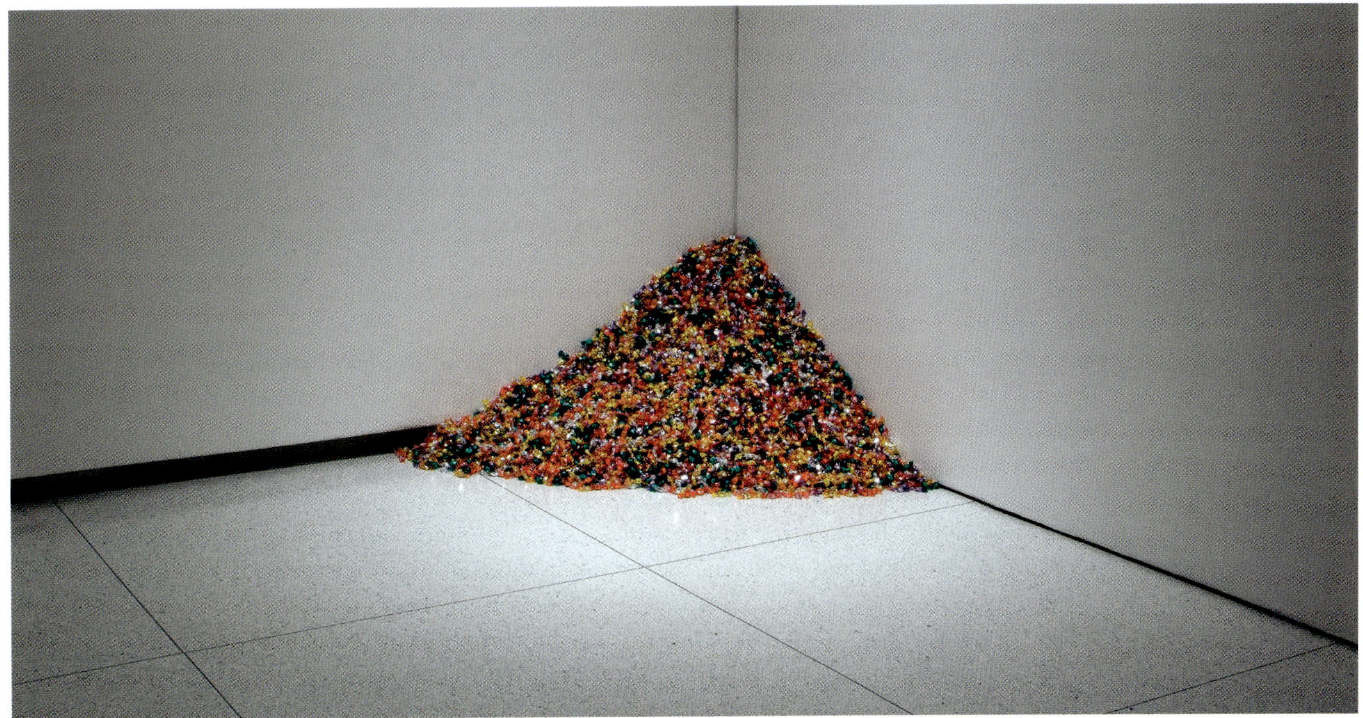

7.22 Felix Gonzalez-Torres, *"Untitled" (Portrait of Ross in LA)*, 1991. Candies individually wrapped in multicolored cellophane, endless supply. Overall dimensions vary with installation. Ideal weight 175 lbs (79 kg). Courtesy of Andrea Rosen Gallery, New York.

first into the candy and then into the viewer's own body. Gonzalez-Torres explained: "I'm giving you this sugary thing; you put it in your mouth and you suck on someone else's body. And in this way, my work becomes part of so many other people's bodies. It's very hot. For just a few seconds, I have put something sweet in someone's mouth and that is very sexy."[16] Whereas Group Material directed our attention to politics in the museum, Gonzalez-Torres here points to the sensual and contemplative potential of art.

Gonzalez-Torres designed candy pieces like *"Untitled" (Portrait of Ross in LA)* in different shapes and sizes, and using different candies. These pieces were the artist's way of working through his struggle with the disease that would take his lover and then himself. Gonzalez-Torres explained: "In a way this 'letting go' of the work, this refusal to make a static form, a monolithic sculpture, in favor of a disappearing, changing, unstable, and fragile form was an attempt on my part to rehearse my fears of having Ross disappear day by day right in front of my eyes."[17] As viewers, we leave the artwork with the taste of it in our mouths. We may then wonder at the experience afterward, and perhaps mention it to a friend or family member. In this way, the artwork extends from the museum into the hands, mouths, bodies, and minds of those who encounter it, and beyond into the wider community.

Despite its disappearing form, *"Untitled" (Portrait of Ross in LA)* is surprisingly permanent. And despite the self-destructive quality of Gonzalez-Torres's sculptures, his work is designed to survive even as it disappears. In another echo of the 1960s, this time of Conceptual art, Gonzalez-Torres developed Certificates of Authenticity and Ownership entrusting owners with rights and responsibilities in regards to the work. In the case of *"Untitled" (Portrait of Ross in LA)*, each time the work is installed the owner may choose the configuration in which the work is assembled, and whether or not to replenish the candy to maintain its "ideal weight." The consequences of the contract for our understanding of the absent body are profound: The object of love that could not be saved in life can be perpetuated forever in art, or lost, depending on the choices of the owner. Gonzalez-Torres, however, does not discuss this tactic in emotive terms. In a return to the type of discussions initiated by Group Material, he spoke of the legal arrangements in political terms. In a conversation with veteran Conceptual artist Joseph Kosuth (b. 1945), he declared: "At this point I do not want to be outside the structure of power, I do not want to be the opposition, the alternative. Alternative to what: To power? No. I want to have power … I want to be like a virus that belongs to the institution."[18] Through his Certificates, as much as much as through the works themselves, Gonzalez-Torres presented himself as a contagion of difference within the institutions of culture.

By the mid-1990s, museums were increasingly open to displaying symbols of difference. The success of Gonzalez-Torres's viral occupation of the institution was confirmed by the prominent role he played in late-century art theorizing and by the selection of his work to represent the United States posthumously at the 52nd Venice Biennale in 2007. By that date, his work had come to represent a shift from self-interest to sociability that was the central component of French theorist, critic, and curator Nicolas Bourriaud's concept of "relational aesthetics." Bourriaud featured

Gonzalez-Torres prominently in his extended argument, developed in his book *Relational Aesthetics* (1997), that important contemporary art created situations for the viewer that approximated forms of sociability that were being pushed out of daily life. Though the particulars of a work like *"Untitled" (Portrait of Ross in LA)* remain important, what mattered most to Bourriaud were the interactions initiated by the piece and carried to fruition by the viewer. New York-, Berlin-, and Chang Mai, Thailand-based Rirkrit Tiravanija's (b. 1961) transformation of gallery spaces into *ad hoc* kitchens in which he cooked and served his audience Thai curry are the most complete example of relational aesthetics. Looking at *"Untitled" (Portrait of Ross in LA)*, one can see that the balance that Gonzalez-Torres struck between exploring personal content and pointing to the social context was tipped in favor of the latter by Bourriaud's emphasis on the shifting nature of the audience rather than on the biography of the artist. An oeuvre that had begun deeply invested in society in its particulars with Group Material and that had then made use of the metaphors of art history to link the personal to the social was now being understood as itself a metaphor for interconnectedness in a global society.

Janine Antoni

At first glance, the early works of Janine Antoni (b. 1964) look like updated versions of Expressionist painting, Minimalist sculpture, and Process art. But what may initially appear to be appropriated Modernist styles are in fact something more. Antoni created *Butterfly Kisses* (1993) (**fig. 7.23**) with short delicate brush marks made by blinking her mascara-covered eyelashes against the page. *Loving Care* (1992) is a gestural abstraction on a gallery floor; to create it, Antoni submerged her hair in dye and then painted the floor using her hair. In their gestural expressive marks and all-over abstract compositions, both works pay homage to postwar Abstract Expressionist painting while the materials and means of creation allude to critical examinations of domestic labor and body image in feminist art of the 1970s.[19] Antoni's work creates a clear distance between the art object and the body. The marks are indexical traces of the body, but they resist identification as such, thus encouraging the viewer to find meaning beyond the specificity of the artist's body.

The complexity of Antoni's combination of body politics and Modernist form is evident in *Gnaw* (1992) (**fig. 7.24**), a two-part installation featuring two 600-pound cubes, one of chocolate, the other lard, and a room titled *Lipstick/Phenylethylamine Boutique* featuring mirrored vitrines, glass shelves, and a display of lipstick and chocolate. The cubes are a variation on a Minimalist trope. However, a close look at *Gnaw* reveals that the body, repressed in Minimalism, has returned here: At the corners of the chocolate cube are teeth marks. The cube of fat, deteriorating at the edges, has also been chewed. Like the Neo-Geo works that layered the sublime perfection of Minimalist geometry with social significance (see Chapter 5), Antoni's chocolate and fat cubes speak of desire, excess, and fragility as well as 1960s abstraction. Antoni cast the two forms and then spent months gnawing and biting at the blocks and spitting bits aside. After carving the blocks with her teeth in this way, Antoni reconstituted the discarded lard as lipstick and the chocolate as heart-shaped candy boxes, displayed in the *Lipstick/Phenylethylamine Boutique.* Phenylethylamine is the chemical in cacao beans that contributes to the pleasure we take from eating chocolate. With this boutique, Antoni gives the results of her corporeal

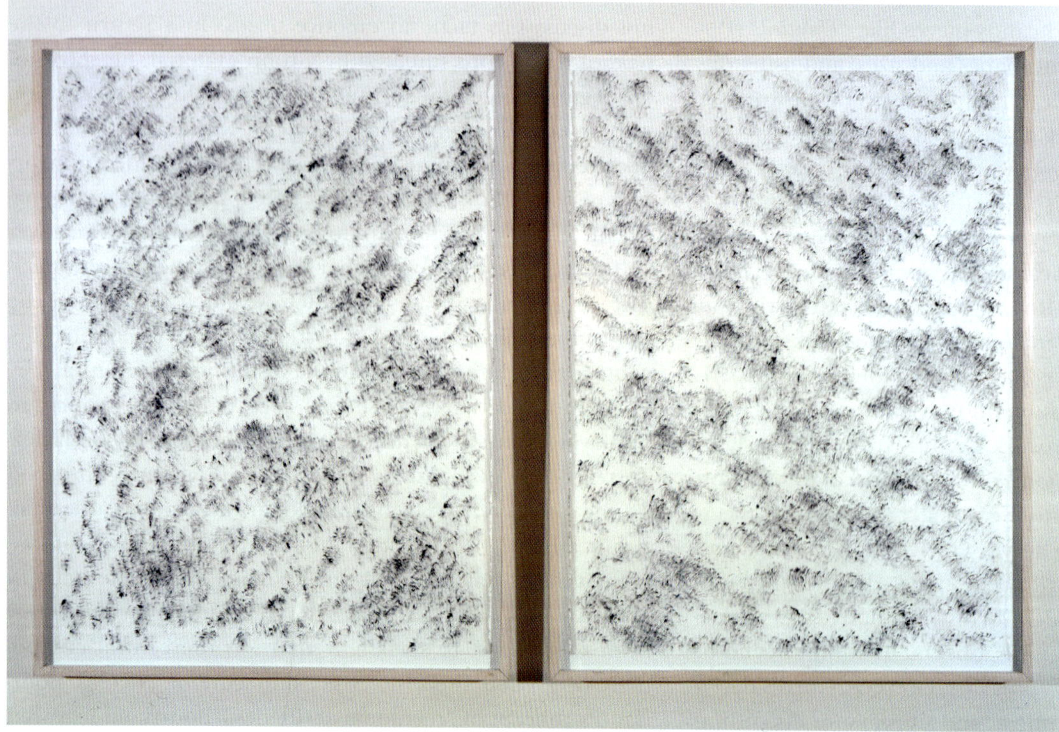

7.23 Janine Antoni, *Butterfly Kisses*, 1993. Cover Girl Thick Lash mascara, 1,124 winks per eye. Diptych, each 22⅛ × 15" (56.19 × 38.1 cm). The Museum of Modern Art, New York. Courtesy of the artist and Luhring Augustine, New York.

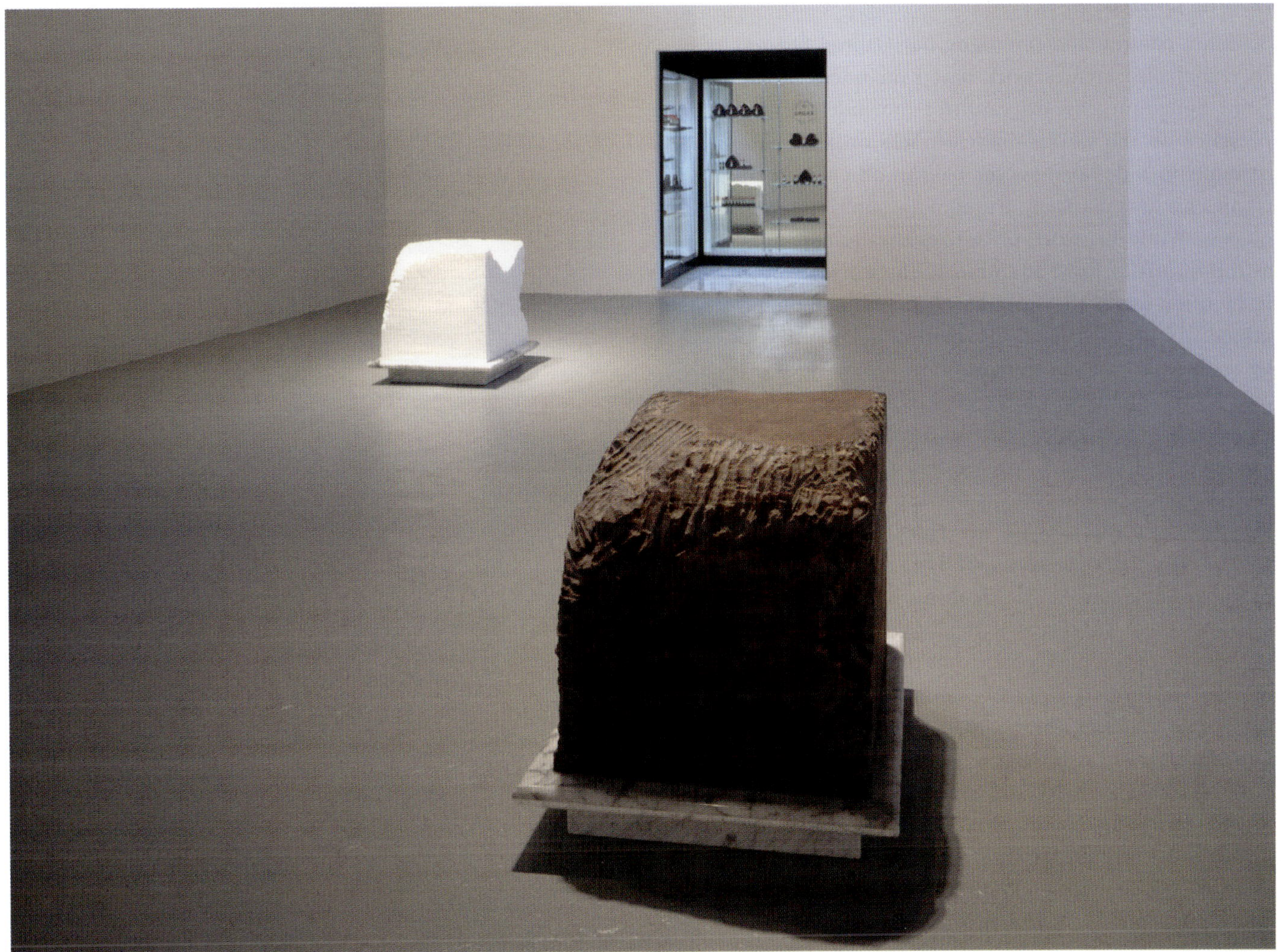

7.24 Janine Antoni, *Gnaw*, 1992. Installation shot. 600 lbs (272 kg) of chocolate gnawed by the artist (24 × 24 × 24"; 60.96 × 60.96 × 60.96 cm); and the same weight and size of lard, also gnawed by the artist. In the background, *Lipstick/Phenylethylamine Boutique* comprising 45 heart-shaped packages for chocolate made from chewed chocolate removed from the chocolate cube and 150 lipsticks made with pigment, beeswax and chewed lard removed from the lard cube. The Museum of Contemporary Art, Los Angeles. Courtesy of the artist and Luhring Augustine, New York.

engagement with Minimalist form an enticing veneer of consumer culture.

Butterfly Kisses, *Loving Care*, and *Gnaw* speak of obsession, compulsion, and even masochism by engaging processes that mimic the symptoms of psychological disorders. *Butterfly Kisses*, for instance, enacts a painful repetition-compulsion of the kind that might be brought on by the insecurities preyed upon by the cosmetics companies that provided Antoni's materials here. The work represents, but is not, symptomatic behavior. Antoni did apply mascara and blink against the page over a thousand times, but she measured out the process over weeks. Likewise, *Gnaw* orients a complex array of references—art history, economics, self-image, desire, and repulsion—around the actions of the artist's body. Unlike similarly structured works, however, such as ORLAN's surgeries or Abramović's *The Biography*, *Gnaw* does not make the artist's body available to the viewer. Antoni carefully designs indexical traces that allude to the body that is not there and in the process generates content that exceeds the autobiographical.

Antoni's interest in the body as a social signifier came from experience. Born and raised in the Bahamas, when she moved to the United States she realized that people misconstrued her body language. The simple act of moving among crowds in a new city exposed the culturally determined nature of the human body. In order to use this insight without focusing on the individual, Antoni sought out materials that might convey the trace of the body without evoking the traditions of self-expression, as abstract painting, modeling in clay, or traditional performance would. In addition to hair dye, mascara, lard, and chocolate, Antoni used soap, plaster drywall, rawhide, wool, and recordings of her rapid eye movements while dreaming. Faced with the traces of an absent body, the viewer is left with processes and objects that take satiric jabs at Minimalism and consumer culture. Not all of her work excludes the autobiographical investigation, but throughout the 1990s and into the new millennium, Antoni enlisted the body and a phenomenal range of materials to draw attention to the social and psychological forces that surround the self.

Gabriel Orozco

Sculptor, painter, and photographer Gabriel Orozco (b. 1962) also creates work based on traces of the body. Sometimes his art captures the index of our presence on the world—bicycle tracks on pavement or dents in a deflated soccer ball; in other cases he creates his own marks by arranging or altering found objects. While his work prioritizes the human body as the means to draw attention to the world around it, he often leaves the specifics of that body undetermined. As he explained: "In my work, I wanted to leave the mark of the human body, the mark of my own body, but I wasn't interested in affirming a particular race, gender, creed, or anything like that. I wanted to leave that space open, to be occupied by that someone else who is looking at my work."[20] His photographic diptych *My Hands Are My Heart* (1991) (**fig. 7.25**) presents the bare arms and torso of a man, first squeezing clay in his hands and then opening them to reveal a heart-sized object. The impression of the man's hands on the soft surface of the clay expresses a protective generosity lavished on the fragile material, the heart it represents, and the individual for whom it is a metaphor.

Orozco has created and discovered diverse surrogates for the body and poetic visions of its passage through the world. Another variation on Minimalist form, *Yielding Stone* (1992) (**fig. 7.26**) is a gray ball, approximately 16 inches in diameter, slightly misshapen, and marred by bits of debris stuck in its surface. Orozco created the work by rolling a mass of Plasticine equal to his own weight through the streets. As it encountered obstacles, it changed shape and

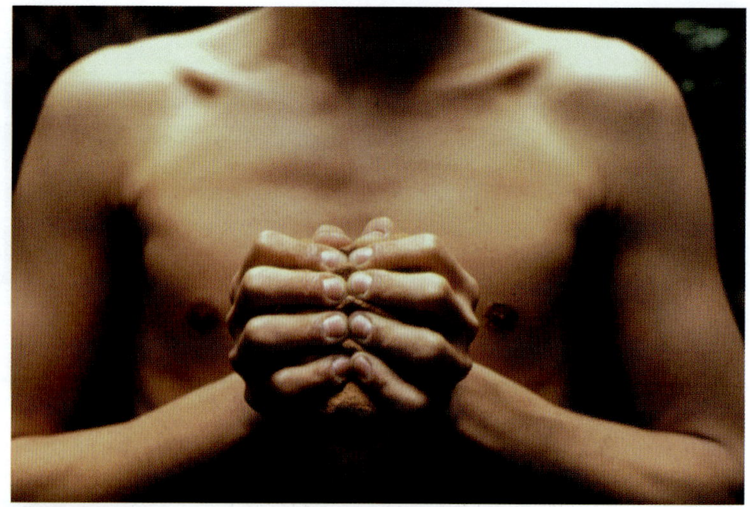

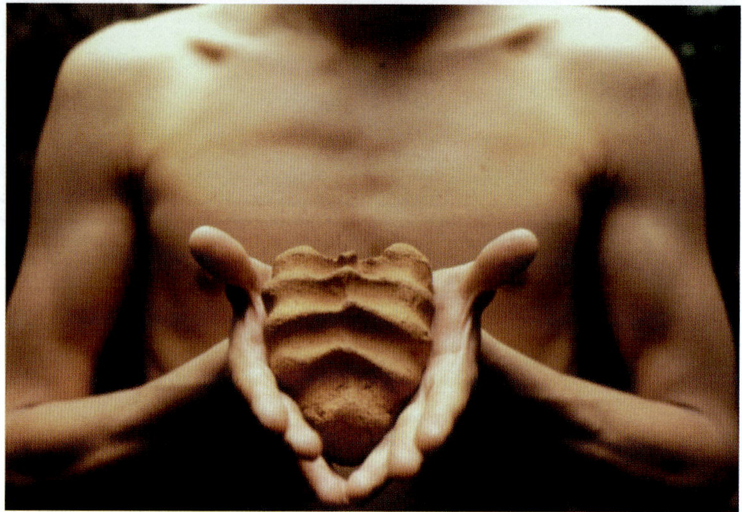

7.25 Gabriel Orozco, *My Hands Are My Heart*, 1991. Silver dye bleach print, 9⅛ × 12½" (23.1 × 31.7 cm). Courtesy of the artist and Marian Goodman Gallery, New York/Paris.

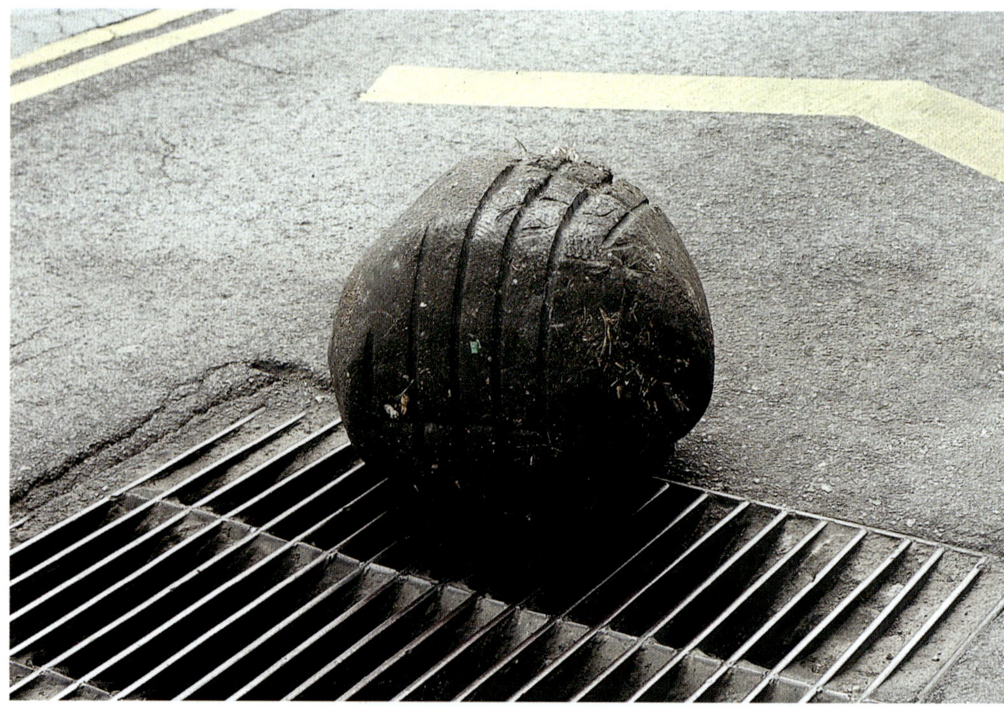

7.26 Gabriel Orozco, *Yielding Stone*, 1992. Plasticine, 14 × 17 × 17" (35.6 × 43.2 × 43.2 cm). Walker Art Center. Courtesy of the artist and Marian Goodman Gallery, New York/Paris.

so a record of its experience became etched into its surface. Plasticine is a common material in a sculptor's studio. It is strong but malleable and so is almost exclusively used to generate forms that are quickly cast in a more durable medium. Orozco by contrast has embraced it as "a material in a state of constant mutability, every time that it is touched it changes."[21] Plasticine is just one of the many materials that serve Orozco's phenomenological and metaphorical expressions of the body in its environment: Motorbikes, cars, breath, groceries, water, wood, and many other objects record the traces made and impressions felt by the body.

Yielding Stone can also be seen as a metaphor for Orozco's life and artistic practice. Born in Jalapa, Veracruz, Mexico, residing in various cities in different countries, and creating work and curating exhibitions in many more besides, Orozco has had a career defined by his near-constant movement through the world. He has no studio and rarely brings materials from one place to another, preferring to make art with the world as he finds it. As with *My Hands Are My Heart*, the results of his artistic wanderings are at once intimate and open-ended, telling the viewer about the kind of world he sees and his relation to it, but providing few details about his personal life. Art historian Margaret Iversen has argued that Orozco's work involves creating objects that redirect the viewer's pursuit of meaning away from the art object and toward its context. In Iversen's view, a work such as *Yielding Stone* reverses the expectation that art provides the meaning, order, and logic that are otherwise missing from the world. Instead, like the clay that reveals the shape of the clasped hands in *My Hands Are My Heart*, *Yielding Stone* is a significant absence, inviting the viewer to look to the world that shaped it for meaning. The redirection Iversen describes is more than a subterfuge, it is a complex metaphor for self and society that captures the intuition of all the artists discussed in this chapter: The body and the self are defined by their malleability, not by a core identity, and we must attend to the forces that act upon them.

Beyond the "I"

It has been a presumption of all the work discussed in this chapter that there is an "I" who experiences his or her body: a self that is affected by and accessed through the experience of the body. The last two artists to be discussed here, Teresa Margolles and Santiago Sierra, both based in Mexico City, shocked audiences in the late 1990s and early 2000s with work that reminded viewers that the body often has more to do with politics and economics than selfhood. Sierra paid unemployed men to tattoo their bodies, Margolles taxidermied parts of human cadavers. Living or dead, the body in both artists' work has political, economic, and cultural value, but is not a conduit to self-understanding or transcendence. Margolles, born in Culiacán, a Mexican city troubled by the drug trade, and Sierra, a Spanish sculptor who moved to Mexico City early in his career, share little of the lyric attitude that runs through the art discussed thus far in Chapter 7. Both address how the meaning of the human body has become wholly dependent on its circulation within the economies of global capitalism.

Teresa Margolles

Margolles (b. 1963), who trained in forensic medicine as well as art, describes her work as an examination of the "sociocultural implications" of the human corpse.[22] Her exploration of the body began in earnest in 1990, when she, Arturo Ángulo Gallardo, Juan Luis García Zavaleta, and Carlos López Orozco formed SEMEFO, an artist group named after the acronym for the Mexico City morgue, Servicio Médico Forense. In addition to acting as a performance group and a heavy metal band, the artists made objects and installations from materials collected at the morgue. In one installation they displayed the tattoos cut from murder victims who had either remained unidentified or came from families too poor to pay for their burial. After medical examination, the bodies had been treated as medical waste by the state. Margolles collected cremated bones and salvaged bits of hair and blood-stained clothing, as well as the linens and water used to clean the bodies. At times she even made use of body parts. As the Mexican government foundered in the 1990s, violent crime in Mexico City exploded. Margolles's art made the quotidian presence of death in Mexican life grotesquely visible.

Early in her career, Margolles traveled to Europe, where she discovered the work of Joseph Beuys. The apparent hubris of working with materials such as fat, sticks, and felt, and of speaking for all humanity made a profound impression on Margolles. In 2000, while exploring ways to create work that responded to the "collective pain" of humanity, she turned to the bullfight not only as a metaphor but as an event.[23] She was particularly struck by how it was not simply about victory over the animal and the threat it represented, but also about marking the body of the defeated. In the act of forcing the bull to succumb, its body was punctured and disfigured. At the morgue, Margolles came across a male corpse, a casualty of the drug wars. It was adorned with tattoos and had several piercings, including one in its tongue. She described the encounter: "I found a boy in the morgue, a murder victim who was marked in exactly the same way as a defeated bull … I had to go talk to the family, but they helped me because we understood each other. I work with emotion, not reason. So the piece is the tongue itself. It has an initial impact of shock, but what's important is that after death the tongue keeps talking."[24] Margolles provided a funeral for the boy, but his tongue has since traveled beyond Mexico City to art exhibitions, mounted on a rod and a plinth. It sits like a specimen, separated from the individual who once used it and even from any form that suggests a body. The finality of its alienation from the person for whom it once spoke diverts our attention from any relationship between the body and the self to the forces that have made

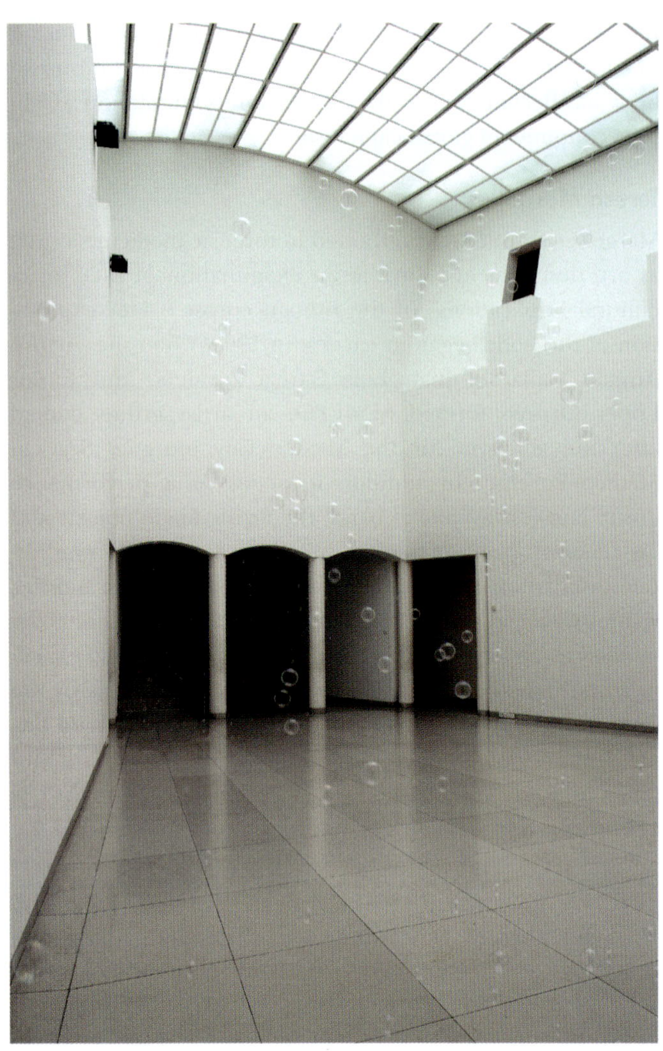

7.27 Teresa Margolles, ***En el Aire (In the Air)***, 2003. Bubbles made using morgue water used during autopsy procedures. Exhibition view at "Muerte sin Fin," Museum für Moderne Kunst, Frankfurt am Main, Germany, 2004. Courtesy the artist and Galerie Peter Kilchmann, Zurich.

it possible for us to stand in a museum and contemplate a severed human tongue.

In considering the morgue as a source of art materials, Margolles has not only looked at corpses. She also directs our attention to the rituals that even the destitute and anonymous dead are still granted. All bodies at the morgue, like the dead in cultures all over the world and throughout history, are cleaned, and Margolles has made a variety of works with the water used to wash the cadavers. She cleans the water and then uses it to fill rooms with mist, bubbles, or condensation. Visitors to the installation *In the Air* (2003) (**fig. 7.27**) watch the gallery fill with bubbles made from the water and feel the liquid as it bursts on their skin. They even breathe in the water, thus facilitating a most intimate relationship with the bodies and lives of the dead. In a formal inversion of such immaterial works, Margolles has also used the morgue water to mix concrete that is then shaped into sculptures. In 2006, at the Jardin Botánico Culiacán in the city where she was born, Margolles fabricated a suite of benches, shaped like chaise longues. Four years later, she created six more benches for the public space around the Los Angeles County Museum of Art (**fig. 7.28**). For this incarnation of the piece, Margolles made it clear that the water used in the works had cleaned the bodies of men killed

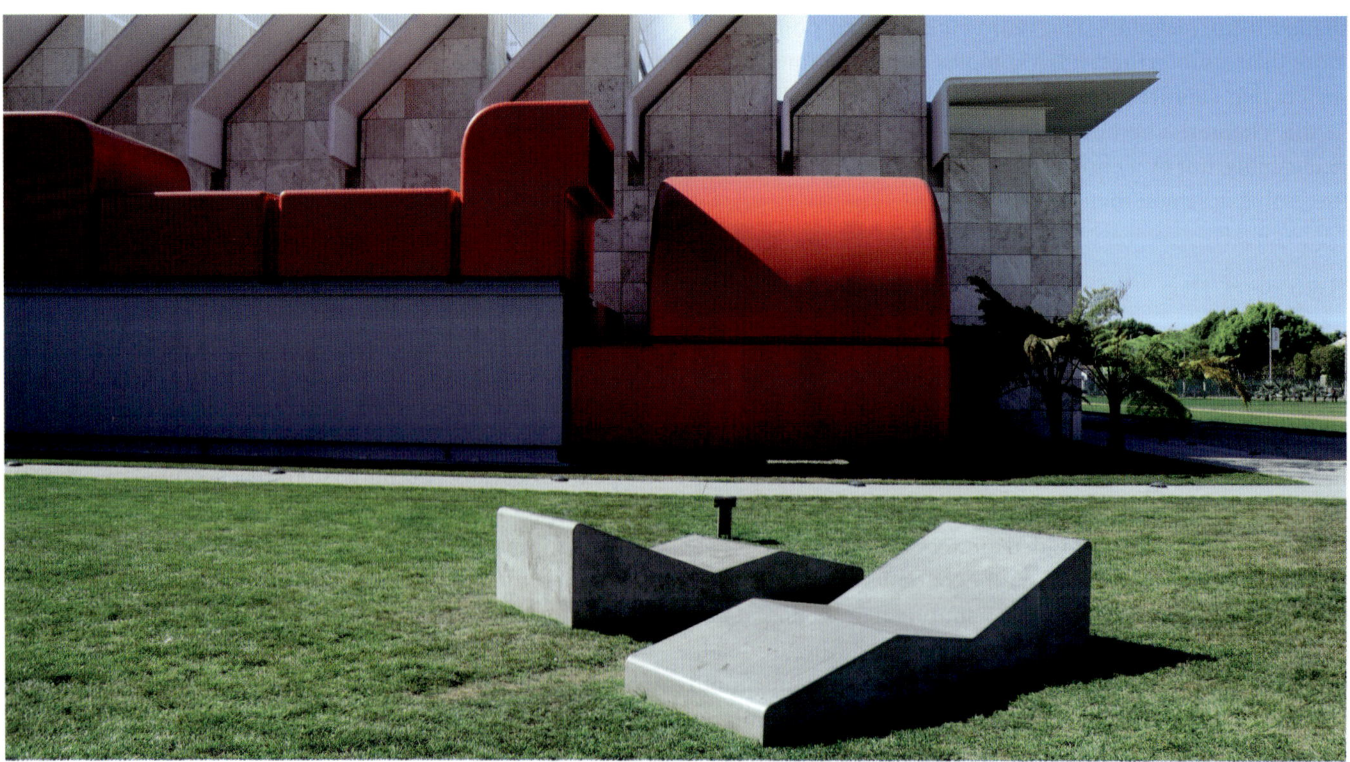

7.28 Teresa Margolles, ***Untitled***, 2010. Concrete and morgue water used during autopsy procedures. Shown installed at Los Angeles County Museum of Art. Courtesy of the artist and Y Gallery, New York.

in drug-related violence. Thus the restful function of the sculpture/furniture, essential to the project as she had conceived it in Mexico, was overlaid with the politics of the drug trade that embroils Southern California and Latin America.

Santiago Sierra

Santiago Sierra's (b. 1966) earliest work in Mexico City seems to have more to do with art history than the body or the political economy. In *Fardo de 1000 × 400 × 250 cm* (*1000 × 400 × 250 cm Bundle*) (1997) he strapped vast quantities of urban refuse to the outside of a gallery, suspending it above the sidewalk until complaints were raised. The emphasis on process, both gravitational and social, relates the work to Process and Conceptual art by sculptors such as Robert Smithson and Hans Haacke (see Chapter 1), while hanging garbage in public responds to more contemporary interests in abjection and waste. From work such as *Fardo*, Sierra focused his attention more clearly on social processes, passing over formal references in his work to concentrate on problems of poverty and the treatment of impoverished laborers in Mexico. In a seminal essay on contemporary Mexican art, performance artist and critic Coco Fusco praised Sierra and Margolles for turning away from aesthetics that made their work immediately legible to the international art community in favor of contextual specificity. As a result, Mexico City, Fusco declared, was now fostering art that risked incomprehension on the global stage in order to respond directly to its local environment.[25] Sierra's turn from form to labor was, to Fusco, evidence of this choice.

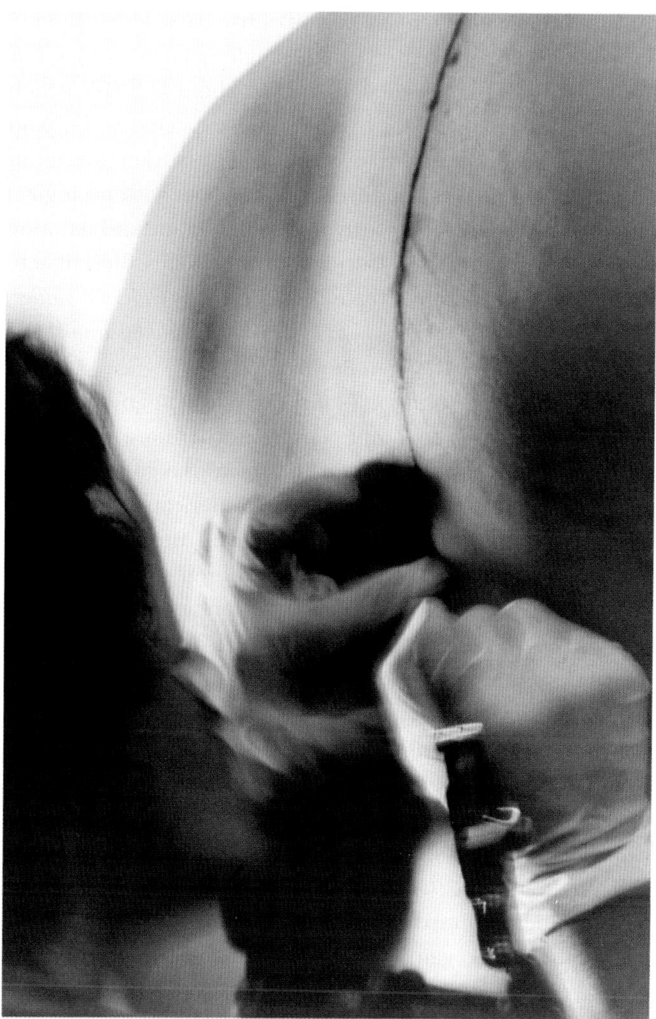

7.29 Santiago Sierra, ***Line of 30 cm Tattooed on a Remunerated Person***, 1998. Performance at 51 Regina Street, Mexico City, May 1998. Courtesy the artist and KOW, Berlin.

To put issues relating to wage labor in Mexico on view, Sierra hired people to work for him. He took apart his sink and paid someone to put it back together. A few months later, he created *Line of 30cm Tattooed on a Remunerated Person* (1998) (**fig. 7.29**). For this, Sierra found a person who had no tattoos or any plan to get one but who needed money. He then paid him $50 to have a vertical line tattooed on his back. Rather than conveying insights into personality, Sierra's manipulations of the human form tell us about the social status of the person and the economic difficulties of his or her community. In Old Havana, Cuba, Sierra paid six unemployed men to stand side by side and have a 250-cm line tattooed across their backs; in Salamanca, Spain, he paid four heroin-addicted prostitutes to have a 160-cm line tattooed across theirs. The Cubans were paid $30, the Spaniards with a shot of heroin. In each case the remuneration corresponded to an amount that was extravagant in its immediate geographic context but insufficient in the terms of Sierra's Western art audience. The sum of $30, for instance, may seem paltry to a viewer in New York who has paid $20 for museum admission to see photographs documenting the work, but in Cuba it was nearly the equivalent of a doctor's monthly salary. Not only do these works put need on display, they also reveal the discrepancy in quality of life and value of labor between the audiences and subjects of Sierra's work.

Sierra's display of people compelled by poverty to submit their bodies to his art has been viewed as a radical means of representing the desperation created by capitalism. Bodies are treated by the individuals to whom they belong as nothing more than a means to make money, and by the artist as a means to make a point—and, to skeptics, a career. Fusco notes that, in Mexico City, Sierra's critique appears quite pointed, focusing as it does "on economic exploitation, in which many educated Mexicans participate through their employment of servants and day laborers, rather than the political corruption, from which most Mexicans can distinguish themselves."[26] That Sierra's art was so site-specific—that is, that it was tied to the conditions of the working class in Mexico City or Old Havana—led Fusco to question whether travel would destroy the efficacy of his critique. Such concern over contextually specific work continues to be relevant for many twenty-first-century artists. In April 2000, in Mexico City, Sierra hired five of the thousands of day laborers who look for work every morning. He directed them to a gallery which had had one of its walls pulled away. Four of the men were instructed to support the now freestanding wall at an angle of 60 degrees for four hours a day across a period of five days. The fifth man was responsible for making sure the angle remained exact. For the week, each man earned 700 pesos, about U.S.$65, which is approximately what they would have expected to be paid if they had been hired by anyone else. The workers were put on view as they exerted effort for money, but with no logical or productive end. The clarity with which labor and its value were displayed attracted German curator Klaus Biesenbach, who invited Sierra to re-create the piece, *The Wall of a Gallery Pulled Out, Inclined 60 Degrees from the Ground and Sustained by 5 People* (2000) (**fig. 7.30**), in Berlin.

Performing *The Wall of a Gallery Pulled Out* in another location would have been simple enough. There are day laborers in every city and the Berlin Kunste-Werke gallery, unlike many of Sierra's Mexican and Latin American venues, had plenty of money to pay them. However, the Mexico City piece, by displaying the bodies of underemployed laborers in an expensive shopping district, responded to the specific economic and political concerns of Mexico City. Berlin was a very different context and demanded a different work. Sierra arrived in the city already familiar with Germany thanks to the time he had spent in Hamburg as a student in the late 1980s and early 1990s. In 2000, he concluded, the bodies most compromised by economic conditions in Berlin were Chechen immigrants fleeing war and civil unrest in Russia and emigrating to Germany in increasing numbers. Once in their new country, they were classed as illegal aliens: Hiring them was against the law, punishable by a fine for the employer and deportation for the worker. For the Kunst-Werke gallery, then, Sierra produced *Workers Who Cannot Be Paid, Remunerated to Remain Inside Cardboard Boxes* (2000), in which unidentified Chechen refugees were given money in exchange for hiding themselves in cardboard boxes for a specified period. Sierra described the resulting work as a collaboration between himself and the museum that addressed the specific economic and political situation in Berlin by enveloping the bodies, stripped of all signs of individuality, of those at the bottom of the capitalist ladder, victims of poverty and politics.

Sierra and Margolles bring us to a point at which the connection between body and self is not so much severed as rendered a point of debate. Both artists make it clear that the connection between the self and body is dependent on political and moral assumptions that are contextually determined. The bodies under observation here are so comprehensively commandeered by politics and economics as to become ill-suited to addressing issues of the self. It is the alienation of the body from the self that is therefore at issue. While most of the work discussed in this chapter enlists the body to delve deeper into nuances of the self, Margolles and Sierra leave us considering the ramifications of presuming a connection between self and body in societies that devalue both.

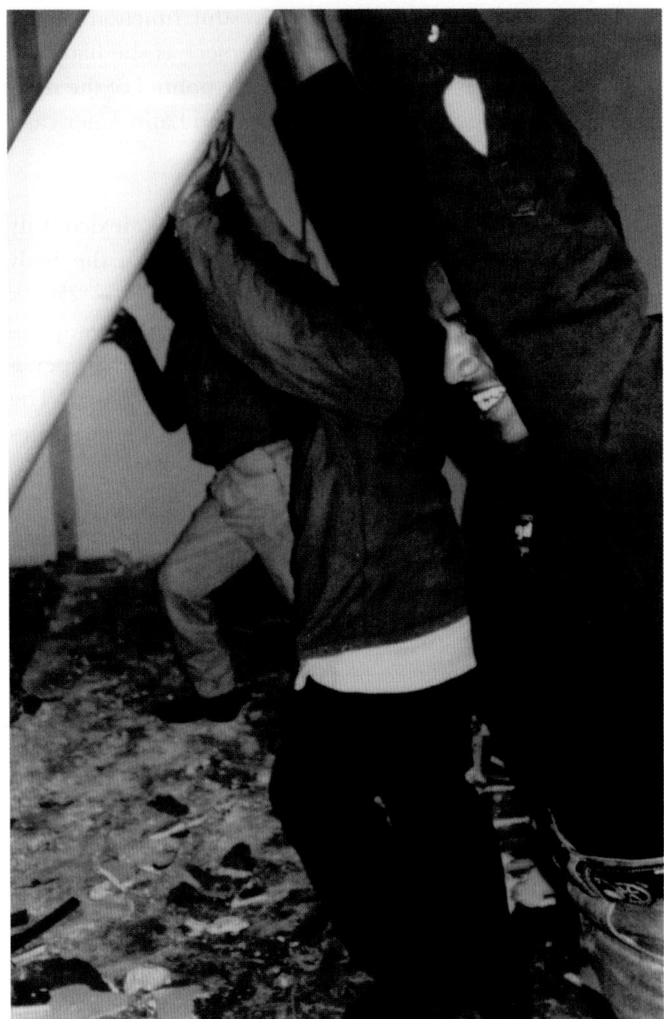

7.30 Santiago Sierra, *The Wall of a Gallery Pulled Out, Inclined 60 Degrees from the Ground and Sustained by 5 People*, 2000. Galería Acceso A, Mexico City, April 2000. Courtesy the artist and KOW, Berlin.

8

Eastward Expansion: Contemporary Art in Russia and China

By the mid-1980s, the world was getting a glimpse of a post-Cold War future. One could look at the reform policies of the Soviet Union and the increasing investment and privatization opportunities in China and see the beginnings of a world that was less and less structured around the binaries of East and West, Communist and capitalist. By the end of the decade, the Berlin Wall had come down, the Soviet Union was on the verge of collapse, and what has become known as the "global era" had begun. The defining feature of this new era was that the political divisions that had served as an obstacle to the global spread of capitalist investment and consumerism had, by and large, disappeared. There would now be McDonald's franchises in Moscow and U.S. corporations in Beijing, and there would also be Russian oil powering U.S. cars and Chinese labor manufacturing consumer goods for the whole world. With this increasingly fluid exchange of money, goods, and labor came cultural contacts that would have an equally profound impact on the art world. Artists were embroiled in these economic and political changes, often serving as witnesses to the profound social shifts at the end of the century as well as to the transformation of the very shape and meaning of their art. Dissident artists in the former Soviet Union who had previously exhibited their work only for an audience of close friends discovered that it was interpreted very differently in the context of an international exhibition. Likewise, a painting or sculpture shown to an art-starved audience under the watchful eyes of the authorities in Beijing held very different power when it was transported to a museum in Paris or a gallery in New York. Beginning with a discussion of the transformation of Russian and Chinese art during the fall of the U.S.S.R. and the strategic Westernization of the Chinese economy, Chapter 8 introduces a series of artists who have reflected upon the events and issues that have become the history of our global present. The next chapter will continue the discussion of artists from around the world who have reacted to globalization and its effects.

Russia

In the 1980s, the Cold War was ending, and with it the era defined by U.S.–Soviet antagonism and the threat of bilateral nuclear war drew to a close. The anxiety of Mutually Assured Destruction was giving way to the uncertainties of a new world order of unchecked capitalism. In 1985, under its new general secretary, Mikhail Gorbachev, the Communist Party of the Soviet Union initiated a set of economic reforms aimed at rebuilding the U.S.S.R.'s long-neglected infrastructure. Cultural reforms, including increased freedom for the press and culture more broadly, followed. Gorbachev hoped a more open society empowered by the policies of *perestroika* ("restructuring") and *glasnost* ("openness") would produce a more efficient government. The effects were exhilarating. Newspapers began to investigate all aspects of Soviet society, revealing individual accomplishments and exposing corruption. Laying bare the workings of the government, however, turned out to be politically costly. Gorbachev had opened Pandora's box—with unforeseen consequences for the U.S.S.R. and the rest of the world.

Both inside and beyond the Soviet borders, the political terrain changed dramatically. Now lacking both the economic resources and the military resolve it had once possessed, Moscow was no longer able to support or control its former allies. Cuba was struck particularly hard when the Soviet subsidies on which it had relied for decades stopped in the late 1980s: The island went into economic freefall. Despite the crisis, it remained committed to Communism. In this, it would be exceptional among Soviet satellite states. In Poland, the Solidarity movement led a successful challenge against the Communist government while other East European nations began to assert their independence from the Soviet Union. Individual Soviet republics began to call for independence. With the threat of dissolution looming, Gorbachev created and assumed the post of president, hoping in this way to circumvent challenges both from those inside the Communist Party seeking to roll back reforms and from nationalists seeking to disband the Soviet Union entirely. The move did not work and in August 1991 Gorbachev resigned. By the end of the year the U.S.S.R. had collapsed.

Perestroika and *glasnost* had a profound effect on the arts, transforming an active but previously sequestered Soviet avant-garde into players in the international art market. Art in the post-World War II Soviet Union had been characterized by a division between state-sponsored "official" art (Socialist Realism) and privately produced and exhibited "unofficial" art (often known as "apartment art," because it was largely displayed in private apartments). In many cases the artists making these works, official and unofficial, were the same. Unofficial art was created in moments of free time and shown only to small groups of friends who simultaneously acted as audience, critics, and collaborators. Throughout Moscow—the center for unofficial culture in these years—these groups supported a loose network of varied artistic activities. When the latter entered the Western market in the late 1980s, however, two styles came to the fore. The first was a conceptually based installation practice most widely seen in the works of Ilya Kabakov. The second was Sots Art, an appropriation-based painterly practice drawing on Socialist Realism, propaganda arts, Western Pop art, and advertising. Sots Art was introduced to the West through the work of the partnership of Vitaly Komar and Aleksandr Melamid, as well as by painters Alexander Kosolapov and Erik Bulatov.

In August 1988, the London-based auction house Sotheby's held a sale of contemporary Soviet Art in Moscow, placing the hitherto-insular artistic community firmly on the international stage. Sotheby's involvement accelerated the flow of collectors to the former Soviet Union and quickly imposed a hierarchy on the Russian artistic community based on Western prestige. The artists themselves began to travel abroad, many of them emigrating and starting to create work that responded to their new lives away from the former U.S.S.R. Though the excitement about and investment in Soviet art would lessen as the market discovered other Communist avant-gardes in Cuba and China, the Soviet and post-Soviet experience set the pattern for the integration of local art from around the world into the global market of the late-twentieth and early-twenty-first centuries.

Apartment Art: Ilya Kabakov

Ilya Kabakov (b. 1933) was the first of the unofficial Soviet artists to attain international prestige. He graduated in the 1950s from the Moscow Art School and the V.A. Surikov Art Academy—Moscow schools that taught artists to paint images showing national accomplishments in the state-sanctioned style—and began an official career as a children's book illustrator. Kabakov has described the academies as places where students and professors treated education as a chore, deadening to creativity but necessary for employment. As a student, he and a group of young artists including Erik Bulatov, Oleg Vassiliev, Ivan Chuikov, and Mikhail Mezhaninov provided their own unofficial education to supplement what the state was willing to give them. In addition to teaching themselves what they could about philosophy, poetry, and art, they discovered role models in a group of Modernist recluses, including Robert Falk (1886–1958), Vladimir Favorsky (1886–1964), and Artur Fonvizin (1882–1973), whose work fell out of favor as the propaganda needs of the Soviet government came to determine the success of Russian artists. Falk in particular, who had continued to paint

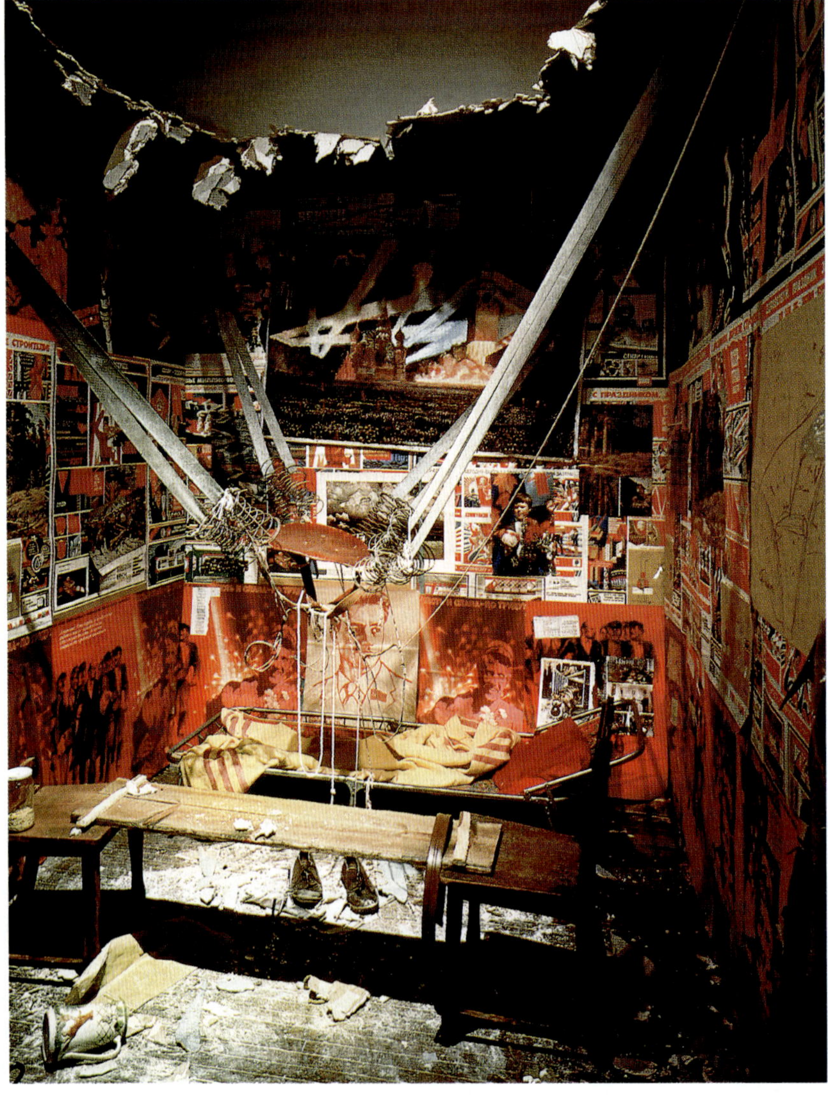

8.1 Ilya Kabakov, *The Man who Flew into Space from His Apartment*, 1985–89. Installation from ***Ten Characters*** series. Six poster panels with collage, furniture, clothing, catapult, household objects, wooden plank, scroll-type painting, two pages of Soviet paper, diorama. Room dimensions 8' × 7' 11" × 12' 3" (2.44 × 2.41 × 3.7 m). Courtesy Centre Pompidou.

Postimpressionist-inspired still lifes, landscapes, and figure studies, appeared radical in his disregard for state-sanctioned art. His commitment to being irrelevant to a system that had rejected him proved inspirational. Kabakov and his peers concluded that their work should be equally removed from anything approaching Soviet definitions of art: Their art would be "non-art."

Kabakov's earliest unofficial activities included creating albums of drawings and paintings that mingle the minutiae of daily life with the fantasies of imagined Muscovites. The collision of fantasy and mundane reality in his work was rooted in life in the shared apartments of Soviet-era Moscow, which by the mid-1980s had also become the locus of privately hosted exhibitions. "[A] person living in a Russian communal apartment," Kabakov later commented, "is charred, burned from all sides in this social communal body, and he dreams not only of a social project where we will all be happy, but he also dreams of having his own individual project where he will build something for himself."[1] This interest in the individual as dreamer and actor would become the foundation for the complex installations that define Kabakov's mature work.

In 1988, Kabakov came to New York to present *Ten Characters* (1985–88), a series of single-room installations detailing the lives and dreams of "The Man Who Collected the Opinions of Others," "The Man Who Flew into Space from His Apartment," "The Collector," "The Composer," and six other characters. Kabakov had begun work on the project in the early 1970s, and by the 1980s had constructed entire scenarios in his own apartment. *The Man Who Flew into Space from His Apartment* (**fig. 8.1**) centers on a homemade spring-released contraption which has seemingly propelled its creator out of his bedroom and up into space. When installed in Moscow, Kabakov's scene spoke to the lives of the many Russians seeking to carve a portal to another existence out of their few moments of private time and tiny amounts of personal space. In that context, the work offered a poignant commentary on the personal cost of Soviet utopianism. Taking *Ten Characters* out of Russia changed the work, however. On the one hand, the series could now be presented together, imitating the communal apartments of Moscow rather than actually occupying one. More significantly, in New York, the sense of intimacy that had been so evident when the work was viewed in Kabakov's home was lost. Seen in Moscow, the boundary between art and life was blurred; living space and sculpture merged into one another. Framed by a New York gallery, however, *Ten Characters* was Art. The question now became whether it was representational or allegorical, both artistic means that create distance between art and life. Such a transformation seemed to run counter to Kabakov's entire artistic project. He had opposed such distinctions in favor of "non-art" which rejected the obligation either to reflect or to reject reality. His work was to be "an action in life itself," "formless" and "inseparable from life."[2] The experience of watching his installations ossify into art might therefore have proven traumatic, but instead his success in New York demonstrated the flexibility and even the universality of *Ten Characters*. Kabakov would henceforth develop this open quality in his work, letting the Soviet elements recede and new ones, often specific to the new contexts, come to the fore.

In the Soviet context, *The Man Who Flew into His Picture* (sketch **fig. 8.2**), another of the *Ten Characters*, which shows the supernatural absorption of a man into his art, might be interpreted as a melancholic reflection on a figure like Falk, isolated and consumed by his painting. When Kabakov met Falk, the older artist was almost entirely dependent on his wife and his paintings to be able to communicate with his guests. In the installation, Kabakov's Man takes refuge in his art to such a degree that he is physically transported into his painting. The room is small and divided diagonally by a wall supporting a large white panel. In front of this panel—the picture mentioned in the title—sits an unoccupied wooden library chair, behind which documents labeled "communication" and "voices" hang in frames or are filed on shelves. In these accompanying texts Kabakov tells us how the Man stared at the white canvas until he finally drew a very small figure on it. As the Man then stared at the drawing—a self-portrait visible in the installation—he became the image and traveled through the field of white into "infinite" and "blinding" depth. The unification of the man and his art, however, is matched by his alienation from it. Kabakov explains: "At

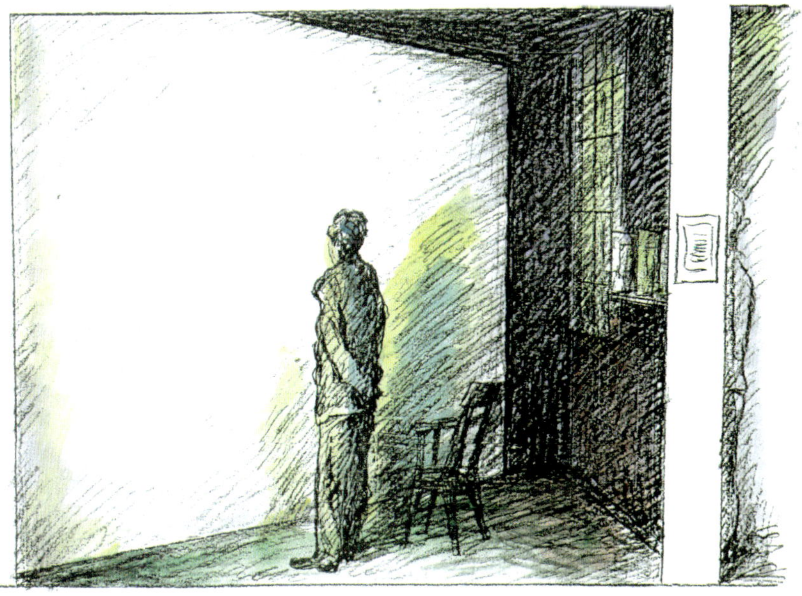

8.2 Ilya Kabakov, *The Man who Flew into His Picture*, 1988. Watercolor, lead pencil, ballpoint pen on paper, 10⅛ × 11¼" (25.5 × 28.6 cm). Collection of the artist. Courtesy the artist.

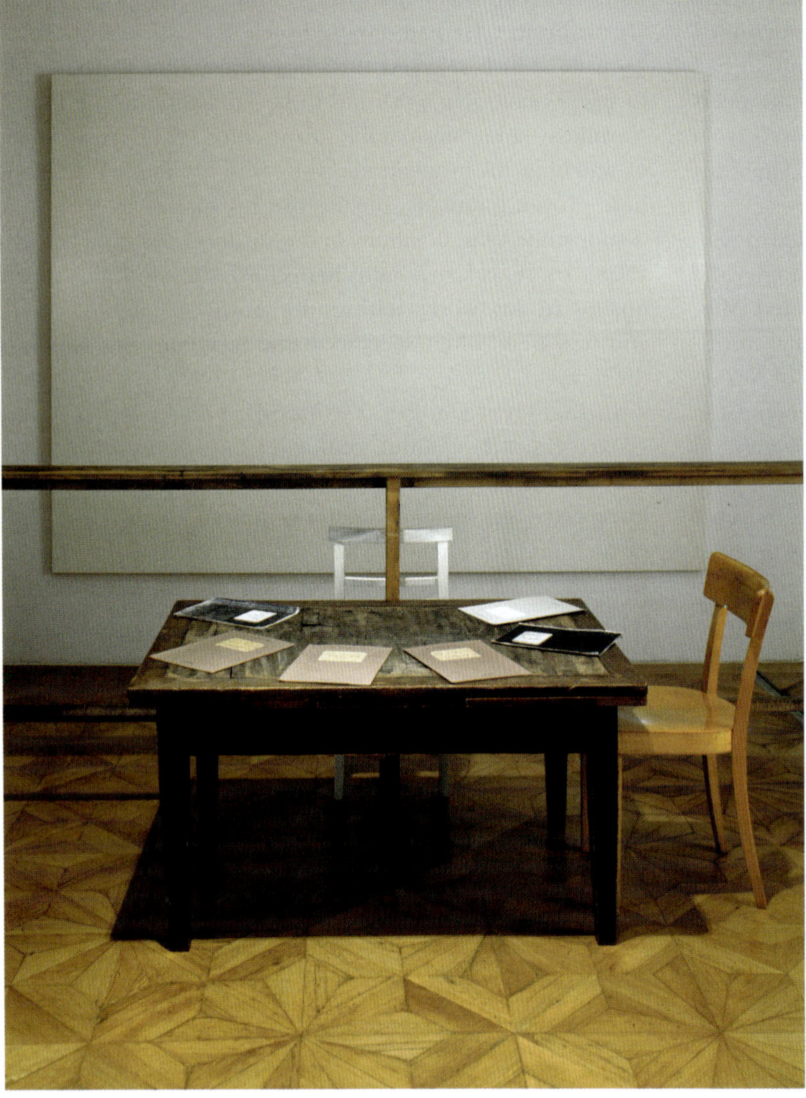

8.3 Ilya Kabakov, *The Man who Flew into His Picture,* 1989. Mixed media. Installation at the Sigmund Freud Museum, Vienna, 1989.

the same time that he is moving with all his soul and is following the departing figure, in a strange way understanding that he is also going there himself, the other half of his consciousness clearly realizes that he is sitting completely immobile in his lonely room, sitting alone in front of an enormous, poorly painted white board."[3]

In 1989, Kabakov re-created *The Man Who Flew into His Picture* for the Sigmund Freud Museum in Vienna (**fig. 8.3**), changing the work to fit its new context. Instead of reconstructing the room, as he had done in New York, Kabakov made Freud's apartment—the location of the museum—the setting. As the context of the work changed from a Soviet communal apartment to the birthplace of modern psychoanalysis, different aspects of the piece took center stage. In the last paragraphs of the Man's story, he pleads for a witness to his journeys into the picture. A silent companion, he believes, will help him stay sane. In Russia, that guest might be a fellow artist, in New York an art critic or collector, but at the Freud Museum one imagines a psychoanalyst. Here medical advice rather than friendship or fame will help the Man. There were other changes, too. Though the five basic elements outlined in Kabakov's 1988 design for the *Ten Characters* installation remained, there was an additional one in the new installation: With no wall to hang from, the texts now rested on a table that, with accompanying chairs, belonged to a family who had occupied Freud's home after the Nazis forced him to leave Vienna in 1938. Kabakov thereby transformed *The Man Who Flew into His Picture* from a meditation on the plight of artists in Soviet Russia into an essay about the relationship of the individual to major developments in modern European intellectual and political history.

Ten Characters demonstrates Kabakov's agility in orchestrating multiple layered narratives and his sensitivity to their changing connotations. Such concerns fit well with the increasing skepticism toward master narratives and unified truths expressed in the Postmodern theorizing of the likes of Michel Foucault, Laura Mulvey, and Jean Baudrillard (see Chapters 1, 2, and 5). As Soviet work of the 1980s was exhibited in the West late in that decade and into the early 1990s, its attention to modes of expression and means of representation, to style as much as if not more than content, drew comparison to appropriation art and the Western criticism that supported it.[4] As Kabakov explained in 1995, several strands of unofficial art in the Soviet Union rebelled against the univocal authority of Soviet official culture, but not all of them would appear valuable to the West. Kabakov's art and the Sots Art discussed below manipulated and broke apart the stories and styles of Soviet history and culture to create an art rooted in the experience of daily life. Such strategies of appropriation and manipulation were clearly consistent with forms of contemporary European and U.S. art and art theory.

Sots Art: Kosolapov, Komar and Melamid, and Bulatov

While Kabakov rejected official art to create non-art, Sots artists, including his friend and fellow illustrator Erik Bulatov, challenged official art from within. Sots Art, a name invented by Komar and Melamid from the elements of "Socialist Pop Art," was based on the bold graphic style of state propaganda and the heroic figuration of Socialist Realism, the official Soviet painting style. The latter accented clear compositions that foregrounded assertive human actors in readily understood narratives that conformed to the political content promoted by the government. Every country had its own form of nationalist realism, rooted in the styles of the 1930s, though the degree to which national leaders were lionized by the style was far greater in the Communist East than the capitalist West. Nonetheless, *Three Soldiers* (1982–84) by Frederick Hart, erected in tandem with Maya Lin's *Vietnam Veterans Memorial* (see figs. 6.1–6.3), provides a populist Western counterpart to the Communist Socialist Realism so objectionable to the Soviet avant-garde.

Sots paintings such as Alexander Kosolapov's (b. 1943) *Manifesto* (1983) (**fig. 8.4**) neutralized the power of official imagery by separating the icons of Soviet power from their ideological functions, creating a distance between artistic form and its state-sanctioned meanings. In Sots Art, the appearance of heroic figures such as Marx and Lenin or monumental Soviet landscapes ceased to convey messages about national stability and power. In *Manifesto*, a colossal bust of Lenin depicted in rich tones of red with black shadows rests on a plinth next to a toppled Classical column. In the foreground, three cherubs relax among flowers and curiously examine a piece of newsprint with the words "The Manifesto" across its top. Mixing ancient and modern was a familiar device in Socialist Realism, used to imbue the events of the present with the glamorous aura of history. In Kosolapov's image, however, the flow of time is disrupted. The age of the ancients has come to an end and been replaced by that of the Communists, but they too have fallen and the cherubs have returned from a mythical past to muse over the ruins of modernity. All of history has turned to rubble in this arcadia, and past and present, utopia and reality, have been folded over one another. Margarita Tupitsyn, curator of several U.S. exhibitions of Sots Art in the 1980s, noted: "Its critical importance lay in the fact that the Sots artists proposed to view Socialist Realism not as mere kitsch or as simply a vehicle for bureaucratic manipulation and state propaganda, but as a rich field of stereotypes and myths which they could transform into a new contemporary language, one able to deconstruct official myths on their own terms."[5] Kosolapov assembled the symbols of Soviet ideology, the style of Soviet propaganda, and the narratives of Neo-Classical art in such a

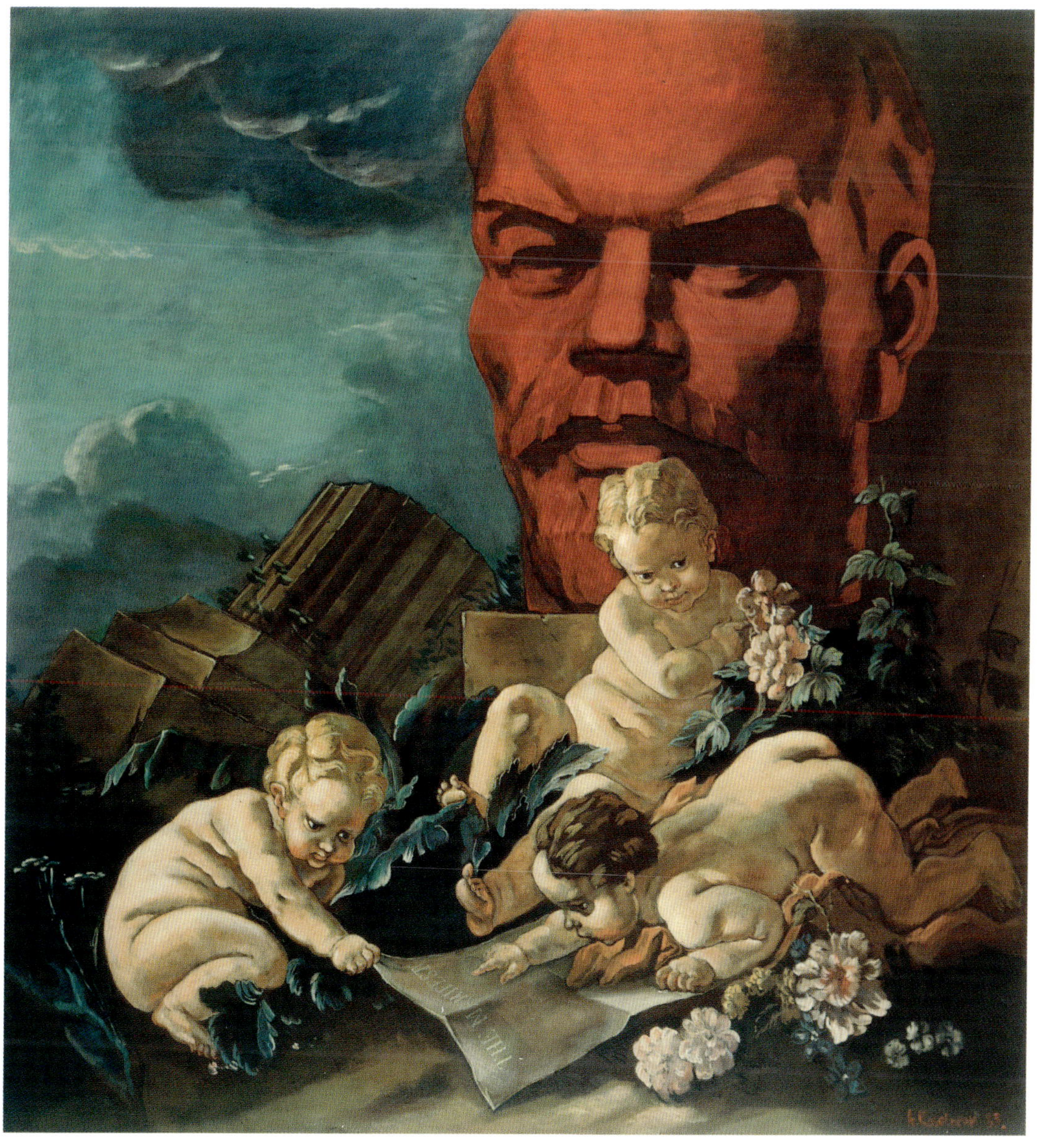

8.4 Alexander Kosolapov, *Manifesto*, 1983. Oil on canvas, 76 × 72" (193 × 182.8 cm). Image courtesy the artist.

way that the past envelops the future that Communism promised. In this way, *Manifesto* not only challenges the promise of Marx and Engels's *Communist Manifesto,* but all later Modernist proclamations that history is an inevitable progressive march toward a utopian future.

Kosolapov painted *Manifesto* in New York. By the 1980s, few of the Sots artists remained in the U.S.S.R. The Soviet authorities as well as art historians recognized their manipulations of the language of power as political critique and made it difficult for such unofficial artists to show their work, leaving this new avant-garde with only the apartments of their friends as exhibition spaces. Moreover, Soviet officials threatened the more outspoken artists with deportation and destroyed their art. The government did, however, permit many artists to obtain exit visas. Emigrating first to Israel and then to the U.S., Vitaly Komar (b. 1943) and Aleksandr Melamid (b. 1945), the instigators of the movement in 1970s Moscow, became its stars in exile in the 1980s. Their images presented Western audiences with visions of the Soviet experiment that were full of humor, irony, longing, and tragedy, bound up in elaborately crafted allegorical narratives, and painted in their variation on the official Socialist Realist style. *The Origin of Socialist Realism* (1982–83) (**fig. 8.5**) recasts the Neo-Classical topos of the birth of painting in which a maiden traces the shadow of her sleeping lover on the wall. Komar and Melamid's version takes place in richly appointed chambers where the muse of Socialist Realism traces the silhouette of an alert and carefully posed Joseph Stalin. In the U.S.S.R., the painting argues, Socialist Realism was only ever about expressing Soviet power, not socialist reality.

The most prominent of the artists to stay in Moscow was Erik Bulatov (b. 1933). His *Danger* (1972–73), a sly juxtaposition of "danger" signs and a bucolic scene painted in a Socialist Realist style, conveys a sense of urgency by disrupting an image of a peaceful picnic with threatening text and by refusing to indicate either the source of the danger or the steps we might take to nullify it. Are the picnicking pair under threat, or are they the threat itself? In either case, a scene that should evoke calm has been turned upside down. In the later *Perestroika* (1989) (**fig. 8.6**), Bulatov again combined representational imagery and text to unsettling effect, transforming the word *perestroika* (which, as stated above, means literally "restructuring") into a great pyramid, silhouetted against a dramatic sky. Strong male hands hold the central letters aloft and lock them together to produce the shape of a hammer and sickle, the Communist symbol used on the flag of the Soviet Union. The word is made monumental—but what this means is pointedly unclear. One can see in the stylization of the text and its integration with the classic symbol of Soviet power a linking of the reformed present with the unreformed past. This connection could be read as a critique, suggesting that Gorbachev's reforms were simply more of the same: Such a message, dispelling claims of Soviet progress, would be in keeping with other Sots works such as *Manifesto.* However, in 1989, many members of

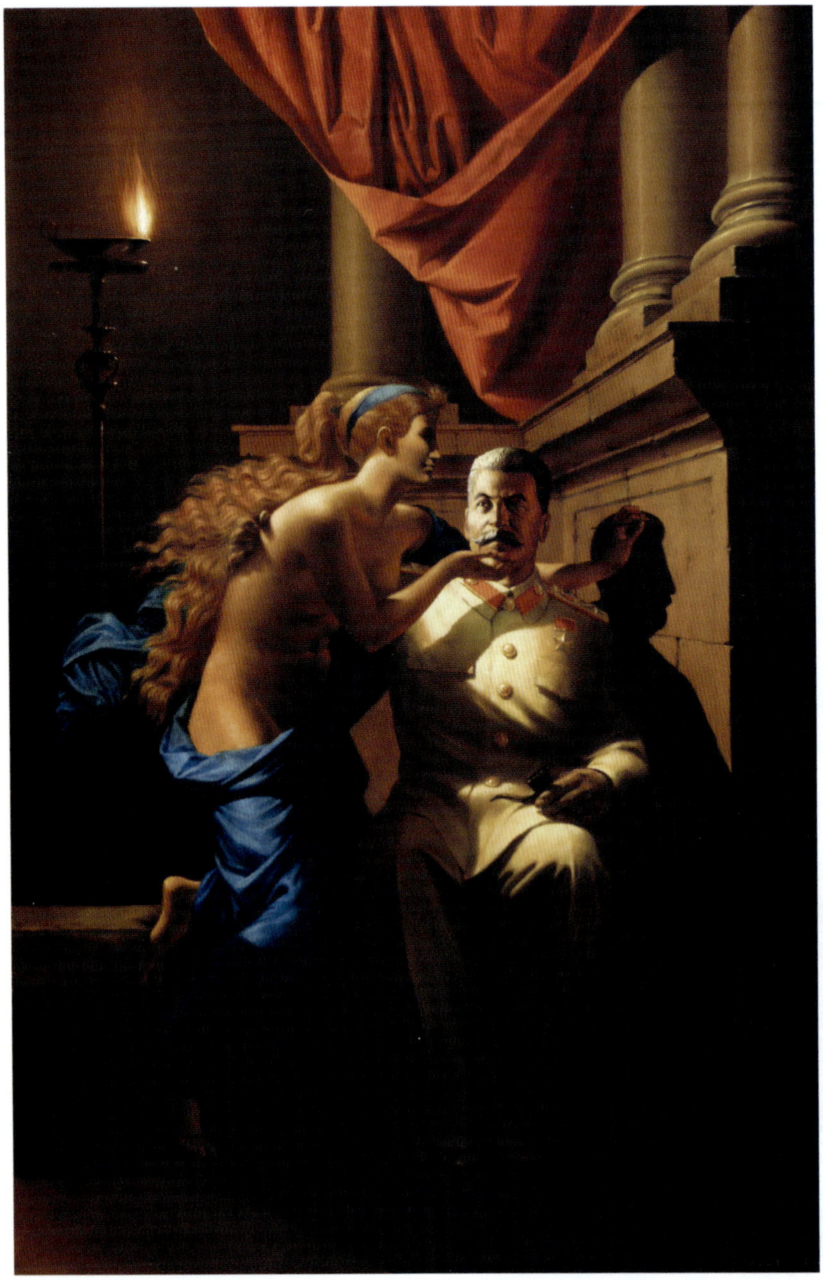

8.5 Vitaly Komar and Aleksandr Melamid, *Origin of Socialist Realism*, 1982–83. Oil on canvas, 72 × 48" (182.88 × 121.92 cm). Courtesy Ronald Feldman Fine Arts, New York.

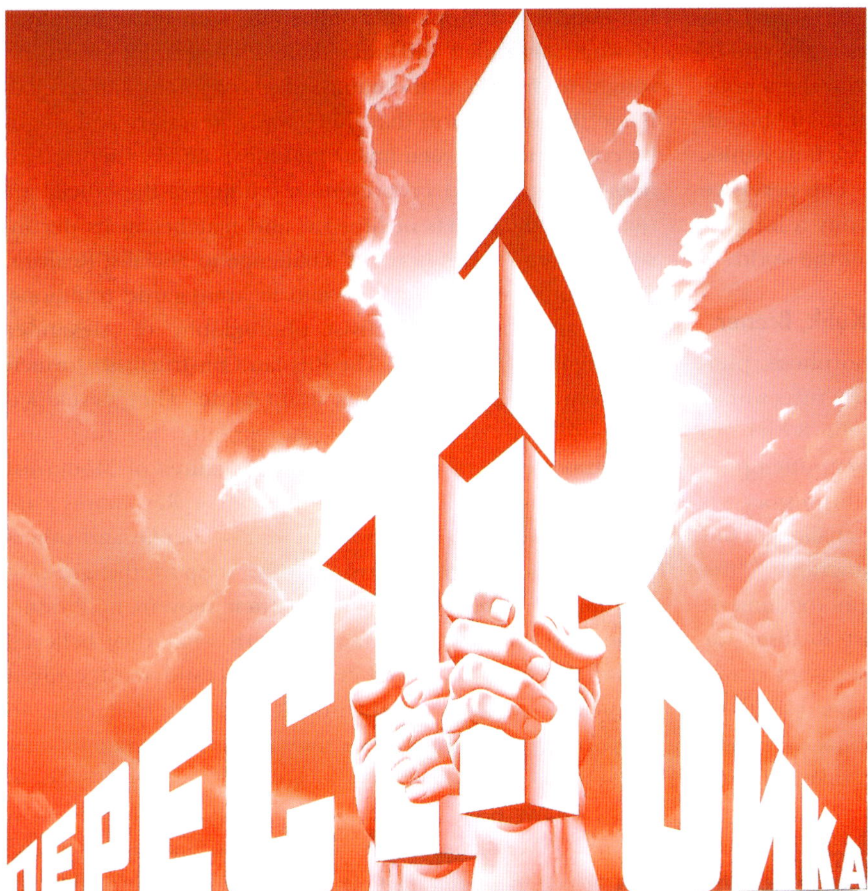

8.6 Erik Bulatov, *Perestroika*, 1989. Oil on canvas, $105\frac{7}{8} \times 107\frac{7}{8}$" (269 × 274 cm).

the Communist Party were looking to *perestroika* as a means of guiding the nation into a brighter, better future. In this case, a connection to the heroic Communist past would be a symbol of fidelity to Soviet ideals. Bulatov's *Perestroika* thus uses the materials of "official" Soviet culture to reach ambiguous conclusions.

As they became more immersed in Western capitalism, Russian artists incorporated Western icons into Sots-style work. Pop art, a style that symbolized capitalist society just as Socialist Realism stood for Soviet power, took on special importance. In the 1980s, Kosolapov developed a series of images that juxtapose icons and logos of East and West. On the left-hand side of *Symbols of the Century* (1982) (**fig. 8.7**) is the head of Lenin, familiar from Communist propaganda, shown facing a Coca-Cola logo that floats on the right. Below the logo is the catchphrase associated with the drink, "It's the real thing," and below that the name "Lenin." Beyond the joke of a Marxist revolutionary selling Coke, *Symbols of the Century* is a poignant expression of the degree to which the idealism of Communism is underwritten by the reality of capitalism. But, the painting also suggests that the reality of free-market capitalism is not so different from that of state-controlled Communist economies; one's options are limited to the choices provided by those in power. The artist's intentions for the work, however, were at least as much autobiographical as they were critical. He explained: "When I was a little boy, the first exhibition of American industry was held in Moscow. Every visitor to the exhibition was served Coke or Pepsi, symbols of the American Paradise for every Soviet person."[6] When he immigrated to the U.S., however, Kosolapov discovered that "Coca Cola was really only a sweet beverage, sometime, though not often, pleasant to drink." This realization that in daily experience the symbol of paradise was, at best, rather mundane paralleled his earlier disappointment about the reality of "the 'paradise' that operated under the sign of

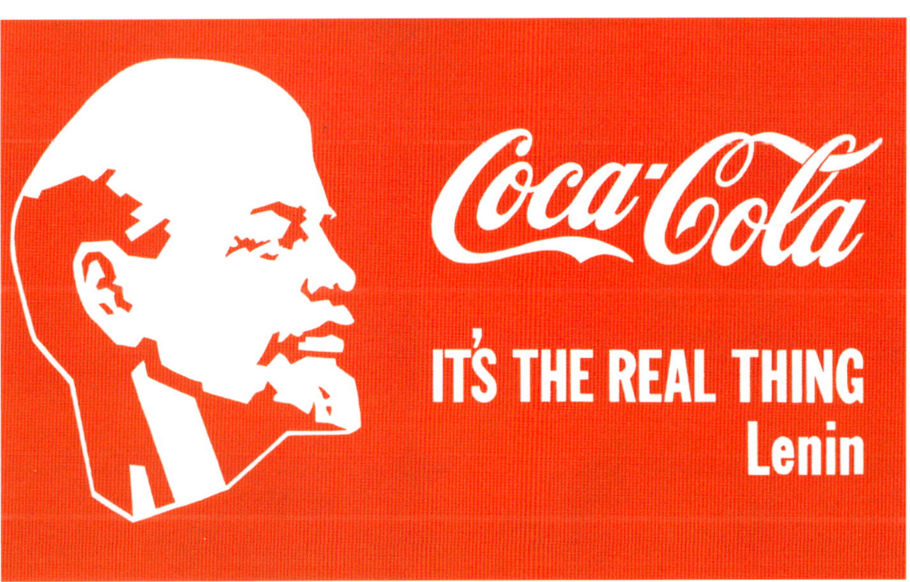

8.7 Alexander Kosolapov, *Symbols of the Century*, 1982. Acrylic on canvas, 72 × 40" (182.88 × 101.6 cm). Image courtesy the artist.

Lenin." The work, taking the images of Lenin and Coca-Cola as a concise means to represent the adversaries at the end of the Cold War, also uses icons and logos to write the autobiography of the artist in a fashion not dissimilar to the brand-conscious compositions of commodity artists such as Ashley Bickerton and Sylvie Fleury (see Chapter 5). The pervasive influence of capitalism rendered the commodity a form of artistic communication that was relevant all over the world.

Photography and Performance: Moukhin, Kulik, Brener

As the Communist world underwent a metamorphosis, photography and performance art came to play new roles within it. Photography had been used throughout the Soviet era to forward party politics. Now, photographers attempted to disentangle their medium of choice from this history. Of course, painters and sculptors faced a similar challenge, but the greater truth claims associated with photography ("the camera never lies") complicated the issue for photographers. Unofficial painters had condemned Socialist Realism for being ideologically complicit with Soviet power, but it was the particular style, not painting itself, that was critiqued. For photographers, the situation was more extreme: It was their medium, rather than any particular style, that had been crucial to state power.

During the period of the Soviet collapse and the rise of an independent Russia, Igor Moukhin (b. 1961) created the series *Last Soviet Monumental Art* (1992) (**fig. 8.8**), which presents fragmented views of public monuments erected to celebrate the strength of Soviet society. Paint peels from the torsos of agile youths, patinas crack, and sculpted bodies collapse under the weight of neglect. Moukhin's photographs can be readily interpreted as companion pieces to Kosolapov's *Manifesto*. The demise of the Soviet empire, however, is not Moukhin's only story. With other members of what was called the Immediate Photography group, he sought to investigate the nature of photography and to challenge the assumption that there was a necessary and singular connection between image and meaning. As a series, *Last Soviet Monumental Art* represents a critique of the official art that filled the streets of Moscow and matches in its deconstructive urge the Sots artists' challenge to Socialist Realism. The photographer also took aim at avant-garde traditions, specifically the Constructivist photography of Alexander Rodchenko (1891–1956). The Russian Constructivists formed the heart of the early Soviet avant-garde. They developed compositional strategies for photography, painting, and sculpture based on the plans and structures of Modernist architects and engineers. As the Russian Revolution consolidated itself into the Soviet state, Rodchenko and others oriented their Constructivist style to support the growing Communist society and renamed their movement Productivism, producing art in tandem with what they believed to be the most advanced technologies and most evolved political science. It was this ideological turn that came to concern contemporary artists such as Moukhin. Rather than being praised as an artist who applied cutting-edge art to revolutionary politics, Rodchenko is held accountable here for using Modernist forms to promote Stalinist policies.[7] *Last Soviet Monumental Art* features a collection of oblique-angled and fractured compositions that mimic Rodchenko's style. Moscow critic and curator Yekaterina Dyogot has noted that Moukhin enlisted the abstractions the earlier photographer discovered in the radio towers, athletes, and engineering projects of Soviet society to document its demise. In Moukhin's photographs, the Socialist Realist style of the decaying monuments no longer communicates state power,

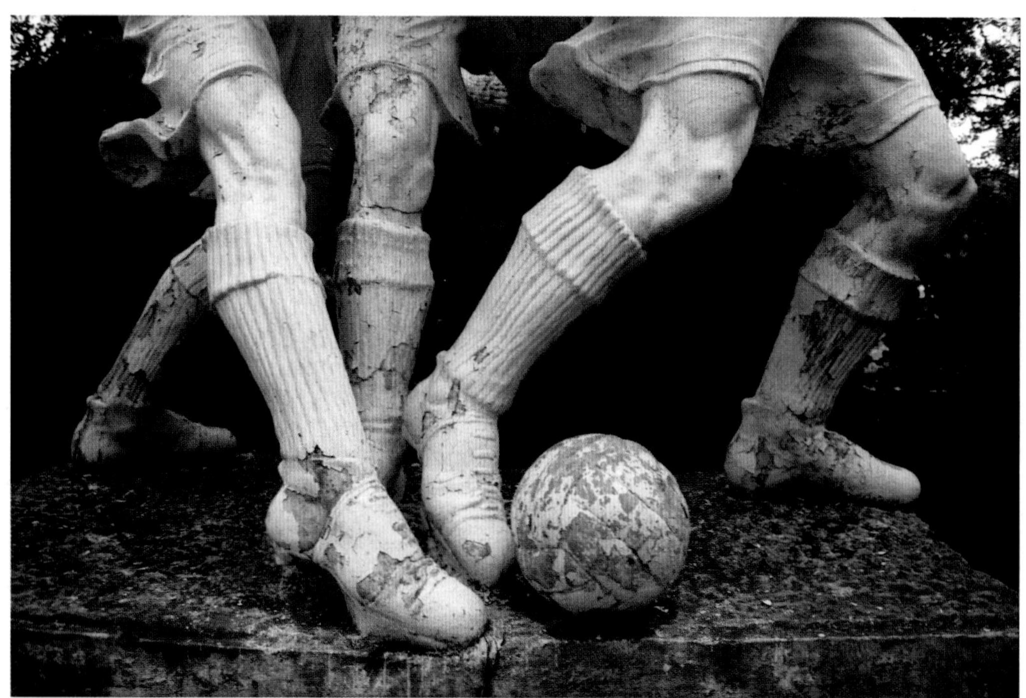

8.8 Igor Moukhin, ***"Footballers,"*** from ***Last Soviet Monumental Art***, 1992. Black and white photograph, Zheleznovodsk, Russia. Image courtesy the artist.

and the Constructivist Modernism of Rodchenko no longer conveys progress. Deconstructing both the avant-garde and official state art in the same image, Moukhin produces an uncomfortable equation in which meaning and style are joined by politics alone.

The Russian art market flourished between the Sotheby's sale in 1988 and the first years of the post-Soviet era. A number of new Muscovite galleries opened, selling Russian art not only to Westerners, but also to individual and corporate Russian collectors who were also investing in Western work. By 1993, however, with the nation undergoing a series of political and financial crises, the market had flattened out. In 1994, President Boris Yeltsin dissolved parliament and curtailed free speech. Meanwhile, oil companies and organized crime bosses accumulated vast fortunes: It became clear that Westernization was not an antidote to corruption. The generation of artists now coming of age confronted the uncertain domestic political situation, but also looked abroad with a far more comprehensive understanding of the West than their predecessors. If Moukhin's photographs exhibit a contemplative analysis of the history of Russian art and the status of Russian society, the performance art of Oleg Kulik (b. 1961) and Alexander Brener (b. 1957) reveals a more belligerent side of 1990s Russian art.

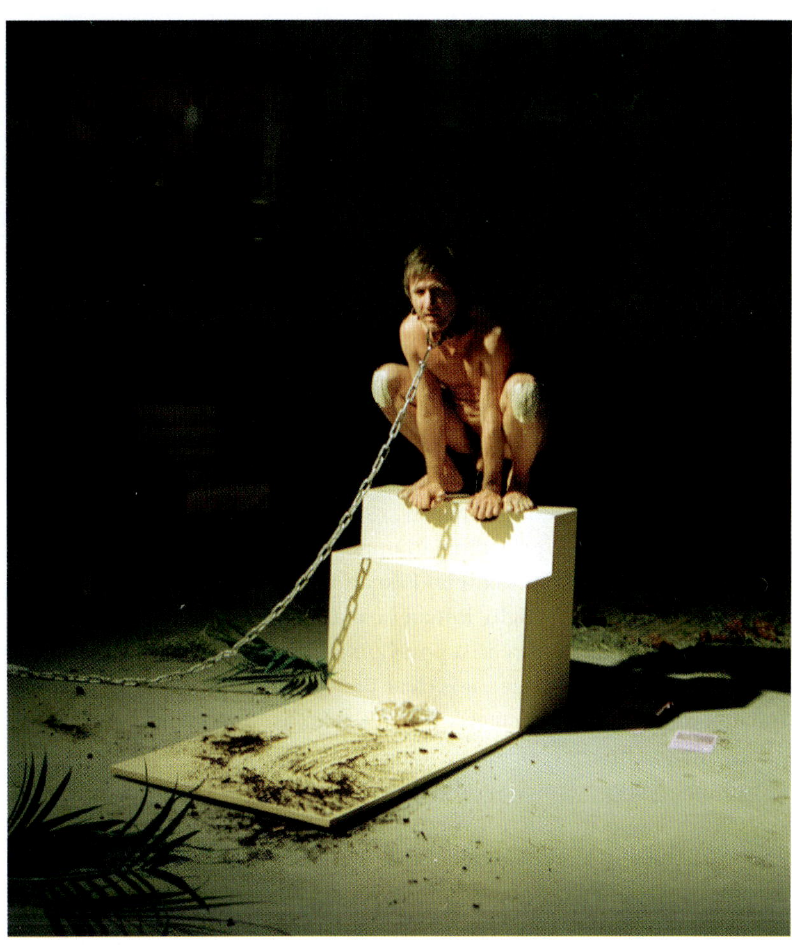

8.9 Oleg Kulik, *Dog House*, 1996. Performance at the "Interpol" exhibition, Center for Contemporary Art and Architecture, Stockholm. Courtesy Regina Gallery.

Performance art was popular among Russian artists in the 1990s because it permitted expressions of a kind that seemed to match the extremity of their situation while resisting the Western market—because there was no end product to sell—that had so rapidly consumed the work of the earlier generation. The history of unofficial art in Moscow also included several precedents for this turn to performance including the work of the Collective Actions group. Active from the mid-1970s and recently representing Russia at the 54th Venice Biennale in 2011, this group staged events for audiences of collaborators and friends in a spirit similar to the exhibitions of apartment art occurring at the same time. For one such performance, *Appearance* (1976), Collective Actions invited an audience to come at a given time to a field, where they were given a certificate acknowledging their attendance. For *Gazing at the Waterfall* (1981), a group was brought to a snowy field where a performer ran about before finally coming to a standstill. The path of the running man formed the image of a fifteenth-century Chinese painting for which the event was named. Such poetic and humorous, if somewhat oblique, assertions of artists' and audiences' rights to meet where they liked and to define art as they chose were accompanied by other Moscow performances of a more explicitly political nature. Sergei Mironenko's (b. 1959) 1988 satiric campaign for the presidency of the U.S.S.R. falls into this latter category. Taking advantage of a relaxation of censorship, Mironenko posted campaign posters for himself, boldly brandishing the slogan "Bastards! What Have They Turned This Country Into!" Kulik and Brener's brand of performance adopts this more abrasive attitude.

Oleg Kulik became infamous in the second half of the 1990s for being walked as a dog around Moscow and other cities by his wife and "keeper," Mila Bredikhina. He often presented himself chained or caged in galleries and museums, and on more than one occasion defended himself against visitors who came too close (**fig. 8.9**). Kulik's first canine performances featured the artist lunging and barking, expressing the violence and corruption that was coming to dominate Russian society. His performances presented Russian life as being in a state of decay, reinforcing the sense of desperation felt by many Russians, but also mimicking how the country appeared in the eyes of the West. "When Independent Russia became open, Western illusions about it disappeared—we became a malign[ed], loveless creature, like a mad dog," Kulik explained.[8] Rather than simply ignoring such chauvinism, Kulik embraced the stereotype. Though the sensationalism of his performances conveys the hyperbolic and anxious character of post-1991 Russia, the descent to the status of a canine was a path Kulik found relevant to all of society.[9] "For me, human stopped being associated with the notions 'alive,' 'feeling,' and 'understanding' and started to be associated with the notions 'artificial' and 'dangerous,'" he wrote.[10] The animal world, he felt, offered the opportunity to experience the world more directly: He became a dog in order to communicate from the position of an authentic animal rather than an artificial human.

Western audiences were able to view Kulik's dog as well as Alexander Brener's confrontational style of performance in a controversial exhibition, "Interpol," held at the Center of Contemporary Art, Stockholm, in 1996. The show was conceived as providing an opportunity for artistic collaborations between East and West European artists who might initiate a dialogue about international culture in a post-Communist age. Though accounts differ, it is clear that these collaborations failed to materialize and that, as guests arrived for the opening, "Interpol" was indistinguishable from any other international survey exhibition in which invited artists deposited works already completed elsewhere or were assigned spaces in which to create their discrete contributions. Kulik had arrived as a dog and found himself in a highly compromised position. His art was based on its distance from the conventional means of creating and presenting art, but here he was trapped in a conventional exhibit, isolated and displayed for the edification and entertainment of the viewer. Possessing the artist's desire to communicate, but limited to a dog's means of communication, Kulik became what any neglected and confined animal becomes: desperate and violent. Like Kabakov's protagonist in *The Man Who Flew into His Picture*, both slipping away and self-aware, Kulik recognized what was happening and tried to stop it. He put up signs in his space to warn visitors of the danger. When one ignored the sign to get a closer look, Kulik bit him. The artist was arrested and the intruding visitor was taken to hospital.

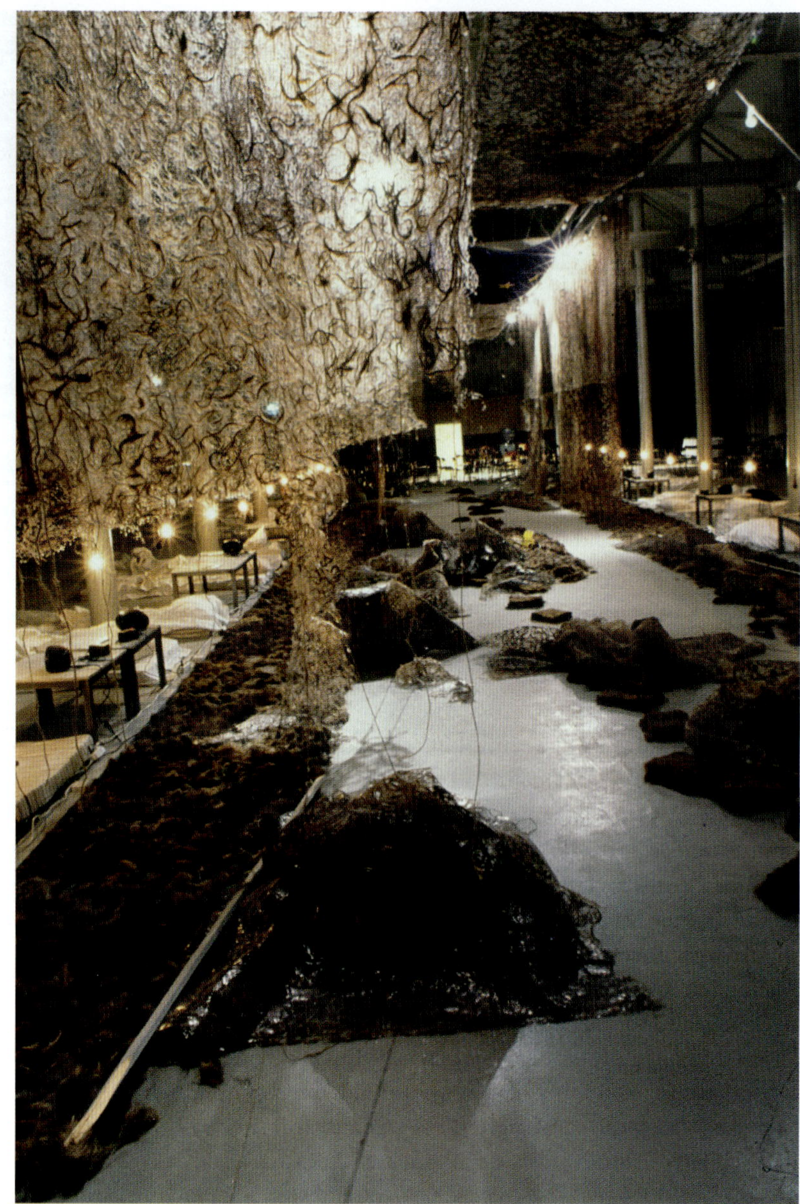

8.10 Wenda Gu, ***united nations—sweden & russia monument: interpol***, 1996. Site-specific installation showing damage done by Alexander Brener, 1996, at the "Interpol" exhibition, Center for Contemporary Art and Architecture, Stockholm. Swedish hair tunnel measuring 84' (25.6 m), a rocket from the Swedish royal airforce, and the European Community flag. Image courtesy the artist.

Kulik and Brener had voiced concern in the weeks and months before "Interpol" opened that the exhibition was failing to develop its announced collaborative structure. Brener characterized the turn of events as a dangerous shift from artistic process to art objects: This change appeared to echo the transformation of the unofficial Soviet artists in the late 1980s from dissidents into producers of luxury goods for the Western market. At the show's opening, therefore, Brener decided to force the idea of process back into the exhibition. Collaborating in the other artists' projects at this point, after the works had been completed, necessarily meant destroying them as they had originally been conceived and executed. Brener decided to make this fact explicit. He singled out Wenda Gu's *united nations—sweden & russia monument: interpol* (1996) (**fig. 8.10**), a large corridor made of human hair. After playing a solo on a drum kit he had set up in the galleries, Brener attacked Gu's piece, tearing it from its tethers on the ceiling and reducing it to formless heaps. The work was part of a larger project for which Gu was collecting hair from across the planet and weaving it into symbols such as flags, iconic images, and calligraphic texts written in his own meaningless alphabet. The "Interpol" installation was one of the first showings for the work. Gu sees the project as a whole, titled *united nations* (see also fig. 8.19), as "a great 'utopia' of the unification of mankind [that] probably can never exist in our reality but it is going to be fully realized in the art world."[11] *united nations—sweden & russia monument: interpol* was featured prominently at "Interpol," apparently confirming the Russians' concern that actual collaboration had given way to representations of it. Though inclusive, Gu's work is hierarchical: The artist controls the conception and the execution. Brener's act rejected such autocratic visions and destroyed the piece in solidarity with the original intentions of "Interpol" that artists should create new models of art making that diverged from those already established and authorized by the West. Though Gu expressed some understanding of the action in the days following the event, he, like most of the European participants in the exhibition, voiced strong objections to the way Brener chose to make his point.

The problem that had come to a head in Stockholm related to diverging visions of the role and place of contemporary art—whether it was a process with social, intellectual, and emotional consequences or a product aimed at a market. Brener's and Kulik's performances represent a significant change in strategy for Russian artists seeking to challenge the status quo. "Soft subversion, a heritage inherited from the 1980s, is no longer adequate, and the hidden undermining of the political context of the enemy is obsolete," Brener wrote with fellow artist Barbara Schurz (b. 1973). "'War is necessary!' was our answer to the question 'What to do?'"[12]

In place of Sots artists' stylistic infiltration or Kabakov's allegorical and site-specific narratives, Brener and the Austrian Schurz advocated an ever-changing strategic assault. Their war would be waged across the post-Communist East as well as in the West. Six months after the opening of "Interpol," Brener was arrested in Amsterdam for spraypainting a green dollar sign on a canvas by the Russian avant-garde painter Kazimir Malevich (1878–1935). Even once-radical art such as Malevich's was now part of an economic and political network that Brener and others were struggling to expose. Sometimes, Brener and Schurz argued, leaflets and demonstrations are what is required of a political artist; at other times, art demands that you bark and bite like a hungry dog, deface famous paintings, heckle academics, spit on art critics, and even drop your pants and defecate—all actions that were carried out by Russian performance artists in the 1990s.

In addition to challenging received notions of art, Oleg Kulik engaged in a more traditional quest to explore what makes us human. Three years after "Interpol," he traveled to Deitch Projects in New York to create a variation on the most famous artistic dialogue between the animal and human worlds of the twentieth century, Joseph Beuys's *I Like America and America Likes Me*. In 1974, Beuys had locked himself and a coyote in the René Block Gallery in New York for three days to enact a reconciliation between the violent and humane aspects of U.S. society. By so doing, Beuys sought to heal the self-inflicted wounds of civilization, a task Kulik set for himself as well. Kulik's dog project was begun as a means of giving form to the anxiety of Russian life. For *I Bite America and America Bites Me* (1997), Kulik locked himself in a cage in Deitch Projects for two weeks. The gallery filled with a musky odor, more animal than human, and at least one person was bitten. The artist reported that the performance led him from the violence and frustration he had felt and shown in Stockholm to a sense of cathartic freedom and openness. In 1974, Beuys had achieved an understanding with a dangerous wild animal; almost a quarter of a century later, Kulik reached peace with the animal of his own making.

Via his performances as a dog and other animals as well as photographic and film works, Kulik imagines multiple integrations of the human and the animal under the banner of "Zoocentrism." In political terms, Zoocentrism promotes population control and equality of rights between people and animals. While *I Bite America* represents a more violent side of this exploration, much of Kulik's work seeks more gentle intimacy. In *Gobi Test* (2004) (**fig. 8.11**), a video about life in Mongolia, Kulik presents a society in "symbiosis" with nature.[13] The film turns on the relationship between human beings and nature—sometimes showing magnificent animals, horses, or oxen, at others detailing the efficient slaughter of

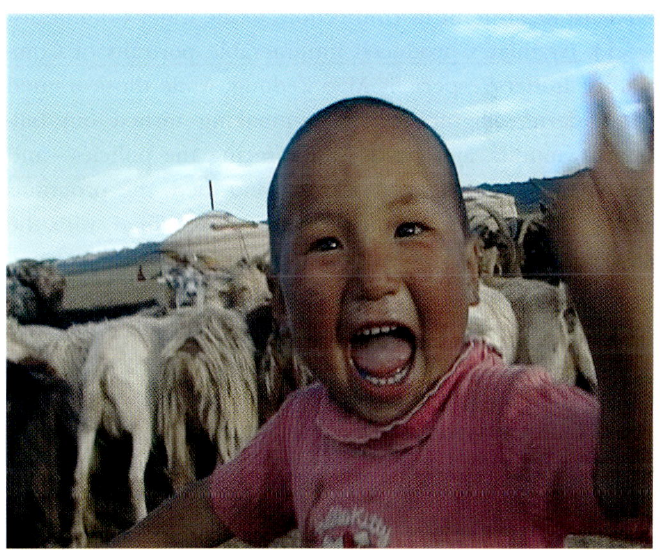

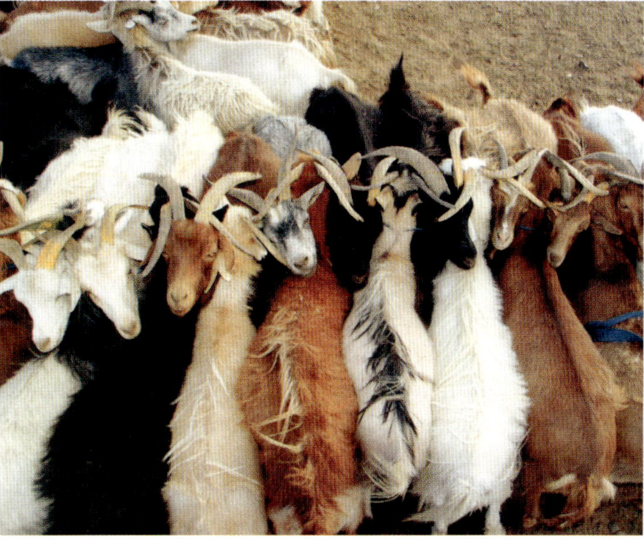

8.11 Oleg Kulik, *The Gobi Test*, 2004. Film, 31 minutes. Courtesy Regina Gallery.

a goat—with neither animal nor human declared superior. *Gobi Test* is a plea for balance. Kulik explains: "'Civilised man' cannot survive in Mongolia. No way. Any kind of business is possible here only if it does not destroy the natural balance."[14] Experiencing life in Mongolia impressed upon Kulik the depth of Western ignorance and hubris in its dealings with the natural world. Far more than the dangers of Westernization to the Moscow art world, Kulik's work conveys the profound need for a balance between humanity and nature.

China

Though confronting very different economic realities, Chinese artists in the last decades of the twentieth century faced aesthetic and political issues similar to those encountered by the Russians. As in Soviet Russia, the visual arts had been shaped by politically determined art education and careers exclusively devoted to the production of official art and propaganda. During the Cultural Revolution (1966–76), art schools rejected traditional Chinese arts in favor of Socialist Realism for its connections to the wider Communist world. Graduates produced innumerable portraits of Communist leaders, especially Mao Zedong, while those trained in modern calligraphy and printmaking turned out billboards, murals, and posters announcing the policies—and the enemies—of the state. When Mao died, the programs of the Cultural Revolution were quickly modified, with the state warming to Western capitalist markets and in some degree relaxing its control of culture. The few artists who had been experimenting with abstract and individual styles in private were suddenly able to discuss and even show their work, while many artists and intellectuals criticized during the Cultural Revolution were rehabilitated. While not open to all forms of dissent, the government under the leadership of Deng Xiaoping permitted a far greater amount of free speech than ever before. This new state of affairs as well as its limits was put on display in September 1979 in a park just outside the China Art Gallery, now the National Art Museum of China in Beijing. Sharing the enthusiasm and urgency of the moment, a group of twenty-three art students and teachers set up the "Stars Art Exhibition" to display their efforts to represent and critique contemporary reality. The announcement for the show, written by one of its organizers Huang Rui (b. 1952), declared: "We have used our own eyes to know the world, and our own brushes and awls to join in it."[15] The artists were outspoken in their rejection of existing state ideology and their desire to participate in building a new China. Art displayed in the show included abstract and representational work, sculpture, and oil and ink painting. Opening on September 27, the "Stars" organizers intended to honor the thirtieth anniversary of the founding of the People's Republic of China, celebrated on October 1, 1979. On the morning of the 29th, however, police confiscated the art and shut down the exhibition. Artists and supporters gathered on October 1 for a peaceful protest against the closure and charged that the police had violated civil rights guaranteed in the constitution. The show was not reopened but, in 1980, twelve of the participating artists formed the Stars Painters Society and were granted an officially sanctioned exhibition at the China Art Gallery.[16]

As the "Stars Art Exhibition" demonstrated, the process of warming to the West and opening Chinese public culture up to increased dissent and debate was not a smooth one. In 1982, fearful of excessive Westernization, the state initiated the Anti-Spiritual Pollution Campaign, targeting "individualism," "art for art's sake," and "abstraction."[17] Pressure to temper the politics of their work compelled the Stars Painters Society to disband and nine of the original twelve members to leave China.[18] Despite the campaign, artists were still able to expand their knowledge of traditional Chinese arts as well as Western Modernism through exhibitions, publications, and even experimental programming in the educational system. Though there continued to be few opportunities to exhibit, let alone to sell, unofficial art, there grew up a community of like-minded artists and intellectuals as well as a supportive network of writers within the state-sanctioned publishing industry. The Anti-Spiritual Pollution Campaign was ended in 1984 and the following year Chinese openness to Western art culminated in the highly influential 1985 exhibition of work by Robert Rauschenberg at the China Art Gallery of Art, Beijing.[19]

During the 1980s, Chinese artists negotiated a variety of stylistic and political influences, both domestic and international. There were a number of important collectives and movements, including: New or Rustic Realism, which represented common subjects in an almost Photorealistic manner; Current of Life, a movement based in Western China which harnessed the expressive gestural abstraction of traditional Chinese ink painting and the spirit of rural and naïve arts to create emotive and representational imagery; and Rationalist Painting, a more conceptual and analytic approach to representation shared by a number of east Chinese artists' groups. The vibrancy of these movements, particularly the various collectives that fell within Current of Life and Rationalist Painting, contributed to what has been called the '85 New Wave Movement. Several conceptually based movements also formed in the 1980s, including the Dada- and Zen-inspired excursions into art and chance of Xiamen Dada and the text-based work of artists including Wenda Gu and Xu Bing.[20] By the close of the decade, performance-based work, particularly from artists working in Beijing, was also reaching critical mass.

"China/Avant-Garde"

As the restrictions of the Anti-Spiritual Pollution Campaign were relaxed, a number of artists, critics, and curators recognized the need to exhibit the new Chinese art publicly. As early as 1985, Wang Guangyi (b. 1957) and Shu Qun (b. 1958), members of the Northern Arts Group, organized the "Zhuhai Conference," a symposium that featured as its highlight a slide show of work by artists and collectives from all over China. The experience of viewing such a great variety of contemporary work proved compelling. Gao Minglu and a team of curators and critics that would come to include Li Xianting and Hou Hanru among others set about creating what in 1989 became the controversial "China/Avant-Garde" exhibition at the China Art Gallery, Beijing. The result of three years of preparation and the participation of numerous Chinese arts organizations and over 150 individual artists from all over China, the show introduced Beijing audiences to artists who have since become major figures in the contemporary art world. Paintings by Current of Life painter Zhang Xiaogang could be compared to those of northern Rationalist painter Wang Guangyi. Xu Bing's monumental *Book from the Sky* (1987) was shown, as was work by Wenda Gu and Xiamen Dada's Huang Yong Ping. The energy and spirit of innovation of Chinese art in the post-Cultural Revolution years were amply on view, as was national pride. In the catalogue, Gao describes contemporary China as "a country opening its door to the world" and presenting its art as the site of "conflicts between the beautiful and the ugly, the new and the old, the true and the false, and the [confrontation of] existing complicated values."[21] Contemporary Chinese artists and their supporters were bidding farewell, he concluded, "to the ideas of art meant to [please] human sense organs alone or instruct people with dogmas."[22] Just as they had in the "Stars Art Exhibition," contemporary artists were presented as leading an engaged populace in a democratic China.

China was, perhaps, not quite ready for Gao's vision of Chinese art. The sponsors of the exhibition were fined and it was shut down twice, so that in the end it was only open to the public for eight days. The two closures were quite dramatic. In the first case, artist Xiao Lu (b. 1962) brought a gun into the museum and fired two shots at the installation that she and Tang Song (b. 1960) had made. This violent and surprising gesture took place just hours after the opening, without the prior knowledge of the curators or the authorities. Officials closed the exhibition and took Xiao and Tang into custody. Under the pretext of a spring holiday, the gallery stayed closed for five days. Upon its reopening, the authorities received an anonymous letter claiming that a bomb would go off in the museum if the show was not closed again. For two more days the doors were shut. It is not known who sent the threat, but the combination of violent gestures and the readiness of officials to shut the exhibition down turned "China/Avant-Garde" into the swansong of the '85 New Wave Movement. In retrospect, this suppression of contemporary art foreshadowed the silencing of the democracy movement in Tiananmen Square four months later and the beginning of a period of tightened restrictions on artistic opportunities in China.

Wang Guangyi

"China/Avant-Garde" captured the vibrancy of the 1980s Chinese art scene and also presented many artists at a turning point in their careers. Wang Guangyi (b. 1956), one of the most internationally recognized of the '85 New Wave Movement, is a case in point. Wang was represented in the Beijing show by examples of his work with the Northern Arts Group, which he had co-founded with Shu Qun in 1984 in Harbin after rejecting the art-school education he had received during the Cultural Revolution. Wang's work captured the Rationalist aesthetic with its characteristically flat, clearly delineated compositions painted with a

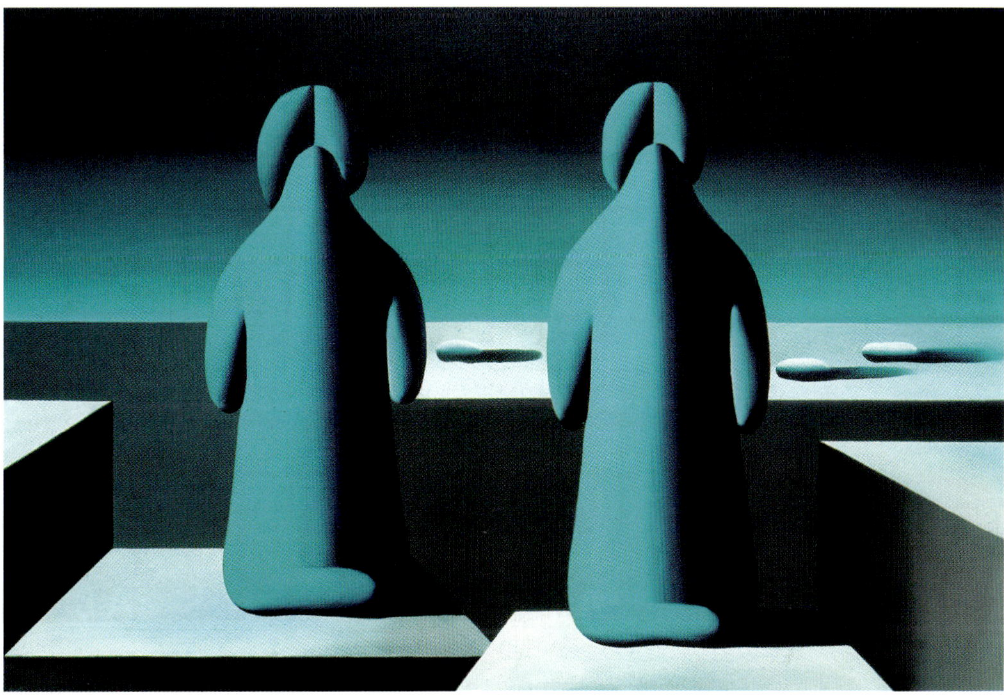

8.12 Wang Guangyi, *Frozen North Pole no.28*, 1985. Oil on canvas, 39⅜ × 59" (100 × 150 cm). Artist collection. Courtesy Wang Guangyi Studio.

highly reduced palette. Works such as *Frozen North Pole no. 28* (1985) (**fig. 8.12**), one of a series represented in "China/Avant-Garde," were intended to provide an analysis of daily life stripped down to its bare essentials by strong, disciplined individuals. The Northern Arts Group was a collection of artists and intellectuals who were interested in the intersection of art with philosophy, literature, and society, and who believed that reductive abstractions such as Wang's scenes could move the viewer beyond the material world to access the sublime character of the region. It was in this milieu that Wang began to conceive of his style as "an objective attitude toward past cultural facts."[23] Soon after painting the Northern scenes, Wang applied his Rationalist lens and abstract style to iconic examples of past Western art, as if seeking through his analysis of them to discover an essence that might equate to the sublime character of the North. The lesson of these "Post-Classical" paintings, Rationalist variations on works including the *Death of Marat* (1793) by Jacques-Louis David and *The Return of the Prodigal Son* (ca. 1666–68) by Rembrandt, was that it was in history, even more than in geography, that one finds the source of one's personal and artistic identity.

In 1988, Wang turned away from imaginary landscapes and Western masterpieces to examine the image bank of contemporary Chinese history. *Mao Zedong—AO* (1988) (**fig. 8.13**), one of a series of portraits of the Chinese leader, exemplifies Wang's Rationalist approach to contemporary Chinese history. The painting consists of three black-and-white portraits of Mao copied in oil from an official state portrait and placed side by side. The faces lighten slightly as the images are repeated from left to right and what appear to be clouds in the background shift position. Wang overlaid the faces with a grid as though the painting was being marked up to be enlarged, as was the practice when creating the mural-sized portraits that dominated Chinese public spaces. Wang has explained that the grid was a means to scale the symbol of Mao down to that of "normal person."[24] By painting the image of Mao with the grid still visible, Wang was attempting to reverse the propagandizing process and thus restore Mao's humanity. Despite the artist's intention being to disrupt the mystifying power of the image, rather than to disrespect the man himself, audiences were shocked. Wang's Mao paintings were among the most controversial shown in "China/Avant-Garde." In fact Wang changed the letters to AC because censors thought AO was a disrespectful reference to a current pop song.

The pressures created by the censorship of the exhibition led to the dissolution of the Northern Arts Group. Wang reacted by becoming more assertive. Paintings such as *Great Criticism—Coca-Cola* (1990–93) (**fig. 8.14**), from his *Great Criticism* series, begun in 1990 and continuing into the twenty-first century, join the visual language of Chinese political propaganda with that of U.S. advertising. In this work, labeled "Political Pop," stalwart workers appropriated from Mao-era imagery raise fists, tools, and eyes toward the logos of Marlboro cigarettes or Coca-Cola. Wang's imagery can be read as depicting Communism branded by corporate sponsors and capitalism, and exalted by the masses. Capitalist advertising and Communist propaganda appear as two sides of the same coin, each subverting the

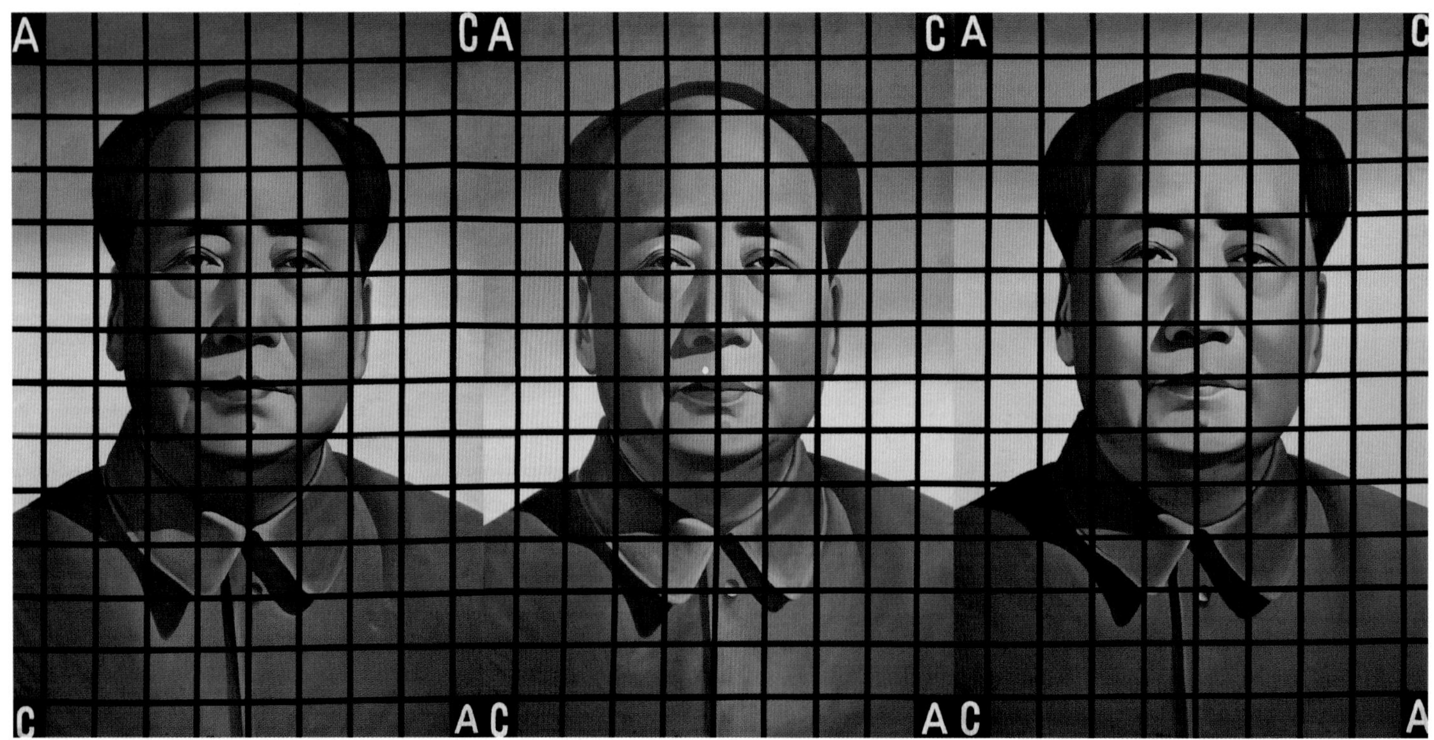

8.13 Wang Guangyi, *Mao Zedong—AO*, 1988. Oil on canvas, 141¾ × 47¼" (360 × 120 cm), triptych. Created in Zhuhai, China. American private collection. Courtesy Wang Guangyi Studio.

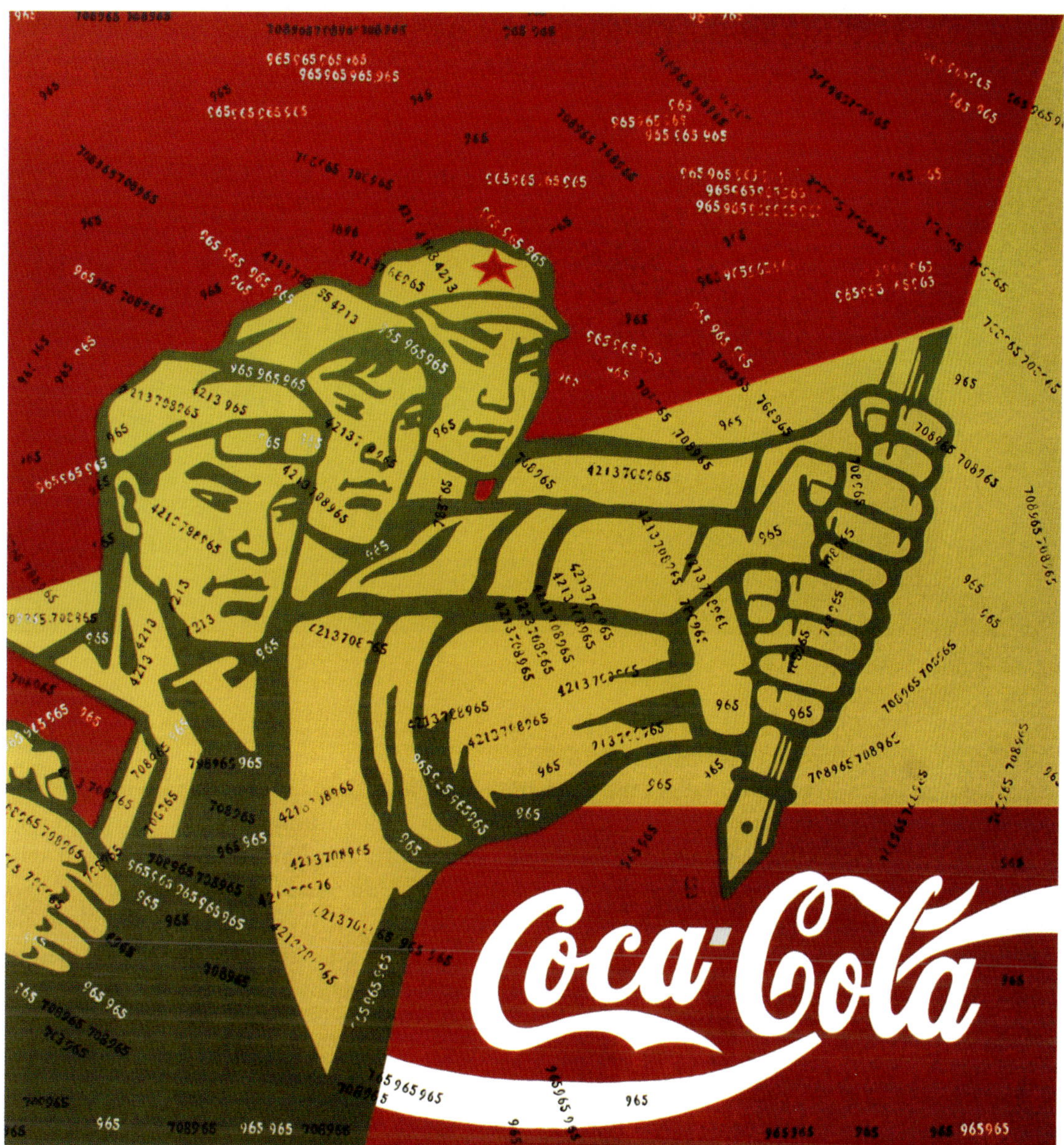

8.14 Wang Guangyi, *Great Criticism—Coca-Cola,* 1990–93. Oil on canvas, 78¾ × 78¾" (200 × 200 cm). Created in Wuhan, China. American private collection. Courtesy Wang Guangyi Studio.

individual in favor of the few in power. Despite such an apparently controversial equation of Communism with capitalism, it is central to the complexity of Wang's art that by the 1990s the idea that the two systems were mutually exclusive existed only in the realm of propaganda. Relationships between the products and ideologies of East and West had been developing for decades. The China of Deng Xiaoping, who dominated Chinese politics from 1976 until he stepped out of political life in 1992, was based on the compatibility of these supposedly antagonistic political systems. Deng initiated liberalization in the late 1970s, formalizing a more open relationship with the West, meeting with President Carter in 1979, negotiating from 1982 to 1984 the return of Hong Kong from Britain (to take place in 1997), and transforming features of the Chinese economy by selectively adapting Western models. Political Pop enlisted the languages of Communist and capitalist propaganda to point to the similarities between East and West that had become central tenets of post-Maoist policies.

Zhang Xiaogang

Zhang Xiaogang (b. 1958), who formed the Southwest Arts Group, one of the Current of Life collectives, has described the 1980s as the moment when he was able to "armor up" with Modernism.[25] For Zhang, with the relative flood of information about the West that followed the end of the Cultural Revolution, there came the romantic and mystical idea of living as a bohemian artist that contrasted with the more ascetic attitude of the Northern Arts Group. By the mid-1980s, Zhang had begun teaching at the Sichuan Academy and taking an interest in Western Expressionism and Surrealism. He was also deeply involved with Eastern traditions of Buddhism and ancient Chinese painting and mysticism. His contribution to "China/Avant-Garde," *Forever Lasting Love* (1988) (**fig. 8.15**), represents the culmination of his interest in combining these cross-cultural aesthetic and religious references.[26] The painting is a large triptych, integrating figural groups that are rich in symbolic allusions to Western and Eastern traditions. Different family groups populate the

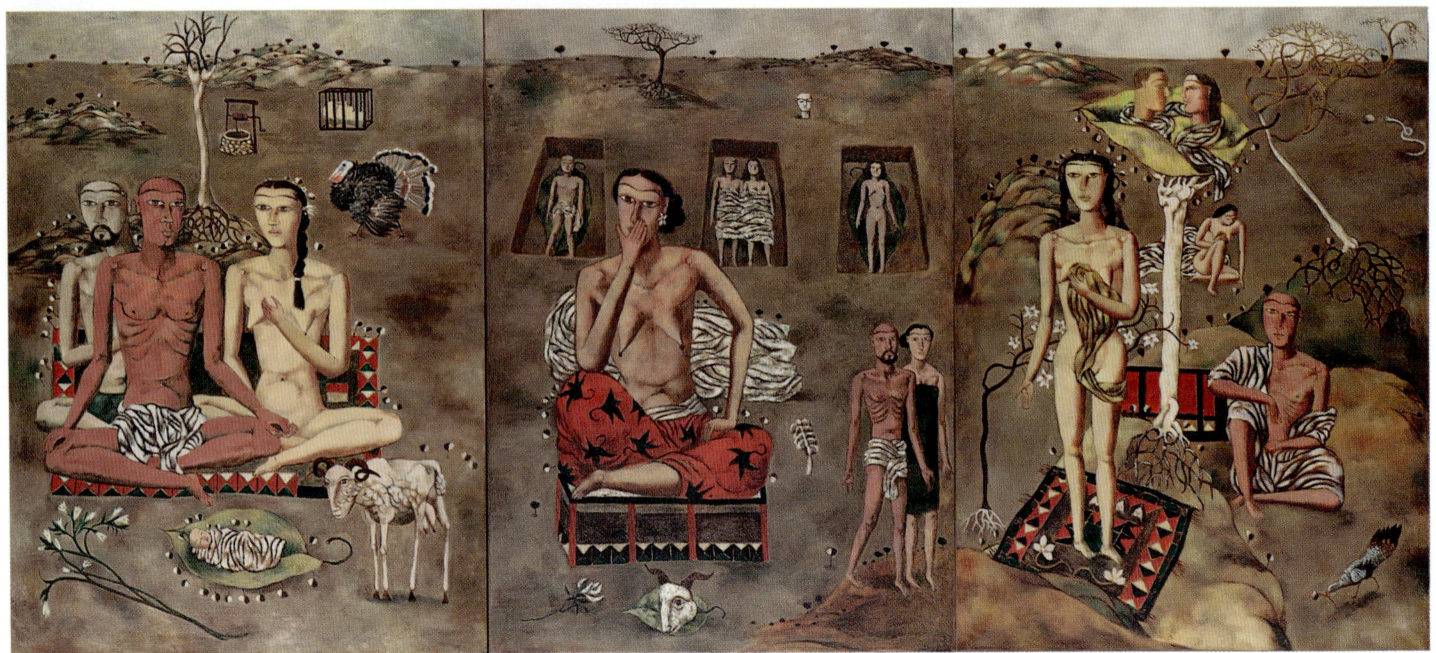

8.15 Zhang Xiaogang, *Forever Lasting Love*, 1988. Oil on canvas, 51³⁄₁₆ × 39⅜" (130 × 100 cm). © Zhang Xiaogang, courtesy of Zhang Xiaogang Studio.

canvases, meditating and contemplating in a barren landscape populated only with an occasional animal, bonelike tree, and—in the central panel—what appear to be three graves. The narrative is not logical or linear, there is no beginning or end, but rather the scenes evoke thoughts of life and death, parenthood, love, discomfort, and isolation. The bodies have the awkward flat quality of folk art for which the Sichuan region was known, yet they are also informed by the work of modern Western artists such as Van Gogh and Picasso who looked to rural communities for access to spiritual truths. After 1989, the synthesis represented by *Forever Lasting Love* ceased being of such interest to Zhang as he sought ways to connect his painting more directly to his lived experience rather than to his mystical intuitions.

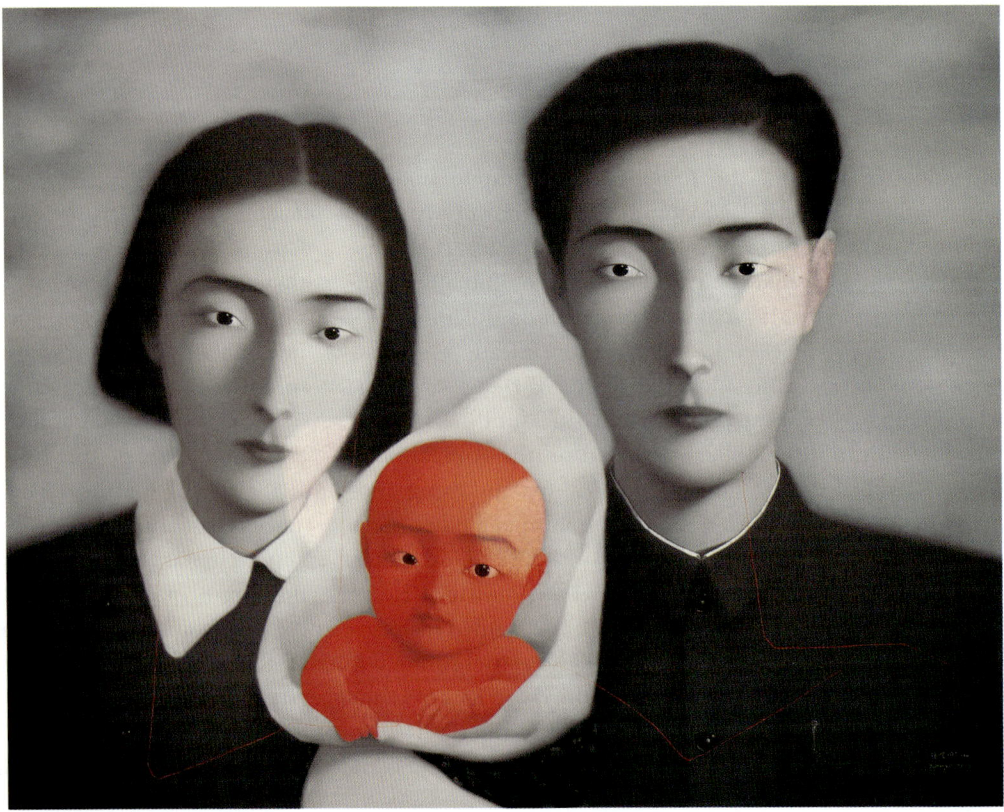

8.16 Zhang Xiaogang, ***Bloodline: Big Family No. 9 (red baby)***, 1996. Oil on canvas, 59 × 74¹³⁄₁₆" (150 × 190 cm). Asiart Archive. © Zhang Xiaogang, courtesy of Zhang Xiaogang Studio.

In the early 1990s, Zhang traveled to Germany and France. This European trip proved transformative. Though he had learned about Western art in China, the experience of seeing so much of it in person created a personal crisis for him. Facing a political landscape transformed by the June 4, 1989 events at Tiananmen Square and the aesthetic revelation he had had in Europe, Zhang was left to search for ways to make art that was true to himself as a contemporary Chinese citizen. For all of 1992, he did not paint. When he began to work again he started in a very different direction from *Forever Lasting Love.* Still interested in the poetic and allusive quality of his 1980s work, he now developed several portrait-based series in which the paint begins to look more and more like muted scrims of translucent color and where the faces are rendered with a slightly blurred effect. The soft, even tender, painted surface of the canvas is interrupted with occasional passages marked by brighter colors and a sharper focus. In a reversal of his practice in *Forever Lasting Love,* Zhang now resisted the mixing of Western with local traditions that he felt had become the *lingua franca* of contemporary international art. Instead he focused on family portrait photography from previous decades. The *Bloodlines* series—from which *Bloodline: Big Family No. 9 (red baby)* (1996) (**fig. 8.16**) is taken—began with posed photographs dating from the Cultural Revolution. Shortly after starting the series, however, Zhang decided to base the paintings more loosely on source photographs. He therefore began inventing his own groupings, individual characters, and the relationships between them. The men tend to be intellectuals and the women variations on the artist's mother. He painted the children at approximately the age he himself had been at the start of the Cultural Revolution; the girls are often inspired by his daughter.[27] Zhang sometimes paints the eyes slightly crossed or directed off into the distance, disrupting the cohesion of the group portrait. Cutting through the slightly out-of-focus heads of *Bloodlines* are red lines asserting the familial relationships between the characters and insisting on connections that the isolating gazes and soft focus suggest have been forgotten. History infuses the paintings, connecting contemporary viewers to a childhood in the Mao era. Politics hovers like a ghost, casting a pervasive melancholy over the atmosphere and attitude of the paintings. In place of the analysis and critique demanded by work such as Wang Guangyi's, Zhang's appeals are first and foremost to memory—partial and perhaps failing, but present nonetheless.

Huang Yong Ping

"China/Avant-Garde" was accompanied by a bilingual (English/Chinese) catalogue, thereby revealing the curators' interest in promoting Chinese art internationally. In the event, the exhibition provided a number of participants with a stepping stone to successful careers outside China. One example is the Xiamen Dada artist Huang Yong Ping (b. 1954). Shortly after he displayed *"A History of Chinese Painting" and "A Concise History of Modern Painting" in a Washing Machine for Two Minutes* (1987) (**fig. 8.17**), two art-history books, written by Wang Bomin and Herbert Read respectively, reduced to a small pile of pulp, at "China/Avant-Garde," Huang accepted an invitation to exhibit in Jean-Hubert Martin's "Magiciens de la Terre" exhibition in Paris (see Introduction and Chapter 9). "Magiciens" was a groundbreaking 1989 exhibition that sought to present contemporary work by artists from all over the globe. Huang's Dada-inspired gesture of comically cleansing art history while metaphorically representing the commingling of cultures shared common cause with Martin's efforts. In Paris, Huang created a room-sized installation of reptilian forms built from machine-washed books, photographs, and newspapers and symbolizing longevity. After the show he relocated to the city.

Huang began his career interrogating art-making processes. For instance, as a student he had accepted conventional themes such as the lives of Chinese factory workers, but rejected the practice of using oil paints to elevate such populist content. Instead he used spraypaint to create images of labor, employing industrial materials to match his

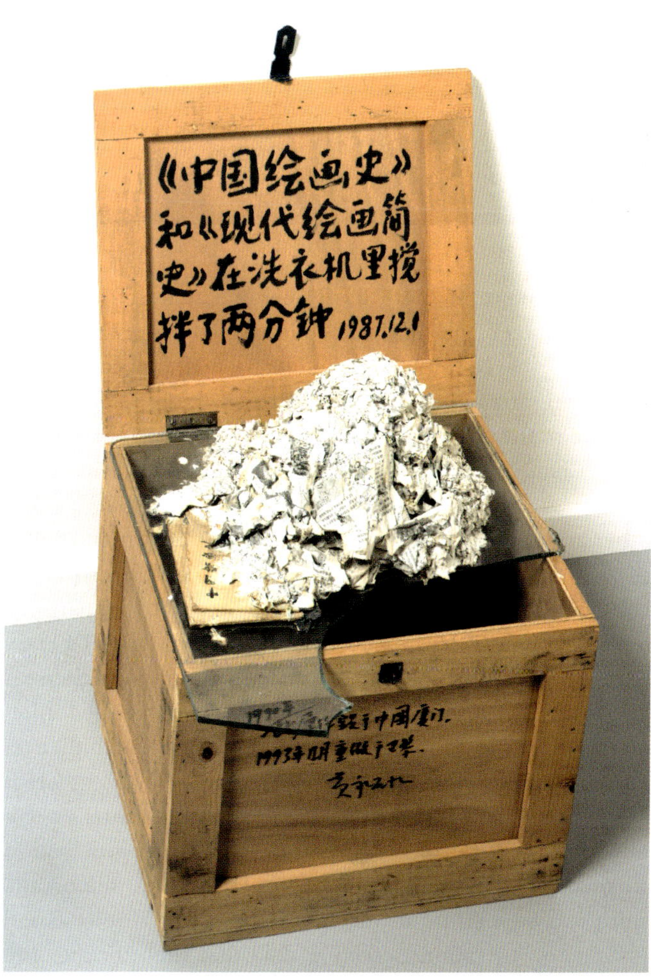

8.17 Huang Yong Ping, *"A History of Chinese Painting" and "A Concise History of Modern Painting" in a Washing Machine for Two Minutes*, 1987. Chinese tea box, paper pulp, and glass, 30¼ × 19 × 27½" (76.8 × 48.3 × 69.9 cm). Walker Art Center, Minneapolis © Huang Yong Ping.

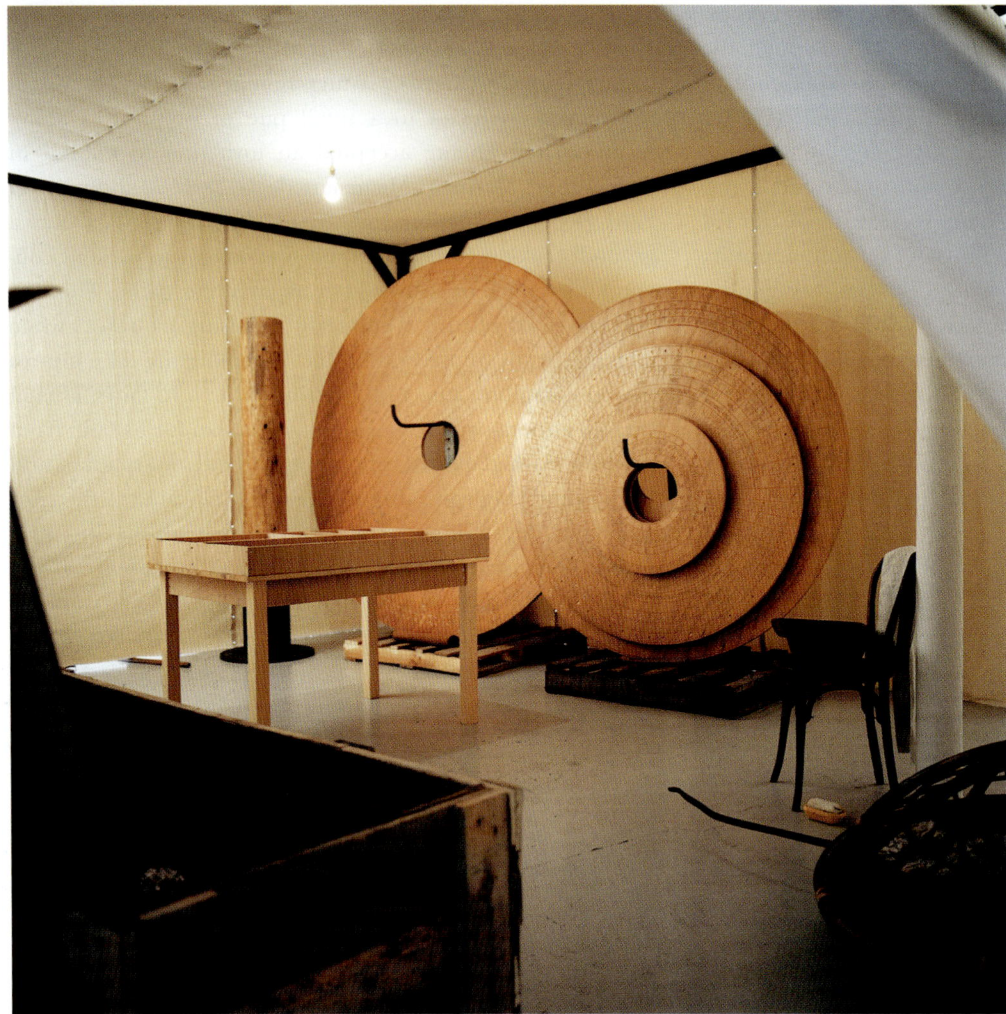

8.18 Huang Yong Ping, *House of Oracles*, 1992. Tent and related objects of metal, cloth, water, wood, brass, and papier-mâché, overall installation 10½ × 15¾ × 15¾' (3.2 × 4.8 × 4.8 m). Collection of the Fondation Cartier, France © Huang Yong Ping.

industrial subject matter. He also became interested in Dada, reading Marcel Duchamp and collecting copies of Dada texts which he shared with like-minded friends and colleagues. In a 1986 statement explaining Xiamen Dada, Huang clarified the philosophical and historical significance of his interests. "Chan is Dada, Dada is Chan. Postmodernism is the modern renaissance of Chan Buddhism," he wrote.[28] While other artists, particularly John Cage (1912–92), whom Huang singled out, have drawn connections between Eastern mysticism and Western Dada, Huang noted that such comparisons have particular relevance in the Chinese context. His essay cites Duchamp, Beuys, and Rauschenberg among others as important because, like Buddhism, they dismantled hierarchies in order to incorporate the everyday, the audience, and meaninglessness into the practice of art making. Great art, Huang writes, "stops being about an individual's accumulation of masterpieces; it is now about the participation ... of the public."[29] Huang's expression of this democratic spirit can be seen in his machines—discs that revolve based on chance operations, creating data that then dictates the production of abstract paintings. Built on a massive scale and assembled into the *House of Oracles* (1989–92) (**fig. 8.18**), the machines become the source of sculptural expressions of the artist's desire to relinquish control over the production of objects. *House of Oracles* is based on the tools Huang uses in his studio practice, but, built at the scale of an industrial machine, it suggests collective rather than solitary creation. Such reimaginings of the artistic process are deeply concordant with Gao's claims that the '85 New Wave Movement was oriented toward the people. Rather than turn the Dada/Chan into a private affair, Huang's claim that artworks have become participatory events parallels the agitation for increased democracy as advocated by the Stars Painters Society.

Wenda Gu and Xu Bing

The conjunction of Conceptualist strategies and Chinese traditions can also be seen in the works of Wenda Gu (b. 1955) and Xu Bing (b. 1955), who both engage the political and expressive power of the written word. Calligraphy plays a central role in Chinese art history and was enlisted by the Communist state to accompany and often substitute for official imagery. Banners and posters dominated by what is called "big character" calligraphy were used to report governmental accomplishments and to denounce political enemies. Gu and Xu were both well versed in traditional arts, and during their training had used their skills to create propaganda of this kind. Both artists went on to create their

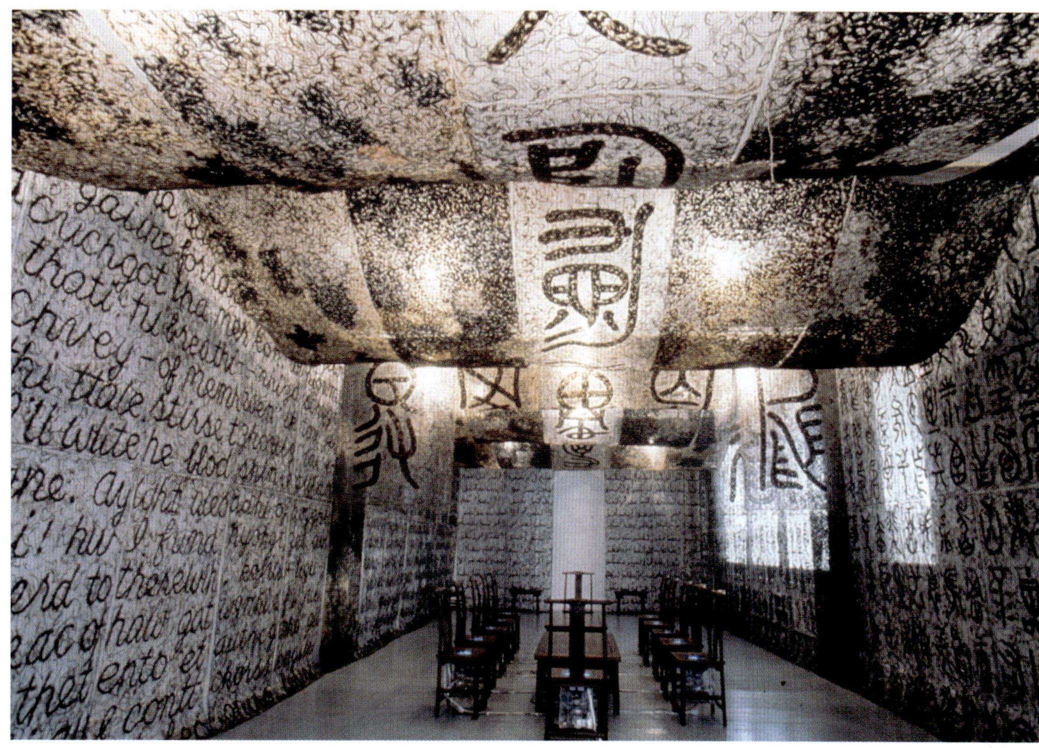

8.19 Wenda Gu, ***united nations—china monument: temple of heaven***, 1998. Site-specific installation commissioned by San Francisco Museum of Modern Art & Asia Society New York, Wenda Gu studios, Shanghai & New York, 1997–98. Temple of pseudo-English, Chinese, Hindi, and Arabic made of human hair curtains collected from all over the world; 12 Ming-style TV chairs, 2 Ming-style tables, 13 × 20 × 52' (3.96 × 6.1 × 15.86 m). Permanent collection of the Hong Kong Museum of Art, China. Courtesy the artist.

first mature work out of invented letters, thus appropriating the authority of calligraphy while destroying its ability to carry "official" meaning.

Gu's earliest invented characters appeared in large installations and evocative landscape paintings. He received traditional training in calligraphy and ink painting from a master at the China National Academy of Art in Hangzhou and supplemented his formal education by privately learning about various Western styles. This artistic education supplemented his experience in the Red Guard writing "big character posters." This political task, Gu explained, impressed him for the passion and invention with which his colleagues carried it out. Most of the poster writers were ordinary young people and laborers who brought their fervent belief in Marxism, rather than any formal artistic training, to their calligraphy. The results, Gu said, "had their own identity and creativity," and constituted "the new form of Chinese words."[30] In his art, Gu drew on this idea of creating new words as well as traditional calligraphic styles and history. To create his first mature work he fragmented, inverted, abstracted, and otherwise distorted traditional calligraphic forms, appealing to but ultimately frustrating the viewer's desire for meaning. Gu started to convey the content of his fictitious language through the materials with which he wrote, most famously in his sculptures made of human hair (see also fig. 8.10). In his series of installations, titled *united nations*, for which he used hair from all over the world in a symbolic expression of the compatibility of all peoples, Gu integrated pseudo-versions of different languages. *united nations—china monument: temple of heaven* (1998) (**fig. 8.19**), created for an exhibition in New York and now in the collection of the Hong Kong Museum of Art, combines Gu's invented variations of Chinese, English, Hindi, and Arabic. By eliminating the specific meaning of language, Gu enlists the long tradition in China of valuing the emotive quality of calligraphy and applies the abstract communicative power of language to the utopian project of bringing together the peoples of the world.

While Wenda Gu crafted his invented characters in luminescent curtains of human hair, Xu Bing printed books. His *magnum opus* is *Book from the Sky* (1987–91) (**fig. 8.20**), an installation comprising four books, three scrolls, and several individual pages, all printed with characters that have no meaning. Xu started the project writing in his own hand, but soon settled on movable type as a way to connect his work to historic traditions of printmaking as well as to more modern newspaper production. He invented over a thousand characters, all studiously modeled on a Song Dynasty style of calligraphy. The characters looked so much like actual writing that when *Book from the Sky* was first exhibited viewers spent hours looking for actual words, to be rewarded only very rarely when they stumbled on an obscure word that Xu had unintentionally reinvented. Xu described the effect of courting and obstructing comprehension as connected to Zen Buddhism, but the result for audiences when the work was shown in Beijing at "China/Avant-Garde" was more frustration and bewilderment than transcendence. The artist's skill was on view, as was his enormous time commitment, but what this book was and why it existed remained obscure. The confusion was only further aggravated by the title under which Xu first exhibited the piece, *The Mirror of the World—An Analyzed Reflection of the End of This Century*, suggesting that this was some kind of realist project presenting a true image of the world.[31]

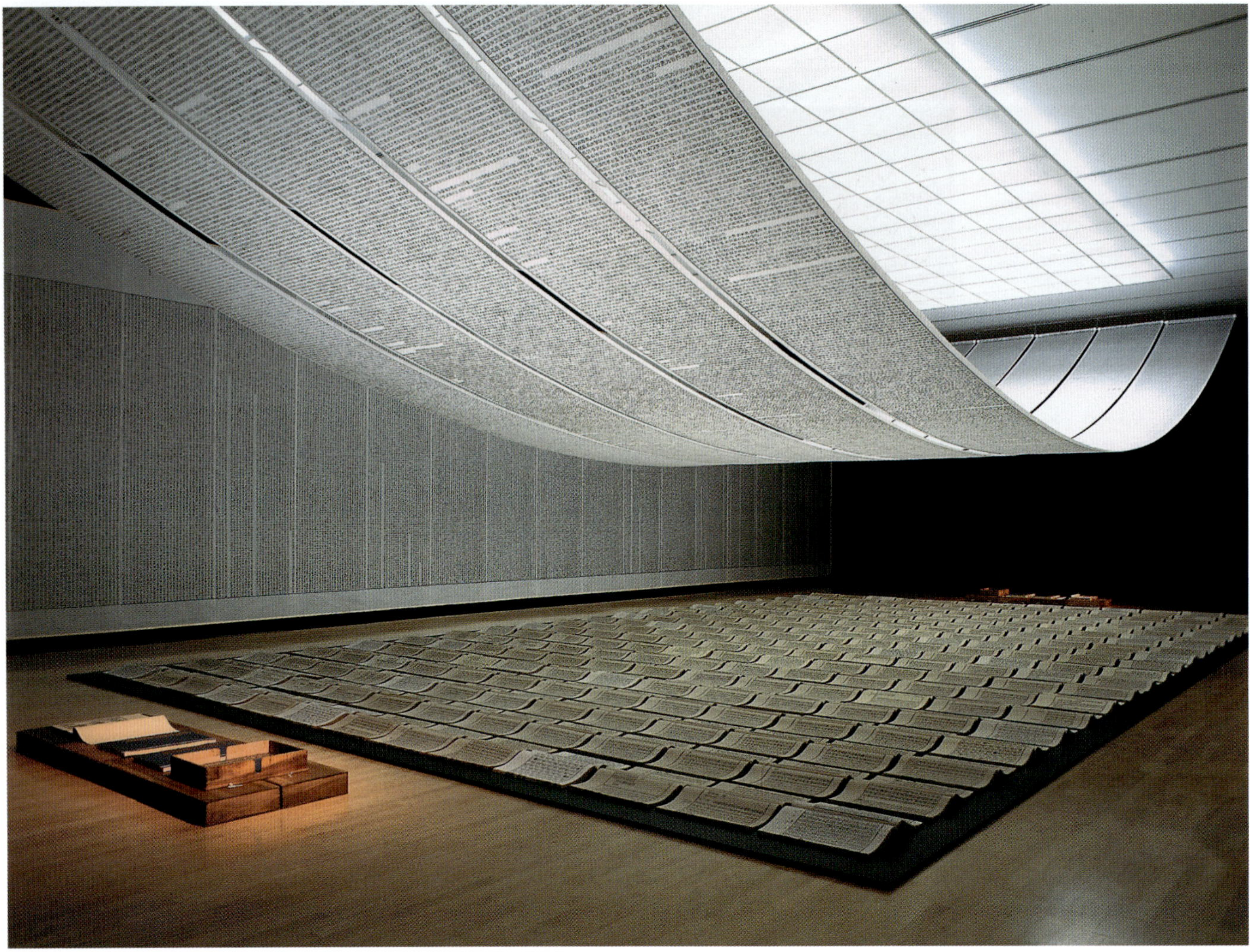

8.20 Xu Bing, *Book from the Sky*, 1987–1991. Handprinted books, ceiling and wall scrolls printed from wood letterpress type using false Chinese characters, dimensions variable. Installation view, "Crossings," National Gallery of Canada, Ottawa, 1998. Courtesy Xu Bing Studio.

Installed with the scrolls hanging from the ceiling, the printed sheets of *Book from the Sky* billowed above the audience. Visitors strained to make out the writing, as though reading clouds. Rendering the printed word senseless was profoundly disturbing to both ordinary spectators and government officials. When the government closed "China/Avant-Garde," Xu's work was singled out for official censure: *Book from the Sky* was said to devote too much time and energy to meaninglessness, and was held up as evidence that young Chinese artists were rootless at best, and pandering to Western collectors at worst. In the tense atmosphere after the suppression at Tiananmen Square, the official attack on Xu's work sent out a message that there were lines that an artist should not cross. Xu left China in the summer of 1990 and resettled in New York.

Ai Weiwei

When Xu Bing moved to New York he met fellow expatriate Ai Weiwei (b. 1957), who in 1981 had been the first of the Stars Painters Society group to leave China. Ai lived in the East Village where he created a modest body of sculpture and photographed his daily life, which included visits from Chinese artists whom he graciously hosted and trips to New York artworld events. More than anything, however, he was seeing art. While his compatriots in China were reading and debating about Western art newly available to them in books, Ai was able to experience directly nearly every gallery show in the city. He saw the early appropriation, Neo-Expressionist, and commodity art exhibitions, and was in New York for the rise and fall of the East Village scene. Duchamp, Andy Warhol, and Jeff Koons became liberating influences, convincing him that making objects was secondary to creating a lifestyle, a discovery that would prove increasingly incendiary for Ai. When he arrived in New York, he also met Tehching Hsieh (see Chapter 7), with whom he became close and to whom he introduced Xu in the early 1990s.

In 1993, Ai returned to China to see his ailing father and decided to stay. He now found himself in a Beijing art world still shaken by the events of the late 1980s and once again deprived of information, not only from the West but also about different art directions within China. As if continuing to play the role of host, Ai set about sharing with

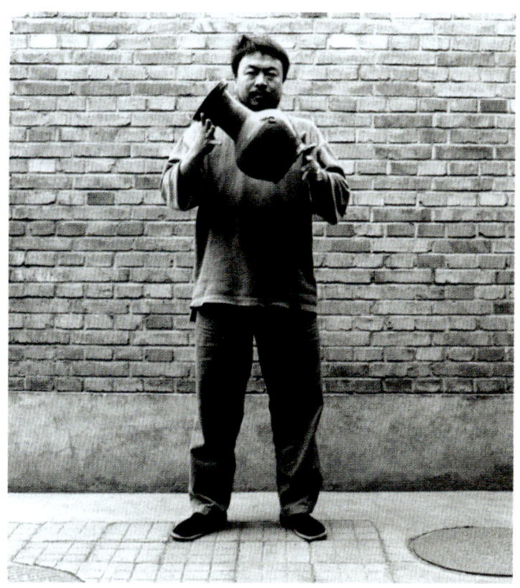 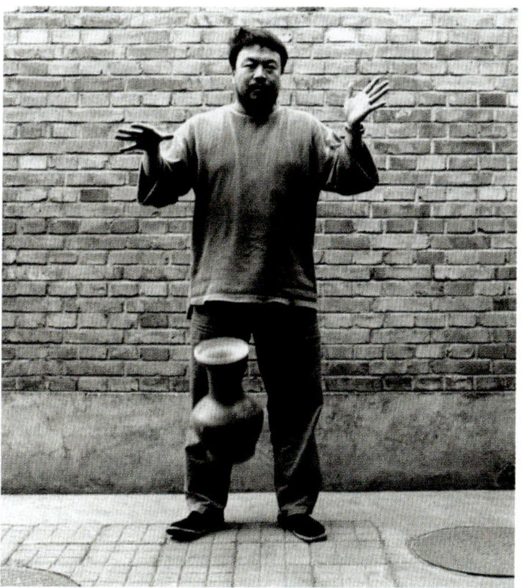 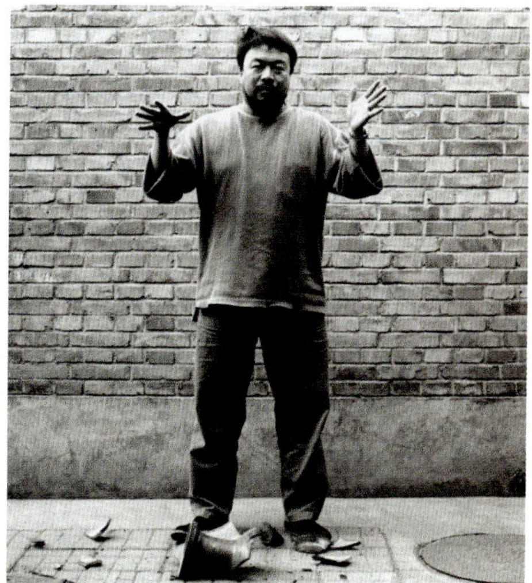

8.21 Ai Weiwei, ***Dropping a Han-Dynasty Urn***, 1995. Three black-and-white prints, each 58¼ × 47⅝" (148 × 121 cm). © Ai Weiwei.

his new community his knowledge of the art and artists he had discovered in the U.S., as well as of the Chinese artists whom he had met abroad. He published three contemporary art-history books featuring interviews with Chinese artists and illustrated articles about artists from abroad, including Duchamp, Warhol, and Koons. The volumes, known as the *Black Cover Book* (1994), *White Cover Book* (1995), and *Gray Cover Book* (1997), represent a renewed dialogue among Chinese artists about global contemporary art. The *Black Cover Book*, which included an interview with Tehching Hsieh, was co-produced by Feng Boyi and Xu Bing, the latter providing materials from New York.

Ai's practice in China began to emulate the Dada, Pop, and commodity art he had admired in New York, though incorporating content and materials specific to China. His most notorious early work is the triptych *Dropping a Han-Dynasty Urn* (1995) (**fig. 8.21**), which documents the artist letting a 2,000-year-old vessel fall to the ground. Ai's gesture is a curious combination of Dadaesque nihilism and a rather straightforward form of realism that points to the indifference to anything but the present that seemed to characterize contemporary life in China. Despite the context of the pervasive destruction of the Chinese past seen in the razing of historical buildings in Beijing and other cities, controversial public works projects such as the Three Gorges Dam flooding huge areas of the south, and the Mao-era rejection of the "Four Olds"—old ideas, old culture, old customs, and old habits—Ai's willful shattering of an ancient artifact remains shocking. The calculated transformation of historical objects, bordering on vandalism, has become a signature artistic act for Ai. Though rarely breaking things, he has variously dipped prehistoric pottery in industrial paint, cut apart and creatively reassembled Ming and Qing furniture, as in *Table with Three Legs* (2009) (**fig. 8.22**), and built installations out of the towns and temples that have been lost thanks to the rapid industrialization and urbanization of contemporary China. Pieces such as *Han Dynasty Urn with Coca-Cola*

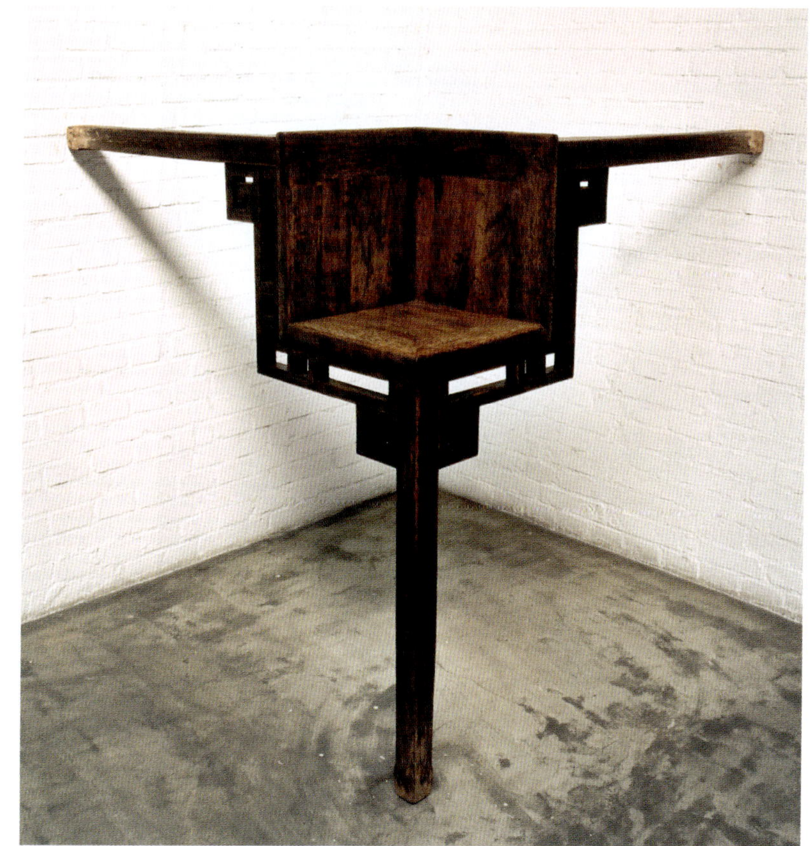

8.22 Ai Weiwei, ***Table with Three Legs***, 2009. Table, late Ming or early Qing Dynasty (1368–1911). Wood, 48$\frac{7}{16}$ × 48$\frac{7}{16}$ × 48$\frac{7}{16}$" (123 × 123 × 123 cm). © Ai Weiwei.

Logo (1994), for which Ai carved and painted the Coca-Cola logo on an ancient vessel, suggest that there is an economic motive and corporate agent that we can blame for the obliteration of history. Ai has been outspoken in saying that the forces of capital, as they are currently being harnessed by the Chinese state, are causing great harm.

Zhang Huan

The swift official response to Xiao Lu's gunshots at "China/Avant-Garde" and the subsequent tightened restrictions placed on the Chinese art world made clear that confrontational tactics would no longer be tolerated. Performance artists by and large retreated to more protected venues and more private acts. The performance-based work of Beijing artists Zhang Huan and Ma Liuming demonstrated the fertility of this approach in the 1990s. Zhang Huan (b. 1965), born in Anyang, was trained in *Su*, or Soviet-style painting, and came to Beijing to pursue graduate study. Within two years he had ceased painting and turned to the body as his medium, explaining, "The body is the only direct way through which I come to know society and society comes to know me."[32] From 1994 until he moved to the United States in 1998, Zhang created an oeuvre of performances that use the body—always his own, sometimes other people's as well—to draw attention to the often confrontational relationship between human beings and the world. The pieces are variously painful, terrifying, and funny. Using his body as "proof of identity," Zhang said he immediately related to the work of Tehching Hsieh and Marina Abramović when he learned about it in the 1990s.[33]

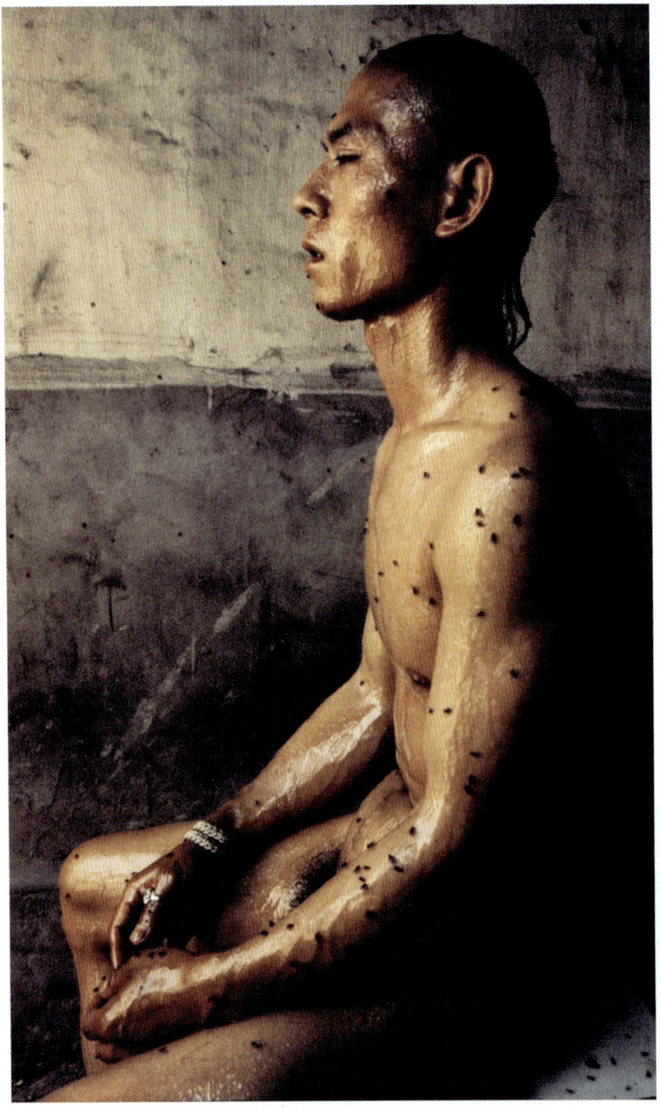

8.23 Zhang Huan, *12 Square Meters*, 1994. Performance, Beijing, China. Courtesy of Zhang Huan Studio.

Though his very first performance had a confrontational style, Zhang quickly adopted an experiential, endurance-based practice. He also chose to create his art in and around his home in the squalid neighborhood of Dashan Village, Chaoyang, in eastern Beijing. Choosing to live and work in this location represented a deliberate anti-establishment gesture that placed Zhang in opposition to the established artist neighborhood of Yuanmingyuan in western Beijing. To further emphasize its bohemian credentials, Zhang christened his neighborhood the "East Village" after learning about the East Village in New York from Ai Weiwei. Zhang's East Village performances fall into two general categories: those that focus attention on the artist's body and tend toward what Zhang called "self-torture"; and those that point outward to the environment, often evolving around a central image of the landscape. In *12 Square Meters* (1994) (**fig. 8.23**), an early solo work, Zhang covered his body in fish sauce and honey and sat for an hour in 100-degree heat in the middle of a badly neglected public restroom. The stench of ammonia and waste from the bathroom plus the fish odor emanating from Zhang was so pungent that photographer Rong Rong, who documented much of the East Village art scene, had to wrap his face in rags. Zhang recounted his sensations:

> I just felt that everything began to vanish from my sight. Life seemed to be leaving me far in the distance. I had no concrete thought except that my mind was completely empty. I could only feel my body, more and more flies landing and crawling over my nose, eyes, lips, ears, forehead, every part of me. I could feel them eating the liquid on my body. Some were stuck but did not stop eating ... The very concept of life was then for me the simple experience of the body.[34]

In *12 Square Meters*, Zhang deliberately heightened the sensations felt by anyone who has recoiled from the heat and stench of a poorly kept public toilet. By taking the material at hand and choreographing it into a performance, he transformed a daily event into a "quest to discover how we relate to the environment we exist in."[35] After enduring sixty minutes in the bathroom, Zhang rose and walked slowly to a pond not far away. In the film of the event, the image of his naked fly-covered body descending gracefully into the

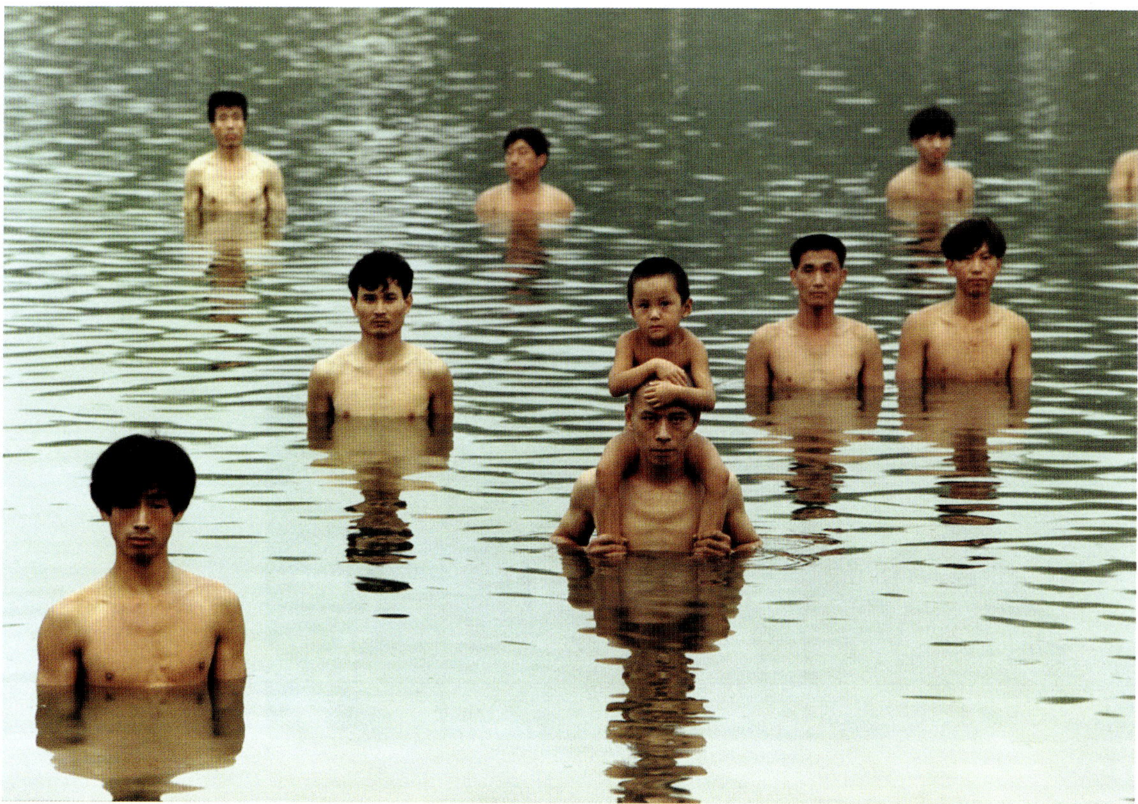

8.24 Zhang Huan, *To Raise the Level of a Fish Pond*, 1997. Performance, Beijing, China. Courtesy of Zhang Huan Studio.

pool is cathartic. The unpleasant sight of the flies floating on the water and the fact that Zhang's head does not re-emerge at the end of the film suggest, however, that bathing in the water is not necessarily an antidote to sitting in the latrine. In fact, the pond was heavily polluted, offering something less than the cleansing experience Zhang's performance implies.

On August 15, 1997, he created his landscape performance *To Raise the Level of a Fish Pond* (**fig. 8.24**). This took place at a small manmade fishpond and involved forty-six migrant laborers, a child, and Zhang walking into the water. For the piece, the artist turned to men who, like himself, had come to the city and found almost no means of making a living there. He had them encircle the pond and on a signal walk slowly into the water before turning to face forward as Zhang himself walked into the pond with a young boy on his shoulders. *12 Square Meters* was composed of three elements: the artist's body, the city as represented by the toilet, and the pond. In *To Raise the Level of a Fish Pond*, these three elements are again present, though here the city is represented not by a failed piece of urban infrastructure but by struggling people. As one looks at each face and watches each person move, it becomes evident that there is individuality within this community. Each person's identity is articulated in relation to his body, the bodies of other people, and nature—which, in this case, is also a product of humanity. In 1998, the photograph shown here of *To Raise the Level of a Fish Pond* was featured prominently in the exhibition "Inside Out: New Chinese Art." Zhang followed the show to New York and moved there.

Ma Liuming

Like Zhang, Ma Liuming (b. 1969) trained as a conventional oil painter. Ma completed his initial training at Hubei Institute of Fine Arts in Wuhan in 1991 before leaving for Beijing and settling in the East Village in 1993. A visit to his Beijing studio by the London-based duo Gilbert and George, who had been among the most significant British performance artists in the 1960s and who continued to create new work—primarily photography based on images of their own bodies—inspired Ma to take performance seriously. Both Ma and Zhang, with whom he sometimes collaborated, identified the body as the most important factor shaping their experience of the world. But where Zhang described how, when he was growing up, physical force seemed to be the only way he could communicate, Ma said that he found his body confused those around him. In fact, other people's presumptions about his body kept intruding into his life. He repeatedly had to field questions about his gender—even friends would grow curious about whether he was hiding something from them. This confusion about who he was and his own curiosity led him to ask broader questions about masculinity, femininity, and gender ambiguity.

In 1993, Ma created an alter ego, Fen Ma Liuming, and turned these questions into art. In China, Liuming is a typical male name and "Fen" is a common element in women's names. Together Fen Ma Liuming signaled the transgender subject matter of the performance. Ma hired a professional stylist to make him up so that his face looked as much like a woman's as possible, thus joining male and female in his own form as well as his name. Ma also pointed out that, in

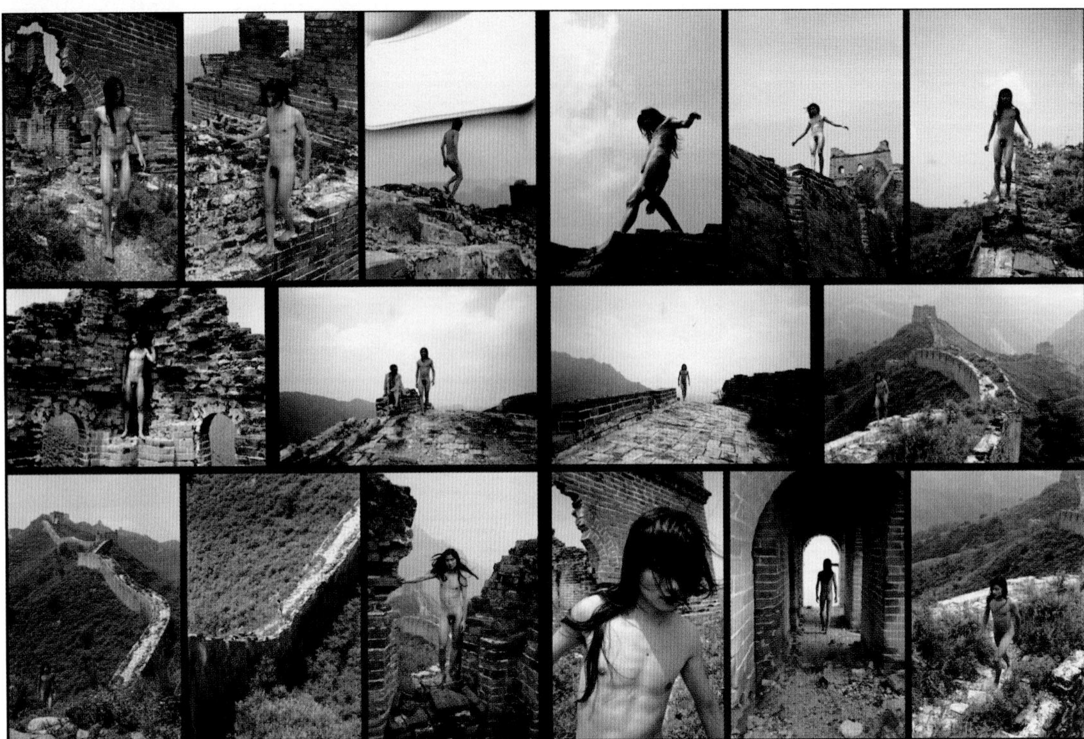

8.25 Ma Liuming, *Ma Liuming Walking the Great Wall*, 1998. Gelatin silver print, 47¾ × 72½" (121.2 × 184.1 cm). Courtesy Xin Dong Cheng Gallery.

addition to meaning "fragrance" and being a female name, *fen,* a homophone for Fen, means "separation." Thus Ma's name incorporates ideas about gender differentiation even as his persona and performances convey connections. In his new persona, Ma created photographs and performances presenting Fen Ma Liuming in both male and female dress, though most often naked, and in a variety of contexts, including a marriage ceremony, walking the Great Wall of China (**fig. 8.25**), and posing for photographs with spectators. In the performances, the gender clues created by cosmetics might be echoed or undermined by his clothes and activities, but in either case are complicated by the evidence of his naked body with its male genitalia and feminine physique. In the public portrait performances, Ma presents himself as an object, in some cases even drugged, while participants walk up to him, strike a pose, and have their photograph taken with him. The results range from humiliating to romantic—some people even undress in solidarity with the nude artist. In performances such as these, Ma initiated a set of changing relationships by making his body the focus of actions that others performed. He ceased performing as Fen Ma in 2003.

The Rising Art Market

As is evident from the examples cited above, Chinese artists responded in very different ways to the political changes and opportunities they encountered at the end of the Cold War. The "Stars" artists' assertion of their right to experiment with form and content was amply exploited by the artists who followed them—but there were costs. Periodic repressive acts, including the Anti-Spiritual Pollution Campaign of the early 1980s and the 1989 crackdown, curtailed the kind of public communication and experimentation that foster art communities. However, unlike the implosion taking place in the former Soviet Union, China's mechanisms for incorporating ideas from the outside, though imprecise and inconsistent, were porous enough to maintain a relatively steady production of art and a comparably stable art community. Many artists left the country, but many stayed, and others, including Zhang Xiaogang and Ai Weiwei, traveled away and then returned. In the early twenty-first century Xu Bing and Zhang Huan were both working in China, Xu also serving as a vice-president of the Central Academy of Fine Arts in Beijing. Despite inconsistent and often oppressive government actions, China was never without an artistic and intellectual community able to knit together memories of past works to inform the production of new ones.

What was not present in China until the late 1990s, at least to any meaningful degree, was an art market, domestic or international. Individual collectors did occasionally surface. Much of the work in the "China/Avant-Garde" exhibition was sold to an unnamed and now apparently missing Chinese collector, and a few Western collectors, notably Uli Sigg and Guy Ullens, were collecting in the 1980s, but there was no system in place to facilitate or promote investment in contemporary Chinese art.[36] In 1989, the Hong Kong-based Hanart TZ Gallery, under the direction of Johnson Chang (Chang Tsong-zung), presented "The Stars: Ten Years," a retrospective of the "Stars" artists, and in 1993, Chang, with Li Xianting, curated "China's New Art, Post-1989." Initiated by the gallery, both shows then traveled, the latter in abbreviated form to venues in Australia, Canada, and the U.S. International interest in Chinese art thus grew, and national representatives were included in international biennials starting in 1993 in

Venice. Individual expatriate Chinese artists also began to attract attention and higher prices. In 2004, Sotheby's finally negotiated a sale inside China, in Hong Kong, comparable to the 1988 Moscow sale. China itself was slow to recognize the importance of supporting its artists. Only as late as 1996, with the first Shanghai Biennial, was there a concerted Chinese attempt to recognize the value being generated by its art community. For the first two incarnations of the Shanghai event, its curators focused on Chinese artists only. Then, in 2000, they opened the exhibition up to the rest of the world, effectively transforming what had been a local platform into an international forum like the biennials held in the West. To critics, the change was an example of the government's cynical use of the arts to soften its international image in the face of its unpopular policies relating to other things such as currency control and human rights. For artists, the message was sent out that Western taste would be setting the agenda. Art critic Wang Nanming, notoriously critical of Chinese artists working abroad, summed up the issue in the title of his critique: "The Shanghai Art Museum Should Not Become a Market Stall in China for Western Hegemony."

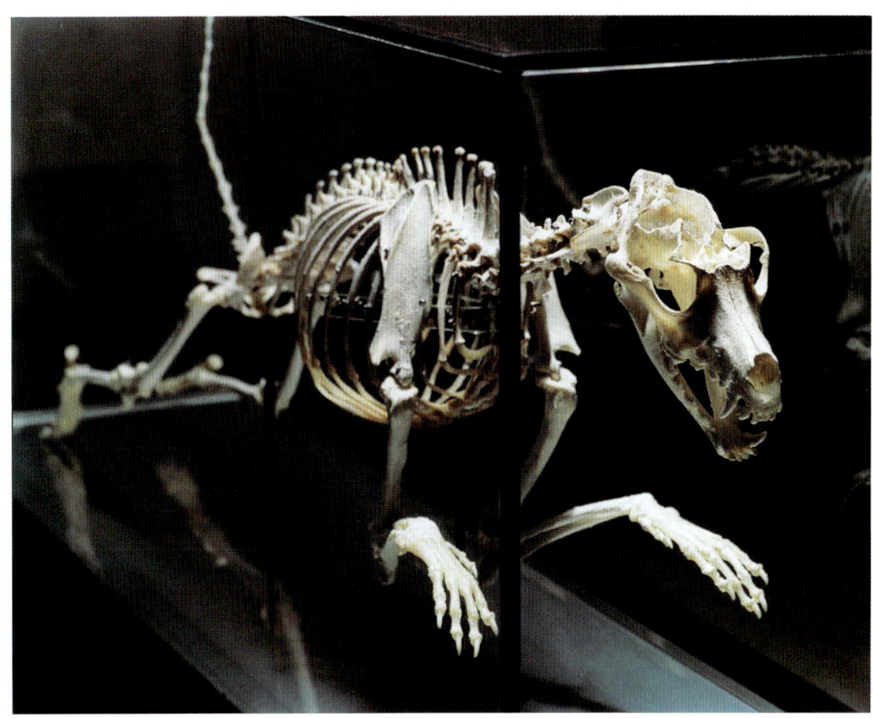

8.26 Sun Yuan, *Solitary Animal*, 2000. Dog skeleton in barium chloride solution, 15¾ × 21⅝ × 59½" (40 × 55 × 150 cm). Exhibited at "Fuck Off!," Donglang Art Gallery, Shanghai, China. Courtesy the artist.

The most dramatic response to the Shanghai Biennial's decision was Ai Weiwei and curator and critic Feng Boyi's concurrent exhibition of challenging Chinese contemporary art, bluntly titled "Fuck Off!" The accompanying catalogue begins with two of Ai's *Perspective* photographs in which the artist photographed his outstretched hand with his middle finger raised at various monuments, as if making perspectival measurements for a drawing. Ai gestures first toward the White House in Washington, D.C. (*Perspective*, 1995), and then toward Tiananmen Square in Beijing (*Perspective*, 1996). The exhibition opened at the Eastlink Gallery in Shanghai during the opening festivities of the 2000 biennial; thanks to its English title, it generated plenty of press attention, as intended. The curators' statement explained that the exhibition "emphasizes the independent and critical stance that is basic to art existence ... It tries to provoke artists' responsibility and self discipline, [and] search for the way in which art lives as 'wildlife.'"[37] Though the catalogue included much work that was not displayed in the show, including a number of pieces that made use of human and animal corpses, the exhibited work, including *Inflated—A Horse* (2000) by Beijing painter and sculptor Yang Maoyuan (b. 1966)—a horse, its hide blown up to the point where it began to suggest the form of a ball—and *Solitary Animal* (2000) (**fig. 8.26**)—a dog's skeleton enclosed in a vitrine purported to be filled with poisonous gas—by Beijing sculptor Sun Yuan (b. 1974), amply demonstrated that the artists were taking seriously the Chinese name of the show: "An Uncooperative Approach." Ai continued, well beyond the 2000 event, to be an outspoken critic of the Chinese government, shifting his concern from the cultural politics challenged in "An Uncooperative Approach" to address a spectrum of national and international issues. In the subsequent decade he appeared to spend as much energy on publishing his opinions on the Internet as on making objects; by 2010, his Twitter account had 48,000 followers who could read up to 100 messages a day. "For the first time in over 1,000 years, Chinese people can exercise their personal freedom of expression," Ai explained. In March 2010, in what appeared to be a fresh wave of attacks on free speech in China, officials arrested Ai, his studio was demolished, and all his means of communication were shut down. After an 81-day detention, Ai was released and soon after fined 15 million yuan (2.5 million dollars) for tax evasion. As in 1979, when the "Stars Art Exhibition" was closed, there was an outcry—but this time, after over two decades of growing integration of China with the international art world, many of the voices calling for the expansion of free speech and the release of the artist came from outside the country.

9

Engaging the Global Present

By the 1990s, it had become clear that grappling with contemporary life required communicating along the global networks that define it. While artists as different as Mona Hatoum and Wang Guangyi made art rooted in the contact and conflict between cultures and nations, exhibition practice also demonstrated that the contemporary art world was changing. In this respect, the 1989 exhibition, "Magiciens de la Terre," curated by Jean-Hubert Martin at the Centre Pompidou and the Grand Halle at the Parc de la Villette, Paris was a signal event, revealing much about the urgency and challenge of rewriting the map of contemporary art. Martin had taken seriously critiques that Western curators consistently relegated non-Western art to anonymous source material for Western masters. He further conceded that, with regard to contemporary art, European and U.S. museums effectively excluded the creative efforts of 80 percent of the world. "Magiciens de la Terre" was thus designed to be a "planetary" exhibition, including living artists from all over the globe. Visitors were confronted with an incredibly wide range of objects and practices providing irrefutable evidence that global artistic production far exceeded the contents of contemporary Western art auctions. To its detriment, however, "Magiciens" placed undue emphasis on authorship, exoticism, and mysticism, the very features that so much contemporary theory, art criticism, and art in the West had been challenging for decades. Despite intending otherwise, many of the stereotypical binaries of West and non-West were reinforced: For instance, viewers were met at the door by a Kruger text piece asking "Who are the Magicians of the Earth?" and entered to find the answer in the form of Tibetan and Yuendumu sand paintings on the floor. Authority, intellect, and technology appeared still to be the preserve of the West, while community, environment, and spirit were the priorities of the non-Western arts. Such failures notwithstanding, the show marked a significant step in the direction of acknowledging the biases of Western curating and opening up the field to the global character of contemporary art.

In the decades following "Magiciens," the art world has taken on global dimensions, developing around a network of biennial and triennial exhibitions held in cities all over the world. Thus an artist working on one aspect of globalization can count on his or her work being shown alongside that of an artist from another part of the world examining a different one. There are challenges, however, especially as the biennial system has come to mimic the flow of global capital, in some cases quite directly. At the turn of the millennium one could see emerging a repetition of the pattern demonstrated in the 1950s promotion of Abstract Expressionism (see Introduction) whereby culture followed in the footsteps of economic and political power. Now, however, artists and curators working within the contemporary network have an awareness about the intersections between art, economy, and politics that only began to be explored in the 1960s. The reshaped art world, like the specific examples of art discussed in this chapter, has the potential to provide artists and audiences with a map of contemporary life that includes an analysis of the power that has gone into making it.

Chapter 9 will address the expanded vision of the art world from a variety of perspectives beginning with a selection of art and events from Cuba that articulate individual and communal identities within competing personal, national, and international frameworks. Cuban art has a long history of reflecting cultures from across the spectrum of political power, including those of the indigenous populations of the Caribbean, European colonial powers, and forced slave-trade migrations. After the revolution in 1959, the nation became a nexus of Cold War tension as well. For Cuban artists, Western artistic movements including Abstract Expressionism and Pop art, as well as Afro-Cuban and Latin American influences, were readily consumed alongside socialist politics. Artists showing in Havana have been consistently in dialogue with the capitalist West, the Communist East, and the developing world in Latin America and Africa. In the 1980s, as Cuba struggled to survive the Soviet collapse, it stepped up to lead the postcolonial world through the initiation of the Havana Biennial. Started in 1984, the biennial asserted the strength of art outside the U.S. and European umbrella. As the climate continued to change after the fall of the Soviet Union, Cuban artists faced another chapter in their history of navigating the global pressures of politics and art. After introducing themes in contemporary Cuban art, Chapter 9 will examine a variety of different perspectives and approaches from other nodes on the network of contemporary art. The artworks included here range from interpretations of the Indian miniature tradition and Japanese animation to documentary imagery of street life in southern China, home-building in Israel, and the global shipping industry. This work treats the fact of globalization through individual case studies, sometimes localized in a single city, at other times identified through an industry or cultural phenomenon.

Cuban Experiments

Cuban art has been cultivating relationships with the outside world—whether the U.S., Europe, the Soviet Union, Latin America, or Africa—since the revolution in the late 1950s. Much more than their counterparts in Eastern Europe or China, Cuban artists have been consistently well informed about the international avant-garde and eager to enlist its radicalism for the utopian aims of the revolution. In the 1960s, Abstract Expressionism and Pop art were used to address issues relating to social and individual identity in Cuba. The various Caribbean, Latin American, and African traditions found in Cuba were promoted and examined by artists who, like contemporary politicians, were seeking to demonstrate the breadth and depth of Cuban society. In the early 1970s, Cuba strengthened its ties to the Soviet Union and the arts endured their "Gray Period." The experimentation that had flourished in the early years after the revolution suddenly faltered, though by the middle of the decade formal innovation was once again accepted—as long as it did not directly oppose state policies. Arts education, a priority in the early days of the revolutionary government, also suffered during the early 1970s. Then, in 1976, the government founded the Instituto Superior del Artes (ISA), a graduate school that renewed the official Cuban commitment to the arts and fostered students and teachers who encouraged, and themselves produced, socially engaged, aesthetically experimental, and conceptually challenging art. Though issues of censorship and control did not disappear, it was once again possible to create meaningful art within the Cuban system. In contrast to the stultifying experience of Soviet artists, art students in Cuba left graduate school in the early 1980s with a sense of purpose and community.

The "Volumen" Generation

The first fruits of the relaxation of art policies went on display in January 1981 at a small exhibition in Havana called "Volumen I." Three of the eleven participating artists, José Bedia, Flavio Garciandia, and Rubén Torres Llorca, were products of the first ISA intake. The show was eclectic, including work in abstract, realist, Minimalist, performance, and expressionist styles. Over 8,000 people came to see it in only two weeks. In retrospect, it marked the beginning of a renaissance in Cuban art and introduced several modes that have since become popular, in particular an assemblage-based sculptural practice rooted in Afro-Cuban religious practices, a Conceptual investigation of the visual culture of contemporary Cuban life, and an interest in performance.

JOSÉ BEDIA José Bedia (b. 1959) set the tone for the 1980s generation with large-scale installations rooted in Afro-Cuban spirituality and directed to international as well as local audiences. Bedia was among the first Cuban artists of his generation to have an impact on the international art world in the 1980s. His paintings and installations featured prominently at "Magiciens de la Terre" and, throughout the international art world, engaged signs of pre-modern cultures, post-modern aesthetics, and contemporary geopolitics in an exceptional way. Bedia's art drew on his own experience of the Palo Monte Mayombe faith. When he was initiated into it in 1983, he has explained, his art went from being distanced and representational to becoming fully integrated with his life. His 1994 installation at the Philadelphia ICA in the U.S., *Kakuisa el Songe, Vuela el Hierro* (*Kakuisa of Songe, Flight of Iron*) (**fig. 9.1**), refers directly to Palo. Rising from behind a small iron bowl, a reference to the *nganga*, the site of a Palo initiate's spiritual power,

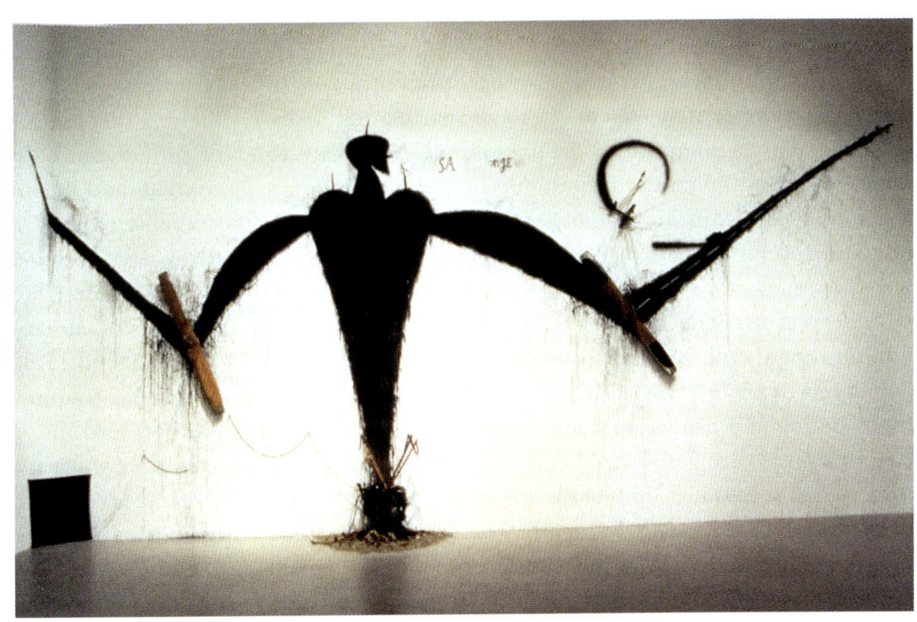

9.1 Jose Bedia, *Kakuisa el Songe, Vuela el Hierro (Kakuisa of Songe, Flight of Iron)*, 1994. Installation at the Institute of Contemporary Art, Philadelphia. Courtesy George Adams Gallery, New York.

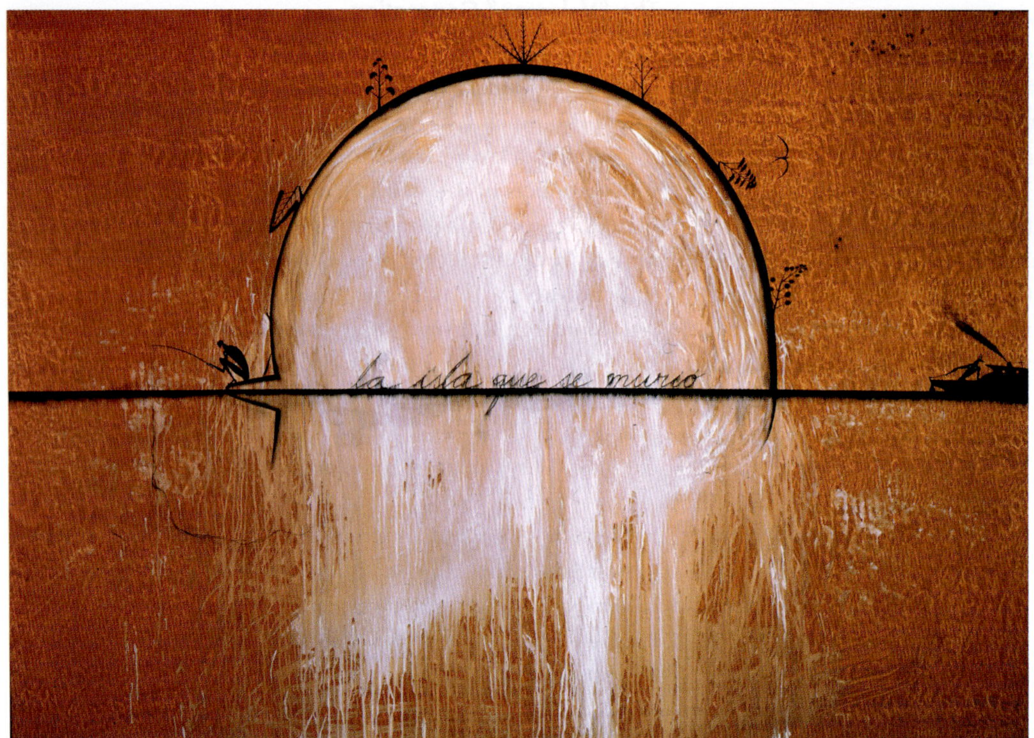

9.2 Jose Bedia, ***The Island That Died***, 1996. Acrylic on canvas, 71½ × 103" (181.61 × 261.62 cm). Private collection, Buenos Aires. Courtesy George Adams Gallery, New York.

is a towering figure painted directly on the wall. This floating body is the spirit Sarabanda, Bedia's patron spirit and a motif repeated throughout his oeuvre. *Kakuisa el Songe* presents the protection and power of faith, but it is also about problems of the material world. Two propellers extend from the arms of the great spirit, drawing on Sarabanda's traditional association with metal and evoking flight and emigration. Economic challenges at home and increased opportunities abroad led Bedia to leave Cuba in 1990, going first to Mexico City, then in 1993 to Miami. He has spent much of his professional life creating installations in museums and galleries around the world, acting as an ambassador for his culture and a historian of the Americas. Many of his works present motifs of travel: ships journey from sea to sky, roads vanish into the distance. Sarabanda often rises, as he does in *Kakuisa el Songe*, to watch over the itinerant artist and outsider. In all of Bedia's work, religious icons and symbols from capitalist, Communist, and developing nations guide the individual along his or her way.

Observers of Bedia's art have interpreted his tactics in different ways. One reading focuses on the artist's frequent depictions of an "everyman" figure. Such characters include the reclining and fishing men in *The Island That Died* (1996) (**fig. 9.2**), who are generalized enough in their appearance to serve as surrogates for nearly any viewer. Art historian and curator Charles Merewether has described how these figures anchor Bedia's work in viewers' sense of self while all around them whirl "historical and contemporary encounters between cultures and countries" and "between the every day and the sacred sphere."[1] Gods, ships, spirits, and people inhabit Bedia's world. In Merewether's interpretation, Bedia's work is an exploration of conflict in contemporary life and an invitation to participate in spiritual and personal growth. A second interpretation of Bedia's work hinges on what art historian Robert Farris Thompson has defined as "primalism," which, in its attitudes to non-Western art, stands in stark contrast to primitivism.[2] Pablo Picasso's use of the materials that he found in the anthropology museum in Paris and elsewhere in the first years of the twentieth century is a famous example of primitivism. The North African masks' "exotic" origins and formal invention provided Picasso with an important inspiration for his painting *Les Demoiselles d'Avignon* (1907) and invested the figures with a mysterious and troubling sexual energy, but their precise meanings were of little interest to him and of no significance in his use of them. Primalism, Thompson argues, reverses the priorities of primitivism by embracing such works' original function, context, and meanings. To be a primalist thus requires considerable cultural education and experience; in this regard Bedia was obviously amply suited to the task. In addition to Palo, Bedia's work makes reference to African religions that he encountered while serving with the Cuban army in Angola, Native American religion, which he learned about during his training with a Lakota shaman, and Christianity. Furthermore, he draws inspiration from his extensive collection of African, Native American, Pre-Columbian, and Oceanic art. Bedia's practice, Thompson argues, "blends contemporary art with sacred impulses from beyond the West" in a manner that "involves direct sacrifice, a giving back, rigorous tests of body and mind, and the nurturing of trust and friendship with native artists and philosophers." Rather than focusing on the "common man" and other aspects of Bedia's work that will be immediately comprehensible to most viewers,

Thompson's primalism emphasizes features, such as the *nganga* in *Kakuisa el Songe*, that will remain incomprehensible to the uninitiated. While the universal fishing man in *The Island That Died* awaits the viewer to join him, the primalist *Kakuisa el Songe* announces how long and hard that journey may prove, and what special knowledge and study will be required to survive it.

ELSO "Volumen I" also featured the work of Juan Francisco Elso Padilla (1956–88), another young artist who positioned his work at the intersection between fine arts and indigenous religion. It is a characteristic of Afro-Cuban practices, unlike their African antecedents, that they incorporate features of different religions. Elso, like Bedia, found inspiration in Native American, Christian, and Afro-Cuban traditions. In addition to religious content, he also addressed the history of Cuba and Latin America and his own biography in sculpture that mixed materials such as sticks, twine, blood, iron, wood, and paint. *Por América* (*For America*) (1986) (**fig. 9.3**), a polychrome wood statue of the Cuban hero José Marti, exemplifies Elso's ability to intertwine political history, spirituality, and aesthetics. The sculpture presents Marti, author of *Our America* (1891), regarded by many as the founding manifesto of Latin American politics and Cuban identity, as frail and wounded. Wooden blades puncture his body and the ground around him. The paint that colors his flesh and clothing is abraded. Mud is caked on his torso. The figure raises a machete in his right hand as his eyes stare out intensely. Marti, killed in the war of independence fought with Spain, is the father-figure of the Cuban nation. Elso's subject matter in the work, however, is spiritual as well as political and historical.

The most powerful invocation of the spirit in *Por America* is not visible to the viewer. Elso practiced Santería, a Cuban religion rooted in the African Yoruba faith. Before completing the sculpture, Elso and his wife performed a Santería rite of fidelity and love. As part of the ceremony they made offerings of their blood and mixed them together. After the ritual, Elso took some of the blood and placed it in a cavity he had carved in the back of *Por America.* The rite sanctifies the relationship of the lovers and the blood that they have offered together. By placing the sacred substance inside the sculpture, Elso seems to enlist the help of the Cuban poet-revolutionary to safeguard his oath of love. Elso's act also invests the sculpture with the sacred power rooted in Santería. Marti had written that the key to creating a strong, successful society in Latin America was awareness of the region's complexities and knowledge of its history and traditions. "Our Greece must take priority over the Greece which is not ours," he wrote, arguing that the region's past and not European history be used as the example for creating a strong modern Latin America.[3] "Our America," as he said, would survive only by rejecting racism and embracing the variety of indigenous cultures as well as external resources that proved useful for local needs. Elso's act echoes such sentiments. When he died at age thirty-two of leukemia, he left a body of work that in its poetic and philosophical breadth remains a touchstone for contemporary Cuban art.

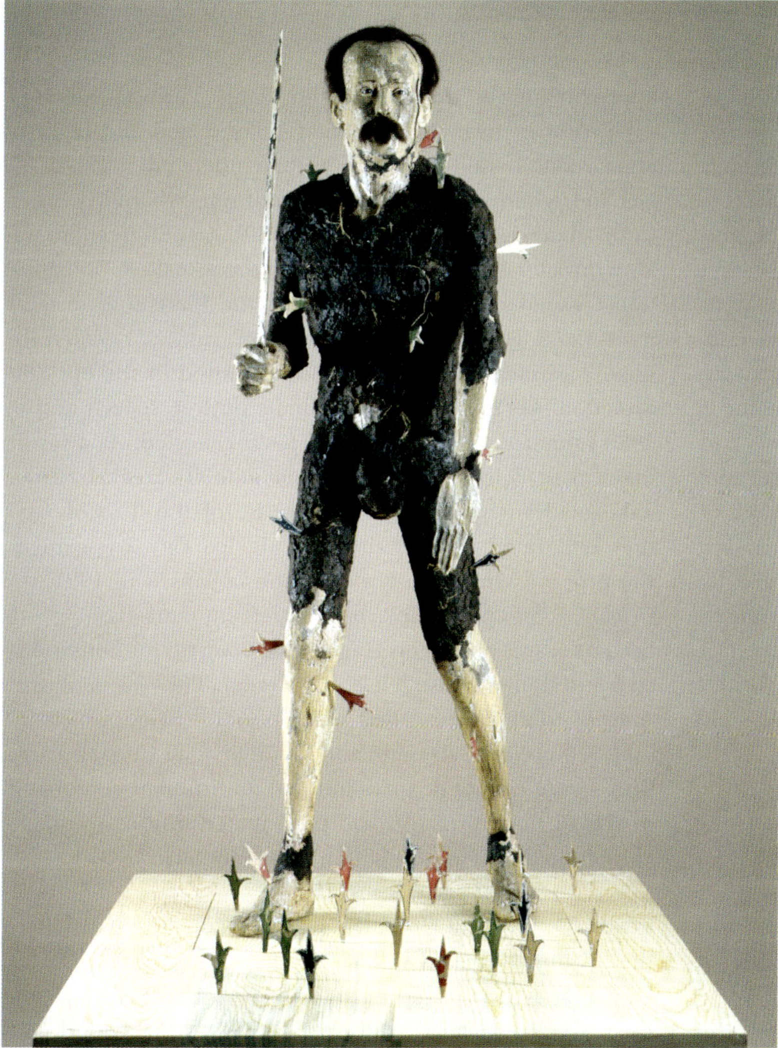

9.3 Juan Elso, *Por América (For America)*, 1986. Carved wood, plaster, and earth, figure approx. three-quarter life size. Entire piece, dimensions variable. Collection Hirshhorn Museum and Sculpture Garden Collection, Washington, D.C. Courtesy George Adams Gallery, New York.

FLAVIO GARCIANDIA Spiritualism and assemblage were not the only themes or approaches on display in "Volumen I." Flavio Garciandia (b. 1954) crafted paintings from irreverent combinations of political and popular symbols. Like his Russian Sots Art contemporaries (see Chapter 8), Garciandia composed his works by rearranging the iconography and typography of official propaganda, mixing it with other features of visual culture including kitsch and graffiti.

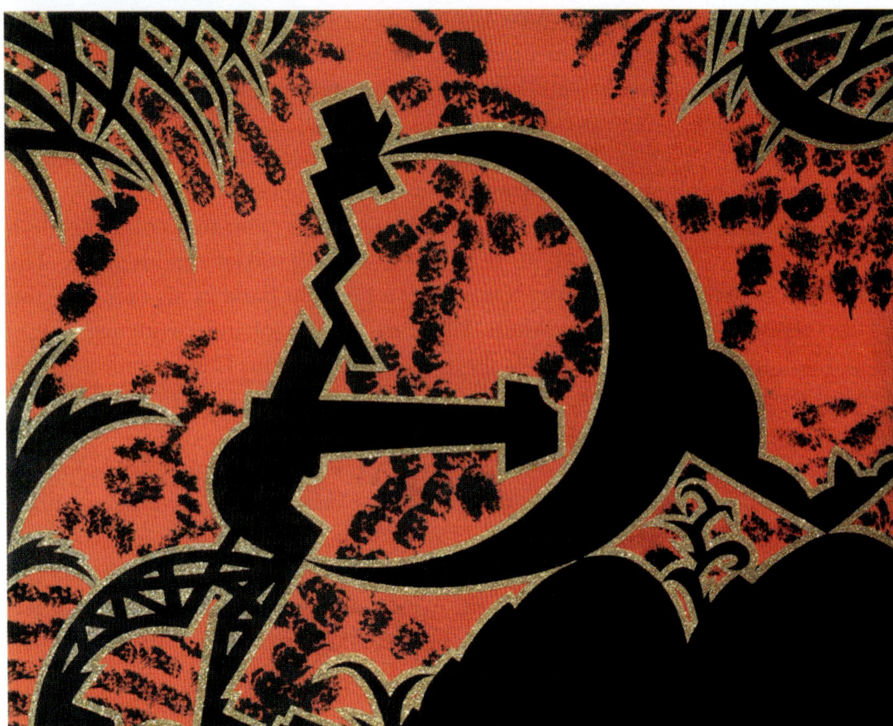

9.4 Flavio Garciandia, *Untitled*, 1990. Acrylic and glitter on canvas, 59½ × 66⅞" (150 × 170 cm). Collection Krings-Ernest, Cologne, Germany. Courtesy the artist.

Garciandia's goal was to represent the visual life of ordinary Cubans without repeating the ideological hierarchy that prioritizes the expressions of the state. Hence, in paintings such as *Untitled* (1990) (**fig. 9.4**), all manner of objects—hammers, sickles, amulets, palm trees, girders, penises, and stars intertwine and overlap in a flat, clear style that uses a bright palette and is suggestive of a stylistic amalgamation of elements drawn from advertising, propaganda, and wallpaper. Garciandia presents Cuban visual culture in what he calls an "uncontrollable kaleidoscope,"[4] his works staging a "clash between provocative sexual and political symbols and a perverse decorativism."[5] In the United States and Europe, the barrage of advertising created an ambiguous chaos out of which artists such as Ashley Bickerton and Sylvie Fleury (see Chapter 5) created their maps of identity and adventure. By way of contrast, working in a politically authoritarian context, Garciandia took an ordered environment and turned it upside down, creating new relationships between high and low, official and alternative.

The Second Generation

In 1984, the Cuban government invited the world to visit the first Havana Biennial. President Fidel Castro himself was credited with initiating the event and its mission of spotlighting Third World artists. The results successfully demonstrated the vitality of art outside the U.S. and European centers and Cuba's leadership of Third World culture. During the 1960s, Cuba had pronounced itself the revolutionary leader for the Third World and played a significant role in political and military struggles in Latin America and Africa. During the 1970s, this international role gave way to tightening bonds with the Soviet Union. Now, after approximately a decade of the "Gray Period," ideological pressures from Moscow had relaxed and the biennial appeared to herald a revival of Cuban independence.

Later editions of the biennial went somewhat awry owing to the financial crisis of the later 1980s. Artistic freedom was also threatened by ideological mandates, called "Rectification," issued in 1986. Troubled by the increasing instability in the Soviet Union, the Cuban government rejected the idea of *glasnost* (see Chapter 8) and moved in the opposite direction. Rectification placed limits on free speech and by 1989 numerous exhibitions had been canceled. As a result, many artists felt they could not pursue their careers in Cuba. Taking advantage of the relative ease of travel to Mexico, they emigrated, invigorating the Mexico City art scene in the process. When the Soviet Union collapsed in 1991, the Cuban economy shrank by 35 percent and basic goods became scarce almost overnight. Fuel reserves for both industrial and domestic use fell by 90 percent. This was the beginning of what Castro called the "Special Period," which, he said, required the strength and sacrifice of all Cubans. Faced with severe economic privation and government censorship, nearly all the artists who had participated in the "Volumen" exhibition and who were still in Cuba now left.

KCHO One of the first artists to step into the gap left by the "Volumen" artists was Alexis Leyva Machado (b. 1970), known as Kcho (pronounced Kah-cho). His nickname and carpentry skills came from his father; informality and craft are integral to his art, which constitutes an effective, flexible, and legible metaphor for Cuban life. By the early 1990s, Kcho had developed an assemblage technique similar to Elso's, combining natural and manmade materials to represent nationally meaningful symbols and scenes. In *Seal* (1990), he created a monumental version of the Cuban national seal out of sticks, branches, leaves, and twine. In place of the key that occupies the central panel of the crest, Kcho set a machete, a symbol for the Cuban sugar economy. Sugar is the primary export of Cuba and itself a symbol of Cuban history, identity, and ambition. It is also intimately connected to the lives of ordinary Cubans, many of whom have participated in the exhausting work of harvesting it. In addition, the sugar harvests are part of the political imagery of revolutionary heroes such as Castro and Che Guevara, as well as of the history of colonial occupation. Kcho's nuanced use of materials and symbols brings together the cultural and natural identities of his homeland while evoking the struggle for survival that has marked the country's history.

At the fifth Havana Biennial in 1994, Kcho presented *Regatta* (1993) (**fig. 9.5**), a flotilla of small boats roughly crafted from debris found on a beach and placed like toys on the floor of the historic Morro Castle. As a country, Cuba is often conceived of as a vessel afloat on a difficult sea. *Regatta* modifies the metaphor slightly to present a community of individuals joined together by their common relationship to the sea. While all of Cuba is bound to the ocean, Kcho's childhood on the Isla de la Juventud, a small island approximately four hours from Havana by boat, lends added biographical relevance to the theme. In Morro Castle, Kcho's fleet faced north from Havana Harbor toward Miami, issuing what appeared an ambiguous challenge: Was the work presenting a challenge to the U.S. or a threat of mass emigration to the Cuban government? Life in Cuba was getting increasingly difficult in the "Special Period"; *Regatta* certainly expressed a longing for something better. Less than two months after the close of the biennial, 35,000 people set out for Miami on makeshift boats in what was the largest exodus from the island since the Mariel Boatlift in 1980. Many died in the attempt. The U.S., concerned about its ability to support the sudden influx of immigrants, ended its thirty-five-year policy of welcoming Cuban citizens—at the same time President Castro announced he would not prevent Cubans from leaving. These changes in U.S. and Cuban policy led to claims that Castro was emptying his prisons into the sea and horrific images of U.S. Coast Guard vessels chasing down and arresting Cubans who had survived for days on rafts. Though, in retrospect, *Regatta* appears presciently political and even potentially critical of the government, in the spring of 1994 it did not encounter trouble from Cuban officials. In fact, the piece marked the start of Kcho's career as an art star in Cuba and abroad. He has since enjoyed the full support of the government and even of Castro personally. After the biennial, Kcho was invited to take part in a residency at the Ludwig Foundation in Germany, for which he created a circular assembly of small lead boats. Rather than oriented so as to suggest a destination or confrontation, this fleet faces inward toward itself.

Kcho continued developing his imagery of the sea in a large installation. In *Speaking of the Obvious Was Never a Pleasure for Us* (1997) (**fig. 9.6**), a *balsero*, the sort of makeshift boat used by Cubans to flee to Florida, is integrated into a composition balancing the shelter of a tent with the forward motion of a flotilla. A single boat, suspended a few feet in the air, supports a pyramidal arrangement of furniture. Below, a small cluster of bottles huddle together like a liquid shadow. Sandbags and a wooden scaffold adorned with garments, chairs, nets, oil drums, and small figures frame the scene.

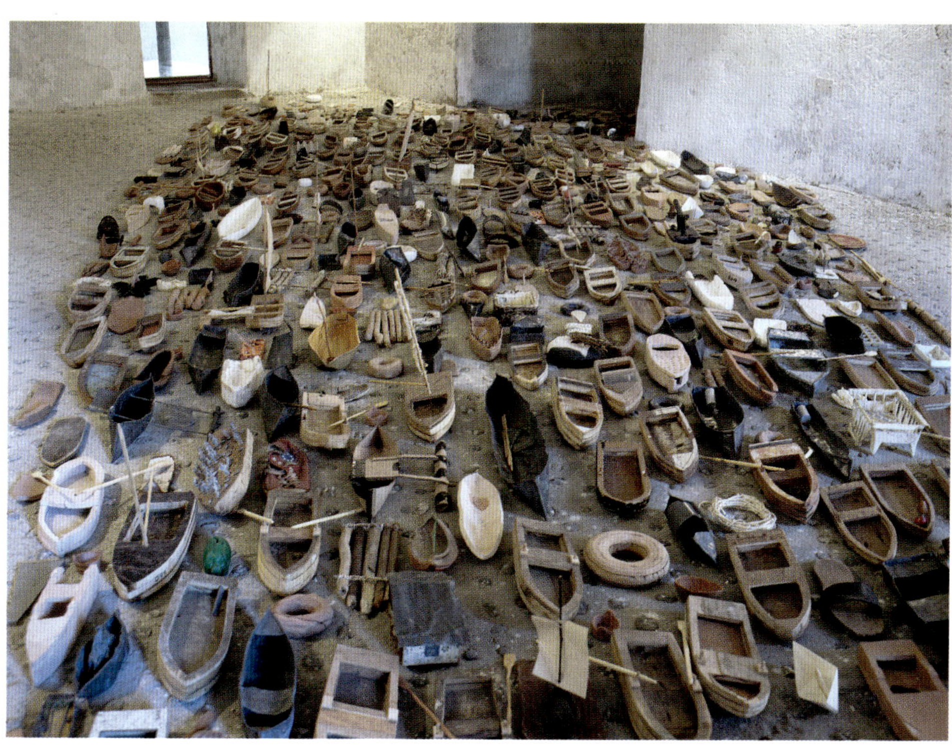

9.5 Kcho, *Regatta*, 1994. Small boats crafted from driftwood, overall ca. 19' 8" × 9' 10" (6 × 3 m). Ludwig Collection, Germany.

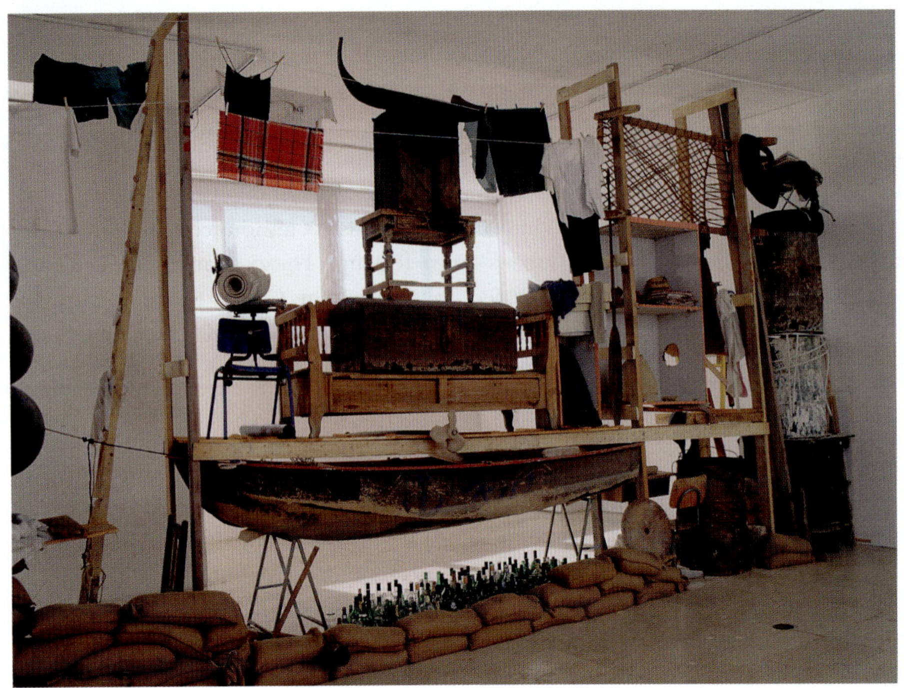

9.6 Kcho, ***Speaking of the Obvious Was Never a Pleasure for Us***, 1997. Detail. Mixed media. Installation view at the Billy Rose Pavilion, the Israel Museum, Jerusalem, summer 1997.

9.7 Ibrahim Miranda, ***Vida Disipada II (Dissipated Life II)*** from ***Metamorphosis*** series, 2010. Mixed media on maps, dimensions variable. Installation view at Servando Art Gallery, Havana, 2011. Courtesy Estudio Ibrahim Miranda.

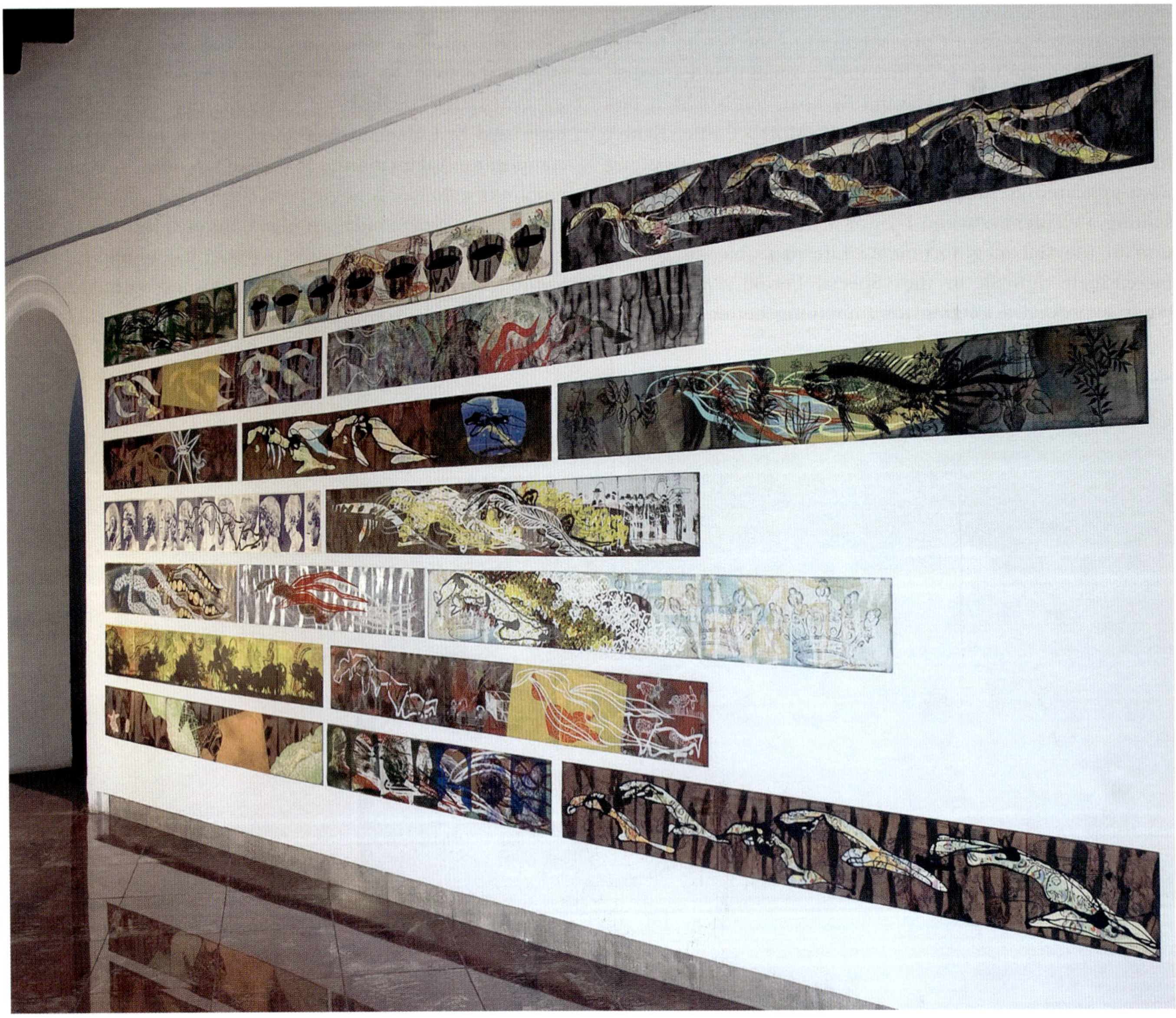

This is neither an image of moving forward nor of staying still; its meaning does not conform to a utopian vision or to contemporary social criticism. Rather, Kcho's installation evokes transitional states. The small figures that roam the work must make do in the spaces between progress and stasis. Raised in the period of Rectification, Kcho creates art that evokes situations, but does not point the finger of blame or even offer critique; that is left to the viewer.

IBRAHIM MIRANDA One of the most beautiful and (as in *Regatta*) poetic uses of the Cuban geography as a metaphor for the character and condition of Cuban culture is a series of prints by Ibrahim Miranda (b. 1969) called *Metamorphosis* (2010) (**fig. 9.7**). Miranda is a painter and printmaker of Kcho's generation who has been active in Havana since the mid-1990s. *Metamorphosis* is a suite of mixed-media prints depicting an evolving map of Cuba. In one image the island drifts in the current like seaweed, in another it swims. Flora and fauna are printed over it on one page while an image of Adam and Eve is stamped across it on another. Miranda's island changes character as it moves from the deep sea to the Hebrew Bible, evoking different aspects of Cuban history, culture, and tradition. Throughout all the transformations Miranda creates in the *Metamorphosis* imagery, cartographic inscriptions remain, asserting that the island, like all mapped territories, is always a social and historical fact, as political as Kcho's seal.

RENÉ FRANCISCO RODRIGUEZ The Havana 1994 biennial was underwritten in large part by international funds, provided chiefly by the Ludwig Foundation of Cuba, a cultural development organization established by German entrepreneur and collector Peter Ludwig. Ludwig had become interested in Cuban art after learning about it on trips to the Soviet Union in the late 1980s. In 1990, he sponsored "KUBA OK," the first major exhibition of contemporary Cuban art in Europe, and subsequently purchased two-thirds of the work in the show. He also funded exhibitions and cultural activities in Cuba before finally establishing the Ludwig Foundation in Havana in 1994, which provided important contacts between Cuban artists and the outside world. Such ties necessarily created dilemmas. Artists of the 1990s, for instance, faced a temptation to cater to visiting collectors and curators. The artist team of Eduardo Ponjuan (b. 1956) and René Francisco Rodriguez (b. 1960) captured the threat from foreign investment to Cuban identity in *Dream, Art and Market (Portrait of Peter Ludwig)* (1993–94) (**fig. 9.8**), which appeared in the 1994 biennial. Eschewing the styles discussed thus far and disregarding traditional Cuban themes, Ponjuan and Francisco created a portrait of Peter Ludwig in a Photorealistic style surrounded by a series of attributes: examples of Pop art, an exhibition catalogue, and a view of Havana. Ludwig sits like a svengali, transforming the young Cuban portraitists into international artists fluent in the *lingua franca* of Western styles. The anxiety about participating in the international market was all the more intense because support such as that provided by Ludwig was the primary way artists were able to survive the "Special Period."

In the late 1980s, Francisco had initiated a series of projects that started with conversations and then developed into collaborations with other artists and the communities in which he lived and worked. Basing his artistic practice on the needs of his audience became the foundation of what Francisco called his "Pragmatic Pedagogy," and it had as much to do with his teaching at the ISA as with making art. In the classroom, Francisco adopted a horizontal rather than vertical structure that dispensed with the traditional hierarchical roles of master and pupil. Pragmatic Pedagogy defines art

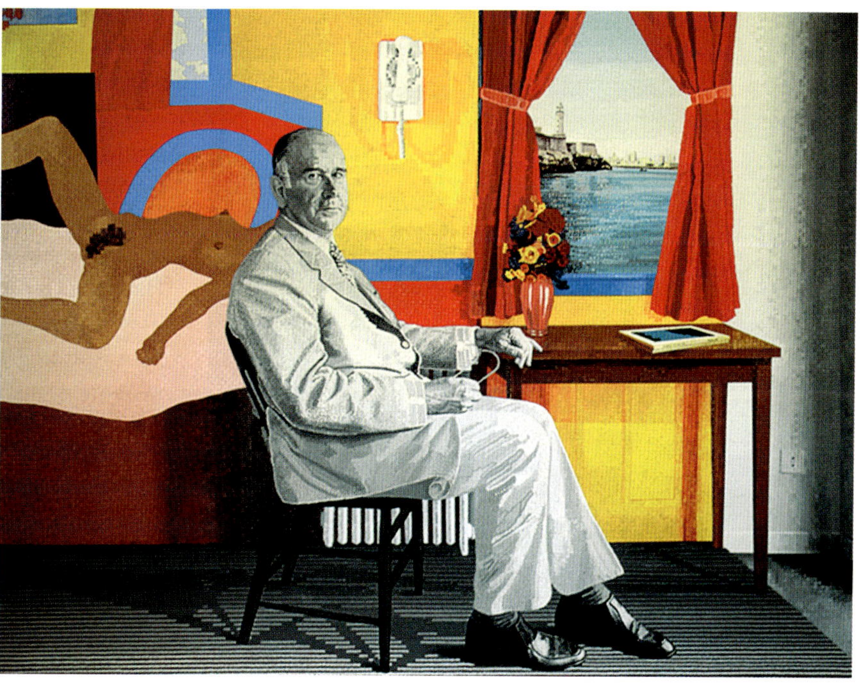

9.8 René Francisco Rodriguez & Eduardo Ponjuan, *Dream, Art and Market (Portrait of Peter Ludwig)*, 1993–94. Pencil and oil paint on primed canvas, 70⅞ × 79 × 1⅝" (180.3 × 200.7 × 4 cm). Daros Latinamerica Collection, Zurich. Courtesy the artist.

and education as means of transmitting knowledge between those who make art and those who live with it, and between teachers and students. Knowledge is constantly in flux and each side of the equation is in need of the other throughout the conception, execution, and reception of art. Everyone involved is an artist. In addition to responding to the practical needs of the ordinary Cubans during the "Special Period," Francisco, like many of his generation, was deeply influenced by Joseph Beuys (see Chapter 1). For Francisco and his peers and students at the ISA, Beuys's definition of art as social sculpture and belief in the creative power of every person were key ideas.

In 1989, Francisco and his students formed the artist group DUPP, which stood for *Desde Una Pedagogica Pragmatica* ("From a Pragmatic Pedagogy"). Their intention was to put their teaching philosophy into action, stepping out of the classroom to make art in stores, streets, and apartments as well as in studios and galleries. An early DUPP project, *La Casa Nacional* (1990) (**fig. 9.9**), began with the group interviewing residents of Old Havana to see what services they could provide for them. The answers varied: Some people requested art objects, others wanted assistance with home repairs. If DUPP's proposed services were accepted, members would take up residence with the families while they produced the desired environment or finished the required task. The project redefined artistic practice for those who participated. Members developed their plumbing and plastering skills as much as their painterly ones. Moreover, the creative process was shaped by conversations with people far outside the traditional art world, people whose aesthetics were often guided more by kitsch and patriotism than design theory, art history, or investment potential. Reflecting on the formation of DUPP, Francisco has explained that the privations and political pressures of the "Special Period" rendered the example of the "Volumen" generation, with its objects, exhibition schedules, and poetic metaphors, irrelevant. What was required instead was Pragmatic Pedagogy and the creation of processes, objects, and aesthetics that responded to the new political and economic circumstances.

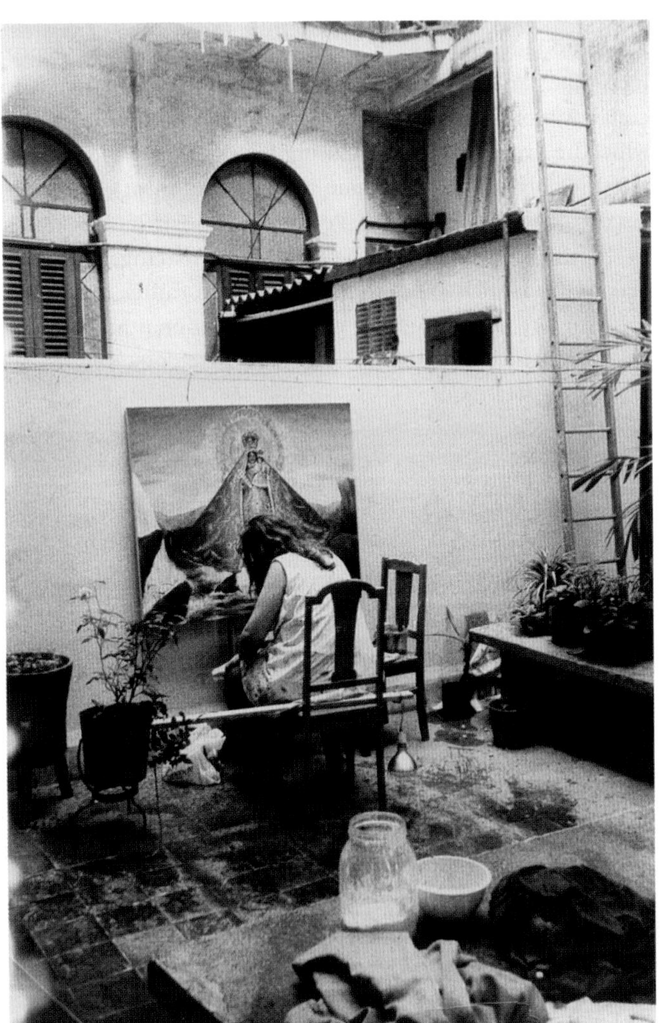

9.9 DUPP, *La Casa Nacional*, 1990. A DUPP artist at work, Old Havana. Courtesy Galería DUPP.

CARLOS GARAICOA René Francisco was not the only artist to feel that the "Special Period" had rendered existing modes of art making insufficient. He was also not the only one to turn to the city to help him define a relevant new artistic practice. The streets of Havana, however, inspired dreams as well as activism, as is abundantly evident in the photography, sculpture, and drawing of Carlos Garaicoa (b. 1967). Garaicoa graduated from the ISA in 1991 and quickly found inspiration in Havana's architecture. In the 1960s, the revolutionary government effectively nationalized large portions of the city. The mansions of affluent supporters of the deposed regime became state buildings or were divided into multifamily homes. Religious buildings were taken over, and in the famous instance of the founding of the ISA, a golf club became an art school. The result of this forced reattribution of functions was to render the visual cues of the existing architecture unreliable. Compounding the confusion, the hasty collectivization of Havana was done with the expectation that as the nation moved forward, the city would be rebuilt. Cuba failed to find economic prosperity, however, and the temporary solutions of the 1960s became permanent. As such, an aesthetic of decay and contingency came to dominate the capital.

Garaicoa found metaphors for self and society in the symbolic confusion and idiosyncratic form of post-revolutionary Havana. The inspiration for *About the Construction of the Real Tower of Babel* (1994–95) (**fig. 9.10**) came from one of his many photographs of the scaffolding that collects around weakened buildings in his neighborhood of Old Havana. These temporary structures once indicated construction work, but had metamorphosed into semi-permanent structural supports, holding up buildings awaiting perpetually deferred repairs. From these street scenes Garaicoa created fantasies in which magic gardens and gentle giants support the crumbling façades of Havana. In *About the Construction*, a compromised foundation supports a gold-banded pyramid that reaches high above the endangered streets. Here is a

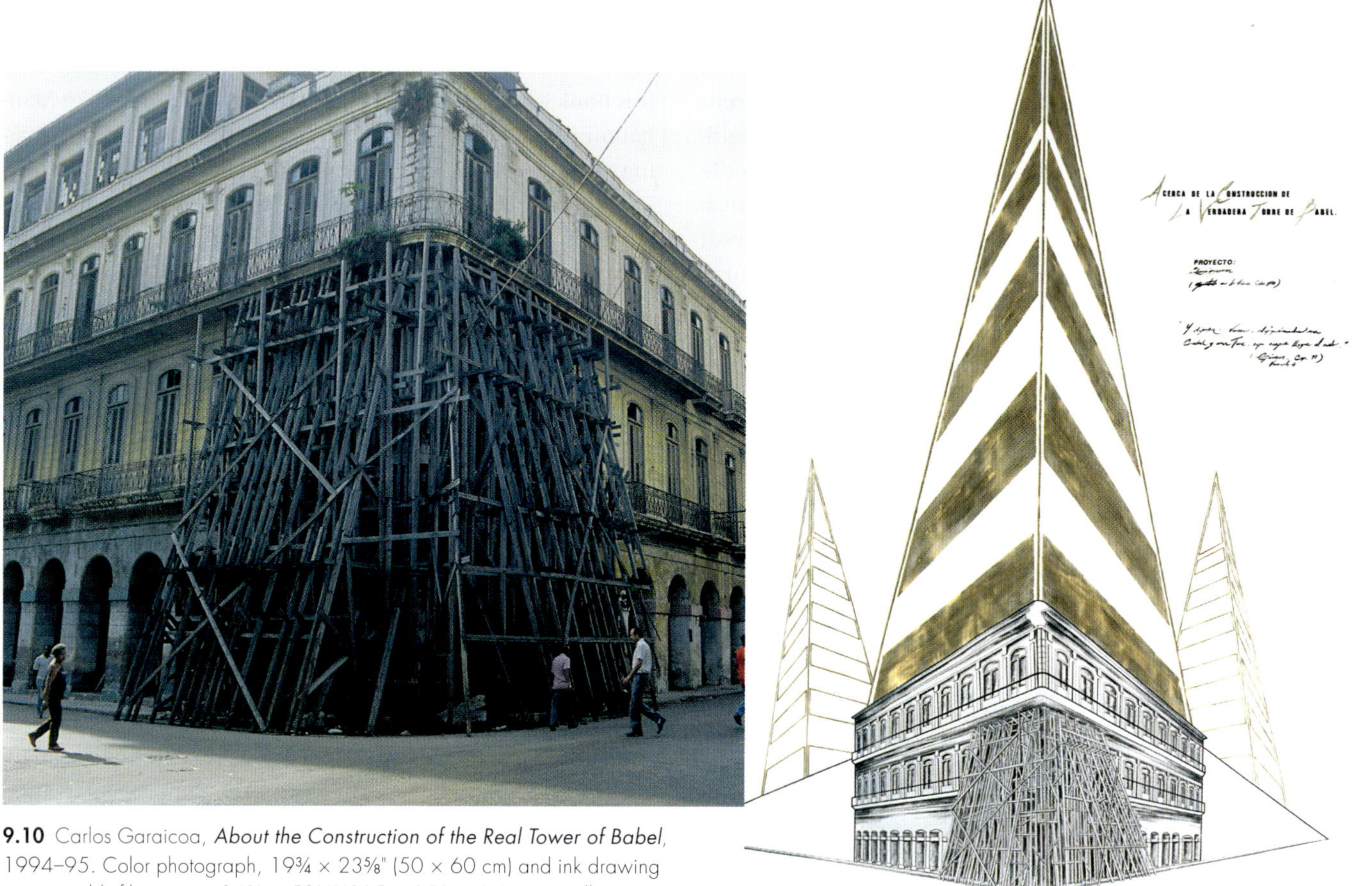

9.10 Carlos Garaicoa, *About the Construction of the Real Tower of Babel*, 1994–95. Color photograph, 19¾ × 23⅝" (50 × 60 cm) and ink drawing on vegetable-fiber paper 84⅝ × 59⅛" (215 × 150 cm). Private collection. Courtesy the artist.

contemporary Tower of Babel, a monument built on unstable ground and conveying the pathos and desperation of failed utopian dreams. Garaicoa observed that his generation "never got the chance of a life beyond politics," but their work is not clearly partisan and their attitude toward political solutions is ambiguous.[6] Kcho invests contemporary situations with mythological dimensions similar to the narratives of Bedia, but without the specificity of the older artist's faith; Francisco turns to the community with appeals for collaboration not unlike the ones that have consistently inspired Cubans to make sacrifices for the nation since the revolution; and Garaicoa has cultivated a careful balance between general allegorical evocations and judiciously placed, specifically Cuban details. The utopian vision of the Cuban nation, the unsteady alliance with the Soviet and post-Soviet world, and its antagonistic relationship with the Unites States have contributed to the complex political attitudes taken toward the challenges of Cuban life. Likewise the insight and inspiration shown in the first Havana Biennial was real, and represented the culmination of a long-standing Cuban project of drawing on the historical and cultural heterogeneity of the nation to lead a truly diverse and oppressed world. The Cuban example provides instructive evidence of the complexity of mapping the global turns of contemporary art and has had great resonance.

Mapping the Global Present

The poignancy of Garaicoa's *About the Construction of the Real Tower of Babel* lies in the directness with which it projects the limits of comprehension. The viewer, like the artist, sees the dilapidation of reality and dreams of imaginary supports to hold up the collapsing city. In another piece from the series, Garaicoa drew the first hallucinogenic mushroom farm in Havana, again juxtaposing reality with an invented and escapist remedy. Finding a way to respond in the realm of the real is difficult. Francisco found one solution, but he has admitted that few of his students follow his example. The Cuban situation is extreme, yet it is also representative of a large part of the world. The paths of the global economy have transformed the geography of production and distribution, creating dramatic demographic shifts. The political and cultural responses to such changes have profoundly impacted individual lives and been a source for a great variety of art. The section that follows introduces three artists—Shirin Neshat, Shahzia Sikander, and Yinka Shonibare, MBE—whose lives and art chart three very different paths through the global present. Unlike the previous discussion, these three do not form a group and do not share common background, media, or subject matter. Rather, each is representative of a growing number of prominent artists who were raised and trained largely outside the West, whose art has been exhibited primarily in Western museums and international biennials, and highlights the variety of traditions and meanings at play in the contemporary art world. The photography, film, painting, sculpture, and installation of these very different artists connect and juxtapose a wide variety of cultural traditions, artistic styles, and political convictions from the Middle East, South Asia, West Africa, Europe, and North America. Mapping this global present and grappling with the losses it creates, the options it provides, and the identities it produces have become projects of a great significance to the new millennium and its art.

Shirin Neshat

In 1975, at age seventeen, Iranian-born photographer and video- and filmmaker Shirin Neshat arrived in California. By 1982, when she had completed her MFA at University of California, Berkeley, the Iranian Revolution (1979) and the Iran–Iraq War (1980–88) had transformed her homeland, so that Neshat deemed it unsafe to return there. Instead, she moved to New York, but, unlike the many artists discussed in this book who followed a similar path from art school to Manhattan in the 1980s, Neshat found the experience debilitating. It would take her eight years and a long-awaited return trip to Iran in 1990 before she started making art again. Upon returning to the U.S. from her visit home, Neshat began *Women of Allah* (1993–97), a series of staged photographs of veiled women, occasionally shown in groups or accompanied by children or men, but most often pictured alone and with weapons (**fig. 9.11**). Dressed in what had become the legislated public attire for women in Iran, Neshat's subjects, often played by the artist herself, appear in provocative poses. A woman sits with the barrel of a gun projecting from under her hair or between her bare feet. Bullets are held in open hands. On the photographs, where the skin of the women is not covered by clothing, Neshat lettered Farsi poetry by women writers connected to very different aspects of Iranian feminist thought. The lines of Forough Farrokhzād (1935–67) addressing the difficulty of living under the traditional restrictions of Persian society decorate the flesh of one woman. Other images bear the poetry of Tahereh Saffarzadeh (1936–2008), which celebrates the revolution and the liberating power of the traditions of Islam. Neshat's images juxtapose sensuality, spirituality, power, and violence, and, particularly in light of their inclusion of texts, complicate any stereotypical notions of Iranian femininity. *Women of Allah* renewed Neshat's capacity and commitment as an artist, and initiated what she has called "a visual discourse on the subject of feminism and contemporary Islam—a discourse that puts certain myths and realities to the test, claiming that they are far more complex than most of us have imagined."[7]

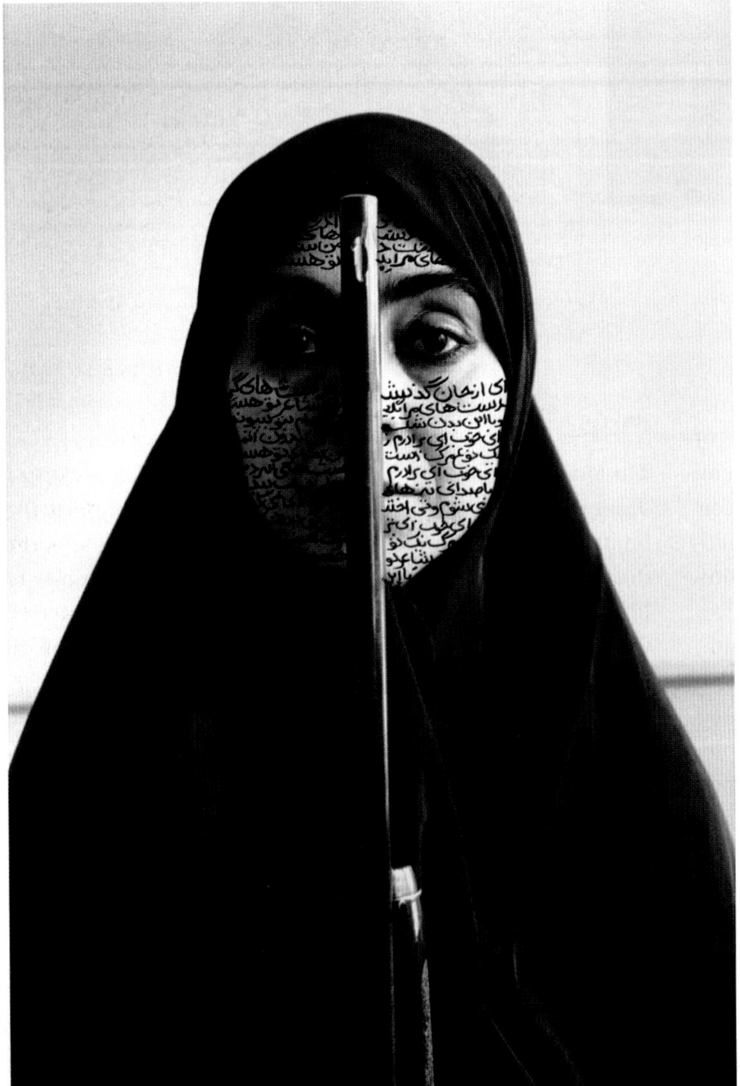

9.11 Shirin Neshat, ***Rebellious Silence*** from the ***Women of Allah*** series, 1994. Black and white resin-coated print and ink. Photograph by Cynthia Preston. © Shirin Neshat. Courtesy Gladstone Gallery, New York and Brussels.

To create *Women of Allah*, Neshat acted as director, producer, and even actor. She composed the images, created the sets, arranged the models or posed herself, but hired professional photographers to work behind the cameras. In 1997, she took what in retrospect looks like the next logical step, turning to film, a move that coincided with a growing interest in video art in the wider art world. By the late 1990s, it was common to see exhibitions dominated by video installations. *Turbulent* (1998) (**fig. 9.12**) is the first of three black-and-white, two-channel projections that Neshat created to examine gender dynamics in Iranian culture. It was followed by *Rapture* (1999) and *Fervor* (2000).

Turbulent consists of facing projections which begin on one side with a man singing a traditional thirteenth-century Sufi love song to a rapt audience of men. On the other screen a silent woman stands

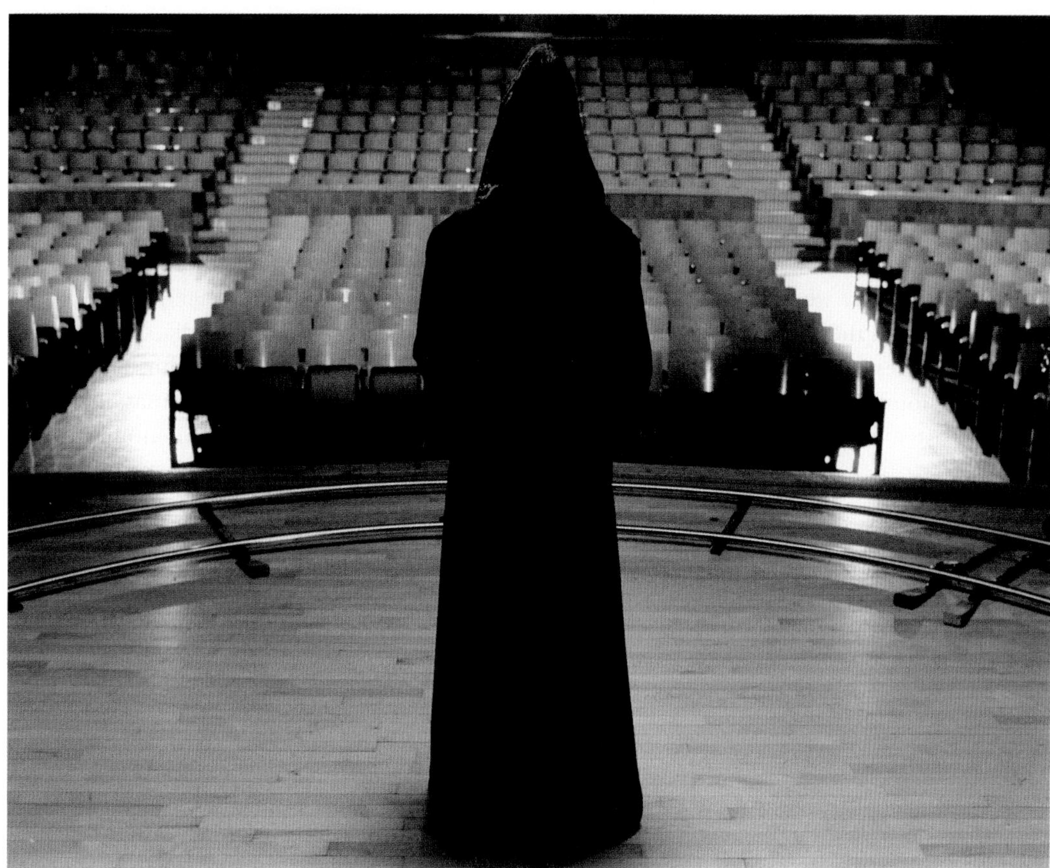

9.12 Shirin Neshat, *Turbulent*, 1998. Production still. © Shirin Neshat. Courtesy Gladstone Gallery, New York and Brussels.

on the stage of an empty theater. The male figure is Neshat's frequent collaborator Shojoa Youssefi Azari but the voice is that of a popular Iranian singer. For those few in her audience of primarily Western museum- and gallery-visitors who recognize the music, there is therefore a distance between what is seen and heard. This discrepancy becomes more pointed in the second half of the piece. Throughout the man's performance the woman, played by composer and recording artist Sussan Deyhim, waits silent and still. She stands veiled with her back to the camera as the man strives, as Neshat has explained, to reach mystical revelation through song. When the man has finished and his audience has given him a warm ovation, Deyhim begins a wordless melody. The song, which Deyhim composed herself, is an acrobatic vocal feat that sounds nothing like the music we were listening to before. The camera circles the woman as the urgency and intensity of her singing increase. When she then falls silent, the man and his audience stand aghast. Women were not permitted to perform in Iran. One challenge Neshat posed with *Turbulent* was to represent women reaching the spiritual heights music provides for men by cleverly circumventing the restrictions of contemporary society: The woman sings but her music is not recognizable as song and as there is no audience in the concert hall it does not constitute a performance. Neshat has portrayed what Laura Mulvey described in her essay on "the Gaze" (see Chapter 2): "The thrill that comes from leaving the past behind without rejecting it, transcending outworn or oppressive forms, or daring to break with normal pleasurable expectations in order to conceive a new language of desire."[8]

The presence of oppositional dichotomies defines the structure and content of Neshat's videos into the early 2000s. She has explained that her intent in works such as *Turbulent* was to approach gender in contemporary Iran through binaries, in this case "empty theater/full theater, rational/irrational, traditional music/nontraditional music, and communal/solitary."[9] As Deyhim's unprecedented song suggests, however, while binaries might determine the normative relationship between men and women, they do not limit how individuals can act, think, or create. With *Soliloquy* (1999) and *Fervor* (2000), Neshat continued to investigate the place and power of individuals in Iranian society. Projections including *Rapture* (1999) and *Passage* (2001) further examine the power of ritual and collective behavior. *Rapture* includes footage only of large numbers of men or women, with no close-ups on individuals. It contrasts the actions of a hundred men dressed in contemporary attire as they occupy a medieval fort with those of the same number of women beyond the fortified walls. The viewer is invited to extrapolate from the actions a narrative in which women create spaces and patterns beyond the existing social order. In 2009, Neshat, again with Azari, created a feature-length film, *Women Without Men*, which gave historical specificity to the philosophical, emotional, and cultural concerns conveyed in the earlier videos. Based on the 1990 novel of the same name by Shahmush Parsipur, it follows the lives of four women in Iran during the collapse of the democratically elected government in 1953. As the populist government falls to a British- and U.S.-supported military coup, Neshat utilizes the aesthetics of her videos—with their saturated palettes, slow pacing, graceful choreography and staging, and contrast of open landscapes with confined architecture—to imagine women's attempts to create identities and homes for themselves.

If the 1980s were dominated by art that in one way or another took aim at universalizing discourses, whether by critiquing practices of representation (as did the appropriation artists), reimagining means of expression (the Neo-Expressionists), or displaying an ambiguous fascination with capitalist culture (the commodity artists), the 1990s were marked by a desire to start from the particular. As has been addressed in Chapters 6 and 7, work that explored histories and identities outside the dominant narratives of Western power were finding audiences in the art world. Neshat's *Women of Allah* was quickly integrated into exhibitions and her films were enthusiastically received.

Shahzia Sikander

In the late 1990s, Shahzia Sikander (b. 1969) began building an art of layered icons, styles, and media. Her work in miniature and large-scale painting, installation, and digital animation has produced a complex representation of the interconnecting cultures, histories, and phenomena that

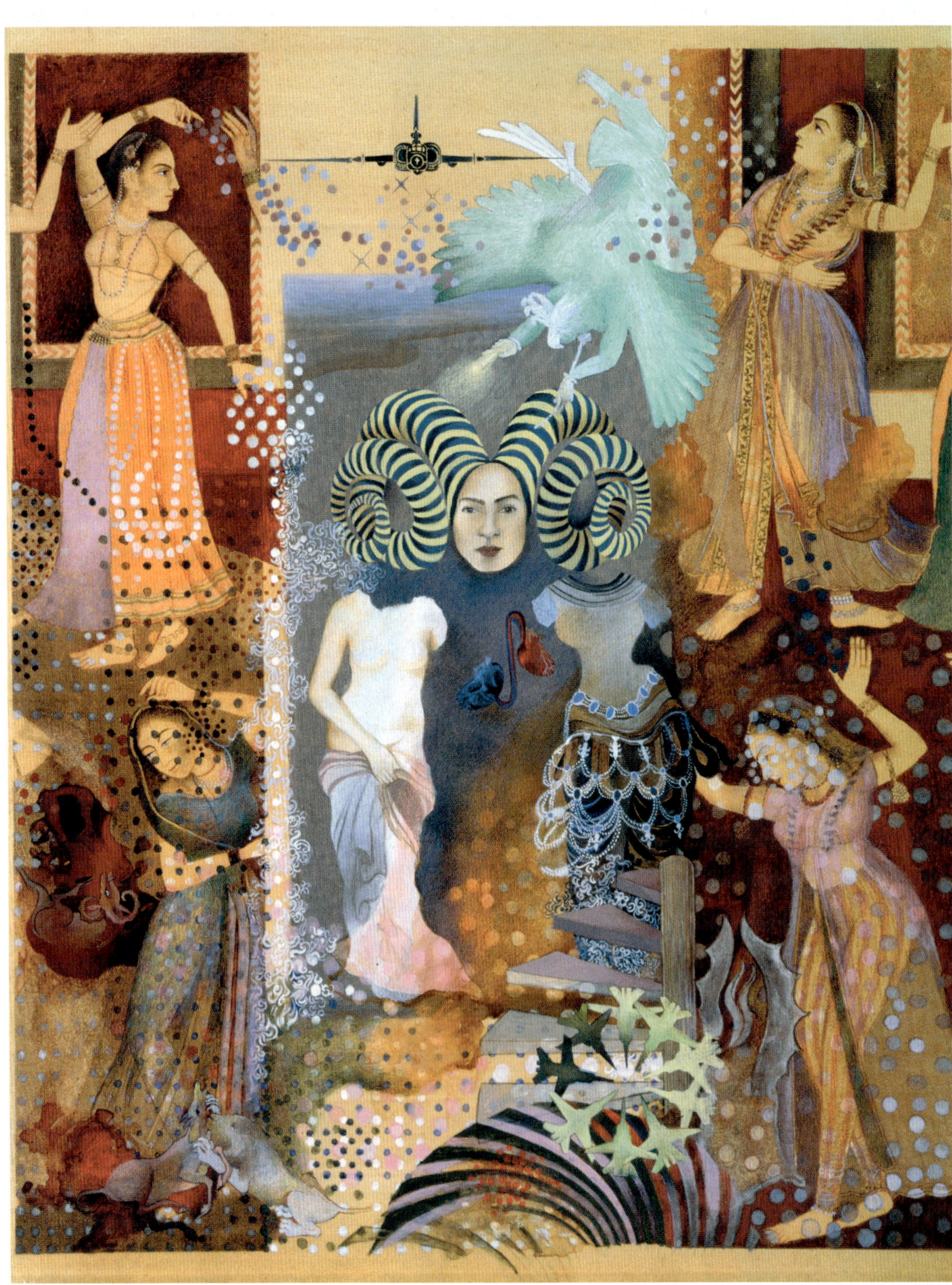

9.13 Shahzia Sikander, ***Pleasure Pillars***, 2001. Vegetable color, dry pigment, watercolor, ink, and tea on wasli paper, 12 × 10" (30.5 × 25.4 cm). © 2012 Shahzia Sikander. Image courtesy of Sikkema Jenkins & Co., New York.

constitute her experience of contemporary life. Sikander was born in Pakistan and trained as a miniaturist at the National College of Arts, Lahore. While nearly all of her peers were immersing themselves in Western traditions, Sikander followed a workshop-style curriculum that demanded a deep historical and practical understanding of Persian, Indian, and Pakistani art. Though intimately connected to centuries-old traditions and a craft-oriented practice, miniature painting proved surprisingly in tune with contemporary art theory. As Sikander noted, all traditions of miniature painting rely on copying and appropriation and thus have little to do with the concept of originality that was being so forcefully critiqued at the time. Across her oeuvre, and often in a single image, one can see references to the staged romances popular in Kangra miniatures, the refined control of Mughal draftsmanship, and the open, raw appearance of Rajput painting. Each of these styles in turn exhibits various integrations of Hindi, Muslim, and Sikh cultures and alludes to many nationalities—including Persian, Indian, Chinese, Pakistani, and even European ones. Upon moving to the United States in 1993, first to study at the Rhode Island School of Design and then to do postgraduate work in Houston, Sikander incorporated into her work references to Western abstraction and Expressionism, as well as U.S. symbols such as cowboy boots and fighter planes. She cultivated various means of layering forms and styles so that every element was recontextualized without losing its original significance. As she explained: "Physical, emotional, geographical, cultural and psychological boundaries among cultures exist. But, being an artist means pointing to the shifting nature of such boundaries."[10]

Pleasure Pillars (2001) (**fig. 9.13**), painted using watercolor, dry pigment, vegetable color, tea, and ink, provides an example of Sikander's layering of forms and histories as well as of her technical prowess. It is part of an extended project on which she was working in New York in late 2001 when the World Trade Center was destroyed. She described how, in the aftermath of the violence, objects and experiences that had meant one thing before the event seemed to take on new meanings afterward. The phenomenon of familiar things accruing new and changing significance in the wake of the crisis resonated with Sikander's use of symbols and styles as hinges between different traditions and cultures. *Pleasure Pillars* represents a moment at which her practice, though essentially unchanged, acquired a specific relevance to the political realities of the twenty-first century. The image is an assembly of spaces and figures evoking different cultures, histories, and artistic traditions.

In a 2008 interview, Sikander described the core of her practice as the production of "interstitial spaces" that serve as a "third space," a "political space," "a transgressive space," and "a space of the ideal, the fantastical, the subliminal."[11] Such spaces begin in the art and extend out into the experience of the viewer and the artist. At the four corners of *Pleasure Pillars* are dancers from the historic text the *Badshahnama*; their representation evokes their original Mughal context and their movements seem to carve out room for themselves in the painting. In the center, a delicately rendered portrait based on the artist herself supports a fantastic horned headdress and floats over two headless figures, one based on the Greek goddess Venus and the other on a Hindu *devata*, or deity. Between them, two hearts, one red and one blue, are connected by a single artery. Sikander has called these two central figures outcasts from the canon, female characters standing for those people ignored in the dominant historical narratives of East and West. The two appear as the central part of a larger series, *Maligned Monsters*, begun around 2000. In 2002, they were painted on banners hanging outside the Museum of Modern Art in New York. In the lower left of *Pleasure Pillars*, Sikander rendered a dying deer and a lion feasting on a bull, allegories of power in traditional hunting scenes. At the top of the scene, a fighter jet flies toward the viewer while at the lower left Sikander has painted a circular seal of similar warplanes, their arrangement transforming a threatening object into a pattern alluding to floral designs and invoking thoughts of gardens, which in Urdu poetry signify exile and also revolution and rebirth. Such mutable forms are of particular interest to Sikander. Dots cascade across the surface of the picture, alluding to bombs as well as Modernist abstractions. Next to the jet is a second flying figure, part human, with great open wings and the head of an eagle, who swoops in from the right: This is Garuda, who in the Hindu tradition is said to be powerful enough to obliterate the world, provides protection, and most importantly carries on his back the supreme deity, Vishnu. Sikander depicts his movement across the surface of the composition in opposition to the approaching path of the warplane, juxtaposing the divine path of the spirit with the secular course of the plane. Consistent with Sikander's interest in forms and symbols that migrate between cultures and resist any singular identification or meaning, Garuda appears in both the Hindu and Buddhist traditions as well as being used as a state symbol for different South Asian nations.

Just four years after arriving in the U.S., Sikander had already been included in the 1997 Whitney Biennial. Her work immediately captured the art world's attention for its intricacy and the international character of its references. Cultural theorists embraced the way Sikander articulated difference in her work. Most notably, Homi Bhabha, who had been theorizing hybridity as the natural state of the contemporary global citizen, adopted Sikander as a prime example of this tendency. Rather than appealing to any essential cultural identity, Bhabha's hybrid citizen is a traveler constituted by the many influences that surround him or her. Within a fragmented global experience, one responds to the traditions, practices, and meanings that one encounters with personal experiences, emotions, and ideas in order to create a home in a "third space."[12] This space, full of cultural, historical, and ideological content, fosters the production of one's own culture and identity, neither of which, Bhabha asserts,

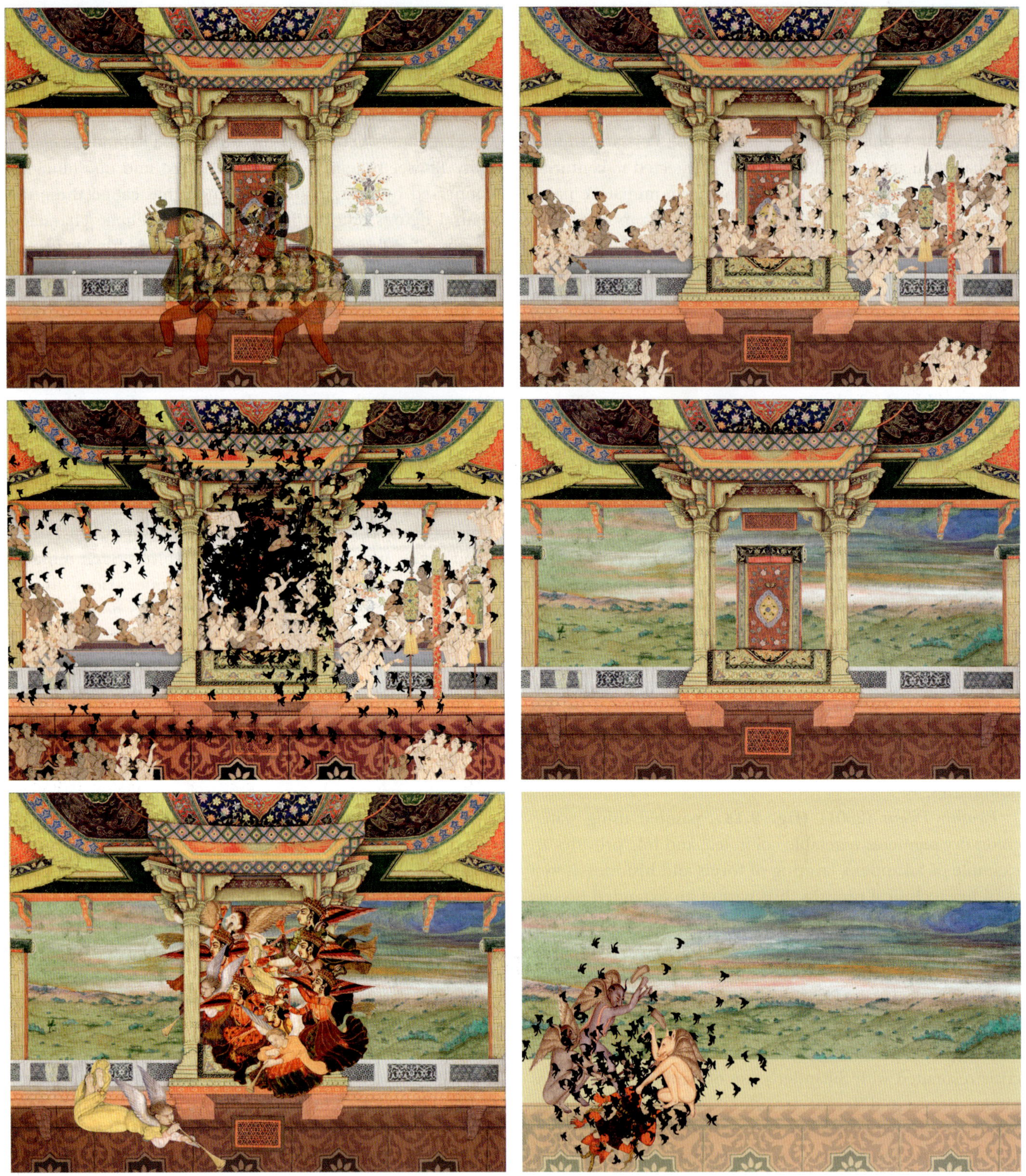

9.14 Shahzia Sikander, ***spiNN***, 2003. Six film stills. Digital animation (color, sound), 6 minutes 38 seconds.

is ever whole, but is always open to integration with others' cultures and to translation into others' practices. Sikander elaborates that the "third space" she strives to create is "constructed not simply within the piece but also through a larger set of relationships that surround the work" and address the question of "[h]ow to be between."[13] In this context, Sikander's multivalent collections of sources and styles offer a map of hybrid experience and her practice a model for living in the contemporary world.

Sikander has expanded the physical element of her art into three-dimensional space in the form of large-scale installations in which she paints on walls and on overlapping sheets of papers and fabrics that move in the gentle breezes in the gallery, drawing her work closer to the viewer's body. She has also collaborated with choreographer and dancer Sharmilla Desai, confronting the spaces of theory with those of the body. In contrast, animated work such as *spiNN* (2003) (**fig. 9.14**) integrates the tradition of the miniature with digital innovations, suggesting the links between traditional aesthetics and histories and virtual technologies. To make *spiNN*, the artist scanned painted images into digital animation software and set the parts in motion across a flat screen. Sikander has embraced multiple styles and media as a means of opening her art to systems of meaning that locate the "inbetween" of our corporeal, cultural, and technological identities.

Yinka Shonibare MBE

A very different presentation of the network of cultures, traditions, and aesthetics linking former colonies with colonial powers can be seen in the work of Yinka Shonibare MBE (b. 1962). Raised in Lagos, Nigeria, and London, England, Shonibare has created abstract and representational practices that initiate often surprising dialogues between Africa and the West. *Double Dutch* (1994) (**fig. 9.15**) typifies his juxtaposition of recognizably European and African aesthetic tropes—in this case, the Western Minimalist grid contrasts with the African textile-inspired abstractions. The binary structure that seems to pit rational Western order against syncopated African rhythms starts to falter, however, as one learns the rather complicated and global history of the seemingly "African" source of the textiles.

The fabric Shonibare uses as source material and support in *Double Dutch* is Dutch wax fabric, which most viewers would identify as characteristically African. Its history, however, charts a rather circuitous route through Africa, Southeast Asia, and Europe. In the nineteenth century, Manchester textile mills began producing copies of Dutch machine-made versions of handmade Indonesian batiks. The British then sold these second-generation imitations in West Africa, where they became very popular, leading English producers to design further examples specifically for the African market. In the 1960s, clothing made of Dutch wax fabric was worn in Africa as a sign of anti-colonialist nationalism and was adopted as a sign of pan-African pride by expatriate and diasporic Africans around the world. Thus *Double Dutch*, which appeared initially to be a juxtaposition of Western avant-garde and African craft traditions, is in fact a product of a complex exchange of forms, cultures, and money in both colonial and postcolonial society. In the artist's words, it is all about "pretend authenticity"—a sense of meaning that is rooted in what we make of the world rather than any inherent or essential truth.[14]

Shonibare also uses the fabrics more directly in his work, for instance in tableaux showing headless mannequins caught indulging in the typical pursuits of the English

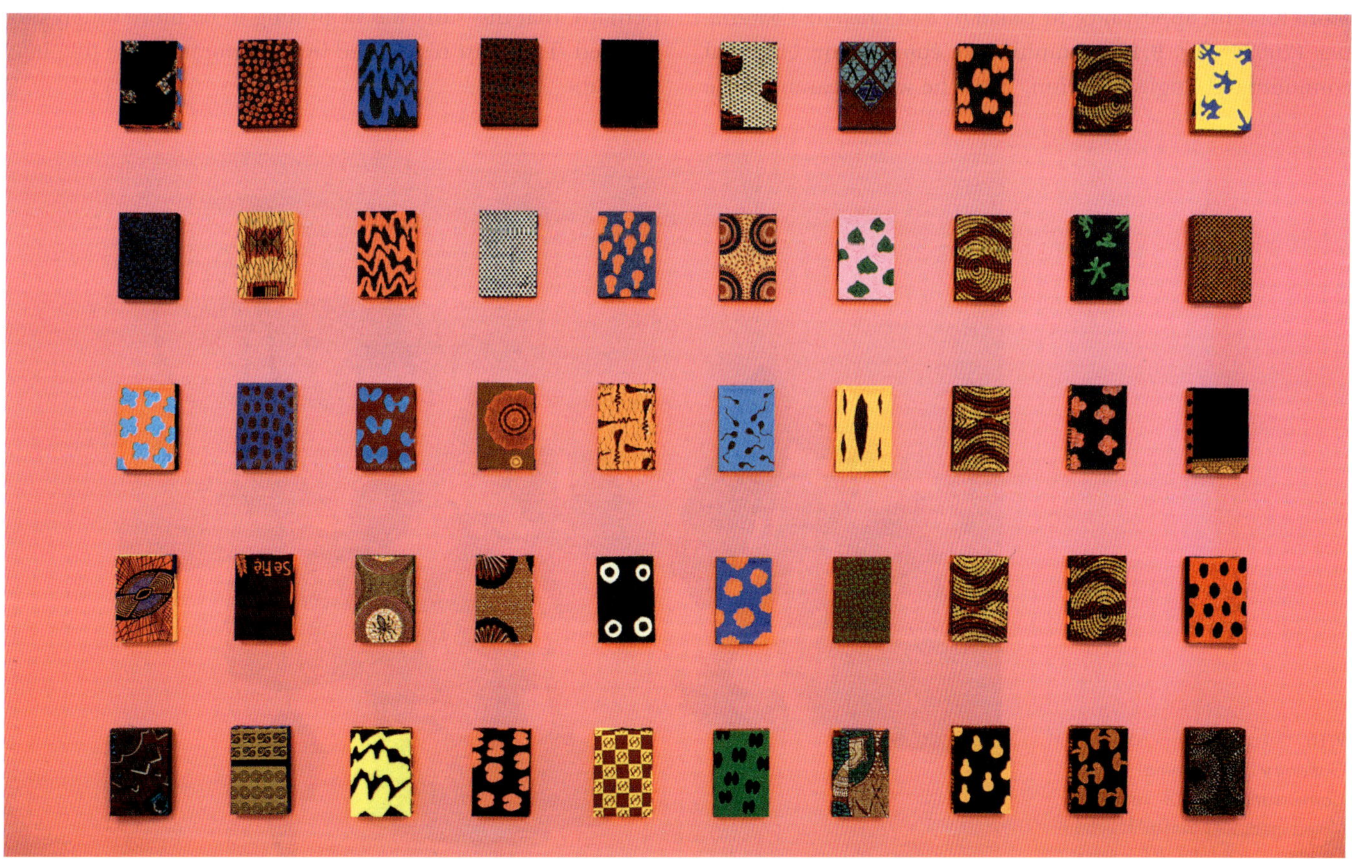

9.15 Yinka Shonibare MBE, ***Double Dutch***, 1994. Emulsion, acrylic on textiles, 50 panels. Overall dimensions 131 × 231½" (332 × 588 cm); each panel 12½ × 8¾ × 1¾" (32 × 22 × 4.5 cm). © Yinka Shonibare. Courtesy the artist and Stephen Friedman Gallery, London.

aristocracy. The figures ice-skate, hunt, invent, duel, and have sex while dressed in Victorian fashions—all tailored to perfection, by the artist, in Dutch wax fabrics. The "skin" pigment of the mannequins, seen at the hands and necks, is gray or tan, conveying a mixture of races to match the integration of cultures signified by the clothing. Though the opposition of colonizer and colonized remains overt, Shonibare's vision of society undermines the dichotomy of Europe and Africa. The artist revels in the conundrum that, in so far as his work reads as African, there is nothing that could be called indigenous about it. Likewise, its apparent Englishness is dependent on myths of national character that are consumed as readily by the English as the fabrics were consumed by Africans.

Within Shonibare's tableaux, souvenirs, symbols, and representations of Europe, Africa, modernity, and tradition circulate freely among the bodies of fancifully dressed mannequins and through the space of the museum. The intent is to be "critical of the relations of power through parody, excess, and complicity," Shonibare has explained.[15] His is not a frontal critique; political issues, he has reflected, had already been "well-raised, and I felt that it had been done. Wouldn't it be good to just surprise people?"[16] Assuming a level of political awareness in his audience that earlier generations of artists could not, Shonibare raises issues of colonialism with a sense of theatricality that is often entertaining, but also quite bleak. The specter of violence that lurks in the background of all his scenes with headless actors makes a more forceful appearance in *Gallantry and Criminal Conversation* (2002) (**fig. 9.16**), a multifigure composition of sexual conquest and English tourism. While he was researching the Grand Tour—the name given to the trips to Italy members of the British upper classes customarily took to visit the great cultural sites of antiquity and the Renaissance, beginning in the late seventeenth century—Shonibare learned that it had also served as an important rite in the sexual education of the aristocracy.

While *Gallantry and Criminal Conversation* presents sexual conquest as analogous to the cultural intermixing enacted in the costumes, other installations suggest that the fluid boundaries within European and non-European cultures were not all carnal. *The Age of Enlightenment* series (2008) includes portraits of Enlightenment figures including the German philosopher Immanuel Kant (**fig. 9.17**) and the Scottish political economist Adam Smith dressed in Shonibare's couture, but this time afflicted with disabilities as well as missing their heads. Kant, for instance, has no legs. These great thinkers, minus their heads and many of their limbs and wrapped in Shonibare's signs of miscegenation, fill journals and muse over their writings. The production of knowledge arises from thinkers built out of the fragments of African and European culture. In 1990, sociologist Paul Gilroy wrote that the histories related by black British artists revealed that "our story is not the other story after all but the story of England in the modern world."[17] The story Shonibare tells is an English history of crossing of boundaries rather than enforcing them. In 2004, Shonibare was granted and accepted the title of MBE (Member of the Most Excellent Order of the British Empire), suggesting, perhaps, that this story was beginning to be more widely recognized. The artist responded by incorporating the title into his name.

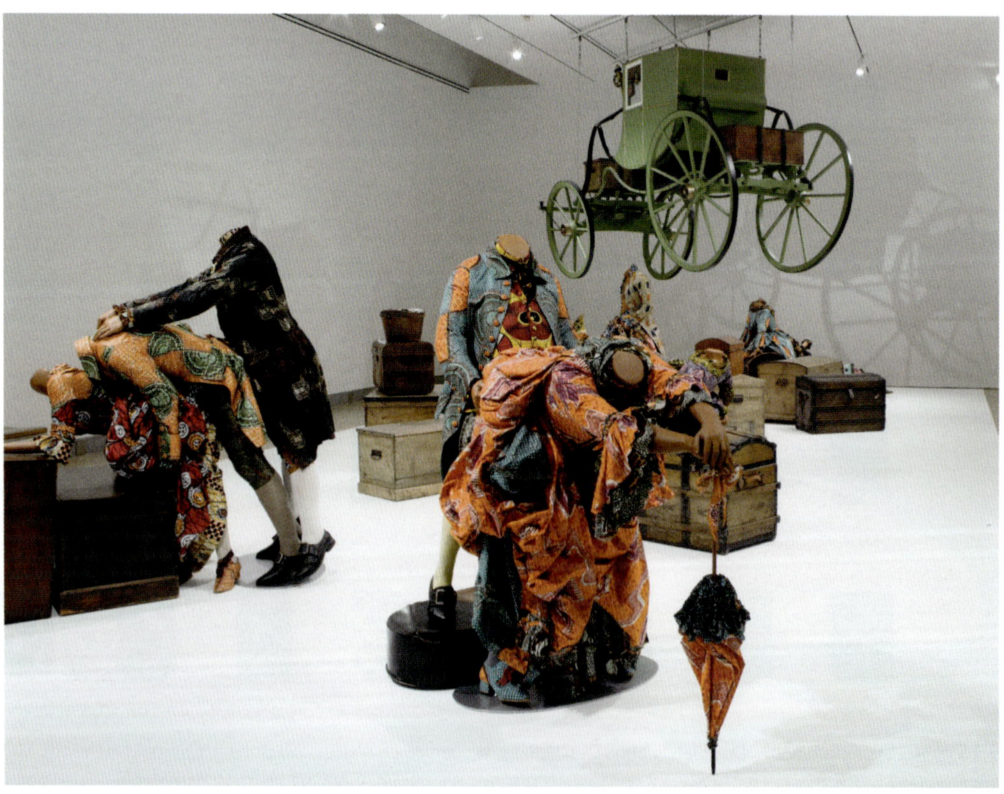

9.16 Yinka Shonibare MBE, ***Gallantry and Criminal Conversation***, 2002. Installation. Mixed media. © Yinka Shonibare. Courtesy the artist and Brooklyn Museum, New York. Photography by Christine Grant.

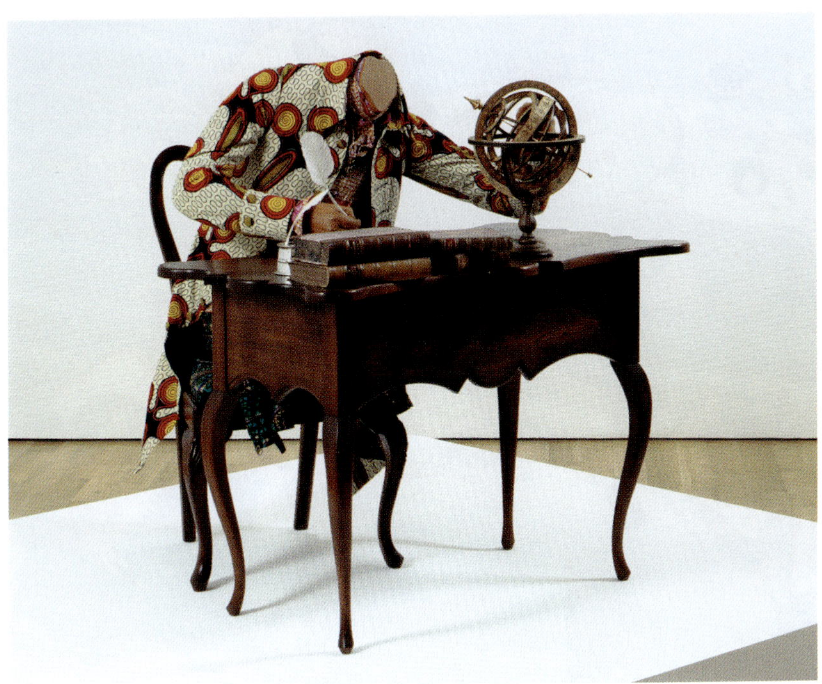

9.17 Yinka Shonibare MBE, *The Age of Enlightenment—Immanuel Kant*, 2008. Installation. Mixed media. Copyright the artist. Courtesy the artist, Stephen Friedman Gallery, London, and James Cohan Gallery, New York.

Youth Culture as a Measure of Global Change

While Neshat, Sikander, and Shonibare engaged history and art history to address the complex interchanges between cultures and nations, Japanese artist, art historian, and cultural impresario Takashi Murakami (b. 1963) argued that the intersections of personal, national, and global identity are best addressed through the aesthetics of entertainment with particular attention to youth. The increasing deferral of adulthood, due in large part to the difficulty of securing employment, and the pressure this put on young people was one effect of the economic changes at the end of the millennium: The future promised to children was disappearing as they reached it. Murakami was not alone in identifying this difficult transition as a subject that might provide insight into many contemporary anxieties. Along with a number of artists, including Yoshitomo Nara and Chiho Aoshima, Murakami has generated a beautiful and searching inquiry into what it means to come of age in contemporary Japan. Artists around the world have also identified adolescents and the culture they support as a means to grapple with the changes wrought by globalism. Cao Fei in the Pearl River Delta and Yang Fudong in Shanghai look at the ramifications of change in China on the younger generations, while two European artists, Phil Collins and Rineke Dijkstra, capture the similarity of experience and temperament among young people across cultures. Dijkstra's portraits in locations as distant as the Ukraine and North Carolina, and Collins's videos of karaoke in Indonesia and Colombia suggest that attention to mass culture and its adolescent consumers is a vital means of learning about—and learning from—the rapid changes at the turn of the millennium.

Takashi Murakami

Since the 1990s, Takashi Murakami has appropriated the style, content, and production practices of popular youth culture to articulate a national aesthetic, comment on post-World War II history, and develop an engaging and commercially successful oeuvre. In 1993, he created DOB, a mouselike creature whose large ears and round face spell out the letters of his name, which is derived from a nonsense phrase beginning *dobozite* ("why"). Murakami imbued DOB with the enigmatic allure of Hello Kitty and the prankster energy of Mickey Mouse. The character appeared in paintings and sculptures, as well as on toys and clothing, revealing a personality that was irrepressibly cute, or *kawaii*, a Japanese term referring to the prevalent taste, shaped by pre-teen girls, for flowers, ponies, and big-eyed, pastel-colored cartoon characters. Murakami also cast DOB in the roles of hero and monster. Paintings such as *Tan Tan Bo Puking—a.k.a. Gero Tan* (2002) (**fig. 9.18**) demonstrate Murakami's ability to transform his pop-culture references into an expression of turn-of-the-millennium anxiety. DOB, still recognizable by his round head and with the "D" and "B" still legible on his ears, has grown to a gargantuan size, sprouted abscesses of smaller DOBs that push through his skin, and lost all control of his body. The carefully rendered contours fail to contain the leaking fluids that DOB projects onto the *kawaii* landscape of flowers and hills. An inscription reads: "As my tongue flays to pieces, my headache intensifies and my eyes have become blind. As shit and piss flow, an excruciating pain runs through my entire body and I sense death is near."[18] Through Murakami's fantastic compositions and vibrant surfaces, DOB's ultimate prank appears to be to seduce the viewer into a world of pain and anguish.

In addition to drawing on the iconic sensibility of the Disney and Sanrio corporations, creators of Mickey Mouse and Hello Kitty respectively, Murakami adopted their production methods by setting up a large workshop-cum-factory and various merchandising outlets for his work. The name Murakami gave to his studio initially—the Hiropon Factory (renamed Kaikai Kiki Co., Ltd. in 2001)—alludes to Andy Warhol's Factory , but as an operation it goes well beyond art-historical homage: It variously creates art, represents artists, develops and distributes merchandise, publishes books, and even produces the art fair GEISAI. By the twenty-first century, Murakami had achieved a global reach and, like Warhol before him, had successfully stepped outside the framework of the art world.

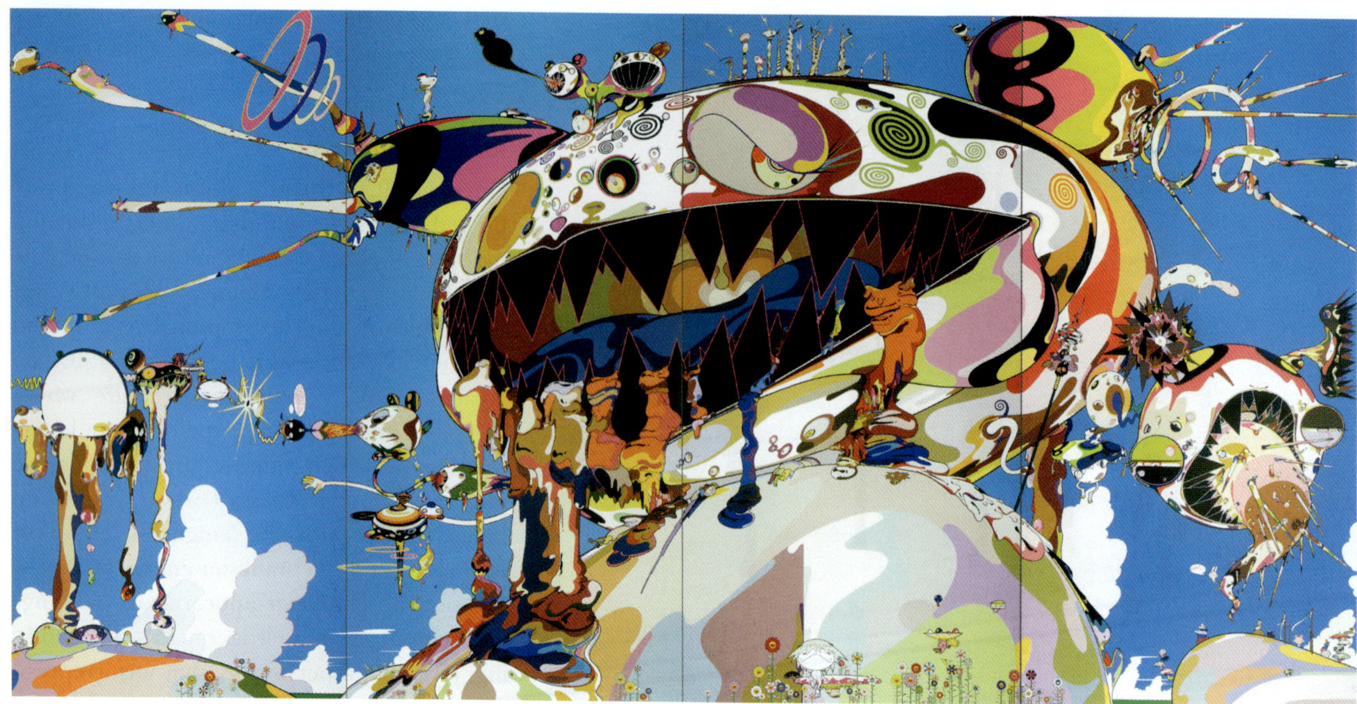

9.18 Takashi Murakami, *Tan Tan Bo Puking—a.k.a. Gero Tan*, 2002. Acrylic on canvas mounted on board, 141¾ × 283½ × 2⅝" (360 × 720 × 6.7 cm). Courtesy Galerie Emmanuel Perrotin, Paris & Miami.

While Murakami was introducing DOB to the world, he remained attentive to audiences at home, particularly the *otaku*, devoted fans and obsessive collectors of Japanese animation (*anime*) and comic books (*manga*). His work enlisted *otaku* culture to address identity, desire, emotion, and sexuality in the Japanese context and in explicitly Japanese terms. By the 1990s, the *otaku* had become a sizable group, shaping the image of Japanese culture inside and outside the country. Many younger Japanese found in such pursuits a means of escape and accomplishment not available to them elsewhere. They also found themselves at the center of a media frenzy. In 1993, police captured Tsutomu Miyazaki, a serial killer who had targeted young girls and photographed their dead bodies. Miyazaki's home was searched and his room was found to be full of *anime*, *manga*, and related figurines. As a result, the mass media associated the obsessions of the *otaku* with the pathology of the murderer. Across Japan, millions of parents looked into the rooms of their teenage children and saw collections identical to Miyazaki's (Murakami's own room was not dissimilar). In 1995, the Aum Shinrikyo cult released lethal Sarin gas into the Tokyo subway system, injuring thousands and killing eleven. The terrorists' headquarters were raided and typical *otaku* objects were found among their weaponry and propaganda. Again the media connected the *otaku* with criminality. Murakami felt that this perception, though unfairly made in the news, was important. "Most of the newly developed cults consist of people like the *otaku*," he explained, "so severely ... alienated that they either choose to join these cults or create new cults."[19] In Japanese culture, which Murakami felt was really a collection of isolated subcultures, the *otaku* revealed the anti-social reflex of a large portion of Japanese youth—but, he insisted, they stood in contrast to the violence of Miyazaki or Aum Shinrikyo.

Murakami's complicated relationship with the *otaku* is evident in a series of sculptures completed between 1997 and 2000 which appear to be *manga* figurines enlarged to human scale. The culminating piece is the *Second Mission Project Ko²* (1997–2000) (**fig. 9.19**), a female figure metamorphosing from a sexualized combatant into a fighter plane. This three-part installation was created with the designer Bome, famous for his own line of highly finished figurines, and Vi-Shop, a professional *manga* manufacturer. Collaboration with top-level *otaku* creators was essential if the work was to assume the qualities of *otaku* paraphernalia while existing as art. Joining these two categories of material culture at a level of parity, rather than using one to provide expertise or inspiration for the other, proved very difficult. When it was completed, the high level of detail and finish in the *Second Mission Project Ko²*, the narrative complexity of its transformation from human to machine, and its emotionally evocative quality engaged *otaku* viewers. The producer of *Second Mission Project Ko²*, Masahiko Asano, described the *otaku* figurine as an "object of love, an assertion of identity that says 'look what I have created,' and an outlet for sexual desire."[20] *Second Mission Project Ko²* recontextualizes this drive for love, self, and sex in artworld terms. While the *otaku* admired Murakami's sincerity and professionalism, when it was exhibited many were appalled that the object of their desire had been put on display so publicly. The word *otaku* means "home," and it is a central tenet of *otaku* culture that collections are safely protected from the outside world. Murakami's project put that intimate,

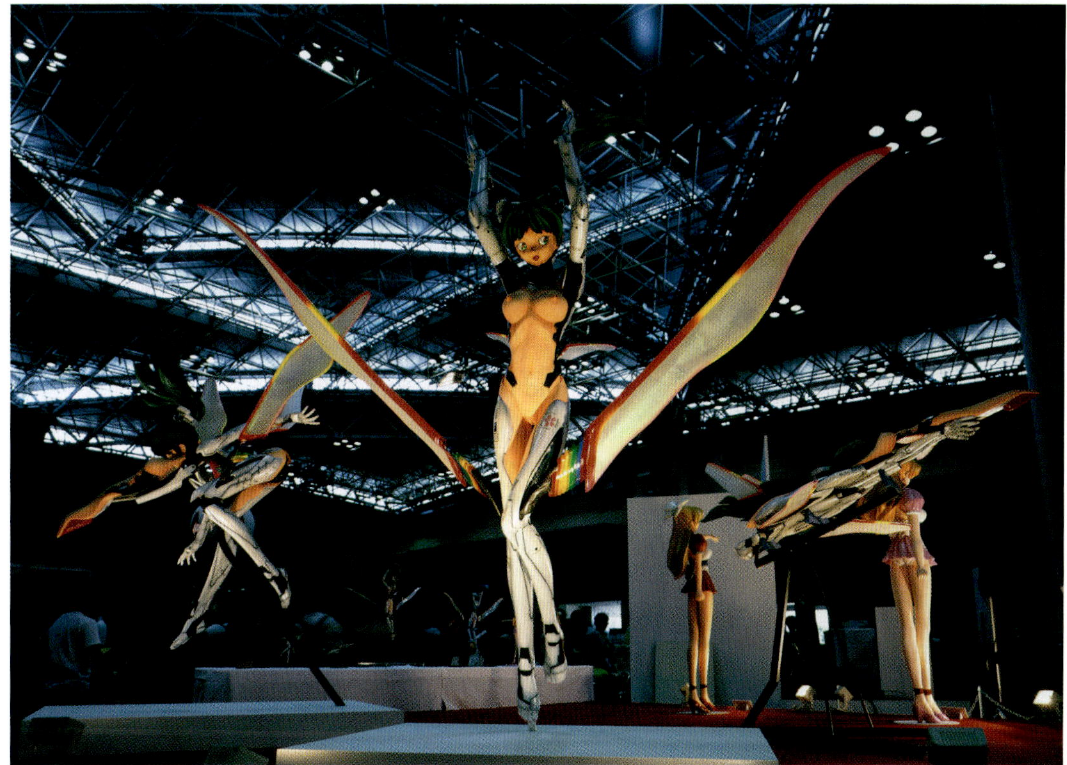

9.19 Takashi Murakami, *Second Mission Project Ko²* *(ga-walk type)* in foreground and *Second Mission Project Ko² (human type)* in background, 1997–2000. Original Design Model BOME; Arrangement Director Masahiko Asano; Macquette Production MODEL KINGDOM; Life-sized figure production Fuyuki Shinada (Vi-shop). Wonder Festival Installation view/Tokyo BigSite, Tokyo, 2000 © 1997–2000 Takashi Murakami/Kaikai Kiki Co., Ltd. All Rights Reserved. Special thanks to KAIYODO Co., Ltd.

sheltered space in the spotlight, allowing it to be discussed in relation to the concerns of art and history.

Murakami, who has a PhD in art history from the Tokyo National University of Fine Arts and Music, provided a historical reading of the *otaku* and of his own art. In his "Tokyo Pop Manifesto" (1999), Murakami associated adolescent obsessions and the history of postwar Japan: "Postwar Japan was given life and nurtured by America. We were shown that the true meaning of life is meaninglessness, and were taught to live without thought. Our society and hierarchies were dismantled. We were forced into a system that does not produce 'adults.'"[21] The *otaku* were one of many manifestations of the enforced infantilization of Japanese society by the West. Social scientists throughout the 1980s and 1990s identified aspects of Japanese culture, including its technological savvy and the role of teenage girls in popular culture, as part of this history. Murakami continued his analysis to argue that such phenomena were also a source of creativity: "Three apparently negative factors, including 1) a value system based on an infantile sensibility, 2) a society without any definitive standard of wealth, and 3) amateurism, are now helping to engender a new world of creativity."[22]

In the essay "A Theory of Super Flat Japanese Art" (2000), Murakami provided an art-historical lineage for what is known as Tokyo Pop that extends back through eighteenth- and nineteenth-century prints to seventeenth-century screen paintings. The defining characteristic of Japanese art, Murakami concludes, is its insistent two-dimensionality. This "Superflat" style is an aesthetic and a cultural attitude that rejects hierarchies of high and low and is open to influences from other cultures. Chinese painting, European Surrealism, and U.S. animation are among important sources for Japanese artists. Murakami compares the Superflat style to the "Flatten Image" function in Photoshop, which compresses all the layers on which one composes into a single digital surface. This device provides a metaphor for the appearance of Japanese art and its manner of integrating other traditions. Murakami presented his art-historical argument in three exhibitions, "Superflat" (2000), "Coloriage" (2002), and "Little Boy" (2005), which included everything from sculptures and paintings to posters and toys by a wide range of designers and artists including Murakami himself. "Little Boy"—the codename of the atom bomb dropped by the U.S. on Hiroshima in 1945—included "Article 9," the provision in the Japanese constitution written after World War II which forbids the rebuilding of the Japanese military, printed across a gallery wall, so maintaining the centrality of politics in the world of art and play.

Yoshitomo Nara and Chiho Aoshima

Among the artists Murakami has featured in his exhibitions, Yoshitomo Nara (b. 1959) and Chiho Aoshima (b. 1974) represent different takes on the integration of youth culture and fine art. Nara began populating his work with disruptive little girls whose wide-eyed *kawaii* appearance was infused with a touch of punk-rock irony and knowing violence while he was in Cologne in the 1990s. With her diminutive size, surly gaze, and violent temper, the protagonist of *Dead Flower* (1994) (**fig. 9.20**) is characteristic of his work. Nara's European experience encouraged a different combination of subcultures and art than is found in Murakami's work; his aesthetic leans to a comparatively painterly approach. Nevertheless,

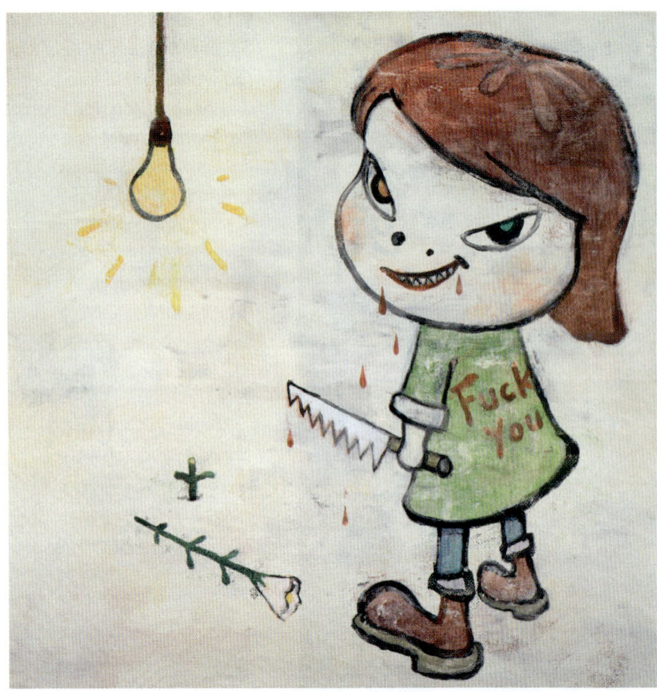

9.20 Yoshitomo Nara, *Dead Flower*, 1994. Acrylic on cotton, 39¼ × 39¼" (100 × 100 cm). © Yoshitomo Nara, courtesy Pace Gallery. Photograph courtesy the artist and Pace Gallery.

he shares Murakami's conviction that the *otaku* sensibility is a suitable foundation for contemporary Japanese art.

Aoshima had no formal artistic training when Murakami included her in "Tokyo Girls Bravo," (1999) the first of three exhibitions of that title featuring the work of young female artists. Shortly after, she joined Murakami's studio. Her work, initially produced entirely on a computer using Illustrator software, and more recently including sculpture and drawing, embraces the linear clarity of Murakami's style while exploring pictorial space and filling it with narrative inventions that revolve and evolve around a range of female protagonists. If Murakami points forcefully to subculture fantasies as a source of insight into contemporary society, Aoshima expands our understanding of what such visions might include. In paintings such as *Magma Spirit Explodes: Tsunami Is Dreadful* (2004) (**fig. 9.21**), she places doe-eyed nymphs at the center of the fiery demise of civilization. Other scenes lavish attention on the characters' erotic reveries. Though the settings shift from urban dreams to natural disasters to Arcadian idylls, Aoshima's characters exhibit a consistent ambivalence toward whatever surrounds them. Fire may lick their flesh, ropes may bind their limbs, but the girls gaze out past their surroundings, as though the scenes we see exist only in their or our imaginations.

Cao Fei and the U-theque Collective

Facing economic and cultural transformation in her home city of Guangzhou, China, Cao Fei (b. 1978) also turned to domestic youth culture and found a source of creative community-building. Cao made her international reputation while still in her mid-twenties with a body of work about Chinese teenagers engaged in live-action role-playing games in Guangzhou, the capital of Guangdong Province in the Pearl River Delta (PRD). The PRD is at the heart of China's unprecedented industrial, technological, and urban expansion. Cao's subjects, such as the two figures depicted in *A Mirage* (2004) (**fig. 9.22**), are COSPlayers, young men and women who traverse the city in costume, enacting adventures inspired by the digital avatars they have created in computer and online games. Cao explains the appeal of such games with reference to contemporary modernization: "China is growing at high speed and the development of the new cities in pace with the global economy is confusing. On many levels, all of us, young and old, lose our way. Costume players, or COSPlayers, juxtapose their fantasy world as an expression of alienation from traditional values. They represent the marginality of my generation."[23] Cao Fei's COSPlayers have appropriated an element of global culture—in this case, Japanese animated fantasy characters—and used them to create a community for themselves at home. Cao collaborated with her subjects to convey the character and significance of the cosmology they created.

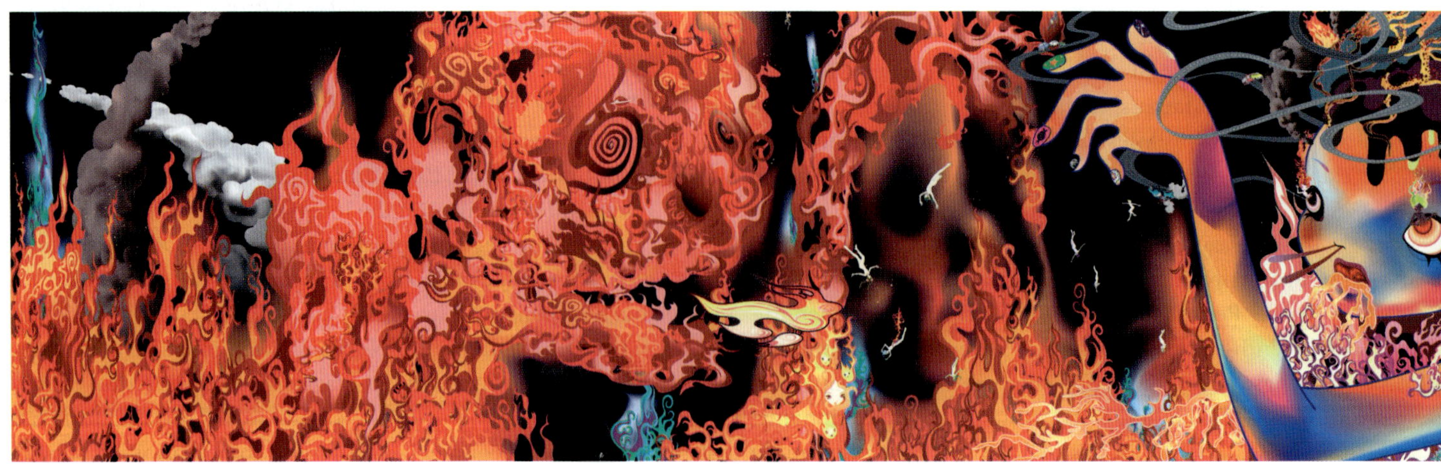

9.21 Chiho Aoshima, *Magma Spirit Explodes: Tsunami Is Dreadful*, 2004. Chromogenic print, 34¼ × 231⅞" (87 × 589 cm). Carnegie Museum of Art. Courtesy Blum & Poe, Los Angeles/Galerie Emmanuel Perrotin, Paris & Miami. © 2004 Chiho Aoshima/Kaikai Kiki Co., Ltd. All Rights Reserved.

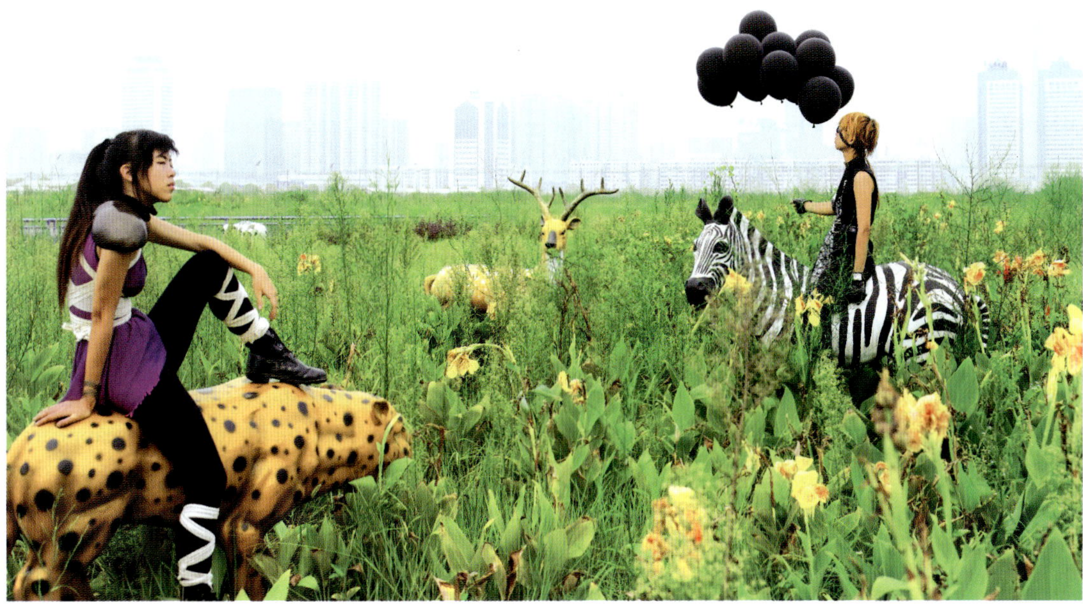

9.22 Cao Fei, ***A Mirage*** from ***COSPlayers*** series, 2004. Digital C-print, 29¼ × 39¼" (74.3 × 99.7 cm). Courtesy the artist and Lombard Freid Gallery.

A Mirage, a photograph Cao created in conjunction with her video *COSPlayers* (2004), depicts a moment in the fantasy. In a field of tall grass and flowers outside the city, a leopard stalks a zebra and a gazelle. The animals are all fiberglass. A young girl dressed as an *anime* warrior rests on the back of the predator while her counterpart, a slight male dressed in black, rides the zebra. The boy holds a cluster of black balloons. The video reveals that the boy and girl had previously met in combat, but in *A Mirage* they are at peace, distracted but connected in an artificial Serengeti. Soon these tranquil heroes will fight, die, and be resurrected to return home, he to clean his sword while his father watches television, she to send text messages while her father or grandfather reads the paper. Compared to their fantasy life with its action, risks, and camaraderie, the scenes of reality that conclude the film are poignantly vacant.

Pop culture and fantasy are not the only means to create meaning and community in Cao's China. Together with filmmaker, curator, and critic Ou Ning (b. 1969) and the collective U-theque, she has documented other strategies for surviving the development of Guangzhou. The district of San Yuan Li has been of particular interest. Once famous for providing shelter to the anti-British resistance during the nineteenth-century Opium Wars, the village is now surrounded

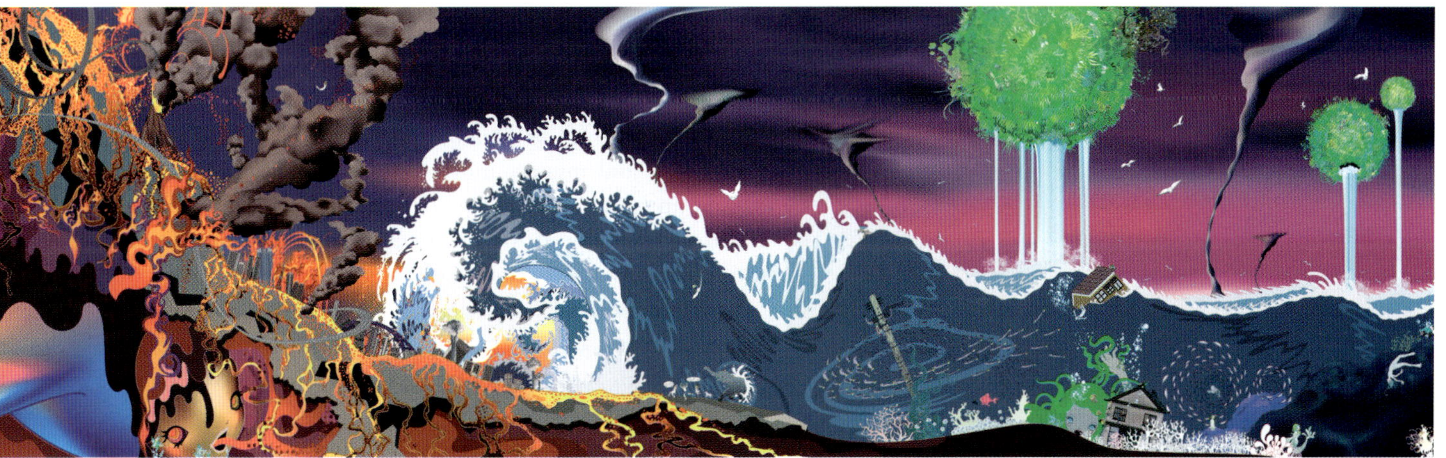

by metropolitan expansion. As a legal entity, however, it has remained outside the zoning and development oversight of the city that encircles it. This means that it is also without input into the urban change that affects it. The residents have responded by supporting a layered black-market economy and an organic pattern of architectural growth. To explore the survival of San Yuan Li, Cao Fei and U-theque took digital video cameras into the streets, following individuals and alleyways to create informal video diaries that were then edited into a short film, *San Yuan Li* (2003) (**fig. 9.23**).

While working on *San Yuan Li,* the filmmakers made the neighborhood their home, learning its stories and how to read the environment. Here, peasants who had lost their livelihoods in the country found that with a little ingenuity they could become landlords. Rising real-estate prices outside the village encouraged renters to move to San Yuan Li, so local property owners found themselves pushing the physical limits of their homes to generate fresh income: New units were put on top of old ones, rooms were cantilevered over alleys, and porches became apartments. In the process of editing the film, Cao and Ou combined footage, often increased the speed of segments, and repeated moments in which the camera spins through the narrow alleys or pinpoints details of architecture or urban activity. The effect of this digital post-production transports the eye thorough the space of San Yuan Li in a very different way than that in which the body is forced to walk through its narrow streets and steep stairwells. In its desperate accommodation of the encroachment of the metropolis, San Yuan Li is shown to have transcended the scale of a village. With the ground level cut off from the sun by the telescoping architecture, the U-theque filmmakers discovered that nature had reappeared nearer to the sky. On top of the city, on the terraces and roofs of San Yuan Li, residents had planted gardens, installed goldfish ponds, and built aviaries. *San Yuan Li* appears as a both a parody of the ebullient claims of economic and architectural growth that surround it, and an alternative to the escapist response to societal change chronicled in *COSPlayers.*

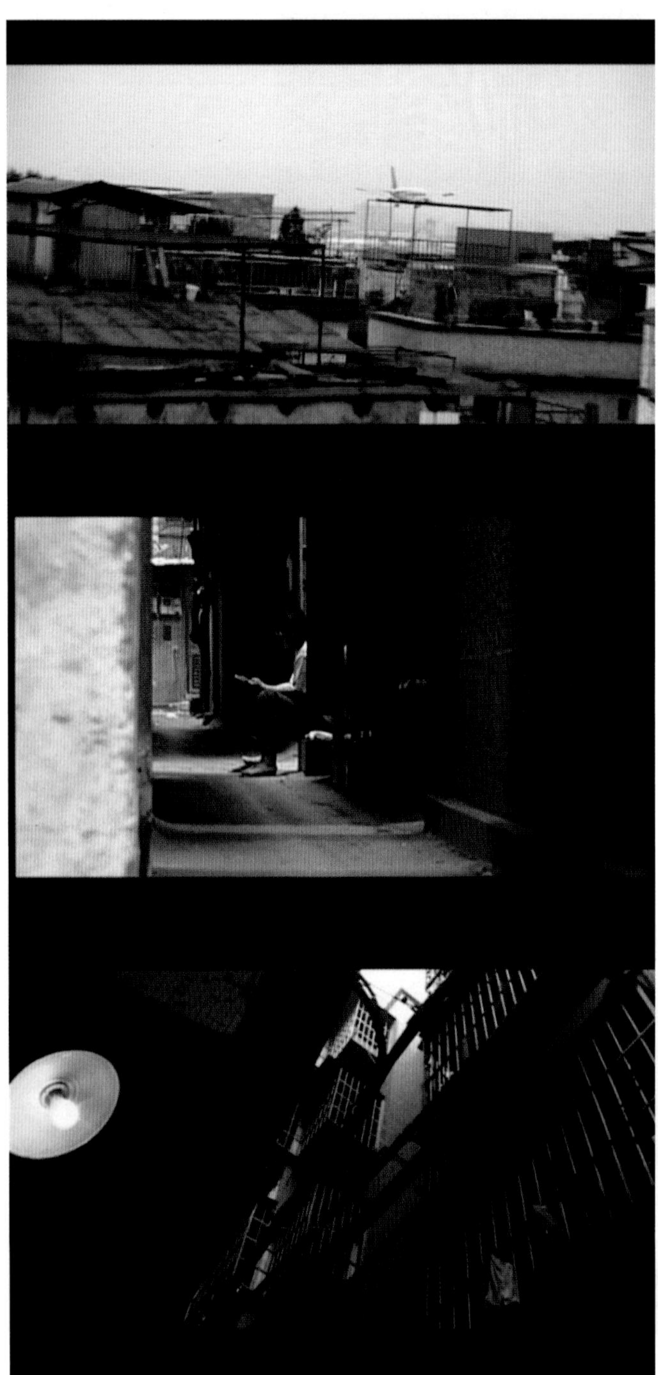

9.23 U-theque, *San Yuan Li,* 2003. Film directed by Ou Ning and Cao Fei. Running time 40 minutes.

Yang Fudong

To the north, in Shanghai, filmmaker and photographer Yang Fudong (b. 1971) also turned his attention to the challenges facing young people in a changing China. In a series of works, Yang created intricate scenarios expressing the melancholy and anxiety experienced by a generation of Chinese youth who felt that the realization of their dreams had been deferred by forces they could not even identify. The conflicted emotions of his generation, Yang felt, corresponded to an ambiguity in the national reform movement encapsulated by Deng Xiaoping's famous 1992 pronouncement "To get rich is glorious," made in praise of Western economic values, just three years after the brutal suppression of the Western-inspired democracy movement in Tiananmen Square. Yang moved to Shanghai in 1998 to work as a game designer but soon decided that film was the perfect tool for speaking to the concerns of his generation. His memories of watching detective and mystery movies at the military base where he grew up, and his knowledge of film history, gleaned primarily through reading, made the medium appear rich in ambiguities, partial answers, and poetic gaps. As a result, Yang's work has developed an aesthetic of lacunae and allusion—so different from Cao Fei's use of digital media—that is perfectly suited to his sense both of film and of alienation in contemporary China.

Yang's monumental five-part film *Seven Intellectuals in a Bamboo Forest* (2003–07) (**fig. 9.24**) speaks to the personal and psychological challenges of entering the global

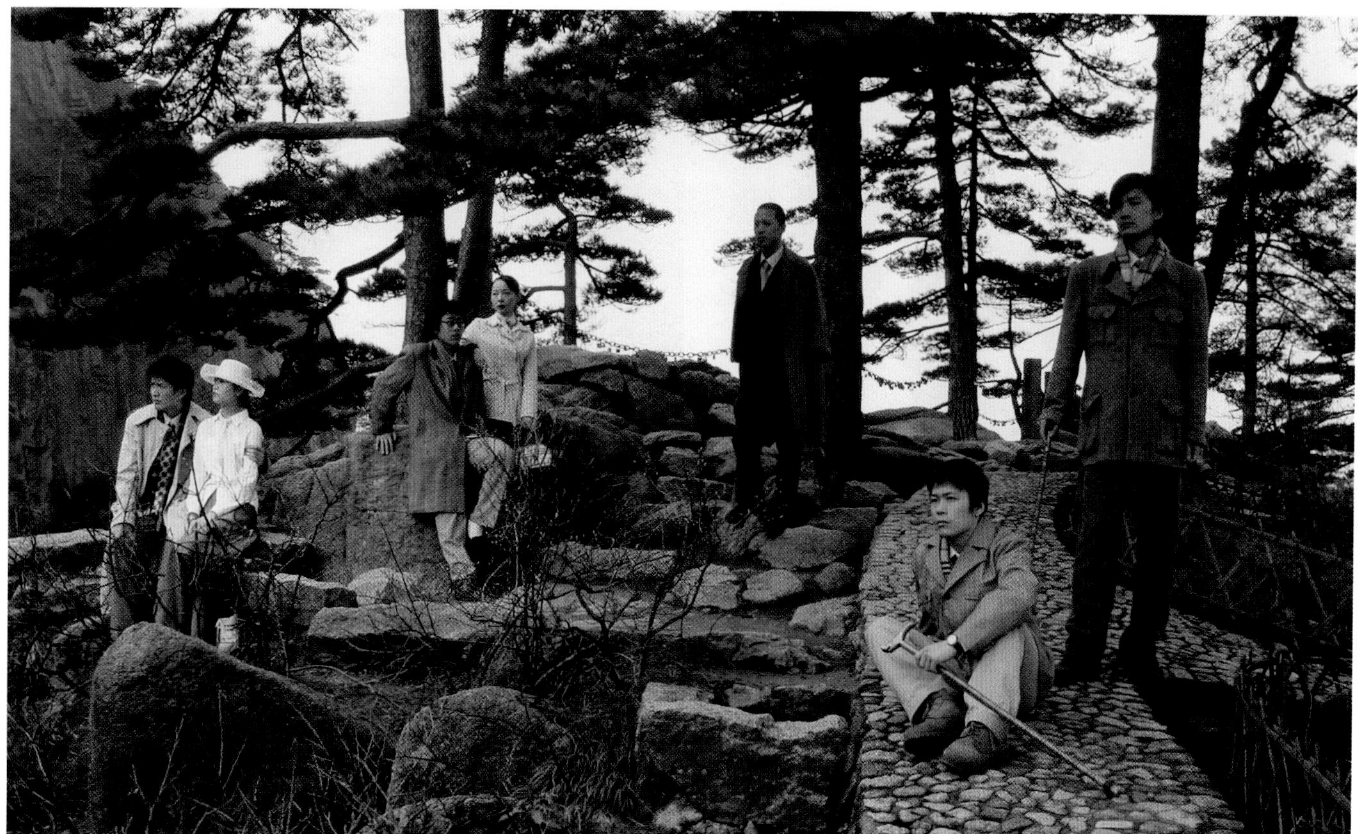

9.24 Yang Fudong, ***Seven Intellectuals in a Bamboo Forest***, 2003–07. Photograph.

economy. It is an extended portrait of a generation that has compromised its dreams in order to enter a society that has no place for it. The protagonists journey through the woods and streams of the Yellow Mountain in Anhui Province, southwest of Shanghai. They wander through rural villages and city streets, often pining for earlier moments in history. Dressed in costumes from the 1940s, but speaking a thoroughly contemporary Chinese, Yang's seven intellectuals mimic the revolutionary exile of the Seven Sages of the Bamboo Grove in the third century, who protested the politics of their day by fleeing to the mountains to practice free speech and live unfettered lives. Though Yang's characters share the discontent of their predecessors, they lack their passion and creative energy. These young men and women are not angered by life so much as estranged from it. One muses: "Sometimes having belief is a mistake … it also leads you to confusion … I just want to follow my heart though it is vulnerable, filled with frustrations and failures. I am far away from my existence." The conversations and journeys of the seven intellectuals are marked by cycles of assertion and doubt. Yang tells us that his characters, like himself and the actors, who are his friends, had dreams and ideals but lost them due to something unknown, an internal problem within themselves or an external social one—they cannot say.

Yang expresses the characters' indecision and disappointment through their languorous journey from the contemporary Chinese city up into mountains that have served as a retreat for millennia. Of the function of landscape, Yang explains: "Sometimes I feel landscape is kind of thinking by your heart, or a kind of emotional state. When you lose your heart, you shall not see the landscape even if it is beautiful."[24] The protagonists of Yang's film do not find a home or even reach a conclusion about what they should do next, but they do see the landscape. The film's first lines of dialogue are a musing on the paucity of representation in the face of direct experience. One of the women speaks: "The days when I had never been to the Yellow Mountain it was no more than a postcard to me. Those strange rocks and stones and huge pine trees did not look real. But when I was finally in the Yellow Mountain I had a different feeling. That moment I was standing on the top of the mountain. Surrounded by the pervasive clouds and mist, I felt I was flying in the sky." The speaker encounters the landscape as a catalyst for sensing her heart, her past, and her present. In the experience of the real place, there is a sensation of unity and purpose. It is followed, however, by nihilism as the speaker recounts that her next impulse is to leap to her death. Yang's film does not conclude with any such clear or tragic resolution. In the end, the group find themselves back where they started. "They return to the city, devoid of identity. Perhaps they are many people, perhaps they are seven. Perhaps they are in a dream. From beginning to end, they cannot find their position. They are still a collective of youth, a future, unknown collective," Yang writes.[25]

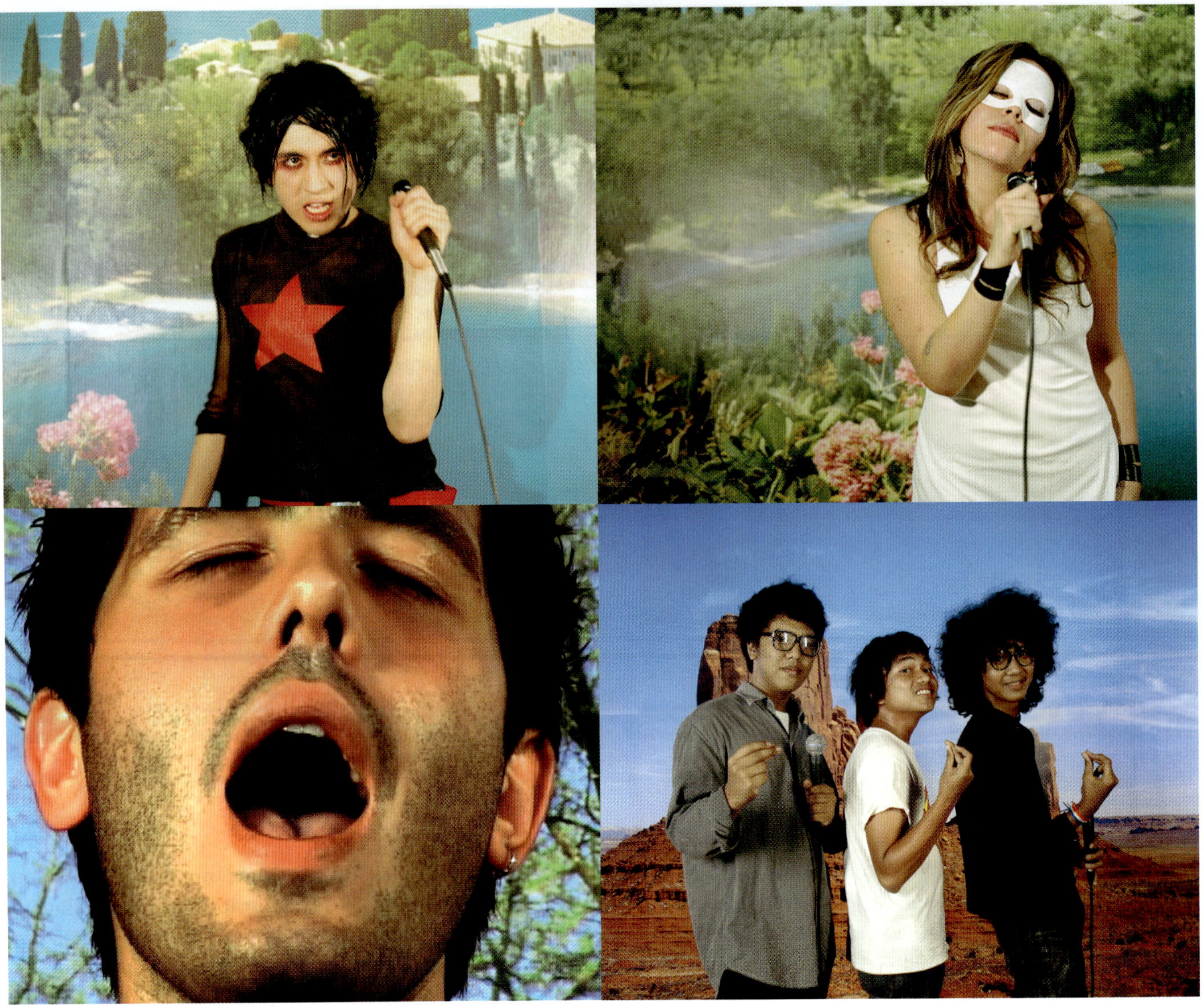

9.25 Phil Collins, ***the world won't listen***, 2004–07. Film stills. Synchronized three-channel color video projection with sound, ca. 60 minutes. Courtesy Shady Lane Productions and Tanya Bonakdar Gallery, New York.

Phil Collins

Murakami's "Superflat" concept argued that the foundations for contemporary Japanese art, whether they lay in historical traditions or the *otaku*, were inherently multicultural. East and West, Disney and Sanrio, were layered and flattened in Murakami's art to build a national aesthetic for the twenty-first century. Likewise, Cao Fei observed the Chinese present as integrating cultural forms from abroad. English-born photographer and videomaker Phil Collins (b. 1970) took another hybrid cultural form, karaoke, to examine the community-building of millennial teenagers. Collins's three-channel projection *the world won't listen* (2004–07) (**fig. 9.25**) features teenagers and young adults in Bogotá, Colombia, Istanbul, Turkey, and Jakarta and Bandung, Indonesia, singing the melancholic, angst-ridden songs of the 1980s U.K. pop band The Smiths. Collins created the audio tracks with the guitarist of Aterciopelados, one of the most significant Latin American pop bands of the 2000s. The performers take the microphone and demonstrate the potency of pop culture in creating community and identity in places distant in space and time from Thatcherite Britain, home to the original fans of the band. Collins's installation juxtaposes simultaneous performances, thereby highlighting the global nature of pop culture. These young participants, many of whom know the lyrics without actually being able to speak English, sing with invigorating and contagious abandon. They perform solo or with friends; they laugh and cry and, most of all, use Western pop culture to propel themselves beyond their isolation and circumstances.

Karaoke has been of interest to many artists of Collins's generation. U.S. mixed-media artist Andrea Bowers (see Chapter 11) has filmed karaoke performers while Korean sculptor Lee Bul (b. 1964) has created customized karaoke booths and projections. In each case, it is the individual singer and his or her immediate context that are under scrutiny—in Bowers's work, by elaborating on the give-and-

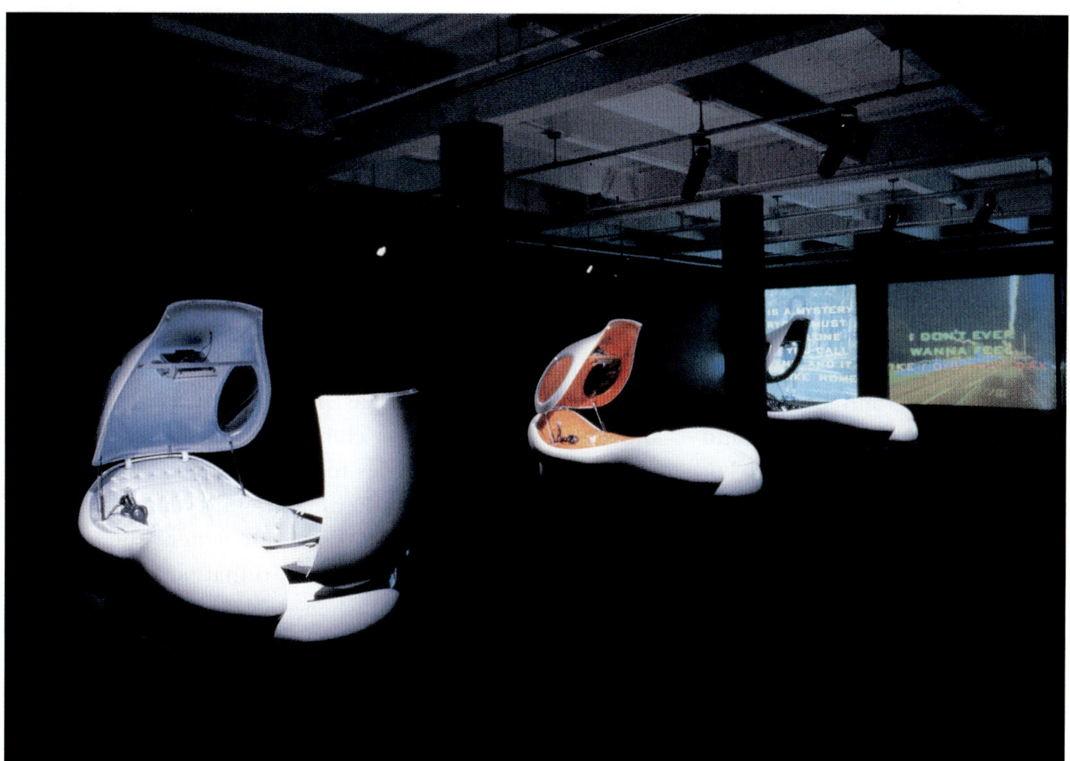

9.26 Lee Bul, *Live Forever, I, II and III*, 2001. Installation view. Mixed media. Fabric Workshop and Museum, Philadelphia, 2001. Courtesy the artist and Lehmann Maupin Gallery, New York and Hong Kong.

take of performer and audience, in Lee's, by isolating the performer from his or her audience. Lee's *Live Forever* (2001) (**fig. 9.26**), with its futuristic racing-car design and cyborg aesthetic, suggests the power of karaoke to transport the performer into another realm entirely. Collins's empathetic filmmaking in *the world won't listen*, with its close-up yet sympathetic cinematography and generous sound quality, transforms the singers into stars, alone in the spotlight. At the same time *the world won't listen*, its title taken from a 1987 collection of Smiths' songs, steps out of England to explore the extent to which the world *does* listen. The contours and character of the world mapped by the work are very different from the alienated shelter The Smiths provided for their first fans in the U.S. and Europe of the 1980s. Collins presents a community of listeners, extending from Jakarta to Dallas, Texas, where the piece was first shown in its entirety, to Glasgow, where it received its first European screening.

Accompanying the installation, Collins exhibited enlargements of the letters written by Smiths frontman and lyricist Morrissey to music magazines in the years before he formed the band. They reveal a writer consumed by the minutiae of his subculture and committed to rigorously defending its quality and its borders. There is a sense of embattlement in these letters that has nothing to do with the outward reach and aesthetic carelessness of Collins's subjects. In the face of the bunker mentality that supported The Smiths' original fanbase as they raged against Thatcherite Britain and the Reaganite U.S. and sought allies among other members of the alienated and disenfranchised youth, Collins projects a network of interrelated communities not obviously connected by class, race, nationality, or politics.

Collins has spoken about his art as a means of investigating the changing character of politics and identity "in the flexible framework of desire, consumerism, or popular culture."[26] *the world won't listen* is a case study of such change. Not only does Collins's work illustrate the changing function and context of culture, it anticipates the responses to such change. At first glance, the piece invites the Western viewer to indulge in a patronizing smile at the quaint failures of non-Westerners trying to sing in English. The international appeal of black hair dye, goth clothes, and Morrissey's persona appears to demonstrate the steamroller effect of globalization by which middlebrow Western mass media crushes local cultures. Places such as Colombia, Turkey, and Indonesia are struggling to articulate their own economies and politics in the shadow of neighboring powers, whether North American, European, or Asian, and are most vulnerable to such hegemonic Western universalism. *the world won't listen*, however, layers such presumptions with its celebration of a global youth culture that claims ownership of whatever pieces of culture it finds relevant. Collins's *they shoot horses* (2004), a seven-hour, two-screen projection of a dance marathon staged in Ramallah, Palestine, presents another view of such cultural appropriation. In the video, nine teenagers dance to U.S. R&B and European pop until they are no longer able to stand. Like the singers in *the world won't listen*, these dancers are compelling to the point of being heartbreaking as they give themselves over to the music. Collins is explicit in his desire to make us fall in love, as he did, with his subjects—but we are also meant to wonder why it might seem strange to European or U.S. viewers that kids from Jakarta, or Istanbul, or Bogotá, or Ramallah, would care about The Smiths or choose to dance to European pop. The Western origins of these bits of global culture are less significant than their creative manipulation by kids all over the world.

Rineke Dijkstra

Dutch photographer Rineke Dijkstra (b. 1959) has taken a similar interest in, and shown a matching empathy with, adolescents on the cusp of adulthood. In 1992, Dijkstra left a career as a commercial photographer and began photographing teenagers at beaches in the U.S., Poland, and Ukraine (**fig. 9.27**). Her approach remained close to what it had been when she was being paid to take portraits of businessmen. The subjects are positioned in the center of the image, tightly framed, and caught in a very shallow depth of field that limits the focus to little more than the person and the ground on which they stand. Looking out from this narrow envelope of space, the teenagers appear caught between the proportions of children and adults and exhibit expressions and body language that convey attitudes in flux between confidence and profound insecurity. Despite the intimacy of the portraits and the clear connection between photographer and subject, we do not get to know these young people. There is a compelling uniformity about the swimmers in Ukraine and at Coney Island. As we view image after image, we witness an apparently universal sense of distance shared by Dijkstra's adolescent subjects. In addition to the bathers, Dijkstra has photographed Israeli military inductees, teenage British clubbers, young bullfighters, and new mothers. Several series follow the same person, returning to document them as they mature into young adulthood. Dijkstra captures, in the words of one writer, "the desire to arrest youth, to distill and study it so that perhaps we might know it as we never could when we were in between things

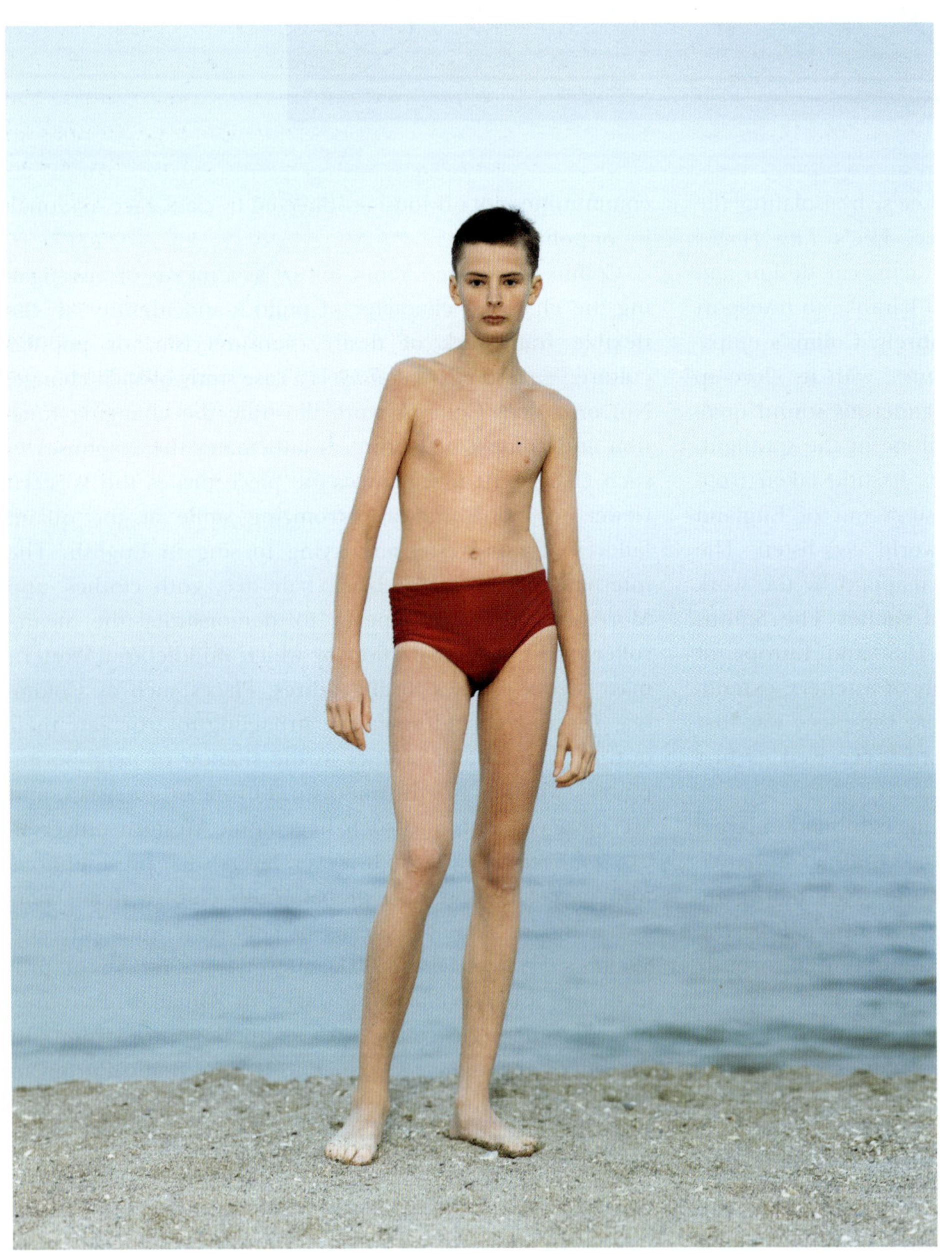

9.27 Rineke Dijkstra, ***Odessa, Ukraine,*** August 4, 1993. Chromogenic print 60¼ × 50¾" (153 × 129 cm). The Museum of Modern Art, New York. Courtesy of the artist and Marian Goodman Gallery, New York/Paris.

ourselves."[27] For the artist, the portraits expose what adults learn to hide; she might have added that they even show the act of hiding.

Adolescence as a shared as well as symbolic experience is the subject of Dijkstra's two-track video *The Buzz Club, Liverpool, England/Mysteryworld, Zaandam, Netherlands* (1996–97). For the piece, Dijkstra traveled to dance clubs in working-class towns. The Buzz Club and Mysteryworld are not trend-setting nightclubs filled with the rich and famous. Rather, these are places where ordinary kids grow up. For the work, she filmed her subjects in an area separate from the bar and dancefloor; as a result, they are shown surrounded by the sounds of the club, but not by other clubgoers. At first they stand there, nearly as static as the subjects of Dijkstra's photographs. Then, as they get more comfortable or bored, their bodies start to move with the music; occasionally they dance as if no one were watching. The transformation from anxiety to action, even of the most limited kind, is compelling, all the more so since the adolescent self-consciousness never disappears from Dijkstra's subjects. Unlike the adults who performed for Andy Warhol's screen tests, an obvious precedent for Dijkstra's film, these kids do not flourish in the excitement of playing a movie star—instead, they slowly reveal flashes of confidence and insecurity as they enact what amounts to an allegory for the awkward, ill-defined passage into adulthood.

Imaging the Global Economy

Since its beginnings in the nineteenth century, photography has proved a particularly effective cartographic art form, providing evidence of the world beyond to viewers left behind at home. *Fish Story* (1988–95) (**fig. 9.28**), an image-and-text installation and book on sea commerce by U.S. photographer Allan Sekula (b. 1951), developed this tradition in a distinctly contemporary direction by combining mid-twentieth-century photojournalism, Conceptual art, and an interest in the aesthetics of the commonplace to depict the realities of late twentieth-century economic networks. Though often formally beautiful, juxtaposing messy human activity with the formal rigor provided by the horizon or the geometry of cargo containers and ports, Sekula's photographs favor signs of economic and cultural exchange over the romantic myths of the ocean. His photography and writing established a model for what amounts to a genre of related work by artists all over the world, that applies the technology of the camera to reflect on the economic and political exploitation of the planet.

Zoe Leonard

With her series *Analogue* (1998–2007) (**fig. 9.29**), U.S. photographer Zoe Leonard (b. 1961) created a similar map charting the collapse of what used to be called the "rag trade" and the survival of its shadow economy in the collection and sale of used clothes in developing nations. The textile industry had supported immigrant populations in the U.S. throughout much of the twentieth century, but by the turn of the millennium small-scale clothiers had been almost entirely replaced by corporate manufacturing, so dramatically changing the face of the industry. Leonard charts the latter-day fate of the original rag trade. *Analogue* begins with photographs of the repair shops, run-down boutiques, and corner stores that at one time supported a thriving garment trade in Leonard's Lower Manhattan and includes 400 images (selected from over 10,000) that document a network of connections that pass from the

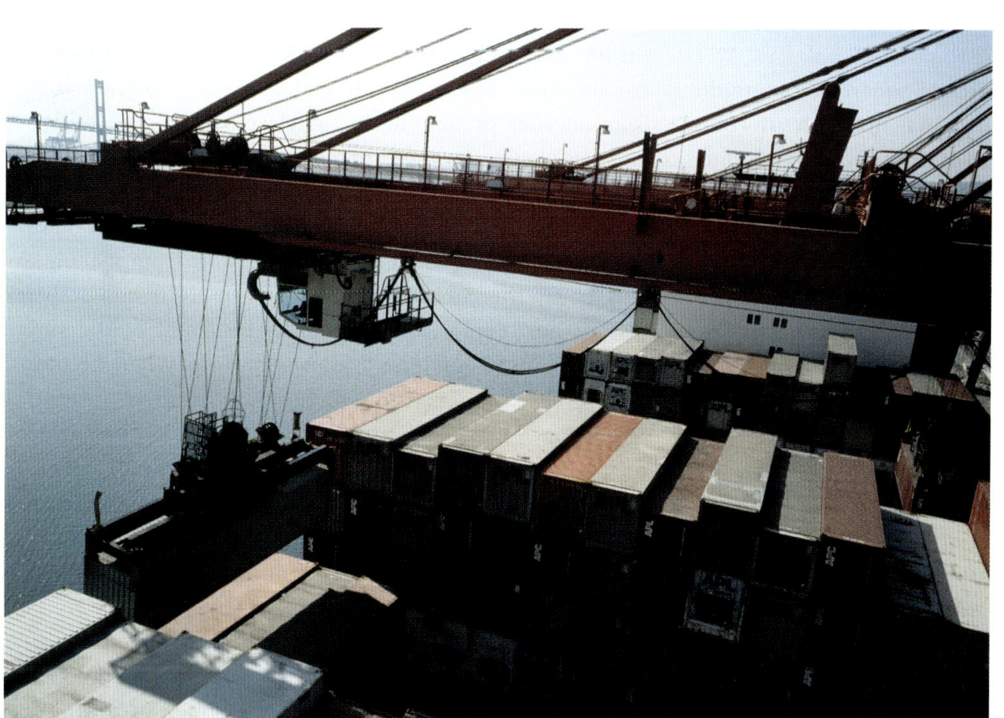

9.28 Allan Sekula, *Hammerhead crane unloading 40-foot containers from Asian ports. American President Lines terminal, Los Angeles harbor. San Pedro, California,* November 1992, from the series *Fish Story* (1988–95). Dye destruction color print, 24¾ × 31¼ × 1¾", framed (62.8 × 79.3 × 4.4 cm). Courtesy of the artist and Christopher Grimes Gallery, Santa Monica.

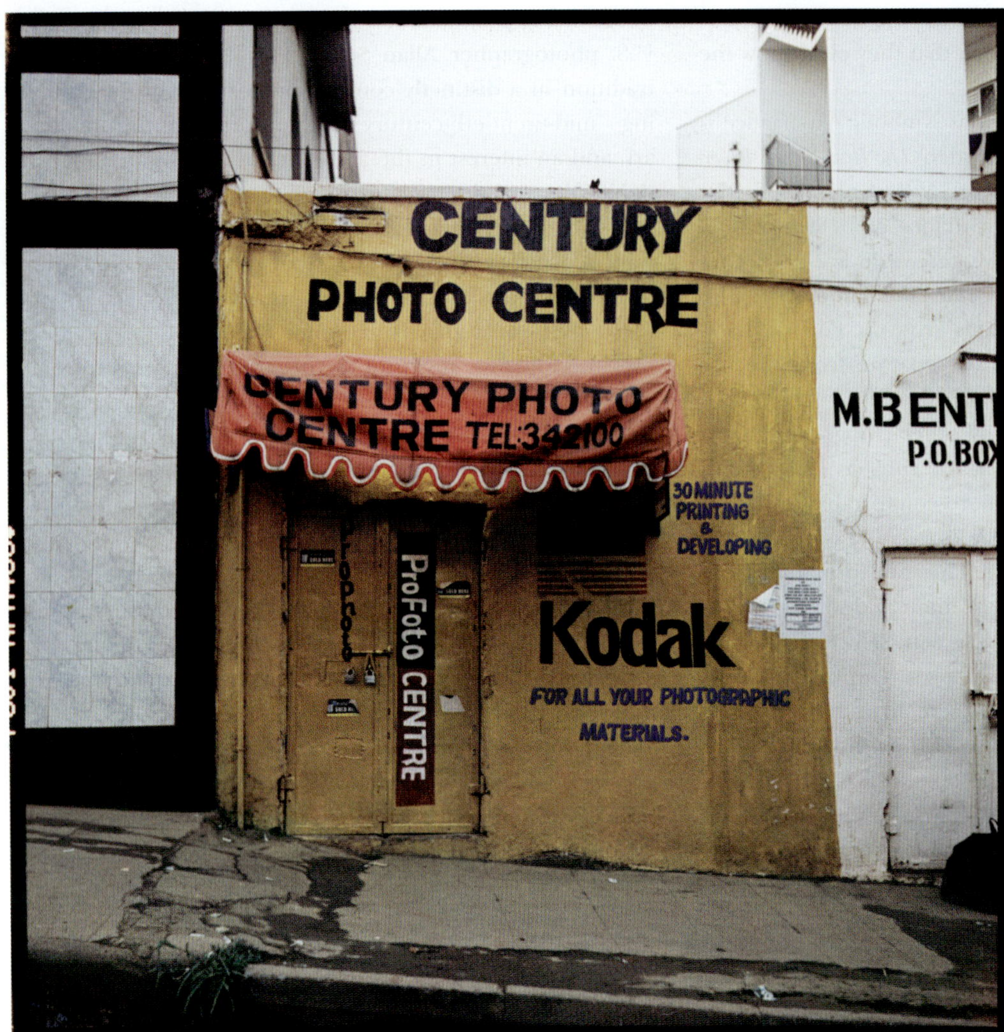

9.29 Zoe Leonard, ***Analogue***, 1998–2009. Detail. Whole series contains 412 C-prints and gelatin-silver prints, each 11 × 11" (28 × 28 cm). Edition of 3. © the artist. Courtesy Galerie Gisela Capitain, Cologne.

U.S. into Latin America and Africa. In pursuit of this faltering economy, Leonard has incorporated images of a variety of other low-end trades such as repair shops and dry-goods stores into *Analogue.*

Analogue consists of a long series of square photographs that recall the serialism of Conceptual art seen in Hans Haacke's *Shapolsky et al.* (see fig. 1.18) or the typological photography of Berndt and Hilla Becher. Both precedents established serial presentation as a sign of political and intellectual concern. A longer look at *Analogue,* however, reveals not just a historian's interest in a fading economy, but a more personal, tactile attachment to outdated technologies. *Analogue* is a collection of gelatin silver and C-prints: The technology involved is analogue as opposed to digital. Many of the images depict photography shops and photographs, linking Leonard's outmoded medium with her subject matter. By celebrating the fragile survival of print photography in the context of an investigation into economic hardship, Leonard alludes to the social traditions of Modernist photography. What some might perceive as a romantic attraction to historic media is also a link binding the social, spiritual, and emotional gravity of past art with the political concerns of the present.

Chen Chieh-jen

Factory (2003) (**fig. 9.30**) by Taiwanese photographer and filmmaker Chen Chieh-jen (b. 1960) is a study of one place on the networks suggested by Sekula's and Leonard's work. In the early 1990s, Taiwan had just come out of almost four decades of martial law, declared at an end in 1987, and was also enduring a dramatic downturn in its economy. In tandem with these developments there was a notable increase in the creation of art addressing political themes.[28] It was at this time that Chen took a hiatus from making art and began researching his family and local and military history, and exploring as much as he could of the physical remnants of modern Taiwanese history. When he began making art again in the late 1990s, he started creating a "genealogy," he explained, of those "who are suppressed, cut off by the multiple, soft structures of … exclusion that collaborate with the new world of … contemporary consumer culture."[29] This twofold concern—on the one hand with the histories that have been excised, and on the other with the consequences of embracing global capitalism—took on particular importance as the country was going through its first presidential elections. Questions about the domestic and international character of this next chapter in the history

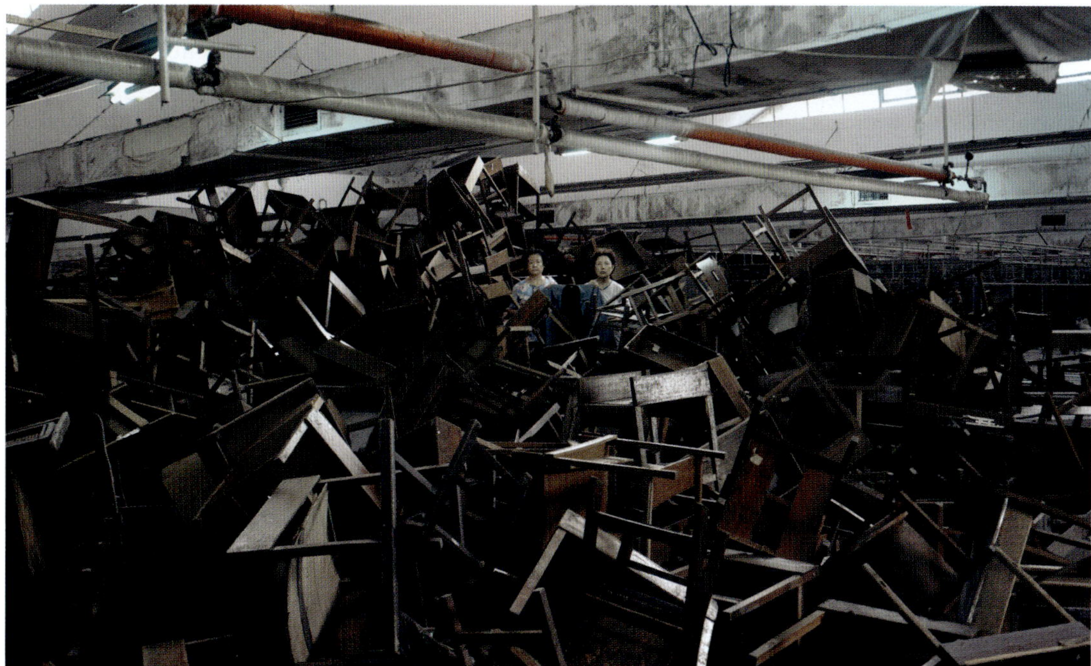

9.30 Chen Chieh-jen, *Factory*, 2003. Production still, 41⅜ × 70⅞" (105 × 180 cm). Courtesy of the artist and Chi-Wen Gallery.

of Taiwan were thus of pressing concern. Chen began by looking at historical examples of the exercise of power in the region, completing a series of photography and a video based on images of war and torture. He then turned to contemporary history with a series of films that examine the cost of Taiwan's willingness to turn itself into "a downstream processing site for multi-national capital."[30] *Factory* (2003) is one of these films.

Following the dramatic downturn in the economy in 1987 and in the face of the increasing collaboration between Chinese manufacturing and Western economic interests, many Taiwanese factories went bankrupt. During his explorations in the 1990s, Chen visited a number of disused industrial sites. He also discovered the Lien Fu garment workers who had been abruptly dismissed from their jobs, some after over twenty years of service, when the factory lost business in the mid-1990s. Severance packages and retirement benefits that had been promised were never paid. The workers protested, but to no avail. Chen created *Factory* by inviting some of the women back to their place of work to be filmed in slow long shots in the now-abandoned space. They are shown standing among the old desks and chairs, some piled to the ceiling, or seated at sewing machines, rented by the artist, to evoke the space as it was a decade before. The women did not want to talk publicly about their situation, so Chen took their silence as a formal conceit: *Factory* has no audio track, the silent passing of time creating an aural complement to the vast empty spaces of the building.

In addition to capturing the vacant spaces of the economic collapse, *Factory* is an effort at overcoming the consumer-induced historical amnesia that the artist saw all around himself. Into the contemporary footage Chen splices propaganda material from the 1960s showing productive workers and satisfied investors parading through a factory not unlike the Lien Fu operation. The scenes remind the viewer that it is not only the flows of capital being funneled to China now instead of Taiwan that have brought about the economic collapse—it is also the history of the policies of the Taiwanese state. The lesson is meant to be broadly applicable. "In places all over the world," Chen writes, "labourers have had similar experiences—a production relationship between the 'transplanted' and the 'untransplanted.' In order to find low-priced labour, factories constantly shift locations. But after being abandoned, unemployed workers have no choice but to linger on in the same place."[31] Chen's subsequent films have looked at the difficulty of travel out of Taiwan as well as at U.S. support of the Taiwanese state during the period of martial law. Chen's work thus elaborates on the history of internationalism in Taiwan, beginning in the colonial period when it was under Chinese and Japanese rule, through the period of the Kuomintang when U.S. support maintained the state, and into the present period in which Taiwan faces the impact of global capitalism.

Nodes on the Global Network: Israel and Palestine

As Chen Chieh-jen's work demonstrates, contemporary postcolonial globalization has very particular local consequences that are rooted in historical internationalism. Mapping the global present requires an exploration in time as well as space. This chapter concludes with two works that invite us to reflect on the geographical and historical dimensions of the Arab-Israeli conflict. The first, *Where We Come From* (2001–03) by U.S.-Palestinian artist Emily Jacir, pays particular attention to the political geography of exile by focusing on the restrictions placed on the movements of Palestinians. The piece highlights the degree to which it is the state, through passports and citizenship laws, that determine our relationship to home and family. The second work, *Summer Camp* (2007) by Israeli Yael Bartana, narrows the geographical focus to a single Palestinian home, and with documentary footage and references to Zionist cinema of the 1930s alerts the viewer to the history of Israeli nation-building and the complexity of creating homes and communities that challenge the existing politics of place.

Emily Jacir

Emily Jacir's (b. 1970) *Where We Come From* (**fig. 9.31**) is a simply conceived and executed performance piece. It is rooted in an artistic tradition dating from the 1960s and 1970s which stages, documents, or otherwise draws attention to ordinary activities, and in so doing shows them to be politically or personally significant (see Chapter 1). The point is not to create new objects, but to invite the audience to look again at what already exists. Jacir's activity here is travel. Having lived all over the world, in Saudi Arabia, Italy, the U.S., and the West Bank, and possessing a U.S. passport, she has spent her whole life, she says, "going back and forth between Palestine and other parts of the world."[32] She has enjoyed a freedom of movement that is not granted to her fellow Palestinians, either those in the West Bank, Gaza, or in exile. Drawing attention to the exceptional nature of her mobility, she approached Palestinians inside and outside their homeland and asked, "If I could do anything for you, anywhere in Palestine, what would it be?" Answers include visiting grave sites, meeting with relatives, going on a date, and other personal and rather mundane tasks. The artwork consists of the requests, written in Arabic and English, and photographs documenting Jacir's fulfillment of the errands framed and displayed in pairs. The artist satisfied the desires of others in a fashion that further restrictions enacted in 2004 have made impossible to repeat. Her work presents, as Edward Said suggested, "a creative juxtaposition of wish, [and] wish fulfillment ... that Palestinians cannot experience in the present."[33] Hanging in a gallery as a series of prosaic documents, *Where We Come From* recalls work such as Hans Haacke's *Shapolsky et al.* (see fig. 1.18) and Mary Kelly's *Post-Partum Document* (see fig. 1.29) and thus conveys its identity not only as a narrative of exile but as information to be integrated into a larger argument for political action.

Yael Bartana

Yael Bartana's (b. 1970) *Summer Camp* (**fig. 9.32**) shows one modest, yet symbolically significant, political action. The work consists of a makeshift auditorium specially constructed to screen a short film documenting the Israeli Committee Against House Demolition (ICAHD) rebuilding a Palestinian home. The home had been demolished by Israeli Defense Forces (IDF) and, since ICAHD lacked official authorization for its action, once rebuilt, it would likely be destroyed again. Building homes in the unforgiving desert lies at the heart of Israeli national identity, whether as a historic reminder of the formation of the nation in the 1940s or, more recently, as a political statement in the action of constructing settlements in the occupied territories. ICAHD is a group of Israelis, Palestinians, and others who are investing this patriotic act with critical meaning. Opposing the actions of the IDF represents

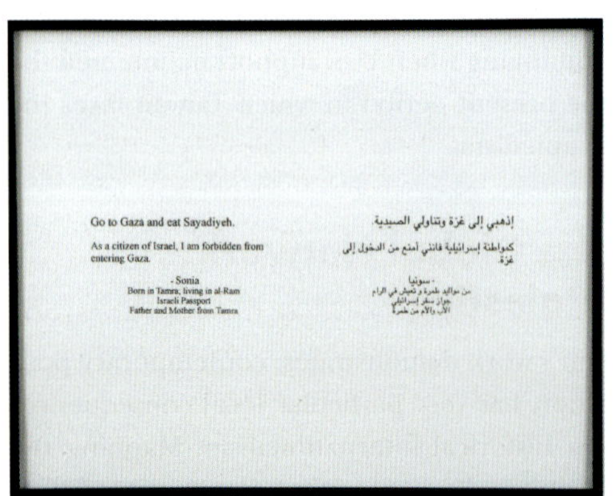

Go to Gaza and eat Sayadiyeh.

As a citizen of Israel, I am forbidden from entering Gaza.

- Sonia
Born in Tamra, living in al-Ram
Israeli Passport
Father and Mother from Tamra

إذهبي إلى غزة وتناولي الصيدية.

كمواطنة إسرائيلية فانني أمنع من الدخول إلى غزة.

- سونيا
من مواليد طمرة و تعيش في الرام
جواز سفر إسرائيلي
الأب والأم من طمرة

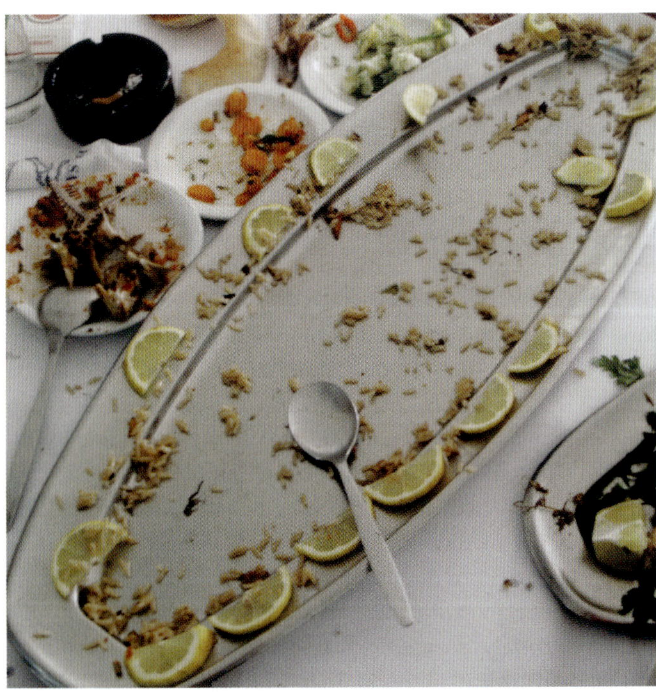

9.31 Emily Jacir, *Where We Come From*, 2001–03. Detail (*Sonia*). One American passport, 30 texts, 32 C-type prints, and 1 video; text (*Sonia*): 9½ × 12" (24 × 30.5 cm); photo (*Sonia*): 15 × 15" (38 × 38 cm). © Emily Jacir, courtesy of Alexander and Bonin, New York.

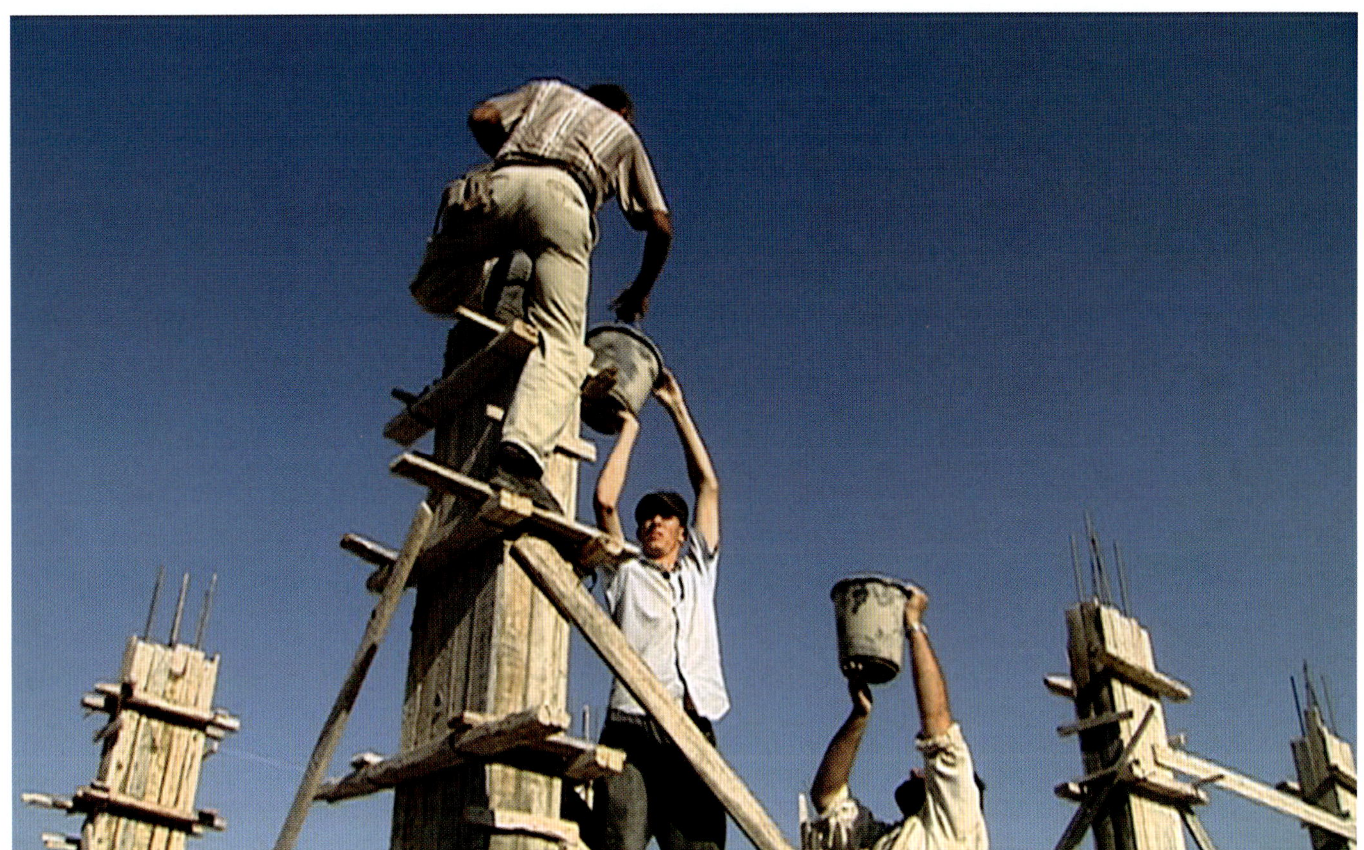

9.32 Yael Bartana, ***Summer Camp***, 2007. Film still. One-channel video and sound installation, 12 minutes. Courtesy Annet Gelink Gallery, Amsterdam.

a direct criticism of existing Israeli policies toward Palestinians. With its focus on Jews and Palestinians building together, Bartana's work's subject appears to be a new chapter in the construction of the nation. The film and soundtrack of *Summer Camp* imitate iconic Zionist propaganda films of the 1930s, specifically Helmar Lerski's *Avodah* (1935). Though using only footage of the contemporary volunteers, Bartana appropriated the style and in parts the sequencing of the earlier film when it came to editing and assembling her own work. On the outside of the theater hang posters for *Summer Camp* that use the heroic poses and fragmented aesthetic of 1930s avant-garde film. Both Lerski's and Bartana's films are glosses on the Zionist slogan "We have come to the land to build and be rebuilt in it," and in each case the filmmakers aim to create a catalyst within the larger political theater of the Middle East. Just as the success of the Zionist state supported by Lerski depends on the political will of the participants, the multicultural Israel proposed by Bartana and ICAHD will be the product not of house-builders but of the wider society in which they build.

Once completed, the house featured in *Summer Camp* enters into multiple narratives. It is simultaneously a home, an act of political resistance, a statement of ethical and philosophical intent, a crime, and part of an artwork. It is different from the homes to which those building it will return, which are, in turn, different from each other. Above all, this home is a fragile object that is constructed less out of concrete and rebar than it is out of the intersecting forces of political will and individual commitment. The original home was not strong enough to withstand the political actions of the Jerusalem municipality that oversees the region in which it is located or the IDF, which enacts the government's policy of home demolition. As an object, it was clearly not physically strong enough to withstand the bulldozers. In the film it is being rebuilt in the full knowledge that it will likely survive only in the work of art that itself, as presented at Documenta 12 in 2007, is housed in a temporary structure at a temporary exhibition.

Much of the work discussed in this chapter approaches the question of how to represent the realities of globalism by attempting to visualize the economic, cultural, biographical, and political networks that connect different parts of the world. Jacir's *Where We Come From* shares with works by Allan Sekula, Phil Collins, Zoe Leonard, and José Bedia, among others, an interest in describing and mapping such connections. Bartana's *Summer Camp*, like Flavio Garciandia's *Untitled*, René Francisco and DUPP's *Casa Nacional*, Shahzia Sikander's *Pleasure Pillars*, and Cao Fei's *COSPlayers*, presents a sense of the character of locations that are defined by their existence as contingent meeting points of different political, economic, and social forces. All places might be similarly viewed as intersections. These works are models for understanding the nodes and networks that make up the cartography of the present.

10

New Metaphors and New Narratives

In many ways, Chapter 10 revisits issues already raised in Chapter 1: At the beginning of the new millennium, artists were again concerned with creating new metaphors out of the materials in their studios and out of what they saw in the world, just as James Rosenquist did in *F-111* (see fig. 1.1) or Nancy Spero in *Notes in Time on Women* (1979) (see fig. 1.26). The first half of the chapter addresses a variety of painters and sculptors whose work highlights the particularities of their chosen media, but who, unlike strict formalists, are intent on using aesthetic decisions to signify social, political, and philosophical content. The second half of the chapter examines the work of artists, several working in video and new media, for whom the complexities of storytelling capture the viewers' attention as much if not more than the content of the those stories. There is more to this art than formal questions, of course, but my concern in the final chapters is to demonstrate that the broadened perspectives and critical visions brought to art making since the late 1970s have created an environment in which aesthetic concerns, from color choices to how one tells a story, are understood to intersect with open networks of meaning that are, in turn, inflected by an artist's means of presentation. Contemporary art is the result of a life lived, to use Jean-François Lyotard's formulation, with a "sensitivity to differences" and an ability to "tolerate the incommensurable." The art of the previous two chapters has, in many ways, pointed to difference and incommensurability. The art of this chapter and the next invites a discussion of what it means to experiment with the building blocks of any art—form, narrative, and experience as discussed in Chapter 11—in a world defined by such instability.

The artists discussed in this chapter began their careers while the battles over painting begun in the late 1970s were raging (see Chapters 2 and 3). The debates over the supposed "end of painting" and critiques of conventional forms of narrative had sharpened the theoretical tools with which artists, critics, and audiences dissected art and culture. By the turn of the millennium, the polemical brinkmanship characteristic of the 1980s had relaxed, but more importantly the call to take seriously the consequences of artistic conventions had been internalized. Matthew Ritchie, a British-born painter, noted that his generation no longer faced the "obligation to perpetuate or dismantle ... We [could] just go off and start to build new structures."[1] The impulse to create new forms had been felt with great urgency by the artists with whom this book began. Robert Rauschenberg's *Thaw* (see fig. 0.6), Helio Oiticica's *Tropicalia* (see fig. 1.8), and the Fluxus and feminist recontextualizations of everyday actions were all such efforts at creating new structures expressive of the changing world. The post-World War II generation, however, was also vigorously rejecting the priorities of the previous era, and this need to clear the ground continued to drive much political art up to and including appropriation in the early 1980s. By the 1990s, however, as Ritchie suggested, museum and gallery visitors all over the world witnessed increasingly constructive rather than deconstructive practices. The applicability of Pop art and appropriation practices to Russian, Chinese, Cuban, and Japanese, as well as U.S. and European, artists, and the evident compatibility of Minimalism with body art or historical content demonstrated that all-or-nothing positions were no longer necessary. Form and content were understood to be in an ongoing relationship that demanded critical attention, and audiences could be counted on to provide it. Certainly, art and art-history students were now being provided with critical tools that had been unavailable twenty years before.

This chapter focuses on a group of artists, primarily from the U.S. and Europe, who interrogate the relationship of abstraction and representation and who experiment with permutations of narrative. Many others could have been included. A glance back at earlier chapters reveals artists, including Shahzia Sikander, Yinka Shonibare, and Zhang Xiaogang, who were just as concerned with the signifying potential of painting as the artists discussed here. Likewise, numerous challenges to narrative traditions have already been presented through the work of Yang Fudong, Cao Fei, Kara Walker, and Walid Raad, among others. The division that becomes obvious in such lists, in which non-Western and non-white artists enter the discussion of contemporary art due to the explicit content of their work, is consistent with patterns evident in larger artworld institutions, from museums to auctions and academia. Does this mean that Shahzia Sikander cares more about addressing her experience as a Pakistani woman living in the West than the affective and intellectual power of painting? Certainly not, and neither were Cao Fei and Ou Ning indifferent to the signifying power of digital video as they shot footage for *San Yuan Li* (see fig. 9.23). The experimentation with form and narrative discussed in this chapter explores a familiar problem shared by many artists—that of making one's formal practice relevant to the contemporary environment. The legacy of over twenty years of incorporating and building upon the deconstructions and demystifications of the 1960s and 1970s put artists in a position to create new metaphors that would be meaningful in a changed world and new forms of narrative suited to the new millennium.

Relearning to Paint

The renewed attention to the formal aspects of art—the properties of particular media, the character of abstraction, the structures of narrative—found critical outlets in the work of writers including Dave Hickey in Las Vegas, Jeremy Gilbert-Rolfe in Los Angeles, and David Batchelor in London, who argued forcefully for a heightened appreciation of visual pleasure in art and popular culture. Exhibitions celebrating a veritable renaissance of visual expression and narrative painting includd "Beau Monde," SITE Santa Fe, New Mexico (2001) curated by Dave Hickey, "The Mystery of Painting," Sammlung Goetz, Munich (2001), "Painting at the Edge of the World," Walker Art Center, Minneapolis (2001), "Dear Painter, Paint Me," Centre Pompidou, Paris (2002), and "Remote Viewing (Invented Worlds in Recent Painting and Drawing)," Whitney Museum of American Art, New York (2005), and the continued support and promotion of painting by the Saatchi Gallery, London, throughout the 1990s culminating in "The Triumph of Painting" (2005).

The phenomenon extended beyond painting to include sculpture, photography, and video. Though this critical and curatorial focus on painting was concentrated in the West, work by artists such as Sikander and Takashi Murakami (see Chapter 9), as well as the international range of the participants in the shows noted above, indicated that if the end of painting had been glimpsed in many locales, it had never been reached. What this means for contemporary art remains unresolved to this day. Unlike the return to painting announced in the early 1980s which struck a decidedly anti-historical tone, the artists discussed here have explicitly considered their craft and its past. As a result, viewers are often encouraged to think critically about the aesthetic choices made by the artist and to find meaning as well as beauty in the results.

Amy Sillman

Amy Sillman (b. 1956) finished her undergraduate education at the School of Visual Arts, New York in 1979. Painting had become unfashionable over the preceding decade or so owing to its alleged complicity with the structures of power or its mere "decorativeness," or both. But it was during this very time at the School of Visual Arts that Keith Haring and Jean-Michel Basquiat were beginning to breathe life back into painting by taking it out of the studio and into the streets. Far beyond the classrooms of the School of Visual Arts, artists such as Martin Kippenberger and Mike Kelley, were simultaneously integrating critique and celebration in their painting through their extravagant combinations of excess, virtuosity, and travesty. Sillman, a very different personality, hunkered down, supported herself by taking a variety of jobs, and painted. She showed intermittently in the 1980s but waited until 1995 to return for a graduate degree in painting. Her work since the late 1990s evokes sources in Abstract Expressionism and children's art, and enlists figurative styles from cartoons to life studies.

Before her time at the School of Visual Arts, Sillman's commitment to painting had already been shaped by the eclectic art scene in her hometown of Chicago. Instead of viewing the medium as a hegemonic force of Modernism, Sillman learned from the Chicago Imagists including Ed Paschke (see fig. 5.1) and the Hairy Who, a group of painters interested in unorthodox conjunctions of abstractions and representation and also associated with the school of the Art Institute of Chicago, that painting could address content ranging from strip clubs to the psyche, in styles that evoke both Cubism and comic books. In the galleries of the Art Institute of Chicago, she was also exposed to what might be called art's "minor histories," a term popular in the theoretical writings of the 1970s and 1980s that designates the many events that give nuance to and even contradict the dominant narratives of official history. Here, Sillman began her lifelong connection to the art of Florine Stettheimer (1871–1944) and Yves Tanguy (1900–55); the Arts and Crafts designs of William Morris (1834–96), Indian miniatures, and Early Renaissance Sienese painting also became important sources for her. Once in New York, she worked for May Stevens, a painter and co-producer of the feminist arts journal *Heresies*. Exposure to the artists and writers associated with the journal further directed Sillman to painting at the margins of art history.

Sillman's *Bed* (2006) (**fig. 10.1**) features a couple lying close together, arms intertwined, their bodies cupped like spoons. The figures are half-covered with sheets and pillows, greens and blues. The paint hovers on the canvas in layers that alternately reveal and hide a yellow ground brushed irregularly across the canvas. Floating above and beside the couple is a shadowy outline of a third figure, all limbs and head, extending its reach across the bed. Compared to a painting such as Francesco Clemente's *Abbraccio* (1983) (see

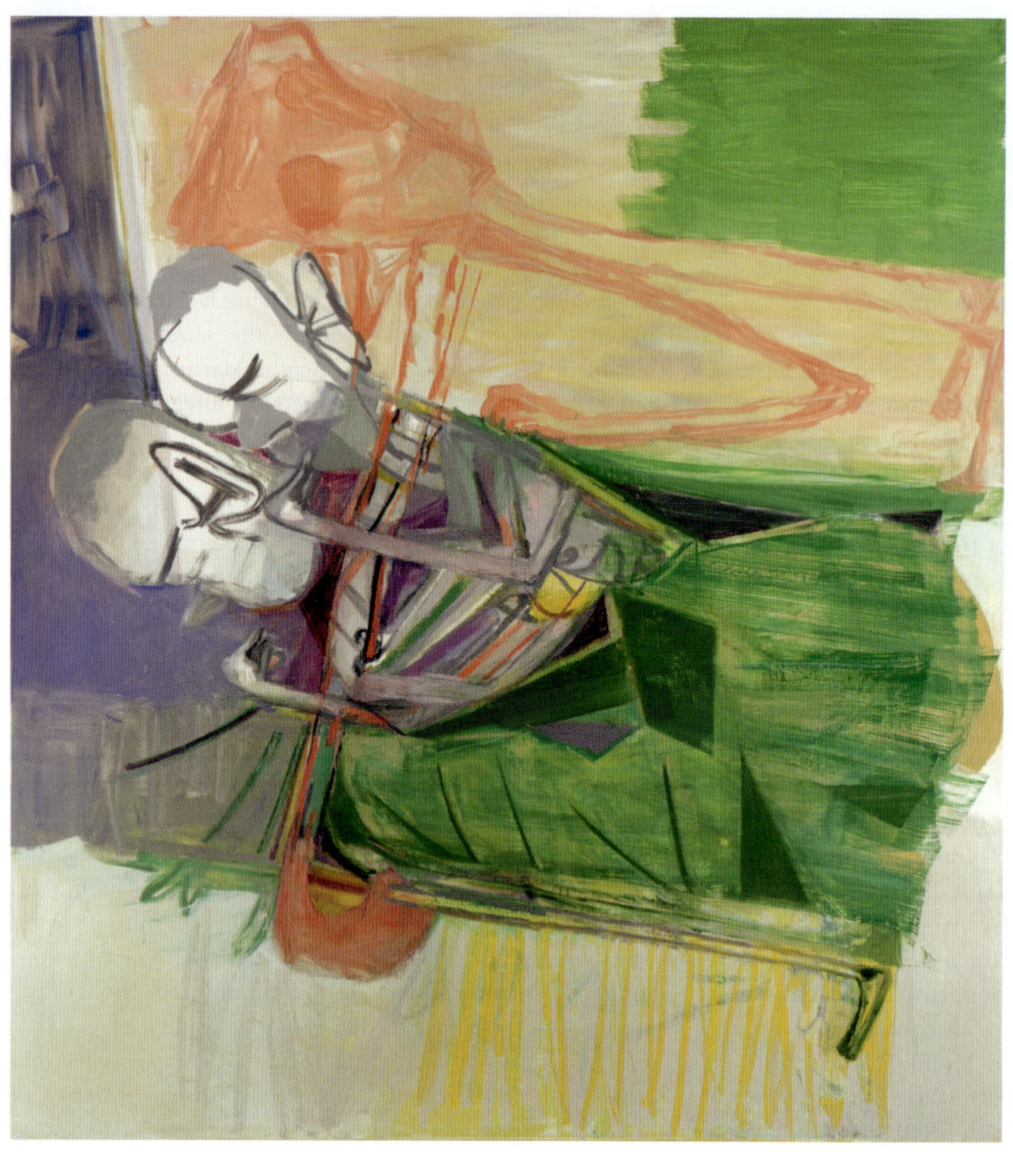

10.1 Amy Sillman, ***Bed***, 2006. Oil on canvas, 91 × 84" (231.1 × 213.4 cm). © 2013 Amy Sillman. Image courtesy of Sikkema Jenkins & Co., New York.

10.2 Amy Sillman, ***P & H 2 (Behemoth)***, 2007. Oil on canvas, 84½ × 93" (214.6 × 236.2 cm). © 2012 Amy Sillman. Image courtesy of Sikkema Jenkins & Co., New York.

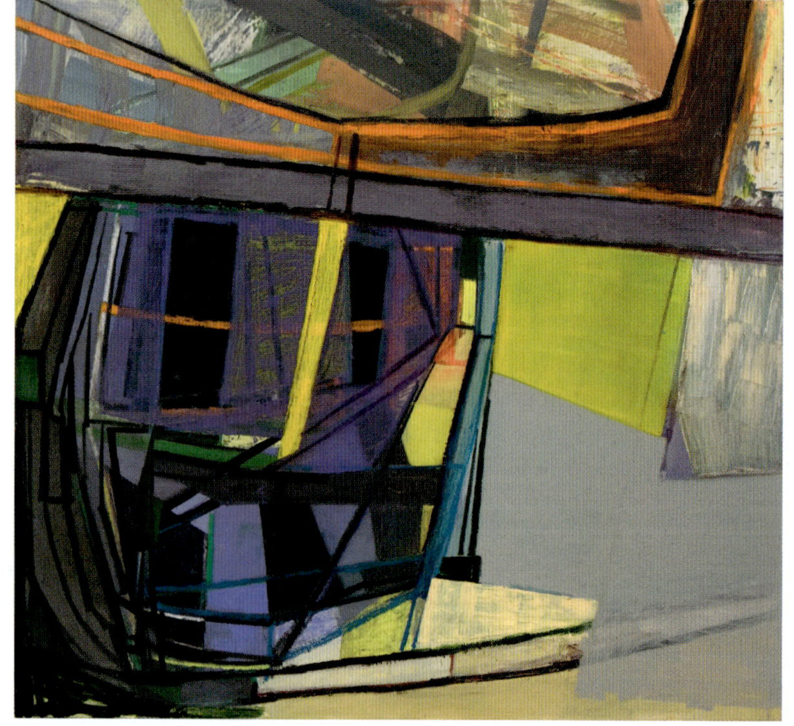

fig. 3.12), in which the artist enlists the expressive power of paint to clarify the psychological weight and ecstasy of two bodies becoming one, *Bed* is decidedly ambiguous. "This is not just fragmentary imagery but also fragmentary process and fragmentary consciousness," Sillman explains.[2] The narrative, protagonists, emotional content, and paint are all in flux and bound, she says, to "subconscious structure[s]" that are themselves merely evocative fragments.[3] Sillman's paintings include representation, abstraction, and text, all of which seem to extend the promise of meaning. In each case, however, the artist withholds clarity through distortion, fragmentation, erasure, and obliteration, confronting the signifying function of the picture with the physical properties of paint: "To scrape it, move it, to push it around, and water it down and wipe it off because it has got such a good procedural durability. I don't think oil painting would be

all that interesting if you weren't going to essentially use its materiality as one of your tools."[4] Her intent is to pursue and inspire free association unbounded by the limits of speech.

It was only after completing *Bed* and feeling she needed more information about the figure that Sillman began working with models. She asked couples with whom she was close to pose for her, first drawing from life and then improvising. The ultimately abstract nature of the paintings, such as *P & H 2 (Behemoth)* (2007) (**fig. 10.2**), reveals Sillman's priorities. Observation joins formal invention and personal expression as one more means of linking the painting with source material in the world. Sillman compares the continual shift between sensual, emotional, conceptual, and aesthetic references to a "crazy loop with your body of feeling, auto-feeling, seeing and auto-seeing and not quite knowing where a thing or a body ends and begins."[5] The results, to use the language of the artist and her critics, are teetering, imperiled, tipping, slightly wrong, abject, off, awkward. Painting is a means of responding to a world in flux and a way of revealing, in Sillman's words, "estrangement and otherness as ... profound pleasures."[6]

Cecily Brown

Sillman's re-entry in the art world in the late 1990s coincided with an explosion of figurative art that restaged a variety of approaches to picture making. John Currin (b. 1962) reflected on Old Master compositions and techniques, Elizabeth Peyton (b. 1965) exhibited seemingly effortless and emotionally penetrating portraits based on celebrity photos, and Cecily Brown (b. 1969) reveled in sexually delirious forays into expressive figuration. Brown described her experience as she finished her training at the Slade School in London and moved to New York to start her career in the early 1990s: "I was ashamed of my pleasure in painting, my predilection for emotionally charged subjects and for my love of dead painters. I eventually gave up painting; unable to come up with a good reason to be doing it, or to justify it, I seized up."[7] By the end of the decade, however, it had become "an intoxicating time to be painting, and New York an exhilarating and sympathetic climate; the mood is generous and open and eclectic."[8] Paintings such as *Night Passage* (1999) (**fig. 10.3**) feature dramatic painterly surfaces that stage scenes of erotic seduction and psychoanalytical revelation. Brown's oeuvre engages bodies, sex, and pleasure as

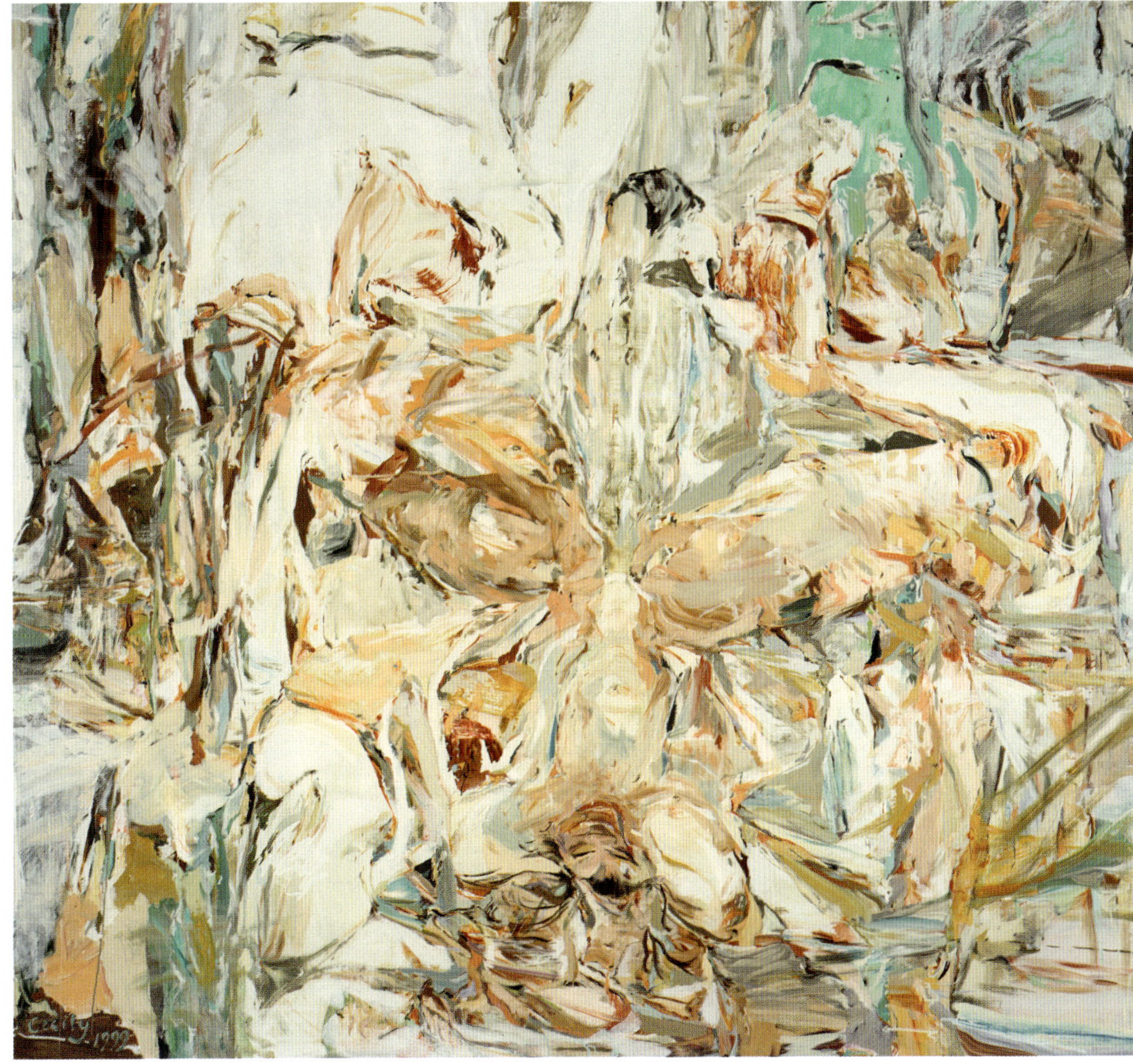

10.3 Cecily Brown, ***Night Passage***, 1999. Oil on linen, 100 × 110" (254 × 279.4 cm). © Cecily Brown. Courtesy Gagosian Gallery.

well as the history of post-World War II figurative abstraction in the form of William de Kooning and Francis Bacon. The breadth of Brown's references and the assertive manner in which she makes them her own turned her work into statements of a late-century feminist art. Painting, figurative and abstract, appeared once again to be an exciting and productive means of advancing one's art.

Franz Ackermann

In 1991, Franz Ackermann (b. 1963) finished graduate studies in painting at the Hochschule für bildende Künste, Hamburg, and won a DAAD scholarship to travel to Hong Kong. He spent his time there exploring the city before returning to his very small apartment to create what he called *Mental Maps* of the world outside (**fig. 10.4**). These drawings, which came to include motifs taken from his travels all over Asia, are small abstracted visions of landmarks, incidents, objects, streets, and journeys that represent "a retrospective recording of the dynamism and energy" or the "boredom and melancholy" of a location.[9] The *Mental Maps* are cartographic abstractions that address the emotional traces and physical impact of urban space. Upon his return to Germany in 1992, Ackermann would devote himself to paintings and large-scale installations that integrate painting, assemblage, and sculpture into the conceptual project of the drawings.

Mapping and travel have a long relationship with modern and contemporary art. Starting with the roots of Modernism in the seventeenth century and captured in works such as Vermeer's *Art of Painting* (1666), cartography, exploration, and art have often been inseparable. Works by Daniel Buren, Suzanne Lacy, Anselm Kiefer, Nari Ward, and Zoe Leonard illustrate how mapping has been a bedrock of contemporary political and Conceptual art. With Ackermann's work—as well as that of Odili Donald Odita and Ingrid Calame (see below)—mapping provides the foundation for increasingly expansive forms of art. Upon completing numerous *Mental Maps*, Ackermann "discard[ed] the watercolor as a sketch, as an impression—discarding this brevity,"[10] and turned to the materiality of the everyday. Paintings and installations, he explained, move from cartographic abstractions to more direct and representational engagement with the real. "I am quite certain," he said, "a painterly aspect [can] be found in any hotel room, in any dormitory of the world."[11] In his new work, the fluctuations of information and the perambulations of the artist meet the architecture and design of the real.

After the attacks of September 11, 2001, the meaning and context of travel changed dramatically. Ackermann observed:

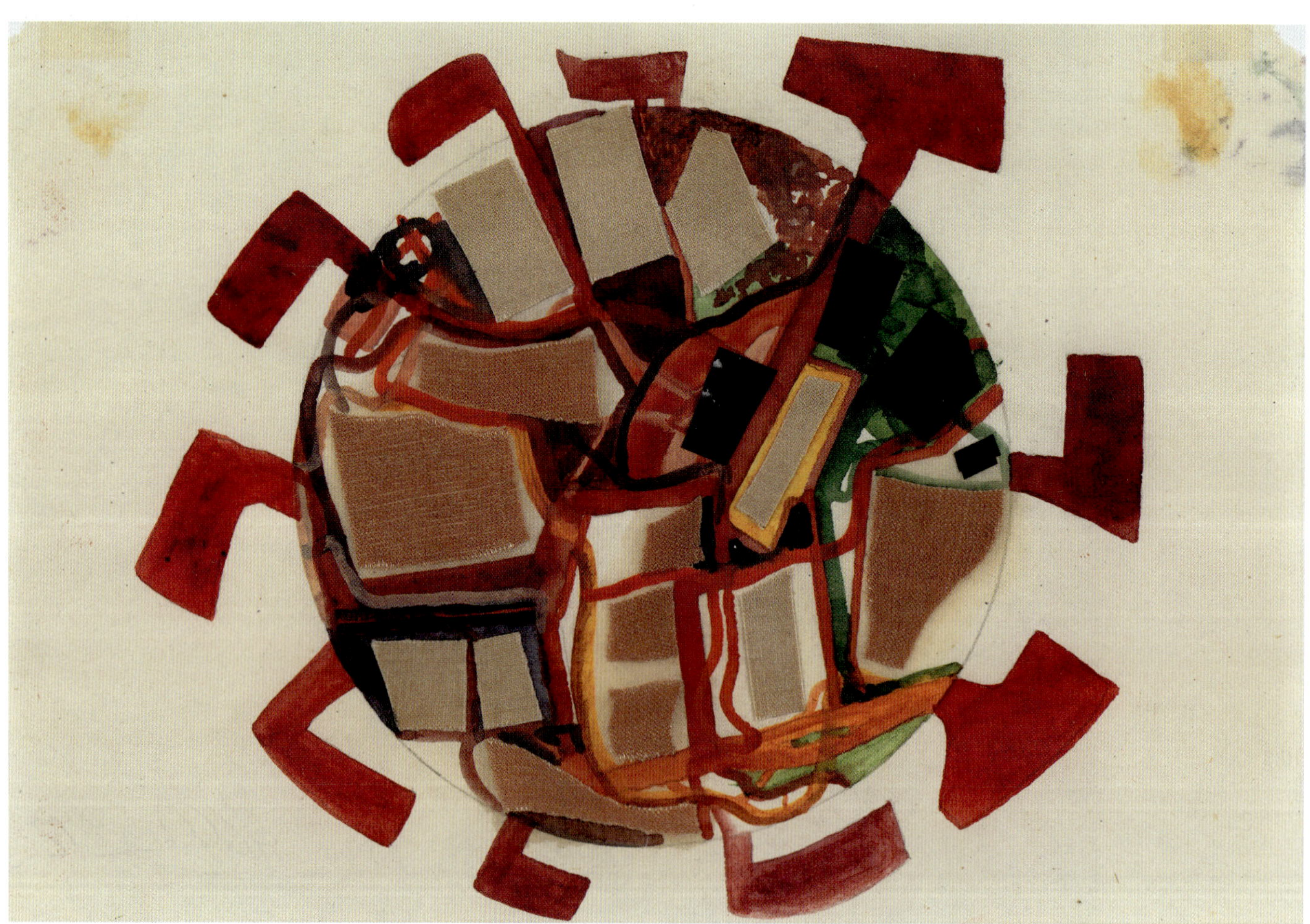

10.4 Franz Ackermann, ***Untitled (Mental Map: no. 10, public parking lots)***, 1994. Mixed media on paper, 5⅛ × 7½" (13 × 19 cm). Courtesy White Cube.

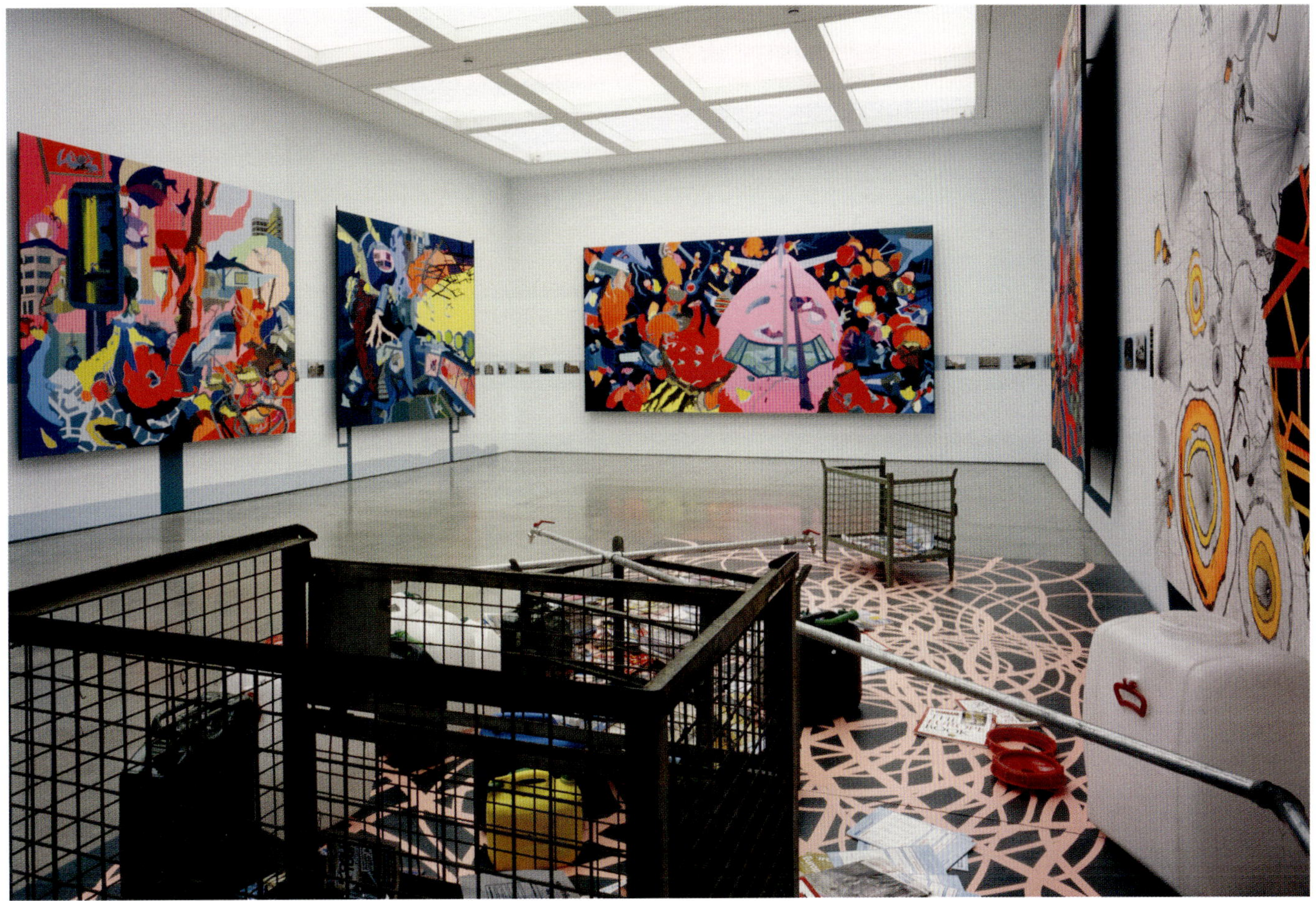

10.5 Franz Ackermann, ***Home, Home Again***, 2006. Installation view at White Cube, Hoxton Square, London, April 21–May 20, 2006. © Franz Ackermann. Courtesy White Cube.

"Suddenly you couldn't move around freely anymore. Traveling became a political act. And all at once we were forced to realize that at every moment, somewhere in the world, wars are being fought for territorial gain, a fact that had been almost forgotten amid all the globalization hype."[12] Ackermann's work after 2001 has admitted a sense of foreboding that tempers the romance inherent in the *Mental Maps* of the 1990s. In his installation at the White Cube gallery in London in 2006, *Home, Home Again* (**fig. 10.5**), he included a row of eighty-eight photographs of hotels over which he had drawn lines as if the buildings were caught in the cross hairs of a gun sight. The allusion to sniper fire provides an uncharacteristically literal connection to the visually explosive paintings that dominated the exhibition. Architectural features suggesting waiting rooms and even detention chambers were built in the gallery, confronting the expansive spaces of the paintings and the implied threat of the photographs with signs and spaces of interrogation and incarceration. In this installation, viewers were not encouraged to let their minds wander as freely as in Ackermann's earlier paintings or the *Mental Maps*. Ackermann's insistence on the continued relevance of objects and circumstances on the ground in a world proudly proclaiming itself deterritorialized reminds the viewer that our virtual digital networks include analogue regions and corporeal travelers. Things as well as ideas, presence as well as appearance, remain critical.

Odili Donald Odita

The integration of representation and abstraction that constitutes Ackerman's practice is given a different spin in the work of Nigerian-born, U.S.-raised and -trained Odili Donald Odita (b. 1966). Signifying the breadth of his concerns, Odita's early installations often combined collaged and appropriated images with the abstract paintings that have since become the heart of his practice. These installations—including his first New York show, "Color Theory," in 1999, which juxtaposed photo-based work integrating fashion, advertising, and news imagery—link consumer culture with global and racial politics, but also with his abstract paintings. In the context of the overtly political representations, abstractions such as *Present Tense* (1999) (**fig. 10.6**) invite the viewer to search out the common ground between the paintings and the photographs. One answer lies in Odita's observation that "all visual materials are culturally grounded, and it is important to recognize where their meaning is derived."[13] This is a familiar point, rooted in the re-evaluation of geometric abstraction that began in the 1980s, but Odita's juxtapositions are both forceful and quite open-ended.

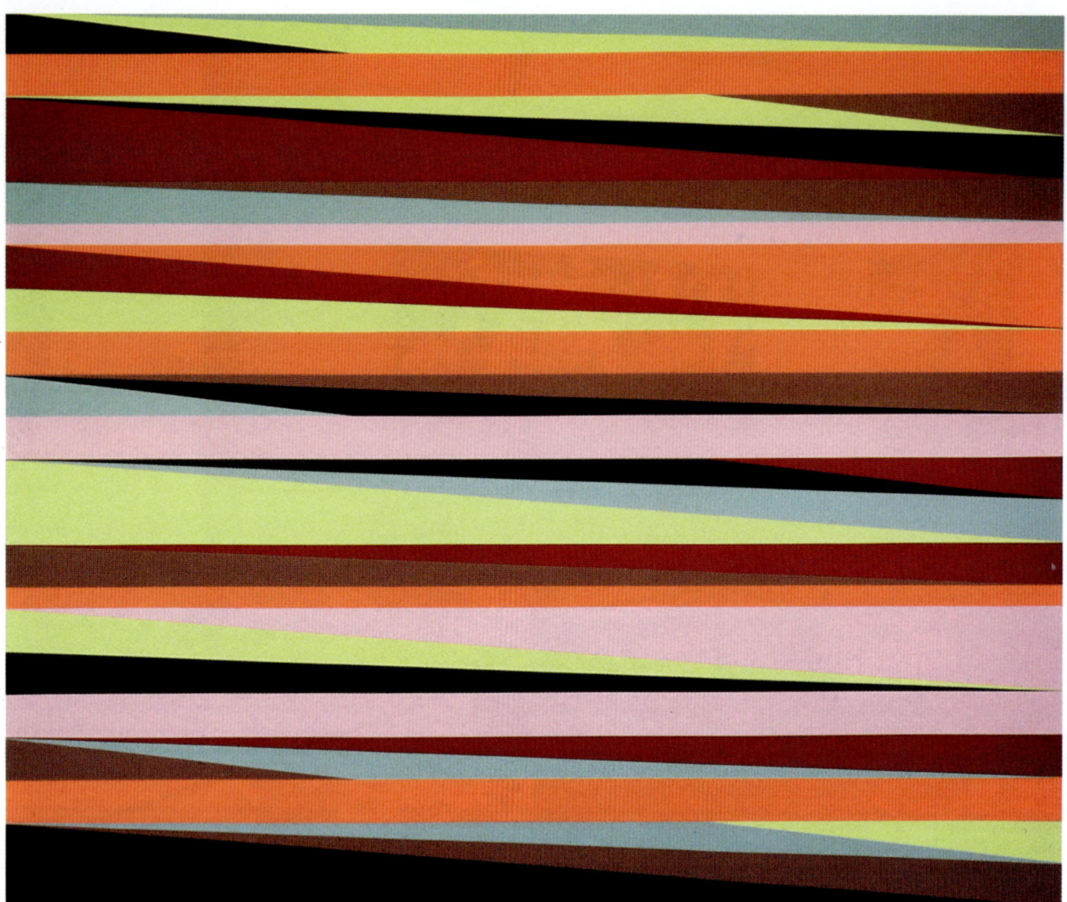

10.6 Odili Donald Odita, *Present Tense*, 1999. Acrylic on canvas 84 × 104" (213.36 × 264.16 cm). Image courtesy the artist.

Unlike the Neo-Geo focus on power, meaning in Odita's paintings lies in a variety of personal, social, geographical, and historical sources. The angular network of browns, pinks, yellows, and blues in *Present Tense* is inflected with references to African textiles and landscapes, as well as to computer screens and the mass media. Color for Odita is a means of invoking other places, many paintings using a palette based on trips the artist made to Africa, as well as to his childhood home in Ohio. In addition, he selects colors that evoke television screens, thus mapping the real and the virtual across the surface of his canvases. The collision of these sources, like the fractured compositions themselves, generates a dialogue across cultures and borders in which technology, craft, city, and nature are all points of contact.

Ingrid Calame

The sensitivity to the cultural meaning of abstraction finds a very literal example in the 1:1 scale vision of Ingrid Calame's indexical abstractions. The LA-based Calame (b. 1965) has made fidelity to the shape (and scale) of the world the defining feature of her work. In 1994, while making more traditional oil-on-canvas paintings, she looked down at the studio floor. The shapes of the dripped and spilled paint she saw there inspired her to devise a practice based on finding rather than making marks. Calame traces stains. Laying sheets of translucent Mylar on sidewalks, streets, playgrounds, and parking lots, as well as on floors and walls, she meticulously records the marks left by oil, tires, footsteps, the weather, and machinery. In addition to ordinary streets, Calame has traced in the New York Stock Exchange, churches, and abandoned playgrounds and factories. In some instances, such as *From #258 Drawing (Tracings from the Indianapolis Motor Speedway and the LA River)* (2007) (**fig. 10.7**), the final work references multiple sites. After she or her assistants have traced the stains, Calame labels the documents and assembles them, layering the tracings in what she calls "constellations," which are then retraced onto sheets of Mylar or painted in enamel on aluminum. The painted constellations carry with them the aesthetic appeal of chaos, the refined control of Calame's steady hand and considered palette, and the narrative mystery of reconstructing the actions that produced the stains in the first place. Stains, she says, "index events," and with each new tracing her archive of forms and associations grows richer.[14]

Calame's works on the speedway accumulate "events" from throughout the history of the track. Captured prominently among the skidded tire tracks and dripped residues of motor oil, coolant, and fuel are very specific marks, including the doughnut-shaped skid marks made by Indy 500 winners in celebration of victory. The vibrant and artificial colors of the logos and details that cover the cars inspired the palette of *From #258 Drawing*. Calame's tracings from the LA River, a space identified with different subcultures than those that use the speedway, record the residue left by water that flows

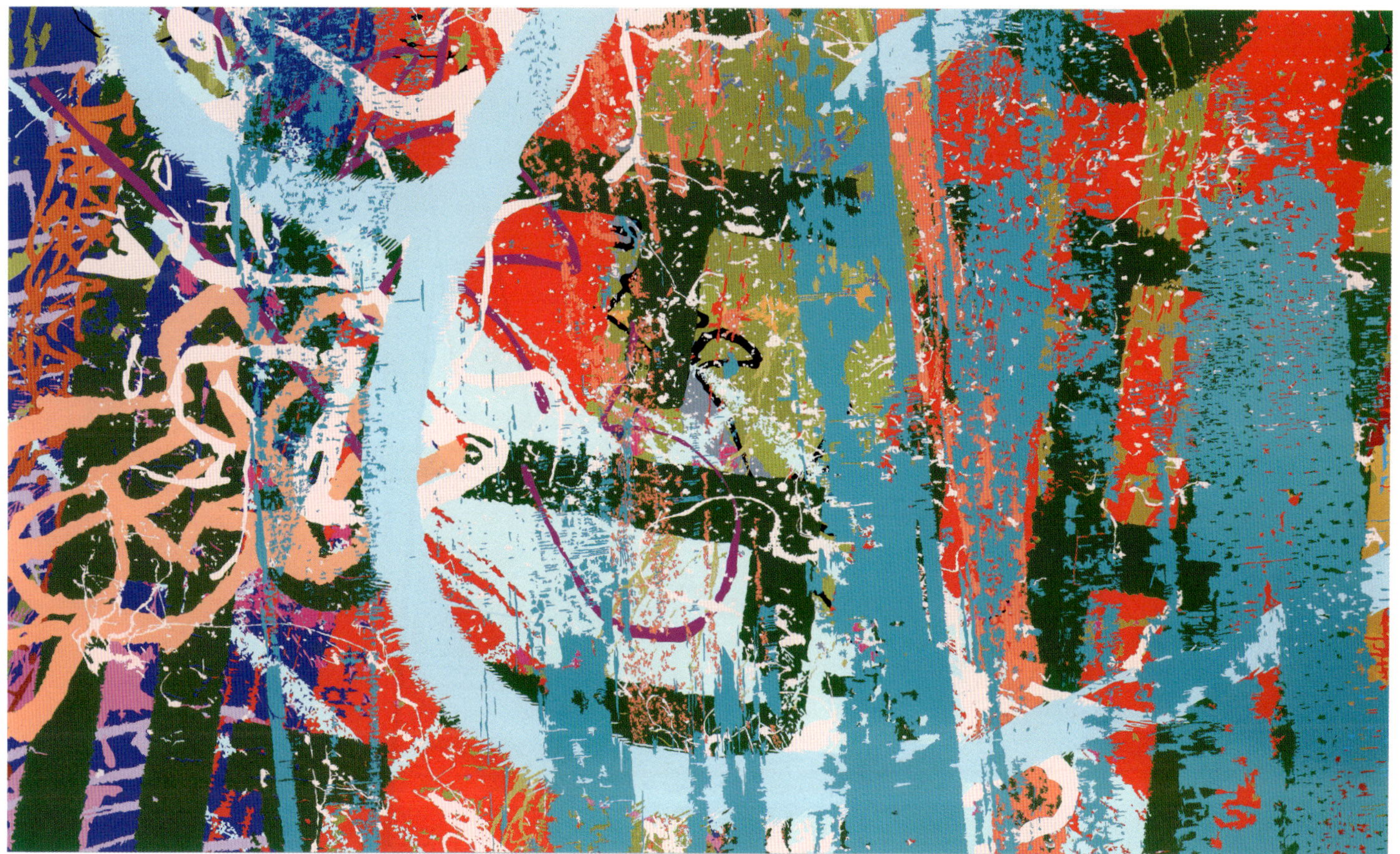

10.7 Ingrid Calame, ***From #258 Drawing (Tracings from the Indianapolis Motor Speedway and the LA River)***, 2007. Enamel paint on aluminum, 71 × 119 × 1⅛" (180.34 × 302.26 × 2.8 cm). Indianapolis Museum of Art, Carmen & Mark Holeman Contemporary Fund 2008.3 © the artist. Image Courtesy James Cohan Gallery, New York & Shanghai.

through the culverts as well as deliberate signs of human presence. One can make out fragments of graffiti among the broad vertical bands of *From #258 Drawing*. Calame's paintings and drawings of the Indianapolis Motor Speedway and the Los Angeles River together cover hundreds of square feet, mimicking the scale of the sites as well as the appearance of their surfaces.

The all-over fluid indexicality of Calame's abstractions has been compared to Jackson Pollock's signature drip paintings: Her works share much with the mesmerizing weblike quality of Pollock's brand of Abstract Expressionism. Nevertheless, Calame's work is striking for its distance from Abstract Expressionism's gestural immediacy. Each of her paintings, regardless of its aesthetic seduction, is also an archive of marks in the world, each one studiously copied and filed away in the artist's studio. This encyclopedic and analytic quality mediates the more emotive aspects of the work in a way foreign to her mid-century predecessors. Calame shares with all the artists discussed in this section a commitment to art that is referential, indexical, and even semiotic at the same time as being abstract, evocative, and visually poetic. John Yau (b. 1950), poet, critic, and longtime ally of painters, wrote of Calame's work: "The forms begin to float free from their literalness, while the staccato colors and asyndetic transitions [those without conjunctions] bounce you all over the place."[15] As much as we are brought face to face with the precise record of human presence in this or that factory, street, racetrack, or neighborhood, Calame's signs achieve an independence from their referents in the world and a visual and emotional identity within the networks of her art.

Albert Oehlen

As Franz Ackermann traveled the world, painters in Germany continued to have a strong impact on late-twentieth-century painting. Gerhard Richter and Sigmar Polke dominated discussions of painting and the circles based around Martin Kippenberger in the west and Leipzig-based Neo Rauch (b. 1960) in the east were drawing considerable attention. Rauch's personal combination of Socialist Realism, theatrical narration, and painterly abstraction in paintings such as *Schicht (Shift)* (1999) (**fig. 10.8**) set the tone for a new generation of painters from the former East Germany. The work of Albert Oehlen (b. 1954), born in the western city of Krefeld, adds nuance to explorations into the properties and possibilities for painting at the turn of the millennium. Before attending art school at the Hochschule für bildende Künste, Hamburg, in the mid-1970s, where he studied with Polke and met Kippenberger, Oehlen worked at a bookstore and created performances. He prepared a legal brief against his previous teachers for the intellectual damage he considered

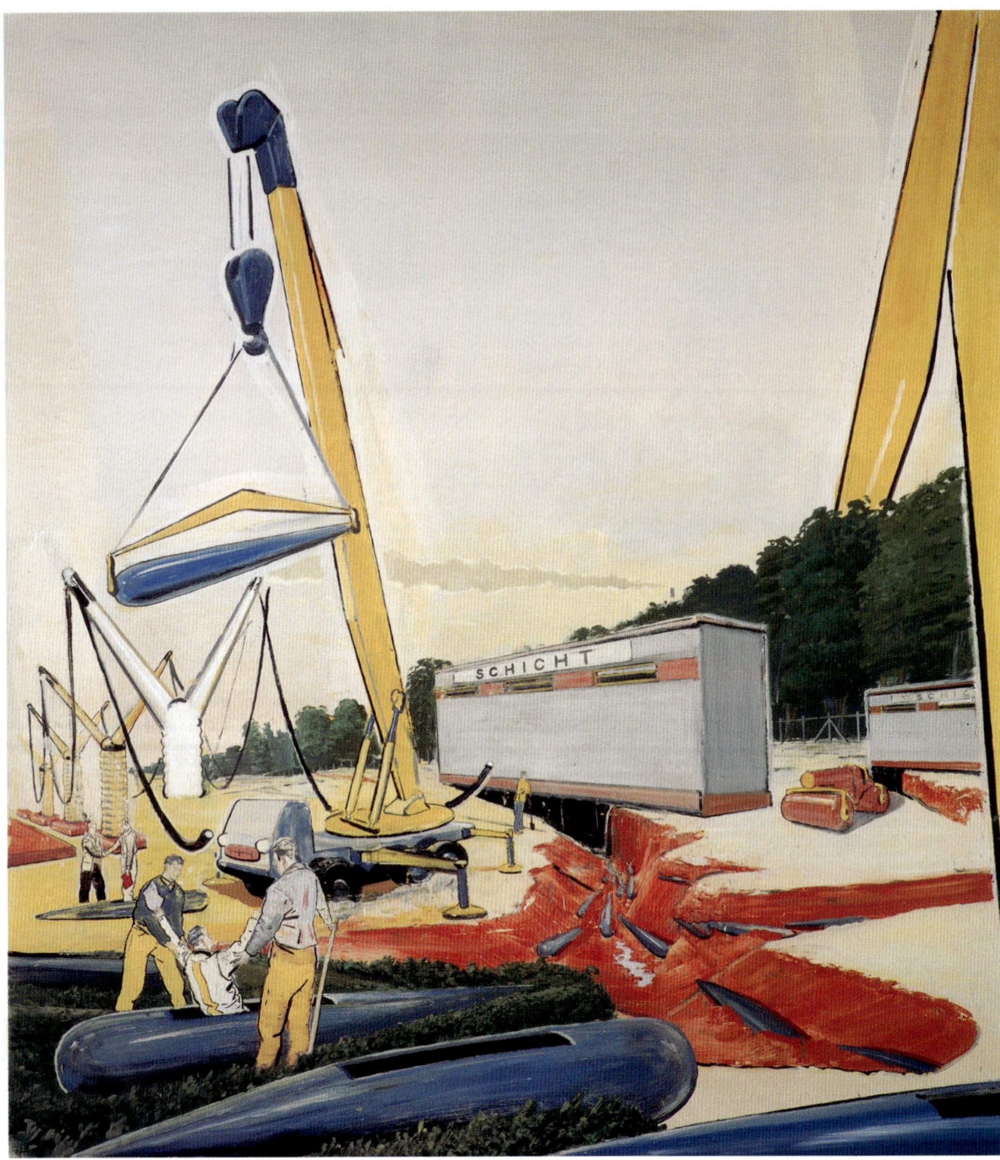

10.8 Neo Rauch, *Schicht (Shift)*, 1999. Oil on canvas, 78¾ × 70⅞" (200 × 180 cm). Courtesy Galerie EIGEN + ART Leipzig/Berlin and David Zwirner, New York.

himself to have incurred in their courses and performed the *Bread Roll Initiative*, in which he and fellow artist Werner Buttner threw ham rolls over the Berlin Wall. The sandwiches were a gesture of solidarity with the East, serving as both food and a metaphor for the divided city. After art school, Oehlen returned to Berlin, where he continued to collaborate with Buttner and others, including his own brother Markus Oehlen, Kippenberger, A.R. Penck, Jörg Immendorf, and the band Red Krayola. The Berlin scene was vibrant and competitive, with artistic and social jousting between Oehlen's group, led by Kippenberger, and the *Neue Wilde* (Young Wild Ones) painters such as Helmut Middendorf and Rainer Fetting (see Chapter 3). Comparing the art of the two groups, Oehlen remarked: "We were much more devious ... We mixed up techniques, introduced things those people wouldn't have used and played other tricks ... We weren't worried whether it was coherent and comprehensible."[16] Their art recorded the collision between any number of styles, genres, images, and materials. Oehlen left Germany for Andalucía, Spain, with Kippenberger in 1987, moving to Madrid the following year. Since 1992, he has maintained a home and studio in Spain and, like Kippenberger, Oehlen has created work in which cultural as well as aesthetic and personal references collide.

Maintaining a sense of incoherence was quite difficult for Oehlen. Recounting a discussion with friend and writer Rainald Goetz, he remarked: "It became obvious [by the mid-1990s] that I had convinced myself I was producing work that was clear and precise. [Goetz] told me that believing yourself to have achieved clarity was a stupid state to be in. The tone of his comments was along the lines of 'More is more'—that you shouldn't abandon content."[17] In response, Oehlen redoubled his efforts to treat his canvas as a site of inconsistency and chaos. Using paint, collage, and computers, Oehlen borrowed from the history of art, the appearance of graphics software, and all manner of visual culture. Oehlen's *El Pez Roncando (The Fish Snoring)* (2001) (**fig. 10.9**) presents laser-printed patterns designed with computer software and a mouse, lines and fields copied from computer monitors, spills and gestural flourishes achieved with the energy and technique of expressionist painting, carefully

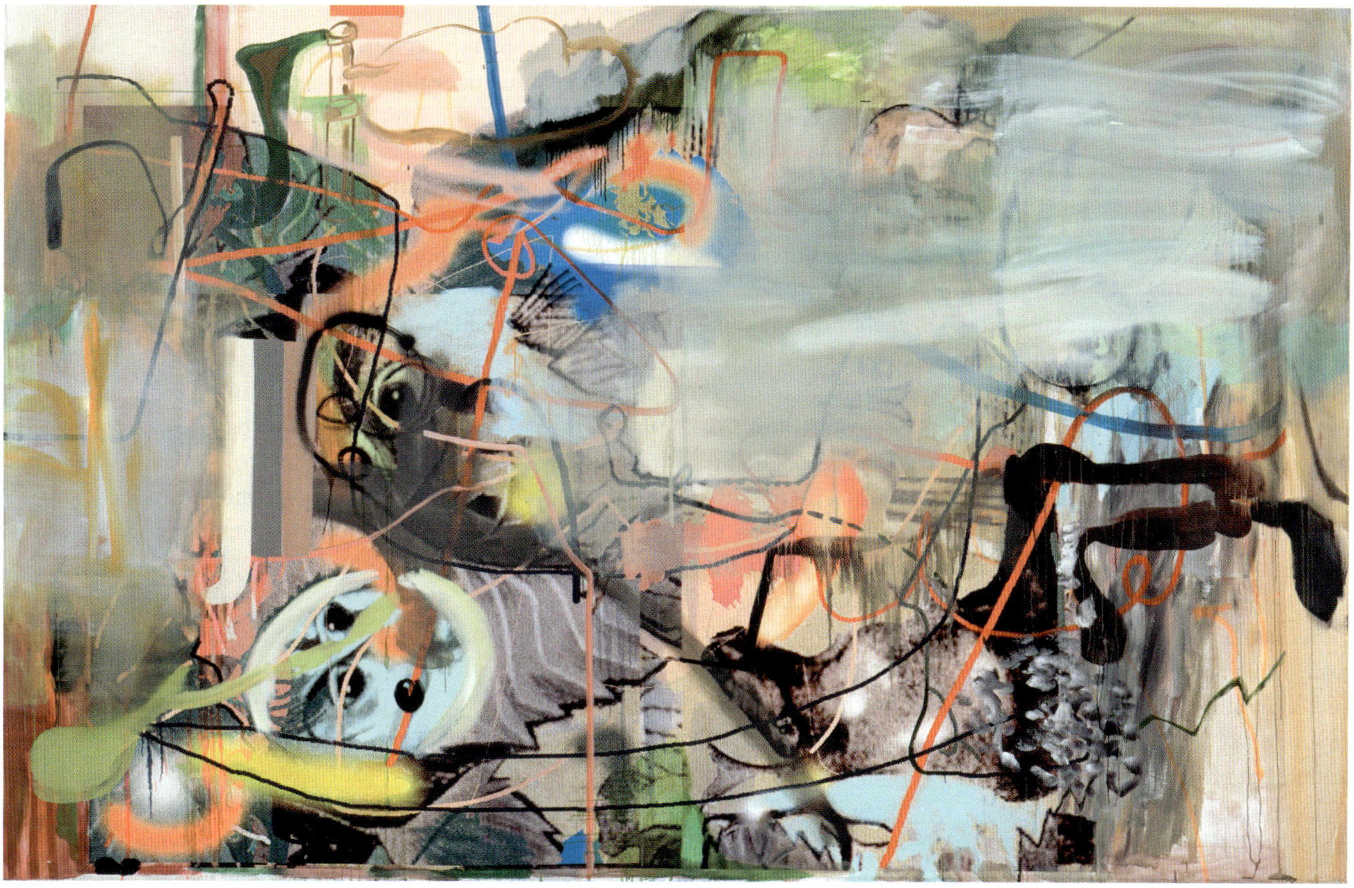

10.9 Albert Oehlen, ***El Pez Roncando (The Fish Snoring)***, 2001. Mixed media on canvas, 94½ × 149⅝" (240 × 380 cm). © Albert Oehlen. Courtesy Gallery Grässlin, Frankfurt.

rendered features and forms, stylized images of animals, people, and things, and photographs. Many of these elements are compatible with one another and unite the composition formally and conceptually. More often than not, however, each passage appears to have only a coincidental relationship with the ones above and below it, creating a sense of disjunction or indifference across the canvas. When Oehlen wants coherence, he chooses a unifying element, such as a consistent expressionist style or a uniform gray palette as in *Bad (Bath)* (2003) (**fig. 10.10**), into which he then introduces features such as a heavily outlined profile,

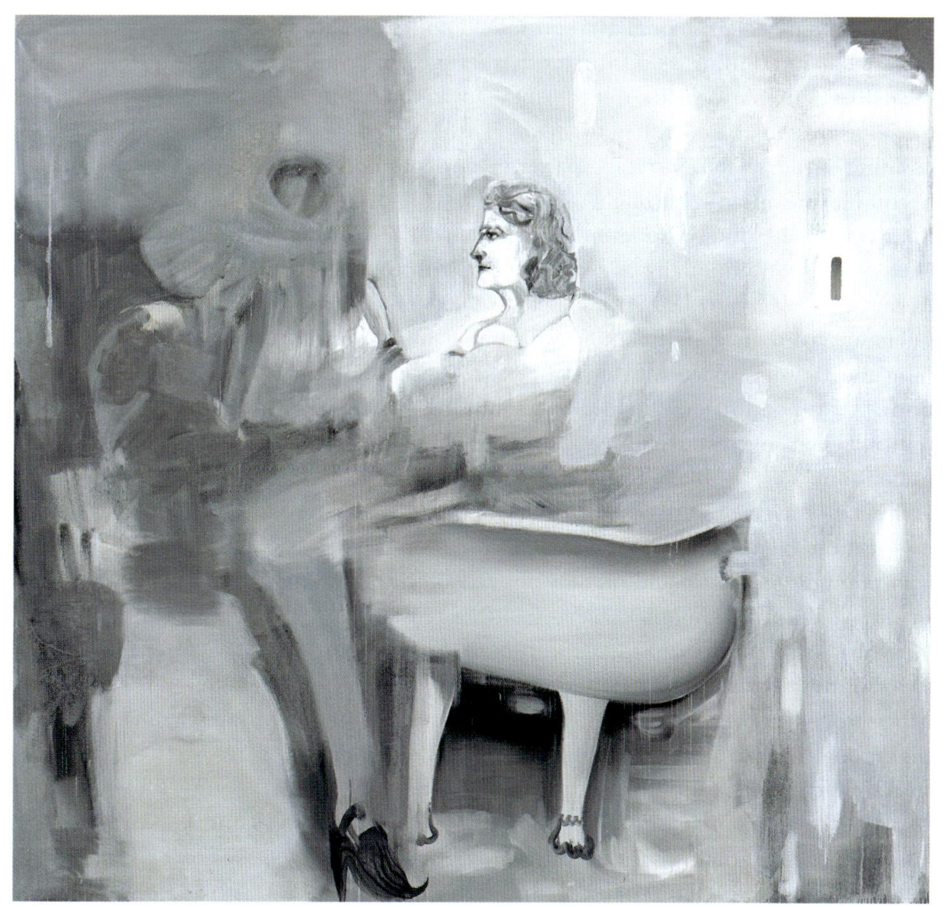

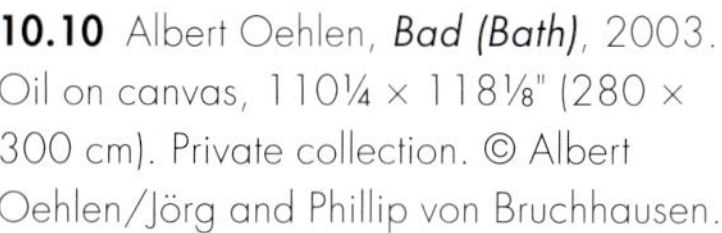

10.10 Albert Oehlen, ***Bad (Bath)***, 2003. Oil on canvas, 110¼ × 118⅛" (280 × 300 cm). Private collection. © Albert Oehlen/Jörg and Phillip von Bruchhausen.

the partially rendered bath for which the work is titled, and floating geometric forms that fight against the cohesion of the painting.

Painting has survived, Oehlen comments, because it permits "the visible working through of inferences, misunderstandings, ideas to be criticized, and also your own mistakes. It's not a principle, not a justification—it's work. It means nothing else."[18] Like Thomas Lawson's argument in "Last Exit: Painting" (1981), a pro-painting manifesto written to counter the dire polemics being leveled against the medium at the time, Oehlen asserts that painting is powerful to the degree that it is enmeshed in the social forces that shape daily life and the mass media: Painting does not transcend life. Like the other artists discussed in this chapter, materiality as well as referentiality are critical to his work. The emotive reactions we have toward the washes or the flourishes of sprayed or violently brushed paint are as important as the associations we bring to the reindeer, eyes, and computer-generated lines in *El Pez Roncando.* Oehlen's juxtaposition of mutually exclusive meanings and effects on a single surface testifies to the flexibility of painting in the twenty-first century and to the willingness of audiences to see it as a medium of instability and flux. For Oehlen, art in the new millennium is not a place to create clarity and refinement, nor is it an excuse to reject them. Rather, a painting is a field in which to work with the complexity of contemporary life.

Space and Sculpture

The work that began Chapter 10 represented both a renewed investment in painting as a source of visual pleasure and a means to connect with life outside the canvas. Most often, the allusions to the world were made in the language of painting—colors, compositions, patterns, and even images becoming meaningful through their relation to sources in the world. Increasingly, however, artists could be seen using devices more traditionally associated with sculpture as in Ackermann's *Home, Home Again.* By the 2000s, Odita and Calame were both experimenting with wall-painting—wrapping the viewers' space with evocative and sensual abstractions. It was not a stretch then to find that some of the most optically rich and even painterly works of the turn of the millennium were as likely to be identified as sculpture and architecture as they were to be called painting. The following section begins with a discussion of the simultaneous utilization of geometric and organic abstraction in museum-quality sculpture, domestic objects, and restaurant décor. Work by Jorge Pardo represents the extreme flexibility of styles of abstraction to join, sometimes uncomfortably, territory from the overtly artistic to the mundane. The artists that follow, Katharina Grosse and Jessica Stockholder, create self-conscious interventions into museum space applying vibrant color to complex installations and to walls, windows, and doors dematerializing the architecture of the gallery and materializing the space within it.

Jorge Pardo

Los Angeles-based sculptor Jorge Pardo (b. 1963) calls his work "unmanageable."[19] It is not that the work itself is unwieldy, dense, or overly complicated. On the contrary, Pardo's output, which has included lamps, chairs, and houses as well as murals, paintings, and prints, is not only easily incorporated into daily life, but is also unfalteringly beautiful. Its unmanageability, like the open-ended character of Oehlen's painting or the awkward expressionism of Sillman's, lies in the exponentially multiplying contexts that inform each object. Faced with a sculpture that doubles variously as a lamp, a chair, or even a house, the viewer confronts many contradictory meanings. A sculpture based this closely on a cabinet or a chair maintains its link to the kitchen whether it is displayed in a museum or a private house. The viewer chooses the significance and even function of the object without the help of an authoritative guide. The lamps that fill the *Mountain Bar, Los Angeles,* which Pardo designed in 2003 (**fig. 10.11**), refer through their abstract organic forms to sculpture by Jean Arp (1886–1966) or Constantin Brancusi (1876–1957) as well as to the critical legacy of Neo-Geo. Nonetheless, the *Mountain Bar* lamps are also lighting fixtures and as such participate in a discourse of design and utility that relates as much to IKEA as it does to Modernism. This active relationship to diverse contexts permits the artist to reach out to meanings and associations produced in the homes, restaurants, libraries, bookstores, museums, and even malls that house his art.

Raised in Havana and Chicago, Pardo moved to Los Angeles for art school, finishing an MFA at the Art Center in 1988. One of the earliest exhibitions in which he participated, at the Bliss Gallery in Pasadena, California in 1987, involved Pardo and his friends going door to door to invite neighbors to contribute art or objects that they thought should be shown in a gallery in the manner of Group Material's "The People's Choice" show (see Chapter 4). For his first solo show, Pardo turned for inspiration to the mundane spaces found in every home—closets, garages, basements—exhibiting a group of sculptures that took their form, though not their substance, from ordinary objects. For *Ladder* (1989), he disassembled a ladder purchased at a hardware store and replaced parts of it with bits of expensive African bubinga wood, local redwood, fir, and cheap particle board. Each of these different woods has its own aesthetic, cultural, and emotive associations, and market value. The history of Marcel Duchamp's readymades lurks close to the surface of Pardo's objects while the relationship between pre-existing forms and handmade processes in his work reflects similar conundrums found in Jasper Johns's flags, targets, and ale and coffee cans from the 1950s and 1960s. But unlike Duchamp, who asserted that his readymades were about choice alone, or Johns, who rejected the real-world connotations of the flags and targets, Pardo welcomes every extra-artistic connection his objects make. As one sits down to order a drink under a Pardo lamp or buy a book at a Pardo-designed bookstore, it

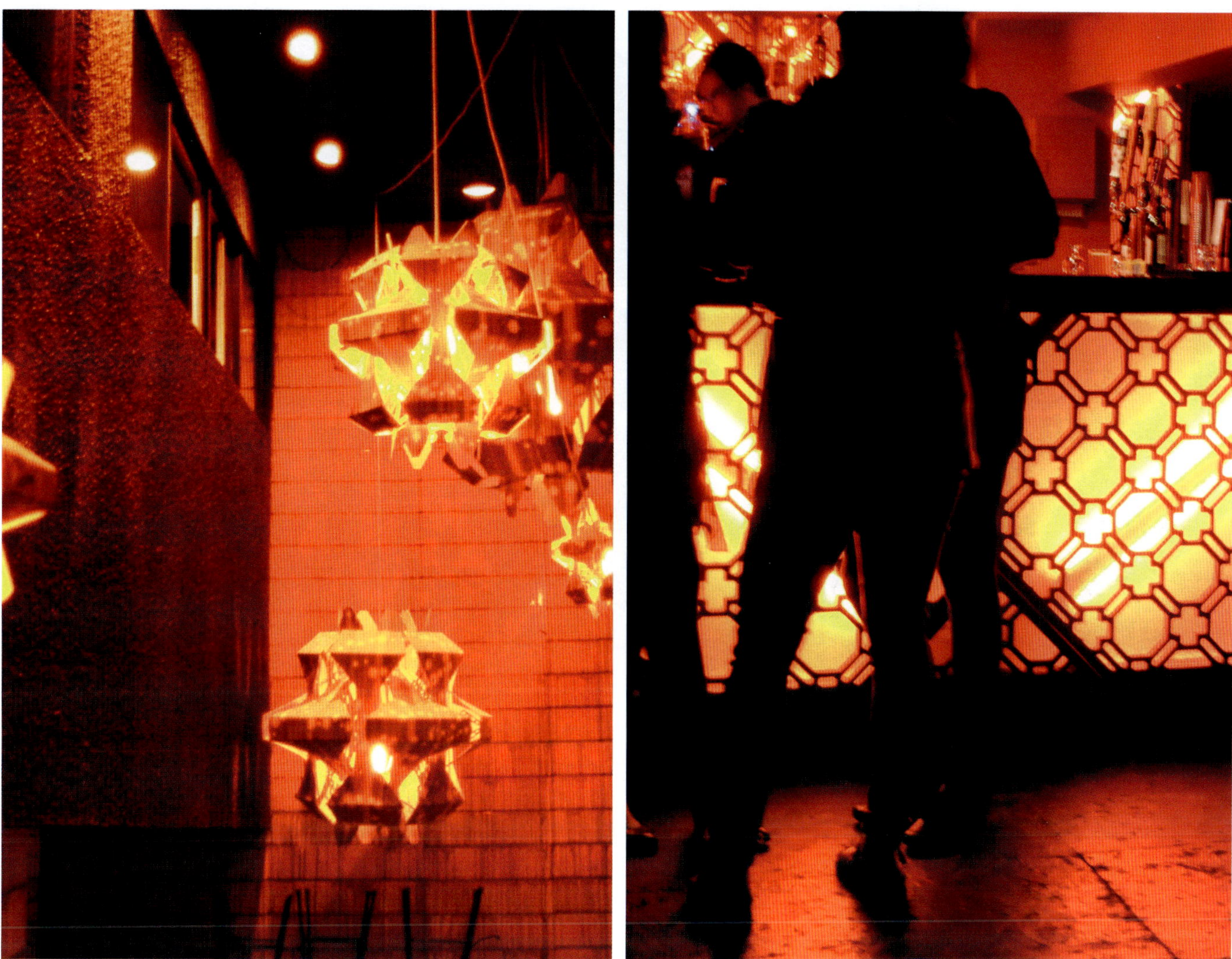

10.11 Jorge Pardo, ***Mountain Bar, Los Angeles***, 2003. Courtesy Friedrich Petzel Gallery, New York.

can be difficult, if not impossible, to distinguish the art from the design or the intellectual inquiry from the commercial appeal. The expected status of art as discursive intervention or aesthetic addition is under siege from the multiple contexts in which the work takes on meaning.

In the mid-1990s, the Museum of Contemporary Art, Los Angeles, invited Pardo to produce a solo exhibition. Having worked with domestic objects as a source of inspiration, Pardo decided to up the ante for the MoCA show and proposed building a house. The museum agreed and contributed the funds it would have spent on a more traditional exhibition, around 10 percent of the total cost of the structure; Pardo raised the rest on his own. In 1998, *4166 Sea View Lane* (**fig. 10.12**) finally opened. Audiences were invited to tour the house during specific hours, chosen to avoid disturbing the neighbors. When the show closed, Pardo moved in. *4166 Sea View Lane* mingles discourses on domesticity, art, architecture, real estate, construction, and community, raising questions about the intellectual merit of the project, the formal beauty of the house, the structural integrity of the foundations, the potential value of the property, and the possibility that the whole thing was a scam on Pardo's part to get a "free" house. Controlling these conversations proved, to use Pardo's term, "unmanageable."

4166 Sea View Lane is a residential structure with guest quarters and studio space. It is approximately 3,000 square feet in area, well within the average size for properties in the Mount Washington neighborhood of Los Angeles where it is located. Unlike neighboring homes that rise to acquire ocean views, Pardo's home hugs the gentle slope of the landscape. It is also unusual in expanding right to the edge of the property line, where it displays a solid exterior wall. The interior of the house, Pardo explains, is an exercise in creating "interestingly made space."[20] Pardo laid out the rooms in a long angular path, with several abrupt turns and oblique views that contrast with the necessarily horizontal and vertical character of the walls and floors. These geometric features contrast with the organic abundance of a central garden that is visible from nearly every point in the house. Pardo also designed furniture, paintings, and fixtures that accent the contrast between geometric and organic systems in the architecture.

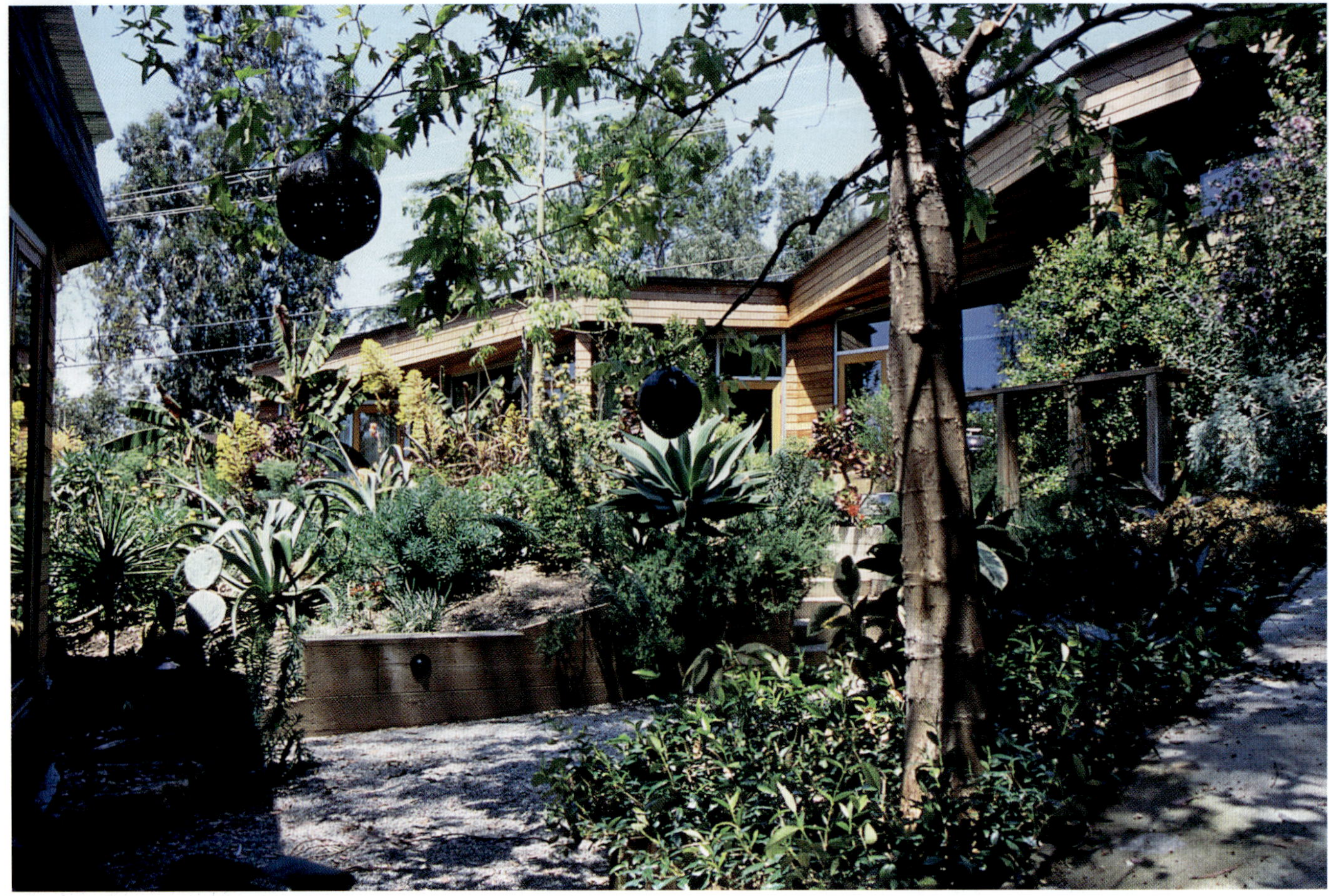

10.12 Jorge Pardo, ***4166 Sea View Lane***, 1998. Courtesy Friedrich Petzel Gallery, New York.

Like the historical Modernist homes that dot the Los Angeles cityscape and the Latin American villas that color California vernacular architecture, *4166 Sea View Lane* provides abundant intrusions of exterior and interior. However, as critic Chris Kraus has remarked, in contrast to his architectural forebears, Pardo does not treat the outside as the vibrant and final element necessary for the completion of the more passive interior space. In *4166 Sea View Lane*, one sees the landscape through glass walls. Standing securely inside the home, Kraus argues, forecloses the sensation produced by open widows that there is a way, and therefore a need, to escape. Inside and outside are conceived as different and independent elements and designed with "an equivalent balance that is active."[21] *4166 Sea View Lane* possesses, Kraus continues, "a strange absence of longing," in which one doesn't pine for an elsewhere.[22] The house finds its *raison d'être* in the careful attention to composition, surface, shape, and color, and the proposition that a house, like a painting, is informed by the world but also significant on its own.

Katharina Grosse

In 1992, Berlin-based painter Katharina Grosse (b. 1961) won the Villa Romana Award, a residency and fellowship in Florence, and as a result changed her practice to more actively engage space. In Italy, her interest turned away from the painting as an object and toward color and space independent of canvas support. Grosse was inspired by Renaissance palazzi and the attention their designers had given to every square inch of the interior. Returning to her studio, she experimented with ways of activating the environment around the work as well as inside it. Her solution was an air compressor set to propel 270 liters of paint per minute. Attaching an airbrush and tanks of paint to the machine, Grosse took aim and sent jets of paint across walls, floors, ceilings, furniture, windows, and anything else that caught her eye—even other artworks.

Grosse began spraypainting with rather formalist interests in the properties and potential of her medium. She explained: "I was making wall paintings with paintbrushes, following the format of the wall itself. It occurred to me that I was working as if with objects and I thought that my painting should be more independent from the space and its surface. This is what spray-painting allowed."[23] Mural painting demands that the artist address the surface of the wall, attending to its limits, carefully maneuvering around corners and edges. Spraypainting, on the other hand, shifts the priority to the pigment and the painter. Wall, window, floor, ceiling, stairs—anything in the path of the spraygun gets painted. Though her first spray piece, *Inversion* (1998), at the Bern Kunsthalle, was monochrome, subsequent pieces such as *Cincy* (2006) (**fig. 10.13**) at the Contemporary Arts Center, Cincinnati, lavish their host institution with vibrant hues of luminescent paint. Liberated from canvas and frame, Grosse's paint possesses its own spatial qualities that effectively dematerialize the surfaces it strikes. Walls and floors cease to securely define the end of a room when jets of red, yellow, blue, and green careen across them. The depth suggested by hot and cool color fields on the floor has nothing to do with the limits of the room, while the yellow, green, and orange sprayed on the windows close in a space that the architecture had left open.

To create her installations, Grosse seals the room around her and approaches the walls, ceiling, and floor in a full-body suit and helmet. Photographs of her at work look like images taken in outer space or deep under water. Because of the force of the spray, the limited visibility allowed by her protective gear, and the twists and turns of the architecture, Grosse is never able to see more than a fragment of the work as she creates it. With only a rough idea of what the finished work will look like, she composes in the moment, spontaneously playing fresh fragments off against those laid down before it. The artist experiences a heightened awareness of the relationship of adjacent parts, but it is the viewer who encounters the work as a simultaneous whole. Painting, in Grosse's words, "allows you [the viewer] a panoptical structure with regard to the gaze and a synoptic structure with regard to time."[24] While the artist invents her relationship to space, feeling her way around the rooms and slowing or quickening her movements as she sees fit, the viewer, with a clear vision of the environment and an immediate apprehension of the complete work, is in control of the temporality of his or her experience. The viewing experience reverses the balance of time and space experienced by the artist. Though this contrast is relevant to all painting, Grosse's practice takes it to extremes.

Grosse has described her creative process as the reification in paint of the act of looking. As the contrast between the temporal and spatial features of the work indicates, seeing and painting are categorically differentiated in her work. She notes: "A picture cannot share the reality from which it comes." It may begin with observations in the world but the process of art making must lead to an image "independent enough, not only from the process of its manufacture but also from the initial idea and the theory that surrounds it."[25] The continued appeal of the aesthetic solutions created for the Florentine palazzi, and their ability to inspire Grosse's twenty-first-century spraypainted response, demonstrate the impact of the interiors, independent of the context in which they were created. Likewise, Grosse asserts that, to be successful, her own work must not be too bound to its sources.

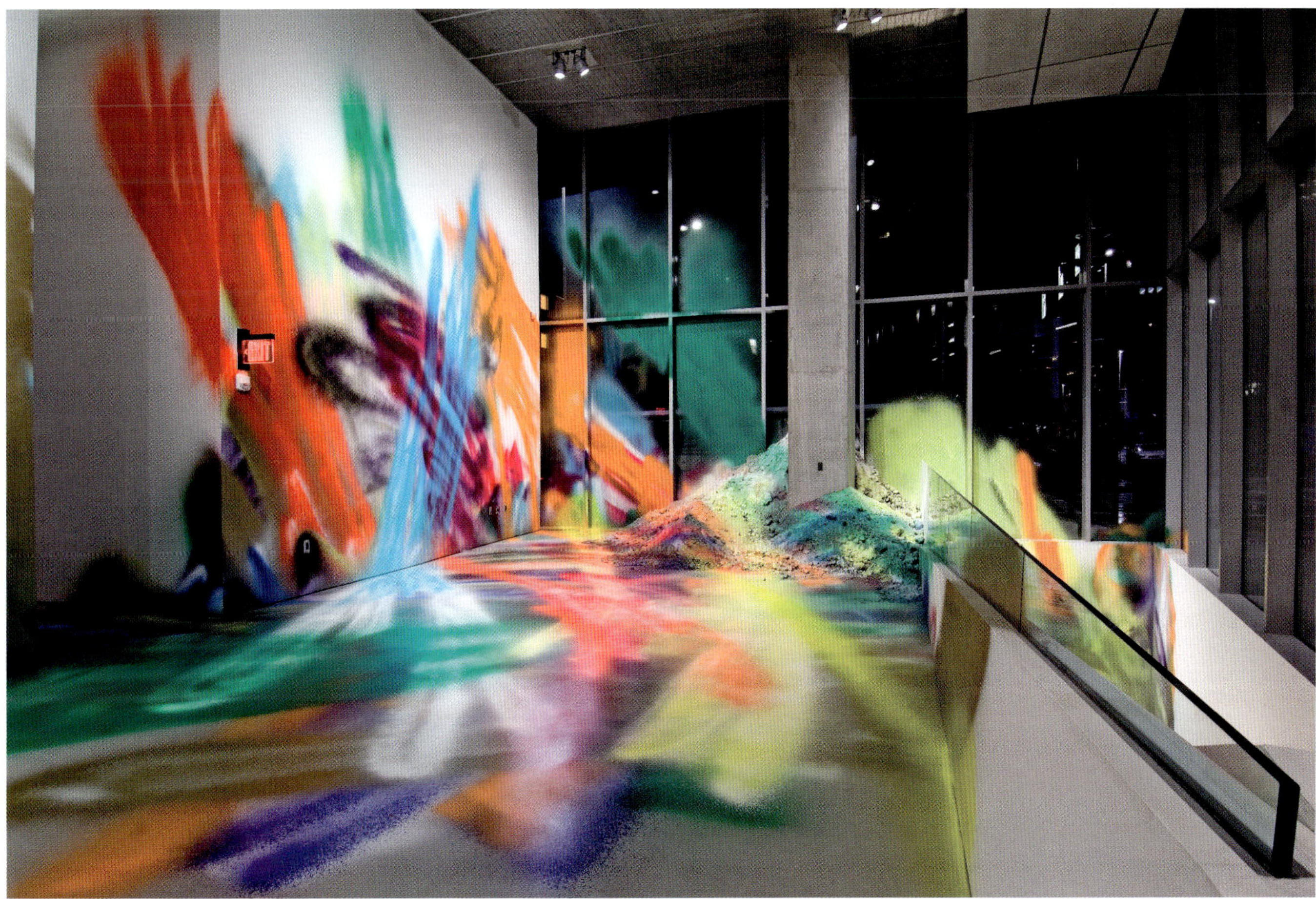

10.13 Katharina Grosse, *Cincy,* 2006. Installation at the Contemporary Arts Center, Cincinnati, Ohio. Spraypaint, styrofoam, and soil. Image courtesy BUREAU N.

Curator, critic, and museum director Ulrich Loock (b. 1953) developed the relationship between looking and spraypainting in Grosse's work, arguing that the latter is an extension of the institutional critique work of artists such as Hans Haacke and Andrea Fraser (see Chapter 1). Skeptical of the opticality favored by Greenbergian formalism, institutional critique rejected the effects of paint in favor of a critical appreciation of painting, directing viewers' attention away from the art object itself to focus on the cultural institutions that determine its value. Grosse, Loock wrote, is painting in the space of this redirected gaze. Jorge Pardo expressed a similar impulse to use the insights of institutional critique to expand the arena in which one can paint to include many new contexts, from museums to kitchens. Grosse has focused primarily on cultural institutions as a place to explore the visual and intellectual power of paint.

In addition to connecting Grosse's sprayed paint with the deflected gaze of institutional critique, Loock helpfully distinguished between the opticality praised by the formalists and the visuality embraced by this new generation of painters. Opticality tended to be confined to the work of art—the artist learned the properties of his or her medium and the viewer's attention remained focused on the artwork. Visuality is opticality diverted to anything the eye might find before it. Like Oehlen copying and pasting across his computer screen or Ackermann collecting views and memories from all over the world, Grosse encourages viewers to relish the visual properties of her paint, the aesthetics of the surfaces on which it falls, and any associations that either might conjure. She associates metallic pigments and spraypainting with the popular arts of auto-body detailing and graffiti, but, like Oehlen, refuses to describe the effect of the work in terms of its sources or their styles. Grosse's work follows the path set out by institutional critique but, unlike her Conceptual art predecessors, she is committed to the visual pleasures and capacities of paint. The opposition of the open-ended references of Grosse's materials and the emotive and even destructive character of her style within the rigid structure of the museum suggests the critical potential of her work.

Jessica Stockholder

The work of U.S. sculptor Jessica Stockholder (b. 1959) offers a useful point of comparison. As both artist and educator, Stockholder has been influential in asserting the expansive potential of paint divorced from the brush and canvas. Installations such as her *Your Skin in This Weather Bourne Eye-Threads & Swollen Perfume* ... (1995) (**fig. 10.14**) spread out to occupy all available space, with orchestrated assemblages that display a sense of the theatrical and the logic of painting in three dimensions. Stockholder paints with things—plastic tubs, extension cords, ropes, fruit, carpets, lumber—to produce stages and objects through and around which spectators travel. A work such as *Your Skin* appears as a fragmented assembly of layered vistas to be collected and experienced as one might on a walk through a city or the woods. Taking a few steps offers the spectator a fresh scenic view that more often than not renders the last one not only impossible to see, but hard to remember. A shift in

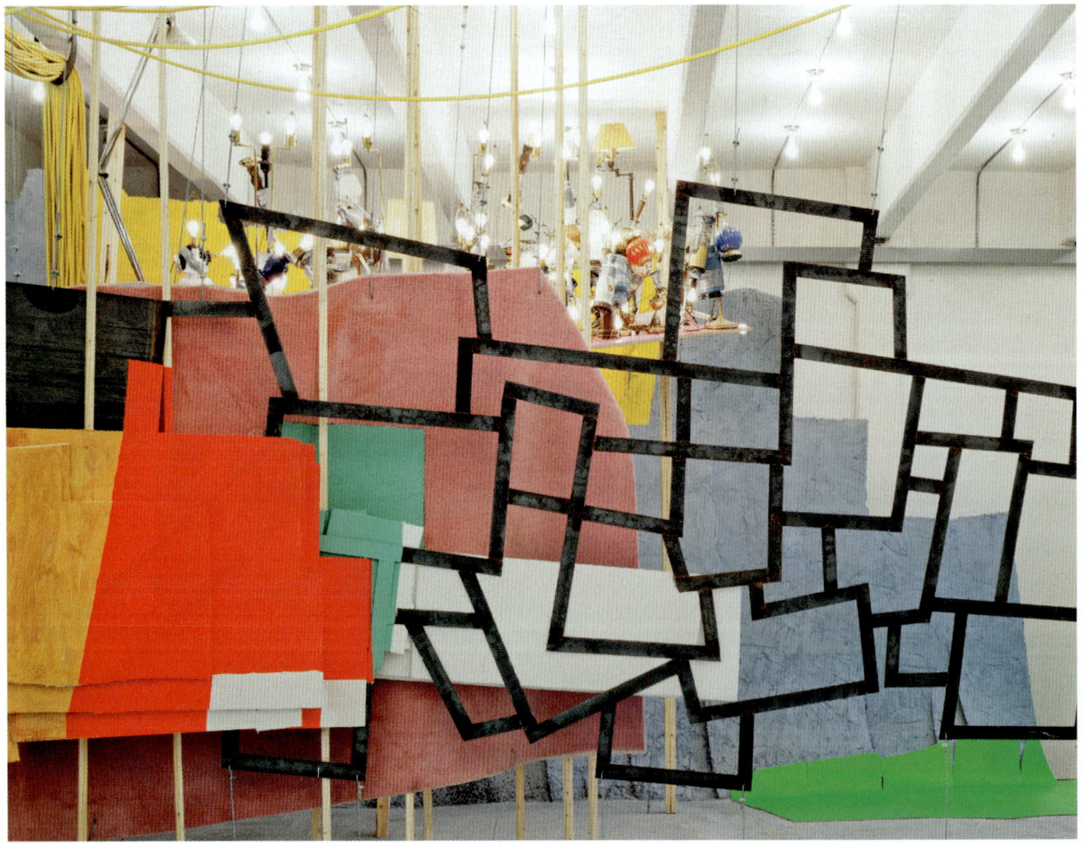

10.14 Jessica Stockholder, *Your Skin in this Weather Bourne Eye-Threads & Swollen Perfume* ..., 1995. Paint, concrete, structolite, miscellaneous building materials, carpet lamps, electrical cord, purple plastic stacking crates, swimming-pool liner, welded steel, stuffed pillows, papier-mâché, balls. DIA Center for the Arts. Courtesy Mitchell-Innes & Nash.

perspective and the yellow extension cords that cascade through the wind generated by electric fans become the frame for another view. On a website accompanying the installation, Stockholder prominently featured snapshots of objects and environments in nature, thus introducing information from the landscape to the sculpted spaces inside the gallery. She created fluid transitions for *Your Skin* between the space and materials of the sculpture and the information and images provided through the architecture of the website. Unlike Grosse's practice, in which each work threatens to violate the integrity of the institution that supports it, Stockholder's remains loyal to the museum as a stage for individual and aesthetic experience, even extending the peripatetic character and exploratory logic established in the gallery into the virtual realm of cyberspace.

The Power of Fiction

As painters and sculptors have been re-examining their media, another group of artists have been thinking hard about the utility of fiction. Art has always provided viewers with new worlds, places of alternative systems of logic and order in which to take refuge from the chaos of the outside world. For some artists, fiction provides distance from the world, while for others it is a space in which to reimagine the potency of storytelling for life in the new millennium. By the end of the century, there was a sense that striking down the teleological necessity of Modernist claims was a progressive act that, regretfully, had functioned less as a corrective to Western Modernist hegemony than as a means to substitute one power for another. If artists, art historians, and critics were to avoid letting the power of the past determine the parameters of the resistance that faced it, a trap outlined by Laura Mulvey in *Visual Pleasure and Narrative Cinema* in the 1970s, the properties of narrative communication as well as those of formal expression had to be reconsidered. The fictive potential of art thus came to be explored with an intensity that matched the examination of media demonstrated by the painters and sculptors discussed above. The last sections of this chapter will examine first a few examples of cosmological art, which proposes that the artist's task is to create a world with enough internal coherence to provide motivation and logic for the elements within it, and then less systematic excursions into fiction and the spaces of contemporary life.

A cosmology relies on a division between art and life such that the systems presented in the former realm are not undermined by those in the latter. Both religious and Modernist art are typically cosmological as each proposes to offer clear systems to viewers, who are encouraged to accept them and the values they promote. For most critics in the 1970s and early 1980s, attention to fictive systems and hermetic narratives appeared not only retrograde, but also potentially dangerous. Fears that such qualities were complicit with conservative politics underlay the rejection of Neo-Expressionist storytelling in the early 1980s. As examples in this book suggest, however, there were instances in which fiction continued to be of interest to the art world. Narrative and even cosmological art was embraced when it was the product of Soviet, Chinese, or African-American cultures, where the production of alternative worlds and systems was perceived to be a defensive gesture rather than the hegemonic one it appeared to be when it came from the Western mainstream. Such practices could also be comfortably celebrated when the stories being told were clearly imbricated in systems outside the image—the works of Leon Golub and Kara Walker serve as very different examples of this. In these cases, narrative could be understood as a political instrument. At the other end of the spectrum, some artists chose to label their work as cosmological as a way of insisting that, no matter how much a work of art seemed indistinguishable from a moment in life, it was in fact art. Nicolas Bourriaud's theorizing of relational aesthetics and artworks as "models of sociability" engaged cosmological thinking.[26] Artists Liam Gillick and Rirkrit Tiravanija, both of whom are central to Bourriaud's discussions, have described their work in terms of models and cosmologies to insure that interactions we might have with and within it are not confused with real life, but rather are recognized as artistic experiences.

Matthew Ritchie

In 1995, when asked to explain his first solo show, U.K.-born, U.S.-based painter Matthew Ritchie (b. 1964) said his goal was to create an "independent system and a model of models" that could "describe the internal architecture of making paintings."[27] He had chosen painting, he explained, because it "most closely resembles the internal operations of the mind, in its conjunction of the fantastic and the mundane suspended in an organic delirium."[28] Paintings such as *Mr. Universe* (1998) (**fig. 10.15**) are explosive convulsions of color and form, and map out the activities of a cast of characters rooted in biblical narratives, popular culture, archaic legends, Classical literature, and science. They also represent thought. Each character represents abilities, personality traits, convictions, and states of being. Ritchie is a prolific writer who publishes accounts of his characters and analyses of the scientific theories that give form to the terrain and plots that they inhabit. In the end, he aims to visualize not only how we make art, but also how we think and how the physical world—from cell growth to the Big Bang—functions.

Ritchie's cosmology revolves around the adventures of forty-nine characters he introduced in groups between 1995 and 2002. The first were the seven Watchers, forced to flee Heaven for sexually enticing Adam's children. Mulcifer, the builder, symbol of the frontal lobe of the brain, was the "matrix of information" for the Watchers and the index for the entire project.[29] Upon being thrown down to Earth, the Watchers broke apart, sending their attributes into the world. Seeking out the attributes that had formerly belonged to the Watchers, and chronicling the addition of new features to life

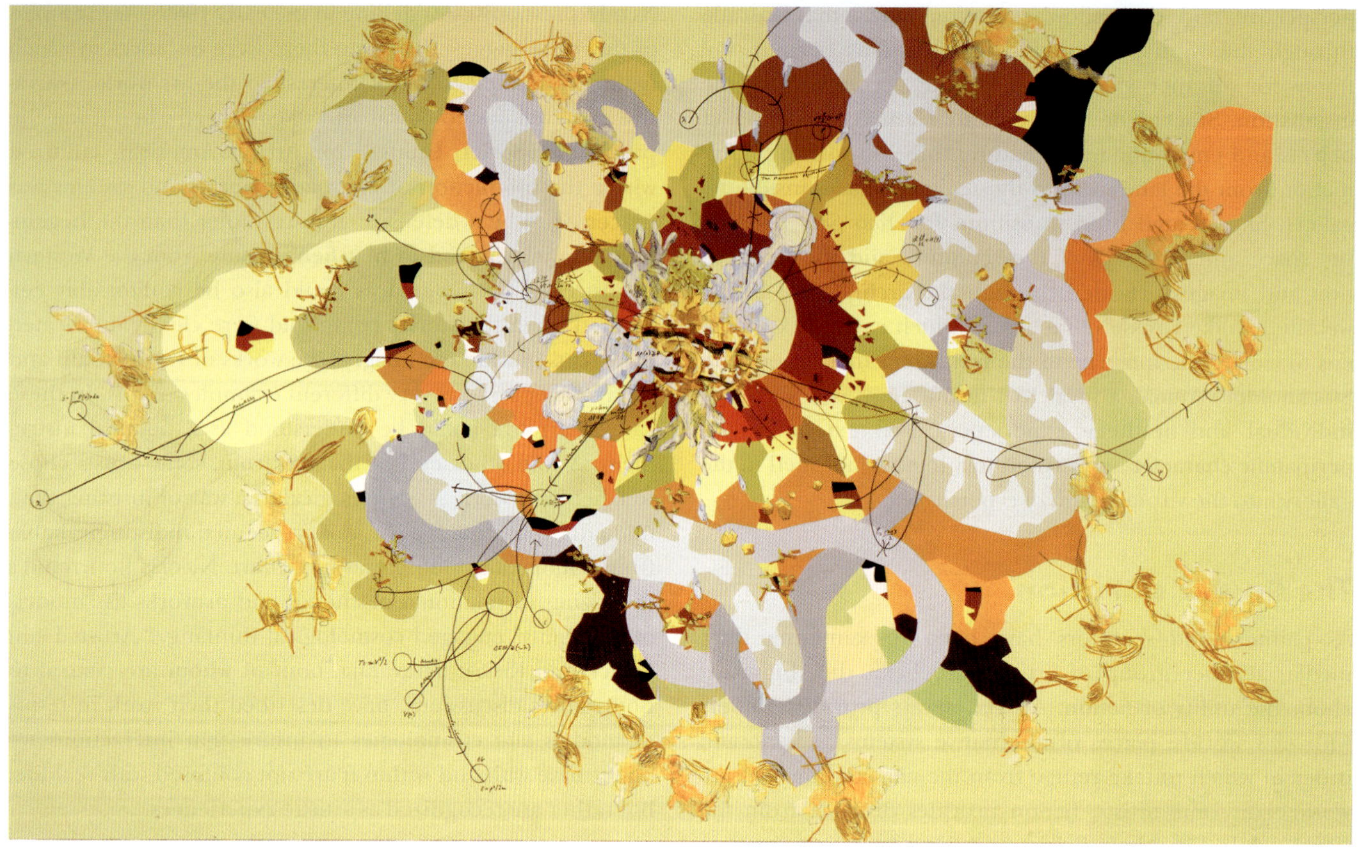

10.15 Matthew Ritchie, ***Mr. Universe***, 1998. Oil and marker on canvas, 84 × 138" (213.36 × 350.52 cm). © Matthew Ritchie. Courtesy Andrea Rosen Gallery, New York.

on Earth, led Ritchie to create more characters. There are ordinary subjects—including an actress, an astronaut, and a swimmer—but most are rather extraordinary. We meet the seven Gamblers, personifications of quantum-mechanical forces of the universe who play a game symbolizing the beginning of time. Ritchie also imagines the Golem and a collection of superheroes, angels, and mythical creatures, each of which is its own reification of ideas, emotions, and qualities.

Ritchie's oeuvre includes geological and crystalline assemblies of Sintra, a plastic membrane, affixed directly to the wall

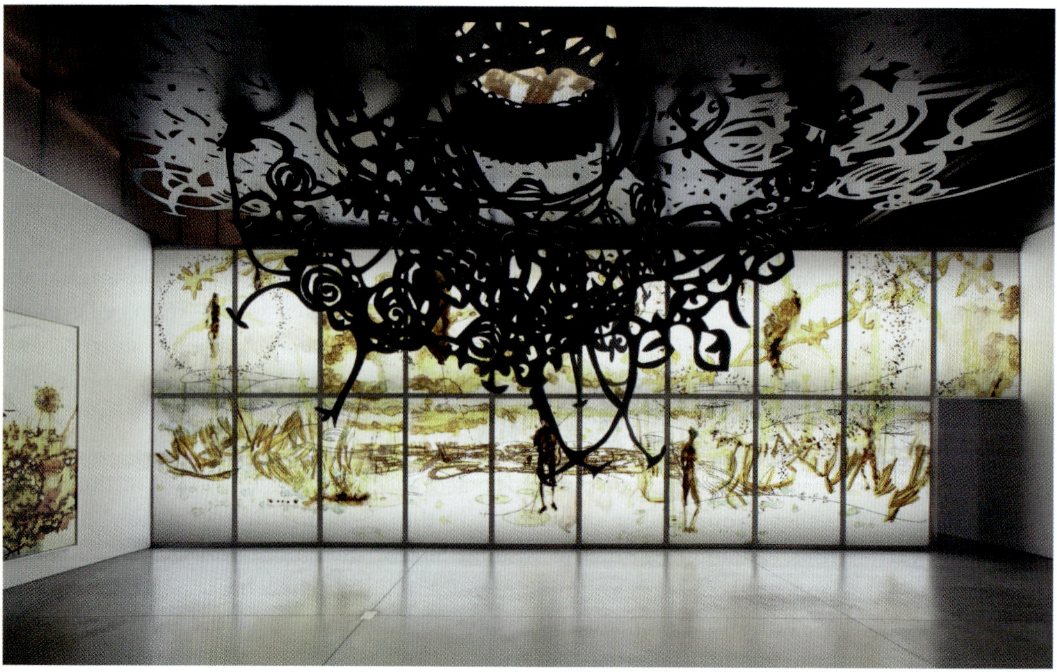

10.16 Matthew Ritchie, ***Universal Adversary***, 2006. Mixed media. Installation view, Andrea Rosen Gallery, 21 September–28 October, 2006. © Matthew Ritchie. Photo by Tom Powel. Courtesy Andrea Rosen Gallery, New York.

and spreading across the floor, architectural structures made of laser-cut metal sheets, lightboxes, computer animations, and many works on paper and canvas. Drawing, however, remains the foundation of his studio practice. *Mr. Universe,* which is oil and marker on canvas, presents a scenario typical of Ritchie's work of the 1990s. There is a central form painted with interlocking polygons of flat pigment overlaid with various forms of notation sketching out objects or textures and suggesting geometries and theorems. Like most of Ritchie's work, *Mr. Universe* is a map and an image; it is an ideogram describing a moment in the history of the universe, with notations indicating features of its growth or character and a depiction of a landmass in the throes of geological change. The duality of maps and pictures, ideas and things, corresponds to the dual nature of Ritchie's protagonists as characters and symbols. This conjunction of cartographic or conceptual descriptions with representational and physical qualities is amplified in later works such as *Universal Adversary* (2006) (**fig. 10.16**), in which the viewer is surrounded by illuminated screens and ornamented scaffolding, and is even sent up a staircase to a crow's-nest from which to view scenes of a maritime apocalypse.

The visual and narrative complexity of Ritchie's work ensures the cosmological integrity of the system. Simultaneously, however, it is the correlation of certain elements with aspects of reality that ensures the relevance of the work. The notation across the surface of *Mr. Universe,* which resembles scientific data, or the title "Universal Adversary," which is lifted from U.S. military jargon, links the invention in the art to exploration of the real world, reminding the viewer that the purpose of this cosmology is to produce a model for how we think about our universe and how we create within it.

Matthew Barney

Ritchie invented and complicated his cosmological structures to visualize processes of intellectual, artistic, and even planetary creation. U.S. artist Matthew Barney (b. 1967), whose work consists of films, sculptures, installations, drawings, and performances, turned to cosmologies with a similarly abstract aim: to give sculptural form to the potential for transformation in the absence of its resolution. In other words, the challenge is to represent change as a process without resorting to sculpting states of before and after. His monumental *Cremaster Cycle* (1994–2002) is a five-film series that explores gender differentiation without resolving its protagonists into either male or female positions. The films and related photography and sculpture explore the ability to become one or another gender without showing the results of such differentiation. Within the cosmology of *The Cremaster Cycle,* Barney weaves webs of people, things, places, sounds, colors, shapes, and movements, all of which signify and actualize indeterminacy.

Despite the centrality of film to Barney's career, he considers himself first and foremost a sculptor. Each of the films features sustained examinations of sculptures and sets built with unstable substances including petroleum jelly, ice, beeswax, and tapioca. Such materials suggest entropy and link Barney's work to the Process art of Eva Hesse (1936–70) and Robert Smithson as well as the work of Joseph Beuys (see Chapter 1). Like these earlier artists, Barney forced his entropic materials to meet with resistance as provided by materials as varied as the body, architecture, geography, and even film. The plot of *The Cremaster Cycle* reiterates the perpetual play of give and take, transformation and obstruction, and entropy and containment performed by his materials.

Cremaster 4 (1994) (**fig. 10.17**) was the first film in the cycle to be made, and its storyline is the clearest. Barney plays the Loughton Candidate, a satyr on the cusp of adulthood whose impending maturation is the centerpiece of

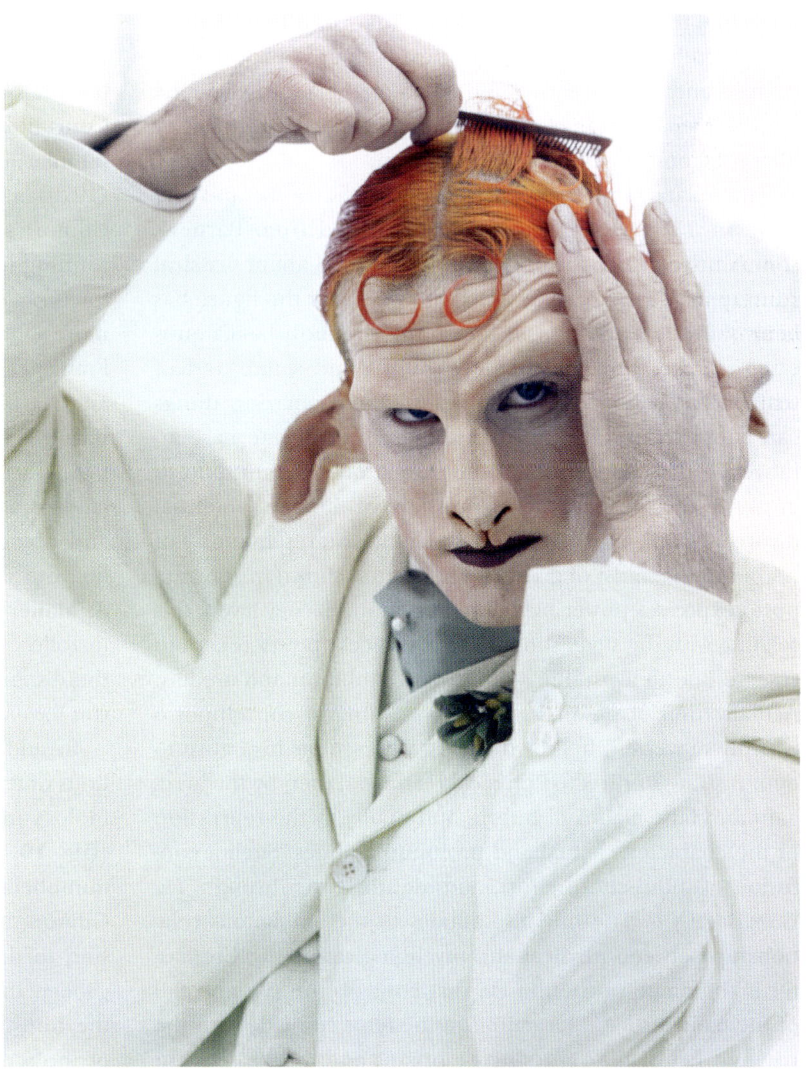

10.17 Matthew Barney, ***Cremaster 4, The Loughton Candidate,*** 1994. Production still. © 1994 Matthew Barney. Courtesy Gladstone Gallery, New York and Brussels.

the plot. During the film, he examines the roots of horns on his head which may grow and so mark his sexual maturity as male, or they may not, thus stabilizing his gender as female. He dances and finally submerges himself first in the ocean and then in a narrow underground fissure that ends with a long tunnel lined with petroleum jelly. Objects such as the tunnel and jelly, and motorcycles that race around the Isle of Man, U.K., (where the film was shot) carry the plot as much as the actors do. The urgency of the protagonist's development is conveyed by the speeding vehicles, the difficulty by the narrow passageway, and the sexual nature of the process emphasized by the highly masculine yet clearly female bodies of a collection of cross-dressing Sibyls that bring to mind Michelangelo's Sistine Chapel ceiling. In other episodes of the cycle the potential for change is expressed by characters including architects, masons, nymphs, queens, and bees, objects such as cars, buildings, and furniture, and scenes including horse races, séances, executions, and the slow arrangement of grapes inside a blimp. Every object in the films is, in fact, a character and every character is, in Barney's words, a "physical state."[30] Elaborating states of being while shortcircuiting narrative resolution subverts the classic Hollywood film that relies, as Laura Mulvey theorized (see Chapter 2), on both the delectation of details, amply provided by Barney, and the cathartic resolution of the plot, which he denies. *Cremaster 4,* like all the films in the cycle, ends with the protagonist's gender still in question.

The relationship between narrative, the body, and the mind in *The Cremaster Cycle* can be gleaned from Barney's comments on Greek art: "There's something about classical contrapposto [the pose in which the weight of the figure has been shifted to one foot in preparation to move]—it's quivering on the threshold between hubris and some kind of real but repressed omnipotence. All these amazing things can happen on that threshold, these powerful internal narratives."[31] The conventional interpretation of contrapposto presents the pose as an expression of human potential divorced from any specific task. Unlike representations of heroes in the midst of great deeds, a figure shown in contrapposto expresses power by deferring action. Barney layers this reading with the suggestion that the subject's power is kept in reserve due to a psychic confusion of ambition and anxiety. Actualization of power in Barney's reading of contrapposto is triply subverted, first by the artist who sculpts his figure to demonstrate undirected physical readiness, then by the arrogant and false claims of hubris, and finally by the repression of the character's actual and profound abilities. Such a confusion of indirection, effort, and identity runs through *The Cremaster Cycle.* The title also alludes to the ambiguous relationship between physical and psychological power. Cremaster is the name of the muscle that controls the rise and fall of the male testicles. Its actions in the fetus coincide with the rise and fall of the reproductive organs and the subsequent determination of sex. Barney points out that the cremaster muscle does not control gender differentiation. Like the movies named for it, the cremaster muscle fulfills a real function that imitates, symbolizes, and even represents a transformation that it nonetheless does not effect. Barney conceives of video and film in a similar fashion, as a means to represent power and also to create skepticism about the things it depicts. He has listed his exposure to the performance videos of Marina Abramović and Ulay (see Chapter 7) as an important influence on his work, both for the impact of the performances and also for the sensation that he felt, while watching them of examining evidence, that as such invited suspicion as well as inspiration. This potential of video and film to fictionalize their contents like the obscure and extravagant plots provides a means of insulating Barney's cosmology from the real world of the viewers to whom it is addressed.

Barney has said that the *Cremaster Cycle* "could be considered a system that seeks freedom by decentralizing its energy, attempting to hybridize itself into a web of available cultural vehicles."[32] The web extends to biological and geological phenomena, popular culture, history, sports, and Barney's own narrative inventions. *Cremaster 2* (1999) illustrates the breadth of its creator's cosmology. This film revolves around the execution on January 17, 1977 in Salt Lake City, Utah of convicted murderer Gary Gilmore, the performances of Harry Houdini, and the life of bees. Gilmore was the first person to be executed in the United States after the Supreme Court lifted its 1972–76 ban on the death penalty. He entered popular lore through Norman Mailer's *The Executioner's Song* (1979), a Pulitzer Prize-winning account of the last months of Gilmore's life that Mailer then adapted into an Emmy Award-winning television movie in 1982. Barney approached Mailer for *Cremaster 2* and cast the writer as Harry Houdini, who Gilmore's grandmother claimed was the father of Gary's father, Frank. The paternal triad of Frank Gilmore, Norman Mailer, and Harry Houdini is one of the associative networks that fill Barney's films. Gilmore's parents, his victims, his girlfriend, the police, the country singer Johnny Cash, as well as the landscape of Utah, the life of bees, and many other symbols and objects intertwine to illuminate the end of Gilmore's life, but they never define a clear plot or stable resolution. As Mailer said of Barney's filmmaking: "For people who want to follow the story, it's hopeless, they'll hate the work. But there's an intensity of perception, and a visceral experience you have when you watch his stuff which is extraordinary."[33]

In addition to screening the films, Barney exhibits portions of the sets and related sculpture, thus extending his cosmology into the gallery. *The Cabinet of Harry Houdini* (1999) (**fig. 10.18**) from *Cremaster 2* suggests power through the dumbbells while the Mormon context that permeates the Gilmore narrative is symbolized by the honeycomb, an allusion to the bee, a symbol of the religion. Displayed in the gallery, the work is an inverted reflection of the objects in the films. Full cosmological and even aesthetic elaboration of the sculpture requires knowledge of the films. Attention to potentiality and particularity is shared by Barney's contemporaries, who often present the self in perpetual flux. Unlike

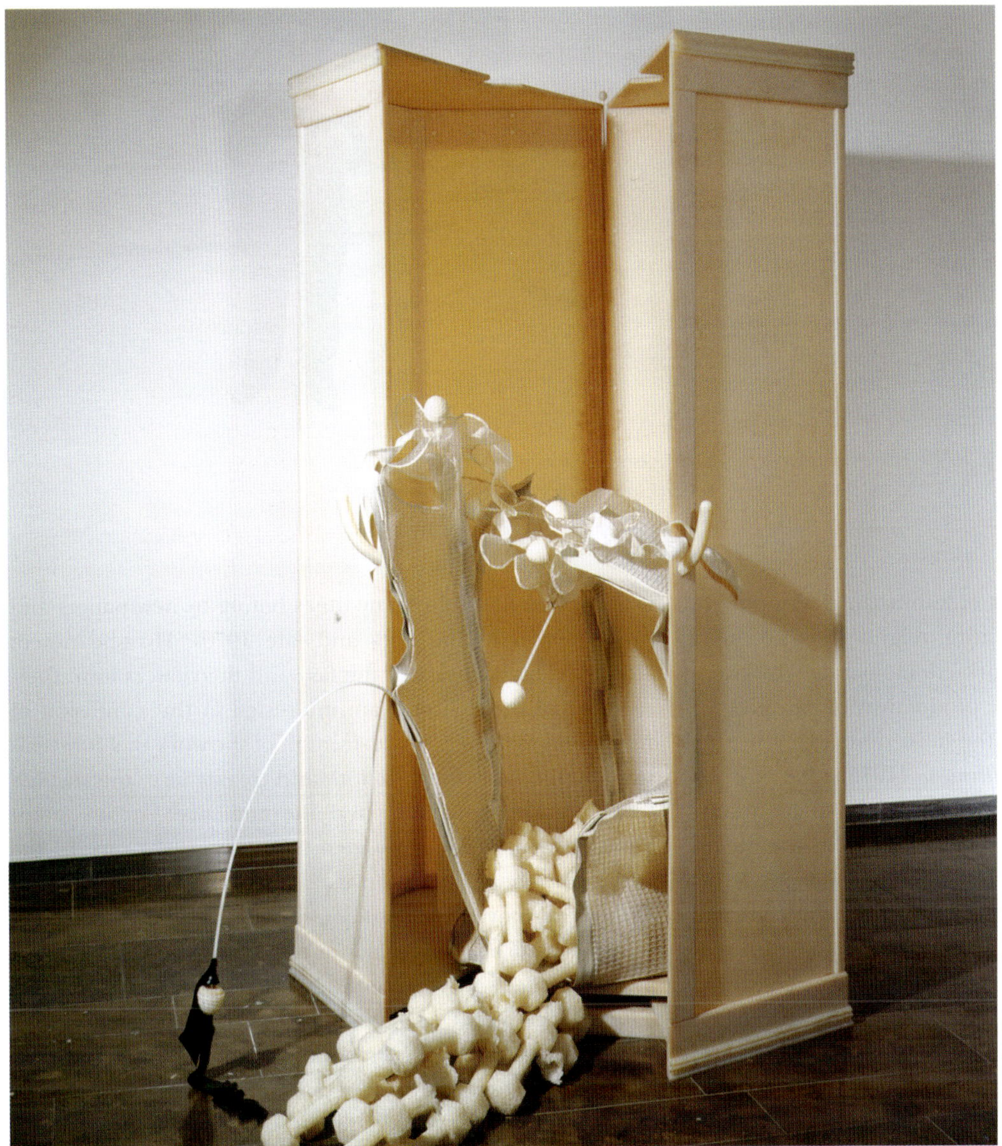

10.18 Matthew Barney, *The Cabinet of Harry Houdini*, 1999. Cast nylon, salt epoxy resin, woven polypropylene, prosthetic plastic, and beeswax, 83⅝ × 60 × 73" (212.4 × 152.6 × 185.4 cm). Astrup Fearnley collection, Oslo. © 1999 Matthew Barney. Courtesy Gladstone Gallery, New York and Brussels.

the identity art of the 1980s and 1990s, Barney's system and the shifting identity positions within it are contained by the cosmology of the films. Barney's choice of cosmological storytelling provides a setting in which to develop artistic ideas that, like medical experimentation, require a sterile environment uncontaminated by the variables of real life.

Pierre Huyghe

French artist Pierre Huyghe (b. 1962) shifts the discussion from self-contained cosmologies that signify their relevance to the outside world as models or analogies, to strategies for dissolving the boundaries between artistic narrative and actual reality. He begins with an understanding of narrative in which "[e]verything that resembles a narrative refers to an elsewhere, an elsewhere that is also a before, where things had a real existence."[34] Unlike the cosmologies of Ritchie or Barney, Huyghe's stories are significant in the degree that they point to real opportunities outside the narrative. In fact, Huyghe's ambition is even greater. He proposes to "investigate how a fiction, how a story, could in fact produce a certain kind of reality."[35] The challenge is to create narratives that open up fissures to the "parallel scenarios," the "utopias, negotiations, and failures," that are found in the "elsewhere" of "real existence." In his words: "to actualize this narrative, we must inhabit it."[36]

Though Huyghe creates films, photographs, installations, and sculptures, his primary medium is narrative. He offers fragmented and layered segments of stories to collaborators who use them to create new narratives which, in turn, provide material to audiences and to new collaborators. In interviews, he refers to the stories as "scores" or "the scenario," terms that indicate performativity, reproducibility, and even chance: One writes the score for others to interpret. Likewise, a scenario—as opposed to a plan—is partial and opens itself to unknown elements that may appear during the execution of the work. *The Third Memory* (1999) (**fig. 10.19**), a two-channel re-enactment of a bank robbery, looks to Hollywood movies, television news, autobiography, and reality TV as sources, and puts authorial power in the hands of the bank robber. *Streamside Day Follies* (2003) adds traditional community

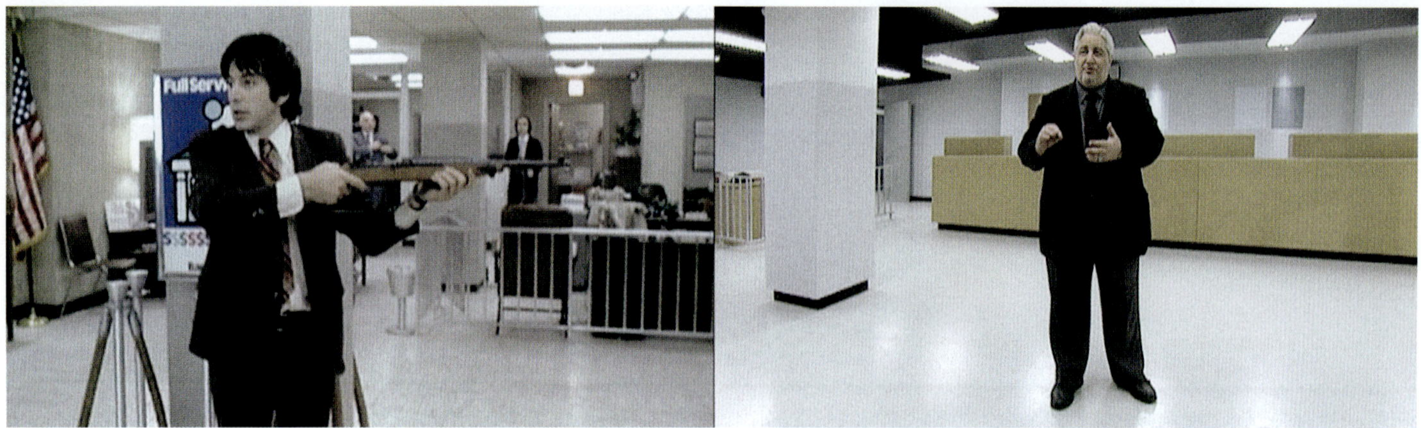

10.19 Pierre Huyghe, ***The Third Memory***, 1999. Film stills. Double projection, beta digital video monitor. Solomon R. Guggenheim Museum, New York. Courtesy of the artist and Marian Goodman Gallery, New York.

festivals and contemporary tales of suburban development into the mix while inviting an entire neighborhood to take ownership of the tale. Both works demonstrate Huyghe's scoring and are case studies of the productivity of narrative.

The Third Memory reimagines the heist dramatized in the Sidney Lumet film *Dog Day Afternoon* (1975), starring Al Pacino as lead gunman John Wojtowicz, renamed Sonny Wortzik in the movie. Huyghe saw the movie in the 1990s and invited the real Wojtowicz, who served fourteen years for the crime, to Paris to recount his memories of the robbery. Wojtowicz accepted and was filmed directing a cast of hired actors to reenact the crime with him on a set Huyghe built to resemble the bank in the movie. Several times during the work, Huyghe uses the second screen to show Al Pacino playing Wojtowicz or period news footage of the real Wojtowicz during the robbery. The event itself—as Wojtowicz tells it and as Pacino acted it—was highly theatrical. The 1975 movie poster declared: "The robbery should have taken 10 minutes. 4 hours later, the bank was like a circus sideshow. 8 hours later, it was the hottest thing on live T.V. 12 hours later, it was all history. And it's all true." The inherent drama of the event, however, is less significant for Huyghe than the manner and consequences of its retelling. The robbery was one of the first crimes to be committed in front of television cameras. Almost as soon as the police arrived, camera crews were on the scene, transforming the Brooklyn sidewalk into a stage and Wojtowicz and the police into actors. News of events at the bank was broadcast throughout the day, even interrupting a nationally televised speech by President Richard Nixon. Wojtowicz deftly stepped into his role of leading man, darting in and out of the bank, confronting the police, and talking to the cameras. His actions, as well as the news broadcasts of them, constitute the first narrative in Huyghe's work. They provide part of the "score," not only for *The Third Memory*, but also for *Dog Day Afternoon*, which provides the second and most familiar element of the "score."

Wojtowicz's retelling of the crime, his arrest, and his involvement with *Dog Day Afternoon* constitutes a third narrative. It is a story he had told many times before to newspapers and on television in the mid- and late 1970s. Huyghe noted: "John has his memory of the fact and the viewers have their memory of the fiction. I am interested in this confusion of reality and fiction."[37] It is a strength of the work that it reveals the degree to which fiction and reality are intertwined for both the protagonist and the audience. At one point Wojtowitz says: "The cops keep trying to provoke us. In the real movie the cops fire on us." Describing the actual event as the "real movie" is a Freudian slip that underlines the complicated nature of our experience of the past. It also serves as a reminder that an event and its representation are categorically different, though the experience of each is real, with consequences for our understanding of the world and ourselves. One does not leave *The Third Memory* with a sense of truth about what really happened. Rather, we experience a reality that combines the events that occurred with the stories that carry them.

Reflecting on the diversity of his projects, Huyghe has noted that with every work a new poetics of production is invented. Of *Streamside Day* (2003) (**fig. 10.20**) he says: "I occupy both sides of a divide: I build up a fiction and then I make a documentary of this fiction. The point is: we should invent reality before filming it. We need to 're-scenarize' the real."[38] *Streamside Day* centers on Streamside Day, a festival initiated, or scored, by Huyghe to commemorate the founding of a housing development, Streamside Knolls, in the Hudson River Valley in New York. In consultation with the residents, Huyghe set a date and posted announcements: "Welcome to Streamside Day Celebration." Elements included: "Parade and Costumes, Balloons and T-Shirts, Lemonade and Green Cotton Candy, Donuts and 'Streamside Day Cake.'" Also planned were: "Cookie decorating, building houses out of cardboard boxes and a Wild Pet Parade." In addition Huyghe retooled the sound system on an ice-cream truck, assembled an artificial moon, and set up a stage. The town supervisor, a position akin to mayor, and the real-estate developer responsible for the site were invited to speak, and a musician sang

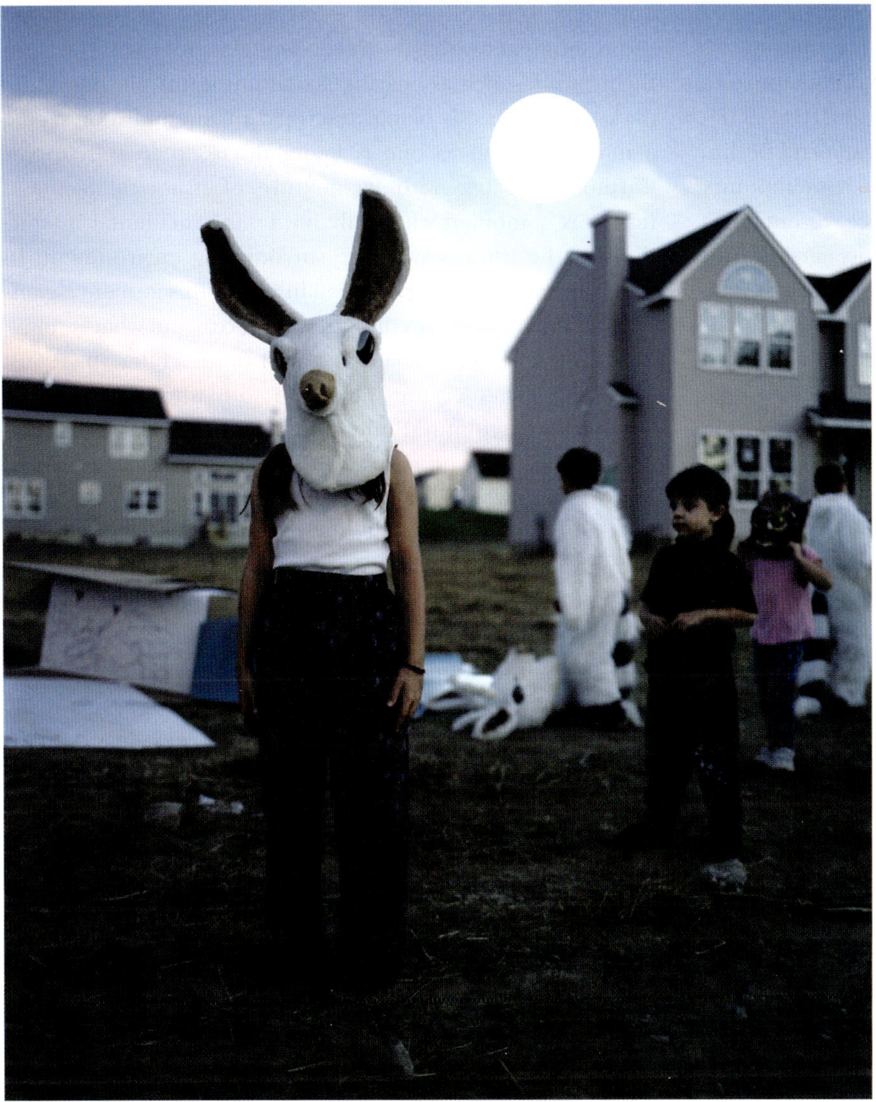

10.20 Pierre Huyghe, ***Streamside Day***, 2003. Film still. Digital video projection from film and video transfers, 26 minutes. Courtesy of the artist and Marian Goodman Gallery, New York.

an original composition, "Streamside Celebration." Having placed these elements into the setting like objects in an interactive installation, Huyghe then picked up the camera. Most of the resulting film records what happened as the new residents of Streamside Knolls marched through their still-unfinished neighborhood, played music, dressed up, ate, danced, and made Streamside Day into an event. Huyghe hoped that future residents would replay the fiction he had created, making it an annual celebration. When he discussed the project, he was careful to say that he did not think artists should own the burden of fixing the world, but that the narratives they create should add something to reality. In addition to the celebration itself and any possible tradition it may give rise to, the song and programming for a community center were real products that came out of Huyghe's fiction.

The Streamside Day celebration became the "score" for Streamside Day Follies, a temporary cinematic and architectural installation. To view the work, one enters what appears to be an empty room, around the edges of which hang walls that have been painted metallic hues of green, alluding, for Huyghe, to the Emerald City in *The Wizard of Oz*. The walls soon start moving along tracks in the ceiling to form a shimmering pentagon in the center of the room. This structure is one of Huyghe's follies—small whimsical elements of garden architecture designed to decorate the landscape of an estate. A film is then projected on the inside of these walls, presenting a short documentary that culminates in a musical performance, a second folly. The story *Streamside Day* presents begins with idyllic scenes of nature. A fawn and a bunny lie together in the woods. A waterfall cascades into a quiet pond. The fawn then makes its way into the nearly finished neighborhood of Streamside. Meanwhile, a young couple and their two daughters drive to their new home. They are shown a model of the development that includes their new house and the girls set off to play in the nearby woods. Above them, the vines and trees take on an ominous aspect of looming figures, but before the fantasy turns black the celebration begins. This new introduction is not part of the Streamside Day Celebration; it is, instead, part of the fantasy created for the gallery audience. Providing the viewer with an architectural space akin to an emerald jewel box, along with visions of nature straight out of a Disney movie, frames Huyghe's film with conventional cultural constructions regarding nature. The documentary scenes of the celebration that follow are thus doubly undermined, first, by the artifice of Huyghe's deliberate planning and, second, by the architectural and cinematic fictions in the gallery. For the viewer, the status of any "reality" here is impossible to determine. As the fake moon grows brighter in the sky, even the wall text that explains the reality of Streamside Knolls in Fishkill, New York is not enough to dispel the feeling that everything here is fake. If we return to Huyghe's discussion of the function of narrative, we realize that it is just at the moment when the work most clearly resembles a narrative that we are alerted to the "elsewhere" that surrounds the story we are being shown. For the gallery viewer, the narratives of *Streamside Day* point to "utopias, negotiations, and failures" of cities, suburban developments, small towns, or even Kansas and Oz.

Janet Cardiff

The next artists to be discussed incorporate into their explorations of narrative explicit appreciation for the pleasure of being entertained. Canadian artist Janet Cardiff (b. 1957), who splits her time between rural western Canada and Berlin, has created one of the most striking formats in contemporary art. Speaking into a binaural recording device, essentially a dummy head with microphones mounted in its ears, Cardiff creates audio walks, providing her audience with a soundtrack while the real world supplies the visuals. In headphones provided by the artist, Cardiff's voice speaks gently as though she is standing just behind us. Birds sing to the left, a man approaches and walks by us on the right, his footsteps getting softer as he passes into the distance. Just beyond the tunnel we are standing beneath, it rains. These sonic and spatial effects compete with our sensual apprehension of the actual spaces through which we walk. Sometimes Cardiff's excursions pass through crowded public spaces, sometimes they lead one on nearly solitary strolls. Often fragments of her stories are synchronized with what is occurring in the landscape. The people that pass in the recording correspond with those on the street beside you, or an object described in the story appears in front of you. These instances of synchronicity amplify the effect of being, as Cardiff describes it, "inside the filmic experience."[39]

Like many of the visual artists discussed in this chapter, Cardiff describes her process as "layering." She will go over and over a site, walking through it, videotaping it, learning as much as she can from the location and researching its history. In *Munster Walk* (1997), she imagines a German man traversing the sidewalks where his dead daughter once walked. As Cardiff relays details from the environment and narrates fragments of a story about a daughter, or a mother, we hear other voices—of a boy and an older man. In *Her Long Black Hair* (2004), a walk through Central Park in Manhattan, Cardiff layers the sounds of musicians who seem to be near the listener with gunshots fired, she tells us, to control the goats and pigs grazing in the park—a detail from the city's past. Soon after, we hear strollers and nannies, along with the consistent rhythm of footsteps, which we are instructed to follow with our own. In this fashion the listener keeps pace with Cardiff's tour, hearing moments in the narrative at particular places in the park and on occasion being prompted to compare the scene with photographs provided at the start of the journey. Discussing her creative process, Cardiff has said: "Actually the way we approach audio is also very similar to printmaking ... You can take different sources from all over, and then you collage them together. Conceptually I always found that interesting; you can take something recorded now and footage that was recorded 20 years ago, and you can seamlessly put them together in audio. It's like a mixture of time and space."[40] Drawing on what she sees as a societal instinct to reframe experiences in terms of stories, Cardiff relies on her audience to collaborate with her in turning the layered fragments into a narrative experience, one that is necessarily different for each participant. At those moments when the recording coincides with facts on the ground—such as hearing actual musicians playing in the park while music is being described in the audio or seeing a man approach as one is being discussed in the story—Cardiff's narrative with its mixture of historical fact and fiction is combined with daily life by the incidental interactions of the listener with the surrounding environment. In the process of listening and walking, Cardiff's audience gains a heightened awareness of both what is real and what is not.

Cardiff and her husband, George Bures Miller (b. 1960), who helps produce the walks and with whom Cardiff collaborates on sculptural and sound installations, have listed movies, theaters, and amusement parks as influences. These are all places where the viewer suspends control in exchange for entertainment. Cardiff has responded to the common critique of her work that it is manipulative: "Everything in our culture is about manipulation. Our behavior is always modified, and that was one of the subtexts of my walk pieces. It is a manipulation—but it's also like a child's game in that you have the freedom to give up your power, it's really about that pleasure."[41] Cardiff's audio walks suggest that one of the pleasures we can afford ourselves in the early twenty-first century is that of stepping into a story delivered in such a way as to meddle with our ability to distinguish fact from fiction.

Francesco Vezzoli

At the opening of the 2005 Venice Biennale and again at the 2006 Whitney Biennial, long lines formed outside a small screening room built into the galleries. Inside, there were plush velvet seats, red curtains, and a silver screen. Dramatic music with crisply edited voiceover and frequent screams of pleasure and distress surrounded the spectator and bled teasingly into the neighboring rooms. The film being screened was *Trailer for a Remake of Gore Vidal's Caligula* (2005) (**fig. 10.21**) by the Milan-based artist Francesco Vezzoli (b. 1971) and it advertised a blockbuster movie based on Vidal's script dramatizing the life of the Roman emperor and infamous tyrant Caligula (12–41 CE). The original film had become mired in creative conflict and was eventually released in 1979 with Vidal's name removed. It failed badly at the box office. Vezzoli's trailer promised finally to bestow upon Vidal, Caligula, and a cast of stars the glory they deserved. However, *Trailer for a Remake of Gore Vidal's Caligula* was a preview for a film Vezzoli had no intention of making. The five-minute spectacle joined other Vezzoli projects: a completed pilot for a reality TV show that never aired, an election campaign for candidates who did not exist, a premiere of a play that never opened, promotion for an exhibition that did not exist, and an advertising campaign for a perfume with no scent.

The trailer opens with Gore Vidal sitting outside a villa in Los Angeles and speaking: "What is the point of telling the story of someone who is somewhat insane at a very dark point in human history? I think the answer to that is: Every

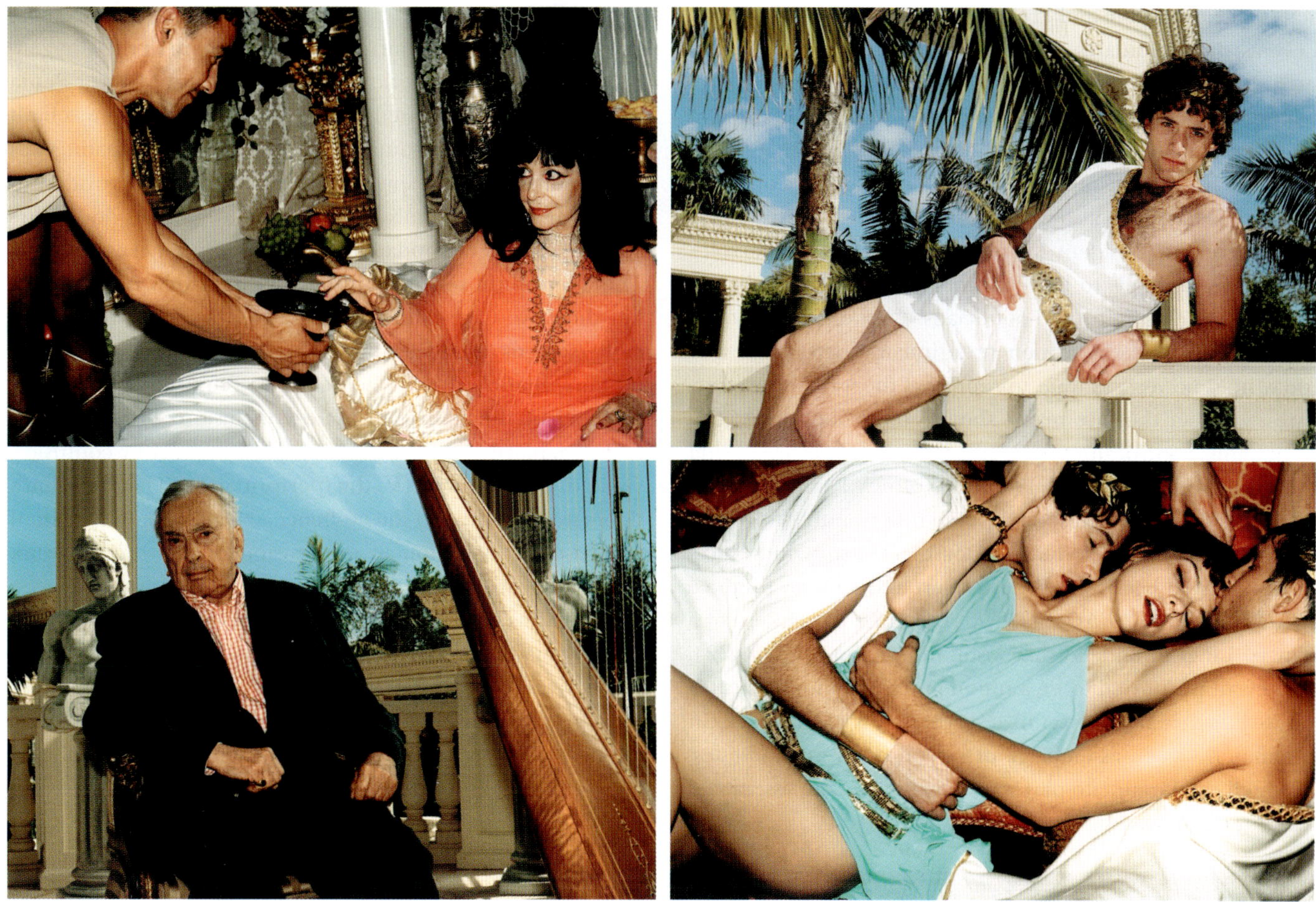

10.21 Francesco Vezzoli, ***Trailer for a Remake of Gore Vidal's Caligula***, 2005. Film stills featuring Adriana Asti (top left), Gore Vidal (bottom left), and Milla Jovovich (bottom right). © Francesco Vezzoli. Courtesy Gagosian Gallery.

point in human history is dark." Then titles fill the screen, the volume increases, and a second voice intones: "Throughout the course of human history there have been only three truly great stories … The first was the immaculate birth of Christ. The second was the untimely death of Christ. And the third and greatest by far belonged to this man. Caligula." The anticipated remake promises to be "so passionate in its extremes you can literally feel it coating you in the taboo" and stocked "with an international cast of superstars more decadent than your wildest dreams." The latter is most certainly true. Like all of Vezzoli's productions, his *Caligula* is indeed stocked with stars, all of whom agreed to work on the project for free. Helen Mirren, who was in the original film, Benicio Del Toro, Adriana Asti, Milla Jovovich, Karen Black, and Courtney Love are all featured. Donatello Versace designed the costumes. Vezzoli has said that the melodramatic story of the Roman emperor was attractive as an allegory for the excesses of George W. Bush's presidency. But the *Trailer* is hardly a cautionary tale. This is a romp through Hollywood in which history, fiction, fame, and sexual fantasy comically and seductively collide. After Vezzoli began enlisting the help of film icons in the late 1990s, he was critiqued for being too much of a fan. His response was that his art reflected upon the way we wrap our imaginations in melodrama and wealth. "I wanted to create something that contained the visual richness of an opera, something stuffed with quotations, loaded with references and details," he explained.[42] Once viewers have been seduced, there is ample opportunity to ask them to reflect on the specious presentation of stars and sex or on the hubris of empire, whether in Rome or Hollywood.

Since graduating from Central Saint Martins in London in 1995, Vezzoli has drawn attention to a remarkable variety of the narrative strategies that permeate contemporary culture, including televised drama, reality television, classic and experimental film, movie advertising, avant-garde theater, entertainment news, soap operas, and biography. He uses narrative to invite the viewer into what he considers the core of his artistic project—the investigation of sites of power, entertainment being only one. In 2007, he demonstrated his interest in moving into other realms of power with *Democrazy*, dueling promotional videos supporting two fictional presidential candidates. Vezzoli enlisted the services of political strategists who had advised U.S. presidents George W. Bush and Bill Clinton. By using political professionals, Vezzoli insured that the spoken lines would be real, as authentic as if they had genuinely been uttered on the campaign trail. It was simply that in this case the politicians were fake. Vezzoli cast U.S.

actress Sharon Stone and French philosopher Bernard-Henri Lévy as the candidates. The prevalence of actor-politicians such as Ronald Reagan or Arnold Schwarzenegger in contemporary politics, however, contributes to the confusion of reality and fiction in *Democrazy*, as does the fact that Stone and Lévy have each contributed to public dialogues on international issues. Lévy also worked in a limited advisory capacity for French president Jacques Chirac. Both of Vezzoli's actors were as likely to be real candidates as any number of genuine celebrities-turned-politicians. "My true purpose," Vezzoli explained, "is to penetrate into the structures that today hold power ... I want to represent the ways these structures, whether they are reality shows, Hollywood, or elective campaigns, control the media and seduce the masses so that they can manipulate them. With *Democrazy* I wanted to go where a lot of people thought I would never be able to go."[43]

A few months after the opening of *Democrazy* in Venice, Vezzoli turned back to the world of art and fame to produce *RIGHT YOU ARE (IF YOU THINK YOU ARE)*, a premiere of a play by Luigi Pirandello that would never run (**fig. 10.22**). The event purported to be a unique production of a theatrical work originally written to tests the limits of narrative. In actuality it was an assemblage of several different storylines, of which the Pirandello play was only one. Vezzoli assembled a cast including Cate Blanchett, Abigail Breslin, Natalie Portman, David Straithairn, and Anita Ekberg at the Guggenheim Museum, New York. John Galliano and Miuccia Prada designed and contributed several costumes. A stage was built in the center of the rotunda around which VIP seating was arranged. Additional special viewing areas were provided to guests in the museum's upper levels, while the downstairs auditorium accommodated the remaining ticket holders. The auditorium seating offered no direct view of the stage, but did have Cate Blanchett seated on its stage in front of eight screens broadcasting a live feed of the production upstairs. Blanchett left when she was required to make her entrance on the main stage at the conclusion of the play.

The fanfare of the production was matched by confusion created at the night of the performance. The museum's doors were opened to the audience about an hour later than advertised. In addition to the tension caused by this delay, there was considerable upset because the event had been advertised as free to the public, but few if any tickets were actually made available. Attendance was largely a matter of being invited or, one might say, being cast in the role of audience member. The scenario appeared to repeat the pattern of entitlement by which stars and socialites get the privileged seats while the rest watch from a distance or read about it in

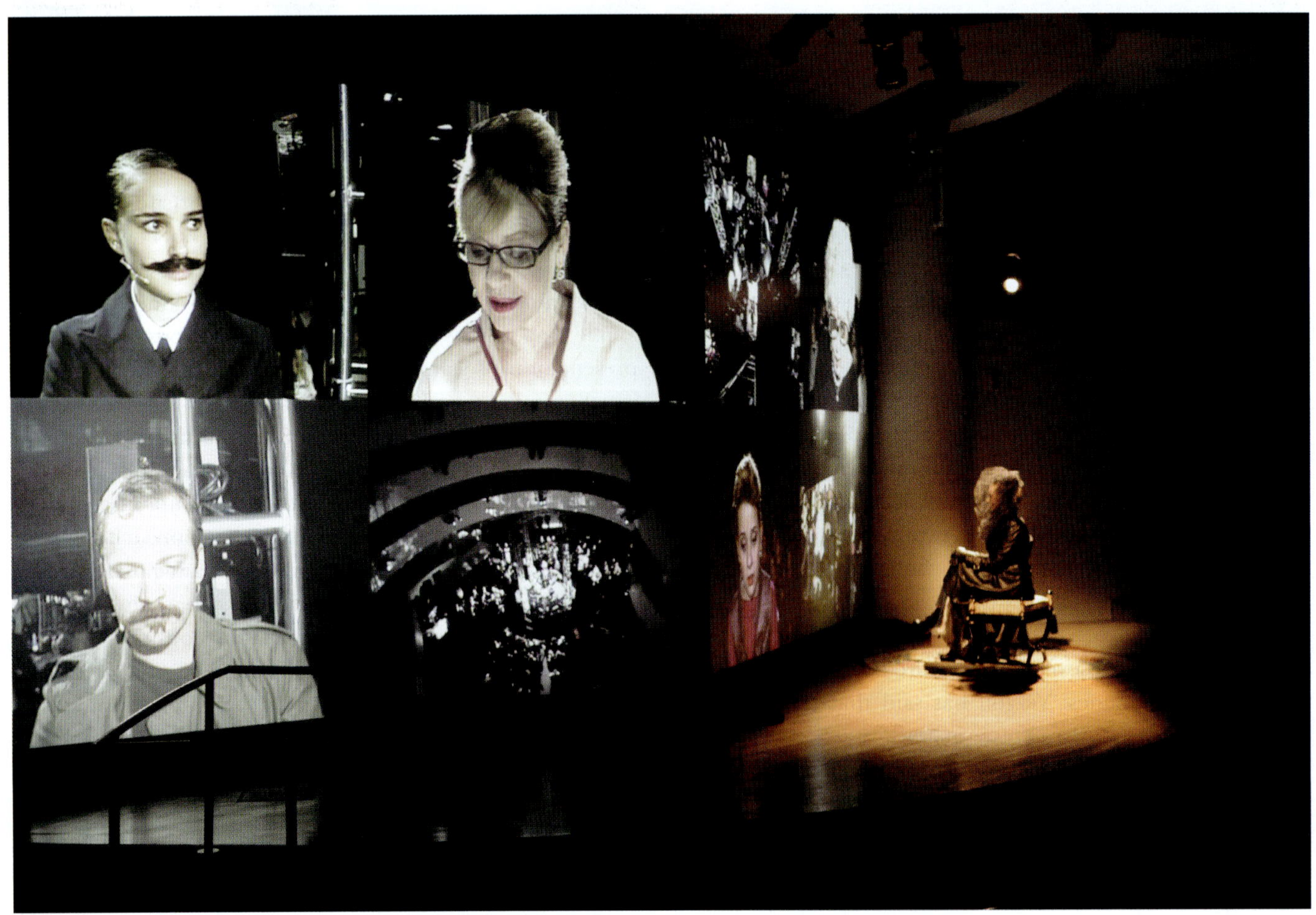

10.22 Francesco Vezzoli, *RIGHT YOU ARE (IF YOU THINK YOU ARE)*, 2007. Live performance at the Solomon R. Guggenheim Museum, New York (Performa07). © Francesco Vezzoli. Courtesy Gagosian Gallery.

the papers. Once the play began, however, it became evident that this narrative of privilege, like the narrative of the play and the drama of the event itself, was part of a composition best viewed from afar. The actors sat in a circle, with their backs to the audience, and performed the play as a reading. They had neither rehearsed nor memorized their lines. The VIPs could see very little and were being filmed for the audience in the theater below, alongside the actors, all of whom were performing for the camera. Vezzoli recounted: "That night at the museum the real art was the gathering of all those people (artists, actors, curators, critics, journalists, and socialites) as symbols of their social and public roles and their interaction with themselves."[44]

Vezzoli's claim was essentially that everybody upstairs at the Guggenheim was part of his work, assembled, indeed appropriated, from their personal and professional lives to be re-presented for the viewing public downstairs. The overflow guests, no doubt disappointed not to have the VIP seats, turned out to be the ones who not only got the clearest picture of the play, but also the only view of the "real art" in its entirety. Questions were raised about who looks at whom, how power functions to permit access (in this case to the stars), and also how it can be subverted by vision, both the directorial gaze of the artist and the surveilling eyes of the audience downstairs. Narrative here, as in the work of Huyghe and Cardiff, was presented so that the seduction of the plot was disrupted by a self-consciousness regarding the mechanics and social meaning of its telling. As with the painters in this chapter, beauty and absorption are accompanied by connections to the real world. Work such as Vezzoli's demonstrates how the critiques of the previous decades—from Laura Mulvey's analysis of cinema and "the Gaze," to deconstructions of painting and mass media—have not prevented contemporary artists from turning to traditional genres and conventional forms. Artists still paint and stories are still told. Both are done, however, with an awareness of their limits and, often, an eagerness to reject purity of form or the exclusivity of narrative.

Narrativity 2.0

As the references in the work discussed earlier in this chapter to computer graphics, networked systems, and the aesthetics of the Internet demonstrate, the impulse to think through form and narrative is being transformed by digital and online technologies. Two very different artists, Cory Arcangel and Ryan Trecartin, work in close dialogue with traditional media while being clearly immersed in the aesthetics and experience of YouTube, Photoshop, and Web 2.0, as the increasingly interactive Internet is called. Much as Pop artists of the 1960s expanded their artistic vocabulary by drawing on the aesthetics of pop culture, Arcangel and Trecartin make work that is both formally and conceptually embedded in the style and culture of commercially defined modes of representation.

Unlike those artists with whom this chapter began, whose art remains rooted in painting or sculpture, Arcangel and Trecartin mine the computer monitor and television screen for content and form, and then return their creative energies to those very same screens and even their original audiences. The results further develop the visual and metaphoric potential of computer-based and online communication for conveying the character and aesthetics of the new century. Arcangel's interest in entertainment technologies such as early video games, the storage capacity of the Internet, especially as evidenced in blog and Twitter feeds, and the way each deteriorates with age and use, suggests very different meanings from Trecartin's manipulations of Internet communication to generate fragmented, centrifugal, and metamorphosing expressions of emotion, personality, and even social analysis. This discussion will start with Arcangel's appropriation-based, abstract, and often contemplative work before addressing Trecartin's high-speed and expressive videos.

Cory Arcangel

In early 2000, Cory Arcangel (b. 1978), recently graduated from the Oberlin Conservatory of Music in Ohio, began creating an eclectic body of work that seemed to fit no genre. As he described it: "When I graduated from school, I investigated all the different outlets for my work and participated in them all. That included underground film festivals, performance spaces, non-profits, museums, galleries, the web, and even self-organized tours. So I pretty much made work for any context that existed and still do to this day."[45] The question of labels, for himself or what he was making, was set aside. Arcangel found his first bit of artworld fame thanks to a rather rudimentary computer animation of white clouds slowly and uniformly crossing a sky-blue field. Many viewers, particularly those who were children of middle-class homes in the 1980s, could be counted on to recognize the scene as coming from the Super Mario Brothers video game manufactured by Nintendo. Arcangel created the piece, called *Super Mario Clouds* (2002), by hacking into a game cartridge and removing everything except for the sky and the clouds. The process of winnowing the game down to its background highlights its formal qualities: its ability to present fields of color produced by light and to include objects and colors in motion. Arcangel makes clear his formalist, even Greenbergian (see Introduction) attention to media specificity in the tutorial "How to Make Super Mario Clouds." This text, posted online, provides instructions for replicating the work as well as a history of Arcangel's source material. The Nintendo Entertainment System (NES) games including Super Mario Brothers, he explains, constituted a technological advance in the gaming industry because they utilized two chips, one containing the graphics and the other the programming that directs where and when the imagery appears. Arcangel created *Super Mario Clouds*, and an extensive body of related works, by appropriating the graphics chip and modifying the programming chip. Limiting his intervention to manipulating the assembly language of the program gave Arcangel "control over the machine and assure[d] me that aesthetic choices are based on the hardware of the machine."[46] *Super Mario Clouds*, like the game itself, looks as it does because it takes full advantage of the graphics capability of the NES. In Greenberg's terms, Arcangel demonstrated the "irreplaceability" of his medium, ironically one destined for rapid obsolescence. He then made *Super Mario Clouds 2k3* (2003), for which the animated sky took on cinematic dimensions for projection in museums; *The Making of Super Mario Clouds* (2004), a silent, real-time documentation of the artist cracking the NES Super Mario Brothers game; and finally, with Paper Rad (a collective of three like-minded artists), the *Super Mario Movie* (2005) (**fig. 10.23**), a virtuosic fifteen-minute display combining music and animation created within the media limitations of the NES system. These works and a host of related video-game modifications have been compared to Minimalism for their reduced geometric compositions, Pop art for their sources, Conceptual art for their use of instructions, and Fluxus for their fascination with the everyday.

Arcangel's debt to 1960s traditions, particularly avant-garde music and Fluxus art, is made explicit in his *Structural Film* (2007), a variation on Nam June Paik's *Zen for Film* (1964–65) (see fig. 1.3). For the piece, Archangel simulated the empty celluloid of Paik's film using the "Aged Film" filter on iMovie software and then had the digital file saved in a second program, QuickTime, and transferred to 16mm film. The transfer process produced an image quality that not only evokes the analogue experience of watching the light pass through Paik's film and land on the silver screen, but also interrupts the illusion with pixelated irregularities that reveal Arcangel's digital medium. *Structural Film* stakes out a historical reference for Arcangel's interest in media technology, but it is only one such source. A very different tradition—one linked to the early 1980s practice, called cracking, of breaking through the copyright codes of game cartridges to insert personalized features into the software—is another important source for his work. The DIY aesthetic of cracking shares a spirit of individuality and anti-authoritarianism with graffiti art, which was gaining visibility at the same moment (see Chapter 4). Arcangel made this legacy explicit in *Low-Level Allstars* (2003), a compilation of period crack tags—introductions literally graffitied into the software. The tags appear as several seconds of animation advertising the prowess of the digital intruder. Created for the Commodore 64 system, a lower-resolution, single-chip predecessor of the NES, the tags are character-based and black-and-white. As assertions of individuality within the digital architecture, these tags set

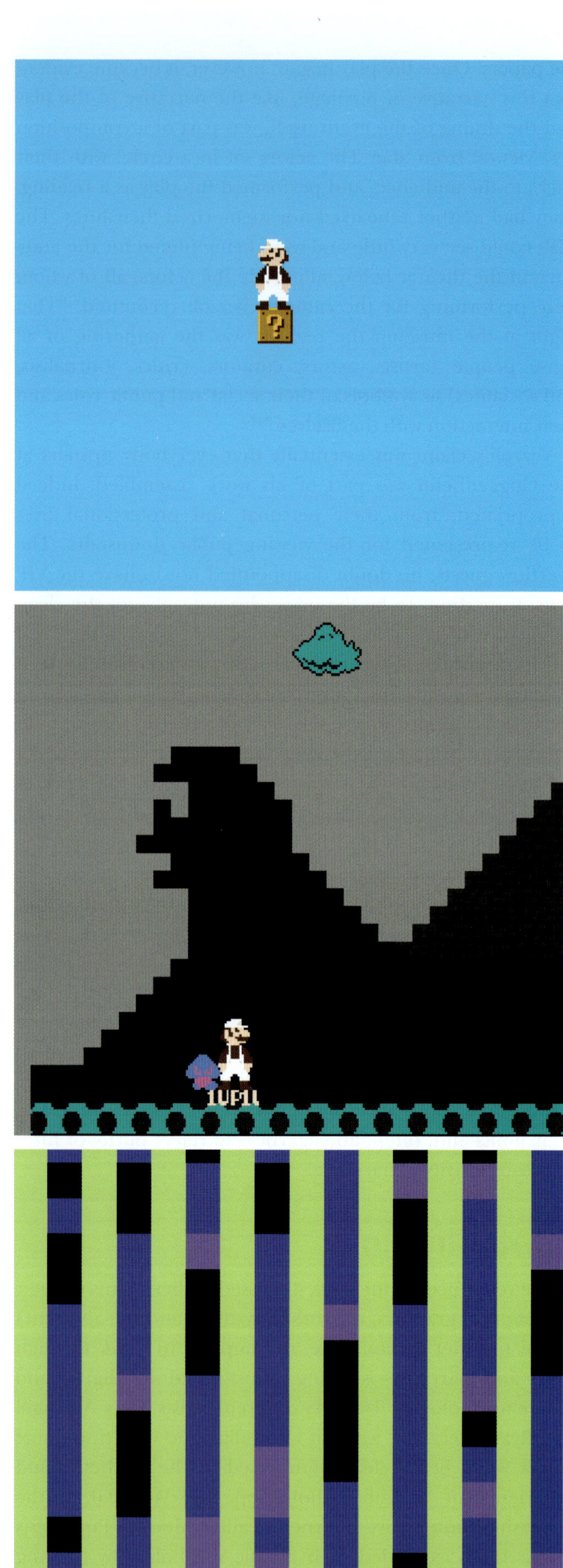

10.23 Cory Arcangel in collaboration with Paper Rad, ***Super Mario Movie***, 2005. Hacked Nintendo Entertainment System Super Mario Brothers cartridge, Nintendo Entertainment System game console, and artist software. © Cory Arcangel. Courtesy of Cory Arcangel and Lisson Gallery.

the stage for such twenty-first-century projects as those of IAA and Hasah Elahi (see Chapter 11), or the attempts of hacker groups such as Anonymous to leave their mark on contemporary cyberspace.

Arcangel has described his art as a means of finding open spaces within technology that are not defined by its conventional rules and limits. Praising his success, critics have made much of the meditative repetition of clouds in *Super Mario Clouds* or the unending open road in *F1 Racer Mod* (2004), for which Arcangel removed everything but the road and distant mountains from an automobile racing game: Here, it appears, is the open space of technology awaiting our entry. *Super Mario Movie* raises the bar for aesthetic tension and narrative drama in Arcangel's work, but also suggests that technology might offer something more somber than empty space. It begins with the Mario logo which is followed by the words: "As a video game grows old its content and internal logic deteriorate. For a character caught in this breakdown problems affect every area of life." The scenes that follow stretch the technical limits and opportunities of the Nintendo game system to chronicle Mario's path through a virtual landscape that explodes in vibrant colors and loud music, also generated by the game system, and degrades into collections of icons, colored squares, and letters. More text appears periodically but soon likewise degrades into illegible collections of characters. The theme of deterioration through repetition or the passage of time is a common theme in Arcangel's oeuvre. His essay "On Compression" (2007–08) describes how the data loss that occurs in the compression provided by JPEG technology has created the recognizably pixelated images that characterize the aesthetic of the first decade of the new millennium. His 2009 retrospective at the Nederlands Institute voor Mediakunst, Amsterdam, was called "Depreciated," linking the information loss to economics and extending the significance of deterioration from an influence on style to a metaphor for social conditions.

It is not only animated surrogates who struggle through virtual space to maintain familiar forms of productivity; real people populate Arcangel's televisual arena as well. Following the example of appropriation artists of the 1980s, Arcangel has enlisted the Internet as an archive of attempts, both successful and not, to create and communicate within the technologies provided by contemporary culture. These works, including *Working On My Novel* (2010 and 2012 editions) (**fig. 10.24**), *Sorry I Haven't Posted* (2010), and *follow my other twitter* (2011), consist of reposting entries submitted to social media sites that include the title phrase of the work. *Working On My Novel* is a list of Tweets—short messages of no more than 140 characters posted on the Twitter website—announcing their authors' involvement with a creative activity from which they are taking at least a short break. The immediate impact is, of course, humor—though it can also be overwhelming to be confronted by hundreds of paused novelists or a cascade of apologies. Arcangel's appropriations, however, are much more than a joke; these works point to an archive of shared experience that, due to the connectivity of the Internet, can be shared, even if only marginally. We are also being shown a collective portrait of effort and desire, produced like the

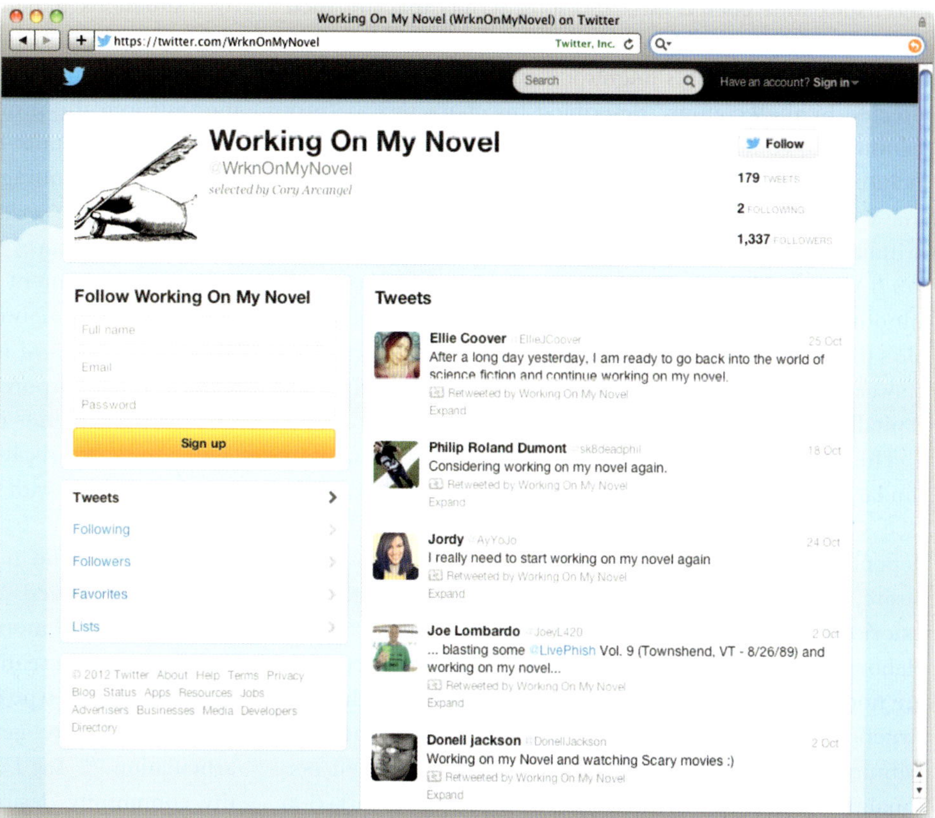

10.24 Cory Arcangel, *Working On My Novel*, 2012. Twitter feed. © Cory Arcangel. Courtesy of Cory Arcangel and Lisson Gallery.

paintings and sculptures discussed earlier through layers of associative fragments—albeit Tweets rather than colors, images, or objects. While the novel sits unfinished and the author posts, we learn of many other things occupying people's lives: writers express pride and disappointment, families are raised, riots are broadcast on TV ... Despite or perhaps because of the standardization and limited detail, the instances of difference appear quite starkly, drawing attention to individuality within the technological space. Of *Sorry I Haven't Posted,* for which he was reposting up to fifty contributions a day, Arcangel wrote on his own website: "There are some really touching ones out there. Enjoy!"

Ryan Trecartin

With an aesthetic shaped by the Internet and a sensitivity to the impact of global economics and social media on the early twenty-first century, U.S. video artist Ryan Trecartin (b. 1981) has submitted old-fashioned face make-up, costumes, and sets to digital editing software and produced results that generate physical and metaphoric power that recalls the impact of James Rosenquist's *F-111.* Like Rosenquist, Trecartin has integrated the style and technology of contemporary media to replicate the most representative qualities of contemporary life. In 1965, Pop artists concentrated on the collision of advertising, urban growth, and the threat of the military-industrial complex; in 2010, Trecartin addressed the integration of digital video, telecommunications, and global capitalism. Unlike Rosenquist, Trecartin begins his projects with words, not images. His high-keyed, fast-paced video works, such as the nearly four-hour, seven-part *Any Ever* (2009–10) (**fig. 10.25**) that includes all the works discussed here, start with poetry, lists, and long scripts that are then transformed into scenes and sets for the camera. Trecartin has emphasized that this linguistic foundation is profoundly affected by the economy, describing his characters as "projections that come out of [capitalist] word systems."[47] Names including Able, Y-Ready, Wait, and Free Lance indicate a character's position in the workforce while those such as Britta and Adobe identify favored objects of consumption. In *Ready (Re'Search Wait'S)* (2009–10) Wait, played by the artist, announces: "I love learning about myself through other people's products," concisely explaining thereby the relationship between the individual, the self, and society in contemporary capitalist culture.

The embrace of consumption-fueled self-actualization, similar to that examined in Sylvia Fleury's work of the 1990s (see Chapter 5), led Trecartin to conceive of identity as dependent primarily on individual impulses such as taste and desire, which are more subject to choice and change than exterior forces of history or essential traits of character. He elaborates: "As people explore and expand into spaces that are not dependent on the body, but rather the mind, the construction and use of one's personality can become the most defining aspect to identify. And the thing I love about personality is that it can be added to, changed or re-worked at will, while not being classified or grouped very easily."[48] In order to avoid the traps of definition, Trecartin composes with what he calls situations, configurations of experience, environments, and relationships built from details of normative and alternative constructions of family, identity, friendship, and work. *Any Ever* is full of awkward family encounters, dominating co-workers, ambitious artists, and melodramatic friends, presented in fractured episodes and with dialogue delivered in a transfixing if not fully comprehensible fusion of corporate-speak and youth slang; the situations include vignettes of the business operations of K-CoreaINC., a hierarchically organized corporation perpetually promising the horizontal structure of a friendship group as its employees, called Koreas, spread from offices to airplanes and hotels. In *The Re'Search (Re'Search Wait'S)* (2009–10) we meet Told, a teenage rock band that models creative collaboration and friendship, and participates in a larger mass-culture situation defined by the collective infatuation for suicidal reality star Sammy B. In *Sibling Topics (Section A)* (2009), Trecartin created a family with similarly fluid qualities. In this work, three quadruplets receive a video message from their dead mother telling them about their murdering absent father who had a fetish for threes—hence the estrangement of their fourth sibling. The perpetual motion of the work's layered organization, as situations lead to and interrupt others over the four hours of *Any Ever,* as well as the overlapping information within the frames of the video and layered audio tracks, is dizzying and invites repeated viewing, facilitated by the artist's choice to make all his work available online.

The motivation for Trecartin's situation-based practice lies in its power to subvert the determinism of linear narrative; situations generate infinite opportunities for characters to align and realign within the work and for viewers to make fresh connections throughout. Careers, kinship, and interests join the protagonists of *Any Ever,* while similarities between the details of their personalities, possessions, or even names encourage viewers to link temporally disparate scenes within the series, much as color or shape can join spatially distant features of architecture, painting, or sculpture. In form and content, situations match contemporary existence. "We're all networked and we're maintaining our own discrete networks of multiple selves, too. And we're moving towards more corporeal expressions of this. Versions of yourself layered together might actually be an emerging form of collaboration," Trecartin explains.[49] Such layering has particular importance with regard to gender and sexuality. When pressed about the frequent merging of tropes of masculinity, femininity, and hetero- and homosexuality in his work, Trecartin explained: "I see it less as a lack of distinction in binary terms and more as an exploration of territories within infinite gender creation, individualization and specificity. I imagine this as a type of multiplex space. I'm often interested in realities where gender takes a back-seat to personality articulation."[50] *Any Ever* presents life on a stage where identity, community, desire, and values are in a constant state of

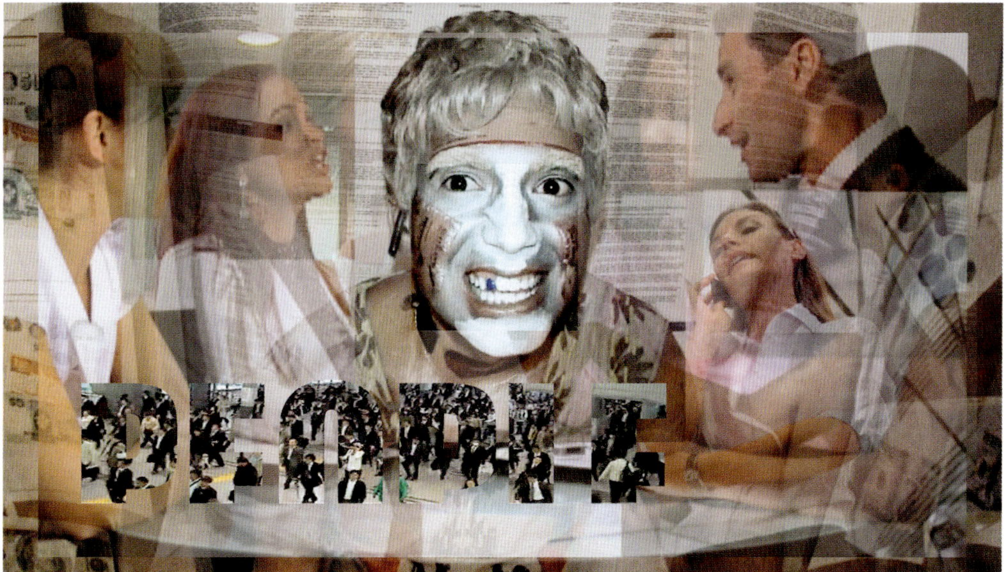

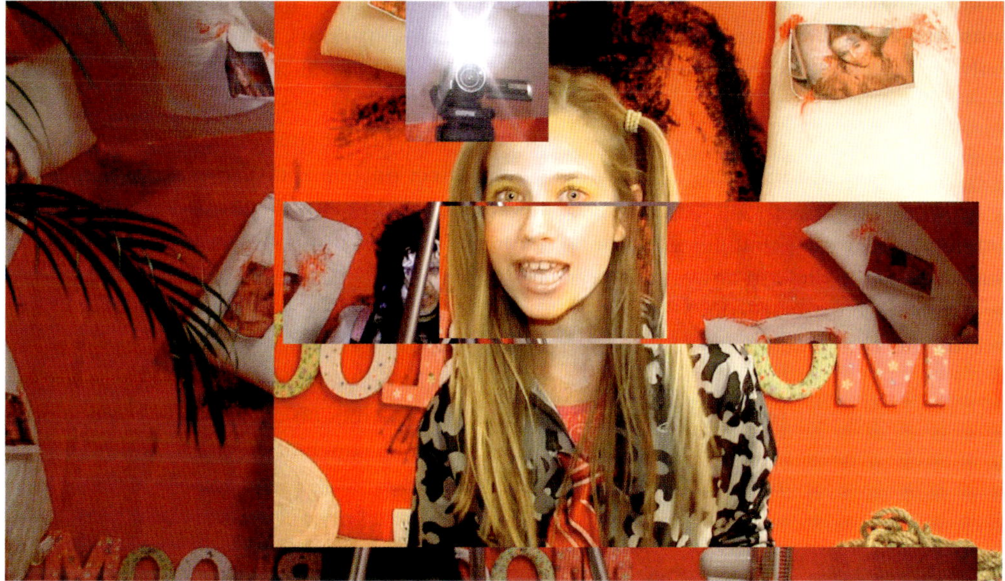

10.25 Ryan Trecartin, ***Roamie View: History Enhancement (Re'Search Wait'S)*** (top) and ***The Re'Search (Re'Search Wait'S)*** (bottom), 2009–10, from ***Any Ever*** series. Film stills. Courtesy of the artist and Elizabeth Dee, New York.

generation through language (descriptions of selves, others, and circumstances), bodies (refined through surgery, prosthetics, costumes, and cosmetics), and art (sculptures, paintings, and interior decoration), as well as undergoing an almost simultaneous destruction.

The value Trecartin places on individual capacity and the opportunity for change can be gleaned from his studio practice. After the initial script has been written and delivered to the actors, artist and actors collaborate to interpret the words into events for the camera. Actors are limited to takes as short as single lines or actions, often changing and repeating them until they lose any relation to their context. Talking with Cindy Sherman, Trecartin explained that the "performances are made to be cropped, altered, repurposed, and enhanced. Each line is said, on average, about twenty-five times ... everything is performed for the edit."[51] This compulsion to repeat destroys any dependence the single parts may have upon a framing narrative, and thus emphasizes the individuality of any remark or gesture. Such a focus resonates with the concerns of artists within art movements as diverse as Minimalism, appropriation, and feminism whose practice aimed to separate the objects of their attention, whether a form, an image, or a person from the contexts that had over-determined their meanings and limited their potential (see Chapter 1). After isolating parts of speech and activities, Trecartin devotes enormous energy to post-production. In the editing process, for which he favors consumer-ready software such as iMovie and Adobe After Effects rather than high-end products, and where he makes heavy use of animation and audio manipulation, he gives the situations their individual character and connective potential. The process that began with writing, and continued in the analogue practices of set-building, costuming, and acting, reaches completion in a practice defined by contemporary technology. *Any Ever* is not only saturated in the social and technological facts of the present but is also a manifestation of the digitally mediated and physically direct means with which we experience them.

11

The Art of Contemporary Experience

Historian of science Bruno Latour (b. 1947) has argued that observations about the environment, like the conclusions we draw about ourselves and others, are in perpetual flux and depend not only on objective changes in the world, but also on the shifting perspective of its viewers. What we need, he says, is "a test to measure our bearings accurately."[1] As Latour turned his eye to art, writing perceptively on Danish-Icelandic sculptor and photographer Olafur Eliasson, he clarified the entanglements that complicate such a test: "If there's one thing we don't believe in any more it's the possibility of being emancipated, freed from all attachments, blissfully unaware of the consequences of our actions."[2] Artists in this chapter provide us with different means of finding our bearings in a world that requires awareness. The art discussed in this chapter, whether a simulated electrical storm as in Eliasson's *Your strange certainty still kept* (1996) (see fig. 11.1) or a cardboard and aluminum foil cavern as in *Cavemanman* (2002) by Swiss-born, Paris-based sculptor Thomas Hirschhorn (see fig. 11.12), is explicitly conceptual—signifying within arguments about art, society, nature, and self—and also phenomenological, to be experienced as directly as rain. This work demands that viewers layer their sensual apprehension of form with an intellectual analysis of content, or vice versa, envelop their conceptual appreciation with a physical response. French sculptor and video artist Pierre Huyghe (see Chapter 10) explained that, coming of age in the 1980s and 1990s, "we all became extremely self-conscious and aware about the consequences of our actions."[3] The lesson for the twenty-first century, he determined, was that "conclusions should be suspended but the tension should remain."[4] Not every artist in this chapter would agree with Huyghe about the necessity of suspending conclusions. All, however, demonstrate a self-conscious attention to consequences and produce art that visualizes, conceptualizes, and even amplifies rather than resolves tension.

Chapter 11 is divided into three sections starting with a discussion of art that celebrates the complexities of experience, and the virtue of paying close attention to the sensations we feel, the associations they evoke, and the ideas they generate. This largely liberating and often meditative work is followed in a second section by art addressing the ideological and technological constraints placed on experience by its surveillance. The theoretical and technological discussions of power raised in part two are complemented by a final section that offers artistic analyses of a wide variety of media and their effect on our ability to make sense of our interactions with the world. As with the art discussed in the previous chapter, the material presented here revisits some of the issues regarding art and life that were introduced in the 1960s and 1970s. It is work that either self-consciously produces experiences or critically examines the nature of our experience in light of questions raised over the last few decades. Hirschhorn describes his art as a "tool to encounter the world,"[5] and this book concludes with a selection of work about such encounters.

The Experience of Experience

Asking viewers to be wholly engaged with the material world while simultaneously critically examining what they find there is not new. Seventeenth-century Baroque art typically juxtaposed the physicality of the here-and-now with the ethereal realm of the divine, or celebrated the effects of the natural world while simultaneously using them to express civic and nationalist politics. An immediate precedent for twenty-first-century artists concerned with perception and contemplation is the art of the 1960s California-based Light and Space artists. Robert Irwin (b. 1928), one of the central figures of the movement, described his work to Eliasson in terms of "perceiving yourself perceiving."[6] Irwin created works in which shadows and reflections appear to share the same visual and physical properties as objects in space. Unlike their peers Hans Haacke, Terry Fox, and Gregory Battcock, who alerted the viewer to the politics of process (see Chapter 1), Light and Space artists strove to exclude specific cultural or historical references, enlisting only abstract effects of lights, color, and space. James Turrell (b. 1943) cut openings in gallery roofs, creating rectangular planes that appear to be both windows and wall paintings. The open sky appears flat like a painted screen. As the color of the sky above changes throughout the day, Turrell's works are transformed: An unarticulated composition of pale blue, for instance, might take on vibrant striations of red and orange. Suddenly a bird or plane might cross the scene, breaking the illusion of flatness, and we see the new protagonist flying through deep space. Such art is not about fooling the eye, but rather creating opportunities for viewers to arrive at different yet accurate perceptions about the physical world. Shadows, reflections, and solid objects are all equally real; color expanding in two dimensions and light moving through space are both facts in our environment. In the spaces he has created in Roden Crater, Arizona, Turrell has expanded the scale of his work from the built environment to the Earth and stars. One looks out from the basin of this extinct volcano to see the sky alternately appear as infinite space and finite surface. Such sensations provide a point of reference for the nature of self-conscious perception in art of the early twenty-first century.

Olafur Eliasson

Unlike the earlier Light and Space artists, Olafur Eliasson (b. 1967) is committed to muddying the experience of seeing oneself seeing with cultural cues. When selected to represent Denmark at the Venice Biennale in 2003, he outlined a programmatic investigation: "I would like to think about the conditions of our orientation when confronted with partial or total absence of the sources that support our orientation."[7] When our senses, memory, expectations, perspective, logic, and emotions fail us, how might we regain our bearings? Eliasson sculpts by recontextualizing fragments of natural phenomena. He gives us rooms of rain, mist, clouds, and light. He creates waterfalls, rainbows, electric storms, and ice plates. The visual, aural, and physical sensations created by the work are familiar from our experiences in nature, but they are displaced in the art. *Your strange certainty still kept* (1996) (**fig. 11.1**) invites the viewer to be confused and amused by a wall of water droplets suspended in midair, and also to examine the hoses, pump, plastic-covered basin, and strobe light that create the illusion. By inserting the hardware of the sculpture among the constituent elements of the landscape—in this case, the flash of light and the gentle fall of rain—Eliasson represents the sensations created by nature but divorces them from the means that generally produce them. Though the artifice involved in creating the effect is revealed, the sense of wonder is no less powerful and, in fact, the chains of associations are enhanced. Flashing lights and splashing water will remind some viewers of a lightning storm, while others, entranced perhaps by the rhythm of the

11.1 Olafur Eliasson, *Your strange certainty still kept*, 1996. Water, strobe lights, acrylic, foil, wood, hose, and pump. Installation view at Tanya Bonakdar Gallery, New York, 1996. Courtesy of The Dakis Joannou Collection, Athens, Greece.

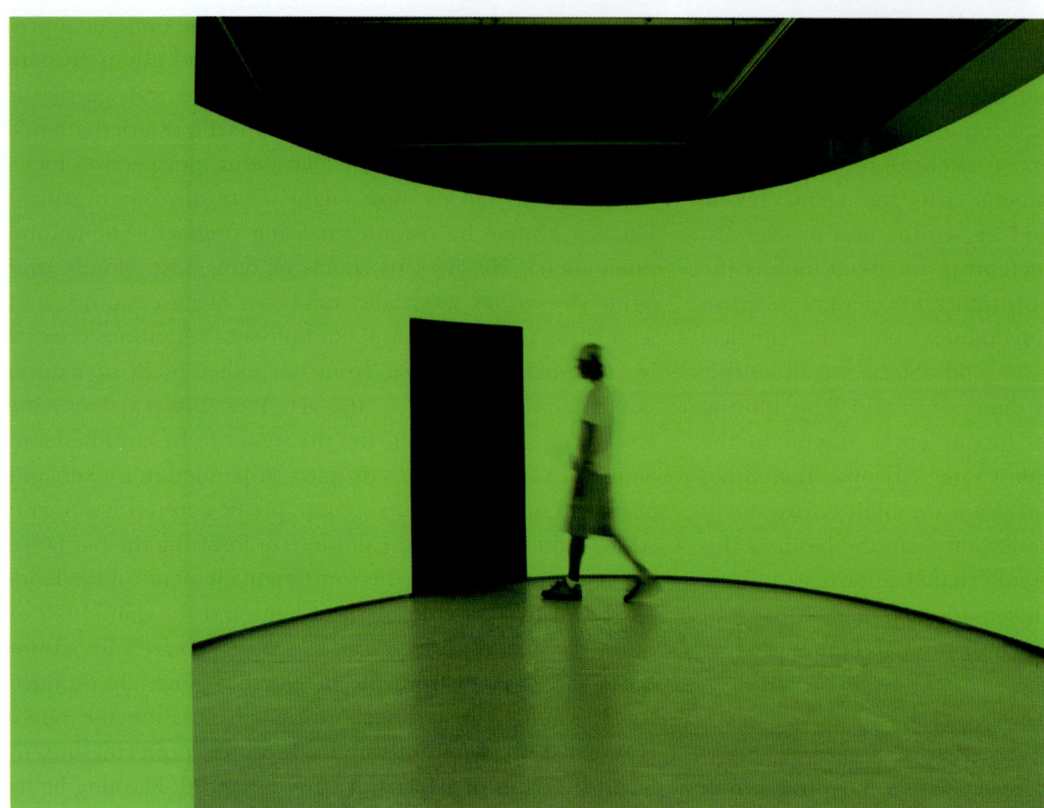

11.2 Olafur Eliasson, ***Your colour memory***, 2004. Stainless steel, wood, fluorescent lights, color filter foil (red, green, blue), projection foil, fabric, and control unit. Installation view at Arcadia University Art Gallery, Glenside, Pennsylvania, 2004. Photographer: Aaron Igler. Courtesy of Astrup Fearnley Museet for Moderne Kunst, Oslo, Norway.

strobe, will think of nightclubs. Eliasson's sublime isolation of time, motion, and gravity and his overt presentation of mechanics, technology, and artifice integrate phenomenology and technology, nature and culture.

Light and Space artists heighten our awareness of the human being as a sensing body; Eliasson treats such sensual experiences as conduits to social meaning. A large part of his oeuvre comprises photographs of islands, fissures, rivers, basalt crystals, waterfalls, and the horizon in Iceland. When asked directly what nature means to him, however, Eliasson explains, "I don't believe that 'nature' as such—as a fundamentally truthful or 'natural' state of things—exists."[8] His work is about engagement, a term he uses in its physical, intellectual, and ethical meanings. Art historian Mieke Bal has historicized Eliasson's concerns, describing his art as a reinvention of the Baroque attitude in which "subjects must engage with their environments, neither detached nor immersed but active, on innovative, creative and responsible terms."[9] Eliasson explains: "Engagement has consequences and these entail a heightened feeling of responsibility."[10] Standing in front of *Your strange certainty still kept*, a viewer observes both the effects of the weather and the signs of artifice and so gains insight into our experience of nature and art. *Your colour memory* (2004) (**fig. 11.2**), a curved room whose walls glow with a slowly changing spectrum of colors, solicits an engagement with community and time as well as nature and the senses. The space of the work fills with a color—deep red or magenta, yellow, blues, greens—which changes every thirty seconds. After approximately fifteen seconds in the red light, the retina produces a green afterimage that soon overwhelms the perception of the red. At this point, the red of the wall changes and the green of the afterimage competes with the new color that produces a second corresponding afterimage. As Eliasson points out, each viewer's experience is dependent on when he or she entered the piece, and the combinations of color and afterimage will be different for everyone. Viewers can reset their vision by stepping inside a small dark room built off the main room. Eliasson concludes an essay he wrote to accompany *Your colour memory* by asserting that "in preserving the freedom of each visitor to experience something that may differ from the experiences of others, art can continue to have a significant impact on both the individual and society as a whole."[11] This ethical imperative, he insists, should be shared by individual viewers and also by institutions that presume to engage art and audiences. To this end, Eliasson has developed a new type of art school that he has begun to realize through a variety of seminars and workshops in his studio and around the world. In 2009, at the Universität der Künste in Berlin, he established the Institut für Raumexperimente (Institute for Spatial Experiments) which serves as a "laboratory for experience."[12] Aiming to cultivate a pedagogy of experimentation, the Institut invites participants to invent means of creating, activating, and analyzing actions and phenomena that occur in all manner of spaces, from urban to natural, architectural to personal. The goal, like the experience of *Your colour memory*, is to encourage experience and its analysis in order to "strengthen our ability to re-negotiate our surroundings," and to "co-produce society."[13]

Ernesto Neto

Working on nearly the other side of the world, Brazilian sculptor Ernesto Neto (b. 1964) approaches the problem of art making in a similarly enveloping, if rather more romantic, fashion than Eliasson. The working assumption of art that invites us to see ourselves seeing, as Eliasson has put it, is that there is a distinction between body and mind, between experience and perception. The role of the artist is to connect these two aspects of our being. Neto creates from the position that there is no duality in our being, that, on the contrary, it is as "body-minds that we connect the things in this world, in life—the way we touch, the way we feel, the way we think and the way we deal."[14] The ideal work of art to address the human as a fully sentient and sensual being is an environment that resembles, in Neto's discussions, a party or a dance. *Anthropodino* (2009) (**fig. 11.3**) was one such environment.

Occupying the Park Avenue Armory in New York City from May 14 to June 14, 2009, *Anthropodino* was a network of navelike rooms, skeletal corridors, small caverns, and open pools and pads filled with cushions and balls. The structure was constructed primarily using Lycra and polyamide gauze, stretched to form walls and supported by an intricate system of pulleys and teardrop-shaped gauze counterweights filled with heavy pellets, spices, or Styrofoam balls. The installation, occupying nearly 2,000 square feet, took on the appearance of a biomorphic, amoebalike cathedral, glowing as light passed through its lilac, blue, and gold walls. The scents of the spices—including clove, cumin, ginger, and pepper—and most of all the movement and clear pleasure of the audience filled the space. *Anthropodino*, like most of Neto's work, was made to be entered—people walked through the gently enclosing corridors of its ethereal domes, pausing to lie on a bed of pillows and gaze up into a collection of hanging pendulums. Orifices stitched into the walls gave the piece a decidedly corporeal quality while also serving as an invitation to peer, and even reach through, from one space to another. Children and adults played in the ball pool and a sense of wonder pervaded the installation. The mere fact of hearing laughter and seeing kids running happily around an artwork is enough to make one aware of the striking quality of Neto's art.

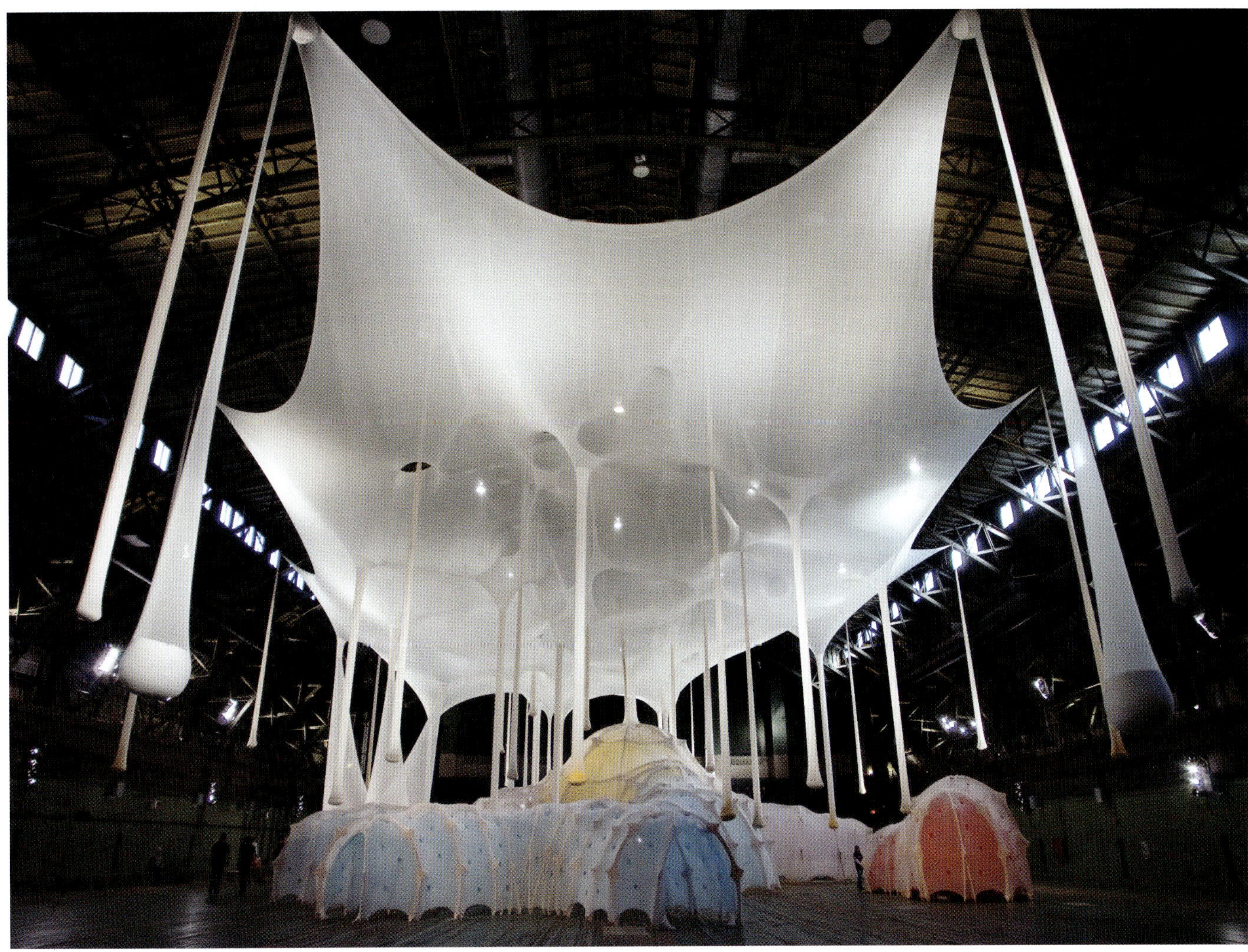

11.3 Ernesto Neto, *Anthropodino*, 2009. Mixed media installation, dimensions variable. Commissioned by Park Avenue Armory for Wade Thompson Drill Hall. Courtesy the artist, Tanya Bonakdar Gallery, New York, and Galeria Fortes Vilaça, São Paulo.

The array of sensations Neto marshaled for *Anthropodino* was remarkable. Even his small individual sculptures integrate the viewing mind with the smelling, touching, and hearing body. Neto discusses this movement of eye and body across and even through the surfaces of his work as a dance intended to bring the viewer to a state in which customary divisions of mind and body, self and other, are weakened and life can be experienced without dualities. Like Neto's understanding of the mind-body, his perception of the world we encounter, either in the artwork or outside it, is as a "cultural-physical" entity.[15] It is the artist's responsibility, he claims, to engage the viewer with the "physical, psychological and mental ... field of events where the relationship between the individuality of men and their world occurs."[16] This art experience is one in which judgment and knowledge are created by "thinking through our pores."[17] It is significant that such thinking is not only about the self, and that pleasure can be experienced through criticality or analysis. In fact, Neto has devoted considerable time to more evidently social and political issues. In 2003, with fellow artists Marcio Botner (b. 1970) and Laura Lima (b. 1971), he opened a gallery in his hometown of Rio de Janeiro called A Gentil Carioca (which, roughly translated, means "Gentle People of Rio") to provide a meeting place and exhibition spaces for artists in the region. A Gentil Carioca programs events in different sites from bars to performance spaces and has provided a platform for political and pedagogical activity. As in the creation of a sculpture or installation, so in curating an exhibition, producing a symposium, or hosting a party, the art lies in our ability, Neto asserts, to "create conditions of possibility."[18]

Roni Horn

Ernesto Neto has said that his goal in making work is to produce a sensation akin to "that moment [in seduction] when both of your faces change into something else because the erotic charge is so high, when your bodies move towards each other."[19] Olafur Eliasson has described the content of his work as the moment his audience is transformed "from a state of indifference to a state of difference."[20] U.S. sculptor Roni Horn (b. 1955) has also defined her work in terms of its ability to produce, rather than represent or record, experience. "The acquiring of an actual experience is," Horn asserts, "the content of the work."[21] Horn's work includes Minimalist-inspired sculptures, serial photography of people, buildings, and water, installations of letters and words, columns of glacial water, and many books. Horn enlists materials such as glass, rubber, and gold which produce sculpture that has, in her words, "credible ... physical reality."[22] All of her work depends on an "integral use of the world ... a necessary inclusion of circumstances."[23] Horn's appeal to the materiality of everyday life and the circumstances surrounding the artwork leads to an experience for the viewer that connects him or her to a network of associations drawn from life as much as from art. By the twenty-first century, art as experience could be literal. *Test Site* (2006) (**fig. 11.4**), by Sweden-based Belgian sculptor Carsten Höller (b. 1961), is a series of multistory slides on which visitors at the Tate Modern museum in

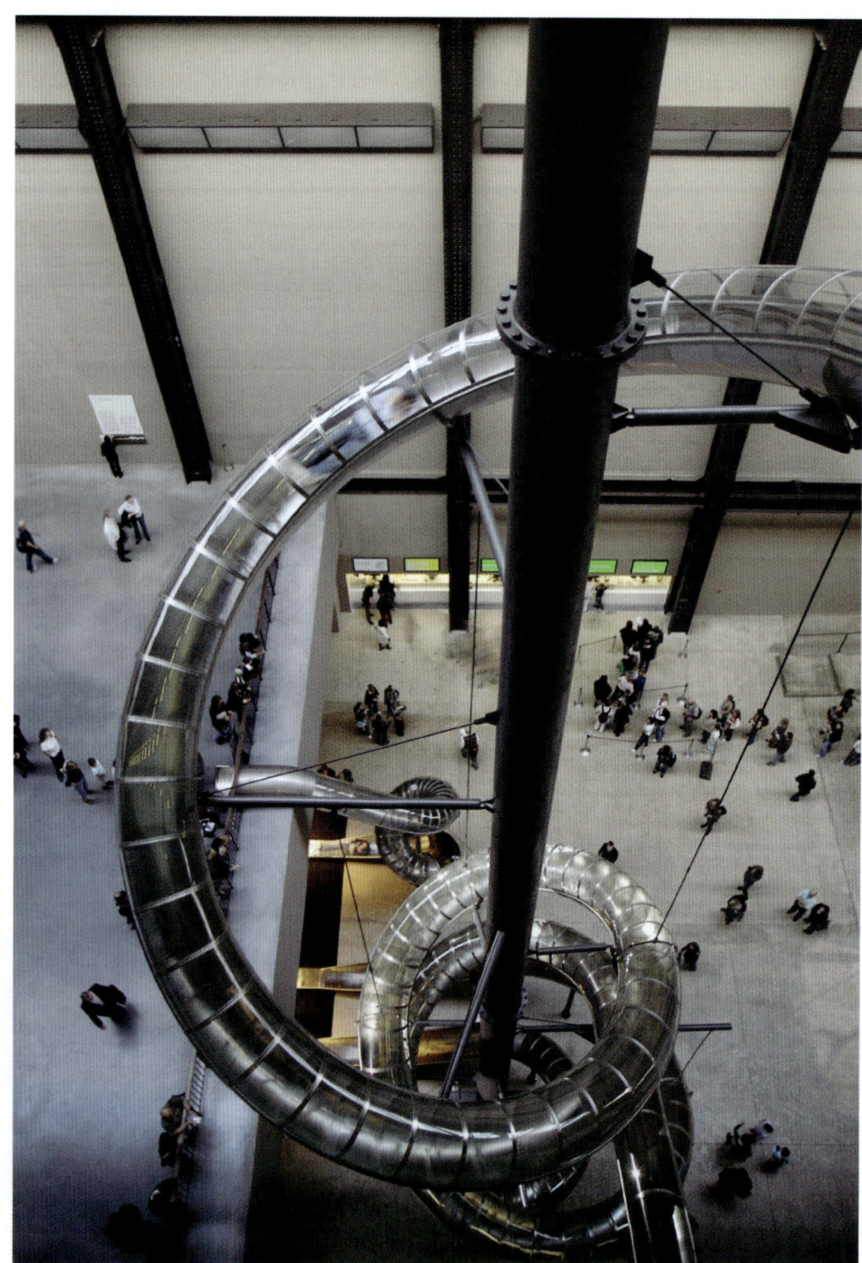

11.4 Carsten Höller, *Test Site*, 2006. Five slides. Installation view "Unilever Series: Carsten Höller." Turbine Hall, Tate Modern, London, 2006. Courtesy of the artist/Air de Paris, Paris.

London were invited to play. A popular sculpture, Höller's piece prompted viewers to tap into their inner child and move through the museum in a spirit of adventure, sociability, and fun. In the early 1980s, when Horn was leaving graduate school, the kinds of experience of particular interest to artists were defined in more overtly political terms by works such as Barbara Kruger's billboards and Jenny Holzer's displays (see Chapter 2). In 1979, Donald Judd (see Chapter 1) began the construction of a specially designed exhibition space for his own work and that of John Chamberlain and Dan Flavin. The facility, in Marfa, Texas, opened to the public in 1986, reinserting the transcendent Minimalist experience into the 1980s art world. Each of these examples treats the viewer differently: On Höller's slides we are a child, in front of Kruger's billboard we are citizens, and in Marfa we are eyes and a soul. Horn's oeuvre and the meaning and experiences it produces draw on all of these identities.

"Piece for Two Rooms" (1986)—one of four paired "identities," or ways of presenting the works, that make up *Things That Happen Again* (1986–91) (**fig. 11.5**), one of which is in Marfa—consists of two identically machined sections of forged copper cones. The two pieces are placed in adjacent rooms so that when visitors encounter the first object they cannot see the second. Unlike a Minimalist work by Judd, which one experiences entirely in the present tense, Horn's sculpture takes time. Comparing the two parts requires moving between the spaces and is dependent on the viewer's patience and memory. Even the presence of other people moving around the gallery and the sculpture can make determining the relationship between the two parts difficult. The work "unfolds."[24] Horn explains:

> You go into a space and see a simple disc. It doesn't look like much: it isn't, until you walk in and see that it is a three-dimensional cone-shaped object which is familiar but has certain subtle formal qualities which make it different, which take away from it being familiar. It becomes memorable. Then you go into the next room and enact exactly the same experience, but of course it's unexpected and it's so many minutes later; it's a slightly younger experience in your life. Whereas when you walked into the first room, you had the experience of something unique, you can't have that a second time.[25]

The first object is the premise for considering the relationship between the familiar and the strange, between what one knows from habit and memory and what one learns from exploration and novelty. The second object, because it makes itself known seconds after the first, elicits different questions and different reactions. In common with much of Horn's

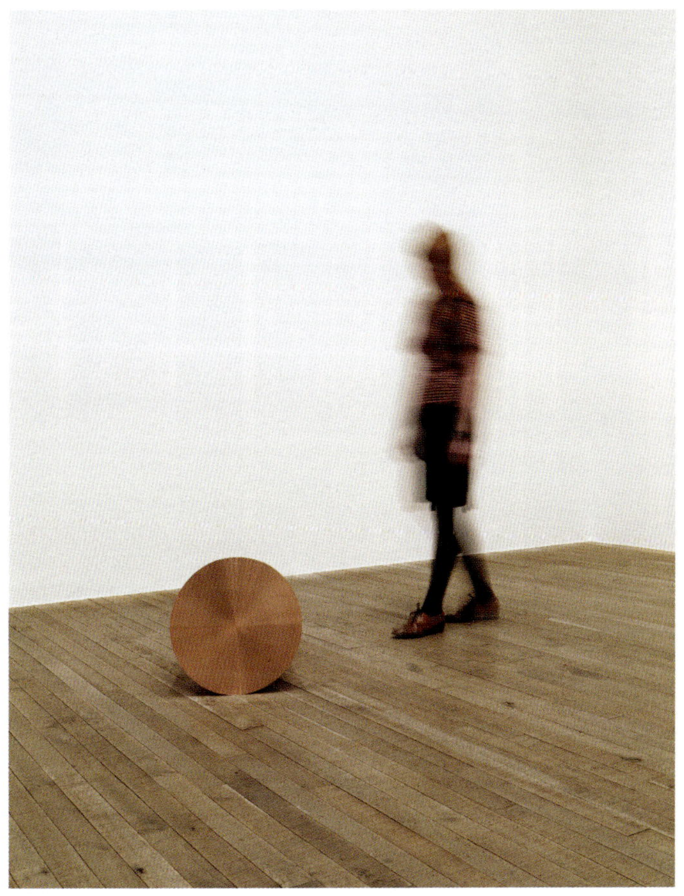
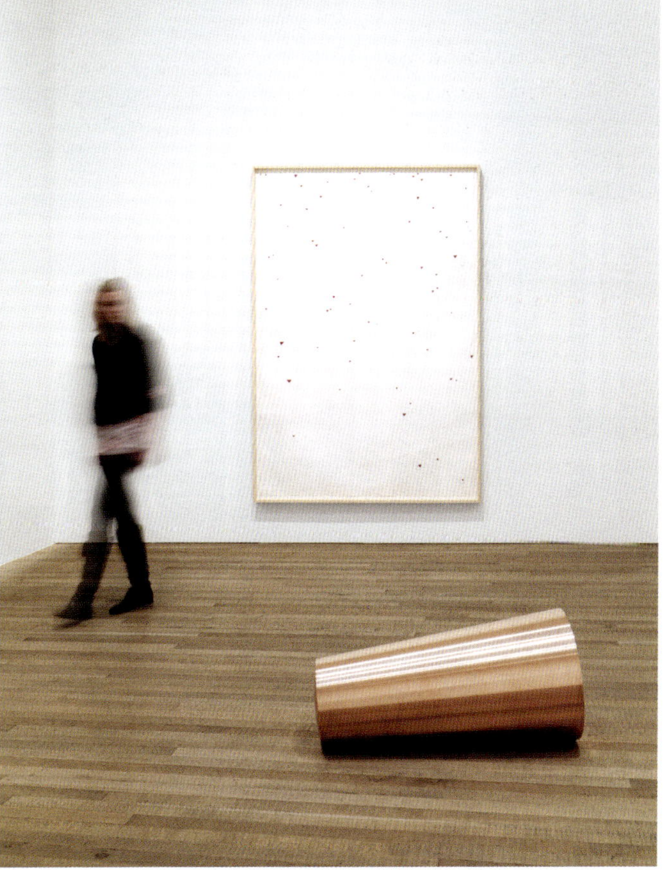

11.5 Roni Horn, ***Things That Happen Again***, 1986. Here shown presented as "Piece for Two Rooms," with two solid copper forms installed in separate rooms. Diameter 11½ × 17" (29.1 × 43.2 cm) each, length 35" (88.9 cm) each. Installation view at Tate Modern, London, 2009. Courtesy Hauser & Wirth.

oeuvre, *Things That Happen Again* muses on how sameness, repetition, and doubling can be means of sensing and contemplating difference. She writes: "the idea of the identical is a paradox since you always have a here and a there, a now and a then."[26] The here-and-now of experience and the there-and-then of memory are prompted by the object and lead the viewer, Horn says, "to the foundation of identity."[27] In an unusually direct discussion of the personal meaning in her work, Horn describes her interest in pairs, copies, and mimicry as "profoundly (although not exclusively) related to my sexuality and androgyny."[28] As in many works by Felix Gonzalez-Torres (see Chapter 7), with whom Horn became close in the early 1990s, *Things That Happen Again* invites reflection on the deeply personal and individual experience of difference and similarity.

Complementing the unstable heart of the presumably stable concept of sameness, Horn creates moments of stasis in the flow of water. Her impossible project of staying water has included documenting glaciers, rivers, mist, the changing atmospheric conditions of Iceland, and even the appearance and emotions of people as they endure and indulge in the sensations associated with water. In 1998, she was invited to London to consider a project on the Thames that led to *Still Water: The River Thames for Example* (1999). The Thames is a particularly dramatic urban waterway. In addition to its long, often violent history as the central artery of London, it is tidal and moves through the city with considerable force. The river continues to attract suicides and violent deaths. When Horn arrived in London she looked closely at the water. She interviewed people who lived and worked on or near it and did historical research. She photographed the surface of the water, avoiding cityscape traditions that present rivers as symbols of nature harnessed for the power of culture. In *Still Water*, the Thames appears as a substance and a surface with changing properties, one day luminescent, the next flatly opaque, variously rippled and reflective. Across the images of *Still Water*, Horn typed small numbers that annotate the eddies, small waves, and patches of still water. At the bottom of the photographs are footnotes: passages from descriptions concerning the river, lines from songs, snippets of overheard conversations, poems, thoughts. While the footnotes assign meaning, they also contain it, stilling the streams of

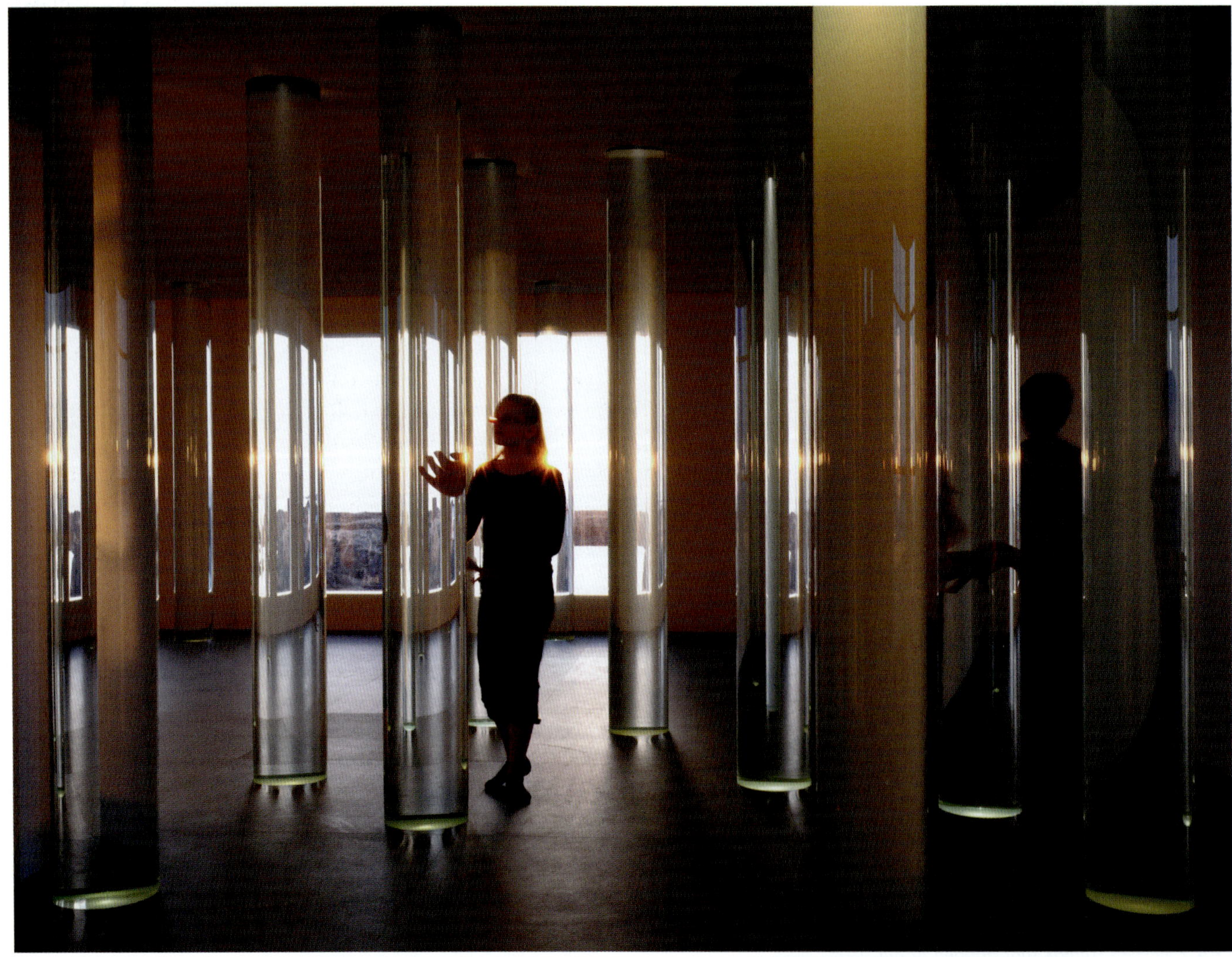

11.6 Roni Horn, *Vatnasafn/Library of Water*, 2007. Permanent installation, since 2007, initiated by Artangel. Stykkishólmur, Iceland. Courtesy Hauser & Wirth.

association the river provokes just as the photographs freeze its current. *Still Water* forms an encyclopedia of moving water, an index to the Thames. In 2001, Horn made the reference-book metaphor explicit by publishing ninety-five of the images without footnotes as *Dictionary of Water*.

Horn started traveling to Iceland in the mid-1970s and has often described the country as her studio and her medium. In 2003, she acquired an abandoned library perched high above Stykkishólmur harbor. To create *Vatnasafn/Library of Water* (2007) (**fig. 11.6**), she made some architectural modifications and installed twenty-four glass columns, each filled with water from one of the island's major glaciers. Standing inside the structure and facing out of the windows that Horn enlarged to extend from floor to ceiling, one looks out to the sea and sky that envelop Iceland. It was the Icelandic landscape and culture that helped Horn figure out how to integrate matter with the ephemeral nature of experience. She explains: "Iceland taught me to taste experience. Because that's possible here—possible because of the intensely physical nature of experience on this island. This palpable quality has been one lesson. Sensual experience balances the intellect and here the best of both worlds exists in provocative union."[29] Empowered by the landscape, Horn built *Vatnasafn* into a lighthouse illuminated by the very elements—water, stone, and light—that had made her own experience of Iceland personally transformative. The columns of water, which at the bottom reveal sediment from the glaciers, deliver the substance of the view from the library into its interior. Horn set into a dense rubber floor English and Icelandic words describing the weather, thus juxtaposing, as in *Still Water*, the flux of water and the flow of language. Horn has been outspoken about the risk of global warming to the Icelandic landscape, and the library is a means to draw attention to political as well as sensual realities. Horn positions the viewer as a light in this beacon able to encounter art and the world with a balance of the senses and the intellect.

Mark Dion

The artists discussed thus far have created, through their work, a syntax for sensual and intellectual engagement with the world. U.S. sculptor Mark Dion (b. 1961) begins with the scientific means we already have to contemplate our place in the world. He dons a lab coat and steps into the roles of botanist, ichthyologist, entomologist, biologist, herbalist, archeologist, and, ultimately, in a new outfit, curator. Though his work addresses specific locales, from the Amazon Rainforest to New England, art historian Miwon Kwon has persuasively argued that Dion's art is primarily discursive, meaning that its most important context is an intellectual discourse rather than a geographic site. As such, a work such as *On Tropical Nature* (1991), which involved collecting specimens from the rain forest, signifies most directly within a discussion of the natural sciences and museology and then, only secondarily, with regard to the rainforest. Dion's education illustrates Kwon's thesis. In the early 1990s, he pursued two paths, enrolling as an art student in the Whitney Studio Program and taking biology at the City College of New York. Dion kept his two interests separate until he perceived, he says, "that nature is one of the most sophisticated arenas for the production of ideology."[30] Having recognized the social, intellectual, and political function of nature, he incorporated the environment as both the subject and the site of his art. His subsequent work maintained his original love of nature while exploring the dual identity of the environment as both self-evident and socially inscribed.

On Tropical Nature (1991) characterizes Dion's early environmental art. Playing the role of explorer/naturalist, Dion spent three weeks in the rainforest near the source of the Orinoco River in Venezuela. Here, he collected specimens and sent them back to the Sala Mendoza art museum in Caracas. Once a week, the curators who had commissioned the work received crates of butterflies, soil samples, branches, seedpods, shells, and more. Dion also sent artifacts gathered from members of his party including lanterns, clothes, trowels, notebooks, plastic tubs, a camera, and shoes. The collection fell well outside the normal disciplinary boundaries of either art or science museums. Without taxonomic guides or instructions from the artist to transform the collection into a cohesive, not to mention coherent, exhibition, the curators had to display the materials based on improvised criteria. The viewer was left to muse over the specimens and puzzle out the logic of an exhibition. Dion had forced the Sala Mendoza curators to liberate their practice from the conventions of both the history of art and scientific display.

Dion has continued to give considerable attention to museums and strategies of display. It is a telling aspect of Dion's work, exemplified by *New England Digs* (2001) (**fig. 11.7**), for which Dion and his assistants collected and presented artifacts from sites in rural and industrial New England, that as it disregards best practices or even archeological common sense it balances a critique of disciplinary categories with pleasure in the historical record. Dion, who was born and raised in New Bedford, Massachusetts, returned to New England to excavate a riverbed, a tavern, and a farm. The resulting display exhibits little regard for provenance and no respect for chronological distinctions. Instead, Dion creates a contemporary version of the *Wunderkabinett*, the German name for the "cabinets of curiosities" filled with all manner of natural and scientific wonders by collectors in earlier centuries. The cabinet built for *New England Digs* is filled with all manner of ordinary things. Mid-nineteenth-century broken glass from O'Malley's Tavern is displayed with twentieth-century litter. Long objects might be displayed with similarly shaped items, or blue things put together regardless of date or original location. A drawer full of neatly arranged swizzle sticks, beads, combs, lightbulbs, buttons, and broken dolls' heads, though emotionally suggestive, lacks any of the chronological or typological precision demanded of a

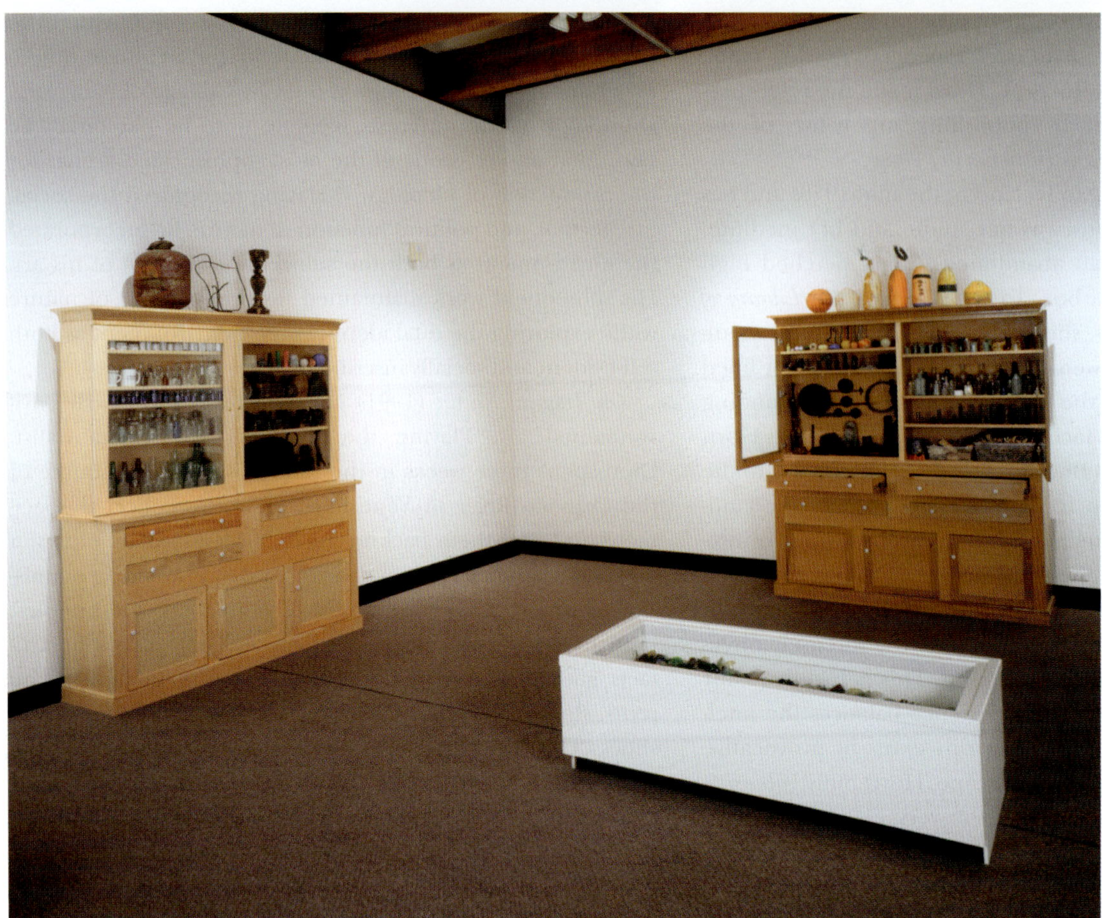

11.7 Mark Dion, *New England Digs*, 2001. Mixed media. Courtesy the artist and Tanya Bonakdar Gallery, New York.

contemporary archeological display. This encounter with the past, similar to the dialogue with nature presented in *On Tropical Nature*, asks us to reflect on the customary means by which museums and viewers turn experience of the world into knowledge.

Through his art and statements Dion makes it clear that his work is driven by experience and wonder. No amount of theoretical analysis and self-scrutiny is allowed to overwhelm the record of insect, plant, animal, and human life his work presents. Provoked by Dion's talk of wonder, Kwon asked him rather pointedly, "How do you provoke a sense of the marvelous or generate curiosity in our day and age?" Dion's response was to simply cite truth and biodiversity, and the opportunity to experience both is nowhere more on display than in his *Vivarium Neukom* (2004–06) (**fig. 11.8**) in Olympic Park, Seattle, Washington.[31] The *Vivarium* is a fallen 60-foot western hemlock tree, known as a nurse log, housed in a climate-controlled enclosure that simulates its original ecosystem. The tree, found in an area of old-growth forest near Seattle, began its life about the time the city was settled by European explorers. When such massive trees expired in the then-thickly forested region, they became hosts to vibrant ecosystems that perpetuated the development of the forest. Now, of course, the forest has been largely cleared for lumber and urban development. Dion found his particular hemlock tree on protected land, where it had been resting for over a decade. It was already home to a variety of wildlife. For the work, Dion carefully transported the tree and the life growing under its protection to the renovated Seattle waterfront. The *Vivarium* now provides visitors with an encounter with a cross section of nature, functioning as it would in the forest.

Docents and kiosks provide the educational component in the *Vivarium*, but it is the effect of defamiliarization that is the work's most singular achievement. Inside the room, Dion has installed green tinted-glass roofing panels to simulate the effect of light passing through the canopy of the forest. The space mimics the shape of the fallen tree with its towering root system and tapering trunk. State-of-the-art water-filtration and temperature-control systems replicate the atmosphere of the forest. In an urban park, however, just yards away from a major road intersection and railroad tracks, the features that emulate the forest "enhance the uncanniness of nature," as Dion describes it.[32] The emerald light and moist air are otherworldly. The angular plan of the architecture creates a sense of acceleration as one looks down the length of the trunk lying prone on its plinth like a massive cadaver on an examination table. Visitors look directly into the decaying body of the hemlock as though they were among the species living off the tree. True to the Romantic tradition, there is strong sense of the sublime here, but Dion's space is colored by the absurdity and even the cruelty of putting a tree on life support. The artist is quick to point out the tragic and farcical element of the project. The

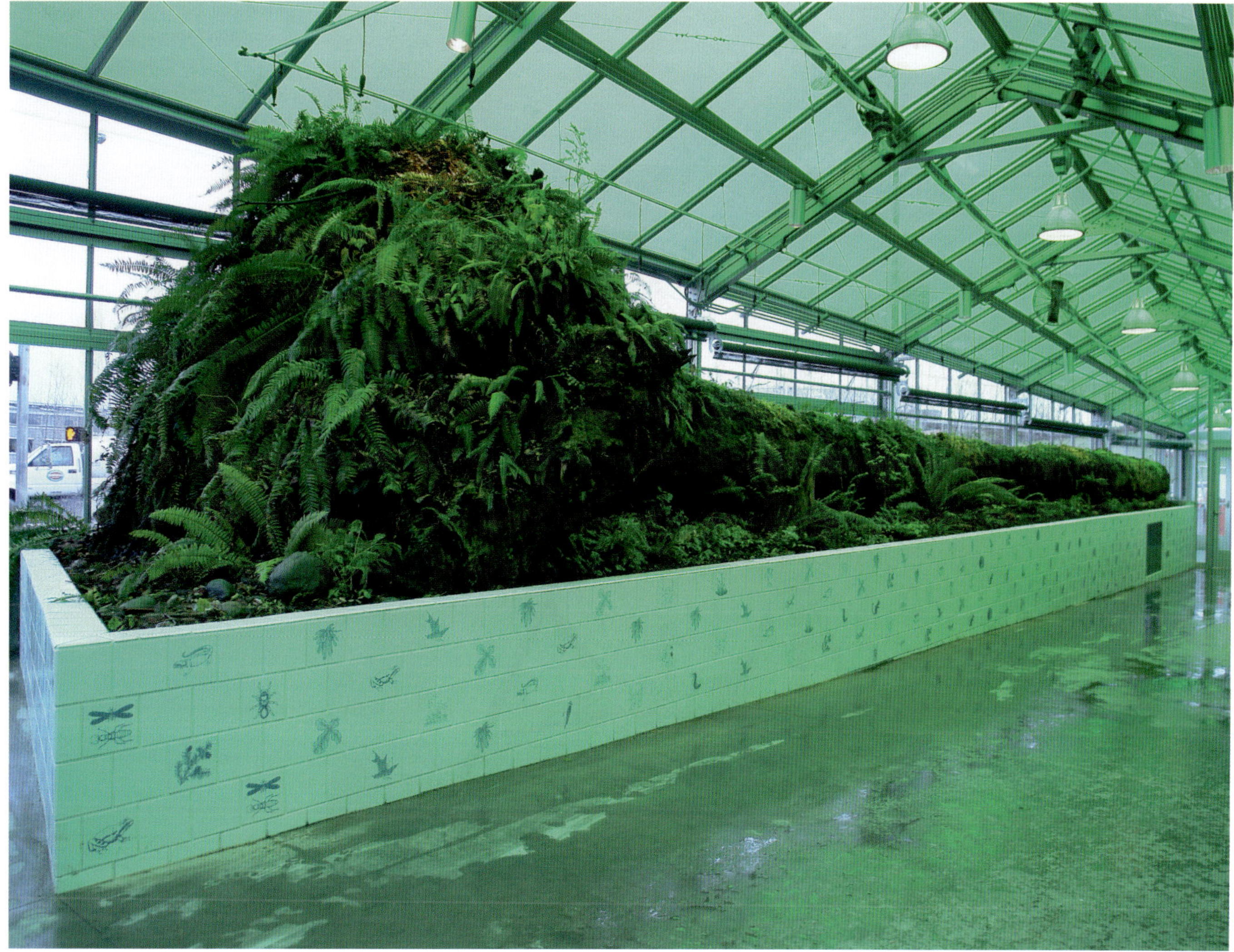

11.8 Mark Dion, ***Vivarium Neukom***, 2004–06. Hemlock tree. Greenhouse length 80' (24.38 m). Olympic Park, Seattle. Seattle Art Museum. © Mark Dion.

Vivarium can sustain the nurse log for decades, but bringing the tree under the protection of society as an object of artistic and educational interest limits its productive capacity. Isolated from the ecosystem of the forest, the hemlock tree can display its role as host to a complex ecosystem, but cannot contribute to the environment from which it came. Dion has created a space in which one can be educated about the environment, but in which one is also overwhelmed by the strange beauty of entering botanical time and arboreal space. In his notes, he wrote: "This is a knock-out piece, with an accessible core and a rich poetic resonance."[33] The poetry of Dion's work addresses nature as defined and confined by human actions, as well as as an ecological phenomenon beyond the grasp of comprehension.

Tom Sachs

Tom Sachs (b. 1966) entered the New York art scene in the late 1990s with an interest in social constructions of knowledge and power quite different than those of Dion's biologists and curators. His first exhibitions included, among other things, fully functional hand-built guns. His most notorious show ensured his then-gallerist, Mary Boone, was arrested on weapons-possession charges. The guns, like all of Sachs's subsequent work, were constructed from found materials in a process he called "American Bricolage." Sachs credits British sculptor Richard Wentworth (b. 1947), whom he encountered in London while studying architecture in the late 1980s, with inspiring his practice. Wentworth's work celebrates "Making do and getting by," by which he means the contingent, *ad hoc*, and DIY solutions we devise when faced with immediate problems and are pressed for time and money. No effort is made to hide the mechanics of an object or to beautify it. Sachs has been rather explicit about embracing Wentworth's pragmatism in his own practice. His rules, circulated in one of his self-published manuals, include "Paint first, cut second" and "Be thorough … no detail should be left unacknowledged or unattended." These insure that he, his assistants, and the viewer are continually attentive to the processes of making.[34] In the guns, we see how the wood—salvaged from police barricades—fits together with

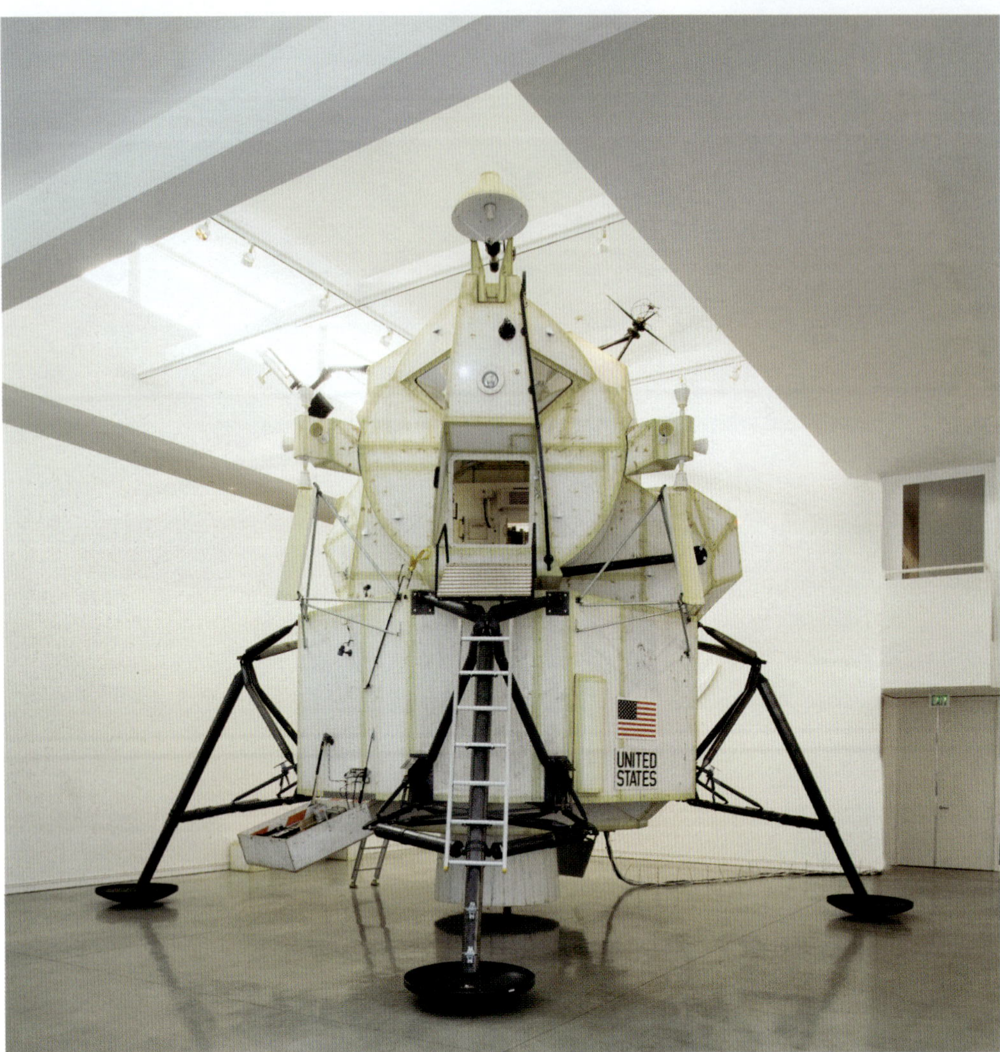

11.9 Tom Sachs, *Apollo Lunar Excursion Module (LEM)*, 2007–2012. Installation. Courtesy the artist.

springs, screws, and pipes purchased from a hardware store. *Apollo Lunar Excursion Module (LEM)* (2007–12) (**fig. 11.9**), a 1:1 scale model of the Apollo 11 Lunar Exploration Module with customized Mission Control, displays the plywood, PVC piping, extension cords, iPods, and police barricade lumber that keep the work together and functioning. These sculptures and installations become models for the transformation of thought into action and desire into objects. They are also explorations of the myths of U.S. identity in which bootstrap resourcefulness and rugged individualism meet an uneasy balance between idealism and violence.

Sachs's Space Program captures the breadth and depth of his project and returns our discussion to the intersections of nature and culture, science and art. In addition to the *Lunar Excursion Module,* this work includes space suits with functional circulation and filtration systems, provisions, reconnaissance and communication devices, shotguns, side arms, and headquarters for technicians operating outside the vehicle. A wall of monitors in Mission Control connected to closed circuit television (CCTV) cameras in and on the *Lunar Excursion Module* displays all parts of the voyage. Sachs uses a wide variety of televisual technology. In addition to the bank of monitors, there are fully functioning handmade Hasselblad cameras such as were on board the actual NASA Lunar Exploration Module, a variety of interior monitors for the astronauts, and a landing computer outfitted with the 1979 Atari video game *Lunar Lander.* The entire mission has also been edited into a short film, available for viewing online. When Sachs's Space Program was shown at the Gagosian Gallery in Los Angeles, after the exterior-mounted *Modular Equipment Stowage Assembly* of the *LEM* had opened and one of the Hasselblads had begun taking photographs, Sachs's team dug up samples of the gallery floor. Pieces of concrete were collected, catalogued, and preserved. Watching the scene, the viewer marvels over Sachs's encyclopedic knowledge of NASA's work and the innumerable ways in which he re-creates its solutions. The problem facing NASA was putting a man on the moon. Sachs's Space Program addresses quite different circumstances and in so doing raises the question: What exactly is being simulated?

The Apollo space program of the 1960s and early 1970s expressed the limitless reach of the national imagination and provided evidence of U.S. ingenuity. For many of Sachs's generation, the image of Neil Armstrong stepping onto the lunar surface suggested a future full of possibilities. His Space Program generates the kind of awe one feels

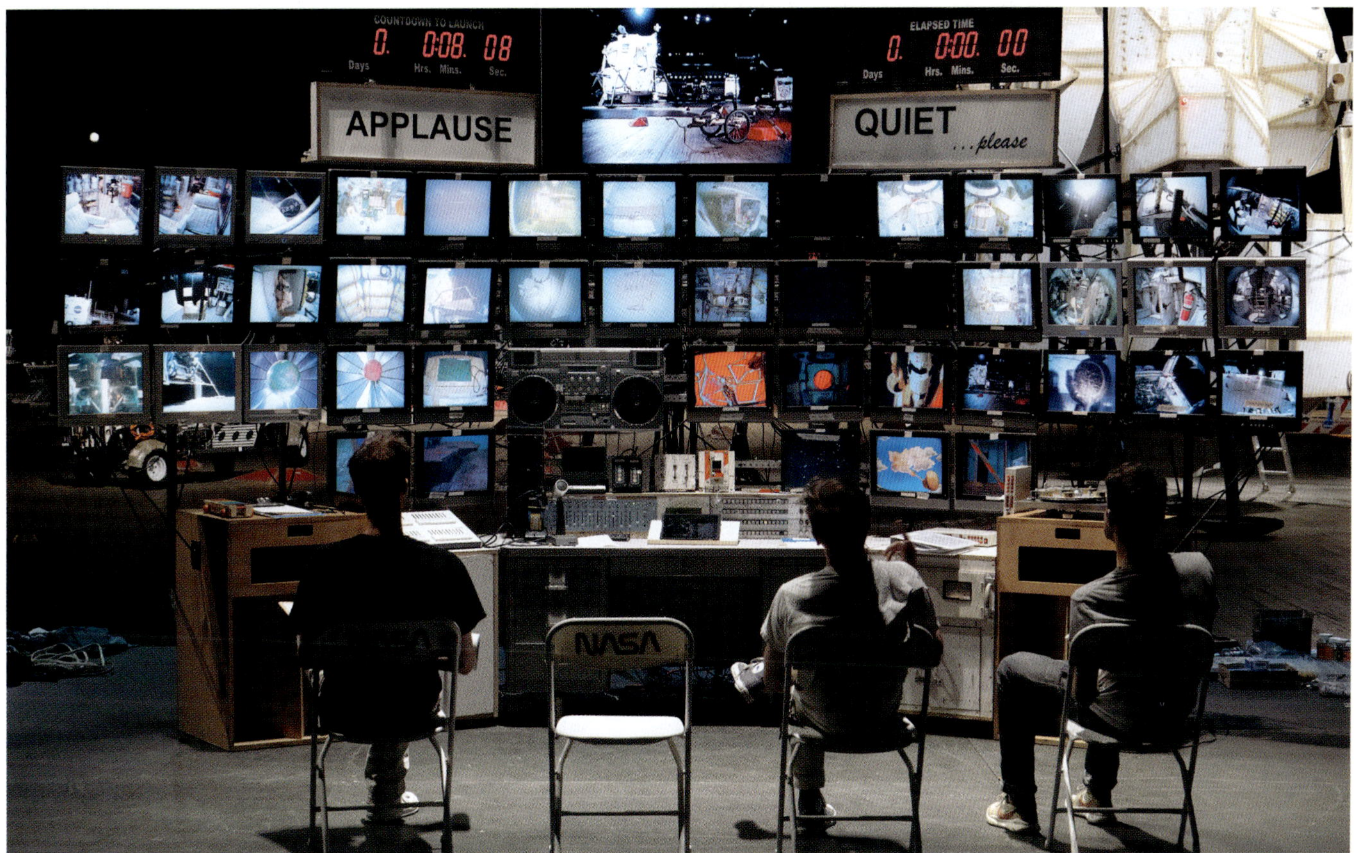

11.10 Tom Sachs, Installation view of Mission Control (2007–12) at *Space Program 2.0: MARS*, 2012. Courtesy the artist.

encountering the real relics of manned space flights at the National Air and Space Museum in Washington, D.C. With cargo units filled with Jack Daniel's whiskey, baked beans, cigarettes, a collection of LPs, and a turntable, however, it's clear that this voyage isn't going to end in the Sea of Tranquility. Outfitting his meticulously fabricated details of space travel with accouterments of distinctly earthly pleasures, Sachs invites reflection on the meaning the Apollo mission had for us here on Earth. In the spring of 2012, Sachs's *Space Program 2.0: MARS* touched down on Mars with a mission to find life (**fig. 11.10**). Convinced by engineers at the Jet Propulsion Lab to abandon a second voyage to the moon and to follow President Barack Obama's orders to direct attention to the red planet instead, Sachs set about repurposing as much of his lunar technology as possible and investigating what was required for the new journey. Less an anthropological and somewhat nostalgic expedition through the science of the past, the Martian mission involves a close look at what we now know about space travel. Sachs has held whiteboard sessions detailing the challenges of reaching, orbiting, entering, and exiting Martian airspace, as well as surviving on the planet's surface. Because of the timing of the orbits of Earth and Mars, once an expedition team reaches its destination it has to remain there for nearly a year until it is possible to return. The landing took place at the Armory building on the Upper East Side of Manhattan, where Neto's *Anthropodino* had been installed a few years earlier, and at least some familiar forms of life were on hand to witness it. Sachs's Space Program, like the smallest of his objects, reminds the viewer that science and technology are ultimately instances of making do and getting by, inspired by and shaped according to the needs, desires, and limitations of the here-and-now.

Experience Observed

Experience in the work discussed thus far has been variously intimate, sensual, humorous, and intellectual. Artists have striven to connect viewers to a renewed sense of themselves and others, and have drawn attention to our environment or even to outer space. There are times when the viewer's involvement is limited, but even then we are reminded by the work that its primary aim is not representational. We are not invited into *Your colour memory* to see the colors Eliasson has created, but to experience their effect. Likewise, though Sachs's *Space Program 2.0: MARS* as a model has much to say about the meaning of the NASA space program, it is a fully independent project, justified not by its resemblance to the JPL or NASA experiments but by the satisfactory execution of its own mission. Such investments in the production of experiences in the museum, however, like any traditional works of art, have the side effect of prioritizing the spaces of art over those of life. By contrast, the

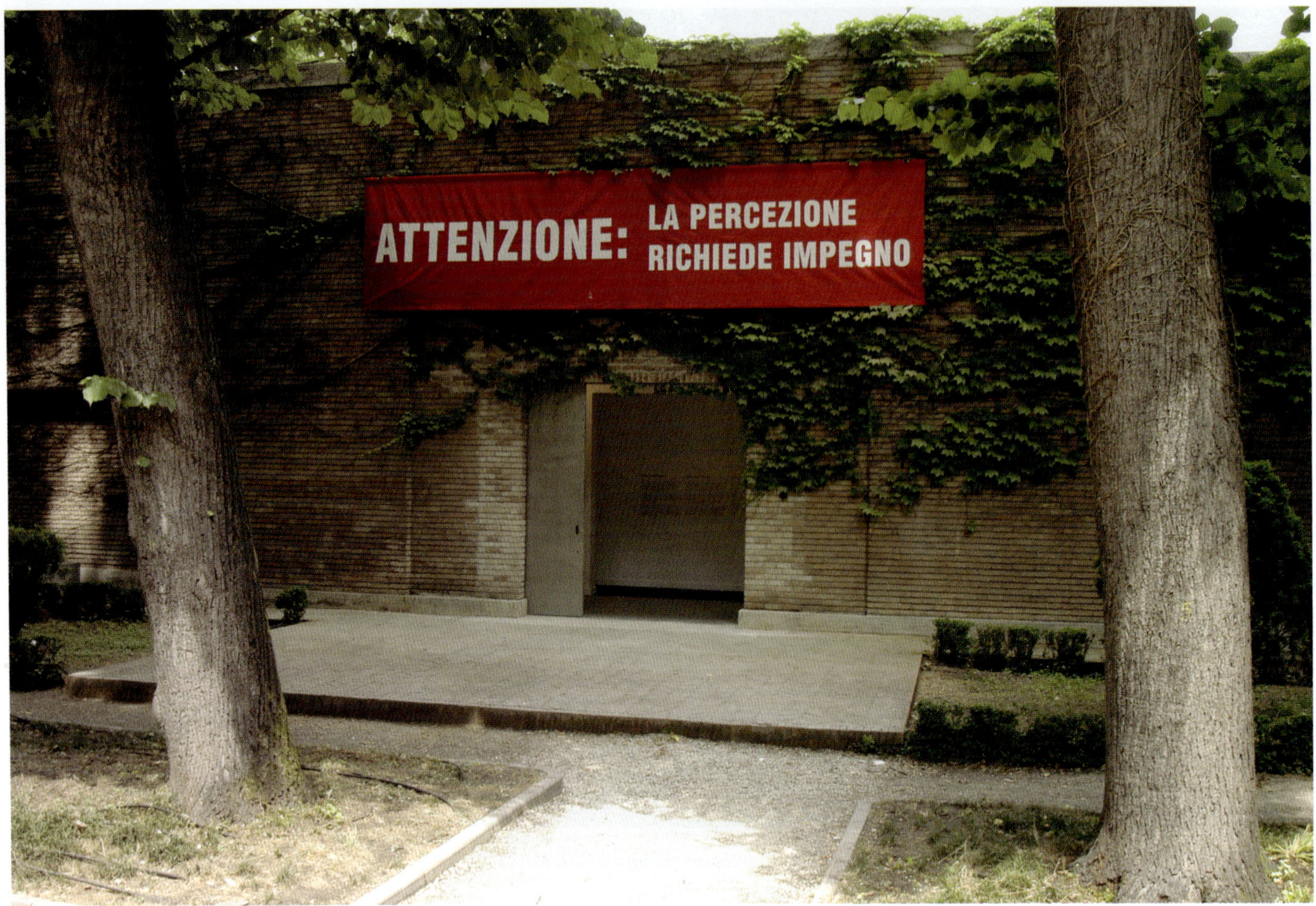

11.11 Antoni Muntadas *On Translation: Warning*, 1999–2005. Installation at the Spanish Pavilion, Venice Biennale, 2005. Courtesy the artist.

artists discussed in the final portion of this book develop a variety of strategies to look at how we experience our lives outside the gallery. These works address questions of surveillance and power in the first section, and the media and representation in the second. This art responds in different ways to the injunction that Spanish video and installation artist Antoni Muntadas (b. 1942) has plastered on billboards and museums: "Warning: Perception requires Involvement" (**fig. 11.11**).

Thomas Hirschhorn

The work of Thomas Hirschhorn (b. 1957) can be seen as a political inquiry into the operations of contemporary culture and a philosophical version of Sachs's and Wentworth's making do and getting by. Filled with allusions to political and critical theory, intellectual history, and philosophy, Hirschhorn's art provides a centrifugal invitation to reimagine the world. *Cavemanman* (2002) (**fig. 11.12**), the result of intensive accumulation and apparently manic assemblage characterized as much by haste as by desire, typifies Hirschhorn's art. For the piece, the artist and a team of assistants transformed a gallery into corridors and caves of cardboard, packing tape, and two-by-fours. White walls disappeared and the new surfaces were quickly covered with graffiti and posters that made it look like a mix of the Paleolithic-era Lascaux Caves in France, contemporary Times Square, and a college dorm room. Books on political theory, globalization, economics, and culture lined shelves hung too high to be reached. Gargantuan versions of similar texts lay stacked on the cave floors. Charts, tables, and pages copied from essays were plastered on the walls. Empty beer and soda cans littered the floor. Finally, there were bodies: aluminum foil-covered mannequins and cardboard cutouts, many headless and most connected to each other and the walls with twists of foil. Explosive charges, made of paper and foil, were laid throughout the rooms and connected to the texts and figures. Hirschhorn has described *Cavemanman* as the abandoned home of a reclusive philosopher who has indulged in his "all-consuming preoccupation with the achievement of equality between all human beings, all over the world."[35] "1 Man = 1 Man" is scrawled over and over throughout the rooms, expressing the democratic impulse of Hirschhorn's philosopher. The philosophical clutter recalls Ilya Kabakov's *The Man Who Flew into Space from His Apartment* (see fig. 8.1). Rather than retreating from the precise Soviet experience of Kabakov's Man, however, Hirschhorn's philosopher appears to have sought respite and resolution from a more generalized and globalized condition.

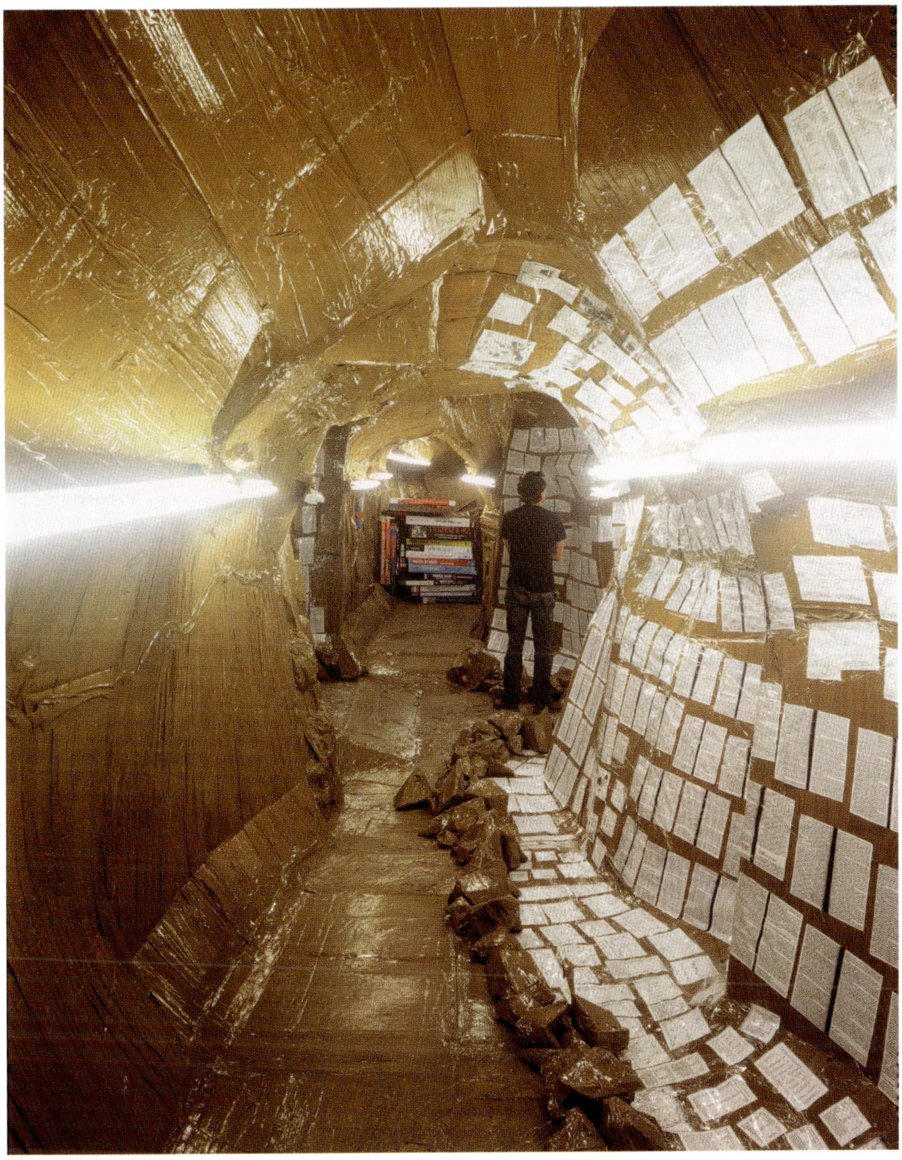

11.12 Thomas Hirschhorn, ***Cavemanman***, 2002. Mixed media installation. Barbara Gladstone Gallery, New York.

The formal and intellectual excess of *Cavemanman* is typical of Hirschhorn's work. It presents his signature mix of heady intellectual content—books in the cave are authored by the likes of Noam Chomsky, Simone Weil, Alexis de Tocqueville—and mass-cultural favorites represented by posters of The Beatles, Madonna, and Che Guevara. Even more important than the intellectual and political arguments placed in front of the viewer is the continual presentation of options of all sorts—spatial and visual as well as political and intellectual. This collision of information is based on Hirschhorn's insistent rejection of singularity of any sort, particularly representational. For every crisis, event, or idea that he addresses, he collects many images. Discussing his work with art historian Benjamin H.D. Buchloh, Hirschhorn takes the example of the September 11, 2001 attacks on the World Trade Center in New York:

> I don't believe in the superiority of the single image because I know that the single image is utilized as a tool of exerting power. Let's take the example of 9/11—this single image of the collapsing towers, and the resulting ruins—and how this single image wants to have power over me. Although we know perfectly well that there are ruins in Grozny, and that there are ruins in Palestine, and that there are ruins all over the world, this picture alone claims to have the greatest power over me. I want to combat this power by producing a huge number of other images.[36]

Hirschhorn seeks to undermine the hegemonic power of the isolated single image with a multiplicity of representations—not to reduce the consequences of any one tragedy or to conflate New York, Grozny, and Gaza, but rather to put the crises of contemporary life in context. Hirschhorn's aim is to demonstrate that there are relationships between the different ruins and to initiate a dialogue between writers who have thought about such things and viewers who step into and around Hirschhorn's work.

Like Sachs and Eliasson, Hirschhorn deliberately reveals his process. However, the wonder of *Space Program 2.0: MARS*

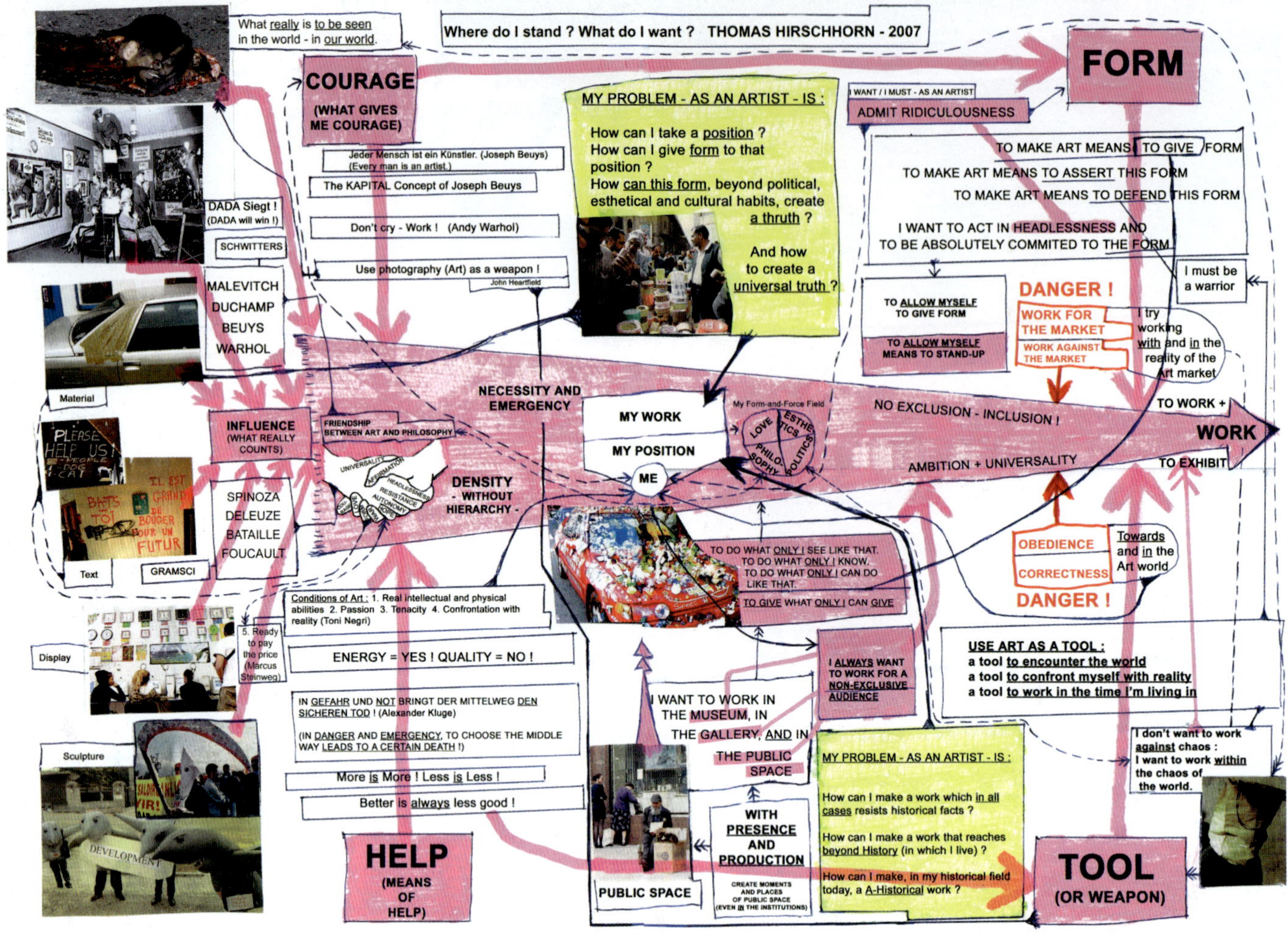

11.13 Thomas Hirschhorn, *Where Do I Stand? What Do I Want?*, 2007. Mixed media. Courtesy the artist.

or *Your strange certainty still kept* is irrelevant to *Cavemanman.* Mind, body, and world come together in the latter with little mystery. Hirschhorn's materials have no inherent value and his technique requires no special skills. "Quality, no! Energy, yes!" he often says. The cave, with its accumulation of objects and ideas knit together in a precarious network of tape and foil, both mimics Hirschhorn's process of wrestling with ideas and provides space for active reflection. "I want to implicate the viewer," he says, "not so much in my work as in the issues that my work deals with. I hope that I can make people think and relate to the world as human beings."[37] The goal of reflection, for Hirschhorn, is change. He explains: "Without serious thought there obviously can't be any meaningful political action, and I hope that I can make people feel involved in the world."[38] Every object, book, poster, and scrap of cardboard has a link to reality. Thus, thinking about *Cavemanman* or any of Hirschhorn's work is necessarily a matter of both art and life. Without the signs of value imparted by precious materials, white-walled galleries, or directive artist's statements, viewers are left to confront the parts of the work and the juxtapositions Hirschhorn creates on their own. Hirschhorn's manifesto *Where Do I Stand? What Do I Want?* (2007) (**fig. 11.13**) spells out the power of art to create "density without hierarchy," "ambition + universality," and "truth."[39]

Hasan M. Elahi

One of the most common, if often invisible, instances of politics intruding upon daily experience is state- and corporate-sponsored surveillance, and numerous artists have taken this infringement on privacy as the subject of their work. Though surveillance art, focusing on the technology, imagery, and infrastructure of covert observation of public and private spaces, was established by the late 1990s, it took on a particular urgency after the September 11, 2001 attacks on the World Trade Center in New York and the Pentagon in Washington, D.C., when local and national governments as well as private organizations in the U.S. and Europe dramatically increased their use of CCTV surveillance of public space. Legislation such as the U.S. Patriot Act authorized less visible forms of intrusion, and restrictions were tightened worldwide on travel, immigration, and the granting of visas and asylum.

U.S. video and new-media artist Hasan M. Elahi (b. 1972) captured the post-September 11 anxiety in his web-based

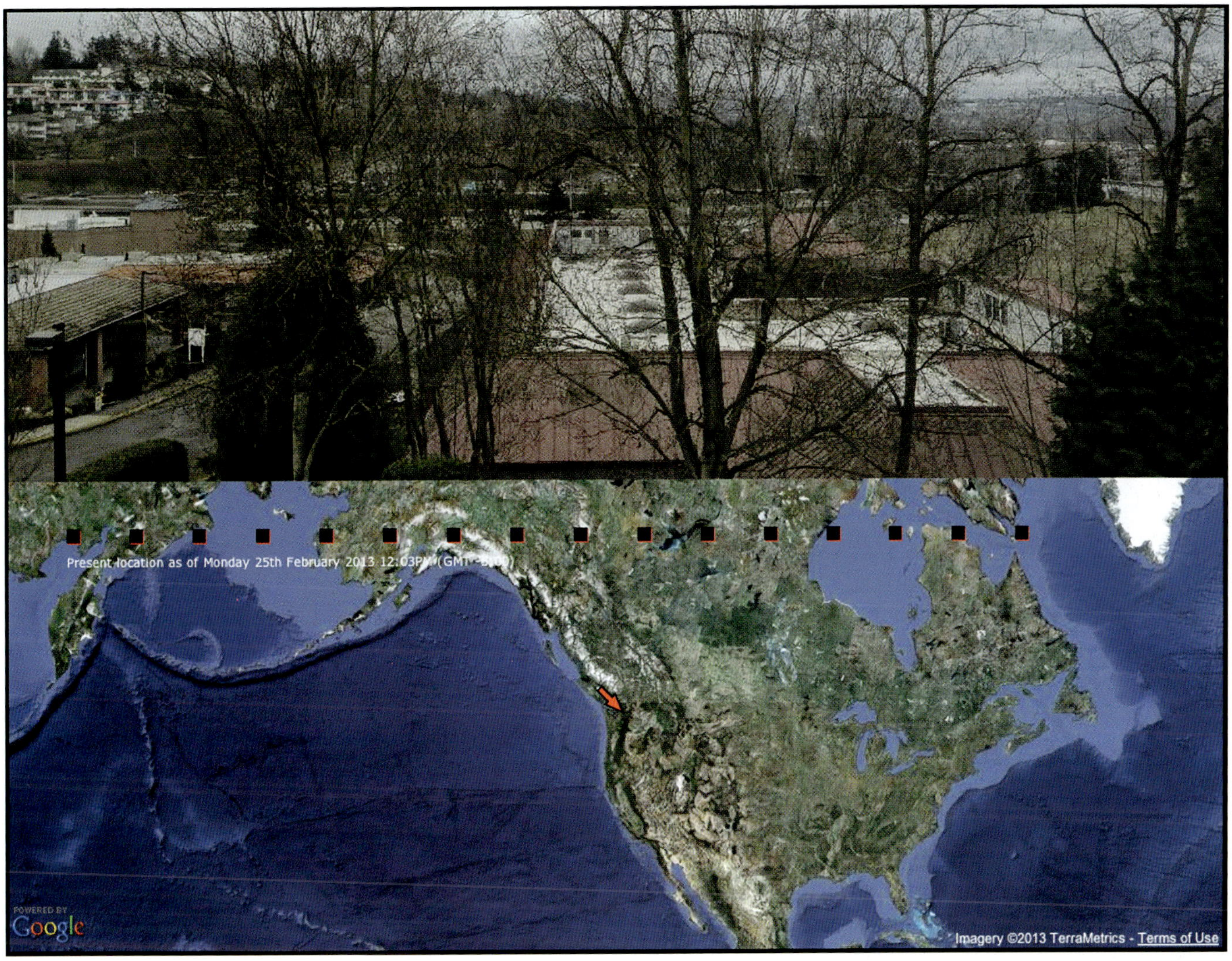

11.14 Hasan M. Elahi, *Tracking Transience: The Orwell Project*, 2003–ongoing. Blog trackingtransience.net, access date February 25, 2013. The six small images are archive images. Courtesy the artist.

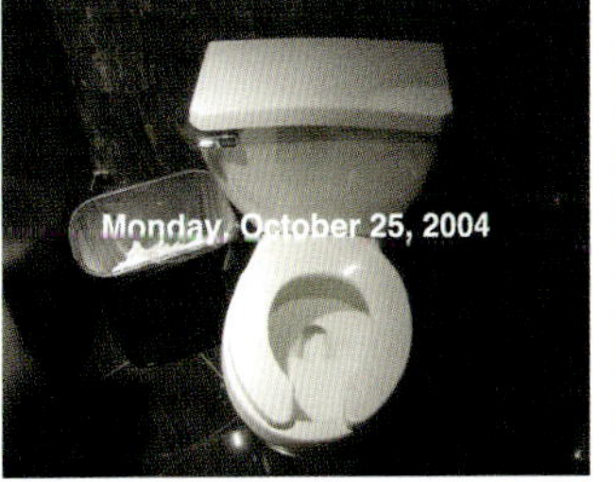

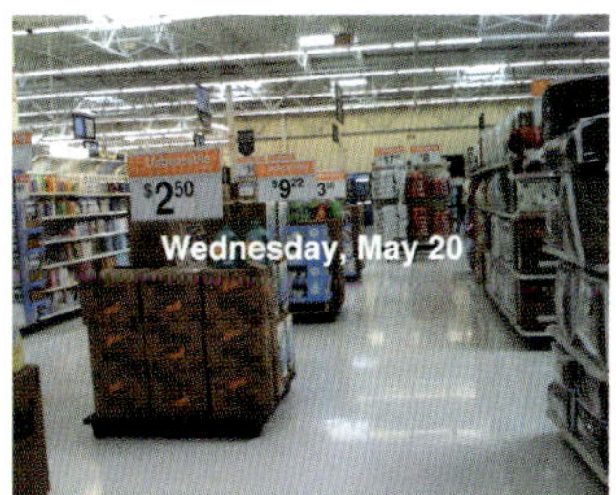

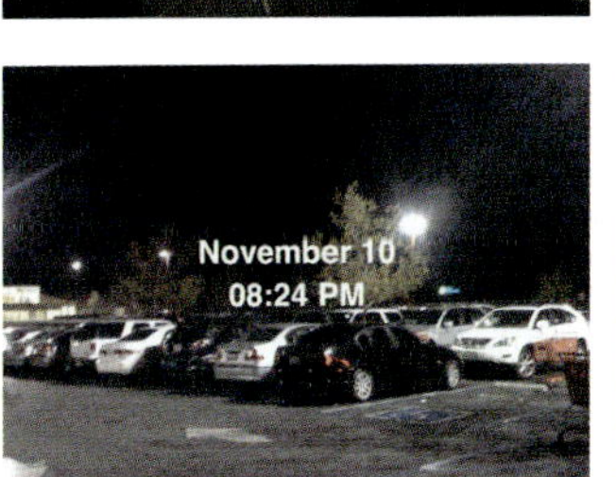

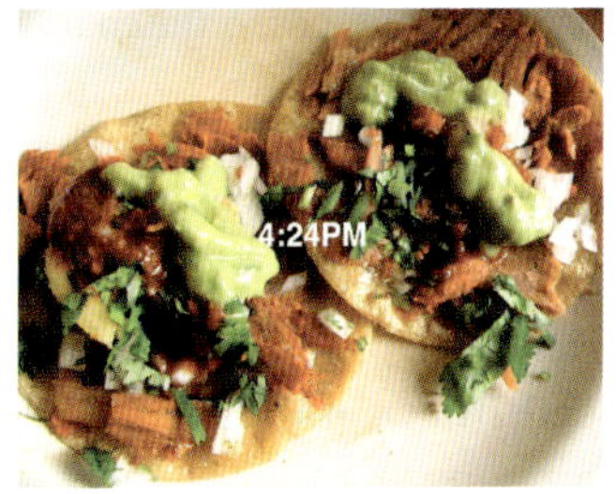

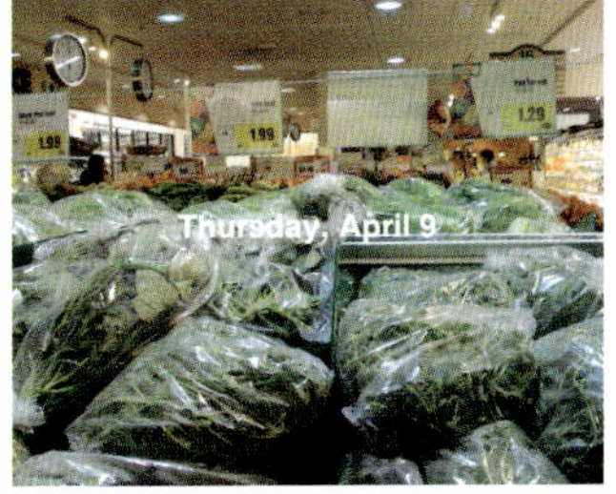

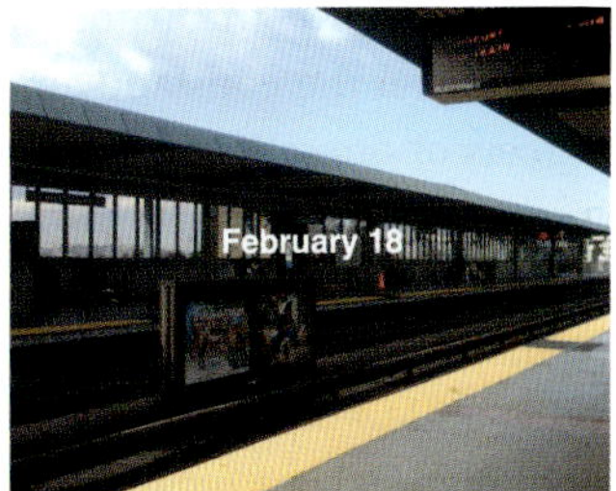

Tracking Transience: The Orwell Project (2003–ongoing) (**fig. 11.14**). Returning to the U.S. from the Netherlands in June 2002, Elahi was detained by the Federal Bureau of Investigation on suspicion of engaging in terrorist activities. Born in Bangladesh, Elahi was interrogated regarding his travels abroad and his activities around the time of the September 11 attacks. By way of response, he decided to turn surveillance technologies on himself to create a twenty-four-hour alibi for himself. He began recording nearly every aspect of his life, maintaining a log of all the credit-card transactions and phone calls he made and even taking photographs of his meals and the toilets he used. He also developed software that used Global Positioning System (GPS) satellites to document his whereabouts and upload details to the publicly accessible website, trackingtransience.net. The logs of Elahi's website indicate it has had many visits from the FBI and even from the President's office. Elahi mines this database of information and images to create additional video and installation work, also under the title *Tracking Transience: The Orwell Project*, that prompts reflection on the afterlife of

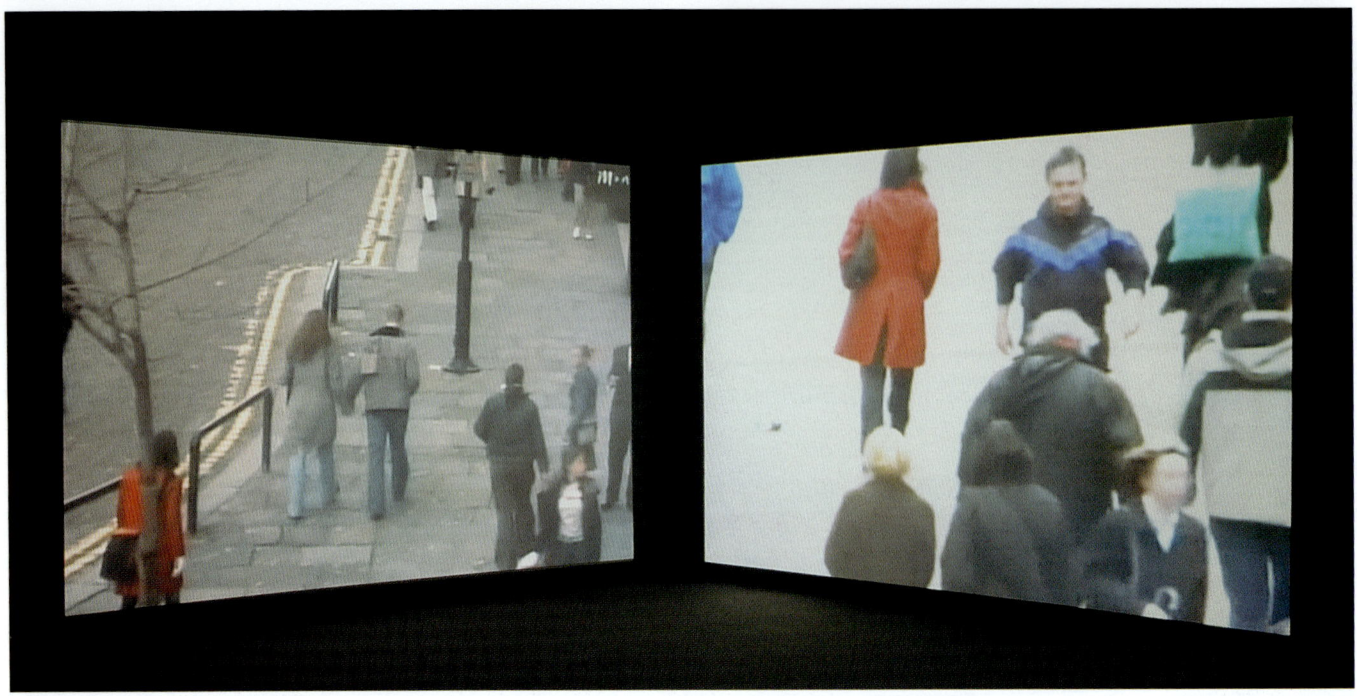

11.15 Jill Magid, ***Evidence Locker***, 2004. Film stills. DVD, edited CCTV footage and audio, 18 minutes. Courtesy of the artist and Yvon Lambert.

the Panopticon (see Chapter 5) and the production of self under conditions of constant observation. The excessiveness of his project suggests that relinquishing privacy is not the key to security. If everyone facilitated the state's scrutiny of our lives in this way, the quantity of data would overwhelm the system. A digital uprising, overwhelming the authorities through data overload, however, is not the point of Elahi's work. The character of life for millions of people has been transformed in the last decades. For everything from socializing to protesting, the Internet and cell-phone technology have opened up expansive new networks. These technologies, as Elahi's work suggests, are as useful for keeping track of us as they are for facilitating our connections. Cell phones, GPS devices, credit cards, key cards, shopping cards, even library cards produce new forms of visibility. *Tracking Transience* invites us to pay attention to this virtual experience and its consequences in the material world.

Jill Magid

Video artist and writer Jill Magid (b. 1973) has noted of the increase in municipality-sponsored surveillance: "The camera in its static position seems to favor its context over the pedestrians passing though it. It seems to say: The city is permanent, the civilian ephemeral."[40] Magid has taken advantage of the theatrical potential of this situation to become an actor on the constantly monitored urban stage. There are aspects of oneself, she explains, that are only accessible if we internalize the role of the observer. Role-playing, a central aspect of identity theories in the 1990s, is the conceptual and formal foundation of *Evidence Locker* (2004) (**fig. 11.15**), a video and web project that Magid created for the 2004 Liverpool Biennial in England.

To begin, Magid, like Elahi, established herself as the target of surveillance. She enlisted the help of City Watch, a surveillance system of over 200 CCTV cameras that monitor public spaces in Liverpool. She dressed in red so she would be easy to spot and maintained contact with an operator who followed her movements through the city. We see her sitting at a café, walking through the streets, and often looking up at the cameras. In one segment she is on the phone with the camera operator and closes her eyes as we hear his voice guide her slowly through a crowd. City Watch accumulates footage in thirty-one-day blocks that are then archived in an evidence locker for seven years. Magid's segments have themselves become part of the public record, available in thirty-one short segments accessible via evidencelocker.net. Each episode is accompanied by a letter to the operator, reporting her daily activities in detail far exceeding what is visible in the video. Magid's missives are personal and at times read like love letters. In making *Evidence Locker*, she reported: "My body became part of the system ... It was the most intimate experience of my life."[41] Despite being the hero of the story, Magid is not the sole surrogate for the viewer. One of the City Watch operators develops a prominent supporting role, becoming, as the letters reveal, an object of the artist's affection. She even meets him toward the end of the performance. Magid notes: "Some viewers identify with the controller and some identify with me."[42] *Evidence Locker*, like much of Magid's work, explores the effects of surveillance on subjectivity and relationships in contemporary life.

The Institute of Applied Autonomy

Elahi and Magid both use the means of surveillance to connect with others, Elahi reaching out through his website

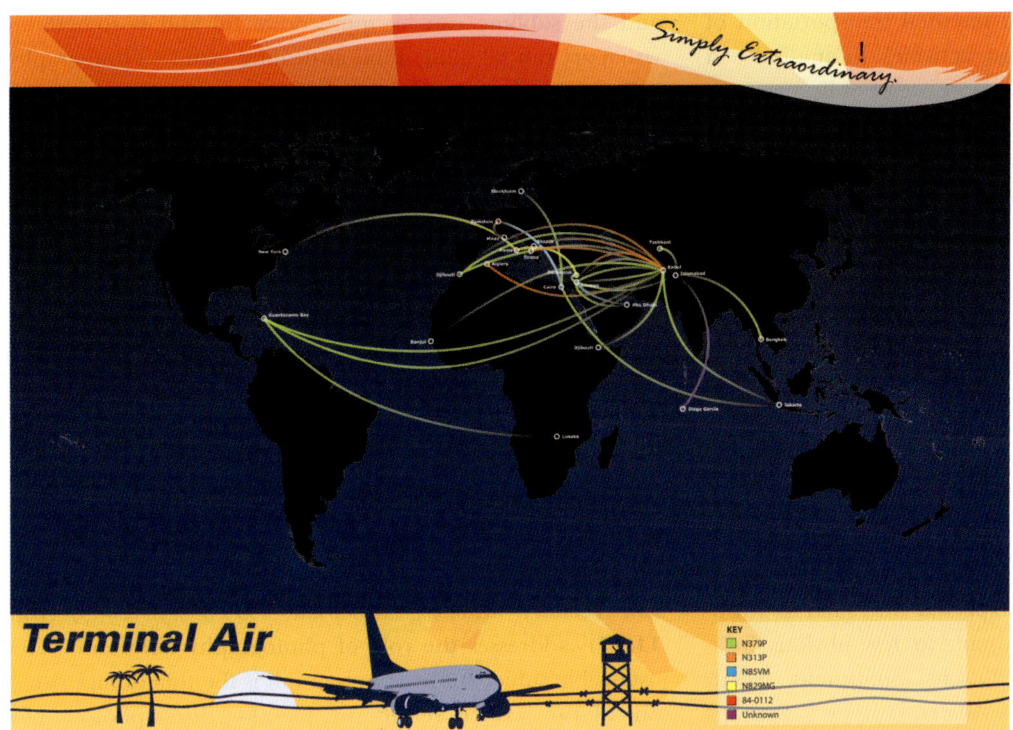

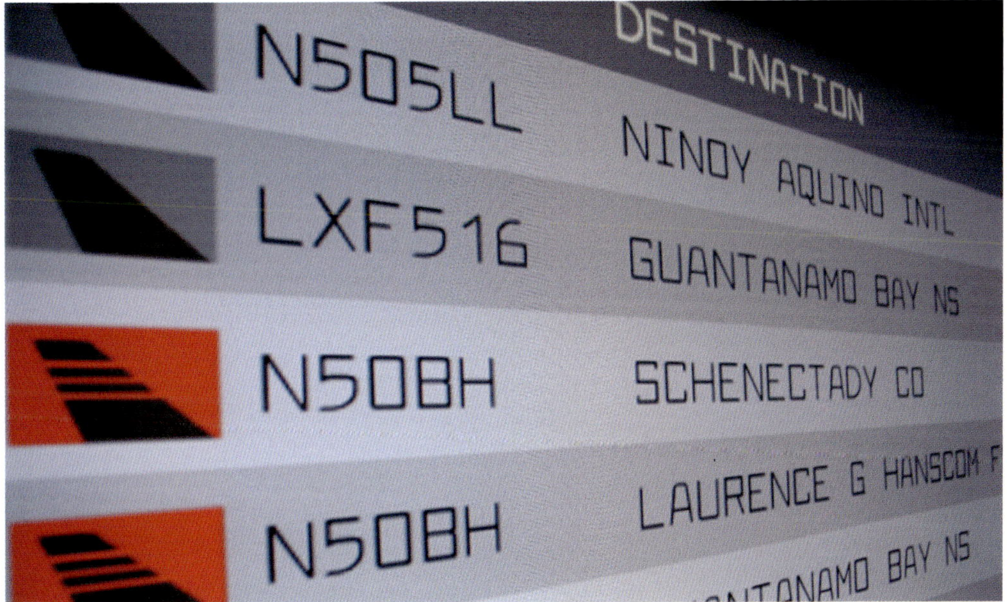

11.16 Institute of Applied Autonomy with Trevor Paglen, *Terminal Air*, 2007. Screen grab and details of air-traffic tracking program. Courtesy the artist.

and Magid letting the cameras lead her to a brief meeting with one of her watchers. These limited and fleeting moments of contact, however, ultimately serve to emphasize the isolation inherent in a culture of surveillance. The Institute of Applied Autonomy (IAA) proposes a collective public with the desire to overcome the isolating function of surveillance. Founded in 1998, the IAA is a research and development organization "dedicated to the cause of individual and collective self-determination." It creates and shares "technologies which extend the autonomy of human activists."[43] IAA hardware and software are designed to allow the public to challenge state and corporate control of technologies of surveillance and secrecy. Its *iSee* (2001) is an interactive map that allows users to plot routes through Manhattan that avoid CCTV cameras. In fact, there is almost no way to cross Manhattan without being observed by devices in banks, corporate offices, and even lumber yards. The maps generated by *iSee* can be used for navigating the island relatively unseen, but are just as significant for illustrating the degree to which public space is monitored and revealing what properties are being most carefully observed.

If *iSee* is directed at subverting surveillance and reclaiming urban space, *Terminal Air* (2007) (**fig. 11.16**) attempts to repurpose the technologies of surveillance to undermine state secrecy. The program logs the movements of airplanes that have been used by the United States government for extraordinary rendition, one of the most controversial practices of George W. Bush's "War on Terror"-related foreign policy, which involves the undocumented transportation of individuals suspected of terrorist activities to undisclosed locations outside the U.S. for the purpose of enlisting interrogation procedures that violate U.S. law. The IAA is limited in its ability to track this clandestine practice. Nonetheless, *Terminal Air* trains a public eye on its mechanisms.

Trevor Paglen

IAA created *Terminal Air* in collaboration with geographer and photographer Trevor Paglen (b. 1974), whose projects highlight the aesthetic and political applications of technologies of observation. Paglen has found and photographed classified military bases, spy satellites, and secret CIA prisons, as well as the geography of extraordinary rendition, including the airplanes tracked in *Terminal Air*, law offices, administrative office buildings, airports, and detention facilities.[44] This "American geography of secrecy" extends, as Paglen notes, all over the world, from expected sites such as Washington, D.C. and Kabul, Afganistan, to less obvious locations such as Dedham, Massachusetts, Smithfield, North Carolina, Rabat, Morocco, and Adana, Turkey.[45] Perhaps the most shocking feature of Paglen's work is that the vast networks of covert operations he has uncovered have been found through ordinary means. He explains: "This secret state has to intersect the visible world in all sorts of different places, because it can't be a completely self-contained thing, and those intersections … in the materiality of the surface of the earth" can be seen and represented.[46] While researching these intersections, Paglen reaches out to plane-spotters who log the comings and goings of aircraft all over the world, similar groups of satellite observers, and amateur investigators of all sorts who maintain records, often online. Like Paglen, these communities are alert for aberrations such as planes landing in irregular locations and at odd times or objects orbiting the Earth outside registered flight paths. Combining research, travel, and the use of telescopic lenses, Paglen's oeuvre serves as an archive of information he has been able to uncover about the Black Ops run by the U.S. government.

Paglen diverges from the plane-spotters or IAA in his commitment to exceeding a documentary or political function and creating a critical engagement with the history of art and aesthetics. He is particularly interested in the power of art as a tool to encounter the sublime, defined by Paglen as "those moments where we can sense that we cannot sense, let alone understand something."[47] In response to reaching the limits of understanding, one has recourse, Paglen asserts, to "aesthetics," which have "often been linked to notions of freedom: ambiguity and the sublime can be quite powerful and is something visual art can be quite good at dealing with."[48] Photography is Paglen's primary tool for pushing the limits of understanding, though it is one toward which he shows great skepticism. His *Limit Telephotography* presents the discrepancy between the promise of photography to reveal the truth and its inherent limits. For these works, Paglen points telescopic lenses developed for photographing outer space at classified military sites up to 40 miles away. The images indubitably show soldiers and military operations but, despite their supposedly extraterrestrial powers, the cameras produce often blurry and awkwardly cropped results that confirm little else. The photographs provide only partial knowledge—photographing the secret world does not exactly expose its secrets in detail.

Paglen's *The Other Night Sky*, a series begun in 2007 and including *DMSP 5B/F4 from Pyramid Lake Indian Reservation (Military Meteorological Satellite; 1973-054A)* (2009) (**fig. 11.17**), addresses the role of photography differently. The ostensible subject of the photograph is the tufa domes rising out of the lake. It recalls nineteenth-century photographs

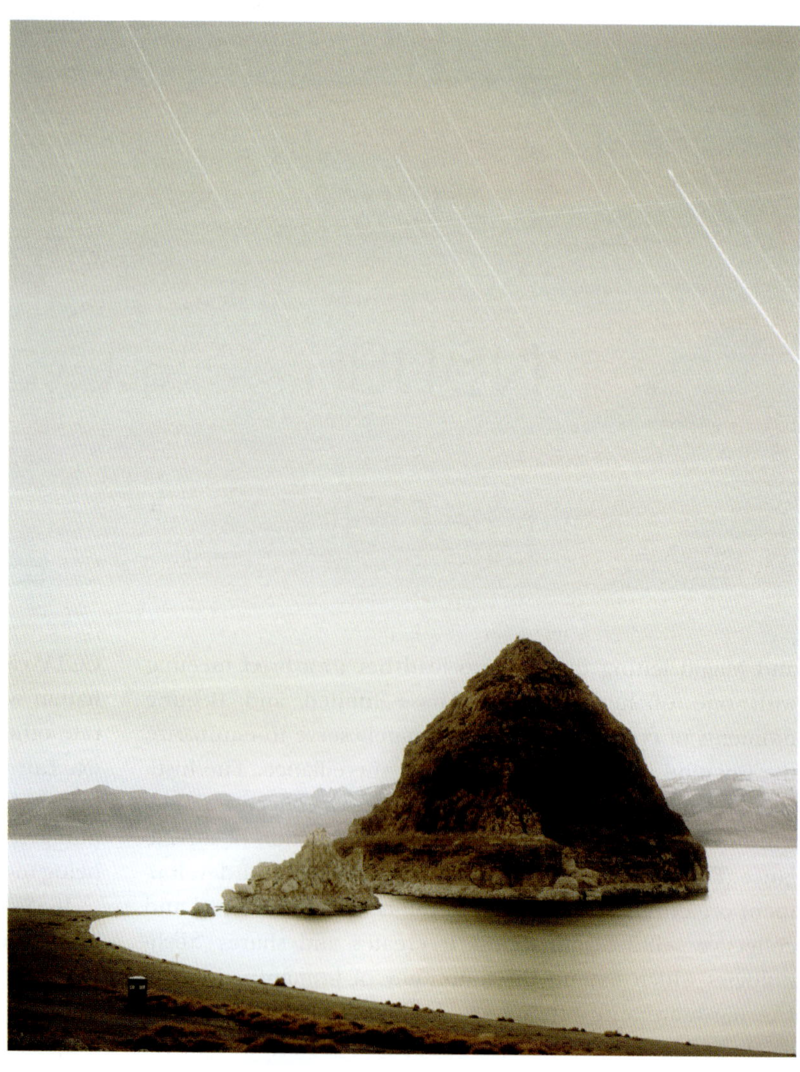

11.17 Trevor Paglen, *DMSP 5B/F4 from Pyramid Lake Indian Reservation (Military Meteorological Satellite; 1973-054A)*, 2009. Photograph. Courtesy the artist.

of the site taken by Timothy H. O'Sullivan (1840–82) for the U.S. government-sponsored King Survey in the 1860s.[49] O'Sullivan had been employed to document the breadth of the continent, demonstrating the geographical expanse and natural resources available to the U.S. nation and laying the groundwork for its westward expansion. These first photographs of the American landscape were both aesthetically and politically motivated. In *DMSP 5B/F4*, Paglen documents a light horizontal line cutting across the sky, above the tufa domes that had captured O'Sullivan's attention. This is the reflection of the sun in the body of a reconnaissance satellite captured by the long exposure of Paglen's camera, itself computer-controlled to locate the path of the officially nonexistent object. *DMSP 5B/F4* is a representation of the landscape being observed. With images such as O'Sullivan's as its art-historical source, *The Other Night Sky* unites historical and contemporary efforts to observe and represent the landscape. *DMSP 5B/F4* is a beautiful photograph, with its limited palette of luminescent earth tones and contrast between the heightened detail on the dome that had been O'Sullivan's subject and the blurred lines of the satellite that is Paglen's. It elegantly merges the surveilling eye of the classified satellite, the documentary gaze of Paglen as investigator, and the imperialist view of O'Sullivan, to present a history of ways of seeing and a window into the secret geography of the twenty-first century.

Mass Media, Personal Experience, and Politics

Surveillance art drew attention to the fact that in our world all spaces, and the experiences that occur in them, are subject to and possess political power. In this work, daily life is the object of a technology of observation extending from the stars to our bedrooms. The politics of experience, however, is not only a matter of policing society or subverting control. Beginning with the work of German filmmaker Harun Farocki, the last section of this book examines work that treats the body as a tool for action and understanding. Like the surveillance artists, Farocki and the collection of painters, photographers, film and video artists, sculptors, and performance artists discussed in the following section contemplate experience as connected and understood predominately through its representation in various forms of mass media from newspapers and television to computer simulations and virtual reality. The earliest work discussed in this section is a film from the 1960s in which Farocki, in the guise of a television newscaster, burns himself in an attempt to more accurately report on the war in Vietnam. The works of Belgian painter Luc Tuymans, U.S. video artist Silvia Kolbowski, and Israeli/U.S. video artist Omer Fast discussed here, like those of Farocki, analyze different forms of imagery and provoke sensual as well as intellectual and visual appreciation of topics relating to the experience and representation of global politics, particularly of war. The chapter, and the book, ends with a discussion of artists whose work presents and promotes transformative action—often no more complicated than locking arms or more radical than raising a child. The drawings and videos by Los Angeles-based Andrea Bowers capture moments in the history of non-violence that, like the photography of Catherine Opie, end the chapter with images of the experience of politics at the beginning of the twenty-first century.

Harun Farocki

Paglen's *DMSP 5B/F4* is the product of pointing a camera at the underside of U.S. democracy, at the eyes that observe the Earth in secret. It documents one means of producing what German filmmaker Harun Farocki (b. 1944) has called "operational imagery": "Images that do not try to represent reality but are part of a technical operation."[50] Beginning with *Eye/Machine* (2000–03) (**fig. 11.18**), a series of three two-channel installations, and *War at a Distance* (2003), its single-channel version, Farocki has examined such operational imagery as it appears in both manufacturing and military technology.

In *Eye/Machine* and *War at a Distance*, Farocki juxtaposes assembly-line production and weapons technology with a particular concern for how both have been transformed to rely on images. Scenes from the factory floor show the use of sensory robotics to guide the assembly of machine parts. Of particular interest to Farocki is the ubiquity of image-recognition technology. In place of the crowded shop floors of the first Industrial Revolution, Farocki presents the fully automated and nearly emptied factories that typify contemporary production. Contrasting the presence of products with the absence of people, these works pursue a question that art historian Georges Didi Huberman (b. 1953) has proposed anchors all of Farocki's practice: "Why, in which way, and how does the *production of images* take part in the *destruction of human beings*?"[51] *Eye/Machine* and *War at a Distance* detail the second half of this proposal by showing imagery used to sell weapons systems and footage recorded by missile-mounted cameras, the latter dating from between World War II and the Gulf Wars. Created entirely with found footage, *Eye/Machine* and *War at a Distance* are composed of imagery produced by the military-industrial complex, edited to convey Farocki's political and philosophical perspective. At the end of the film Farocki's narrator points to the common economic foundation for the depopulated fields of industrial production and those of military destruction: "Manual work is being abolished here and at the same time being displaced to poorer countries. Today wars too are more likely to take place in poorer countries than in rich ones. The rich countries' highly developed weapons no longer find an enemy who is their equal."

Despite delivering a clearly critical message regarding the unobstructed escalation of the military and the role of images within that rise, Farocki's intent is not strictly didactic. As Huberman again points out, Farocki's work since the late 1960s has required participation: not in terms of sharing

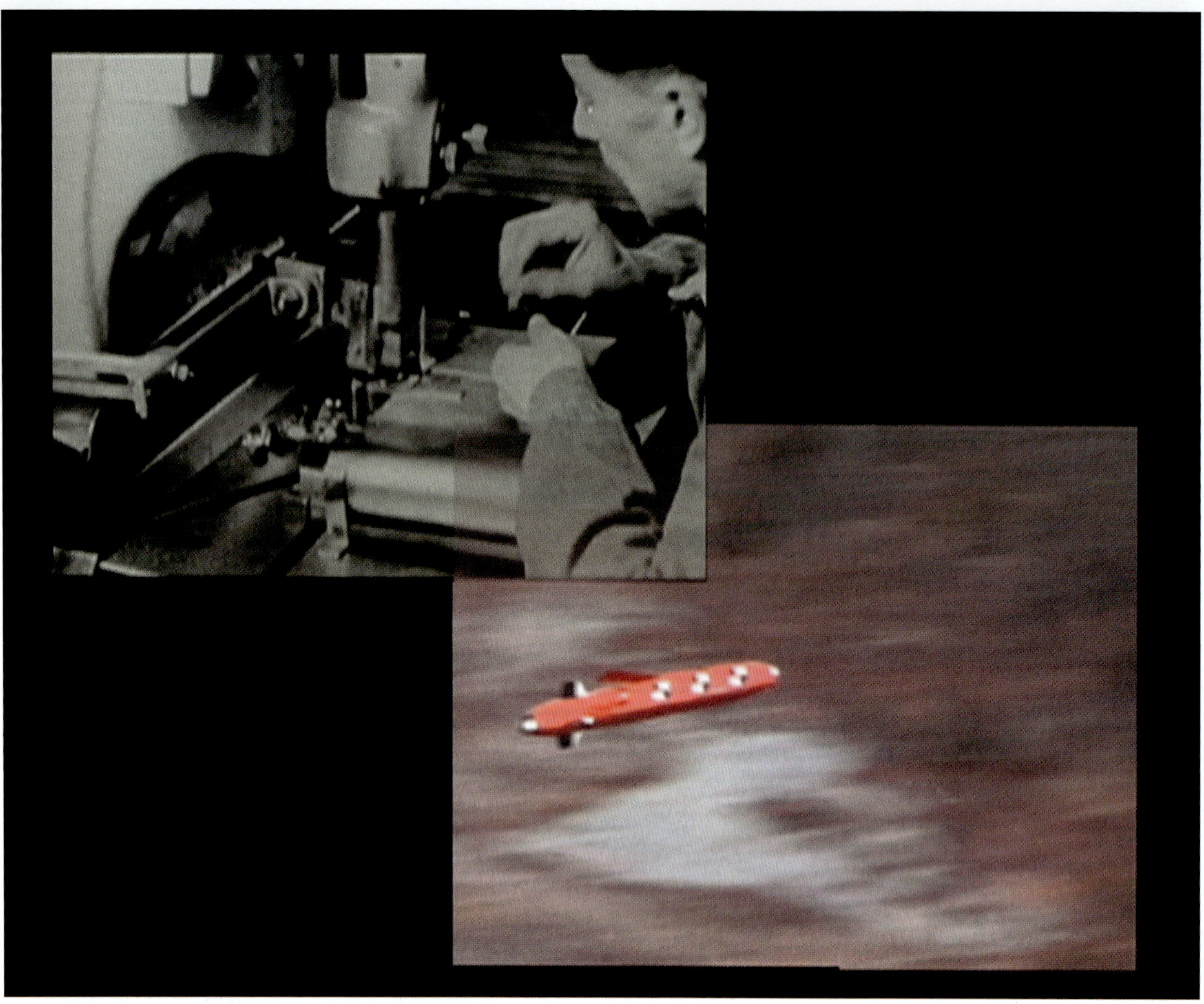

11.18 Harun Farocki, *Auge/Maschine (Eye/Machine) I–III,* 2001–03. Video. Double channel installation, sound, color, 25/17/15 minutes. © Harun Farocki. Courtesy: Galerie Thaddaeus Ropac Paris/Salzburg.

meals or manipulating the artwork as in the genre of "relational aesthetics" (see Chapter 7), but by demanding the viewer share in the analysis and critique of the facts before her or him. No image is trusted to speak on its own. In one of his earliest and most shocking films, *Inextinguishable Fire* (1969), Farocki initiated a discussion about the culpability of the scientific community in relation to the Vietnam War by drawing attention to the logistics of napalm production, the political utility of dividing the labor involved, and the limitations of representation in addressing the issue. Farocki begins the film by showing himself reading a translated testimony of a Vietnamese civilian recounting a napalm attack. He then poses the question of how this atrocity can be addressed in film. Images of flesh burning or wounded bodies, Farocki calmly explains, will cause the viewer to look away, feel assaulted, and dismiss the issue entirely. Farocki then takes a lit cigarette from off-screen and presses it into the bare skin of his forearm. The action, though surprising and distressing, is not explained by either the disruption it creates or the pain it causes. As an image alone, it "calls for an appraisal within ... language," to use Huberman's characterization of all images in Farocki's work. Words are needed and an off-screen narrator speaks them: "A cigarette burns at 400 degrees, napalm burns at 3,000 degrees." With this detail Farocki's action becomes anchored not in his pain or the reactions of the viewer but in the recounted, though not represented, reality of the war in Vietnam. Throughout his career, Farocki has developed multiple strategies for juxtaposing images that draw attention to their necessarily interdependent character. As the rest of *Inextinguishable Fire* repeatedly demonstrates, it falls to the individual to carefully examine as many fragments of information and imagery as possible in order to comprehend and respond to social products of all kinds, from politics to science and technology.

Farocki's work is motivated by an ethical commitment to exposing the mechanics of representation in contemporary society. Recent examples include *Deep Play* (2007), a twelve-channel video installation based upon the broadcast of the 2006 Soccer World Cup Final, and *Serious Games* (2009–10), a four-part, multichannel installation documenting virtual-reality combat simulations used for U.S. operations in Afghanistan. Both works develop the analysis of operational imagery through calculated juxtapositions of appropriated representational footage with virtual images, including a range of computer-generated, image-recognition, artificial-intelligence, and video-game materials. Commissioned for Documenta 12, *Deep Play* uses a great variety of operational imagery generated in contexts other than factory production and military destruction. On one monitor Farocki shows the telecast of the World Cup Final, which extended to a penalty shootout that gave Italy the victory over France. The other eleven monitors present a range of imagery produced in conjunction with the game. There is footage generated by security cameras, filmed analysis of the game, video of commentators, displays showing individual players' movements and energy expenditure, and computer-rendered representations of the players for video-game development, to name but a few of the examples Farocki found. The results demonstrate the degree to which moving-image production, well beyond broadcast material, is integral to the sports and entertainment economies. More important to questions about the social function of representations, *Deep Play* suggests that deciphering how images function and how meaning is created in our society requires understanding a vast reservoir of material, much of which circulates far from the general public's gaze. To look at it through the lens of Guy Debord's writing (see Chapter 5), which was fundamental to Farocki's early thinking, images are not only the face of the spectacle but also its unseen machinery, and artists are in a unique position to provide insight into both.

Though virtual reality appears in *Eye/Machine*, *War at Distance*, and *Deep Play*, these works rely primarily on representational images captured in the real world. *Serious Games*, on the other hand, addresses the complex relationship between experiences had in virtual reality and in life outside it. Farocki began the project when one of his collaborators, producer and sound engineer Matthias Rajmann (b. 1965), started researching the military use of immersive virtual-reality software for pre- and post-tour-of-duty training. The programs, developed by the University of Southern California's Institute for Creative Technologies (ICT), simulate Afghani and Iraqi terrain and a variety of probable combatant exchanges. *Serious Games* juxtaposes computer-generated scenarios with Farocki's own footage of military personnel operating the systems. *Serious Games I: Watson Is Down* (2010) follows a team of four infantry soldiers along a virtual transport route in Afghanistan. The trainees function as a unit learning to maneuver the vehicle, navigate away from IEDs (Improvised Explosive Devices), coordinate with friendly units, and return enemy fire. Unable to adequately defend themselves, the gunner, Watson, is shot and killed, at which point a new category of problem arises: What is to be done with a virtual cadaver? After a pause in which the driver asks what they should do with Watson, the unit moves on in silence as the living Watson leans back in his chair, red-faced, and lets out a frustrated sigh. *Watson Is Down* demonstrates that virtual reality not only simulates spaces and events but also stimulates real-life camaraderie and adrenalin. In the confusing moment of virtual death, the body asserts itself—reborn in the death of the image.

In addition to presenting virtual reality as a staging ground in which to learn tactics, *Serious Games* also utilizes ICT systems created to help GIs process experiences of trauma and death. Unlike the preparatory function of the training materials in *Watson Is Down* or *Serious Games II: Three Dead*, the environments in *Serious Games III: Immersion* (2009) and *Serious Games IV: A Sun with No Shadow* (2010) (**fig. 11.19**) were programmed to enhance memory of real experiences rather than to anticipate them. The ICT software in these cases was created to help the soldier relive traumatic

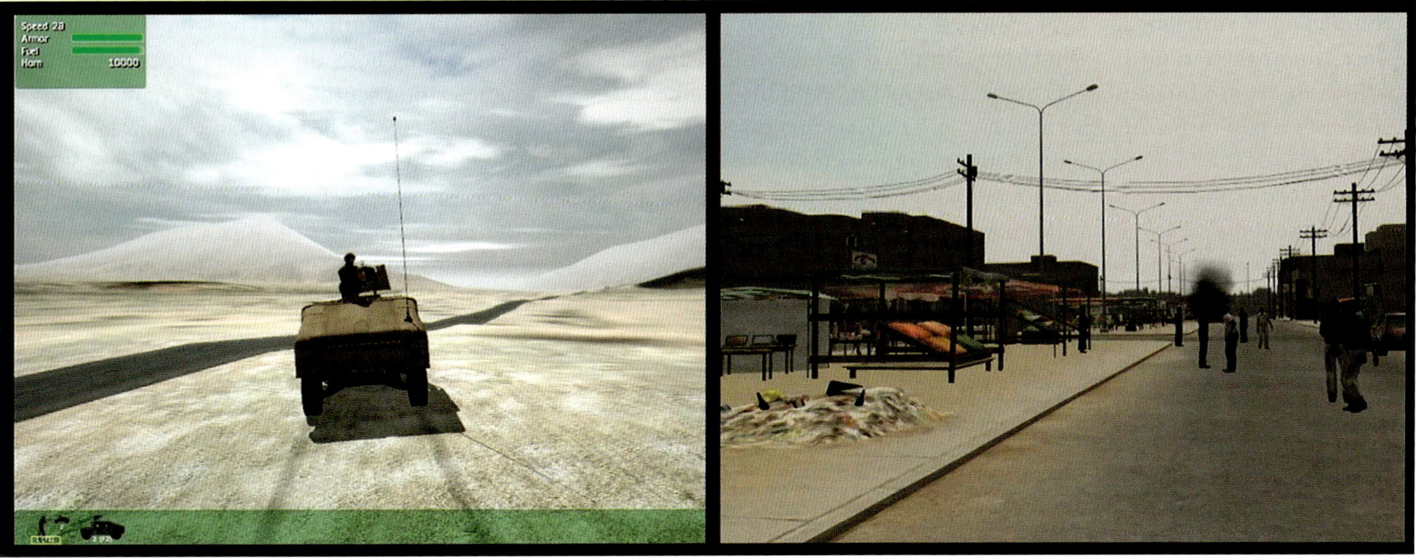

11.19 Harun Farocki, *Eine Sonne ohne Schatten (A Sun with No Shadow)—Serious Games IV*, 2010. Video. Installation, sound, color, 7 minutes 39 seconds, col. A+B. © Harun Farocki 2012. Image courtesy Galerie Thaddaeus Ropac.

experiences for therapeutic sessions with a councilor or psychologist. Like the imagery in *Eye/Machine* and Farocki's earlier work, the operational capacity of these simulations is enhanced by their ability to approximate the appearance of the world. The simulations, however, are not dependent on any sources in the material world. On one screen of *Immersion*, we see a war zone not unlike the setting of popular video games. The software was, in fact, adopted from *Full Spectrum Warrior*, a training system and X-Box video game developed previously by ICT. On the second screen of *Immersion*, Farocki shows footage he has taken of a soldier walking us through a clearly traumatic mission in which the commanding officer was dismembered by an explosive device. The soldier recounts being paralyzed with fear and describes feeling nauseous and almost unable to speak about it. The emotional intensity of *Immersion* reaches a critical point near the end of the twenty-minute video when the soldier crouches down as if to get out of the virtual terrain and away from the memory. When he finally does rise, he removes the headset on which he has been viewing the simulated terrain and with a grin and a laugh acknowledges a round of applause. Farocki had not taken his camera crew into an actual therapy session, but instead documented a demonstration of the software by military therapists and ICT developers, staged to show the efficacy of simulated imagery as a therapeutic tool. *Immersion* places the viewer in front of a copy for which there is no original, a truly Baudrillardian simulacrum (see Chapter 5).

Farocki provides a side-by-side comparison of pre- and post-deployment virtual spaces in *Serious Games IV: A Sun with No Shadow*. Copied segments of the training session from *Watson Is Down* appear again, this time coupled with scenes from PTSD (Post-Traumatic Stress Disorder) therapy sessions. Without the drama the actor provided in *Immersion*, *A Sun with No Shadow* concentrates on the character of the simulations, revealing the degree to which the soldiers trained in a virtual-image bank stripped of actual people, face, upon their return, a similarly neutralized territory in which to begin post-combat recovery. The operational function of images in *Eye/Machine* and *War at a Distance* that dispensed with the body to facilitate the smooth operation of the factory or war machine here eliminates real places so as to help soldiers survive what they have experienced in them. As Jan Verwoert wrote of this piece: "The before and after match to such a degree that it is as if the in between [the war] never happened."[52] *A Sun with No Shadow*, however, points to this in-between in a way that is at once mundane and horrifying. Looking over the pre-deployment training and post-tour-of-duty therapy simulations, Farocki noticed that in the second there were no shadows, an occurrence he supposed to be simply the result of needing to save money on programming costs. Cost-benefit analyses notwithstanding, the loss of shadow remains a potent metaphor for war as the event in which the solid matter and living beings that cast them are destroyed.

Luc Tuymans

In the late 1970s and early 1980s, it appeared to artists that the mass media either prevented the unmediated experience of reality *à la* Guy Debord's *Society of the Spectacle*, manipulated the viewer as in Foucault's analysis of power, or replaced reality altogether *à la* Baudrillard's simulacra. Artists responded by approaching the image world variously with the theoretical precision of appropriation, the cavalier humor of a Kippenberger, or the nihilism of Neo-Expressionism. Artists in the twenty-first century have continued dissecting the power of representation. Critique, however, has been contextualized with a sense that the mass media, like the world it purports to represent, is open for mediation. In the words of Belgian painter Luc Tuymans (b. 1958): "There are no more images that come across as a totality, no more universal images."[53] In fact, Tuymans argues, painting highlights the fissures in what still purports to be universal by enveloping the photographic images we "digest" with the physicality that "shakes loose the emotional element within the viewer," inviting us to "decipher and decode."[54]

Tuymans's paintings address a range of dramatic and often upsetting subject matter, including the Holocaust, postcolonial liberation struggles, resurgent nationalisms, and war generally. Nonetheless, they are not, he asserts, "witnessing elements" created to convince the viewer of anything.[55] Instead, each work presents fragments that must be fitted into contexts whose relevance is determined by the viewer. The viewer must convince him- or herself. Tuymans selects topics and sources that are so overdetermined by history or contemporary politics that his paintings draw upon competing political and social discourses. Moreover, it is one of Tuymans's accomplishments that his paintings refer to explicit political content while also being open to other narratives. *The Secretary of State* (2005) (**fig. 11.20**), a portrait of U.S. secretary of state Condoleezza Rice, is one of his more celebrated portraits. The painting is based on a televised appearance and references both the camera that produced the image and the television set that carried it. We recognize that the tightly cropped face is the result of a zoom lens on a television camera, and the pale cast of the painting evokes the light of a television screen. Tuymans provides only the slightest indication of personality—Dr. Rice's slightly squinting eyes and pursed lips add a somewhat anti-social cast to her expression. The iconic presentation of the isolated head is a product of the style of news broadcasting, but it also reflects the role played by the secretary of state as one of the few "faces" of U.S. policy during the Second Gulf War.

Though much can be gleaned from *The Secretary of State*, much is missing. Tuymans reproduced his subject's iconic presentation but not the circumstances that give it importance. We recognize the televisual format but do not know the specific events being reported. The reason for Dr. Rice's expression is unknown and we are not shown her whole face, nor the rest of her body. Each detail Tuymans paints seems to

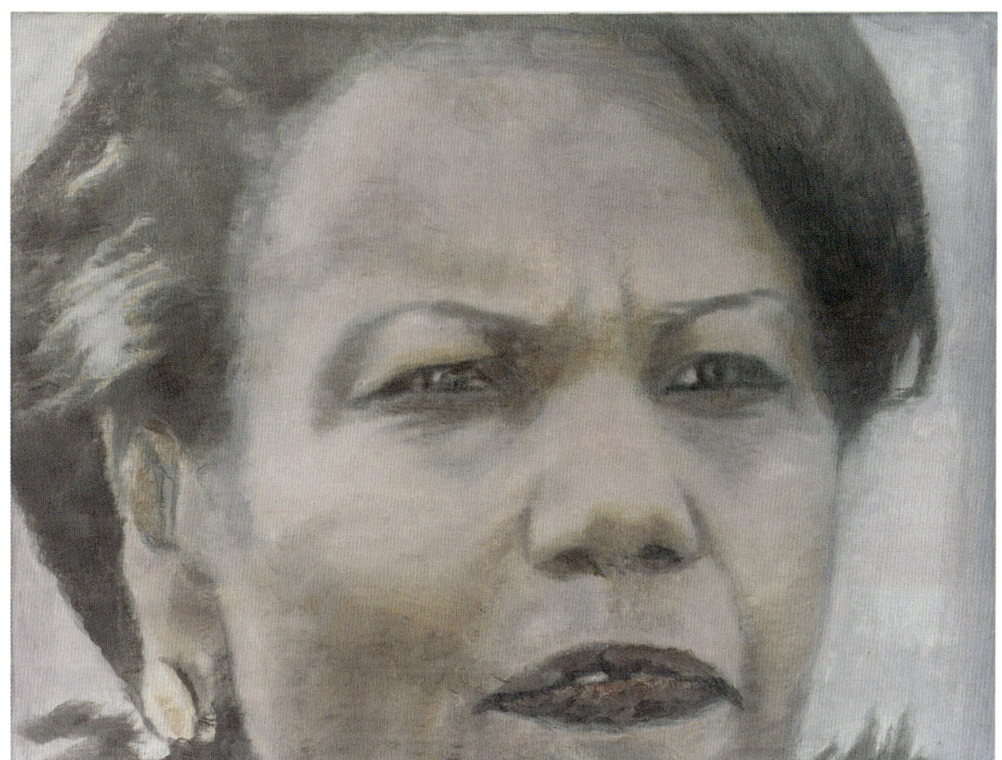

11.20 Luc Tuymans, ***The Secretary of State***, 2005. Oil on canvas, 18 × 24¼" (45.7 × 61.9 cm). The Museum of Modern Art, New York. Courtesy Studio Luc Tuymans.

limit what we can say with certainty about the subject, forcing the viewer away from the canvas to grapple with its context. This reduction of the image, Tuymans says, "is frightening, very powerful ... Then you know and you can see at once that you can't see everything. This non-experience of the image is something very important, especially because you are asking the viewer to make up for this lack."[56] Like the hysterical documents of Raad and the Atlas Group (see Chapter 6), Tuymans's paintings distinguish themselves from mimetic representations, and ask the viewer to reconstruct the paths that connect the image to constellations of political, historical, emotional, and aesthetic facts.

Tuymans's formal challenge, like his conceptual one, is to paint images that are demonstrably incomplete—the surfaces often only lightly covered, the compositions fragmentary, and even the subject matter, as in *The Secretary of State*, only partially defined—yet that are clearly finished as works of art. The viewer must recognize the work as a fragment or a presentation of lack, rather than as an empty composition or a half-done canvas. Tuymans begins most of his paintings by making quick sketches or watercolors from images he has found or photographs he has taken. He then paints from these small studies, putting significant distance between the photographic source and the final work. Like Cindy Sherman (see Chapter 2), Tuymans implies a narrative context for his images by quoting cinematic conventions including the cropped view, the close-up, the camera pan, and artificial lighting. He also relies heavily on television aesthetics: the light of the screen, the extreme, often arbitrary close-ups produced by news crews, the abrupt transitions as the camera is trained and retrained on the heart of an event, and the quickly edited sequences in a news report or sporting event. Even the dimensions of *The Secretary of State* (18 by 24¼ inches) allude to the standard size of a television screen rather than the traditional, much larger, vertically oriented state portrait. Having established the mass-media aesthetic, Tuymans then contrasts the televisual source of his imagery with his painterly style. The brushstrokes on the small painting are visible, as are the layers of paint and even the texture of the canvas below them. Tuymans paints with subtle modulations of color exemplified in the passages of warmer ocher hues that breathe volume into the subject's face. *The Secretary of State* is typical of a body of work in which Tuymans confronts the ubiquitous generality of the televised image with the material individuality of painting, thereby locating his subject at the intersection of the globalized flow of information and the localized experience of daily life.

Silvia Kolbowski

Writer and curator Nato Thompson has argued forcefully that understanding the relationship between sensation and representation is essential to the urgent task of articulating how images work in and out of works of art. "In order to understand contemporary politics," Thompson claims, "we must understand that a war of affect is being played out across a landscape of spectacle."[57] Theorists writing about the spectacle since Debord (see Chapter 5) have consistently predicted that global citizenry would be numbed and overwhelmed by the mass media. Thompson, on the other hand, and a host of others including Jacques Rancière and Bruno Latour, have found in contemporary society new forms of sensation with the potential to engage spectacle critically.

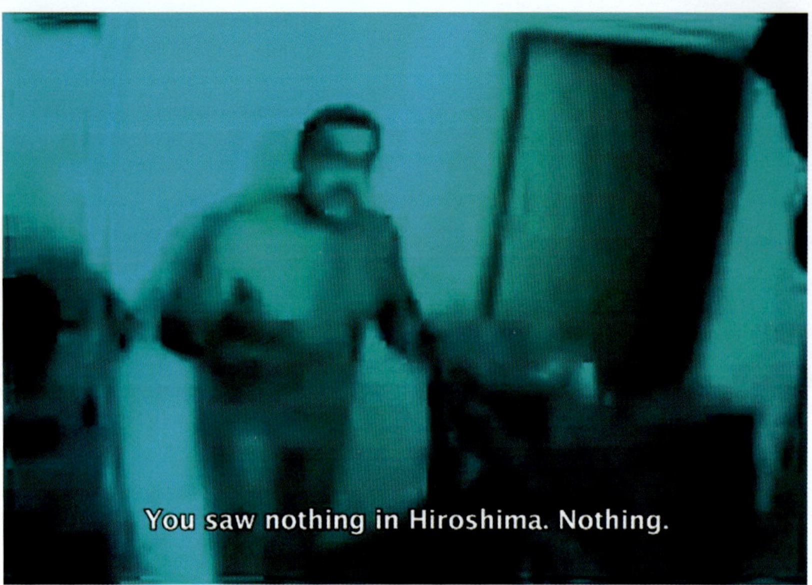

11.21 Silvia Kolbowski, *After Hiroshima Mon Amour*, 2008. Video still of projection loop. Video, 16mm, 22 mins. Courtesy the artist.

Visual artists at the turn of the millennium were well positioned to assess the political and personal consequences of living as much with representations of the material world as with actual experiences in it. In the new millennium Silvia Kolbowski (see Chapters 2 and 6) continued to address the collision of body, psyche, and mass media with a critical eye toward the dominance of television and cinema. Like many of the artists discussed in this chapter, she upholds fiction as an important means to subvert the dominant narratives of power and to process experiences of war and trauma.

Silvia Kolbowski has been addressing the political and psychological impact of media representations since the beginning of her career in the early 1980s. Her twenty-two-minute projection *After Hiroshima Mon Amour* (2008) (**fig. 11.21**) borrows its plot from the 1959 Alain Resnais film *Hiroshima Mon Amour* and appropriates its imagery from uploaded footage taken by U.S. troops on active duty in Iraq, first-person reportage of the devastation in post-Hurricane Katrina New Orleans, and fragments of Resnais's film. As she had in her earlier work, including *Model Pleasure* (see fig. 2.10), Kolbowski practices an impure form of appropriation, at one moment representing the original untouched and at the next submitting it to dramatic modification. She removed individual frames from the Resnais original to give her version a choppier, more abstracted appearance. For several scenes that use contemporary video footage, she dramatically altered the color and layered the imagery to present Iraq and New Orleans as related examples of U.S. hubris and indifference. *After Hiroshima Mon Amour* also includes several re-enacted scenes that, like the rest of the film, rely on Margaret Duras's screenplay and synopsis for *Hiroshima Mon Amour* for their dialogue but take license with its directions and staging. The result of Kolbowski's assemblage is a bold presentation of the aggression and indifference of U.S. power and a nuanced examination of the role of various forms of representation in the creation and contemplation of crisis.

Both the Duras/Resnais film and Kolbowski's *After Hiroshima Mon Amour* begin with an image of hoarfrost before slowly shifting to ash-covered flesh and then to the naked skin of two lovers. *After Hiroshima Mon Amour* then introduces action in Iraq and the dialogue, given in the form of subtitles but not actually spoken, begins. The first two lines are those of the Duras/Resnais original but their order is reversed. "I saw everything," we read as we see a soldier's perspective as he forcibly enters an Iraqi home. The scene is tense and confusing. Then a second subtitle, "You saw nothing in Hiroshima. Nothing," transports us back from the early twenty-first-century Middle East to mid-twentieth-century Japan. Kolbowski continues to intercut her sources, connecting the present with 1959 and 1945, and Iraq and New Orleans with Hiroshima, and also linking up film, video, Internet, and fine art. By triangulating Katrina, Iraq, and Hiroshima, Kolbowski proposes that there are important similarities between the internal and international politics in and beyond the West as well as between those after World War II and today; her formal choices, however, indicate that there have also been significant changes since *Hiroshima Mon Amour* was made.

The Duras/Resnais film is about the inevitability of having to confront the spiritual, psychological, and political aftermath of the bombing of Hiroshima and the impossibility of reconciling oneself to it or its impact: One can neither avoid it nor engage it. This condition corresponds to what Jalal Toufic described as post-crisis status in his discussion of Hiroshima, Auschwitz, and Beirut in *Undying Love or Love Dies* (2002) (see Chapter 6). Resnais and Duras demonstrated how art can give form to this contradiction, even if it cannot resolve it. In their story, the historical trauma of the nuclear attack on Japan is approached obliquely through the fleeting relationship between two lovers, a visiting French actress and a Japanese architect. When Kolbowski integrates the love story into her film, she casts ten actors of different races and ethnicities in the roles of the fictional protagonists. The two lovers and the many actors complement the unseen subjects who recorded the imagery of Baghdad and New Orleans. Duras and Resnais had invited the viewer to identify with the actions or inactions of the protagonists. Kolbowski, by multiplying the actors who play the couple and the photographers who document the scenes, collectivizes the experience that was so individuated and personalized in the original. Duras and Resnais, like Adorno, Fautrier, and Pollock, answered the question as to whether art would survive human barbarism; it did, but in the hands of the first post-World War II generation it tended to place the burden of experience and expression on the individual, whether it was the painter in the studio or the viewer alone before the work. It has become critically important to Kolbowski that her work should convey the fact that historical events and the means through which they occur and are made known have "psychical dimension[s]." Her art, she explains, "draws out an affective response," and thus instigates an inquiry into the connection between the individual and society.[58] Kolbowski, like Farocki and the artists who will close this chapter, suggests that we can and must grapple with the cost of barbarism as it is experienced, in communities and using our capacities as both thinking and feeling subjects.

Omer Fast

Israeli/U.S. video artist Omer Fast (b. 1972) has approached questions of history, memory, and trauma through single- and multiple-channel projections of appropriated material, documentary film, and fully scripted drama. Since completing his MFA at Hunter College in New York in 2000, he has been creating work that examines the impact on our "consciousness" of encountering the world with "screens and cameras as very much part of our sensory/memory apparatus."[59] He began his investigation by thinking about the spaces of actual experience in relation to those of its representation—that is, the difference between sites and sets. Projects such as *Spielberg's List* (2003), filmed in Kraków, Poland, near the collapsing, abandoned set of Steven Spielberg's movie *Schindler's List* (1993), and *Godville* (2005), shot at Colonial Williamsburg, a living-history museum in Virginia, began as considerations of places in which site and set were confused, "kind of super-space[s] ... that conflate ... historical events with their later representations."[60] These works evolved from interviews with people who lived and worked between history and its representation. *Spielberg's List*, a two-channel video, features Polish residents of Kraków who had worked as extras on the set of *Schindler's List.* The documentary style of much of the footage and Fast's careful editing suggest that we are listening to Holocaust survivors, but when a woman's story of being captured by the SS ends with a laugh, or a photograph of the concentration camps is time-stamped "March 3, 1993," it becomes apparent that the occupation being recollected is of Poland by Hollywood, not Nazis. Though many of the speakers take pleasure in reminiscing about the film and make no connections to the war itself, others discuss the sincere emotional conflict raised by the decision to participate in Spielberg's retelling. One young man poignantly describes how troubling he found his own preference to be cast as a German instead of a Jew. *Spielberg's List* presents and provokes the experience of emotional conflict that is layered upon the traumas of history by our attempts to represent them.

In 2006, Fast set out for another "super-space," a training facility at Fort Irwin, California, that included simulations of Iraqi and Afghan terrain. While waiting at Fort Hood military base in Texas to be granted access permission, Fast interviewed GIs recently returned from the war in Iraq. When authorization to go to Fort Irwin failed to arrive, these conversations became the basis for *The Casting* (2007) (**fig. 11.22**), a four-screen projection dramatizing two events from a GI's deployment to the Middle East, and the casting of the film about it. The work consists of two two-sided projections that hang side by side. On the front are scenes of actors frozen in *tableaux vivants* illustrating the narration of then-Sergeant Ronn Cantu. The production values are high and

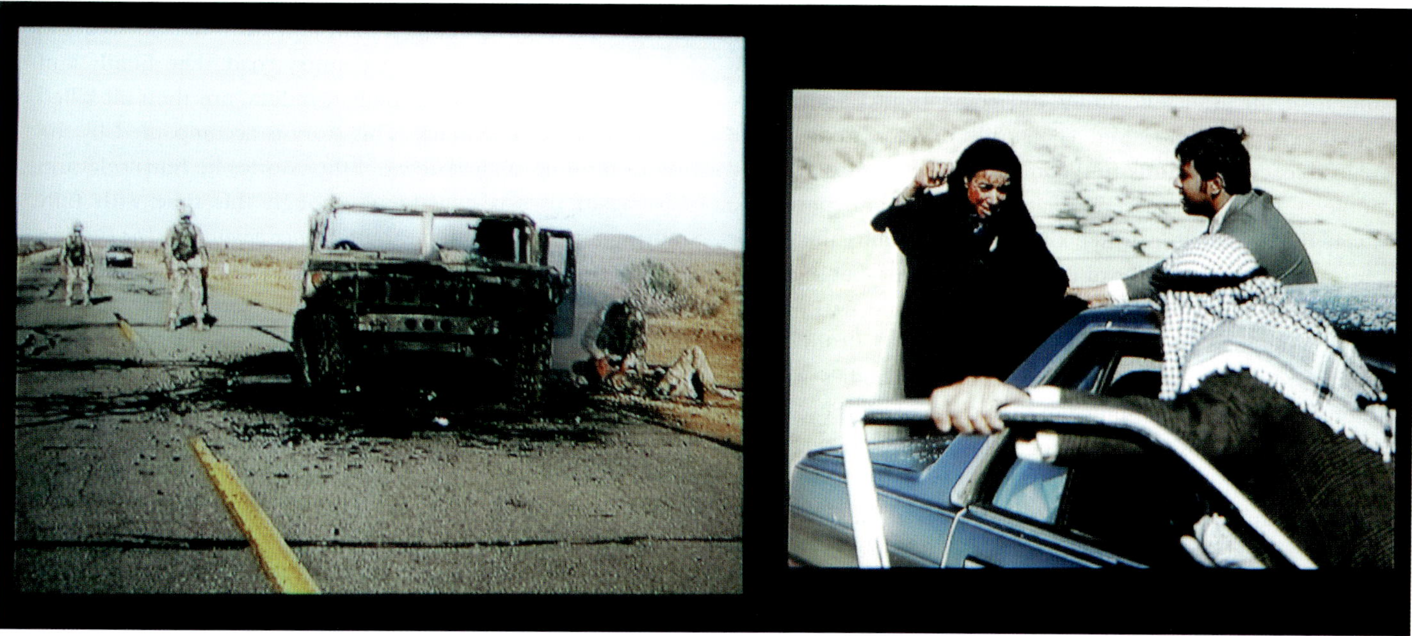

11.22 Omer Fast, *The Casting*, 2007. Film still, 4 channels, 14 minutes, 35mm transferred to video/sound. Commissioned by Museum moderner Kunst, Stiftung Ludwig, Wien. Collection: Indianapolis Museum of Art. Courtesy of the artist, Arratia Beer, Berlin and gb Agency, Paris.

the scenes look like they might be stills until an actor moves a bit or smoke and sand blow by, thus reminding the viewer that the medium is moving film. Cantu describes the accidental killing of a boy on a highway outside Baghdad as the actors tense with the effort of remaining still. Fast explains that "instead of substituting the pathos of the soldier's story with the pathos of actors acting, I am going to give you the pathos of the body under duress."[61] Folded into this story is a second one about a Christmas Day date with a German girl whom Cantu met while he was stationed in Bavaria. This narrative includes an awkward introduction to her family and the revelation that the girl cuts herself. "It's not painful at all," she says of the act. "It just helps me to remember things that happen to me." Discussing the self-harming and the accidental murder is clearly upsetting to the soldier. Toward the end of the film, he comments that, due to the intensity and chaos of the experience, he remembers everything that occurred, but that he cannot be trusted to put the events in the right order—his memories and the story that is being made from them are two different things.

The projections that play on the rear of the screens reveal how much editing was required to create the narration heard on the front. We see Sergeant Cantu being interviewed before his second tour of duty in Iraq, after which he would be promoted to the rank of staff sergeant and become an outspoken critic of the war. A sentence or two are uttered and then we see the image jerk as the film is cut to incorporate a different sentence, phrase, word, or even syllable into the narration: The footage of the speaking subject is a constantly shifting series of fragments cut and pasted together. Shot over several days, the Sergeant is seen in different clothes, often changing appearance from word to word, making Fast's editing clearly visible. The overt presentation of the artifice here suggests the possibility that the entire narrative is a fabrication—and the story of the girl cutting herself was indeed the invention of the artist. Study of the interview reveals that much of the Iraqi encounter did come from Cantu's personal experience, however. The stories in *The Casting* sound plausible, convey truths, and come from the mouths of Fast's subjects, but have uncertain relationship to their experience. Even the sentence in which the Sergeant admits that he is not sure about the order of events, a comment that seems so natural for someone retelling a traumatic event, was not his own. Fast says of his working process: "Often I'm dealing with people who have experienced things in their bodies and are then forced at some distance in time to recollect those experiences. So the loss of experience, the wanting to recapture its immediacy, this is articulated in the work, both explicitly [though the narrative] and through the editing."[62] "Compulsive cutting," as Fast refers to his own editing, becomes a means and a metaphor for the effort required to transform the miasma of experience into stories and histories that can be remembered and retold.

5000 Feet Is the Best (2011) (**fig. 11.23**), a thirty-minute single-channel video about the operation of Unmanned Aerial Vehicles (UAVs) by the U.S. military, strikes a different balance between documentation and drama, interview and editing. Named for the most effective distance from the ground for carrying out satellite surveillance, the video intertwines three variations of a fictional interview with the pilot of a Predator Drone with three fragments of an actual conversation with its sensor operator, the second member of the two-person team that controls the plane. The sensor operator, identified by Fast only as Brandon, was stationed in the U.S. while he executed surveillance and combat missions in Afghanistan remotely. He provided Fast with details about Predator surveillance capacities, combat protocol, soldiers' daily lives, and some specifics about individual missions. Over the course of the piece, the sensor operator also discusses "virtual stress," the impact of engaging in real warfare from within the realm of representation. Despite serving from a room safe in Las Vegas, the soldiers operating the warplane with a camera and remote controls, as both Brandon and his fictional pilot counterpart declare, are nonetheless active in the war zone every day. Soldiers in the virtual theater of war confront death and experience symptoms of PTSD every bit as real as if they had been stationed in Iraq or Afghanistan. *5000 Feet*, like *After Hiroshima Mon Amour*, draws attention to the psychological impact of historical events and the means of representation by which we encounter and engage them. The operating modes of global war, maintained by virtual realities, have brought us out the other side of the simulacra theorized by Baudrillard in the 1980s. It is not that Kolbowski and Fast, and certainly not the soldiers their work features, are announcing the return of any historically distant or nostalgically imagined real. Instead, contemporary life is shown to be real in both its virtual and material forms.

The war story told by the pilot, played by U.S. actor Denis O'Hare (b. 1962), follows a man and his family as targeted combatants stop them on a country road. The family and the soldiers, identified as Taliban militia, are then all killed in the U.S. missile attack. This story is accompanied by the pilot's musings on a variety of other stories he finds relevant. Fast again uses re-enactment, though this time with fully moving actors rather than the *tableaux vivants* of *The Casting*. He cast the scene with what look like middle- and working-class whites and located the action in terrain evoking the outskirts of a generic U.S. suburb. When O'Hare describes the dress of the suspected enemy as typical of the south, Fast somewhat comically shows his actors dressed in plaid shirts, work boots, and baseball caps. This is but one detail that illustrates how all stories, from personal ones to news accounts, are dependent on associative chains made by the listener. In a related piece, *Her Face Was Covered, Part 2* (2011), Fast clarifies his interest in such incidental connections. Presented as a slide show with alternating images and texts, *Her Face Was Covered* tells the story of another drone attack. Sometimes the images provide the expected visual information: "So, basically there's a truck," is followed by a slide

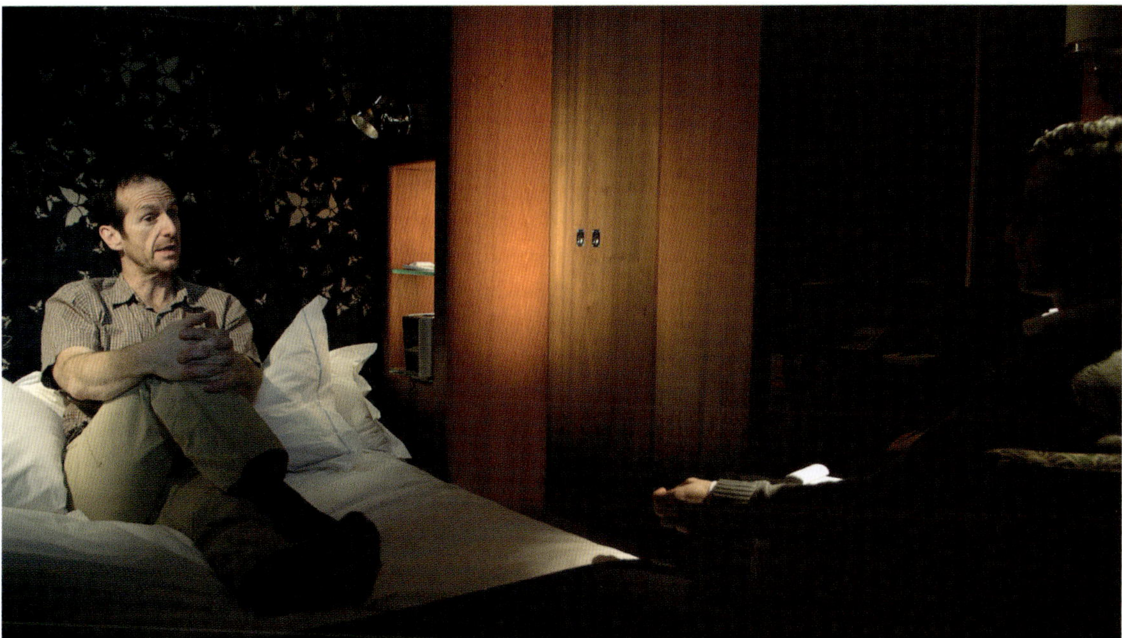

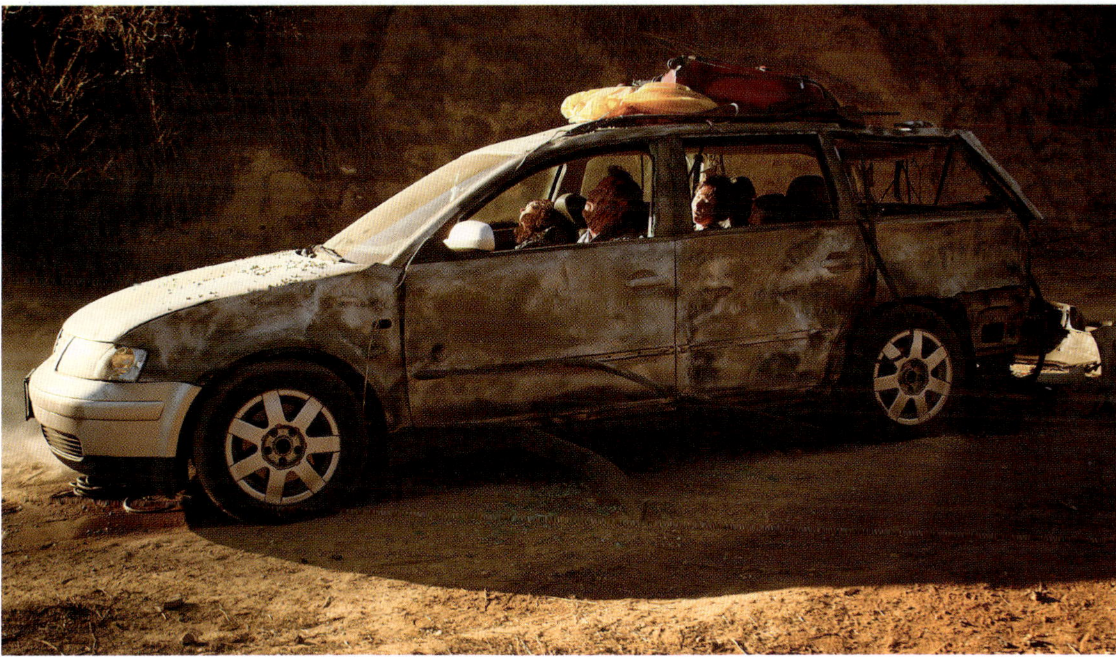

11.23 Omer Fast, *5000 Feet Is the Best*, 2011. Film still, digital video, 30 minutes. Courtesy of gb agency, Paris and Arratia Beer, Berlin.

of a yellow moving truck. Often, however, as when "and the order is given to stop the convoy" is followed by an image of a waitress, words and image do not coincide as expected. These works convey some of the complexity of how experience is filtered through the personal and cultural databanks of representations.

Fast's own craft plays a major role in *5000 Feet Is the Best.* Its scenes are richly and meticulously staged, professionally acted, and exquisitely edited. Unlike in the previously discussed work, however, Fast does not use editing to fabricate the narration. Instead, the readily apparent and virtuosic edits are enlisted for aesthetic and emotional impact. By the third time the pilot submits to his interviewer, the room feels like it has filled with cameras, each one frenetically feeding images into the central eye of the editor, picking out and amplifying details such as lights, shadows, and colors that were dormant throughout the first telling. The effect is breathtaking and draws attention not only to the artifice of filmmaking but also to the variety of details that at any moment can be brought to bear on fleshing out our memories and turning them into stories and history.

Andrea Bowers and Catherine Opie

Since her first exhibitions in the late 1990s, Los Angeles-based Andrea Bowers (b. 1965) has been focusing on community and activism, producing what amounts to an archive of protest and democratic actions. Bowers was born and raised in a small working-class town in northern Ohio. She received a traditional studio training in college before immersing herself in the conceptual and political environment of CalArts in the early 1990s. Interested in crowds, Bowers began making drawings of moments of connection between strangers as well as portraits of individuation. Her protagonists become themselves as they join together in celebration or even simple fandom. In 2003, she began drawing a history of democratic protest. "It had just been a matter of time," she explained, "before documenting people's actions turned into documenting people's activism."[63] Bowers has since made compelling work about undocumented citizens, at-risk populations, abortion, the environment, feminism, and AIDS that addresses political empowerment in the face of crisis. Her material comes primarily from interviews, many of which she films and incorporates into the final work, and archives. Though the lives and events she focuses on are often dramatic and complex, her staging and presentation are controlled and simple: People read letters, write notes, teach, watch, and speak. At times her subjects might dance, or sing, or hold each other.

Bowers's work on activism began with series of drawings and video works about non-violent civil disobedience that present a philosophical and practical guide to resistance and self-determination at the turn of the millennium. She executed the drawings, including *Nonviolent Protest Training: Abalone Alliance Camp, Diablo Canyon Nuclear Power Plant, 1981 and San Luis Obispo County Telegraph-Tribune, Sept 14, 1981* (2004) (**fig. 11.24**), in a Photorealist style, isolating the activists from their context and surrounding them with vast fields of white paper. The exhaustive detail invites the viewer to peer closely at bodies suspended in poses of action and collapse. Protestors rally but the site of their demonstration is revealed only outside the drawing in the titles or, as in the unusual case of *Nonviolent Protest Training: Abalone Alliance Camp*, in an accompanying clipping. In other drawings, the demonstrators are drawn hanging limply, with their bodies descending unsupported toward the ground, the result of Bowers excluding the arresting officers, the surrounding architecture, landscape, and witnesses from the images. These are portraits of resistance separated from the agents of authority. Bowers has described her labor-intensive method of meticulously transcribing the source photograph in minute detail as a means of letting the body transmit information to the mind.[64] The physicality of her process, like the imagery itself, offers a conduit from protestors' acts of resistance to viewers' acts of perception.

Nonviolent Civil Disobedience Training (2004), a two-channel video related to *Nonviolent Protest Training*, further develops Bowers's thinking about the integration of bodies and politics. For the film, Bowers enlisted a group of ten dancers to take a course in non-violent civil disobedience. Political action groups typically offer such training sessions to educate themselves and others in the forms their resistance takes and to build a sense of purpose and community. At the start of the video, the two anonymous facilitators present a history of non-violence and prompt the dancers to think about the

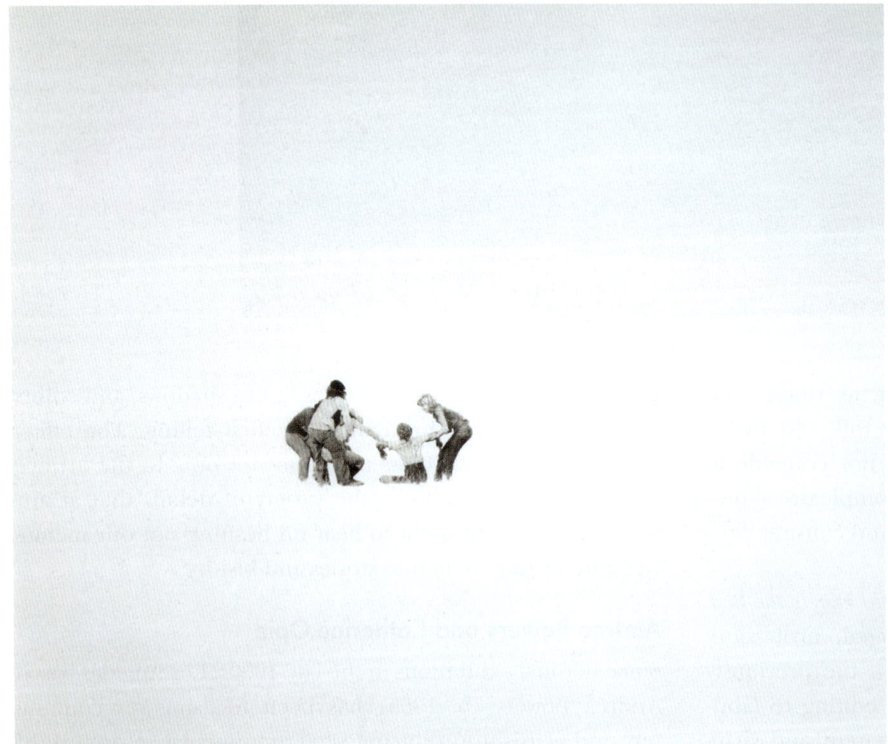

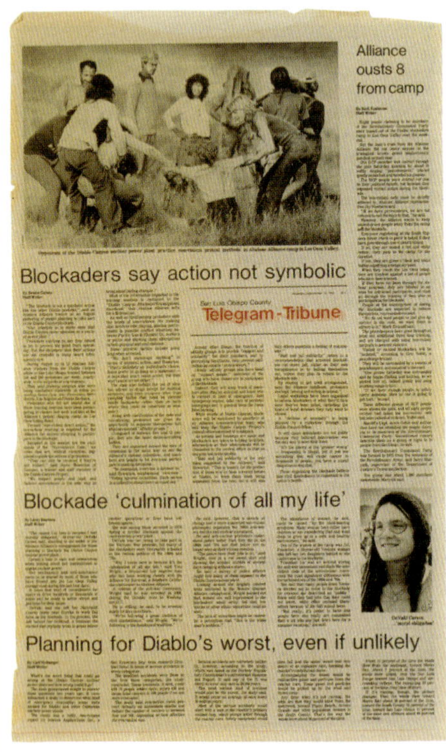

Alliance ousts 8 from camp

Blockaders say action not symbolic

San Luis Obispo County Telegram-Tribune

Blockade 'culmination of all my life'

Planning for Diablo's worst, even if unlikely

11.24 Andrea Bowers, *Nonviolent Protest Training: Abalone Alliance Camp, Diablo Canyon Nuclear Power Plant, 1981 and San Luis Obispo County Telegraph-Tribune, Sept 14, 1981*, 2004. Graphite on paper and newspaper page, diptych; graphite 38 × 49¾" (96.5 × 126.36 cm), newspaper 23 × 14" (58.42 × 35.56 cm). Whitney Museum of American Art, New York. Partial and promised gift of Steven G. Perelman. Courtesy of Susanne Vielmetter, Los Angeles Project.

meaning and purpose of violence and its alternatives. In terms analogous to those used by political theorists, they spell out the organizational structure of resistance in the twenty-first century while detailing ground operations of the World Trade Organization protests in Seattle, Washington in 1999. They describe the non-hierarchical structure, compared often by observers to swarms or insect colonies, by which thousands of individuals from hundreds of different interest groups were able to coordinate actions in a common pursuit. The instruction is presented primarily in the left-hand projection. On the right, though not exclusively, the dancers become students; they share their ideas about violence and protest, and then enact non-violent actions. The video balances the didactic content with a demonstration of the physical aesthetics of protest.

Unlike the facilitators or their usual students, the dancers did not identify themselves as activists; they were simply on a job, in essence playing the role of young activists. Toward the end of the film, Bowers presents the dancers sitting cross-legged on the floor with their arms intertwined as the facilitators approach the group in the role of police officers. The students' bodies become obstructions that have to be carried away, and as viewers watch one can nearly feel their weight being dragged across the floor. Bowers has captured the physicality of the experience, and also the new social relationship of the dancers, who, regardless of their politics or reason for being in the training session, have become a community. As in the work of Fast or Huyghe (see Chapter 10), the line between actor and subject, reality and representation, is left intentionally vague. By presenting the dancers' experience of the training, Bowers encourages the viewers to identify with them as subjects, while she also uses them as representations of politically engaged citizens.

Since *Nonviolent Civil Disobedience Training*, Bowers has mined contemporary politics for her archive of non-violent resistance. *The United States v. Tim DeChristopher* (2010) (**fig. 11.25**) continues her investigation of experience and representation as well as chronicling political agency in the twenty-first century. The film is a single-channel projected video that cuts between panoramic vistas of the desert landscape, most often snow-covered and under cloudy skies, footage of climate activist Tim DeChristopher shot relatively close up as he tells his story, and scenes of Bowers walking into the foreground of the landscape and writing a number on a chalkboard. The film repeats combinations of these scenes, with slightly different views, numbers, and moments from the narrative. The story DeChristopher tells is of his successful bid, despite having no money or intention to possess, to buy fourteen parcels of public land in the Southwest U.S. being sold at auction by the Bush administration in the last days of 2008. The fact that he won the 22,000 acres (at $1.8 million) prevented private oil interests from acquiring the land, disrupted the sale, and publicized the auction, which was later declared to have been illegal. By his action, DeChristopher successfully re-presented the land as part of the nation to be preserved rather than as a mapped commodity to be sold.

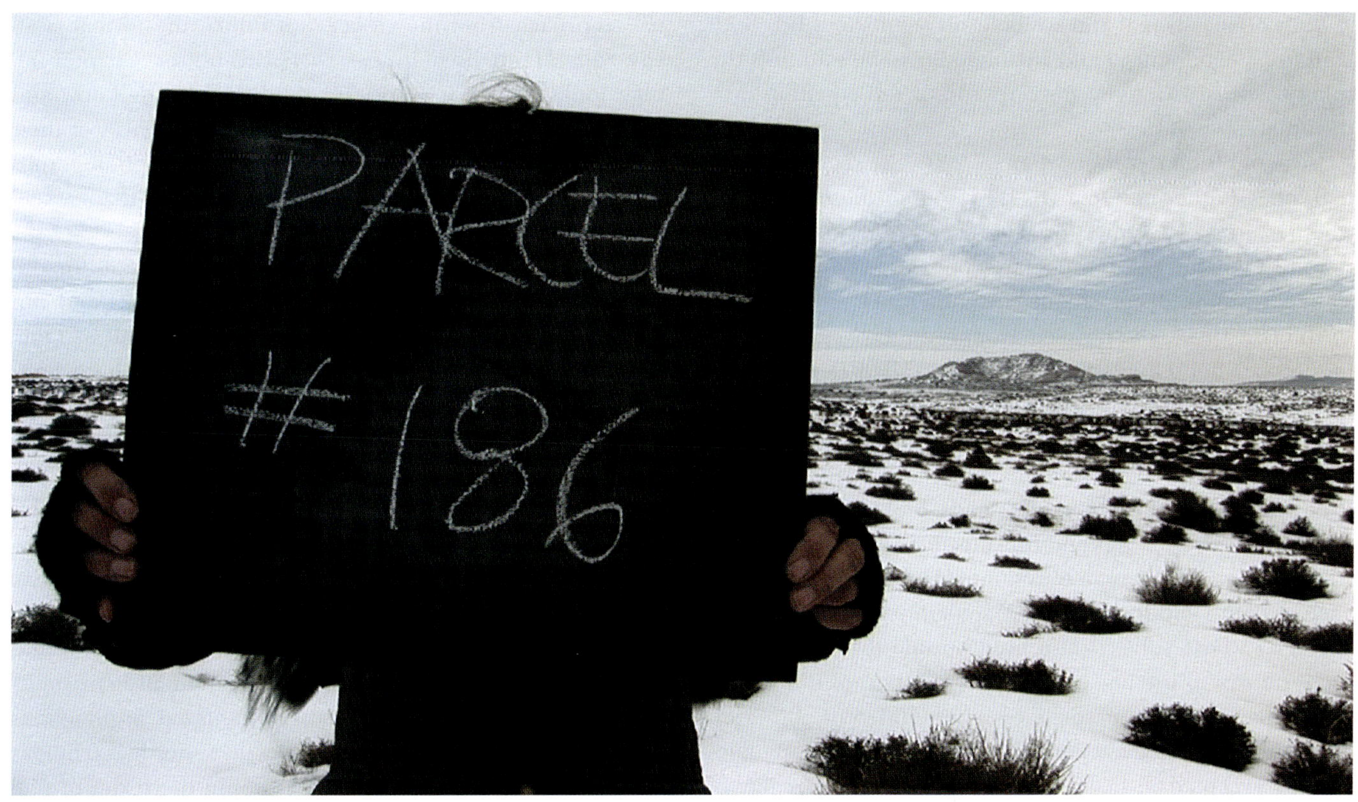

11.25 Andrea Bowers, *United States v. Tim DeChristopher*, 2010. Single-channel HD video (color with sound), 16:15 minutes looped. Utah Museum of Fine Arts. Courtesy of Susanne Vielmetter, Los Angeles Projects.

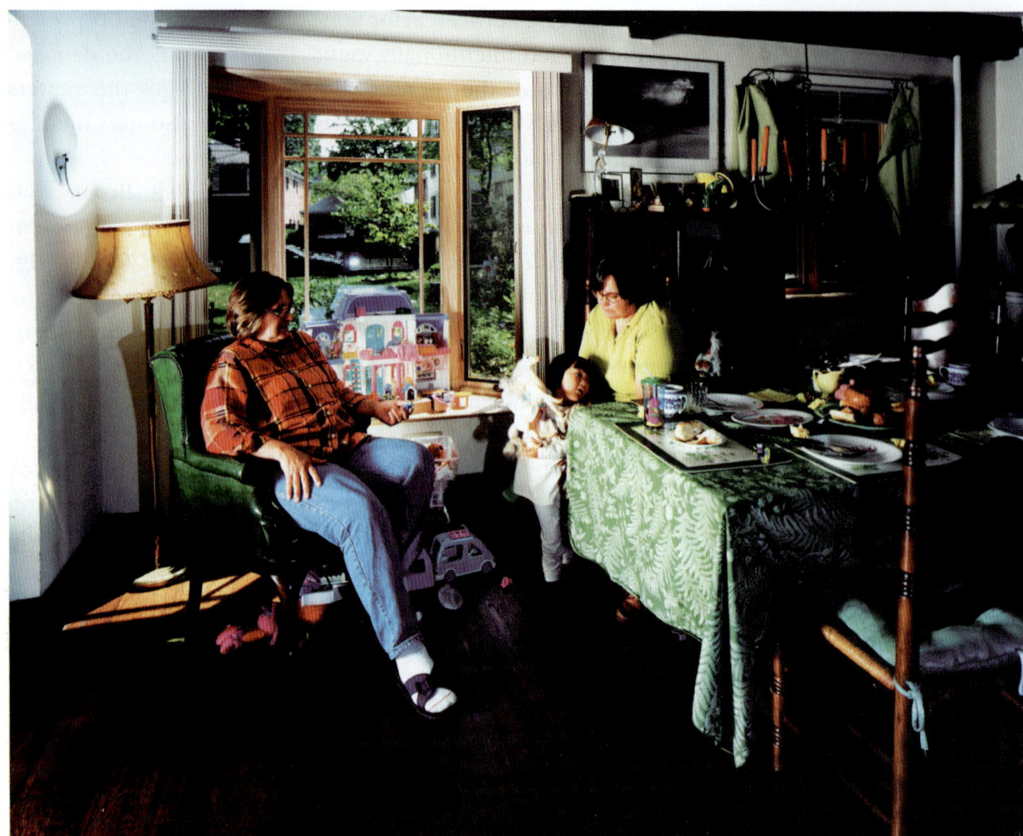

11.26 Catherine Opie, ***Joanne, Betsy & Olivia, Bayside, Queens***, 1998. Chromogenic print, 40 × 50" (101.6 × 127 cm). Edition of 5 + 2 APs. Courtesy Regen Projects, Los Angeles. © Catherine Opie.

As he speaks in the film, it becomes clear that the numbers Bowers writes are the lot numbers of the land on which she stands. With these numbers raised between the space of the gallery and those of the landscape, Bowers presents the land as both physically real and symbolically significant: It is both land to be experienced and a commodity to be sold. It is the role of activists to argue for one side of the equation over the other.

In a published conversation in 2007, Bowers and photographer Catherine Opie (b. 1961) posed the question of whether artists have the power to change the world.[65] Like Bowers, Opie has produced a large body of work that invites viewers to think deeply about both difference and activism. In the late 1990s, she traveled around the U.S. photographing lesbian households for a series she called *Domestic*. The scenes, including *Joanne, Betsy & Olivia, Bayside, Queens*, 1998 (**fig. 11.26**), are casually posed pictures of couples and families in mostly middle-class homes. Parents hold their children, couples hold each other's hands, looks are exchanged or avoided. The settings and the affections are familiar from households everywhere in the country. Unlike photographers such as Nan Goldin or Robert Mapplethorpe (see Chapters 4 and 7) whose subjects also lived outside the mainstream, Opie refuses to use any of the expected signs of difference. These particular domestic scenes are different, however: Though the idea of lesbian parents and alternative families may be accepted in many parts of the world, the reality of it is often met with prejudice and it is most certainly not the norm. Secondly, while composed to look like snapshots taken from any family photo-album, they are large-format photographs that require significant forethought and deliver a heightened degree of detail and luminescence. Opie's deliberately produced images foster a contemplative approach from the viewer, not unlike the formal strategy Sally Mann used in *Immediate Family* (see Chapter 7). One looks longer at scenes we think we already know and search the details of the sitters' homes, the nuances of their body language, and the light and color of the photographs to glean insight into lives defined by far more than sexual orientation.

Opie's work, in its creation of a visual language for difference that is rooted in the lives of her subjects and not the fears of society, is clearly political. Nonetheless, Opie comments to Bowers that it has become difficult to be a political artist at a time in which idealism seems to have no place. Opie's photographs of demonstrations and public celebrations, including *Untitled #1 (Jan. 20th, 2009)* (2009) (**fig. 11.27**) from the *Inauguration* series provides a record of this "aporia," the sense of emptiness and doubt within twenty-first-century politics, even at its moments of greatest success. Bowers strikes a more optimistic position, claiming "that art can have an effect on people's political philosophies, and that has to occur before their participation in activism."[66] As much as consciousness-raising and moral argument is part of Bowers's work, it is notable that she, like Thomas Hirschhorn, thinks that her success lies in the realm of philosophy. Opie, too, acknowledges that, regardless of however one answers the question of whether art changes the world,

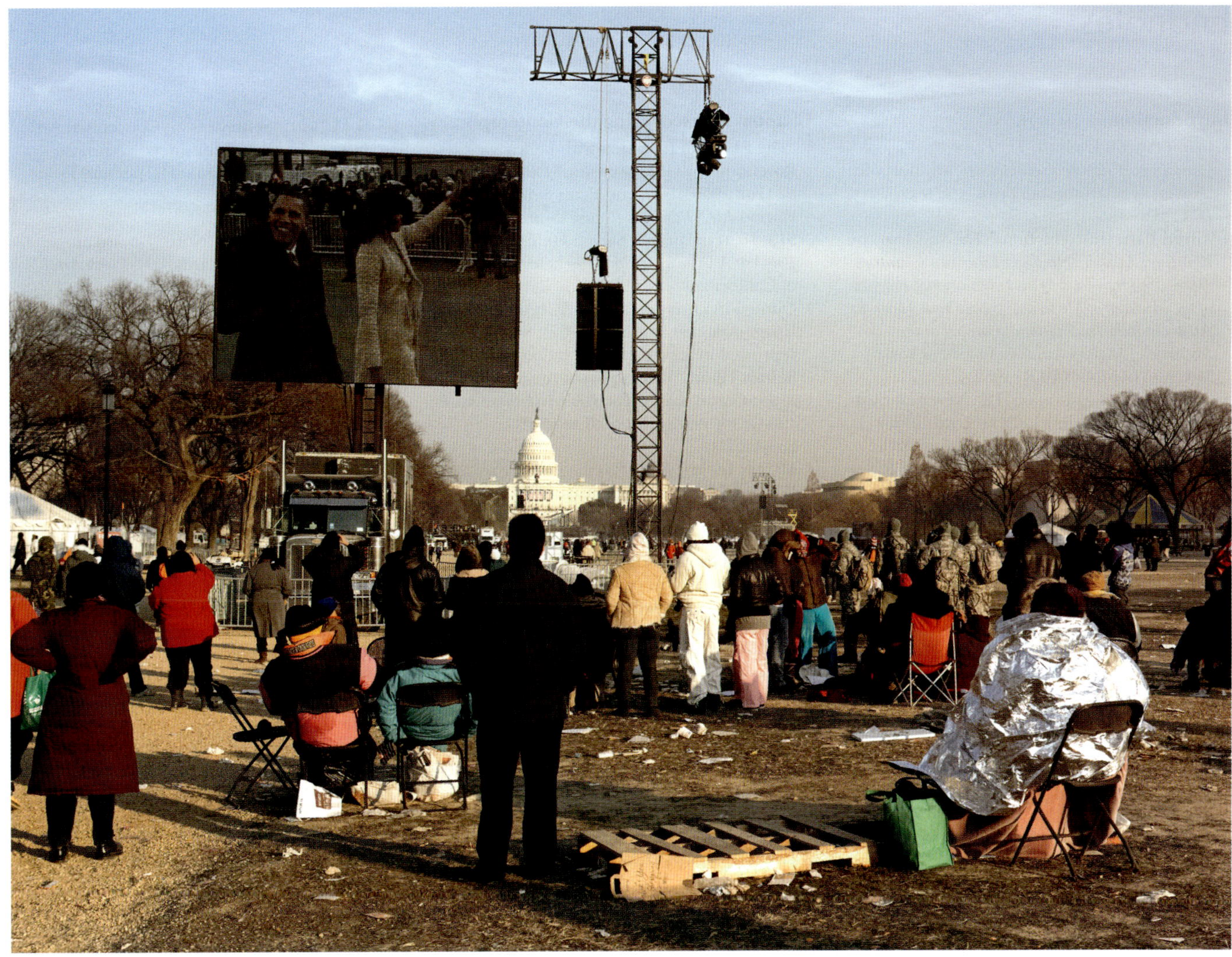

11.27 Catherine Opie, *Untitled #1 (Jan. 20th, 2009)* from the *Inauguration* series, 2009. C-print, 37.5 × 50" (95.3 × 127 cm). Edition of 5 + 2 APs. Courtesy Regen Projects, Los Angeles. © Catherine Opie.

one can make work that "creates the recognition of the possibility of change," and that is the foundation for political and social transformation.[67]

Bowers's work, in which movement, speech, and sensation, community, education, and maturation, and even parenthood and friendship constitute political action, extends the 1970s feminist notion that the personal is political. Her work also elaborates the related Foucauldian insight that political power is not limited to regulation or discipline but has evolved into a process for shaping social life and subjectivity. Foucault used the term "biopolitics" to describe the mechanisms by which life was so affected, and it has become central to political theory in the twenty-first century. Family, work, and school are key sites where human life is politically shaped; they are also sites where human beings can act to remake the world based on the kind of life they want to lead. Bowers's work, like most of the work discussed in this chapter, and throughout this book, proposes an art and politics of resistance. Bowers's and Opie's dialogue, like that between Kolbowski and Raad, or the political and pedagogical considerations of many of the other artists discussed in this chapter, testifies to the seriousness with which artists are taking the creative potential of occupying the intersections between contemporary art and life. The art of the 1970s discussed in Chapter 1 drew attention to the critical lenses through which we might view the confrontation between life and power, focusing particularly on issues of gender, race, and class. As the art world has extended its networks and become less securely tethered to the local politics of artworld centers, the legacy of the critical analyses refined in the late 1970s and early 1980s, and inflected by the art and theory of the 1990s, can be felt in the twenty-first-century appeal to see and feel with sensitivity, to think openly, and to be active in the studio, museum, and the world beyond.

Endnotes

Introduction

1 Jean-François Lyotard, *The Postmodern Condition: A Report on Knowledge*, Minneapolis: University of Minnesota Press, 1984, xxiii.

2 *Ibid.*, xxv.

3 Alfred Barr, "Introduction," *The New American Painting: As Shown in Eight European Countries 1958–59: Organized by the International Program of the Museum of Modern Art, New York under the Auspices of the International Council at the Museum of Modern Art, New York*, New York: Museum of Modern Art, 1959.

4 The critical reception of "The New American Painting" was chronicled in the exhibition catalogue published on the occasion of the final stop of the show, in London in 1959. See "As the Critics Saw It," in *The New American Painting*, 7–14.

5 Serge Guilbaut, one of the earliest historians to draw attention to the adoption of U.S. art for Cold War political purposes, called his account *How New York Stole the Idea of Modern Art*, Chicago: University of Chicago Press, 1983. The author explains that the body of the text was completed between 1975 and 1978, ix.

6 Hugo Ball, "Statement, May 15, 1916, Zurich," facsimile and translation in Robert Motherwell, ed., *The Dada Painters and Poets*, 2nd ed., Cambridge: Harvard University Press, 1981, xxv, 30.

7 Cited in T.J. Clark, *Farewell to an Idea*, New Haven: Yale University Press, 1999, 234.

8 Kazimir Malevich, "The Non-Objective World," (1926), selections reprinted in Herschel Chipp, ed., *Theories of Modern Art*, Berkeley: University of California Press, 1968, 337–646: 43, 346.

9 Alfred Barr, *The New American Painting*, *ibid.*, 68.

10 Michel Tapié, "The Necessity of an Autre Esthetic," (1953), in Tapié, *Observations*, ed. Paul and Ester Jenckins, New York: George Wittenborn, Inc., 1956, 19.

11 *Ibid.*

12 Claes Oldenburg, "I Am for an Art" (1961), reprinted in Ellen Johnson, ed., *American Artists on Art*, New York: Harper and Row, 1982, 97–101:98.

13 This and the following citations from "Avant-Garde and Kitsch" (1939) are from Clement Greenberg, *Art and Culture*, Boston: Beacon Press, 1961, 3–21.

14 Clement Greenberg, "American-Type Painting," *Partisan Review* (Spring 1955), reprinted and revised in Greenberg, *Art and Culture*, 208.

15 *Ibid.*

16 Leo Steinberg, "Jasper Johns: The First Seven Years of His Art" (1962), in Steinberg, *Other Criteria*, New York: Oxford University Press, 1972, 17–54:22.

17 *Ibid.*

Chapter 1: Discovering the Contemporary

1 "The F111: An Interview with James Rosenquist by G.R. Swenson," *Partisan Review*, 32 (Fall 1965), 599, and Peter Selz, "The Flaccid Art," *Partisan Review* (Summer 1963), 313–16, reprinted in Steven Henry Madoff, *Pop Art: A Critical History*, Berkeley: University of California Press, 1997, 85.

2 Quoted in unsigned article "Everything Clear Now?" *Newsweek* (Feb. 26, 1962), 86–87, reprinted in Steven Henry Madoff, *ibid.*, 187.

3 Sidney Tillim, "Rosenquist at the Met: Avant-Garde or Red Guard?" *Artforum* (April 1968), 46–49, reprinted in Madoff, 258–62:258.

4 Marcia Tucker, *James Rosenquist*, New York: Whitney Museum of American Art, 1972, *passim.*

5 Leo Steinberg, "Other Criteria," based on a lecture at the Metropolitan Museum of Art, 1968, published in part (including his discussion of flatbed painting) in Steinberg, "Reflections on the State of Criticism," *Artforum* (March 1972), 37–49, and then in full in Steinberg, *Other Criteria*, New York: Oxford University Press, 1972, 55–92:82.

6 Dick Higgins, "A Child's History of Fluxus" (1979), in Achille Bonita Oliva, Gabriella De Mila, and Claudio Cerritelli, eds., *Ubi Fluxus Ibi Motus 1990–1962*, Milan: Mazzotta, 1990, 172–74.

7 Donald Judd, "Specific Objects," in Judd, *Complete Writings 1959–1975*, Halifax: The Press of the Nova Scotia College of Art and Design, 2005, 181.

8 Bruce Glaser, "Questions to Stella and Judd," reprinted in Ellen Johnson, ed., *American Artists on Art from 1940 to 1980*, New York: Harper and Row, 1982, 117.

9 Robert Smithson, "Donald Judd," in Philadelphia Institute of Contemporary Art, *7 Sculptors* (Philadelphia: ICA, 1965), reprinted in Jack Flam, ed., *Robert Smithson: The Collected Writings*, Berkeley: University of California, 1996, 4–6:4

10 Robert Morris, "Notes on Sculpture" (1966), in Gregory Battcock, ed., *Minimal Art: A Critical Anthology*, Berkeley: University of California Press, 1995, 222–35:232.

11 Cited in Guy Brett, "Lygia Clark: Six Cells," in Le Fundacio Antoni Tapiès, *Lygia Clark*, Barcelona: Le Fundacio, 1998, 22.

12 Lynn Gumbert, Ned Rifkin, and Marcia Tucker, *Early Work: Lynda Benglis/Joan Brown/Luis Jiminez/Gary Stephan*, New York: The New Museum, 1982, 11.

13 Accessed online at http://www.ubu.com/concept/serra_verb.html.

14 Robert Smithson, "Spiral Jetty (1972)," in Jack Flam, ed., *Robert Smithson: The Collected Writings*, *ibid.*, 143–53:146.

15 Gilles Deleuze and Felix Guattari, *Anti-Oedipus: Capitalism and Schizophrenia*, Minneapolis: University of Minnesota Press, 1983, 109.

16 Susan Sontag, "Against Interpretation," in Sontag, *Against Interpretation and Other Essays*, New York: Farrar, Strauss and Giroux, 1969, 14.

17 Sol Lewitt, "Sentences on Conceptual Art" (1969), in Ellen Johnson, ed., *American Artists on Art*, New York: Harper and Row, 1982, 125.

18 *Ibid.*

19 Willoughby Sharp, "Notes Toward an Understanding of Earth Art," *Earth Art*, Ithaca, N.Y.: Office of University Publications, Cornell University, 1970, n.p., reprinted in Jeffrey Kastner, ed., *Land and Environmental Art*, New York: Phaidon Press: 1998, 199–200:199.

20 *Ibid.*

21 Allan Kaprow, "The Shape of the Art Environment: How Anti-Form Is Anti-Form?" *Artforum* (April 1968), 32–33:33

22 Gregory Battcock, "The Politics of Space," *Arts* (Feb. 1970), 40–43:41.

23 *Ibid.*, 42.

24 *Ibid.*, 43.

25 Willoughby Sharp, "Elemental Gesture: Terry Fox," *Arts* (May 1970), 48–51:48.

26 Caroline Tisdall, *Joseph Beuys*, New York: Solomon R. Guggenheim Foundation, 1979, 86.

27 Joseph Bueys, "Interview with Willoughby Sharp," *Artforum* (Dec. 1969), 47.

28 Joseph Beuys, "I Am Searching for Field Character" (1973), trans. Caroline Tisdall in *Art into Society, Society into Art*, London: Institute of Contemporary Art, 1974, 48, reprinted in Charles Harrison and Paul Wood, *Art in Theory 1900–2000*, Malden, MA: Blackwell Publishing, 2003, 929.

29 Joseph Beuys, "Untitled Statements,"(ca. 1973) in Kristine Stiles and Peter Selz eds., *Theories and Documents of Contemporary Art: A Sourcebook of Artists' Writings*, (Berkeley: University of California Press, 1996), 633.

30 Jon Bird, *Leon Golub: Echoes of the Real*, London: Reaktion, 2000, 55.

31 Jack Burnham, "Hans Haacke's Canceled Show at the Guggenheim," *Artforum* (June 1971), 67–71:71.

32 *Ibid.*, 70.

33 Adrian Piper, "In Support of Meta Art," *Artforum* (Oct. 1973), 79–81:79.

34 Statement in "Politics," a column in *Artforum* (May 1971), 12.

35 Larry Neal "The Cultural Front," *Liberator* (June 1965). Neal met with AfriCOBRA members at the 1970 Congress on Functional Aspects of Black Art (CONFABA), organized by students on Donaldson's African-American art-history course at Northwestern University. Others groups, notably Latino and Chicano ones, enlisted the same logic to underscore their own mural projects.

36 Barbara Jones-Hogu, "The History, Philosophy and Aesthetics of AfriCOBRA," in *AFRICOBRA III*, Amherst: University of Massachusetts, 1973, n.p.

37 Wadsworth Jarrell in Robert L. Douglas, *Wadsworth Jarrell: The Artist as Revolutionary*, San Francisco: Pomegranate Art Books, 1996, 29.

38 Barbara Jones-Hogu, "The History, Philosophy and Aesthetics of AfriCOBRA," *ibid.*

39 *Ibid.*
40 *Ibid.*
41 Jeff Donaldson, "Artist Statement," in *AfriCOBRA III*, *ibid.*, n.p. and reprinted in Donaldson, "AfriCOBRA Manifesto? Ten in Search of a Nation," NKA 30 (Spring 2012), 83: 81.
42 Barbara Jones-Hogu, "The History, Philosophy and Aesthetics of AfriCOBRA," *ibid.*
43 Emory Douglas, "Revolutionary Art/Black Liberation" (1968), in Philip Sheldon Foner and Clayborne Carson, eds., *The Black Panthers Speak*, Cambridge: Da Capo Press, 1995, 16.
44 *Ibid.* Douglas notes Newton's perception of the black community as being visual in St. Clair Bourne, "An Artist for the People: An Interview with Emory Douglas," in Sam Durant, ed., *Black Panther: The Revolutionary Art of Emory Douglas*, New York: Rizzoli 2007, 200.
45 Louis Althusser, "Ideology and Ideological State Apparatuses (Notes Towards an Investigation)" (Jan.–April 1969), in Althusser, *Lenin and Philosophy and Other Essays*, New York: Monthly Review Press, 1971, 127–86:133.
46 *Ibid.*
47 Nancy Spero, "Interview with Jo Anna Isaak," in Jon Bird, Jo Anna Isaak, and Sylère Lotringer, *Nancy Spero*, New York: Phaidon, 2006, 18.
48 Hélène Cixous, "The Laugh of the Medusa," in Elaine Marx and Isabelle de Courtivron, *New French Feminisms*, New York: Schocken Books, 1980, 245–64:250.
49 *Ibid.*, 253.
50 Judy Chicago and Miriam Schapiro, *Womanhouse*, Valencia: Feminist Art Program, California Institute of the Arts, 1972, n.p.
51 *Ibid.*
52 Anne-Marie Sauzeau-Boetti, "Negative Capability as Practice in Women's Art," *Studio International*, 191:979 (1976), 24–25, in Rozsika Parker and Griselda Pollock, eds., *Framing Feminism*, London and New York: Pandora, 1987, 279.
53 *Ibid.*
54 *Ibid.*, 278.
55 Martha Rosler, "The Private and the Public Feminist Art in California," *Artforum* (Sept. 1977), 66–74:70.
56 Cindy Nemser, "Interview with Members of AIR," *Arts* (Dec.–Jan. 1973), 58–59:59.
57 Martha Rosler, "The Private and the Public Feminist Art in California," *ibid.*, 68.
58 *Ibid.*, 68–69.
59 Cindy Nemser, "Four Artists of Sensuality," *Arts* (March 1975), 73–75.

Chapter 2: Taking Pictures

1 See Douglas Crimp, "Pictures," *October* 8 (Spring 1978), 75–88.
2 Michael Fried, "Art and Objecthood," *Artforum* (June 1967), reprinted in Gregory Battcock, ed., *Minimal Art: A Critical Anthology*, Berkeley: University of California Press, 1995, 147.
3 Craig Owens, "The Allegorical Impulse: Towards a Theory of Post-modernism (Parts 1–2), *October* 12–13 (Spring and Summer 1980).
4 Douglas Crimp, "Pictures," *ibid.*, 85.
5 See Rosalind E. Krauss, *The Originality of the Avant-Garde and Other Modernist Myths*, Cambridge, MA: MIT Press, 1985.
6 Jeanne Siegel, "After Sherrie Levine," *Arts* (Summer 1985), 141–44.
7 *Ibid.*
8 Douglas Crimp, "Appropriating Appropriation," in *Image Scavengers: Photographers* (Philadelphia: Institute of Contemporary Art, 1983), 30, cited in Crimp, "Boys in My Bedroom," *Art in America* 78 (February 1990), 47–49:47.
9 Abigail Solomon-Godeau, "Winning the Game When the Rules Have Changed," *Screen*, 26:6 (Nov.–Dec 1984), 90.
10 Douglas Crimp, *On the Museum's Ruins*, Cambridge: MIT Press, 1993, 13.
11 "In the Picture: Jeff Rian in Conversation with Richard Prince," in Rosetta Brooks et al., *Richard Prince*, London: Phaidon, 2003, 12.
12 *Ibid.*, 9.
13 Lisa Phillips, *Richard Prince*, New York: Whitney Museum of American Art, 1992, 25.
14 "In the Picture," 16.
15 Richard Prince, *Why I Go to the Movies Alone* New York: Tanam Press, 1983, 11.
16 *Ibid.*, 11.
17 *Ibid.*, 13.
18 Carter Ratcliff, "Art and Resentment," *Art in America* 70 (Summer 1982), 9–13.
19 Laura Mulvey, "A Phantasmagoria of the Female Body," *New Left Review* 188 (July/August 1991) 136–51 on Sherman and Crimp, "Boys in My Bedroom," *Art in America* 78 (February 1990), 47–49 are good examples of this.
20 "Untitled Statement" (1982) and "Interview with Els Barents" (1982), reprinted in Kristine Stiles and Peter Selz, eds., *Theories and Documents of Contemporary Art*, Berkeley: University of California Press, 1996, 791–94.
21 Sandy Nairne, *State of the Art: Ideas and Images of the 1980s*, London: Chatto & Windus, 1987, 132. Sherman emphasized her concern with reaching a wide public in 2003, saying that she "wanted to find something that anyone could relate to without knowing about contemporary art": "Cindy Sherman Talks to David Frankel," *Artforum* (March 2003), 54.
22 Sandy Nairne, *State of the Art*, *ibid.*, 133, and "Cindy Sherman Talks to David Frankel," *ibid.*, *passim.*
23 Rosalind Krauss, "The Originality of the Avant-Garde," in Krauss, *The Originality of the Avant-Garde and Other Modernist Myths*, *ibid.*, 162.
24 *Ibid.*, 168.
25 *Ibid.*, 168–70.
26 Walter Benjamin, "A Short History of Photography" (1931), reprinted in Alan Tractenberg, ed., *Classic Essays of Photography*, Stony Creek, CT: Leete's Island Books, 1980, 199–216.
27 Peter Schjeldahl, "Shermanettes," *Art in America* (March 1982), 110–11.
28 Peter Schjeldahl, "The Oracle of Images," in *Cindy Sherman*, New York: Whitney Museum of American Art, 1987, 8.
29 Ken Johnson, "Cindy Sherman and the Anti-Self: An Interpretation of her Imagery," *Arts* (Nov. 1987), 47–53.
30 Judith Williamson, "Images of Women," *Screen* (Nov. 1983), 105.
31 Therese Lichtenstein, "Cindy Sherman," *Arts* (Jan. 1983), 3.
32 Abigail Solomon-Godeau, "Suitable for Framing: The Critical Recasting of Cindy Sherman," *Parkett* 29 (1991), 112–21.
33 Laura Mulvey "Visual Pleasure and Narrative Cinema," in Brian Wallis, ed., *Art After Modernism*, New York: The New Museum, 1984, 363.
34 Laurie Anderson. "Language is a Virus from Outer Space," on *United States Live*, New York: Warner Brothers, 1983. The phrase is, in fact, William Burroughs's, used by Anderson in her own form of appropriation.
35 The risk that art, even modern art, might resist this inclination to become another attribute of power was illustrated in a press conference at the UN on Feb. 5, 2003 in which U.S. Secretary of State Colin Powell explained why war must be waged against Iraq. Behind the podium was a tapestry of Picasso's 1937 work *Guernica*. To avoid the possibility that this work might not be turned into an innocuous monochrome by the cameras, the UN publicity team had the tapestry covered.
36 Allan McCollum, "In the Collection Of ...," *Wedge* (Winter–Spring 1985), 64.
37 Andrea Fraser, "In and Out of Place," *Art in America* (June 1985), 122.
38 Cited in Dan Cameron, "Four Installations: Francesc Torres, Mierle Ukeles, Louise Lawler/Allan McCollum and TODT," *Arts* (Dec. 1984), 70.
39 Craig Owens, "From Work to Frame, or, Is There Life After 'The Death of the Author,'" in Owens, *Beyond Recognition*, Berkeley: University of California Press, 1992, 122–39, makes clear that critics and advertisers in the 1980s identified the U.S. and even the global imagination in the same terms. Kruger and Stallone were two sides of the same coin. Owens even suggests that the art world was also infected with the need for the hero worship that Kruger critiques.
40 Rosalyn Deutsch, "Breaking Ground: Barbara Kruger's Spatial Practice," in Ann Goldstein et al., *Barbara Kruger: Thinking of You*, Los Angeles: Museum of Contemporary Art, 1999, 77.
41 Lynn Tillman, "Interview with Barbara Kruger," in *ibid.*, 196.
42 Gary Indiana, "The War at Home," in *ibid.*, 9.
43 Kate Linker, *Love For Sale*, New York: H.N. Abrams, 1990, 17.
44 Bruce Ferguson, "Wordsmith: An Interview with Jenny Holzer," *Art in America* 74 (Dec. 1986), 109–14:113.
45 In Jeanne Siegel, "Jenny Holzer's Language Games," *Arts* (Dec. 1985), reprinted in Siegel, *Artwords 2: Discourse on the Early 80s*, Ann Arbor: UMI Press, 1988, 285–97.
46 Bruce Ferguson, "Wordsmith: An Interview with Jenny Holzer," *ibid.*
47 See David Joselit, "Voices, Bodies and Spaces: The Art of Jenny Holzer," in Joselit et al., *Jenny Holzer*, London: Phaidon, 1998, 48–54.
48 Benjamin H.D. Buchloh, "Allegorical Procedures," *Artforum* 21:1 (Sept. 1982), 48.
49 Hal Foster, "Subversive Signs," *Art in America* 70:10 (Nov. 1982), 88–92: 88.
50 Craig Owens, "The Medusa Effect, or, The Specular Ruse," in Owens, *Beyond*

Recognition, Berkeley: University of California Press, 1992, 191–200.
51 *Ibid.*, 88.

Chapter 3: Back to the Easel

1 Christos M. Joachimides, "A New Spirit in Painting," in Joachimides, Norman Rosenthal, and Nicolas Serota, eds., *A New Spirit in Painting*, London: Royal Academy of Art, 1981,14.
2 *Ibid.*
3 Martin-Gropius-Bau, *Zeitgeist*, New York: George Braziller, Inc., 1983, 9.
4 René Ricard, "Julian Schnabel's Plate Paintings at Mary Boone," *Art in America* (Nov. 1979), 125–26:125.
5 Jeff Perrone, "Boy Do I Love Art or What?" *Arts* (Sept. 1981), 72–78:72.
6 Christos M. Joachimides, "A New Spirit in Painting," *ibid.*, 14.
7 So titled in the 1987 Whitechapel show, Julian Schnabel, *Julian Schnabel: Painting 1975–87*, London: Whitechapel Gallery, 1987.
8 *Ibid.*, 104. See Pincus-Witten, "Julian Schnabel: Blind Faith," *Arts* (Feb. 1982), 152–55:155: "I am interested in madness or paranoia or angst—as they are emotional states that are meditations on death."
9 Statement, July 11, 1986, in Julian Schnabel, *Julian Schnabel: Painting 1975–87*, *ibid.*, 104.
10 *Ibid.*, 105.
11 Jeff Perrone, "Boy Do I Love Art or What," *ibid.*, 77.
12 Eric Fischl, *Eric Fischl*, New York: Vintage Books, 1987, 33.
13 *Ibid.*
14 Constance W. Glenn, "Conversation with the Artist," in Constance W. Glenn and Lucinda Barnes, *Eric Fischl: Scenes Before the Eye*, Long Beach, CA: University Art Museum, 1986, 17.
15 1981 statement reprinted in Peter Schjeldahl, "Witness," in David Whitney, ed., *Eric Fischl*, New York: Art in America, and Stewart, Tabori, & Chang, 1988, 22–23
16 Eric Fischl, *ibid.*, 43.
17 Schnabel, cited in Christian Hubert et al., "Post-Modernism: A Symposium," *Real Life Magazine* (Summer 1981), 9, and Salle in Salle, "The Paintings Are Dead," *Cover* (May 1979), reprinted in Brian Wallis, ed., *Blasted Allegories*, New York: The New Museum, 1987, 325.
18 Walter Robinson, "David Salle," *Art in America* (March 1980), 117–118; cf. Georgia Marsh interview with David Salle, *Bomb* (Fall 1985), reprinted in Jeanne Seigel, *Artwords 2: Discourse on the Early 80s*, Ann Arbor: UMI Press, 1988, 173–75. Salle's denial is from Robert Pincus-Witten, "Pure Painter: An Interview with David Salle," *Arts* (Nov. 1985), 79.
19 Peter Schjeldahl, "David Salle," in Jeanne Siegel, *Artwords 2: Discourse on the Early 80s*, *ibid.*, 165, and Pincus-Witten, "Pure Painter," *ibid.*, 80.
20 Christian Hubert et al., "Post-Modernism: A Symposium," *Real Life Magazine* (Summer 1981), 4–10:4.
21 *Ibid.*
22 Robert Pincus-Witten, "Pure Painter," *ibid.*, 80.
23 *Ibid.*
24 Mira Schor, "Appropriated Sexuality," *M/E/A/N/I/N/G* (Dec. 1986), reprinted in Susan Bee and Mira Schor, eds., *M/E/A/N/I/N/G: An Anthology of Artists' Writings, Theory, and Criticism*, Durham, NC: Duke University Press, 2000, 24–36:29.
25 *Ibid.*, 32.
26 Douglas Crimp, "End of Painting," in Crimp, *On the Museum's Ruins*, Cambridge: MIT Press, 1993, 90.
27 Thomas McEvily, "Royal Slumming: Jean-Michel Basquiat Here Below," *Artforum* (Nov. 1992), 96, and bell hooks, "Altars of Sacrifice: Re-Membering Basquiat," *Art in America* (June 1983), 70.
28 Achille Bonito Oliva, *The International Trans-avantgarde*, Milan: Giancarlo Politi Editore, 1982, 40–42.
29 *Ibid.*, 50.
30 *Ibid.*, 50.
31 *Ibid.*, 56.
32 *Ibid.*
33 Francesco Clemente, *Clemente*, New York: Vintage Books, 1987, 17.
34 Photo in Danny Berger, "Sandro Chia in His Studio: An Interview," *Print Collectors Newsletter* (Jan.–Feb. 1982), 168; quote in Jamey Gamrell, "Sandro Chia at Castelli Green," *Art in America* (Oct. 1983), 188.
35 Carter Ratcliff, "On Iconography and Some Italians," *Art in America* (Sept. 1982), 152–59:154. Ratcliff traces a variety of precedents of the water-carrier figure.
36 Danny Berger, "Sandro Chia in his Studio: An Interview," *ibid.*, 169.
37 Ann Percy, *Francesco Clemente: Three Worlds*, Philadelphia: Philadelphia Museum of Art, 1990, 20.
38 *Ibid.*, 50.
39 Danny Berger, "Francesco Clemente at the Metropolitan: An Interview," *Print Collectors Newsletter* 13 (March/April), 1982:12.
40 Robert Storr, "Realm of the Senses," *Art in America* (Nov. 1987), 134.
41 Merope Lolis, "Francesco Clemente," *Arts* (Sept. 1981), 23, and Donald Kuspit, "Francesco Clemente at Mary Boone and Sperone Westwater," *Art in America* (Nov. 1983), 227.
42 Michael Cannell, "Francesco Clemente," *Arts* (June 1983), 4.
43 Thomas Lawson, "Last Exit: Painting," *Artforum* (Oct. 1981), reprinted in Brian Wallis, ed., *Art after Modernism*, New York: The New Museum, 1984, 160.
44 Julia Kristeva, *Powers of Horror*, New York: Columbia University Press, 1982, 1–2.
45 Edit DeAk, "A Chameleon in a State of Grace," *Artforum* (Feb. 1981), 37.
46 Robert Storr, "Realm of the Senses," *ibid.*, 140.
47 Benjamin H.D. Buchloh, "Figures of Authority, Ciphers of Regression," *October* 16 (Spring 1981).
48 Calvin Tompkins "The Art World: An End to Chauvinism," *The New Yorker* (Dec. 7, 1981), 146–54. Tompkins notes Ileana Sonnabend, Marian Goodman, and Mary Boone at the German Pavilion and details the surge of European Neo-Expressionist exhibitions in New York in the previous few years.
49 The connection between the rhetoric of political normalization and the critical enthusiasm for the new painting is made in Douglas Crimp, "The Post Modern Museum," *Parachute* 46 (March–May 1987), in Crimp, *On the Museum's Ruins*, 313, and Andreas Huyssen, "Anselm Kiefer: The Terror of History, the Temptation of Myth," *October* 48 (1989), 25–26.
50 See A. Wildermuth, "Crisis of Interpretation," *Flash Art* (March 1984), 8–18, and Achille Bonito Oliva, *The International Trans-avantgarde, ibid.*
51 See Lisa Saltzman, *Anselm Kiefer and Art after Auschwitz*, Cambridge: Cambridge University Press, 1999, 107–10, for a summary of the German reactions, and Huyssen, "Kiefer in Berlin," *October* 62 (Fall 1992).
52 Donald Kuspit, "Flak from the Radicals: The American Case Against German Painting," in Jack Cowart, ed., *Expressions: New Art from Germany*, St. Louis: St. Louis Art Museum, 1983, 46.
53 Peter Schjeldahl, "Our Kiefer," *Art in America* (March 1988), 116–27.
54 Theodor Adorno, "Cultural Criticism and Society" (1967), in Adorno, *Prisms*, Cambridge, MA: MIT Press, 1981, 17–34:34.
55 Lisa Saltzman, *Anselm Kiefer and Art after Auschwitz, ibid.*
56 Steven Henry Madoff, "Anselm Kiefer: A Call to Memory," *Art News* (Oct. 1987), 129.
57 *Ibid.*
58 Andreas Huyssen, "Anselm Kiefer: The Terror of History, the Temptation of Myth," *October* 48 (1989), 25–45:39.
59 Donald Kuspit, "Anselm Kiefer," in Siegel, *Artwords 2* (1987), 89.
60 Laurie Attias, "Anselm Kiefer's Identity Crisis (the Artist and Post-Reunification Germany)," *Art News* 96 (June 1997), 110.
61 Theodor Adorno, *Aesthetic Theory*, 444, cited in Lisa Saltzman, *Anselm Kiefer and Art after Auschwitz, ibid.*, 20 in an extended discussion of Celan, Adorno, and Kiefer.
62 Daniel Arasse, *Anselm Kiefer*, New York: Harry N. Abrams, 2001, 140.
63 Armin Wildermuth, "A Crisis of Interpretation," *Flash Art* 116 (March 1984), 12. Fetting confirms the anti-conceptual stance in Helena Kontova, "Rainer Fetting Interview," *Flash Art* 115 (Jan. 1984), 16.
64 Paul Maenz, "Interview with Paul Maenz," *Flash Art* 117 (April 1984). Maenz characterizes the various regions of the German art scene, assigning a particular media focus to the Berlin painters in contrast to others.
65 Dorothea Dietrich, "A Conversation with Markus Lüpertz," *Print Collectors Newsletter*, 12, for Immendorff's critique of Lüpertz's apoliticality, and Douglas Crimp, "The Post Modern Museum," *ibid.*, for a more substantial critique. cf. Dietrich, "Allegories of Power: Markus Lüpertz's 'German Motifs,'" *Art Journal* 48 (Summer 1989), 164–70.
66 Ernst Busche, "Violent Painting," *Flash Art* 101 (Jan. 1981), 27–31:29.
67 Rosalyn Deutsche, "Alienation in Berlin: Kirchner's Street Scenes," *Art in America* (Jan. 1983), 65–72.
68 Donald Kuspit, "Acts of Aggression: German Painting Today, Part II," *Art in America* (Jan. 1983), 132.
69 "My Brain Is Hanging Upside Down (Bonzo Goes to Bitburg)," Ramones, *Animal Boy* (1986).

70 A.R. Penck, "From My Vantage Point," in *A.R. Penck*, New York: Mary Boone/Michael Werner Gallery, 1984, reprinted in John Yau, *A.R. Penck*, New York: Abrams, 1993, 117.

71 Statement of May 1978, reprinted in Barbara Theimann, "Jörg Immendorff works in the Ludwig Collection (1978–1987)," in State Russian Museum & Ludwig Museum in the Russian Museum, *Jörg Immendorff: All Things Have the Tendency to Change*, St. Petersburg: State Russian Museum, 2001, 36.

72 Heinz Althofer, "The Morality of Painting," in Tayfun Belgin, ed., *Immendorff: Bilder*, Heidelberg: Edition Braus, 2000, 155–68:158.

73 Donald Judd, "Local History," *Art Year Book 7* (1964), in Judd, *Donald Judd:Complete Writings 1959–1975*, Halifax: The Press of the Nova Scotia College of Art and Design, 1975, 151.

74 Jutta Koether, "Who Is Martin Kippenberger and Why Are They Saying Such Terrible Things About Him?" *Artscribe International* (Jan.–Feb. 1989), 52–57:53.

75 Stephen Prina, "Kippenberger's Tact," in Daniel Bauman et al., *Martin Kippenberger*, Basel: Kunsthalle Basel, 1998, 96–125: 98.

76 Jutta Koether, "Who Is Martin Kippenberger ...?" *ibid.*, 53.

77 Jutta Koether, "Martin Kippenberger," *Flash Art* 156 (Jan.–Feb. 1991).

Chapter 4: Into the Streets

1 Included in the group were John Fekner, Keith Haring, Jenny Holzer, Tom Otterness, Kenny Scharf, Christie Rupp, and Kiki Smith, nearly all of whom would make their way inside the art world during the 1980s.

2 Coosje van Bruggen, the curator delegated to oversee the U.S. contributions, was supportive of Holzer's plan to invite Fashion Moda.

3 Jeffrey Deitch, "Report from Times Square," *Art in America* (Sept. 1980), 59. The most acute analysis of the show came from Lucy R. Lippard, writing under a pseudonym, Anne Ominous, "Sex and Death and Shock and Shlock," *Artforum* (Oct. 1980), 50–55.

4 Carlo McCormick, "Guide to East Village Artists," supplement to Phyllis Plous, *Neo-York: Report on a Phenomenon*, Santa Barbara: University Art Museum, 1984, 1.

5 Carlo McCormick and Walter Robinson, "Slouching Toward Avenue D," *Art in America* (Summer 1984), 137.

6 David Wojnarowicz, *Close to Knives*, New York: Vintage Books, 1991, 122–23.

7 *Ibid.*

8 John Carlin, "Angel with a Gun: David Wojnarowicz, 1954–1992," in Dan Cameron et al., *Fever: The Art of David Wojnarowicz*, New York: The New Museum, 1999, 93.

9 Mark Holborn, "Nan Goldin's Ballad of Sexual Dependency: Interview by Mark Holborn," *Aperture* (Summer 1986), 38–45:41.

10 Group Material, Statement (1985), reprinted in Kristine Stiles and Peter Selz, eds., *Theories and Documents of Contemporary Art: A Sourcebook of Artists' Writings*, Berkeley: University of California Press, 1996, 895.

11 Artists' statement, reprinted in Alan Moore and Marc Miller, eds., *ABC No Rio Dinero: The Story of a Lower East Side Gallery*, New York: ABC No Rio and Collaborative Projects, 1985, 22.

12 "Reflections of a Long Distance Runner: Conversation between David Hammons and Deborah Menaker Rothschild," in *Yardbird Suite*, Williamstown, MA: Williams College Museum of Art, 1994, 48.

13 Joan Acocella, "Plastic Heaven," *Artforum* (Jan. 1992), 64–67:65.

14 "Roundtable for Education and Democracy," in Brian Wallis, ed., *Democracy: A Project by Group Material*, Discussions in Contemporary Culture, Number 5, New York: Dia Art Foundation, 59.

15 "Gran Fury," April 12, 1989 interview with David Deitcher in Russell Ferguson, William Olander, Marcia Tucker, and Karen Fiss, *Discourses: Conversations in Postmodern Art and Culture*, New York: The New Museum of Contemporary Art, 1990, 196–208:198.

16 "On Site Specificity: A Discussion with Hal Foster, Renée Green, Mitchell Kane, Miwon Kwon, John Lindell, Helen Molesworth," *Documents* 2 (Spring 1994), 11–22, 14–15.

17 Cylena Simonds, "Public Audit: An Interview with Elizabeth Sisco, Louis Hock, and David Avalos," *Afterimage* (Summer 1994), 8–11:8.

18 "David Avalos and Jean Parisi," in *Art Out There*, Chicago: School of the Art Institute of Chicago, 1996, 62.

19 To clarify the question of taxes paid by non-citizens, Avalos, Sisco, and Hock note that when you buy something you automatically pay taxes: Sales taxes and luxury taxes, for instance, do not require citizenship.

20 Cylena Simonds, "Public Audit," *ibid.*, 9.

Chapter 5: Commodities and Consumerism

1 Peter Nagy, "From Criticism to Complicity," *Flash Art* 129 (Summer 1986), 46–49:46.

2 John M. Armleder, Spark Vett, Parker Williams, and Sylvie Fleury, "John Armleder at any Speed," *Parkett* 50:50 (1997), 36–42.

3 Jeff Koons, *Jeff Koons Handbook*, New York: Rizzoli, 1992, 36.

4 Monika Spruth and Rosemarie Trockel, "Do women and men really want the same thing?" *Eau de Cologne* (November 1985), 29.

5 Jeff Koons, *Jeff Koons Handbook*, 33.

6 *Ibid.*, 48.

7 *Ibid.*, 78.

8 Germano Celant, "Haim Steinbach's Wild Wild West," *Artforum* 26:4 (Dec. 1987), 75–79:77.

9 *Ibid.*, 75.

10 *Ibid.*

11 Mike Kelley, *Minor Histories: Statements, Conversations, Proposals*, Cambridge, MA: MIT Press, 2004, frontispiece.

12 See Robert Storr, "An Interview with Mike Kelley," *Art in America* (June 1994), 90–93:92, and Jutta Koether, "Interview with Mike Kelley," *Journal of Contemporary Art* (Cologne, Germany) (Summer 1994), 7–24, reprinted in John C. Welchman, ed., *Mike Kelley: Interviews, Conversations and Chit-Chat (1986–2004)*, Zurich: JRP Ringier, 2005, 95–117.

13 Isabelle Graw, "Interview," in John C. Welchman et al., *Mike Kelley*, London: Phaidon, 1999, 8–41:16.

14 Mike Kelley, *Minor Histories*, *ibid.*, 62.

15 Peter Halley, "Statements (1983)," reprinted in Peter Halley, *Collected Essays 1981–1987*, Zurich: Bruno Bischofberger Gallery, 1988, 25.

16 *Ibid.*, 256.

17 *Society of the Spectacle* was published with no copyright. It can be fully accessed online at a number of sites including http://www.marxists.org/reference/archive/debord/.

18 Jean Baudrillard, "The Precession of Simulacra," reprinted in *Art after Modernism: Rethinking Representation*, New York: The New Museum, 1984, 253.

19 "Ross Bleckner," interview with Peter Drake, *Flash Art* 129 (Summer 1986), 66–67:66.

20 "Talking Abstract: Part Two," interview with Lilly Wei, *Art in America* (Dec. 1987), 114.

21 Constance Lewallen, "Sherrie Levine," *Journal of Contemporary Art* 6 (1993), available online at http://www.jca-online.com/slevine.html.

22 Jeanne Siegel, "Geometry Desurfacing: Ross Bleckner," *Arts* magazine (March 1986), reprinted in Siegel, *Artwords 2: Discourse on the Early Eighties*, Ann Arbor: UMI, 1988, 230.

23 Martha Buskirk, "Interviews with Sherrie Levine, Louise Lawler, and Fred Wilson," *October* 70 (Fall 1994), 99–112:100.

24 Clive Robertson, "Reconstructing Futures," in General Idea, *General Idea's Reconstructing Futures*, Toronto: General Idea, ca. 1978, n.p.

25 *Ibid.*

26 General Idea, "Glamour," *FILE Megazine* 3:1 (1975), 21.

27 *Ibid.*, 22.

28 General Idea, *General Idea, 1968–1984*, Basel: Kunsthalle, 1985, 25.

29 General Idea, *General Idea's Reconstructing Futures*, *ibid.*, n.p.

30 *Ibid.*

31 "Conversation between John Armleder and Raphaela Platow," in Martin Engler, *John M. Armleder: Everything Is Not Enough*, Waltham: Rose Museum of Art, 2006, 96–114:107.

32 "Rosemarie Trockel talks to Isabelle Graw," *Artforum* (March 2003), 225.

33 Jutta Koether, "Interview with Rosemarie Trockel," *Flash Art* 134 (May 1987), 40–42:41.

34 Sidra Stitch, *Rosemarie Trockel*, New York: Prestel, 1991.

35 "Rosemarie Trockel Talks to Isabelle Graw," *ibid.*, 273.

36 Jutta Koether, "The Nonchalance of Continuous Tense-ness," *Parkett* 58 (2000), passim and cf fn 4.

37 *Ibid.*, 104–08:104.

38 *Ibid.*, 108.

39 Peter Schjeldahl, "Loony Koons," *7 Days* (Dec. 14, 1988), 66.

40 Cited in Negar Azimi, "Fluffy Farhad," *Bidoun* (Spring 2010), 32–37:32–33.

41 *Ibid.*, 37.

Chapter 6: Memory and History

1 "Report of the Vietnam Veterans Memorial Design Competition," Records of the Vietnam Veterans Memorial Fund Container 3/66 Manuscripts Division, Library of Congress, cited in Daniel Abramson, "Maya Lin and the 1960s: Monuments, Time Lines, and Minimalism," *Critical Inquiry* 22:4, (Summer 1996), 679–709:687.

2 Doris von Drateln, "Jochen Gerz's Visual Poetry," trans. Ingeborg von Zitzewitz, *Contemporanea* 2 (Sept. 1989), 47.
3 Michael Gibson, "Hamburg: Sinking Feelings," *ARTnews* 86 (Summer 1987), 106–07:107, cited in James E. Young, "The Counter-Monument: Memory Against Itself in Germany Today," *Critical Inquiry* 18:2 (Winter 1992), 267–96:283. Young elaborated the discussion of the counter-monument in James Young, *At Memory's Edge*, New Haven: Yale University Press, 2002.
4 Jochen Gerz, "Toward Public Authorship," *Third Text* 18:6 (2004), 649–56:652.
5 Jacques Rancière, *The Politics of Aesthetics*, London: Continuum, 2006, 13.
6 Jacques Rancière, "The Work of the Image," in Lisa LeFeuvre et al., *Esther Shalev-Gerz*, Paris: Jeu de paume, 2010, accessible from the artist's website http://www.shalev-gerz.net/DE/15-09-2006/work_image.pdf.
7 Leslie Camhi, "Christian Boltanski: A Conversation with Leslie Camhi," *The Print Collector's Newsletter* 23:6 (Jan.–Feb. 1993), 201–06:202.
8 Susan Tumarkin Goodman, "Eight Artists: A Cultural Context," in The Jewish Museum, *From the Inside Out: Eight Contemporary Artists*, New York: The Jewish Museum, 1993, 22–39:25.
9 Howard N. Fox, *Eleanor Antin*, Los Angeles: Los Angeles County Museum of Art, 1999, 132.
10 Transcript of acceptance speech at the National Foundation for Jewish Culture Awards held at the Hudson Theater, New York City, May 18, 1998.
11 "In Conversation: Whitfield Lovell with John Yau," *Brooklyn Rail* (July–Aug. 2006), accessed online at http://www.brooklynrail.org/2006/07/art/whitfield-lovell.
12 "Whitfield Lovell in Conversation with Leslie King-Hammond," in Whitfield Lovell, *The Art of Whitfield Lovell: Whispers from the Walls*, San Francisco: Pomegranate Press, 2003, 53–65:53.
13 James Hannaham, "Pea Ball Bounce: Interview with Kara Walker," *Interview* 28:11 (Nov. 1998), 114–19:119.
14 The letter was circulated widely. Sections including this passage are reprinted in numerous discussions of Walker's work including Mark Reinhardt, "The Art of Racial Profiling," in Ian Berry, Darby English, Vivian Patterson, and Mark Reinhardt, eds., *Kara Walker: Narratives of a Negress*, Cambridge: MIT Press, 2003, 108–29:119.
15 "Reading Black Through White in the Work of Kara Walker: A Discussion Between Michael Corris and Robert Hobbs," *Art History* 26:3 (June 2003), 422–41:440.
16 Kara Walker, "The Debate Continues: Kara Walker's Response," *International Review of African American Art* 15:2 (1998), 48–49:49.
17 Charles H. Rowell , "An Interview with Kerry James Marshall," *Callaloo* 21:1 (Winter 1998), 263–72:265
18 *Ibid.*, 270.
19 Carlos Basualdo, "Interview: Carlos Basualdo in Conversation with Doris Salcedo," in Nancy Princenthal, Carlos Basualdo, and Andreas Huyssen, *Doris Salcedo*, London: Phaidon, 2000, 6–35:14.
20 *Ibid.*
21 Katya Garcia-Anton, "Silent Witnesses: Doris Salcedo at the Tate Gallery," *The Art Newspaper* 94 (July–Aug. 1999), 21.
22 Corinne Diserens, "William Kentridge: Unwilling Suspensions of Disbelief," *Art Press* 255 (March 2000), 26.
23 Carolyn Christov-Bakargiev, "Interview: Carolyn Christov-Bakargiev in Conversation with William Kentridge," in Dan Cameron et al., *William Kentridge*, London: Phaidon, 1999, 14.
24 *Ibid.*, 31.
25 Jessica Dubow and Ruth Rosengarten, "History as the Main Complaint: William Kentridge and the Making of Post-Apartheid South Africa," *Art History* 27:4 (Sept. 2004), 679.
26 Artist statement, www.theatlasgroup.org.
27 Alan Gilbert, "Walid Ra'ad," *Bomb* 81 (Fall 2002), accessed at www.bombsite.com/issues/81/articles/2504.
28 Waled Sadek, "A Matter of Words. (Art and Artists in Beirut, Lebanon)," *Parachute* (Oct. 2002), 34.
29 *Ibid.*
30 *Ibid.*
31 Description of the Berlin event in André Lepecki, "'After All, the Terror Was Not Without Reason': Unfiled Notes on the Atlas Group Archive," *TDR: The Drama Review*, 50:3 (T191) (Fall 2006), 97.
32 Alan Gilbert, "Walid Ra'ad," *ibid.*
33 *Ibid.*
34 Silvia Kolbowski and Walid Raad, *Between Artists: Silvia Kolbowski, Walid Raad*, New York: A.R.T. Press, 2006, 26.
35 Jalal Toufic, *Undying Love or Love Dies*, Sausalito, C.A.: Post-Apollo Press, 2002, quoted in Silvia Kolbowski and Walid Raad, *Between Artists*, ibid., 55.
36 Jalal Toufic, *Undeserving Lebanon*, online at http://www.jalaltoufic.com/downloads/Jalal_Toufic_Undeserving_Lebanon.pdf: Forthcoming Books, 2007, 9.
37 André Lepecki, "In the Mist of the Event: Performance and the Activation of Memory in the Atlas Group Archive," in Kassandrea Nakas and Britta Schmitz, eds., *The Atlas Group (1989–2004): A Project by Walid Raad*, Köln: Walther König, 2006, 61–65:62.

Chapter 7: Culture, Body, Self

1 From an unpublished manuscript, cited in Petra Barreras del Rio, "Ana Mendieta: A Historical Overview," in Barreras del Rio and John Perreault, eds., *Ana Mendieta: A Retrospective*, New York: New Museum, 1987.
2 Cited in Kaira M. Cabanas, "Ana Mendieta: Pain of Cuba, Body I Am," *Woman's Art Journal* 20:1 (Spring–Summer, 1999), 12–17:14.
3 Laura Roulet, "Ana Mendieta and Carl Andre: Duet of Leaf and Stone," *Art Journal* 63:3 (Fall 2004), 90.
4 Adrian Piper, "In Support of Meta Art," *Artforum* (Oct. 1973), 79–81:79.
5 Hans Ulrich Obrist, "Interview with Tehching Hsieh," in Paula Orrell, ed. *Marina Abramovic and The Future of Performance*, New York: Prestel, 2010, 96.
6 Quotes in this paragraph are from "The Year of the Rope: An Interview with Linda Montano and Tehching Hsieh," in Linda Frye Burnham and Steven Durland, eds., *The Citizen Artist: 20 Years of Art in the Public Arena. An Anthology from High Performance Magazine, 1978–1998*, Gardiner, NY: Critical Press, 1998, 29–39.
7 Cited in Jill O'Bryan, "Saint Orlan Faces Reincarnation," *Art Journal* (Winter 1997), 52.
8 Janet A. Kaplan, "Deeper and Deeper: Interview with Marina Abramović," *Art Journal* (Summer 1999), 7.
9 *Ibid.*
10 David Frankel, "In Her Own Words: Interview with David Frankel," in Helene Posner, *Kiki Smith*, New York: Monacelli, 2005, 38–39.
11 Claudia Gould, "But It Makes You Think About What You Think About Too: Conversation with Kiki Smith," in Linda Shearer and Claudia Gould, *Kiki Smith*, Williamstown, MA: William College Museum of Art and Columbus and Ohio: Wexner Center for the Arts, Ohio State University, 1992, 66. (It was jointly published by the two institutions.)
12 Mona Hatoum, *Mona Hatoum*, London: Phaidon, 1997, 122.
13 "Mona Hatoum Interviewed by Janine Antoni," *Bomb* 63 (Spring 1998), reprinted in Laura Steward Hoen, ed., *Mona Hatoum: Domestic Disturbance*, North Adams, MA: Mass MOCA and Santa Fe, NM: SITE Santa Fe, 2001, 26.
14 Laurel Berger, "Mona Hatoum: In Between, Outside, and in the Margins," *Artnews* (Sept. 1994), 149.
15 Edward W. Said, "The Art of Displacement: Mona Hatoum's Logic of Irreconcilables," in Tate Gallery, *Mona Hatoum: The Entire World as a Foreign Land*, London: Tate Gallery, 2000, 17.
16 Nancy Spector, *Felix Gonzalez-Torres*, New York: Guggenheim Museum, 1995, 147–50.
17 Tim Rollins, "Felix Gonzalez-Torres," in Lucinda Barnes et al., eds., *Between Artists: Twelve Contemporary American Artists Interview Twelve Contemporary American Artists*, Los Angeles: A.R.T. Press, 1996, 81–101:88.
18 Cited in Ad Reinhardt, Joseph Kosuth, and Felix Gonzalez-Torres, *Symptoms of Interference, Conditions of Possibility*, London: Camden Arts Centre, 1994, 76.
19 Janine Antoni, "Janine Antoni: Biting Sums Up My Relationship to Art History," *Flash Art* 26:171 (Summer 1993), 104–05, and Ewa Lajer-Burcharth, "Antoni's Difference," in Dan Cameron et al., *Janine Antoni*, Kusnacht, Switzerland: Ink Tree, 2000, 44–45.
20 Carmen Boullosa, "Gabriel Orozco," *Bomb* 98 (Winter 2007), accessed online at www.bombsite.com/issues/98/articles/2862.
21 Artist's notebook, reproduced and translated in Gabriel Orozco, *Photogravity*, Philadelphia: Philadelphia Museum of Art, 1999, 160–63.
22 "Interview with Gerard Matt," in Lucas Gehrmann et al., *Teresa Margolles*, Vienna: Kunsthalle Wien Project Space, 2003, 19–20.
23 "Santiago Sierra by Teresa Margolles," *Bomb* 86 (Winter 2004), accessed online at http://www.bombsite.com/issues/86/articles/2606 March 2009.
24 *Ibid.*
25 Coco Fusco, "The Unbearable Weightiness of Beings: Art in Mexico after NAFTA," in

Fusco, *The Bodies That Were Not Ours*, New York: Routledge, 2001, 61–77.
26 *Ibid.*, 67.

Chapter 8: Eastward Expansion: Contemporary Art in Russia and China

1 Robert Storr, "An Interview with Ilya Kabakov," *Art in America* (Jan. 1995), 68.
2 " 'With Russia on Your Back': A Conversation Between Ilya Kabakov and Boris Groys," *Parkett* 34 (1992), 30–41:38.
3 http://www.ilya-emilia-kabakov.com/text/10_2.html.
4 Margarita Tupitsyn introduced this comparison to Western audiences in her Sots Art exhibition at the New Museum in New York in 1986 and it was developed with point-by-point comparisons in David A. Ross et al., *Between Spring and Summer: Soviet Conceptual Art in the Era of Late Capitalism*, Boston: Institute of Contemporary Art, 1990. See particularly Tupitsyn, "U-Turn of the U-topia," in *ibid.*, 35–51.
5 Margarita Tupitsyn, "Sots Art: The Russian Deconstructive Force," in the New Museum, *Sots Art*, New York: The New Museum, 1986, 4–15:4.
6 Quotes in this paragraph are from Gerald Pirob, "Art and Ideology: Excerpts from an Interview with Alexander Kosolapov," in *New Directions: Essays on Aspects of the Permanent Collection by Members of the Rutgers University Faculty in Honor of the 25th Anniversary of the Jane Voorhees Zimmerli Art Museum*, New Brunswick, NJ: The Museum, 1991, 3–7:6.
7 See Jo Anna Isaak, "The Future of Disillusion: Sex, Truth, and Photography in the Former Soviet Union," *Art Journal* 53:2 (Summer 1994), 47. This issue of *Art Journal* is devoted to Russian photography and offers a good overview of the subject as well as some in-depth discussions.
8 Oleg Kulik in S. Khripoun, "Empire Bites Back: Oleg Kulik's 'Canine Performance' at Deitch Projects," *Thing Reviews* (April 27, 1997), 1.
9 See the discussion of the body in post-Soviet art in Pat Simpson, "Peripheralizing Patriarchy: Gender and Identity in Post Soviet Art: A View from the West," *Oxford Art Journal* 27:3 (2004).
10 Oleg Kulik, "Why Have I Bitten a Man?" in *Primary Documents: A Sourcebook for Eastern and Central European Art Since the 1950s*, New York: MoMA, 2002, 349.
11 Wenda Gu, "the divine comedy of our times—a thesis on united nations art project & its time and environment," posted on the artist's website, http://www.wendagu.com/home.html, 1995.
12 Alexander Brener and Barbara Schurz, *Anti-Technologies of Resistance*, 2000, http://subsol.c3.hu/subsol_2/contributors/brenertext.html. See also Brener and Schurz, *The Art of Destruction*, Ljubljana: Blossom v. Fruit SAMIZDAT, 2004.
13 Oleg Kulik, "The Gobi Test, or the Unbearable Charm of Mongolia," in *La Biennale di Venezia 51: Always a Little Further*, Venice: Fondazione La Biennale di Venezia, 2005, 178.
14 Oleg Kulik, "The Gobi Test, or the Unbearable Charm of Mongolia," in *La Biennale di Venezia 51, ibid.*
15 Huang Rui, "Preface to the First Stars Art Exhibition (Xingxing Meizhan) (1979)" in Wu Hung, ed., *Contemporary Chinese Art: Primary Documents*, New York: Museum of Modern Art, 2010, 7
16 The twelve were Huang Rui, Ma Desheng, Yan Li, Wang Keping, Yang Yiping, Qu Leilei, Mao Lizi, Bo Yun, Zhong Ahcheng, Shao Fei, Li Shuang, and Ai Weiwei.
17 See Gao Minglu, *The Wall: Reshaping Contemporary Chinese Art*, Buffalo, N.Y. : Albright Knox Art Gallery, 2005, 370.
18 Bo Yun, Mao Lizi, and Yang Yiping remained in China, and Ai Weiwei, though the first to leave, has since returned.
19 Li Xianting (co-curator of the 1989 "China/Avant-Garde" show), writing under the pseudonym Li Jiantun, claimed that half the young Chinese artists working in the 1980s did so under a style influenced by Rauschenberg. See "The Significance Is Not the Art" (1986) in Wu Hung, *Contemporary Chinese Art: Primary Documents*, 62–63. Gao Minglu, the chief curator of "China/Avant-Garde" and signatory of the introduction, also described the Rauschenberg exhibition as "the most provocative foreign exhibition" of the period, though he claimed that interest in a Rauschenberg-like collage aesthetic could be found in pre-1985 Chinese art. See Gao Minglu, "The '85 Movement" (1986) in Wu Hung and Peggy Wang, *Contemporary Chinese Art: Primary Documents*, New York: The Museum of Modern Art, 2010, 61.
20 Because Wenda Gu has adopted the Western custom of placing his given name first and family name second, I refer to him as Wenda Gu. When he exhibited in "China/Avant-Garde," however, he was referred to as Gu Wenda.
21 Gao Minglu et al., *China/Avant-Garde*, China Art Gallery: Beijing, 1989, n.p.
22 *Ibid.*
23 "Wang Guangyi in Conversation with Paul Gladston" (Nov. 2007), interview in Paul Gladston, *Avant-Garde Art Groups in China, 1979–89*, Bristol: Intellect—University of Chicago Press, forthcoming 2013. The Northern Arts Group included Shu Qun, Liu Yan, Ren Jian, Gao Minglu, Li Xianting, Wang Xiaojian, Zhou Yan, and Huang Zhuan. Wang Guanyi was the vice-chairman.
24 artasiapacific.com/Magazine/77/ReasoningWithIdolsWangGuangyi, accessed January 2013
25 Jérôme Sans, *China Talks: Interviews with 32 Contemporary Artists*, Hong Kong: Timezone, 2009, 187.
26 *Forever Lasting Love* is the English title of the work as it appeared in the 2011 Sotheby's Hong Kong sale of the Ullens collection. It was published by Gao Minglu as *Eternal Life*: see Gao, *The Wall, ibid.*, 99.
27 Zhang explains the history of these paintings in Sans, *China Talks, ibid.*, 186–93.
28 Huang Yongping, "Xiaming Dada—Postmodern?" (1986), excerpt reprinted in Walker Art Center, *House of Oracles: A Huang Yong Ping Retrospective*, Minneapolis: Walker Art Center, 2005, 76–77:77.
29 *Ibid.*
30 Melissa Chiu, "The Crisis of Calligraphy and the New Way of Tea: An Interview with Wenda Gu," *Orientations* 33:3 (March 2002), accessed at http://www.wendagu.com/publications/wenda-gu-interiews/melissa-chu.html.
31 Translated in Britta Erickson, *Words Without Meaning, Meaning Without Words: The Art of Xu Bing*, Washington, D.C.: Smithsonian, 2001, 38.
32 Qian Zhijian, "Performing Bodies: Zhang Huan, Ma Liuming, and Performance Art in China," *Art Journal* (Summer 1999), 63.
33 *Ibid.*
34 *Ibid.*, 65–66.
35 Gao Minglu, "Private Experience and Public Happenings: The Performance Art of Zhang Huan," in Zhang Huan, *Pilgrimage to Santiago*, Barcelona: Xunda de Galicia and Cotthem Gallery, 2001. Accessed online at http://www.zhanghuan.com/ListText.asp?id=1 March 2009.
36 On the sale of work from "China/Avant-Garde," see Maggie Ma, "Memories of 1989," *Artzine*, http://www.artzinechina.com/display_vol_aid252_en.html, accessed July 16, 2010.
37 Ai Weiwei and Feng Boyi, *Fuck Off*, Shanghai: Eastlink Gallery, 2000, n.p.

Chapter 9: Engaging the Global Present

1 Charles Merewether, "Preface: The Encounter," in Judith Bettleheim et al., *Crónicas Americanas: Obras de José Bedia*, Monterrey, Mexico: Museo de Arte Contemporáneo de Monterrey, 1997, 30–36:33.
2 Quotes in this paragraph are from Robert Farris Thompson, "Sacred Silhouettes," *Art in America* (July 1997), 64–71:70.
3 José Marti, "Our America," translated and reprinted in Aviva Chomsky, Barry Carr, and Pamela Maria Smorkaloff, eds., *The Cuba Reader: History , Culture, Politics*, Durham, NC: Duke University Press, 2003, 122–27:124.
4 Artist statement, Sixth Biennial of Sydney, cited in Charles Merewether, "Light Me Another Cuba: Late Modernism After the Revolution," in Merewether, *Made in Havana: Contemporary Art from Cuba*, Sydney: Art Gallery of New South Wales, 1988, 6–17:10.
5 *Ibid.*, 25.
6 Lorenzo Fusi, "A Conversation with Carlos Garaicoa," in Carlos Garaicoa, *Carlos Garaicoa: Capablanca's Real Passion*, Prato, Italy: Gli Ori, 2005, 101–15:106.
7 Interview by Gerald Matt, in *Shirin Neshat*, Serpentine Gallery: London, 2000, 27, cited in Bill Horrigan, ed., *Shirin Neshat: Two Installations*, Horrigan: Bill Wexner Center, 2000, 10.
8 Laura Mulvey, "Visual Pleasure and Narrative Cinema," in Brian Wallis, ed., *Art After Modernism*, New York: The New Museum, 1984, 363.
9 Bill Horrigan, ed., *Shirin Neshat: Two Installations, ibid.*, 21.
10 Bridget L. Goodbody, "From Lover to Foe and Back Again," *Art Asia Pacific* 43 (Winter 2005), 62.
11 "Shahzia Sikander in Conversation with Fereshteh Daftari," in Shahzia Sikander, *Shazia Sikander: Intimate Ambivalence*, Birmingham, U.K.: Ikon Gallery, 2008, 53–64:58.
12 Jonathan Rutherford, "The Third Space: Interview with Homi Bhabha," in

Rutherford, ed., *Identity: Community, Culture, Difference*, London: Lawrence and Wishart, 207–21:211.

13 "Chillava Klatch: Shahzia Sikander Interviewed by Homi Bhaba," in Sikander, *Shahzia Sikander*, Chicago: Renaissance Society, University of Chicago, 1999, 16–21:21.

14 Kobena Mercer, "Art That Is Ethnic in Inverted Commas," *Frieze* 25 (Nov.–Dec. 1995), accessed online at http://www.frieze.com/issue/article/art_that_is_ethnic_in_inverted_commas/June 2012.

15 Yinka Shonibare, "Poetic License," in D. Burrows, ed., *Who's Afraid of Red, White and Blue?*, Birmingham: Article Press, 1998, 73.

16 Lori Waxman, "Yinka Shonibare: Interview," *New Art Examiner* 28:3 (2000), 36–37:37.

17 Paul Gilroy, "The Art of Darkness: Black Art and the Problems of Belonging to England," *Third Text* 10 (Spring 1990), 52.

18 Cited in Mika Yoshitake, "The Meaning of the Nonsense of Excess," in Paul Schimmel et al., *©Murakami*, Los Angeles: The Museum of Contemporary Art, 2007, 111–27:111.

19 Mako Wakasa, "Takashi Murakami," *Journal of Contemporary Art* (2000), accessed online at http://www.jca-online.com/murakami.html.

20 Masahiko Asano, "Special Interview: Figures 4," in Takahashi Murakami, *Summon Monsters? Open the Door? Heal? Or Die?*, Tokyo: Museum of Contemporary Art, 2001, 94–95:95.

21 Takashi Murakami, "Greetings, You Are Alive: Tokyo Pop Manifesto," in *Kōkoku hihyō (Advertisement Criticism)* 226 (April 1, 1999), selection reprinted in Murakami, ed., *Little Boy: The Arts of Japan's Exploding Subculture*, New York: Japan Society 2005, 152.

22 *Ibid.*

23 Carolee Thea, "Cao Fei: Global Player," *Art Asia Pacific* (Fall 2006), 66–67:66.

24 Questions for interview with Yang Fudong, Copenhagen, June 2008, Shanghai: ShangART Gallery, 2008. http://www.shanghartgallery.com/galleryarchive/texts/id/1115.

25 Yang Fudong, "*Seven Intellectuals in the Bamboo Forest: Postscript by Yang Fudong*" (2009), http://www.shanghartgallery.com/galleryarchive/texts/id/1382.

26 Michelle Roecchi and Massimiliano Gioni, "Phil Collins: Face Value," *Flash Art* (Jan.–Feb. 2002), 84–86:84.

27 Jan Avgikos, "Rineke Dijkstra: Marian Goodman Gallery," *Artforum* (Nov. 2003), 188.

28 See Hsiao Chong-ray, "From Radical Criticism to Gradual Sedimentation—The Current Mentality of Contemporary Art in Taiwan (1988–1999)," in Victoria Lu, ed., *Visions of Pluralism: Contemporary Art in Taiwan 1988–1999*, Kaohsiung, Taiwan: Mountain Art Culture and Education Foundation, 1999.

29 Chen Chieh-jen, "About the Form of My Works," www.asa.de/magazine/iss2/3chen.htm.

30 Amy Cheng and Chen Chieh-jen, "On Lingchi: Echoes of a Historical Photograph," *Yishu* (March 2003), 81.

31 Artist statement, http://www.iniva.org/exhibitions_projects/2009/chen_chieh_jen/introduction.

32 Stella Rollig and Emily Jacir, "Interview," in Stella Rollig and Genoveva Rückert, eds., *Emily Jacir—Belongings*, Linz: O.K. Centrum für Gegenwartskunst Oberösterreich, 2004, 6–19:4.

33 Edward S. Said, "Emily Jacir," *Grand Street* 72 (Fall 2003), 206.

Chapter 10: New Metaphors and New Narratives

1 Matthew Ritchie, "Information, Cells & Evil," *Art:21*, online edition, http://www.pbs.org/art21/artists/ritchie/clip1.html.

2 Phong Bui, "Brooklyn Rail: Amy Sillman with Phong Bui," *Brooklyn Rail* (April 2006), online at http://brooklynrail.org/2006/04/art/amy-sillman-with-phong-bui.

3 Ian Berry, "Ugly Feelings: A Dialogue with Amy Sillman," in Berry and Anne Ellegood, *Amy Sillman: Third Person Singular*, Saratoga Springs, New York: The Frances Young Tang Teaching Museum and Art Gallery, 2008, 5–23:5.

4 Phong Bui, "Brooklyn Rail," *ibid.*

5 *Ibid.*

6 Amy Sillman and Gregg Bordowitz, *Amy Sillman and Gregg Bordowitz: Between Artists*, New York: Art Resources Transfer 2007, 41.

7 Cecily Brown, "Painting Epiphany," *Flash Art* (May/June 1998), 76–79:76.

8 *Ibid.*, 78.

9 Aneta Panek, "Franz Ackermann, Voyages Parallèles/Franz Ackermann: What a Long, Long Trip It's Been," *Art Press* 14 (2005), 38–43:41.

10 Stephan Urbaschek, "What Is a Dream Sequence in Painting? An Informal Conversation with Franz Ackermann in a Garden in Karlsruhe, April 2005," in Rainald Schumacher, ed., *Imagination Becomes Reality Part 1: Expanded Paint Tools*, Munich: Sammlung Goetz, 2005, 44–55:48.

11 *Ibid.*

12 Aneta Panek, "Franz Ackermann," *ibid.*, 43.

13 Olu Oguibe, "Artists on Artists," *BOMB* 89 (Fall 2004).

14 Cited in Margo A. Crutchfield, "Secular Response 2 A.M.," *MOCA Cleveland* (May 2003).

15 John Yau, "Ingrid Calame Constellations," *Brooklyn Rail* (Oct. 2007), accessed online at http://www.brooklynrail.org/2007/10/artseen/ingrid-calame-constellations.

16 Jorg Heiser and Jan Verwoert, "Ordinary Madness: An Interview with Albert Oehlen," *Frieze* 78 (Oct. 2003). Accessed online at http://www.frieze.com/issue/article/ordinary_madness/.

17 *Ibid.*

18 Diedrich Diederichsen, "The Rules of the Game," *Artforum* 33:3 (Nov. 1994), 66–71:71.

19 Lane Relyea, "Interview," in Christine Végh et al., *Jorge Pardo*, New York: Phaidon, 2008, 22.

20 Fritz Haeg, "Interview with Jorge Pardo," *Index Magazine*, LA Design Special Supplement (May–June 1999), n.p.

21 Chris Kraus, "Focus: *4166 Sea View Lane*," in Végh et al., *Jorge Pardo*, 105–14:108.

22 *Ibid.*, 112.

23 Louise Neri and Katharina Grosse, "Painting in the Expanded Field" in Louise Neri, ed., *Antipodes: Inside the White Cube*, London: White Cube, 2003, 58–69. Accessed online at http://www.katharinagrosse.com/info.php.

24 *Ibid.*

25 Katharina Grosse and Ulrich Loock, "Katharina Grosse in Conversation with Ulrich Loock: Painting on Three-Dimensional Supports," in *Katharina Grosse: Atoms Outside Eggs*, Museu Serralves: Porto, 2007, 19–71, accessed online at http://www.katharinagrosse.com/info.php.

26 Nicolas Bourriaud, *Relational Aesthetics*, Dijon: Les Presses du Réel, 1998, 70.

27 Owen Drolet, "Matthew Ritchie Interview," *Urban Desires* (1995), http://desires.com/1.3/Art/docs/ritchie.html

28 *Ibid.*

29 Jennifer Berman, "Matthew Ritchie," *Bomb* (Spring 1997), accessed online at http://www.bombsite.com/issues/59/articles/2035.

30 Hans Ulrich Obrist, "Artist Project: Matthew Barney," *Tate Magazine* 2 (Nov.–Dec. 2002), accessed online at http://www.tate.org.uk/magazine/issue2/barney.htm.

31 Thyrza Nichols Goodeve, "Travels in Hypertrophia: Thyrza Nichols Goodeve Talks with Matthew Barney,"*Artforum* (May 1995), 66–69:68–69.

32 Matthew Barney and Arthur C. Danto, "A Dialogue on Blood and Iron: Matthew Barney and Arthur C. Danto on Joseph Bueys," *Modern Painters* (Sept. 2006), 62–69:65.

33 Calvin Tomkins, "His Body, Himself: Matthew Barney's Strange and Passionate Exploration of Gender," *The New Yorker* (Jan. 27, 2003).

34 Pierre Huyghe in "Artist Questionnaire: 21 Responses," *October* 100 (Spring 2002), 6–97:34.

35 George Baker, "An Interview with Pierre Huyghe," *October* 110 (Fall 2004), 80–106:84.

36 Pierre Huyghe in "Artist Questionnaire: 21 Responses," *ibid.*

37 Adrian Dannat, "Where Fact and Fiction Meet," *The Art Newspaper* (March 31, 2005).

38 George Baker, "An Interview with Pierre Huyghe," *ibid.*, 106.

39 Atom Egoyan "Janet Cardiff," *Bomb* 79 (Spring 2002), 60–67:62.

40 Michael Juul Holm and Mette Marcus, eds., *Louisiana Contemporary: Janet Cardiff and George Bures Miller*, Humlebæk: Louisiana Museum of Modern Art, 2006.

41 Carolee Thea, "Inexplicable Symbiosis: A Conversation with Janet Cardiff," *Sculpture* (Jan.–Feb. 2003), accessed on the artist's website.

42 Helena Kontova and Massimiliano Gioni, "Francesco Vezzoli: Group Portrait with a Lady," *Flash Art* 219 (2001).

43 Marcella Beccaria, "Francesco Vezzoli: Portrait of the Artist as a Young Man," in Cristina Garbagna, ed., *Francesco Vezzoli: Democrazy*, Milan: Electa, 2007, 180.

44 Francesco Vezzoli, "Francesco Vezzoli and Nancy Spector in Conversation," in Vezzoli, *Right You Are (If You Think You Are) by Luigi Pirandello*, Milan: Edizioni Charta, 2009, 105–08.

45 Interview with Cory Arcangel by Petra Heck, Aug. 25, 2009, at http://nimk.nl/eng/cory-arcangel-depreciated/interview-cory-arcangel.

46 Cory Arcangel, "Super Mario Clouds" (2002/2003) in Raphael Gygax and Heike Munder, eds., *Cory Arcangel (BEIGE)*, Zurich: JRP Ringer, 2005, 106–15:107.
47 Katie Kitamura and Hari Kunzru, "Ryan Trecartin in Conversation," *Frieze* 142 (Oct. 2011), 202.
48 Whitney Ford, "The Q & A: Ryan Trecartin, Video Artist," *The Economist* at http://moreintelligentlife.com/blog/whitney-ford/qa-ryan-trecartin.
49 Katie Kitamura and Hari Kunzru, "Ryan Trecartin in Conversation," *ibid.*, 203.
50 Whitney Ford, "The Q & A," *ibid.*
51 Cindy Sherman, "Cindy Sherman Interviews Ryan Trecartin," in Ryan Trecartin et al., *Any Ever: Ryan Trecartin*, New York: Skira Rizzoli, 2011, 144.

Chapter 11: The Art of Contemporary Experience

1 Bruno Latour "Atmosphère, Atmosphère," in Susan May, ed., *Olafur Eliasson: The Weather Project*, London: The Tate, 2003, 35.
2 *Ibid.*
3 George Baker, "An Interview with Pierre Huyghe," *October* 110 (Fall 2004), 80–106:99.
4 *Ibid.*
5 Thomas Hirschhorn, *Where Do I Stand? What Do I Want?*, London: Art Review Ltd., 2007, 23.
6 Olafur Eliasson "Take Your Time: A Conversation, Olafur Eliasson and Robert Irwin," in Madeleine Grynsztejn, ed., *Take Your Time: Olafur Eliasson*, San Francisco: San Francisco Museum of Modern Art, 2007, 51–61:55.
7 Olafur Eliasson, ed., *Olafur Eliasson: The Blind Pavilion*, Ostfildern, Germany: Hatje Cantz Publishers, 2004, n.p.
8 Angela Rosenberg, "Olafur Eliasson: Beyond Nordic Romanticism," *Flash Art* (May–June 2003), 110–13:110.
9 Mieke Bal, "Light Politics," in Madeleine Grynsztejn, ed., *Take Your Time, ibid.*, 153–81:156–57.
10 Olafur Eliasson, "Your Engagement Has Consequences," in Emma Ridgway, ed., *Experiment Marathon: Serpentine Gallery*, Reykjavik: Reykjavik Art Museum, 2009, accessed online from the artist's website.
11 Olafur Eliasson, "Some Ideas About Colour," in Ismail Soyugenc and Richard Torchia, *Olafur Eliasson: Your Colour Memory*, Glenside, Pennsylvania: Arcadia University Art Gallery, 2006.
12 Olafur Eliasson, "Nothing Is Ever the Same," mission statement for the Institut für Raumexperimente, http://www.raumexperimente.net/text-en.html.
13 *Ibid.*
14 Bill Arning, "Ernesto Neto," *Bomb* 70 (Winter 2000), http://www.bombsite.com/issues/70/articles/2274.
15 *Ibid.*
16 *Ibid.*
17 *Ibid.*
18 Fernanda Gomes, "Fernanda Gomes and Ernesto Neto," *Bomb* 102 (Winter 2008), http://www.bombsite.com/issues/102/articles/3039.
19 Bill Arning, "Ernesto Neto," *Bomb* 70 (Winter 2000), http://www.bombsite.com/issues/70/articles/2274.
20 Hans Ulrich Obrist, *Hans Ulrich Obrist & Olafur Eliasson: Conversation Series 13*, Koln: Walter Konig, 2008, 157.
21 Lynne Cooke, "Interview: Lynne Cooke in Conversation with Roni Horn," in Louise Neri et al., *Roni Horn*, London: Phaidon, 2000, 6–25:23.
22 *Ibid.*, 22.
23 Mimi Thompson, "Roni Horn," *Bomb* 28 (Summer 1989), reprinted in *Speak Out!: The Best of Bomb Magazine's Interviews with Artists*, New York: New Art Publications, 1997, 80–86:85.
24 Lynne Cooke, "Interview," *ibid.*, 20.
25 *Ibid.*
26 Collier Schorr, "Weather Girls Interview with Collier Schorr," *Frieze* 32 (Jan.–Feb. 1997), 43–47, http://www.frieze.com/issue/article/weather_girls/. This sentiment is repeated almost word for word in undated notes published in *Roni Horn aka Roni Horn*, New York: Whitney Museum of American Art, 2009, 137.
27 *Ibid.*
28 *Ibid.*
29 Keynote Speech, Graduating Class of 2006, Iceland Academy of the Arts, Reykjavik, accessible on the artist's website.
30 Miwon Kwon, "Interview: Miwon Kwon in Conversation with Mark Dion," in Lisa Graziose Corrin et al., *Mark Dion*, London: Phaidon, 1997, 8–33:9.
31 *Ibid.*, 18.
32 Mark Dion, "Neukom Vivarium," Art 21 interview, http://www.pbs.org/art21/artists/dion/clip1.html.
33 Mark Dion, "Notes: Seattle Art Museum—Olympic Sculpture Park Proposal II," reproduced in Mark Dion et al., *Mark Dion: The Natural History of the Museum*, Paris: Archibooks, 2007.
34 The last two quotes are in Tom Sachs and John Furgason, *Ten Bullets*, 2005, published by the artist.
35 Press release for *Cavemanman*, Barbara Gladstone Gallery, 2002.
36 Benjamin H.D. Buchloh, "An Interview with Thomas Hirschhorn," *October* 113 (Summer 2005), 77–100:93.
37 Thomas Hirschhorn, "1000 Words: Thomas Hirschhorn Talks About His *Critical Laboratory*," Artforum (March 2000), 109.
38 *Ibid.*
39 Thomas Hirschhorn, *Where Do I Stand? What Do I Want?* 2007, 22–23.
40 Geert Lovink, "Surveillance, Performance, Self-Surveillance Interview with Jill Magid," *Institute of Network Cultures* (Oct. 29, 2004). Accessed online at http://www.networkcultures.org/weblog/archives/2004/10/surveillance_pe.html.
41 Eva Wiseman, "Is It Art? Search Me ... Why Artist Jill Magid Loves an Authority Figure," *The Observer* (Sept. 27, 2009), "Features" section 14.
42 Geert Lovink, "Surveillance, Performance, Self-Surveillance," *ibid.*
43 www.appliedautonomy.com/mission.html.
44 For details, see Trevor Paglen and A. C. Thompson, *Torture Taxi: On the Trail of the CIA's Rendition Flights*, New York: Melville House, 2006, and Alexis Bhagat and Lize Mogel, eds., *An Atlas of Radical Cartography*, Los Angeles: The Journal of Aesthetics & Protest, 2008.
45 "Ida Hiršenfelder—Interview with Trevor Paglen," in *Trevor Paglen: Contradictions of the Hidden Landscapes*, exhibition brochure accompanying "Trevor Paglen: A Hidden Landscape," Aksioma Project Space, Ljubljana, April 2011.
46 *Ibid.*
47 Seth Curcio, "Seeing is Believing: An Interview with Trevor Paglen," Daily Serving (Feb. 24, 2011), http://dailyserving.com/2011/02/interview-with-trevor-paglen/.
48 *Ibid.*
49 See Timothy O'Sullivan, *Tufa Domes, Pyramid Lake, Nevada (King Survey)*, 1867, Smithsonian American Art Museum Museum purchase from the Charles Isaacs Collection made possible in part by the Luisita L. and Franz H. Denghausen Endowment, 1994.91.142.
50 Georges Didi Huberman, "How to Open Your Eyes," in Haroun Farocki, *Against What? Against Whom?*, London: Koenig Books, 2009, 46 and Harun Farocki, "Le Point de Vue de la Guerre," *Trafic* 50 (2004), 449.
51 Georges Didi-Huberman, "How to Open Your Eyes," in Haroun Farocki, *ibid.*
52 Jan Verwoert, "See What Shows—On the Practice of Haroun Farocki," in Yilmaz Dziewior, ed., *Haroun Farocki: Soft Montages*, Bregenz, Austria: Kunsthaus Bregenz, 2011, 16–32:27.
53 Éric Suchère, "Luc Tuymans: More than a Medium," *Art Press* (July–Aug. 2002), 26–31:31.
54 Wilhelm Sasnal and Luc Tuymans, "When Luc Tuymans met Wilhelm Sasnal ...," *Art Review* (Feb. 2008), 42–49:45.
55 Yasmine van Pee, "Unnatural Resources: Luc Tuymans," *Modern Painters* (Oct. 2007), 66–75:69.
56 Éric Suchère, "Luc Tuymans: More Than a Medium," *ibid.*, 31.
57 Nato Thompson, "Spectacular Feelings: The Rise of Affect in Contemporary Politics," blog entry, March 19, 2012, http://natothompson.wordpress.com/2012/03/19/spectacular-feelings-the-rise-of-affect-in-contemporary-politics/.
58 Emily Apter, "In Conversation: Silvia Kolbowski with Emily Apter," *Brooklyn Rail* (Oct. 2011), online at http://brooklynrail.org/2011/10/art/silvia-kolbowski-with-emily-apter.
59 Omer Fast, "Back to the Present," *Displayer* 03 (2009), 115.
60 *Ibid.*, 114.
61 Marcus Verhagen, "Pleasure and Pain: Omer Fast Interviewed by Marcus Verhagen," *Art Monthly* 330 (Oct. 2009), 4.
62 *Ibid.*, 3.
63 Andrea Bowers, "Interview with Sam Durant and Monica Bonvicini," *Neue Review* (Dec. 2003), 5.
64 Andrea Bowers and Catherine Opie, *Between Artists: Andrea Bowers and Catherine Opie*, New York: Art Resources Transfer, 2008, 33.
65 *Ibid.*
66 *Ibid.*, 53.
67 *Ibid.*, 54.

Select Bibliography

Introduction

Barthes, Roland. *Image, Music, Text.* New York: Hill and Wang, 1977.

Carter, Curtis L. et al. *Jean Fautrier 1898–1964.* New Haven: Yale University Press. 2002.

Chipp, Herschel, ed., *Theories of Modern Art.* Berkeley: University of California Press, 1968.

Clark, T.J., *Farewell to an Idea.* New Haven: Yale University Press, 1999.

Elderfield, John. *De Kooning: A Retrospective.* New York: Museum of Modern Art, 2011.

Foucault, Michel. *The Archeology of Knowledge.* New York: Pantheon Books, 1972.

Frascina, Francis, ed. *Pollock and After: The Critical Debate.* 2nd. New York: Routledge, 2000.

Greenberg, Clement. *Art and Culture.* Boston: Beacon Press, 1961.

Guilbaut, Serge. *How New York Stole the Idea of Modern Art.* Chicago: University of Chicago Press, 1983.

Jenckins, Paul and Ester, eds. *Observations,* by Michel Tapié. New York: George Wittenborn, Inc., 1956.

Johnson, Ellen, ed. *American Artists on Art.* New York: Harper and Row, 1982.

Kamuf, Peggy, ed. *A Derrida Reader: Between the Blinds.* New York: Columbia University Press 1991.

Lyotard, Jean-François. *The Postmodern Condition: A Report on Knowledge.* Minneapolis: University of Minnesota Press, 1984.

Martin, Jean Hubert. *Magiciens de la Terre.* Paris: Centre Georges Pompidou, 1989.

Meyer-Hermann, Eva. *Andy Warhol: A Guide to 706 Items in 2 Hours 56 Minutes. Other Voices, Other Rooms.* Rotterdam: NAi Publishers, 2008. (Includes annotated select bibliography of Warhol scholarship.)

Miller, Dorothy. *The New American Painting: As Shown in Eight European Countries 1958–59: Organized by the International Program of the Museum of Modern Art, New York under the Auspices of the International Council at the Museum of Modern Art, New York.* New York: Museum of Modern Art, 1959.

Naumann, Francis M., ed. *How, When, and Why Modern Art Came to New York,* by Marius de. Zayas. Cambridge, MIT Press, 1996.

Naumann, Francis M. with Beth Venn. *Making Mischief: Dada Invades New York.* New York: Whitney Museum of American Art, 1996.

Orton, Fred. *Figuring Jasper Johns.* Cambridge: Harvard University Press, 1994.

Rabinow, Paul, ed. *The Foucault Reader.* New York: Pantheon Books, 1984.

Shapiro, Cecile and David, eds. *Abstract Expressionism: A Critical Record.* Cambridge: Cambridge University Press, 1990.

Steinberg, Leo. *Other Criteria.* New York: Oxford University Press, 1972.

Sylvester, David et al. *Willem de Kooning: Paintings.* Washington DC: National Gallery of Art, 1994.

Varnedoe, Kirk. *Jackson Pollock.* New York: Museum of Modern Art, 1998.

Varnedoe, Kirk. *Jasper Johns: A Retrospective.* New York: Museum of Modern Art, 1996.

Chapter 1

Althusser, Louis. *Lenin and Philosophy and Other Essays.* New York: Monthly Review Press, 1971.

Battcock, Gregory, ed., *Minimal Art: A Critical Anthology.* Berkeley: University of California Press, 1995.

Battcock, Gregory. "The Politics of Space." *Arts* (February 1970).

Beuys, Joseph. "Interview with Willoughby Sharp." *Artforum* (December 1969).

Bird, Jon, Jo Anna Isaak, and Sylère Lotringer. *Nancy Spero.* London: Phaidon, 2006.

Bird, Jon. *Leon Golub: Echoes of the Real.* London: Reaktion, 2000.

Burnham, Jack. "Hans Haacke's Canceled Show at the Guggenheim." *Artforum* (June 1971).

Butler, Cornelia. *WACK! Art and the Feminist Revolution.* Los Angeles: Museum of Contemporary Art, 2007.

Campbell, Mary Schmidt, ed. *Tradition and Conflict: Images of a Turbulent Decade 1963–1973.* New York: The Studio Museum in Harlem, 1985.

Chicago, Judy and Miriam Schapiro. *Womanhouse.* Valencia : Feminist Art Program, California Institute of the Arts, 1972.

Cixous, Hélène. "The Laugh of the Medusa." In *New French Feminisms,* edited by Elaine Marx and Isabelle de Courtivron. New York: Schocken Books, 1980, 245–64.

Deleuze, Gilles and Felix Guattari. *Anti-Oedipus: Capitalism and Schizophrenia.* Minneapolis: University of Minnesota Press, 1983.

Donaldson, Jeff. "Artist Statement." In *AfriCOBRA III.* Amherst: University of Massachusetts, 1973.

Douglas, Emory. "Revolutionary Art/Black Liberation" (1968). In *The Black Panthers Speak,* edited by Philip Sheldon Foner and Clayborne Carson. Cambridge: Da Capo Press, 1995.

Douglas, Robert L. *Wadsworth Jarrell: The Artist as Revolutionary.* San Francisco: Pomegranate Art Books, 1996.

Durant, Sam, ed. *Black Panther: The Revolutionary Art of Emory Douglas.* New York: Rizzoli 2007.

Flam, Jack, ed. *Robert Smithson: The Collected Writings.* Berkeley: University of California Press, 1996.

Gumbert, Lynn, Ned Rifkin and Marcia Tucker. *Early Work: Lynda Benglis/Joan Brown/Luis Jiminez/Gary Stephan.* New York: The New Museum, 1982.

Haacke, Hans. *Hans Haacke: Unfinished Business.* New York: The New Museum, 1986.

Jones-Hogu, Barbara. "The History, Philosophy and Aesthetics of AfriCOBRA." In *AfriCOBRA III.* Amherst: University of Massachusetts, 1973.

Kaprow, Allan. "The Shape of the Art Environment: How Anti-Form Is Anti-Form?" *Artforum* (April 1968).

Kelly, Mary. *Post-Partum Document.* London: Routledge and Kegan Paul, 1983.

Le Fundacio Antoni Tapiès. *Lygia Clark.* Barcelona: Le Fundacio, 1998.

Lippard, Lucy R. *Pop Art.* New York: Praeger, 1966.

Madoff, Steven Henry, ed. *Pop Art: A Critical History.* Berkeley: University of California Press, 1997.

Merewether, Charles and Rika Iezumi Hiro, eds. *Art, Anti-Art, Non-Art: Experimentations in the Public Sphere in Post War Japan, 1950–1970.* Los Angeles: Getty Research Institute, 2007.

Meyer, James. *Minimalism: Art and Politics in the Sixties.* New Haven: Yale University Press, 2001.

Munroe, Alexandra and Jon Hendricks, eds. *Yes: Yoko Ono.* New York: Japan Society, 2000.

Nemser, Cindy. "Four Artists of Sensuality." *Arts* (March 1975).

Nemser, Cindy. "Interview with Members of AIR." *Arts* (December–January 1973).

Oliva, Achille Bonito, Gabriella De Mila and Claudio Cerritelli, eds. *Ubi Fluxus Ibi Motus 1990–1962.* Milan: Mazzotta, 1990.

Parker, Rozsika and Griselda Pollock, eds. *Framing Feminism.* London and New York: Pandora, 1987.

Piper, Adrian. "In Support of Meta Art." *Artforum* (October 1973).

Piper, Adrian. *Out of Order, Out of Sight,* 2 vols. Cambridge: MIT Press, 1999.

Rosler, Martha. "The Private and the Public Feminist Art in California." *Artforum* (September 1977).

Sharp, Willoughby. *Earth Art.* Ithaca, N.Y.: Office of University Publications, Cornell University, 1970.

Sharp, Willoughby. "Elemental Gesture: Terry Fox." *Arts* (May 1970).

Sontag, Susan. *Against Interpretation and Other Essays.* New York: Farrar, Strauss and Giroux, 1969.

Spero, Nancy. *Torture of Women.* Los Angeles: Siglio Press, 2010.

Steinberg, Leo. *Other Criteria.* New York: Oxford University Press, 1972.

Stiles, Kristine and Peter Selz, eds. *Theories and Documents of Contemporary Art: A Sourcebook of Artists' Writings.* Berkeley: University of California Press, 1996.

Tisdall, Caroline. *Joseph Beuys.* New York: Solomon R. Guggenheim Foundation, 1979.

Tucker, Marcia. *James Rosenquist.* New York: Whitney Museum of American Art, 1972.

Chapter 2

Benjamin, Walter. "A Short History of Photography" (1931). In *Classic Essays of Photography,* edited by Alan Tractenberg. Stony Creek, CT: Leete's Island Books, 1980.

Wallis, Brian, ed. *Art After Modernism.* New York: The New Museum, 1984.

Brooks, Rosetta et al. *Richard Prince,* London: Phaidon, 2003.

Buchloh, Benjamin H.D. "Allegorical Procedures." *Artforum* (September 1982).

Cameron, Dan. "Four Installations: Francesco Torres, Mierle Ukeles, Louise Lawler/Allan McCollum and TODT." *Arts Magazine* (December 1984).

Crimp, Douglas. "Boys in My Bedroom." *Art in America* (February 1990).

Crimp, Douglas. *On the Museum's Ruins.* Cambridge: MIT Press, 1993.

Crimp, Douglas. "Pictures." *October* 8 (Spring 1978).

Cruz, Amada and Elizabeth A. T. Smith. *Cindy Sherman: A Retrospective*. New York: Thames and Hudson, 1997.

Eklund, Douglas. *The Pictures Generation, 1974–1984*. New York: Metropolitan Museum of Art, 2009.

Ferguson, Bruce. "Wordsmith: An Interview with Jenny Holzer." *Art in America* (December 1986).

Foster, Hal. "Subversive Signs." *Art in America* (November 1982).

Foster, Hal. *The Anti-Aesthetic*. Seattle: Bay Press, 1983.

Frankel, David. "Cindy Sherman Talks to David Frankel." *Artforum* (March 2003).

Fraser, Andrea. "In and Out of Place." *Art in America* (June 1985).

Fried, Michael. "Art and Objecthood." *Artforum* (June 1967).

Goldstein, Ann et al. *Barbara Kruger: Thinking of You*. Los Angeles: Museum of Contemporary Art, 1999.

Joselit, David et al. *Jenny Holzer*. London: Phaidon, 1998.

Kardon, Janet. *Image Scavengers: Painters*. Philadelphia: Institute of Contemporary Art, 1983.

Kolbowski, Silvia. *Silvia Kolbowski: Inadequate … Like … Power*. Köln: Verlag der Buchhandlung Walther König, 2004.

Krauss, Rosalind E. *The Originality of the Avant-Garde and Other Modernist Myths*. Cambridge, MA: MIT Press, 1985.

Lichtenstein, Therese. "Cindy Sherman." *Arts* (January 1983).

Linker, Kate. *Love For Sale*. New York: Harry N. Abrams, 1990.

Marincola, Paula. *Image Scavengers: Photographers*. Philadelphia: Institute of Contemporary Art, 1983.

Mulvey, Laura. "A Phantasmagoria of the Female Body." *New Left Review* 188 (July/August 1991).

Mulvey, Laura. *Visual and Other Pleasures*. Bloomington: University of Indiana Press, 1989.

Nairne, Sandy. *State of the Art: Ideas and Images of the 1980s*. London: Chatto & Windus, 1987.

Owens, Craig. *Beyond Recognition*. Berkeley: University of California Press, 1992.

Phillips, Lisa. *Richard Prince*. New York: Whitney Museum of American Art, 1992.

Prince, Richard. *Why I Go to the Movies Alone*. New York: Tanam Press, 1983.

Ratcliff, Carter. "Art and Resentment." *Art in America* 70 (Summer 1982).

Schjeldahl, Peter. "Shermanettes." *Art in America* (March 1982).

Siegel, Jeanne. "After Sherrie Levine." *Arts* (Summer 1985).

Siegel, Jeanne. *Artwords 2: Discourse on the Early 80s*. Ann Arbor: UMI Press, 1988.

Solomon-Godeau, Abigail. "Suitable for Framing: The Critical Recasting of Cindy Sherman." *Parkett* 29 (1991).

Solomon-Godeau, Abigail. "Winning the Game When the Rules Have Changed." *Screen* 26:6 (November/December 1984).

Wallis, Brian. *Blasted Allegories: An Anthology of Writings by Contemporary Artists*. New York: The New Museum, 1987.

Whitney Museum of American Art, *Cindy Sherman*. New York: Whitney Museum of American Art, 1987.

Williamson, Judith. "Images of Women." *Screen* (November 1983).

Chapter 3

Adorno, Theodor. *Aesthetic Theory*. London: Continuum International Publishing Group, 2004.

Adorno, Theodor. *Prisms*, Cambridge, MA: MIT Press, 1981.

Arasse, Daniel. *Anselm Kiefer*. New York: Harry N. Abrams, 2001.

Attias, Laurie. "Anselm Kiefer's Identity Crisis (the Artist and Post-Reunification Germany)." *Art News* 96 (June 1997).

Bauman, Daniel et al. *Martin Kippenberger*. Basel: Kunsthalle Basel, 1998.

Bee, Susan and Mira Schor, eds. *M/E/A/N/I/N/G: An Anthology of Artists' Writings, Theory, and Criticism*. Durham, NC: Duke University Press, 2000.

Belgin, Tayfun. ed. *Immendorff: Bilder*, Heidelberg: Edition Braus, 2000.

Belgin, Tayfun et al. *Jörg Immendorff: All Things Have the Tendency to Change*. St. Petersburg: State Russian Museum, 2001.

Buchloh, Benjamin H.D. "Figures of Authority, Ciphers of Regression." *October* 16 (Spring 1981).

Busche, Ernst. "Violent Painting." *Flash Art* 101 (January 1981).

Cannell, Michael. "Francesco Clemente." *Arts* (June 1983).

Clemente, Francesco. *Clemente*, New York: Vintage Books, 1987.

Cowart, Jack, ed. *Expressions: New Art from Germany*. St. Louis: St. Louis Art Museum, 1983.

Crimp, Douglas. *On the Museum's Ruins*. Cambridge: MIT Press, 1993.

Whitney, David, ed. *Eric Fischl*. New York: Art in America, and Stewart, Tabori, & Chang, 1988.

DeAk, Edit. "A Chameleon in a State of Grace." *Artforum* (February 1981).

Dietrich, Dorothea. "Allegories of Power: Markus Lüpertz's 'German Motifs.'" *Art Journal* 48 (Summer 1989).

Fischl, Eric. *Eric Fischl*. New York: Vintage Books, 1987.

Gamrell, Jamey. "Sandro Chia at Castelli Green." *Art in America* (October 1983).

Glenn, Constance W. and Lucinda Barnes. *Eric Fischl: Scenes Before the Eye*. Long Beach, CA: University Art Museum, 1986.

hooks, bell. "Altars of Sacrifice: Re-Membering Basquiat." *Art in America* (June 1983).

Hubert, Christian et al. "Post-Modernism: A Symposium." *Real Life Magazine* (Summer 1981).

Huyssen, Andreas. "Anselm Kiefer: The Terror of History, the Temptation of Myth." *October* 48 (1989).

Huyssen, Andreas. "Kiefer in Berlin," *October* 62 (Fall 1992).

Joachimides, Christos M. and Norman Rosenthal. *Zeitgeist*. Berlin: Martin Gropius Bau, 1983.

Joachimides, Christos M., Norman Rosenthal, and Nicolas Serota, eds. *A New Spirit in Painting*. London: Royal Academy of Art, 1981.

Judd, Donald. *Donald Judd: Complete Writings 1959–1975*. Halifax: The Press of the Nova Scotia College of Art and Design, 1975.

Koether, Jutta. "Who Is Martin Kippenberger and Why Are They Saying Such Terrible Things About Him?" *Artscribe International* (January–February 1989).

Kontova, Helena. "Rainer Fetting Interview." *Flash Art* 115 (January 1984).

Kristeva, Julia. *Powers of Horror*. New York: Columbia University Press, 1982.

Kuspit, Donald. "Acts of Aggression: German Painting Today, Part II." *Art in America* (January 1983).

Lawson, Thomas. "Last Exit: Painting," (1981). In *Art after Modernism*, edited by Brian Wallis. New York: The New Museum, 1984.

Mayer, Marc. *Basquiat*. New York: Merrell, 2005.

McEvily, Thomas. "Royal Slumming: Jean-Michel Basquiat Here Below." *Artforum* (November 1992).

Noever, Peter, ed. *Martin Kippenberger The Last Stop West*. Ostfildern-Ruit, Germany: Cantz Verlag, 1998.

Oliva, Achille Bonito. *The International Trans-Avantgarde*. Milan: Giancarlo Politi Editore, 1982.

Penck, A.R. *A.R. Penck*. New York: Mary Boone/Michael Werner Gallery, 1984.

Penck, A.R. *A.R. Penck Retrospective*. Düsseldorf: Richter Verlag, 2007.

Percy, Ann. *Francesco Clemente: Three Worlds*. Philadelphia: Philadelphia Museum of Art, 1990.

Pincus-Witten, Robert. "Julian Schnabel: Blind Faith." *Arts* (February 1982).

Pincus-Witten, Robert. "Pure Painter: An Interview with David Salle." *Arts* (November 1985).

Ratcliff, Carter. "On Iconography and Some Italians." *Art in America* (September 1982).

Ricard, René. "Julian Schnabel's Plate Paintings at Mary Boone." *Art in America* (November 1979).

Saltzman, Lisa. *Anselm Kiefer and Art after Auschwitz*. Cambridge: Cambridge University Press, 1999.

Schjeldahl, Peter. "Our Kiefer." *Art in America* (March 1988).

Schnabel, Julian. *Julian Schnabel: Painting 1975–87*. London: Whitechapel Gallery, 1987.

Seigel, Jeanne. *Artwords 2: Discourse on the Early 80s*. Ann Arbor: UMI Research Press, 1988.

Storr, Robert. "Realm of the Senses." *Art in America* (November 1987).

Wallis, Brian, ed. *Blasted Allegories*. New York: The New Museum, 1987.

Williams, Gregory H. *Permission to Laugh: Humor and Politics in Contemporary German Art*. Chicago: University of Chicago Press, 2012.

Chapter 4

Acocella, Joan. "Plastic Heaven." *Artforum* (January 1992).

Ault, Julie, ed. *Cultural Economies: Histories from the Alternative Arts Movement, NYC*. New York: The Drawing Center, 1996.

Ault, Julie, ed. *Show and Tell: A Chronicle of Group Material*. London: Four Corners Books, 2010.

Buchloh, Benjamin H. D. "Documenta 7: A Dictionary of Received Ideas." *October* 102 (Autumn 1982).

Cameron, Dan. *East Village USA*. New York: The New Museum, 2004.

Cameron, Dan et al. *Fever: The Art of David Wojnarowicz*. New York: The New Museum, 1999.

Crimp, Douglas and Adam Rolston. *AIDS Demographics.* Seattle: Bay Press, 1990.
Crimp, Douglas, ed. *AIDS: Cultural Analysis/ Cultural Activism.* Cambridge: MIT Press, 1988.
Crimp, Douglas. "Mourning and Militancy." *October* 15 (Winter 1989).
Crimp, Douglas. "The Art of Exhibition." *October* 30 (Autumn 1984).
Deitch, Jeffrey. "Report from Times Square." *Art in America* (September 1980).
Ferguson, Russell, William Olander, Marcia Tucker, and Karen Fiss. *Discourses: Conversations in Postmodern Art and Culture.* New York: The New Museum of Contemporary Art, 1990.
Deutsche, Rosalyn and Fara Gendel Ryan. "The Fine Art of Gentrification." *October* 31 (Winter 1984).
Foster, Hal et al. "On Site Specificity: A Discussion with Hal Foster, Renée Green, Mitchell Kane, Miwon Kwon, John Lindell, Helen Molesworth." *Documents* 2:4–5 (Spring 1994).
Frank, Peter and Michael McKenzie. *New, Used and Improved: Art for the 80s.* New York: Abbeville Press, 1987.
Goldin, Nan et al. *I'll Be Your Mirror.* New York: Whitney Museum of American Art, 1996.
Goldin, Nan. *The Ballad of Sexual Dependency.* New York: Aperture Foundation, 1986.
Hager, Steven. *Art After Midnight: The East Village Scene.* New York: St. Martin's Press, 1986.
Hammons, David. *David Hammons Rousing the Rubble.* New York: Institute for Contemporary Art, 1991.
Hammons, David. *Yardbird Suite.* Williamstown, MA: Williams College Museum of Art, 1994.
Holborn, Mark. "Nan Goldin's Ballad of Sexual Dependency: Interview by Mark Holborn." *Aperture* (Summer 1986).
Kardon, Janet. *The East Village Scene.* Philadelphia: Institute of Contemporary Art, University of Pennsylvania, 1984.
Linker, Kate. "Melodramatic Tactics." *Artforum* (September 1982).
Lurie, David V. and Krzysztof Wodiczko. "Homeless Vehicle Project." *October* 47 (Winter 1988).
McCormick, Carlo and Walter Robinson. "Slouching Toward Avenue D." *Art in America* (Summer 1984).
Moore, Alan and Marc Miller, eds. *ABC No Rio Dinero: The Story of a Lower East Side Gallery.* New York: ABC No Rio and Collaborative Projects, 1985.
Ominous, Anne (Lucy Lippard). "Sex and Death and Shock and Shlock." *Artforum* (October 1980).
Osorio, Pepón. *Pepón Osorio: De Puerta en Puerta = Door to Door.* San Juan, Puerto Rico: EAP Press, 2000.
Plous, Phyllis. *Neo-York: Report on a Phenomenon.* Santa Barbara: University Art Museum, 1984.
Simonds, Cylena."Public Audit: An Interview with Elizabeth Sisco, Louis Hock, and David Avalos." *Afterimage* (Summer 1994).
Wallis, Brian, ed. *Democracy: A Project by Group Material.* Discussions in Contemporary Culture, Number 5. New York: Dia Art Foundation, 1999.
Wodiczko, Krzysztof. *Critical Vehicles: Writings, Projects, Interviews.* Cambridge: MIT Press, 1999.
Wojnarowicz, David. *Close to Knives.* New York: Vintage Books, 1991.
Wojnarowicz, David. *Fever: The Art of David Wojnarowicz.* New York: The New Museum, 1999.
Wong, Martin. *Sweet Oblivion: The Urban Landscapes of Martin Wong.* New York: The New Museum 1998.
Wye, Deborah and Jean Fulton. *Art Out There.* Chicago: School of the Art Institute of Chicago, 1996.
Zeitlin, Marilyn A. *South Bronx Hall of Fame Sculpture by John Ahearn and Rigoberto Torres.* Houston Contemporary Arts Museum 1991.

Chapter 5

Armleder, John M., Spark Vett, Parker Williams, and Sylvie Fleury. "John Armleder at any Speed." *Parkett* 50/51 (1997).
Azimi, Negar. "Fluffy Farhad." *Bidoun* (Spring 2010).
Baudrillard, Jean. *Simulations and Simulacra.* Ann Arbor: University of Michigan Press, 1981.
Bordowitz, Gregg. *General Idea: Image Virus.* London: Afterall Books, 2010.
Buskirk, Martha. "Interviews with Sherrie Levine, Louise Lawler, and Fred Wilson." *October* 70 (Fall 1994).
Celant, Germano. "Haim Steinbach's Wild Wild West." *Artforum* (December 1987).
Debord, Guy. *Society of the Spectacle* (1967) was published with no copyright. It can be fully accessed online at a number of sites including http://www.marxists.org/reference/archive/debord/ (accessed November, 16, 2012).
Drake, Peter. "Ross Bleckner, interview with Peter Drake." *Flash Art* (Summer 1986).
Engler, Martin. *John M. Armleder: Everything Is Not Enough.* Waltham: Rose Museum of Art, 2006.
Foucault, Michel. *Discipline and Punish: The Birth of the Prison.* New York: Vintage, 1979.
Fleury, Sylvie. *Sylvie Fleury: Identity, Pain, Astral, Projection.* Paris: Les Presses Du Réel. 2001.
Foster, Hal. *The Return of the Real: The Avant-Garde at the End of the Century.* Cambridge: MIT Press, 1996.
Frenssen, Birte and Rosemarie Trockel. *Rosemarie Trockel: Bodies of Work 1986–1998.* Hamburg: Hamburger Kunsthalle. 1998.
General Idea. *General Idea, 1968–1984.* Basel: Kunsthalle, 1985.
General Idea. *General Idea's Reconstructing Futures.* Toronto: General Idea, 1978.
Graw, Isabelle. "Rosemarie Trockel talks to Isabelle Graw." *Artforum* (March 2003).
Halley, Peter. *Collected Essays 1981–1987.* Zurich: Bruno Bischofberger Gallery, 1988.
Kelley, Mike. *Minor Histories: Statements, Conversations, Proposals.* Cambridge, MA: MIT Press, 2004.
Koether, Jutta. "Interview with Rosemarie Trockel." *Flash Art* (May 1987).
Koether, Jutta. "The Nonchalance of Continuous Tense-ness." *Parkett* 58 (2000).
Koons, Jeff. *Jeff Koons Handbook.* New York: Rizzoli, 1992.
Lewallen, Constance. "Sherrie Levine." *Journal of Contemporary Art* 6 (1993), at http://www.jca-online.com/slevine.html (accessed July 16, 2011).
Nagy, Peter. "From Criticism to Complicity." *Flash Art* (Summer 1986).
Ruf, Beatrix, ed. *General Idea: FILE Megazine 1972–1989.* Zurich: JRP|Ringier, 2008.
Siegel, Jeanne. *Artwords 2: Discourse on the Early Eighties.* Ann Arbor: UMI, 1988.
Singerman, Howard. *Art History, After Sherrie Levine.* Berkeley: University of California Press, 2012.
Stals, José Lebrero. *Mike Kelley 1985–1996.* Barcelona: Museu d'Art Contemporani, 1997.
Steinbach, Haim. *Haim Steinbach: Recent Works.* Bordeaux: Musée d'Art Contemporain, 1988.
Stitch, Sidra. *Rosemarie Trockel.* New York: Prestel, 1991.
Storr, Robert. "An Interview with Mike Kelley." *Art in America* (June 1994).
Wei, Lilly. "Talking Abstract: Part Two." *Art in America* (December 1987).
Welchman, John C. ed. *Mike Kelley: Interviews, Conversations and Chit-Chat (1986–2004).* Zurich: JRP Ringier, 2005.
Welchman, John C. et al. *Mike Kelley*, London: Phaidon, 1999.

Chapter 6

Abramson, Daniel. "Maya Lin and the 1960s: Monuments, Time Lines, and Minimalism." *Critical Inquiry* 22:4 (Summer 1996).
Attie, Shimon. *The Writing on the Wall: Projections in Berlin's Jewish Quarter.* Heidelberg: Edition Braus, 1994.
Berry, Ian et al. *Kara Walker: Narratives of a Negress.* Cambridge: MIT Press, 2003.
Boltanski, Christian. *Christian Boltanski: Lessons of Darkness.* Chicago: Museum of Contemporary Art, 1988.
Cameron, Dan et al. *William Kentridge.* London: Phaidon, 1999.
Corrin, Lisa G. *Mining the Museum: An Installation by Fred Wilson.* New York: New Press, 1994.
Corris, Michael and Robert Hobbs. "Reading Black Through White in the Work of Kara Walker: A Discussion Between Michael Corris and Robert Hobbs." *Art History* 26:3 (June 2003).
Dubow, Jessica and Ruth Rosengarten. "History as the Main Complaint: William Kentridge and the Making of Post-Apartheid South Africa." *Art History* 27:4 (September 2004).
Fox, Howard N. *Eleanor Antin.* Los Angeles: Los Angeles County Museum of Art, 1999.
Gerz, Jochen. *Jochen Gerz Res Publica: The Public Works 1968–1999.* Ostfildern: Hatje Cantze, 1999.
Gerz, Jochen. "Toward Public Authorship." *Third Text* 18:6 (2004).
Gilbert, Alan. "Walid Ra'ad." *Bomb* 81 (Fall 2002), accessed at www.bombsite.com/issues/81/articles/2504.
Goodman, Susan Tumarkin. *From the Inside Out: Eight Contemporary Artists.* New York: The Jewish Museum, 1993.
Kolbowski, Silvia and Walid Raad. *Between Artists: Silvia Kolbowski, Walid Raad.* New York: A.R.T. Press, 2006.
LeFeuvre, Lisa et al. *Esther Shalev-Gerz.* Paris: Jeu de paume, 2010.
Lepecki, André. "'After All, the Terror Was Not Without Reason': Unfiled Notes on the Atlas Group Archive." *TDR: The Drama Review*, 50:3 (Fall 2006).
Lovell, Whitfield. *The Art of Whitfield Lovell: Whispers from the Walls.* San Francisco: Pomegranate Press, 2003.

Marshall, Kerry James. *Kerry James Marshall.* New York : Harry N. Abrams, 2000.
Mullins, Charlotte. *Rachel Whiteread.* London: Tate Publishing, 2004.
Nakas, Kassandra et al. *The Atlas Group (1989–2004): A Project by Walid Raad.* Köln: Verlag der Buchhandlung Walther König, 2006.
Novakov, Anna. *Veiled Histories The Body, Place and Public Art.* New York: San Francisco Art Institute, 1997.
Princenthal, Nancy et al. *Doris Salcedo,* London: Phaidon, 2000.
Raad, Walid. *Scratching at Things I Could Disavow.* Köln: Verlag der Buchhandlung Walther König, 2007.
Rancière, Jacques. *The Politics of Aesthetics.* London: Continuum, 2004.
Rowell, Charles H. "An Interview with Kerry James Marshall." *Callaloo* 21:1 (Winter 1998).
Sadek, Waled. "A Matter of Words. (Art and Artists in Beirut, Lebanon)." *Parachute* (October 2002).
Semin, Didier et al. *Christian Boltanski.* London: Phaidon, 1997.
Toufic, Jalal. *Undeserving Lebanon.* Online at http://www.jalaltoufic.com/downloads/Jalal_Toufic_Undeserving_Lebanon.pdf: Forthcoming Books, 2007.
Townsend, Chris ed. *Art of Rachel Whiteread.* New York: Thames and Hudson, 2004.
Trinh T. Minh-Ha. *Elsewhere, Within Here: Immigration, Refugeeism and the Boundary Event.* New York: Routledge, 2011.
Walker, Kara. *Kara Walker: Narratives of a Negress.* Cambridge: MIT Press, 2003.
Walker, Kara. "The Debate Continues: Kara Walker's Response." *International Review of African American Art* 15:2 (1998).
Young, James E. "The Counter-Monument: Memory Against Itself in Germany Today." *Critical Inquiry* 18:2 (Winter 1992).
Young, James E. "The US Holocaust Memorial Museum: Memory and the Politics of Identity." In *The Jew in the Text,* edited by Linda Nochlin and Tamar Garb. New York: Thames and Hudson, 1995.
Young, James E. *At Memory's Edge.* New Haven: Yale University Press, 2002.

Chapter 7

Abramović, Marina and Germano Celant. *Public Body: Installation and Objects, 1965–2001.* Milan: Charta, 2001.
Abramović, Marina. *Student Body: Workshops, 1979–2003: Performances, 1993–2003.* Milan: Charta, 2003.
Archer, Michael et al. *Mona Hatoum.* London: Phaidon, 1997.
Barnes, Lucinda et al., eds. *Between Artists: Twelve Contemporary American Artists Interview Twelve Contemporary American Artists.* Los Angeles: A.R.T. Press, 1996.
Boullosa, Carmen. "Gabriel Orozco." *Bomb* 98 (Winter 2007), accessed at www.bombsite.com/issues/98/articles/2862.
Burnham, Linda Frye and Steven Durland, eds. *The Citizen Artist: 20 Years of Art in the Public Arena. An Anthology from High Performance Magazine, 1978–1998.* Gardiner, NY: Critical Press, 1998.
Cabanas, Kaira M. "Ana Mendieta: Pain of Cuba, Body I Am." *Woman's Art Journal* 20:1 (Spring–Summer, 1999).
Calle, Sophie et al. *Sophie Calle, m'as-tu vue.* Munich: Prestel Verlag, 2003.
Calle, Sophie. *Sophie Calle—Take care of yourself.* Arles: Actes Sud, 2007.
Cameron, Dan et al. *Janine Antoni.* Kusnacht, Switzerland: Ink Tree, 2000.
Fusco, Coco. *The Bodies That Were Not Ours.* New York: Routledge, 2001.
Gehrmann, Lucas et al. *Teresa Margolles.* Vienna: Kunsthalle Wien Project Space, 2003.
Golden, Thelma et al. *Black Male: Representations of Masculinity in Contemporary American Art.* New York: Whitney Museum of American Art, 1995.
Hatoum, Mona et al. *Mona Hatoum: The Entire World as a Foreign Land.* London: Tate Gallery, 2000.
Hoen, Laura Steward ed. *Mona Hatoum: Domestic Disturbance.* North Adams, MA: Mass MOCA, and Santa Fe, NM: SITE Santa Fe, 2001.
Iversen, Margaret. "Readymade, Found Object, Photograph." *Art Journal* (Summer 2004).
Johnston, Jill. "Tehching Hsieh: Art's Willing Captive." *Art in America* (September 2001).
Kaplan, Janet A. "Deeper and Deeper: Interview with Marina Abramović." *Art Journal* (Summer 1999).
Kleeblaat, Norman L., ed. *Too Jewish? Challenging Traditional Identities.* New York: The Jewish Museum, 1996.
Lovelace, Carey. "Orlan: Offensive Acts." *Performing Arts Journal* (January 1995).
Mann, Sally. *Immediate Family.* New York: Aperture Books, 1992.
Margolles, Teresa. "Santiago Sierra by Teresa Margolles." *Bomb* 86 (Winter 2004), at http://www.bombsite.com/issues/86/articles/2606 (accessed March 2009).
O'Bryan, Jill. "Saint Orlan Faces Reincarnation." *Art Journal* (Winter 1997).
Orozco, Gabriel. *Photogravity.* Philadelphia: Philadelphia Museum of Art, 1999.
Perreault, John and Petra Barreras del Rio. *Ana Mendieta: A Retrospective.* New York: New Museum of Contemporary Art, 1987.
Piper, Adrian. "In Support of Meta Art." *Artforum* (October 1973).
Posner, Helene. *Kiki Smith.* New York: Monacelli, 2005.
Reinhardt, Ad, Joseph Kosuth, and Felix Gonzalez-Torres. *Symptoms of Interference, Conditions of Possibility.* London: Camden Arts Centre, 1994.
Shearer, Linda and Claudia Gould. *Kiki Smith.* Williamstown, MA: William College Museum of Art, and Columbus, Ohio: Wexner Center for the Arts, Ohio State University, 1992.
Spector, Nancy. *Felix Gonzalez-Torres.* New York: Guggenheim Museum, 1995.

Chapter 8

Ai Weiwei and Feng Boyi. *Fuck Off.* Shanghai: Eastlink Gallery, 2000.
Brener, Alexander and Barbara Schurz. *Anti-Technologies of Resistance* (2000), at http://subsol.c3.hu/subsol_2/contributors/brenertext.html (accessed November 2012).
Brener, Alexander and Barbara Schurz. *The Art of Destruction.* Ljubljana: Blossom v. Fruit SAMIZDAT, 2004.
Bulatov, Erik. *Erik Bulatov.* London: ICA, 1989.
Chang Tsong-zung. *China's New Art, Post-1989.* Hong Kong: Hanart T Z Gallery, 1993.
Chiu, Melissa. "The Crisis of Calligraphy and the New Way of Tea: An Interview with Wenda Gu." *Orientations* 33:3 (March 2002).
Erickson, Britta. *On the Edge: Contemporary Chinese Artists Encounter the West.* Hong Kong: Time Zone, 2004.
Erickson, Britta. *Words Without Meaning, Meaning Without Words: The Art of Xu Bing.* Washington, D.C.: Smithsonian, 2001.
Gao Minglu et al. *China/Avant-Garde.* China Art Gallery: Beijing, 1989.
Gao Minglu et al. *Inside Out: New Chinese Art.* San Francisco: San Francisco Museum of Modern Art, 1998.
Gao Minglu. *The Wall: Reshaping Contemporary Chinese Art.* Buffalo, N.Y.: Albright Knox Art Gallery, 2005.
Gladston, Paul. *Avant-Garde Art Groups in China, 1979–89.* Bristol: Intellect—University of Chicago Press, 2013.
Groys, Boris. "'With Russia on Your Back': A Conversation Between Ilya Kabakov and Boris Groys." *Parkett* 34 (1992).
Gu, Wenda. "The Divine Comedy of Our Times—A Thesis on United Nations Art Project & Its Time and Environment." Posted on the artist's website at http://www.wendagu.com/home.html.
Hoptman, Laura and Tomas Pospiszyl. *Primary Documents: A Sourcebook for Eastern and Central European Art Since the 1950s.* New York: Museum of Modern Art, 2002.
Huang Yongping. *House of Oracles: A Huang Yong Ping Retrospective.* Minneapolis: Walker Art Center, 2005.
Isaak, Jo Anna. "The Future of Disillusion: Sex, Truth, and Photography in the Former Soviet Union." *Art Journal* 53:2 (Summer 1994).
Jane Voorhees Zimmerli Art Museum. *New Directions: Essays on Aspects of the Permanent Collection by Members of the Rutgers University Faculty in Honor of the 25th Anniversary of the Jane Voorhees Zimmerli Art Museum.* New Brunswick, NJ: The Museum, 1991.
Kabakov, Ilya. *Ten Characters.* London: ICA 1989.
Kosolapov, Alexander et al. *Alexander Kosolapov: Sots Art.* Bielefeld: Kerber Art, 2009.
Kulik, Oleg. "The Gobi Test, or the Unbearable Charm of Mongolia." In *La Biennale di Venezia 51: Always a Little Further,* edited by María de Corral and Rosa Martínez. Venice: Fondazione La Biennale di Venezia, 2005, 178.
Ma, Maggie. "Memories of 1989." *Artzine* at http://www.artzinechina.com/display_vol_aid252_en.html (accessed July 16, 2010).
Qian Zhijian. "Performing Bodies: Zhang Huan, Ma Liuming, and Performance Art in China." *Art Journal* (Summer 1999).
Ross, David A. et al. *Between Spring and Summer: Soviet Conceptual Art in the Era of Late Capitalism.* Boston: Institute of Contemporary Art, 1990.
Sans, Jérôme. *China Talks: Interviews with 32 Contemporary Artists.* Hong Kong: Timezone, 2009.
Simpson, Pat. "Peripheralizing Patriarchy: Gender and Identity in Post Soviet Art: A View from the West." *Oxford Art Journal* 27:3 (2004).
Storr, Robert. "An Interview with Ilya Kabakov." *Art in America* (January 1995).
Tolnay, Alexander, ed. *Contemporary Photographic Art from Moscow.* New York: Prestel 1995.
Tupitsyn, Margarita et al. *Sots Art.* New York: The New Museum, 1986.
Wu Hung, ed. *Contemporary Chinese Art: Primary Documents.* New York: Museum of Modern Art, 2010.

Zhang Huan. *Pilgrimage to Santiago.* Barcelona: Xunda de Galicia and Cotthem Gallery, 2001.

Chapter 9

Berry, Ian et al. *Shahzia Sikander: Nemesis.* Saratoga Springs, N.Y.: Frances Young Tang Teaching Museum and Art Gallery at Skidmore College, 2004.
Bettleheim, Judith et al. *Crónicas Americanas: Obras de José Bedia.* Monterrey, Mexico: Museo de Arte Contemporáneo de Monterrey, 1997.
Block, Holly. *Art Cuba: The New Generation.* New York: Harry N. Abrams, 2001.
Camnitzer, Luis. *New Art of Cuba.* Austin: University of Texas Press, 2003.
Cheng, Amy and Chen Chieh-jen. "On Lingchi: Echoes of a Historical Photograph." *Yishu* (March 2003).
Dijkstra, Rineke and Katy Seigel. *Rineke Dijkstra: Portraits.* Boston: Institute of Contemporary Art, 2001.
Garaicoa, Carlos. *Carlos Garaicoa: Capablanca's Real Passion.* Prato, Italy: Gli Ori, 2005.
Gilroy, Paul. "The Art of Darkness: Black Art and the Problems of Belonging to England." *Third Text* 10 (Spring 1990).
Goodbody, Bridget L. "From Lover to Foe and Back Again." *Art Asia Pacific* 43 (Winter 2005).
Horrigan, Bill ed. *Shirin Neshat: Two Installations.* Columbus, Ohio: Wexner Center, 2000.
Hu Fang. *Cao Fei: Journey.* Guangzhou: Vitamin Creative Space, 2008.
Lu, Victoria, ed. *Visions of Pluralism: Contemporary Art in Taiwan 1988–1999.* Kaohsiung, Taiwan: Mountain Art Culture and Education Foundation, 1999.
Marti, José. "Our America." Translated and reprinted in *The Cuba Reader: History , Culture, Politics,* edited by Aviva Chomsky, Barry Carr, and Pamela Maria Smorkaloff. Durham, NC: Duke University Press, 2003.
Mercer, Kobena. "Art That Is Ethnic in Inverted Commas." *Frieze* 25 (November–December 1995).
Merewether, Charles. *Made in Havana: Contemporary Art from Cuba.* Sydney: Art Gallery of New South Wales, 1988.
Murakami, Takahashi. *Summon Monsters? Open the Door? Heal? Or Die?* Tokyo: Museum of Contemporary Art, 2001.
Murakami, Takashi, ed. *Little Boy: The Arts of Japan's Exploding Subculture.* New York: Japan Society 2005.
Neshat, Shirin. *Shirin Neshat.* London: Serpentine Gallery, 2000.
Neshat, Shirin. *Shirin Neshat.* Milan: Charta, 2001.
Oguibe, Olu and Okwui Enwezor. *Reading the Contemporary: African Art from Theory to the Marketplace.* Cambridge: MIT Press, 1999.
Rollig, Stella and Genoveva Rückert, eds. *Emily Jacir—Belongings.* Linz: O.K. Centrum für Gegenwartskunst Oberösterreich, 2004.
Rutherford, Jonathan. "The Third Space: Interview with Homi Bhabha." In *Identity: Community, Culture, Difference,* edited by Jonathan Rutherford. London: Lawrence and Wishart, 1990, 207–21:211.
Schimmel, Paul et al. *©Murakami.* Los Angeles: The Museum of Contemporary Art, 2007.
Shonibare, Yinka et al. *Yinka Shonibare MBE.* New York: Prestel, 2008.
Shonibare, Yinka et al. *Yinka Shonibare.* New York: The Studio Museum in Harlem, 2002.
Sikander, Shahzia. *Shazia Sikander: Intimate Ambivalence.* Birmingham, U.K.: Ikon Gallery, 2008.
Sikander, Shahzia. *Shahzia Sikander.* Chicago: Renaissance Society University of Chicago, 1999.
Thea, Carolee. "Cao Fei: Global Player." *Art Asia Pacific* (Fall 2006).
Thompson, Robert Farris. "Sacred Silhouettes." *Art in America* (July 1997).
Wakasa, Mako. "Takashi Murakami." *Journal of Contemporary Art* (2000), accessed at http://www.jca-online.com/murakami.html.
Waxman, Lori. "Yinka Shonibare: Interview." *New Art Examiner* 28:3 (2000).
Weaver, Suzanne and Sinisa Mitrovic, eds. *Phil Collins: the world won't listen.* Dallas: Dallas Museum of Art, 2007.
Yang Fudong. *Seven Intellectuals in Bamboo Forest.* Stockholm: Jarla Partilager, 2008.
Yang Fudong. *"Seven Intellectuals in the Bamboo Forest: Postscript by Yang Fudong"* (2009), accessed at http://www.shanghartgallery.com/galleryarchive/texts/id/1382.

Chapter 10

Baker, George. "An Interview with Pierre Huyghe." *October* 110 (Fall 2004).
Barney, Matthew and Arthur C. Danto. "A Dialogue on Blood and Iron: Matthew Barney and Arthur C. Danto on Joseph Beuys." *Modern Painters* (Sept. 2006).
Barney, Matthew. *Matthew Barney—Drawing Restraint 1987–2007.* Köln: Verlag der Buchhandlung Walther König, 2007.
Batchelor, David. *Chromophobia.* London: Reaktion, 2000.
Berman, Jennifer. "Matthew Ritchie." *Bomb* (Spring 1997), accessed at http://www.bombsite.com/issues/59/articles/2035.
Berry, Ian and Anne Ellegood. *Amy Sillman: Third Person Singular.* Saratoga Springs, New York: The Frances Young Tang Teaching Museum and Art Gallery, 2008.
Bourriaud, Nicolas. *Relational Aesthetics.* Dijon: Les Presses Du Réel, 1998.
Brown, Cecily. "Painting Epiphany." *Flash Art* (May–June 1998).
Bui, Phong. "Brooklyn Rail: Amy Sillman with Phong Bui." *Brooklyn Rail* (April 2006), accessed at http://brooklynrail.org/2006/04/art/amy-sillman-with-phong-bui.
Calame, Ingrid. *Constellations.* New York: James Cohan Gallery, 2007.
Christov-Bakargiev, Carolyn, ed. *Pierre Huyghe.* Milan: Skira 2004.
Christov-Bakargiev, Carolyn et al. *Janet Cardiff: A Survey of Works Including Collaborations with George Bures Miller.* New York: P.S. 1 Contemporary Art Center, 2001.
Clearwater, Bonnie et al. *Jorge Pardo: House.* North Miami: Museum of Contemporary Art, 2007.
Egoyan, Atom. "Janet Cardiff." *Bomb* 79 (Spring 2002).
Garbagna, Cristina, ed. *Francesco Vezzoli: Democrazy.* Milan: Electa, 2007.
Gilbert-Rolfe, Jeremy. *Beauty and the Contemporary Sublime.* New York: Allworth Press, 1999.
Grosse, Katharina. *Katharina Grosse: Atoms Outside Eggs.* Porto: Museu Serralves, 2007.
Gygax, Raphael and Heike Munder, eds. *Cory Arcangel (BEIGE).* Zurich: JRP Ringier, 2005.
Haeg, Fritz. "Interview with Jorge Pardo." *Index Magazine, LA Design Special Supplement* (May–June 1999).
Heiser, Jorg and Jan Verwoert. "Ordinary Madness: An Interview with Albert Oehlen." *Frieze* 78 (October 2003).
Hickey, Dave. *Air Guitar: Essays on Art and Democracy.* Los Angeles: Art Issues Press, 1997.
Hickey, Dave. *The Invisible Dragon: Essays on Beauty.* Los Angeles: Art Issues Press, 1993.
Holm, Michael Juul and Mette Marcus, eds. *Louisiana Contemporary: Janet Cardiff and George Bures Miller.* Humlebæk: Louisiana Museum of Modern Art, 2006.
Neri, Louise, ed. *Antipodes: Inside the White Cube.* London: White Cube, 2003.
Oehlen, Albert. *I will Always Champion Good Painting I Will Always Champion Bad Painting.* London: Whitechapel Gallery, 2006.
Panek, Aneta. "Franz Ackermann, Voyages Parallèles / Franz Ackermann What a Long Long Trip It's Been." *Art Press* 14 (2005).
Ritchie, Matthew. *Matthew Ritchie: Proposition Player.* Houston: Contemporary Arts Museum, 2003.
Schumacher, Rainald, ed. *Imagination Becomes Reality Part 1: Expanded Paint Tools.* Munich: Sammlung Goetz, 2005.
Sillman, Amy and Gregg Bordowitz. *Amy Sillman and Gregg Bordowitz Between Artists.* New York: A.R.T. Press, 2007.
Spector, Nancy. *Matthew Barney: The Cremaster Cycle.* New York: Guggenheim Museum, 2002.
Stockholder, Jessica et al. *Jessica Stockholder.* London: Phaidon, 1995.
Thea, Carolee. "Inexplicable Symbiosis: A Conversation with Janet Cardiff." *Sculpture Magazine* (January–February 2003).
Tillman, Lynne, Jessica Stockholder et al. *Your skin in this weather bourne eye-threads & swollen perfume.* New York: Dia Center for the Arts, 1996.
Tomkins, Calvin. "His Body, Himself: Matthew Barney's Strange and Passionate Exploration of Gender." *The New Yorker* (January 27, 2003).
Trecartin, Ryan, et al. *Any Ever: Ryan Trecartin.* New York: Skira Rizzoli, 2011.
Végh, Christine et al, *Jorge Pardo.* London: Phaidon, 2008.
Vezzoli, Francesco. *Right You Are (If You Think You Are) by Luigi Pirandello.* Milan: Charta, 2009.

Chapter 11

Apter, Emily. "In Conversation: Silvia Kolbowski with Emily Apter." *Brooklyn Rail* (October 2011) accessed at www.brooklynrail.org/2011/10/art/silvia-kolbowski-with-emily-apter
Arning, Bill. "Ernesto Neto." *Bomb* 70 (Winter 2000), accessed at http://www.bombsite.com/issues/70/articles/2274.
Blessing, Jennifer. *Cathering Opie: American Photographer.* New York: Guggenheim Museum, 2008.
Bowers, Andrea. "Interview with Sam Durant and Monica Bonvicini." *Neue Review* (December 2003).
Bowers, Andrea and Catherine Opie. *Between Artists: Andrea Bowers and Catherine Opie.* New York: A.R.T. Press, 2008.
Bowers, Andrea. *Andrea Bowers: Nothing Is Neutral.* Los Angeles: California Institute of the Arts / REDCAT, 2006.
Buchloh, Benjamin H.D. "An Interview with Thomas Hirschhorn." *October* 113 (Summer 2005).
Corrin, Lisa Graziose et al. *Mark Dion.* London: Phaidon, 1997.

Deutsch, Rosalyn. *Hiroshima after Iraq: Three Studies in Art and War.* New York: Columbia University Press, 2010.

Dion, Mark et al. *Mark Dion: The Natural History of the Museum.* Paris: Archibooks, 2007.

Dion, Mark. *New England Digs.* Brockton, MA: Fuller Museum of Art, 2001.

Dziewior, Yilmaz, ed. *Harun Farocki: Soft Montages.* Bregenz, Austria: Kunsthaus Bregenz, 2011.

Ehmann, Antje. *Harun Farocki, Against what? Against whom?* London: Koenig Books, 2009.

Eliasson, Olafur, ed. *Olafur Eliasson: The Blind Pavilion.* Ostfildern, Germany: Hatje Cantz Publishers, 2004.

Eliasson, Olafur. "Nothing Is Ever the Same." Mission statement for the Institut für Raumexperimente, accessed at http://www.raumexperimente.net/text-en.html.

Farocki, Harun. *Nachdruck/Imprint: Texte/Writings.* New York: Lukas und Sternberg, 2001.

Fast, Omer. *The Casting.* Köln: Verlag der Buchhandlung Walther König, 2007.

Gielen, Pascal. *The Murmuring of the Artistic Multitude: Global Art, Memory and Post-Fordism.* Amsterdam: Valiz, 2009.

Gomes, Fernanda. "Fernanda Gomes and Ernesto Neto." *Bomb* 102 (Winter 2008), accessed at http://www.bombsite.com/issues/102/articles/3039.

Grynsztejn, Madeleine, ed. *Take Your Time: Olafur Eliasson.* San Francisco: San Francisco Museum of Modern Art, 2007.

Hanhardt, John C. et al. *Tom Sachs Nutsy's.* New York: Guggenheim Museum, 2002.

Hirschhorn, Thomas et al. *Thomas Hirschhorn.* London: Phaidon, 2004.

Hirschhorn, Thomas. *Jumbo Spoons and Big Cake.* Chicago: The Art Institute, 2000.

Hirschhorn, Thomas. *Where Do I Stand? What Do I Want?* London: Art Review Ltd., 2007.

Horn, Roni. *Roni Horn aka Roni Horn.* New York: Whitney Museum of American Art, 2009.

Kwon, Miwon. *One Place After Another: Site-Specific Art and Locational Identity.* Cambridge: MIT Press, 2002.

Lovink, Geert. "Surveillance, Performance, Self-Surveillance: Interview with Jill Magid." *Institute of Network Cultures* (October 29, 2004), accessed at http://www.networkcultures.org/weblog/archives/2004/10/surveillance_pe.html

May, Susan, ed. *Olafur Eliasson: The Weather Project.* London: The Tate, 2003.

Mogel, Lize and Alexis Bhagat. *An Atlas of Radical Cartography.* Los Angeles: Journal of Aesthetics & Protest Press, 2007.

Neri, Louise et al. *Roni Horn.* London: Phaidon, 2000.

Obrist, Hans Ulrich. *Hans Ulrich Obrist & Olafur Eliasson: Conversation Series 13.* Köln: Verlag der Buchhandlung Walther König, 2008.

Opie, Catherine. *Catherine Opie: 1999 [&] In and Around Home.* Ridgefield, Conn.: Aldrich Contemporary Art Museum, 2006.

Ridgway, Emma, ed. *Experiment Marathon: Serpentine Gallery.* Reykjavik: Reykjavik Art Museum, 2009.

Sachs, Tom and John Furgason. *Ten Bullets.* New York: published by the artist, 2005.

Sachs, Tom. *Tom Sachs: Space Program: Mission Guide and Experience Report.* Beverly Hills: Gagosian Gallery, 2008.

Sasnal, Wilhelm and Luc Tuymans. "When Luc Tuymans Met Wilhelm Sasnal ..." *Art Review* (February 2008).

Schorr, Collier. "Weather Girls Interview with Collier Schorr." *Frieze* 32 (January–February 1997).

Soyugenc, Ismail and Richard Torchia. *Olafur Eliasson: Your Colour Memory.* Glenside, Pennsylvania: Arcadia University Art Gallery, 2006.

Sussler, Betsy, Suzan Sherman, and Ronalde Shavers, eds. *Speak Art! The Best of Bomb Magazine's Interviews with Artists.* New York: New Art Publications, 1997.

Tuymans, Luc et al. *Luc Tuymans.* San Francisco: San Francisco Museum of Modern Art, 2009.

Verhagen, Marcus. "Pleasure and Pain: Omer Fast Interviewed by Marcus Verhagen." *Art Monthly* 330 (October 2009).

Wiseman, Eva. "Is It Art? Search Me ... Why Artist Jill Magid Loves an Authority Figure." *The Observer* (September 27, 2009), "Features" section.

Picture Credits

Laurence King Publishing, the author, and the picture researcher wish to thank the institutions and individuals who have kindly provided photographic material. While every effort has been made to trace the present copyright holders we apologize in advance for any unintentional omission or error and will be pleased to insert the appropriate acknowledgment in any subsequent edition if informed.

Collections and some copyright credits are given in the captions alongside the illustrations. Sources for the remaining copyright credits are given below. Bold numbers indicate figure numbers.

0.1 Image copyright The Metropolitan Museum of Art/Art Resource/Scala, Florence © Succession Picasso/DACS, London 2013 **0.2** Digital image, The Museum of Modern Art, New York/Scala, Florence **0.3** © ADAGP, Paris and DACS, London 2013 **0.4** Digital image, The Museum of Modern Art, New York/Scala, Florence © The Willem de Kooning Foundation, New York/ARS, NY and DACS, London 2013 **0.5** © Jasper Johns/VAGA, New York/DACS, London 2013 **0.6** © Estate of Robert Rauschenberg. DACS, London/VAGA, New York 2013 **0.7** Getty Images © The Andy Warhol Foundation for the Visual Arts/Artists Rights Society (ARS), New York/DACS, London 2013 **0.8** © Centre Pompidou, Mnam Kandinsky Library, Constantinos Ignatiadis **1.1** Digital image, The Museum of Modern Art, New York/Scala, Florence © James Rosenquist/DACS, London/VAGA, New York 2013 **1.2** © The Estate of Roy Lichtenstein/DACS 2013 **1.5** Art Center Acquisition Fund, 1969 © Judd Foundation. Licensed by VAGA, New York/DACS, London 2013 **1.6** © ARS, NY and DACS, London 2013 **1.7** Photo: César Oiticica Filho © Projeto Hélio Oiticica **1.8** © Projeto Hélio Oiticica **1.9** © Lynda Benglis. DACS, London/VAGA, New York 2013 **1.10** Robert Morris © ARS, NY and DACS, London 2013. Rudy Burckhardt © ARS, NY and DACS, London 2013 **1.11** Digital image, The Museum of Modern Art, New York/Scala, Florence © ARS, NY and DACS, London 2013 **1.12** © Estate of Robert Smithson/DACS, London/VAGA, New York 2013 **1.14** © ARS, NY and DACS, London 2013 **1.16** © DACS 2013 **1.17** © Tate, London 2013 © Estate of Leon Golub, DACS, London/VAGA, New York 2013 **1.18** © Centre Pompidou, MNAM-CCI, Dist. RMN-Grand Palais/Bertrand Prévost © DACS, London **1.19** © DB-ADAGP Paris and DACS, London 2013 **1.20** © Romare Bearden Foundation/DACS, London/VAGA, New York 2013 **1.23** © Emory Douglas/DACS 2013 **1.24** © Yoko Ono **1.25** Photo: Yoko Ono © Yoko Ono **1.26** © Estate of Nancy Spero. DACS, London/VAGA, New York 2013 **1.27** Photo: Lloyd Hamrol **1.28** © ARS, NY and DACS, London 2013 **1.31** Photo: Tara Sterling **1.32** www.feldmangallery.com, photograph by D. James Dee © Marsie, Emanuelle, Damon and Andrew Scharlatt/DACS, London/VAGA, New York 2013 **2.1** Courtesy © The Estate of Jack Goldstein **2.3** Gift of the artist, 1995 (1995.266.7) © Walker Evans Archive, The Metropolitan Museum of Art **2.5** © Richard Prince **2.6** © Richard Prince **2.9** 20th Century Fox/The Kobal Collection/Penn, Robert **2.12** Digital image, The Museum of Modern Art, New York/Scala, Florence **2.18** © Guerrilla Girls www.guerrillagirls.com **2.19** © 1977 Jenny Holzer © ARS, NY and DACS, London 2013 **3.1** © The Andy Warhol Foundation for the Visual Arts/Artists Rights Society (ARS), New York/DACS, London 2013 **3.2** © Gerhard Richter, 2013 **3.4** © 2013 Julian Schnabel/ARS, New York/DACS **3.5** © Eric Fischl **3.6** Digital image, The Museum of Modern Art, New York/Scala, Florence © David Salle/DACS, London/VAGA, New York 2013 **3.7** © The Estate of Jean-Michel Basquiat/ADAGP, Paris and DACS, London 2013 **3.8** © The Estate of Jean-Michel Basquiat/ADAGP, Paris and DACS, London 2013 **3.9** © The Estate of Jean-Michel Basquiat/ADAGP, Paris and DACS, London 2013 © The Andy Warhol Foundation for the Visual Arts/Artists Rights Society (ARS), New York/DACS, London 2013 **3.10** © Tate, London 2013 © Sandro Chia. DACS, London/VAGA, New York 2013 **3.20** © DACS 2013 **3.21** © Digital image, The Museum of Modern Art, New York/Scala, Florence © The Estate of Sigmar Polke, Cologne, DACS 2013 **3.23** © DACS 2013 **4.1**, **4.2**, **4.3** Photo: Lisa Kahane **4.11** Image © The Metropolitan Museum of Art/Art Resource/Scala, Florence **4.12** Image courtesy Four Corners Books **4.15**, **4.16** www.feldmangallery.com **4.19** Photo: Ivan Dalla Tana **4.20** Digital image, The Museum of Modern Art, New York/Scala, Florence © 2013 Tim Rollins and K.O.S. **4.22**, **4.23** The New York Public Library **4.24** Photo: Elizabeth Sisco **4.26** Photo: Elizabeth Sisco **5.4** Photo: David Lubarsky **5.8** Photo: Fredrik Nilson **5.14**, **5.15** Photo: © Zindman/Fremont **5.16** Photo: © Cheryl O'Brien **5.17** Installation image from John M. Armleder: Too Much is not Enough, 26 April–29 July 2007. Rose Art Museum, Brandeis University **5.19** © DACS 2013 **5.20** © DACS 2013 **5.23** Photo: Laurent Lecat, assisted by Ruy Ribière **6.1** © Ron Sachs/dpa/Corbis **6.2** © Aurelie and Morgan David De Lossy/cultura/Corbis **6.3** © Melvyn Longhurst/Alamy **6.5** Photo: Kulturbehörde, Hamburg © DACS 2013 **6.6** © ADAGP, Paris and DACS, London 2013 **6.7** © ADAGP, Paris and DACS, London 2013 **6.8** © 1993 Rachel Whiteread **6.9** © 2000 Rachel Whiteread © Travel Library Limited/SuperStock **6.10** © DACS 2013 **6.11**, **6.12** www.feldmangallery.com **6.20** Denver Art Museum Collection: Funds from Polly and Mark Addison, the Alliance for Contemporary Art, Caroline Morgan, and Colorado Contemporary Collectors: Suzanne Farver, Linda and Ken Heller, Jan and Frederick Mayer, Beverly and Bernard Rosen, Annalee and Wagner Schorr, and anonymous donors, 1995.77 Photo © Denver Art Museum **6.22** Photo: Robert Pettus **7.7** © Adrian Piper Research Archive Foundation Berlin **7.10**, **7.11** © ORLAN/ADAGP, Paris and DACS, London 2013 **7.12**, **7.14** © Marina Abramović. Courtesy of Marina Abramović and Sean Kelly Gallery, New York © DACS 2013 **7.13** Photo: Alessia Bulgari © Marina Abramović. Courtesy of Marina Abramović and Sean Kelly Gallery, New York © DACS 2013 **7.15** Photo: Todd-White fine art photography © Tracey Emin. All rights reserved, DACS 2013 **7.16** © ADAGP, Paris and DACS, London 2013 **7.17** © ADAGP, Paris and DACS, London 2013 **7.20** Photo: Edward Woodman **7.21** Photo: Philippe Migeat **7.25** © DACS 2013 **7.26** © DACS 2013 **7.27** Photo: Axel Schneider **7.29** © DACS 2013 **7.30** © DACS 2013 **8.1** Image courtesy of the artist and Sprovieri Gallery, London © DACS 2013 **8.3** Photo: Margherita Spiluttini © DACS 2013 **8.2** © DACS 2013 **8.4** © ARS, NY and DACS, London 2013 **8.5** www.feldmangallery.com Photo: D. James Dee **8.7** © ARS, NY and DACS, London 2013 **8.8** © Igor Moukhin **8.17** T. B. Walker Acquisition Fund, 2001 © ADAGP, Paris and DACS, London 2013 **8.26** © DACS 2013 **9.2**, **9.3** Photo: Adam Reich **9.5** Photo: Anne Gold **9.6** Exhibition made possible by the Lindy and Ed Bergman Visiting Artist's Fund with the support of the Jerusalem Center for the Visual Arts. Photo © The Israel Museum, Jerusalem by Oded Antman **9.7** Photo: Johan Vogel **9.10** © DACS 2013 **9.31** Photo: Bill Orcutt **10.4** Photo: Todd-White Art Photography **10.5** Photo: Stephen White **10.8** Photo: Uwe Walter, Berlin. © Neo Rauch courtesy Galerie EIGEN+ART Leipzig/Berlin/DACS, 2013 **10.13** Photo: Tony Walsh © Katharina Grosse and VG Bild-Kunst, Bonn 2013/DACS 2013 **10.17** Photo: Michael James O'Brien **10.19** © ADAGP, Paris and DACS, London, 2013 **10.20** © ADAGP, Paris and DACS, London, 2013 **10.21** © DACS 2013 **10.22** Photo by: Jason Schmidt. © DACS 2013 **11.1** © 1996 Olafur Eliasson **11.2** © 2004 Olafur Eliasson **11.3** Photo: Jean Vong **11.4** Photo © Attilio Maranzano/VG Bild Kunst, Bonn © DACS 2013 **11.6** Photo: Stefan Altenburger Photography Zürich **11.8** Gift of Sally and William Neukom, American Express Company, Seattle Garden Club, Mark Torrance Foundation and Committee of 33, in honor of the 75th Anniversary of the Seattle Art Museum, 2007.1. Photo: Paul Macapia **11.9** Photo: Josh White **11.10** Photo: Genevieve Hanson **11.11** Photo: Claudio Franzini © Antoni Muntadas/DACS 2013 **11.12** © ADAGP, Paris and DACS, London 2013 **11.13** © ADAGP, Paris and DACS, London 2013 **11.23** Still by Yonn Thomas **11.24** Photo: Hermann Feldhaus **11.25** Film credits: Editor Fil Rüting; Producer and Director Andrea Bowers; Camera Andrea Bowers and Steve Smith; Guide David Russell; Production Assistant Alex Olson

Index